Highlighting the most relevant topics...

W9-CFB-835

ETHICAL PERSPECTIVES

INTERNATIONAL PERSPECTIVES

DIFFERENT POINTS OF VIEW

Human Resource Management

Fifth Edition

Cynthia D. Fisher

Bond University

Lyle F. Schoenfeldt

Appalachian State University

James B. Shaw

Bond University

HOUGHTON MIFFLIN COMPANY

Boston   New York

This book is dedicated, with much love and appreciation, to our parents:
  Hazel, Eleanor, and Roland Fisher
  Jeannette and Robert Schoenfeldt
  James and Wanza Shaw

Editor-in-Chief: George T. Hoffman
Associate Sponsoring Editor: Joanne Dauksewicz
Senior Production/Design Coordinator: Jill Haber
Senior Manufacturing Coordinator: Priscilla J. Bailey
Marketing Manager: Steven Mikels

Cover image: *Gears and People Interlocking* by David Ridley/© The Stock Illustration Source, Inc.

Printed in the U.S.A.

Library of Congress Control Number: 2001133251

ISBN: 0-618-12329-6

123456789–QUV–06 05 04 03 02

Brief Contents

Contents

PART 2   Planning for Organizations, Jobs, and People   53

● **4**   *Job Analysis: Concepts, Procedures, and Choices*   *142*

PART 3   Acquiring Human Resources   **179**

5   *Equal Employment Opportunity: The Legal Environment*   *180*

● 8   *Assessing Job Candidates: Tools for Selection*   *318*

PART 4   Building Individual and Organizational Performance   367

● 9   *Human Resource Development*   *368*

PART 5   Rewarding Employees   **479**

● 12   *Compensation System Development*   *542*

● 13   *Incentive Compensation and Benefits*   *596*

PART 6   Maintaining Human Resources   **657**

14   *Safety and Health: A Proactive Approach*   *658*

● **15** *Labor Relations and Collective Bargaining*   *702*

● 16   *Employment Transitions*   *742*

PART 7   Multinational Human Resource Management   797

17 *Managing Human Resources in Multinational Organizations*   *798*

Preface

The Fifth Edition of *Human Resource Management* offers students a comprehensive, current, and research-based introduction to the human resource management function. The book is designed for a survey course in human resource management at the junior, senior, or graduate level, but it also serves as a useful reference for practicing managers and HR professionals in search of sound advice on most human resource issues. Drawing from more than seventy years of combined experience in teaching human resource management, as well as from findings reported in the most recent literature, we have produced a text that we believe to be logically organized, clearly presented, fully substantive, and quite interesting as well.

Important Themes

Several themes have guided our discussion of the subject matter. The first theme is strategic human resource management. Chapter 2 is devoted entirely to strategic issues and their impact on the choice of human resource practices. Most subsequent chapters begin with further discussion of how the organization's strategy should affect choices with respect to the activities described in that chapter.

The second theme is the international dimension of human resource management. Human resource management in multinational organizations is introduced in the first chapter and discussed extensively in Chapter 17, which is devoted entirely to multinational human resource management. Further, thirteen International Perspective boxes provide comparative information on how other nations and cultures deal with human resource management issues. The authors are well qualified to discuss international HRM, as all three have led study-abroad tours related to human resource management, and Drs. Fisher and Shaw have held teaching posts in Singapore and Australia as well as in the United States.

The third theme focuses on the human resource manager's responsibilities for facilitating ethical behavior by employees and for dealing ethically with employees. This theme is introduced in the first chapter and reinforced throughout the book via twelve Ethical Perspective boxes. Topics include whistleblowing, civil liberties inside the organization, procedural and distributive justice in reward systems, ethics in recruiting, privacy, and other ethical dilemmas confronting practitioners.

A fourth theme is benchmarking and utility or cost-benefit analysis. Human resource programs can produce quantifiable returns for organizations, but the results of programs are seldom evaluated carefully in monetary terms. Utility is discussed in connection with recruiting, selection, training, performance appraisal, and employee-assistance programs. Benchmarking against what leading firms are doing is also discussed in a number of chapters as a way of assessing human resource department performance.

A final theme is represented in the Point of View boxes that appear throughout the text. These reflect our opinion that the world is a complex place, and that there are a variety of potentially useful ways to look at any given problem. These boxes point out inherent contradictions or alternative or potentially controversial positions on aspects of human resource management. As the text is designed for more advanced students, we think there is value is presenting alternative points of view that may start students questioning received wisdom.

In addition to the above themes and thorough coverage of basic human resource management activities, this book contains much more extensive treatment of the role of human resource managers in improving productivity and quality than other textbooks at this level. It also contains an entire chapter on mechanisms by which employees leave organizations, both voluntarily and involuntarily.

Content and Organization

The book is organized into seven parts and seventeen chapters, logically following the progression of individuals into, through, and out of the organization.

The first part, Overview and Introduction, defines human resource management and briefly reviews its history. It outlines the plan of the book; introduces the international, strategy, ethics, and utility themes; explores differing expectations of the multiple constituencies of the human resource management function; considers trends and challenges that have been affecting the practice of human resource management; and explores career tracks and preparation for the human resource profession.

The second part, Planning for Organizations, Jobs, and People, is comprised of three chapters. Chapter 2 is devoted to strategic issues in human resource management. This chapter is intended to capture the interest of the general business student by demonstrating that appropriately chosen human resource management practices are critical for successful strategy implementation. It also shows that the human resource manager is a vital part of any management team. In addition, Chapter 2 deals with the issue of converting a traditional personnel department to a fully participating human resource management unit capable of making a valuable strategic contribution to the organization. Some instructors may prefer to use Chapter 2 as a final capstone chapter, putting together what students have learned throughout the course. (After much debate, we decided to place this chapter early in the book because it can also set the stage for all the material to come. It clearly demonstrates how effective management of the human resource functions to be studied can make a significant difference to the success of the organization as a whole.)

Chapter 3 discusses forecasting the demand for and the supply of human resources, planning programs to deal with anticipated shortfalls or surpluses, and planning managerial succession. Chapter 4 contains a thorough discussion of job analysis techniques and the practical and legal issues involved in planning and conducting job analysis projects. Strategic considerations in job analysis are also presented.

The third part of the book, Acquiring Human Resources, is devoted to organizational entry. It begins with Chapter 5, which provides a thorough presentation of the latest Equal Employment Opportunity legislation, court decisions, and enforcement procedures. Chapter 6 presents internal and external recruitment techniques, describes how to plan and evaluate recruiting efforts, and cites the latest research on how job applicants respond to recruiters and make decisions about job offers. Chapter 7 discusses procedures for validating selection devices. Decision making in selection and evaluating the utility of a selection system round out the chapter.

Chapter 8 begins with a discussion of the relationship of strategy to staffing, then describes a number of specific selection tools. Recent research on personality testing for selection is included. The interview is thoroughly discussed, including particularly effective techniques of behavior description and situational interviewing. A number of methods for managerial selection are also described, and the chapter closes with a discussion of criteria that must be considered in choosing selection devices.

The fourth part of this text, Building Individual and Organizational Performance, consists of two chapters. Chapter 9 provides a complete discussion of human resource development, from needs assessment through training design through evaluation. It includes recent research on trainee motivation and adult learning, provides extensive information on transfer of training, explores high-tech training delivery, and discusses the utility of training programs. Chapter 10, Human Resource Approaches to Improving Competitiveness, focuses on the human resource manager's expanding role in facilitating productivity, quality, service, speed, and learning improvements in organizations. Several major approaches to improving competitiveness through people are explicated, with an extensive discussion of high involvement work practices. The chapter also describes a number of specific interventions such as open book management, goal setting, suggestion systems, job redesign, and self-directed work teams. The chapter closes with a discussion of how specific human resource activities might be modified to facilitate quality improvement efforts.

Part Five, Rewarding Employees, covers performance appraisal and reward systems. Chapter 11 is now entitled Performance Assessment and Management. The chapter still provides in-depth coverage of performance appraisal methods and issues, but also considers the performance assessment and management process in a larger context, bringing to the reader's attention the interconnections among selection, training, productivity improvement, and performance appraisal. Chapter 12 outlines the basics of developing a compensation system, beginning with the concepts of internal and external equity and motivation. The chapter goes on to describe job evaluation methods, wage surveys, creating wage grades, the trend toward broadbanding, and the laws that regulate compensation. Chapter 13 explores individual and group pay-for-performance systems and includes expanded coverage of executive compensation. It also discusses strategic issues and new variable pay approaches. The second part of this chapter describes a variety of employee benefits and related issues.

The sixth part, Maintaining Human Resources, includes three chapters. Chapter 14 addresses safety and health, including occupational safety and health laws, standards, and enforcement procedures. This chapter has been substantially revised to maximize readability and relevance. Chapter 15 addresses the role of unions and the human resource manager's activities in dealing with organized employees. It also clearly describes the legal environment of labor relations, the process of certification, preparation for and the conduct of collective bargaining, strikes and other dispute resolution procedures, and the grievance process. Current topics, such as the trend toward hiring permanent replacements for strikers, the quasi-union role of some professional associations, and global issues in labor relations are now discussed. Much of the material on the history of the labor movement in the United States has been removed from this edition. Chapter 16, now called Employment Transitions, has been extensively modified. This chapter begins by considering career paths and career planning within an organization, culminating in a decision to retire. The chapter then turns to the issue of employee turnover. An extensive new section considers the causes and costs and benefits of voluntary employee turnover. Retention management programs are discussed. We then turn to involuntary turnover, including issues such as employment-at-will, discipline systems, discharge for cause, and managing layoffs effectively.

The seventh part of this textbook, Multinational Human Resource Management, raises issues particular to multinational corporations. A good portion of Chapter 17 focuses on the special problems of managing expatriate employees—their selection, training, compensation, and repatriation. The remainder of the chapter considers culture and related issues in selecting, appraising, and compensating host-country nationals when conducting business abroad.

New in the Fifth Edition

- All chapters have been thoroughly updated with the most recent developments in law, practice, and research.

- Chapter 10, Human Resource Approaches to Improving Competitiveness, has been greatly updated and features a substantial new case.

- Chapter 11, Performance Assessment and Management, has been revised to focus on the entire process of performance management as well as performance appraisal.

- Chapter 14, Safety and Health: A Proactive Approach, has been extensively updated. There is increased discussion of management's role in developing and implementing safe work practices, and issues of workplace violence and mental health in the workplace receive more attention.

- Chapter 15, Labor Relations and Collective Bargaining, has been streamlined to improve its relevance to a survey course on HRM. The material on the history of unions in the United States has been further reduced in this edition.

- Chapter 16 is now called Employment Transitions. Material on career planning that appeared in Chapter 3 in previous editions now leads this chapter. Information on why employees quit jobs and how to reduce dysfunctional turnover has been added. This information is especially timely as many organizations have experienced increasing turnover in a very tight labor market. The remainder of this chapter provides advice on managing involuntary turnover in the form of disciplinary discharge and layoff.

- Several new Point of View boxes raise controversial and thought-provoking issues.

- Several new Ethical Perspective boxes and ten revised boxes keep important ethical concerns at the forefront of students' minds.

- Two new International Perspective boxes join eleven revised boxes to expand students' appreciation of the way HR functions are conducted beyond our boundaries, and the special problems that can arise in multinational HRM.

- There are several new cases and a number of new end-of-chapter exercises.

- PowerPoint slides have been updated by the authors and professionally formatted for each chapter.

Pedagogical Features

- A number of pedagogical features enhance the learning experience:
- The chapter outline introduces students to text material and provides an overview of important concepts and topics.
- Each chapter opens with an HR Challenge vignette. These brief case scenarios pose a realistic question or problem related to chapter content and serve to stimulate student interest.
- Numerous figures and tables highlight important points and expand upon text discussion to aid in the understanding of key concepts.
- A complete chapter summary reviews the major topics discussed.
- Questions for Discussion encourage recollection of information as well as the application of concepts to real-world situations and problems.
- End-of-chapter cases and exercises help students develop skills and integrate human resource management concepts with their own knowledge and work experience. Internet exercises appear in each chapter.
- A Manager's Vocabulary list appears at the end of each text chapter to encourage students to check their mastery of terms presented in the chapter.
- An extensive subject and author index facilitates many uses of the book.

New Student Web Site

A new web site for students provides study aids such as chapter learning objectives and chapter outlines, as well as self-assessment quizzes. In addition, Internet and Excel exercises, unique to the web site, encourage students to take a hands-on approach to solving HR problems and making HR decisions.

Complete Instructor Support

The teaching package for the Fifth Edition includes the *Instructor's Resource Manual with Test Bank,* a computerized test bank, transparencies, videos, a complete set of color PowerPoint slides, and an Instructor web site.

- The *Instructor's Resource Manual with Test Questions* contains instructional resources as well as a complete test bank of questions. For each chapter in the textbook, the resource manual includes a chapter synopsis, chapter objectives, an overview of the HR Challenge, an extensive lecture outline, suggested answers to the end-of-chapter discussion questions, teaching notes for the end-of-chapter cases and exercises, summaries of the boxed text features, additional lecture topics, sources for further reading, and suggested research paper topics. For users of previous editions, the *Instructor's Resource Manual* also includes a detailed transition guide describing changes in the text.
- *Test Bank and Computerized Test Bank.* The test bank includes a pre-lecture quiz as well as true/false, multiple choice, and essay questions for each chapter. An electronic version of the printed *Test Bank* allows instructors to edit or add questions, select questions, or generate randomly selected tests. The program also includes an Online Testing System, which allows instructors to ad-

minister tests via a network system, modem, or personal computer, and a grading function that lets instructors set up a new class, record grades from tests or assignments, and analyze grades to produce class and individual statistics.

- *Overhead transparencies.* 100 transparencies illustrate every major topic in the text.
- *Videos.* A new video package highlights real companies and key themes in human resources management.
- The *PowerPoint program* for this edition has been professionally prepared for instructors who wish to use computer projection and/or customize our slides to fit their own lectures.
- *Instructor web site.* This password-protected site features sections from the Instructor's Manual that can be downloaded for customization, teaching notes for the student web-based Internet and spreadsheet exercises, and PowerPoint slides for previewing and downloading.

Acknowledgments

We would like to thank everyone who adopted the first four editions of this text, and we trust that you will find this fifth edition even more satisfying.

A number of individuals provided reviews and suggestions that helped in improving this text. We appreciate their time and effort.

Yohannan Abraham
Southwest Missouri State University

Peggy Anderson
University of Wisconsin—Whitewater

Alan Cabelly
Portland State University

Anne C. Cowden
California State University, Sacramento

Joseph Culver
University of Texas at Austin

Thomas Daymont
Temple University

Mildred Doering
Syracuse University

Walter O. Einstein
Southeastern Massachusetts University

David M. Hegedus
University of Wisconsin, Oshkosh

Brenda Johnson
St. Mary's University of Minnesota

Bruce H. Johnson
Gustavus Adolphus College

Brian Klaas
University of South Carolina

Michael Koshuta
Purdue University, North Central

Dianne R. Layden
University of Redlands

Nancy McDaniel
Hocking College

Jeff Mello
Golden Gate University

Marsha P. Miceli
Ohio State University

Elaine King Miller
Colorado State University

R. LaVelle Mills
Tarleton State University

Karen Minchella
Baker College

Jonathan S. Monat
California State University, Long Beach

William M. Moore
Drake University

Earl C. Nance
Brewton Parker College

Robert Paul
Kansas State University

Gary C. Raffaele
The University of Texas at San Antonio

Hyman Sardy
Brooklyn College

Dale Scharinger
University of Wisconsin, Whitewater

Charles N. Toftoy
George Washington University

Thomas R. Tudor
University of Arkansas at Little Rock

Steve Werner
University of Houston

Paul L. Wilkens
Florida State University

Arthur Yeung
University of Michigan

We would also like to thank the following individuals for special contributions.

Hal Aikens of the University of Tennessee for advice on Chapter 10, and for writing a new HR Challenge and an end-of-chapter case on productivity issues.

Huge Hindman of the Appalachian State University, for updating the Labor Relations chapter.

Jerry Fox of Appalachian State University for his review and feedback on Chapter 5. (EEO is Jerry's litmus test for any HR book).

Peter Villanova of Appalachian State University for his review and feedback on Chapter 11, Performance Appraisal.

Samir Shrivastava for updating the *Instructor's Resource Manual* and the *Test Bank*.

Peter Howes of HRM Consulting Ltd., Brisbane, for permission to modify and reprint the Jumbuck Enterprises case at the end of Chapter 2.

Drs. James H. Browne and Stuart H. Warnock of the University of Southern Colorado for the Internet and Excel exercises that appear on our student web site.

Lyle would like to thank his family—Wanda, Beth, Todd, and Sarah—for their special support during the writing of this book.

All of the authors express their appreciation to Joanne Dauksewicz and Amy Johnson of Houghton Mifflin Company for their support during this revision. It can't be easy when two of the three authors are halfway around the world!

PART ONE

Overview and Introduction

1. An Introduction to Human Resource Management

An Introduction to Human Resource Management

HR Challenge

How does a company become second ranked on Fortune *magazine's list of the "100 Best Companies to Work For?"[1] According to Jim Goodnight, CEO of Cary, North Carolina's SAS Institute, the second firm on* Fortune's *list, "The well-being of our company is linked to the well-being of our employees. Employees determine whether we flourish or fail. If we make the effort and invest resources in our employees' professional welfare, everyone wins—the employee, the customer, and the company."[2]*

The 100 Best Companies have in common a commitment to their employees. They have nice perks, 26 (of the 100) offer on-site day care; 29 offer concierge services, like dry-cleaning pickup; nearly half offer domestic-partner benefits to same-sex couples; and 31 offer fully paid sabbaticals. However, despite these killer benefits, the oft repeated motto was, "Nice perks may help somewhat in recruiting, but to keep people here we've got to demonstrate that we offer a culture where they are respected and treated as adults, one that shows people that we really do care about them."[3]

The SAS Institute is well known for its statistical analysis and decision support software. Founded in 1976, SAS is in its third decade of double-digit annual growth and remains the world's largest privately held software company, serving more than 33,000 customer sites in 110 countries. Some 4,135 employees serve 3.5 million users in turning raw data into refined insights.[4]

Some of the employee benefits that set SAS Institute apart are low-cost day-care facilities for 700 kids, a cafeteria outfitted with highchairs so employees can eat lunch with their children, free access to a 36,000-square-foot gym, a putting green, and on-site massages. There are also an on-site health center and flexible work schedules. In addition, SAS pays a huge 15-percent-of-pay contribution to employee retirement plans. Most important, SAS's approach shows up in their bottom-line financial performance. For example, employee turnover at SAS is a paltry 3 percent, one-tenth of the industry average of 30 percent per year.[5] All of this concern for employees is part of the reason that SAS has over 30,000 applicants for less than 500 jobs it was seeking to fill.[6]

Does it surprise you that SAS Institute's human resource practices are credited with the major role in its success? Did you expect that CEOs would view working with people as the key to SAS Institute's success? How can other organizations be human resource champions and join SAS Institute as among America's Best Companies to Work For?

Organizations require a number of things to be effective:

1. Physical resources, including the manufacturing facilities and equipment to produce a product or service
2. Financial resources, including equity, leverage (debt), and retained earnings
3. Marketing capability to connect whatever products or services are created with customers
4. Human resources, including the experience, skills, knowledge, judgment, and creativity belonging to the organization, along with the means of organizing, structuring, and rewarding these capabilities

While all these are important to organizational effectiveness, the factor that is most likely to provide potential competitive advantage is human resources and how these resources are managed. The production technology, financing, and customer connections (marketing) can all be copied. The basics of managing people can also be copied, but the most effective organizations find unique ways to attract, retain, and motivate employees—a strategy that is harder to imitate.[7]

In a recent book, *The Human Equation: Building Profits by Putting People First*, Jeffrey Pfeffer outlined his blueprint for organizational success (profitability).[8] Front and center is Pfeffer's belief that organizational success is based not on conventional factors such as large size, a unique image, the right market niche, dominant market share, being in the right industry (e.g., high tech), and so forth, but on how employees are treated. Pfeffer believes that there are seven human resource practices that, taken together, lead to organizational success, profitability, and survival.[9] The seven practices include:

- Employment security as a way of building commitment to employees[10]
- Selective hiring to recruit the right people for the organization
- Self-managed teams and decentralization as basic elements of organizational design
- Higher compensation contingent on organizational performance
- Extensive training so that employees can use their skill and initiative to identify and resolve problems
- Reduced distinctions based on status
- Extensive sharing of information

Consider Southwest Airlines, one of many companies committed to the practices described by Pfeffer. Most think of Southwest Airlines as a small low-fare carrier. However, according to Herb Kelleher, Southwest's CEO, "Southwest has been kind of like a little puppy that gets fat off the table scraps of other airlines."[11] Today, Southwest is the big dog on the block in many respects:

- Southwest, whose stock soared 90 percent in the year 2000, is the nation's most valuable airline, with a market capitalization of $16 billion, more than American's, United's, and Delta's combined.
- Southwest is the nation's number-two domestic carrier, with 57.5 million passengers in the United States in 1999 versus Delta Airlines' 58 million.
- At its current growth rate, Southwest could become the number-one domestic airline by 2005.[12]
- Southwest is the most profitable airline in the industry, showing annual profits since its inception in 1971.[13]
- Southwest has even done well post-September 11, 2001. For example, in November 2001 Southwest's passenger traffic fell 1 percent compared to declines of more than 20 percent for the country's top carriers, American Airlines and United Airlines.[14]

Southwest's success has nothing to do with competitive advantage in the traditional sense. It has the same access to capital, the same planes (Boeing 737s), and the same technology as all other airlines. It sells what is essentially a commodity product—low-cost, low-frills airline service at prices its competitors have difficulty matching. Most of Southwest's success comes from its very productive, very motivated, work force.

For example, in its thirty years of operation, Southwest has never laid off an employee. In the early 1990s, when the airline industry was going through a crisis, 120,000 people were laid off, but none at Southwest.[15] Southwest is extremely selective in who it hires. Recent trends are such that they have received 140,000 applications a year for 4,000 to 5,000 positions.[16]

The preceding illustrations of SAS Institute and Southwest Airlines provide vivid examples of the role that people—human resources—play in determining the competitiveness and effectiveness of organizations in meeting the challenges of the twenty-first century. The success of both organizations comes from managing people effectively, a combination of a number of important but less visible aspects of operations. From these examples it is clear that most of the changes and challenges facing organizations have to do with their employees. In organizations as diverse as *Fortune* 500 corporations, nonprofit universities, NFL football teams, and local restaurants, CEOs are seeing the results of employee involvement, of having the right people to do the job, and of getting managers to care about their people. The successful organizations of the recent past have adopted a professional approach to human resource management that will ensure continued success in the twenty-first century.

What are the challenges facing organizations, and therefore human resource managers? As a part of the celebration of its fiftieth anniversary, the Society of Human Resource Management considered these future organizational and human resource challenges. Professionals came up with the five challenges shown in Table 1.1. The challenges seen by human resource (HR) professionals parallel those facing organizations: acting strategically, changing, decentralizing, dealing with more complex laws and regulations, and keeping up with changing technology.[17] Clearly, the issues facing organizations in the twenty-first century involve better coordination and more effective use of human resources.

It is one thing to look at the challenges in Table 1.1 and another to more fully visualize how these challenges might impact a top-level HR executive. A recent article entitled "Jack the Job-Killer Strikes Again" outlined four changes underway at General Electric.[18] The changes were as follows:

- The closing of Montgomery Ward, a subsidiary of GE Capital, and the resulting loss of 28,000 jobs.

● TABLE 1.1

Top Challenges for Organizations and the HR Profession

Challenge	Notable Characteristics
HR professionals as strategic business partners	• Making HR a partner in assisting corporate leaders in navigating the uncharted waters of the new business realities • Integrating people strategies with business strategies • Having HR professionals create new options and possibilities—thinking outside the box
Leading change in the organization	• Leading organizations in adapting to a faster pace of change • Continually changing relationships between organizations and employees • Driving diversity into all aspects of the organization • Assisting organizations in analyzing, planning, and implementing change
Teaching HR competencies to line managers	• Downsizing HR • Decentralizing HR • Moving important "people" tasks to front-line managers • Having front-line managers with HR competencies
Coping with more complex laws and labor shortages	• Understanding increasingly complex labor laws • Grasping the impact of government policies on the basic needs and demands of working people • Working within and beyond public education and government training to fill critical positions in the organization
Keeping up with changing technology	• Leveraging technology in the delivery of HR services to employees • Using technology to track applicants' and employees' skills and experiences • Allowing technology to handle administrative aspects of HR so that HR professionals can devote time to other aspects of their organizational role

Source: Adapted from "Future Challenges and Opportunities for the HR Profession," *HRMagazine*, Vol. 43 (3), 1998, pp. 69–75.

- The acquisition of Honeywell International and its 120,000 workers. The article suggests that GE is likely to cut up to 50,000 Honeywell jobs.
- The paring of as many as 10,000 jobs from GE units sensitive to the slowing economy.
- The "digitization" of GE through the moving of "reams of administrative work" to the Web. As a result, GE expects to save $1.6 billion in 2001 and eliminate 11,000 jobs.

Although on the surface the article seems to be about the elimination of roughly 100,000 jobs, or more than 15 percent of the work force, it is about four very different business challenges facing a major global organization. The business moves along with some of the major HR moves are described in Table 1.2. As can be seen, HR professionals need many skills as part of GE's vast strategic moves.

A look at Malden Mills shows how product and human resource management innovation can be combined. Not much was known of Malden Mills before a mid-1990s story about the factory owner in Massachusetts who, on having his business devastated by fire, pledged that he would continue paying salary and benefits to his approximately 1,000 employees. It took Aaron Feuerstein almost three months to rebuild Malden Mills, and, in the process, he kept his promise to his employees—but this is just part of the story.

Malden Mills has operated as a family-owned venture since President Aaron Feuerstein's grandfather founded it in 1907. It was a thriving firm through the 1970s as the nation's largest producer of carpet pile fabrics, only to see its fortunes turn in the 1980s as a result of a recession and a failed effort to produce and mar-

● **TABLE 1.2**

Business and HR Challenges Facing General Electric

Business Challenge	A Sample of Key Activities Associated with the HR Challenge
Closing of Montgomery Ward	• Being a strategic partner in planning for closing • Using familiarity with laws and regulations to manage the severance process • Determining whether key employees at Ward should be placed elsewhere in GE
Acquisition of Honeywell International	• Being a strategic partner in planning for the acquisition • Identifying duplicated positions in the two organizations and setting in place a process to determine to whom position will be offered • Using familiarity with laws and regulations to manage the merger process • Determining whether excess employees should be placed elsewhere in Honeywell or in other GE units
Job loss due to slowing economy	• Identifying units and positions most impacted by the economy • Determining positions to be eliminated • Using familiarity with laws and regulations to manage severance • Working to bolster the morale of employees being retained
Elimination of jobs by moving administrative work to the Web	• Familiarity with technology and how it can impact administrative process in general and delivery of HR services in particular • Identifying administrative jobs to be eliminated • Driving organizational change, namely the reliance on the Web for administrative service

Source: Adapted from Pamela L. Moore, "Jack the Job-Killer Strikes Again," *Business Week*, February 12, 2001, p. 12.

ket "fake fur." After bottoming out in 1981, when it filed for bankruptcy protection, Malden Mills enjoyed a resurgence through its trademarked Polartec, a popular fabric that is made from recycled plastic soft-drink bottles. A synthetic fleece, Polartec allows skiers and hikers to look sharp and stay warm in freezing weather. Some of the biggest names in outdoor fashion, including L. L. Bean, Eddie Bauer, and Ralph Lauren, sell the Malden product. Malden Mills shrewdly pushed to create brand-name awareness for Polartec, a strategy that has allowed the company to fight off low-cost imitators.[19]

Polartec's brand image enabled Malden Mills to pay above-industry wages to its employees. Workers' salaries average $12.50 an hour, compared with the textile industry's average of $9.50. Malden Mills' labor costs are higher, its energy costs are higher, and its taxes are higher, so it has to rely on high-quality products and a skilled work force; hence Feuerstein's desire to keep his valued employees while he rebuilt.[20] In a recent interview, Feuerstein was asked why he continued to pay workers during the reconstruction. He answered:

> It's the right thing to do because I think a business, yes, must maximize the profitability to the shareholder, but it means something more than that. There is a right way to treat employees; to treat them with respect and not as a pair of hands, and to give them the loyalty and trust that they expect and to treat them as human beings.[21]

How many enterprises have such a genuinely symbiotic relationship between management and employees? Ultimately, organizations that are most successful over an extended period of time are those that are both innovative—as places to work and in the products and services they offer—and profitable. Yet, as seen from the Malden Mills example, innovation does not just happen but requires continual vigilance, flexibility, change, and leadership. Of course, not all human resource management is cutting edge. See A Different Point of View for an alternative view of human resource management.

The general purpose of this text is to explore the range of practices that defines human resource management and its relationship to other organizational objectives, such as quality of the product or service and financial success. This chapter examines some of the general issues related to human resource management, including the following:

- The scope of human resource management
- Themes and perspectives that define human resource management
- Challenges facing human resource management
- Professional opportunities in human resource management

A DEFINITION OF HUMAN RESOURCE MANAGEMENT

Human resource management (HRM) involves all management decisions and practices that directly affect or influence the people, or **human resources,** who work for the organization. In recent years, increased attention has been devoted to how organizations manage human resources. This increased attention comes from the realization that an organization's employees enable an organization to achieve

Blow the Sucker Up

Clearly, this text takes the stance that HR is a necessary function with the capacity to add greatly to an organization's competitive position. While this is the dominant view, it is not universal. In a much-discussed article entitled "Taking on the Last Bureaucracy," Thomas Stewart suggested that most HR departments are 80 percent routine administration with little value added. Stewart's vivid suggestion for HR was:

> Why not blow the sucker up? I don't mean improve HR. Improvement's for wimps. I mean abolish it. Deep-six it. Rub it out; eliminate, toss, obliterate, nuke it; give it the old heave-ho, force it to walk the plank, turn it into road kill.

Stewart's characterization, while accurate for many companies, is the HR department of the past. Consider the situation of a new HR professional. As a first job assignment, she was asked to meet with department managers to gain their perspective on the role of HR. In one of those meetings she is told:

> In this organization, HR does nothing more than churn paper. I call them "the boulder in the road to progress." All we hear from HR is what we cannot do. Somebody from HR is always rattling the old saber about going to jail or getting sued for something. We never hear constructive ideas from them about how to help us better manage our people, develop our talent, build our bench strength, achieve business results, or deal realistically with the people-oriented problems we face on a minute-to-minute basis. It would certainly be refreshing if we had someone in HR who would help us drain the swamp of problems while we fight off the alligators.

To be sure, Jim Goodnight's HR department (see the HR Challenge) is a value-adding partnership that contributes to the SAS Institute at each step of the business cycle, product development, marketing/sales, and customer support. At SAS, HR is not a "boulder in the road to progress"; it is a bridge connecting major sections of the business highway. The value-added paradigm for HR includes the following:

- Focusing on deliverables, such as customer (employee) understanding, operational excellence, and profitability
- Understanding *why* things work in the particular organization instead of just copying what works for others
- Mastering HR competencies, some of which are not yet defined
- Extending boundaries, such as involving suppliers and customers in the design and delivery of HR services
- Measuring the impact of HR practices on the market value, the intellectual capital, or the maneuverability of the firm

The excitement and challenge of an HRM career in the twenty-first century is one of understanding business, understanding what it takes to maximize the contributions of employees at all levels, and bringing the two together. The new HRM paradigm is a true partnership between top corporate officers and senior HR executives to meet the exciting challenges facing the nation's organizations. There is no excuse for the HR alluded to by Stewart in a progressive organization; in its place is the new HR partnership paradigm.

Sources: Thomas A. Stewart, "Taking on the Last Bureaucracy," *Fortune,* January 15, 1996, pp. 105–108; Jac Fitz-enz and Jack J. Phillips, *A New Vision for Human Resources* (Menlo Park, Calif.: Crisp Publications, 1998); Dave Ulrich, *Human Resource Management,* Vol. 36 (1), Spring 1997, pp. 5–8; W. Warner Burke, "What Human Resource Practitioners Need to Know for the Twenty-First Century," *Human Resource Management,* Vol. 36 (1), Spring 1997, pp. 71–79; and William J. Rothwell, Robert K. Prescott, and Maria W. Taylor, *Strategic Human Resource Leader: How to Prepare Your Organization for the Six Key Trends Shaping the Future* (Palo Alto, Calif.: Davies-Black Publishing, 1998).

its goals and the management of these human resources is critical to an organization's success.[22]

The term "world class," meaning ranking among the foremost in the world, is frequently mentioned as the aspiration of organizations. In the context of HRM, world class is indicated by an HR group with a shared vision as to its constituents and how best to serve them. Excellence in HRM is characterized by a service orientation and a willingness to be in partnership with constituents. Specific earmarks of world class HRM include the following:

- Having an HR vision oriented to the strategic needs of the organization
- Having a philosophy and values consistent with those of the organization
- Being seen as a business unit within the firm and operating in the same way as other units: having customers and quality management and so forth
- Being organized in a way that brings maximum service to the customer and maximum motivation to the HR staff
- Having the best HR products available to customers
- Championing HR programs that fulfill the agendas of the HR professionals and customers
- Having an HR vision that is actively shared by the HR professionals in the organization
- Being a proactive, not reactive, group
- Being involved in the key business issue discussions
- Being seen as successfully creating a great place to work[23]

The number of activities involved in human resource management is potentially large, depending on the size of the organization and its needs. For the purposes of the present discussion, human resource activities are organized into six general areas that constitute the sections of this text. Those general areas, along with related topics that constitute the chapters of this text, are shown in Table 1.3.

Figure 1.1 is a human resource management model that illustrates how HRM activities come to bear on an organization's environment, employees, jobs, job outcomes, and organizational outcomes. All these forces are in turn affected by the organization's external environment. Note that the HRM activities in the model represent the sections and chapters of this text as listed in Table 1.3.

A BRIEF HISTORY OF HUMAN RESOURCE MANAGEMENT

The utilization of people, at least in a rudimentary form, can be traced to ancient times. Efforts to best use talents, even though informal in nature, were undertaken whenever people came together in a community. The change has been that during the course of the last century efforts to best manage human resources have become more formal and specialized. The history of HRM can be characterized in two ways. First, as moving through four broad phases: the craft system, scientific management, the human relations approach, and the current organizational science–human resource approach. Second, through the twentieth century time line illustrated in Table 1.4. The transformation to its present form, HR Management, was the result of business and social dynamics of the 1960s and 1970s—the rise of

Human Resource Management: Major Areas and Related Topics

Major Areas	Related Topics
Planning for Organizations, Jobs, and People	
Strategic management of human resources	Human resource management practices for a retrenchment strategy
Human resource planning	Strategic compensation
Job analysis: Procedures and choices	Forecasting the demand for labor
	Career and succession planning
	Methods of job analysis
	Purposes of job analysis
Acquiring Human Resources	
Equal employment opportunity: The legal environment	Title VII of the Civil Rights Act
Recruiting and job search	Affirmative action
Measurement and decision-making issues in selection	Evaluating recruiting sources
Assessing job candidates: Tools for selection	Realistic job previews
	Determining the validity of a selection device
	Interviews
	Selection tests
Building Individual and Organizational Performance	
Human resource development	Principles of learning
Human resource appoaches to improving competitiveness	Training methods
	Total quality management
	Employee participation schemes
Rewarding Employees	
Performance appraisal	Methods of appraisal
Compensation system development	Providing feedback to employees
Incentive compensation and benefits	Evaluating the worth of jobs
	Gain sharing programs
	Controlling benefit costs
Maintaining Human Resources	
Safety and health: A proactive approach	Occupational Safety and Health Act
Labor relations and collective bargaining	Stress at work
Managing transitions	How unions are formed
	Collective bargaining
	Employment-at-will
	Reductions in force
	Career management
	Retention programs
Multinational Human Resource Management	
Managing human resources in multinational organizations	Staffing of foreign plants
	Selection and training of expatriates

● FIGURE 1.1

Human Resource Management Model

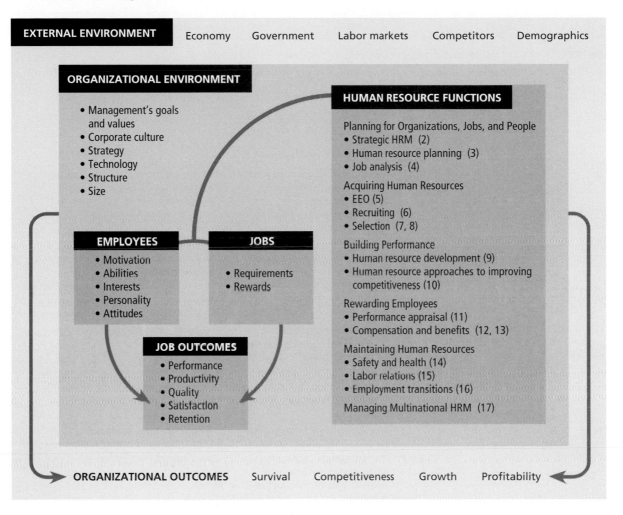

new employment laws and the emergence of organizational science as a guiding force in the workplace.[24]

The Craft System

From the earliest times in Egypt and Babylon, training in craft skills was organized to maintain an adequate supply of craft workers. By the thirteenth century, craft training had become popular in Western Europe. Craft guilds supervised quality and methods of production and regulated conditions of employment for each occupation. The master crafts worker controlled the craft guilds, and the recruit entered after a period of training as an apprentice. The **craft system** was best suited

●**TABLE 1.4**

Evolution of HR Management

Time Period	HR Focus	HR Activity	Example Event
Before 1890	Industrial technologies	Disciplinary systems	
1900–1910	Employee well-being	Health and safety programs	National Cash Register (NCR) forms first personnel department to handle employee issues
1920s	Task design, efficiency, and impact of work groups on individual workers	• Time and motion studies • Employee counseling and testing	Period of scientific management
1930s	• Union of workplace • Passage of major labor laws	• Communication programs • Anti-union campaigns • Personnel becomes staff support to operational line units	Major labor relations legislation • Norris–LaGuardia Act • National Labor Relations Act (Wagner Act)
1940s	Employee benefits and compensation	• Wage increases • Cost-of-living adjustments • Pension, health, and other benefit plans	General Motors and the United Auto Workers sign first contract with "escalator" clause
1950s	• Employee relations • Specialized personnel functions	• Training and development • Separate divisions within personnel established: recruitment, labor relations, training, benefits, etc.	The Hawthorne studies from the human relations movement find widespread applicability
1960s	Employee participation	• Employee involvement • Management by objectives, quality circles, sensitivity training	Peter Drucker's encyclopedic *The Practice of Management* (1954) finds widespread applicability
1970s	Government intervention	Employee rights issues now regulated in areas of discrimination, equal opportunity, safety and health, and various benefit reforms	*Griggs v. Duke Power,* the first U.S. Supreme Court employment discrimination case
1980s	• Employee recognition • Displacement	Enrichment of employee knowledge, skill, abilities through: • Job rotation • Formation of integrated task teams • Outplacement	William Ouchi's *Theory Z* examines the applicability of Japanese employment practices to Western companies
1990s	• Changing demographics of work force • Technology	• Diversity programs • Employees rights issues • Global perspective • Information technology	About 70% of married women are employed, more than double the 1960 rate
2000 and beyond	• Strategic HR planning	Transition from service and support to consultative and leadership role	Exemplified by David Ulrich's book *Human Resource Champions,* which examines the role of HRM in the twenty-first century

Source: Adapted from William J. Rothwell, Robert K. Prescott, and Maria W. Taylor, *Strategic Human Resource Leader: How to Prepare Your Organization for the Six Key Trends Shaping the Future* (Palo Alto, Calif.: Davies-Black Publishing, 1998) and Michael Losey, "HR Comes of Age," *HRMagazine,* Vol. 43 (3). 1998, 40–52.

to domestic industry, which the master operated on his own premises, with his assistants residing and working in the same house.

Scientific Management

The Industrial Revolution and mass production emerged in the nineteenth and early twentieth centuries and led to the deterioration of the craft guilds. The development of mass production transformed the organization of work in two important ways. First, tasks were subdivided into very simple parts that could be performed by unskilled workers. Second, manufacturing grew to such an extent that a large hierarchy of supervisors and managers became necessary. Along with mass production came the assembly line and a scientific approach to an analysis of work in terms of its constituent parts.

The basis of **scientific management** is that there is one best way to do a job. The best way will be the most efficient and therefore the fastest and least expensive. The founder of this new field of scientific management was an American mechanical engineer, Frederick W. Taylor (1856–1915). Two of Taylor's contemporaries, Frank Gilbreth (1868–1924) and his spouse Lillian Moeller Gilbreth (1878–1972), joined in becoming the proponents of scientific management or industrial engineering.[25]

In the decade after 1910, the principles of scientific management were applied on a wholesale basis in the United States. Taylor and his disciples assumed that workers wanted to be used efficiently and were motivated by money. This philosophy proved to be incorrect because it ignored feelings and other motives. Workers were left dissatisfied with their jobs. Union opposition grew as union organizers condemned Taylorism for depriving workers of a voice in the conditions and functions of their work. One result was the emergence of welfare secretaries as organizational employees to oversee programs for the welfare of employees. These programs included recreational facilities, employee assistance programs, and medical programs. The welfare secretary position was the beginning of the professional personnel (now human resource) function.

As antiquated as scientific management seems now, some would argue that many of the basic principles still apply today.[26] For example, the many special incentive systems organizations use to motivate employees and reward performance are adapted from Taylor's ideas. The ideas of scientific management are adaptable, and its basic principles continue to have relevance after almost 100 years.

Human Relations

The first important discovery about the social context of mass production occurred in the famous experiments undertaken by U.S. social scientists Elton Mayo (1880–1949) and Fritz Roethlisberger (1898–1974) between 1924 and 1932 at Western Electric's Hawthorne plant in Chicago. Mayo and his colleagues sought to study the effects of changes in illumination on productivity. The investigators chose two groups of employees working under similar conditions. The level of illumination was varied for the test group but kept constant for the control group. To Mayo's surprise, the output of both groups rose. Even when the researchers told the workers in one group that the light was going to be changed but then did not change it, the workers expressed satisfaction, and productivity continued to increase. Mayo saw that the significant variable was not physical but psychological. The reason for the increase in productivity was the workers' attitudes toward their jobs and Western Electric. Because their cooperation had been requested, the workers now felt themselves part of an important group whose help and advice were being sought by the company.[27]

The discovery of the "Hawthorne effect" led to further research on the social factors associated with work. Results of these studies led to the **human relations movement,** with its emphasis on the fact that employees need to be understood in order to be satisfied and productive. However, the idea that good human relations in and of themselves will increase productivity failed to be consistently supported, and many of the movement's ideas were abandoned.

Organizational Science

Following realization of the limitations of the human relations approach, academic researchers from various behavioral disciplines, such as psychology, political science, economics, and sociology, began studying organizations. The **organizational science** approach focuses more on the total organization and less on just the individual. HRM, as we currently know it, grew out of the organizational science trend and combines learning from the previous movements with current research in the behavioral sciences.

HUMAN RESOURCE MANAGEMENT FUNCTIONS

Within each functional area of human resource management, many activities must be accomplished so that the organization's human resources can make an optimal contribution to the organization's success.

Planning for Organizations, Jobs, and People

● **The Strategic Management of Human Resources**   Associated with the increased attention HRM is receiving is top management's realization that HR needs to be closely integrated with managerial planning and decision making. Increasingly, top management is aware that the time to consider organizational HR strengths or limitations is when strategic business decisions are being formulated, not after critical policies have been decided. For instance, a decision to open a new facility should be made only after considering the availability of labor at the new location and the availability of experienced managers to run the facility. Furthermore, closer integration can result in HR practices that help to elicit and reward the types of behavior necessary for the organization's strategy. Suppose an organization is planning to become known for its high-quality products. Ideally, HR practitioners will design appraisal and reward systems that emphasize quality in order to support this competitive strategy. **Strategic human resource management** is discussed in more detail in Chapter 2 and throughout the text.

● **Human Resource Planning**   The planning process is essential to meet the staffing needs that result when complex and changing organizations encounter a dynamic business environment. The planning process involves forecasting HR needs and developing programs to ensure that the right numbers and types of individuals are available at the right time and place. Organizations depend on what-if scenarios that look at future needs in the context of work force demographics, economic projections, anticipated technological changes, recruitment success, retention goals, and shifts in organizational strategy. Specific **human resource planning** procedures are discussed in Chapter 3.

Careful descriptions and analyses of current jobs are needed to plan for future selection systems and training programs and to ensure that appraisal and compensation systems are rationally based on job demands. The development and use of job analysis information are the topics of Chapter 4.

Acquiring Human Resources

Once HR needs are determined, the next step is filling positions, or **acquiring human resources.** Staffing activities include recruiting applicants, screening and selecting the most qualified candidates, and filling some positions through transfer or promotion.

Staffing is a far more complex activity than in previous times, when employment managers could rely on a "help wanted" sign in front of the plant or recommendations from current employees. Equal employment opportunity (EEO) laws, along with the increased complexity of positions to be filled, require more sophisticated procedures to identify and select prospective employees. The legal environment—specifically EEO laws—associated with organizational entry and progression is discussed in Chapter 5.

The selection process includes several important steps. The first is carefully defining the open position and determining which skills are needed to hold the job successfully. Having determined the specific skills and competencies, employment managers frequently go to great lengths to increase applicant flow, through a variety of recruitment strategies. These activities are the subject of Chapter 6.

The employment manager must then use carefully developed and validated procedures in screening and evaluating job candidates. These may include application blanks, interviews, ability tests, and reference checks, to name a few of the possibilities. Information from several of these procedures is then combined into a judgment of the potential of the applicant as an employee. These activities constitute the measurement and decision-making process in selection, the topics addressed in Chapters 7 and 8.

Building Individual and Organizational Performance

Human resources are unique in their potential to grow and develop to meet new challenges. Many individuals look at the chance to develop and move up as important in where they will seek employment. In order to facilitate employee progression, many organizations choose to spend substantial sums to train and develop their employees.

Employee **training and development** may be implemented by formal or informal procedures. Formal training is often associated with the introduction to a new job; it is also a means of keeping up with technological or procedural changes. Formal training can be coordinated and taught by HR or technical professionals in the organization, or employees may be sent to training programs offered by professional associations or universities.

Informal training occurs on the job and is administered by superiors and peers. The HR department may provide train-the-trainer courses and coordinate on-the-job-training (OJT) opportunities with employee career plans and the organization's forecast of HR needs. Procedures for determining training needs and then constructing, delivering, and evaluating HR development programs to meet these needs are the topics of Chapter 9.

Some organizations undertake other interventions that operate through the human element and are aimed at enhancing productivity, quality, or service. The need to be competitive in a global economy, along with changing demographics and values of workers, has resulted in the realization that traditional ways of structuring work may need to be reconsidered. Recently, some of the most popular HR innovations have focused on improving motivation and involving employees in the decision-making process. For example, many U.S. corporations have implemented quality circles and their more involved successor, total quality management programs. Still other successful organizations are allowing autonomous teams of workers to manage themselves, taking responsibility for the planning, coordinating, and quality control activities traditionally reserved for supervisors.[28] A number of productivity- and quality-enhancing innovations are discussed in Chapter 10.

Rewarding Employees

Performance assessment and management are a crucial link in the HRM process: They are the means by which organizations assess how well employees are performing and determine appropriate rewards or remedial actions. The HRM role in **performance assessment and management** is one of working with line managers to establish performance standards, the performance dimensions to be measured, as well as the appraisal procedures to ensure accuracy. Also included in performance assessment and management are the requirements for the use of results to coach and develop employees.

Another important HR role in the performance assessment and management of employees is to monitor the process and its results. Performance assessment is not a favorite managerial activity, yet it is important that it be undertaken in a timely manner and be done as accurately as possible. Issues relating to performance assessment and management are discussed in Chapter 11.

A logical result of the performance assessment process is determining which employees most deserve rewards. Allocating rewards is a complex and specialized activity. Rewards include both the **direct compensation** (salary or hourly wages) and **indirect compensation** (benefits) that organizations offer to employees in return for their effort.

Intuition would suggest that the higher the compensation an employee receives, the greater that employee's satisfaction would be. Indeed, this tends to be the case, although the relationship is not a strong one.[29] In addition to the level of pay, a successful compensation system is based on fairness: the perceived equity of pay differentials for different jobs within the organization, the perceived equality of pay for similar jobs either within the organization or in competitor companies, and the perceived fairness of the differences in pay between employees who are in the very same job. Employees bring a variety of perspectives to bear in deciding whether they are satisfied with the compensation they receive, thus making the management of compensation a particularly challenging HR activity.[30]

As if this were not enough of a challenge, compensation practices are also affected by legal requirements of equal pay for equal work, minimum wage and overtime provisions, and required benefits such as Social Security. Finally, compensation systems do not exist in a vacuum. They need to be designed to mesh with the strategic objectives of the organization. They also need to integrate the realities of prevailing pay levels in the labor market with an organization's profitability and ability to pay. The general issues related to developing reward systems are the subject of Chapter 12, while specific concerns associated with performance-based reward systems and benefits are covered in Chapter 13.

Maintaining Human Resources

The job of the HR manager does not stop once employees are hired, trained, and paid. Additional issues relate to retaining and maintaining a healthy, willing work force—**maintaining human resources.** The fifth major section of this book focuses on employee health and safety, industrial relations, and the management of **organizational transitions.**

An important source of workplace change has been the desire to promote a safer and more healthful work environment. Part of the concern for health and safety is a result of the Occupational Safety and Health Act of 1970. A second source of such change has been societal concern about exposure to hazardous substances or stress in the workplace. Organizations are taking more responsibility for helping employees deal with problems caused by stress or substance abuse. These issues are discussed in Chapter 14.

A part of the HRM function is establishing and maintaining effective relationships with employees. The process of **collective bargaining** requires unionized companies to negotiate with employee representatives on wages (e.g., base pay, increases, overtime), benefits (e.g., vacations, holidays, pensions), hours (e.g., breaks, cleanup time), and other conditions of work, such as seniority, discipline, and discharge procedures. A unionized work force can be an asset, as evidenced by Southwest Airlines, or a liability, as is the case of Northwest, Delta, American, and United (at the present time).[31] Companies with nonunionized employees generally find it necessary to display equal concern for these issues in order to maintain a positive nonunion relationship with their employees.

For organizations with unions certified to represent employees, the union contract is an important document. Those involved in human resource management must be intimately familiar with the contract and the issues it covers. This familiarity is important both for the contract negotiation process and for using the contract to guide day-to-day HR activities. The topics of labor relations and collective bargaining are covered in Chapter 15.

Another issue of importance to HR managers is **managing employee transitions.** This includes career structures and career planning systems for managing internal promotions and transfers, as well as transitions at the boundary of the organization in the form of exits. Most employees desire some form of career planning or career progression, but patterns of growth and movement over a career have been changing as organizations adopt leaner, flatter structures. In terms of exit, individuals and organizations part company for a number of reasons. Nonvoluntary terminations may occur in the case of underperforming individuals. Acquisitions, mergers, divestitures, or other economic circumstances may require reductions in force, in which surplus employees are retrenched and remaining employees optimally redeployed. Even when unemployment is low, there exists a shifting of jobs because many U.S. companies are still shedding workers; for example, the GE plan to lay off almost 100,000 workers discussed earlier in the chapter or the report of 454,000 jobs lost in manufacturing and services in late 2000 and early 2001 (91,000 jobs per month in a five-month period).[32]

In recent years there has been greater emphasis on the right of individuals to due process, dignity, and self-expression in the workplace. This trend is especially apparent in the case of **employment-at-will,** a legal theory that states that either the employee or the employer can terminate the employment relationship at any time for any reason. Recent state laws and court decisions have limited an employer's right to terminate an employee at will. These changes indicate that an implied contract or promise of fair treatment may exist as part of an employment relationship.

Voluntary turnover of staff is also an important concern for many employers. Employee turnover skyrocketed during the boom of the late 1990s, with many retail and fast-food organizations having turnover rates in excess of 100 percent per year. Talent wars in the high-tech field have resulted in many employees jumping ship. When valued, scarce, and skilled employees quit, work is disrupted, growth plans may be derailed, and extensive costs are incurred in locating and training replacements. Leading employers are now seeking to actively manage the retention process by understanding why employees might leave and acting to prevent or reduce turnover of valuable staff. Career planning, employee retention, reductions in force, discharge for cause, and the associated HR challenges are the topics of Chapter 16.

Multinational Human Resource Management

Chapter 17 extends the concerns of the previous chapters to an international arena through a discussion of **multinational human resource management.** More than ever before, U.S. companies are drawing on and contributing to a global economy. Foreign firms are establishing operations in the United States, and increasing numbers of both large and small U.S. firms are establishing plants and operations outside the borders of the United States. In conjunction with the 1992 formation of the European Union (EU), many U.S. firms entered joint ventures or built production facilities in Europe. Eastern Europe, the Commonwealth of Independent States (formerly the Soviet Union), and Russia are being dramatically reshaped and represent potential international opportunities for firms of other nations, including the United States. China's entry into the World Trade Organization (WTO) in 2001 offers additional opportunities for investment by U.S. firms in that economy.[33] North America is fast becoming an open trade region, as evidenced by the North American Free Trade Agreement, enacted in 1993. Other global expansions are also taking place, including new opportunities in the Pacific Rim and South America, to name a few.

Examples of internationalized corporate operations and their impact on human resource management abound. Many of the foreign automobiles on U.S. highways were manufactured in this country. The challenge to organizations such as Nissan Motor Company is in selecting and training a U.S. labor force to fit the standards and procedures preferred by the foreign parent company. To what extent can or should Japanese HR practices be imported and applied at plants in the United

States? To what extent can or should HR practices of the United States be exported and applied to plants in China?

On the other side of the coin, with over 28,000 restaurants in 120 countries, McDonald's is growing far faster outside the United States than within its borders.[34] For example, McDonald's went from a single location to over 130 restaurants in Beijing in just three years. McDonald's has 58 restaurants in Moscow and surrounding areas, with the Pushkin Square location having the distinction of being the busiest McDonald's in the world.[35] In both countries—the People's Republic of China and Russia—the McDonald's operations are joint ventures with local partners. From an HRM perspective, the objectives of these and other international joint ventures are the following:

- To develop U.S. managers who are ready and willing to work effectively abroad
- To select foreign nationals as employees for these overseas sites
- To develop foreign nationals with broad training and background to assume management responsibility in the overseas locations
- To develop and implement HR policies and practices that optimally merge the concerns of both the home country and the host country

RECURRING THEMES IN HUMAN RESOURCE MANAGEMENT

Four general concerns span all functions of human resource management in organizations: the strategic approach; the increasing globalization of HR activities; maintaining ethical policies and behavior within the organization; and the need to benchmark, measure, and evaluate the **cost-benefit utility** of HR endeavors. These themes are addressed throughout this book in a variety of ways.

Strategic Approach

Business organizations use the resources available to compete with other companies. These include physical resources (e.g., plant, equipment, technology), organizational advantages (e.g., structure, coordinating systems), and human resources. The human resources include the experience, skill, training, and commitment of the employees. It is the allocation and integration of these resources that provides a company with a competitive advantage.

Human resources are directly or indirectly related to all organizational processes and thus are important in allowing an organization to gain and sustain a competitive advantage. To be maximally effective, the human resource management function must be integrally involved in any company's strategic management process. This means that people-related issues should be a primary concern in any organizational decision. Further, an accumulation of important research now demonstrates that when strategically linked, HR practices have an economically significant impact on both employee outcomes (turnover and productivity) and short- and long-term measures of corporate financial performance.[36]

Some of the most interesting aspects of human resource management are not just acquiring human resources, building performance, rewarding employees, and maintaining human resources, but the fusion of these elements with the strategic goals of the organization. In any organization, the challenge is managing the interplay of resources, including human resources, to gain and sustain a competitive advantage.[37]

Chapter 2 examines the process by which organizations respond to business pressures and opportunities and the role of human resource management in this process. Subsequent chapters examine the link between various HR functions and the successful implementation of organizational strategies.

International Human Resource Management

The impact of the dynamic international economy has become a major force in business in general and in human resource management in particular. Much of this book describes state-of-the-art HR practice in North America; however, other nations have sometimes chosen different approaches to dealing with the human side of organizations. For instance, in some countries a condition of doing business is a government mandate on the number of individuals who must be employed. Obviously, this alters many HR practices, including HR planning, selection, compensation, and job design, to name a few. Although interesting in their own right, these varied practices are also important realities faced by multinational firms doing business overseas. Thus many chapters of this text include an International Perspective box comparing HRM practices in the United States with those in other countries. The specific issues of managing human resources in multinational organizations are the focus of Chapter 17.

Maintaining Ethical Policies and Behavior

It has long been recognized that managers have a duty to serve the interests of the business and its owners (shareholders). In the last two decades, however, there has been an increasing realization that profit cannot be the only goal—that managers and corporations have a duty to behave in a responsible fashion toward a set of **stakeholders,** which goes well beyond owners. These stakeholders include customers, the community in which the business is located, employees, and even nonhuman entities such as the environment.

The HR manager has a special role in ensuring that the organization deals fairly and ethically with its employees and that employees deal fairly with one another, the organization, and clients. Some theories of ethics list the duties that human beings owe to one another in general. Although organizations are not necessarily subject to all the **ethical duties** to which persons are, at least some of these duties might be applied to businesses to guide their dealings with employees and applicants.[38] These duties include the following:

- Respecting persons and not using them solely as means to one's own ends
- Not doing any harm
- Telling the truth
- Keeping promises
- Treating people fairly and without discrimination
- Not depriving people of basic rights, such as the right to free speech and association

In organizational terms, fulfilling these duties may translate into the following:

- Instituting careful health and safety practices, informing employees of potentially hazardous working conditions, and taking responsibility for occupational disease and stress-related illnesses traceable to working conditions (see Chapter 14)
- Being truthful in recruiting (see Chapter 6)
- Avoiding the use of invalid and discriminatory selection, appraisal, and advancement systems (see Chapters 5, 7, 8, and 11)
- Providing equal pay for work of comparable worth (see Chapter 12)
- Providing ways for employees to voice their concerns and not illegally constraining employees from exercising their right to form a union (see Chapter 15)
- Following fair policies with regard to discipline, termination for cause, and reductions in force (see Chapters 3, 15, and 16)

Clearly, as an intermediary between the organization and the employee, the HR professional has a large role to play in ensuring fair treatment. In fact, the Society for Human Resource Management (SHRM) has recognized this role by adopting a Code of Ethics to guide the activities of HR professionals. This code is reproduced in Figure 1.2.

The HR function is also charged with protecting the organization from potentially unethical employees. According to the "bad apple" perspective, some individuals are simply predisposed to behave unethically and should be weeded out by the selection process. Applicants who are likely to steal from their employer, take bribes, demand kickbacks, violate the law, or work under the influence of drugs sometimes may be identified by careful background investigation, reference checks, or paper-and-pencil honesty testing (see Chapter 8). More recently, after several horrific incidents, there is ever-increasing concern with violence in the workplace.[39]

Although there is some merit to the "bad apple" perspective, it is far from the whole story. Employees do not make ethical choices in a vacuum or entirely on the basis of their preexisting values and ethical upbringing. Instead, they behave within a context that includes organizational training, role models, formal rules and policies, and appraisal and reward systems. It is the responsibility of the HR manager to ensure that these influences are positive and consistent with the ethical values desired by the top managers of the organization. The Ethical Perspective box lists some ways in which HR staff can help to elicit and maintain ethical behavior among employees. Ethical Perspective boxes in subsequent chapters will raise additional issues of concern to the responsible HR practitioner.

Benchmarking, Measuring, and Evaluating Human Resource Results

Another ever-present reality in today's organizations is the need to strive for the best practices (i.e., **benchmarks**) and to then substantiate the cost-effectiveness of programs, approaches, and policies. HR benchmarking is the process of comparing one's HR practices with those of another firm, particularly a competitor, as a way to outperform the competition.[40]

● **FIGURE 1.2**

Code of Ethics of the Society for Human Resource Management

Source: Reprinted with permission from *HRMagazine,* published by the Society for Human Resource Management, Alexandria, VA.

SOCIETY FOR
HUMAN
RESOURCE
MANAGEMENT

Code of Ethics

As a member of the Society for Human Resource Management, I pledge myself to:

❋ Maintain the highest standards of professional and personal conduct.

❋ Strive for personal growth in the field of human resource management.

❋ Support the Society's goals and objectives for developing the human resource management profession.

❋ Encourage my employer to make the fair and equitable treatment of all employees a primary concern.

❋ Strive to make my employer profitable both in monetary terms and through the support and encouragement of effective employment practices.

❋ Instill in the employees and the public a sense of confidence about the conduct and intentions of my employer.

❋ Maintain loyalty to my employer and pursue its objectives in ways that are consistent with the public interest.

❋ Uphold all laws and regulations relating to my employer's activities.

❋ Refrain from using my official positions, either regular or volunteer, to secure special privilege, gain or benefit for myself.

❋ Maintain the confidentiality of privileged information.

❋ Improve public understanding of the role of human resource management.

This Code of Ethics for members of the Society for Human Resource Management has been adopted to promote and maintain the highest standards of personal conduct and professional standards among its members. Adherence to this code is required for membership in the Society and serves to assure public confidence in the integrity and service of human resource management professionals.

Top management wants to know in bottom-line (i.e., dollar) terms the extent to which the benefits of a policy or program outweigh the costs. Although HR programs can have a significant impact on profits, little has been done thus far to evaluate HR programs in these terms. The benchmarking perspective is basically a method that allows a manager to strive for the best practices and then compare the costs associated with selecting, training, and rewarding employees to the dollar benefits resulting from these efforts. For example, many training programs are proposed and undertaken without examining the extent of increased productivity (benefit) as opposed to the costs of training material, time away from the job for those being trained, salary of the trainer, and so forth.

There is an ever-increasing need for HR managers to speak the language of business and, in so doing, to justify the economic value of existing or proposed programs. The key question decision makers must answer with respect to all programs is this: How can we best allocate our limited resources in the most cost-effective way? As with international considerations, the concept of cost-benefit utility spans all areas of human resource management and thus is considered in many chapters of this text.

ALTERNATE VIEWS OF HUMAN RESOURCE MANAGEMENT

Multiple Constituencies

Although it has been traditional to organize HRM activities by function (such as staffing, compensation, and labor relations), another way to look at human resource management is in terms of the **multiple constituencies** served by the HRM department and what each values as important. The HRM department plays a support or service role in the organization, and, as such, it interacts with a variety of constituencies. (A "constituency" is defined as any group of supporters, customers, or clientele.) At least five internal constituencies can be identified, including the following:

- Board of directors
- Executives
- Managers and supervisors
- Professional employees
- Hourly employees

Constituencies external to the organization include (1) unions, (2) public interest and community groups, (3) regulatory agencies, (4) dealers, (5) suppliers, (6) customers, and (7) stockholders. Except for the first three (unions, public interest and community groups, and regulatory agencies), HR programs generally do not have a direct impact on external constituencies. Of course, there is a potential indirect effect. To the extent that HR programs help ensure the success of the organization, all the internal and external constituencies benefit.

A recent study provides an interesting look at how the HR activities were viewed by managers and HR professionals. Table 1.5 (see p. 26) lists sixteen HR outcomes in order of greatest to least difference in perceived HR impact by managers and HR professionals. Practices were rated on a nine-point scale. Outcomes

How Organizations Encourage Ethical Behavior

 Ethical or unethical behavior is not entirely a matter of the character of individual employees; it is determined at least in part by factors in the organization. People are influenced by the forces surrounding them—their peers, their superiors, the reward system, group norms, and organizational policies and values. Ethical behavior in organizations can be encouraged in a number of ways, many of which involve the HRM department through its roles in training, employee communication, and discipline. In some organizations, the HR department is assigned primary responsibility for managing and monitoring ethical behavior. In others, a separate ethics office takes the lead in this endeavor.

Since a number of defense industry scandals were exposed in the 1980s, organizations have become more sensitive to ethical issues, and many have implemented corporate ethics programs. A further spur to such programs was a set of guidelines issued by the United States Sentencing Commission in 1991. The guidelines introduced heavier penalties for corporate wrongdoing but allow for reduced penalties if the offending organization has made formal, active efforts to ensure ethical behaviour and legal compliance. A well-run and comprehensive corporate ethics program would meet this standard. Such a program should include six components:

1. A formal code of ethics or code of conduct.
2. Ethics committees to develop ethical policy and investigate alleged violations by employees.
3. Ethics communication systems to allow employees to make queries, get advice, or report wrongdoing. Ideally, several means of inquiry will be available (telephone hotlines, e-mail, suggestion boxes, ethical ombudsman, etc.), and at least one of them should permit anonymous contact.
4. Ethics officer(s) and an ethics office to oversee the process and help communicate policy to employees. Ethics Officer has become a recognized job title, and there is now a professional association for such individuals.
5. Ethics training programs to help employees understand the ethical issues likely to arise in their work and how to deal with these issues.
6. A disciplinary system to promptly and decisively deal with violations. Employees expect inappropri-

covered such areas as employee attitudes (morale, loyalty, commitment), behaviors (individual performance, turnover, tardiness, absenteeism), and impact on the firm (customer service, product quality, efficiency). On average, both sets of respondents viewed HR's impact as positive. Interestingly, both groups—managers and HR professionals—viewed HR credibility as the greatest outcome. HR professionals rated the strength of positive impact over 7.00 in six areas. The least positive rating for managers, and the second lowest for HR professionals, was in the area of product quality.[41] This study is illustrative of the range of outcomes on which HR can be judged and the differing perceptions about effectiveness that can result when surveying multiple constituencies.

Strategic Impact of Human Resource Management

Traditionally, the major perspective on human resource management has been a functional one, with HR departments being organized into subunits for recruitment and selection, training, compensation, and labor relations. The multiple-ate behavior to be disciplined. Failure to respond to unethical behavior may lead to feelings of inequity on the part of ethical employees and threaten the entire social system that supports ethical behavior in the organization.

Not all organizations have equally comprehensive ethics programs. A survey in the late 1990s found that 78 percent of responding firms had codes of ethics, 51 percent had telephone lines where employees could raise ethical concerns, and 30 percent had formal ethics offices to foster education and compliance. It is important that codes of ethics be customized to each organization. The company's values and the types of ethical issues likely to arise in its industry should be reflected in the code and in the associated training for employees. For instance, Lockheed Martin's ethics training is based on thirty-four case scenarios representing real problems that have arisen in their organization. When managers conduct the training for their own employees, they choose the scenarios most relevant to their particular work setting.

The vast majority of companies with codes of ethics report that these codes are conveyed to new hires during orientation training. Some companies, such as Raytheon, require an annual one-hour refresher program on ethics for all employees, from the CEO on down. Lockheed Martin reinforces its code with a self-study CD-ROM, an ethics calendar, and a screen saver featuring the company's twelve important values—their "building blocks of trust." Texas Instruments provides employees with ethics training, a booklet, and a wallet card containing a mini-ethics test. The card instructs employees to review the following points before taking an action:

- Is it legal?
- Does it comply with our values?
- If you do it, will you feel bad?
- How will it look in the newspaper?
- If you know it's wrong, DON'T DO IT!
- If you're not sure, ask.

In sum, ethics has become an important issue in many corporations, and HR managers are often at the forefront of efforts to instil and enforce ethically appropriate behavior among employees.

Sources: J. T. Delaney and D. Sockell, "Do Company Ethics Training Programs Make a Difference? An Empirical Analysis," *Journal of Business Ethics,* Vol. 11, 1992, pp. 719–727; G. R. Weaver, L. K. Treveno, and P. L. Cochran, "Corporate Ethics Programs as Control Systems: Influences of Executive Commitment and Environmental Factors," *Academy of Management Journal,* Vol. 42, 1999, pp. 41–57; and S. J. Wells, "Turn Employees into Saints?" *HRMagazine,* December 1999, pp. 48–58.

constituency perspective represents an alternate approach. One way of integrating the functional and multiple-constituency approaches is by looking at human resource management as a vehicle for bringing to reality the organization's strategic objectives.

Many organizational decisions are not seen as affecting employees, but, in fact, they have a critical impact on them. Examples of business decisions made by operating managers and their impact on human resources are shown in Figure 1.3. It is clear that various HR functions would be needed to fully implement the intended action. As an example, the top management decision of a major airline to purchase new jumbo jets will be discussed in detail. The airline has flown the more than 6,000-mile intercontinental route, nonstop from the United States to Asia for a number of years. To serve this route, the airline has used a fleet of Boeing 747–400s, a class of airplane with long range and a capacity of approximately 375 passengers. Business has been good, and projections are for even more passenger traffic in the future. As a result of the importance of Asia as a destination and the business prospects, the airline has decided to purchase four of the new Airbus A380s, the 600-seat to 800-seat "superjumbo" aircraft recognized as the largest

● **TABLE 1.5**

Outcomes and Results of HR Practices as Rated by Managers and HR Professionals[a]

	Mean Ratings by:	
HR Outcomes	**Managers**	**HR Professionals**
HR credibility	7.19	7.74
Employee morale	6.59	7.44
Employee knowledge/skill base	6.81	7.31
Accident and safety record	6.97	7.30
Employee loyalty and commitment	6.41	7.18
Employee career advancement	6.60	7.01
Customer service	6.26	6.89
Firm performance and profitability	6.56	6.84
Employee teamwork/cooperation	6.46	6.82
Individual employee performance	6.38	6.65
Work force diversity	6.55	6.63
Cost reduction and efficiency	6.33	6.60
Employee turnover	6.46	6.60
Tardiness and absenteeism	6.50	6.58
Product quality	6.10	6.45
Team performance	6.46	6.42

[a]Managers and HR professionals were asked to assess the impact of sixteen HR practices using a nine-point scale. Outcomes areas are listed in descending order of perceived impact by HR professionals.
Source: "Ideas and Trends in Personnel," *Human Resource Management,* June 18, 1997, pp. 89–96.

commercial craft. The $220-million-plus flying palace will be spacious enough to feature sleeping quarters, shops, and exercise rooms.[42]

Such a decision has major HR implications that will ripple throughout the organization. To begin with, pilots chosen to fly the new class of equipment, generally the most experienced captains with the airline, will need extensive training on the new aircraft. Of course, this will create training needs throughout the cockpit ranks as other captains move up to more sophisticated equipment, first officers (copilots) qualify as captains, and flight engineers move up to first officer. Cabin attendants will need training in service and in the safety features of the airplane. Ground crews will need to be trained in any new procedures for loading and unloading the airplane. Maintenance mechanics will need training in routine and special servicing requirements of planes previously unfamiliar to them. For purchasing agents, different parts and supplies will need to be ordered to support the equipment. Construction will need to be undertaken to alter the airport gates from which passengers will enter and leave the plane. Marketing representatives will need to know the airplane's special features to promote travel on it. What is not realized is the fact that the seemingly straightforward decision to purchase the new class of aircraft, a sound decision in light of business projections, has set in motion a vast series of HR activities that affects many parts of the organization.

● **FIGURE 1.3**

Strategic Decisions and
Their Implications for
Human Resource
Management

The manner in which HR decisions are made and carried out will have a profound effect on the employees. At the same time, these decisions will affect the long-range evaluation of the decision to fly the routes, the decision on the purchase of aircraft, and the success of the organization. A sound business decision will not be successful if HR difficulties make implementation problematic. The airline will be borrowing over $200 million for each plane and has payments of approximately $20 million per plane each month. If the plane remains idle as a result of failure in the HR chain outlined previously—for example, because maintenance mechanics have not yet completed their certification or too few cockpit crew members have been trained—the cost to the airline is a whopping $670,000 for one day, with no offsetting income. Furthermore, the passengers scheduled to fly that day, all 600 to 800 of them, must make other arrangements and may be reluctant to return to travel on an airline that previously disappointed them.

In summary, there is increased realization of the critical importance of human resource management in organizational effectiveness. Simply put, HRM is the set of functions and activities designed to bring the employee and organization together so that the goals of both are met.

A Political Influence Perspective

Another perspective, which is frequently the topic of cynical discussion, is that of the political considerations that enter into organizational and HR decisions. In this context, "politics" refers to "the methods or tactics involved in managing" an organization.[43]

As Gerald Ferris and Timothy Judge have pointed out, organizations are generally thought of as efficient, machinelike entities.[44] Of course, such is not the case. Politics is the space between the perfect workings of a rational and efficient organization and the messiness of the interaction of people. The greater the gap, the more political tactics become a way of life in achieving job and organizational outcomes.[45]

Such a realization is important for HR managers. Some HR activities tend inherently to be less rational and efficient than others and hence subject to tactics and potential manipulation.[46] For example, contrast HR planning and performance assessment. HR planning involves gathering data in important areas and making assumptions about the future. It is data oriented and one of the more rational HR activities. Consequently, one would expect fewer political tactics to be involved. Performance assessment involves every member of the organization. Although the intention is to be data oriented, the data generally consist of performance information on people and are subject to a wide range of potential perceptual distortions. Yet the impact of how individuals are evaluated has important implications for future rewards and career progression. Therefore, systems of performance assessment and management, unless carefully structured and carried out, will be subject to political manipulation.

CURRENT AND FUTURE CHALLENGES TO HUMAN RESOURCE MANAGEMENT

As we move into the twenty-first century, there can be little doubt that human resource management faces some of the greatest challenges since its definition as a separate staff function almost a century ago. This renewed vigor stems from numerous influences, such as the changing nature of the economy and governmental-legal influences, new organizational forms, global competition, and the increased feeling that organizations are vehicles for fulfilling societal goals. Some of the factors that have forced human resource management to be transformed from a narrowly defined specialty into a more strategic function are discussed in the sections that follow.

Corporate Reorganizations

The last two decades have been characterized by acquisitions and mergers of almost unbelievable proportions as well as other forms of corporate reorganization. Hardly a week goes by without one or more instances of one corporation purchasing another, two corporations joining forces, or companies undergoing massive reorganizations. Each year a new record is set, with one of the current records for a merger being America Online's purchase of Time Warner.[47] The purchase was with AOL stock, which made the value of the deal at $181.9 billion when announced, but closer to $100 billion (still a large amount) when the acquisition was finally consummated in early 2001.[48] In virtually every major industry, the number of major players is shrinking. The reorganizations continue in an effort to improve competitiveness, either by cutting layers of managers and restructuring the work forces or by gaining economies through combining efforts.

As can be seen from Table 1.6, the megamergers of recent years all involve related companies seeking to gain an advantage by entering new markets. For example, AOL's $100-billion purchase of Time Warner is a way for both companies to achieve much greater penetration in the growth markets of telecommunications and entertainment. Other large mergers involved overlapping companies, such as Hewlett-Packard and Compaq, seeking economies of scale through combined efforts.

It is difficult to imagine circumstances that pose a greater challenge for human resource management than the reorganizations that have characterized the last twenty years. Such reorganizations inevitably affect many organizational levels and employees. Furthermore, given the complexities of the situation, decisions may be slow in coming. In the meantime, employees are left wondering what, if any, role they will play in the "new organization."[49] As a result of reorganizations, employees may face these potential changes:

- Loss of job, pay, and benefits
- Job changes, including new roles and assignments
- Transfer to a new geographic location
- Changes in compensation and benefits

● TABLE 1.6
Megamergers of Recent Years

Acquirer	Target	Date Announced	Transaction Value When Announced ($ billions)	Comment
American Online	Time Warner	January 2000	$181.9	Worth approximately $100 billion when consummated
MCI WorldCom	Sprint	October 1999	$127.3	Blocked because of regulatory concerns
Pfizer Inc.	Warner-Lambert	November 1999	$87.9	
Exxon	Mobil	December 1998	$86.4	
American Home Products	Warner-Lambert	November 1999	$76.1	
Travelers Group	Citicorp	April 1998	$72.6	
SBC Communications	Ameritech	May 1998	$72.4	
Bell Atlantic	GTE	July 1998	$71.3	
AT&T	Tele-Communications	June 1998	$69.9	
Hewlett-Packard	Compaq	September 2001	$25	

Source: Adapted from "Big Deal: Ten Largest Mergers and Acquisitions," *Washington Post,* available at: http://www.washingtonpost.com/wp-srv/business/images/topdeals.htm.

- Changes in career possibilities
- Changes in organizational power, status, and prestige
- Staff changes, including new colleagues, bosses, and subordinates
- Change in corporate culture and loss of identity with the company

There is little indication that the pace of corporate reorganizations will slacken in the near future. To a greater extent than ever before, corporations consider reorganizations (acquisitions, mergers, divestitures, downsizing) as routine business transactions. Yet an important key to the success of almost any reorganization is the management of human resources.

Global Competition

A long-term trend with profound and far-reaching implications for HR professionals is that of a global economy. International competition in goods and services is forcing major economies into a global affiliation. Rather than being the dominant economic force, the United States is one of a small (and changing) group of economically strong countries. In addition, the United States is no longer an isolated national economy but part of a world economic community.

The transition has not been an easy one for U.S. industry. For example, even in recent times, the United States had strong textile and apparel industries. U.S. companies supplied many parts of the world with finished cloth products. As competition with Third World countries increased, U.S. manufacturers insisted that their products were superior to the less expensive imports. Consumers soon realized, however, that imported textile and apparel products were as good as the domestic counterparts and also cheaper. The result can be seen simply by examining the labels of the apparel in your wardrobe or of other finished textile products. The U.S. textile industry is much diminished at this time.

What has transpired in the textile industry is an example of a trend toward a global economy. From an HR perspective, this trend has represented a monumental challenge. Relationships between employees and employers have been shaken in industries that have been reduced dramatically in the United States, such as the shoe, automobile, steel, and electronics industries. The readjustment for workers in these industries has usually involved switching from the declining manufacturing sector of the economy to the service sector.

As a response to increasing international competition, many **international joint ventures (IJVs)** have been formed. IJVs are a way for U.S. corporations to have an international presence without establishing a wholly owned subsidiary abroad. An IJV is achieved when a new organization or partnership is formed by two or more companies from different countries for the purpose of conducting a new business. As such, IJVs have become the most widespread form of U.S. multinational investment.

One study identified seventeen HR issues related to IJVs. These issues were categorized into the nine subject areas indicated in Table 1.7. In general, these issues arise from the somewhat different goals of the host and foreign partners or from the different organizational climates or procedures within the IJV and either the host or foreign parent.

● **TABLE 1.7**

HR Challenges Associated with International Joint Ventures (IJVs)

Human Resource Management Area	Example of Human Resource Management Challenge
Staffing	Management at the host country partner may perceive providing jobs for their citizens as a more important objective than increasing profits.
Promotion	Blocked promotion of host country nationals in the IJV may result from reserving top positions for expatriates from the foreign parent.
Loyalty	Because of the multiplicity of entities involved in the IJV, loyalty conflicts may occur.
Delegation	Parent companies limit the delegation of authority to the IJV and/or disagree on the desired extent of autonomy.
Decision making	Decision making is a particularly complicated process because of the conflicting expectations of the entities involved.
Unfamiliarity	Each employee group may experience feelings of strangeness and lack of familiarity with the employees of the other entities.
	Expatriates may be unfamiliar with the environment and culture of the host country.
Communication	Communication blockages can result because of interpersonal problems between geographically dispersed managers.
Information	Information flow from the host or foreign parent to the IJV may be restricted because of suspicion regarding the intentions of the other parent.
Compensation	Dissatisfaction with compensation gaps between host country nationals and expatriates can develop.
	Difficulties in assessing the performance of IJV staff stem from the different procedures and performance standards of the parent companies.

Source: Adapted from Oded Shenkar and Yoram Zeira, "Human Resources Management In International Joint Ventures: Directions for Research," *Academy of Management Review,* Fall 1987, pp. 546–557. Reprinted by permission.

More and more, HR professionals are becoming primarily responsible for helping to make the efforts at business globalization effective. The need to identify and place U.S. employees, mainly managerial and professional personnel, in foreign subsidiaries or joint ventures is one of the important challenges of the global economy. The problems associated with the selection, training, and compensation of expatriate managers will be discussed in Chapter 17.

Cyclical Growth

Cyclical organizational growth as a result of both market shifts and competitive factors has resulted in a redefinition of the workplace. In the past, people entered an organization and then progressed as they gained new skills and as expanded business created opportunities for advancement. Now employees are being asked to prepare for a radical new condition of permanent insecurity—a future full of endless efforts to upgrade job skills, perpetual recombining of work teams, and, when business wanes, sporadic layoffs. The example of approximately 100,000 layoffs by General Electric is a good example.[50] Those GE employees who remain have experienced the feeling of permanent insecurity as they seek to continually upgrade job skills just to stay in place.

At the same time, this is not a saga about rampant unemployment but one about an emerging redefinition of employment. The movement to cyclical growth is a long-term trend that is driven by some of the following changes:

- The use of information technology in place of human resources
- Continued automation, requiring fewer workers
- Flatter organizations, with fewer layers between top and bottom, thus cutting out unneeded managers
- Plant closings to bring production capacity in line with business realities
- Redesigning of the work force to be more flexible, such as by using temporary workers[51]

Clearly, managing human resources in times of slower or negative growth will be a significant challenge for the HR professional throughout our new century.

Increasing Diversity in the Work Force

Another major challenge for human resource management is the changing nature of the work force. Figure 1.4 illustrates the dimensions of **diversity**, with six primary elements at the core surrounded by secondary dimensions. Taken together,

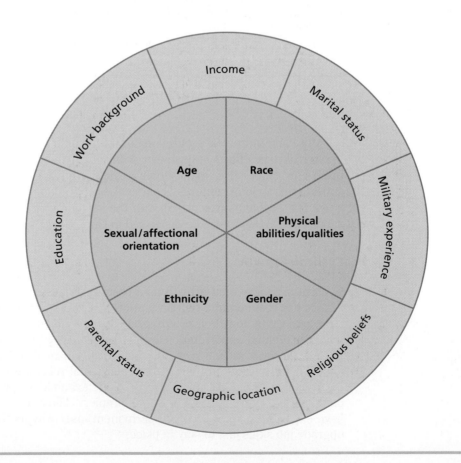

FIGURE 1.4

Primary and Secondary Dimensions of Diversity

Source: Marilyn Loden and Judy B. Rosener, *Workforce America: Managing Employee Diversity as a Vital Resource,* p. 20. © 1991 by Business One Irwin. All rights reserved. Reproduced with permission of The McGraw-Hill Companies.

the increased diversity of the work force has caused organizations to reexamine policies, practices, and values. The important earmarks of the increased diversity are as follows:

- The nature of work has changed, with almost all jobs today being done as easily by women as by men. As a result, the percentage of American women who participate in the work force has increased significantly over time, with the figure now just over 61 percent. This is almost double the rate of participation in 1950.[52]

- Women now account for about 47 percent of the work force and will approach parity with men in the near future.[53] This shift has led to fundamental changes toward family-friendly working conditions and benefits, changes to be discussed in Chapter 13.

- The minority share of the work force will continue to grow from 24 percent in 1995 to approximately 32 percent by the year 2020 (see Figure 1.5).[54] In some regions the minority work force is already the majority. For example, in California, 40 percent of the state population is minority, which means that in many communities blacks, Hispanics, and Asian/Pacific Islanders are already the majority.[55] It is estimated that by 2020, 42 percent of the population will be Hispanic and 18 percent Asian. Whites will constitute only one-third of California's population in 2020.[56]

- Hispanics are the fastest-growing segment of the minority population in the United States, having grown 38.8 percent to 31.3 million between 1990 and 2000.[57]

● **FIGURE 1.5**

Changes in the Ethnic Composition of the American Work Force

Source: From Richard Judy and Carol D'Amico, *Workforce 2020: Work and Workers in the 21st Century,* (Indianapolis: Hudson Institute, 1997) p. 109.

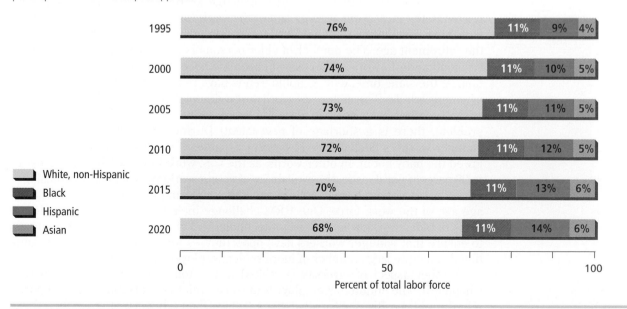

- Asian-Americans, although constituting only 5 percent of the U.S. work force, tend to be affluent and well educated and are outperforming North American whites in the classroom and the workplace.

- Work force demographics are about to implode. By 2006, nearly 80 million aging baby boomers will total a little less than one-third of the U.S. population. By 2025, the proportion of all Americans who are elderly will be the same as the proportion in Florida today. America, in effect, will become a nation of Floridas. In the twenty-year period from 2010 to 2030, the proportion of the U.S. population over age 65 is expected to grow by as much as it had grown in the previous eighty years.[58]

Progress in accommodating employee diversity has already been dramatic, and many readers will think that most organizations have climbed the learning curve with respect to opportunities for the diverse groups that now make up the work force. However, lasting improvements have been slow in coming. How many organizations have women and minorities in executive roles? Even organizations with a substantial record of progress do not have them in significant numbers at higher levels. An example of this situation is the recent concern with the underrepresentation of minorities in managerial roles in professional sports.

Another challenge that has resulted from changing work force demographics concerns dual-income couples—that is, couples where both partners are actively employed. The growth of the number of women in the work force has led to the result that almost two-thirds of families with children have two wage earners.[59] Organizations have been accustomed to using job moves and physical relocation as important means of developing talent. Men or women moving through organizational ranks to upper-level positions need experience in a variety of roles in different organizational units. Frequently, physical relocation has been required. The increasing number of dual-income families limits individual flexibility in accepting such assignments and may hinder organizational flexibility in acquiring and developing needed talent.

Still another trend that is posing a challenge for human resource management relates to the increasing average age of the work force. The "graying of the work force" is a result of two trends. First, legislation pushed back and then eliminated the retirement age. The number of older persons is increasing, and some of them are continuing to work, either out of economic necessity or for personal gratification. At the same time, demographic trends have resulted in a smaller percentage of young adults. The nature of work force demographics was described previously—another baby boomer turns fifty every eight seconds.[60] To compound the problem, there is a shortage of new talent. During the 1990s, the number of younger workers declined by 14 percent because of the lower birth rate that followed the baby boom. In other words, as the U.S. work force continues to grow 15 to 20 percent per decade, the availability of young workers is actually decreasing.[61] There is a shrinking base of college-age individuals and hence an increasing average age of the work force. One HRM challenge includes training to upgrade the skills of older workers in the face of technological change. A second challenge is to ensure that younger workers have opportunities for career growth and promotion despite the large number of more senior employees in the organization.

Another aspect of diversity is related to the topic of affirmative action (see Chapter 5). The notion that employers must commit to equal employment opportunity through positive, affirmative steps (action) has a history of more than thirty years. Despite this long-standing policy, the idea that employers (and educational institutions) must adopt a specific set of results-oriented procedures to achieve equal employment is now being debated in the public and in the courts.[62] For many organizations, affirmative action has become an integral part of their diversity initiatives. Thus the current unsettled nature of the concept is now causing rethinking and readjustment.

Each of these dimensions and trends related to work force diversity can be examined as an isolated aspect of the challenge facing HR managers; however, it is the interconnectedness and dynamic interaction of these forces that is reshaping organizations and how they relate to the work force.

Employee Expectations

As levels of education have increased among the population, values and expectations among employees have shifted. At present, fully one-quarter of the work force has a college degree. The result has been an emphasis on increased participation by employees at all levels. Previous notions about managerial authority are giving way to employee influence and involvement, along with mechanisms for upward communication and due process.

The UPS strike in August 1997 brought to the fore another set of employee expectations, that is, the part-time versus full-time job issue. UPS's HR practices became the vivid illustration for millions of workers who remain stuck in temporary or part-time jobs that pay less, offer fewer (or no) benefits, and offer fewer routes for advancement despite soaring profits, plentiful jobs, and rising wages. Many workers perceive an inherent inequity in their part-time status as employees of companies making record profits.

Another expectation by employees is that the electronics and telecommunications revolutions will improve the quality of work life. Innovations in communications and computer technology will accelerate the pace of change and as a result lead to many innovations in human resource management. In a bold experiment and effort to give employees an intimate feel for this revolution, Ford Motor has announced that it will offer a desktop computer, printer, and Internet access to its 350,000 employees worldwide for a $5 fee. Ford figures that as a result of this program employees will not only be savvier about using computers at work but will also catch on faster to the new instant-gratification mindset among e-consumers.[63]

Finally, employers are taking steps to support employees' family responsibilities. Once able to assume that the demands of male employees' home lives were taken care of by their wives, employers are now being pushed to pay attention to family issues, such as day care, sick children, elder care, schooling, and so forth. One result is that more employees are enjoying the opportunity to work at home.

Organizations as Vehicles for Reaching Societal Goals

During the past two decades, there has been an increasing trend toward viewing organizations as vehicles for achieving social and political objectives. The beginning of this trend was signaled by the adoption of the 1964 Civil Rights Act by the U.S. Congress. This legislation required organizations to deal fairly with minorities—including women and racial and religious minorities—in hiring, promotion, and other aspects of human resource management. Other legislation followed, including requirements that organizations provide reasonable accommodations for the disabled and for employees with the HIV virus. Another law prohibits discrimination against employees over the age of forty. More recently, the U.S. Congress approved legislation mandating such benefits as family leave for the birth or adoption of a child and certain family emergencies. A further issue discussed as a legislative possibility is comparable worth—that is, mandating equal pay for women doing jobs equivalent in value but different in content from jobs typically held by men (see Chapter 12).

Such legislative requirements generally follow a realization that important issues need national attention. As entities within the larger society, organizations are influenced by the ideology and culture around them. As changes occur in the larger society, organizations also must adapt and change. The results of social and legislative changes are added pressures on organizations. HR practices are not formed in a vacuum but must represent the societal ideology in which they are embedded.

All this adds up to extensive economic, social, political, and technological changes that affect what organizations do and the expectations of their employees. Procedures used in the past to handle the human side of business are no longer effective. The net result is a tremendous challenge for HR managers.

JOBS AND CAREERS IN HUMAN RESOURCE MANAGEMENT

Jobs and careers in human resource management can be both challenging and rewarding. The purpose of this section is to examine HRM jobs, typical compensation, and future HRM career opportunities.

What competencies are required if one is to be effective as an HR professional? A recent study has suggested that in the twenty-first century HR professionals will be expected to contribute to the strategic direction of the organizations that employ them by helping to create and sustain the competitive advantage of the firm.[64] The following competencies are considered critical to this expanded role:

- *Business capabilities*—having knowledge of financial, strategic, and technological aspects of business marketing and sales, computer information systems, customer relations, and production capabilities

- *Human resource practices*—attracting and promoting appropriate people, designing development programs, developing effective appraisal programs and feedback processes, communicating organizational and HR policies, and providing a mechanism for integrating different business units

- *Managing the change process*—establishing trust, providing vision, putting problems in the context of larger systems, clarifying roles and responsibilities, encouraging creativity, and being proactive in bringing about change

These competencies represent a mix of skills that can be acquired through education (e.g., general business knowledge, functional HR expertise) and experience. The HR professional of the twenty-first century is viewed as a strategic partner in running the business.

Types of Jobs

Opportunities vary across organizations, and they vary within organizations depending on the level at which one is working. Professional positions can be divided into three categories: HR specialist, HR manager, and HR executive. In addition, there are numerous support positions (e.g., clerical personnel and computer programmers).

● **Human Resource Specialist** **Human resource specialist** jobs are usually the entry-level positions for an HRM career. Included would be such roles as interviewer, compensation analyst, benefits coordinator, job analyst, and trainer. In larger organizations, there may be promotional opportunities within the specialized functions. For example, a new specialist might begin as an interviewer, move up to coordinating college recruiting in a region, and progress to supervising all college recruiting.

Alternately, an entry-level specialist might work in a smaller company or plant as one of two or three professionals providing HR services. In this case, the specialist might do a little of everything. For example, on any given day, the specialist might run an orientation program for new employees, interview applicants, develop information for contract negotiations, or check with other companies in the area regarding hourly wages.

HR specialists typically have formal college training in human resource management or a related area, such as industrial-organizational psychology, adult education, or industrial relations. Some organizations hire business or liberal arts graduates with excellent interpersonal skills to start in a specialist role while continuing their education in an HR program at the master's degree level.

● **Human Resource Manager** The **human resource manager** is a generalist who administers and coordinates programs spanning several functional areas. The HR manager is usually a top-ranked person at a plant or facility and, as such, is expected to be knowledgeable about all areas of human resource management, to oversee the implementation of organizational human resource policies at the facility, and to advise line managers on human resource issues.

Another role for the HR manager would be to head a functional personnel activity at the corporate level. Many large organizations are organized into relatively autonomous divisions. Typically, such organizations have functional specialists at the corporate level to translate corporate strategy into HR policy and to coordinate this policy throughout all divisions. For example, the corporate headquarters may have a manager of affirmative action to develop a comprehensive plan based on corporate objectives and commitments. The manager would then coordinate with divisional HR managers to make sure that plans at the local level are consistent with corporate objectives.

The HR manager is an experienced professional, usually someone who has served in several specialist positions. The individual in such a position will have obtained knowledge and skills through experience but may or may not have a degree in human resource management.

● **Human Resource Executive** The top-level **human resource executive,** usually a vice president of the organization, has the responsibility of linking corporate policy and strategy with human resource management. The top HR executive would also be expected to have input into organizational goals, especially as these goals affect or are affected by personnel activities. It is important to consider HR opportunities and limitations in establishing overall organizational directions.

Compensation for HR Professionals

The Society for Human Resource Management conducts an annual survey of compensation for HR professionals. The 2000 survey included approximately 1,100 organizations with a combined total of more than 8 million employees.[65] The thousands of respondents constitute a cross section of industries, representing both small and large employers, with the largest share falling into the categories of health care, banking and financial services, professional services, and manufacturing. These results are presented in three ways: (1) base pay, also called total cash compensation, for various HR executives (Table 1.8), (2) base pay for various HR managers (Table 1.9), and (3) base pay by company size (employees and revenue) and industry for three HR professional jobs (Table 1.10).

In Table 1.8, average base pay for top HR executives in the respective area is given. On average, top HR executives for large companies earn just over $200,000 (before incentive compensation). Top executives in specialty areas had average earnings of between $124,500 (training executives) and $157,000 (labor/industrial relations) depending on the specialty.[66]

Average base pay for HR managers is given in Table 1.9. Average cash compensation (before incentive pay) for HR managers ranges from $62,600 for payroll managers to almost $100,000 for labor relations managers. Of interest is the fact that labor relations managers are approximately $13,000 above the next highest manager specialty, HR generalists.[67]

Obviously HR pay varies by size of company (number of employees or revenue) and industry. Variations in HR pay are shown in Table 1.10. For example, HR directors average $112,000. This varies from $99,700 for companies with fewer than 1,000 employees to $115,200 for companies with more than 10,000 employ-

● TABLE 1.8

HR Executive Base Pay (Total Cash Compensation)

Top Corporate HR Executive Jobs in:	Cash Compenstation
HR management	$201,500
Labor/IR	$157,000
International HR management	$149,000
Compensation and benefits	$143,200
Organizational development	$141,500
Compensation	$132,900
Benefits	$127,400
Employee relations	$125,200
Total quality	$125,200
Training	$124,500

Source: Adapted from: Patricia Schaeffer, "HR Pay Keeps Rising," *HRMagazine,* October 2000, pp. 78–83.

● **TABLE 1.9**

HR Management Base Pay (Total Cash Compensation)

HR Management Jobs in:	Cash Compenstation
Labor relations	$99,200
Human resources (generalist)	$86,600
Compensation	$86,000
EEO/diversity	$80,700
Benefits	$80,000
HR information systems	$77,800
Employee communications	$77,000
Employee relations	$76,700
Training	$71,400
Safety/security	$64,500
Payroll	$62,600

Source: Adapted from: Patricia Schaeffer, "HR Pay Keeps Rising," *HRMagazine,* October 2000, pp. 78–83.

ees. Interestingly, HR directors average $114,000 in companies with $1 billion to $5 billion in revenue, and just over $100,000 for either larger or smaller companies. Finally, HR directors are most rewarded in manufacturing ($129,000) and least rewarded in government/nonprofit ($87,300). Although average pay is lower, similar variations are also shown for training and employee relations specialists.[68]

Although not covered in the latest survey, other summaries of HR pay have shown that short-term incentive pay (i.e.., bonus pay) is popular in rewarding HR professionals. For example, a recent survey found that the vast majority (81 percent) of top HR executives are eligible for short-term incentive compensation. On average, 55 percent of the HR professionals are eligible for incentive compensation.[69]

Career Opportunities

The career outlook for HR professionals is reasonably strong. The external factors discussed previously—events related to corporate reorganizations, global competition, and changes in work force demographics—represent long-term trends that have transformed the way organizations interact with employees. HR professionals are in a pivotal position in terms of these challenges.

An even more promising trend is the strategic role played by HR professionals. More and more, organizational effectiveness is being determined by the degree to which strategic objectives are formulated in light of HR considerations. This means that HR professionals must look ahead with respect to corporate objectives—whether they involve a new line of business, a possible acquisition, or a new corporate emphasis—and make sure that the HR policy is consistent with the overall objectives.

The increased status of human resource management can be illustrated by tracking HR reporting relationships over the past several years. Ten to fifteen years ago, senior HR executives typically reported to the third level of

● **TABLE 1.10**

HR Base Pay (Cash Compensation) for Three Job Titles

Average Cash Compensation	Selected HR Jobs		
	Human Resource Director	Trainer	Employee Relations Specialist
Overall average	$112,000	$42,200	$55,000
By Number of Employees			
Small companies (<1000 employees)	$99,700	$44,500	N/A
Medium companies (1000–10,000 employees)	$108,100	$46,850	$50,000
Large companies (>10,000 employees)	$115,200	$39,400	$60,100
By Company Revenue			
Small companies (<$1 billion)	$110,150	$38,000	$48,500
Medium companies ($1–$5 billion)	$114,000	$48,650	$57,050
Large companies (>$5 billion)	$110,350	$44,750	$60,050
By Industry			
Banking/financial	$124,800	$40,500	$54,500
Government/nonprofit	$87,300	$38,700	$42,700
Health care	$105,300	$52,000	$54,200
Hospitality/entertainment	$95,600	$45,000	$43,200
Insurance	$102,600	$42,800	$50,100
Manufacturing	$129,000	$51,400	$60,200
Professional services	$117,000	$48,700	$51,000
Retail/wholesale	$105,300	$35,700	$43,000
Telecommunications	$107,300	$42,800	N/A

Source: Adapted from Patricia Schaeffer, "HR Pay Keeps Rising," *HRMagazine*, October 2000, pp. 78–83.

management—for example, to an administrative vice president. Now senior HR managers often report to first- or second-level managers—for example, to the president or executive vice president. Today many senior HR executives are officers of the corporation and represent the HR point of view as members of the board of directors.

Career Progression

● **Entry**   The HR competencies discussed earlier in this section give an idea of how one can build a career in this area. Technical knowledge is essential. For most, the **career entry point** with a college degree is the position of **HR specialist.** Many business schools have a specialization in human resource management, including courses in most of the major areas addressed as topics in this text. One also can major in the social sciences—for example, in psychology, sociology, or economics, perhaps with a minor in business—and then gain further learning on the job as a technical specialist. The Society for Human Resource Management (formerly called the American Society for Personnel Administration) has student chapters at many colleges and universities. Campus chapters of SHRM provide speakers, field trips, and internship opportunities for participating students.

Many institutions of higher education have graduate programs in human resource management. Such a program normally would lead to a master's degree in business, with a specialization in human resource management. A typical curriculum would include courses in business (accounting, finance, marketing, organizational sciences) and graduate-level study in major HRM areas. Frequently, students would be encouraged to hold an internship as an HR assistant for a semester.

A final entry route is as a line employee who transfers into human resource management. After gaining experience as a supervisor, for instance, it may be possible to switch areas and become an HR specialist.

The competition for entry-level HRM jobs is often quite stiff. These jobs attract new graduates, internal candidates, and would-be career changers from other human service areas, such as teaching and social work. The key to getting interviews and landing the first job is experience: Students who have completed one or more personnel internships have much greater success in the HRM job market.

● **Advancement**   Career advancement is earned by gaining experience in the major areas of human resource management and at different levels within the organization. Hypothetical organizational structures within typical HR departments are shown in Figure 1.6. Table 1.11 illustrates how one might progress. These department structures show the different specialist, managerial, and executive roles that might exist in a large corporate environment.

It is not necessary to rotate through all major areas and levels of an organization when pursuing a career in human resource management, although it is important to gain experience in most areas. Progression is not always stepwise, from plant to division to corporate headquarters. It is possible to start at the plant, move to the division or headquarters, and then move back for further experience at the plant.

Certification as an HR Professional

The Human Resource Certification Institute (HRCI), an affiliate of the Society for Human Resource Management, is a nonprofit corporation that recognizes and accredits individuals who have met experience requirements and have demonstrated a mastery of the HR body of knowledge. The levels of **human resource certification** offered by the institute and the requirements for each level are as follows:

- *Professional in Human Resources* (PHR): Four years of professional HRM experience or two years of HRM experience and a related bachelor's degree or one year of HRM experience and a related graduate degree

- *Senior Professional in Human Resources* (SPHR): Eight years of professional HRM experience or six years of HRM experience and a related bachelor's degree or five years of HRM experience and a related graduate degree; the most recent three years of experience must include policy-developing responsibility

In addition to meeting the educational and experience requirements, applicants must pass an intensive four-hour examination to demonstrate mastery of the

● **FIGURE 1.6**

Organization Charts for Typical Human Resource Departments

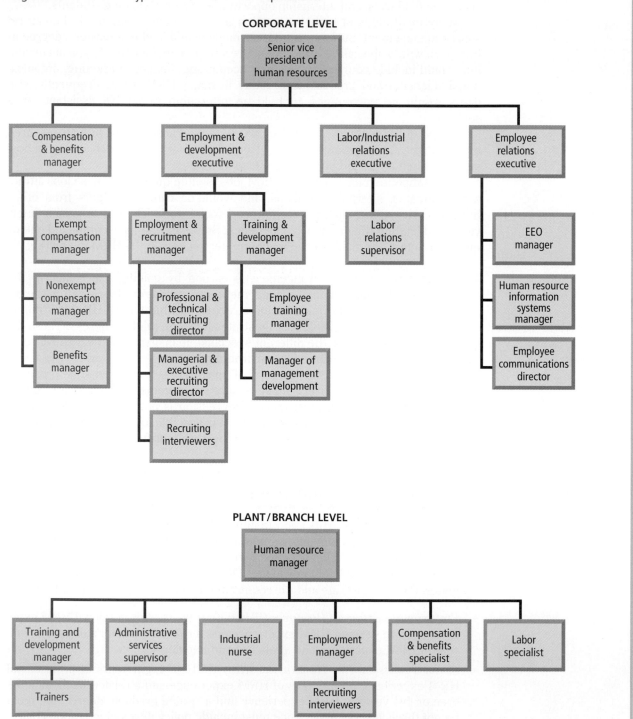

● **TABLE 1.11**

Typical Job Activities in Human Resource Management

Experience Area	Possible Job Activity		
	Plant	**Division**	**Corporation**
Planning	Analyze jobs for compensation decisions	Analyze human resource considerations associated with plant expansion	Analyze human resource considerations associated with new line of business
Organizational entry	Visit technical schools to recruit hourly workers	Visit colleges to recruit graduates	Develop company-wide EEO plan
	Test applicants for hourly positions	Develop affirmative action goals	Develop succession plan for key executives
Developing employees	Orient new employees	Establish quality circle program for productivity improvement	Plan job rotation of experienced managers for further training
	Monitor plantwide suggestion system for productivity improvement		
Performance, evaluation, and reward systems	Apply job evaluation procedure to new job titles	Develop policy for annual wage and salary increases	Plan bonus system for corporate executives
	Supervise performance evaluation		
Maintaining human resources	Resolve employee grievances	Negotiate contract with union	Develop plans for organizational retrenchment
	Conduct exit interviews		

various types of knowledge. The exam covers the six areas shown in Table 1.12. As indicated, the greatest weight goes to general management and HR practices, followed by compensation, selection, and employee/labor relations.

The certifications serve largely to indicate the qualifications of the recipients and ensure the professionalism of the HR field. The certification exam has become popular among professionals. For example, in 1990, just over 2,000 candidates took the certification exam, whereas in 2000, 20,000 candidates completed the exam. Over 44,000 HR professionals are now certified.[70]

Other types of specialist certification are possible. The American Compensation Association, through a series of seven three-hour examinations, allows a qualified professional to be designated as a Certified Compensation Professional. The International Foundation of Employee Benefit Plans, through a series of ten two-hour examinations, authenticates a professional as a Certified Employee Benefit Specialist. The Board of Certified Safety Professionals certifies an individual as an Associate Safety Professional or a Certified Safety Professional (a separate examination for each designation). Finally, the American Board of Industrial Hygiene, through a single examination, certifies an individual as an Occupational Health and Safety Technologist.

● **TABLE 1.12**

Content Areas Covered for HR Certification

Content Area	Example Topics[1]
Strategic Management (12%, 26%)[2]	• Lawmaking and administrative regulatory processes • Environmental scanning techniques • Strategic planning process and implementation • Organizational social responsibility • Management functions
Work Force Planning and Employment (26%, 16%)	• Legal and regulatory factors • Quantitative techniques in HR • Recruiting and staffing • Selection methods • International HR
Human Resource Development (15%, 13%)	• HR training and organizational development theories and applications • Training methods, programs, and techniques • Employee involvement strategies • Performance appraisal and performance management methods • Instructional methods, program delivery, and program effectiveness
Compensation and Benefits (20%, 16%)	• Tax and accounting treatment • Economic factors affecting compensation • Compensation philosophy, strategy, and policy • Compensation and benefit programs • Executive compensation
Employee and Labor Relations (21%, 24%)	• Union representation of employees • Employer unfair labor practices • Union unfair labor practices, strikes, and boycotts • Collective bargaining • Individual employment rights issues and practices
Occupational Health, Safety, and Security (6%, 5%)	• Health • Safety • Security

[1]Topics listed in descending order of coverage within the section.
[2]Percentage weighting PHR and SPHR exams, respectively.
Source: Certification Information Handbook, 1998 edition. Copyright © 1997 by Assessment Systems, Inc. Reprinted by permission of the HR Certification Institute, Society for Human Resource Management, Alexandria, VA.

Summary of Key Points

Human resource managers perform an identifiable set of activities that affect and influence the people who work in an organization. These activities include HR planning, job analysis, recruitment, selection, placement, career management, training, designing performance assessment and compensation systems, and labor relations.

The current challenge of human resource management is to integrate programs involving human resources with strategic organizational objectives. More and more, organizations are under tremendous competitive pressure worldwide. HR managers must find ways to develop effective international programs to meet this challenge. Another important aspect of human resource management is the need to ensure the cost-effectiveness of programs and policies through the optimal utilization of human resources.

Since the HR department plays a support role within the organization, it interacts with a variety of constituencies. It is important to note that the needs of these constituencies are likely to vary. Research offers a useful framework for understanding the conflicting demands on HR professionals.

The challenges to human resource management for the remainder of this century and into the next involve setting directions and formulating policies to address current and future business trends. The challenges of corporate reorganizations, global competition, competitive markets, increasing diversity in the work force, employee expectations, and legal and governmental requirements will allow HR managers to play a dynamic and pivotal role in meeting organizational goals.

Career opportunities are many and varied. The entry-level position is often that of technical specialist. In this role, one would assume responsibility for handling and coordinating well-defined HR programs in a single area. Progression would be to HR manager, a generalist responsible for administering programs across activity areas. The final step would be that of HR executive. In this role, one assumes responsibility for overseeing major areas of activity and for integrating organizational and HR objectives.

The Manager's Vocabulary

acquiring human resources
benchmarks
career entry point
collective bargaining
cost-benefit utility
craft system
direct compensation
diversity
employment-at-will
ethical duties
HR specialist
human relations movement
human resource certification
human resource executive
human resource management (HRM)

human resource manager
human resource planning
human resource specialist
human resources
indirect compensation
international joint ventures (IJVs)
maintaining human resources
managing employee transitions
multinational human resource management
multiple constituencies
organizational transitions
organizational science
performance assessment and management
scientific management
stakeholders
strategic human resource management
training and development

Questions for Discussion

1. What did Mr. Goodnight, CEO of SAS Institute, mean when he said, "The well-being of our company is linked to the well-being of our employees. Employees determine whether we flourish or fail"? What does this say about the role of HRM at SAS Institute?
2. Of Dr. Pfeffer's seven human resource practices indicative of organizational success, which do you think is most important? Why?
3. What is it about Southwest Airlines' success that is so difficult to duplicate? Why?
4. Think of the jobs you have had in the past or expect to seek in the future. What two features of this employment did you (or will you) value most? How can HRM activities contribute to the presence and success of these employment features?
5. If you were the executive in charge of HR at General Electric, what are the first five steps you would take in the goal of paring up to 10,000 jobs from GE units sensitive to the slowing economy? Describe each step and the reason for taking it.
6. Describe the major types of HRM activities.
7. How does the HR function become involved with business ethics concerns in the organization?
8. Should HRM programs have to be justified on a cost-benefit basis? Why or why not? What

problems does the need to justify activities from a cost-benefit perspective pose for HRM?

9. Describe the major constituencies served by the HR function. Why and to what extent do the constituencies differ as to which activities they consider most important?

10. A medium-sized manufacturing company is considering a major business decision to upgrade its technology by purchasing computer-driven equipment. What are some HR considerations that need to be factored into the decision?

11. In what ways has increased international competition influenced human resource management? What types of organizational changes have resulted from increased international competition, and how has the field of human resource management helped achieve these changes?

12. Identify three ways in which HR can add value to an organization.

13. What are some of the factors that have increased the organizational status of the HR function?

14. What do you think will be the two most important challenges to HR managers in the next five years? Why did you pick these two?

15. What types of careers are available in human resource management? What kinds of entry-level positions are available? What should an individual do to prepare for a career in HRM?

16. What are some of the things that make a career in human resources attractive? What are some of the drawbacks? How would a career in HR fit your abilities, interests, and personality?

17. On the basis of your own part-time or full-time work experiences, how do you think the HR function could be improved?

● Case 1.1
Human Resources at Leah's Bakery

While out shopping, you decide to stop in at a friend's business, Leah's Bakery. Leah recognizes you and invites you into her office. She is eager to talk about her work, and in the conversation that follows, she tells you that she is about to mark the second anniversary of what has turned out to be a remarkable business. In terms of the breads, pastries, and other baked goods, customers cannot seem to get enough. On the other hand, Leah has the feeling that she is working harder than is ideal and that the bakery is less profitable than expected. Being a people-oriented person yourself, you pick up on Leah's comment on her difficulty in finding good employees. The following aspects of Leah's Bakery emerge:

1. It takes fifteen employees to staff the bakery for a full week.
2. Leah defines six different positions: two bakers (pastries and breads), one cake decorator, a retail clerk, and a shift supervisor who also works behind the counter.
3. Leah has employed 240 people in the two years of operation. The shortest tenure was two hours and the longest was twelve weeks.

4. Pay for the employees ranges from $6.50 per hour (retail clerk) to $9.50 per hour (shift supervisor). There are no benefits.

Having 240 employees within a two-year period seems to you extraordinary; it represents an 800 percent turnover—equivalent to a new set of employees every six weeks. Yet the information Leah has provided jibes with your observations. Even though you visit the bakery at least once a week, you seldom see familiar faces. The "help wanted" sign is a permanent fixture in the front window. On several occasions, you have even seen the shift supervisor interviewing applicants at the end of the counter. As a frequent customer, you have noticed that the employees are pleasant and are obviously trying their best. At the same time, they frequently do not appear to understand certain common aspects of their jobs—for example, the functions of the cash register, how to enter special orders, the schedule for baking, ingredients of special items, and so forth.

1. What are some possible causes of the high turnover Leah's Bakery is experiencing?

2. If you were asked to help put human resources on a more even footing, on what HR activities would you concentrate?

3. What are three or four human resource programs Leah could implement to reduce the high turnover?

● Exercise 1.1
Human Resource Management in the News

Divide the class into groups of three or four students each. Assign one of the following types of publications to each group:

- **Business magazines** *Business Week* (last three months), *Fortune* (last three months), *Harvard Business Review* (last six issues)
- **Newspapers** (last two weeks) *Wall Street Journal, New York Times,* or other major daily newspaper
- **News magazines** (last three months) *Time, U.S. News & World Report, Newsweek*

Each group is to go to the library and search the assigned sources for the following:

1. Articles directly relevant to HRM, such as layoffs, union activities, recruiting and selection practices, employment law developments, compensation practices, training and development programs, productivity improvement techniques, turnover, performance appraisal, discipline and discharge, and so forth
2. Articles about aspects of the environment that have indirect implications for HRM, such as changing social values, demographics, technological change, trends in the economy, and so on

Each group of students should then organize its materials and prepare an oral summary of what it has found. (Presentation materials, such as PowerPoint, flip chart pads, and/or blank overhead transparencies and markers, should be made available to students in each group as they prepare their presentation.)

International Option Additional groups may be assigned to search recent English-language publications from a specific country or geographic region. Their task would be to look for articles related to human resource management that might be of interest to a multinational organization with operations in the target country or region. The following are examples of regions and sources:

- **Europe** *London Times, International Herald Tribune;* major English-language dailies in France, Germany, Spain, and other countries
- **Pacific Rim** *Asian Wall Street Journal, Asian Business Week, Far Eastern Economic Review;* major English-language dailies in Tokyo, Hong Kong, Taiwan, Singapore, and Seoul
- **Australia** *The Australian* (newspaper), *Business Review Weekly*

Presentation Option 1: Time permitting, each group will make a five- to seven-minute presentation of its findings to the entire class.

Presentation Option 2: Combine groups into triads (quartets if international groups were formed), each triad consisting of a newspaper group, a business magazine group, and a news magazine group (and an international group). Each triad (quartet) should move to a separate room (or corner of the classroom). Then each group should present its summary to the other groups in the triad (quartet).

● Exercise 1.2
Jobs in Human Resource Management

Form the class into groups of four to five students each. Read the brief descriptions of different human resource management jobs given below. In groups, discuss the following questions:

1. Which job does each of you prefer, and why?
2. What do you see as the advantages and disadvantages of each job?
3. What skills, experience, and formal education would be needed to do each job well?
4. How do you suppose each job has changed in the past thirty years? How might each change further between now and 2015?

Manager, Human Resources Plans and carries out policies relating to all phases of HR activity: Recruits, interviews, and selects employees to fill vacant positions. Plans and conducts new employee orientation to foster positive attitude toward company goals. Keeps record of insurance coverage, pension plan, and personnel transactions, such as hires, promotions, transfers, and terminations. Investigates accidents and prepares reports for insurance carrier. Conducts wage survey within labor market to determine competitive wage rate. Prepares budget of HR operations. Meets with shop stewards and supervisors to resolve grievances. Writes separation notices for employees separating with cause. Conducts exit interviews to determine reasons behind voluntary separations. Prepares reports and recommends procedures to reduce absenteeism and turnover. Represents company at HR-related hearings and investigations. Contracts with outside suppliers to provide employee services, such as canteen, transportation, or relocation service. May prepare budget of HR operations using computer terminal. May administer manual and dexterity tests to applicants. May supervise clerical workers. May keep records of hired employee characteristics for governmental reporting purposes. May negotiate collective-bargaining agreement with business representative, labor union.

Manager, Compensation (Alternate Title: Wage and Salary Administrator) Manages compensation program in establishment: Directs development and application of techniques of job analysis, job descriptions, evaluations, grading, and pricing in order to determine and record job factors and to determine and convert relative job worth into monetary values to be administered according to pay-scale guidelines and policy. Analyzes company compensation policies, government regulations concerning payment of minimum wages and overtime pay, prevailing rates in similar organizations and industries, and agreements with labor unions, in order to comply with legal requirements and to establish competitive rates designed to attract, retain, and motivate employees. Recommends compensation adjustments according to findings, utilizing knowledge of prevailing rates of straight-time pay, types of wage incentive systems, and special compensation programs for professional, technical, sales, supervisory, managerial, and executive personnel. Approves merit increases permitted within budgetary limits and according to pay policies. Duties may also include administration of employee benefits program.

Manager, Employment (Alternate Title: Employment Supervisor) Manages employment activities of establishment: Plans and directs activities of staff workers concerned with such functions as developing sources of qualified applicants, conducting screening interviews, administering tests, checking references and background, evaluating applicants' qualifications, and arranging for preliminary indoctrination and training for newly hired employees. Keeps records and compiles statistical reports concerning recruitment, interviews, hires, transfers, promotions, terminations, and performance appraisals, utilizing knowledge of job requirements, valid selection processes, and legislation concerning equal employment practices. Coordinates employment activities, such as those concerned with preparing job requisitions; interviewing, selecting, and hiring candidates; conducting on-the-job indoctrination and additional training; providing supervisory follow-up, development, and rating of employees; and conducting exit interviews. Analyzes statistical data and other reports concerning all aspects of employment function in order to identify and determine causes of personnel problems and to develop and present recommendations for improvement of establishment's employment policies, processes, and practices.

Manager, Labor Relations (Alternate Title: Labor Relations Representative) Manages labor relations program of organization: Analyzes collective-bargaining agreement to develop interpretation of intent, spirit, and terms of contract. Advises management and union officials in development, application, and interpretation of labor relations policies and practices, according to policy formulated by the industrial relations director. Arranges and schedules meetings between workers with grievances, supervisory and managerial personnel, and the labor union's business representative to investigate and resolve grievances. Prepares statistical reports, using records of actions taken concerning grievances, arbitration and mediation cases, and related labor relations activities, in order to identify problem areas. Monitors implementation of policies concerning wages, hours, and working conditions, in order to ensure compliance with terms of labor contract. Furnishes information, such as reference documents and statistical data concerning labor legislation, labor-market conditions, prevailing union and management practices, wage and salary surveys, and employee benefits programs, for use in review of current contract provisions and proposed changes. May represent management in labor contract negotiations. May supervise employees and be known as Labor Relations Supervisor. May be employed by firm offering labor relations advisory services to either management or labor and be known as Labor Relations Consultant. May be employed by governmental agency to study, interpret, and report on relations between management and labor and be known as Industrial Relations Representative.

Training Representative (Alternate Title: Training Instructor) Develops and conducts training programs for employees of industrial, commercial, service, or government establishment: Confers with management to gain knowledge of work situation requiring training for employees to better understand changes in policies, procedures, regulations, and technologies. Formulates teaching outline and determines instructional methods, utilizing knowledge of specific training needs and effectiveness of such methods as individual training, group instruction, lectures, demonstrations, conferences, meetings, and workshops. Selects or develops teaching aids, such as training handbooks, demonstration models, multimedia visual aids, computer tutorials, and reference works. Conducts training sessions covering specified areas such as those concerned with new employee orientation, on-the-job training, use of computers and software, apprenticeship programs, sales techniques, health and safety practices, public relations, refresher training, promotional development, upgrading, retraining of displaced workers, and leadership development. Tests trainees to measure progress and to evaluate effec-

tiveness of training. May specialize in developing instructional software.

Employment Interviewer (Alternate Title: Placement Interviewer) Interviews job applicants to select people meeting employer qualifications: Reviews employment applications and evaluates work history, education and training, job skills, compensation needs, and other qualifications of applicants. Records additional knowledge, skills, abilities, interests, test results, and other data pertinent to selection and referral of applicants. Reviews job orders and matches applicants with job requirements, utilizing manual or computerized file search. Informs applicants of job duties and responsibilities, compensation and benefits, work schedules and working conditions, company and union policies, promotional opportunities, and other related information. Refers selected applicants to person placing job order, according to policy of organization. Keeps records of applicants not selected for employment. May perform reference and background checks on applicants. May refer applicants to vocational counseling services. May conduct or arrange for skills, intelligence, or psychological testing of applicants. May evaluate selection and placement techniques by conducting research or follow-up activities and conferring with management and supervisory personnel. May specialize in interviewing and referring certain types of personnel, such as professional, technical, managerial, clerical, and other types of skilled or unskilled workers. May search for and recruit applicants for open positions. May contact employers in writing, in person, or by telephone to solicit orders for job vacancies for clientele or for specified applicants and record information about job openings on job order forms to describe duties, hiring requirements, and related data.

Job Analyst (Alternate Title: Personnel Analyst) Collects, analyzes, and prepares occupational information to facilitate personnel, administration, and management functions of organization: Consults with management to determine type, scope, and purpose of study. Studies current organizational occupational data and compiles distribution reports, organization and flow charts, and other background information required for study. Observes jobs and interviews workers and supervisory personnel to determine job and worker requirements. Analyzes occupational data, such as physical, mental, and training requirements of jobs and workers, and develops written summaries, such as job descriptions, job specifications, and lines of career movement. Utilizes developed occupational data to evaluate or improve methods and techniques for recruiting, selecting, promoting, evaluating, and training workers and administration of related personnel programs. May specialize in classifying positions according to regulated guidelines to meet job classification requirements of civil service system and be known as Position Classifier.

● Exercise 1.3
Professional Ethics

Figure 1.2 gives the Code of Ethics of the Society for Human Resource Management. Using an Internet browser (e.g., Netscape or Internet Explorer), examine the codes of ethics of two of the three professions listed at right that also serve business or nonprofit organizations.

After examining the SHRM Code of Ethics and those of two of the professions listed, answer the following questions:

1. What are the similarities in these codes to that of the SHRM?
2. What are the differences?
3. Using the codes of other professionals, what changes would you suggest for the SHRM?

Profession	Internet Address for Code of Ethics
Environmental professionals	*http://www.customcpu.com/ professionalscommercial/ aaep/code.htm*
Industrial hygienists	*http://www.aiha.org/ ethics.html*
International Webmaster Association	*http://www.iwanet.org/about/ ethics.html*

Notes and References

1. Robert Levering and Milton Moskowitz, "100 Best Companies to Work For," *Fortune,* January 8, 2001, pp. 148–159.
2. Cited in Nicholas Stein, "Invasion of the Body Snatchers: Winning the War to Keep Top Talent," *Fortune,* May 29, 2000, pp. 132–138.
3. Cited in Levering and Moskowitz, "100 Best Companies to Work For."
4. "Our Company" available at: http://www.sas.com/corporate/index.html
5. "Overworked and Overpaid: The American Manager," *The Economist,* January 28, 1999, pp. 55–56.
6. Levering and Moskowitz, "100 Best Companies to Work For."
7. Jay B. Barney and Patrick M. Wright, "On Becoming a Strategic Partner: The Role of Human Resources in Gaining Competitive Advantage," *Human Resource Management,* Vol. 37 (1), 1998, pp. 31–46.
8. Jeffrey Pfeffer, *The Human Equation: Building Profits by Putting People First.* (Boston: Harvard Business School Press, 1998).
9. Jeffrey Pfeffer and John F. Veiga, "Putting People First for Organizational Success," *Academy of Management Executive,* Vol. 13 (2), 1999, pp. 37–48.
10. See also, Fred Reichheld, *Loyalty Rules! How Today's Leaders Build Lasting Relationships.* (Boston: Harvard Business School Press, 2001).
11. Cited in "The Southwest Train," *USA Today,* December 12, 2000, pp. 9–10.
12. Ibid.
13. Joanne Cole, "Flying High at Southwest," *HR Focus,* May 1998, Vol. 75 (5), p. 8.
14. Brad Foss, "Low-Fare Carriers Rebounding: Low-Fare Carriers Growing While Biggest Airlines Remain in a Funk After Sept. 11," December 14, 2001. Available at: http://biz.yahoo.com/apf/011214/airlines_low_cost_1.html
15. H. Kelleher, "A Culture of Commitment," *Leader to Leader,* 1997, Vol. (1), p. 23.
16. Cole, "Flying High at Southwest"; and Pfeffer, *The Human Equation.*
17. "Future Challenges and Opportunities for the HR Profession," *HRMagazine,* Vol. 43 (3), 1998, pp. 69–75.
18. Pamela L. Moore, "Jack the Job-Killer Strikes Again," *Business Week,* February 12, 2001, p. 12.
19. "Malden Mills: What a Great Place to Work," *National Association of Working People,* November 28, 1997. (Available at:

http://www.beachworks.com/nawptest/greatplace/maldcn.html)

20. Shelly Donald Coolidge, " 'Corporate Decency' Prevails at Malden Mills," *Christian Science Monitor*, March 28, 1996. (Available at: http://plweb.csmonitor.com/plweb-turbo/cgi-bin/fastweb?getdoc+plain1+archives+171374+0++Malden%20Mills)

21. Cited in Susan Stamberg, "Loyalty at Work," *Morning Edition*, March 20, 2001. (Available at: http://search.npr.org/cf/cmn/cmnpd01fm.cfm?PrgDate=3%2F20%2F2001&PrgID=3)

22. Dave Ulrich, "Judge Me More by My Future Than by My Past," *Human Resource Management*, Vol. 36 (1), Spring 1997, pp. 5–8.

23. Dave Ulrich, *Human Resource Champions* (Cambridge, Mass.: Harvard Business School Press, 1997).

24. William J. Rothwell, Robert K. Prescott, and Maria W. Taylor, *Strategic Human Resource Leader: How to Prepare Your Organization for the Six Key Trends Shaping the Future* (Palo Alto, Calif.: Davies-Black Publishing, 1998).

25. Edwin A. Locke, "The Ideas of Frederick W. Taylor: An Evaluation," *Academy of Management Review*, January 1982, pp. 14–24.

26. Michael Freeman, "Scientific Management: 100 Years Old; Poised for the Next Century," *Sam Advanced Management Journal*, Spring 1996, pp. 35–41.

27. Fritz J. Roethlisberger and William J. Dickson, *Management and the Worker* (Cambridge, Mass.: Harvard University Press, 1939).

28. David I. Levine, *Reinventing the Workplace: How Business and Employees Can Both Win* (Washington, D.C.: Brookings Institution, 1995).

29. H. G. Heneman III, "Pay Satisfaction," in *Research in Personnel and Human Resources Management*, Vol. 3, ed. K. Rowland and J. Ferris (Greenwich, Conn.: JAI Press, 1985).

30. R. W. Scholl, E. A. Cooper, and J. F. McKenna, "Referent Selection in Determining Equity Perceptions: Differential Effects on Behavioral and Attitudinal Outcomes," *Personnel Psychology*, Vol. 40, 1987, pp. 113–124.

31. George Edmonson, "Bush's Weight Felt in Airline Affairs Unprecedented Vow: His Determination to Keep 'Strikes from Happening' Loomed Large in Talks with Delta Pilots," *The Atlanta Journal-Constitution*, April 24, 2001, p. D–4.

32. Moore, "Jack the Job-Killer Strikes Again"; and "Will the Smokestack Slump Spread?" *Standard & Poor's Global Report*, March 9, 2001. (Available at http://www.businessweek.com/investor/content/mar2001/pi2001039_044.htm

33. "China's Economic Power," *The Economist*, March 10, 2001, p. 23–25.

34. McDonald's Worldwide Corporate Site. (Available at: http://www.mcdonalds.com/corporate/index.html) Of interest, The McDonald's worldwide corporate site notes that despite their global presence, "On any day, even as the market leader, McDonald's serves less than one percent of the world's population." (You can be sure, McDonald's looks at this as a tremendous opportunity, 1 percent down and 99 percent to go.)

35. McDonald's Worldwide Corporate Site. (Available at: http://www.mcdonalds.com/countries/russia/index.html)

36. Mark A. Huselid, "The Impact of Human Resource Management Practices on Turnover, Productivity, and Corporate Financial Performance," *Academy of Management Journal*, Vol. 38 (3), 1995, pp. 635–672; John T. Delaney and Mark A. Huselid, "The Impact of Human Resource Management Practices on Perceptions of Organizational Performance," *Academy of Management Journal*, Vol. 39 (4), 1996, pp. 649–696; and Mark A. Huselid, Susan E. Jackson, and Randall S. Schuler, "Technical and Strategic Human Resource Management Effectiveness as Determinants of Firm Performance," *Academy of Management Journal*, Vol. 40 (1), 1997, pp. 171–188.

37. Pfeffer, *The Human Equation;* Reichheld, *Loyalty Rules!*

38. Kenneth Goodpaster and John B. Matthews, Sr., "Can a Corporation Have a Conscience?" *Harvard Business Review*, January–February 1982, pp. 132–141.

39. Mary Williams Walsh, "Lessons from the Battle to End Workplace Violence," *New York Times*, December 31, 2000. (Available at: http://www.nytimes.com/2000/12/31/business/31FIVE.html)

40. Dave Ulrich, "Benchmarking and Competitor Analysis," in *The Blackwell Encyclopedic Dictionary of Human Resource Management* (Oxford, U.K.: Blackwell, 1997).

41. "Ideas and Trends in Personnel," *Human Resource Management*, June 18, 1997, pp. 89–96.

42. John Rossant, "Airbus: Birth of a Giant," *Business Week* (International Edition), July 10, 2000. (Available at: http://www.businessweek.com:/2000/00_28/b3689015.htm)

43. *The American Heritage Dictionary*, 3d ed. (Boston: Houghton Mifflin, 1992).

44. Gerald R. Ferris and Timothy A. Judge, "Personnel/ Human Resources Management: A Political Influence Perspective," *Journal of Management*, Vol. 17(2), 1991, pp. 447–488.

45. Pamela L. Perrewé, Gerald R. Ferris, Dwight D. Frink, and William P. Anthony, "Political Skill: An Antidote for Workplace Stressors," *The Academy of Management Executive*, Vol. 14 (3), 2000, pp. 115–123.

46. Ferris and Judge, "Personnel/Human Resources Management."

47. "The Net Gets Real," *The Economist*, January 13, 2000, pp. 22–24.

48. "The Great Merger Wave Breaks," *The Economist*, January 25, 2001, pp. 59–60.

49. Matthew Boyle, "Gearing Down: The Not-So-Fine Art of the Layoff," *Fortune*, March 19, 2001, pp. 209–210.

50. Moore, "Jack the Job-Killer Strikes Again."

51. Joseph F. Coats, Jennifer Jarratt, and John B. Mahaffie, *Future Work: Seven Critical Forces Reshaping Work and the Work Force in North America* (San Francisco: Jossey-Bass, 1990).

52. Richard W. Judy and Carol D'Amico, *Workforce 2020: Work and Workers in the 21st Century*. (Indianapolis: Hudson Institute, 1997), p. 53; and "The Employment Situation," U.S. Department of Labor, Bureau of Labor Statistics. (Available at: http://stats.bls.gov/news.release/empsit.toc.htm)

53. "The Employment Situation," U.S. Department of Labor, Bureau of Labor Statistics. (Available at: http://stats.bls.gov/news.release/empsit.toc.htm)

54. Judy and D'Amico, *Workforce 2020*, p. 108.

55. "State-by-State Breakdown of Population Estimates," CNN.com, August 29,2000. (Available at http://www.cnn.com/2000/US/08/29/minority.growth.glance.ap/index.html)

56. Judy and D'Amico, *Workforce 2020*, p. 108.

57. "Census Figures Show Dramatic Growth in Asian, Hispanic Populations," August 30, 2000. (Available at: http://www.cnn.com/2000/US/08/30/minority.population/)

58. Watson Wyatt Worldwide, *A Nation of Floridas.* (Available at: http://www.watsonwyatt.com/homepage/us/res/workmgmt1-tm.htm)

59. U.S. Department of Commerce, *Statistical Abstract of the United States: 2000.* (Washington: U.S. Government Printing Office, 2000), Table 655.

60. Watson Wyatt Worldwide, *A Nation of Floridas.* (Available at: (http://www.watsonwyatt.com/homepage/us/res/workmgmt1-tm.htm)

61. Ibid.

62. Theresa Forsman, "Affirmative Action's Latest, Greatest Challenge," *Business Week*, April 9, 2001. Available at: http://www.businessweek.com/smallbiz/content/apr2001/sb2001049_420.htm

63. Kathleen Kerwin, Peter Burrows, and Dean Foust. "Workers of the World, Log On," *Business Week*, February 21, 2000, p. 52.

64. Karen E. May, "Work in the 21st Century: The Changing Role of Human Resources," *The Industrial-Organizational Psychologist*, Vol. 35 (3), January 1998, pp. 28–31.

65. Patricia Schaeffer, "HR Pay Keeps Rising," *HR Magazine*, October 2000, pp. 78–83.

66. Ibid.

67. Ibid.

68. Ibid.

69. Mark J. Avery, "Rising Salaries Reflect HR's New Role," *HR Magazine*, November 1997, pp. 87–92.

70. Human Resource Certification Institute. (Available at: http://www.shrm.org/foundation/directory/default.asp?page=human.htm)

Planning for Organizations, Jobs, and People

Strategic Human Resource Management

HR Challenge

Uluru Energy is a seventy-five-year-old Australian public utility company that supplies electrical power to a large region of central and northwestern Australia. There are 500 Uluru employees. The company generates the bulk of its energy supplies from burning locally produced coal. Like many utility firms around the world, Uluru has experienced a long period in which most of its operations have been heavily regulated by the Australian federal government, and it has enjoyed the role of sole provider of power in its region. Following the early pattern set by the firm's first CEO, Oliver Bourke, the management of Uluru is paternalistic, hierarchical, and bureaucratic. There are ten hierarchical levels between the lowest-level utility worker and the CEO. The firm has tended to fill vacant job positions from within the firm, hiring externally only for entry-level positions or for jobs that require highly specialized training and experience that cannot be gained readily from on-the-job training at Uluru. Because of its highly regulated and comfortable market position, Uluru has been able to provide essentially lifetime employment for most of its employees.

Uluru is a heavily unionized firm, with the Australian Public Utility Workers' Union (APUWU) representing 90 percent of nonmanagerial staff. Wages paid to most of the staff at Uluru are based on national "award wages" determined by negotiations between the federal government and national officials of the APUWU. These awards apply to workers in all public utility companies throughout the country.

Thanks to this highly stable environment, the role of the human resources department at Uluru Energy primarily has been that of a bureaucratic administrator, making sure that all government rules and regulations are followed, administering the highly structured pay system, conducting very focused job-related training programs for employees, managing employee health and safety programs, and screening applicants for the relatively few entry-level positions that come available each year. The implicit philosophy of the HR department is "everyone gets treated exactly the same." There are no incentive pay schemes operating at Uluru, nor is there a performance appraisal system, since most wages and other working conditions are strictly set by national wage awards or historical precedent in the case of managerial employees.

Each year for as long as anyone at the firm can remember, Uluru has posted a nice profit. Nothing brilliant, but sizable enough to make everyone in the firm have a warm and somewhat arrogant sense of contentment and satisfaction with their organization. Unfortunately for Uluru, this stable business environment is about to change dramatically, with the election of the new John Boward government. One of the primary election pledges of Mr. Boward was to establish a new industrial relations and business environment in Australia. Among the hallmarks of the government's new policies are the full or partial privatization of public utilities and the establishment of an "enterprise bargaining" process in labor negotiations. Enterprise bargaining allows individual firms to negotiate labor contracts with their own employees (as they do in the United States), rather than having wages and other working conditions set by national government union negotiations. Pay incentive schemes tied to productivity levels, profit-sharing programs, and other forms of compensation systems will become possible under enterprise bargaining. Downsizing and other types of organizational reengineering are also likely to be integral parts of the new Australian business environment.

Jeff Bennett, CEO of Uluru Energy, has received a call from John Boward. Prime Minister Boward informs Jeff that 51 percent of Uluru Energy has been sold to Bodral Mining and Energy. Mr. Boward tells Jeff that the Bodral board of directors has asked that he, Jeff Bennett, remain as CEO of Uluru Energy, although a new vice president of operations will soon be appointed. Following his conversation with the prime minister, Jeff grabs his telephone and dials the number of his recently hired vice president of human resources, Pauline Ranson. In a calm voice he announces the change in the firm's status to Pauline. Both Jeff and Pauline discuss the fact that while their employees are skilled in their jobs and dedicated to the company, they have never faced anything quite like this. For the first time they will face real competition. Other privatized utilities will be battling for their share of the limited Australian market. In addition, new alternative energy firms like Northwestern Alternative Energies from the United States, makers of low-cost solar-powered generators, *have already begun to take away some of Uluru's market. Pauline and Jeff agree that the challenges Uluru will face over the next few years will involve significant changes in how human resources are managed and what sort of human resources the firm needs. Jeff says to Pauline, "How the devil are we going to do this, Pauline? Where do we start? What do we do?"*

The problems faced by Uluru Energy are not unlike those faced by many firms, both public and private, that undergo major changes in the nature of their business environments. In the United States, large companies such as AT&T and IBM immediately come to mind, but there are many others, both large and small, that have faced similar circumstances since the 1980s. The idea that constant change is a fact of organizational life has become widely accepted among practicing managers, organizational consultants, and business academics. One of the common themes in books and articles on organizational change is the important role that human resource management plays in the change process. The view that human resource managers are simply "paper pushers" is rapidly disappearing, to be replaced by the notion that they play a key role in determining the competitive success of firms.

In a generic sense, the new view of human resource management has been referred to as **strategic human resource management (SHRM).** This chapter takes a look at this concept. Specifically, the business factors that contribute to the increased importance of human resources as a source of a firm's strategic competitive advantage are discussed. Several theoretical perspectives on what strategic human resource management actually involves are described. Then the key elements needed to develop strategic human resource management practices within an organization are discussed in detail. Examples are given of how these aspects of SHRM have been operationalized by firms that have undergone or are currently undergoing the transformation from a traditional to a more strategic view of human resource management. The chapter also examines the question of whether strategic HRM practices actually enhance bottom-line financial measures in firms. Is the move from traditional to strategic HRM really worth all the effort required? Evidence supporting the value-adding effects of strategic HR practices is discussed.

This chapter plays a critical role in establishing the context for all subsequent chapters. Following Chapter 2, the text explores a variety of HR functional areas and issues and introduces a large number of sophisticated HR techniques. Some believe that practicing good HRM requires a firm to use the most advanced and sophisticated HR methodologies. As is shown in this chapter, however, simply using the most advanced techniques will not necessarily add the greatest value to a firm's operations or ensure its long-term success. Within the framework of strategic human resource management, effectively managing human assets in a firm requires a far broader view of what is good or bad, efficient or inefficient. What is required is an understanding of the complex interactions among the unique characteristics of the firm, its customers, the business environment in which it operates, its products or services, and the nature of its employees. This chapter provides this broader, more strategic and complex view of managing human resources for long-term competitive success. It is from this broader perspective that the reader must view the methodologies and techniques discussed throughout the remainder of the text.

WHY IS MANAGING HUMAN RESOURCES SO IMPORTANT?

In the past decade, increasing attention has been paid to the importance of human resource management in determining a firm's competitive advantage. Wayne Brockbank notes that this increasing attention is evidenced in several ways.[1] First, in an increasing number of firms, the chief HR executive reports directly to the organization's CEO, indicating higher HR status within the organization. Second, CEOs in major companies like Sears, General Electric, Ford, and Allied Signal are encouraging a greater focus on HR issues as part of programs to enhance competitive advantage. Finally, HR contributions are increasingly being given credit for playing a critical role in improving the performance of major firms (e.g., Baxter International, Harley Davidson, Quantum, Unilever, Arco).

Why is this so? What factors have caused businesses to focus increased attention on HRM? In summarizing the results of a Laborforce 2000 survey involving face-to-face interviews of HR executives in 406 firms, Philip Mirvis noted that the most significant factors identified as affecting HR policies were changing demands from customers or the marketplace, changes in the job mix (i.e., proportion of permanent versus casual workers), new technology, and increasing pressure from competitors.[2]

Randall Schuler identified several similar changes in the basic business environment that place increased importance on human resources. Among these were the following:

- Rapid change
- High levels of uncertainty about basic business conditions
- Rising costs
- Rapid technological change
- Changing demographics
- More limited supplies of highly trained labor
- Rapidly changing government legislation and regulations
- Increased globalization of industries[3]

In his 1997 book, *Human Resource Champions*, Dave Ulrich argues that these changes in the business environment present a number of competitive challenges that are quite different from those faced by firms in earlier times.[4] Each places additional pressure on firms to be innovative and create new ways of doing business with new technologies, new products, and new services to meet an increasingly diverse and demanding customer base. The enhanced value of innovation in determining competitive advantage requires firms to attract, train, and retain employees of the highest quality. Over time and throughout rapidly changing circumstances, firms must be able to sustain the competitive advantage that the skills of these employees provide. Contrary to the situation in the past, when sustained competitive advantage could be gained through finding better, cheaper access to financial capital, or marketing a new product, or inventing some new technological gizmo, the business environment of the twenty-first century requires a greater focus on the human element in organizations. From this realization has come the approach to managing human resources referred to as SHRM.

WHAT IS STRATEGIC HUMAN RESOURCE MANAGEMENT (SHRM)?

Before one can understand what SHRM is, it is essential to have a clear picture of the "traditional" view of HR because it is still the prevalent form of HR activity in most organizations. David Lepak and Scott Snell cite a 1998 Hackett Group survey of 1050 companies that indicates HR professions still devote less than one-third of their time to strategic HR activities.[5] Most of their time is spent on traditional HR activities such as:

- Human resource planning
- Recruiting staff
- Job analysis
- Establishing performance review systems
- Wage, salary, and benefits administration
- Employee training
- Personnel record keeping
- Legislative compliance (affirmative action, EEO, etc.)
- Labor relations

The traditional personnel department is often both physically and psychologically separated from the "real work" of the organization. A visual representation of the traditional role of the personnel department in organizations is shown in Figure 2.1a. The key points represented in Figure 2.1a are that the traditional personnel orientation involves a limited number of functional tasks and that personnel activities and staff are relatively isolated from the "profit-making heart" of the organization.

Strategic HRM: Some Theoretical Perspectives

In the strategic view of HRM, the functional duties described earlier remain important. Certainly hiring, training, and providing pay and benefits to employees are essential tasks that must be accomplished in any organization. However, given the changes in the business environment discussed earlier, many organizations are developing new structural and cultural patterns to meet the competitive demands of their dynamic and international marketplace, and the role of HR in these organizations has had to change to meet these challenges as well.

As a result, a new strategic view of HR has tended to emerge (see Figure 2.1b for a representation of this integrated view of HRM). In these firms, HR plays a central role in helping the organization reach its strategic objectives and interacts fully with other functional areas within the firm.

James Walker has suggested that the new role of HR can be described most simply as one of helping managers maximize the contribution of employees in achieving **competitive advantage.** Ian Clark defines strategic HRM as being ". . . concerned with the promotion of efficiency and profitability. . . . Strategic HRM centers on how organizations can improve their competitive performance by considering and utilizing their human resources more effectively."[6] While these definitions seem straightforward, there is considerable debate about

● FIGURE 2.1

Traditional and Strategic
Views of HRM

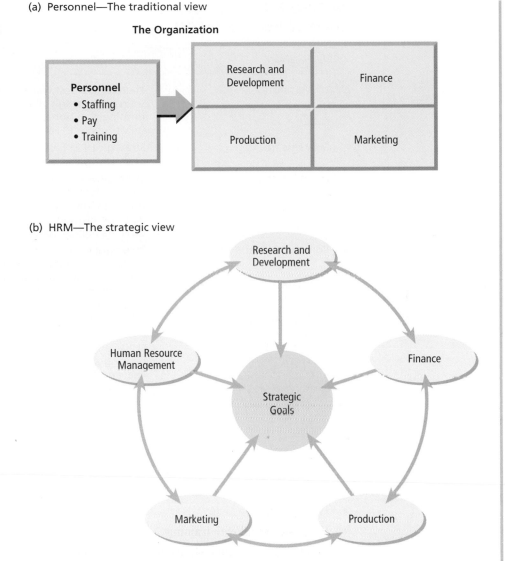

(a) Personnel—The traditional view

(b) HRM—The strategic view

what "helping managers maximize the contribution of employees" or "utilizing their human resources more effectively" really involves. A number of theoretical models have been developed to explain exactly what SHRM requires in an organization and the processes by which SHRM contributes to the bottom-line success of a firm. A summary of these theoretical perspectives is given in Table 2.1.

John Delery and Harold Doty describe a **universalistic approach** to strategic HRM in which HR managers focus on adopting a set of universally effective HR practices.[7] For example, in his book *The Human Equation*, Jeffrey Pfeffer noted strong evidence for a set of HR practices that have a positive effect on organizational performance, regardless of a firm's particular business environment and strategy.[8] This set of HR practices include the following:

● **TABLE 2.1**

Theoretical Perspectives on SHRM

Perspective	Description
Universalistic	There is one best way to manage human resources. Strategic HRM is the process of transforming traditional HR practices into a limited set of "correct" HR procedures and policies.
Strategic fit	Strategic HRM involves matching specific HR practices to the firm's overall business strategy.
HR as internal service provider	Strategic HRM involves HR professionals providing HR services to business units within the firm. The HR goal is to enhance the effectiveness and efficiency of the operations of their business unit customers.
Configurational	There are various configurations, or "bundles," of HR practices that go together and, collectively, can improve business performance. Certain bundles are effective in certain industries and/or in certain business conditions, while other bundles should be used in other industries or under different business circumstances.
Resource based	SHRM engenders organizational success by enhancing a firm's ability to acquire, develop, utilize, and retain employees with high competence levels relevant to firm activities.

- High levels of employment security
- Selective hiring practices
- A focus on teams and decentralized decision making
- High pay levels
- Extensive employee training
- Practices that reduce status distinctions among employees
- High levels of information sharing

Contrary to the universalistic view, the **strategic-fit perspective** of SHRM suggests that "firm performance will be enhanced to the degree that firms adopt human resource management practices that complement and support both other HR policies and practices and the other elements of the organization's strategic plan."[9] Key to this view of SHRM are the notions of horizontal, vertical, and external fit. *Horizontal fit* refers to the consistency among various HR practices within a firm. Thus, if a firm's selection procedures seek to hire highly innovative, risk-taking employees, the firm's performance appraisal and reward systems also should assess and reward innovation and risk taking. *Vertical fit* is the degree to which HR practices are consistent with the firm's overall business strategy. For example, suppose that a firm has decided to enhance its competitive standing relative to other firms in its industry by becoming highly "customer focused." HR training programs that help employees develop better customer relations skills would be consistent with this overall business philosophy. If training programs in the firm concentrated solely on the acquisition of highly technical skills unrelated to employee–customer interactions, such a training system would be inconsistent with the customer-oriented business strategy. *External fit* refers to how well HR practices align with specific aspects of the external environment. For example, in the United States and Australia, there are demographic changes occurring that are causing the work force to become far more multicultural in nature. Diversity management training, remedial language training, or new approaches to selection of employees from nonmajority cultures may be required as part of the overall HR system in order to fit this new external environment and enhance the competitive value of employees.

Another view of SHRM is as an **internal service provider** to a firm's individual business units.[10] In this approach, the role of HR professionals is to improve the quality and cost-effectiveness of HR services provided and to increase the satisfaction of management "customers" in various business units within the firm. Typically in firms with this sort of HR orientation, the budget for HR comes less from a centrally funded source at company headquarters and depends more on a "user pays" model for services provided to business unit "customers." In this model, HR professionals work closely with business unit managers to help solve their people-related business problems and increase the overall effectiveness of their units.

Within the **configurational approach** to SHRM, the effectiveness of HRM in enhancing a firm's competitive advantage depends on a set, or bundle, of HR practices rather than on any single HR program or policy.[11] Over the years, programs such as "quality circles" have been heralded as a cure-all for many organizational ills. Few of these single-program approaches have resulted in the kind of improvements in organizational performance that were promised by their proponents. The configurational view of HR focuses on implementing **HR bundles** rather than single, "magic bullet" programs. The configurational approach to SHRM is consistent with the long-held view that employee performance is determined by a number of factors, such as motivation and ability. Thus, to increase employee performance, HR programs are needed that enhance both motivation (e.g., reward systems) and ability (e.g., hiring or training systems). One could argue that the configurational view is simply an extension of the universalistic approach described above. As noted earlier, Jeffrey Pfeffer found a set (or bundle) of HR practices that seemed to have universally positive effects on employee performance.[12] On the other hand, in a study of sixty-two manufacturing firms, John MacDuffie found that team-based, high-commitment HR practices increased the performance of manufacturing firms using flexible production systems but did not necessarily enhance performance in firms with more traditional mass-production systems.[13] Contrary to Pfeffer's findings, this study suggests that there is no single HR bundle that works universally. So, the universalistic and configurational views may not be the same after all. One of the major contributions of the configurational approach is that research associated with it has identified a number of different "bundles" of HR practices that contain individual HR elements that are internally consistent with one another. Some of these different types of HR systems are described in Table 2.2.

In a 1995 article, Jay Barney discussed a **resource-based model** of strategic HRM. This model is based on the idea that organizations gain competitive advantage when they possess resources that are valuable, rare, difficult for competitors to imitate, and organized in such a way as to maximize their overall value to the firm.[14] In a more recent article, Barney and Patrick Wright expand on the notion

● **TABLE 2.2**

Types of HR Systems

Source	Types of HR Systems		
Dyer and Reeves (1995)	Control systems: • Centralization of decision making • Low employee involvement • Tight controls through rules, policies, appraisal	Commitment systems: • Decentralized decision making • High employee involvement • High levels of autonomy and empowerment	
Snell and Youndt (1995)	Behavior control systems: • Standardized responsibilities set by management • Employee accountability for actions regardless of results • Supervisor-conducted behavior-based appraisals • Use of feedback to fix problems	Output control systems: • Mutually set performance targets • Results-based appraisals • Monetary rewards for achieving results	Input control systems: • Rigorous selection and training; ensuring of requisite skills • Systems to ensure that employees understand and internalize firm's values
Delery and Doty (1996)	Market-type systems: • Hiring from outside • Little training • Evaluation of performance through the use of results measures • Little employment security • Little voice • Narrowly defined jobs	Internal systems: • Internal labor market • Extensive socialization and training • Performance assessment through behavior • Appraisal feedback for developmental purposes • High degree of employment security • Great deal of voice • Employees as excellent sources of information • Broadly defined jobs	

Lepak and Snell (1999)	Developing human capital: Commitment system	Acquiring human capital: Market-based system	Contracting human capital: Compliance system	Creating human capital: Collaborative system
	• Internal development • Loosely defined jobs • Training to develop unique skills • Career development and mentoring systems • Developmental appraisal • Extensive information sharing	• Acquisition of human capital from the market • Development of symbiotic relationship between firm and employees • Selection for skills with immediate use • Not a lot of training • Externally equitable wages	• Contract with external suppliers • Development of transactional relationship between firm and employees • Focus on terms and conditions of employment to ensure compliance • Lots of rules and procedures • Reliance on good selection procedures • Little training	• Use of both internal and external selection • Development of partnership relationship between firm and employees • Encouragment of and reward cooperation • Lots of information sharing • Little training • Possible use of exchange programs and job rotation

Sources: Adapted from information in Lee Dyer and Todd Reeves, "Human Resource Strategies and Firm Performance: What Do We Know and Where Do We Need to Go?" *The International Journal of Human Resource Management,* Vol. 6 (3), 1995, pp. 656–670; Scott Snell and Mark Youndt, "Human Resource Management and Firm Performance: Testing a Contingency Model of Executive Controls," *Journal of Management,* Vol. 21 (4), 1995, pp. 711–737; John Delery and Harold Doty, "Modes of Theorizing in Strategic Human Resource Management: Tests of Universalistic, Contingency, and Configurational Performance Predictions," *Academy of Management Journal,* Vol. 39 (4), 1996, pp. 802–835; David Lepak and Scott Snell, "The Human Resource Architecture: Toward a Theory of Human Capital Allocation and Development," *Academy of Management Review,* Vol. 24 (1), 1999, pp. 31–48.

of a resource-based view of strategic HRM. They conclude that, from this perspective, strategic HRM involves HR managers in solving four basic questions about human resources. These four questions are:[15]

1. How can the HR function aid in either decreasing costs or increasing revenues in the firm, that is, adding value?
2. How can the HR function identify and take advantage of the rare skills and characteristics of employees?
3. How can the HR function help create a labor force that is very difficult for other competitors to imitate?
4. How can the HR function help structure the firm so that it can best exploit its human resource advantage?

Barney and Wright describe actions taken by several firms to deal with these four issues. For example, Federal Express increased revenues by using employee attitude surveys to identify managers with poor employee relations skills. FedEx then used the survey information to improve managerial skills, which eventually led to improved customer service by employees. Nordstrom has taken advantage of rare skills by developing selection and compensation systems that select highly customer-oriented employees (a rare employee) and reward customer service (a rare skill). Southwest Airlines' extensive selection procedures identify flight attendants who contribute to the "fun" atmosphere of the airline. Top management empowers employees to "be inconsistent" and create new, fun, and interesting ways to satisfy customers. These selection and empowerment systems, and the employee behavior that they engender, are difficult for other firms to imitate. Finally, General Motors has developed extensive employee involvement programs to allow employees to contribute their knowledge more easily to help the firm enhance its competitive standing.

Theoretical Perspectives: Conclusions About SHRM

As is often the case with theories about human behavior in organizations, the question for HR practitioners is "Which theoretical approach is correct and, from a practical perspective, what does it suggest are the important aspects for creating a strategically oriented HR function?" Unfortunately, the answer to this question is not a simple one. Like many theories about organizations, none are completely correct. Rather than being right or wrong, each approach points to different aspects of the process needed for developing an effective strategic HR function. Taken collectively, these perspectives seem to identify six key elements required in developing SHRM within a firm. The essential elements of SHRM are as follows:

1. Internally transforming HR staff and structure
2. Enhancing administrative efficiency
3. Integrating HR into the strategic planning process
4. Linking HR practices to business strategy and to one another
5. Developing a partnership with line management
6. Focusing on the bottom-line impact of HR and measurement of that impact

Although these essential processes are listed as if they were independent of one another, there is obvious overlap among the concepts as there are overlaps among the various theoretical perspectives from which they are derived.

Since traditional HR remains the predominant perspective in most organizations, the first ingredient for creating an SHRM perspective is the internal transformation of existing staff who perform HR duties and the structure within which they operate. It is these individuals who must champion and enact the change to SHRM. New skills are usually needed, as are new perspectives about the structure and processes of HRM. Within an SHRM perspective, traditional administrative tasks remain important. Employees must receive their pay and benefits, safety programs must be developed and administered, and EEO laws must be obeyed. However, the focus becomes one of performing these administrative tasks in as efficient and cost-effective a manner as possible.

The third and fourth elements of SHRM are derived from the strategic-fit perspective. The integration of HR into the strategic planning process is critical. Only by being part of the strategic planning process can HR practitioners link business strategy and HR practices to one another. Borrowing concepts from the configurational perspective, the focus of SHRM is not on linking single HR programs to business strategy. Rather, to enhance a firm's strategic effectiveness, SHRM must develop bundles of internally consistent HR activities that contribute to the achievement of the firm's strategic goals and objectives. In addition, as highlighted by the service model of SHRM, the development of an effective partnership between line managers and HR staff is critical. It is impossible for HR activities to have a value-adding effect if those performing the HR function do not work closely with line managers. The sixth essential SHRM element, the importance of a bottom-line, value-adding impact of HR practices, is drawn from all theoretical perspectives. The competitive business environment that most firms face today precludes the luxury of engaging in HR practices that simply "feel good" or "look good" or happen to be the latest HR fad. Human resource management activities must add value to the firm. In the following pages, each of these elements of SHRM is discussed, along with examples of how firms have operationalized them in their own transformation to a strategic approach to human resource management. However, before moving to a detailed discussion of the six elements for HR transformation, a brief discussion of a critical "pretransformation" activity is needed.

Michael Beer has suggested that one key barrier to effective HR transformation is the attitude of many CEOs, who still see HR as primarily an administrative function. Thus, before any true transformation of HR can occur, top management (and particularly the CEO) must be brought "on board."[16] A number of authors have examined this issue, and several consistent themes have developed about how best to achieve top management "buy-in" to an HR transformation.[17] First, the leader of any HR change effort must be a highly competent and credible leader within the organization. Second, those hoping to lead the HR transformation must create a shared need for change among top managers. A compelling business reason for change must be built with which the CEO and other top managers can easily identify. Ideally, this rationale will link HR change directly to changes in overall business strategy. Third, those leading the HR change process must be able to articulate a clearly defined "end-state vision" for HR and the major steps that will be needed to achieve that vision. This should involve an interactive process between HR and other top managers who help HR define that end state. This involvement of top managers will help ensure their commitment to the HR change process. Finally, measures must be developed to monitor the progress of the changes. These measures should be focused on the value added by HR. Such measures will not only help *get* the CEO and top management team "on board" the HR transformation train, but will help *keep* them on board as the train weaves through what will likely be a difficult, challenging landscape.

TRANSFORMING HR STAFF AND STRUCTURE

In order to create a strategic HRM philosophy within a firm, attention must be paid to the transformation of HR staff and the organizational structure in which these people carry out their HR activities. There are two aspects of this transformation: (1) transforming the people and (2) transforming the structure.

Transforming HR People

There are significant differences in the skills needed by HR staff to function effectively in the traditional and strategic orientations to HRM. In the traditional role, staff members need to be specialists in certain personnel functional areas and must hone skills needed for performing traditional personnel activities such as training or recruitment interviewing. In contrast, Warren Wilhelm cites a recent survey of HR professionals indicating that the largest skill component needed by staff taking on a strategic HRM role is change management.[18] A survey of senior HR managers by Drake Beam Morin, Inc., found that 82 percent of the respondents felt that their future role would focus on strategic planning, team building, quality improvement, and diversity management and training. Among the skills that these HR managers indicated they would need to perform their future HR roles effectively were team leadership skills, the ability to have a global perspective, financial and marketing literacy, and good consulting and presentation skills.[19] Table 2.3 summarizes some of the differences in skills needed by staff operating under the traditional and strategic views of HRM.

The information in Table 2.3 presents a "universalistic view" of HR skills, that is, that all HR staff will need these skills in order to enhance HR's strategic role in the organization. This may not be the case. In her 1997 article on "Training HR Pros to Fit Your Culture," Connie Freeman suggests that the competencies that HR professionals need will vary (as for other employees) depending on the stategy of the firm.[20] Freeman's view represents a strategic-fit approach to the specific issue of HR competencies. For example, Freeman suggests that in firms whose strategy is focused on delivering highly reliable, low-cost products and services, HR professionals need particular skill in procedural knowledge, self-control, and attention to detail. On the other hand, for HR professionals in customer service–oriented firms, critical competencies include service orientation, team building, achieving consensus, and communication. However, regardless of whether strategic HR competencies are universal in nature or require a strategic-fit approach, most HR units will face a significant transformation in order to manage human resources with a new strategic view.

The processes by which firms have attempted to transform HR staff from traditional specialists to strategic generalists are quite varied. For example, David

● **TABLE 2.3**

Differences between Key HR Skills in Traditional HRM and SHRM

Traditional HRM	Strategic HRM
Specialist	Generalist
A good policy and procedure writer	A good communicator
Current focus	Current and future focus
Monolingual (speaks "HR-ese")	Speaks the language of business
Management-hierarchy focused	Customer-focused, good customer relations skills
Few financial or marketing skills	Understanding of these aspects of the business
Stays "within the box"	Thinks "outside the box"
Focused on the internal organization	Focused on the internal organization and the broader society
Factual communicator	Persuader
A nationalist	An internationalist

Sources: Adapted from James B. Shaw, "Course Notes for Management 800: Strategic HRM," Bond University, Queensland, Australia, 1997; Valerie Stewart, "Human Capital Issues in Organizational Change," *Asia Pacific Journal of Human Resources,* Vol. 30 (1), 1992, pp. 53–64; Jill Conner and Jeana Wirtenberg, "Managing the Transformation of Human Resources Work," *Human Resource Planning,* Vol. 16 (2), 1993, pp. 17–34.

Jones reports on the efforts of the University of Nebraska Medical Center (UNMC) to transform its HR function.[21] Following a series of focus groups, along with surveys of 300 managers, the nine-member HR redesign team identified a number of aspects of HR practices and HR staff that were in need of transformation. In a somewhat radical move, UNMC essentially "fired" all its current HR staff and then allowed them to reapply for their positions. Behavioral interviews were conducted on these "reapplicants," with each being assessed against a new set of strategic HR skills criteria. As part of Colgate's HR transformation, the company grooms HR talent within the organization by hiring only the best university graduates, with some practical experience, and then rotating them through various functional areas within Colgate and also within specific HR functional areas (typically fifteen to eighteen months of rotation).[22]

Jill Connor and Jeana Wirtenberg have described the process by which AT&T implemented its HR Professionalism program as part of a transformation of the HR function.[23] The focus of the 1988 development effort was to initiate a program to identify, coach, develop, and foster high-level professional skills in AT&T's HR staff. The objective of the program was to enhance the skills of HR professionals so that they could contribute to strategic business success. Extensive research was done on what line managers needed from HR, using surveys and focus groups to collect the data. The results of this research indicated that line managers needed HR to do the following:

- Share responsibility for performance and profitability
- Be customer driven and a business partner with a broad focus
- Focus on solutions, not activities

- Be creative and strategic
- Initiate, lead, and facilitate change
- Help develop global managers
- Act with urgency

Literature reviews were done, and a survey of 150 HR people was conducted to zero in on the behavioral skills that helped differentiate the top-performing HR staff members in AT&T from more average performers. The skills and behaviors identified from this process are presented in Table 2.4. Once the new HR skills and behaviors were identified, a program for marketing the vision of HR Professionalism was implemented using videos, brochures, and a talk by the CEO. In addition, a Professional Development Profile (PDP) procedure was developed. In the PDP process, HR staff self-assessed against the new professional standards. Then each HR professional was asked to distribute an assessment survey to five of his or her customers. The customers assessed the individual against the new professional standards, and an individual feedback report comparing the manager's self-assessment with that of his or her customers was provided. This feedback was backed up by Professional Development Workshops to help individuals close any gaps between the new professional standards and their self-assessed or customer-rated performance. The final step in the development of AT&T's HR Professionalism program involved a one-day meeting of HR leaders, followed by half-day training sessions to ensure that the HR leaders could use the PDP process in their own locations.

The AT&T program for transforming HR is by no means the only approach that is effective. What AT&T's efforts indicate, however, is the complexity of transforming HR skills within a large organization. Time, effort, money, and patience are needed. Although the large size of AT&T's HR staff increased the overall magnitude of the transformation process, there are some essential elements of their process, as well as those used by Colgate and UNMC, that are applicable to medium-sized and small firms. First, the HR transformation was part of and directly linked to an overall strategic reorientation of the organizations involved. This helped to enhance motivation, provide direction, and give a real sense of importance to the transformation process. Second, active participation of HR person-

● **TABLE 2.4**

Skills and Behaviors of Top-Performing HR Staff at AT&T

Accountability for Business Results	Self-Image	Managing Interpersonal Relationships
Is results oriented	Sees self as catalyst for change	Builds information networks
Engages in strategic thinking	Sees self as member of a leadership team	Is effective at influencing others
Develops a business partnership with line managers	Demonstrates self-confidence	Exhibits interpersonal flexibility
Is customer-focused		Is effective at building and managing teams
Uses HR expertise		Energizes and empowers others

Source: Adapted from information in Jill Conner and Jeana Wirtenberg, "Managing the Transformation of Human Resources Work," *Human Resource Planning,* Vol. 16 (2), 1993, pp. 17–34.

nel in the transformation took place, and there were individuals who took on the role of "champion" of the program's objectives. Third, critical emphasis also was placed on getting line managers involved in defining the new skills and behaviors needed in HR staff. Fourth, the transformation was considered as a major change effort. In the case of UNMC, rather drastic action (forcing everyone to reapply for their positions) was taken to overcome the resistance and inertia associated with the change effort. Finally, Colgate's process of hiring and grooming HR staff through job rotations indicates the patience needed in bringing about a true transformation of HR.

Transforming HR Structure

In conducting the transformation of traditional personnel to SHRM, it is quite common for the structure of the HR unit to be transformed as well. In some cases, as for Tampella Power Company, the organization had to set up for the very first time a separate, centralized human resource department. At Northern Telecom, all HR staff members were consolidated into a single corporate unit under a senior vice president of HR. At Benetton in Italy, various recruiting and development activities were centralized. In the case of Siemens Rolm, a team-based structure was implemented.[24]

As with many other forms of organizational restructuring, a key issue in designing a new strategic HRM unit is to determine which activities should be centralized and which should be decentralized. Gregory Kesler notes that during the 1990s new roles were created around partnering approaches for HR. Companies like Warner-Lambert, Motorola, Coca-Cola, and Whirlpool have created new HR-organization structures to realign roles in order to separate transactional-fulfillment work (administrative role) and consultative, business-partnering work (strategic role). These and other companies have reported significant improvements in delivering strategic results when traditional roles are replaced with more consultative organization-effectiveness roles, supported by small centralized staffs of expert resources. These companies have also directly assigned HR partners to front-line business units while aggressively consolidating delivery of employee services.[25] The specific roles normally performed by the three subunits of an HR organization—Expert Resource Teams, Front-Line Business Partners, and Central Service Center—are listed in Table 2.5. Looked at another way, the task of Expert Resource Teams is *effective strategy formulation*, the task of a Central Service Center is *efficient delivery of transactions*, while that of Front-Line Business Partners is *effective and efficient strategy implementation*. Occasionally, however, front-line HR partners may also have to formulate HR strategies specifically for their own business units.

The restructuring of HR at Northern Telecom produced a structure similar, though not identical, to that described by Kesler. Northern Telecom's HR structure, along with brief descriptions of the role of each unit, is shown in Figure 2.2. The Business Unit HR performs the front-line partnering role. The HR Services in Northern Telecom provides cost-efficient service on issues that go across individual business units and is therefore akin to what Kesler calls a Central Service Center. The Corporate HR Unit provides services that make it analogous to Kesler's Expert Resource Team. One issue that Northern Telecom had to deal with in restructuring HR was how to keep the various individual HR teams integrated and communicating with one another. Because it was a global company, Northern

TABLE 2.5

Three Roles in the New HR Organization

Expert Resource Teams	Front-Line Business Partners	Central Service Center
• Develop top management's strategies for new policies and practices • Become thought leaders in the field—specialists/designers • Manage development projects • Benchmark functional excellence • Develop HR know-how • Assure alignment of total HR system with company strategy • Support roll out of programs: Teach others how • Support consultants with "best practices" • Exchange best practices	• Manage client expectations—contracting and execution • Develop people strategies for their operating units—with line leaders • Become decentralized, business unit-aligned "generalists" • Stay close to the business • Tailor and implement new practices/programs to fit • Identify new applications • Manage client projects • Provide linkage between business units and the focus on HR issues	• Meet all current service obligations • Manage all "transactional" support processes • Drive consolidation and productivity • Direct projects to eliminate work • Enable work force access to information tools • Apply information systems to automate all necessary services • Consult in systems design and information requirements

Source: Adapted from Gregory Kesler, "Four Steps to Building an HR Agenda for Growth: HR Strategy Revisited," *Human Resource Planning*, Vol. 23 (3), 2000, p. 35.

Telecom formed networks of HR staff into "geographic councils" to help unite HR employees operating in different localities. Functional networks were also formally designed to promote learning and information dissemination among functional specialists in the various HR teams.

Obviously, the appropriate structure for the HR function will depend on the nature of the firm's business activity, its size, and its overall business strategy. In some organizations, a more centralized structure for HRM may be appropriate to ensure quality of HR products and gain economies of scale in their development and delivery. In other situations, highly decentralized HR units may be necessary. Regardless of which particular structure is used, the key element in successfully transforming traditional HR functions into SHRM units is to find a structure that meets the pressing needs of the business strategy of the organization and allows the HR unit to provide services designed to help the firm achieve strategic objectives. This newly acquired strategic focus of HR does not mean that the function can afford to relegate administrative efficiency to the background. On the contrary, given the focus on cost savings in today's competitive environment, there is increasing pressure on HR to become even more efficient. The next section deals with this issue.

FIGURE 2.2

Northern Telecom's HR
Structure and Roles

Source: Adapted from James
Kochanski and Phillip Randall,
"Rearchitecting the Human
Resources Function at Northern
Telecom," *Human Resource
Management,* Vol. 33 (2),
1994, p. 304.

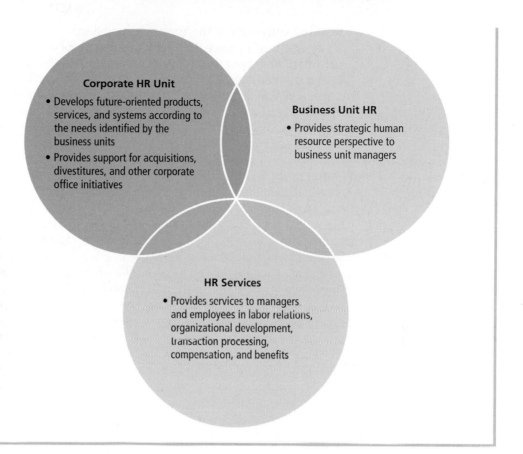

Corporate HR Unit

- Develops future-oriented products, services, and systems according to the needs identified by the business units
- Provides support for acquisitions, divestitures, and other corporate office initiatives

Business Unit HR

- Provides strategic human resource perspective to business unit managers

HR Services

- Provides services to managers and employees in labor relations, organizational development, transaction processing, compensation, and benefits

ENHANCING ADMINISTRATIVE EFFICIENCY

Dave Ulrich has suggested that one of the key roles of HR staff is to be "administrative experts." As administrative experts, HR staff members must take an active role in reengineering administrative and other processes within the firm and find ways to share services more effectively throughout the organization.[26] The objectives here are to increase HR service efficiency and to save money. For example, the Hackett Group conducted a survey to identify characteristics of "best" versus "typical" HR units and found that the average cost per employee of HR services in the best firms was around $800, whereas the per-employee cost in typical firms was $1675. One possible factor contributing to the lower HR costs in the best firms was that their HR administrative services (payroll, benefits, etc.) tended to be highly integrated and shared, whereas these services were more often rather fragmented and duplicated in typical firms.[27]

According to Ulrich, several processes are needed to enhance the administrative expertise of HR units. The first of these focuses on improving **administrative efficiency** by targeting *current* processes for improvement. The role of the HR unit is to examine the gaps between the "as is" process and what the system "should be." Once these gaps are identified, programs can be developed to close them. This could involve dropping a traditional HR program. For example, Alcatel Network Systems in Richardson, Texas, got rid of its managerial performance appraisal system since there was clear evidence that the system did not improve managerial performance.[28] In implementing new programs, the HR unit must market them throughout the organization and then measure whether efficiency has indeed been enhanced. For example, ERTL, Inc., a toymaker in Diresville, Iowa, had considerable difficulty in recruiting new employees. There was an average 128-day lag between the time a position was identified as vacant and the arrival of a new employee to fill that position. There were also excessive costs associated with the recruiting and relocation processes. ERTL's HR unit interviewed new hires to find out what had attracted them to ERTL and then produced a video for use in the recruiting process. In addition, ERTL formed partnerships with specific recruiting firms and also did a careful analysis of the individual components of relocation expenses. As a result of these efforts, the average time between a position's becoming vacant and being filled dropped from 128 to 31 days. Fees paid to external recruiting firms were cut almost in half, and average relocation costs dropped from $12,871 to $10,356.[29]

As suggested earlier, administrative efficiency can also be enhanced through the development of **centralized HR services** that are shared throughout an organization. For example, UNMC developed a **"one-stop shop"** for all its payroll, benefits, and other HR administrative services, while at Siemens Rolm, two forms of shared services were established. Like UNMC, Siemens Rolm set up a centralized processing unit for all basic HR services. In addition, and as part of the firm's overall restructuring of the HR unit, a "core team" of experts in various HR functional areas was established. These experts could be called on for assistance by HR staff throughout the organization.[30]

A final process involved in HR staff members' becoming "administrative experts" requires them to completely rethink how they create value for the firm through their administrative activities. The focus here is for the HR unit to create programs that give value as perceived by the customers of the program, not as perceived by the provider of the program (HR). For example, many of the tasks performed by the HR unit at Northern Telecom involved maintaining information about employees, such as benefits and home addresses. The organization developed a "self-service" concept in which employees became responsible for their own information input and retrieval. The HR Services Unit took on the task of developing information input-and-retrieval systems that would provide the right information to employees in an easily accessible and understandable manner and allow them to update basic information in the system. In looking for news ways to create value within the organization, the HR unit at Northern Telecom assessed employee needs first; then systems were developed to support those needs. Information was to be made available when the employee needed it, not when it was convenient for the system to provide it. The development of these information input-and-retrieval systems moved HR from its traditional clerical role to one of information system developer—a new, more effective way for HR to create value within the organization.[31]

INTEGRATING HR INTO STRATEGIC PLANNING

Strategic integration of HR requires (1) that a strategic planning process occur in the organization and (2) that HR managers play an important role in that process. The requirement that a strategic planning process occur before strategic HRM can develop is one that is often not met in small and medium-sized firms. In a university course conducted by the third author of this book, students are required to analyze several different aspects of HR activities within a local firm. The students try to determine whether the firm is engaging in strategic HRM and then make suggestions as to how the firm can become more strategic in its HR approach. The first part of this assignment asks students to describe the strategic plan of the firm, including its mission, values, and strategic objectives. In at least 75 percent of cases, students find that the firms they have chosen to analyze have no written strategic plan and have a mission and set of strategic objectives that state simply "to make money and not go bankrupt." The next section of this chapter presents a brief description of the strategic planning process. Following that, examples of how HR, specifically, can be integrated into the strategic planning process are provided.

The Strategic Planning Process

The development of a strategic plan typically involves top management, sometimes with the aid of outside consultants, sitting down together to analyze the current and future state of the organization. The process involves answering some pretty basic questions, such as "Where do we want to be as an organization in the next five years, what are our strengths and weaknesses, what opportunities exist in the business environment, and what challenges are we likely to face?"

● **Mission, Goals, and Values Statements**   The **mission statement** delineates the organization's reason for existing. It is important to operationalize a mission and ensure buy-in if a mission statement is not to degenerate into mere rhetoric. The leadership center of General Electric, for example, trains its managers to operationalize a mission or an initiative by frequent use of an exercise based on a valuable concept that has become known by many names over the years, including visualization, backward imaging, and "starting with the end in mind." Managers are asked to imagine themselves at a party six months or a year hence, the purpose of which is to celebrate the achievement of some mission or corporate initiative. They are asked to describe, in very specific terms, how their leaders', peers', and subordinates' behavior has changed—what they are actually doing more of and less of—in the future compared to in the present. This process is used to ensure that GE's vision and mission statements are operational, rather than being merely sweet words or numbers.[32] A mission statement using Uluru Energy (the organization described earlier in the HR Challenge) as an example is shown in Figure 2.3 From Figure 2.3 we know that Uluru is in the business of energy products and services. It is committed to providing the highest level of value-for-dollar to its customers. Uluru Energy sees itself as a team, is committed to its customers, aspires to leadership (markets, financial returns, and the quality of work life for its employees), and is dedicated to continuous improvement.

Uluru's mission statement also describes the key values by which it will operate. There are multiple benefits to be gained from the articulation of a **values statement.** First, a statement of fundamental beliefs can guide strategic change. For example, the strategic transformation of General Electric during the 1980s from a sluggish, diverse set of businesses into a lean, cohesive market leader was guided by a set of values designed to animate the strategy for change.[33] Second, just as individual behavior is shaped by a personal value system, organizational behavior and success are influenced by employee perceptions of corporate beliefs.

● **FIGURE 2.3**

Mission, Goals, and Values for Uluru Energy

The Framework for Uluru's Success as a Private Company

Uluru Energy will be a leader in energy products and services. Uluru conducts business through a strategic framework and with a participative management process that provides vision and direction. The strategic framework guides us in where we want to go (our mission), what we need to get there (our goals), and the behaviors we want to exhibit as we face the day-to-day challenges of private enterprise (our values).

The strategic framework unites us with a shared purpose and a consistent approach to business for all who are employees of Uluru Energy.

Mission

- We are a team committed to pursuing in Australia and in Southeast Asia opportunities that take advantage of our unique commitment to the greatest level of value-for-dollar and highest level of service for all our energy customers.
- We measure our success by the standard of market leadership and financial returns, as well as the extent to which we can create an environment of trust and personal growth among Uluru employees.
- We accomplish this through our dedication to quality and continuous improvement in all that we do.
- We are committed to conducting business according to the highest ethical standards and to being an outstanding corporate citizen.

Goals

- **People.** Develop and maintain a team of motivated and talented individuals working in an environment that fosters accomplishment, involvement, creativity, mutual respect, and the opportunity for each individual to realize his or her fullest potential.
- **Product/cost leadership.** Develop cost-competitive products that result in superior customer satisfaction so as to achieve and sustain market leadership.
- **Marketing excellence.** Establish a market-driven organization that preempts our competitors at identifying and responding to customer needs.
- **Resource utilization.** Ensure the most effective and efficient use of all company resources.
- **Corporate citizen.** Conduct our affairs so that we are known to ourselves, to our customers, and to our communities as a trusted company with high standards, integrity, and concern for the environment in which we operate.
- **Growth and profitability.** Create a business that will achieve growth and profitability and provide superior return on investment to our shareholders.

Values

- **We are a winning team.** We believe that we will succeed only as a team and that everyone's full participation is essential to the fulfillment of our mission. It is imperative that we create an environment of mutual respect, candor, and trust, where all can reach their highest potential, where individual initiative and performance are recognized and rewarded, where all identify with the success of the company, and where a winning attitude prevails.

- **We are customer-driven.** We believe that the success of our business depends on understanding and satisfying the needs of the customer. Market needs must drive our choice of products and services and the way we deliver them. At the same time, success in delivering those products and services requires that the recipients of internal services and staff work deserve the same consideration so that all our activities create value.

The degree to which values create desired organizational outcomes is a function of the extent to which such beliefs are clearly articulated, successfully communicated, and integrated into the way of doing business.[34]

● **Environmental Threats and Opportunities**   Another integral step in the development of a strategic plan is the analysis of environmental factors that influence organizational objectives. **Environmental threats** are features of the external surroundings that may prevent the organization from achieving its strategic goals. For example, it is obvious from reading the HR Challenge that Uluru Energy must attend to threats from new, foreign competitors. **Environmental opportunities** are aspects of the surroundings that may help the organization to achieve its goals. Uluru's long association with the region in which it operates provides it with intimate knowledge of its customers and the conditions in which they live and work. For any firm preparing a strategic plan, an environmental scan should include an analysis of technology, economic factors, the legal/political environment, international markets, competitors, the labor supply, and its customers. Some features of the environment will have more influence on the organization than others. In any case, a strategic planning process should help managers develop as complete an understanding as possible of all the features of the organization's environment and how they come together to affect the enterprise.

● **Organizational Strengths and Weaknesses**   *Organizational strengths* are positive internal characteristics on which an organization can draw to achieve its strategic goals. *Organizational weaknesses* are characteristics that may stand in the way of particular accomplishments. The analysis of strengths and weaknesses typically focuses on specific functions such as marketing, finance, production, and research and development (R&D). Management philosophy and human resources are areas that also may be considered in an analysis. Returning to our HR Challenge example, Uluru Energy has several notable strengths, including finance (return on investment and ability to obtain credit), marketing (distribution channels and customer knowledge), and human resources (trained and committed employees). Uluru's most notable weakness is its long history in a stable, monopoly market. Its employees and managers have never had to operate in a dynamic, highly competitive situation. Also, given its semibureaucratic, hierarchical structure, Uluru very likely has a number of staff members who do not truly add value to the organization's bottom-line activities. These individuals spend much of their time controlling and monitoring the behavior of others, which, in a more competitive environment, might be unnecessary and too costly to maintain.

● **Goals and Objectives**   After an organization has defined its mission and analyzed both external opportunities and threats and internal strengths and weaknesses, it can realistically establish goals and **objectives** that will further its mission. In the case of the Uluru Energy example in Figure 2.3, these goals are rather general in nature: They have to do with people, products, marketing, resources, citizenship, and profitability. Eventually these goals must be translated into specific tactical and operational goals.. For example, Uluru's first goal, which focuses on people, refers to a team orientation that emphasizes accomplishment, involvement, and the opportunity for employees to reach their full potential. These general goals have specific implications for the structure of work (team orientation), the appraisal of performance (emphasis on accomplishment), rewards (involvement), and career progression (achievement of full potential). The definition of goals has several important benefits to an organization and its employees. First, goals are a source of motivation. They describe the purpose of the organization to all involved. Second, goals also provide the basis for decisions. Managers and employees must make many decisions in their day-to-day activities. Knowing the goals, they can make decisions with the desired outcome in mind. Finally, goals become the basis for performance measurement. Comparing performance and goals helps managers guide their future actions.

● **Formulation of Strategies**   Only after the mission has been defined, environmental threats and opportunities analyzed, organizational strengths and weaknesses considered, and goals established can management undertake strategy formulation. The task is to select the most effective game plan or course of action to achieve the organization's goals and objectives. Strategy may be formulated and implemented at the corporate level and for individual business units and functions. Regardless, the HRM function will likely be a critical element in the overall success of any strategy formulation and implementation process. To ensure the success of the overall strategic planning process, HRM will have to be completely integrated and a full partner in the strategic planning team.

How to Strategically Integrate HRM: Some Ideas and Examples

Integration does not simply mean that HR managers are allowed to provide HR-related information to those making strategic decisions. To achieve full integration, HR managers must have the ability to influence the development and selection of information used in making a decision, as well as the ability to make or strongly influence the decision itself.[35] The process of integrating HR into the strategic decision-making process can occur through a variety of actions.

At Australian Global Insurance (AGI), the process of HR integration began by changing the hierarchical position of the senior HR manager so that it was equivalent to that of a chief general manager. This automatically made the top HR person a member of the senior executive committee of AGI. Once on this committee, the top HR person was in a position to make sure that HR issues were incorporated into the **strategic planning process.**[36]

While such actions are both symbolically and substantively useful, the process of integration is not always that easy. Tampella Power Company in Finland hired its first personnel manager in 1988 and placed that individual on its top management team in 1989.[37] A corporate-wide strategic management project called "From Vision to Action" was initiated, and the new personnel manager was named Tampella Power's representative. These actions were to have ensured that HR issues would have a status similar to the status of other functions within the organization and that the senior representative of HR would be placed in a position to represent HR issues in strategic decision making. Unfortunately, the transformation of the role of HR did not occur as easily as expected.

In 1990, a new manager of HR activities was hired, and to increase that individual's status within the company, her title was changed to vice president of human resources. In addition, she had a background in law, and lawyers had always held a high place in Tampella's culture. The new vice president of HR was energetic, aggressive, determined, and patient. At almost every top management meeting, she pressed issues related to training, performance appraisal, wage developments, safety and health, and so forth. Thanks to her consistent efforts and some innovative changes in the functions and focus of the HR department, true changes in the level of HR integration began to take place.

In addition to having a powerful representative on the top strategy-making committee, integration of HR into the strategic planning process also requires HR to gather and present information relevant to the making of overall business strategy. In the case of GE Medical Systems, when the company had to decide whether to acquire a French company, its HR officials participated in early reviews of that company, including assessment of key talent, review of the firm's benefits structure, and assessment of the differences between the French business culture and GE Medical's culture. This information played an important role in the acquisition decision. In a similar vein, Novell was considering setting up a technical support system in either Australia or Singapore. HR employees evaluated local employment laws, the cost and availability of housing, and what it would cost to recruit multilingual employees to staff the center. They also researched tax issues, competitive salary structures, medical facilities, and the health care system. As it happened with GE Medical, this HR-related information played an important part in the making of a critical strategic decision by the firm; it might have proved too late were this information collected after the decision had been made.[38]

FITTING HR PRACTICES TO BUSINESS STRATEGY AND TO ONE ANOTHER

The issue of *fitting* HR practices to business strategy is becoming increasingly relevant in modern business and is perhaps the most important HR issue for HR staff and line managers.[39] HR fit involves making sure HR activities "make sense" and help the organization achieve its goals and objectives. As noted earlier in this chapter, there are three aspects of HR fit.[40] The first aspect, **vertical fit,** concerns the match between HR practices and overall business strategy. The second aspect, **horizontal fit,** relates to the interrelationship among HR activities; that is, the extent to which they are mutually consistent. Consistency ensures that HR practices reinforce one another. HR consistency means that all programs send a common message to all employees, which makes it easy for workers to understand what behaviors are required of them. There are also technical advantages of HR practice consistency; for example, a firm that invests heavily in training programs will likely benefit from also having a good selection system that reduces the likelihood of employee turnover.[41] The third aspect of fit is **external fit,** which concerns how well HR activities match the demands of the external environment. If vertical fit occurs, then horizontal fit should follow. However, it seems useful to think of these two aspects of fit separately so as to ensure that both are managed effectively within the organization. To achieve external, horizontal, and vertical fit, HR staff members, working closely with line managers, must make correct choices about the nature and specific type of HR programs that are used in an organization.

Human Resource Practice Choices

The process of ensuring external, vertical, and horizontal fit requires that HR practices result in and continuously reinforce behaviors needed to accommodate specific aspects of the external environment and to help achieve an organization's objectives.[42] For example, Uluru Energy's goal is to orient HR practices to produce desired results in quality and market development, to respond to customer needs, to effectively utilize resources, and to manage through teamwork and cooperation. Like many organizations, to achieve this goal Uluru will probably need fewer employees and fewer management levels—in other words, the need is to downsize and delayer the organization.

Figure 2.4 organizes **HR practice choices** into six categories. Figure 2.4 defines opposite ends of each practice continuum, such as promoting entirely from within versus filling all openings from the external labor market. Clearly, an intermediate choice is also possible for most of the practices. Furthermore, for large organizations, different units could use different practices, or the practices might vary by level or job category.[43] The challenge is to develop internally consistent configurations of HR practice choices that help implement the organization's strategy and advance its competitiveness. In order to accomplish this successfully, a clear understanding of the nature of the HR choices available is needed.

● **Staffing**   Many staffing decisions have implications for strategy implementation. For example, whether the firm hires from external sources or relies primarily on promoting people from within the organization to fill vacant positions will determine opportunities for current employees and in this way influence rewards (promotion is a reward), training and development, and employment commitment.[44] A related issue is whether recruitment and career decisions will be open or closed. In some organizations, notices of job opportunities are posted, resulting in an extremely open process. In others, decisions are made by a relatively small group of upper-level managers and are simply announced.

● **Appraising**   Performance appraisal is a linchpin in strategic management. Once strategic goals are established, it is important that the performance appraisal system be adjusted to evaluate the behaviors needed to achieve these objectives. Methods of appraisal should vary with the organization's strategy. For example, Richard Beatty and Craig Schneier suggest that firms following an "operational-excellence" strategy (low-cost producer) should have performance measures focused on such things as total cost of production, errors, waste, net sales, and so forth. On the other hand, firms following a "customer-intimacy" strategy (unique solutions and high levels of product customization) will need to assess performance in terms of things like customer retention rates and number of referrals from current customers.[45]

● **Compensating**   Perhaps more than any other area of human resource management, the reward structure communicates the overall philosophy and strategy of the organization. Furthermore, choices with respect to rewards overlap many other areas of human resource management. As with performance appraisal systems, Beatty and Schneier suggest that different reward systems are needed for different strategies. Operational-excellence firms should focus on team productivity, profit sharing, and skills-based pay, while customer-intimacy firms should focus on individual rewards, nonfinancial rewards, and service award programs.[46]

● **Training and Development**   Some organizations do not train and develop their work force but instead seek to hire skilled employees from the outside. At times, as a result of either fast growth or rapidly changing technology, this is the only way to acquire the needed expertise. Other organizations prefer to develop expertise in-house, although training and developing employees is both costly and time

● FIGURE 2.4

Uluru Energy's HR Practice Choices

☐ Choices before strategic planning for redirection
◼ Reorientation of choices to achieve quality strategy

STAFFING CHOICES

Internal sources	External sources
Narrow paths	Broad paths
Single ladder	Multiple ladders
Explicit criteria	Implicit criteria
Limited socialization	Extensive socialization
Closed procedures	Open procedures

APPRAISING CHOICES

Behavioral criteria	Results criteria
Low employee participation	High employee participation
Short-term criteria	Long-term criteria
Individual criteria	Group criteria

COMPENSATING CHOICES

Low-base salaries	High-base salaries
Internal equity	External equity
Few perks	Many perks
Standard, fixed package	Flexible package
Low participation	High participation
No incentives	Many incentives
Short-term incentives	Long-term incentives
No employment security	High employment security
Hierarchical	High participation

TRAINING AND DEVELOPMENT

Short term	Long term
Narrow application	Broad application
Emphasis on productivity	Emphasis on quality
Spontaneous, unplanned	Planned, systematic
Individual orientation	Group orientation
Low participation	High participation

EMPLOYEE INFLUENCE

Collective bargaining	Individual bargaining
Formal due process	Informal (or no) due process
No employee input	Broad employee participation
No employee ownership	Partial or complete employee ownership
Employee compliance	Employee empowerment

WORK SYSTEMS

Job simplification	Job enrichment
Explicit job analysis	Implicit job analysis
Individual orientation	Team orientation
Narrowly defined jobs	Broadly defined jobs
Directive management	Participative management
Specialized jobs	Rotation among jobs
Close supervision	Peer- or self-supervision

consuming. To be effective, training and development must be tied to the overall strategic objectives of the organization and to other HR systems. For example, due to tight labor-market conditions and the need to keep its costs low as part of a cost-leadership strategy, an organization may need to develop its nonmanagerial workers for managerial jobs. One step toward this goal would be to have them work with and learn from current managers. However, if existing managers are not rewarded for helping to develop others, they probably will devote little time and energy to the task. In addition, development efforts will be counterproductive unless promotional opportunities are available for those who complete the program. If employees cannot use what they have learned in-house and/or are not rewarded for doing so, the best of them will tend to depart for opportunities in other organizations.

● **Employee Influence**   One of the rediscoveries of the 1990s was that empowered employees tend to manage their performance in support of business objectives. The concept of employee influence has evolved from superficial participation (e.g., suggestion systems) to responsibility for direct input into the decision process, accountability for outcomes, and sharing in the wealth created by these outcomes. As a result, one of the HR practice issues that continues to be prominent is the amount of influence accorded to employees in such matters as organizational goals, rewards, working conditions, and the work itself. Organizations are finding that **empowered employees**—that is, employees with a feeling of involvement in the results of their efforts—strengthen the organization.[47]

● **Work Systems**   Another factor in individual productivity and organizational effectiveness is the design of work. Jobs have greater motivational value when they give individuals greater responsibility and control of their work as opposed to simplification or overspecialization.[48] The use of **work systems** to influence productivity has also been manifested in an emphasis on teams. The team approach is consistent with **delayering**—that is, the trend for fewer management levels and fewer managers. As a result, more authority and responsibility are delegated to self-managed teams or autonomous work groups to plan, organize, supervise, and evaluate their own work.[49]

HR Practices and Strategic Fit at Uluru Energy: An Example

Different choices about HR practices may be made following a strategic planning process. Returning to Figure 2.4, we see the choices Uluru Energy made before and after the development of its new mission statement and strategic plan. As the squares in the figure indicate, the emphasis at Uluru had been on a traditional bureaucratic organization with a hierarchical structure. Employees were hired for entry-level jobs and then slowly moved up through relatively narrow, specialized internal career paths. Employees were expected to perform their individual jobs under close supervision, with little team orientation or involvement. It is likely that Uluru Energy would need to undertake a very different approach to many HR activities in conjunction with the firm's privatization and strategic redirection, such as delayering and downsizing, developing more extensive communication channels within the firm, building a team orientation, enhancing management development activities and cross-training, implementing new strategy-consistent incentive systems, and generally encouraging higher levels of employee involvement in organizational decision making.[50]

HR Practices and Strategic Fit: Putting It All Together

The AT&T Global Business Communications Systems (GBCS) process of transforming traditional HRM into SHRM is a fine example of how aspects of HR fit can be managed. In 1991, during a period of declining sales and low employee morale, Jerre Stead became president and set about developing a new set of strategic business principles for the organization:

- Make people a key priority.
- Win customers for life.
- Use the total quality management approach to run the business.
- Profitably grow by being the leader in customer-led applications of technology.
- Rapidly and profitably globalize the business.
- Be the best value supplier.[51]

Once these general strategic principles had been established, the development of a more strategic and integrated HR function became possible.

The process of transforming HRM at GBCS is represented in Table 2.6. Step 1 resulted in identifying the basic business principles described above. In step 2, a set of "HR strategic imperatives" were derived directly from the business principles. These HR imperatives helped translate the business principles into a set of HR-related outcomes pertaining to the daily operation of GBCS. Thus, in order to "make people a key priority," HR programs needed to ensure that employees (as sociates) gained a sense of ownership in making the business a success. In order to globalize successfully, GBCS had to become sensitive to differences in cultures and in people with whom GBCS might attempt to do business. In step 3, the HR unit used these imperatives to develop its own internal mission statement, which identified those areas on which it was most essential to focus HR activities.

At GBCS, the critical focus areas for HR were cultural change, rewards and recognition, and the development of ownership among employees. Once the HR mission and focus areas were clarified, the HR unit could then develop, in partnership with management and employees, specific programs to adapt to a new external environment, accomplish its mission, and contribute to the overall strategic success of the organization while at the same time ensuring that specific HR programs were consistent with and enhanced one another. Culture-change programs focusing on communicating the new vision of the organization were developed, along with incentive and recognition programs that rewarded those who exhibited culturally appropriate behaviors. Employee surveys were conducted to identify trouble spots in areas essential to the new culture and business strategy. The surveys also helped enhance the sense of ownership and participation by employees in the organizational transformation.

From the actions taken by GBSC, it is obvious that horizontal, vertical, and external fit of HR practices requires a step-by-step analysis of the overall mission, goals, and objectives of the organization. In addition, to be truly effective, the fit process requires not only the active involvement of individuals in charge of HR practices and policies but also the meaningful participation of line personnel

● TABLE 2.6

AT&T Global Business Communications Systems' HR Transformation Process

Step 1: Establish GBCS Business Principles	Step 2: Identify HR Strategic Imperatives	Step 3: HR Mission	Step 4: Focus Areas	Step 5: Programs
Make people a key priority	Employees must take ownership and responsibility for business success.			Learning forums
Use total quality management	Improve product quality and customer satisfaction to increase shareholder value.		Cultural change	Multiple communications program
Rapidly and profitably globalize	Ensure that GBCS is ready to globalize, which requires sensitivity to different cultures and people.	To create an environment where the achievement of business goals is realized through an acceptance of individual accountability for each associate and by his or her commitment to performance excellence		Special long-term plan recognition program
			Rewards and recognition	
Profitably grow through technology innovation	HR plans are integrated into GBCS's strategic plans, and HR attracts, develops, rewards, and retains people who accept accountability for business success.			Performance excellence partnership
Be the best value supplier	HR provides a level of service to internal and external customers that establishes HR as their value-added business partner.		Ownership	Associate surveys
	HR is competent to provide leadership and support for HR initiatives that contribute to GBCS's success.			Organizational effectiveness monitoring

Source: Adapted from Martin Plevel, Sandy Nellis, Fred Lane, and Randall Schuler, "AT&T Global Business Communications Systems: Linking HR with Business Strategy," *Organizational Dynamics*, Winter 1994, p. 64.

throughout the firm. Before we turn our attention to this issue of building a partnership between HR and line management, one final issue associated with strategic fit must be discussed—the apparent conflict between strategic fit and strategic flexibility in HR practices.

HR Practices: Strategic Fit Versus Strategic Flexibility

So far in this chapter, strategic fit has been portrayed as a highly desirable end state for HR managers to achieve in their organizations. However, as with many things in life, too much of a good thing might have bad consequences. As Gerald Ferris and his colleagues state in a 1999 article, the "fact that organizational environments are dynamic has evoked much speculation about the prescription for tight fit of HRM systems with any particular strategic goal. Chadmick and Cappelli (1999) pointed out the dysfunctionality of external fit in arguing that as fit to external conditions becomes closer or tighter, this can become more problematic as competition changes. Embedded systems and structures are difficult to change under any circumstances, and the greater the intermeshing of fit of such systems, the more entrenched they become, and the more difficult they are to modify." [52] What Ferris and colleagues are pointing out is the danger of HR systems becoming too well "fitted" to a particular business environment and strategy. They suggest that an organization could become like the wooly mammoth: a fantastic, successful creature until the weather changed and—boom!—it died.

Several researchers point out that both fit and flexibility are needed for long-term competitive advantage. [53] Patrick Wright and Scott Snell argue that fit and flexibility are independent concepts, with HR managers needing to pay close attention to both. [54] They describe fit as a *temporary state* in an organization. Fit may exist at time 1, but not at time 2. On the other hand, flexibility is a *characteristic* of an organization related to its ability to meet the demands of a dynamic environment. Wright and Snell distinguish between two types of flexibility. **Resource flexibility** is the extent to which an organization can apply its resources to a variety of uses and purposes. Resource flexibility also involves the cost, difficulty, and time needed to switch resources from one use to another. For example, an organization hires employees who possess a particular skill needed for their current business strategy. There is a good fit between the skills of employees hired and current strategy. At the same time, the organization includes in its selection process measures of "trainability" or "ability to learn" that allow the hiring of employees who can more easily develop new skills if they were needed. In this case the organization has both resource fit and resource flexibility.

Coordination flexibility concerns the extent to which an organization has decision-making and other systems that allow it to quickly move resources from one use to another. For example, AT&T's Resource Link is a database of employee skills to which line managers have ready access. This database provides information about the skills of current employees in other areas of the firm. If "new skills" are needed in one area of AT&T, Resource Link increases the likelihood that these skills can be quickly obtained from areas where they already exist. Resource Link provides enhanced coordination flexibility within AT&T. [55] As with the development of strategic fit, the establishment of HR practices that provide both fit and flexibility is something that HR managers cannot do alone. They can accomplish this difficult task only by developing a strong **partnership** between themselves and line managers.

PARTNERSHIP

Janice Tomlinson argues that to become a business partner, the HR manager must (1) learn as much about the firm's business as possible, (2) be more responsive to and more aware of the organization's needs and direction, (3) shift away from traditional HR functions, (4) become more involved in supportive, collaborative relationships with managers throughout the organization, and (5) demonstrate how critical HR is to the success of the business.[56]

A good example of HR's developing a better partnership role in an organization can be found at Colgate Palmolive.[57] In the late 1980s, due to the increasing size of its international operations and the number of different products it produced and marketed, Colgate engaged in substantial organizational restructuring. Part of that effort involved developing a partnership relationship between HR and line staff worldwide. The development of this partnership was a complex, multistage process. The first step involved the creation of a Global Human Resources Strategy Team made up of twenty-five members, half HR leaders and half senior managers. After initial discussions, this team set a global vision for HR:

> We care about people. We are all part of a global team, committed to working across functions, across countries and throughout the world. We are committed to getting better every day in all we do, as individuals and as teams.[58]

The vision was then circulated to seventy-five general managers and the entire senior management team for buy-in. Once agreement on the new vision was achieved, interviews and discussions were held with line managers worldwide; from this process, HR staff members identified several areas in which business managers needed HR support. Of particular importance were career planning, education, and training. Given a widely accepted vision for HR and information about the needs of line managers, HR staff then created an HR strategy focusing on (1) generating organizational excellence through selection and training, (2) reinforcing organizational excellence through performance management and reward systems, and (3) sustaining organizational excellence through continuous improvement initiatives and constant communication of Colgate's vision. Individual programs, which were to be used worldwide, were developed within each of these three main focus areas. To end the development of the new HR vision and begin its implementation, a kickoff conference was held for all senior HR people worldwide.

Lucent Technologies provides a more recent example of a major firm's focus on the partnership between HR and line management.[59] Lucent has developed a model of HR services that focuses on three client service levels—individual employees, supervisors, and senior leaders. The critical role for value creation in Lucent's new HR approach is that of "HR Business Partner"; that is, HR leaders who work directly with top line managers to implement the organization's strategy. All levels of client services are measured against strict client-service standards. However, the overriding goal of HR Business Partners is to have senior executives view HR as helping them solve *their* problems in *their* businesses for *their* clients and, at the end of the year, for the executives to say that "We were very successful and couldn't have done it without HR."[60] Examples of how HR at Lucent Technologies has gone about transforming itself into a true business partner include the following:

- HR staff attend staff meetings so as to better understand the nature of the business.

- A cadre of 58 HR staff whose job is to find and remove HR practices that do not add value has been developed.

- Top executives from other areas of the firm have been brought in to discuss their areas with HR staff and help identify ways for HR to help grow those areas.

- A new competency model for HR staff has been developed to identify the skills they need to be more effective business partners.

The Colgate and Lucent Technologies examples relate most clearly to Tomlinson's first four points about what it means for HR to become a business partner. Tomlinson's fifth point—demonstrating how critical HR is to the success of the business—is not so clearly demonstrated in the preceding examples, although it is certainly implied in both. The ability of HR to measure its contribution to the organization's bottom line or other relevant measures of firm effectiveness is, however, an essential final ingredient in the development of a lasting, meaningful partnership between HR and line managers. Measurement of HR's contribution to the organization also underlies all other aspects of SHRM. Strategic HRM is really about HR practices adding value to the organization. The next section looks closely at this issue of measuring HR's contribution to organizational competitiveness and success.

MEASURING HRM

HR departments have long been criticized for not providing bottom-line results for the organization. Although some have argued that such criticism is unwarranted and that measuring HR's impact is often unnecessary and sometimes detrimental (see A Different Point of View), there has been increasing pressure on HR departments to evaluate their return on investment.[61] In order to show how HR contributes to overall business success, the first requirement is to identify means of measuring HR's performance. A number of authors have suggested typologies of HR measurement systems, and literally dozens of individual indices have been developed to measure HR effectiveness.[62] However, most of these typologies relate to four basic questions about HRM:

1. What did the customers of the HR practice or those who have some stake in an HR activity think of it?
2. Did the HR activity have a measurable impact?
3. If the HR activity did have an impact, then what was the bottom-line dollar benefit to the organization?
4. How do our HR activities compare with the HR activities of others (an issue of **HR benchmarking**)?

Customer Reactions

The customer/stakeholder approach to measuring HRM effectiveness involves identifying those who have a stake in the activities of HR in the organization or are direct users of HR products—such as managers, unions, customers, employees,

Pitfalls on the Road to Measurement

 In a 1997 article in *Human Resource Management*, Jeffrey Pfeffer challenges the idea that HR managers must justify HR practices using "bottom-line," cost-versus-benefit measures. Pfeffer asks:

When was the last time you, the reader, saw the corporate General Counsel's office justify its use of resources—not whether or not it was less expensive than using outside counsel, but whether the total expenditure on legal bills was reasonable? Legal fees are seen as something necessary and inexorable. . . . Ask your friends in management consulting who do strategy work the last time a corporation's strategy formulation process and associated expenses were measured in a way comparable to the measurement of human resources. (p. 359)

Pfeffer uses practices in two highly successful organizations to support his point. He notes that Singapore International Airlines (SIA) spends about $80,000,000 a year on training. Among the thirty-two participants in one of SIA's most expensive senior-level management training programs are six or seven pilots. These pilots have limited managerial responsibility. When asked why the pilots were included in this high-level *managerial* training class, the SIA people said that it was important to make pilots feel a part of the organization and to understand how it worked—therefore they were included. There was no "bottom-line" answer to the question of how SIA could justify spending managerial training resources on the pilots. SIA really did not care. Including the pilots in the program "made sense," and so they were included.

At AES Corporation, a firm that develops and operates power plants around the world, there is no formal HR staff at all. Money is spent on HR-related issues when employees, working in teams, deem it necessary. While AES measures aggregate results (e.g., profit), it does not have highly complex processes for approving HR expenditures, nor does it invest time and energy micromeasuring the cost-benefit ratio of HR activities.

Pfeffer points out that one of the major problems with the current focus on measuring HR is that "unfortunately, in almost all aspects of organizational operations, what is most easily measured and what is important are often loosely related." (p. 360)

HR managers, due to cost pressures, cannot afford to spend money developing good measures of what is important. Instead they often use measures produced by the firm's accounting systems (e.g., cost of operating an HR system) or measures of the level of HR activity (e.g., number of people hired, transactions processed). Why? Because they are easy to get and to track over time.

Pfeffer identifies a number of problems with the measures that are typically used to assess HR effectiveness. Among these problems are the following:

• They don't tell us if the money is spent wisely, (e.g., whether a training budget is spent on the most critical training needs).
• They are easy to manipulate and play games with.
• They tend to encourage a drive for efficiency, which ends up as a drive for shrinkage.
• There is an assumption that somehow "less" = "better," (e.g., Volvo is more efficient than Toyota because it employs fewer people).
• Such measures don't take into account exactly what is being done with the resources.
• The time horizon of many of these measures is extremely short term.
• They measure specific "parts" of the organization, but do not help us understand the organization as a complete system.
• They tend to measure too many things to be effective in influencing individual behavior.
• They often measure things that HR cannot really influence (e.g., in the auto industry how much training is done in a particular plant is heavily determined by the nature of the technology of the production process in that plant).

Pfeffer (1997) argues that firms like SIA and AES are more likely to show high levels of economic performance than those that chase precision of cost-benefit analysis at the expense of understanding what is really important. To Pfeffer, efforts directed toward micromeasuring the impact of HR programs in an organization are futile, since, as he states in his article, "To measure everything is, at the end, equivalent to measuring nothing." (p. 362)

Source: Jeffrey Pfeffer, "Pitfalls on the Road to Measurement: The Dangerous Liaison of Human Resources with the Ideas of Accounting and Finance," *Human Resource Management,* Vol. 36 (3), 1997, pp. 357–365.

suppliers, or even company shareholders. These individuals are surveyed to assess their perception of whether HR is supplying the right kinds of HR products, in the right way, and at the right time. Jac Fitz-enz, in his 1995 book, *How to Measure Human Resources Management*, suggests that it is important for HR to regularly survey its customers to measure the level of satisfaction with each of the various functions that HR performs (e.g., payroll, training, benefits) as well as the process by which HR delivers its service. It is also important for HR to understand the relative importance of the various aspects of service delivery to each customer. Fitz-enz has identified six measures of HR service delivery satisfaction.[63] These factors, which are presented in Table 2.7, are applicable to any form of customer service, be it HR services or services one might receive in a hotel. The factors deal with basic issues relating to the quality and speed of service as well as the ability of service providers to anticipate (not simply react to) the needs of those they serve.

HR Impact

A wide variety of "impact" measures are being used in organizations. For example, the results of a 1997 survey conducted by the Society of Human Resource Management (SHRM) and CCH, Inc. identified a number of commonly used HR assessment measures. Survey respondents indicated whether they used each of the measures and how important they felt the measure was in assessing the overall effectiveness of HR. The survey results are shown in Table 2.8.[64] Measures that would fall into the "HR impact" category are shown in the top portion of the table.

In order to properly evaluate the impact of HR programs, human resource units must develop a strategic framework for assessing the effectiveness of their

● **TABLE 2.7**

Six Measures of HR Service Delivery

Measure	Definition
Reliability	The dependable and accurate performance of activities related to the HR activity, for example, making sure that medical claims related to worker injuries on the job are filed using proper procedures with all information in the file being accurate
Responsiveness	Indications of a willingness to help and provide prompt service, for example, providing training on interviewing techniques to a new manager when that individual is suddenly faced with recruiting new staff
Assurance	Displaying skills and knowledge that generate trust and confidence within the customer, for example, an HR staff person who is expert in equal employment opportunity law shares this information with managers who are recruiting new staff
Empathy	Providing caring, individual attention, that is, adding the personal touch to service and through specific actions indicating to customers that you care about them and their problems or issues
Tangibles	Appearance of facilities and staff and the appearance and usefulness of the published materials, for example, having clean, comfortable, well-equipped training rooms
Anticipation	Anticipating customer needs, for example, communicating regularly with potential customers to find out what is happening in their work environment and then trying to help them identify potential problems and prevent the problem from actually occurring

Source: Adapted from lecture materials presented by Jac Fitz-enz at the 1996 HR Benchmarking Conference in Sydney, Australia, organized by HRM Consulting of Brisbane. Reprinted by permission of HRM Consulting.

● **TABLE 2.8**

HR Assessment Measures and Their Importance and Use

Measure	Importance (5-Point Scale)	% of Firms Who Used
HR Impact		
Accident rate	3.94	88
Employee turnover rate	3.52	97
Employee attitude surveys	3.50	74
Attendance/absentee rate	3.28	93
Formal appeal/grievance rate	3.09	78
Formal HR program evaluation	2.89	64
Average time to fill positions	2.88	86
Ratio of acceptances to job offers	2.54	70
Ratio of hires to applicants	2.37	79
Dollar Value		
Benefits as % of total compensation	3.80	97
Labor contract costing	3.34	63
Return on HR investment	3.15	67
Cost per hire	2.70	86
Sales revenue per employee	2.62	65
HR cost per sales dollar	2.51	72
Cost per employee training hour	2.45	76
Market pricing of HR services	2.38	51

Source: Adapted from Nancy Kaylor, Susan McLane, and Susan Schechter, "Ideas and Trends in Personnel," *Human Resources Management*, Vol. 408, June 1997, p. 92.

services.[65] The strategic objectives of organizational units should be identified, along with the human resource activities needed to accomplish those objectives. For example, an organizational unit may depend on the development of innovative products for its market growth. The selection of R&D scientists who can regularly achieve product innovations would be a key human resource activity needed for achieving market-growth objectives. If HR staff developed an "improved" selection interview intended to increase the number of innovative R&D scientists hired, the extent to which the new interview actually yielded a greater percentage of innovative scientists would be a measure of HR program impact.

Dollar Value of HR Programs

The third issue in assessing HR practices relates to the monetary costs and benefits of HR activities—the **dollar value of HR programs.** Several dollar-value indices used to assess HR are shown in the lower portion of Table 2.8.[66]

Wayne Cascio, in *Costing Human Resources: The Financial Impact of Behavior in Organizations*, describes more direct ways to assess HR cost-benefit ratios.[67] The first step, obviously, is to figure out how much some undesirable HR-related situation in the organization is costing. For example, Cascio suggests that the cost of employee absenteeism can be assigned a dollar value using the following formula:

> Costs of absenteeism = [hours lost to absenteeism × (average of wage per hour per absent employee + average of benefits per hour per absent employee)] + (total supervisory hours lost due to absenteeism × average hourly wage of supervisors) + all other incidental costs resulting from absenteeism (such as extra wages paid to hire temporary workers to replace the absent employee or wages paid in overtime to employees who have to work extra time because of the absent employee)

Using formulas similar to Cascio's, some researchers have suggested that for employees earning $15,000 per year, the average cost of absenteeism per employee-day is around $207.48.[68] Suppose that a firm has a 3 percent absenteeism rate, which means that each employee is absent about 7.8 days per year. If there are fifty employees earning $15,000, then the firm can expect these employees to have a total of about 390 days of absenteeism per year. At $207.48 per day, this level of absenteeism would cost the firm $80,917.20!

Once the firm knows what absenteeism is costing, the next step becomes one of estimating the costs of the HR program developed to fix the problem. Suppose, for example, that the firm decides to implement an incentive program to reduce absenteeism. Workers who have a perfect attendance record each week have their names placed into a "lotto draw" in which one person wins $50. At the end of the year, each employee is given a lotto ticket—one for each week of perfect attendance. These tickets are then placed into a large drum. Three names are drawn randomly from the drum, with the first person receiving $1000, the second $500, and the third $250. The costs of this program would include the following:

- 52 weeks × $50 weekly prizes = $2600
- Materials used in the drawings such as tickets, drum, and so forth = $250
- Administrative time associated with running the program; for example, one person earning $100 per day (wage + benefits) working the equivalent of two days each month × 12 months = $2400
- Other overhead costs estimated at 30 percent of the program administrator's salary = $720

The total cost of the program would be $5970. If this program resulted in a 20 percent decrease in absenteeism, the benefit gained from the program would be 20 percent × $80,917.20 = $16,183.44. Subtracting the cost of running the incentive program would result in total savings to the firm of $10,213.44!

The preceding absenteeism example seems relatively simple and straightforward. Unfortunately, assessing the dollar costs and benefits of HR practices is not always so easy. Despite the difficulty, the pressures of a more competitive business environment will increasingly place HR practitioners in the position of having to justify the **bottom-line impact** of their practices on the organization. We will not go into great detail on the costing of HR programs here; rather, most chapters in the remainder of this book will include a section that describes some of the methods and formulas that may be used to assess the costs and benefits of HR programs discussed in that particular chapter.

Combining Customer Reaction, HR Impact, and Dollar Value: An Eastman Kodak Example

Eastman Kodak provides an excellent example of a firm that assesses HR using a variety of measures. Kodak developed three clusters of measures for use in assessing the impact and value of HR programs. Examples of these are described below:[69]

Cluster 1: Internal operational measures (how well HR does what it does)

- Cycle time of HR practices (how long it takes to develop and run programs)
- Quality and cost of practices
- Result measures, such as acceptances versus offers in hiring
- HR client satisfaction measures
- Measures such as the ratio of HR expenses to total operating expenses of the company

Cluster 2: Internal strategic measures (how well HR practices serve strategically important initiatives in the organization)

- Leadership diversity in terms of race, gender, and so forth
- 360-degree measures of leadership competency
- Percentage of employees with documented development plans
- Number of hours devoted to development by employees
- Results of development activities assessed using four levels of training evaluation (see Chapter 9)
- Clarity of performance expectations and adequacy of performance feedback

Cluster 3: External strategic measures (to assess how well HR practices satisfy customers and shareholders)

- Incremental sales and earnings
- Changes in customer satisfaction and commitment

The two critical elements of the Kodak system are that (1) it uses a variety of measures of customer reactions, HR impact, and dollar value and (2) it approaches the measurement of HR effectiveness from different strategic perspectives.

Benchmarking HR Practices

As we indicated earlier, the fourth aspect of measuring the effectiveness of HR programs is through HR benchmarking. Benchmarking is important because to determine the true *competitive* advantage of HR, an organization must assess HR practices not only against some internal standard but also against the HR practices of key competitors and firms that exemplify HR excellence. **Benchmarking** is a generic term that can be defined as "a comparison with selected performance indicators from different organizations, typically in the same industry, or with comparable organizations that are considered to be 'best in class.'"[70] Benchmarking has been conducted on a wide variety of organizational practices, often relating to production methods or technology, but for the remainder of this section, we will use the term only as it applies to the comparison and evaluation of HR practices.

There are several different types of benchmarking.[71] **Internal benchmarking** occurs when a firm compares practices in one part of the organization against those in other internal units. For example, work and safety practices in a firm's operations in the southwestern United States might be compared with those in its New England operations. **Competitive benchmarking** is conducted against external competitors in the same markets. Firm A might compare itself with four of its competitors in terms of its employee turnover rate, ratio of HR staff to production employees, and percentage of total operating budget spent on employee training. **Generic HR benchmarking** involves the comparison of HR processes that are the same, regardless of industry. Sheraton Hotels could compare aspects of its HR practices with the HR practices at Ford Motor Company, IBM, Lucent Technologies, and Bond University.

Regardless of which type of benchmarking is conducted, the process is essentially the same.[72] The firm must first *understand its own performance* by developing measures of customer reactions, HR impact, or dollar value (for example, like those shown in Table 2.8). The firm must then *decide exactly what to benchmark,* since more aspects of HR performance may be measurable than need to be benchmarked. Measures that are obtainable in the comparison firms or business units should be identified and then prioritized relative to their overall strategic importance to the role of HR in the company. An overall *plan for the program* should be developed, including the allocation of sufficient resources for the project and the establishment of a clear project calendar. The next step is to *identify firms* (or in the case of internal benchmarking, parts of the firm) that will be in the study, persuade them to participate, and then collect data. *Analyzing the data* collected involves looking for "gaps" between your firm's (unit's) practices and those of other firms (units) in the study. Recommendations on how to close these gaps should be made and then implemented.

The number of different indices of HR performance that can be benchmarked is almost limitless. Table 2.8 provides only a few examples. What benchmark indices should be used will depend on the specific strategy and circumstances of the firm involved. However, in the United States, twenty-five HR measurement "national standards" were developed in 1984 by the Saratoga Institute. A review of these twenty-five measures would be useful for any firm contemplating an HR benchmarking process.[73] Additionally, throughout the remainder of this book, we will identify relevant benchmark indices associated with HR practices discussed in many chapters.

IS STRATEGIC HRM REALLY WORTH ALL THE TROUBLE?

Because of the magnitude of the differences between the traditional personnel perspective and strategic HRM, it is not surprising that many organizations have yet to make the leap into SHRM. There are a variety of reasons why the transformation from traditional HRM to SHRM is not made. (See the International Perspective box for reasons that the transition is slow in Europe.) The adoption of SHRM requires a highly competent and persistent SHRM leader as well as committed and supportive top management. Many firms simply do not have this type of HR leader or top management support. Political forces within the organization, accompanied by competing coalitions with different self-interests, may preclude the adoption of many SHRM practices. For example, HR systems that could help achieve particular organizational objectives may not be supported by unions. Also, firms that are not labor-intensive may be less likely to make the effort to move to a strategic HR orientation, since human resources are perceived to make up a relatively small portion of the organization's potential competitive advantage.

Firms experiencing very stressful business conditions (either rapid expansion or sudden decline) often feel that they are "up to their ears in alligators" and do not have the time or resources to invest in an HRM transformation. Unfortunately, for many of these firms, the lack of attention to HR issues may be one of the primary factors contributing to their business stress. For example, firms undergoing downsizing often cut HR staff, since they are viewed as nonessential to the core business. However, after downsizing, employees often need extensive training to manage expanded jobs and the selection of any new staff becomes particularly critical. Thus, at a time when HR services are most needed, they are often reduced. Additionally, highly decentralized organizations made up of autonomous business units may view the move to a corporate-wide, relatively unitary model of SRHM as both unfeasible and potentially undesirable.

The traditional role that HR has played in many organizations may have established a vicious cycle that makes the transition to SHRM extremely difficult.[74] Unless HR managers are involved directly in the process of strategy formulation, any attempt by senior management to link HR activities with business strategy simply creates a cycle in which HR cannot implement the HR components of the strategy effectively, which causes HR to lose credibility with non-HR managers, thus further isolating HR from the strategic planning process, making it increasingly difficult to implement strategy and so forth.

Transforming traditional HR into strategic HRM is a complex and time-consuming process. Top managers and HR practitioners are right in questioning the overall value of the SHRM transformation process. Just as we can evaluate the effectiveness of a single HR practice, we also must examine the issue of whether strategic HRM is really "worth all the trouble."

There is evidence that HR practices do have a direct bottom-line effect on organizational profitability.

In a 1997 study, Mark Huselid and his colleagues assessed the level of HR "technical" and "strategic" effectiveness in 293 U.S. firms. Firm performance also was measured based on share price, net sales per employee, and gross rate of return on assets. The results of the study indicated that an increase of one standard deviation in overall HR effectiveness was associated with a 5.2 percent increase in per-employee sales volume valued at $44,380, a 16.3 percent increase in cash flow valued at $9,673 per employee, and a 6 percent increase in market value valued at $8,882 per employee. These findings were consistent with the results of an earlier study of 968 U.S. firms in which Huselid found that "high-performance work practices" were also related to increased levels of sales, profits, and market value as well as a 7.05 percent decrease in employee turnover.[75] Other findings also suggest that improved HR practices resulting from a transformation to a strategic HR perspective can have a bottom-line impact. For example, Sears found that for every 5 percent improvement in employee attitudes (resulting from various HR

INTERNATIONAL PERSPECTIVE

Making It Happen in Europe: Harder, yet Easier

 European HRM scholars have pointed out that somewhat different assumptions and environments surround the practice of strategic HRM in Europe as compared with the United States. One study found that American HRM textbooks are full of references to strategy and the strategic role that must be played by the modern HR manager, whereas European texts seldom mention this topic. Chris Brewster of the Cranfield School of Management in England suggests that European HR managers may place less emphasis on a strategic role because these managers in general have less control and autonomy than is assumed in American models. This is due to greater government involvement in regulating work life in many European nations. At the same time, however, European managers enjoy a greater level of government support for the labor market, and in some ways this gives them more choices in the strategic HRM arena. The following environmental factors differentiate the European HRM context from that in America:

1. More collectivist national cultures, on average, than in the United States.

2. More government regulation of the employment relationship—both at the national level and at the European Community (EC) level. At the EC level, a Social Charter pertaining to a number of employee rights has been adopted, and more detailed programs for specifying and ensuring these rights in the member nations are being negotiated.

3. More concentrated patterns of ownership, with greater governmental ownership in many industries and ownership of public firms tending to be concentrated in fewer hands, often those of powerful banks. The banks realize that businesses are in business to stay in business rather than to just turn a profit in the next quarter. This longer-term perspective means that takeovers and mass retrenchments are less common responses to temporarily flagging performance.

4. Greater unionization and much greater recognition of unions as legitimate and necessary partners in the process of running a business.

5. Mandated employee involvement in some European countries. Employers may be required to consult both the employees and the union before making some kinds of decisions.

6. More centralized bargaining and wage setting. More so than in the United States, wage rates in European countries are set by law or by multiemployer or industry-level bargaining rather than by organizational-level talks with a local union.

7. More government involvement in the labor market. Governments spend much more in some European nations on vocational and apprenticeship training and retraining than is the case in the United States. The Social Charter contains language asserting workers' rights to continued training so that their skills do not become obsolete. There is also greater government support for employees who are temporarily or partially unemployed. The highly qualified labor force gives employers in Europe greater freedom to recruit either internally or externally, while support for the unemployed makes part-time and contract labor more feasible and popular.

Sources: Chris Brewster, "European Human Resource Management: Reflection of, or Challenge to, the American Concept?," invited paper presented at the Third Conference on International Personnel and Human Resource Management, Berkhamsted, England, July 1992; Martyn Wright, "Is There a European Theory of HRM? An Empirical Comparison of European and American Texts," in *Proceedings of the Third Conference on International Personnel and Human Resource Management, Berkhamnsted, England*, July 1992; Dennis R. Briscoe and Gregory M. Gazda, "Human Resource Management and the Single European Market 1994: An Update," in *Proceedings of the Fourth Conference on International Human Resource Management, Gold Coast, Australia* July 1994; and Paul Teague, "Between Convergence and Divergence: Possibilities for a European Community System of Labour Market Regulation," *International Labour Review*, 1993, pp. 391–406.

initiatives), customer retention rates increased by 1.3 percent and profits by 0.4 percent.[76]

Research like Huselid's on the financial impact of HR practices remains suggestive rather than conclusive. However, if these results are combined with data like that collected by the Hackett Group on HR costs in best versus typical HR units and the practical dollar-saving experiences of firms like ERTL (discussed earlier in the chapter), there seems to be a strong case for promoting the improvement of HR activities as a means of affecting the financial results of many organizations. The business environment that has caused organizations to focus on human resources as a potentially enduring source of competitive advantage is likely to continue for many years. To the extent that HR practitioners become more adept at measuring aspects of customer reactions, HR program impact, and the dollar value of HR practices and at comparing their own HR practices with those of their best competitors, the importance of strategic human resource management is likely to continue to grow. Is strategic human resource management really worth all the trouble? The answer is almost certainly yes.

Summary of Key Points

This chapter discussed the process of how an organization can move from a traditional personnel management perspective to a strategic HRM approach. This move is necessitated by a modern business environment that is constantly changing, where technology, finance, and products can be imitated easily by competitors. Human resources are one of the few enduring sources of competitive advantage that remain for many firms. The traditional view of HR is that of an isolated, record-keeping function within the organization. Although strategic human resource management can be considered simply as the process of helping an organization achieve competitive advantage through its people, there are many different perspectives on this seemingly simple definition.

Some believe that there is a universal set of HR practices that will always contribute to a firm's success, regardless of the business environment or the company's strategy. The role of strategic human resource managers is one of incorporating these universally effective HR practices into their firm. Others believe that SHRM involves a process of matching specific HR practices to particular aspects of the firm's strategy. Here the HR practitioner's role is to ensure a fit between HR practices and business strategy. Also, HR practices must fit with the external environment and one another. Another view of SHRM is as that of a service provider whose

role is to solve the problems and serve the HR needs of managers within different business units in a firm. Other SHRM specialists believe that SHRM involves a process of putting together configurations of HR practices that are logically consistent with one another and are appropriate for the particular type of industry or business environment in which a firm operates. The final view of SHRM is as a means of gaining competitive advantage by putting together a unique group of human skills and abilities that other firms are unable to imitate and that give the firm special capabilities relative to its competitors.

Each of these perspectives adds to an overall view of SHRM. Taken collectively, these theoretical perspectives suggest that SHRM is a process that involves (1) internally transforming HR staff and structure, (2) enhancing HR administrative efficiency, (3) integrating HR into the strategic planning process, (4) linking HR practices to business strategy and to one another, (5) developing a partnership with line management so that HR programs meet real business needs, and (6) measuring the bottom-line impact of HR activities. Although each of these parts of the SHRM process is complex, time-consuming, and difficult, research indicates that real financial benefits result from more progressive, strategic, and efficient use of human resources within modern organizations.

The Manager's Vocabulary

administrative efficiency
benchmarking
bottom-line impact
centralized HR services
competitive advantage
competitive benchmarking
configurational approach
coordination flexibility
delayering
dollar value of HR programs
empowered employees
environmental opportunities
environmental threats
external fit
generic HR benchmarking
horizontal fit
HR benchmarking
HR bundles
HR practice choices
integration
internal benchmarking
internal service provider
mission statement
objectives
"one-stop shop"
partnership
resource-based model
resource flexibility
strategic-fit perspective
strategic human resource management (SHRM)
strategic planning process
universalistic approach
values statement
vertical fit
work systems

Questions for Discussion

1. Defend this statement: "The business environment now makes human resources one of the few enduring sources of competitive advantage for many firms."

2. Discuss the environmental changes faced by Uluru Energy as described in the HR Challenge. What are Uluru's organizational strengths and weaknesses? Explain how these changes will affect the basic business strategy Uluru will need to follow.

3. Compare and contrast the universalistic, configurational, and resource-based approaches to strategic human resource management.

4. Pick a specific large organization with which most people are familiar. As best as you can determine, what business strategy is the organization following? What implications does this strategy have for human resource management? What HR practice choices might make the most sense for this firm?

5. Discuss an organization you have worked for. In what ways did its HR practices facilitate or inhibit meeting the organization's goals?

6. What typical aspects of the structure of the HR function are changed when firms move to SHRM?

7. How are the skills needed by staff in a strategic HRM environment different from those needed by staff in a more traditional personnel/HR environment?

8. What is meant by the statement "Integration is a key part of the process of developing a SHRM perspective"? How would you go about integrating HR into the strategic planning process of a firm?

9. What do the terms "vertical fit," "horizontal fit," and "external fit" mean?

10. Describe how some organizations have gone about building a partnership between HR and line managers.

11. How can we measure the effectiveness of an HR program?

12. Defend this statement: "Developing a tight fit between HR practices and a firm's business strategy and external environment can be detrimental to a firm's long-term success."

13. Is SHRM really worth all the effort it requires?

● **Case 2.1**
Jumbuck Enterprises

You are the vice president of HR at Jumbuck Enterprises. The new CEO of Jumbuck, Harry (also known as "Chainsaw") Price has called you into his office one fine Monday morning. Harry says to you: "[Your name], times are tough here at Jumbuck Enterprises. Things have got to change, and change in a big way. All this warm-and-fuzzy human resource management stuff is great—as long as you have the profits to spend on it. When you don't, well, then I reckon I can save the firm quite a bit of money by sacking the whole HR Department. After all, a couple of decent clerks can handle the payroll."

You gape at Chainsaw with a look of total disbelief in your eyes. You catch your breath and say, "But Chain . . . , I mean Harry, the HR Department is one of the most critical groups in the firm. How can Jumbuck Enterprises be productive and successful without a motivated, highly trained, and talented work force? Every year the efforts of the HR Department result in hundreds of thousands of dollars in added profit for the firm."

Harry raises his eyes up toward the ceiling, gives a little laugh, and says, "Oh yeah, well prove it. You've got until Friday at noon to show me how the HR Department affects the bottom-line profits of this organization. I want a ten-minute presentation from you about HR's great value to this firm. It better be good. Otherwise, by Friday at 5:00 you'll all have received your last paychecks from Jumbuck Enterprises."

You hurry back to your office and rummage through a stack of reports one of your assistants has just prepared for you from a benchmarking study. In these data your firm is compared with 200 firms in all industries in the local area. Of these 200 firms, twenty were in your industry. Given the data below, justify your existence as an HR unit within Jumbuck Enterprises. How have you increased profits either directly or indirectly? How have you added value?

Some Hints
Average cost of an operative leaving the firm is estimated at one-half to one times the operative's annual salary. Average cost of a manager leaving the firm is estimated as one to

two times the manager's annual salary. Average cost of a day's absence by an employee earning $20,000 per year is $210 per day.

HR Expense Factor

HR operating expenses/total organization operating expenses

	Jumbuck			All Industry Median	Your Industry Median
	2000	2001	2002		
	1.1%	.98%	.94%	1.3%	1.1%

HR Staffing Factor

Total number of full-time employees/number of full-time HR employees

	Jumbuck			All Industry Median	Your Industry Median
	2000	2001	2002		
	54	56	55.26	55	58

Operative Absence

Total days absence/total work days

	Jumbuck			All Industry Median	Your Industry Median
	2000	2001	2002		
	3.2%	3%	2.9%	3.77%	3.19%

Average Position Tenure in Years (the average number of years an employee has been in current position)

	Jumbuck			All Industry Median	Your Industry Median
	2000	2001	2002		
Managerial	8	4	3	3.5	3.8
Operative	12	10	9	11	10

Labor Turnover Rate

	Jumbuck			All Industry Median	Your Industry Median
	2000	2001	2002		
Managerial	18%	14%	12%	14%	13%
Operative	22%	18%	14%	15%	16%

Managerial and Professional Start Time (time from job becoming vacant to job being filled)
Time to start in days/number of recruits

Jumbuck			All Industry Median	Your Industry Median
2000	2001	2002		
65	52	45	65.24	57

Managerial and Professional Hiring Costs (average cost of hiring managerial and professional staff)
Cost in dollars of hires/number of hires

Jumbuck			All Industry Median	Your Industry Median
2000	2001	2002		
$1020	$890	$850	$1200	$1000

Recruitment Source Ratio (ratio of positions filled from within the firm to positions filled by external recruits)

Jumbuck			All Industry Median	Your Industry Median
2000	2001	2002		
1:5	1:4	1:2	1:3	1:4

Managerial and Professional Career Path Ratio (e.g., in 1996, for every one promotion, there were twelve horizontal transfers within the firm for managerial and professional staff)
Promotions/horizontal transfers

Jumbuck			All Industry Median	Your Industry Median
2000	2001	2002		
1:12	1:8	1:5	1:6	1:8

Average Cost of Sick Leave Days Due to Accidents on the Job (includes employee absences from work plus medical costs associated with the accident)

Jumbuck			All Industry Median	Your Industry Median
2000	2001	2002		
$1850	$1730	$1520	$1475	$1550

Company Operating Expenses = $81,000,000 This has been the same for the last 3 years, along with the following:

Total employees	1000
Total operative employees	800
Total management employees	200
Average operative salary	$20,000
Average management salary	$40,000
Average HR salary	$25,000
Revenue per employee	$86,000
Gross profit per employee	$5,000
Number of management hires	16

Source: Adapted from a case prepared by Pat Foley and Peter Howes and presented at the 1996 Benchmarking Conference, HRM Consulting, Ltd., Sydney, Australia 1996. Reprinted by permission of HRM Consulting.

● **Exercise 2.1**
HR Strategy: E-Commerce Comes to Bojangles' Book and Music Company

You are the HR director for Bojangles' Book and Music Company (BBMC) in Springhill, Louisiana. Bojangles has been a family-owned business since 1925. It has been very successful over the years, providing a wide range of books and music to its customers. Bojangles prides itself on its very high level of customer service and an ability to fully live up to its motto of "You Want It , We Got—Or We Can Get It Fast." Bojangles' operations have spread from its single store in Springhill to a total of thirty stores in Louisiana, Mississippi, Alabama, and Georgia. Bojangles locates its stores in medium-sized towns because it found competition in the larger cities was too great. It has a highly efficient distribution system to ensure that all stores can live up to the BBMC motto.

BBMC's work force is hired from the local store areas. Stores provide part-time work for local high school students, while full-time employees tend to range in age from the mid-twenties to the late thirties. BBMC provides a profit-sharing scheme to all of its full-time employees. Turnover among these staff members is relatively low, with most staying with BBMC for several years.

Over the past couple of years, BBMC's profits have been dropping. Market research conducted by a professor from Western Central Louisiana University has indicated that much of Bojangles' loss in revenue can be attributed to book and music sellers operating on the Internet. After much soul searching, Beauregard B. Goree, Bojangles' current CEO, has decided "to take Bojangles' Book and Music Company onto the World Wide Web!"

Initially, BBMC will run all of its e-commerce operations from its home site in Springhill and use its existing distribution center. As to what this move to e-commerce means for BBMC's existing storefront operations, Beauregard B. Goree will only say, "Well, we'll just have to wait and see about that!"

1. Outline BBMC's strengths and weaknesses related to this change in mode of operation.

2. Outline the opportunities and threats associated with this change in business strategy.
3. Outline the HR practice implications for staff of such a change in operations. Specifically,
   a. what changes, if any, would be needed in how people are hired and what kinds of skills and qualifications they would need to have?
   b. how would you appraise the performance of staff in the new e-commerce operations and how would that differ from staff in the storefront sites?
   c. what changes would be required in how you paid staff?
   d. what new training and development programs would be required?

● Exercise 2.2

Changes in Business Strategy, Changes in HR: A Group Project

Students work in groups of four to five. Each group is to identify an organization that has undergone a major "strategic shift" in the recent past—for example, AT&T during its breakup and deregulation of the telecommunications industry. Students may also focus on any local firm that has undergone some major shift in strategy.

The task of each group (this may be done in or outside class) is to do the following:

- Outline the basic nature of the old and the new strategies of the firm.
- Identify the human resource implications of this strategic shift in terms of the selection, training, performance appraisal, and compensation of employees.
- Identify the major problems that the firm has or will likely experience in implementing these new HR activities.
- Prepare a report for presentation to the class.

For example, an organization that moves from being a mass producer of low-cost items to a maker of luxury-niche market products would need to focus more on quality, customer orientation, and reliability of service. Employees would need to be more quality focused and have better interpersonal and communication skills when dealing with customers. This would have an impact on both selection and training activities. Instead of speed and efficiency of production being the primary focus of performance appraisal, quality and customer-relations behaviors would become more important. Pay and incentive systems would need to reflect these new priorities. One major problem that is likely to face HR managers is the need to terminate employees who are unable to develop new and necessary skills. Pay and incentive systems to motivate performance may be difficult to implement if the firm is highly unionized or has low profit levels that make increased incentives not unfeasible.

In their reports, students should stress the fit between HR activities and the firm's new strategy, as well as the horizontal fit among the various HR activities, to show that they are consistent with one another.

● Exercise 2.3
Benchmarking Resources on the Web

Your company is thinking about beginning a benchmarking program in human resource management. Use the Internet to locate data and articles about benchmarking human resource management. Prepare a report to your manager on what you have learned about the advantages and disadvantages of benchmarking, how to select comparison organizations, and whether you should obtain the services of any of the benchmarking organizations or consultants you encounter on the Web.

Notes and References

1. Wayne Brockbank, "If HR Were Really Strategically Proactive: Present and Future Directions in HR's Contribution to Competitive Advantage," *Human Resource Management*, Vol. 38 (4),1999, pp. 337–352.

2. Philip Mirvis, "Human Resource Management: Leaders, Laggards, and Followers," *Academy of Management Executive*, Vol. 11 (2), 1997, pp. 43–56.

3. Randall S. Schuler, "Repositioning the Human Resource Function: Transformation or Demise," in *HRM Reality: Putting Competence in Context*, eds. P. J. Frost, V. F. Mitchell, and W. R. Nord (Cincinnati: Southwestern, 1992), pp. 8–21.

4. Dave Ulrich, *Human Resource Champions* (Cambridge, Mass.: Harvard Business School Press, 1997).

5. David Lepak and Scott Snell, "Virtual HR: Strategic Human Resource Management in the 21st Century," *Human Resource Management Review*, Vol. 8 (3), 1998, pp. 215–234.

6. James Walker, *Human Resource Strategy* (Sydney: McGraw-Hill International Editions, 1992); and Ian Clark, "HRM: Prescription, Description and Concept," *Personnel Review*, Vol. 22 (4), 1993, pp. 20, 23.

7. John Delery and Harold Doty, "Modes of Theorizing in Strategic Human Resource Management: Tests of Universalistic, Contingency, and Configurational Performance Predictions," *Academy of Management Journal*, Vol. 39 (4), 1996, pp. 802–835.

8. Jeffrey Pfeffer, *The Human Equation: Building Profits by Putting People First* (Boston, Mass: Harvard Business School Press, 1998).

9. John Delery, "Issues of Fit I Strategic Human Resource Management: Implications for Research," *Human Resource Management Review*, Vol. 8 (3), 1998, pp. 289–309; and Patrick M. Wright, "Strategy—HR Fit: Does It Really Matter?" *Human Resource Planning*, Vol. 21 (4), 1998, pp. 56–57.

10. Russell Eisenstat, "What Corporate Human Resources Brings to the Picnic: Four Models for Functional Management," *Organizational Dynamics*, Vol. 25 (2), 1996, pp. 7–22.

11. David Lepak and Scott Snell, "The Human Resource Architecture: Toward a Theory of Human Capital Allocation and Development," *Academy of Management Review*, Vol. 24 (1), 1999, pp. 31–48.

12. Pfeffer, "Pitfalls on the Road to Measurement: The Dangerous Liaison of Human Resources with the Ideas of Accounting and Finance," *Human Resource Management,* Vol. 36, (3), 1997, pp. 357–365.

13. J. P. MacDuffie, "Human Resource Bundles and Manufacturing Performance: Flexible Production Systems in the World Automotive Industry," *Industrial and Labor Relations Review*, Vol. 48 (2), 1995, pp. 197–221.

14. Jay Barney, "Looking Inside for Competitive Advantage," *Academy of Management Executive*, Vol. 9 (4), 1995, pp. 49–61.

15. Jay Barney and Patrick Wright, "On Becoming a Strategic Partner: The Role of Human Resources in Gaining Competitive Advantage," *Human Resource Management*, Vol. 37 (1), 1998, pp. 31–46.

16. Michael Beer, "The Transformation of the Human Resource Function: Resolving the Tension Between a Traditional Administrative and a New Strategic Role," *Human Resource Management*, Vol. 36 (1), 1997, pp. 49–56.

17. Ibid.; Wayne Brockbank, "If HR Were Really Strategically Proactive: Present and Future Directions in HR's Contribution to Competitive Advantage," *Human Resource Management*, Vol. 38 (4), 1999, pp. 337–352; and Timothy Galpin and Patrick Murray, "Connect Human Resource Strategy to the Business Plan," *HRMagazine*, Vol. 42 (3), 1997, pp. 99–104.

18. Warren Wilhelm, "Revitalizing the Human Resource Function in a Mature, Large Company," *Human Resource Management*, Vol. 29 (2), 1990, pp. 129–144.

19. Cited in William Morin, "HR as Director of People Strategy," *HRMagazine*, Vol. 39 (12), 1994, pp. 52–54.

20. Connie Freeman, "Training HR Pros to Fit Your Culture," *HRFocus*, Vol. 74 (5), 1997, pp. 9–10.

21. David Jones, "Repositioning Human Resources: A Case Study," *Human Resource Planning*, Vol. 19 (1), 1996, pp. 51–53.

22. Dawn Anfuso, "Colgate's Global HR Unites Under One Strategy," *Personnel Journal*, October 1995, pp. 44–54.

23. Jill Conner and Jeana Wirtenberg, "Managing the Transformation of Human Resources Work," *Human Resource Planning*, Vol. 16 (2), 1993, pp. 17–34.

24. Information concerning Tampella Power from Arja Ropo, "Towards Strategic Human Resource Management: A Pilot Study in a Finnish Power Industry Company," *Personnel Review*, Vol. 22 (4), 1993, pp. 35–53; information about Northern Telecom from James Kochanski and Phillip Randall, "Rearchitecting the Human Resources Function at Northern Telecom," *Human*

Resource Management, Vol. 33 (2), 1994, pp. 299–315; information on Benetton from Arnaldo Camuffo and Giovanni Costra, "Strategic Human Resource Management—Italian Style," *Sloan Management Review*, Vol. 34 (2), 1993, pp. 59–67; information about Siemens Rolm from Gillian Flynn, "On Track to a Comeback: Siemens Rolm Models Reengineering Done Right," *Personnel Journal*, Vol. 75 (2), 1996, pp. 58–69.

25. Gregory Kesler, "Four Steps to Building an HR Agenda for Growth: HR Strategy Revisited," *Human Resource Planning*, Vol. 23 (3), 2000, p. 24–37.

26. Ulrich, *Human Resource Champions*.

27. Cited in "Going First Class," *HRFocus*, Vol. 73 (7), 1996, p. 11.

28. Described in Beer, "The Transformation of the Human Resource Function."

29. Elizabeth Sheley, "Share Your Worth: Talking Numbers with the CEO," *HRMagazine*, Vol. 41 (6), 1996, pp. 86–95.

30. Gillian Flynn, "On Track to a Comeback: Siemens Rolm Models Reengineering Done Right," *Personnel Journal*, Vol. 75 (2), 1996, pp. 58–69; and Jones, "Repositioning Human Resoures."

31. Kochanski and Randall, "Rearchitecting the Human Resources Function at Northern Telecom."

32. Stephen Kerr, "Organizational Rewards: Practical, Cost Neutral Alternatives That You May Know, But Don't Practice," *Organizational Dynamics*, Vol. 28 (1), 1999, pp. 61–70.

33. Noel Tichy and Ram Charan, "Speed, Simplicity, Self-Confidence: An Interview with Jack Welch," *Harvard Business Review*, September–October 1989, pp. 112–120.

34. Richard L. Osborne, "Core Value Statements: The Corporate Compass," *Business Horizons*, September–October 1991, pp. 28–34.

35. J. Thibault and L. Walker, *Procedural Justice: A Psychological Analysis* (Hillsdale, N.J.: Erlbaum, 1975); and "A Theory of Procedure," *California Law Review*, Vol. 66, 1978, pp. 541–566.

36. Peter Howes and Pat Foley, "Strategic Human Resource Management: An Australian Case Study," *Human Resource Planning*, Vol. 16 (3), 1993, p. 64.

37. Information concerning Tampella Power from Ropo, "Towards Strategic Human Resource Management."

38. Information about GE Medical and Novell taken from Shari Caudron, "HR Leaders Brainstorm the Profession's Future," *Personnel Journal,* Vol. 73(8), 1994, pp. 54–61.

39. Melody Jones, "Four Trends to Reckon With," *HRFocus*, Vol. 73 (7), 1996, pp. 22–23.

40. Delery, "Issues of Fit I Strategic Human Resource Management."

41. James Baron and David Kreps, "Consistent Human Resource Practices," *California Management Review*, Vol. 41 (3), 1999, pp. 29–53.

42. Richard Beatty and Craig Schneier, "New HR Roles to Impact Organizational Performance: From 'Partners' to 'Players,'" *Human Resource Management*, Vol. 36 (1), 1997, pp. 29–37.

43. P. Boxall, "Strategic HRM: Beginning a New Theoretical Direction," *Human Resource Management*, Vol. 2 (3), 1992, pp. 61–79.

44. J. N. Barron, A. Davis-Blake, and W. T. Bielby, "The Structure of Opportunity: How Promotion Ladders Vary Within and Among Organizations," *Administrative Science Quarterly*, Vol. 2, 1986, pp. 248–273.

45. Beatty and Schneier, "New HR Roles to Impact Organizational Performance."

46. Ibid.

47. William C. Byham, *Zapp: The Lightning of Empowerment* (Pittsburgh: Development Dimensions International Press, 1989); and Robert Frey, "Empowerment or Else," *Harvard Business Review*, September–October 1993, pp. 80–94.

48. Michael A. Campion and Paul W. Thayer, "Job Design: Approaches, Outcomes, and Tradeoffs," *Organizational Dynamics*, Winter 1989, pp. 66–78.

49. "Who Needs a Boss?" *Fortune*, May 7, 1990, pp. 52–60; and Cresencio Torres and Jerry Spiegel, *Self-Directed Work Teams* (San Diego: University Associates, 1991).

50. Richard Blackburn and Benson Rosen, "Total Quality and Human Resources Management: Lessons Learned from Baldrige Award-Winning Companies," *Academy of Management Executive*, Vol. 7 (3), 1993, pp. 49–65.

51. Information about AT&T's Global Business Communications Systems obtained from Martin Plevel, Sandy Nellis, Fred Lane, and Randall Schuler, "AT&T Global Business Communications Systems: Linking HR with Business Strategy," *Organizational Dynamics,* Winter 1994, pp. 59–72.

52. C. Chadwick and P. Cappelli, "Alternatives to Generic Strategy Typologies in Strategic Human Resource Management," in *Research in Personnel and Human Resource Management, Supplement 4, Strategic Human Resources Management in the 21st Century*, eds. P. Wright, L. Dyer, J. Boudreau, and G. Milkovich (Greenwich, Connecticut: JAI Press, 1999), pp. 11–29; and Gerald Ferris, Wayne Hochwarter, Ronald Buckley, Gloria Harnell-Cook, and Dwight Fink, "Human Resources Management: Some New Directions," *Journal of Management*, Vol. 25 (3), 1999, pp. 385–415.

53. Chadwick and Cappelli, "Alternatives to Generic Strategy Typologies in Strategic Human Resource Management"; Ferris et al., "Human Resources Management"; and J. Milliman, M. Von Glinow, and M. Nathan, "Organizational Life Cycles and Strategic International Human Resource Management in Multinational Companies: Implications for Congruence Theory," *Academy of Management Review*, Vol. 16, 1991, pp. 318–339.

54. Patrick Wright and Scott Snell, "Toward a Unifying Framework for Exploring Fit and Flexibility in Strategic Human Resource Management," *Academy of Management Review*, Vol. 23 (4), 1998, pp. 756–772.

55. Ibid.

56. Janice Tomlinson, "Human Resources—Partners in Change," *Human Resource Management*, Vol. 32 (4), 1993, pp. 545–554.

57. Anfuso, "Colgate's Global HR Unites Under One Strategy."

58. Cited in ibid., p. 47.

59. B. Becker and M. Huselid, "Overview: Strategic Human Resource Management in Five Leading Firms," *Human Resource Management*, Vol. 38 (4), 1999, pp. 287–301.

60. Ibid.

61. Pfeffer, "Pitfalls on the Road to Measurement."

62. See, for example, Wayne Cascio, *Costing Human Resources: The Financial Impact of Behavior in Organizations* (Boston: PWS-Kent, 1987); Jac Fitz-enz, *How to Measure Human Resources Management* (New York: McGraw-Hill, 1995); Jean Hiltrop and Charles Despres, "Benchmarking HR Practices: Approaches, Rationales, and Prescriptions for Action," *Interna-*

tional Review of Strategic Management, Vol. 6 (4), 1995, pp. 197–220; Nancy Kaylor, Susan McLane, and Susan Schechter, "Ideas and Trends in Personnel," *Human Resources Management*, Vol. 408, June 1997, pp. 87–97; Edward Rogers and Patrick Wright, "Measuring Organizational Performance in Strategic Human Resource Management: Problems, Prospects, and Performance Information Markets," *Human Resource Management Review*, Vol. 8 (3), 1998, pp. 311–331; and Ulrich, *Human Resource Champions*.

63. Fitz-enz, *How to Measure Human Resources Management.*

64. Kaylor et al., "Ideas and Trends in Personnel."

65. Richard Wintermead and Karen Mattimore, "In the Changing World of Human Resources: Matching Measures to Mission," *Human Resource Management*, Vol. 36 (3), 1997, pp. 337–342.

66. Kaylor et al., "Ideas and Trends in Personnel."

67. Cascio, *Costing Human Resources.*

68. Lyle Spencer, *Calculating Human Resource Costs and Benefits: Cutting Costs and Improving Productivity* (Brisbane, Australia: Wiley, 1986).

69. Arthur Yeung and Bob Berman, "Adding Value Through Human Resources: Reorienting Human Resource Measurement to Drive Business Performance," *Human Resource Management*, Vol. 36 (3), 1997, pp. 321–335.

70. Jean Hiltrop and Charles Despres, "Benchmarking the Performance of Human Resource Management," *Long Range Planning*, Vol. 27 (6), 1994, p. 47.

71. Taken from lecture materials provided by Peter Howes of HRM Consulting, Inc., of Brisbane at the 1996 HR Benchmarking Conference in Sydney, Australia.

72. Ibid.

73. Fitz-enz, *How to Measure Human Resources Management,* pp. 33–34.

74. Dirk-Pieter van Donk and Arnout Esser, "Strategic Human Resource Management: A Role of the Human Resource Manager in the Process of Strategy Formation," *Human Resource Management Review*, Vol. 2 (4), 1992, pp. 299–315.

75. Mark Huselid, Susan Jackson, and Randall Schuler, "Technical and Strategic Human Resource Management Effectiveness as Determinants of Firm Performance," *Academy of Management Journal*, Vol. 40 (1), 1997, pp. 171–188; Mark Huselid, "The Impact of Human Resource Management Practices on Turnover, Productivity, and Corporate Financial Performance," *Academy of Management Journal*, Vol. 38 (3), 1995, pp. 635–672.

76. Yeung and Berman, "Adding Value Through Human Resources."

Human Resource Planning

HR Challenge

Twenty percent of today's registered nurses are expected to retire within the next ten years. The demand for health care is rising with the aging of the population. The number of new entrants into the nursing profession is insufficient to replace those leaving, much less cater to increasing demand. The shortage of nurses is forecast to worsen steadily through 2020.[1] These statistics sounded a warning bell for the New Hanover Health Network, a five-hospital system in southeastern North Carolina. New Hanover was experiencing difficulty in recruiting nurses to service its 800 beds and anticipated even more shortages in the future. The firm's existing HR systems were simply unable to supply their needs. A proactive strategy was needed to equip the firm to acquire critical human resources in an increasingly difficult labor market. New Hanover decided to take a hard look at its staffing sources and practices, and adopt a multipronged, strategic approach to meeting its future needs for nursing staff. Suppose that you were the Director of Human Resources at New Hanover Health Network. What kind of programs and practices might you implement to achieve these goals?[2]

Chapter 3 is about human resource planning, the process by which organizations anticipate future staffing needs and plan programs to ensure that the correct number and type of employees are available when they are needed. The first section of the chapter defines and describes the nature of human resource planning. Then the discussion moves to judgmental and mathematical methods for forecasting the demand for labor within a firm and to the methods planners can use to make forecasts about the future internal supply of labor. External labor trends are highlighted next, with emphasis given to how these affect organizations. The next section of the chapter describes how to plan responses to potential shortages and surpluses so that the organization will have the number and type of human resources required to allow for effective implementation of strategy.

WHAT IS HUMAN RESOURCE PLANNING?

An organization would not build a new plant, conduct the ribbon-cutting ceremony, and then begin to worry about how to staff the facility. A firm cannot hire several hundred engineers and get them on board overnight, nor can it develop management talent in just a few weeks. Foresight is necessary to ensure that appropriately qualified staff will be available to implement an organization's future plans. The tighter the labor market, the more forward planning is required to avoid future problems due to understaffing. On the other hand, planning ahead in a declining economy is also critical in minimizing expensive overstaffing and possible layoffs. **Human resource planning** is concerned with the flow of people into, through, and out of an organization. HR planning involves anticipating the need for labor and the supply of labor and then planning the programs necessary to ensure that the organization will have the right mix of employees and skills when and where they are needed. The forecasting methods described below provide key input for these processes.

Human resource experts can also take on a strategic role in collaboration with the top management team to plan a strategy for the firm that capitalizes on or builds the organization's unique human resource competencies.[3] For instance, Marriott Corporation's goal of being the provider of choice for food and lodging services was supplemented by the goal of becoming the "employer of choice" as well. Executives decided that unless Marriott was a very attractive employer, it would not be able to obtain the number and quality of people it needed for a growth and high-quality service strategy. The company adopted initiatives to broaden its recruiting base, but it also worked hard at retaining and motivating current employees. To that end, changes were made in career paths, job responsibilities, work teams, and reward systems.[4]

At Colgate-Palmolive, a global HR team was formed to help the organization meet its goal of "becoming the best truly global consumer products company." Top HR managers and key senior line managers worked together on the team to translate business plans into human resource plans that would support organizational excellence. As a result, strategic initiatives were adopted in recruitment, selection, development, individual performance management, team performance management, career planning, diversity, employee attitude surveys, and employee communication.[5]

A Model for Human Resource Planning

The first step in HR planning is to collect information. A forecast or plan cannot be any better than the data on which it is based. HR planning requires two types of information: data from the external environment and data from inside the organization (see Figure 3.1).[6] Data from the external environment include information on

● FIGURE 3.1

Human Resource Planning Model

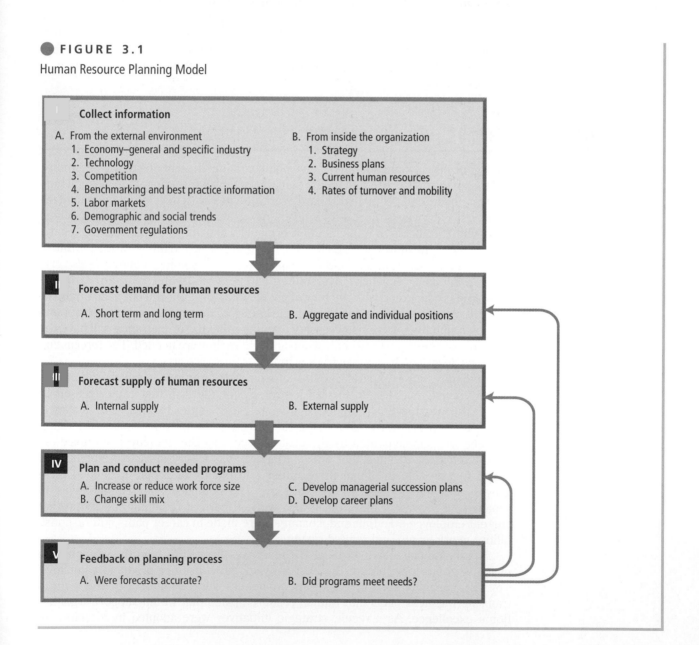

current conditions and predicted changes in the general economy, the economy of the specific industry, relevant technology, and competitor firms. Any of these may affect the organization's business direction and volume and thus the need for human resources.

Human resource planners must also be aware of labor-market conditions such as unemployment rates, skill availabilities, and the age distribution of the labor force. Finally, planners need to be aware of federal and state regulations: those that directly affect staffing practices, such as affirmative action or retirement-age legislation, and those that indirectly affect demand for services or ability to pay staff. As an example, employment in the home health industry rose substantially between the beginning of 1998 and the end of 2000, due to changes in government policy and budget with regard to Medicare payments for home health services.[7] A systematic program of environmental scanning will help an organization anticipate what is likely to happen and prepare for shifts in the external environment.[8]

External benchmarking data also can be useful in human resource planning. One might, for instance, discover that other companies are doing the same work with fewer people, which could lead to a consideration of more efficient ways to work. Benchmarking efforts by Duke Power Company's consulting arm showed them new ways to organize. Historically, they had staffed projects exclusively with highly experienced (and expensive) professionals. Benchmarking showed them that other successful consulting firms used a small number of top-class experts working with a large support staff of less skilled and experienced people, and they were able to replicate this approach successfully.[9]

The second major type of information comes from inside the organization. Internal information includes short- and long-term organizational plans and strategies. Obviously, plans to build, close, or automate facilities will have HR implications, as will plans to modify the organization's structure, buy or sell businesses, and enter or withdraw from markets. A decision to compete on the basis of low cost rather than personalized service also will have staffing implications. Finally, information is needed on the current state of human resources in the organization, such as how many individuals are employed in each job and location, their skill levels, and how many are expected to change positions or depart the organization during the forecast period.

Once planners have the external and internal information they need, they can forecast the future demand for employees. At a minimum, this forecast includes estimating the number of employees who will be needed in the coming year. Longer-term demand forecasts also may be made. Next, planners forecast the supply of labor: the internal supply of employees and their skills and promotability, as well as the probable availability of potential new employees with requisite skills in the external labor market.

The final step in HR planning is to plan specific programs to ensure that supply will match demand in the future. These programs often include recruiting plans and also may include training and development activities, incentives or disincentives to early retirement, modifications of career paths in the organization, or a variety of other HR management programs. Note that the feedback loop shown in Figure 3.1 allows for learning from past planning efforts. If demand or supply forecasts have not been as accurate as desired, forecasting processes can be improved in subsequent years. Similarly, if programs prove to be inadequate or inappropriate, they can be modified.

Who Plans?

Traditional HR planning is usually initiated and managed by the HR department. However, since information is needed from all parts of the organization, line managers must be involved in the HR planning process, with some planning methods requiring more manager involvement than others. Strategic HR planning involves top management as well as HR experts and may rely on information from many levels of management.

Not all organizations engage in HR forecasting and planning, although more and more are doing so each year. As with many other HR activities, larger firms are more likely than smaller ones to have HR planning systems.[10] Because of the large number of individuals involved, the military has been a leader in the development of sophisticated HR planning systems.

Who Is Planned For?

In designing a human resource planning system, there are several choices regarding whom to plan for. One choice is to plan at the **aggregate level,** for jobs or job families. This type of planning is typically used for jobs with multiple incumbents and for jobs at or below the middle-management level. An organization may forecast that thirty-five electrical engineers will be needed at the California development laboratory or that a total of 2,100 registered nurses will be required. The focus is on the number of persons needed for a job or job category, not on identifying the specific individuals who will fill the positions.

Many large organizations plan for each job or job family, but this may not always be necessary. The alternative is to plan only for those jobs that logic or experience indicates are problematic. For instance, a large manufacturer may need to plan carefully for scientists and engineers if there is a chronic shortage of these professionals. But the manufacturer may find that it does not need to engage in long-range planning for janitors or assembly personnel if they can be hired and trained quickly when demand increases.

Duke Power Company has developed a work force planning system that is based on pivotal roles—jobs that have the greatest strategic importance in each of its businesses. All other jobs are considered support roles and are less central to future business success. The pivotal roles identified surprised some employees—traditionally important top management and engineering jobs were not always pivotal in the new competitive environment Duke faces. Instead, the jobs of national account manager, customer service representative, and meter reader were among those identified as critical for planning purposes.[11]

In addition to aggregate planning—or instead of it—many organizations plan at the individual level. For important jobs, particularly upper-management positions, these organizations identify specific employees who are likely successors when a position becomes vacant due to promotion or retirement. A **succession plan** for a top managerial position might identify from one to three possible replacements and specify the additional training and experience each needs to become fully qualified for that position in the future.

When Is Planning Done?

Usually, an organization mounts a major planning effort once a year, but modifications can be made on the basis of new information throughout the year. For instance, an unexpected business downturn would indicate that near-term recruiting plans should be reconsidered. The appearance of a problem in staffing or a new strategic initiative also may trigger the need for further planning. A large organization in the midst of downsizing may run its computerized planning models every few weeks to monitor changes made through voluntary attrition, enhanced retirement packages, and layoffs.

The planning process can focus on one of several time horizons. For example, organizations at the elementary stage of development of the HR planning function typically plan for the short term—just one year in advance and with particular emphasis on recruiting or downsizing needs. Likewise, those operating in a very turbulent and unpredictable environment might limit their planning to the relatively near-term future. Organizations that have more experience in HR planning, have more complex needs, and operate in a more stable environment might also plan for the intermediate term—two to three years out. Some organizations engage in long-range HR planning—more than three years into the future. Plans for executive succession and the development of "high-potential" managers often incorporate these longer time horizons.[12]

FORECASTING THE DEMAND FOR LABOR

Once HR planners have collected information from both internal and external sources, they forecast the **demand for labor.** How many and what type of people will be needed to carry out the organization's plans in the future? These forecasts are grounded in information about the past and present and in assumptions about the future. Different methods of forecasting the demand for labor require different assumptions. Some of the more common assumptions are that past trends and relationships among variables will hold up in the future; that the productivity ratio is constant (or follows a known pattern) as the number of units produced increases; and that the business plans of the organization, sales forecasts, and so on are reasonably descriptive of what will actually happen. In a highly volatile business, these assumptions may not be valid. It is always wise to explicitly list one's assumptions in forecasting and to put no more faith in the forecast than in the assumptions on which it was based.

Demand forecasting methods can be divided into two categories: judgmental and mathematical. In practice, most organizations use some combination of the two methods. For example, expert judges might estimate the values of some variables and then use these values in prediction equations, or experts might integrate the results of mathematical methods with less quantifiable information into a final subjective forecast.

Judgmental Methods

Judgmental methods make use of knowledgeable people to forecast the future. Judgmental methods do consider quantitative data but also allow for intuition and expertise to be factored in. These methods may be used by small organizations or by those new to HR forecasting that do not yet have the database or expertise to use some of the more complex mathematical models. Judgmental methods also may be preferred when an organization or environment is in a state of transition or turmoil; at such times, past trends and correlations cannot be used to make accurate predictions about the future.

Perhaps the simplest judgmental method is **bottom-up,** or **unit, forecasting:** Each unit, branch, or department estimates its own future need for employees. Ideally, managers receive some guidance and information, which they combine with their own perspectives to reach the estimates. The sum of the estimated unit needs is the demand forecast for the whole organization. HR planners may wish to review the unit forecasts carefully before summing so as to control managers' natural tendencies to exaggerate the needed size and importance of their units.[13]

Houston Lighting and Power developed a spreadsheet-based bottom-up planning system that provides line managers with information on current staffing levels in the job classes they supervise, asks for estimated changes in workload and productivity, and requests estimates of HR needs in each of the next five years. The estimates are approved by the next level of management and then forwarded to the HR planning group, which integrates them into an organization-wide forecast.[14]

Another judgmental method involves **top-down forecasting** by experienced top managers and executives. These experts meet to discuss how trends, business plans, the economy, and other factors will affect the need for human resources at various levels of the organization. Besides predicting the most likely future demand, these experts also may make separate forecasts based on best- and worst-case scenarios. For instance, they might forecast what the need for labor will be if almost everything that could go wrong does go wrong (e.g., there is a recession, the organization loses the product liability suit now being tried, the company does not land the government contract it has bid for). After completing such exercises, the experts can be fairly certain that the actual demand for labor will fall somewhere in between their best- and worst-case predictions. Many of the mathematical forecasting methods also lend themselves to this type of what-if assessment.

One highly structured judgmental method of expert forecasting utilizes the **Delphi technique** to achieve group consensus on a forecast.[15] In using this technique, the experts do not meet face to face. This is more economical if they are assigned to different locations; it also can improve the quality of decision making by minimizing disruptive personality conflicts and preventing the loudest group member from dominating the decision process. The first step in the Delphi process is to develop an anonymous questionnaire that asks the experts for an opinion and reasons that they hold that opinion. The results of this questionnaire are compiled and returned to the experts, along with a second anonymous questionnaire. In this way, the experts can learn from one another and modify or elaborate their positions in the second questionnaire. The process continues through several more rounds until the experts agree on a judgment.

In one published test of the Delphi technique, a national retail company predicted the number of buyers needed in one year. The experts were seven managers, who responded to five rounds of questionnaires. In the first round, estimates ranged from thirty-two to fifty-five buyers. By the fifth round, estimates narrowed to between thirty-four and forty-five buyers, with a mean of thirty-eight. The Delphi predictions were not made public or used in recruitment planning that year so that the company could evaluate their accuracy compared with actual end-of-year staffing levels. At the end of the year, thirty-seven buyers were actually employed. The Delphi method proved to be much more accurate than three simple mathematical models also applied to the same forecasting problem.[16]

A complete Delphi process using several rounds of anonymous questionnaires takes time to complete, so this method may not be appropriate if results are needed very quickly. As with any expert forecasting method, participants should be knowledgeable about the topic. Their existing knowledge can be supplemented by providing information on past and current staffing, business performance, business plans, and the like.

Simple Mathematical Methods

The simplest mathematical methods of forecasting use only one factor to predict demand. For example, to predict the need for labor, one could examine staffing levels during the last few years, note the trend, and extend this trend to the upcoming year. A better method would be to use forecasts of the coming year's sales, production, or another business factor related to the need for labor. This information would then be combined with productivity ratios to predict the number of direct labor employees needed.[17]

The **productivity ratio** is the average number of units produced per direct labor employee per year. Suppose a company produces sofas and knows from past history that the productivity ratio is about fifty sofas per furniture assembler per year. If the marketing department expects to sell 10,000 sofas in the coming year, then the company needs 10,000/50 = 200 furniture assemblers.

Direct-to-indirect labor **staffing ratios** are used to calculate the number of individuals required in other jobs. For instance, if the sofa firm generally has one supervisor for every fifteen assemblers, then about thirteen supervisors will be needed for two hundred assemblers. Past experience also may show that two shipping-and-receiving clerks are required for every fifty assemblers. This means that the company needs a total of eight clerks.

Productivity and staffing ratios based on historical data may be modified judgmentally if the ratios are expected to change. For instance, if the union has negotiated a new contract requiring workdays that are thirty minutes shorter and more paid holidays, the expected productivity ratio should be adjusted downward. If an improved order-processing program will be installed in the clerks' computers, the staffing ratio may change, with fewer clerks needed to service the same number of direct workers.

Forecasting with productivity ratios is based on the assumption that the number of employees needed increases linearly with the amount of work to be done. This assumption is not always correct. Envision, for example, a company that has handled increasing demand for its product by having employees work overtime. At some point, the company will not be able to cope with increasing sales in this way and may decide to add a second shift or open a new plant. At this juncture, a large increase in staffing will occur, resulting in a discontinuous relationship between output and labor demand.

A different demand forecast method may be suitable for companies that do a great deal of contract or project work. For these firms, the amount of labor needed depends directly on how many contracts they land or how many projects go ahead. If the firms can calculate the number of people or labor hours needed for each contract, these figures can be multiplied by the estimated probability of receiving each contract and then summed to estimate the most likely aggregate labor-demand figure. Forecasts of this type tend to be accurate only if there are many pending contracts to sum over and if one can correctly estimate the probabilities of receiving various contracts.[18] One high-tech firm plots future research projects through the anticipated phases of development. The number and types of engineers and scientists needed for each phase of each project are estimated, together with the likely duration of each phase and the probability that the project will progress to each additional phase. Adding across projects provides an estimate of the demand for various types of research and development staff for each future time period.

Complex Mathematical Methods

Some forecasting methods use more complicated statistical techniques. Large organizations with a long history of HR planning are likely to employ these methods. One such method, **multiple regression,** uses several factors that correlate with labor demand to forecast future demand. Examples of such factors include sales, profits, capital investments, and gross national product (GNP). Historical data are used to derive an equation describing the relationships of these factors to employment levels; then current or predicted values of the factors are inserted into the equation to predict future demand. This method can be applied only when sufficient historical data exist to allow for the derivation of stable regression equations, when fairly strong relationships exist between the factors and labor demand, and when no dramatic changes in productivity or product mix are anticipated.[19]

A second forecasting method employs **linear,** or **goal, programming** to determine optimal staffing levels given a set of constraints. Constraints might include compensation budgets, minimum and maximum ratios between various kinds of jobs, or minimum and maximum output figures. Further information on these techniques is available in most operations research textbooks as well as in the sources listed in Notes and References at the end of this chapter.[20]

THE INTERNAL SUPPLY OF LABOR

Once the demand for labor is predicted, it is necessary to forecast the supply of labor that the organization will already have available to meet the demand. The **internal supply of labor** consists of all the individuals currently employed by an organization. These employees can help to fill future demands by remaining employed in their current positions or by being promoted or transferred to fill vacancies elsewhere in the organization. The internal supply of labor is constantly changing as new people enter and others resign, retire, or are discharged. The skill mix also changes as people move in and out and as employees develop new capabilities through training or on-the-job experience.

To keep track of the current internal supply and to predict the future supply, planners need some sort of supply information system. At a minimum, this system may consist of simple staffing tables that show the number of incumbents in each job within the organization. For small companies, a manual system may suffice, but increasingly employee information is stored and manipulated in computer programs, some of which have very sophisticated retrieval and analysis capabilities. The next sections describe two such systems: skills inventories and human resource information systems.

Skills Inventories

A **skills inventory** is a manual or computerized system designed to keep track of employees' experience, education, and special abilities. Computerized skills inventories may be freestanding programs or modules of a larger human resource information system (described further below). The skills inventory information form in Figure 3.2 shows what might appear in a typical skills inventory. The key words

FIGURE 3.2

Skills Inventory Information Form

Source: From Richard A. Kaumeyer, Jr., *Planning and Using Skills Inventory Systems* (New York: Van Nostrand Reinhold, 1979). Reprinted by permission.

SKILLS INVENTORY

Employee Name: I. M. Nameless   Date Printed: 1/1/98

Employee Number: 28036   Department: 319

KEY WORDS

Word	Description	Activity
1. Accounting	Tax accounting	Supervising/analyzing
2. Bookkeeping	General ledger	Supervising
3. Auditing	Computer records	Analyzing

WORK EXPERIENCE

From	To	Description
1. 1993	1998	Chief tax accountant at XYZ Stores
2. 1985	1993	Bookkeeper at XYZ Manufacturing
3. 1984	1985	Auditing training at XYZ Bank

EDUCATION

Degree	Major	Date
1. MBA	Business admin.	1984
2. BS	Accounting	1982

SPECIAL COURSES

Course	Date
1. Management theory	1994
2. Business planning	1991
3. Computer audits	1985

MEMBERSHIPS

1. American Accounting Society
2. American Management Association

LICENSES

Name	Date
1. CPA	1985

LANGUAGES

Name	Fluency
1. Spanish	Fluent
2. French	Read

POSITION PREFERENCE

1. Accounting
2. Auditing

LOCATION PREFERENCE

1. San Francisco
2. San Diego

HOBBIES

1. Bridge
2. Amateur radio
3. Boating

Employee Signature: _____ Personnel Department: _____

Date: _____   Date: _____

---

describing the specific occupational area (general ledger bookkeeping) and activities performed (supervising) are drawn from a standardized manual developed for the organization. Planners need comparable information about employees and jobs, and using standard terminology is the surest way to achieve this goal.

The inventory can be used to assess the current supply of employees of various sorts. For instance, an employer might wish to know how many people are presently working as salespersons, how many people have current or past experience in firefighting, or how many certified professional engineers are employed. The inventory also can be used to identify candidates for promotion or transfer. Suppose a large company has an opening for an experienced petroleum geologist who is willing to relocate and who speaks fluent Arabic. A personnel requisition form that describes the opening will be generated using the same standard key words that are used in the skills inventory. The inventory system will then be able to generate a list of all qualified employees in the organization. The inventory can also help to identify individuals who are ready for particular training or development courses. In addition, through the items on location and position preference, the inventory can ensure that employees' own career plans and wishes are considered when the organization makes transfer or promotion decisions.

Clearly, skills inventories can be very useful tools for assessing the internal supply of labor. Any such system, however, must be accurate and current to be maximally useful. Gathering and updating employee information is a large and critical job. Often initial information is collected by questionnaire. Every year thereafter employees receive a copy of their information, which they update as needed.[21] In addition, some updates may be made automatically. For instance, a list of attendees at a company-sponsored training program could be merged with a computerized skills inventory to update the records of those who were trained.

Human Resource Information Systems

A **human resource information system (HRIS)** combines in one system all the information that organizations typically keep on employees and on positions. HRISs can streamline administration and record-keeping tasks as well as provide decision support for managers and HR specialists.[22] The last decade has seen a massive movement toward full-blown, highly integrated human resource information systems that can do much more than simple skills inventory systems.[23] Even quite small firms are finding advantages in automating HR information.[24] Many of the functional components are available in modular form and can be added as demand grows. For instance, a firm might start out with pay and benefits modules, then later add modules for tracking appraisal and training. Most human resource information systems are comprised of the components and capabilities listed below and shown in Figure 3.3.

- A computerized database management system.
- Screens for inputting data.
- Programs for cross-checking data and transaction accuracy.
- Modules for performing specific functions such as tracking applicant flows and for generating regular reports such as monthly compensation costs or positions filled versus those vacant.
- Query programs for requesting special information combinations or what-if analyses.
- Self-serve interfaces. Some systems now allow employees and managers to selectively access and modify records at self-service kiosks. For instance, employees may be able to change their benefit preferences themselves, or a manager may be able to add a new employee to the payroll rather than requiring assistance from an HR clerk to do so.

One issue of concern with HRISs is the fact that organizations can so readily store and access large amounts of information about employees and applicants. Questions may arise about employee privacy, who has access to sensitive information, and whether information used to make decisions about individuals is accurate. The Ethical Perspective box explores these questions in further detail.

● **FIGURE 3.3**

Elements of an HRIS

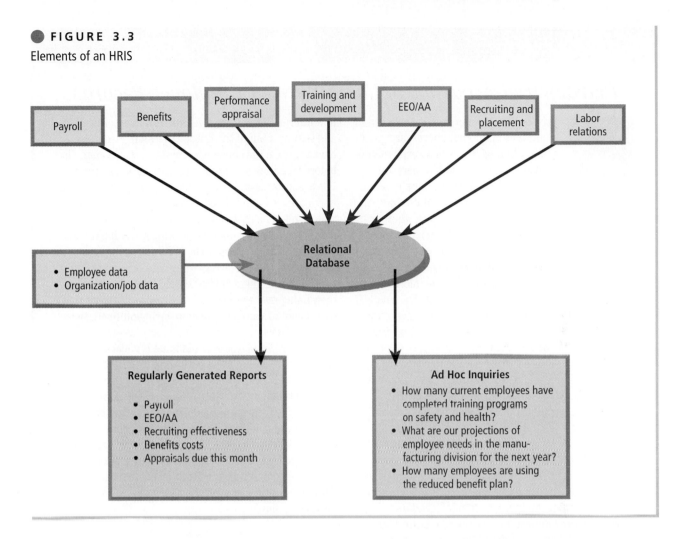

Leading-edge HRISs can support integrated HR record keeping and decision making across multiple locations and even across countries. For instance, SAP boasts that its HRIS user interfaces are available in multiple languages, that local labor law requirements are incorporated into record fields as appropriate for each country, and that salary information can be maintained in both local currency and headquarters currency units simultaneously. Further, internal recruitment searches can be conducted worldwide at the touch of a button. Microsoft recently adopted SAP for its worldwide operations. A single human resource management system residing on one server has replaced the series of customized programs and stand-alone systems on many computers that was previously used in eighteen different subsidiaries in fifty-five countries. Now users need to learn only one system to access up-to-the-minute information on employment around the world.

HRISs are available in a wide range of prices, starting as low as $500 for a simple one-function program. An annual index and reviews of HRIS packages can be found at www.hrcensus.com. Lately, large providers such as PeopleSoft, SAP, and Oracle have made available **enterprise resource planning** systems, which offer

Privacy and Accuracy of Computerized Employee Records

Privacy is an area of growing concern to employees and to human resource managers. Although there is no explicit constitutional right to privacy, certain amendments and federal laws have some relevance to this issue, and some states have enacted privacy laws. Privacy considerations, whether derived from legal requirements or from basic respect for individuals, may constrain the type and amount of information that employers gather about applicants and employees and also the way that the information is stored, used, and disseminated by organizations.

With more and more employee records stored in computers, there is some concern that unauthorized persons could gain access to employee information of a confidential nature, such as performance appraisals, salary data, home addresses, or drug test results. Employers should have privacy policies in place that clearly specify who may access what type of data and for what purposes. Technical approaches should also be used to restrict computer users' access to information that is off-limits to them. HRIS security systems include limiting physical access to terminals by unauthorized persons, such as locking offices after hours, or key card access to the human resource information center. Probably more important is multilevel password protection to limit access to data files. Some individuals will have passwords that allow them to view only selected types of information. Others may be authorized to view a wider range of information, and still others will be allowed to both view and edit information. As access to HRISs becomes more available to individuals outside the HR specialty via various self-serve interfaces, security becomes a more pressing concern.

Firms doing business in the European Union have encountered strict new data privacy rules that apply to both customer and employee databases. They must disclose to the member nation's data protection authority how information on employees is stored, processed, and sent in or out of the European Union. Firms also have to obtain the consent of employee works councils before installing new employee information systems. These approvals add months to the process of adopting new systems. Failure to comply with the privacy rules may result in heavy fines, or even an order to shut down data transmission from Europe altogether. Japan, Australia, and Canada seem to be following in the European Union's footsteps regarding data privacy. U.S. firms doing business abroad should take a hard look at their data privacy policy and procedures to assure that they do not run afoul of the more stringent regulations in place elsewhere.

Another employee records issue is accuracy. Ideally, employees should be permitted to view their personnel records from time to time to make sure that they are timely and accurate. Some HRISs automatically produce "turnaround documents" when employees' files are modified. These are paper copies sent to employees showing the changes made and requesting correction if needed. For instance, if an employee fills out a change in his or her flexible benefits scheme, the HRIS will return a copy of the change to the employee for verification.

Sources: Ellen Messmer, "EU Data-Privacy Laws Bog Down U.S. Firms," *Network World,* December 17, 2001, p. 8; Sandra E. O'Connell, "Security for HR records," *HRMagazine,* September 1994, p. 37; E. R. Eddy, D. L. Stone, and E. F. Stone-Romero, "The Effects of Information Management Policies on Reactions to Human Resource Information Systems: An Integration of Privacy and Procedural Justice Perspectives, *Personnel Psychology,* Summer 1999, pp. 335–358; J. C. Hubbard, K. A. Forcht, and D. S. Thomas, "Human Resource Information Systems: An Overview of Current Ethical and Legal Issues," *Journal of Business Ethics,* September 1998, pp. 1319–1323; and D. L. Stone and E. F. Stone-Romero, "A Multiple Stakeholder Model of Privacy in Organizations," in *Managerial Ethics,* ed. M. Schminke (Mawah, N.J.: Erlbaum, 1998), pp. 35–59.

complete HRISs as well as compatible systems for managing other business functions such as accounts receivable, materials management, and finance.

A further recent advance in such systems is the use of **application service providers,** which host and maintain both hardware and software. Individuals at the company simply log on through a Web browser to access their HRIS or other applications. This approach is said to offer companies faster implementation, predictable costs, high reliability, and expert support compared to the less certain process of installing and maintaining an in-house system.[25]

Whatever its level of complexity, an HRIS should be able to provide information needed in HR planning. Up-to-date reporting of head count, positions budgeted, turnover rates, and the like can assist in forecasting internal supply. Queries might be made to assess, for instance, the number of employees who are eligible for an enhanced retirement package or who might be available to transfer to a location anticipating a skill shortage.

Predicting the Internal Supply of Labor

Given the necessary data in staffing tables, a skills inventory, or a HRIS, human resource professionals can predict the internal supply and distribution of labor in the future.

Markov analysis is a fairly simple method of predicting the internal supply of labor at some future time. The heart of Markov analysis is the **transition probability matrix,** which describes the probabilities of an incumbent's staying in his or her present job for the forecast time period (usually one year), moving to another job in the organization, or leaving the organization. When this matrix is multiplied by the number of people beginning the year in each job, the results show how many people are expected to be in each job by the end of the year.

To develop the transition probability matrix, planners take the following steps:

1. Specify a mutually exclusive and exhaustive set of states that include all jobs between which people can move and an exit state for those who quit, retire, or are fired.

2. Gather data from each of the last several years on what transition rates actually occurred between each state. Such data could show, for instance, that during the past year 15 percent of the people who began the year in job A left the organization, 10 percent were transferred to job B, and 5 percent were promoted to job C.

3. Attempt to develop stable, reliable estimates of expected future transition rates. Some judgment is required at this step. Many organizations use the preceding year's transition rates. However, if the preceding year was atypical (with an unusually high or low rate of movement), planners may find it better to average the rates over the last several years. This third step is very important because the accuracy of prediction depends on using correct transition rates. If movement rates vary widely from year to year, planners may not be able to use Markov analysis to forecast internal supply.[26]

Once the transition probability matrix is developed, applying it is a simple matter (see Table 3.1). To produce predictions, the matrix is multiplied by the vector of the number of incumbents in each state. For instance, job A began the year with sixty-two incumbents. Fifteen percent of those incumbents ($0.15 \times 62 = 9$) left the

● **TABLE 3.1**

Markov Analysis

(Time 1)	Transition Probability Matrix (Time 2)				
	Job A	**Job B**	**Job C**	**Job D**	**Exit**
Job A	0.70	0.10	0.05	0	0.15
Job B	0.15	0.60	0.05	0.10	0.10
Job C	0	0	0.80	0.05	0.15
Job D	0	0	0.05	0.85	0.10

	Matrix Applied to Incumbents[a]					
	Initial Staffing Level	**Job A**	**Job B**	**Job C**	**Job D**	**Exit**
Job A	62	44	6	3	0	9
Job B	75	11	45	4	8	7
Job C	50	0	0	40	2	8
Job D	45	0	0	2	38	5
Predicted end-of-year staffing level		55	51	49	48	29

[a]Numbers have been rounded to whole digits because fractions of employees are not meaningful.

organization, 10 percent ($0.10 \times 62 = 6$) moved to job B, and 5 percent ($0.05 \times 62 = 3$) moved to job C. That leaves forty-four of the original incumbents in job A. However, 15 percent of the seventy-five people ($0.15 \times 75 = 11$) in job B transferred to job A, so the total number of employees in job A at the end of the year is fifty-five ($44 + 11$). (These numbers have been rounded to whole digits because fractions of employees are not meaningful.)

Markov analysis describes what is expected to happen if existing transition rates remain the same. This type of analysis can also be used speculatively to assess the impact of possible modifications in transition rates. For instance, suppose that job D is going to be understaffed because of an unusually large number of retirements. In the past, this job has been filled largely by promotions from job B. Planners might use the Markov model to determine what would happen if the rate of lateral transfers from job C to job D was increased or if the rate of promotion from job B was increased. Planners could experiment with different probabilities until they found a workable solution.

Researchers used Markov analysis to assess the impact of three HR options on the age and rank composition of the faculty of Auburn University's College of Veterinary Medicine. Data from 1984 to 1994 were used to model the transition rates between the states of assistant professor, associate professor, full professor, and

● **TABLE 3.2**

Academic Staff by Rank for School Years 1984 and 1994 Actual and 2004 Projected

	1984	%	1994	%	2004	%
Forecast Based on Transitional Probabilities Alone						
Assistant professor	34	40.0	26	26.5	21	19.6
Associate professor	23	27.1	35	35.7	52	48.6
Professor	28	32.9	37	37.8	34	31.8
Total	85	100	98	100	107	100
Forecast Including Simulation of a Hiring Freeze in the First Two Years						
Assistant professor	34	40.0	26	26.5	12	12.6
Associate professor	23	27.1	35	35.7	43	45.3
Professor	28	32.9	37	37.8	40	42.1
Total	85	100	98	100	95	100
Forecast Including Simulation of an Early Reitrement Option in Years 1 and 4						
Assistant professor	34	40.0	26	26.5	30	28.3
Associate professor	23	27.1	35	35.7	53	50.0
Professor	28	32.9	37	37.8	23	21.7
Total	85	100	98	100	106	100

Source: E. R. Hackett, A. A. Magg, and S. D. Carrigan, "Modelling Faculty Replacement Strategies Using a Time-Dependent Finite Markov-Chain Process," *Journal of Higher Education Policy and Management*, May 1999, p. 87.

exit. Forecasts were subsequently made for 1995 and 2004. Some of the results are shown in Table 3.2. In scenario 1, entry-level hiring continued at the usual rate over the ten-year period. In scenario 2, a hiring freeze on new employees was imposed in the first two planning years, as the newly elected governor was hinting at this course of action. In scenario 3, enhanced retirement packages were offered in the first and fifth years of the plan. The hiring freeze alternative, while saving funds in the short term, had undesirable long-term impacts—the faculty became older, the proportion of people in higher ranks increased disproportionately, and in consequence the average salary increased. Scenario 3, offering an enhanced retirement package twice, reduced the proportion of senior faculty to below what would be desirable. Further experimentation with various scenarios suggested the best combination of actions.[27]

Markov analysis is widely used and easy to apply. However, it has been criticized for certain weaknesses and limitations.[28] Transition probabilities must be relatively stable or able to be estimated for Markov analysis to be accurate. Also, the probabilities will not be reliable if there are only a few incumbents in each job. Generally, Markov analysis works best if there are at least fifty people in each job or state.[29]

A second weakness is conceptual rather than statistical. Markov analysis assumes that the probability of movement is determined solely by the employee's initial job state. The probability of moving to job B depends entirely on where the employee began the year—in job A, C, or D. In actual practice, however, people move within organizations because of the pull of vacancies rather than the push of their current assignments. Thus the true probability of moving to job B also depends on the number of vacancies in job B.

An approach to predicting internal movement and supply that takes this dynamic into account is called **renewal,** or **replacement, analysis.** This method is driven by destination demand—the number of vacancies anticipated in higher-level jobs. Transition matrices help identify how the demand can be filled by internal movements from lower-level positions. These movements create additional vacancies and in turn drive further movement at even lower job levels.[30]

More complex methods of forecasting internal supply are available in goal programming, network analysis, and computer simulation. Simulations may use both replacement and Markov analyses, utilize the age and promotability information stored on each of thousands of employees, and allow a variety of different HR policies and assumptions to be tried out and evaluated.[31]

The U.S. Navy developed a very sophisticated HR forecasting model to help reduce civilian employment levels in eight shipyards that were being downsized. Markov analysis showed that allowing natural attrition and typical transition rates to take their course would reduce overall employment levels, but in a way that was unbalanced across critical shipyard occupations. To keep each of eighteen different occupations staffed at the desired level, attrition needed to be combined with modified transfer rates and carefully planned hiring in some areas. Adding goals to the model and predicting two years into the future on a quarterly basis allowed the reductions to be thoroughly planned and accomplished with minimal disruption of work efficiency.[32]

Choosing Forecasting Methods

A number of methods of forecasting HR demands and internal supply have been presented. Not all are appropriate for all organizations and situations, so the HR practitioner must make choices about which methods best suit the organization in question. The following factors are among those that should be considered in choosing techniques for HR forecasting:

- *Stability and certainty.* It is not feasible to use methods that rely heavily on past data if the organization and environment are changing rapidly and in relatively unpredictable ways. Informed human judgment may be superior in this situation. It will also be useful to forecast several scenarios, each with different sets of assumptions.

- *Availability of data.* How accurate and complete are past data on employee numbers, skills, and flows? If the data are not available, some statistical approaches cannot be used.

- *Number of employees.* Some statistical techniques, such as Markov analysis, are reliable only for large numbers of employees. Smaller numbers might call for judgmental methods.

- *Resources available.* How much time, computing power, and statistical expertise are available to compile the forecast?

- *Time horizon.* Judgmental methods may be superior at anticipating the direction of complex long-term trends, whereas statistical methods may be quite accurate in the short term.

- *Credibility to management.* Will key managers accept the process and believe its predictions? Sometimes simpler methods that involve substantial management input will have more credibility, although in high-tech organizations sophisticated modeling may be readily accepted.[33] Duke Power Company faced the challenge of developing a work force planning system that would satisfy two distinct sets of clients. Managers on the utilities side of the company were used to sophisticated head-count planning models, whereas those in Duke's investment, real estate, and consulting businesses wanted something "so simple it could be outlined on a napkin."[34]

Implications of Internal Supply and Distribution

Whatever methods are chosen to make HR forecasts, the real benefit comes from the way the forecasts are used. Careful study of internal supply and distribution reports allows HR planners to anticipate and head off a variety of problems. For instance, planners might notice that a particular unit or job family contains a high proportion of employees nearing retirement age. This may signal the need to establish a high-volume training program to prepare replacements for these positions.

The Union Oil Company of California developed an internal flow model that produces statistics on the replacement ratio, or the number of employees in a given five-year age bracket who are waiting to fill each job currently held by someone in the next-older age bracket. Ratios that are too high are a concern because they mean that upward progress is blocked and younger employees are likely to become frustrated in their careers.[35] Ratios that are too low indicate a possible future shortage of experienced employees for higher-level jobs.

A British expert on HR planning, Gordon McBeath, points out that recent recruiting trends may create problems with HR flows in the future if organizations fail to anticipate the effects for their organizations. Firms that historically have hired new employees straight from university have shifted to hiring an increasing number of returning homemakers and older graduates as the supply of young graduates shrinks. Some firms have found that these mature workers have different movement patterns, being less eager to move up the hierarchy into management and expecting employment for five to ten years rather than thirty to forty. If most managers of the future will come from today's smaller crop of new college graduates, then a higher than usual percentage of new graduates will advance into management. In anticipation, one organization has raised hiring standards for new graduates to ensure that more of them will have promotion potential, even though a typical response to a shortage of entry-level employees would have been to lower hiring standards.[36]

Duke Power Company had hoped to deal with downsizing by moving surplus midcareer employees from other occupations into vacant entry-level reactor operator positions in their three nuclear power plants. However, their work force planning model showed that this would create a great shortage of fully qualified licensed senior reactor operators and supervisors in the future because it takes ten to nineteen years to move from entry level to supervisor. In response, the company changed its policy from transferring employees to recruiting technical graduates or ex-Navy nuclear operators for vacant slots because these individuals could become qualified supervisors much more quickly.[37]

Benchmarking the Internal Supply and Distribution of Labor

There are a number of ways in which an organization's internal supply and distribution of employees might be compared with that of its competitors to produce useful insights. A simple measure is revenue per employee or, alternatively, profit per employee. This varies widely across industries, so within-industry comparisons are most appropriate. If, for instance, a bank finds that its profit per employee is $20,000, whereas the industry average is $45,000, there is clearly room for improvement. Perhaps there are too many employees or they are not trained and equipped to perform their work efficiently.

Another type of benchmarking measure is the staffing ratio of front-line operating employees to managerial and professional support staff. Organizations that are top heavy and have too many managers for the number of people actually doing productive work compared with industry norms might wish to consider a flatter, less bureaucratic structure. In an Australian benchmarking survey, the finance sector averaged three operatives per manager/professional, while the transport industry averaged twenty-five operatives per manager/profession in transport. The U.S. Army utilizes a similar measure—the tooth-to-tail ratio. This is the number of fighting personnel compared with the number of support staff (logistics, training, medical, maintenance, etc.) required to back them up in the field. Generally, the ratio is about 1:10.[38]

THE EXTERNAL SUPPLY OF LABOR

As they hire new workers, lay off or discharge others, and lose current employees to other firms, organizations continuously interact with external labor markets. Therefore, to plan effectively, HR planners must understand how to assess and adjust to the **external supply of labor.**

Some Definitions

A great deal of data are collected and published monthly about the labor supply, but making sense of these data requires an understanding of a few basic concepts and definitions.[39]

The **civilian labor force** comprises all people sixteen years of age or older who are not in the military and who are employed or seeking work. The civilian labor force does not include **"discouraged" workers** who have given up looking for work or people who are institutionalized in prisons or mental hospitals. In 2002 the labor force comprised nearly 141 million people, and it is forecasted to grow slowly to 155 million by 2008.[40]

The **labor reserve** is made up of people sixteen years of age or older who choose not to work; they include students, full-time homemakers, and retired persons. These people are considered a reserve in the sense that they could conceivably become workers in an emergency or for the right incentive.

The **labor force participation rate** is the percentage of the total working-age population that is currently in the labor force. In 2002, the participation rate of males over age 20 was 76 percent. The participation rate of females in the same age range was 60.7 percent. In the prime working years of ages 24 to 54, the male participation rate is over 90 percent.

The **unemployment rate** is the percentage of the labor force that is seeking work rather than working. When the unemployment rate is high and many people are out of work, the labor market is described as "loose," meaning that employers can find new employees easily. Conversely, a "tight" labor market occurs when unemployment is very low and employers have great difficulty in finding new workers. The overall unemployment rate reached a thirty-year low of 4 percent in 2000, with some metropolitan areas—including Minneapolis/St. Paul, Minnesota, and Raleigh, North Carolina—having unemployment below 2 percent. The nationwide unemployment rate for university graduates was also under 2 percent during 1999 and 2000, sparking a bidding war for technical talent in some fields. A downturn in 2001 followed by the September 11 terrorist attacks increased unemployment to 5.6 percent by the start of 2002.

In the United States, the Bureau of Labor Statistics conducts a monthly Current Population Survey using a representative sample of households nationwide. Each month the bureau reports these labor force statistics in its journal, *Monthly Labor Review.* This journal also contains analyses of new developments and trends in the labor supply. Additional labor force statistics are available at the bureau's web site, www.bls.gov.

Labor Markets

The concept of labor markets is an important one. A **labor market** is the area from which an employer typically recruits to fill a position; this area varies according to the type of job being filled.[41] For instance, the labor market for secretaries, plumbers, cashiers, and so on is usually the immediate, surrounding geographic area. This is so because workers are seldom willing to relocate for these jobs and employers find it unnecessary to mount a nationwide search to fill them. For these jobs, the labor market is defined by how far potential employees are willing to commute to work. For other jobs—such as college professor, top manager, computer engineer, or research chemist—the labor market is nationwide or even international. There also are regional labor markets for skilled jobs for which incumbents are willing to move but for which employers need not search too widely. For example, schools in Texas may recruit teachers at Texas and Oklahoma universities, but they probably feel no need to recruit in New York. In times of employee shortages, labor markets may widen. For instance, the nursing shortage referred to in the HR Challenge has expanded the nurse labor market geographically. American hospitals are now recruiting in Canada, Canadian hospitals are dealing with the ensuing shortage in their own country by recruiting in the United Kingdom, U.K. hospitals have turned to recruiting in South Africa, and South African hospitals find they need to recruit in Asia![42]

Before making decisions, employers must be sure that information is collected on the right labor markets. Knowing that the unemployment rate is very high for the country does not guarantee that a firm will be able to find sufficient new employees at any specific location. Labor markets are based on skills as well as geography. For instance, the nationwide labor market for entry-level electrical engineers may be quite a bit tighter or looser than the local labor market for secretaries or refrigeration mechanics. Data on local and regional labor-market conditions are available from state employment service offices.

In summary, there is a great deal of data available on current labor markets. This information might be quite helpful to the recruiter who is attempting to fill positions right now, but for most HR planning purposes, data projecting the future status of various labor markets will be more useful. Fortunately, the Bureau of Labor Statistics publishes such projections and every two years issues a revised outlook for the next ten-year period.

Demographic Trends in the Labor Supply

The rate of population growth, and thus the number of people potentially available as employees, has not followed a smooth pattern over the last fifty years. The peaks and valleys in the age distribution of the population have created some interesting challenges for employers.

The Depression of the early 1930s and World War II created a **birth dearth,** with relatively few children being born. The **baby boom** occurred when many children were born between 1945 and 1964 to people who had postponed marriage and child-bearing during World War II. (Note that in Australia, the baby boom continued for about ten years longer, with birth rates not dropping off until the early 1970s.) The coming of age of the baby-boom group, plus a huge increase in female participation in the U.S. labor force, accounted for the rapid growth of the labor force by 3 percent per year in the 1970s. However, following the baby boom was a **baby bust,** with relatively few children being born between 1965 and the late 1970s. These children reached working age and entered the labor force in the late 1980s and 1990s, during which time the rate of growth of the labor force averaged only 1.5 percent per year. The characteristics of baby busters, also called generation X and thirteeners (the thirteenth generation since the United States became a nation), have received a lot of attention both from marketers and from employers. Another trend, called the **baby-boom echo,** is the increasing number of babies born to baby boomers from 1979 to 1994. These children are now starting to enter the labor force.[43]

What implications do these demographic trends have for organizations? One effect involves the aging of the labor force (see Figure 3.4). The median age of all employees was 35.9 in 1988 and 38.7 in 1998; it is expected to reach 40.5 by 2008.[44]

● **FIGURE 3.4**

The Aging of the Work Force

Source: Data compiled from H. N. Fullerton, Jr., "Labor Force Projections to 2008: Steady Growth and Changing Composition," *Monthly Labor Review,* November 1999, pp. 19–32.

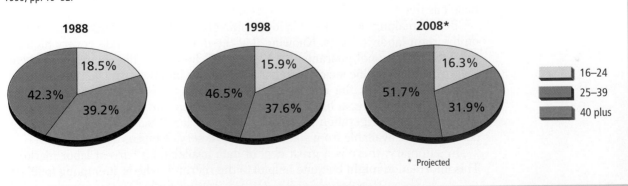

	1988	1998	2008*	
	18.5% / 42.3% / 39.2%	15.9% / 46.5% / 37.6%	16.3% / 51.7% / 31.9%	16–24 / 25–39 / 40 plus

* Projected

The work force hasn't been this old since 1962, when the small birth-dearth generation entered the work force. The large baby-boom generation is now well into middle age. Middle-aged workers want job security, advancement, status, challenge, and interesting work. Organizations have found it hard to provide these conditions to such a large number of employees, especially during the difficult economic climate of the late 1980s and early 1990s. After 2005, as the baby boomers grow old and begin to retire, a brand-new set of social and employment problems may emerge. The solvency of the Medicare and Social Security systems is clearly one issue. Boomers may want (or need) to continue working beyond traditional retirement age, and they may also want different fringe benefits than they did while raising families.[45] Occupations that contain a disproportionate share of older workers may experience labor shortages due to mass retirements. One such occupation is that of schoolteacher. Fewer teachers were needed to educate the baby-bust cohort, so there were fewer young entrants into the profession. In consequence, the average age of teachers is greater than that of the work force generally—fully 50 percent of secondary teachers are over age 45. This occupation may be especially hard hit by retirements because many school districts allow early retirement from age 55.[46]

A second effect of demographic trends has been a labor shortage for organizations that depend primarily on young, part-time workers from the baby-bust generation. Many states have clamped down on the employment hours of teenagers in an effort to boost school performance, making this source of labor even scarcer.[47] HR planners at fast-food chains and grocery stores have had to worry about where their cooks, counter help, checkers, and baggers would come from. Wages for these positions have risen to attract the available young people, and some organizations have successfully turned to less traditional sources of labor to fill the gap.[48] For instance, the Times-Mirror newspapers hired off-duty mail carriers to deliver papers because they were unable to recruit enough school-aged boys and girls for the task, and Kentucky Fried Chicken hired more disabled and retired people.[49]

A third effect also involves the baby-bust generation—not just their numbers, but their attitudes and characteristics as employees. Although any stereotypes are bound to be less than wholly accurate, "busters" are often portrayed in the media as angry, bitter, and disillusioned. They reportedly doubt that applying themselves and working hard will lead to success and that they will be able to enjoy a standard of living equal to that of their parents. Demographers predict that baby busters graduating from college will face increasing competition for good jobs and that many will have to accept jobs far below their ability level.[50] In fact, a new term, "McJob," has been coined to refer to the dead-end service jobs in which many of them will find themselves. Indeed, there is evidence that new job growth through 2008 will be concentrated at both the high (university degree) and low (high school education, minimal training) ends of the spectrum, with low-level service jobs comprising the second-fastest-growing segment.[51]

Boomers are likely to believe that baby busters lack a work ethic, but busters contend that they are interested instead in a reasonable balance among work, family, and community. Busters' supposedly short attention span, need for stimulation, and desire to keep their options open may be satisfied by frequent job changes and seem to have resulted in a decline in loyalty to any one employer.[52] Busters change jobs on average once every eighteen months.[53] They are also considered to have greater affinity and talent for high technology and computers, stronger needs for personal contact and feedback from superiors, more appreciation of diversity, less tolerance for "hype," and more desire for straight, honest facts than their predecessors.[54] Taken together, these characteristics present tremendous leadership challenges for the boomers who manage busters and for the HR managers who design staffing and reward systems to attract and motivate these workers.

Work Force Diversity

Besides changes in the numbers and work values of available workers, shifts are also occurring in the racial and gender composition of the labor force.[55] In all respects, **work force diversity** is increasing. Figure 3.5 shows the expected racial and gender distribution of the labor force predicted to the year 2025. White non-Hispanics will drop from 74 percent of the labor force in 1998 to 64 percent in 2025. By 2010, there will be more Hispanics than blacks in the labor force, and by 2025, Hispanics will comprise 17 percent of the work force. Asian representation is growing rapidly, from less than 5 percent in 1998 to a projected 7.7 percent in 2025. The number of women will also increase, from 46.3 percent in 1998 to 48 percent by 2015.[56]

Awareness of the increasing ethnic diversity of the American work force touched off a "diversity boom" during the 1990s that shows no signs of slowing.

FIGURE 3.5

Composition of the U.S. Labor Force by Race and Ethnic Origin
Source: Data compiled from H. N. Fullerton, Jr., "Labor Force Participation: 75 Years of Change, 1950–98 and 1998–2025," *Monthly Labor Review*, December 1999, pp. 3–12. Values for 2015 and 2025 are estimated.

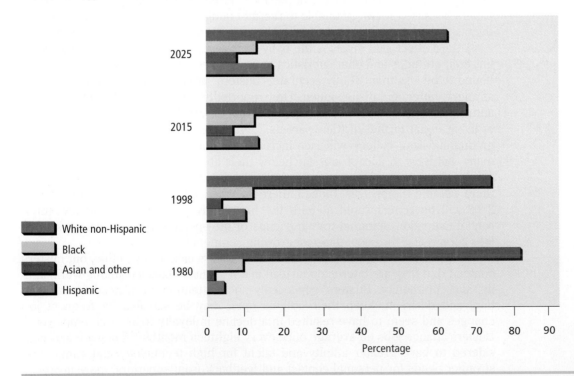

Related books, consulting services, and training programs abound.[57] Their purpose is to enhance tolerance of and sensitivity to workers perceived as different in terms of age, ethnicity, disability, gender, language, education, values, or lifestyle. Organizations are being encouraged to use diversity as an advantage, making use of the variety of viewpoints and skills that come with a widely varied work force in order to better serve a widely varied set of customers. Valuing diversity as a fact of life, rather than reluctantly accepting affirmative action for identified minority groups, seems to be the wave of the future.[58]

The Contingent Work Force

Much has been written in the past decade about the increasing number of **contingent workers.** This term refers to employees who do not have permanent full-time jobs but are called on by companies to work when and as needed. While definitions of "contingent workers" vary, the term is usually considered to include employees working on short-term or project contracts; those working on an on-call basis, such as substitute teachers; those working as independent contractors; and those whose services are acquired from a temporary help or employee-leasing agency.[59] Some definitions also include all part-time workers, although some part-time employees have permanent jobs. Alarmists noted the decline of "good," secure, full-time jobs during the 1990s. However, research suggests that most contingent and part-time employees have chosen this type of job because of the flexibility it offers and are reasonably satisfied with their situations. For organizations, contingent workers allow variations in workload to be managed without the need to lay off permanent employees.[60] As unemployment declined in the late 1990s, the upward trend in contingent workers slowed and began to reverse. Employers become more willing to lock in scarce workers on a permanent basis.[61]

Industry and Occupational Trends

The Bureau of Labor Statistics predicts which occupations and industries will be growing or declining in the near future. The fastest-growing occupations between now and 2008 are expected to be in the professional specialty field, in jobs such as computer engineer, systems analyst, database administrator, desktop publishing specialist, and medical and physician assistant. The largest growth in absolute numbers of new jobs is predicted for systems analyst, retail salesperson, cashier, general manager, truck driver, clerk, registered nurse, and personal caregiver.[62] As mentioned above, the job market is growing at both ends—occupations requiring substantial skill and education, and jobs requiring very little training or education. Some forecasters are worried that America's educational system will fail to provide the large numbers of highly skilled employees needed to fuel future economic growth.[63]

PLANNING HUMAN RESOURCE PROGRAMS

Having made demand and internal supply forecasts and considered the state of the external labor market, the HR planner can anticipate future problems with employee supply and plan programs for offsetting them. The following sections deal with planning for a new start-up and planning for labor shortages and surpluses. The final section considers managerial succession planning.

Planning for a New Establishment: Opening the Mirage

An exemplary exercise in HR planning occurred in connection with the opening of the Mirage hotel and casino in Las Vegas.[64] This property cost $635 million and has 3,049 rooms, a 105,000-square-foot casino, and twelve food and beverage outlets. All these facilities were opened virtually simultaneously. Obviously, a great deal of HR planning was necessary to carry out this feat.

Planning began two years in advance of the opening with the hiring of a vice president for human resources. His first task was to gather data on labor-market demographics, wage trends, competitors' expansion plans, and the opening experiences of other luxury hotels. Then he calculated the number of employees needed to run the facility (initially estimated at 5,000) and adjusted this figure for the expected number of no-shows (those hired before opening who did not turn up), early turnovers, and the lower-than-usual productivity of individuals just learning their jobs. These projections produced a target number of hires and allowed the estimation of the number of applications (47,000) needed to produce that number of qualified staff. Later, estimates of the likely volume of business were increased, so employment projections increased as well. For the opening, 6,200 people were hired from 57,000 applications.

After making the demand forecast, the next task of the HR vice president was to consider sources of applicants. He decided that some experienced employees would come from the company's other Las Vegas casino and that the local labor market would be sufficient to supply the rest. He directed special attention to jobs known to be problematic in the area, such as that of housekeeper. In this case, the organization offered a cash bonus to employees who referred a friend for the job of housekeeper.

In addition to planning for numbers of employees in each job category, the HR vice president had to plan their training and schedule their starting dates. He hired forty-two middle managers early and put them through a half-year training program; he hired and trained supervisors; finally, he had each supervisor conduct training for his or her work group. The hotel and casino opened successfully six weeks ahead of the original schedule.

The careful HR planning that preceded the opening has continued. Three years after the opening, the Mirage employed over 7,000 people in 405 job classifications. Extensive training, excellent employment conditions, and HR services that treat employees like valued customers made the Mirage a continuing success story as an employer. Turnover averages 60 percent per year in the hospitality industry, but the Mirage has an employee turnover rate of only 19 percent per year.[65]

Planning for Shortages

Clearly, the Mirage had to deal with an unusually large initial labor shortage that had to be met primarily from the external labor market. Most existing businesses would also tend to go to the external labor market for new employees when demand exceeds internal supply, though this is not their only option. Figure 3.6 lists a number of potential actions to deal with shortages.

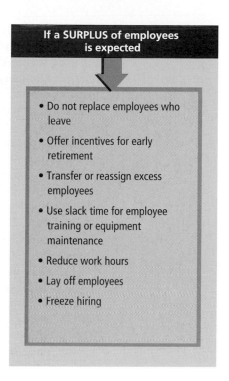

● **FIGURE 3.6**

Program Planning
Options

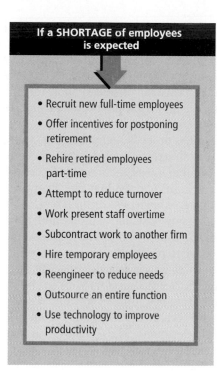

**If a SHORTAGE of employees
is expected**

- Recruit new full-time employees
- Offer incentives for postponing retirement
- Rehire retired employees part-time
- Attempt to reduce turnover
- Work present staff overtime
- Subcontract work to another firm
- Hire temporary employees
- Reengineer to reduce needs
- Outsource an entire function
- Use technology to improve productivity

**If a SURPLUS of employees
is expected**

- Do not replace employees who leave
- Offer incentives for early retirement
- Transfer or reassign excess employees
- Use slack time for employee training or equipment maintenance
- Reduce work hours
- Lay off employees
- Freeze hiring

Employers are finding that recruiting qualified employees from the external environment is not always easy. Innovations in recruiting may be necessary (they are discussed further in Chapter 6), and in some cases employers may have to create qualified workers where none existed before. For instance, Barden, a ball-bearing manufacturer in Connecticut, experienced great difficulty in filling its labor needs in an area with an unemployment rate of only 2.5 percent. Then it discovered the answer to its labor shortage in immigrants whose English was too poor to make them attractive to other employers. The organization retained the Berlitz language-training company to provide four hours of English instruction each day for three weeks. The result was competent, committed, and self-confident employees.[66]

When faced with a shortage, employers should consider other alternatives to hiring additional full-time employees. Some companies reduce labor demand by outsourcing peripheral functions—such as security, cleaning, printing, and account collection—to other firms that specialize in providing these services. Some employers encourage employees who are nearing retirement age to continue working by increasing the pension formula to reward extra years of service more heavily, or they rehire retired employees on a part-time basis. If a shortfall is caused or worsened by high employee turnover, employers should attempt to identify the causes of turnover and act to remedy them (there is a further discussion of retention strategies in Chapter 16). If successful, this course of action would save recruiting and training costs and might substantially improve employees' attitudes.

If the long-range plan suggests that demand will peak quickly and then return to a lower level, hiring new permanent employees would be unwise. For relatively short periods of increased demand, employers could pay for overtime rather than hire additional employees. Overtime work must be compensated at one and one-half times the regular hourly rate, but it may still be more economical than hiring, training, and providing benefits to new employees who are not needed over the long term. Alternatively, employers may choose to subcontract some work to another company during the demand peak or to acquire temporary workers from firms specializing in the provision of skilled short-term labor.[67]

Another response to a tight labor market is to analyze and modify the way work is done so as to achieve greater efficiency and thus require fewer staff. Companies have engaged in "business process reengineering" to eliminate unnecessary steps and activities that do not directly add value for the customer.[68] (This is discussed further in Chapter 10.) In other cases, technology can reduce the demand for employees. Caroline Power & Light is providing electricity services for more customers than ever with 2,000 fewer employees through technology-driven improvements in productivity. The company installed laptops and positioning devices in service trucks; trucks can now be routed to multiple locations on one trip rather than losing time by returning to base to pick up their next assignment. Soon electricity meters will be read remotely by computer, greatly reducing the need for meter readers.[69]

New Hanover Health Network, referred to in the opening HR Challenge, has adopted a number of strategies to meet its anticipated future shortage of nursing staff. Working with the Health Care Division of an HR consulting firm (Bernard Hodes Group, www.hodes.com), New Hanover made changes designed to increase retention of current nursing staff as well as attract an increasing supply of applicants. First, it made applying easier by installing an online application process. Second, it used the consultant's expertise in résumé-mining to locate potential nursing applicants across hundreds of Web job-board sites. Third, it merged recruitment advertising with the firm's other marketing activities with the goal of creating a recognizable brand image in the minds of both customers and potential employees. Recruitment ads now look similar to other advertising done by the firm and benefit more from the image created by other marketing efforts. Fourth, New Hanover made a strategic decision to move away from using contract nursing employees, who tend to stay only a short while, and toward permanent staff employed directly by the hospitals. Contract employment was reduced by 47 percent in less than a year. This has helped to create a climate of long-term commitment among employees. Fifth, New Hanover undertook a "boomerang initiative" in which employees who have recently left the firm are invited to return. As an incentive, there is no loss of benefits or seniority if the return is within one year of departure. Six to eight percent of nurses who quit have been recaptured by this program. Sixth, a full-time staffing position was created to coordinate recruitment and retention efforts. The staffing expert works closely with nursing schools in an attempt to recruit their graduates. Finally, the staffing expert has implemented a mentoring program to ease the school-to-work transition for new nursing graduates. The turnover rate of new graduates has fallen dramatically, from 30 percent to 6 percent, at least partly as a result of the mentoring program. New Hanover Health Network will still need to engage in shorter-term human resource supply and demand forecasting to guide month-to-month hiring, but this series of planned activities has paid off in the form of reduced hiring needs and a larger applicant pool over the long term.[70]

While not feasible in the case of hospitals, one possible response to a shortage of labor is to move work to countries in which qualified employees are more readily available (and in many cases, wages are lower).[71] The maquiladora factories across the Mexican border are an example, as are the numerous factories doing production work for U.S. firms in Asia. Nike is an example of a firm that has contracted out virtually all production of its athletic shoes to manufacturers in Asia. It's not just low-skilled work that is going off-shore to find plentiful, lower-cost labor, however. India has become a popular site for software companies because of the plentiful supply of skilled programmers, and a number of white-collar clerical jobs have been exported to Ireland. In addition to the challenges involved in managing a labor force in another country (see Chapter 17 for more on this), there may be sticky ethical issues involved when poorer nations are used as sources of labor for wealthier nations (see the International Perspective box).

Planning for Surpluses

When forecasts show that internal supply will exceed demand, employers must make plans to reduce supply. If the problem is recognized far enough in advance, a full or partial hiring freeze plus natural attrition may take care of the surplus. This alternative is the least costly in terms of both money and company reputation. If attrition is insufficient, employers can offer incentives for early retirement. (Under the Age Discrimination in Employment Act of 1967, employees cannot be forced to retire, except in individual cases where there is a documented medical or job-performance problem.) A major oil company offered such an incentive program to managers, expecting about 2,000 employees to accept it. To the company's surprise and dismay, nearly 6,000 managers accepted the early retirement package. Needless to say, HR planners and trainers had to scramble to deal with the sudden shortfall of experienced managers.

Depending on the nature of the surplus, a firm may be able to transfer or reassign employees to jobs in parts of the organization that are still experiencing demand. Some firms have set up an internal temporary agency through which surplus employees can be borrowed by other units, allocated to work on special projects, or even sent out as temporaries to work for other organizations.[72] If the firm expects the surplus to be short lived and can afford to keep excess workers on the payroll, it can use the slack time to provide cross-training in related jobs to increase work force skills and flexibility. Alternatively, excess workers can perform equipment maintenance and overhaul or other activities that were postponed when demand was high.[73]

An option that allows retention of all or most employees but still realizes payroll savings is to reduce work hours, perhaps to a four-day, thirty-two-hour workweek. In this way, a company can spread a 20 percent decrease in demand (and in pay) equitably across the whole work force rather than keep 80 percent of employees full time and lay off 20 percent. This alternative has been especially popular in states that permit workers on partial layoff to collect unemployment compensation for the days they do not work.

As indicated in Figure 3.6, the last resort is to lay off excess employees. This action obviously is bad for the employees, but it is also bad for the employer. Laying off workers damages a company's reputation as a good place to work and can be costly. Laid-off workers are entitled to collect unemployment compensation from a state-managed fund. The fund is supported by employer contributions, and the rate at which a firm is required to contribute depends on its past history of employee claims against the fund. Thus layoffs now will convert into higher premiums in the future.

INTERNATIONAL PERSPECTIVE

Manufacturing Overseas

One solution to scarce or expensive workers is to take production abroad, either by building a factory in a low-wage country or, more commonly, by contracting with existing manufacturers there. This approach has been taken by a large number of U.S. organizations as well as by many manufacturers headquartered in Japan, Taiwan, and Hong Kong. Popular sites for overseas manufacturing are the People's Republic of China, Thailand, Indonesia, the Philippines, Mexico, and India.

At first, most U.S. companies ignored any ethical issues involved in using overseas manufacturers to produce their goods. However, the potential ethical pitfalls are numerous: Overseas manufacturers may provide dangerous working conditions, require excessively long hours, hire children, and pay below-subsistence wages. In China, even the inadequate safety rules are often sidestepped because officials are eager to attract new investors or are easily bribed. In Shenzhen, China, eighty-one workers were killed when fire ripped through a handicrafts factory. The factory had illegally housed workshops, workers' dormitories, and a warehouse under the one roof. The situation was worsened by the fact that windows were barred and doors were locked to keep workers inside and prevent theft. A few months earlier, a similar Bangkok factory fire killed nearly 200 workers.

Of course, wages are lower than in the home country, but some foreign manufacturers fail to pay even what is promised. There are reports of Chinese workers hired by foreign firms at the minimum wage of about $100 a month and then routinely "fined" more than half their wages for mistakes in production. There are allegations that a company in Bangladesh supplying shirts to a large U.S. clothing retailer pays garment workers 20 cents per hour, well below the local minimum wage of 33 cents; fails to pay overtime rates; and requires workdays of twelve and a half hours, seven days per week, in violation of local labor laws. The labor cost of clothing made in Haiti and Honduras can be as little as one-half of 1 percent of the retail price of the garment in the United States. Young women from rural areas are often hired in garment factories on the assumption that they are more obedient and easier to exploit than older males. In many cases, children accompany their mothers to work and are themselves put to work at a very young age.

American companies that are seen to exploit workers have come under pressure from Western trade unions, human rights groups, consumers, shareholders, and investigative journalists. Recently, students at more than 175 campuses mobilized to protest against garments bearing their university's logo being made in overseas sweatshops.

In the interest of maintaining their reputations as good corporate citizens, some large U.S. companies have adopted global sourcing guidelines in an attempt to assure that their suppliers' employees are treated

Unfortunately, studies show that layoff is often the option chosen because HR managers usually have less than two months between the time a surplus of employees is first noticed and the time that staff reductions must be completed.[74] Better planning might lengthen this interval and allow the use of other methods to reduce staff. Note that federal law (the Worker Adjustment and Retraining Notification Act) requires employers to give employees sixty days' notice before closing an entire plant or laying off fifty or more people.[75]

Many responsible companies provide outplacement services to employees who must be let go. At a minimum, such services may include sessions on how to prepare a résumé and conduct a job search.[76] Chapter 16 discusses outplacement in more detail. Several recent studies have shown that fair and generous treatment of humanely. Retailing giant Wal-Mart has felt the sting of ignoring the conduct of its suppliers. The company was the subject of a scathing documentary when one of its subcontractors in Bangladesh was found to be employing underage workers. In response, Wal-Mart adopted a groundbreaking supplier code of conduct. In part, the code prohibits workweeks of more than sixty hours and forbids the hiring of children under age fifteen. Levi Strauss also has a stringent sourcing policy and is an acknowledged leader in efforts to raise safety and employment standards in overseas suppliers. The company now prohibits hiring children under fourteen and is paying for schooling for some younger children who were already employed. Nike's athletic apparel products are produced in more than fifty countries in about 704 plants, none of which Nike owns. The company has adopted a detailed code of conduct for the treatment of employees in overseas plants. All plants are audited regularly by both Nike managers and independent experts. Violations of the code result in financial penalties on the supplier and ultimately the termination of the contract to provide goods for Nike. (For more on Nike's code, see http://www.nikebiz.com/labor/toc_stan.shtml). Nevertheless, allegations that large companies routinely exploit poor workers overseas continue to be made.

However, the ethical issues are not as simple as they may first appear. Imposing Western-level safety or pay standards will deter foreign investment in underdeveloped economies, yet foreign investment is desperately needed to improve employment and living standards throughout these countries. Employment in foreign-owned factories is the only source of income for many families and the only source of financial independence for some Third World women—if the firms leave, these individuals suffer. Even child labor has two sides: If education simply isn't available, aren't children better off accompanying their mothers to work in foreign-owned factories than begging in the streets or being employed as virtual slaves in local cottage industries? And some child laborers are the sole supporters of their families: Is it responsible to fire them for being underaged when a sourcing policy comes into effect? Firms from wealthier nations are generally being urged to remain in less developed nations and work with their suppliers to improve the pay and conditions of local workers.

Sources: Mark Clifford, "Social Engineers," *Far Eastern Economic Review,* April 14, 1994, pp. 56–60; Martha Nichols, "Third-World Families at Work: Child Labor or Child Care?" *Harvard Business Review,* January–February 1993, pp. 12–23; C. M. Solomon, "Put Your Ethics to a Global Test," *Personnel Journal,* January 1996, pp. 66–74; M. A. Emmelhainz and R. J. Adams, "The Apparel Industry Response to 'Sweatshop' Concerns: A Review and Analysis of Codes of Conduct," *Journal of Supply Chain Management,* Summer 1999, pp. 51–57; and M. B. Marklein, "Making Them Sweat: Students Step Up Pressure to Hold Colleges Accountable for Apparel," *USA Today,* April 13, 2000, p. 01D. See http://www.business-humanrights.org/Company-Policies.htm for links to many cites containing companies' codes of conduct and http://nt1.ids.ac.uk/eldis/hot/ethics.htm for research on ethics in business related to the above issue.

laid-off employees can sustain morale and performance of the employees who are not laid off. Unfair treatment may cause layoff survivors to suffer from stress, fear, and guilt.[77]

When a company must lay off some but not all employees, it should have a fair procedure for deciding who must go. For unionized employees, layoff procedures are usually specified in the contract, with seniority often being an important factor. All employers should have a **reduction in force (RIF)** policy prepared well in advance of the need to reduce employment levels. While such a policy might reward employees with longer service for their loyalty, it also should reflect what is best for the company. This means that marginal performers or unskilled, easily replaceable employees should be released first. A firm should make every effort to retain good performers and skilled employees; although some of the latter may have to move down to less skilled jobs for a while, at least they will receive paychecks and will be available to move back up when business improves.

A special case of planning for employee redeployment and potential surpluses occurs when there is a merger or acquisition. In 2000, there were a record number of mergers and acquisitions involving U.S. companies, with 9,472 transactions reported, valued at a total of $1.41 trillion.[78] A large percentage of mergers and acquisitions fail altogether or fail to perform as well as expected, and this is most often attributed to problems in dealing with the human side of the deal. Human resource executives and planners need to be involved in potential mergers from the earliest stages right through to the successful integration of the two firms.

During the due diligence pre-merger phase, HR experts need to explore the size and skills of the target's work force, estimate costs and liabilities of compensation and benefit systems, investigate contractual obligations to employees and retirees, investigate potential legal or compliance problems, and assess the culture of the target organization compared to that of the acquirer.

When the decision is made to go ahead with the merger, critical decisions must be made quickly about the new organization's structure and who will staff the executive ranks. But decisions don't stop here. Employees at all levels want to know "how will this affect me?" Retrenchments are common as redundant functions and facilities are centralized. Aside from possible job loss, employees also face changed job responsibilities, derailed career plans, reduced power, and new bosses. HR planners have to work quickly to provide answers to employees who are understandably worried about their future in the new organization. A transparent and objective process based on performance, future capability, and the projected needs of the new organization should be put in place to help determine who stays and who goes. Throughout the merger or acquisition process, frequent and honest communication with the work force is essential.

A common employee response to uncertainty, perceived threat, or poor communication from the company is to quit, yet a significant share of the cash paid in the deal was to obtain the other organization's experienced work force. Thus another important HR function early in the merger process is to identify individuals with critical skills and to implement a program to retain them through the turbulent period of the merger. Retention bonuses or special grants of stock are possible choices. For those who will no longer be needed, severance arrangements and outplacement assistance should be put in place. Gaps that cannot be filled by any current employees also need to be identified so that targeted recruiting and selection can proceed. Finally, there is a great deal of work to be done in harmonizing HR systems and policies in the areas of compensation, benefits, record keeping, and so forth.[79]

Managerial Succession Planning

Regardless of expansion or contraction of the total work force in an organization, the need for good managers is critical and continuous. Many organizations plan for managerial succession and development because they have found that it takes years of systematic grooming to produce effective top managers. Some organizations have extremely detailed and long-range succession plans. For instance, one article reported that Exxon Corporation had already hired and was grooming the individual it expected to be chief executive officer twenty-two years later![80]

How companies practice succession planning varies.[81] Most successful programs, however, seem to include top management's involvement and commitment, high-level review of succession plans, formal assessment of the performance and potential of candidates, and written development plans for individual candidates.[82] Plans should center on especially important jobs and should correctly identify the skill requirements of those jobs. For instance, IBM's Executive Resources Planning System focuses on the job of director and identifies candidates with the potential to move up to this level.[83] At Union Oil Company, planners identify an apex job within each functional area and focus on candidates for future openings in this job. In the marketing function, for instance, the apex job is field division sales manager.[84] At Crocker National Bank, the goal is to develop general bankers able to move into senior positions.[85]

Most managerial succession planning systems rely on committees of higher-level managers to identify high-potential candidates and plan developmental activities for them.[86] Development plans include formal training programs and a series of job assignments leading to the target job. The plans are usually formally presented to yet higher-level managers for review. At Crocker National Bank, interdivisional meetings are also part of the process because general banker candidates need to be transferred across divisions to acquire a sufficiently broad base of experience.

In addition to planning for the development of individuals, these systems also result in the identification of viable near-term replacements for important positions. The traditional format for displaying such information is the **replacement chart.** The chart in Figure 3.7 shows how long an incumbent is expected to remain in his or her present position and lists one to three individuals who are now or soon will be ready to assume the position. In a thorough system, the chart is

● **FIGURE 3.7**

Replacement Chart

Qualification codes for readiness
0: Ready to move up now
1: Ready in a year
2: Ready in two years

Manager of
Human Resource Development
C. D. Schmidt

J. H. Doe	0
G. M. Sanchez	0
C. B. Mills	2

Manager of
Management Development
J. H. Doe

| W. K. Rule | 1 |
| K. A. Marino | 2 |

Training
Manager
G. M. Sanchez

M. W. Field	0
S. B. Moore	0
L. S. Ting	1

Manager of
Exempt Compensation
C. B. Mills

| J. Q. Rumowski | 0 |
| P. L. Shaw | 2 |

A DIFFERENT POINT OF VIEW

Is Traditional Long-Term Succession Planning Feasible?

 Some experts have strongly criticized traditional succession planning systems, stating that "thousands of managerial hours are expended to prepare flashy presentations and lengthy tomes identifying candidates for jobs that probably will not exist in three years. . . . Predicting succession in an era of constant change is fast becoming an impossibility."* Frequent restructuring, mergers, and acquisitions now mean that the nature and number of top jobs at organizations change often. The increasing rate of employee turnover also suggests that candidates identified today may no longer be with the firm when higher-level jobs open up. Succession plans are based on intentions and assumptions in place at the time when the plans are drafted. It is quite likely that the situation, the job, the organization, and the people may change before a succession actually occurs. For example, one *Fortune* 500 company had identified a "perfect" successor for the job of Latin American regional president. However, when the time came to make the appointment, it was found best to appoint a different individual, one who had less Latin American experience but more experience in marketing a major new product scheduled for rollout in the region that year.

Succession planning in the twenty-first century is changing to meet the realities of the labor market and the escalating pace of change, as shown in Figure 3.8. The goal is to build a good depth of leadership talent without the rigidity of traditional replacement charting systems. There is movement away from position-by-position planning, given that the requirements and even existence of positions may change rapidly. The newer approach involves "pools." Managerial jobs (either current or anticipated) are analyzed using a competency framework, and jobs with similar competency profiles are grouped together into position pools. Using the same competency framework, high-potential employees are assessed via 360-degree appraisal, interviews, and possibly assessment centers (see Chapter 8 for details). Employees are then grouped into candidate pools, which are drawn upon when openings occur. As before, written development plans are still prepared for each high-potential candidate. Plentiful feedback is also given so that employees understand what competencies are required in different higher-level jobs and can engage in self-development targeted at those posts.

In some companies, a competency-based approach means that there is less secrecy and greater transparency in the process of identifying the next generation of upper-level managers. For instance, the 3 percent of salaried employees at Boeing who are identified as "high potentials" know who they are, know what skills are required in the jobs they may someday fill, and report more enthusiasm for selfdevelopment than in the past.

*David W. Rhodes, "Succession Planning—Overweight and Underperforming," *Journal of Business Strategy,* November–December 1988, pp. 62–64; quote: p. 62.

Sources: Charles Borwick, "Eight Ways to Assess Succession Plans," *HRMagazine,* May 1993, pp. 109–114; M. Leibman, R. A. Bruer, and B. R. Maki, "Succession Management: The Next Generation of Succession Planning," *Human Resource Planning*, Vol. 19 (3), 1996, pp. 16–29; E. J. Metz, "Designing Succession Systems for New Competitive Realities," *Human Resource Planning*, 1998, Vol. 21 (3), 1998, pp. 31–37; J. W. Walker, "Do We Need Succession Planning Anymore?" *Human Resource Planning*, Vol. 21 (3), 1998, pp. 9–11; and F. Cope, "Current Issues in Selecting High Potentials," *Human Resource Planning*, Vol. 21 (3), 1998, pp. 15–17.

backed up by formal evaluations of performance and potential as well as comprehensive development plans for each possible replacement.

Traditional succession planning, as described above, has come under attack in the last few years. While many of the features listed above are still important in identifying and developing managerial talent, the structure and emphasis of succession planning at pace-setting organizations has changed, as shown in Figure 3.8 and described in A Different Point of View.

How Succession Planning Systems are Changing

Source: E. J. Metz, "Designing Succession Systems for New
Competitive Realities," *Human Resource Planning*, Vol. 21
(3), 1998, p. 33.

BUSINESS SYSTEMS

FROM		TO
Organizational pyramids with multiple layers	→	Flatter organization structures
Desire for "seasoned" leaders	→	Want the "seasoning" developed sooner in careers
Stability	→	Flexibility with faster market responsiveness

SUCCESSION SYSTEMS

FROM		TO
Groom a backup for each position	→	Develop pools of broadly qualified candidates; have position pools
Specialty disciplines in candidates	→	More broadly disciplined candidates
Business unit autonomy	→	More centralization and integration of systems and information
Siloed career growth	→	Cross-boundary fertilization to develop broader skills and perspectives
Largely human resources driven	→	Largely line driven
Subjective and informal criteria: personality/image oriented	→	Strategic competencies and models define success; 360 degree feedback
Technical competence a key factor	→	Cross-functional management capability. quick learner; manage change
Tolerate marginal performers	→	Fewer positions for development requires removing marginal blockers
Company directs and controls career	→	Individual sets career direction
Controlled and confidential process	→	Input from multiple sources; more open planning and development process
"Promises"	→	No "promises"
Focus on training and seminars as primary development vehicle	→	Sequential job assignments provide primary development experience supplemented by specific training
Take advantage of vacancies to promote candidates	→	Create assignments for development (e.g., exchanges, trades, special projects)
Promote from within when fully qualified	→	Promote when about 70% qualified; hire less experienced talent at entry level

Summary of Key Points

Organizations must plan for human resources. Otherwise, they run the risk of having (1) employees of insufficient skill or number to meet the organization's needs or (2) an excess of costly employees whose pay and benefits eat into profits. HR planning is based on information about the organization's internal and external environments and on assumptions about what will happen in these environments in the future. Planning may be at the aggregate level of jobs or job families or at the individual level, as in the planning of managerial succession and development. Strategic human resource planning involves HR experts in formulating and implementing the organization's strategy in the light of HR opportunities and constraints.

HR planners may use judgmental methods, such as unit forecasting or the Delphi technique, to predict a firm's need for labor at a particular point in the future. Mathematical techniques may be used for this same purpose. HR planners predict the future internal supply of labor, drawing on skills inventories, human resource information systems, and Markov analyses to make their forecasts. Planners also gather information on relevant external labor markets to determine the availability of potential new employees.

After both demand and supply forecasts are made, planners reconcile the two to determine areas in which more or fewer employees will be needed. Then they design programs to increase or reduce the size of the work force or to change employees' skills to match the forecasted needs. A number of alternatives for dealing with employee shortages and surpluses are available. Through careful planning, an organization can anticipate needs and implement programs to meet them before the needs actually materialize and cause problems for the organization. Succession planning ensures the supply of qualified and experienced top managers for the future.

The Manager's Vocabulary

aggregate-level planning
application service provider
baby boom
baby-boom echo
baby bust
birth dearth
bottom-up, or unit, forecasting
civilian labor force
contingent worker
Delphi technique
demand for labor
demand forecasting
"discouraged" workers
enterprise resource planning
external supply of labor
human resource information system (HRIS)
human resource planning
internal supply of labor
labor force participation rate
labor market
labor reserve
linear, or goal, programming
Markov analysis
multiple regression
productivity ratio
reduction in force (RIF)
renewal, or replacement, analysis
replacement chart
skills inventory
staffing ratios
succession plan
top-down forecasting
transition probability matrix
unemployment rate
work force diversity

Questions for Discussion

1. Why should organizations engage in HR planning? Why do some organizations need relatively more complex and comprehensive HR planning systems than do others?
2. What are the benefits of strategic HR planning?
3. When are judgmental methods of demand forecasting preferred over mathematical methods? When is the reverse true?
4. Why is the internal supply of labor not static? How can organizations keep track of their internal supply of labor?

5. Describe the advantages and disadvantages of Markov analysis for predicting the future internal supply of labor.

6. A low-tech organization is about to use systematic HR planning for the first time. As yet, the HR function has little power or credibility in the organization, though the head of HR is a well-trained, newly hired MBA. The organization's environment is fairly stable, and good records of past staffing levels are available. What method or methods of human resource planning would you recommend in this situation? Why?

7. What kinds of information might an HR planner want to gather about the external labor market?

8. How are changing age and ethnic demographics likely to affect organizations in the next decade?

9. From your own experience, how do boomers and busters differ from each other in skills, attitudes and work values, and job prospects? How might these differences affect relationships between the two groups in the work setting?

10. Would you like to be part of the "contingent" work force? Why or why not? What are the advantages and disadvantages of contingent positions for employees and for employers?

11. What can an organization do when a shortage of employees is anticipated?

12. What can an organization do when it expects the internal supply of labor to exceed the demand for labor?

13. What purposes are served by managerial succession planning? What are some characteristics of an effective managerial succession planning system? How have succession planning systems changed in the past few years?

● Case 3.1
Brooks Beverage Management, Inc.

Brooks Beverage Management, Inc. (BBMI), is a soft-drink bottler in Holland, Michigan. The market for some of BBMI's cold drinks is expected to dip sharply in winter, when consumers turn to hot beverages. This will result in an excess of about fifty-five production-line employees between September and March. If laid off, these employees would be difficult and costly to replace. Each receives three months of training on the high-tech bottling equipment before being fully qualified. BBMI operates in a labor market with a very low unemployment rate of 3 percent, so anyone laid off would be snapped up quickly by another employer and not be available in the spring when demand picks up at the bottler. BBMI has put together a task force of representatives from all areas of the company to suggest solutions to this anticipated staffing dilemma. What ideas can you think of to ensure that the services of skilled employees are available when they are needed, year after year? Be creative!

Source: V. Frazee, "Share Thy Neighbor's Workers," *Personnel Journal*, June 1996, pp. 81–84. Reprinted by permission.

● Case 3.2
Elite Small Goods

Your firm, Elite Small Goods, supplies specialty food items to delicatessens in major cities. Elite operates two small food-processing plants in New York City to supply its East Coast markets. These plants use old technology in simple and labor-intensive processes. Most of the production employees have limited English-language capability and less than a high school education. However, they are loyal to the firm; turnover is less than 10 percent per year. These operators are managed by traditional supervisors who make all the decisions and issue orders. Equipment maintenance is provided by specialized tradespeople at each plant: an electrician, a boilermaker, and an engine mechanic.

Business is good enough that management is considering modernizing one of the plants. Processing would become much more efficient, with one plant doing more work than both can do together at the present time. The older plant would be closed. The new processing equipment requires sophisticated skills from production operators, including reading technical manuals, operating computers, and performing a wide variety of other tasks. The vendor suggests that the new equipment is most effective when employees are organized into self-managed teams. The modernized plant also will require two multiskilled mechanics who can be trained to maintain all aspects of the complex equipment.

Presently, combined employment at the two plants is sixty-five. The modernized plant will require only fifty-five employees. A manager who strongly favors modernization has been heard to say that "since only ten jobs are affected, the human resource implications are minimal." The CEO has asked you to study and report on the staffing implications of the proposed plant modernization and closure. What do you do now? What information do you seek, and what use do you make of it? What type of staffing actions do you think may be necessary? What cautions might you give management?

● Exercise 3.1
Human Resource Planning and the Internet

Using the Internet, locate the latest figures about the size and composition of the U.S. population, the U.S. labor force, and the unemployment rate. Attempt to locate similar information for your city or state. How might you use this type of information in human resource planning?

Search the Internet for additional information that may be relevant to human resource planning for one of the following types of organizations:

- A large nationwide moving company specializing in employee relocation
- A junior college in Houston
- A group of five hospitals in North Carolina
- A high-tech company in California's Silicon Valley

● Exercise 3.2
Predicting Supply and Demand

It is now January 2003. Your task is to predict supply and demand for each job category as of January 2004 and to plan what to do to meet the demand.

1. Your 700 operatives this year will produce 100,000 products. Improvements to the plant scheduled for completion in December 2003 will enable production of 120,000 products. You plan to hire more operatives in order to utilize this new capacity to the fullest in 2004. The improvements to the plant also will result in an increase in productivity such that each worker will be able to produce 5 percent more next year than this year.

2. The use of a new computerized billing system will increase the productivity ratio of clerks to 135 percent of the current ratio. The workload for the clerks will not change from what it is this year.

3. Because of a large standing order, fewer salespersons will be needed. It is estimated that a sales force of forty people will be sufficient to handle business at the beginning of 2004.

4. The ratio of management and staff to operatives should be the same as it is at present.

SUPPLY

Present Number of Employees (beginning of 2003)	Transition Probability Matrix				
	Operatives	Clerical	Sales	Management/Staff	Exit
700 Operatives	.80	0	0	0	.20
150 Clerical	.10	.80			.10
50 Sales			.80	.10	.10
100 Management/staff				.90	.10

FORECAST

	Operatives	Clerical	Sales	Management/Staff
January 2004 predicted supply	_____	_____	_____	_____
January 2004 predicted demand	_____	_____	_____	_____
Gap	_____	_____	_____	_____

What discrepancies will exist and how will you deal with them for each group (operatives, clerical, sales, management/staff)? Be innovative and suggest several solutions.

Notes and References

1. Todd Raphael, "Behind the Nursing Shortage," *Workforce,* September 29, 2000. (Available at: www.workforce.com/archive/article/001/07/16.xci)

2. "Mounting a Strategic Recruitment Initiative"[paid advertorial], *Workforce.* (Available at: www.workforce.com/feature/00/07/26/)

3. Randall S. Schuler and James W. Walker, "Human Resources Strategy: Focusing on Issues and Actions," *Organizational Dynamics,* Summer 1990, pp. 4–19.

4. Dave Ulrich, "Strategic and Human Resource Planning: Linking Customers and Employees," *Human Resource Planning,* Vol. 15 (2), 1992, pp. 47–62.

5. Brian J. Smith, John W. Boroski, and George E. David, "Human Resource Planning," *Human Resource Management,* Vol. 31, Spring–Summer 1992, pp. 81–93.

6. Emily S. Bassman, "Strategic Use of Environmental Scanning Data," in *Human Resource Forecasting and Strategy Development,* ed. Manuel London, Emily S. Bassman, and John P. Fernandez (New York: Quorum, 1990), pp. 29–37.

7. J. L. Martel and D. S. Langdon, "The Job Market in 2000: Slowing Down as the Year Ended," *Monthly Labor Review,* February 2001, pp. 3–20.

8. Lorenz P. Schrenk, "Environmental Scanning," in *Human Resource Management: Evolving Roles and Responsibilities,* ed. Lee Dyer (Washington, D.C.: BNA Books, 1988), pp. 88–124.

9. J. J. Laabs, "Duke's Newest Power Tool," *Personnel Journal,* June 1996, pp. 44–52.

10. Harvey Kahalas, Harold L. Pazer, John S. Hoagland, and Amy Levitt, "Human Resource Planning Activities in U.S. Firms," *Human Resource Planning,* Vol. 3, 1980, pp. 53–66.

11. Laabs, "Duke's Newest Power Tool."

12. Susan E. Jackson and Randall S. Schuler, "Human Resource Planning: Challenges for Industrial/Organizational Psychologists," *American Psychologist,* February 1990, pp. 223–239; E. H. Burack and N. J. Mathys, *Human Resource Planning: A Pragmatic Approach to Manpower Staffing and Development* (Northbrook, Ill.: Brace-Park, 1996).

13. A. M. Bowey, "Corporate Manpower Planning," *Management Decision,* Vol. 15, 1977, pp. 421–469.

14. Daniel N. Bulla and Peter M. Scott, "Manpower Requirements Forecasting: A Case Example," in *Strategic Human Resource Planning Applications,* ed. Richard J. Niehaus (New York: Plenum Press, 1987), pp. 145–155.

15. Andre L. Delbecq, Andrew H. Van de Ven, and David H. Gustafson, *Group Techniques for Program Planning* (Glenview, Ill.: Scott, Foresman, 1975), pp. 83–107.

16. George T. Milkovich, Anthony J. Annoni, and Thomas A. Mahoney, "The Use of the Delphi Procedures in Manpower Forecasting," *Management Science,* December 1972, pp. 381–388.

17. Burack and Mathys, *Human Resource Planning.*

18. Don R. Bryant, Michael J. Maggard, and Robert P. Taylor, "Manpower Planning Models and Techniques," *Business Horizons,* April 1973, pp. 69–78.

19. Lee Dyer, "Human Resource Planning," in *Personnel Management*, ed. Kendrith Rowland and Gerald Ferris (Boston: Allyn and Bacon, 1982), p. 53. See Robert H. Meehan and S. Basheer Ahmed, "Forecasting Human Resources Requirements: A Demand Model," *Human Resource Planning*, Vol. 13 (3), 1990, pp. 297–308, for an example of using regression to predict demand in a public utility company.

20. Bowey, "Corporate Manpower Planning"; and Bryant, Maggard, and Taylor, "Manpower Planning Models and Techniques" For further information on linear or goal programming, see C. J. Verhoeven, *Techniques in Corporate Manpower Planning* (Boston: Kluwer, 1982); Richard C. Grinold and Kneale T. Marshall, *Manpower Planning Models* (New York: North-Holland, 1977); and Richard J. Niehaus, *Computer-Assisted Human Resources Planning* (New York: Wiley, 1979). An excellent source on planning is D. Ward, T. P. Bechet, and R. Trip, *Human Resource Forecasting and Modeling* (New York: Human Resource Planning Society, 1994).

21. William E. Bright, "How One Company Manages Its Human Resources," *Harvard Business Review*, January–February 1976, pp. 81–93.

22. Michael J. Kavanagh, Hal G. Gueutal, and Scott I. Tannenbaum, *Human Resource Information Systems: Development and Application* (Boston: PWS-Kent, 1990).

23. K. A. Kovach and C. E. Cathcart, Jr., "Human Resource Information Systems (HRIS): Providing Business with Rapid Data Access, Information Exchange and Strategic Advantage," *Public Personnel Management*, Summer 1999, pp. 275–282.

24. R. E. Thaler-Carter, "The HRIS in Small Companies: Tips for Weighing the Options," *HRMagazine*, July 1998, pp. 30–37.

25. "Complete eBusiness Functionality Folded into a Single Reliable Solution." Available at: http://peopletalk.peoplesoft.com/en/new/peopletalk/mar2000/cover/index/html

26. John A. Hooper and R. F. Catalanello, "Markov Analysis Applied to Forecasting Technical Personnel," *Human Resource Planning*, Vol. 4, 1981, pp. 41–47.

27. E. R. Hackett, A. A. Magg, and S. D. Carrigan, "Modelling Faculty Replacement Strategies Using a Time-Dependent Finite Markov-Chain Process," *Journal of Higher Education Policy and Management*, May 1999, pp. 81–93.

28. Herbert G. Heneman III and Marcus B. Sandver, "Markov Analysis in Human Resource Administration: Applications and Limitations," *Academy of Management Review*, October 1977, pp. 535–542.

29. Richard J. Niehaus, "Human Resource Planning Flow Models," *Human Resource Planning*, Vol. 3, 1980, pp. 177–187.

30. For more information, see Guy E. Miller, "A Method for Forecasting Human Resource Needs Against Internal and External Labor Markets," *Human Resource Planning*, Vol. 3, 1980, pp. 189–200.

31. Niehaus, "Human Resource Planning Flow Models"; and Bryant, Maggard, and Taylor, "Manpower Planning Models and Techniques."

32. E. S. Bres III, R. J. Niehaus, F. J. Sharkey, and C. L. Weber, "Use of Personnel Flow Models for Analysis of Large Scale Work Force Changes," in Niehaus (ed.), *Strategic Human Resource Planning Applications*, pp. 157–167; for an update on this system, see R. J. Niehaus, "Evolution of the Strategy and Structure of a Human Resource Planning DSS Application," *Decision Support Systems*, Vol. 14, 1995, pp. 187–204.

33. James A. Craft, "Human Resource Planning and Strategy," in Dyer (ed.), *Human Resource Management*, pp. 47–87.

34. Laabs, "Duke's Newest Power Tool."

35. Bright, "How One Company Manages Its Human Resources."

36. Gordon McBeath, *The Handbook of Human Resource Planning* (Oxford: Blackwell, 1992); example: p. 52.

37. Laabs, "Duke's Newest Power Tool."

38. *The Australian Human Resource Benchmarking Report: 1995 Edition* (Brisbane: Australian Human Resources Institute and HRM Consulting Party, Ltd., Brisbane, 995); L. M. Spencer, Jr., *Calculating Human Resource Costs and Benefits* (New York: Wiley-Interscience, 1986).

39. *Handbook of Methods,* Bulletin 2285 (Washington: Bureau of Labor Statistics, 1988).

40. H. N. Fullerton, Jr., "Labor Force Projections to 2008: Steady Growth and Changing Composition," *Monthly Labor Review*, November 1999, pp. 19–32.

41. M. Duane, *Customized Human Resource Planning* (Westport, Conn.: Quorom, 1996).

42. Raphael, "Behind the Nursing Shortage."

43. George T. Silvestri, "Occupational Employment: Wide Variations in Growth," *Monthly Labor Review,* November 1993, pp. 58–86.

44. Fullerton, "Labor Force Projections to 2008."

45. R. W. Judy and C. D'Amico, *Workforce 2020: Work and Workers in the 21st Century* (Indianapolis, Ind.: Hudson Institute, 1997).

46. Arlene Dohm, "Gauging the Labor Force Effects of Retiring Baby-Boomers," *Monthly Labor Review*, July 2000, pp. 17–25.

47. Richard R. Nelson, "State Labor Legislation Enacted in 1990," *Monthly Labor Review,* January 1991, pp. 41–56.

48. Paul Magnusson and Susan B. Garland, "Jobs, Jobs, Jobs Galore," *Business Week*, April 18, 1988, pp. 26–28.

49. Martin M. Greller and David M. Nee, *From Baby Boom to Baby Bust: How Business Can Meet the Demographic Challenge* (Reading, Mass.: Addison-Wesley, 1989); and Stephanie Overman, "Myths Hinder Hiring of Older Workers," *HRMagazine,* June 1993, pp. 51–52.

50. Kristina J. Shelley, "The Future of Jobs for College Graduates," *Monthly Labor Review,* July 1992, pp. 13–21.

51. D. Braddock, "Occupational Employment Projections to 2008," *Monthly Labor Review*, November 1999, pp. 51–77.

52. Bob Filipczak, "It's Just a Job: Generation X at Work," *Training,* April 1994, pp. 21–27.

53. C. L. Jurkiewicz, "Generation X and the Public Employee," *Public Personnel Management*, Spring 2000, pp. 55–74.

54. Kim Macalister, "The X Generation," *HRMagazine,* May 1994, pp. 66–69.

55. Joseph F. Coates, Jennifer Jarratt, and John B. Mahaffie, *Future Work: Seven Critical Forces Reshaping Work and the Work Force in North America* (San Francisco: Jossey-Bass, 1990).

56. H. N. Fullerton, Jr., "Labor Force Participation: 75 Years of Change, 1950–98 and 1998–2025," *Monthly Labor Review*, December 1999, pp. 3–12.

57. Maria Shao, "Diversity Training: What Is It? Who Does It? Working Together," *Boston Globe,* March 7, 1994, pp. 8–9.

58. R. Rooseveldt Thomas, Jr., "From Affirmative Action to Affirming Diversity," *Harvard Business Review,* March–April 1990, pp. 107–117; Marilyn Loden and Judy B. Rosener, *Workforce*

America! Managing Employee Diversity as a Vital Resource (Homewood, Ill.: Business One Irwin, 1991); David Jamieson and Julie O'Mara, *Managing Workforce 2000: Gaining the Diversity Advantage* (San Francisco: Jossey-Bass, 1991); Lee Gardenswartz and Anita Rowe, *Managing Diversity: A Complete Desk Reference and Planning Guide* (Burr Ridge, Ill.: Irwin Professional Publishing, 1993); R. M. Wentling and N. Palma-Rivas, "Current Status of Diversity Initiatives in Selected Multinational Corporations," *Human Resource Development Quarterly*, Spring 2000, pp. 35–60; and R. M. Wentling and N. Palma-Rivas, "Current Status and Future Trends of Diversity Initiative in the Workplace: Diversity Experts' Perspective," *Human Resource Development Quarterly*, Fall 1998, pp. 235–253.

59. A. E. Polivka, "Contingent and Alternative Work Arrangements, Defined," *Monthly Labor Review*, October 1996, pp. 3–9. Note that this entire issue of *Monthly Labor Review* is devoted to a discussion of the characteristics of the contingent labor market.

60. A. E. Polivka, "Into Contingent and Alternative Employment: By Choice?" *Monthly Labor Review*, October 1996, pp. 55–74; C. von Hippel, S. L. Mangum, D. B. Greenberger, R. L. Heneman, and J. D. Skoglind, "Temporary Employment: Can Organizations and Employees Both Win?" *Academy of Management Executive*, January 1997, pp. 93–104; R. Nardone, "Part-Time Employment: Reasons, Demographics, and Trends," *Journal of Labor Research*, Summer 1995, pp. 275–292.

61. S. Hipple, "Contingent Work: Results from the Second Survey," *Monthly Labor Review*, November 1998, pp. 22–35.

62. G. T. Silvestri, "Occupational Employment to 2005," *Monthly Labor Review*, November 1995, pp. 60–84.

63. Judy and D'Amico, *Workforce 2020*.

64. Information in this section comes from Robert W. Eder, "Opening the Mirage: The Human Resources Challenge," *Cornell Hotel and Restaurant Administration Quarterly*, August 1990, pp. 25–31; quote: pp. 26–27.

65. Bill Leonard, "HR Policies Ensure the Mirage Won't Vanish," *HRMagazine*, June 1992, pp. 85–91.

66. Schuler and Walker, "Human Resources Strategy."

67. Marc J. Wallace, Jr., and M. Lynn Spruill, "How to Minimize Labor Costs During Peak Demand Periods," *Personnel*, July–August 1975, pp. 61–67; Leonard Greenhalgh, Anne T. Lawrence, and Robert I. Sutton, "Determinants of Work Force Reduction Strategies in Declining Organizations," *Academy of Management Review*, April 1988, pp. 241–254; and A. Halcrow, "Temporary Services Warm to the Business Climate," *Personnel Journal*, October 1988, pp. 84–89.

68. Daniel Morris and Joel Brandon, *Re-engineering Your Business* (New York: McGraw-Hill, 1993).

69. Y. J. Dreazen and J. M. Schlensinger, "A Tight Labor Market Can Spur Productivity," *Wall Street Journal Interactive Edition*, March 18, 2000. Available at: www.careerjournal.com/ hrcenter/articles/20000216-dreazen.html

70. "Mounting a Strategic Recruitment Initiative."

71. Robert O. Metzger and Mary Ann Von Glinow, "Off-Site Workers: At Home and Abroad," *California Management Review*, Spring 1988, pp. 101–111.

72. The theme of *Personnel Journal* in June 1996 was strategies to prevent layoffs. The issue contains seven articles about various ways to avoid layoffs.

73. Rene J. Schoysman, "Planning Manpower in a Downturn Economy," *Journal of Systems Management*, May 1980, pp. 31–33.

74. J. T. McCune, R. W. Beatty, and R. V. Montagno, "Downsizing: Practices in Manufacturing Firms," *Human Resource Management*, Vol. 27, 1988, pp. 145–161.

75. "President Lets Plant Closing Become Law Without His Signature," *Ideas and Trends in Personnel*, August 9, 1988.

76. Gary B. Hansen, "Innovative Approach to Plant Closings: The UAW–Ford Experience at San Jose," *Monthly Labor Review*, June 1985, pp. 34–37.

77. Joel Brockner, "The Effects of Work Layoffs on Survivors: Research, Theory, and Practice," in *Research in Organizational Behavior*, Vol. 10, ed. Barry M. Staw and L. L. Cummings (Greenwich, Conn.: JAI Press, 1988), pp. 213–255.

78. "Two Tales Can Be Told About the M&A Market in 2000" (Press release, Dec. 28, 2000, Los Angeles). Available at: http://www.mergerstat.com/

79. J. W. Walker and K. F. Price, "Perspectives: Why Do Mergers Go Right?" *Human Resource Planning*, 2000, Vol. 23 (2), pp. 6–8; R. N. Bramson, "HR's Role in Mergers and Acquisitions," *Training & Development*, October 2000, pp. 59–66; T. A. Daniel, "Between Trapezes: The Human Side of Making Mergers and Acquisitions Work," *Compensation and Benefits Review*, Winter 2000, pp. 19–37.

80. G. L. McManis and M. S. Leibman, "Succession Planners," *Personnel Administrator*, August 1988, pp. 24–30.

81. David W. Rhodes and James W. Walker, "Management Succession and Development Planning," *Human Resource Planning*, Vol. 7, 1984, pp. 157–173; and S. D. Friedman, "Succession Systems in Large Corporations: Characteristics and Correlates of Performance," *Human Resource Management*, Vol. 25, 1986, pp. 191–213.

82. James K. Wellington, "Management Succession at Arizona Public Service," *Human Resource Planning*, Vol. 4, 1981, pp. 157–167; and W. J. Rothwell, *Effective Succession Planning: Ensuring Leadership Continuity and Building Talent from Within* (New York: AMACOM, 1994).

83. Lee Dyer and Nelson O. Heyer, "Human Resource Planning at IBM," *Human Resource Planning*, Vol. 7, 1984, pp. 111–125.

84. Bright, "How One Company Manages Its Human Resources."

85. Jofannie Houk, "Human Resource Planning at Crocker National Bank," *Human Resource Planning*, Vol. 4, 1981, pp. 37–46.

86. See Diana Kramer, "Executive Succession and Development Systems: A Practical Approach," in London, Bassman, and Fernandez (eds.), *Human Resource Forecasting and Strategy Development*, pp. 99–112, for detailed advice on setting up a succession planning system.

Job Analysis: Concepts, Procedures, and Choices

HR Challenge

Alpha Electric (formerly Alpha Defense Systems, Inc.) is converting its plant in Banksia, Tennessee, from military to commercial manufacturing. Alpha is a former defense contractor that made computer components for use in highly sophisticated weapons systems. The Banksia plant will adapt its weapons-systems technology to manufacture components for high-tech communications systems. Alpha will be moving into an extremely competitive business environment where product life cycles are short and innovation, customer orientation, high quality, and cost-effectiveness are necessary to succeed.

Alpha Electric has decided to redesign its manufacturing process. Assembly-line jobs will be relatively similar to those in the old manufacturing process. However, warehousing, shipping and receiving, and most other jobs within the plant will be converted to a team-based approach. The organizational structure will be flattened, and employees will be given more responsibility and broader powers to do their jobs. One of the first problems that Alpha faces is to decide what jobs will have to be performed in the new plant environment. While some are mandated by technology and the manufacturing process, others are not. Given the flatter structure, greater individual and team responsibilities, and higher level of employee empowerment, deciding who does what job has become a much more complex task. For many areas of work, do traditional jobs still exist? As the HR director of Alpha Electric, you are faced with the task of analyzing and helping to design the new work structure. What do you do? Where do you start?

A traditional solution to the preceding HR Challenge would have involved the HR director's developing a job analysis program for Alpha Electric to identify what work needed to be done and who should do it. However, in recent years, the nature and methods of job analysis have been undergoing a transition brought about by dynamic business environments, a more empowered work force, shorter product life cycles, and many other factors. What would have been a fairly straightforward HR problem a few years ago has now become a much more complex and difficult scenario.

This chapter examines the role of job analysis in twenty-first-century organizations. Traditionally, job analysis has been defined as the process of "obtaining information about jobs."[1] . While it has always been a complex area of human resource management to describe, an adequate discussion of job analysis has become even more difficult. This is because the term "job" has become a very contentious term in modern organizations. For example, William Bridges, in his 1995 book *Job Shift*, suggested that jobs "are artificial units superimposed on this field. They are patches of responsibility that, all together, were supposed to cover the work that needs to be done."[2] To fully understand what is discussed in this chapter, the reader must first recognize that modern job analysis has a "split personality."

TRADITIONAL JOB ANALYSIS

Over the past fifty years, an enormous number of methodologies have been developed for use in measuring and understanding the nature of jobs. Part of the discipline of job analysis focuses on these traditional methods. Within this traditional approach, the goal of research and practice has been to identify better methods and measurement procedures to describe the content of jobs. In the traditional view, there is a straightforward assumption that jobs exist and can be measured. In contrast to the traditional view are the **job extinction** proponents, who argue that *jobs* no longer exist in modern organizations due to the dynamic nature of work in rapidly changing business environments. The job extinction view argues that much of what we now know as job analysis is no longer meaningful and must be replaced with drastically different means for understanding what employees do in organizations.

One way of appreciating these two different views of job analysis is to compare how the two perspectives define "a job." Traditionally, a job has been defined using four concepts that have a hierarchical relationship to one another. Thus, a job is comprised of several similar positions. Each position is made up of a set duties, which are comprised of several distinct tasks. A definition for each of these four concepts is given below:

Do We Really Need Job Descriptions, or Even Jobs?

In sharp contrast with traditional human resource management practice, some authors feel that to facilitate the flexibility required in today's rapidly changing environment, companies should do away with job descriptions. Tom Peters, author of the highly influential *Thriving on Chaos* and more recently *Liberation Management: Necessary Disorganisation for the Nanosecond Nineties,* explains:

> Perhaps a case could be made for job descriptions in a stable, predictable, very vertically oriented (functional) organisation. Today, in all cases the job description is a loser. . . . It is imperative today that managers and non-managers be induced to cross "uncrossable" boundaries as a matter of course, day after day. Standing on the formality of a written job description (as an excuse for inaction, or the reason you have to "check up—and up and up—the line") is a guaranteed strategy for disaster.*

An article in *Fortune* magazine makes the point even more strongly—it argues that the entire concept of "job" is becoming obsolete. "In a fast moving economy, jobs are rigid solutions to an elastic problem."† Instead of viewing organizations as a structure of jobs,

they should be viewed as "fields of work," made up of constantly changing activities and projects, with a shifting complement of core and peripheral workers doing whatever needs to be done.

W. L. Gore and Associates, maker of Gore-Tex waterproof fabrics, has proved that such unconventional human resource management can be successful. Bill Gore wanted to avoid stifling his employees' initiative and constraining their interpersonal communications, so he abandoned job titles, hierarchy, and a traditional corporate structure. There are only three job titles in the organization, which employs over 6,000 people: President, Secretary-Treasurer, and Associate. The first two titles are used only because they are required by incorporation law.

Gore's associates are expected to be flexible and adaptable. Rather than being assigned a specific job and having work flow down from above, associates are expected to commit themselves to a team to which they feel they can make the most valuable contribution—or alternatively, initiate a team themselves and lead it toward a new objective. Those who require more regimented and structured working conditions do not stay with the organization for long.

Associates at Gore can recall countless stories of newcomers who have either thrived or failed in their

- A **task** is "a meaningful unit of work activity generally performed on the job by one worker within some limited time period. . . . It is a discrete unit of activity and represents a composite of methods, procedures, and techniques."[3]
- A **duty** is a loosely defined area of work that contains several distinct tasks that are performed by an individual.
- A **position** is the set of tasks and duties performed by a single individual in an organization. Each person in an organization has a position.
- A **job** is "a group of positions that are identical with respect to their major or significant tasks and sufficiently alike to justify their being covered by a single analysis."[4]

In contrast to this highly structured and static view of a job is the description provided by Greg Stewart and Kenneth Carson.[5] They state that, "In general, determinations of what needs to be done and who does it are made as people evaluate themselves and others, and then enter into agreements that bind them to act in unusual working environment. One example is the story of Jack Dougherty. On July 26, 1976, Jack Dougherty, a newly minted MBA from the College of William and Mary, became an associate. Bursting with resolve and dressed in a dark blue suit, he presented himself to Bill Gore, shook hands firmly, looked him in the eye, and said he was ready for anything.

What happened next was the one thing for which Jack was not ready. "That's fine, Jack, fine," Gore replied. "Why don't you look around and find something you'd like to do." Three frustrating weeks later, Jack found that something. Now dressed in jeans, he loaded fabric into the maw of a machine that laminates Gore-Tex membrane to other fabrics. It was Jack's way of learning the business. And by 1982, he had become responsible for all advertising and marketing in the fabrics group.[‡]

Fundamental to the success of Gore's dynamic structure is the firm's system of sponsorship, whereby each new associate is assigned to a more senior associate, or "sponsor," who is expected to take an active interest in the new associate's progress, developing his or her strengths and providing coaching about his or her weaknesses. In the absence of a well-defined job description, such a system ensures that associates can contribute to the fullest extent of their ability and that they are recognized appropriately for their contribu-

tions. Also fundamental to the system is a strong commitment by all employees to follow four guiding principles:

1. Be fair.
2. Make commitments, and keep them.
3. Use your freedom to grow and develop.
4. Consult others when your decisions will have an impact on them or cause a potentially major problem for the company.

By following the principles, associates can regulate their behavior without any need for detailed rules and fixed responsibilities.

* Tom Peters, *Thriving on Chaos* (London: Pan, 1989), pp. 500–501.
[†]William Bridges, "The End of the Job," reprinted in *Time   Australia,* September 19, 1994, pp. 2–7, from *Fortune,* September 19, 1994; quote, p. 4.
[‡]Frank Shipper and Charles C. Manz, "Employee Self-Management Without Formally Designated Teams: An Alternative Road to Empowerment," *Organizational Dynamics,* Winter 1992, p. 57.
Sources: John Huey, "The New Post-Heroic Leadership," *Fortune,* February 21, 1994, pp. 42–50; Tom Lester, "The Gore's Happy Family," *Management Today,* February 1993, pp. 66–68. For more information about W. L. Gore, see http://www.gore.com/careers/us.html; Tom Peters, *Liberation Management: Necessary Disorganisation for the Nanosecond Nineties* (London: Macmillan, 1992); and Frank Shipper and Charles C. Manz, "Employee Self-Management Without Formally Designated Teams: An Alternative Road to Empowerment," *Organizational Dynamics,* Winter 1992, pp. 48–61.

a predictable manner . . . the formation of these agreements is known as behavioral contracting . . . . These contracts psychologically bind individuals to perform specific behaviors . . . behavioral contracts also differ . . . in that they are dynamic, comprehensive, and subjective, rather than static, narrow, and objective."[6] For an example of this sort of **behavioral contracting** in action, see A Different Point of View. Stewart and Carson would label traditional approaches to job analysis as "static, narrow, and objective," and of relatively little use in understanding the real nature of work. Some authors have even argued that traditional job analysis is detrimental to organizational health. As early as 1992, Bob Cardy and Greg Dobbins suggested that the "traditional approach to job analysis assumes a static job environment. Specifically, it must be assumed that the job analyzed today will consist of the same set of duties and tasks tomorrow . . . the reliance on job analysis and the proliferation of resulting job descriptions can cripple an organization's ability to be flexible and adapt rapidly to change."[7]

As with many situations in which proponents of new ideas attack traditional methods, the reality for job analysis research and practice probably lies somewhere between "jobs are dead" and "let's just keep on doing the same old job analysis things." Despite the fact that jobs are more dynamic now than in the past, Michelle Crosby points out that in "most instances, people still have jobs—a definable set of activities that are performed as well as a definable set of competencies that enable their effective performance. The list of activities and competency assessments associated with a particular position may be broader than it was in the past, but it certainly still exists . . . even if 'jobs' as we have traditionally known them are dying, clearly work is not."[8]

For job analysts, the arguments of the job extinction proponents show that there is a need for more dynamic approaches to job analysis. However, traditional methods of analyzing jobs, *if properly adapted,* remain extremely useful.[9] Given this, in the remainder of the chapter we will provide a thorough discussion of traditional methods of job analysis, since they provide a solid foundation on which to develop improved techniques for analyzing twenty-first-century work. Toward the end of the chapter we will elaborate on the *new strategic view of job analysis* and describe some of the more dynamic approaches to job analysis that already exist or are currently being developed.

THE JOB ANALYSIS PROCESS

As noted above, **job analysis** is defined simply as "obtaining information about jobs."[10] A job analysis typically produces a **job description** and the context in which the work activities are performed, that is, a written narrative of the activities performed on a job as well as information about the equipment used and working conditions in which the job is performed. There is also usually a **job specification** that outlines the specific skills, knowledge, abilities, and other physical and personal characteristics that are necessary to perform a job. Note that job specification requires one to infer from the job description the human traits presumed to be necessary for successful completion of a job. The basic job analysis process consists of ten steps, which can be grouped into the four major phases shown in Figure 4.1.

● **FIGURE 4.1**

Job Analysis Process

PHASE 1 **Scope of the Project**	**PHASE 2** **Methods of Job Analysis**	**PHASE 3** **Data Collection and Analysis**	**PHASE 4** **Assessing Job Analysis Methods**
• Decide purposes of project • Decide which jobs to include	• Decide which types of data are needed • Identify sources of job data • Select specific procedures of job analysis	• Collect job data • Analyze data • Report results to organization • Recheck job analysis data periodically	• Evaluate results against criteria of benefits, costs, and legality

PHASE 1: THE SCOPE OF THE JOB ANALYSIS

To determine the scope of any job analysis effort, an organization must first decide what it hopes to accomplish with the job analysis data. It must then identify the jobs or work processes that it wants to include in the analysis program. Top management, both within and outside the HR function, must be involved in these decisions.

Uses of Job Analysis

Knowing what duties a job requires and what skills are needed to perform these duties is critical in setting up an appropriate selection system (test development and validation). Job analysis became even more important in selection thanks to a variety of equal employment opportunity laws, including the Americans with Disabilities Act (ADA) that went into effect in 1992 (discussed more fully in Chapter 5). For some time, U.S. courts have indicated that organizations must clearly show that there are direct links between the duties that employees perform on their jobs and the knowledge, skills, and abilities that are assessed in selection procedures. The ADA outlaws discrimination against mentally and physically handicapped individuals who are able to perform the essential functions of a job, either in the usual way or with reasonable accommodation to their needs, such as workbenches designed to accommodate wheelchairs. To ensure that truly qualified disabled people are not misjudged but that those not able to do the job are properly rejected, organizations can no longer rely on job descriptions that simply list the tasks that must be performed. Instead, the organization must be sure that job descriptions identify the essential functions or fundamental duties of jobs and link these clearly to specific physical and mental requirements.[11] Table 4.1 shows a range of other uses for job analysis.

For prospective employees, job analysis data can provide realistic information about what jobs will be like. Studies have found that such **realistic job previews**

● **TABLE 4.1**

Uses of Job Analysis

Recruiting and Selecting Employees	Developing and Appraising Employees	Compensation	Job and Organizational Design
Human resource planning	Job training and skill development	Determining pay rates for jobs	Designing/redesigning jobs to improve efficiency or motivation
Identification of internal labor markets	Role clarification	Ensuring equal pay for equal work	Determining lines of authority and responsibility
Recruitment	Employee career planning	Ensuring equal pay for jobs of comparable worth	Determining necessary relationships among work groups
Selection	Performance appraisal		
Placement			
Equal employment opportunity			
Realistic job previews			

reduce applicants' unrealistically high expectations about jobs and thus reduce early employee dissatisfaction and turnover.[12] For new hires, job analysis data can help orient them to their positions.

Job analysis data can provide the information needed to develop job-relevant training programs and performance appraisal systems. In addition, such data can help supervisors and employees clarify conflicts and ambiguities in employees' roles.

Job analysis data can be used to determine the similarity of jobs and thus the feasibility of transfers between jobs. In the U.S. Air Force, job analysis data have been used to identify jobs that individuals can transfer to with minimal retraining.[13] Similarly, job analysis data may be used to identify nontraditional career paths for employees. In one study, job analysis data were used to show that the skills, knowledge, and abilities essential for performance in secretarial and clerical positions are very similar to those needed in entry-level management jobs.[14] Since female employees often predominate in secretarial and clerical jobs, such information may provide employers with ways to increase the movement of women into managerial positions. From the employees' perspective, they can use job analysis information to plot career paths and make maximum use of their past experience in moving to different, more challenging jobs.

A traditional use of job analysis has been in the area of job evaluation, to determine the relative worth of jobs and thereby develop equitable compensation structures.[15] The Equal Pay Act of 1963 mandates that employees who are in jobs that require the same skill, effort, and responsibility and that are performed in the same working conditions be paid similarly unless certain exceptions apply.[16] Job analysis provides a way for organizations to determine the relative similarity of two jobs.

Job analysis procedures have been used to design jobs for maximum efficiency. The effectiveness of the Japanese automobile and electronics industries has often been attributed to group management techniques.[17] Some of their successes, however, stem from the use of very detailed job analysis methods to determine the nature of jobs and to design work environments that allow workers to perform those jobs efficiently. In many cases, careful analysis of the actions required to perform a particular task or job has enabled Japanese firms to replace human workers with robots.

One use of job analysis data not included in Table 4.1 is **job classification.** The reason for this omission is that in many of the uses listed, job classification is an intermediate step between the collection and use of the data. In job classification, the job analyst uses information to categorize similar jobs into a job family. The analyst can then develop selection, appraisal, pay, or other procedures for an entire job family rather than for a single job. For example, in the area of personnel selection, research has shown that cognitive ability tests may be extremely useful in selecting among job applicants across a wide variety of jobs. Job analysis data help to identify groups of jobs for which a single cognitive ability test might serve as a predictor of future job performance among job applicants.[18]

Determining Which Jobs to Analyze

A variety of factors determine which jobs in an organization should be analyzed. Likely targets of job analysis are jobs that are critical to the success of an organization, for example, those of quality control specialists in an organization whose business strategy focuses on providing high-quality products. Jobs that are difficult to learn and perform (and thus require extensive training) are also essential to analyze, as are jobs for which the organization is constantly having to hire new employees (since job analysis provides information about how best to select those employees). Legal considerations may also determine which jobs should be analyzed. Jobs that have few minority or female employees should be analyzed to make sure that illegal discrimination is not occurring in hiring practices. In addition, jobs should be analyzed when new technology or other circumstances suggest that the way in which the job is performed needs to be changed. When completely new jobs are added, these should be analyzed. When some jobs are eliminated and their duties distributed to other jobs within the organization, job analysis may be appropriate to clarify the nature of these expanded jobs.[19]

Which types of jobs, the number of jobs, and the geographic dispersion of jobs are important for determining the specific method of job analysis used.[20] For example, one way to collect job information is to observe employees actually performing the jobs. If IBM were to use this procedure for collecting information about all the jobs in IBM worldwide, this job analysis project would cost millions of dollars and take years to complete. If, on the other hand, IBM were interested only in the job of keyboard assemblers at a single plant, this observation method of collecting job information might prove quite useful.

PHASE 2: THE METHODS OF JOB ANALYSIS

To determine which methods of job analysis to use, the job analyst must decide on (1) the types of data to collect, (2) the sources of information from which to get the data, and (3) the specific procedure of job analysis to implement.

Types of Job Data

Several types of data can be collected in a job analysis project. These data relate to various work activities and human abilities as well as to other job characteristics and information about the equipment used on the job. J. W. Cunningham and his colleagues identified three levels of work activities.[21] **Foundation work activities** are free of technological content and are thus applicable to a wide range of occupations. For example, a question such as "How much responsibility for people do you have on your job?" could be asked of employees in almost any type of job. **Intermediate work activities** have some technological content but are applicable across a reasonably wide range of occupations, for example, "How much of your time is spent teaching people?" Although teaching people would not be applicable to every job, there are a wide range of jobs that might involve some level of teaching, for example, professors, personnel trainers, and supervisors in technical fields who might have to instruct subordinates. **Area work activities** are technologically oriented and quite specific to particular occupational groups, for example, nursing. Collecting this type of data would involve questions such as "How much time do you spend cleaning surgical equipment?" In addition to identifying this hierarchy of work activities, Cunningham and his colleagues also described a hierarchy of knowledges and skills that ranged from "fundamental" (e.g., ability to read, think, plan) to "occupation specific" (e.g., the skill needed by a surgeon to use a laser scalpel).

In addition to Cunningham's work, there are a number of taxonomies of human abilities that have been developed over the years and are widely used in job analysis.[22] Taken collectively, these taxonomies identify four major types of abilities:

- **Psychomotor abilities,** such as manual dexterity and arm/hand steadiness
- **Physical abilities,** such as strength and stamina
- **Cognitive abilities,** such as intelligence and verbal comprehension
- **Situational abilities,** such as the ability to work under time pressure and the ability to work alone

There has also been a large amount of recent work to identify "core competencies" of managers and other professionals. Such studies represent efforts to develop lists of human abilities, skills, and knowledge relevant to occupational clusters or specific occupations.[23]

Many other types of information can be collected as part of a job analysis process. A good example of this can be found in the Occupational Information Network (O*NET) that is being developed for the U.S. Department of Labor. Data on worker requirements, worker characteristics, experience requirements, occupation requirements, occupation-specific requirements, and occupation characteristics are all part of the O*NET system. Examples of the types of data in each of these six major categories are presented in Table 4.2.

● **TABLE 4.2**

Types of Data in the Occupational Information Network (O*NET) Database

---

Experience Requirements
1. Experience and training—Specific preparation required for entry into a job and past work experience contributing to qualifications for an occupation
2. Licensing—Licenses, certificates, or registrations that are used to identify levels of skill or performance relevant to occupations

---

Occupation Requirements
1. Generalized work activities—General types of job behaviors occurring on multiple jobs, such as:
   a. Looking for and receiving job-related Information
   b. Information/data processing
   c. Performing complex/technical activities
   d. Coordinating/developing/managing/advising others
2. Organizational context—Characteristics of the organization that influence how people do their work such as:
   a. Decision-making system
   b. Job characteristics
   c. Job stability and rotation
   d. Human resources systems and practices
   e. Social processes & roles
   f. Culture & organizational values
   g. Supervisor role
3. Work context—Physical and social factors that influence the nature of work, such as:
   a. Formality of communication
   b. Job interactions
   c. Responsibility for others
   d. Conflictual contact
4. Physical work conditions, such as:
   a. Work setting
   b. Environmental conditions
   c. Job hazards
   d. Body positioning
   e. Work attire

5. Structural job characteristics, such as:
   a. Criticality of position
   b. Pace and scheduling

Occupation-Specific Requirements

Detailed information describing the characteristics of a particular occupation, such as occupational skills & knowledge, tasks & duties, machines, tools & equipment

Occupation Characteristics

Basic information on the nature of the industry, job opportunities, and pay within the occupation

Worker Characteristics

1. Abilities—Enduring attributes of the individual that influence performance
   a. Cognitive abilities, such as:
      i. Verbal abilities
      ii. Idea generation and reasoning
      iii. Attentiveness
   b. Psychomotor abilities, such as:
      i. Fine manipulative abilities
      ii. Reaction time and speed abilities
   c. Physical abilities, such as:
      i. Endurance
      ii. Flexibility, balance, and coordination
   d. Sensory abilities, such as:
      i. Visual abilities
      ii. Auditory and speech abilities
2. Interests—Preferences for work environments and outcomes, such as:
   a. Holland occupational classification
   b. Occupational values
3. Work styles—Personal characteristics that describe important interpersonal and work-style requirements in jobs and occupations, such as:
   a. Achievement orientation
   b. Social influence
   c. Interpersonal orientation
   d. Conscientiousness
   e. Practical intelligence

Worker Requirements

1. Basic skills—Developed capacities that facilitate learning or the more rapid acquisition of knowledge, such as:
   a. Reading comprehension
   b. Writing
   c. Critical thinking
2. Cross-functional skills—Developed capacities that facilitate performance of activities that occur across jobs, such as:
   a. Social skills
   b. Complex problem-solving skills
   c. Systems skills
3. Knowledge—Organized sets of principles and facts applying in general domains, such as:
   a. Business and management
   b. Manufacturing and production
   c. Arts and humanities
   d. Law and public safety
4. Education—Prior educational experience required to perform in a job

Source: Department of Labor, Occupational Information Network, http://www.doleta.gov/programs/onet.

Regardless of the content of the data collected, the job analyst must also decide whether to collect data in a qualitative or quantitative format. **Qualitative data** are narrative descriptions of the work activities, abilities, characteristics, and equipment associated with the job. **Quantitative data** are numerical values that indicate the extent to which the work activities, abilities, characteristics, and equipment are involved in the performance of the job. For example, a job analyst who collects qualitative data about a job might learn that typing letters is really important on the job. By collecting data in a quantitative format, the analyst might instead find that 70 percent of an employee's time is spent typing letters.

An advantage of quantitative data is that they allow the job analyst to compare different jobs. Using qualitative data, the job analyst might find that for one job "typing letters is very important" and for another job "typing letters is critical." How, then, can the job analyst compare these two jobs? Is "very important" the same as "critical"? If, instead, the job analyst were to collect quantitative data, he or she might find that typing letters is 50 percent of one employee's job but 80 percent of another's.

Sources of Job Data

Although the most direct source of information about a job is the job incumbent, a number of other sources are available. For example, other nonhuman sources could include existing job descriptions, equipment maintenance records, films of employees working, or architectural blueprints of a work area. In addition to job incumbents, job data could be obtained from supervisors or other job experts. These sources might provide information that the average job incumbent cannot, thereby enabling the job analyst to question the incumbent more effectively.

The first place a job analyst should look for information about a job is in job analysis data that already exist. However, the job analyst should view these data with caution. They may have been developed using inadequate procedures, or they may no longer be valid descriptions of present-day jobs.

Although people such as job analysts, trainers, supervisors, and other experts may never have performed a certain job, they may be knowledgeable about the content and context of the work. For instance, an engineer who designed a nuclear reactor probably could offer considerable insight into the job of a nuclear reactor operator. Regardless of which sources are used, the job analyst should ensure that (1) nonhuman sources are the most recent available, (2) any source used is as accurate and reliable as possible, and (3) whenever possible data should be collected from several different sources of information.

Having good job analysis data is important because inaccurate job analyses can cost money.[24] For example, exaggeration of job duties could result in a higher salary than the job is really worth. Inaccurate job descriptions could result in poor hiring decisions that result in lower productivity of employees in the job. The financial costs of poor job analysis data can become very apparent when organizations defend their personnel practices in court (as in the case of a sex, race, or age discrimination suit). Judges are increasingly interested in the adequacy of the sources of job analysis information. This is particularly the case when **subject matter experts (SMEs)**—individuals who provide job analysis information—are involved.[25]

When using subject matter experts, a job analyst should select SMEs who have had an adequate opportunity to perform the job or observe the job being performed. According to several studies, the complexity level of the job being rated, as well as the amount of job knowledge, experience, and competence that SMEs have, will influence the accuracy and reliability of the information they provide. A recent study has found that contextual factors such as firm size may also affect job analysis ratings. [26] Job incumbents who are interviewed should be representative of the types of people who do the job and include both males and females if both sexes perform the job. Significant differences have been found in the job analysis ratings made by males and females. However, these differences may be due in part to women's tending to have less job experience than men.[27] It is also probably best to collect information from both high and low performers and from individuals with varying levels of experience on the job.[28]

Job Analysis Procedures

There are a wide variety of specific procedures that can be used in analyzing a job. They range from very simple qualitative approaches to highly complex and structured quantitative methods. In the next sections we will discuss three major types of job analysis procedures.

● **Narrative Job Descriptions**   **Narrative job descriptions** and specifications are the simplest form of job analysis. The job analyst collects qualitative data from various sources of job data. Most frequently, the analyst interviews employees and supervisors or observes workers performing the job. Narrative job descriptions typically include information on job title; job identification number; name of the department or division where the job is performed; name of the job analyst; brief written summary of the job; list of the job's major duties; description of the skills, knowledge (including education), and abilities needed to perform the job; list of the machines, tools, and equipment used on the job; and an explanation of how the job relates to other jobs in the organization. In writing these descriptions, job analysts try to describe the job in a terse, direct style with concrete, simple language. They avoid technical terms (unless they are widely used on the job) and make minimal use of adjectives, gerunds, and participles. An example of a narrative job description is presented in Figure 4.2.

The uses of narrative job descriptions are relatively limited. The information provided is so general that its use in developing specific performance appraisal or training content is difficult. The same problems exist for use of narrative descriptions in pay determination or job design. However, narrative descriptions are useful for recruiting and orientation, for creating realistic job previews, and for career planning.

● **Engineering Approaches**   **Engineering approaches** involve an examination of the specific body movements and/or procedural steps that are used to perform a particular task. The job analyst collects data by observing actual employees on the job, films of employees working, or both films and live employees. The analyst develops an operation chart to show the actions of an employee performing a task. The chart typically uses symbols to represent the worker's specific actions and the sequence in which they occur; through the use of symbols and brief phrases, a detailed description of the task emerges.

Micromotion studies are a particular type of engineering approach. They are used to analyze jobs that contain very short-cycle, repetitive tasks (e.g., soldering the electrical circuits on the chassis of a television set). The job analyst develops a list of basic body motions and uses it to analyze all the tasks included in the study. Several standard lists of basic body motions have been developed.[29] These lists in-

Job title:	Receptionist	Organization:	Bonwit-Maxwell
ID number:	071-582-911A		Department Stores
Division:	Customer Credit	Job analyst:	Edward Bourgois
		Date analyzed:	November 7, 1999

Job Summary

Answers inquiries and gives directions to customers, authorizes cashing of customers' checks, records and returns lost charge cards, and sorts and reviews new credit applications.

Job Duties

1. Answers inquiries and gives directions to customers. Greets customers at information desk and ascertains reasons for visits to credit office. Sends customers to Credit Interviewer to open credit accounts, to Cashier to pay bills, to Adjustment Department to obtain correction of errors in billing. Directs customers to other store departments on request, referring to store directory.

2. Authorizes cashing of checks. Authorizes cashing of personal or payroll checks (up to a specified amount) by customers desiring to make payment on credit account. Requests identification such as driver's license or credit card from customers, and examines check to verify date, amount, signature, and endorsement. Initials check and sends to Cashier.

3. Answers telephone calls from customers reporting lost or stolen charge cards and arranges details of cancellation of former cards and replacements. Obtains all possible details from customers regarding lost or stolen cards and submits data to Head Authorizer for processing. Notifies Head Authorizer immediately to prevent fraudulent use of missing cards. Orders replacement cards for customers when confirming letters are received.

4. Records charge cards that have inadvertently been left in sales departments and returns them to customers. Stamps imprint of cards on sheets of paper, using imprinting device. Dates sheets and retains for own records. Fills out forms, posting data such as customers' names, addresses, and dates cards were returned. Submits sheets to Head Authorizer.

5. Sorts and records new credit applications daily. Separates regular charge account applications from Budget Accounts. Breaks down charge account applications into local and out-of-town applications and arranges them alphabetically within each group. Counts number of applications in each group and records in Daily Record Book. Binds each group of applications with rubber band and transmits to Tabulation Room.

Skills, Knowledge, Abilities

Education needed: 6th grade
On-the-job training: 3–5 weeks

Machines, Tools, Equipment, Work Aids

Impressing device—small, hand-operated device similar to stapler; used to make credit-card impressions on paper.

Relationships to Other Jobs

Promotion from: This is an entry-level job.
Promotion to: Credit Interviewer
Supervision received: Credit manager
Supervision given: No subordinates of this job
Transfers: None

clude such motions as search, select, grasp, hold, position, inspect, assemble, and disassemble. The analyst films workers performing a task and then analyzes the film to identify the separate motions and the time required to complete each motion. The term **time and motion study,** which derives from this analysis of time and motions, is often used to describe this category of job analysis procedures.

The engineering approaches to job analysis provide detailed information about jobs. These methods concentrate on tasks and/or basic body movements, are relatively objective in their manner of collecting information, and usually result in some form of quantitative data. The data are particularly useful for the design of equipment to be used on the job. However, these procedures provide little of the broader context in which the job is performed. They present little direct information about the environment in which the work takes place or the abilities that are necessary to perform the job.

● **Structured Job Analysis Procedures**   Although there are many different structured job analysis procedures, we will discuss eight that are representative. Each procedure provides a different view of jobs and is suitable for different uses.

Critical Incidents Technique   J. C. Flanagan developed the **critical incidents technique (CIT)** for assembling lists of behaviors that are critical to job performance. The procedure consists of four steps:[30]

1. A panel of experts provides written examples of behaviors that represent effective or ineffective performance on the job. These examples describe a given incident: what led up to it, exactly what the employee did, the consequences of the behavior, and to what extent the consequences of the behavior were under the control of the employee. For example, a critical incident of good performance by a night security guard might be: The security guard heard a strange hissing sound coming from the basement. He investigated the noise and found a gas leak in the building's furnace. He immediately cut off the gas to the furnace, preventing an explosion, and called the utility company to arrange for the repair of the leak.

2. All the examples generated in step 1 are then sorted into groups of similar behaviors (e.g., handling emergency situations). This sorting may be done by either the job analyst or a group of experts on the job.

3. The categories identified in step 2 are defined and named by either the job analyst or job experts.

4. The job behavior categories are rated according to how critical or important they are for job performance. This rating is done by a group of job experts.

Using the CIT, job analysts can identify major types of behaviors that correlate with effective or ineffective performance. The CIT is well suited for developing performance appraisal systems and also for determining the training needs of employees. However, it does not identify the common, routine behaviors performed on jobs. This limitation in Flanagan's approach can be eliminated easily by extending the CIT procedure to include statements concerning average performance and thus provide a better overall view of job behaviors.[31]

Department of Labor Method   The **Department of Labor (DOL) method,** described most recently in the Department of Labor's *Revised Handbook for Analyzing Jobs,* has been used to collect data on thousands of jobs. In previous years this data was regularly published in the ***Dictionary of Occupational Titles (DOT).***[32] However, the U.S. Department of Labor is now developing the **Occupational Information Network** database called **O*NET.** Job data for O*NET is collected using a survey method involving nine questionnaires.[33] Examples of the type of data collected were presented earlier in Table 4.2. The O*NET database system will replace the *Dictionary of Occupational Titles* and will include sophisticated occupational and career information systems. Although the final database for O*NET is still a work in process, a considerable amount of occupation-related information can already be obtained from its web site at http://www.doleta.gov/programs/onet. In terms of the potential uses of O*NET data, Robert Guion states that information on O*NET "is intended for comparing jobs and occupations, nor for providing job-specific or occupation-specific information. Nevertheless, its content includes the kinds of information useful in more narrowly focused job analysis surveys."[34]

Functional Job Analysis (FJA)   In **functional job analysis (FJA),** trained job analysts review written materials, observe workers performing the job, and interview job incumbents and supervisors for information. Others familiar with the job then review all this information to ensure its validity and reliability. The typical steps in the FJA procedure are as follows:[35]

1. The job analyst and top management decide on the goals, purposes, and objectives of the FJA project.

2. Job analysts identify and describe the tasks performed on the job in a standardized written format, outlining what action occurs, to what purpose, and under what specific conditions.

3. Job analysts analyze each task using seven scales: three worker-function scales (see Table 4.3), a worker-instruction scale, and three scales concerning general educational development in reasoning, mathematics, and language. The worker-function scales indicate the type of behavior engaged in toward data, people, and things; these scales also indicate the percentage of time spent on each task involved with data, people, and things. For example, in performing one task, an employee might spend 70 percent of the time working with people, 10 percent working with data, and the remaining 20 percent working with things.

4. Job analysts write performance standards to describe how to assess the performance of workers. For example, for the task of typing letters, the performance standard might read: "Letters are typed with no typographical, grammatical, or spelling errors" or "No more than one spelling error per page of typing."

5. Job analysts identify the training needed by the employee to perform the job. This analysis of training content identifies the functional, specific content, and adaptive skills needed to perform the task. For the job of typist, a worker might need to be trained in how to type (functional skill) and in the proper format of business letters (specific content skill). The training analysis also might indicate that a good typist must be able to "pace his or her work"—an adaptive skill that enables the worker to perform the task properly over time.

The FJA method has been used to analyze many different jobs. It has a wide range of applications but is not particularly useful for job classification or evaluation unless combined with other techniques. One of its main advantages is that it

● **TABLE 4.3**

Worker-Function Scales in Functional Job Analysis

Data	People	Things
1. Comparing	1a. Taking instructions 1b. Serving	1a. Handling 1b. Feeding/off-bearing
2. Copying	2. Exchanging information	2a. Machine tending I 2b. Machine tending II
3a. Computing 3b. Compiling	3a. Sourcing information 3b. Coaching 3c. Persuading 3d. Diverting	3a. Manipulating 3b. Operating/controlling I 3c. Driving/controlling 3d. Starting up
4. Analyzing	4a. Consulting 4b. Instructing 4c. Treating	4a. Precision working 4b. Setting up 4c. Operating/controlling II
5a. Innovating 5b. Coordinating	5. Supervising	
6. Synthesizing	6. Negotiating 7. Mentoring	

Note: The higher the scale number, the more complex is the function. Precise definitions of the worker functions can be found in the source of this table.

Source: S. A. Fine and M. Getkake, *Benchmark Tasks for Job Analysis: A Guide for Functional Job Analysis* (Mahwah, N.J.: Erlbaum, 1995).

analyzes each task separately. This characteristic provides a detailed picture of the job and makes the FJA method applicable for a variety of organizational purposes.

Position Analysis Questionnaire (PAQ)   Designed by E. J. McCormick to analyze a wide variety of jobs, the **Position Analysis Questionnaire (PAQ)** consists of 194 items: 187 items characterize the worker-oriented activities involved in performing a job, and 7 items deal with pay issues.[36] The items of the PAQ are grouped into six divisions. The first division includes items on the sources of information that workers use in performing a job, the second division concerns the mental processes used on the job, and the third division identifies the actual output of the job. The final three divisions of the PAQ deal with relationships with other persons, the job context, and other job characteristics.

To complete the PAQ, a job analyst, supervisor, or job incumbent uses one of six rating scales. (The job analyst usually rates the PAQ items during an interview with a job incumbent or supervisor.) The six scales used to rate PAQ items are (1) extent of use, (2) importance to the job, (3) amount of time, (4) possibility of occurrence, (5) applicability, and (6) special code. The special code scales are constructed for specific items and vary in their exact format. Depending on the nature of the item, each is rated using only one of the scales. Typically, a PAQ analysis is completed for several individual positions with the same job title. The results of these analyses are then averaged to get a better, more reliable picture of the job.

The items on the PAQ can be grouped into thirty-two divisional and thirteen overall job dimensions. Each job dimension represents a category of worker-oriented activities that may occur on the job. The job-dimension scores represent the actual levels of these activities that occur on a particular job. Examples of PAQ job dimensions and sample items within each of the six divisions are shown in Table 4.4. In addition to job-dimension scores, L. D. Marquardt and McCormick have developed procedures using the PAQ to provide scores on seventy-six human attributes.[37] These attribute scores indicate the levels at which various physical, cognitive, and situational abilities are involved in job performance.

The PAQ has been used extensively for personnel selection, job classification, and job evaluation. However, its use in performance appraisal and training systems is limited. The worker-oriented PAQ items make analyzing a wide variety of jobs easier, but they also make it difficult to translate PAQ scores directly into specific performance standards or training content.

Task Inventory Procedure   A **task inventory** is "a form of structured job analysis questionnaire that consists of a listing of tasks within some occupational field . . . and [a] provision for some type of response scale for each task."[38] A task inventory focuses on what gets done on a set of jobs in a particular occupation. Because of this, a task inventory must be developed for each group of jobs that is to be ana-

⬤ **TABLE 4.4**

PAQ Divisions with Example Items and Job Dimensions

Division	Items	Divisional Dimensions[a]
Information input: How and from where does the worker get information used in performing the job?	Use of written materials Near visual differentiation	Interpreting what is sensed Using various sources of information
Mental processes: What reasoning, decision-making, planning, and information-processing activities are used in performing the job?	Level of decision making Coding/decoding	Making decisions Processing information
Work output: What physical activities are performed and what machines, tools, or devices are used?	Use of keyboard devices Assembling/disassembling	Controlling machines/process Performing skilled/technical activities
Relationships with other persons: What interactions with other people are involved in performing the job?	Instructing Contacts with public, customers	Engaging in general personal contacts Performing supervisory/coordination/related activities
Job context: In what physical or social environment is the job performed?	High temperature Interpersonal contact situations	Being in a stressful/unpleasant environment Engaging in personally demanding situations
Other job characteristics: What other activities, conditions, or characteristics are relevant to job performance?	Specified work pace Amount of job structure	Working nontypical vs. day schedule Working in businesslike situations

[a]Divisional PAQ job dimensions were formed by factor analyzing the items within each PAQ division separately. Overall job dimensions were formed by factor analyzing all items of the PAQ together. Only examples of divisional job dimensions are provided.

Source: Data compiled from E. J. McCormick, R. C. Mecham, and P. R. Jeanneret, *Position Analysis Questionnaire (PAQ) Technical Manual (System II)* (Logan, Utah: PAQ Services, Inc., 1977).

lyzed. In contrast to the PAQ, there is no single version of the task inventory. Developing a task inventory involves six major steps:[39]

1. *Determine the jobs to include in the inventory.* Most task inventories are developed for use in analyzing an occupation rather than a single job.

2. *Construct a list of tasks.* Using written materials, as well as interviews with job incumbents and supervisors, the job analyst produces an initial list of tasks performed. A group of individuals familiar with the occupation reviews the list of task statements. A pilot study using job incumbents may be conducted with this list to ensure that all relevant tasks are included and that the wording of the task statements is appropriate.

3. *Plan the survey and analyses.* The job analyst must decide what information about tasks is needed. The analyst may collect several different types of data, such as whether the task is performed on a specific job, the importance of the task to the job, the criticalness of the task, the relative time spent performing the task, the complexity of the task, and the difficulty of learning the task. A portion of a typical task inventory is shown in Figure 4.3. Usually the analyst runs a pilot study to ensure that the instructions are clear and that the format of the inventory is appropriate and easy to use. Once the inventory is ready, the job analyst plans how it will be administered, which job incumbents will be selected to complete the inventory, and what analyses will be conducted on the data that are collected.

4. *Administer the task inventory.* The job analyst administers the inventory by handing it out to select employees during work hours or mailing it to employees.

5. *Process the survey data.* As the inventories are returned, they are checked to make sure that they have been filled out properly. The data are then coded and analyzed to identify important tasks. Once important tasks have been identified, additional data on these tasks may be collected to determine the skills, knowledge, or abilities that are required to perform the tasks. Analyses may also be done to cluster similar jobs into job families.

6. *Report the data.* Once all analyses are complete, the job analyst must write reports that summarize the findings of the project and suggest how the task inventory data may best be used to improve HR practices in the organization.

Task inventories provide a wealth of information about the jobs within a specific occupational field. They are useful when the job analyst needs to collect data from many job incumbents who are spread over a large geographic region. Once designed, the inventories are relatively easy to complete and may be mailed to employees. When only a few employees are involved, however, task inventories are not cost-effective because they are expensive to develop. The information obtained from task inventories is very useful in the design of training programs.

Since no two task inventories are exactly the same, inventory data cannot be used to compare jobs in very different occupational fields. For the same reason, task inventories are not suited for organization-wide job evaluation purposes.

Ability Requirements Scales   Both the PAQ and task inventory methods focus on behavioral or work activities of jobs. The **ability requirements scales,** developed by E. A. Fleishman and his associates, measure abilities needed to perform jobs.[40] Job experts are asked to rate the extent to which fifty-two abilities are required to perform the job. These include abilities such as oral comprehension, number facility, night vision, dynamic flexibility, and selective attention. Job experts rate each

● **FIGURE 4.3**

Sample Task Inventory

Source: Harry L. Ammerman, *Performance Content for Job Training,* Vol. 3 (Columbus, Ohio: Center on Education and Training for Employment, [formerly CVE], The Ohio State University). Copyright 1977. Used with permission.

DATA PROCESSING TASK INVENTORY		*Page 14 of 26 pages*
Listed below are duties and the tasks that they include. Check all tasks that you perform. Add any tasks you do that are not listed, then rate the tasks you have checked.	CHECK IF DONE ✔	TIME SPENT 1. Very much below average 2. Below average 3. Slightly below average 4. About average 5. Slightly above average 6. Above average 7. Very much above average
H. Operating automatic data processing equipment		
1. Analyze job steps to determine data recovery points.		
2. Analyze machine operation through use of messages received from the equipment.		
3. Analyze machine operation through use of conditions displayed.		
4. Determine cause of machine stops and malfunctions.		
5. Interrogate memory locations on the console.		
6. Load programs and data cards.		
7. Locate tapes in storage media or tape library.		
8. Maintain card files (source object, etc.).		
9. Maintain current run tapes.		
10. Maintain levels of data processing supplies.		

ability using scales in which the ability is carefully defined and distinguished from other abilities. The rater uses a seven-point scale, in which each point on the scale is "anchored" with a behavioral example. For example, for rating the ability of static strength, the 1 level on the rating scale is anchored with the statement "Lift one package of bond paper," and the 7 level on the scale is anchored with the statement "Reach over and lift a seventy-pound box onto a table." Once important abilities have been identified, individual tasks on the job that require those abilities can be identified. The ability requirement scales are particularly appropriate for use in job classification and the development of personnel selection systems.

Personality-Related Job Analysis Procedures   There has been a resurgence of interest in personality characteristics as predictors of job performance using the "Big Five" personality dimensions.[41] As a result, attempts are being made to develop job analysis instruments to describe the personality requirements of jobs; that is, **personality-related job analysis procedures.** For example, Patrick Raymark and his colleagues have conducted research on the development of the **Personality-Related Position Requirements Form (PPRF).**[42] The PPRF is designed to identify aspects of jobs that are potentially related to individual differences in personality. The PPRF consists of 107 items divided into five major categories (surgency, agreeableness, conscientiousness, emotional stability, and intellectance). Factor analysis results indicated that these five categories could be divided further into twelve subfactors. The structure of the PPRF is shown in Table 4.5. Items within each of the twelve subfactors of the PPRF have a common format—that is, "Effective performance in this position requires the person to . . ."—with job experts indicating whether the personality characteristic represented by the item is "not required," "helpful," or "essential" to performance on the job.

Managerial Job Analysis Procedures   A number of job analysis procedures have been designed specifically for use with managerial and professional jobs. Two examples of these **managerial job analysis procedures** are described here.

Walter W. Tornow and Patrick R. Pinto developed the **Management Position Description Questionnaire (MPDQ),** a 208-item questionnaire that is used to describe managers' jobs.[43] Based on earlier work by J. K. Hemphill, the MPDQ is completed by incumbent managers, who use a six-point scale to rate each item.[44] Statistical analyses have shown that the 208 items can be grouped into thirteen major categories, such as internal business control, public and customer relations, staff service, supervision, and advanced financial responsibility.

The **Professional and Managerial Position Questionnaire (PMPQ)** consists of ninety-three items, divided into three major sections: job activities, personal requirements, and other information.[45] The first section, job activities, includes items on six major types of activities: (1) planning and scheduling activities, (2) processing information and ideas, (3) exercising judgment, (4) communicating, (5) interpersonal activities and relationships, and (6) technical activities. The second section of the PMPQ concerns the personal requirements needed for job performance. This section contains personal development items dealing with the educational, training, and experience requirements of the job. The section also includes personal characteristics items used to indicate whether traits such as adaptability are needed on the job. The final section of the PMPQ, other information, includes items on the number of personnel supervised by the employee, whether or

● **TABLE 4.5**

Structure of the Personality-Related Position Requirements Form (PPRF)

Category 1: Surgency	**Category 3: Conscientiousness**
1. General leadership	7. General trustworthiness
2. Interest in negotiations	8. Adherence to a work ethic
3. Achievement striving	9. Thoroughness and attentiveness to details
Category 2: Agreeableness	
4. Friendly disposition	**Category 4: Emotional stability**
5. Sensitivity to interest of others	10. Emotional stability
6. Cooperative or collaborative work tendency	**Category 5: Intellectance**
	11. Desire to generate ideas
	12. Tendency to think things through

Source: Adapted from Patrick Raymark, Mark Schmit, and Robert Guion, "Identifying Useful Personality Constructs for Employee Selection," *Personnel Psychology,* Vol. 50(3), 1997, pp. 723–736.

not the employee is a member of professional organizations or has a professional license or certification, and the salary of the employee.

PHASE 3: DATA COLLECTION AND ANALYSIS

The job analyst must deal with several issues related to collecting and analyzing job data. The job analyst may have made all the right decisions up to this point about the scope and method of the job analysis project. However, if the procedures used in collecting the job data and analyzing those data are incomplete or incorrect, the job analysis project will be a failure.

Collecting Job Data

The first important aspect of collecting job data is to get the organization ready. Second, the job analyst must be aware of the sources of bias that may influence the accuracy of the data collected. Finally, the job analyst must be sure that interviews, if used, are conducted in a skillful manner.

● **Getting the Organization Ready**   Before data collection can begin, the job analyst must make sure that members of the organization understand and are committed to the project. Top management should be involved closely in the development of the project. The job analyst must liase closely with the organization's internal HR unit and also with any supervisors whose employees may be involved in the data collection process. Perhaps most importantly, there must be a clearly stated rationale and set of goals for the project that is provided to all organizational members who participate in the project.

● **Sources of Bias**   The primary concern in collecting data about a job is that these data provide an accurate, up-to-date, and representative picture of work activities. One major source of bias that can occur during data collection results from the sampling procedures used to select data sources. As we noted earlier in this chapter in our discussion of the sources of job information, it is important to collect job data from the type of people who actually do the job, since factors such as the gender and experience of the job incumbent can influence how the job is described. Jobs also change over time. For example, the work activities of a farmer in midsummer are quite different from those in midwinter. Thus the job analysis should be sure to identify any changes in the job due to these time factors. Finally, jobs may change due to technology or other situational factors. The job of a person doing architectural drawings by hand is very different from that of a person doing the same drawing using the latest computer-assisted design software. The job of an insurance salesperson in Tampa, Florida, may change dramatically if a hurricane roars through the city. Thus the job data obtained must reflect these situation-determined changes so that they are recognized and incorporated into the overall picture of the job.

● **Job Analysis Interviews**   E. J. McCormick provides a useful set of guidelines for conducting job analysis interviews (see Figure 4.4). Although such guidelines are helpful, there are no simple methods for conducting good interviews. Interviewing is a skill that must be developed through practice.

● **FIGURE 4.4**

Guidelines for Job Analysis Interviewing

Preparing for the interview

Opening the interview

Steering the interview

Closing the interview

- Build the interviewee's interest in advance through well-prepared announcements; be sure that the interviewee is notified in advance about the exact time and place of the interview.

- Select a place for the interview that ensures privacy and comfort.

- Avoid or minimize obvious status symbols that would indicate that the interviewer is of higher status than the interviewee.

- Put the worker at ease. Learn his or her name in advance. Introduce yourself and talk about pleasant topics until the worker is at ease.

- Clearly describe the purpose of the interview, making sure that the worker understands what is to be accomplished and how the information he or she provides will benefit the organization and its workers.

- Encourage the worker to talk. Be courteous and show a sincere interest in what is being said.

- Help the worker talk about job duties in an orderly and logical sequence, according to the time sequence in which the duties occur or in order of their importance to the job.

- Keep the interview alive by probing for more information, using "expectant pauses," asking unobtrusive and neutral questions, or summarizing what the worker has recently said.

- Allow the worker sufficient time to think about and construct a response to a question. Ask only one question at a time and do not rush.

- Avoid questions that can be answered with only a yes or no.

- Avoid leading questions.

- Use simple, easily understood language.

- Do not be aloof or condescending. Show a personal interest in the worker.

- Try to establish a steady, comfortable pace for the interview. Do not let the worker stray from the subject.

- Try to get all the information you need about the job that the worker can provide.

- Indicate that the interview is nearing an end by the kinds of questions you ask and the inflection in your voice.

- Summarize the major information that the worker has provided. Ask the worker if your summary adequately represents what was discussed in the interview.

- Explain to the worker how valuable the information provided will be.

- End the interview on a friendly note.

Analyzing Job Data

Once quantitative job data are collected, numerous methods are available for analyzing them. What statistical analyses will be done should be decided before data are collected; otherwise, the job analyst may find that the data collected are not amenable to the analysis procedure(s) that he or she wants to use.

If job data are collected from several sources (e.g., several job incumbents), the job analyst should always check **inter-rater reliability;** that is, how well these sources agree on the characteristics of the job. A low level of agreement among data sources would indicate that either some sort of bias is present or major differences in the jobs of the data sources exist.

Reporting and Rechecking Job Data

Once all the analyses have been completed, the job analyst must prepare a report that typically includes the purpose and scope of the project, a summary of the specific methods used and why they were used, an explanation of the analyses conducted and what information they provided, and a strategy as to how the information gained from the project can be used in the future. The report should be written in a form that is easy for the average manager (with no technical expertise in job analysis methods) to understand. The very best job analysis project is worthless unless managers can understand what was done and what the results of the project were.

The final part of the job analysis process is to recheck the results of the project periodically. Since jobs are dynamic, the information collected about a job today may not accurately represent the job five years from now. Thus data must be updated periodically to incorporate job changes; otherwise, the organization may find itself selecting, training, or appraising the performance of employees for jobs that no longer exist.

PHASE 4: ASSESSING TRADITIONAL JOB ANALYSIS METHODS

There are several factors that have traditionally been used to assess job analysis methods. Some criteria that serve as the basis for assessments are presented in Table 4.6. Although these criteria can be helpful in comparing different methods, which method is best depends on the particular objectives of the organization, as well as on cost limitations and other factors governing the project. Legality is also a criterion that should be used to assess whether a job analysis method would be acceptable to the courts if it were used as evidence to support the personnel selection, training, performance appraisal, or pay practices of the organization. An organization must make clear why a job analysis is being conducted and must use a method of analysis relevant for that purpose. The results of a job analysis should be used only for the purpose for which it was originally intended. Job data should be collected from several sources. Human sources should be representative of workers associated with the job and should be well acquainted with the job about which they are to provide information. A job analysis should include a listing of all tasks performed on the job but should make clear which tasks are most important.

● **TABLE 4.6**

Ten Criteria for Assessing Job Analysis Methods

Number	Criterion	Definition
1	Purposes served	Can the data collected be used for a variety of purposes?
2	Versatility	Can a method be used to analyze many different jobs?
3	Standardization	Does a method provide data that can be easily compared to data collected by other methods?
4	User acceptability	Do users of the method accept it as a reasonable way to collect job data?
5	Training required	How much training is needed before individuals can use it to collect data in the organization?
6	Sample size	How large a sampling of information sources is needed before an adequate picture of the job can be obtained?
7	Off the shelf	Can the method be used directly off the shelf, or must considerable development work be done to tailor it for use in a particular organization?
8	Reliability	Does the method produce reliable data?
9	Time to complete	How long does it take to analyze a job using the method?
10	Cost	How much does the method cost to implement and use?

Source: From E. L. Levine, R. A. Ash, M. Hall, and F. Sistrunk, "Evaluation of Job Analysis Methods by Experienced Job Analysts," *Academy of Management Journal*, Vol. 26 (1983), pp. 339–348. Reprinted by permission.

When job analysis results are used to justify the use of specific ability, skill, or knowledge tests in selection, there should be a clear and readily justifiable link between specific tasks performed on the job and the skills, abilities, and knowledge tested for in selection.[46] Job analysis data should be checked regularly for reliability and validity, and the results of a job analysis should be reported in a written form that is clear and easily understood. By following these guidelines, the job analyst can greatly increase the likelihood that job analysis procedures will be acceptable from a legal perspective.

Of late there have been calls to concentrate more on the accuracy of the inferences made in the job analysis process than on the accuracy of the data collected. Looked at it another way, the job analysis process essentially involves making some inferences. The "job-descriptive inference" involves the extent to which a job description and lists of tasks and duties adequately represent the work activities that underlie job performance. The "job-specification inference" involves listing knowledge, skills, abilities, and other characteristics (KSAOs) that can be tied to specific behaviors identified in a job description.[47] For example, the job of a salesperson may involve making audiovisual presentations. An inference has to be made in this instance about the extent to which an effective presentation taps into the product knowledge, communication skills, and persuasive skills of a salesperson. An organization that fails to appreciate the fact that making good presentations involves more than merely possessing good communication skills may end up hiring wrong candidates or misdirecting its training effort. The point is that no matter how accurate the data collected, if inferences made are erroneous, then job analysis will not prove useful.

THE "NEW STRATEGIC VIEW" OF JOB ANALYSIS

Critics of traditional job analysis procedures argue that the job analysis methods developed in the past are inadequate for use in the firms of the twenty-first century. The primary reason for this inadequacy is the fact that jobs in organizations have become highly dynamic in response to a rapidly changing business environment. Such criticism is, perhaps, a bit too harsh if we examine the situation more closely. As indicated earlier in this chapter, research and practice in traditional job analysis have focused on developing better methods of measuring the content of jobs. In traditional research, the concept of "better" was typically operationalized as some set of psychometric criteria such as increased inter-rater agreement or more consistent factor structures in items across time and situations. These psychometric criteria remain essential elements of a good job analysis instrument. However, the critics of traditional approaches to job analysis have provided an additional criterion that must be added to our concept of developing "better" methods. That criterion is the extent to which a job analysis method can adequately measure changes in the nature of jobs and predict those changes into the future. In this section we will describe some of the current attempts to develop methods of job analysis that better meet the challenge of measuring what employees do in a rapidly changing organizational environment.

Future-Oriented, Strategic Job Analysis

Benjamin Schneider and Andrea Konz suggest the need for strategic job analysis.[48] The main objective of **future-oriented, strategic job analysis** is to identify the tasks, skills, abilities, and knowledge that will be needed to perform the job in the future. Schneider and Konz used a fairly standard job analysis methodology to look at the future requirements of a job. Their methodology is unique in one important way, however. First, they asked job experts to describe the job as it was currently being performed. Second, the experts were asked to predict changes in technology, population, social values, and other social and business factors that might impinge on the nature of work in their organization. Finally, they asked them to predict how these external changes would affect the nature of jobs performed within the firm. These data were then used to describe the tasks, skills, knowledge, and abilities needed for doing the job in the future.

In another study of 600 employees across a variety of diverse jobs, Richard Arvey and his colleagues used regression techniques to predict the future importance of job tasks and abilities from job data collected using a large inventory of current tasks and abilities.[49]

William George reported a case in which an organization was changing its strategic focus to an increased "customer-conscious" orientation.[50] To help employees understand the nature of this strategic shift, job descriptions were altered to focus more on "what we want to be doing in the future" rather than on what was actually being done in current jobs. In the work by Schneider and Konz and by Arvey and his colleagues, as well as the example reported by George, relatively traditional job analysis methods were used to describe a future job rather than a job as it was currently performed. In all of these examples, traditional job analysis methods were adapted to allow organizations to anticipate the nature of job changes. This would give organizations time to better prepare their current employees for the changes as well as allow the firms to redeploy employees to the new jobs when their old jobs disappeared rather than having to terminate their current work force and hire a new one.[51]

Job Analysis: A More Generic Approach to What We Measure

Another major criticism of traditional job analysis is that it focuses too much on the concrete duties and tasks that a job requires. Jobs in the twenty-first century are more likely to involve "flows" of knowledge, skills, and abilities that change due to technological, business, and other conditions.[52] As a result, Cardy and Dobbins suggested that job analysis should focus more on "generic personal characteristics or work behaviors that are important for competitive success."[53] They refer to this approach as **generic job analysis.** This focus on generic personal characteristics or work behaviors is directly related to the problem of the dynamic nature of twenty-first-century jobs. Proponents of the generic job analysis approach argue that the more dynamic jobs are, the more job analysis procedures must focus on broad and generic rather than narrow and specific measures of job content.

Although many traditional methods of job analysis focus on concrete tasks and duties, several of them include job descriptors that can be used to describe activities that are involved in a wide variety of jobs. For example, data from the Position Analysis Questionnaire (described earlier in this chapter) and the Occupational Analysis Inventory have been used to provide information about the extent to which generic human "attributes" are needed on a job. These attributes include such things as convergent and divergent thinking, intelligence, dealing with people, empathy, working alone, or dealing with concepts and information.[54] In a study of generic work behaviors in the retailing industry, Steven Hunt was able to identify nine generic behavior dimensions (e.g., thoroughness, unruliness, attendance, theft, drug misuse) that were applicable to a wide variety of retail jobs.[55] While the list of attributes or generic work behaviors may need to be broadened and an examination of the future job would be required, the basic methodologies employed above allow us, when we use them imaginatively, to create generic job descriptions like those championed by Cardy and Dobbins.

Another more generic approach to job analysis is **work process analysis.** Wayne Cascio describes a *work process* as "a collection of activities . . . that takes one or more kinds of input and creates an output that is of value to a customer. Customers may be internal or external. Individual tasks are important parts of the process, but the process itself cuts across organizational boundaries and traditional functions."[56] Rather than describing the job that is performed by an individual, work process analysis identifies the individual's current "task cluster"; that is, the group of tasks which that person performs for some (often relatively limited) amount of time.

Competency modeling is a process that has been increasingly popular and, as typically conducted, represents a broader, more generic approach to measuring job characteristics.[57] Timothy Athey and Michael Orth have defined competence as "a set of observable performance dimensions, including individual knowledge, skills, attitudes, and behaviors, as well as collective team, process, and organizational capabilities, that are linked to high performance, and provide the organization with sustainable competitive advantage."[58] Two aspects of this definition are important. First, competencies represent a broad range of characteristics. For example, Patricia McLagan identified a number of major kinds of competencies.[59] These include the following:

- **Task competencies:** Abilities needed to do the tasks and activities on a job, such as sweeping a floor
- **Results competencies:** Abilities needed to achieve some specific result on a job, such as achieving a 15 percent profit
- **Output competencies:** Abilities needed to produce some specified output, such as designing a product
- **Knowledge, skill, and attitude competencies:** Subject matter knowledge, process abilities, attitudes, values, orientations, or commitments needed to be effective
- **Superior performer differentiators:** Abilities rooted in a person's intelligence and personality that are possessed by superior performers but not by other employees
- **Attribute bundles:** A *collection* of knowledge, skills, attitudes, tasks, outputs, and results needed for effective performance, such as a "problem-solving attribute bundle" made up of some knowledge, such as technical know-how and problem-solving techniques; some skills, such as analytical skills and lateral thinking; and some attitudes, values, orientations, and/or commitments, such as achievement orientation and integrity

Second, competencies are those characteristics that differentiate effective from ineffective performers or are in some way critical to particular competitive strategies in which an organization may engage.

As there are many different kinds of competencies, there are also many different methods by which the competency requirements of jobs are determined. In general, however, these competency-modeling methods are very much like those used in more traditional job analysis procedures but are focused on a broader range of job competency requirements and typically have an orientation toward future changes in the nature of the job. Among these competency analysis procedures are the following:[60]

1. Work analysis: The job analyst focuses on high performers, watching them work and recording their results and what they do to achieve them.
2. A critical incident interview: The job analyst looks at critical incidents, then identifies the competencies associated with each incident.
3. Sets of critical incident interviews: The job analyst looks at critical incidents from average and superior performers, lists their competencies, and knocks out any that are possessed by both kinds of performers.
4. Creation of assumptions about the future: The job analyst leads managers and job experts in completing a future environment analysis to identify competencies that will be needed to deal with the new environment.
5. Work planning processes: Job experts identify the work processes that will be needed as a result of changes in strategy or the environment and identify competencies needed by new work processes.

A significant amount of competency research has focused on identifying **managerial competencies** relevant to specific managerial jobs or to the more generic occupation of "manager."[61] A summary of some of the managerial competencies identified is presented in Table 4.7. In addition to research studies on managerial competencies in general, many firms are using competency-modeling procedures to identify the critical competencies for managers in their firm. Often these compe-

● TABLE 4.7

Summary of Research on Core Managerial Skills and Competencies

Study	Managerial Skills and Competencies
Carter et al. (1995)	Dealing with ambiguity and uncertainty
	Cross-cultural skills
	Leadership skills
	Teamwork skills
	Understanding the perceptions and behaviors of others
	Communication skills
Wallace and Hunt (1996)	Strategic and organization-wide management processes associated with change, vision, and environmental awareness
	Problem solving and decision making focusing on judgment, flexibility, and evaluation of decisions
	Administrative and operations management dealing with operational scheduling, inventory administration, purchasing, cost accounting, and productivity monitoring
	Leadership and team building, which involves providing individualized consideration to subordinates, building team morale, and developing aspects of leadership
	Persuasion and influence processes such as forging alliances and understanding the political implications of decisions
Cox and Cooper (1989) and McCall, Lombardo, and Morrison (1988)	Strategic thinking
	Analytical/problem solving
	Decision making
	Action orientation (getting things done)
	Interpersonal and team skills
	Leadership
	Learning from failure (personal reflection)
	Personal attributes relating to maturity, temperament, and personal awareness
Business/Higher Education Round Table in Australia (1992)	Communication skills
	Capacity to learn new skills and procedures
	Capacity for cooperation and teamwork
	Capacity to make decisions and solve problems
	Ability to apply knowledge to the work force
	Capacity to work with minimum supervision
	Theoretical knowledge in a professional field
Karpin Committee, 1995	"Soft" or people skills
	Leadership skills
	Strategic skills, international orientation
	Entrepreneurship
	Broadening beyond technical specializations
	Relationship-building skills across organizations
	Utilization of diverse human resources

Sources: Business/Higher Education Round Table, commissioned Report #2, *Educating for Excellence*. Melbourne, Victoria, Australia; C. Carter, J. Nicholson, and M. Barlow, "The Australian Manager of the Twenty-First Century." Report prepared by the Boston Consulting Group for the Industry Task Force on Leadership and Management Skills, *Enterprising Nation: Renewing Australia's Managers to Meet the Challenges of the Asia-Pacific Century* (Research Report, Vol. 2), pp. 1223–1288; C. J. Cox and C. L. Cooper, "The Making of the British CEO: Childhood, Work Experience, Personality, and Management Style," *The Academy of Management Executive*, Vol. 3, 1989, pp. 241–245; M. W. McCall Jr., M. M. Lombardo, and A. M. Morrison, *The Lessons of Experience* (Lexington, Mass.: Lexington Books, 1988); J. Wallace and J. Hunt, "An Analysis of Managerial Competencies Across Hierarchical Levels and Industry Sectors: A Contemporary Australian Perspective," *Journal of the Australian and New Zealand Academy of Management*, Vol. 2 (1), 1996, pp. 36–47; Karpin Committee, "Enterprising Nation: Reviewing Australia's Managers to Meet the Challenges of the Asia-Pacific Century" (April 1995, Report of the Industry Task Force on Leadership and Management Skills). Canberra Australian Government Publishing Service.

● FIGURE 4.5

Multilevel Corporate Competency Model

Source: Adapted from Elmer Burack, Wayne Hockwarter and Nicholas Mathys, "The New Management Development Paradigm," *Human Resource Planning,* Vol. 80(1), 1997, pp. 14–21.

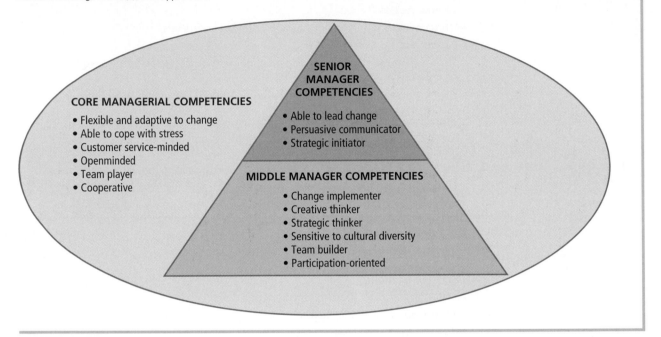

tency models are hierarchical in nature, identifying a set of core competencies that all managers must possess as well as competencies applicable to different managerial levels within the firm. An example of such a model is presented in Figure 4.5.

THE TRADITIONAL AND NEW STRATEGIC VIEWS OF JOB ANALYSIS: WORKING TOGETHER

The area of competency modeling is a good example of how critical aspects of both the traditional and "new strategic view" of job analysis fit well together. As noted, competency modeling focuses on more generic characteristics required by jobs and typically takes a dynamic, future-oriented view of these characteristics. However, within this new approach, researchers have acknowledged that much work needs to be done to ensure that competency-modeling methods also meet the psychometric qualities relating to reliability and accuracy of more traditional methods. Better, easier-to-use, and more reliable methods are needed to assess job competencies and other strategic or generic aspects of jobs.[62] The "new view" of job analysis that is really needed is one that combines the emphasis of the "strategic view" of job analysis with the methodological rigor that has long characterized more traditional methods.

JOB ANALYSIS: ADDING VALUE TO THE ORGANIZATION

Regardless of which approach is taken to job analysis, any job analysis effort must, in the end, add value to the organization. The extent to which job analysis programs add value can be measured in many ways. The essence of any measure of value added by an HR activity is an assessment of the relative costs versus benefits of the activity. The criteria described in Table 4.6 provide insight into the likely value-adding ability of any job analysis project, at least in terms of the costs of any project. Job analysis methods that can serve several purposes, can be used to analyze many different jobs, and are standardized such that comparisons across jobs are made easy, have more value-adding potential than job analysis systems of a more restricted nature. User acceptability relates directly to the reaction of stakeholders in the job analysis program. If users (and those whose jobs are analyzed) react negatively to the process, then the value added to the firm is reduced. Job analysis methods that are off the shelf or require relatively small sample sizes will reduce the dollar cost of job analysis programs considerably. Job analysis methods that require little training of those who use them reduce the direct costs to the organization of any training programs needed. Job analysis methods that can be completed quickly (e.g., paper-and-pencil checklist methods versus extensive interviews) also will have greater potential for adding value due to their lower cost in time and effort. The reliability of the data collected by job analysis methods also affects its value-adding potential, since data that are unreliable have little chance of providing useful information to the organization. The cost of job analysis materials also will determine value added. Job analysis methods that have questionable legality may cost the firm many tens of thousands of dollars if the company is taken to court.

While the preceding criteria can help HR managers determine the likely costs of any job analysis project, the dollar or nondollar benefits of such programs are more difficult to assess. The ultimate value of any job analysis program lies in its ability to help employees perform their strategic roles in the organization more efficiently and effectively. Thus it is critical for an organization to have a clear understanding of how job analysis data are expected to help increase employee productivity. Job analysis data could be used in training programs to "multiskill" employees so that they can perform more varied work roles. The benefits of the job analysis data are then determined by the level to which employees better understand and perform varied tasks. If job analysis data are collected to help reduce conflict in the firm resulting from "territorial overlap," then the benefits of the job analysis data must be assessed on the basis of conflict being reduced and employees having a clearer understanding of what their roles are in relation to others. Job analysis data collected to help employees increase the speed and quality of their performance must be assessed using measures of performance speed and quality, which can then be translated into actual dollar savings. The possible list of criteria for use in determining the benefits of job analysis data is almost infinite. It is obvious from earlier discussion, however, that one of the value-adding criteria that must be included in such a list is the extent to which any job analysis procedure helps an organization anticipate and then adapt quickly to the dynamic evironment that characterizes business life in the twenty-first century.

Summary of Key Points

The nature of jobs is changing. The stable, relatively finite groups of tasks that have made up employees' jobs have become far less stable and considerably less finite. Jobs are broader and subject to frequent alteration. Since jobs are changing, the traditional approaches to job analysis may need to change as well. Greater emphasis must be placed on identifying how jobs are likely to change in the future. In situations of change, job analysis methods may have to focus more on identifying the generic personal characteristics of employees that allow them to function well in a dynamic environment. However, traditional methods of job analysis can serve as the basis for these future-oriented, strategic job analysis procedures.

Given this increasingly complex work environment, conducting a good job analysis is far more complex and difficult than it might seem. It requires that the job analyst make many important decisions. The analyst, in conjunction with management, must decide on the purpose and desired uses of the job analysis data. Job analysis may be used for human resource planning and recruitment. It also may be used to develop sound employee selection and placement procedures. Job analysis serves as the basis for developing training and performance appraisal programs and can be used to set wage rates across different jobs.

Once the organization decides how it intends to use the job analysis data, the job analyst must determine what jobs will be analyzed, what type of information is needed, and the sources of that information. Information about behavioral descriptors, ability requirements, and other job characteristics, such as the motivational nature of the job, can be collected. The job analyst also may want information concerning the machines, tools, and equipment that are used on the job and the working conditions in which the job takes place. The analyst can choose among a variety of human and nonhuman sources to provide these data.

Based on these decisions, the job analyst chooses from a myriad of job analysis procedures, ranging from simple narrative descriptions to highly complex micromotion or structured procedures. The functional job analysis method provides data that are useful in identifying worker traits needed to perform the job, as well as information useful in developing standards for employee perfor-

mance. The task inventory is excellent for collecting data from large numbers of job incumbents and is particularly helpful in developing personnel selection tests and training programs. The Position Analysis Questionnaire is an excellent method for comparing a wide variety of very different jobs.

Once job data are collected, they must be analyzed for reliability and accuracy and then summarized and used within the organization. The job analyst must recheck these data periodically and assess their overall value—their costs and benefits—to the organization, as well as their versatility.

Job analysis methods should be designed so that they can be performed reliably and in a standardized way throughout the organization. Methods should be assessed in terms of the time needed to teach individuals how to do the analysis, the time needed to complete the analysis, and the costs of collecting data. Any method used by an organization also should conform to standards set down in recent legal decisions that have specified what the courts consider a "good" job analysis procedure. It is also important to have clear measures of the expected benefits of job analysis programs, as well as the dollar costs of conducting them, so that the level of value adding achieved through job analysis projects can be assessed.

The Manager's Vocabulary

ability requirements scales
area work activities
attribute bundles
behavioral contracting
cognitive abilities
competency modeling
critical incidents technique (CIT)
Department of Labor (DOL) method
Dictionary of Occupational Titles (DOT)
duty
engineering approaches
foundation work activities
functional job analysis (FJA)
future-oriented, strategic job analysis
generic job analysis
intermediate work activities
inter-rater reliability
job

job analysis
job classification
job description
job extinction
job specification
knowledge, skill, and attitude competencies
Management Position Description Questionnaire (MPDQ)
managerial competencies
managerial job analysis procedures
micromotion studies
narrative job descriptions
Occupational Information Network (O*NET)
output competencies
personality-related job analysis procedures
Personality-Related Position Requirements Form (PPRF)
physical abilities
position
Position Analysis Questionnaire (PAQ)
Professional and Managerial Position Questionnaire (PMPQ)
psychomotor abilities
qualitative data
quantitative data
realistic job preview
results competencies
situational abilities
structured job analysis procedures
subject matter experts (SMEs)
superior performer differentiators
task
task competencies
task inventory
time and motion study
work process analysis

Questions for Discussion

1. Are jobs becoming "extinct"? If yes, why? If no, why not?

2. What is job analysis, and why is it important to an organization?

3. What is the difference between a job description and a job specification?

4. Suppose that your company wants to develop a method for selecting job applicants with the highest potential for doing well on the job. What type of job analysis data (duty and task information, ability requirements, or other job characteristics) would be most useful in setting up this selection system?

5. How do the advantages of quantitative job data compare with those of qualitative job data?

6. What general guidelines should the HR specialist use when deciding how many and what sources of job information to use in a job analysis project?

7. Compare and contrast the Position Analysis Questionnaire and task inventory methods of job analysis. What are the relative advantages and disadvantages of each?

8. Table 4.6 lists ten criteria for assessing job analysis methods. Suppose you are the HR manager of a small company employing 150 people. Which of the ten criteria would you find most important in assessing a job analysis project? Suppose your company had 5,000 employees rather than 150. Would the list of most important criteria change for you? Why or why not?

9. According to the new strategic view of job analysis, job analysis procedures need to be more future-oriented and strategic. Job analysis procedures also need to be more generic in nature. What is meant by future-oriented, strategic job analysis? What kinds of information would be collected in a generic job analysis procedure?

10. What is a "competency"? What is competency modeling and how does it exemplify the new strategic view of job analysis?

● Exercise 4.1
Conducting a Job Analysis

This exercise will give you some hands-on experience in conducting a job analysis. You will interview a job incumbent and then use the information you collect in that interview to describe the job performed by the incumbent. It is important that the job incumbent has held the position long enough to really know what it involves. In conducting the job interview, you should first review the job analysis form and instructions provided here. In your interview, you must collect enough information about the job to complete this form. Before starting the interview, spend some time planning how you will proceed and writing down some of the questions you will ask.

Option: Redo the job analysis you have conducted on the current job, this time describing the job as it will be ten years in the future. How will the job change? What new skills and abilities will be needed? What tasks and duties will no longer be performed or will be performed in a very different manner?

Instructions for Filling Out the Job Analysis Form

1. *Job identification*
   Organization: name of organization
   Incumbent: name of job incumbent interviewed
   Analyst: name of person analyzing job
   Date: date of interview
2. *Job summary*   Provide an overview (one to three sentences) of the job being analyzed. Do not write this job summary until you have completed the remaining parts of this job analysis form.
3. *Duties performed*   Identify the major duties that are performed on the job. Arrange these duties in either chronological order (i.e., in the time sequence in which the tasks are usually performed) or the order of importance to the job. Indicate the percentage of time spent on each duty during a typical workday. You will probably need more space than allowed on this sample form.
4. *Supervision given*   How many subordinates does the job incumbent supervise? What are the titles of those subordinates?
5. *Supervision received*   What is the job title of the job incumbent's supervisor? How closely is the incumbent supervised?
6. *Relationship to other jobs*   Promoted from: What position would the incumbent usually hold prior to this job? Promoted to: What is the most likely position to which the incumbent would be promoted?
7. *Machines, tools, and equipment used*   List these devices, and define any that are not commonly known.
8. *Working conditions*   Indicate the physical environment of the job (e.g., indoors or outdoors, physically hazardous surroundings).
9. *Job specifications*
   Physical requirements: List any special physical skills or abilities needed to perform the job (e.g., being able to lift fifty pounds).
   Educational requirements: Indicate the minimum level of education necessary *to perform the job*. Do not list what the organization specifies as the necessary educational level because organizations often require a higher level of education than is actually needed to perform the job. Also list any certificates or licenses required.
   Special skills: List any special skills needed (e.g., the artistic skills of a musician).
   Experience required: What previous experience is necessary to perform the job? Do not include "experience" that is easily acquired on the job.
   Training required after hire: Indicate any specific job training that is necessary after the employee enters the job.
10. *Unusual terms*   Define any terms used in the preceding analysis that would not be commonly understood.

Job Analysis Form

1. *Job identification*

   Organization _____

   Job title _____

   Incumbent _____

   Analyst _____

   Date _____

2. *Job summary*

   _____

   _____

3. *Duties performed*

   _____

   _____

4. *Supervision given*

   _____

   _____

5. *Supervision received*

   _____

   _____

6. *Relationship to other jobs*

   Promoted from _____

   Promoted to _____

7. *Machines, tools, and equipment used*

   _____

   _____

8. *Working conditions*

   _____

   _____

9. *Job specifications*

   Physical requirements:_____

   _____

   Educational requirements:_____

   _____

   Special skills: _____

   _____

   Experience required: _____

   _____

   Training required after hire: _____

   _____

10. *Unusual terms*

   _____

   _____

● Exercise 4.2
Planning a Job Analysis Project

For each of the following jobs and organizational situations, indicate the type of job analysis method(s) that would be most appropriate, identify from whom information about the job should be collected and what kind of data would be best to collect, and discuss any particular problems that might confront the job analyst. Be sure to indicate how your choices will help to ensure that your job analysis efforts are seen as reliable and valid by members of the organization. You may have to make assumptions about the firm. Feel free to do so, but indicate what your assumptions are.

Scenario A Pangigantic is a large firm that manufactures electronics components. Most of the work is done by assemblers at an assembly line. The jobs tend to be fairly simple and repetitive in nature. The firm has begun an effort to increase productivity by improving the design of the machinery used in manufacture as well as selecting better, more skilled people to work on the line.

Scenario B Archi-Builders, Inc., is a small firm providing architectural and interior design services to customers in a fairly limited geographic area. Projects are typically done using a "team-based" approach involving architects, engineers, interior designers, and building construction specialists. The CEO of the firm has asked you to help analyze the "job" of these project teams with the hope that work design and scheduling as well as employee selection and training can be improved.

Scenario C Bore All, Pty., Ltd., is a medium-sized Australian firm that specializes in the drilling of water wells (known as "bores" in Australia). Profits from the firm have been decreasing over the past four years, and the board of directors has approached you to help them design the job of and help hire the new CEO of Bore All. The chair of the board of directors indicates that in the past the CEO of Bore All has been "one of those engineer-types, great at drilling wells, but not much of an entrepreneur." It is obvious that the job of the new CEO will be very different from the typical CEO job in the past.

● Exercise 4.3
*An Internet Encounter with O*NET*

The U.S. Department of Labor has developed the Occupational Information Network database, called O*NET, which is an advanced technology database system that will replace the *Dictionary of Occupational Titles*. Although O*NET is still a system "in progress," it already includes a significant amount of sophisticated occupational and career information. The Web site for O*NET is http://www.doleta.gov/programs/onet/.

Use the Internet to visit the O*NET site. What sort of information is available from O*NET? Look particularly at the detailed information listed within the major categories of information provided. Does O*NET allow you to link with other databases containing occupational information? How might organizations and individuals make use of this information?

Notes and References

1. E. J. McCormick, *Job Analysis: Methods and Applications* (New York: AMACOM, 1979), p. 20.

2. William Bridges, *Job Shift: How to Prosper in a Workplace Without Jobs* (St. Leonards, Australia: Allen & Unwin, 1995), p. 1.

3. H. L. Ammerman, *Performance Content for Job Training,* Vol. 2 (Columbus, Ohio: Center for Vocational Education, Ohio State University, 1977), p. 21.

4. McCormick, *Job Analysis,* p. 19.

5. Greg Stewart and Kenneth Carson, "Moving Beyond the Mechanistic Model: An Alternative Approach for Contemporary Organizations," *Human Resource Management Review*, Vol. 7 (2), 1997, pp. 157–184.

6. Ibid., p. 164.

7. Bob Cardy and Greg Dobbins, "Job Analysis in a Dynamic Environment," *Human Resources Division News*, Vol. 16 (1), 1992, p. 4.

8. Cited in Allan Church, "From Both Sides Now: The Changing of the Job," *The Industrial Organizational Psychologist*, Vol. 33 (3), 1996, pp. 52–62.

9. Jodi Nelson, "The Boundaryless Organization: Implications for Job Analysis, Recruitment, and Selection," *Human Resource Planning*, Vol. 20 (4), 1997, pp. 39–49.

10. McCormick, *Job Analysis,* p. 19.

11. Equal Employment Opportunity Commission, *A Technical Assistance Manual on the Employment Provisions (Title I) of the Americans with Disabilities Act)* (Washington, D.C.: EEOC, 1992); and Krystin Mitchell, George Alliger, and Richard Morfopoulos, "Toward an ADA-Appropriate Job Analysis," *Human Resource Management Review*, Vol. 7 (1), 1997, pp. 5–26.

12. J. P. Wanous, *Organizational Entry* (Reading, Mass.: Addison-Wesley, 1980).

13. Roger Ballentine, J. W. Cunningham, and William E. Wimpee, "Air Force Enlisted Job Clusters: An Exploration in Numerical Classification," *Military Psychology*, Vol. 4 (2), 1992, pp. 87–102.

14. William Wooten, "Using Knowledge, Skill and Ability (KSA) Data to Identify Career Pathing Opportunities: An Application of Job Analysis to Internal Manpower Planning," *Public Personnel Administrator*, Vol. 22 (4), 1993, pp. 551–563.

15. Steve Urbanek, "Job Analysis: A Local Government's Experience," *Public Personnel Management*, Vol. 26 (3), 1997, pp. 423–429.

16. Equal Pay Act of 1963 (Public Law 88–38) (EPA).

17. W. Ouchi, *Theory Z: How American Business Can Meet the Japanese Challenge* (Reading, Mass.: Addison-Wesley, 1981).

18. Jen A. Algera and Martin A. Greuter, "Job Analysis for Personnel Selection," in *Advances in Selection and Assessment,* ed. Mike Smith and Ivan Robertson (New York: Wiley, 1989), pp. 7–30.

19. William P. Anthony, Pamela L. Perrewe, and K. Michelle Kacmar, *Strategic Human Resource Management* (New York: Harcourt Brace Jovanovich, 1993), pp. 210–211.

20. Ammerman, *Performance Content for Job Training*, pp. 15–16.

21. J. W. Cunningham, D. W. Drewes, and T. E. Powell, "Framework for a Revised Standard Occupational Classification (SOC)," in *Seminar on Research Findings,* ed. Standard Occupational Classification Revision Policy Committee (No. 1995-398-319-40067) (Washington, D.C.: U.S. Government Printing Office, 1995), pp. 57–165.

22. E. A. Fleishman and M. K. Quaintance, *Taxonomies of Human Performance: The Description of Human Tasks* (Orlando, Fla.: Academic Press, 1984), pp. 162–167; E. A. Fleishman and M. D. Mumford, "Individual Attributes and Training Performance: Applications of Ability Taxonomies in Instructional Systems Designs," in *Training and Development: New Frontiers in Industrial and Organizational Psychology,* ed. I. Goldstein (San Francisco: Jossey-Bass, 1990); and L. D. Marquardt and E. J. McCormick, *Attribute Ratings and Profiles of the Job Elements of the Position Analysis Questionnaire (PAQ)* (West Lafayette, Ind.: Department of Psychological Sciences, Purdue University, 1972).

23. Timothy Athey and Michael Orth, "Emerging Competency Methods for the Future," *Human Resource Management*, Vol. 38 (3), 1999, pp. 215–226; Jon Briscoe and Douglas Hall, "Grooming and Picking Leaders Using Competency Frameworks: Do They Work?" *Organizational Dynamics*, Vol. 28 (2), 1999, pp. 37–51; and Elmer Burack, Wayne Hochwarter, and Nicholas Mathys, "The New Management Development Paradigm," *Human Resource Planning*, Vol. 20 (1), 1997, pp. 14–21.

24. Frederick Morgeson and Michael Campion, "Social and Cognitive Sources of Potential Inaccuracy in Job Analysis," *Journal of Applied Psychology*, Vol. 82 (5), 1997, pp. 627–655.

25. J. Hogan and A. M. Quigley, "Physical Standards for Employment and the Courts," *American Psychologist*, Vol. 41 (11), 1986, pp. 1193–1217; and Douglas Pine, "Assessing the Validity of Job Ratings: An Empirical Study of False Reporting in Task Inventories," *Public Personnel Management*, Vol. 24 (4), 1995, pp. 451–460.

26. J. Kevin Ford, Eleanor M. Smith, Douglas J. Sego, and Miguel A. Quinones, "Impact of Task Experience and Individual Factors on Training-Emphasis Ratings," *Journal of Applied Psychology*, Vol. 78 (4), 1993, pp. 583–590; Michael Lindell, Catherine Clause, Christina Brandt, and Ronald Landis, "Relationship Between Organizational Context and Job Analysis Task Ratings," *Journal of Applied Psychology*, Vol. 83 (5), 1998, pp. 769–796; Wendy Richman and Miguel Quinones, "Task Frequency Rating Accuracy: The Effect of Task Engagement and Experience," *Journal of Applied Psychology*, Vol. 81 (5), 1997, pp. 512–524; and Juan Sanchez, Alina Zamora, and Chockalingam Viswesvaran, "Moderators of Agreement Between Incumbent and Non-Incumbent Ratings of Job Characteristics," *Journal of Occupational and Organizational Psychology*, Vol. 70, September 1997, pp. 209–218.

27. Frank J. Landy and Joseph Vasey. "Job Analysis: The Composition of SME Samples," *Personnel Psychology*, Vol. 44 (1), 1991, pp. 27–50.

28. Anda Papadopoulou, Elizabeth Ineson, and Derek Wilkie, "Convergence Between Sources of Service Job Analysis Data," *International Journal of Contemporary Hospitality Management*, Vol. 7 (2/3), 1995, pp. 42–47; and Wendy Richman and Miguel Quinones, "Task Frequency Rating Accuracy: The Effect of Task

Engagement and Experience," *Journal of Applied Psychology,* Vol. 81(5), 1997, pp. 512–524.

29. McCormick, *Job Analysis*, pp. 76–77.

30. J. C. Flanagan, "The Critical Incidents Technique," *Psychological Bulletin*, Vol. 51, 1954, pp. 327–358.

31. S. Zedeck, S. J. Jackson, and A. Adelman, *Selection Procedures Reference Manual* (Berkeley: University of California Press, 1980).

32. U.S. Department of Labor, Employment and Training Administration, *The Revised Handbook for Analyzing Jobs* (Washington, D.C.: U.S. Government Printing Office, 1991); and U.S. Department of Labor, *Dictionary of Occupational Titles,* 4th ed., revised (Washington, D.C.: U.S. Government Printing Office, 1991).

33. Robert Guion, *Assessment, Measurement, and Prediction for Personnel Decisions* (Mahwah, N.J.: Erlbaum, 1998).

34. Ibid., p. 92.

35. S. Fine and M. Getkate, *Benchmark Tasks for Job Analysis: A Guide for Functional Job Analysis* (Mahwah, N.J.: Erlbaum, 1995).

36. E. J. McCormick, P. R. Jeanneret, and R. C. Mecham, "A Study of Job Characteristics and Job Dimensions as Based on the Position Analysis Questionnaire (PAQ)," *Journal of Applied Psychology,* Vol. 56, 1972, pp. 347–368.

37. Marquardt and McCormick, *Attribute Ratings.*

38. McCormick, *Job Analysis,* pp. 117, 119.

39. Ammerman, *Performance Content for Job Training.*

40. E. A. Fleishman, *Manual for the Ability Requirements Scale (MARS, revised)* (Palo Alto, Calif.: Consulting Psychologists Press, 1991); and E. A. Fleishman and M. E. Reilly, *Human Abilities: Their Definition, Measurement, and Job Task Requirements* (Palo Alto, Calif.: Consulting Psychologists Press, 1991).

41. Murray Barrick and Michael Mount, "The Big Five Personality Dimensions and Job Performance: A Meta-Analysis," *Personnel Psychologist*, Vol. 44 (1), 1991, pp. 1–26; and Michael Mount and Murray Barrick, "The Big Five Personality Dimensions: Implications for Research and Practice in Human Resource Management," *Research in Personnel and Human Resource Management*, Vol. 13, 1995, pp. 153–200.

42. Patrick Raymark, Mark Schmit, and Robert Guion, "Identifying Potentially Useful Personality Constructs for Employee Selection," *Personnel Psychology*, Vol. 50 (3), 1997, pp. 723–736.

43. W. W. Tornow and P. R. Pinto, "The Development of a Managerial Job Taxonomy: A System for Describing, Classifying, and Evaluating Executive Positions," *Journal of Applied Psychology,* Vol. 61, 1976, pp. 410–418.

44. J. K. Hemphill, *Dimensions of Executive Positions* (Columbus, Ohio: Bureau of Business Research, Ohio State University, 1960).

45. J. L. Mitchell and E. J. McCormick, *Development of the PMPQ: A Structured Job Analysis Questionnaire for the Study of Professional and Managerial Positions* (West Lafayette, Ind.: Research Foundation, Purdue University, 1979).

46. Juan Sanchez and Scott Fraser, "An Empirical Approach to Identify Job Duty—KSA Linkages in Managerial Jobs: A Case Example," *Journal of Business and Psychology*, Vol. 8 (3), 1994, pp. 309–325; and Andrew Vinchur, Eric Prien, and Jeffrey

Schippmann, "An Alternative Procedure for Analyzing Job Analysis Results for Content-Oriented Test Development," *Journal of Business and Psychology*, Vol. 8 (2), 1993, pp. 215–226.

47. Fredrick P. Morgeson and Michael A. Campion, "Accuracy in Job Analysis: Toward an Inference-based Model", *Journal of Organizational Behavior,* Vol. 21, 2000, pp. 819–827.

48. Benjamin Schneider and Andrea M. Konz, "Strategic Job Analysis," *Human Resource Management*, Vol. 28 (1), 1989, pp. 51–63.

49. R. Arvey, E. Salas, and K. Gialluca, "Using Task Inventories to Forecast Skills and Abilities," *Human Performance*, Vol. 5, 1992, pp. 171–190.

50. William George, "Internal Marketing and Organizational Behavior: A Partnership in Developing Customer-Conscious Employees at Every Level," *Journal of Business Research*, Vol. 20, 1990, pp. 63–70.

51. Bridges, *Job Shift.*

52. From statements made by Donald Davis in Church, "From Both Sides Now."

53. Cardy and Dobbins, "Job Analysis in a Dynamic Environment," p. 5.

54. J. W. Cunningham, R. R. Boese, R. W. Neeb, and J. J. Pass, "Systematically Derived Work Dimensions: Factor Analyses of the Occupational Analysis Inventory," *Journal of Applied Psychology*, Vol. 68 (2), 1983, pp. 232–252; J. W. Cunningham, Thomas Powell, William Wimpee, Mark Wilson, and Roger Ballentine, "Ability-Requirement Factors for General Job Elements," *Military Psychologist*, Vol. 8 (3), 1996, pp. 219–234; and McCormick, Jeanneret, and Mecham, "A Study of Job Characteristics and Job Dimensions as Based on the Position Analysis Questionnaire (PAQ).

55. Steven Hunt, "Generic Work Behavior: An Investigation into the Dimensions of Entry-Level, Hourly Job Performance," *Personnel Psychology*, Vol. 49 (1), 1996, pp. 51–83.

56. Wayne Cascio, "Whither Industrial and Organizational Psychology in a Changing World of Work?" *American Psychologist*, Vol. 50 (1), 1995, pp. 928–939.

57. Michael Harris, "Practice Network: Comptency Modelling: Viagraized Job Analysis or Impotent Imposter," *The Industrial-Organizational Psychologist*, Vol. 36 (2), 1998, pp. 37–41; and Jorgen Sandberg, "Understanding Human Competence at Work: An Interpretative Approach," *Academy of Management Journal*, Vol. 43 (1), 2000, pp. 9–25.

58. Athey and Orth, "Emerging Competency Methods for the Future," p. 216.

59. Patricia McLagan, "Competencies: The Next Generation," *Training & Development*, Vol. 51 (5), 1997, pp. 40–47.

60. Ibid.

61. Briscoe and Hall, "Grooming and Picking Leaders Using Competency Frameworks"; Burack, Hochwarter, and Mathys, "The New Management Development Paradigm"; and Richard Mirabile, "Everything You Wanted to Know About Competency Modelling," *Training & Development*, Vol. 51 (8), 1997, pp. 73–77.

62. Athey and Orth, "Emerging Competency Methods for the Future."

Acquiring Human Resources

Equal Employment Opportunity: The Legal Environment

HR Challenge

What does it take to be the poster company for race bias? How about the largest ever settlement in an equal employment opportunity (EEO) suit, $192.5 million.[1] This is the distinction achieved by Coca-Cola in a settlement called "the largest, and most-sweeping race discrimination class action in United States history."[2]

Yes, Coca-Cola, the same company that has carefully cultivated minority Americans as consumers of its product by public pronouncements, strategic alliances, and specific marketing strategies. The suit with four named employees along with a class of about 2,000 minority employees, accused Coca-Cola of failing to place the same importance on its minority employees as it did on attracting minority consumers.[3] The question became "can the real thing do the right thing?"[4]

Minority employees allege disparities between white and minority employees at Coca-Cola in terms of pay, promotions, performance *evaluations, and dismissals. Citing statistics it says document a big salary gap based on race, the suit, for example, alleges the median salary for black employees at Coca-Cola corporate headquarters in 1998 was about $36,000, compared with $65,000 for whites working there.[5]*

As part of the suit, it was discovered that an internal report presented to Coca-Cola chairman M. Douglas Ivester in 1995 recommended a number of initiatives to enhance diversity, including addressing the fact that there were few minorities in certain areas and levels of the company. The report was prepared by Carl Ware, the highest-ranking black executive at Coca-Cola, and was significant because it indicated that Mr. Ivester, who was Coca-Cola's chairman at the time, was told of the need for greater diversity.[6] The recommendations included the need to:

- *Establish a mentoring program for minority employees.*
- *Develop and communicate a statement of philosophy as a commitment to diversity.*
- *Establish specific diversity goals.*
- *Institute executive accountability for improved diversity results.*

Of course, Mr. Ware's diversity suggestions are good advice to any company, especially a company cultivating minorities as customers. To Coca-Cola's credit, in agreeing to settle the case they belatedly, and at a considerable price, accepted Mr. Ware's sound recommendations.

In addition to paying damages to the plaintiffs in the case, Coca-Cola agreed to a number of stipulations that will lead to increased diversity. For example, they agreed to create a seven-member task force that will review how Coca-Cola pays, promotes, and evaluates minority employees. The task force will be made up of labor and civil rights officials from government, academics, attorneys, consultants, and businesspeople, and can make recommendations that are binding on the company. The task force will also have broad power to investigate and monitor diversity issues.

In the settlement, the current chairman of Coca-Cola, Douglas Daft, stated that the company "recognized that diversity is a fundamental and indispensable value and that the company, its shareholders and all of its employees will benefit by striving to be a premier 'gold standard' company on diversity."[7]

What are the EEO standards needed to prevent being the poster company for EEO? How should organizations respond to EEO complaints? More to the point, how can organizations prevent the types of issues that led to the misfortunes of Coca-Cola? These are important questions that will be addressed in considering the human resource legal environment.

In this chapter the term **equal employment opportunity (EEO)** is used to represent a collection of legal and social policies that state that members of U.S. society should have equal access to and treatment in employment. Since the mid-1960s, EEO laws and regulations have influenced almost every aspect of human resource management. All managers and supervisors must be familiar with EEO policies. Familiar or not, a recent survey showed a great deal of looking the other way. The survey by consulting firm KPMG of 2,300 blue- and white-collar workers in seventeen industries found that, for example, one-third of those surveyed said they had witnessed sexual harassment in the past year.[8] In addition, 36 percent of the respondents said they had observed employment discrimination. Clearly, even after forty years of EEO laws, further work needs to be done.

An organization should develop HR practices consistent with EEO laws and regulations for two reasons. First, equal employment opportunity is the law of the land. Companies that intentionally or unintentionally violate EEO laws are subject to a variety of penalties. These penalties include making back pay settlements of thousands of dollars, paying for the legal defense of the organization in court, paying the legal costs of the person or persons filing the charges of discrimination if the company is found guilty, and losing federal contracts that the company might have. The case of Coca-Cola described earier in the HR Challenge is an example of the monetary cost of discrimination suits.[9] By any standard, $192.5 million is a huge amount of soft drinks and should sound alarm bells in many corporate boardrooms.

The second reason for conforming to EEO laws and regulations is that it makes good sense from an HR perspective. The goal of human resource management is to make maximum use of all human resources available to an organization. By discriminating against individuals because of their race, sex, national origin, disability, or other characteristics, an organization is turning away potential employees who could make valuable contributions to the company. Obviously, the costs to an organization of such potential human resource losses are more difficult to measure than the direct monetary losses associated with court settlements. However, from the perspective of good human resource management, these human resource losses should be considered as significant as direct monetary losses.

This chapter describes the important components of the EEO environment with which all HRM specialists should be familiar. A familiarity with the EEO environment can help organizations avoid both the financial and human costs inherent in violating EEO laws and regulations. In recent years, however, especially with the passage of the Americans with Disabilities Act, EEO laws have become increasingly complex. While the descriptions provided herein should be very helpful, organizations facing specific problems are advised to seek expert assistance.

THE EEO ENVIRONMENT

Several major components make up the EEO environment; they are shown in Table 5.1. Illegal discrimination in our society can take many forms, but this text focuses only on such discrimination in employment situations. Legal and regulatory documents include amendments to the U.S. Constitution; laws passed by the federal, state, and local governments; presidential executive orders; and guidelines prepared by government agencies. These documents define employment discrimination. Agents of enforcement include the Equal Employment Opportunity Commission, the Office of Federal Contract Compliance Programs, the Department of Justice, and the court systems. These agents can take a variety of administrative and judicial enforcement actions against organizations that discriminate illegally. The final component in the EEO environment is management and its preventive and corrective responses to EEO legislation and regulations.

● **TABLE 5.1**

Components of the EEO Environment

	Specific Elements
Employment discrimination	Overt discrimination
	Disparate treatment
	Disparate impact
Legal and regulatory documents	U.S. Constitution and amendments
	State and local laws
	Laws passed by Congress
	Presidential executive orders
	Guidelines of U.S. Government agencies
Agents of EEO enforcement	Equal Employment Opportunity Commission
	Office of Federal Contract Compliance Programs
	U.S. Department of Justice
	Federal and state court systems
Management responses	Preventive actions
	Corrective actions

Source: From *Federal Regulation of Personnel and Human Resource Management,* 2nd edition, by J. Ledvinka and V. G. Scarpello. © 1991. Reprinted with permission of South-Western College Publishing, a division of Thomson Learning. Fax 800-730-2215.

DISCRIMINATION DEFINED

Many people assume that discrimination implies some form of illegal act. In fact, to "discriminate" means simply to distinguish clearly or differentiate. One example of "desirable" discrimination is the effort to achieve a distinction between good and poor workers in a company's performance management system.

Illegal discrimination occurs when unfair actions are taken toward members of a protected class. A **protected class** or group consists of individuals who share some characteristic in common, such as their race, color, religion, sex, national origin, age, disability status, or status as military veterans. These individuals are protected in that laws prevent discriminatory employment actions against them because of the characteristic they have in common. Suppose, for instance, that in the performance management example mentioned previously most white employees were rated as outstanding performers while the majority of Hispanic employees were rated as unsatisfactory performers. Such discrimination would be questionable and, if based solely on race, would be illegal.

Laws preventing discrimination have been passed when Congress or a state legislature has had evidence that individuals with some particular characteristic in common have been treated unfairly in our society. For example, during the civil rights movement of the 1960s, several laws were passed to protect citizens from racial discrimination in housing, employment, and voting rights because strong evidence existed that racial discrimination (left over from pre–Civil War days) still existed.

LEGAL AND REGULATORY DOCUMENTS

The important EEO laws and regulatory documents are summarized in Table 5.2 and described in the following sections.

The Constitution

The **Fifth Amendment** to the U.S. Constitution states that "no person shall . . . be deprived of life, liberty, or property, without due process of law." This amendment relates to the actions of the federal government toward federal employees. The **Fourteenth Amendment** applies due process to actions taken by state governments and provides state employees with "equal protection of the laws." If a gov-

● **TABLE 5.2**

Major EEO Laws and Regulatory Documents

Law or Document	Type of Discrimination Prohibited	Employers Covered
Fifth Amendment—U.S. Constitution	Deprivation of employment rights without due process	Federal government
Fourteenth Amendment—U.S. Constitution	Deprivation of employment rights without due process	State governments
Civil Rights Act of 1866	Racial discrimination in employment	Private employers, unions, employment agencies
Civil Rights Act of 1871	Deprivation of employment rights	State/local governments
Equal Pay Act of 1963	Sex discrimination in pay	All employers, unions
Title VII—Civil Rights Act of 1964 (amended 1972)	Employment discrimination based on race, color, religion, sex, national origin	Private employers, government unions, employment agencies
Age Discrimination in Employment Act of 1967 (amended 1986)	Employment discrimination based on age (ages 40 and above)	Private employers, unions, employment agencies
Vocational Rehabilitation Act of 1973	Employment discrimination based on mental or physical handicaps	Federal contractors, government
Immigration Reform and Control Act of 1986	Discrimination based on citizenship or national origin	Employers generally
Older Workers Benefit Protection Act of 1990	Expands protection of Age Discrimination in Employment Act	Private employers, unions, employment agencies
Americans with Disabilities Act of 1990 (amended 1994)	Discrimination based on physical or mental handicap	Employers generally
Civil Rights Act of 1991	Discrimination based on race, color, religion, sex, or national origin	Employers generally
Family and Medical Leave Act of 1993	Provides unpaid leave for employees under certain circumstances	Larger employers generally
Executive Order 11246 (amended by Executive Order 11375)	Same as Title VII with affirmative action required	Federal contractors
Uniform Guidelines (interpretive document for EEO laws)		

ernment worker is fired without a due process hearing, that worker can possibly file suit in court (1) using either the Fifth or the Fourteenth Amendment as the basis for the case and (2) arguing that he or she is being deprived of property without due process of law.

Federal Legislation

Although many EEO laws have been passed by state and local governments, we will limit our discussion to those passed by the U.S. Congress. Managers, however, should be aware of state EEO laws, since these laws are sometimes more stringent than federal laws. For example, a Texas state law prohibiting age discrimination covers individuals between the ages of twenty-one and seventy. The federal age discrimination law applies only to persons who are age forty and over.

● **Civil Rights Acts of 1866 and 1871**   The **Civil Rights Act of 1866** provides all citizens with the same right to make and enforce contracts as "white citizens" have.[10] This law has been interpreted by the courts as prohibiting racial discrimination by employers, unions, and employment agencies in the making of employment contracts.[11] It is often combined with the **Civil Rights Act of 1871,** which gives all people in the United States the right to sue if deprived of constitutional rights as a result of state action, custom, or conspiracy.[12]

● **Equal Pay Act of 1963**   The **Equal Pay Act** prohibits wage discrimination among employees on the basis of sex when the work requires equal skill, effort, and responsibility and is performed under similar working conditions.[13]

- Skill is defined as the experience, training, education, or other abilities needed to perform the job.
- Effort can be mental and/or physical in nature (e.g., lifting 100-pound sacks of grain or working in a job that requires constant attention to detail). It is the degree or amount, not the nature, of the effort that is considered.
- Responsibility is the degree of accountability for people, equipment, money, or other things that the job entails.
- Working conditions include the physical surroundings and hazards under which the job is performed.

Court cases indicate that jobs need not be identical to be considered substantially equal to one another.[14] These rulings prevent organizations from giving men and women different job titles and paying them different wages even though they do essentially the same work. In other words, if a female executive secretary has essentially the same job duties as a male office manager, she must be paid the same wage. However, in jobs that are substantially equal, pay differentials between some male and female employees may be allowed as long as the differences are based on one of the following factors:

- Bona fide seniority systems
- Differences in the quality of performance
- Piece-rate pay systems, where pay is tied directly to the number and quality of units produced
- Factors other than sex (such as night shifts paying more than day shifts)

Despite the existence of the Equal Pay Act for more than thirty years, general disparities in the rates of pay for men and women still do exist. In 1999, women employed full time earned, on average, seventy-six cents for every dollar earned by men.[15] The issue, though, is quite complex and involves, among other things, the types of work women do and the occupations they are in. (See Chapter 12 for further discussion of the Equal Pay Act and the earnings gap.) The 106th Congress (1999–2000) considered the Paycheck Fairness Act, which would have strengthened pay equity laws and procedures. Hearings were held by the appropriate Senate committee (June 2000), but the Senate voted against this amendment.[16] The outlook for this legislation is uncertain.

● **Civil Rights Act of 1964**   The most important legislation concerning equal employment opportunity is the Civil Rights Act of 1964, amended by the Equal Employment Opportunity Act of 1972, the Pregnancy Discrimination Act of 1978, and the Civil Rights Act of 1991.[17]

Title VII of the Civil Rights Act   **Title VII** is a portion of the **Civil Rights Act of 1964,** as was constituted then and exists today, that is the most important piece of legislation ever enacted by Congress to guarantee American workers equal employment opportunity.[18] The goal of Title VII was economic justice and national well-being. Regarding economic justice, Congress noted that it had been well documented that discrimination forced a marginal existence on minority employees while, at the same time, depriving the nation of the talents and skills minorities possessed. With respect to national well-being, Congress stated that:

> Aside from the political and economic considerations, . . . we believe in the creation of job equality because *it is the right thing to do.* We believe in the inherent dignity of man. He is born with certain inalienable rights. . . . All vestiges of inequality based solely on race must be removed in order to preserve our democratic society. . . .[19] (emphasis added)

Title VII prohibits employment discrimination based on race, color, religion, sex, or national origin. It protects employees from discrimination in such terms and conditions of employment as selection, placement, promotion, discharge, training, and pay and benefits. The Equal Employment Opportunity Commission (EEOC) was created by the 1964 law to enforce the provisions of Title VII.

As amended, Title VII applies to private employers that have fifteen or more employees on each working day of twenty or more calendar weeks in the current or preceding year. Title VII also applies to labor unions, employment agencies, state and local governments and their agencies, colleges, and universities. It protects all employees and applicants for employment in these organizations. There are some exceptions to this coverage, however. Religious organizations are not covered by certain religious discrimination aspects of Title VII. Elected public officials and their staffs and members of the Communist party are not protected. Employees who apply for jobs that require national security clearance are subject to special policies.

Pregnancy Discrimination Act of 1978   This act, which amended Title VII, was passed to protect pregnant women from employment discrimination.[20] The **Pregnancy Discrimination Act** (PDA) of 1978 requires employers to be nondiscriminatory in providing employee benefits such as health insurance, sick leave, pensions, and vacation time. If an employer provides sick leave and health or disability insurance to employees generally, it cannot specifically exclude childbirth and related medical conditions. Other important aspects of the PDA include the following:

- Elective abortions may be excluded from health insurance plans but not from other benefits, such as sick leave. Medical problems resulting from abortions may not be excluded from medical insurance.

- Employers must provide medical benefits to the husbands of female employees if they provide benefits to the wives of male employees.

- Employers must provide leave of absence or sick leave for childbirth on the same basis as for any other medical disability.

- Employers must allow women to work until their pregnancy results in physical disability that (1) interferes with their job performance and (2) is the same level of disability that would cause workers with other medical problems to have to stop working.

- Employers must allow women to return to work after childbirth on the same basis as for other disabilities.

In 1987, the U.S. Supreme Court faced the issue of whether a state statute that required employers to provide leave and reinstatement to employees disabled by pregnancy was preempted, or overridden, by the nondiscrimination mandates of the PDA. At issue in *California Federal Savings & Loan* v. *Guerra*[21] was a California statute providing such pregnancy leave. The employer in the case argued that under the law, pregnant employees are treated differently from other employees and that the California law was thus not consistent with the PDA. Justice Thurgood Marshall, writing the opinion for the Court, disagreed with this assertion and held that the PDA did not preempt this California statute. Justice Marshall wrote that the favorable treatment given to pregnant workers under the California statute was not of the kind that was meant to be outlawed by the PDA. The PDA was meant essentially to prevent harmful discriminatory actions being taken against pregnant employees.

Title VII and Fetal Protection Policies   In the 1991 case of *United Auto Workers* v. *Johnson Controls*, the U.S. Supreme Court examined the validity under Title VII of a company's fetal protection policy that said that all women of childbearing age were excluded from certain jobs involving lead exposure.[22] Opponents of the policy argued that the policy constituted sex discrimination, in that fertile men were given a choice of whether or not they wanted to risk lead exposure but fertile women were not. The Supreme Court upheld this point of view, ruling that the company's fetal protection policy did constitute unlawful sex discrimination and that no valid bona fide occupational qualification (discussed later in the chapter) was advanced. The court rejected arguments that the policy was necessary for safety reasons.

Sexual Harassment   Supreme Court Justice Clarence Thomas, former U.S. Senator Bob Packwood, former President Clinton, and various business leaders have all helped propel **sexual harassment** into the headlines. Because Congress did not discuss on-the-job sexual behavior in its passage of Title VII, the courts originally interpreted this omission to mean that sexual behavior was not a form of sex discrimination. However, in *Barnes* v. *Costle* (1977), sexual harassment was recognized for the first time as a form of sex discrimination under Title VII.[23] The EEOC has defined illegal sexual harassment in the following way: Unwelcome sexual advances, requests for sexual favors, or other verbal or physical conduct of a sexual nature constitute sexual harassment when any of the following conditions apply:

- Submitting to or rejecting such conduct is an explicit or implicit term or condition of employment.
- Submitting to or rejecting the conduct is a basis for employment decisions affecting the individual.
- The conduct unreasonably interferes with an individual's work performance or creates an intimidating, hostile, or offensive working environment.[24]

These EEOC guidelines were upheld by the U.S. Supreme Court in the significant 1986 case of *Meritor Savings Bank* v. *Vinson*.[25] In that case, the employer bank argued that Title VII's prohibition of discrimination with respect to "compensation, terms, conditions, or privileges" of employment involved only "tangible losses" of "an economic character." Essentially, the employer was arguing that only "quid pro quo" sexual harassment—that is, a situation in which continued employment or an employment benefit is conditioned on sexual conduct—should be unlawful under Title VII. Thus the case of an employee's being fired for not having sex with a boss would constitute clearly unlawful quid pro quo harassment. On the other hand, if no clear quid pro quo situation is involved, there is no legal violation.

In the *Meritor* case, the Supreme Court rejected this narrow interpretation of Title VII and held that "environmental" sexual harassment, as defined in the EEOC's guidelines, also was unlawful. In the Supreme Court's opinion, any workplace conduct that is sufficiently severe or pervasive so as to alter the conditions of an individual's employment and create an "abusive" working environment can be unlawful. Thus, under the *Meritor* case, sexual jokes, pornographic pictures, and so forth can, under certain circumstances, constitute unlawful sexual harassment under Title VII.

The Supreme Court also ruled in *Meritor* that the fact that a sexual relationship between parties at the workplace is "voluntary" may be irrelevant. The critical issue in such cases is whether the sexual advances at issue were "unwelcome" and whether they were sufficiently severe to be "abusive." If so, they may be held unlawful under Title VII.

In the *Meritor* case, the Supreme Court did somewhat duck the critical issue of when an employer is responsible for the harassing actions of its employees. A lower court hearing the case had held that employers are strictly liable for the hostile work environment that is created by a supervisor's sexual advances to an employee, even if the employer neither knew nor could have reasonably known of the alleged misconduct. The Supreme Court rejected this notion and held that the lower court had erred in concluding that employers are always automatically liable for acts of sexual harassment committed by their supervisors. On the other hand, the Court also rejected the notion that absence of notice to an employer necessarily insulates the employer from liability. Instead, the Court avoided issuing a definitive ruling on employer liability, holding only that the general rules regarding employer responsibility for the actions of employees should apply.

Finally, the Supreme Court in *Meritor* rejected the bank's argument that the failure of the woman to report the harassment by way of the bank's existing grievance procedure insulated the bank from liability. The Court held that the complainant may have failed to report the violation for a variety of reasons and that such a failure to report does not necessarily alter the bank's liability.

Another defining U.S. Supreme Court case was that of *Harris* v. *Forklift Systems*,[26] which further defined the concept of "environmental" sexual harassment. In that case, the president of the company, while not engaging in any explicit quid pro quo behavior, had clearly created a sexually harassing environment of the kind potentially unlawful under the *Meritor* case. Among other things, he had referred to the plaintiff, Teresa Harris, as a "dumb ass woman," made sexual innuendoes about women's clothing, and asked female employees to get coins from his front pants pocket. The company argued, however, that because Teresa Harris had not shown any concrete psychological harm as a result of these actions, they did not violate Title VII. The Supreme Court disagreed.

The Supreme Court held that workplace conduct need not result in concrete psychological harm in order to be actionable in court as "abusive work environment" harassment. The Court held that such conduct need only be so pervasive and severe that a "reasonable person" would perceive it to be hostile or abusive. Such a determination would turn on all relevant circumstances, including the following

1. The frequency of the discriminatory conduct
2. Its severity
3. Whether it is physically threatening or humiliating or a mere offensive utterance
4. Whether it unreasonably interferes with an employee's work performance

In sum, the Supreme Court stated that Title VII clearly comes into play before harassing conduct leads to a "nervous breakdown." (See the International Perspective box for information on what constitutes cross-cultural sexual harassment or an abusive work environment.)

Because of the vagueness of what constitutes sexual harassment, the fact that the Civil Rights Act of 1991 mandates jury trials in cases of sexual harassment, and the high level of damages permitted under that act, attorneys have become extremely aggressive in their pursuit of evidence in such cases. While questioning of plaintiffs regarding abortion, sexually transmitted diseases, and past sexual activity is not generally permitted in rape cases, such questioning is permissible, and is being conducted, in sexual harassment cases.[27]

Two recent cases have gained notoriety. The first concerns the issue of same-sex sexual harassment. Recent federal district court decisions had been mixed as to whether same-sex sexual harassment is a legitimate claim under Title VII of the Civil Rights Act of 1964. These decisions have now been clarified in the case of Joseph Onscale, a male worker on an off-shore drilling rig. Onscale charged that three male coworkers sexually harassed him with physical attacks, taunts, and threats of rape. The Supreme Court, in the case of *Onscale* v. *Sundowner*, reversed a U.S. appeals court in ruling that the Civil Rights Act of 1964 could not include cases of same-sex harassment.[28] The *Onscale* case thus opened up a new area of sexual harassment litigation—that associated with same-sex harassment.[29]

The second item of note is a record-setting $10 million settlement of sexual harassment charges brought by eighty female employees. The suit against the drug maker Astra was the result of alleged reckless behavior on the part of the former

INTERNATIONAL PERSPECTIVE

Sexual Harassment—Or Is It?

 A Korean salesman hired by a U.S.-based multinational company in Seoul is rotated to a U.S. office for six months of training and work experience. After a few months, an American female co-worker complains of sexual harassment. It seems the Korean has refused to listen to her or respond to her questions even though they need to work closely together, has screamed at her in front of customers, and has publicly addressed her with an obscene term. At one point, she thought he was so angry that he might strike her. He also frequently tells her that women are less important than men in his culture and that he intends to treat her accordingly. The Korean insists that he has not done anything wrong or anything different from what he did while working in Asia in the past.*

A U.S. expatriate working in Mexico is subject to what she sees as unwanted advances by her superior. In addition to his making suggestive comments to her, she complains that he stands too close to her and sometimes touches her while talking. This has continued despite her consistently moving away and displaying a total lack of interest in his advances. A female colleague from Mexico tells her to lighten up—the manager's behavior is normal.

A Middle Eastern–born man is shocked when an American coworker files a formal sexual harassment complaint. He is stunned that any woman would even think of behaving so disrespectfully toward a man.

Because cultures differ in the type of behavior that is acceptable between the sexes, there seems to be considerable possibility of misunderstanding when employees of diverse cultures and genders meet in the workplace. Behavior that Americans would consider unacceptable is especially likely to occur in countries where the sexes are not equal under the law or in society.

It is possible that perfectly innocent local customs might be offensive to hypersensitive Americans. For instance, standing close and touching while speaking to others are common in Hispanic and southern European nations but could be seen as overtly sexual by those accustomed to greater personal distance.

It is clear that U.S. regulations prevail when the employees involved are working in the United States. To reduce the likelihood of incidents, firms should fully brief expatriates posted to the United States on our local practices and regulations regarding male–female behavior at work.

When the harassment takes place in an overseas establishment, it is less clear whose standards should apply—those of the host country or those of the home country. Multinational firms are often admonished to adapt their policies to local customs rather than practice "cultural imperialism." On the other hand, if freedom from unwanted sexual advances or overtly discriminatory behavior is considered a universal human right, then firms should protect this right in their operations worldwide. While relatively few countries have well-developed and enforceable prohibitions against sexual harassment in the workplace, more and more nations are moving in this direction. The European Commission recently adopted a directive to ban sexual harassment that requires member states to formulate their own regulations preventing harassment—though how harassment is defined may be culture-specific.

*This first incident is a true one. The company subsequently established that the offender was a hot-tempered individual with a history of impulsive and possibly abusive behavior. While cultural values undoubtedly contributed to the situation, they were not the whole story, and one would not expect most Korean men to behave in this way.

Sources: Robyn Talbot, Eastern Hemisphere Human Resource Director, personal communication, 1997; and W. Hardman and J. Heidelberg, "When Sexual Harassment Is a Foreign Affair," *Personnel Journal*, April 1996, pp. 91–97.

president, Lars Bildman, and other executives.[30] In an unusual move, Astra has filed a $15 million suit against Lars Bildman, thus attempting to collect the damages from the employee most responsible for the illegal activity.[31]

Finally, two more recent cases, *Faragher* v. *City of Boca Raton* and *Burlington Industries Inc.* v. *Ellerth*, reaffirmed long-established court guidelines.[32] The guidance for employers is:

- If an employer does not have a written policy against sexual harassment, it should get one that includes a clearly stated procedure for filing a complaint.

- Once an employer has a written policy and procedure, it should be made known to everyone in the organization.

- Every complaint should be investigated in accordance with the procedures.

- Every employment decision should be documented.[33]

Even with recent decisions there are unresolved issues. For example, many people are confused about what constitutes sexual harassment and the extent of the employer's obligation to prevent what most often takes place "behind closed doors."[34]

Religious Harassment   In 1993, the EEOC proposed new guidelines dealing with, among other things, "religious harassment" in the workplace. The idea was to develop federal standards that would better protect workers from unlawful on-the-job harassment over their religious beliefs. The proposal, however, drew considerable criticism from various sectors concerned that the EEOC's plan might prompt employers to ban all at-work forms of religious expression, including the wearing of a cross or a Star of David. Amid such controversy, the EEOC, in September of 1994, withdrew its proposal.

● **Age Discrimination in Employment Act of 1967**   The **Age Discrimination in Employment Act** (ADEA) of 1967, amended in 1986, prohibits employment discrimination against job applicants and employees aged forty years or over.[35] The legislation was designed to remedy the stereotypical perceptions and resulting restrictive practices that deemed older workers unsuitable for employment. Leading to the ADEA was a study reporting that applicants over fifty-five years of age were excluded from 50 percent of all private-sector jobs, whereas 25 percent of jobs were closed to applicants forty-five years of age or older.[36] As an effort to protect older workers, the ADEA has taken on additional significance in the twenty-first century as a result of the aging of the work force (see the discussions of work force diversity in Chapters 1 and 3).

The legislation applies to private firms that employ twenty or more people on each working day of twenty or more calendar weeks in the current or preceding year. Employment agencies, labor unions, and federal, state, and local government employees are covered by the law.[37] This law has effectively banished any mandatory retirement age. It also prohibits discrimination based on age in recruiting, hiring, promoting, firing, and laying off employees and in most other terms and conditions of employment. The federal law applies only to persons aged forty and above. A twenty-five-year-old worker is not protected by the act.

A recent court case, *O'Connor* v. *Consolidated Coin Caterers Corp.*, clarifies one important aspect of age discrimination.[38] The plaintiff, James O'Connor, was terminated by Consolidated at age fifty-six and replaced by a forty-year-old. Lower courts ruled that this was not age discrimination because O'Connor's replacement was in the protected class, that is, age forty or above. The Supreme Court ruled that the fact that one person in the protected class has lost out to another person in the protected class is irrelevant.[39] In other words, Mr. O'Connor's claim of age discrimination was valid.

● **Older Workers Protection Act of 1990**   The **Older Workers Protection Act** amended the ADEA to make clear that certain previously permitted age-based distinctions in employee benefits plans are unlawful. More specifically, the new law overturned the Supreme Court's 1989 decision in *Public Employees Retirement System of Ohio* v. *Betts*, which held that employer decisions concerning employee benefits generally were not subject to challenge under the ADEA.[40] The 1990 law also sets very strict standards regarding employee waivers and releases of age discrimination claims—that is, situations in which employees, as a condition for receiving a severance or other payment from their employer, sign a waiver, or release, giving up any future age discrimination claim. Under the new law, employees must be given at least three weeks to consider any waiver or release agreement and even then have a week after signing the agreement to revoke it.

● **Vocational Rehabilitation Act of 1973**   The **Vocational Rehabilitation Act** requires employers who have federal contracts of $2,500 or more to take affirmative action toward qualified handicapped individuals.[41] The laws discussed thus far require only that employers not discriminate against certain types of persons. The affirmative action components of the Vocational Rehabilitation Act and the executive orders (discussed later in the chapter) require employers to develop more active procedures for seeking out and accommodating the needs of workers protected by the laws.

● **Americans with Disabilities Act of 1990**   The **Americans with Disabilities Act** (ADA) went into effect on July 26, 1992. The scope of this law is vast, extending far beyond the employment context. For example, all new apartment and business buildings must be made accessible to the disabled. With respect to employment, the law initially affected all employers with more than twenty-five employees. On July 26, 1994, this requirement was lowered to fifteen employees, making an estimated 400,000 more employers subject to this act. Thus the ADA is significantly broader in application than the Vocational Rehabilitation Act of 1973, which applies only to federal contractors, although the new law does not mandate any affirmative action. Simply put, the ADA prohibits discrimination on the basis of disability—in hiring and in all terms, conditions, and privileges of employment. Unlike the Vocational Rehabilitation Act, which is administered by the Department of Labor, the ADA is administered by the EEOC.

Administration by the EEOC   The EEOC was deluged with charges when the ADA went into effect, receiving more than 35,000 charges from mid-1992 through 1994. The ADA charges during this period constituted about 20 percent of the overall workload of the EEOC. This percentage increased with the extension of coverage to employers with fifteen or more employees, effective July 26, 1994; an additional 9 million employees were thereby protected by the ADA. However, as seen in Table 5.3, disabilities (ADA) charges constituted approximately 16 to 17 percent of all charges received by the EEOC in the period between 1994 and 1999, with the figure dropping to 14.5 percent in fiscal year 2000.

TABLE 5.3

Summary of Charges Received and Resolved by the EEOC

	FY 1994	FY 1995	FY 1996	FY 1997	FY 1998	FY 1999	FY 2000
Charges Received[a]	**117,510**	**115,977**	**105,483**	**110,529**	**108,965**	**105,919**	**109,216**
Racial discrimination	26.9%	25.9%	24.9%	26.4%	26.4%	27.2%	26.5%
Religious discrimination	1.3%	1.4%	1.5%	1.5%	1.6%	1.7%	1.8%
Sex discrimination	22.0%	22.6%	22.6%	22.4%	22.4%	22.4%	23.1%
Sexual harassment	12.3%	13.4%	14.5%	14.4%	14.3%	14.4%	14.5%
Pregnancy discrimination	3.5%	3.5%	3.5%	3.5%	3.9%	3.9%	3.8%
Age discrimination	16.7%	15.0%	14.9%	14.3%	13.9%	13.4%	14.7%
Equal pay discrimination	1.2%	1.1%	0.9%	1.0%	1.0%	1.0%	1.2%
Disabilities discrimination	16.0%	17.1%	17.1%	16.4%	16.3%	16.1%	14.5%
Resolutions[b]	**90,340**	**114,870**	**130,409**	**136,943**	**131,811**	**127,401**	**122,630**
Settlements	6.2%	4.7%	3.8%	4.3%	5.0%	6.7%	8.9%
Withdraw with benefits[c]	7.7%	6.0%	4.5%	4.0%	3.9%	4.4%	4.7%
Administrative closure[d]	38.3%	38.7%	31.6%	29.8%	27.9%	25.2%	21.4%
No reasonable cause	44.9%	48.2%	57.7%	58.0%	58.5%	57.5%	56.4%
Reasonable cause	2.9%	2.4%	2.3%	3.8%	4.7%	6.3%	8.6%

[a]The number for total charges reflects the sum of the individual charge filings. Because individuals often file charges claiming multiple types of discrimination, the actual number of charges for any given fiscal year will be less than the total of the eight types of discrimination listed.

[b]Resolutions include charges received from previous periods; hence resolutions can exceed charges received in a given year.

[c]Charge is withdrawn upon receipt of desired benefits.

[d]Closed for administrative reasons, such as failure to locate charging party; charging party failed to respond, failed to accept full relief, etc.

As Figure 5.1 shows, the most common impairment involved in charges brought under the ADA since its inception has been back impairment, followed by emotional and psychological impairments. Just over half the charges brought have involved allegations of illegal discriminatory discharge.

Defining "Disability"   At the heart of the ADA is the definition of "disability." The act defines **"disability"** as (1) a physical or mental impairment that substantially limits one or more of the major life activities of an individual, (2) a record of such an impairment, or (3) being regarded as having such an impairment. The term "physical or mental impairment" is defined broadly. It includes any physiological disorder or condition, cosmetic disfigurement, or anatomical loss affecting one or more of several body systems, as well as any mental, physical, or psychological disorder.

The definition of "mental or psychological disorder" includes emotional and mental illness, mental retardation, and learning disabilities. This definition is so broad that it includes virtually the entire spectrum of psychological disorders; as such, it prompted considerable debate in Congress during legislative consideration of the bill. At the urging of Senator Jesse Helms of North Carolina, various conditions—including kleptomania, compulsive gambling, sexual behavior disorders, and pyromania—were specifically excluded from the definition of "disability" under the ADA. Homosexuality and bisexuality were also excluded on the grounds that they are not impairments. Nevertheless, the ADA covers hundreds of psychological disorders. The act also specifically states that persons with acquired immune deficiency syndrome (AIDS) and those who are HIV-positive (infected with the human immunodeficiency virus) are protected under the ADA.

Interestingly, the ADA protects only disabilities that "substantially limit one or more major life activities." A common cold, for example, although a disability, does not "substantially limit" any "major life activities." The EEOC in its regulations has stated that it will examine the nature, severity, duration, and impact of the given impairment on a case-by-case basis to determine whether the impairment does substantially limit a major life activity and thus constitute a disability under the law. It should be noted, however, that the ADA covers people who are viewed by employers as having a substantially limiting impairment, even if the impairment does not necessarily have this effect. For example, an executive whose high blood pressure has clearly been controlled by medication probably cannot be denied a promotion for that reason.

Reasonable Accommodation   Although the ADA, unlike the Vocational Rehabilitation Act, does not require affirmative action, it does impose an affirmative obligation on employers to make "reasonable accommodations" to the known disabilities of an applicant or an employee unless the employer demonstrates that this would constitute an "undue hardship." The concept of **reasonable accommodation** is not unique to the ADA. Title VII of the Civil Rights Act, for example, requires employers to reasonably accommodate the religious practices of their employees as long as such accommodations do not constitute an "undue hardship." Such accommodations may include job transfers, work-schedule changes, or other actions that allow workers to meet both their religious and their job responsibilities.

With respect to the disabled, employers are required to make reasonable accommodations of a kind that will allow individuals to perform the essential functions of the job. Reasonable accommodations often involve changes in the work-

EEOC Americans with Disabilities Charges Received[a]

Note: HIV is a subcategory of blood disorders.

Source: http://www.eeoc.gov/stats/notable/ada.html.

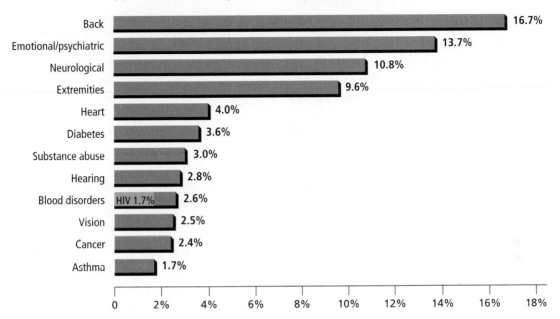

(a) Most common impairments alleged under ADA**

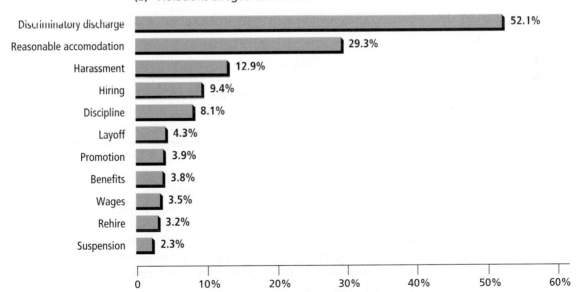

(b) Violations alleged under ADA

* Charges received July 26, 1992 – September 30, 1998.
** This is not a complete list, therefore, percentages do not add up to 100.

[a]Charges received July 26, 1992 to September 30, 1998.

[b]This is not a complete list; therefore percentages do not add up to 100.

place, the job itself, and the equipment used to perform the job. For example, employers may modify elevators to include Braille or voice floor indicators, alter restrooms to meet the special needs of disabled workers, and build ramps to allow wheelchair access to buildings.

Employers are not required to accommodate the needs of handicapped workers in every case. Employers may argue that changes necessary to accommodate a worker would cause undue hardship—that is, the accommodation would be extremely costly to the company and/or would disrupt the efficient, safe operation of the company. Whether or not an accommodation is reasonable or results in undue hardship for the employer depends on several factors:

- The nature of the job itself (whether it can be changed to accommodate a certain type of handicap)
- The size of the company
- Union agreements that might preclude certain types of work-schedule or work-rule changes
- The cost of the accommodation for the employer

Recent ADA U.S. Supreme Court Cases   As with other EEOC issues, the courts have had a great deal to do with defining the scope of the statutes. Even though the ADA is relatively recent in the history of employment law, the courts have already done a great deal to signal both employees and employers as to the nature of the issues involved.

In a recent decision that severely limits the ADA, the Supreme Court ruled that states do not have to make "reasonable accommodations" in the workplace. In the landmark case *Board of Trustees of University of Alabama* v. *Garrett*, the Court ruled that the disabled could not sue state government agencies.[42] The court ruled that states' rights trump the legal rights of people with disabilities.

The case had to do with Patricia Garrett, a nurse who worked at the University of Alabama's medical center. Garrett discovered that she had breast cancer and received a leave of absence while recovering from surgery. When she returned to work, she was demoted in deference to her employer's belief that she had a disability and could no longer perform her duties satisfactorily.[43]

While the merits of Garrett's case could be debated, the decision could seriously undermine the ADA in the future—not only in the public sector but also in the private sector. All told, the Court's decision is a huge step backward for disabled persons seeking a fair chance to work and contribute.

The second case, *PGA Tour, Inc.* v. *Martin*, also had implications beyond the case itself.[44] In this case the Supreme Court ruled decisively in favor of Casey Martin, a professional golfer suffering from a progressive circulatory disorder that has caused his right leg to atrophy such that walking is not only very painful but also poses the risk of severe damage to his health. The court ruled that Martin should be allowed to use a golf cart. Justice Stevens said the PGA Tour's walking rule was "at best peripheral" and "not an indispensable feature" of golf and "thus it might be waived in individual cases without working a fundamental alteration."[45]

The broader implications of this case have to do with the Court's emphasis on the need to evaluate each case on an individual basis. According to Justice Stevens, those for whom the given rules and procedures are "beyond their capacity," not simply uncomfortable or difficult, should be accommodated.

AIDS in the Workplace   As noted earlier, AIDS is clearly defined as a disability under the ADA. Employers cannot require a test for AIDS or any other medical examination as a condition of making an offer of employment. Once an offer of employment has been made, however, employers can make the offer conditional on the taking of such an examination. An employer cannot generally discriminate against a job applicant who is HIV-positive, although such a person may be lawfully excluded from coverage under the employer's health insurance plan if the plan excludes other preexisting conditions. The following are some general guidelines for dealing with the AIDS issue:

- Treat AIDS like any other disease that is covered by state or federal laws against discrimination.
- Educate coworkers about AIDS.
- Maintain confidentiality of all medical records.
- Do not in any way discriminate against a person with AIDS.
- Do not exclude AIDS victims from training or consideration for promotion.
- Accommodate or make a good effort to accommodate the AIDS victim.[46]

Obesity   Evidence of weight-based discrimination has been observed in many studies. In fact, studies assessing the effect of both employee weight and other possible bases for discrimination (sex, specific disabilities, race, etc.) provide evidence that weight-related bias may be greater than that associated with other characteristics.[47] The question of whether being overweight is a legally protected impairment under the ADA remains.

The Rehabilitation Act decision of the U.S. Court of Appeals for the First Circuit in *Cook* v. *State of Rhode Island, Department of Mental Health, Retardation and Hospitals* (1993) has led some commentators to speculate that obesity is probably covered by the ADA.[48] That case involved the refusal of a state mental retardation facility to hire an individual who was five feet, two inches tall and weighed over 320 pounds. The state facility argued that the individual's obesity compromised her ability to evacuate patients in the event of an emergency and also increased the possibility of her developing serious illnesses leading to increased absenteeism and worker compensation claims. The state government also argued that there was, in the plaintiff's obese condition, an element of voluntariness that mitigated against its being accorded legally protected status.

The federal appeals court, however, rejected these arguments. The court held that "morbid obesity," defined as being more than twice the proper body weight or more than 100 pounds overweight, constituted a legally protected impairment even if not caused by an underlying physical disorder. The court stated that a "voluntariness" test was improper, noting that impairments such as alcoholism or perhaps even diabetes could in some sense be seen as "voluntary" conditions.

Genetic Discrimination   Discrimination based on the presence of a disability is illegal under the ADA. But what about discrimination based on genetic characteristics that predispose an individual to developing a disease, condition, or late-onset disorder? (Late-onset disorders are those that may not show visible signs until later in the individual's life.) The ADA may protect against genetic discrimination as well, since the law applies not only to people with a disability but also to people regarded as having a disability. People who experience genetic discrimination are often regarded as having a disability because they have an abnormal gene. The EEOC ruled in 1995 that genetic discrimination in employment is prohibited. More recently, the EEOC issued guidance implementing an executive order that prohibits genetic discrimination by the federal government. While the executive order is limited to federal government employment, it represents a major step in setting the legal standard for addressing genetic discrimination in the workplace.[49]

Workplace Violence   As noted earlier, the ADA clearly covers most psychological disorders. Anger and aggression of the type that are part of some psychological disorders, however, constitute a clear threat of possible workplace violence. Headlines about disgruntled employees gunning down coworkers alarm both employers and other employees.[50] There is, therefore, a question as to how employers are supposed to handle employees with psychological disorders, given potential correlations between workplace violence and some forms of mental illness.

It should be noted, though, that a recent congressional Office of Technology Assessment study found higher correlations between workplace violence and factors other than mental illness. Indeed, the two factors most highly correlated with workplace violence were (1) substance abuse and (2) a prior history of violence.

Nevertheless, this is not an issue employers can easily ignore. An employer may treat a disabled employee prone to violence the same as any other employee, even if the misconduct resulted from the disability. For example, an employee with a mental disability may be disciplined or fired for violence or threats of violence as long as the same discipline would be imposed on an employee without a disability.[51]

● **Immigration Reform and Control Act of 1986**   The **Immigration Reform and Control Act** (IRCA) provides penalties for companies and individuals within the companies who knowingly hire illegal aliens.[52] The IRCA covers companies with three or more employees. For first offenses, fines of $250 to $2,000 per illegal alien may be imposed. A pattern of violation by a company may result in fines of up to $10,000 and six-month jail sentences. Employers must collect sufficient information from job applicants to confirm their legal status within the United States, and both the applicant and the company must fill out an I-9 form. Companies must retain their employment records for three years after hire or for one year following termination, whichever comes first.

English-Only Rules   With increasing numbers of immigrants coming into the United States, an issue of heightened importance is whether an employer can lawfully require employees to speak only English at work. Traditionally, the EEOC has considered such "English-only" work rules unlawful, representing discrimination on the basis of national origin. In June 1994, however, the Supreme Court upheld without comment a decision by the federal appeals court in San Francisco rejecting the EEOC's position that English-only rules are automatically invalid. The appeals court held that employers who require their workers to speak English on the job do not necessarily violate Title VII.

The case of *Garcia* v. *Spun Steak Co.* (1994)[53] involved two employees of San Francisco meatpacker Spun Steak Company who were making derogatory and racist remarks in Spanish, belittling coworkers. In response, the company adopted an English-only rule for the workplace. When the EEOC challenged this rule as automatically invalid and mandated that the employer show some "business necessity" for adopting it, the employer countered that while Title VII protects against discrimination based on national origin, it does not protect the right of workers to express their cultural heritage in the workplace. The appeals court agreed with the employer, noting that the EEOC's traditional policy in this regard created a new right never contemplated by Congress.

Since the *Garcia* case, however, there have been a number of cases and EEOC settlements suggesting that the original EEOC position that English-only policies are, more often than not, employment discrimination may prevail. For example, *EEOC* v. *Premier Operator Services, Inc.*, involved employees who worked as telephone operators. Their ability to speak Spanish was perceived an asset because the company services many Spanish-speaking customers, and many employees were tested for their bilingual abilities. However, Premier had an English-only policy prohibiting speaking Spanish at work except when speaking to a customer on the phone. The court ruled that the English-only policy constituted disparate treatment based on national origin. There was no evidence of business necessity for the English-only policy that was related to performance on the job. Nor was there any evidence that speaking Spanish at work caused discord among the employees.[54]

● **Civil Rights Act of 1991**   One of the fundamental purposes of this legislation was to reverse the U.S. Supreme Court's 1989 decision in *Wards Cove Packing Co.* v. *Antonio.*[55] In *Wards Cove,* the Court made it more difficult for employees to prove discrimination (particularly in "disparate impact" cases, to be discussed later in this chapter). The new legislation overturned *Wards Cove* and essentially put into law the Supreme Court's 1971 decision in *Griggs* v. *Duke Power Co.*, which obliges employers to prove that a practice causing discrimination was required by a "business necessity."[56] The 1991 act also overturned another 1989 Supreme Court decision, which held that the Civil Rights Act of 1866 did not apply to cases in which an employee was discharged but only to those cases relating to the formation of a contract, such as hiring. The 1991 legislation made it clear that the Civil Rights Act of 1866 does indeed apply to discharge cases.

The **Civil Rights Act of 1991** also amends Title VII to provide that an employment practice may be established as unlawful by demonstrating that race, color, religion, sex, or national origin was a motivating factor for an adverse employment decision, even though other legitimate factors also motivated the decision. The act further expands the scope of Title VII and the ADA to apply to U.S. citizens employed in foreign countries by American-owned or American-controlled employers. This provision in the law overturned a 1991 Supreme Court decision, which held that Title VII did not apply outside the United States to U.S. citizens working for American-owned or American-controlled companies.

The Civil Rights Act of 1991 also amended section 703 of Title VII to explicitly prohibit "race norming" of employee or job candidate test scores—that is, altering test scores on the basis of race, sex, national origin, or other criteria. In addition, the law established a formal commission to study the artificial barriers to advancement that women and other minorities face in the workplace—the so-called glass ceiling.

Traditionally, damage awards under Title VII have been limited to back pay, lost benefits, and attorney's fees and costs. The 1991 act, however, provided monetary awards of compensatory and punitive damages in cases of intentional discrimination. Under the 1991 law, compensatory damages can cover emotional pain and suffering and enjoyment of life, but the amount of punitive damages that can be awarded is limited by the size of the given employer. When compensatory or punitive damages are sought, either party may demand a jury trial.

Jury Trials and the Civil Rights Act of 1991   The provision for jury trials for discrimination claims in the Civil Rights Act of 1991 constituted a radical change in the enforcement of Title VII. As noted earlier in the discussion of aggressive legal tactics in sexual harassment cases, employers and their attorneys generally feel at much greater risk in trials before juries as opposed to trials solely before federal judges. It is surmised that juries are more likely to be swayed by visceral or emotional arguments than are federal judges well familiar with Title VII law. Moreover, as Justice Scalia pointed out in his concurrence in the *Harris* v. *Forklift Systems* case discussed earlier, the legal standards being given to juries in such cases are often themselves quite vague and ambiguous. Although the 1991 act limits the amount of monetary award on a sliding scale according to employer size, companies are taking steps to try to keep Title VII cases away from juries.

One way employers are achieving this is by getting employees to agree, in a written agreement before they are hired, that any discrimination claim arising during the course of employment will be submitted for **arbitration** rather than to the courts. The U.S. Supreme Court in the 1991 case of *Gilmer* v. *Interstate/Johnson Lane* upheld such a mandatory arbitration clause in the securities industry.[57]

Recently the U.S. Supreme Court handed employers a further victory by ruling that companies can insist that workplace disputes go to arbitration rather than to court. Thus arbitration is another important enforcement vehicle for disputes that would otherwise go to court.[58] The 5–4 ruling by the U.S. Supreme Court in *Circuit City Stores, Inc.* v. *Adams* means, in essence, that an employer can enforce a signed agreement that obligates an employee to take all employment-related disputes to arbitration under the Federal Arbitration Act (FAA) rather than to court.[59] The case arose when former Circuit City employee Saint Clair Adams sued, claiming that Circuit City had discriminated against him because of his sexual orientation. As a condition of his employment, Adams had signed an agreement to submit all employment-related claims to a neutral arbitrator.[60] Employers who do not now require employment-related disputes to be resolved through arbitration are likely to look at the benefits of such a procedure now that there is no question on the basic issue of enforceability.

● **Family and Medical Leave Act of 1993**   The **Family and Medical Leave Act** (FMLA) was signed into law by President Clinton on February 5, 1993, and became generally effective on August 5, 1993. The law's enactment followed eight years of congressional debate of this controversial legislation and a veto of the bill by President George H. W. Bush. The law applies to all employers with fifty or more employees. To be eligible for coverage under the act, employees must have worked for the given employer for at least 1,250 hours during a minimum of twelve months. Certain highly paid employees are exempt from coverage under the act.

Eligible employees qualify for a total of up to twelve weeks of unpaid leave during any twelve-month period in one or more of the following circumstances:

1. The birth of a child to an employee and the need to care for the child
2. Placement of a child with the employee for adoption or foster care
3. Caring for a spouse, child, or parent with a serious health condition
4. The employee's own serious health condition

Moreover, when an employee returns to work after the leave, he or she generally is entitled to return to the position formerly occupied, if that position remains available. If that position is no longer available, the employee has the right to an "equivalent" position with equivalent pay, benefits, and working conditions. Employees on leave pursuant to the act are entitled to have their health benefits maintained while on leave. However, employees are expected to give their employers thirty days' notice that leave is needed, if such notice is at all practicable. Husbands and wives both working for the same employer can take only a combined total of twelve weeks of leave during a twelve-month period for certain situations, such as the birth of a child. Some individual states have enacted leave legislation that is broader in scope than the federal legislation, and employers in those states are required to follow the state laws.

Numerous policy arguments were raised during the long debate leading to the Family and Medical Leave Act. Proponents of the legislation pointed to the facts that today approximately 65 percent of mothers work outside the home and that many parents head single-parent homes. Without leave legislation, the care of a sick child would be problematic. In addition, proponents of the legislation pointed to the comprehensive leave legislation existing in other countries, such as France's sixteen weeks of leave at 90 percent of normal pay.

Opponents of the legislation primarily objected to the fact that it represented a new government mandate for employers. They argued that this new cost to employers could hurt employees not in need of family leave—and also job seekers in "high-risk" leave categories, since employers would be reluctant to hire such individuals.

The Family and Medical Leave Act is administered by the U.S. Department of Labor, which commissioned a study of the act's effectiveness in 2000. Two surveys were involved: (1) interviews with more than 2,500 employed U.S. residents and (2) interviews with human resource directors of more than 1,800 U.S. private business establishments. Notable findings were as follows:[61]

- One-sixth of all employees (16.5 percent) took leave for a family or medical reason in the eighteen months prior to the 2000 survey.
- Over half (52.4 percent) of all employees who took leave did so because of their own health, while 18.5 percent did so to care for a new baby (newborn, adopted, or foster child), 13 percent to care for an ill parent, and 11.5 percent to care for an ill child.
- Only 2.4 percent of employees needing leave could not take it, the most common reason being the inability to afford the leave (77.6 percent of those needing but not taking leave).
- One-sixth (16 percent) of establishments covered by the FMLA and 41 percent of employees (at both covered and noncovered establishments) were not aware of the act.
- A large majority of those taking leave said that it had positive effects on their ability to care for family members (78.7 percent), their own or family members'

emotional well-being (70.1 percent), and their own or family members' physical health (63.0 percent).

- Two-thirds of those taking leave (65.8 percent) received at least some pay during their leave.

Clearly the FMLA is providing the opportunity for employed individuals to respond to family needs while at the same time protecting their jobs.

Executive Orders

Presidential **executive orders** are another type of document that addresses employment discrimination. **Executive Order 11246,** issued by President Lyndon Johnson in 1965, prohibits discrimination based on race, color, religion, or national origin. **Executive Order 11375,** issued in 1967, prohibits discrimination based on sex. Both these executive orders apply to federal agencies and companies with federal contracts of $10,000 or more. The Office of Federal Contract Compliance Programs (OFCCP) within the Department of Labor ensures that federal contractors comply with the provisions of these executive orders.

Whereas Title VII prohibits discrimination, Executive Orders 11246 and 11375 establish the concept of **affirmative action** for organizations. These executive orders require employers to take the following affirmative actions:

- Treat job applicants and employees without regard to race, color, religion, or national origin.
- State in advertisements that all applicants will be treated equally.
- Tell all labor unions and subcontractors associated with the company about the company's commitments under the orders.
- Include the equal opportunity obligation in all subcontracts and purchase orders.
- Comply with all provisions of the orders and provide information to federal agencies when requested.
- File regular compliance reports describing hiring and other employment practices.

● **"Glass Ceiling" Initiative and Beyond**   On August 9, 1991, the Labor Department issued its "Report on the Glass Ceiling Initiative." This report, the result of an intensive study by the OFCCP of nine corporate work forces, focused on the general paucity of women and minorities in top managerial positions in the nation's largest corporations. This lack of minorities and women in top positions has been termed a "glass ceiling," which women and minorities can see through but not get through. The report made recommendations regarding development, training, and other approaches designed to facilitate the movement of women and minorities into the executive suite. As noted earlier, the Civil Rights Act of 1991 established a special glass ceiling commission to study these issues further.

As concerns regarding workplace diversity have grown, attention has focused not only on invisible barriers (glass ceilings) preventing women and minorities from attaining executive positions but also on invisible barriers that may exist regarding effective communication and working relations within organizations. Clearly, such "glass walls" frequently inhibit positive interaction among individuals with differing backgrounds within organizations. An important objective for the multicultural organization of today is to work toward breaking through such barriers.[62]

Affirmative Action Plans   Companies with federal contracts (of $10,000 or more) must formulate detailed **affirmative action plans (AAPs)** to ensure their compliance. Additionally, nonconstruction contractors with fifty or more employees and contracts of $50,000 or more must develop written affirmative action plans for each of their establishments. These AAPs consist of four parts:

1. A utilization analysis that shows the percentage of men, women, and minorities employed in the company
2. An availability analysis that indicates the availability of men, women, and minorities in the relevant labor market
3. An identification of problem areas (using utilization and availability data) that lists any inequities between the availability and actual representation of men, women, and minorities in the company
4. Corrective actions, with goals and timetables, that outline the employer's plans to achieve employment parity

Utilization Analysis   The employer identifies the number of men, women, and minorities who are employed in each job group (utilized) within the company. The employer also may collect data on the nature of recent hiring decisions (e.g., out of twenty recent applicants hired for the job of carpenter, ten were women) and on the number of offers made to minority applicants (e.g., ten blacks were offered the job of first-line production supervisor, but only one accepted). Other data might include a work force comparison of the employer and similar companies in the same geographic region or a statistical report on the increase in the company's minority or female employees over a designated time period.

Availability Analysis   In its AAP, the employer must indicate the availability of men, women, and minorities in the relevant labor market. Any minority group making up 2 percent or more of the labor market should be considered. There is considerable disagreement over what geographic area constitutes the appropriate labor market from which to collect data. Factors that affect the appropriateness of the geographic region are (1) the area in which the employer presently recruits employees, (2) the area in which current employees and job applicants typically live, (3) the availability of public transportation, and (4) the type of job involved. Even when the appropriate geographic region can be determined, there remains the problem of identifying exactly how many qualified, potentially employable individuals live in that region. As a result, the availability analysis can become a fairly subjective process.

Identification of Problem Areas   The employer examines utilization and availability data for instances of underutilization—that is, where utilization is less than availability—or for instances of concentration—that is, where certain jobs are filled almost exclusively by members of a particular sex or minority.

Table 5.4 presents hypothetical utilization and availability analyses for Acme Electronics Corporation. A comparison of row 2 (percent of utilization) and rows 8 and 10 shows that black women are both seeking work and qualified at a

● **TABLE 5.4**

Hypothetical Utilization and Availability Analyses: Acme Electronics Corporation

Job group: Technicians
Relevant labor area: Standard Metropolitan Statistical Area
Prepared by: J. B. Shaw, EEO Coordinator
Date: 2/6/98

		Total	Male	Female	White Male	White Female	Black Male	Black Female
Utilization	1. Size of utilized population	500	350	150	200	140	150	10
	2. Percent of utilization	100%	70%	30%	40%	28%	30%	2%
Availability	3. Size of available population	100,000	49,000	51,000	20,000	21,000	29,000	30,000
	4. Percent of availability	100%	49%	51%	20%	21%	29%	30%
	5. Size of work force	60,000	36,000	24,000	16,200	14,400	19,800	9,600
	6. Percent of work force	100%	60%	40%	27%	24%	33%	16%
	7. Individuals seeking work	3,500	1,925	1,575	578	709	1,347	866
	8. Percent seeking work	100%	55%	45%	17%	20%	29%	24%
	9. Individuals with requisite skills in reasonable recruiting area	42,000	25,200	16,800	13,104	9,240	12,096	7,560
	10. Percent of individuals with requisite skills	100%	60%	40%	31%	22%	29%	18%

Note: In actual utilization and availability data, information would be presented for total, male, female, white male and female, black male and female, Hispanic male and female, Asian male and female, and American Indian male and female.

Source: Adapted from *EEO Compliance Manual*, 1979. Reprinted by permission of Prentice-Hall, Inc., Englewood Cliffs, New Jersey.

considerably higher rate than their current utilization for the job group of technicians. White men and women are somewhat overutilized. Black male utilization and availability are relatively equal—that is, parity exists for black men. This table also reflects an instance of concentration. Since 70 percent of the technicians are men, men are concentrated in this job group.

Corrective Actions, with Goals and Timetables   If utilization problems exist, the company must develop a set of specific actions that will achieve parity. At Acme Electronics, these actions might include increasing recruitment efforts at predominantly black universities, advertising in women's magazines, or developing special training programs to help current (particularly black) female employees acquire skills that would allow them to become technicians. The employer must specify the goals it hopes to achieve by these actions and the targeted deadlines for their achievement. Acme Electronics, for example, might set the goal of increasing the number of black female technicians by 100 percent (from ten to twenty) within two years.

The Current Debate over Affirmative Action   Almost forty years after the establishment of affirmative action, a debate rages over whether it has done any good or, even if it has, whether its continuation is a necessity. There is little doubt that things have changed in these four decades. In 1964, when affirmative action went into effect, the work force was comprised of 10.7 percent minority workers and 34 percent women. Today minority workers account for 25 percent and women almost 50 percent of the work force.[63] Despite the progress, many would argue that there continues to be a role for affirmative action. The issue today is not so much organizational entry as advancement. In the 500 largest U.S. firms, 97 percent of senior managers are white; an almost equal percentage are male.[64]

Given the past progress and current needs, why is there so much animosity surrounding affirmative action? The idea of affirmative action is an emotional issue to many on both sides of the debate. Some believe that, within reason, a preference should be given to those members of protected groups (e.g., minorities and women) who have been the objects of past discrimination. Those supporting affirmative action are not concerned that the current members of the protected groups may not, themselves, have been victims of discrimination, since the goal is a preference to correct past discrimination.

Those against affirmative action believe that employment policy should not favor one group over another. They believe that affirmative action should not be used to remedy the effects of either actual or historical discrimination in such a way as to benefit nonvictims to the detriment of those who are not members of a protected class.

To date, the most visible anti–affirmative action effort was the successful 1996 California ballot initiative, which stated:

> The state [of California] shall not discriminate against, or grant preferential treatment to, any individual or group on the basis of race, sex, color, ethnicity, or national origin in the operation of public employment, public education, or public contracting.

In addition to the California initiative, the Supreme Court ruled that preferential treatment based on race is almost always unconstitutional. Further, several federal courts have prohibited universities from offering scholarships to minorities

A DIFFERENT POINT OF VIEW

Individualism: The Only Cure for Organizational Racism
By E. A. Locke

It is now taken as a virtual axiom that the way to cure racism is through the promulgation of racial and ethnic diversity within corporations, universities, government agencies, and other institutions. The diversity movement has many facets: diversity awareness, diversity training, diversity hiring and admissions, diversity promotions, and diversity accommodations (e.g., black student organizations and facilities at universities). The common feature in all these facets is: racial preference.

If diversity is the cure, however, why, instead of promoting racial harmony, has it brought racial division and conflict? The answer is not hard to discover. The unshakable fact is that *you cannot cure racism with racism.* To accept the diversity premise means to think in racial terms rather than in terms of individual character or merit. Taking jobs away from one group in order to compensate a second group to correct injustices caused by a third group who mistreated a fourth group at an earlier point in history (e.g., 1860) is ab-surd on the face of it and does not promote justice; rather, it does the opposite. Singling out one group for special favors (e.g., through affirmative action) breeds justified resentment and fuels the prejudices of real racists. People are individuals; they are not interchangeable ciphers in an amorphous collective.

Consider a more concrete, though fictional, example. Suppose that since its creation in 1936, the XYZ Corporation refused to hire redheaded men due to a quirky bias on the part of its founder. The founder now dies and an enlightened Board of Directors decides that something "positive" needs to be done to compensate for past injustices and announces that, henceforth, redheads will be hired on a preferential basis. Observe that (1) this does not help the real victims—the previously excluded redheads; (2) the newly favored redheads have not been victims of discrimination in hiring, yet unfairly benefit from it; and (3) the non-redheads who are now excluded from jobs due to the redhead preference did not cause the previous discrimination and are now unfairly made victims of it.

solely on the basis of race.[65] Opponents of affirmative action think that it makes the goal of a colorblind society more difficult to achieve. Affirmative action started out as a means to attain nondiscrimination and equal opportunity but wound up trying to allocate opportunities on the basis of proportionalism by using only two variables, race and gender.[66] (For a further argument against quotas, see A Different Point of View.)

The fragility of affirmative action at the present time is illustrated by the case of *Board of Education of the Township of Piscataway* v. *Taxman*.[67] In 1989, the Piscataway (New Jersey) school board was faced with the need to lay off one of the ten teachers in the high school business department. Seniority guided the decision, but the two junior teachers, Sharon Taxman and Debra Williams, had been hired on the same day. The board, relying on its affirmative action plan, laid off Taxman, a white, in preference to Williams, the only black teacher in the department. Taxman filed suit, which the U.S. Supreme Court agreed to hear on appeal in mid-1997. Five months later a broad coalition of civil rights groups agreed to pay about 70 percent of the $433,500 needed to pay Taxman's back salary and legal bills to settle the case. The civil rights groups feared that the Court's mere acceptance of

The proper solution, of course, is simply to stop discriminating based on irrelevant factors. Although red-headed bias is not a social problem, the principle does not change when you replace hair color with skin color.

The traditional and essentially correct solution to the problem of racism has always been colorblindness. But this well-intentioned principle comes at the issue negatively. The correct principle is *individuality awareness.* In the job sphere there are only three essential things an employer needs to know about an individual applicant: (1) Does the person have the relevant ability and knowledge (or the capacity to learn readily)? (2) Is the person willing to exert the needed effort? and (3) Does the person have good character, for example, honesty, integrity?

It will be argued that the above view is too "idealistic" in that people often make judgments of other people based on nonessential attributes such as skin color, gender, religion, nationality, and so forth. This, of course, does happen. But the solution is not to abandon the ideal but to implement it consistently. Thus, organizational training should focus not on diversity-worship but on how to objectively assess or measure ability, motivation, and character in other people.

The proper alternative to diversity, that is, to focusing on the collective, is to focus on the individual and to treat each individual according to his or her own merits. Americans have always abhorred the concept of royalty, that is, granting status and privilege based on one's hereditary caste, because it contradicts the principle that what counts are the self-made characteristics possessed by each individual. Americans should abhor racism, *in any form,* for the same reason.

With a few heroic exceptions, such as Nucor and Cypress Semiconductor, which have defied quota pressures, business leaders (following the intellectuals) have been terror-stricken at the thought that there is any alternative to diversity. Their belief—that you can cure racism with racial quotas—is a hopeless quest with nothing but increased conflict and injustice as the end. It is time that business leaders find the courage to assert and defend the only true antidote to the problem of racism: individualism.

Source: "Individualism: The Only Cure for Organizational Racism" by Edwin A. Locke, *The Industrial Organizational Psychologist,* April 1997. Reprinted by permission of the author.

the *Taxman* case signaled its intent to end all voluntary programs designed to achieve a more diverse work force. The civil rights groups viewed the case as "atypical" and were reluctant to see it as the basis for the potential rethinking of all affirmative action in employment.

As one observer stated, "America has been a country that corrects laws in one direction and corrects them in another, then over-corrects and over-corrects."[68] Clearly the correction is underway with respect to affirmative action, and the end result continues to be in the balance.

● **The Problem of Reverse Discrimination**   One problem that organizations often face when specifying goals and timetables for affirmative action programs is **reverse discrimination.** Title VII prohibits discrimination in employment based on race, color, sex, national origin, or religion. Because previous hiring practices have often been discriminatory, many companies have implemented selection procedures designed not only to prevent discrimination but also to make up for and correct for the effects of past discrimination. For example, an organization might have established a hiring quota to increase the number of women in managerial positions; this quota might require that one female manager be hired for every male hired. Inevitably, the question before the courts has become: Do such voluntary quota systems constitute a form of illegal reverse discrimination against nonminority males?

Steelworkers v. Weber   In *Steelworkers* v. *Weber* (1979), the Supreme Court ruled that a quota system used by Kaiser Aluminum and Chemical Corporation to admit persons into a training program did not constitute illegal reverse discrimination because the quota system was designed to correct the effects of the company's past discriminatory practices against blacks.[69] The *Weber* decision has been supported in several later court rulings, which have strongly backed the use of voluntary procedures to correct for past discrimination.[70]

Firefighters Local Union 1784 v. Stotts   One important case indicates that actions taken as part of bona fide seniority systems may take precedence over voluntary quota systems. The city of Memphis, Tennessee, had instituted procedures to increase the number of minority firefighters in its employ. During a period of layoffs, however, a "last hired, first fired" policy was implemented, which had an adverse impact on recently hired black firefighters. In *Firefighters Local Union 1784* v. *Stotts* (1984), the Supreme Court supported the seniority-based layoff policy and ruled that black firefighters could claim protection from the policy only if they had personally and directly been the object of hiring discrimination by the city of Memphis.[71] (Later in this chapter we outline some steps that management can take to minimize the possibility that a quota system set up as part of an AAP will result instead in reverse discrimination.)

City of Richmond v. J. A. Croson   The city of Richmond, Virginia, had enacted an ordinance requiring prime contractors on city projects to subcontract at least 30 percent of the dollar amount to minority-owned businesses. The ordinance was passed in response to the fact that virtually none of the city's contracts had been awarded to minority businesses, even though 50 percent of the city's population was black. No direct evidence, however, was ever uncovered to prove that the city or its prime contractors actually discriminated against minorities. In *City of Richmond* v. *J. A. Croson* (1989), the U.S. Supreme Court ruled that the city of Richmond's program violated the equal protection clause of the U.S. Constitution because no evidence had been presented to demonstrate specific instances of minority discrimination. Set-aside programs of this kind would thus be permissible only if designed to correct demonstrable acts of past discrimination.[72] The Supreme Court's *Croson* decision put into question minority business set-aside programs in nearly forty states and 200 cities and counties throughout the United States.

Adarand Constructors, Inc. v. Pena   The U.S. Supreme Court, in the case of *Adarand Constructors, Inc.* v. *Pena* (1995), ruled that preferential treatment based on race is almost always unconstitutional.[73] The 5–4 ruling was based on a case in Colorado in which Adarand, a white-owned Colorado-based highway construction company specializing in guardrail work, submitted the low bid. Gonzales Construction Company also submitted a bid and was awarded the contract based on its minority status. After losing the guardrail subcontract to Gonzales, Adarand filed suit claiming that the race-based decision violated his right to equal protection. In its decision, the Supreme Court supported Adarand's claim.

Uniform Guidelines

In 1978, the EEOC, along with several other government agencies, issued a set of guidelines for hiring employees. These guidelines, officially called the *Uniform Guidelines on Employee Selection Procedures* (also called the **Uniform Guidelines**), outline what organizations should do to avoid illegal discrimination in selecting employees.[74] The EEOC has also issued special guidelines on sex, national origin, age, and religious discrimination. Although organizations are not required to follow the practices detailed in the *Uniform Guidelines,* the EEOC uses them to determine which charges of discrimination brought to it are legitimate and should be taken to court. In November 1991, a major controversy erupted when the White House "floated" a proposed executive directive dismantling the *Uniform Guidelines.* This proposed directive was quickly rescinded on the personal order of President George H. W. Bush.

ENFORCEMENT OF EEO LAWS AND REGULATIONS

In the majority of EEO cases, individuals who believe that they have been discriminated against bring complaints to the EEOC or to the OFCCP (although the OFCCP usually turns individual discrimination complaints over to the EEOC). These agencies examine the facts of each case, decide whether or not illegal discrimination has occurred, and attempt to arrange a settlement between the individual and the organization. If no settlement is reached, the agencies cannot force a settlement on an employer but may take the issue to federal court. The courts can force an organization to make changes in its selection or other HR practices.

The individual who files a complaint with the EEOC or OFCCP is called the complainant or the charging party. In court, this individual may be called the plaintiff. The organization against which the complaint is filed may be referred to as the respondent or, in court, as the defendant.

As described previously, more and more employers are likely to require employees to sign an agreement to submit all employment-related disputes to a neutral arbitrator under the Federal Arbitration Act. Thus arbitration becomes a further method of enforcing EEO regulations.

Equal Employment Opportunity Commission

Besides Title VII problems, the EEOC handles issues related to the Equal Pay Act, the Pregnancy Discrimination Act, the Age Discrimination in Employment Act, and the Americans with Disabilities Act. The major activity of the agency is to process charges of discrimination related to these laws. Discrimination charges filed with the EEOC increased in the early part of the 1990s but more recently have decreased.

Table 5.3 shows the number of private-sector charges received over a seven-year period. Charges received peaked at 117,510 in fiscal year 1994 and then decreased in subsequent years.[75] Approximately one-quarter of the charges were for racial discrimination, with sex discrimination close behind in the percent of cases filed. Age and disabilities discrimination also accounted for a sizable number of the charges filed. Since resolutions included charges received during previous periods, the number of resolutions exceeded charges in recent years.

Of interest, in each year approximately 80 to 90 percent of the charges filed with the EEOC were determined to have no reasonable cause (approximately 45 to 58 percent) or were dropped administratively (approximately 21 to 39 percent). Administrative closure generally stems from the failure of the charging party to respond to EEOC communications. (Remember, given the EEOC backlog, communication may be many months after the charge was filed, and the problem may have been resolved.) The conclusion of "no cause" means that there is no reason to believe discrimination occurred based on the evidence examined. The charging party may request a review in such "no cause" findings and may exercise the right to bring private court action. Also of interest, the EEOC brings suit in less than 1 percent of cases. An example of such a suit is the case of the drug maker Astra USA, discussed earlier.

A schematic of the EEOC's charge processing procedure is presented in Figure 5.2. Procedural steps must occur within certain time limits after the discriminatory act has occurred; these time limits are included in the figure.

● **The Charge**   A charge is filed against an organization, usually by a private individual. This charge must be made to the federal EEOC or to a state or local EEO agency within 180 days of the occurrence of the allegedly discriminatory act. If the charge is first processed by a state or local agency, and if that agency's actions are not satisfactory to the individual, the individual has up to 300 days from the occurrence, or 30 days after the state or local agency has concluded its investigation and rulings, to file with the federal EEOC.[76]

● **The Investigation**   The EEOC must investigate the charge to see whether discrimination has occurred. The EEOC may interview the complainant and personnel in the organization (e.g., supervisors or coworkers) to determine the facts; the EEOC also may ask the organization to provide data (from personnel files) relevant to the charge. Once the investigation is complete, the EEOC makes a ruling. An example of an EEOC ruling is presented in Figure 5.3. The EEOC may rule that there is reasonable cause to believe that discrimination has occurred. If reasonable cause is found, the EEOC attempts to conciliate the dispute. If no reasonable cause is found, the EEOC dismisses the case. Complainants may then, on their own, file suit against the company in federal court.

● **The Conciliation Meeting**   An EEOC mediator (conciliator) meets first with the complainant to work out an acceptable settlement and then tries to get the employer to agree to it. This process of trying to reach an out-of-court settlement is called **conciliation.** The conciliator then draws up a conciliation agreement, which is signed by the complainant, the employer, and the EEOC. The conciliation agreement is a written document that lists the violations that occurred and the agreed-upon corrective actions that will be taken by the employer. The agreement might include actions such as granting the employee a promotion that had been denied because of discrimination, giving back pay, or instituting new company policies to prevent discrimination in the future. If a conciliation agreement is not achieved, the EEOC may then file suit against the company in federal court or provide a **right-to-sue letter** to the complainant, who can then file suit on his or her own behalf.

● FIGURE 5.2

EEOC Charge-Processing Procedure

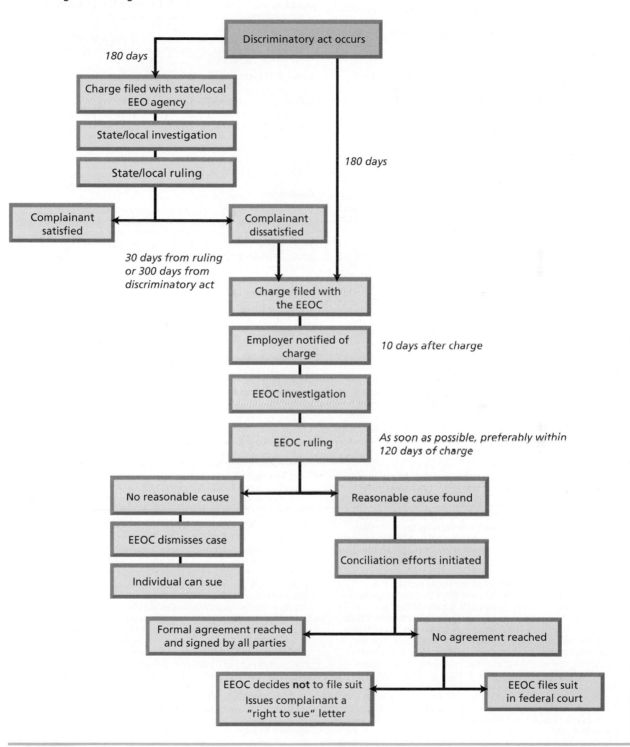

FIGURE 5.3

Example of EEOC Ruling

Summary of Charge

Charging Party, a male, alleges that Respondent unfairly compensated him because of the sex of the students that he coaches in violation of Title VII of the Civil Rights Act of 1964, as amended (the Act), 42 U.S.C. §2000e et seq. (1982).

Summary of Investigation

The Charging Party is a male coaching girls' junior varsity softball who alleges that coaches of boys' sports in comparable positions receive higher compensation for similar work. Charging Party does not allege that he was paid less because of his sex; instead, he claims that he is "being unfairly compensated by the respondent because of the sex of the students that [he] coach[es]."[1] The issue to be resolved is whether Charging Party's allegation that he was unfairly compensated because of the sex of the students he coaches states a claim of discrimination under the Act.

The Charging Party was hired by Respondent school district in 1967 as a school teacher. In the spring of 1980, Charging Party agreed to coach girls' junior varsity softball as a paid extra activity under Respondent's collective bargaining agreement. The agreement provided that persons coaching school sports would be paid $6.93 per hour. Respondent establishes its salary for these positions by estimating the number of hours required to coach each sport for that season and multiplying that estimate by the hourly rate. It bases these estimates upon such factors as number of tournament games, number of pre-season and weekly practice sessions, and additional on-call obligations to serve as assistant or substitute coaches for the school's other varsity teams. Using this formula, girls' junior varsity softball, the sport which Charging Party had agreed to coach, was credited with seventy-five hours and he was paid $519.75 for the season. Boys' reserve baseball was credited with one hundred and fifty hours and its coach was paid $1,039.50 for the season, while boys' freshman baseball was credited with one hundred and twenty-five hours and its coach was paid $866.25 for the season.

Charging party and Respondent agree that all coaches regardless of their sex, the sport they coach, or the sex of the persons they coach, receive the same $6.93 per hour for their coaching duties according to the requirements of Respondent's collective bargaining agreement. There is no dispute between the parties concerning the facts and circumstances which gave rise to this charge.

Section 703(a)(1) of the Act makes it unlawful for an employer "to discriminate against any individual with respect to this compensation, terms, conditions, or privileges of employment, because of such individual's . . . sex[.]"

The issue of whether, under the Act, a claim of disparate treatment in the payment of salaries can be based upon the sex of the students being coached was addressed in *Jackson* v. *Armstrong School District*, 438 F. Supp. 1050 (W.D. Penn. 1977). Accord, *Kenneweg* v. *Hampton Township School District*, 438 F. Supp. 575 (W.D. Penn. 1977). In *Jackson*, female coaches claimed that their employer had violated the Act by denying them higher wages because they coached women's sports. They did not allege that they had been denied positions coaching men's sports because of their sex. The court dismissed the female coaches claim for failure to state a claim of discrimination on the basis of their sex, as Section 703(a)(1) of the Act requires. The court pointed out that "[i]t is clear from the statute that the sex of the claimants must be the basis of the discriminatory conduct. Here plaintiffs are not discriminated against because of *their* sex." *Jackson*, 430 F. Supp. at 1052 (emphasis in original).[2] In reaching its decision that the female coaches had not stated a claim under the Act, the court in Jackson relied on the Fifth Circuit Court of Appeals decision in *Stroud* v. *Delta Airlines, Inc.*, 554 F.2d 892 (5th Cir.), cert. denied, 434 U.S. 844 (1977), where the court stated:

The Supreme Court has noted that the objective of Congress in passing the Civil Rights Act of 1964, of which the sex discrimination provision was a part, was to achieve equality of employment opportunity and to remove certain barriers. These barriers are those which operate to favor one group of employees *identifiable* by race, color, religion, sex, or national origin. *Alexander* v. *Gardner Denver Co.*, 415 U.S. 36 . . . [1974] . . .

Stroud at 893 (emphasis in original).

It is the Commission's view, based upon the plain language of the statute and the courts' interpretation of it, that a change which alleges discrimination on the basis of the sex of the persons that the charging party is coaching does not state a claim of discrimination under the Act. It is necessary that the claim of discrimination be based upon the sex, race, religion, color or national origin of the charging party as required by Section 703(a)(1)[3] or on the basis of retaliation as required by Section 704(a) of the Act.

Conclusion

The Commission is without authority to process this charge because Charging Party has failed to state a claim under the Act. This charge is returned to the District Office for dismissal pursuant to Section 1601.19 of the Commission's Procedural Regulations, 29 C.F.R. §1601.19 (1984) and Section 4.4 of Volume I of the Commission's Compliance Manual.

[1] The Charging Party does not allege, and the evidence does not show, that the coaches of girls' sports are predominantly women and that, because of that fact, the coaches of girls' sports, including the Charging Party, are being discriminatorily compensated. Therefore, that issue is not addressed in this decision.

[2] The court in *Jackson* recognized that if it were to allow the claim of the female coaches, it would also have to allow the claim of the male coaches who might allege that their employers discriminated against them on the basis of the sex of the persons that they were coaching. The court stated:

Following [the female coaches'] argument further[.] the male coaches of women's basketball would be free to lodge the same charge. In turn we envision the anomalous situation of the school district, which shows no sexual preference towards women's basketball coaches, being sued for discriminatory practices. This is not what Title VII says nor contemplates. It was designed to curb discriminatory practices committed against certain classes—e.g., sex, race, or ethnic derivation—of employees with the idealistic goal of engendering parity for all.

Jackson v. *Armstrong School District*, 430 F. Supp. 1050, 1052 (W.D. Penn. 1977).

[3] Claims of persons holding coaching positions alleging discrimination on the basis of their sex have uniformly been recognized by the courts. *Harrington* v. *Vandalia-Butler Board of Education*, 418 F. Supp. 603, 606 (S.D. Ohio), rev'd on other grounds, 585 F.2d 192 (6th cir. 1978), cert. denied, 441 U.S. 932 (1979) (female physical education teacher stated claim when she alleged discrimination on basis of her sex because of her employer's failure to provide her with adequate instruction area, adequate office space, and private shower and toilet facilities, similar to those provided to male physical education teachers); *Strong* v. *Demopolis City Board of Education et al.* 515 F. Supp. 730, (S.D. Ala. 1981) (female coach who alleged she was paid less than a male coach because of her sex stated claim under the Act); and *Burkey* v. *Marshall County Board of Education.* 513 F. Supp. 1084 (N.D. W. Va. 1981) (refusal to hire female coach for male sports and paying equally qualified female coach less than male coaches with comparable duties discriminated against the female coach on the basis of her sex).

● **EEOC and Judicial Enforcement**   The EEOC enforces the laws through conciliation agreements or the federal courts. The courts may order a company to take the following actions:

- Remedy the effects of past discrimination by granting back pay, promotions, or retroactive seniority to specific individuals who have been discriminated against.[77]
- Cease discrimination by modifying discriminatory policies and practices or by using temporary quotas to achieve racial balance.[78]
- Pay the attorney's fees of the complainant.

Office of Federal Contract Compliance Programs

The OFCCP enforces the provisions of executive orders relating to employment discrimination. A primary function of the OFCCP is to conduct reviews to ensure that the affirmative action programs required by executive orders are carried out. The review process used by the OFCCP is outlined in Figure 5.4.

● **Types of Reviews**   The OFCCP may conduct a complaint investigation when an individual files a complaint of discrimination against a company. The OFCCP often turns the complaint over to the EEOC but can choose to investigate the complaint itself. A preaward review of an organization may be conducted before it receives a federal contract. A regular compliance review may be conducted of an organization covered by executive orders, even if no complaint of discrimination has been filed.

● **The Review Procedure**   In the first phase of a review—the **desk audit**—the OFCCP requests the contractor to provide relevant information about its recruitment activities, hiring practices, and the makeup of its present work force. The OFCCP reviews this material to see whether there is evidence of discrimination or whether practices dictated by the executive orders are being followed. If there is no evidence of violations, the review may end. If possible violations are found, the OFCCP conducts an on-site review and seeks other information to confirm or refute the violations. The OFCCP may request additional personnel data and conduct interviews with company employees. When the on-site review is completed, the OFCCP may take additional information from the company and conduct an off-site analysis.

● **OFCCP Decisions**   The OFCCP may take one of three actions:

- Notify the contractor that it is in compliance.
- Find that the contractor is not in compliance and turn the case over to the Justice Department for prosecution in the federal courts.
- Find that the contractor is not in compliance, issue a show-cause statement, and attempt to remedy the violations through additional OFCCP involvement.

A **show-cause statement** includes a list of the violations that the OFCCP has identified, a list of actions that the contractor must take to correct these violations, and a request that the contractor reply in writing as to how it will correct the violations and/or present further evidence to prove that no violations have actually occurred. If a satisfactory agreement is not reached, the OFCCP may enforce its decision using administrative procedures or turn the case over to the Justice Department.

● **FIGURE 5.4**

OFCCP Review Procedure

● **Administrative and Judicial Enforcement**   The OFCCP may enforce its rulings by taking the case to an administrative law judge within the Department of Labor. This judge can rule against the company and (1) cancel the company's federal contract, (2) suspend the company from receiving contracts for a specified time period, (3) permanently prevent the company from receiving federal contracts, or (4) take other appropriate actions.

Alternatively, the OFCCP can turn the case over to the Justice Department at several junctures before or after a show-cause statement has been issued. The Justice Department decides whether the case is strong enough to take to court. The court can provide "injunctive relief"—that is, make the company stop acting in ways that violate the executive orders, suspend or cancel the company's federal contracts, and/or institute other actions similar to the methods of EEOC enforcement discussed earlier.

In the spring of 1994, the OFCCP released a working paper asserting that the agency's current enforcement and sanctions provisions had not been particularly effective in inducing federal contractors to identify problem areas and correct them. Toward this end, various new sanctions were proposed, including (1) imposing remedial monetary fines, (2) withholding contract progress payments, and (3) debarring government contracts for a fixed term.

The Federal Courts

Typically, the federal court system serves as the final step in the enforcement of EEO laws. A discrimination suit may pass through three levels in the federal court system. First, the suit is filed in a federal district court. The Civil Rights Act of 1991 allows discrimination cases to be brought to a jury. Prior to this act, all Title VII cases were decided by judges. If the decision is appealed, then the case goes to the federal district circuit court of appeals, which usually has three or more judges who hear the case as a panel. Finally, from the circuit courts, the case may be appealed to the U.S. Supreme Court.

PROVING ILLEGAL DISCRIMINATION

The court system has a very formal process for establishing guilt in EEO cases. This process is associated with the concept of burden of proof. The plaintiff provides evidence to indicate a **prima facie case** of discrimination. *Prima facie* simply means "on the face of it" or "at first sight." The evidence presented must suggest, at first sight, that the employer has discriminated. Once a prima facie case has been established, the burden of proof shifts to the employer, who has the opportunity to show that its actions were not illegal and are justified by sound business reasons.

The Prima Facie Case

The most direct way to establish a prima facie case is to show that the employer overtly discriminated against a member of a protected class. Statements by the employer such as "We do not hire blacks as managers" or job advertisements such as "Management trainee position: women need not apply" would make a convincing prima facie case. But rarely do such blatant examples of discrimination exist. A prima facie case is usually established by proving disparate treatment or disparate impact.

● **Disparate Treatment (*McDonnell Douglas Corp.* v. *Green*)** **Disparate treatment** occurs when one employee is treated differently from other workers because of his or her race, sex, national origin, or the like. In such a situation, different standards are applied to different types of people. The court case that most clearly describes how illegal discrimination can be proved in a case of disparate treatment is *McDonnell Douglas Corp.* v. *Green* (1973).[79] In this case, Green, a black mechanic/technician at McDonnell Douglas Corporation, was laid off as part of a company-wide work force reduction. Green protested that his layoff was racially motivated and joined protests against McDonnell Douglas that included blocking highway accesses to the McDonnell Douglas plant. Green was arrested for these protest activities. In 1965, McDonnell Douglas placed job advertisements for qualified mechanics/technicians. Green applied for the job but was rejected. He filed a case of racial discrimination against McDonnell Douglas. In deciding this case, the Supreme Court said that, first, Green had to prove a prima facie case of discrimination by showing the following:

- He was a member of a protected class.
- He applied for a job for which he was qualified.
- He was rejected.
- The employer continued to seek applicants for the job.

These criteria for showing a prima facie case of discrimination have become known as the *McDonnell Douglas* v. *Green* rule. Green's situation met the requirements of this rule and indicated a prima facie case of racial discrimination. The Supreme Court stated, however, that simply showing a prima facie case of discrimination did not end the process: The employer had to be given the chance to defend its actions. In this case, McDonnell Douglas defended itself by stating that Green had been rejected because he had participated in illegal actions against the company (the blocking of highways to the plant). The Supreme Court accepted this defense as reasonable. The Court then stated that Green should have the opportunity to prove that the organization's rationale for his rejection was, in fact, a cover-up for a racially discriminatory decision. The Court suggested that data showing that McDonnell Douglas had rehired white workers, but not black workers, who had committed acts of similar seriousness against the company would be useful in invalidating the company's defense. Data showing that McDonnell Douglas had a general pattern of discriminatory practices against blacks (e.g., that McDonnell Douglas hired very few minority workers for any jobs) also would be useful. The Court indicated that Green had not provided sufficient evidence to refute the company's rationale for rejecting his application.

● **Disparate Impact (*Griggs* v. *Duke Power Co.*)** In *Griggs* v. *Duke Power Co.* (1971),[80] the Supreme Court established the concept of disparate impact as a type of discrimination. The Griggs approach was specifically upheld by Congress in the Civil Rights Act of 1991. **Disparate impact,** also called **adverse impact,** occurs when the same standards are applied to all employees but have very different consequences for particular groups. In the *Griggs* case, Willie Griggs, a black man, applied for the job of coal handler at the Duke Power Company. The company, which required that all coal handlers have high school diplomas, rejected Griggs because he did not. Griggs filed a suit against the company, claiming that the diploma requirement had nothing to do with a person's ability to do the job and that it discriminated against blacks, since a lower percentage of blacks had high school diplomas than did whites. In this case of adverse impact, the Supreme Court ruled that in proving a prima facie case of discrimination, Griggs did not have to show that Duke Power Company intended to discriminate against blacks but simply that the policies of the company had an adverse impact on them. The *Griggs* ruling and other court decisions have held that at least three types of data can be used to show a prima facie case of disparate impact.[81] These types of data are presented in Table 5.5.

TABLE 5.5

Types of Data Used to Show Disparate Impact

Comparison/Type of Data	Ratio 1				Ratio 2				Ratio1/Ratio 2
1. Comparison of Actual Impact	*Minorities[a] Hired*	*Minority Applicants*	*Ratio Hired*	*Percent Hired*	*Majorities Hired*	*Majority Applicants*	*Ratio Hired*	*Percent Hired*	*60% Minorities Hired / 68.2% Majorities Hired*
Hiring data	60	100	60/100	60%	75	110	75/110	68.2%	
2. Comparison of Potential Impact	*All Minorities in Labor Market*	*Qualified[b] Minorities in Labor Market*	*Ratio of Potentially Hireable Minorities*	*Percent of Potentially Hireable Minorities*	*All Majorities in Labor Market*	*Qualified Majorities in Labor Market*	*Ratio of Potentially Hireable Majorities*	*Percent of Potentially Hireable Majorities*	*50% Potentially Hireable Minorities / 80% Potentially Hireable Majorities*
Labor-market data	10,000	5,000	5,000/10,000	50%	25,000	20,000	20,000/25,000	80%	
3. Comparison of Work Force to Population	*Minorities in Company Work Force*	*Total Company Work Force*	*Minority Ratio to Total Work Force*	*Minority Percent of Total Work Force*	*Minorities in Local Population*	*Total Local Population*	*Minority Ratio to Population*	*Minority Percent of Population*	*6% Minorities in Work Force / 41.7% Minorities in Population*
Population and company data	30	500	30/500	6%	25,000	60,000	25,000/60,000	41.7%	

[a] "Minorities" means protected classes such as blacks, Hispanics, or women.

[b] In this context, the term "qualified" means that the person has some specific qualification that the employer seeks in hiring workers (e.g., a high school diploma).

A comparison of the actual impact of selection procedures may be used to determine whether disparate impact exists. In comparison 1 of Table 5.5, the minority members hired–minority applicants ratio is compared with the majority members hired–majority applicants ratio. If these ratios are radically different from each other, the difference would indicate that discrimination might have occurred somewhere in the selection process. Alternatively, if an organization had some specific qualification that it required of employees—a high school diploma in the case of Duke Power Company—disparate impact could be shown by looking at the potential effect the requirement would have on minority and majority applicants.

In comparison 2 of Table 5.5, only 50 percent of the minorities in the labor market have a high school education, as opposed to 80 percent of the majorities. A significant adverse impact could occur if an organization used a high school education as a selection requirement. The third type of disparate impact data involves comparing the proportion of minorities in the company's work force with the proportion of minorities in the local population. If minorities comprise 41.7 percent of the local population but only 6 percent of the company's work force, for example, this inequity might constitute a prima facie case of discrimination.

In *Griggs* v. *Duke Power Co.*, the prima facie case of discrimination was established using data that showed the potential impact of the hiring requirement on black applicants (see comparison 2 of Table 5.5). In rebutting the prima facie case, the company argued (1) that the hiring requirement was fair because it was applied to all applicants and (2) that there was no intention to discriminate. The good intent of the company was demonstrated by its practice of helping to fund the education of workers who attempted to complete their high school education. The Court rejected this defense, saying that impact, not intent, was the key issue in determining discrimination. Furthermore, the company had no proof that having a high school diploma had any fundamental relationship to on-the-job performance of employees.

● **Four-Fifths Rule**   A major question related to proving disparate impact is: How do we decide when the impact is adverse enough to be considered discriminatory? The EEOC has developed a rule of thumb for determining adverse impact. It is called the **four-fifths rule.** The EEOC applies this rule to actual impact data to determine whether a prima facie case of discrimination exists.[82] The rule states that if the minorities hired–minority applicants ratio is less than four-fifths (80 percent) of the majority members hired–majority applicants ratio, then a prima facie case of discrimination exists. For example, in comparison 1 of Table 5.5, the minority ratio is 60/100 (60 percent, or .60), and the majority ratio is 75/110 (68.2 percent, or .682). To compare the two selection rates, 0.60 is divided by 0.682, yielding 0.879 (or 87.9 percent). Thus the minority ratio is greater than four-fifths (or 80 percent) of the majority ratio, and no prima facie case exists.

● **Retaliation**   A special form of disparate treatment is **retaliation.** Employers cannot retaliate—by firing, demoting, harassing, or otherwise treating employees unfairly—because employees have filed discrimination charges. In *EEOC* v. *Union Bank of Arizona* (1976), the Court ruled that protection against retaliation should be extended even to employees who suffered retaliation because their employer mistakenly believed that they had filed a charge.[83] In *United States* v. *City of Socorro* (1976), a federal district court ruled that it was illegal discrimination to retaliate against an employee whose spouse had filed a charge of discrimination.[84] Employees who are retaliated against can get injunctive relief from the retaliation.[85]

Section 706 of Title VII of the Civil Rights Act of 1964 allows the EEOC to seek immediate relief from retaliation for an individual filing a charge of discrimination, even though the EEOC has not completed its processing of the charge.

Rebutting a Prima Facie Case

A company can defend itself against a prima facie case of adverse impact or treatment by using the defenses of job relatedness, bona fide occupational qualification, bona fide seniority system, or business necessity.

● **Job Relatedness**   Showing **job relatedness** is a defense that is appropriate in situations in which an apparently neutral practice of the organization has a disparate impact on some protected class. The company must show that its procedures are related to employee performance. For example, an employer may be able to justify the adverse impact on women caused by a six-foot, two-inch requirement by showing that individuals who are less than six feet, two inches tall have difficulty performing the job. The height requirement would not constitute illegal discrimination because it relates directly to the ability of workers to perform their job.

If an employer can show that individuals who score below seventy on an ability test have difficulty performing the job, then hiring only applicants with scores of seventy or above may be justified, even if this selection requirement adversely affects black applicants. However, proving that a particular hiring requirement is job-related is not easy. In *Albermarle Paper Company* v. *Moody* (1975), Albermarle had used test scores of verbal and nonverbal intelligence in selecting job applicants.[86] The company had hired an industrial psychologist to determine the job relatedness of these tests, and the psychologist had found a significant correlation between test scores and supervisor ratings of employee performance. Moody, a black employee of Albermarle, filed a charge of racial discrimination against the company and successfully proved that the tests had an adverse impact on black job applicants. In ruling on the case, the Supreme Court stated that to show job relatedness, a company must first analyze and document the tasks and responsibilities of the job. The Court also stated that performance standards must be clear and unambiguous so as to allow the employer to accurately determine which employees are high (or low) performers. Albermarle had met neither of these requirements. No systematic job analysis had been conducted, and the performance ratings used were highly subjective and ambiguous in nature. The Court ruled in favor of Moody. A detailed description of how an organization can show the job relatedness of hiring requirements is provided in the *Uniform Guidelines* and is discussed further in Chapter 7.

● **Bona Fide Occupational Qualification**   Another defense against a prima facie case of adverse treatment is the **bona fide occupational qualification (BFOQ).** The BFOQ defense has been interpreted narrowly by both the EEOC and the courts and can be based on age, sex, religion, or national origin but not on race or color. An employer claiming its conduct was based on a BFOQ admits sex-based treatment, for example, but maintains that the differential treatment was necessary to promote legitimate business objectives. Thus, requiring that only male actors be considered for the role of Julius Caesar would be justifiable since "maleness" is an inherent part of the character of Julius Caesar. In *Dothard* v. *Rawlinson* (1977), the Supreme Court held that refusing to hire females as prison guards in an all-male prison was justifiable as a BFOQ.[87] Since the BFOQ defense involves the direct use of age, sex, religion, or national origin in making selection decisions, organizations hoping to use this defense must have very convincing evidence to support their cases. In *Diaz* v. *Pan American World Airways* (1971), the company had used sex (only women were hired) as a BFOQ for hiring flight attendants.[88] Pan Am did not have any strong evidence to prove that only women were capable of performing flight attendants' essential duties of serving food and drinks and providing for the safety of the passengers. A federal court ruled that sex was not a BFOQ for the job of flight attendant.

● **Bona Fide Seniority System**   A third possible defense is the **bona fide seniority system.** Organizational actions that result in disparate treatment or disparate impact may be justified if the actions are part of a bona fide seniority system. In *Teamsters* v. *United States* (1977), the Supreme Court decided that seniority systems that had the effect of locking minorities into lower-level jobs were valid as long as the intent of the seniority systems was not to discriminate.[89] The definition of a bona fide seniority system as one that does not intend to discriminate has been supported in other court decisions.[90] In *Firefighters Local Union 1784* v. *Stotts*, discussed earlier, the "last hired, first fired" policy used by the city of Memphis in laying off firefighters had an adverse impact on black employees. Nevertheless, the Supreme Court ruled that the policy was justified because it was part of a bona fide seniority system.

● **Business Necessity**   A final defense is **business necessity.** Employers may justify practices that result in disparate treatment or disparate impact if the actions are essential to efficient and safe operation of the company. In *Furnco Construction Corporation* v. *Waters* (1978), the Supreme Court accepted the company's practice of requiring job applicants to possess certain experience, skills, and training because improper performance of the job could result in serious physical harm to employees.[91] These requirements had an adverse impact on black job applicants but were justified by business necessity. Employers using the business necessity defense generally have been required to prove that there existed an overriding necessity, not simply a convenience for their actions.[92]

MANAGEMENT'S RESPONSE

The final factor in the EEO environment is management and the responses it makes to EEO laws and regulations. In this section we examine the actions that management should take to deal effectively with equal employment opportunity.

Take Control

The most important step in dealing effectively with EEO activities is for management to take control of them in the organization.[93] The key elements of control are information, policy, and communication. An organization should regularly conduct a self-analysis to examine the status of minority, female, and disabled workers. The company may wish to develop and regularly update special logs on a variety of personnel decisions. A sample data log of employee discipline/discharge decisions is presented in Figure 5.5. This information allows the company to identify

● **FIGURE 5.5**

Discipline/Discharge Log

Source: Adapted from
V. Grossman, *Employing
Handicapped Persons:
Meeting EEO Obligations.*
Reprinted by permission of
BNA Books, Washington, D.C.

Location: _____   From: _____   To: _____

Name	Race / Sex	Handi-cap / Age	A. Type of discipline	B. Job-related reason for discipline	C. Job-related reason for discharge	D. Type of separation	Reason for other type of separation	Date recalled or returned if laid off or on leave of absence

Place proper symbols, numbers, or answers in each column.

Race: M—Minority
　　　 NM—Non-minority
Sex:　 F—Female
　　　 M—Male
Handicapped—H
Age—Put age if employee is
　　　40 years of age or older

A. Type of Discipline
1—Verbal warning
2—First written warning
3—Second written warning
4—Demotion
5—Suspension (specify number of days)
6—Discharge

B. Job-Related Reason for Discipline
1—Unsafe work performance
2—Ineffective work performance
3—Failure to obey a supervisor
4—Failure to obey the employer's policy
5—Interfering with the work
　　performance of other employees
6—Unexcused lateness or tardiness
7—Unexcused absences
8—Other (specify)

C. Job-Related Reason for Discharge
1—Did not receive written recommendation to
　　work from drug or alcoholism counselor or
　　physician
2—Did not receive written recommendation to
　　work from physician or counselor because of
　　mental, physical, or emotional condition
3—Unsafe work performance
4—Ineffective work performance
5—Failure to obey a supervisor
6—Failure to obey the employer's policy
7—Interfering with the work performance
　　of other employees
8—Unexcused tardiness
9—Unexcused absences

D. Type of Separation
1—Resignation
2—Layoff
3—Sick leave
4—Other leave of absence
5—Death
6—Retirement
7—Disability
8—Discharge

● FIGURE 5.6
A Corporate Policy
Against Sexual
Harassment of
Employees

Policy of Acme Electronics Corporation

Corporate policy is that all employees have the right to work in an environment free of discrimination. One form of discrimination is sexual harassment. Corporate policy concerning sexual harassment is as follows:

Any employee found engaging in sexual harassment will be subject to:

— Official reprimands that will be placed in the employee's permanent personnel file
— Suspension from work without pay
— Demotion to a lower-paying job assignment
— Discharge from the company
— Other appropriate action

No supervisor shall explicity or implicity threaten that a subordinate's refusal to submit to sexual advances will result in adverse effects on the worker's employment, pay, promotions, assigned duties, or any other condition of employment. Acme employees are prohibited from engaging in behavior of a sexual nature that would create an offensive, unpleasant, or otherwise hostile work environment, e.g., telling jokes of a sexual nature, offensive flirtations, sexual advances or propositions, comments concerning the bodies of members of the opposite sex, or using sexually explicit words that might be considered offensive.

Acme Corporation encourages any employee who feels he/she has been the victim of sexual harassment to report the incident to his/her supervisor or to Bob Farrow, chair of the EEO Compliance Committee (456-2534, Room 423 in the Personnel Office). The incident will be investigated, and corrective action will be taken if appropriate. Acme management is committed to eliminating this type of behavior from our company and will take every step necessary to protect individuals from it.

areas in which disparate impact or disparate treatment may be occurring and provides the basis for a defense of company policies in discrimination suits.

An organization should collect information concerning the potential impact that new HR policies may have on its work force. For example, organizations forced to make layoffs should evaluate the likely impact of these layoffs on minorities, women, and older workers. If need be, the companies could take steps to lessen the adverse effect of the layoffs on these protected groups and thus prevent discrimination complaints.

All organizations should develop formal, written policies concerning equal employment opportunity. An example of such a policy against sexual harassment is presented in Figure 5.6. However, policies are effective only to the extent that they are understood by employees. The Ethical Perspective box addresses another problematic policy area—anti-nepotism rules.

The last element of control is communication. The organization should make sure that EEO policies are displayed widely and prominently throughout the company. The organization should develop special training programs to transmit knowledge of EEO issues and the company's EEO policies to managers, first-line supervisors, and other key employees. The Ethical Perspective box describes problems that can occur when this education effort fails.

Make Procedures Objective and Job-Related

Employers' decisions about hiring, firing, promoting, and providing benefits to employees must be objective and job-related. Testing procedures used to hire employees should be validated using techniques consistent with the EEOC's *Uniform Guidelines*. (These techniques are discussed in more detail in Chapter 7.) When decisions are based on performance evaluations of employees, the procedures used to assess performance should be as objective and directly related to the job as possible. Job analysis should be used to determine the important aspects of job performance. Performance should be assessed by persons who have been trained in performance-rating techniques and have had adequate time to observe the performance of the individual(s) being rated. (The details of how to set up a good performance appraisal system are discussed in Chapter 11.)

Develop Grievance Procedures

In cases of discharges, promotions, or sexual, racial, ethnic, or religious harassment, the availability of formal grievance procedures often aids in resolving complaints of discrimination so that the EEOC's involvement is not necessary. Every employer should have a formal grievance procedure that employees can use to deal with possible cases of discrimination. Such a procedure is usually available in unionized companies. Nonunionized organizations also should develop a formal grievance procedure. Figure 5.7 shows how such a procedure might work. Moreover, as noted earlier, some companies have adopted internal procedures culminating in binding outside arbitration.

Act Affirmatively

If evidence of discrimination exists in the organization, management should develop policies to correct the situation. These plans should be consistent with guidelines set forth by the OFCCP and the EEOC. In developing these plans, organizations should make use of the minority, female, and disabled workers already in the company. These employees, formally brought into the process, can provide useful insights and information about how best to recruit and retain minority, female, and disabled workers. Employers should take into account the Supreme Court decision in *Steelworkers* v. *Weber*, discussed earlier in this chapter. In that case, the Court ruled that voluntary quota systems are acceptable to the extent that employers do the following:

- Avoid quota systems when no evidence of past discrimination exists.
- Develop plans that do not require the discharge of or have other significant ill effects on majority workers.
- Avoid setting minority quotas of greater than 50 percent.
- Develop plans that are temporary in nature and will end once the negative effects of past discrimination are corrected.[94]

Anti-Nepotism Rules—Fair or Unfair?

 "Nepotism is the practice of showing favoritism to relatives and close friends."* Examples would include hiring or promoting a relative largely because of the relationship and at the expense of more qualified candidates who are not related to the decision maker. The authors of a text on business ethics, William Shaw and Vincent Barry, point out that this action "would raise a number of moral concerns; chief among them would be disregard both of managerial responsibilities to the organization and of fairness to all other applicants."†

To prevent this potential conflict of interest and the unfairness that may arise when relatives are hired, a number of organizations have adopted anti-nepotism rules. The most extreme form of rule prohibits the employment of a relative of an employee anywhere in the organization, even at another site. Less extreme rules prohibit the employment of related people at the same site or in the same department. The most limited type of anti-nepotism rule is a no-supervision rule, which states that one may not have decision-making authority (regarding job assignment, appraisal, hiring, or compensation) over a relative.

Anti-nepotism rules were invented to prevent abuses and served this role reasonably well until the explosion in the number of dual-career couples in the 1970s. Suddenly, rules that were intended to prevent the hiring of unqualified relatives were prohibiting the

employment of highly qualified individuals who just happened to be married to current employees. If the spouse is qualified on his or her own merits, a rule intended to ensure fairness in employment now causes unfairness.

A more difficult situation arises when coworkers marry. Presumably both were hired on their own merits, but a no-spouse rule may now decree that one must transfer to another department or leave the organization altogether. Somehow, the presence of one's spouse is presumed to have an immediate and deleterious effect on one's ability to perform the job properly.

Most no-spouse rules are written in sexually neutral language (no spouses, as versus no wives of male employees), but some have been challenged in court. Title VII–based challenges focus on the fact that anti-nepotism rules often have an adverse impact on women. In the case of coworkers who marry, the Fifth and the Fourteenth Amendments, which protect the right to marry, have been invoked. With some exceptions, no-spouse rules have been upheld by the courts. Legality, however, does not guarantee fairness.

Even more complex problems can be created when intimate relationships short of marriage take place between coworkers or between a superior and a subordinate. Should no-spouse rules be applied to coworkers who are cohabiting? Dating? When a boss is romantically involved with a subordinate, perceptions of favoritism may occur, and if the relationship goes sour,

If a Complaint Is Filed

If, despite the best efforts of the organization, an employee files a discrimination complaint with the Equal Employment Opportunity Commission, the actions of management remain critical. Management should make some of the following responses:

1. When notified by the EEOC that a charge has been filed, ask for a copy of the charge to find out precisely what the company has allegedly done.
2. Conduct an internal investigation to see if the charge is valid. During the investigation, take great care not to pressure or harass the individual who made

sexual harassment charges are a possibility. On the other hand, most people feel that legal off-the-job behavior such as dating is a private matter and none of the employer's business.

Some organizations are accommodating dual-career couples by relaxing stringent anti-nepotism rules that were adopted before large numbers of married women entered the labor force. They find that these antiquated rules deny them the services of potentially excellent employees and also complicate the recruiting of professionals, who are often married to other professionals. A sensible policy for many organizations seems to be to emphasize ability and merit, rather than relationship or nonrelationship, in all personnel decisions and, if necessary, to adopt a no-supervision-of-spouses rule. This prevents any suspicion of favoritism and reassures employees who are not related to the boss that evenhanded treatment will prevail. Effective anti-nepotism policies also specify exactly which relationships are covered (stepchildren? third cousins?) and which procedures will be followed should one member of a related pair need to be transferred or terminated.

An alternate approach is taken by firms such as Steelcase, Inc., which intentionally hires married couples and relatives. Usually 10 to 18 percent of new hires are sons or daughters of employees. Quad/Graphics, a large printing company in Wisconsin, reports that over half its employees are related in some fashion. Allowing the employment of relatives helps to create a familylike work atmosphere and may be the only option when a firm is one of few major employers in a small community. However, an exclusive emphasis on hiring relatives might limit diversity and equal opportunity for members of minority groups not traditionally employed by the firm.

Note that in the international arena, nepotism takes on a whole different flavor. In a great many countries, especially those with a collectivist culture, individuals have a positive duty to look after their relatives and friends by employing them. Failing to do so would be a breach of their moral responsibilities. In countries such as Thailand, India, Mexico, Korea, and Indonesia, who you know is said to be more important than what you know, especially in hiring for small and medium-sized organizations. Expatriate managers must be sure they understand the local context before passing harsh judgment on nepotistic practices that would be problematic back home.

*William Shaw and Vincent Barry, *Moral Issues in Business* (Belmont, Calif.: Wadsworth, 1989), p. 240.
†Ibid.
Sources: Len Bierman and Cynthia D. Fisher, "Anti-Nepotism Rules Applied to Spouses: Business and Legal Viewpoints," *Labor Law Journal,* 1984, pp. 634–642; J. M. Steiner and S. P. Steinberg, "Caught Between Scylla and Charybdis: Are Anti-Nepotism Policies Benign Paternalism or Covert Discrimination?" *Employee Relations,* Autumn 1994, pp. 253–267; Richard K. Zuckerman and Sharon N. Berlin, "Romance in the Workplace: Employers Can Make Rules If They Serve Legitimate Needs," *New York State Bar Journal,* September–October 1999; and Bless Stritar Young, "In the Family Way: Drafting Your Anti-Nepotism Policy," *ABA Law Practice Management,* February 2001 (also available at www.abanet.org/lpm/newsarticle11695_front.shtml).

the charge. Such harassment might result in the company's being charged with retaliation.

3. Respond to the charge in writing. The response should be absolutely accurate and clearly state the organization's position. If the internal investigation shows that discrimination actually occurred, management should attempt to reach an equitable settlement with the employee.

4. Cooperate within reasonable limits with the EEOC or the OFCCP. During the EEOC's fact-finding investigation or the OFCCP's compliance review, the agency may ask for a large number and great variety of personnel documents. Management should take the position that it will gladly cooperate but will provide only documents that are relevant to the case at hand. Management need

● **FIGURE 5.7**

EEO Grievance Procedure for Sexual Harassment Complaint

not turn over every available personnel document. Which data are turned over should result from a negotiation between management and the investigators. By providing unrestricted access to personnel data, the saying "Give me enough time and documents, and I'll find something illegal" will surely apply.

Summary of Key Points

There are many different aspects of discrimination under EEO law. These range from broad concepts, such as disparate treatment and disparate impact, to more specific instances, such as sexual harassment, pregnancy discrimination, discrimination against the disabled, and reverse discrimination. The U.S. Constitution, the laws passed by Congress and state legislatures, presidential executive orders, and guidelines of U.S. government agencies all provide protection against these various types of discrimination. The process by which an individual can prove discrimination by an employer has been clearly set out in the courts. This process requires the plaintiff to initially prove a prima facie case of discrimination, using data that show (1) that he or she has been treated differently from other employees because of his or her race, sex, religion, color, national origin, or disabled status or (2) that company policies have an adverse impact on some protected class. The organization then has an opportunity to defend its actions, on the basis of a BFOQ, seniority system, job relatedness, or business necessity.

Along with state and federal court systems, the Equal Employment Opportunity Commission, the Office of Federal Contract Compliance Programs, and the Justice Department help enforce the laws and executive orders that prohibit discrimination. These agents of enforcement have a wide array of potential sanctions that can be used against organizations that discriminate. Increasingly, cases in this area are being subject to jury trials, and partly because of this, there has been a considerable growth in interest in the use of arbitration and other alternative methods to resolve disputes.

The final element in the EEO environment is management. By taking control, making HRM procedures objective and job-related, setting up procedures to handle discrimination complaints when they arise, and acting affirmatively, management can prevent itself from becoming the object of discrimination lawsuits. Companies also may be able to purchase insurance policies to protect themselves against EEO lawsuits. By taking these steps, management can make maximum use of all the human resources available to it.

The Manager's Vocabulary

adverse impact
affirmative action
affirmative action plans (AAPs)
Age Discrimination in Employment Act
Americans with Disabilities Act
arbitration
bona fide occupational qualification (BFOQ)
bona fide seniority system
business necessity
Civil Rights Act of 1866
Civil Rights Act of 1871
Civil Rights Act of 1964
Civil Rights Act of 1991
conciliation
desk audit
disability
disparate impact
disparate treatment
equal employment opportunity (EEO)
Equal Pay Act
Executive Order 11246
Executive Order 11375
executive orders
Family and Medical Leave Act
Fifth Amendment
four-fifths rule
Fourteenth Amendment
Immigration Reform and Control Act
job relatedness
Older Workers Protection Act
Pregnancy Discrimination Act
prima facie case
protected class
reasonable accommodation

retaliation
reverse discrimination
right-to-sue letter
sexual harassment
show-cause statement
Title VII
Uniform Guidelines
Vocational Rehabilitation Act

Questions for Discussion

1. What could Coca-Cola have done to prevent such charges of race discrimination? How would you rate Coca-Cola's handling of the charges? "Did the real thing [Coca-Cola] do the right thing?"

2. What are some of the reasons an organization should be interested in complying with EEO regulations? How is Coca-Cola an example of the necessity to comply?

3. In the context of discrimination laws, what is a protected class? Can someone who is not a member of a protected class claim discrimination in employment?

4. What sorts of practices are prohibited by the Equal Pay Act of 1963?

5. Do you agree with the U.S. Supreme Court's decision in the *Meritor* case? What is "environmental" sexual harassment? How do you prove its existence? To what extent should courts be permitted to hear evidence regarding the private sex lives of plaintiffs bringing harassment charges?

6. Suppose that a friend of yours has been exposed to the AIDS virus and is HIV-positive. Your friend's employer learns about this and fires your friend. Is this illegal employment discrimination?

7. Title VII of the Civil Rights Act of 1964 prohibits discrimination in employment based on race, color, sex, religion, or national origin. Executive Orders 11246 and 11375 require employers with federal contracts to act affirmatively in hiring employees. What is the difference between not discriminating and acting affirmatively?

8. In what ways is the Americans with Disabilities Act of 1990 (ADA) different from other civil rights legislation? In what ways is it the same?

9. A faculty member at your college requests a leave under the Family and Medical Leave Act of 1993 (FMLA) to help her daughter, who is expecting twins. Would such a request be covered by FMLA? How should the college respond?

10. What is affirmative action? Why is it controversial at the present time?

11. What is a bona fide occupational qualification (BFOQ)? Can race be a BFOQ? Why or why not?

12. What are the roles of the Equal Employment Opportunity Commission (EEOC) and the Office of Federal Contract Compliance Programs (OFCCP)?

13. To prove that an organization has illegally discriminated against a person, the individual(s) must first show evidence of a prima facie case of discrimination. How is this done in a situation where disparate treatment has occurred? where adverse impact has occurred?

14. Why are the Supreme Court cases *Griggs* v. *Duke Power Co.* (1971) and *Albermarle Paper Co.* v. *Moody* (1975) important to understanding discrimination in employment?

15. How would you rule if an employee fired for bringing a gun to work sued the employer under the ADA, claiming he had a "mental disability"?

Case 5.1
"Mentoring" the Sales Force

Biff LaFourche, president of Provincial Life Insurance Company of Jackson, returned from lunch to find personnel manager Frank Anderson waiting to see him.

"I think we've got a problem with Bob Snowden and Sally Ambrose," Anderson said, after he closed the door to LaFourche's office.

Bob Snowden, thirty-two, was one of Provincial's three vice presidents and had supervised the company's three regional offices for about five years. Snowden had received excellent performance evaluations ever since he had joined the company and was thought to be one of the company's rising stars. Aside from improving bottom-line results, Snowden was known to have taken a personal interest in helping agents who sometimes had problems with their work. Without exception, these problem agents were attractive women in their twenties.

Recently, Snowden had been spending a great deal of time attempting to improve the performance of Sally Ambrose. Sally, twenty-five, had been employed as a marketing representative (salesperson) in the company's Meridian branch office for less than two years. About three months earlier, Sally had come to the Jackson headquarters to discuss her job performance and future career goals with Snowden as part of a formal company program of job enrichment for marketing representatives. After work that day, LaFourche had run into Sally and Bob at a local bar, where they were having a few drinks. LaFourche talked with them for a few minutes about the company and about their job-improvement discussion.

From that chance encounter, it appeared to LaFourche that Snowden was going to take Sally under his wing and develop her abilities in sales, just as he had with several other young women. Before their meeting, Sally's sales performance had been lagging, and it appeared that she might have to be terminated not too far down the road unless she showed dramatic improvement. In the last two months, however, it appeared to LaFourche that Sally Ambrose was making the improvements that were necessary for her to stay with the company.

LaFourche recognized that Snowden's efforts to improve the performance of these marketing reps was sometimes a tricky matter, because the reps did not directly report to Snowden. For example, Sally Ambrose's direct supervisor was Estelle Landry, manager of the Meridian office. Estelle, in turn, reported to Bob Snowden.

"What seems to be the problem?" LaFourche asked Anderson.

Anderson explained that a company employee had come to him in confidence a few days earlier. The employee had been in the Atlanta airport two Fridays ago on a business trip and had seen Bob Snowden and Sally Ambrose walking down the concourse, holding hands. The employee noticed the pair entering the boarding area for a flight to Orlando.

The employee expressed concern that there appeared to be a romantic relationship between the manager and the marketing rep and was worried about how that might affect the treatment of other employees at the company. Anderson said he checked company records and found that both Snowden and Ambrose had taken that Friday and the following Monday off from work.

"The employee asked not to be identified," Anderson concluded. "I hope you understand."

"Certainly," LaFourche replied. "I assume you believe that the employee was telling the truth?"

Anderson nodded.

Briefly, LaFourche tried to figure out if the employee was one of the twenty people who worked in the Meridian office, one of the fifty employed at the Jackson headquarters, or someone at another branch office of the company. Was the employee a woman, perhaps someone Snowden had jilted? Was the employee a man, upset at possible favoritism toward a female agent? Or was the employee genuinely concerned that the company could be harmed if the apparent relationship between Snowden and Sally Ambrose turned sour and Sally filed harassment charges?

"What do you think we should do about this, Frank?"

Anderson shook his head. "I'm not really certain there is anything we can do. I'm worried, though, that if this gets out, it could affect Snowden's work with other people, particularly Estelle. It certainly puts her in a difficult position."

"Yes, and if we don't do anything, what do you think the employee will do? Spread gossip about what might or might not be going on?"

"I'm not sure," Anderson said. "But I do know that the sexual harassment policy we wrote last year doesn't deal with this sort of thing."

Anderson continued, "You know, there seemed to be a lot of concern on the part of the employee who told me about this. Coming to me like that about one of the top managers around here certainly could put that person out on a limb. That's why I think the story is true."

"Thanks, Frank," LaFourche said. "Let me think about this a bit."

As president of a medium-sized insurance company, Biff LaFourche had other matters to consider that afternoon. Yet his thoughts kept returning to what Frank Anderson had told him about Bob Snowden and Sally Ambrose. Had it been just a coincidence that the marketing reps whose performance had improved after Snowden's help were all attractive young women? Were Snowden's nonwork activities any of LaFourche's business? Could these activities be considered non–work-related, now that another employee was involved? Should he contact the company's lawyer and get some advice?

The next morning, after LaFourche finished his morning coffee, he dialed 283.

"Bob Snowden speaking."

"Bob, this is Biff. Can you step into my office for a couple of minutes?"

Source: This case was written by Roland E. Kidwell, Jr., Department of Commerce, Niagara University, and Amy Laura Oakes Wren, Department of Accounting and Business Law, Louisiana State University at Shreveport. Reprinted by permission.

1. What are the facts that suggest the relationship between Bob Snowden and Sally Ambrose is an issue for Provincial Life and that Biff LaFourche should take action?
2. If the relationship is an issue for Provincial Life, does the policy statement on sexual harassment need revision? If so, what revisions?
3. At what point does a consensual relationship between adults become a work-related problem? Is the relationship between Bob and Sally at that point? What facts suggest that the relationship between Bob and Sally is not a problem?
4. Outline the conversation Biff should have with Bob. How far should he go in probing the nature of the relationship between Bob and Sally? Should the company lawyer be present?

● Exercise 5.1
Interviewing Under the ADA

As discussed throughout the chapter, the Americans with Disabilities Act, which became effective in July 1992, has had a monumental impact on the administration of equal employment opportunity laws. In general, employers may not, under the ADA, make preemployment inquiries as to whether, or to what extent, an individual is disabled. Employers may, however, ask job applicants whether they can perform the "essential functions" of the job. The EEOC recently issued guidelines with regard to preemployment inquiries under the ADA in an attempt to clarify what types of questions may be asked legally of job applicants. Some observers have countered, though, that these guidelines and the sample questions included with them have made matters even more unclear. After each of the following sample questions, mark whether you think the question is legal or illegal.

Legal/Illegal

1. How many days were you sick last year?   _____

2. What physician-prescribed medications are you currently taking?   _____

3. Are you able to lift things?   _____

4. How well can you handle stress?   _____

5. Can you perform this job function with or without reasonable accommodation?   _____

6. When do you expect to recover completely from your broken arm?   _____

● **Exercise 5.2**
Affirmative Action Update

Your employer is interested in keeping up with the latest on affirmative action. As part of your job, you provide quarterly summaries of legislation, lawsuits, and court rulings. Using this Web site, provide this quarter's summary (remember, the focus is on affirmative action only): http://www.shrm.org/hrlinks/legal.htm (HR Links, Society for Human Resource Management).

● **Exercise 5.3**
Affirmative Action Debate

As a class, divide into an even number of groups to debate the proposition: *Affirmative action laws are largely a thing of the past in the modern workplace and mandating affirmative action can now be retired.*

• Odd-number groups should prepare to make a case that affirmative action laws continue to be needed.

• Even-numbered groups should prepare to make a case that affirmative action laws can now be retired.

Notes and References

1. Timothy S. Bland and Robert D. Hall Jr., "Do the Math: A Few Million Here, a Few Million There—It all Adds Up to a Convincing Argument to Prevent Class-Action Lawsuits, *HR Magazine*, June 2001, p. 121–125.

2. "Coca-Cola Agrees to Pay $192.5 Million, Make HR Policy Changes to Settle Lawsuit," *BNA Daily Labor Report*, July 31, 2001. Available at http://my.shrm.org/hrnews/articles/default.asp?page=ban1117a.htm

3. *Abdallah v. The Coca-Cola Company, N.D. Ga., No. 188CV3679.* (Settlement approved 12/22/00)

4. A Race-Bias Suit Tests Coke: Can the Real Thing Do the Right Thing? *The Wall Street Journal*, May 18, 1999, p. B1.

5. *The Wall Street Journal*, May 18, 1999, Ibid.

6. "Coke Was Told in '95 of Need for Diversity," *The Wall Street Journal*, May 20, 1999, p. B1.

7. *BNA Daily Labor Report*, Ibid.

8. Jennifer Gill, "Ain't Misbehaving? Not at Work," *Business Week*, June 7, 2000. Available at: http://www.businessweek.com/careers/content/jun2000/ca2000067_401.htm

9. Joshua M. Javits, "It's the Real thing: $192.5 Million," *Legal Report*, March–April, 2001, pp. 1–2.

10. Civil Rights Act of 1866, Section 1981 (401 FEP Manual 81).

11. *Johnson* v. *Railway Express Agency*, U.S. Supreme Court, 10 FEP 831 839 847 (1975).

12. Civil Rights Act of 1871, Section 1983 (401 FEP Manual 81).

13. Equal Pay Act of 1963 (401 FEP Manual 451).

14. *Schultz* v. *Wheaton Glass Co.*, 421 F. 2d 259 (3rd Cir. 1970).

15. Linda Levine, "The Male-Female Wage Gap: A Fact Sheet," *Congressional Research Service*, December 12, 2000. (Available at: http://www.cnie.org/nle/econ-65.html)

16. Ibid.

17. Civil Rights Act of 1964 (401 FEP Manual 1); 401 FEP Manual 11.

18. Benjamin W. Wolkinson and Richard N. Block, *Employment Law: The Workplace Rights of Employees and Employers* (Cambridge, Mass.: Blackwell, 1996), p. 10.

19. House Judiciary Committee Report, 88th Congress, Report 914, Part 2, December 2, 1963.

20. *General Electric Co.* v. *Gilbert*, 423 U.S. 822 (1976).

21. *California Federal Savings & Loan* v. *Guerra*, 479 U.S. 272 (1987).

22. *United Auto Workers* v. *Johnson Controls*, 111 S. Ct. 1196 (1991).

23. *Barnes* v. *Costle*, 561 F. 2d 983 (D.C. Cir. 1977); *Fisher* v. *Flynn*, 598 F. 2d 663 (1st Cir. 1979); and *Williams* v. *Civiletti*, 487 F. Supp. 1389, 22 FEP 1311 (1980).

24. Discrimination Because of Sex, Title VII of the Civil Rights Act of 1964, as amended; Adoption of Final Interpretive Guidelines, 29 CFR Part 1604, Section 1604, 11(a), 1980.

25. *Meritor Savings Bank* v. *Vinson*, 477 U.S. 57 (1986).

26. *Harris* v. *Forklift Systems*, 114 S. Ct. 367 (1993).

27. See Ellen E. Schultz and Junada Woo, "Plaintiffs' Sex Lives Are Being Laid Bare in Harassment Cases," *Wall Street Journal*, September 15, 1994, p. A1.

28. *Onscale* v. *Sundowner Offshore Services*, U.S. Supreme Court, 96-568, March 4, 1998.

29. Kenneth M. Jarin and Ellen K. Pomfret, "New Rules for Same Sex Harassment," *HRMagazine*, June 1998, pp. 115–123.

30. Mark Maremont, "Abuse of Power: The Astonishing Tale of Sexual Harassment at Astra USA," *Business Week*, May 13, 1996, pp. 86–98.

31. Mark Maremont and Rochelle Sharpe, "Astra Expected to Pay over $10 Million to Settle Charges of Sexual Harassment," *Wall Street Journal*, February 5, 1998, p. A4.

32. *Farager* v. *City of Boca Raton*, 524 US 775 (1998); and *Burlington Industries, Inc.* v. *Ellerth*, 524 US 742 (1998).

33. Debbie Rodman Sandler, "Sexual Harassment Rulings: Less Than Meets the Eye," *HRMagazine*, October 1998, pp. 136–143.

34. Paul Gibson, "The Future of Sexual Harassment Suits," *HRMagazine*, October 1998, pp. 142–143.

35. Age Discrimination in Employment Act of 1967 (401 FEP Manual 351).

36. Daniel P. O'Meara, *Protecting the Growing Number of Older Workers: The Age Discrimination in Employment Act.* (Philadelphia: Wharton School, 1989), p. 13.

37. "Supreme Court Clarifies Proof Required for Age Discrimination Claims," *Employment Law Briefs*, Vol. 4 (2), October 1996, p. 3.

38. *O'Connor* v. *Consolidated Coin Caterers Corp.*, 116 S. Ct. 1307 (1996).

39. Ibid.

40. *Public Employees Retirement System of Ohio* v. *Betts*, 109 S. Ct. 2854 (1989).

41. Vocational Rehabilitation Act of 1973 (401 FEP Manual 501).

42. *Board of Trustees of University of Alabama* v. *Garrett* (99–1240) 193 F.3d 1214, reversed.

43. John M. Williams, "The High Court's Low Blow to the Disabled," *Business Week*, March 7, 2001. Available at: http://www.businessweek.com/bwdaily/dnflash/mar2001/nf2001037_455.htm

44. *PGA Tour, Inc.,* v. *Martin*, 532 U.S. 121 S. Ct 1879 (2001).

45. Cited in Linda Greenhouse, "Golf; Disabled Golfer May Use a Cart On the PGA Tour, Justices Affirm," *New York Times*, May 30, 2001, p. A1.

46. *Cook* v. *State of Rhode Island, Dept. of Mental Health, Retardation and Hospitals*, 2 AD Cases 1476 (1993).

47. Mark V. Roehling, "Weight-Based Discrimination in Employment: Psychological and Legal Aspects, *Personnel Psychology*, Vol 32, 1999, pp. 969–1016.

48. *Cook* v. *State of Rhode Island, Dept. of Mental Health, Retardation and Hospitals*, 10 F. 2d 17, 2 AD 1476 (1st Cir. 1993).

49. "EEOC Accomplishments Report for Fiscal Year 2000." (Available at: http://www.eeoc.gov/accomplishments-00.html)

50. Mike France and Michael Arndt, "Office Violence: After the Shooting Stops," *Business Week*, March 12, 2001, pp. 98–100.

51. "EEOC Enforcement Guidance on the Americans with Disabilities Act and Psychiatric Disabilities" (Available at: http://www.eeoc.gov/docs/psych.html)

52. Immigration Reform and Control Act of 1986, 8 USC 1324 (a).

53. *Garcia* v. *Spun Steak Co.*, 62 FEP 525, FEP 1856 (1994).

54. *EEOC* v. *Premier Operator Services, Inc.*, 113 F.Supp.2d 1066 (N.D. Tex, 2000).

55. *Wards Cove Packing Co.* v. *Antonio*, 109 S. Ct. 2115 (1989).

56. *Griggs* v. *Duke Power Co.*, 401 U.S. 424, 3 FEP 175 (1971).

57. *Gilmer* v. *Interstate/Johnson Lane Corp.,* 500 U.S. 20, 111 S. Ct. 1647 (1991).

58. Linda Greenhouse, "Court Says Employers Can Require Arbitration of Disputes," *New York Times*, March 22, 2001. (Available at: http://www.nytimes.com/2001/03/22/business22BIZC.html)

59. *Circuit City Stores, Inc.* v. *Adams,* (99–1379) 194 F. 3d 1070.

60. Margaret M. Clark, "Supreme Court Supports Arbitration Agreements," *HR News*, Vol 20 (5), May 2001, pp. 1, 20.

61. U.S. Department of Labor, "FMLA Survey," (Available at: http://www.dol.gov/dol/asp/public/fmla/forward.htm and http://www.dol.gov/dol/asp/public/fmla/chapter8.htm)

62. Taylor Cox, Jr., "The Multicultural Organization," *Academy of Management Executive*, May 1991, pp. 34–47.

63. U.S. Department of Labor, Bureau of Labor Statistics "The Employment Situation." (Available at: http://stats.bls.gov/news.release/empsit.toc.htm)

64. Charlene Marmer Solomon, "Affirmative Action: What You Need to Know," *Personnel Journal*, August 1995, p. 60.

65. *Hopwood* v. *The University of Texas,* 95 F. 3d 53 (1996).

66. Solomon, "Affirmative Action," p. 62.

67. *Taxman* v. *Piscataway Township Bd. Of Educ.,* 91 F.3d 1547 1551 (3d. Cir. 1996).

68. Ibid, p. 58.

69. *Steelworkers* v. *Weber*, 443 U.S. 193, 20 FEP 1 (1979).

70. *Edmonson* v. *U.S. Steel Corp.*, District Ct. Alabama, 20 FEP 1745 (1979); *Moseley* v. *The Goodyear Tire & Rubber Co.*, 612 F. 2d 187, 22 FEP 121 (1980); and *Wright* v. *National Archives and Records Service*, 4th District California, 21 FEP 8 (1979).

71. *Firefighters Local Union 1784* v. *Stotts*, U.S. Supreme Court, 34 FEP 1702 (1984).

72. *City of Richmond* v. *J. A. Croson,* 109 S. Ct. 707 (1989).

73. *Adarand Constructors, Inc.* v. *Pena*, 515 U.S. 200 (1995).

74. *Uniform Guidelines on Employee Selection Procedures,* 29 *Code of Federal Regulations,* Part 1607 (1978).

75. U.S. EEOC, "Enforcement Statistics and Litigation." (Available at http://www.eeoc.gov/stats/enforcement.html)

76. On November 20, 1990, the EEOC announced that it would consider charges by "testers" in the investigation and prosecution of job discrimination claims. Testers are individuals who seek employment in an attempt to prove discrimination but without the intention of actually accepting employment if it is offered. Although the use of testers to prove discrimination has become a fairly well accepted practice in the housing discrimination context, the use of such testers in the employment context is quite controversial. The U.S. Chamber of Commerce, for example, has expressed concern over the EEOC policy, noting that it will cause employers to expend needless time, effort, and money interviewing individuals who are not really interested in employment.

77. *Albermarle Paper Co.* v. *Moody*, 422 U.S. 405, 10 FEP 1181 (1975).

78. *Clark* v. *American Marine Corp.*, 437 F. 2d 959, 3 FEP 155 (1971).

79. *McDonnell Douglas Corp.* v. *Green*, 411 U.S. 792, 5 FEP 965 (1973).

80. *Griggs* v. *Duke Power Co.*, 401 U.S. 424, 3 FEP 175 (1971).

81. The other court decisions include *Hazelwood School District* v. *United States*, 433 U.S. 299, 15 FEP 1 (1977), and *Teamsters* v. *United States*, 431 U.S. 324, 14 FEP 1514 (1977).

82. Although the concept of a prima facie case was developed in the court system, the type of evidence that indicates a prima facie case is also the type that the EEOC and OFCCP look for in their own investigations of organizations. The agencies look for evidence of disparate treatment and disparate impact. Of course, the OFCCP also examines the extent to which organizations are following the actions set forth in their affirmative action programs.

83. *EEOC* v. *Union Bank of Arizona,* 12 FEP 527 (D. Arizona), 1976.

84. *United States* v. *City of Socorro*, 25 FEP 815 (D. New Mexico), 1976.

85. *Drew* v. *Liberty Mutual Insurance Co.*, 480 F. 2d 69, 5 FEP 1077 (1973).

86. *Albermarle Paper Co.* v. *Moody*, 422 U.S. 405, 10 FEP 1181 (1975).

87. *Dothard* v. *Rawlinson*, 433 U.S. 321, 15 FEP 10 (1977).

88. *Diaz* v. *Pan American World Airways*, 442 F. 2d 385, 3 FEP 337 (1971).

89. *Teamsters* v. *United States*, 431 U.S. 324, 14 FEP 1514 (1977).

90. *Pullman-Standard* v. *Swint*, 456 U.S. 273, 28 FEP 1073 (1982); and *American Tobacco Co.* v. *Patterson*, 456 U.S. 63, 28 FEP 713 (1982).

91. *Furnco Construction Corp.* v. *Waters*, 438 U.S. 537, 17 FEP 1062 (1978).

92. *Robinson* v. *P. Lorillard Co.*, 444 F. 2d 829, 3 FEP 653 (1971); and *Bethlehem Steel Co.* v. *United States*, 446 F. 2d 652, 3 FEP 589 (1971).

93. R. Peres, *Dealing with Employment Discrimination* (New York: McGraw-Hill, 1978), p. 133.

94. L. S. Kleiman and R. H. Faley, "Voluntary Affirmative Action and Preferential Treatment: Legal and Research Implications," *Personnel Psychology*, Vol. 41, 1988, pp. 481–496.

Recruiting and Job Search

HR Challenge

Your organization, Health Source, Inc., owns four large drugstores in Houston, Texas, and will open two more stores in the next year. One of the new stores will be located in suburban Houston, and the other will represent your first venture into the Dallas market. Each store will require about twenty-five employees at the start, including five pharmacists, four cosmeticians, a manager, an assistant manager, and a number of clerks.

How would you go about locating and recruiting the fifty employees needed for the new stores? What are your options? How do the recruiting methods you considered compare with one another in terms of cost, and how effective do you think each will be? How long will the recruiting process take? Are there any possible legal or ethical ramifications to think about? Would your recommendations for recruiting be the same or different if (1) Health Source plans no further expansion after these two new stores, and (2) if Health Source plans to pursue an aggressive expansion policy for several years?

Recruiting is the process by which organizations locate and attract individuals to fill job vacancies. Most organizations have a continuing need to recruit new employees to replace those who leave or are promoted, to acquire new skills, and to permit organizational growth. Recruiting is an even more important activity when unemployment rates are low and economic growth is strong, as firms compete to attract the qualified employees they need to succeed. Recruiting can be quite expensive. Companies spend, on average, over $1,000 recruiting each nonexempt employee, about $7,000 recruiting each exempt employee, and over $23,000 recruiting each executive from the external labor market.[1]

Recruitment follows HR planning and goes hand in hand with the selection process by which organizations evaluate the suitability of candidates for various jobs. Without accurate planning, organizations may recruit the wrong number or type of employees. Without successful recruiting to create a sizable pool of candidates, even the most accurate selection system is of little use. This chapter concentrates on how to plan and conduct a successful and cost-effective recruiting effort. It highlights methods that can be used to locate candidates from within the organization and from the outside labor market. It also focuses on the job applicant and the ways in which a candidate looks for and chooses a job. The chapter closes with a discussion of the measures that can be used to evaluate the effectiveness of the recruitment process.

OVERVIEW OF THE RECRUITMENT PROCESS

Figure 6.1 presents an overview of the recruitment process from the perspectives of the organization and the candidate. This flow chart displays the process as it unfolds over time. When a vacancy occurs and the recruiter receives authorization to fill it, the next step is a careful examination of the job and an enumeration of the skills, abilities, and experience needed to perform the job successfully. Existing job analysis documents can be very helpful in this regard. In addition, the recruitment planner must consider other aspects of the job environment—for example, the supervisor's management style, the opportunities for advancement, pay, and geographic location—in deciding what type of candidate to search for and what search methods to use. After carefully planning the recruiting effort, the recruiter uses one or more methods to produce a pool of potentially qualified candidates.

A firm can generate candidates *internally*, from among its present employees who desire promotion or transfer, or *externally*, from the labor market. The organization then screens the candidates, evaluates some of them more thoroughly, and offers the best the position. Throughout the recruitment process, the organization attempts to "sell" itself to the more promising candidates—that is, to convince them that the organization is a good place to work and that it offers what they want in the way of both tangible and intangible rewards.

Candidates searching for an employer go through a parallel set of activities— first acquiring occupational skills and experience, next searching for job openings through a variety of methods; and then applying for jobs that appear to be a suitable match for their qualifications. As the process continues, applicants attempt to "sell" organizations on their abilities while at the same time collecting information that allows them to evaluate companies and jobs. Eventually, they decide to accept or reject job offers.

● **FIGURE 6.1**

The Recruitment Process

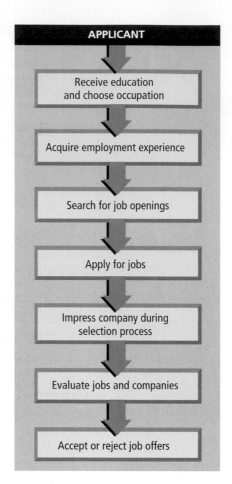

In the recruitment and selection process, the organization's and the individual's objectives may conflict. The organization is trying to evaluate the candidate's strengths and weaknesses, but the candidate is trying to present only strengths. Conversely, although the candidate is trying to ferret out both the good and the bad aspects of the prospective job and employer, the organization may prefer to reveal only positive aspects. In addition, each party's own objectives may conflict. The organization wants to treat the candidate well to increase the probability of job-offer acceptance, yet the need to evaluate the candidate may dictate the use of methods that may alienate the prospect, such as background investigations or stress interviews. Analogously, the applicant wants to appear polite and enthusiastic about the organization to improve the probability of receiving an offer, but he or she may also want to ask penetrating questions about compensation, advancement, and the company's financial health and future.[2]

STRATEGIC ISSUES IN RECRUITING

The nature of a firm's recruiting activities should be matched to its strategy and values as well as to other important features such as the state of the external labor market and the firm's ability to pay or otherwise induce new employees to join. In

● FIGURE 6.2

Strategic Decisions in Recruiting

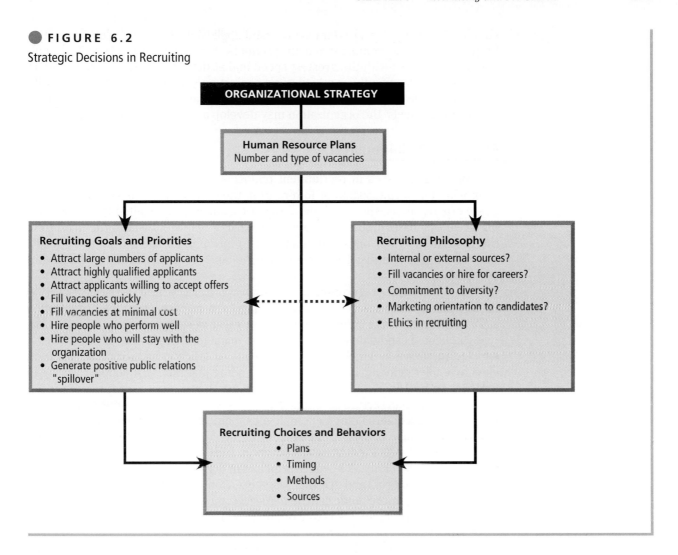

this section we will discuss the varied goals that can be served by recruiting, how a recruitment philosophy based on corporate values can guide recruiting choices—including the critical choice of whether to recruit internally or externally—and how innovative recruiting can achieve a competitive advantage in attracting scarce employee resources. Many of the issues to be discussed below are summarized in Figure 6.2.

Recruitment Goals

A good recruiting program needs to serve many and sometimes conflicting goals. A commonly mentioned goal is to attract a large pool of applicants, but applicant pools can be too large and thus costly to process. Recruiting must also attract a high proportion of well-qualified candidates who are seriously interested in accepting a job offer. Post-hiring goals also must be considered—the recruiting process must yield workers who are good performers and who will stay with the organization for a reasonable length of time. An additional goal is that recruiting efforts should have beneficial "spillover" effects; that is, the organization's general image should be enhanced, and even unsuccessful applicants should develop positive attitudes toward the company and its products. Further, all the preceding goals should be reached with the greatest speed and at the least possible cost to the organization.[3] Balancing these varied goals against one another should be done with reference to the organization's overall strategy and values. As a part of this process of prioritizing goals, the organization may develop a recruitment philosophy.

Recruitment Philosophy

One of the key issues in recruitment philosophy is whether to promote largely from within the organization or to hire from the outside for vacancies at all levels. Some organizations, such as General Electric Company and United Parcel Service, put great emphasis on developing and socializing managers within the firm, from the ground up. Other organizations prefer to hire proven talent from the outside. The advantages and disadvantages of internal and external recruiting will be discussed further below.

A second aspect of recruitment philosophy concerns where the emphasis is: on merely filling vacancies or on hiring for long-term careers. Does the organization seek people with skills sufficient for present vacancies, or does it try to attract the type of talented candidates who can feed the management pipeline of the future? A short-term view may emphasize filling vacancies quickly, whereas a longer-term view may tolerate delay in the interests of finding just the right people to bring in for the long haul.[4]

A third aspect of recruitment philosophy concerns depth of commitment to seeking and hiring a diverse range of employees. Some firms are still at the EEO/affirmative action stage of mere compliance with the law, whereas others, like Corning Incorporated, Digital Equipment Corporation, and Avon Products, Inc., have graduated to valuing diversity as a central principle of organizational life. Their recruiting practices, both internal and external, actively encourage participation by all types of people. Perhaps more important, extensive training and consultative processes strive to create a climate that is welcoming to and supportive of all candidates.[5]

A fourth aspect of recruitment philosophy is whether applicants are viewed as commodities to be purchased or as customers to be wooed. Organizations that adopt a **marketing orientation** with respect to recruiting will spend substantial time and money to determine what their customers (potential applicants) want and to tailor their recruiting practices and messages to various segments of the market. For instance, NEC Information Systems hired a research firm to explore what systems analysts and marketing graduates wanted in a job and then incorporated these features successfully into the company's advertising campaign.[6] Swiss Bank and Ingersoll-Rand have used focus groups of university students to obtain a better understanding of the needs of the campus recruiting market.[7]

A fifth aspect of recruitment philosophy has ethical overtones, in terms of fairness and honesty in the recruitment process. This theme is further developed in the Ethical Perspective box.

Internal or External Sources?

Deciding whether the position is to be filled internally or externally is often an early task in recruitment planning for a specific vacancy. In some cases, there is no decision to be made. For instance, entry-level jobs must be filled externally, but for other positions, the company's policy or union contract may require that internal sources be used first. Most organizations use a mixture of internal and external sources—promoting from within when qualified employees are available and recruiting from external sources when new skills are needed or growth is rapid. Each type of source has its advantages and disadvantages.

● **Advantages of Internal Recruiting**   When **internal recruiting** is used, the vacancy is filled by a person of known ability. Since the employer has observed the employee in one position, there is less guesswork involved in assessing his or her suitability for a second position. In contrast, assessments of external recruits are based on less reliable sources, such as references, and on relatively brief encounters, such as interviews. Another advantage of promoting from within is that doing so motivates current employees. Skilled and ambitious employees are less likely to quit and more likely to become involved in developmental activities if they believe that promotion is likely.[8] Also, training and socialization time is reduced when openings are filled internally because a current employee has less to learn about the organization and its idiosyncratic procedures than a newcomer. Recruiting may also be faster and less expensive if an internal candidate can be found. Finally, in times of impending retrenchment, filling as many jobs as possible internally maximizes job security for present employees.

● **Disadvantages of Internal Recruiting**   If the organization is expanding rapidly, there may be an insufficient internal supply of qualified individuals above the entry level. This situation may result in people's being promoted before they are ready or not being allowed to stay in a position long enough to learn how to do a job well. Also, when one vacancy is filled internally, a second vacancy is created—the position of the individual who was promoted or transferred to fill the first vacancy. If this slot is also filled internally, then another vacancy occurs. This movement of personnel is called the **ripple effect.** In one organization, 195 initial vacancies eventually resulted in 545 job movements.[9] Another disadvantage of internal recruiting is that some organizations' internal recruiting procedures are extremely cumbersome. They may involve a bureaucratic nightmare of forms, waiting times, eligibility lists, and requirements of permission to interview from the candidate's current superior.[10] Still another disadvantage of internal recruiting is that an organization can become inbred and lose flexibility if all its managers are homegrown. Finally, meeting affirmative action goals usually can be accomplished only by aggressive external recruiting.

● **Advantages of External Recruiting**   **External recruiting** can bring in new ideas and viewpoints, avoid the confusion that accompanies the ripple effect, meet affirmative action goals, and cope with the demands of rapid growth without overusing inexperienced personnel. Another advantage may be savings in training costs. Hiring experienced workers away from other companies may cut down on the need for a comprehensive training and development program in-house. Finally, there may be instances that require a severe shakeup or turnaround. Particularly at the upper-management level, an outsider with no prior commitment to present employees or ongoing projects may be the only individual with enough objectivity (and even ruthlessness) to bring about needed changes and enunciate a new vision for the organization.[11]

Ethics in Recruiting and Job Search

A number of ethical challenges can arise in the recruiting process. Both parties to recruiting may be motivated to present their best sides while concealing their weaknesses, and this may lead to a temptation to lie or mislead by omission or commission. Applicants may engage in résumé fraud, though most organizations have a policy of firing employees if significant résumé fraud is later detected. Firms sometimes emphasize the most positive aspects of jobs while failing to mention less pleasant aspects, and in extreme cases, firms have been sued for fraudulent recruiting. In one case, a firm enticed an individual to relocate with promises of a bright future. However, the firm knew that its financial condition was very shaky and that there was a good probability that the new employee would soon be laid off. A jury later awarded the employee damages of $250,000

Honesty is a central value in most ethical systems, so blatant lying would probably be regarded by both employers and applicants as unacceptable. However, the morality of other recruiting behaviors is not so clear-cut and may be defined situationally by common practice in the industry. Theft of property would be rejected by most people, but what about theft of employees and their organization-specific knowledge? When one organization raids a competitor by hiring away its best talent, has an unethical act been committed by the raider? What if the new hire passes on critical insider knowledge of the strategies, customers, or technology of the former employer? "Noncompete" agreements signed on hiring are efforts to prevent employees, if they later quit, from using their organization-specific knowledge to the disadvantage of their former employer, but such agreements are not always legally enforceable. Recently, firms including Wal-Mart and PaineWebber have filed corporate-raiding lawsuits against other firms they claim have made attempts to damage them by wholesale poaching of important staff. In another case, an employer sued their former director of recruiting, who they allege tried to use his insider knowledge of the firm's compensation system to lure staff to his new employer.

In some industries, raiding is commonplace and accepted. But do some firms go too far? Recruiters in the information technology industry have been known to loiter in the parking lots of competitors to pitch job opportunities to employees as they leave work. Others pay

● **Disadvantages of External Recruiting**   One disadvantage of external recruiting is the cost. Because the external labor market is much larger and harder to reach than the internal one, recruiting externally usually takes longer and costs more. With external recruiting, there is also the risk of hiring a candidate who does not live up to the apparent high potential displayed during the selection process. Finally, too much external recruitment is discouraging to current employees because it reduces their chances to move up in the organization.

Countercyclical Hiring

One strategic issue relevant to external recruiting is when to do it. Most firms recruit each year to meet that year's needs. They attempt to hire many people in a boom year and hire very few during years when the industry, economy, or company is on a down cycle. Human resource planners at Union Oil Company of California realized that such short-range recruitment planning was not efficient. In boom years, the company was attempting to hire many people at the same time thousand-dollar bribes to obtain in-house phone directories. Some recruiters have been known to telephone companies and lie about their identity as they try to obtain names and contact details for valuable employees. One recruiter represented himself as a producer from *The Larry King Show* and asked for the company's chief financial officer's name and phone number, ostensibly so he could be interviewed on the program.

A firm called Advanced Internet Recruitment Strategy (AIRS) runs popular seminars designed to teach recruiters how to search company Web sites and associated links to locate potential candidates. Techniques such as "X-ray," "peelback," "flipping," and "domain search" enhance access to employee information not intended for the public. Companies are advised to keep employee information and company directories behind firewalls and to supply only generic contact information (such as sales@companyname.com) rather than specific employee names on public Web sites. De-Paul University ethicist Laura Hartman argues that the onus shouldn't be solely on the employer to protect employee data behind firewalls. Rather, she contends that it is unethical for recruiters to use advanced search techniques to poach employees, just as it would be unethical to steal from a person's home just because they forgot to lock their door.

A recent survey of human resource specialists asked which of a number of questionable recruiting methods they thought were ethical. The survey was provoked by an incident in which twenty employees of one retailer were caught cruising the aisles of a competitor's store trying to lure away employees. Only 8 percent of respondents thought that this was ethical. Ten percent thought that recruiting in a competitor's parking lot was ethical, 13 percent felt that contacting employees via e-mail addresses found on the employer's intranet was acceptable, and 17 percent had no problems with calling employees at home using phone numbers obtained from an ex-employee of the competitor. Fifty-one percent of respondents felt that all four actions were unethical.

Sources: John Andrews, "Résumé Liars Are Abundant, Experts Assert," *Wall Street Journal,* April 24, 1981, p. 25; M. Geyelin and W. Green, "Companies Must Disclose Shaky Finances to Some Applicants," *Wall Street Journal,* April 20, 1990, p. B8; S. Kuczynski, "You've Got Job Offers," *HR Magazine,* March 1999, pp. 50–58; G. Flynn, "Raid the Competition for Workers, Not Their Secrets," *Workforce,* December 1998, pp. 121–123; Eilene Zimmerman, "Fight Dirty Hiring Tactics," May 16, 2001, www.workforce.com/feature/00/17/14; and "What Types of Recruiting Are Ethical," *Workforce,* May 30, 2001, www.workforce.com/cgi-bin/iu.pl.

that its competitors were also recruiting heavily. This high demand drove up starting salaries and resulted in lower-quality hires. During the leaner years of the cycle, top graduates were willing to work for lower starting salaries and were readily available, since competitors were not hiring. Consequently, Union Oil began to plan campus recruiting on a five-year schedule, spreading its hiring evenly over the period and thus maximizing applicant quality while controlling salary costs.[12] Research suggests that the firms most likely to engage in **countercyclical hiring** emphasize human resource planning to avoid shortages, strive to maintain a regular age distribution of managers, and value training and development. They also are firms that can afford to hire in downturns, since they are among the stronger financial performers.[13]

Alternatives to Traditional Recruiting

Traditional recruiting is not always the answer to a firm's human resource needs. This section explores a number of options that may either replace or supplement what we normally think of as "recruiting." Suppose, for example, that a recruiting campaign brings in too few qualified applicants. A traditional approach is to intensify essentially similar recruiting efforts—to run yet another advertisement, extend a contract with an employment agency, or recruit in a larger geographic region. Sara Rynes, a leading recruitment researcher, suggests that in this situation organizations should broaden their focus from recruiting activities to the concept of applicant attraction.

In addition to doing "more of the same" in the way of recruiting, firms can attempt to attract applicants by improving or changing the nature of inducements, perhaps increasing wages or providing flexible work arrangements or stock options. New benefits in the race to attract technical professionals have included signing bonuses of up to $20,000, paid sabbaticals, casual dress codes, concierge services, being allowed to bring one's pet to work, reduced summer hours, and massages in the office. Public-sector organizations have had to work very hard to attract information technology professionals, as they cannot offer stock options and sky-high salaries. Fairfax County, Virginia, has had success attracting new employees by offering flextime and job sharing, as well as playing up the facts that very little travel is required and that working hours are reasonable (as opposed to the travel, very long hours, and weekend work common in the private sector).[14]

A third strategy is to change the focus of recruiting to labor pools that are relatively more plentiful and underutilized; for example, to recruit from retirees, people with disabilities, disadvantaged urban residents, mothers with young children, and so on. Inducements as well as recruiting methods and messages will have to be tailored to the needs and desires of these groups. In some cases, employees from these pools may need assistance with adaptive devices or arrangements, transportation to work, or extra training.[15]

Another alternative for finding scarce professionals in technical fields is to sponsor their immigration from other countries. A number of visa programs are available in the United States. The H-1B temporary professional worker visa (lasting one year to six years if renewed) has been especially popular, with the cap recently raised to 195,000 entrants per year.[16] Britain is also experiencing shortages of skilled staff, with two-thirds of companies finding recruiting difficult. In response, the government announced plans to reduce work permit processing time from three months to a week for non–European Union applicants.[17]

Cisco Systems has used yet another approach to acquire talent on a large scale. It has purchased entire companies (twenty-five in 2000 alone), largely to obtain the intellectual capital and product development expertise embedded in these organizations' work forces.[18]

There are even more distinct alternatives to traditional recruiting, which include not hiring at all. Many firms have no desire to repeat the painful retrenchments of the 1980s and early 1990s and are reluctant to recruit enough full-time staff to meet all their needs. Instead, they have adopted the staffing strategy of keeping a small cadre of permanent employees (who are relatively insulated from layoff), along with a buffer of temporary or contract workers. This strategy is also employed in large Japanese companies and has allowed them to offer lifetime employment to selected groups of employees.

Several alternatives to recruiting and hiring employees directly have increased in popularity. The first is to use temporary workers obtained from a temporary help agency. The temporary help industry has been expanding rapidly since the 1970s.[19] **Temporaries** are especially helpful for covering peak demand periods, especially in an uncertain economic climate when demand could drop precipitously. Temporaries may cost more per hour worked, but they are paid only for the time they actually work. Another advantage of using temporaries is that they are quickly and easily available; therefore, recruiting costs are minimal. In addition, the temporary help agency has already selected and trained the temporaries; thus training costs are low because the temporaries require only a brief orientation to the company. It is not uncommon for firms to offer successful temporaries a permanent position. Essentially, firms can "try before they buy" to be sure a candidate is qualified and fits in. Some temporary agencies charge a "conversion fee" when their employees are hired within thirty to ninety days of initial placement.[20]

Historically, temporaries have been used primarily in jobs such as assembler, laborer, secretary, clerk, or truck driver. In today's work environment, however, they are available for a variety of other professions, including nursing, computer programming, engineering, and accounting.[21] There is even a trend toward "interim executives"—high-caliber, experienced managers who can be brought in for a few months to oversee a turnaround, liquidation, or special project.[22]

Employee leasing is a way to obtain the services of individuals over a longer time period than would normally be the case with temporaries. An employee-leasing firm recruits, hires, trains, and compensates employees, and the organization that leases them provides their work facilities, direct daily supervision, and duties. For example, a nursing services firm employs many nurses and provides them to hospitals on a contract basis. This arrangement relieves the hospitals of a great deal of HRM responsibility. In the future, a number of HR professionals may find themselves working in employee-leasing firms rather than in large production-oriented companies. Employee leasing provides the organization with flexibility to change the number of employees easily and without actual layoffs.[23]

Yet another alternative to recruiting and hiring to staff a function within the organization is to hire an outside firm to perform the entire function, either on or off the organization's premises. Strategic management experts suggest that unless an organization can perform a support function extremely well, it should consider subcontracting that function so that the organization can concentrate all available resources on building unique core competencies. By hiring out such functions as maintenance, security, and office services, the organization can achieve greater efficiency by having these activities performed by specialists. Also, the organization can place competitive pressure to perform on the supplier, in that the supplier can always be replaced by another supplier. This type of incentive is not present when the function is performed in-house.

A similar solution is for the organization to contract with a single individual or consultant on a project basis. For instance, a firm may award a contract to a freelance computer consultant to do a piece of programming rather than hire an additional full-time programmer. Not infrequently, the individuals providing these services are former employees who have become self-employed.[24]

All these options—temporaries, employee leasing, subcontracting—reduce an organization's employment levels and thus its recruiting needs. Another approach to reducing the need to recruit is to attempt to increase the retention of current employees. Loss of talented, experienced staff to voluntary turnover can be very costly and disruptive to an organization. Chapter 16 discusses strategies to enhance employee retention.

INTERNAL RECRUITING

Most companies fill vacancies internally whenever possible. A number of internal recruiting methods are used for different levels of jobs. Lower-level jobs such as manual and clerical jobs are often called **nonexempt** jobs because their incumbents are not exempt from the minimum wage and overtime provisions of the Fair Labor Standards Act (discussed more in Chapter 12). These people typically are paid an hourly wage. In contrast, higher-level administrative, managerial, and professional employees are paid on a salary basis and are **exempt** from the overtime provisions of the Fair Labor Standards Act. The following discussion considers the internal recruiting methods used for each category of job in turn.

Internal Recruiting for Nonexempt Positions

Some small or nonunionized companies have an informal system for locating promotable employees. When openings occur, the hiring manager may rely on memory to suggest candidates or may ask supervisors to recommend employees who appear qualified. The obvious drawbacks of such a system are that (1) good candidates may be overlooked, (2) favoritism may be displayed, and (3) qualified candidates may be hoarded by a supervisor who prefers to keep them in the department rather than recommend them for deserved promotions elsewhere. A more systematic method would involve the use of a skills inventory system to locate all viable candidates. Figure 6.3 is an example of the many steps in an internal recruitment process in one organization. In this situation, the human resource department searches the organization's records to locate possible candidates; then a long series of steps is followed to determine whether or not the candidate fits the opening.

The most commonly used system for internal recruitment is that of **job posting and bidding.** The HR manager posts openings on bulletin boards, publishes them in an in-house newspaper, and/or posts them on the company's intranet. Employees nominate themselves if they are interested in being considered for an opening. Many large or unionized companies use this method, and all but the very top civil service jobs are filled internally by this method.[25]

Job postings describe the positions, locations, pay rates, and qualifications and encourage all interested employees to apply. The hiring manager and an HR representative evaluate the candidates and make the selection decision. Employees who apply but are not selected often receive feedback. This feedback loop demonstrates that the system operates in an open and fair manner and helps rejected candidates understand how to improve their qualifications for future openings.[26]

In unionized companies, the basis of selection and other details of the posting-and-bidding process are spelled out in the union contract. Two types of clauses are common. The first type says that the hiring manager will select the applicant with the most seniority if he or she is at least minimally qualified. The second type says that the hiring manager will select the most qualified person but that if there are two equally qualified candidates, the hiring manager will choose the one with more seniority. In nonunionized organizations, policies may state that the selection decision will be based primarily on the applicant's ability to do the vacant job and secondarily on the applicant's performance, attendance, and seniority in his or her present job.[27]

● **FIGURE 6.3**

Internal Recruitment
Process

Source: Reprinted with
permission from Bernhard
Welle, Vice President, Human
Resources, Dial Corp., Phoenix,
Ariz.

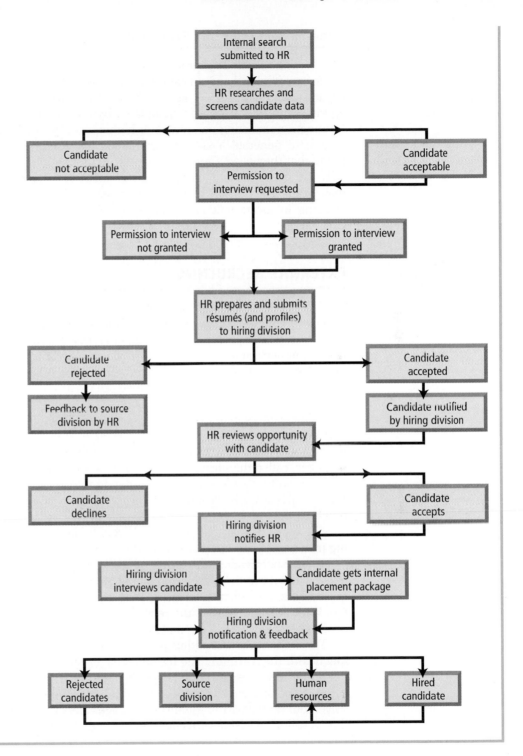

Internal Recruiting for Exempt Positions

The posting-and-bidding process is relatively rare as a method of internal recruiting for professional and managerial positions in the private sector, although a few organizations have used it successfully.[28] Organizations trying to fill vacant managerial slots might identify candidates by consulting replacement charts or by forming a nominating committee of higher managers who would pool their information to generate a slate of candidates. Larger organizations, however, have found that they need a more systematic method of identifying candidates, particularly if they wish to encourage transfers across divisional lines. These firms use managerial succession–planning processes and human resource information systems to locate suitable candidates. (Succession planning was discussed in Chapter 3.)

EXTERNAL RECRUITING

A successful external recruiting effort requires careful planning and coordination. In most medium-sized and large organizations, HRM professionals do most of the recruiting. These people may be human resource generalists who spend some of their time performing recruitment activities or full-time recruiters who specialize in seeking and screening potential new employees. A separate recruiting function with at least one full-time recruiter tends to exist in organizations that have a continuing need to recruit a minimum of fifty to one hundred exempt employees each year.[29] Recruiters may make hiring decisions for some lower-level jobs, but ordinarily they locate, evaluate, and then refer the most qualified candidates to the manager (or sometimes the team) of the unit in which the vacancy exists. This manager, called the hiring manager, makes the final hiring decision, often in consultation with other managers. In order to find the right kind of candidates, recruiters must work closely with hiring managers throughout the recruitment process.

The recruiter's first step after receiving an assignment is to meet with the hiring manager to find out more about the position to be filled. The two of them must work out specifications in terms of what education, skills, and experience are needed and desired.[30] Besides obtaining the needed information about the job's requirements, the recruiter must also identify what might attract candidates to the job. With this information, the recruiter can begin to plan where to look for applicants, how many to look for, and how to screen them.

Throughout the recruiting process, the hiring manager should stay in close touch with the recruiter. The hiring manager should examine résumés or applications that have passed initial screening by the recruiter and should also review some of the applications that the recruiter rejected during the first step. Such involvement on the part of the hiring manager allows feedback as to whether or not the recruiter's decisions are consistent with the hiring manager's preferences.

Planning for External Recruiting

Before beginning the recruiting effort, the recruiter must plan which methods to use, how intensively to use them, and when to begin recruiting to produce the required number of candidates at the time they are needed. As a rule, higher-level positions take longer to fill. Several other factors, including the following, may make recruiting more difficult or time-consuming:

- The need for a confidential search and/or the requirement that no advertising be done
- A technically complex position for which qualified individuals are hard to find
- Competition in the marketplace for the type of candidates needed
- A poor industry, company, or division reputation
- Low pay relative to what other firms are offering to similarly qualified individuals
- An unclear job description or confusing reporting relationships
- No housing assistance or relocation costs paid by the company
- An undesirable location

These factors either make it difficult to locate candidates or make candidates less willing to entertain offers.[31] Under any of these conditions, recruiters should begin the search early, consider using a wider than usual range of recruiting methods, and perhaps target nontraditional segments of the labor market.

If data from past recruiting efforts are available, recruiters should calculate, for different types of positions, the average time between the first contact with an applicant and the first day on the job. Such data can help in determining how far in advance to begin the recruiting process.[32]

An article by Robert Armacost and Rohne Jauernig contains a sophisticated example of recruitment planning in a large city. The municipality authorized a single position, that of pension financial manager, in early November and requested that it be filled by the first or second week of January. This was a high-level position that involved managing a $14 billion pension fund. The city's civil service rules specified a complex set of recruiting and selection steps. The recruiter assigned to the project first estimated the time required to complete each step, determined which steps could occur concurrently, and identified steps that were critical in that they could slow down the entire project. The recruiter applied the Critical Path Method (CPM) and the Program Evaluation Review Technique (PERT) to identify the quickest way to move through the set of activities to the final step of producing a ranked eligibility list of candidates. The recruiter also identified activities that could be speeded up over their expected duration by overtime work ("crashed"). Ultimately, the recruiter forwarded the eligibility list to decision makers just forty-one days after the project began. Table 6.1 shows the activities involved, the estimated and actual time in days to complete each one, and the activities that were "crashed" through overtime to keep the recruitment plan on schedule when other activities took longer than expected.[33]

More commonly, recruitment planning uses somewhat less sophisticated methods. Recruiting goals are usually expressed in terms of the number of positions to be filled. However, knowing that the firm needs to hire fifteen engineers does not immediately tell a recruiter how extensively to search. What the recruiter really needs to know is how many applications or initial interviews will be needed to locate fifteen engineers who are not only able to pass all the selection hurdles but also willing to accept a job offer. Based on past experience in similar situations, the recruiter may be able to calculate yield ratios for different jobs or recruiting methods. A **yield ratio** is the number of candidates who pass each stage of the

● **TABLE 6.1**

Finding a Pension Financial Manager: Time in Days for Recruitment and Selection Activities

Activities	Expected Time	Actual Time	Crash Time	Crash Cost
Job analysis and announcement sheet	2.33	2.0		
Education and experience questionnaires	1.0	0.5		
Advertisement/legal notice	1.0	3.5		
Recruitment/accepting applications	20.17	23.0		
Application review	2.33		1.0	$124
Oral board list development	1.92	3.0		
Lining up raters	1.25		0.5	$69
Questionnaire rating form	1.08	0.5		
Oral examination and rating form	4.83		1.0	$263
Ranking questionnaires	7.17	6.0		$155
Scheduling oral examinations	1.92	0.5		$132
Oral examination	2.0	2.0		
Eligibility list development	2.0		1.0	$94

Source: Adapted from Robert L. Armacost and Rohne L. Jauernig, "Planning and Managing a Major Recruiting Project," *Public Personnel Management,* Summer 1991, p. 123. Reprinted with permission of *Public Personnel Management,* International Personnel Management Association, Alexandria, Va.

selection process and enter the next stage compared with the number who entered each stage to begin with. For instance, suppose that (1) 25 percent of the applicants who submitted résumés in response to a newspaper advertisement meet the criteria for being invited to a screening interview, (2) about 50 percent of those who are screened are invited back for further interviews, (3) about 20 percent of those invited back decline to pursue their applications, (4) 33 percent of the remaining candidates receive job offers, and (5) 75 percent of the candidates who are offered jobs accept (see Figure 6.4). On the basis of yield ratios for past recruiting, the HR professional could calculate that the firm has to attract 600 candidates to apply to produce fifteen eventual hires. Previous experience data could also help the recruiter plan how many campuses to visit or how many ads to place to produce 600 applicants. Of course, dramatic changes in the unemployment rate may make projections based on previous recruitment data inaccurate.

Recruitment Information and Résumé-Tracking Systems

Before beginning to recruit candidates, the HR professional must have a system for tracking applicants as they move through the recruitment and selection process. The system may be manual or computerized, depending on the number of applicants handled. An efficient recruitment information system must ensure that candidates do not get lost but instead move through the process and stay informed of their status. An applicant who is deemed unsuitable should receive a polite letter to that effect as soon as possible after the decision. Good candidates who

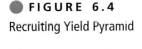

FIGURE 6.4

Recruiting Yield Pyramid

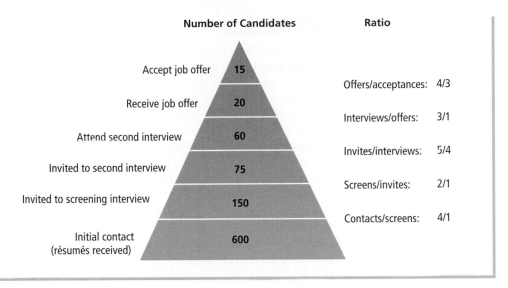

are pending should receive encouraging letters or e-mails to keep them interested in the organization. Such conscientious communication enhances an organization's image, even among candidates who are eventually rejected.[34]

The recruitment information system must be able to generate reports on applicant characteristics to determine whether adverse impact is occurring or affirmative action efforts have broadened the applicant pool as intended. The statistics generated must cover the percentages of black, other minority, and female applicants to various job categories. The recruitment information system also should be able to provide data necessary to calculate yield ratios, average time from first contact to first day on the job, and other indices helpful in planning and evaluating recruiting.[35]

The pace of recruiting and the volume of applications received have skyrocketed with the spread of Internet recruiting. Recruiters need help to quickly screen out resumes of the many individuals who are not qualified and to enable a very fast response to the most promising candidates. The best candidates may be hired by someone else unless a telephone interview is arranged within twenty-four to seventy-two hours of the electronic submission of a resume.[36] In the past few years, **résumé-tracking software** programs such as Restrac, Recruit-soft, and Resumix have been developed to store and search résumés electronically. Résumés are either submitted by e-mail or scanned in from paper copies.[37] An artificial intelligence program picks out and catalogs key words from the documents. Recruiters can search their résumé database for needed qualifications, and the programs create ranked lists of potentially qualified candidates. The U.S. Navy has adopted Resumix to help manage the more than 1,000 Internet resumes it receives every day.[38] Recently, more advanced **hiring management systems** have been developed to facilitate internal and external posting of jobs, sort and manage incoming resumes, and integrate corporate recruiting Web sites with commercial job boards. Some of the more frequently mentioned hiring management systems are provided by Hire.com, Hotjobs.com, Personic, Webhire, and BrassRing Systems.[39]

Informal Methods

External recruiting methods are often grouped into two classes: informal and formal. **Informal recruiting methods** tap a narrower labor market than formal methods. Informal methods include rehiring former employees or former cooperative education students, hiring people referred by present employees, and hiring from among those who have applied without being solicited (such applicants are called walk-ins or **gate hires**). **Formal recruiting methods** search the labor market more widely for candidates with no previous connection to the company.

Employee referral, also known as **word-of-mouth advertising,** is quick, effective, and usually inexpensive. Because employees who refer their friends and acquaintances as candidates have their own credibility on the line, they tend to refer people who are well qualified and well motivated and then to mentor these individuals once they are hired. APX International, an engineering firm in Michigan, finds 80 percent of its new hires by employee referral. Each time employees receive their paycheck, they are given information about current job openings. In essence, the firm has as many recruiters as it has employees.

Some companies give bonuses to employees who refer a good candidate. For example, the pharmaceutical company McGaw pays $2,000 for a successful referral for a sales job. Half is paid after the first month of employment and the remainder after six months if both the new hire and the referrer are still working for the company.[40] PeopleSoft has paid as much as $5,000 for referrals in hard-to-find specialties, and Canadian technology giant Nortel has run a $1 million cash and prizes scheme to encourage employee referrals. At Texas Instruments, employees who successfully refer others receive cash bonuses as well as entry into a raffle for a new car.[41] Referral bonuses became both more common and more generous as unemployment rates fell to near-record lows in the late 1990s.

One significant drawback of word-of-mouth advertising is that this method may reduce the likelihood of a firm's meeting its affirmative action goals. If a firm's work force is primarily nonminority, then the friends referred by present employees are likely to be nonminority as well. Thus companies should supplement informal methods with formal methods that reach a more diverse audience. Word-of-mouth advertising is also unlikely to generate the large numbers of candidates that might be needed for a major expansion.

Formal Methods

Formal methods of external recruiting entail searching the labor market for candidates who have no previous connection to the firm. These methods traditionally have included newspaper advertising, use of employment agencies and executive search firms, and campus recruiting. Posting job ads on the Internet, either on the company's own site or a commercial job board, has also become extremely popular in the last few years. Figure 6.5 shows the primary recruiting sources used by a sample of HR professionals in a 1996 survey (the Internet data are from another survey in 2000). Historically, newspaper advertising has been the most commonly used method of recruiting. Table 6.2 shows the effectiveness of various recruiting methods as perceived by HR executives in 1996 (while Internet recruiting was in its infancy). On a scale from 1 (not effective) to 5 (extremely effective for producing high-performing employees), it is clear that three methods were considered superior: employee referrals, university recruiting, and executive search firms.

● FIGURE 6.5

Recruiting Sources Used by HR Professionals

Source: Based on a survey of 303 HR professionals published in "HRdatafiles.hrm: Ways Companies Find and Recruit People," *HRMagazine*, December 1996, p. 53.

[a]Data on internet recruiting is from "More Pros and Cons to Internet Recruiting," *HR Focus*, May 2000, p. 8.

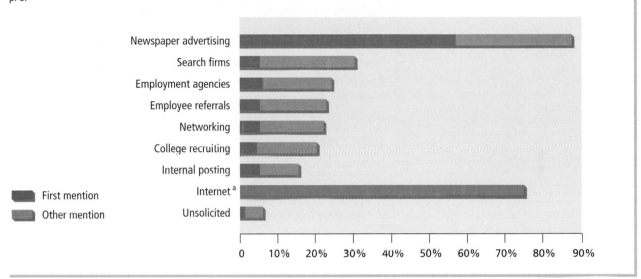

The most commonly used method at that time, newspaper advertising, was rated only average in effectiveness.[42]

● **Recruitment Advertising**   A very common formal recruiting method is newspaper advertising. This method, which is used by virtually all organizations, accounted for 70 percent of recruitment advertising expenditures in 1998.[43] Ads placed in newspapers are accessible to everyone and thus do not discriminate against any groups in disseminating information about job openings. Recruitment advertising has an obvious target—people who are seeking work—and an obvious goal—attracting these job seekers to apply for a job at a particular company. Newspaper ads, however, reach a much wider audience. Estimates are that only 10 to 20 percent of the readers of help-wanted ads are currently seeking work. Other readers are not actively looking for jobs but skim the ads regularly to see what is available. These readers are unlikely to apply immediately but are developing images of the employers whose ads they see. A well-designed, informative advertisement may help convince these people to consider the company at some later date when they are interested in a new job. Another audience for ads includes clients, stockholders, brokers, activists, and regulators, all of whom may have some interest in an organization's activities. The final audience for ads is a company's own employees. When one company discontinued its regular recruitment advertising, it found that its employees were suddenly nervous and that rumors of layoffs were circulating.[44] A well-designed advertising campaign can reinforce confidence and pride

● TABLE 6.2

Mean Rated Effectiveness of Recruiting Sources in a Survey
of 201 HR Executives

Source	Effectiveness
Employee referrals	3.84
College recruiting	3.81
Executive search firms	3.71
Professional associations	3.08
Newspaper advertisements	3.05
Direct (unsolicited) applications	2.86
Private employment agencies	2.78
Public employment agencies	1.92
Unions	1.64

Scale: 1 = Not good
     3 = Average
     5 = Extremely good

Source: Reprinted by permission of the publisher, from *HRFocus*, May 1996. © 1996
American Management Association, New York. http://www.amanet.org. All rights reserved.

among current employees. However, the U.S. Army found that the reverse can also occur. Soldiers reported uniformly negative reactions to the Army's "Be All You Can Be" ad campaign, feeling that it was misleading and unrealistic and failed to emphasize such important values as patriotism and self-sacrifice.[45]

The main purpose of a recruitment ad is to generate a **qualified response**—that is, to produce applications from candidates who are at least minimally qualified for the job. A good ad should also make screening of applications easy by clearly telling applicants what sort of information to provide in their application package. To elicit a qualified response, the ad must contain enough information about the job, necessary qualifications, location, and pay rate to allow uninterested or unqualified people to make the decision not to apply. At the same time, the ad must attract qualified candidates by conveying a good impression of the company or division and by emphasizing the advantages of the particular job. To achieve its objectives, an ad must not misrepresent the job and raise unrealistic expectations in candidates. Rather, it should clearly describe the legitimate attractions of the job.[46]

One form of advertisement is a **blind ad,** in which the company does not identify itself but rather asks candidates to reply to an anonymous post office box. A company may use blind ads when it does not want competitors to know that it is planning an expansion, when it does not want its own employees to know that one of them may be replaced, or when it has a poor reputation as an employer. Blind ads typically yield a significantly lower response rate than nonblind ads and should not be used unless there is a very good reason. A survey conducted in Europe in the late 1980s discovered that 75 percent of job ad readers said that the organization's name was a crucial piece of information that should always be included in a job advertisement.[47]

The greatest concentration of ads usually appears in Sunday newspapers in larger cities. For a firm seeking a person whose skills are relatively common in the general population (such as a bookkeeper, secretary, laborer, or salesperson), the newspaper is a good place to advertise. Local papers may be most appropriate if the firm does not expect to assist in employee relocation. If, however, a company is seeking a person with a specialized skill or unusual knowledge in a geographically dispersed labor market (such as a nuclear physicist), it should choose advertising sources that specifically target the population of qualified persons, such as publications and conventions of professional organizations.[48] For example, universities looking for new faculty for the management department could advertise in the Academy of Management Placement Roster, the academy's placement web site and conduct screening interviews at the academy's annual professional meeting.

● **Internet Recruiting   Internet recruiting** has grown at a phenomenal rate over the past few years. Seventy-nine percent of *Fortune*'s Global 500 companies recruited on the Internet in 2000, and 100 percent were expected to do so by 2002.[49] Entire new job titles—such as Internet Sourcer, Internet Recruiting Specialist, and Internet Recruiting Manager—have come into being in the past few years. Companies find that Internet recruiting is much less expensive and much faster than traditional methods. It is by far the most economical way to reach a nationwide or worldwide audience of job candidates. Further advantages of Web-based recruiting, as seen by HR managers and search consultants, are shown in Figure 6.6. A drawback can sometimes be the very large number of resumes that are submitted, many of which are not at all suited to the positions listed.[50]

At first, Internet recruiting was used largely to reach candidates in the information technology and engineering fields. Each year, as more and more people have gained access to the Web, a wider and wider range of jobs have been advertised and successfully filled via this recruitment medium. New graduates are especially active in using the Web to locate job opportunities, apply online, and research companies as potential employers. There are a number of ways in which the Internet is used by both job seekers and employers, including the following:

- Résumé bulletin boards on which candidates can list their qualifications and availabilities
- Sites that provide online access to the help-wanted sections of many major newspapers
- Sites that seek both original job listings from employers and résumés from applicants and provide search and matching services for a fee
- Company web sites that contain job listings and facilities for online submission of résumés

When Internet recruiting first began, recruiters used the Web much as they would use a newspaper—they posted job ads on Internet **job boards,** the e-equivalent of the classified section of the Sunday paper. While job boards attract a great deal of traffic, some recruiters feel that many of the résumés posted are out of date and that the best candidates have already been taken or have not posted their resumes in the first place. Companies are increasingly customizing their Internet recruiting, combining some use of job boards with their own careers site.

Cisco.com/jobs is considered a state-of-the-art recruiting web site. It contains a searchable database of thousands of jobs in the Cisco organization around the

● FIGURE 6.6

Why Recruit on the Internet? Opinion of HR Managers and Headhunters

Source: A. S. Kay, "Recruiters Embrace the Internet," *Informationweek*, March 20, 2000, pp. 72–80.

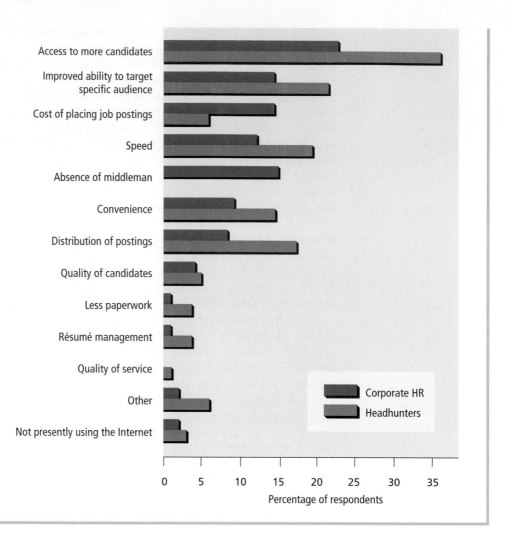

world. Job seekers can put job listings of interest in their "shopping basket" and then submit a résumé by e-mail or use the Profiler system on the site to build a résumé. On request, users can receive a weekly e-mail update of job listings matching their qualifications and location preferences. Users can also use the "Make Friends at Cisco" program to be introduced to a Cisco employee in a similar location and job who can give them the lowdown on what it's like to be an employee.

Some sites include surveys to allow job candidates to self-assess their value fit to the organization's culture. A good example is Texas Instrument's www.ti.com/recruit/docs/fitcheck.shtml. Other model recruiting sites include GE Power Systems' www.gepowercareers.com, Advanced Micro Devices' www.amd.com, Booz Allen & Hamilton's www.bah.com, NationsBank's www.nationsbank.com, and Eastman Kodak's www.kodak.com.[51] Wetfeet.com, a Web recruitment consulting firm, gives a monthly award for the best corporate recruiting web site. Its criteria for assessing sites can be found in Table 6.3.

Despite its popularity, Internet recruiting still accounts for a modest percentage of hires for most companies.[52] While Internet recruiting may initially attract

● **TABLE 6.3**

Criteria for an Effective Recruitment Web Site

Navigation:

1. An obvious link to the careers section from the company home page.

2. A clear navigation structure that guides users through the site.

3. Intuitive organization of content has priority over flashy applications.

Content:

1. Current and credible content that supports the company's recruitment brand.

2. Detailed company information on products and services, unit descriptions, management, and office locations.

3. Discussion of company culture and the value proposition to candidates.

4. Content that is designed for Web presentation.

Functionality:

1. Online resume submission, or a clear explanation of how to apply.

2. List of open jobs, searchable on multiple levels (specialty, location, experience, etc.).

3. Personalization features such as résumé builders, culture tests, etc.

Other Features:

1. Five mouse clicks or less from the company home page to a specific job opening.

2. E-mail acknowledgment of résumé submissions within 48 hours.

3. For some companies, a subsite for students/new graduates is very helpful. The Texas Instruments site provides extra advice on the job search and selection process for those who are relatively new to this activity.

Source: Courtesy of Texas Instruments Incorporated.

candidates to apply, this is only an early step in the recruiting process. Candidates still need face-to-face time with company representatives before they make a decision to switch employers, and employers also need to meet the candidate in person in order to assess the individual's suitability to the job and the company.

Internet recruiting is certainly not the best choice for all recruiting needs. Jobs requiring lower levels of education, paying less, and likely to be filled from a single local labor market are probably better suited to newspaper ads, local employee referrals, or a public job service agency. For example, gift catalog company Lillian Vernon Corp. uses Internet recruiting for management information systems and engineering jobs but uses local newspaper and television ads, billboards, and an airplane towing a banner to recruit locally each year when its employment swells from 1,000 to 5,000 for the Christmas rush.[53]

There were concerns about equal employment opportunity when Internet-based recruiting first began, because individuals who used the Net in the mid-1990s were largely white, male, and under forty years of age. Some firms were worried that Internet recruiting would skew their applicant pool well away from population demographics and make it harder to meet diversity goals. This has become less of an issue each year as a larger and larger percentage of the population gain ready access to the Net, but the issue may still merit consideration.[54]

● **Employment Agencies**   Another formal method of recruiting is to use an employment agency. An agency finds and prescreens applicants, referring those who seem qualified to the organization for further assessment and final selection. An agency can screen effectively only if it has a clear understanding of the position it is trying to fill. Thus it is very important that an employer be as specific and accurate as possible when describing a position and its requirements to an employment agency.

Employment agencies are covered by Title VII of the Civil Rights Act and thus are forbidden to discriminate in screening and referring candidates on the basis of race, color, sex, religion, or national origin. Sometimes, however, agencies have been known to discriminate at the request of firms. For instance, in a survey of recruiters for executive search firms, 14 percent reported having been asked not to refer Jewish candidates for certain positions.[55]

Alternatively, an employment agency may discriminate without the client organization's knowledge if the agency's recruiters mistakenly believe that a certain race or sex of candidate is more likely to be welcomed or if the agency uses an invalid selection device with an adverse impact in screening. In this case, both the agency and the client organization could face discrimination charges.[56]

Agencies that provide employment services can be publicly funded or for-profit agencies. On occasion, unions provide employment services as well.

● **Public Job Service Agencies**   Every state has a publicly funded agency that is affiliated with the U.S. Employment Service (USES). These **public job service agencies** have a number of offices throughout each state. In addition to administering unemployment compensation, public job service agencies attempt to find jobs for those seeking work. In most cases, able-bodied persons who are collecting unemployment compensation must register with the job service agency; however, anyone who is seeking work may register as well.

State job service agencies interview job seekers to find out about their skills, experience, and preferences. Employers call in their vacant jobs and describe the job specifications. The agency then matches applicants and refers qualified persons to the employer for interviews. State job service agencies may also test applicants when requested to do so by employers.

Public job service agencies fill primarily blue-collar and clerical positions. Sometimes, however, the agencies are able to fill higher-level openings. They are also able to recruit nationally through their web site, America's Job Bank (www.ajb.dni.us). This site lists both openings and résumés of job seekers. One day in February 2002, America's Job Bank listed 397,799 individuals seeking work and 929,198 jobs to be filled. State and USES employment agencies offer their services with no direct charge to either the job seeker or the employer.

● **Private, For-Profit Agencies**   Organizations use for-profit, **private employment agencies** to produce a set of prescreened candidates; job seekers use them to locate a suitable position. For each successful placement, agencies charge a fee that can range from 10 to 30 percent of the employee's first-year pay. The fee may be paid by either the applicant or the employer, depending on the labor market. Employment agencies specializing in administrative support personnel typically

● **TABLE 6.4**

Examples of Employment Agency and Executive Search Fees

Position	Salary	Fee	Fee Type
Administrative assistant	$ 30,000	$ 6,000	Contingency
Small company controller	$ 65,000	$16,250	Contingency
Director of business development	$200,000	$66,000	Retained
Underwriter	$ 58,000	$18,000	Contingency
Receptionist	$ 19,000	$ 3,600	Contingency

Source: Information from www.bankrate.com/brm/news/biz/tcb/19990916a.asp

handle jobs paying under $40,000 per year, while those filling professional/technical jobs in accounting, finance, data processing, retail, software engineering, and technical sales cover jobs paying $40,000 to $80,000 annually.[57] Private employment agencies are presently under threat from Internet job boards and the ability of companies to recruit directly through their own Web sites. Table 6.4 shows the fees charged for some specific positions by selected agencies in 1999. A contingency fee means that the fee is payable only if the position is successfully filled. The "retained" fee listed against the Director of Business Development position is paid for a search by an executive recruitment (headhunter) firm, regardless of the outcome of the effort.

● **Unions**   Unions sometimes provide employment services for their members. For construction workers and stevedores, labor contracts may specify that employers first seek candidates at the union hiring hall before recruiting elsewhere. The union hall refers union members seeking jobs to companies for evaluation and selection.

● **Additional Recruiting Methods**   As employers have had to contend with labor shortages in some regions and occupations, they have used more innovative recruitment methods. Some of these include job fairs, TV or radio ads, direct mail, point-of-sale recruitment advertising (on the assumption that those who buy your product may be interested in making or selling it), and employment hotlines to provide job information twenty-four hours a day. Another increasingly common method is "telecruiting," whereby potential candidates who are already employed are phoned in an effort to build their interest in changing employers. Table 6.5 shows additional methods of attracting employees that complement traditional recruiting activities.

Another way to innovate when job candidates are scarce is to consider bringing them in from an area where employees are more readily available. An example of a company that did this effectively is the Opryland Hotel in Nashville. When the hotel doubled in size in 1996, 1,500 more workers were needed. With 3 percent unemployment in the local labor market, traditional recruiting sources and methods would not yield the required number of qualified employees. Therefore, Opryland Hotel went to a place where unemployment stood at 12 percent—Puerto Rico. Two

● **TABLE 6.5**

Innovative External Recruiting Methods

Telecruiting Phone calls to potential candidates, with names obtained from mailing lists of professional associations, schools, and mailing list companies.

Direct mail Using lists from above sources.

Point-of-sale recruiting messages (posters, literature, messages on the back of cash register tapes) Useful if customers are potentially qualified applicants.

Talent scout cards One organization in need of customer-oriented service staff gave its managers "talent scout" cards inviting prospective candidates to apply for jobs. Managers were asked to distribute the cards to exceptionally friendly, helpful customer service personnel they encountered while doing their shopping.

Posters Displayed on community bulletin boards, parks, laundromats, banks, etc.

Door hangers Useful for recruiting in a specified geographic area.

Radio Alone or to refer candidates to open houses or large newspaper ads.

Billboards Fixed highway displays or electronic billboards with varying messages.

Hotlines and 800 numbers Telephone lines with either recorded job vacancy messages or live interviewers. Live lines are increasingly being made available on Sundays, when most newspaper ads appear and candidates have the time to follow up on openings.

Information seminars On job-hunting skills or on topics specific to one's industry, such as new developments in artificial intelligence. The latter may attract qualified professionals who would be reluctant to attend an open house or job fair, where the recruiting purpose is more explicit.

Welcome Wagon, relocation consultants, realtors These organizations are aware of newcomers to the community. Increasingly, spouses of individuals transferred into the community are seeking work and can be located through these sources.

Referral program Employee referral systems are common, but now some firms are encouraging their customers and suppliers to refer candidates as well.

Outplacement firms and local layoffs Skilled employees who have lost their jobs through no fault of their own may be found by contacting outplacement firms and by monitoring the local paper for layoffs at other establishments in the community.

Event recruiting Attend or sponsor or supply free refreshments or gifts at trendy events such as bike races, marathons, and grand openings of microbreweries. Cisco Systems has successfully used event participation to establish a reputation as a "cool" place to work by participating in the types of events popular with the people they wish to employ.

Re-recruiting of former employees Especially in high tech, good individuals may be recruited away by a new challenge or more money. A few years later, they may again be willing to move and can bring their newly honed skills back to a former employer. This requires companies to get over any hangups about "disloyal" employees and face the new realities of career paths in the twenty-first century.

Source: Compiled from Catherine D. Fyock, "Expanding the Talent Search: 19 Ways to Recruit Top Talent," *HRMagazine*, July 1991, pp. 32–35. Reprinted with permission from *HRMagazine*, published by the Society for Human Resource Management, Alexandria, Va. Additional ideas from K. Wheeler "Non-Traditional Recruiting Methods, Revised: Some Ideas and Examples," November 29, 2000, www.erexchange.com/articles

hundred and fifty employees were hired and relocated in the first year. Because Puerto Rico has a strong hospitality industry and relatively high unemployment, the company was easily able to find qualified staff.[58]

Recruiting Targeted Groups

In this section we will further discuss directing recruiting methods to specific segments of the labor market, such as executives, new college graduates, the disadvantaged, minorities, and older workers. In each case, these groups are better served with focused methods than with generic newspaper advertising. The more carefully one can specify the group being targeted, the better aimed one's recruitment methods can be. One example of excellent targeting is provided by United Airlines at Boston's Logan Airport. The company was having a hard time filling food service jobs in the late 1980s. Because the airline could offer free travel as a benefit, it decided to target people who would have a particular desire to fly: immigrants who had family members overseas. To reach this audience, the airline used recruiting posters placed along mass-transit routes serving immigrant sections of the city. The method was a great success, and the airline's applicant shortage was relieved.[59]

● **Executive Search Firms**   **Executive search firms** recruit managerial talent for positions paying over $80,000 per year. They view the organization rather than the candidate as their client. In fact, most executive search firms are not interested in receiving unsolicited applications or résumés. Instead, they conduct a separate nationwide or even international search for each position that they contract to fill.

Most of the *Fortune* 1,000 companies and many public-sector organizations make some use of executive search firms, or **headhunters**.[60] These firms charge employers substantial fees, usually equal to one-third the estimated first-year cash compensation (salary and bonus) for the position, plus search expenses. Many headhunters charge this fee whether or not the search results in a candidate's being hired. They see themselves as professionals who are paid to use their skills to make the search rather than to guarantee its outcome.

One survey showed that about 40 percent of all executive searches were completed successfully within the time specified by the contract. An additional 15 to 20 percent were eventually completed, and 40 percent failed.[61] Among the many reasons why a search might fail to produce an acceptable candidate are the following:

- Unclear or unrealistically high job specifications
- Poor company or industry reputation
- Internal politics in the hiring organization
- Insufficient research staff at the search firm
- Use of an overly specialized search firm[62]

Most of these reasons need no further explanation, but it might be helpful to understand a little more about overly specialized search firms. Typically, a firm that is hired to conduct a search agrees not to raid the client organization for a period of two years. The agency is barred from calling on that organization's employees as prospects in subsequent searches for other organizations. Executive search firms that have been very successful in writing a lot of contracts or that are highly specialized in a discipline (e.g., data-processing management) or in an industry (e.g., the petroleum industry) eventually may find themselves forbidden to recruit from the most likely sources of candidates, compromising their ability to conduct effective searches.

Firms use executive search firms for several reasons. First, search firms are better at locating candidates who are already employed and who may not be actively considering a job change. Second, they are very good at the "high-touch" relationship building that is necessary to woo executives from one company to another. Third, using search firms tends to be faster for a company than if it were to do its own recruiting. The search firm may already have extensive files of possible candidates and is experienced in locating additional names. Search firms claim they can fill a position in about half the time that a company would need to do its own recruiting. Fourth, the search firm can keep the hiring company's name a secret until the final referral stage if the company does not want others to know that staffing changes are contemplated in important positions. A final reason is that directly seducing a competitor's employees is considered bad form, but hiring a third party to do it is more acceptable.

The search process consists of several steps. Most search firms begin by drawing on the files accumulated in previous searches. Some firms claim to have extensive databases. Executive recruiters also search published sources, such as business periodicals and alumni directories of prestigious schools.[63] In addition, they contact organizations, trying to acquire information about managers who may fit the profile they are looking for.[64] Finally, recruiters phone prospects and try to interest them in the job. Recruiters proceed to interview the better prospects and check references before referring the top candidates to the hiring company for final selection. Occasionally, the search firm may continue its involvement in the process by serving as a mediator while the chosen candidate and the employer negotiate the details of the employment contract.[65]

The executive search industry grew rapidly in the 1990s but is now facing significant challenges. Perhaps the largest of these is the rise of the Internet, which allows savvy computer users to replicate search firms' extensive proprietary databases with relative ease. While high-end recruiting will continue to require a personal touch, big search firms like Korn/Ferry, Heidrick & Struggles International, and LAI Worldwide are hedging their bets by entering the Internet market themselves. Korn/Ferry's Internet subsidiary, Futurestep Inc., promises searches completed in four weeks rather than the months usually allowed.[66]

● **Campus Recruiting**   **Campus recruiting** is widely used by large and medium-sized firms that need highly educated entry-level employees. Campus recruiting can be very productive for an organization, since many good candidates can be interviewed in a short period of time and at a single location. Furthermore, it is convenient because the university recruitment center provides both space and administrative support.[67] Campus recruiting is moderate in cost. It is more expensive than word-of-mouth recruiting, gate hiring, or limited advertising, but it can be less expensive than using employment agencies (when the company pays the fee). A survey of employers in 2000 found that the cost per hire was about $6,200 and that firms generally interviewed about four to five candidates for each one they hired.[68]

One disadvantage of campus recruiting is that candidates are available to start work only at certain times of the year. Other disadvantages include the lack of experience and the inflated expectations often held by new graduates, the high cost of hiring graduates for positions that may not really require a college degree, and the difficulty of evaluating candidates who do not possess much relevant work history. In the last few years, another cost of campus recruiting in fields such as information technology, engineering, and accounting has been the hefty signing bonuses required to attract candidates. Bonuses ranged from $1,000 to about $10,000 and averaged $3,500 for these fields in 1999.[69]

The campus recruiting cycle can mean that candidates are interviewed and given job offers up to nine months before they are expected to begin work. In 2001, firms such as Intel and Cisco Systems made offers to candidates early in the year before an unexpected downturn in the information technology industry. When these new graduates were ready to report to work in June through September, they were no longer needed. Some firms asked students to defer reporting to work for several months; others offered "unsigning bonuses" to those who relinquished their offers.[70]

In planning a firm's university recruiting program, the recruiter must first decide how many schools to visit. Experts advise that more intensive recruiting at a smaller number of appropriately selected schools tends to be more effective than brief visits to a larger number of schools. Recruiters usually choose universities on the basis of the company's past experience with their graduates, the degrees offered, the reputation of the school, the demography of the student body (e.g., sex, age, and minority composition), the geographic location, and the quality of the college placement office.[71]

After targeting a subset of schools, the recruiter makes an effort to build up the company's reputation with students and disseminates detailed information on the types of careers available before making the interview visit. A key role in attracting students may be played by the recruiting brochure distributed prior to the interview visit. A British survey has found that a good brochure addresses students' most pressing information needs: what the job duties will be, starting salary ranges, where the company is located, training and career development policies, opportunity for promotion, and the disciplines and degrees required.[72] Making other company literature widely available on campus, awarding scholarships and prizes, employing students in internship and work/study programs, and sending executives into the classroom as guest speakers are additional ways to increase a company's visibility on campus. By visiting the same schools year after year, the firm can develop visibility and maintain an ongoing relationship with placement center officials. Recent research also suggests that a top-class company Web site is important in attracting university students to events both on and off campus.[73]

Although campus interviewers may be full-time HR professionals, they often are people who work in some other capacity during most of the year. For instance, engineering managers may be pressed into service to conduct campus interviews with engineering students for a few weeks each year. J.C. Penny sends younger staff members to recruit on campus on the assumption that they will relate better to students.[74] Candidates usually value the opportunity to be interviewed by someone in their own specialty, but this practice can backfire if the interviewer is not well trained for the role.[75] Before embarking on recruiting tours, managers should receive in-depth training on how to conduct interviews and should be made aware of EEO issues. They also need to be able to sensibly answer candidates' questions about career opportunities, the company's compensation and benefits packages, and procedures during the remainder of the selection process.

Campus interviews are usually followed by site-visit or plant-trip invitations to the best candidates. The firm should plan these visits carefully to make a good impression. For instance, the firm should pay all travel expenses in advance. The trip itself should be well organized, with interviews, meals, and tours carefully scheduled so that candidates are not left at loose ends. Candidates particularly enjoy having a sponsor to shepherd them through the entire trip. They also like talking to employees in positions similar to the one for which they are being considered.

Some organizations are dropping the term "campus recruiting," which implies a one-dimensional activity conducted a few weeks a year, in favor of the concept of a "university relations program." The latter brings home the importance of maintaining year-round visibility on selected campuses using a variety of methods.[76]

University cooperative education programs or internships are excellent methods of recruiting that provide companies with the opportunity to assess the ability of new professionals and get an inside track on hiring the best ones. Young professionals can be very impressed by a properly structured internship experience and may strongly desire to return to the same company full time after graduation. Kraft General Foods hires 300 interns each year and finds that the internship program provides a competitive edge in attracting top graduates.[77] A side benefit of cooperative and internship programs is that they keep the company well publicized on campuses at no additional cost.[78] The International Perspective box describes the lengths to which some British companies are going to recruit top candidates into internship and sponsorship programs early in their studies.

● **Recruiting Older Workers**   Older workers are often mentioned as a possible solution to labor shortages. Individuals are retiring at younger ages but are remaining in the work force in some fashion for years after their formal retirement.[79] Some older workers want full-time employment; others seek part-time work to keep them busy, renew social contacts, or supplement income; and still others are looking for opportunities to develop new skills and experience personal growth. Some individuals stay with their preretirement employer under different terms, while others seek different employers and/or different types of work. Employers say they value older workers because of their skills, scheduling flexibility, low absenteeism, high motivation and loyalty, and ability to mentor younger workers.

Older workers may not be reached by traditional recruitment advertising because they tend to assume that employers are not interested in them. Thus recruitment messages should specifically mention the value placed on experience and maturity, the chance to build a second or third career, the opportunity for flexible scheduling, and the opportunity to work while keeping one's Social Security benefits. These messages can be delivered through the senior employment networks in operation in many areas; through clubs, organizations, and publications for seniors; and also through more general advertising outlets.[80] One expert suggests holding "unretirement" parties or "second-career fairs" as well as including pictures of older workers on recruiting literature.[81]

● **Recruiting Disabled Workers**   The 43 million Americans with some form of disability comprise another large but often neglected source of workers. Some of these have become disabled in adulthood and have valuable prior work experience. If a disability does not interfere with a person's ability to perform the essential function of the job (either with or without accommodation), the employer may not discriminate against the person. In fact, people with disabilities often make excellent employees, displaying a high level of motivation and commitment and possessing skills commensurate with those of the nondisabled population. McDonald's hired over 9,000 physically or mentally disabled people as part of a special recruiting and development program.

As with older workers, recruiting the disabled is a matter of getting information about jobs to them and making them feel welcome as applicants. This may mean supplementing standard methods with contacts, advertising, and visits to organizations, networks, rehabilitation facilities, and training schools for various disabilities, as well as making sure that recruiting literature portrays acceptance of workers with disabilities. When assessing disabled candidates, it is critical to test

INTERNATIONAL PERSPECTIVE

Graduate Recruiting and Sponsorship in England

Competition for top university graduates is keen in the United Kingdom. Some companies are recruiting fewer graduates but looking for very high quality with a view to having these excellent candidates take on greater responsibilities. Many large firms have discovered that recruiting when students are in their final year of study is too late. They are undertaking sponsorship programs to reach the highest-potential candidates considerably sooner.

Proctor & Gamble U.K. targets students in their second year of university study. BAT, a tobacco company, signs up 300 first-year students in its "BAT—We Challenge You" scheme, with a view to hiring many of them when they graduate three years later. This program offers paid internships, scholarships, and an "ongoing relationship" with the organization during university studies. The company's graduate recruitment manager says that the program helps them identify "the 30 percent with moral qualms about working in our industry" before they are actually hired.

Arthur Andersen begins its recruiting even sooner—developing relationships with the most promising seventeen- and eighteen-year-olds in sixth form (final year of high school). These students are offered a scholarship of £12,000 per year for tuition and expenses and paid holiday work. They even receive £1,000 to travel the world and discover themselves. The program takes fifty students each year. There is no obligation to remain in the program or to commit to Arthur Andersen, but most do. Participants also provide great word-of-mouth advertising to a wide circle of university friends.

One survey showed that about 26 percent of firms surveyed sponsor university students for recruitment purposes. Sponsorship programs are particularly popular among manufacturing organizations, which target engineering students. Most programs offer paid internships or holiday work together with a modest bursary (scholarship), averaging £1,179 per year. Only one in four sponsoring companies begins its arrangements with students in their final year of study—the others begin earlier.

Does it work? Over 60% of sponsored students join their sponsoring organization after graduation. However, one-third of companies report success in hiring every one of the sponsored students to whom they offered a job. Note that failing to hire a sponsored student is not necessarily a failure of the program—it might be that the student and company have mutually decided that the "match" between them is not good enough to be continued long term. This could very well be a sound decision.

Sources: "Employers in Rush to Capture Young Talent," *People Management,* September 12, 1996, p. 9; "Firms Alter the Way They Recruit Top Prospects," *People Management,* January 11, 1996, pp. 8–9; and "Graduate Recruitment and Sponsorship: The 1996 IRS Survey of Employer Practice," *IRS Employment Review,* November 1996, pp. 9–10.

them only on "essential functions" of the job and to provide necessary accommodation during assessment so that applicants can display their capabilities fully.[82]

Crestar Bank of Richmond, Virginia (now SunTrust Bank Mid-Atlantic), has received an award for its efforts to hire disabled employees for its call centers in Richmond and Norfolk. The bank worked extensively with the Virginia Department of Rehabilitative Services and other public agencies to identify candidates and assess the accommodations needed to allow them to perform the job. The vast majority of accommodations (such as changing the height of a desk to suit a wheelchair) cost less than $1,000. In cases where the cost was higher (for example, to provide special software for a blind employee), the public agency partner was able to assist.[83]

● **Recruiting Disadvantaged Workers**   One largely underutilized source of workers is people in inner cities who may lack some job skills and also lack convenient employment opportunities, since many jobs have migrated to suburban areas. With training and attention to other needs such as transportation, these individuals can make fine employees. For instance, when Pizza Hut in New Jersey couldn't find enough local people to staff its suburban stores, it recruited in nearby cities where youth unemployment was high and then organized transportation from the city to the suburban stores.[84]

Urban youth, the homeless, and individuals recently released from prison have a very high unemployment rate. These employees may also need considerable training and support, with respect to both on-the-job behavior (why it is necessary to report to work on time, why and how to be polite to customers, how to dress for work) and off-the-job living arrangements (rent money during the transition to employment, transportation to work, etc.). Firms that have successfully hired from these labor pools recommend partnering with a nonprofit social service agency that can provide the extra training, support, and counseling that may be needed.[85] For instance, United Parcel Service installations in northern New Jersey successfully hired 1,500 employees through the Main Street Counseling Center, a community-based organization in Essex, New Jersey.[86] In some cases, employers are eligible for tax credits or subsidies for a portion of initial wages and training costs when hiring from specified groups.

● **Affirmative Action Recruiting**   Organizations with government contracts of over $100,000 must have a written affirmative action plan (AAP). This document includes goals for increasing the number of women and minorities in job classes in which they are currently underutilized by the organization. Thus many organizations are attempting to increase their hiring of women for upper-level or nontraditional jobs and their hiring of minorities for a wide range of jobs.

In order to hire minorities, firms must first find and attract applicants. Advertising is one way to do this. Firms should design ads carefully so that they do not convey stereotypes or preferences for male or nonminority applicants; the ads should also carry a line about the employer's commitment to equal employment opportunity. When seeking candidates for jobs not usually performed by one sex, companies should run ads that are sexually neutral or, from time to time, ads that are specially worded for affirmative action.[87] Figure 6.7 is an example of a T. J. Maxx ad that celebrates diversity and is designed to attract a wide variety of candidates. The Maryland State Police found that using a picture of a black officer on a recruiting billboard produced more minority applicants in two months than all other methods combined had produced during the preceding two years.[88]

In addition to advertising content, location is very important. Firms should place ads in minority and foreign-language newspapers, as well as in major dailies in cities with large minority populations. Firms also should consider advertising in military publications because the armed forces are disproportionately nonwhite and individuals finishing a tour of duty often make excellent employees. Other effective locations for ads are on minority or foreign-language radio stations, as well as in newsletters of professional organizations (e.g., the Association of Black Psychologists or the Society of Women Engineers) that reach a desired audience.

Other affirmative action recruiting methods include recruiting on predominantly minority or female junior college and college campuses, using the public job service office, placing banner ads on web sites that cater to minority interests, and using pri-

● **FIGURE 6.7**

Diversity Message in a Recruitment Advertisement

Source: Reprinted courtesy of T. J. Maxx.

If You Built
A $2.9 Billion
Company
By Offering All
Kinds Of
Merchandise
Would You Want
Only One Kind
Of Employee?

Of course not.

At T.J. Maxx, diversity is one of the mainstays of our $2.9 billion business, not only in our merchandise, but also in the Associates that make up our team at locations all across the country. Our Home Office – the corporate support center for all our activities nationwide – shares the company-wide commitment to diversity in all of its forms. We currently have wide-ranging opportunities for professionals at all levels with backgrounds in Finance, Human Resources, Systems, Merchandising, Marketing, Purchasing, Loss Prevention, or Administration. All in a corporate environment which includes a fitness center, on-site day care, and other amenities which reflect our concern for the well-being of every Associate. We feel this makes our Home Office a "one-of-a-kind" setting where our Associates can grow and succeed.

Send your resume to: T.J. Maxx, Dept. HM0895, 770 Cochituate Road, Framingham, MA 01701. Fax: (508) 390-2650. We are an equal opportunity employer committed to workforce diversity.

MAXXIMIZE YOUR POTENTIAL

vate employment agencies that specialize in minority placement. For example, His-panData is a database resource service specializing in providing Hispanic candidates for professional positions. Inroads is a nonprofit organization that identifies high-per-forming minority university students and places them in paid internships. Organiza-tions such as IBM, Chubb Corp., AT&T, and Proctor & Gamble have found that this program is an excellent way to attract top minority candidates.[89]

Once candidates are attracted to apply, it is important to convey the feeling that the company is seriously committed to valuing diversity. Recruiting teams should include minority-group members, and interviewers should be trained to communi-cate effectively with all kinds of people and focus on job-relevant abilities rather than on race- or gender-related attributes.

● **Recruiting Passive Job Seekers**   Potential job candidates can be categorized as to their level of activity in seeking a new job, according to a recent survey of 3,000 professionals and executives. Some are actively seeking employment, either be-cause they are currently unemployed (2 percent) or employed but looking for a change (9 percent). These candidates will proactively read job ads in newspapers and on the Web, use informal contacts to obtain job leads, post their résumés on job boards, and readily apply for jobs. Most traditional recruiting activities are aimed at this group of active candidates. Other people (53 percent) are not looking to make a job move—they are happy where they are or for some other reason not at all interested in pursuing employment alternatives. There is little point in target-ing recruiting efforts at this group. However, there is increasing interest in recruit-ing from among what have been called **passive job seekers.**[90] These individuals are not actively looking but would change jobs within the next six months if the right opportunity came along. They will not post their résumés on job boards, list with an employment agency, or regularly read employment ads, yet they are often highly desirable as employees. Methods that attract this group most effectively are probably employee referral, networking, general PR releases about the company, banner ads for the company's recruitment web site at other web sites likely to be visited by individuals in the desired profession, and headhunters. Some companies have developed skills in locating potential passive candidates on the Web—by using meta–search engines to locate résumés on individuals' homepages, lurking in newsgroups and e-forums to see who sounds clever, finding posted professional association membership rosters, and accessing electronic in-house directories of competitors.[91]

THE APPLICANT'S POINT OF VIEW

This section discusses the methods candidates use to search for jobs, the ways ap-plicants evaluate job offers and make decisions about accepting jobs, and a tech-nique that helps applicants make better decisions and produces more suitable em-ployees for organizations.

Job Search

Research on the methods job seekers use to find work indicates that the majority of jobs are obtained through informal sources. One survey determined that 60 to 90 percent of blue-collar employees found their jobs informally, as did 60 to 84 percent of managers, professionals, and technicians. Contacting employers directly (in person, by phone, or by letter) and seeking help from friends and relatives seem to be the most effective methods of job search for many types of candidates.[92] Private employment agencies are also effective in finding jobs.[93] Generally, using multiple search methods, using them frequently, beginning to search for work as early as possible, making many contacts, and not interrupting one's search for a vacation or other reason all help to reduce the duration of unemployment.[94] Being financially insecure and/or having a family to support are also correlated with speed of job finding, probably because individuals in such situations are more likely to take the first offer they receive.[95]

Job Choice

How do people decide which of several job offers to accept? There has been a fair amount of theorizing on this topic over the years. Early work in this field assumed that job offers were simultaneous and so candidates simply picked the best job. In real life, however, candidates seldom have more than one or two offers at the same time. Thus their decision process is more complicated; it is sequential rather than simultaneous. As a result, it seems likely that job seekers "satisfice," or take the first offer that is at least minimally acceptable on all important dimensions, rather than optimize, or engage in a very long and costly search to find the best possible job.[96]

Which factors do job seekers look at when evaluating a job offer? The research literature offers three views:

1. Individuals make rational choices based on objective factors such as pay, location, and opportunity for advancement.

2. People form gut-level preferences for one organization over another based on subjective factors that they may not even be aware of.

3. Job seekers do not have enough information to differentiate on the basis of either objective or subjective factors about the company or job; consequently, they tend to be unduly influenced by certain recruiting factors, such as the interviewer's skill or politeness.[97]

● **Objective Factors Approach**   According to the **objective factors approach,** candidates evaluate job offers on their merits. If a firm wishes to take a marketing orientation toward recruiting, it is necessary to find out which aspects of jobs are desirable to candidates and then provide and publicize those aspects. Table 6.6 shows how 1,000 American employees ranked the importance of ten job factors. Note that pay was ranked only fifth. Other studies also have found that pay comes in at about fifth when individuals rank their own preferences but is almost always ranked first in importance to "other people" or to "subordinates." Researchers agree that pay is probably quite important to most people but that it may be socially undesirable to admit this publicly.[98] In the study cited in Table 6.6, male and female employees had very similar preferences. However, there were pronounced differences in the ranks given to various job characteristics by employees of different age groups and income levels. Employees under age thirty ranked pay at the top of their list. Those aged thirty-one to forty ranked job security first, those aged forty-one to fifty felt that "being in on things" was most important, and those over age fifty most preferred interesting work. Employees earning less than $25,000 per

● **TABLE 6.6**

Average Ranks of the Importance of Ten Job Characteristics to American Employees

Job Characteristic	All Employees	Under Age 30	Ages 31–40	Ages 41–50	Age Over 50	Earnings < $25,000	Earnings $40,000–$50,000
Interesting work	1	4	2	3	1	5	1
Full appreciation of work done—others show appreciation of my work	2	5	3	2	2	4	3
A feeling of being "in on things," being well informed and involved	3	6	4	1	3	6	2
High job security	4	2	1	4	7	2	4
Good wages	5	1	5	5	8	1	6
Promotion and growth in my skills within the organization	6	3	6	8	9	3	5
Good working conditions	7	7	7	7	4	8	7
Personal loyalty to employees from superiors and the organization	8	9	9	6	5	7	8
Tactful discipline from superiors	9	8	10	9	10	10	9
Sympathetic help with personal problems from superiors	10	10	8	10	6	9	10

Source: Data compiled from: K. Kovach, "Employee Motivation: Addressing a Crucial Factor in Your Organization's Performance," 1994. Reprinted by permission of Dr. Kenneth A. Kovach, George Mason University, Fairfax, Virginia.

year placed good wages and job security at the top of their list, whereas those earning $40,000 to $50,000 put interesting work and being in on things in the top two positions. A 1999 survey of graduating college students asked which of four items respondents valued most in making a career decision. The winner by a large margin, selected by 42 percent of respondents, was balancing work and personal life. This was followed by money (26 percent), advancement potential (23 percent), and location (9 percent).[99]

Research generally supports objective job factors as the primary determinants of applicants' final job choice decisions.[100] The recruiting implications of the objective job factors approach are straightforward. Organizations and recruiters need to find out which job factors are important to most candidates and then attempt to make these factors available. The most important and influential factors should receive the most emphasis in recruiting literature and in other communications with candidates. In other words, recruiters need to apply market research techniques to the task of selling the organization's merits to job candidates and also to improving the "product" they are trying to sell.[101]

● **Subjective Factors Approach** Those favoring the **subjective factors approach** say that applicants evaluate the "perceived ability of a firm to provide satisfaction for [their] deep-seated and often unrecognized emotional needs."[102] There is some support for the idea that individuals are attracted to organizations whose images or climates match their personality and values.[103] For instance, security-minded individuals might gravitate toward paternalistic organizations. From a recruiting standpoint, this approach suggests that applicants must have enough contact with the organization to assess whether or not the subjective aspects of the organization fit their own needs. Recruiting literature also might discuss the organization's culture and prevailing values to help applicants assess the fit with their own preferences.

Recent research verifies that graduates are more likely to apply for an interview with firms that have a good image or reputation. Among the determinants of image were previous contact with the firm, use of the firm's product, studying the organization in class, and amount of useful information in the recruiting literature.[104] This research confirms our earlier recommendation that firms should try to be highly visible on campus in a variety of ways in order to support their campus recruiting efforts.

● **Recruiting Factors Approach**   Those who take the **recruiting factors approach** hold that candidates do not usually acquire enough knowledge of either organizations or jobs to make a rational decision between job offers. This lack of discriminating information causes job seekers, particularly inexperienced ones, to be unduly influenced by recruiting factors such as the interest and concern the recruiter shows or the smoothness with which the recruiter handles paperwork. These recruiter behaviors are taken as indicators of the likely characteristics of the rest of the organization.[105]

A great deal of research verifies that recruiting factors do have some impact on job choice decisions. For instance, students are more impressed when the recruiter has the title Director of Recruiting than when the same person uses no title. Students are unfavorably impressed by interviewers who are lacking in verbal fluency (who pause, repeat themselves, or stumble when asking questions).[106] Other studies have found that interviewers who are pleasant, conduct interviews in an organized fashion, are knowledgeable about the job, have read the applicant's résumé before the interview, and show interest in the candidate make a better impression and increase the probability of job offer acceptance.[107] Interviewers who present a balanced (positive and negative) picture of the job are perceived as being more credible and trustworthy than those who present only positive information.[108] Long time lags between selection steps (e.g., a wait of two months after a screening interview before the applicant is invited on a plant trip), poorly organized site visits, and stress interviews tend to sour applicants on a company. Finally, a recruiter who stays in touch with a candidate after an offer is extended helps increase job offer acceptances and increase the rate at which candidates who have accepted actually show up to begin work.[109]

The recruiting factors approach to job choice clearly points to the importance of a highly professional recruiting function. Interviewers need to be trained or selected for both style and substance. More specifically, it has been suggested that effective recruiters "must possess an image and appearance that reflects favorably on the organization: an outgoing nature; flexibility, willingness to take necessary risks, ability to think on one's feet, skill in setting priorities; self-motivation, and salesmanship," as well as communication, interpersonal abilities, and familiarity with the organization.[110] In addition to these personal traits and skills, which aid in making a good impression, recruiters must be sure that contacts with candidates are timely and informative and that site visits are well choreographed.

● FIGURE 6.8

Factors Affecting Job Choice

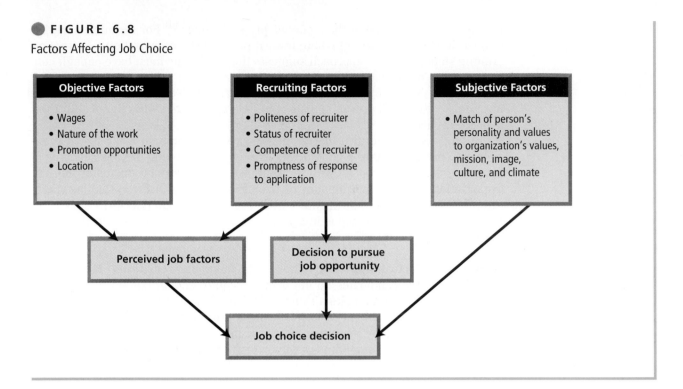

Computerized hiring management systems can also assist by providing candidates with regular e-mailed updates on their progress and the company's continuing interest in them.

The three views of the applicant decision process are beginning to be integrated, as shown in Figure 6.8. It appears that recruiting factors have their greatest impact on applicant reactions early in the recruiting process, at the initial inquiry and first interview stage. Good treatment here means that candidates are more likely to decide to pursue their application with the organization. Also, a competent recruiter can influence candidate perceptions of the objective factors in the job by providing greater amounts of relevant information. Objective factors are not always accurately perceived by applicants, but these factors and the candidate's perceptions of them become much more important as candidates learn more and move closer to their final decision about which job to accept.[111] Although recruiting factors may not always directly affect final job choice decisions, a professional approach to recruiting is necessary to attract and sustain the interest of desirable job candidates.

Realistic Job Preview

Once a new employee has been recruited and selected, he or she must adjust to the new job and organization. There may be problems at this step, as evidenced by the high rate of turnover among new hires in their first few months. One reason for the turnover may be that the job did not match the newcomer's expectations or desires.[112] The recruitment process may be partly responsible for this mismatch,

● **TABLE 6.7**

A Comparison of a Realistic Job Preview Film and a Traditional Recruiting Film

Material in Both Films	Material in Traditional Film	Material in RJP Film
Customers can be quite unfriendly at times; work is fast-paced; helping customers can be satisfying; dealing with others is a large part of the job. Action shots of operators handling an emergency call, a "wise-guy" call, a credit-card call, an overseas call, a "nasty" customer, and a directory-assistance request.	Everyone seems happy at work; the work is exciting, important, and challenging.	The job is routine, lacks variety, and may become boring. Supervision is close so that there is little freedom and limited opportunity to make friends with coworkers. Employees are criticized for poor performance but seldom praised for good performance. The job is challenging at first, but once it is learned, it is easy.

Source: Reprinted from *Personnel*, July/Aug. 1975. Copyright © 1975 American Management Association. Used with permission of the publisher, American Management Association, New York, NY. All rights reserved. http://www.amanet.org.

since recruiters tend to present jobs in very favorable terms in order to increase candidates' offer acceptance rate.

One way to prevent these problems is to use a **realistic job preview (RJP),** a down-to-earth presentation of both the favorable and unfavorable aspects of the job. Ideally, each stage of recruiting is honest and realistic. An RJP may take the form of a booklet or film about the job, realistic information delivered by an interviewer, or a work-sample test that exposes the candidate to actual job conditions and activities. Table 6.7 contrasts the contents of an RJP recruiting film with the contents of an unrealistically positive film that was shown to telephone operator applicants.

Many studies have compared the attitudes and behaviors of realistically recruited employees with those of unrealistically recruited persons. Overall, these studies show that RJPs sometimes reduce turnover, lower recruits' expectations about the job, slightly reduce the job offer acceptance rate, and slightly increase job satisfaction and commitment to the organization among new hires.[113] While the beneficial effects of RJPs are not always pronounced, the cost of forestalling just a few early turnovers may justify the use of the technique. Several reasons for the effects of RJPs have been suggested and have received varying degrees of support in the literature:[114]

1. *Self-selection*: If the RJP helps the applicant realize that the job will not be personally satisfying, the applicant may choose not to take the job or select him- or herself out of the organization's selection process. Without this realistic information, the applicant might have accepted the offer and could have become an early turnover statistic.

2. *Commitment to the decision*: When the RJP is presented before the candidate accepts or rejects the job offer, the candidate feels that he or she has made an informed decision about the job. Having accepted a job known to include difficult moments or distasteful duties, a newcomer feels less justified in reversing the decision and quitting when an unpleasant event actually occurs.

3. *Lowered expectations*: The aim of an RJP is to lower, or make more realistic, the expectations that the newcomer holds about the job. One theory of job satisfaction states that dissatisfaction is a function of the discrepancy between what one expects on a job and what one actually gets. Lowering expectations reduces the gap between expectations and reality; consequently, dissatisfaction decreases. Since dissatisfaction is one cause of turnover, this mechanism can explain both attitudinal and behavioral differences between RJP and no-RJP groups.

4. *Coping*: Research has shown that unpleasant events are less stressful and dealt with more effectively if they are expected than if they are surprises. It is possible that the RJP operates by improving the ability of new hires to cope with negative aspects of the job. The RJP may stimulate newcomers to mentally rehearse their reactions to anticipated job problems and so increase their ability to deal with problems when they occur.

RJPs are most useful when recruiters present them early in the recruiting process (so that the self-selection and commitment processes can occur). RJPs are particularly effective for jobs in which there tends to be early high turnover and for complex jobs in which applicants are unlikely to have an accurate picture of the job or occupational field prior to applying.[115] RJPs make the most sense when there are plenty of applicants for the available openings; if some decide to decline offers, the jobs can still be filled. Finally, RJPs are most effective in reducing turnover when unemployment is low. In this situation, applicants will be most likely to turn down a job offer that does not suit them because other jobs are readily available.[116]

EVALUATION AND BENCHMARKING OF RECRUITMENT

A firm should evaluate its recruitment process along with all its other human resource management activities. Collecting appropriate evaluation measures on past recruiting efforts can help an organization to predict the time and budget needed to fill future openings, identify the recruiting methods that yield the greatest number or the best quality of candidates, and evaluate the job performance of individual recruiters. Benchmarking against similar firms can also be informative. The granddaddy of all recruiting evaluation measures is cost per hire, though speed of filling vacancies is also an important measure.

Nationwide Insurance, a large insurance and financial services firm, recently benchmarked its recruiting methods and subsequently made a number of improvements to the process. Its time to hire averaged forty-five days, and a survey showed that hiring managers were not particularly satisfied with the service they were receiving. Fifteen to twenty thousand applications were received per month. With this volume, there were delays in processing, some candidates fell through the cracks, and most did not receive a timely acknowledgment of their application. Hiring managers were receiving lists of fifteen candidates per position, placing too much of a burden of assessment and rejection on them. Improvements to the recruitment system included online résumé submission with instant acknowledgment and another e-mail thanking the candidate for his or her interest within twenty-four hours. Those who haven't been invited for an interview for their job of choice receive a later e-mail asking whether they are still interested in Nationwide and would like to remain in the candidate pool for future jobs. Recruiters are doing more prescreening, and now hiring managers are sent only the top three candidates. At some job fairs, Nationwide is almost hiring on the spot. Candidates can talk to a prescreener, then have a complete interview, then talk to the head of the hiring unit in a single day. If they pass these hurdles, they are told that Nationwide is very interested in hiring them. The required drug tests and background checks are undertaken within the next forty-eight hours, and a final offer is made within just a few days. The time to hire has come down substantially, and hiring managers report much greater satisfaction with recruiting services since these changes were instituted.[117]

Measures Used to Evaluate Recruiters

In appraising the performance of individual recruiters, the HR manager must keep in mind the difficulty of the search assignments as well as the number of positions the recruiter filled. A recruiter will be able to locate ten qualified laborers more quickly than ten engineers and ten engineers more quickly than ten executives.[118] After allowing for differences in assignment difficulty, the appraiser might count the number of applications the recruiter processed, the hires the applications produced, and the eventual job successes of those the recruiter recommended for hire. Finally, the appraiser might survey applicants who both accepted and rejected offers to see if their treatment by various recruiters could have been improved.[119]

Measures Used to Evaluate Recruiting Sources

When a number of sources or methods of recruiting have been used, it makes sense for the HR manager to evaluate each to see whether some are consistently superior to others. Inefficient sources can be dropped from future recruiting efforts. Some of the criteria that are used to evaluate sources and methods are total cost, cost per hire, number of applicants generated, yield ratios, and eventual job tenure and performance of hires. Table 6.8 shows some hypothetical evaluation results. As a rule, gate hires and employee referrals tend to be quick and low in cost. Advertising and campus recruiting take the longest and cost more. Recruiting through agencies is intermediate in terms of the time it takes to fill positions, but it is often the most costly method.[120]

Differences in the Quality of Recruiting Sources

Research on the quality of different recruiting sources offers some interesting viewpoints. Stephen Mangum asserts that the best jobs are filled internally or through informal recruiting methods, such as word of mouth, and that the best candidates also find new jobs informally, through a network of contacts who are aware of their abilities. He suggests that only the least desirable jobs and least employable people are left to be matched through formal methods, such as newspaper ads, employment agencies, and Internet job boards.[121] Although this argument may be overstated, there is a body of research to support the idea that informal sources do produce the best candidates. A series of studies of employee tenure indicate that candidates who are referred by a current employee, who are rehired, or who turn in an unsolicited application stay in their new jobs significantly longer than those hired through agencies or newspaper ads.[122] The research on the job

● **TABLE 6.8**

Example of Recruiting Source Evaluation Data

Recruiting Source	Cost per Hire	Contacts per Hire	Offers per Hire	Time to Fill in Days	Turnover in First Year
Unsolicited applications	Low	6	1.5	18	10%
Employee referrals	Low-moderate[a]	1.4	1.2	23	6%
Campus recruiting	Moderate	4.5	3	110	20%
Private employment agencies	Moderate–high	4	2	35	12%
Newspaper Advertising	Moderate	12	2	35	15%
Internet	Low	20	5	20	25%

[a]depending on whether referral bonus is paid

performance of hires from different sources is less extensive and less conclusive than that on turnover, but some evidence for similar differences does exist.[123]

Two rationales for differences in the applicant quality of recruiting sources have been advanced. One, based on RJP research, suggests that informal sources, such as rehires and employee referrals, yield candidates who have been told about both the good and bad aspects of the job and thus have a lower turnover rate. The second explanation is that sources may simply tap into different kinds of people in terms of ability level, motivation, or experience. Anyone can read a newspaper or surf the Net, but perhaps it takes a candidate with a bit more initiative to research a company enough to make an unsolicited application or to find out about an opening from contacts. In addition, more experienced employees may be more likely to have and use a network of informal sources, whereas new labor force entrants may tend to use newspapers and agencies to find positions; we know that younger people also have higher turnover rates.[124] There is some support in the research literature for all these propositions.[125]

Ideally, each firm should conduct its own analysis of source quality for each type of job. Recruiting sources that are of low quality can be used less intensively or eliminated altogether in future recruiting. In one study of recruiting sources for bank tellers, the researcher estimated that by discontinuing use of the three worst sources, the bank could save $180,000 over four years in reduced turnover, recruiting, and training costs.[126]

Summary of Key Points

Individuals seeking jobs and organizations seeking good employees may have conflicting objectives during the recruiting process. These may lead each side to emphasize the positive and conceal the negative about itself.

Organizational recruiting plans should be guided by good human resource planning and keyed to the strategy and values of the organization. A company's recruiting philosophy and goals will influence the approach it takes to recruiting. In some cases, recruiting may not be necessary if a company explores creative ways of dealing with labor shortages, such as outsourcing, temporaries, or employee leasing.

One of the first decisions a company must make in filling a vacancy is whether to seek a current employee through internal recruiting or seek a new hire from the external labor market. Internal and external recruiting have their own advantages and disadvantages. A firm that chooses internal recruiting has several methods available, including the job posting-and-bidding (self-nomination) process, nomination by superiors, and searches of the human resource information system.

Recruiting should be planned carefully so that the correct scope and timing of activities can be undertaken. Companies also need a means of tracking applicants, searching résumés, and producing applicant flow statistics. These activities can be accomplished manually or by computerized systems of varying levels of sophistication.

If a firm chooses external recruiting, it must plan carefully and may consider a wide variety of methods. Informal methods, such as gate hires and employee referrals, are inexpensive and often produce very good candidates. Formal methods include recruitment advertising (either in print or on the Internet), using employment agencies, and campus recruiting. Advertising makes vacancies known to a large number of potential applicants. Properly written ads can produce qualified applicants, help a firm meet its affirmative action goals, and enhance a company's public image. Employment agencies and executive search firms may be used to locate and prescreen applicants. Using private agencies and search firms is costly but may bring a company results significantly faster than if the company did its own recruiting. Campus recruiting is used by many organizations to hire entry-level professional and technical employees. A carefully planned university relations program can make campus recruiting very effective. Special recruitment campaigns targeting, for example, older people or the disadvantaged also have proven effective in attracting employees in tight labor markets.

From the job seeker's point of view, organizations and jobs may be evaluated on the basis of objective factors of a job, subjective factors such as an organization's image or culture, or recruiting factors such as recruiter behavior and informativeness. Ideally, job seekers should be given realistic job previews that help them to select jobs they will like and to reduce turnover and dissatisfaction due to unmet expectations.

After a company completes a recruiting effort, it should evaluate the outcomes, its recruiters, and the sources and methods used. In this way, the firm can improve the quality, success, and cost-effectiveness of future recruiting efforts.

The Manager's Vocabulary

blind ad
campus recruiting
countercyclical hiring
employee leasing
employee referral
executive search firm
exempt job
external recruiting
formal recruiting methods
gate hires
headhunters
hiring management systems
informal recruiting methods
internal recruiting
Internet recruiting
job board
job posting and bidding
marketing orientation to recruiting
nonexempt job
objective factors approach
passive job seeker
private employment agency
public job service agency
qualified response
realistic job preview (RJP)
recruiting factors approach
résumé-tracking software
ripple effect
subjective factors approach
temporaries
word-of-mouth advertising
yield ratio

Questions for Discussion

1. Explain how the organization's and candidate's objectives in the recruiting process might conflict. How might these conflicts affect the eventual success of the recruiting and job search process?
2. What factors might go into a company's recruiting philosophy? How might the recruiting philosophies of a major international accounting firm and a small family-owned convenience store differ?
3. What are the pros and cons of using some form of temporary or leased employees rather than hiring permanent employees?

4. Suppose that a regional sales manager who needs to hire four salespeople delegates recruiting and initial screening to the regional HR office. What types of information must be exchanged between the sales manager and the recruiter to maximize the likelihood of a successful recruiting effort?

5. How are yield ratios used in recruitment planning?

6. How does internal recruiting for a nonexempt position typically differ from internal recruiting for an exempt position?

7. Think of a job that seems hard to fill in your local labor market. Using a wide variety of methods, design a recruitment campaign to attract candidates to this job.

8. Describe the ways in which companies and applicants can use the Internet for recruitment and job search.

9. Describe the services provided by various types of employment agencies and search firms. Why might a company use these organizations rather than doing its own recruiting?

10. Suppose that an organization plans to recruit at your university on a regular basis. What sorts of activities might it pursue to maximize recruiting success? Are there companies that are particularly visible and effective in recruiting on your campus? How did they get that way?

11. Pick one nontraditional labor market and plan a campaign to reach members of this market in your area.

12. Describe three views of how candidates evaluate organizations when choosing among job offers. What are the recruiting implications of each view?

13. Based on the data in Table 6.6, write a recruiting ad for a job paying $75,000 per year and requiring twelve to fifteen years of postuniversity experience (probably meaning that many candidates would be in their mid-thirties). Now rewrite the ad supposing that the same job paid $27,000 and was likely to be filled by someone just graduating from a junior college. How will you modify the contents of the ads to appeal to the likely job characteristic preferences of these different groups of candidates?

14. What is a realistic job preview? Describe the effects it has and the four possible explanations for these effects. Have you ever had a realistic job preview? What effect did it have on your decision to accept the job? What effect did it have on your decision to stick with the job if you accepted it?

15. How and why should recruiting methods and sources be evaluated?

16. What are some of the ethical issues that can arise in recruiting? Have you observed what you consider to be either bad manners or bad ethics on the part of companies seeking employees? What effect did this have on you?

● Case 6.1
Inova Health System

Inova Health System is a Falls Church, Virginia, provider of health care. Its 10,000 employees provide services in three hospitals, seven outpatient centers, and two long-term-care facilities and also provide home nursing visits. Historically, each of these units has managed its own recruiting. As health care budgets tightened, HR administrators at Inova wondered whether decentralized recruiting was still appropriate. Some of the problems encountered with each unit doing its own recruitment advertising and screening were the following:

• Duplication of advertising expenses—$500,000 in the past year
• Units competing with one another to recruit from the same labor market
• Candidates interested in jobs common to several facilities (such as nursing) needing to apply and interview separately at each facility
• Lack of internal mobility for current employees across units due to lack of knowledge of openings

- A less-than-consistent corporate identity projected to candidates and the community by unit-specific recruitment advertising
- Inability to measure recruiting effectiveness or keep accurate EEO/AA statistics because of varying record-keeping systems across units
- Inefficiencies because each unit is too small to support sophisticated recruitment technologies such as a twenty-four-hour jobs hotline or a computerized résumé-scanning and -tracking system

You are part of a task force of experienced recruiters drawn from Inova's larger units. The task force is charged with recommending what, if anything, should be done to improve the recruitment function at Inova.

1. How would you begin to study this problem?
2. Might you use benchmarking in any way? How?
3. Do you think you would choose to centralize the recruitment function? Why or why not?
4. If you do recommend a centralized recruiting office, what services would it provide?
5. If you centralize recruiting, what benefits would you anticipate for (a) the company and (b) the applicants?
6. What barriers might you encounter in implementing a centralized system?

Source: "HR at Inova Reengineers Recruitment Process" by Phyllis A. Savill, copyright June 1995. Used with permission of ACC Communications Inc. *Personnel Journal* (now known as *Workforce*), Costa Mesa, California. All rights reserved.

● Exercise 6.1
Creating Effective Recruitment Ads

1. Write a recruitment ad for a job you have held.
2. Explain where you would place this ad.
3. In groups, consider each ad and try to rewrite it to improve its appeal and likelihood of generating a qualified response. Consider layout and artwork as well as text.
4. Pick one ad and rewrite it to appeal especially to older workers.
5. Could some disabled people perform this job? Rewrite the ad to appeal to this audience, and discuss how you could go about finding disabled candidates.

● Exercise 6.2
Developing Recruiting Plans

Design a recruiting campaign for several of the situations described below. Include an explicit definition of the labor market you intend to reach; then select the method(s) you would use to reach this target audience. How would you attract qualified candidates to apply? Justify why your recruiting plan is appropriate and cost-effective for the particular job you are trying to fill. Explain why your recruiting plans differ from one another.

1. Toy World is opening a new superstore in Seattle in six months. The store manager and half the supervisors will come from other Toy World stores in the Pacific Northwest. All other employees will be new hires. A large number of stockroom workers and clerks are needed.[127]

2. A rapidly growing software company needs to hire about ten software engineers per month for the next year.
3. A U.S.-based manufacturer of agricultural chemicals needs to appoint a regional manager to spearhead its entry into the Southeast Asian market.
4. A seventy-outlet women's clothing store chain needs to fill two middle-management positions at its headquarters. The HR director realizes that all the current middle managers are white males.
5. The local 7-Eleven store needs two part-time clerks.

● Exercise 6.3
Recruiting on the Internet

1. For the occupation and job of your choice, search the Net for employment opportunities. Which sites seem most useful for a job seeker in this occupational area? What advice would you give to a novice user who is seeking job opportunities via the Internet?

2. Suppose you would like to work for a specific major company. Search the Net for that com-pany's advertisements or any other information about the company that would be useful to you as a job seeker. How many different locations did you find and use?

3. Suppose you are the director of recruiting for the company you chose in item 2. How would you strengthen your company's presence and recruiting effectiveness on the Internet?

Notes and References

1. Employment Management Association Annual Staffing Metrics Surveys.

2. Lyman W. Porter, Edward E. Lawler III, and J. Richard Hackman, *Behavior in Organizations* (New York: McGraw-Hill, 1975).

3. Sara L. Rynes and Alison E. Barber, "Applicant Attraction Strategies: An Organizational Perspective," *Academy of Management Review,* April 1990, pp. 286–310.

4. The first two aspects are based on James A. Breaugh, *Recruitment: Science and Practice* (Boston: PWS-Kent, 1992).

5. R. Rooseveldt Thomas, "From Affirmative Action to Affirming Diversity," *Harvard Business Review*, March–April 1990, pp. 107–117.

6. Steven D. Maurer, Vince Howe, and Thomas W. Lee, "Organizational Recruiting as Marketing Management: An Interdisciplinary Study of Engineering Graduates," *Personnel Psychology,* Winter 1992, pp. 807–833; and Albert H. McCarthy, "Research Provides Advertising Focus," *Personnel Journal,* August 1989, pp. 82–87.

7. S. P. Talbott, "Boost Your Campus Image to Attract Top Grads," *Recruitment Staffing Sourcebook* (supplement to the March 1996 issue of *Personnel Journal*), pp. 6–8.

8. Dave R. Dahl and Patrick R. Pinto, "Job Posting: An Industry Survey," *Personnel Journal,* January 1977, pp. 40–42; and W. Chan, "External Recruitment Versus Internal Promotion," *Journal of Labor Economics,* Vol. 14 (4), 1996, pp. 555–570.

9. Elmer H. Burack and Nicholas J. Mathys, *Human Resource Planning: A Pragmatic Approach to Manpower Staffing and Development* (Lake Forest, Ill.: Brace-Park Press, 1980); and D. Geoffrey John, "Staffing with Temporary Help," *Personnel Administrator,* January 1987, pp. 96–99.

10. J. Scott Lord, "Internal and External Recruitment," in *Human Resource Planning, Employment, and Practice,* ed. Wayne F. Cascio (Washington, D.C.: Bureau of National Affairs, 1989), pp. 73–102.

11. K. H. Chung, M. Labatkin, R. C. Rogers, and J. E. Owers, "Do Insiders Make Better CEOs Than Outsiders?" *Academy of Management Executive,* November 1987, pp. 325–331; and A. Gupta, "Contingency Perspectives on Strategic Leadership: Current Knowledge and Future Research Directions," in *The Ex-ecutive Effect: Concepts and Methods for Studying Top Managers,* ed. D. C. Hambrick (Greenwich, Conn.: JAI Press, 1988).

12. William E. Bright, "How One Company Manages Its Human Resources," *Harvard Business Review,* January–February 1976, pp. 81–93.

13. Charles R. Greer and Timothy C. Ireland, "Organizational and Financial Correlates of a 'Contrarian' Human Resource Investment Strategy," *Academy of Management Journal,* December 1992, pp. 956–984.

14. C. Cunningham, "Reeling in IT Talent in the Public Sector," *InfoWorld,* May 15, 2000, pp. 78–79.

15. Rynes and Barber, "Applicant Attraction Strategies." See Margaret L. Williams and George F. Dreher, "Compensation System Attributes and Applicant Pool Characteristics," *Academy of Management Journal,* August 1992, pp. 571–595, for evidence that firms improve their pay and benefit systems when they have had trouble filling vacancies.

16. L. A. West, Jr., and W. A. Bogumil, Jr. "Foreign Knowledge Workers as a Strategic Staffing Option," *Academy of Management Executive*, November 2000, pp. 71–83.

17. A. Turpin, "Moving in for the Skill," *Director,* July 2000, p. 23.

18. R. Barner, "Talent Wars in the Executive Suite: Six Trends Shaping Recruitment," *The Futurist,* May–June 2000, pp. 35–41.

19. Gladys Fazio Garlitz, "Temporary Workers: A Changing Industry," *Personnel Administrator,* March 1983, pp. 47–48; and J. L. Simonetti, N. Nykudym, and L. M. Sell, "Temporary Employees: A Permanent Boom?" *Personnel,* August 1988, pp. 50–56.

20. V. Frazee, "The Try-Before-You-Buy Method of Hiring," *Recruitment Staffing Sourcebook* (supplement to the August 1996 issue of *Personnel Journal*), pp. 6–8.

21. Garth Mangum, Donald Mayall, and Kristin Nelson, "The Temporary Help Industry: A Response to the Dual Internal Labor Market," *Industrial and Labor Relations Review,* July 1985, pp. 599–611; and Max Messmer, "Right-Sizing Reshapes Staffing Strategies," *HRMagazine,* October 1991, pp. 60–62.

22. Stephenie Overman, "Hired to Take Charge Temporarily," *HRMagazine,* June 1993, pp. 52–53.

23. John Ross, "Effective Ways to Hire Contingent Personnel," *HRMagazine,* February 1991, pp. 52–54.

24. Martin M. Greller and David M. Nee, *From Baby Boom to Baby Bust: How Business Can Meet the Demographic Challenge* (Reading, Mass.: Addison-Wesley, 1989), chap. 4.

25. Sharon M. Tarrant, "Setting Up an Electronic Job-Posting System," *Training & Development,* January 1994, pp. 39–42.

26. Dahl and Pinto, "Job Posting."

27. Garry G. Wallrapp, "Job Posting for Non-Exempt Employees: A Sample Program," *Personnel Journal,* October 1981, pp. 796–798.

28. James T. Gunn, "An Open Job-Bidding System for Professionals and Managers: Fact or Fiction," *Human Resource Planning,* Vol. 2, 1979, pp. 187–195.

29. Lord, "Internal and External Recruitment."

30. Robert Half, *Robert Half on Hiring* (New York: Crow, 1985).

31. Donn L. Dennis, "Evaluating Corporate Recruiting Efforts," *Personnel Administrator,* January 1985, pp. 21–26.

32. Roger H. Hawk, *The Recruitment Function* (New York: American Management Association, 1967).

33. Robert L. Armacost and Rohne L. Jauernig, "Planning and Managing a Major Recruiting Project," *Public Personnel Management,* Summer 1991, pp. 115–126.

34. M. Gibelman, "Managerial Manners—Notably Lacking in Personnel Recruiting," *Administration in Social Work,* Vol. 20, 1996, pp. 59–72.

35. This section draws on Christine White and Abbie W. Thorner, *Managing the Recruitment Process* (New York: Law and Business, 1982).

36. Scott Hays "Hiring on the Web," *Workforce,* Vol. 78 (8), August 1999, pp. 76–84.

37. W. H. Baker, K. DeTeinne, and K. L. Smart, "How *Fortune* 500 Companies Are Using Electronic Resume Management Systems," *Business Communication Quarterly*, September 1998, pp. 8–19.

38. S. P. Talbott, "Get the Most from Automated Résumé-Tracking Software," *Recruitment Staffing Sourcebook* (supplement to the March 1996 issue of *Personnel Journal*), pp. 18–20.

39. J. Meade, "Where Did They Go?" *HR Magazine,* September 2000, pp. 81–84.

40. K. Tyler, "Employees Can Help Recruit New Talent," *HRMagazine,* September 1996, pp. 57–60.

41. J. D. McCool, "Harnessing the Power of Employee Referrals," August 2, 2000. (Available at: www.wetfeet.com/employer/articles)

42. D. Terpstra, "The Search for Effective Methods," *HRFocus,* May 1996, pp. 16–17.

43. A. S. Kay, "Recruiters Embrace the Internet," *Informationweek,* March 20, 2000, pp. 72–80.

44. Van M. Evans, "Recruitment Advertising in the 80's," *Personnel Administrator,* December 1978, pp. 21–25, 30.

45. L. Shyles and J. E. Hocking, "The Army's 'Be All You Can Be' Campaign," *Armed Forces & Society,* Spring 1990, pp. 369–383.

46. Margaret Magnus, "Recruitment Ads That Work," *Personnel Journal,* August 1985, pp. 42–63; Martin Asdorian, Jr., "Drowning in Résumés," *HRMagazine,* September 1992, pp. 59–62; and Karel De Witte, "Recruitment Advertising," in *Assessment and Selection in Organizations,* ed. Peter Herriot (Chichester, England: Wiley, 1989), pp. 205–217.

47. De Witte, "Recruitment Advertising."

48. Robert A. Martin, "Employment Advertising—Hard Sell, Soft Sell, or What?" *Personnel,* May–June 1971, pp. 33–40.

49. Recruitsoft.com/iLogos Research, "Global 500 Web Site Recruiting 2000 Survey." (Available at: www.recruitsoft.com)

50. Scott Hays, "Hiring on the Web," *Workforce,* Vol. 78 (8), August 1999, pp. 76–84.

51. This list of cites is recommended in M. N. Martinez, "Get Job Seekers to Come to You," *HR Magazine,* August 2000, pp. 45–52.

52. "Online Recruiting: What Works, What Doesn't," *HR Focus,* March 2000, pp. 1, 11+.

53. Marlene Piturro "The Power of e-cruiting" *Management Review,* Vol. 89 (1), January 2000, pp. 33–37.

54. T. Hatlevig, "Internet Demographics Cause Recruiting Headaches," *Personnel Journal,* September 1995, pp. 157–158; and J. M. Stanton "Validity and Related Issues in Web-Based Hiring," *The Industrial Psychologist*, January 1999, pp. 69–77.

55. S. L. Slavin and M. A. Pradt, *The Einstein Syndrome: Corporate Anti-Semitism in America Today* (Lanham, Md.: University Press of America, 1982).

56. Stephen Rubenfeld and Michael Crino, "Are Employment Agencies Jeopardizing Your Selection Process?" *Personnel,* September–October 1981, pp. 70–77.

57. P. Falcone, "Maximize Your Recruitment Resources," *HR Magazine,* February 1999, pp. 92–93.

58. S. P. Talbott, "Creative Staffing Drives Success," *Recruitment Staffing Sourcebook* (supplement to the March 1996 issue of *Personnel Journal*), pp. 12–13.

59. T. Chauran, "Get High Mileage from Your Advertising Dollar," *Recruitment Today,* February–March 1989, pp. 48–51.

60. C. Rush, "Executive Search: Recruiting a Recruiter," *Public Management,* July 1995, pp. 20–22.

61. William Dee, "Evaluating a Search Firm," *Personnel Administrator,* March 1983, pp. 41–43, 99–100.

62. Loretta D. Foxman and Walter L. Polsky, "Career Counselor," *Personnel Journal,* February 1985, pp. 21–22, and March 1985, pp. 14–16. See also John Wareham, "The Search," *Across the Board,* September 1979, pp. 28–31.

63. Florence Berger, "Executive Search: The Headhunter as Matchmaker," *Cornell Hotel and Restaurant Administration Quarterly,* May 1983, pp. 55–61.

64. John C. Perham, "How Recruiters Get the Lowdown," *Dun's Business Month,* May 1985, pp. 60–61.

65. Larry Reibstein, "Offers and Counteroffers: Attitudes Change in Executive Search Game," *Wall Street Journal,* May 5, 1986, p. 21. For more information about executive search firms, see Stephanie Jones, *The Headhunting Business* (London: Macmillan, 1989).

66. J. Reingold, E. C. Baig, L. Armstrong, and W. Zellner, "Headhunting 2000," *Business Week,* May 17, 1999, p. 74.

67. This section draws on Stephen D. Bruce, *College Recruiting* (Stamford, Conn.: Bureau of Law and Business, 1983). See also B. Leonard, "The Sell Gets Tough on College Campuses," *HRMagazine,* June 1995, pp. 61–63; J. Phillips, *Recruiting, Training, and Retaining New Employees* (San Francisco: Jossey-Bass, 1987); M. E. Scott, "A Case for College Relations and Recruitment," National Association of Colleges and Employers, 62 Highland Avenue, Bethlehem, PA, 18017.

68. "National Association of Colleges and Employers (NACE) Year 2000 Employer Benchmark Survey," National Association

of Colleges and Employers, 62 Highland Avenue, Bethlehem, PA, 18017.

69. A. C. Poe, "Signing Bonuses: A Sign of the Times," *HR Magazine,* September 1999, pp. 104–112.

70. *The Sunday Oregonian*, May 6, 2001, pp. B1, B4.

71. Maury Hanigan, "Key Campus Strategies," *HRMagazine,* July 1991, pp. 42–44.

72. Philip Schofield, "The Difference a Graduate Recruitment Brochure Can Make," *Personnel Management,* January 1991, pp. 36–39.

73. Jobtrak.com survey, June 12, 2000. Available at: http://static.jobtrak.com/mediacenter/press_poll_061200,html.

74. A. C. Poe, "Face Value," *HR Magazine*, May 2000, pp. 60–68.

75. John W. Boudreau and Sara L. Rynes, "Giving It the Old College Try," *Personnel Administrator,* March 1987, pp. 78–83; and Sara L. Rynes and John W. Boudreau, "College Recruiting in Large Organizations: Practice, Evaluation, and Research Implications," *Personnel Psychology,* Vol. 39, 1986, pp. 729–757.

76. Lord, "Internal and External Recruitment."

77. Harriet Edleson, "Innovative Internships," *HRMagazine,* July 1991, pp. 39–41; and Talbott, "Boost Your Campus Image to Attract Top Grads."

78. Robert E. Hite, "How to Hire Using College Internship Programs," *Personnel Journal,* February 1986, pp. 110–112.

79. D. C. Feldman and S. Kim, "Bridge Employment During Retirement: A Field Study of Individual and Organizational Experiences with Post-Retirement Employment," *Human Resource Planning,* Vol. 23 (1), 2000, pp. 14–25.

80. This section draws on two publications by the American Association of Retired Persons: *How to Recruit Older Workers* (1993) and *The Older Workforce: Recruitment and Retention* (1993).

81. Catherine D. Fyock, "Finding the Gold in the Graying of America," *HRMagazine,* February 1994, pp. 74–76.

82. Mary Cook, *The AMA Handbook for Employee Recruitment and Retention* (New York: AMACOM, 1992), pp. 57–61; Susan J. Herman, *Hiring Right: A Practical Guide* (Thousand Oaks, Calif.: Sage, 1994); and V. Frazee, "Focusing Your Recruiting Efforts on Disabled Workers," *Recruitment Staffing Sourcebook* (supplement to the August 1996 issue of *Personnel Journal*), pp. 10–12.

83. S. Overman, "Winning Ways," *HR Magazine*, July 2000, pp. 87–96.

84. J. A. Tannenbaum, "Firms Try Busing to Ease Labor Shortage," *Wall Street Journal,* December 30, 1988, p. B2.

85. S. Overman, "Put Overlooked Labor Pools on Your Recruiting List," *HR Magazine,* February 1999, pp. 87–90.

86. Andrew S. Bargerstock and Gerald Swanson, "Four Ways to Build Cooperative Recruitment Alliances," *HRMagazine,* March 1991, pp. 49–51, 79.

87. Sandra L. Bem and Daryl J. Bem, "Does Sex-Biased Job Advertising Aid and Abet Sex Discrimination?" in *Contemporary Problems in Personnel,* ed. W. Clay Hamner and Frank L. Schmidt (Chicago: St. Clair Press, 1977), pp. 445–455.

88. The remainder of this section is based on Robert Calvert, Jr., *Affirmative Action: A Comprehensive Recruitment Manual* (Garrett Park, Md.: Garrett Park Press, 1979).

89. M. N. Martinez, "Looking for Young Talent? Inroads Helps Diversify Efforts," *HRMagazine,* March 1996, pp. 73–76.

90. L. Sewell, "Passive Candidates: Who They Are and How to Find Them". (Available at: http://www.wetfeet. com/employer/articles/article.asp?aid=377)

91. S. Boehle, "Online Recruiting Gets Sneaky," *Training*, May 2000, pp. 66–74.

92. Michael C. Keeley and Philip K. Robins, "Government Programs, Job Search Requirements, and the Duration of Unemployment," *Journal of Labor Economics,* July 1985, pp. 337–362; Bradley R. Schiller, "Job Search Media: Utilization and Effectiveness," *Quarterly Review of Economics and Business,* Winter 1975, pp. 55–63; and Samuel J. Yeager and Thomas Vocino, "Sources of Information Used by Professionals in Government to Find Jobs: Effectiveness and Impact," *Review of Public Personnel Administration,* Fall 1983, pp. 100–113.

93. Steven M. Bortnick and Michelle Harrison Ports, "Job Search Methods and Results: Tracking the Unemployed, 1991," *Monthly Labor Review,* December 1992, pp. 29–35.

94. Lee D. Dyer, "Job Search Success of Middle-Aged Managers and Engineers," *Industrial and Labor Relations Review,* April 1973, pp. 969–979; and Graham L. Reid, "Job Search and the Effectiveness of Job Finding Methods," *Industrial and Labor Relations Review,* July 1972, pp. 479–495.

95. Dyer, "Job Search Success of Middle-Aged Managers and Engineers," pp. 479–495.

96. Donald P. Schwab, "Recruiting and Organizational Participation," in *Personnel Management,* ed. Kendrith M. Rowland and Gerald R. Ferris (Boston: Allyn and Bacon, 1982), pp. 103–127; Donald P. Schwab, Sara L. Rynes, and Ramon J. Aldag, "Theories and Research on Job Search and Choice," in *Research in Personnel and Human Resources Management,* ed. Kendrith M. Rowland and Gerald R. Ferris (Greenwich, Conn.: JAI Press, 1987), pp. 129–166; and A. E. Barber, C. L. Daly, C. M. Giannantonio, and J. M. Phillips, "Job Search Activities: An Examination of Changes Over Time," *Personnel Psychology,* Vol. 47, 1994, pp. 739–766.

97. Orlando Behling, George Labovitz, and Marion Gainer, "College Recruiting: A Theoretical Base," *Personnel Journal,* January 1968, pp. 13–19.

98. Clifford E. Jurgenson, "Job Preferences (What Makes a Job Good or Bad?)," *Journal of Applied Psychology,* June 1978, pp. 267–276.

99. JobTrak.com Career Value Poll. (Available at: http://static.jobtrak.com/mediacenter/press_polls/poll_121499.html>)

100. Sara L. Rynes, "Recruitment, Job Choice, and Post-Hire Consequences: A Call for New Research Directions," in *Handbook of Industrial and Organizational Psychology,* Vol. 2, 2d ed., ed. M. D. Dunnette and L. M. Hough (Palo Alto, Calif.: Consulting Psychologists Press, 1991), pp. 399–444.

101. Hanigan, "Key Campus Strategies."

102. Behling, Labovitz, and Gainer, "College Recruiting."

103. Victor R. Tom, "The Role of Personality and Organizational Images in the Recruiting Process," *Organizational Behavior and Human Performance,* September 1971, pp. 573–592; D. M. Cable and T. A. Judge, "Person–Organization Fit, Job Choice Decisions, and Organizational Entry," *Organizational Behavior and Human Decision Processes,* September 1996, pp. 294–311; A. M. Saks and B. E. Ashforth, "A Longitudinal Investigation of the Relationships Between Job Information Sources, Applicant Perceptions of Fit, and Work Outcomes," *Personnel Psychology,* Summer 1997, pp. 395–426; T. A. Judge and D. M. Cable, "Applicant Personality, Organizational Culture, and Organizational Attraction," *Personnel Psychology,* Summer 1997, pp. 359–394; and J. D. Werbel and S. W. Gilliland, "Person–Environment Fit in the Se-

lection Process," *Research in Personnel and Human Resources Management,* Vol. 17, 1999, pp. 209–243.

104. Robert D. Gatewood, Mary A. Gowan, and Gary J. Lautenschlager, "Corporate Image, Recruitment Image, and Initial Job Choice Decisions," *Academy of Management Journal,* April 1993, pp. 414–427.

105. Sara L. Rynes, Robert D. Bretz, Jr., and Barry Gerhart, "The Importance of Recruitment in Job Choice: A Different Way of Looking," *Personnel Psychology,* Autumn 1991, pp. 487–521.

106. Donald P. Rogers and Michael Z. Sincoff, "Favorable Impression Characteristics of the Recruitment Interviewer," *Personnel Psychology,* Autumn 1978, pp. 495–504.

107. Neal Schmitt and Brian W. Coyle, "Applicant Decisions in the Employment Interview," *Journal of Applied Psychology,* April 1976, pp. 184–192; Daniel B. Turban and Thomas W. Dougherty, "Influences of Campus Recruiting on Applicant Attraction to Firms," *Academy of Management Journal,* December 1992, pp. 739–765; and Steven D. Maurer, Vince Howe, and Thomas W. Lee, "Organizational Recruiting as Marketing Management: An Interdisciplinary Study of Engineering Graduates," *Personnel Psychology,* Winter 1992, pp. 807–833.

108. Cynthia D. Fisher, Daniel R. Ilgen, and Wayne D. Hoyer, "Source Credibility, Information Favorability, and Job Offer Acceptance," *Academy of Management Journal,* March 1979, pp. 94–103.

109. Thomas Bergmann and M. Susan Taylor, "College Recruitment: What Attracts Students to Organizations," *Personnel,* May–June 1984, pp. 34–46; and Sara L. Rynes, Herbert G. Heneman III, and Donald P. Schwab, "Individual Reactions to Organizational Recruiting: A Review," *Personnel Psychology,* Autumn 1980, pp. 529–542.

110. Lord, "Internal and External Recruitment," p. 82.

111. Michael M. Harris and Laurence S. Fink, "A Field Study of Applicant Reactions to Employment Opportunities: Does the Recruiter Make a Difference?" *Personnel Psychology,* Vol. 40, 1987, pp. 765–784; M. Susan Taylor and Thomas J. Bergmann, "Organizational Recruitment Activities and Applicants' Reactions at Different Stages of the Recruitment Process," *Personnel Psychology,* Vol. 40, 1987, pp. 261–286; and Gary N. Powell, "Applicant Reactions to the Initial Employment Interview: Exploring Theoretical and Methodological Issues," *Personnel Psychology,* Spring 1991, pp. 67–83.

112. Robert J. Vandenberg and Vida Scarpello, "The Matching Model: An Examination of the Processes Underlying Realistic Job Previews," *Journal of Applied Psychology,* February 1990, pp. 60–67; L. M. Shore and L. E. Tetrick, "The Psychological Contract: An Explanatory Framework in the Employment Relationship," in *Trends in Organizational Behavior,* Vol. 1, ed. C. L. Cooper and D. M. Rousseau (eds.), (Chichester, England: Wiley, 1994), pp. 91–109.

113. Steven L. Premack and John P. Wanous, "A Meta-Analysis of Realistic Job Preview Experiments," *Journal of Applied Psychology,* November 1985, pp. 706–719; and J. M. Phillips, "Effects of Realistic Job Previews on Multiple Organizational Outcomes: A Meta-Analysis," *Academy of Management Journal,* Vol. 41, 1998. pp. 673–690.

114. James A. Breaugh, "RJPs: A Critical Appraisal and Future Research Directions," *Academy of Management Review,* October 1983, pp. 612–619.

115. Richard R. Reilly, Barbara Brown, Milton R. Blood, and Carol Z. Malatesta, "The Effects of Realistic Previews: A Study

and Discussion of the Literature," *Personnel Psychology,* Winter 1981, pp. 823–834.

116. John P. Wanous, *Organizational Entry* (Reading, Mass.: Addison-Wesley, 1992), p. 60.

117. Todd Raphael, "Nationwide Speeds Up Hiring, Increases Satisfaction," *Workforce,* May 23, 2001.

118. See Dennis, "Evaluating Corporate Recruiting Efforts," for guidance on the relative difficulty of searches and how to take this difficulty into account in evaluation.

119. Hawk, *The Recruitment Function.*

120. Ibid.

121. Stephen L. Mangum, "Recruitment and Job Search: The Recruitment Tactics of Employers," *Personnel Administrator,* June 1982, pp. 96–104.

122. James A. Breaugh, "Relationships Between Recruiting Sources and Employee Performance, Absenteeism, and Work Attitudes," *Academy of Management Journal,* March 1981, pp. 142–147; Martin J. Gannon, "Source of Referral and Employee Turnover," *Journal of Applied Psychology,* June 1971, pp. 226–228; Phillip J. Decker and Edwin Cornelius III, "A Note on Recruiting Sources and Job Survival Rates," *Journal of Applied Psychology,* August 1979, pp. 463–464; C. J. Simon and J. T. Warner, "Matchmaker, Matchmaker: The Effect of Old Boy Networks on Job Match Quality, Earnings, and Tenure," *Journal of Labor Economics,* Vol. 10, 1992, pp. 306–329; and G. S. Taylor, "The Relationship Between Sources of New Employees and Attitudes Toward the Job," *Journal of Social Psychology,* Vol. 134, 1994, pp. 99–110.

123. Breaugh, "Relationships Between Recruiting Sources and Employee Performance, Absenteeism, and Work Attitudes"; David F. Caldwell and Austin Spivey, "The Relationship Between Recruiting Source and Employee Success: An Analysis by Race," *Personnel Psychology,* Spring 1983, pp. 67–72; and J. D. Werbel and J. Landau, "The Effectiveness of Different Recruitment Sources: A Mediating Variable Analysis," *Journal of Applied Social Psychology,* Vol. 26, 1996, pp. 1337–1350.

124. De Witte, "Recruitment Advertising."

125. James A. Breaugh and R. B. Mann, "Recruiting Source Effects: A Test of Two Alternative Explanations," *Journal of Occupational Psychology,* Vol. 57, 1984, pp. 261–267; Maureen A. Conard and Steven D. Ashworth, "Recruiting Source Effectiveness: A Meta-Analysis and Re-Examination of Two Rival Hypotheses," paper presented at the First Annual Conference of the Society for Industrial and Organizational Psychology, Chicago, April 1986; and Philip G. Swaroff, Lizabeth A. Barclay, and Alan R. Bass, "Recruiting Sources: Another Look," *Journal of Applied Psychology,* November 1985, pp. 720–728. Some studies report differences in applicant characteristics from different sources but do not find differences in subsequent performance or tenure; see R. P. Vecchio, "The Impact of Referral Sources on Employee Attitudes: Evidence from a National Sample," *Journal of Management,* 1995, pp. 953–965; C. R. Williams, C. E. Labig, Jr., and T. H. Stone, "Recruitment Sources and Posthire Outcomes for Job Applicants and New Hires: A Test of Two Hypotheses," *Journal of Applied Psychology,* Vol. 78, 1993, pp. 163–172.

126. Gannon, "Source of Referral and Employee Turnover."

127. For information on "mass hiring" exercises, see Stephenie Overman, "Hiring Bakers by the Dozens," *HRMagazine,* February 1994, pp. 55–58.

Measurement and Decision-Making Issues in Selection

Statistical Methods in Selection

Reliability

Validity

Decision Making in Selection

Utility of a Selection System

HR Challenge

Dingo Doggie Bites (DDB) is an Australian dog food manufacturer that has been operating primarily along the eastern seaboard of Australia; that is, in Sydney, Brisbane, Rockhampton, and Cairns. DDB is planning to expand operations significantly and open new production facilities in other areas of Australia—specifically, Melbourne, Adelaide, Darwin, and Alice Springs. The company is family owned and has, in the past, hired production workers on the basis of an interview, a thirty-item test of basic math skills, a standardized verbal ability test, and a "work task-simulation" that the developers, Aussie Psychometrics, Ltd., have assured DDB's management will test the essential psychomotor skills needed to perform production line jobs. Job applicants tend to be relatives or friends of current employees.

There are approximately 200 production workers in the four existing production plants. The new CEO of Dingo Doggie Bites, Kerry Skase, is concerned about the effectiveness of current selection procedures. Considerable competitive pressure is being placed on DDB by American and British firms entering into the Australian dog food market. To put it bluntly, workers at DDB generally perform at an "adequate" level, but productivity almost certainly will have to improve to meet the new threat from foreign competitors. Antidiscrimination laws and legislation on "unfair dismissals" provide additional incentives for firms such as DDB to improve their selection procedures. In the Melbourne and Adelaide plants, job applicants are expected to come from a wide variety of ethnic groups, including Chinese, Vietnamese, Greeks, Croatians, Serbs, and individuals from a variety of Arab nations. A significant proportion of applicants in Darwin and Alice Springs will likely be Australian Aborigines.

You are a widely respected expert on EEO and personnel selection issues in the United States. Although EEO legislation in Australia is somewhat less extensive than that in the United States, there are many similarities between the two countries in their basic approach to equal employment opportunity. An Australian friend of yours, Tom Fischer, has invited you to join him for a round of golf at Le Grande Tres Cher Country Club. Playing with you that day is Kerry Skase. After finding out what you do for a living, Kerry starts telling you about his situation and seeks your help. What should he do? Where should he start? What are the critical issues he should seek advice about from local HR consultants?

Personnel selection is a process of measurement, decision making, and evaluation (see Figure 7.1). The goal of a personnel selection system is to bring into an organization individuals who will perform well on the job. A good selection system also should be fair to minorities and other protected groups.

To have an accurate and fair selection system, an organization must use reliable and valid measures of job applicant characteristics. Although such a statement would seem obvious—any HR practitioner would want a reliable, valid selection process—some research indicates that what happens in the real world is not as ideal as one might like. For example, a research study done in New Zealand found that the *more* valid a selection test was, the *less* likely personnel consultants in New Zealand were to use it! Thirty-three percent of those surveyed did not even understand what the term "validity" meant in reference to personnel selection.[1] In addition to validity and reliability, a good selection system must combine information about applicant characteristics in a rational way and produce correct hire

● **FIGURE 7.1**

The Selection Process

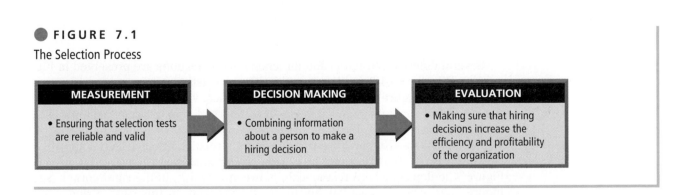

and no-hire decisions. Finally, a good personnel selection system should add to the overall effectiveness of the organization.[2]

This chapter addresses each of these areas in turn. First, it introduces the statistical methods needed to understand reliability and validity. Next, it considers why reliability of selection instruments is important and offers examples of several common methods of assessing reliability. Then the discussion moves to the several ways in which selection tests can be validated so that the results can be used to make hiring decisions. The chapter describes several methods of using test scores to make these decisions. The final sections examine the factors that affect the costs of selection systems and describe the many benefits that can be realized from a properly designed selection process.

STATISTICAL METHODS IN SELECTION

To understand reliability and validity, one must first understand two statistical methods—correlation and regression. Correlation is used to assess the strength and direction of a relationship between variables, whereas regression makes use of the relationship to predict scores on one variable from scores on one or more other variables. Only a brief discussion of these methods is offered here; those desiring more detail should refer to a basic statistics textbook.

Correlation Analysis

Correlation analysis is used to determine the degree of relationship between two variables. For example, an HR specialist may wish to know whether the mechanical ability of employees is related to their job performance. If a relationship exists, then a mechanical ability test given to job applicants might be useful in deciding who should be hired.

The **Pearson product moment correlation coefficient** (represented by the symbol r) is a numerical index that indicates the direction and degree of linear relationship between two variables. The Pearson correlation coefficient has several important characteristics, among them the following:

- The numerical value of r ranges from -1.0 to $+1.0$.
- The sign of the correlation ($-$ or $+$) indicates the direction of the relationship.
- The magnitude of r indicates the strength of the relationship.
- This numerical index is appropriate only for describing linear (straight-line) relationships.

Several different strengths and directions of correlations are presented in Figure 7.2. When $r = +1.0$, a perfect positive linear relationship exists between two variables (see Figure 7.2a). As variable X increases, variable Y increases in some exactly proportional manner. When $r = -1.0$, a perfect negative relationship exists, but in this case, as variable X increases, variable Y decreases (see Figure 7.2b). When $r = +.70$ or $-.70$ (see Figures 7.2c and d), a relationship between X and Y exists, but it is not as strong (not as exactly proportional) as when $r = +1.0$ or -1.0. Figure 7.2e depicts a zero relationship between X and Y. In the right corner (see Figure 7.2f), r also equals 0.0, but for another reason. In this case, X and Y are

● **FIGURE 7.2**

Examples of Strengths and Directions of Correlations

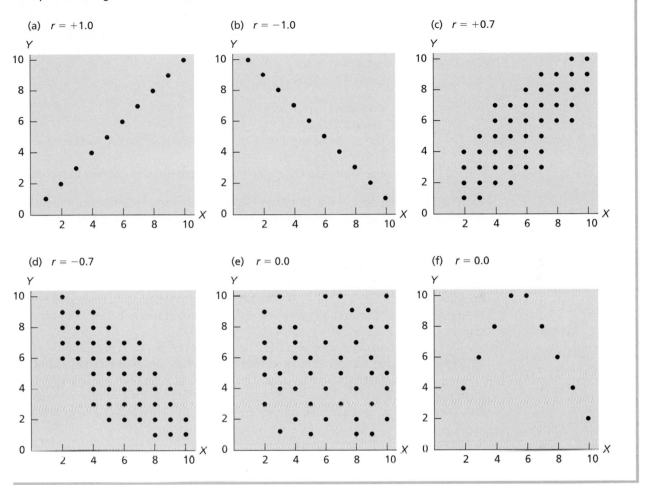

related, but the relationship cannot be represented by a straight line. (The Pearson correlation coefficient is appropriate only for describing linear relationships.)

Regression Analysis

Regression analysis allows HR specialists to use a known relationship between variables to predict an individual's future behavior. The Pearson correlation coefficient indicates how close to a straight line the relationship between two variables is. Regression analysis answers this question: To which straight line is the relationship closest? Regression analysis does this by identifying the equation for the line that best fits a set of data (data for several individuals on two variables, X and Y). If a correlation exists between mechanical ability and job performance, HR specialists can use regression analysis to predict the future performance of an individual whose mechanical ability is known.

The job performance and mechanical ability levels of ten individuals are represented in Figure 7.3. In Figure 7.3a, the line that best fits these data has been drawn. In Figure 7.3b, a non-best-fitting line has been drawn. A complex mathematical formula is used to compute the equation for the best-fitting line. By means of this formula, the HR specialist would find that the equation for the best-fitting line (shown in Figure 7.3a) is

$$Y_p = .128X + 1.9$$

where Y_p = predicted performance
       X = mechanical ability
     .128 = the slope of the line (i.e., for every unit that X increases, Y increases .128 units)
      1.9 = the Y-intercept (i.e., the point where the line crosses the Y-axis).

The HR specialist can use the regression equation to predict performance of a job applicant by inserting the measured mechanical ability of the applicant into the formula. If Joe scored 35 on the mechanical ability test, then Joe's predicted performance would be Y_p = .128(35) + 1.9 = 6.38. How accurately the regression equation actually predicts Joe's performance depends on the strength of the relationship between mechanical ability and performance. As the strength of the relationship increases (r approaches +1.0 or –1.0), the accuracy of prediction increases. If r = 0.0, then predictions based on a regression equation would be no better than random guesses.[3]

Rarely in personnel selection do HR specialists predict the performance of job applicants by using information about only one ability or characteristic. Information used in selecting employees usually includes data from multiple sources, such as interviews, application blanks, references, and ability tests. Multiple correlation and regression analyses are simply extensions of the correlation and regression

● **FIGURE 7.3**

Best-Fitting and Non-Best-Fitting Regression Lines

(a)   Best-fitting

(b)   Non-best-fitting

analyses described above. A multiple correlation indicates the degree of relationship between one variable (e.g., job performance) and a set of other variables, whereas multiple regression analysis allows the HR specialist to develop a "best-fitting" equation using these multiple variables to predict later job behavior.

RELIABILITY

An organization's personnel selection system should use reliable and valid measures of a job applicant's characteristics in order to make correct hiring decisions. **Reliability,** discussed in this section, refers to consistency of measurement.[4] For instance, an individual should get about the same score if his or her intelligence is measured with the same test twice, a few weeks apart. If the person scored 75 on Monday and then scored 145 three weeks later, would this test be a good measure of the person's general intelligence? The answer—not at all! Validity, discussed in the next section, has to do with whether or not the test measures what it is supposed to measure (intelligence) and whether test scores are significantly correlated with job performance (e.g., does intelligence correlate with success in the job of college professor? shoemaker? truck driver?).

In our discussion, the terms "test," "measure," or "instrument" may apply to any form of measurement that takes place in the selection process. Thus an interview is considered as much a test as a paper-and-pencil measure of intelligence. The concept of reliability applies equally to both.

Systematic Error Versus Random Error

Anytime a measure is taken of an individual, there will be some error in that measurement. For example, if a thermometer were used to take the temperature of a patient, the observed temperature could consist of the true body temperature of the patient, some systematic error or bias in the temperature reading, and/or random error affecting the reading.[5] For example, **systematic error** could occur if the thermometer were faulty and thus always measured the temperatures of patients one degree higher than their true temperatures. **Random error** would occur if a patient did not hold the thermometer in the right place in the mouth for the appropriate length of time or if a patient had taken a hot or cold drink just before measurement. At different times, a patient could get a temperature reading lower or higher than his or her true internal body temperature.

The key difference between systematic error and random error is that systematic error affects measurement in a consistent, predictable fashion, whereas random error, by definition, is inconsistent or variable in its effect. Ideally, the HR specialist wants tests that have neither systematic nor random error. However, from the viewpoint of reliability, random error, due to its inconsistent nature, is the greatest problem.

Methods of Measuring Reliability

The most important methods of assessing reliability for HR specialists are test–retest, inter-rater, and internal consistency.[6] In each of these methods, the correlation coefficient is used as the index of reliability. Typically, a correlation of about .80 or higher is considered good reliability. Not all these methods must be used in every situation, and in some instances a particular method may be totally inappropriate.

● **Test–Retest**   The **test–retest method** examines the consistency of a test over time. A single group of people takes a test (time 1). Later, the same people take the same test again (time 2). The correlation (called the **coefficient of stability**) is computed between the time 1 and the time 2 scores. Test–retest reliability is important when we are measuring something that we normally would assume is a relatively stable trait of an individual. For example, intelligence is a fairly stable characteristic of a person, and we would not normally expect that a person's intelligence would vary wildly from one time to another. As we noted earlier, an intelligence test that indicated a dramatically different level of intelligence for a person from one time to another would be a pretty suspect measure of intelligence.

● **Inter-rater Reliability**   Suppose a job applicant is interviewed by several different interviewers. The interviewers rate the applicant separately on several dimensions. In this case, each interviewer can be viewed as a form of "interview test." It is therefore important to know how one interviewer's rating of the candidate correlates with the other interviewers' ratings of the same candidate. This correlation among evaluators who are sizing up the same set of applicants is referred to as **inter-rater reliability.** One caution should be noted about inter-rater reliability: Sometimes inter-rater reliability is low, and that is okay. Suppose that an applicant is being interviewed by three different people—a midlevel manager, a technical specialist, and a person who would be a subordinate of the applicant if the applicant were hired. The inter-rater agreement among these three interviewers could be quite low because they bring to the interview situation different perspectives of the job for which the applicant is being considered. A low level of agreement among the interviewers would not necessarily mean that our interview procedure is faulty. On the other hand, if all three interviewers were technical specialists, a lack of agreement would probably indicate reliability problems.

● **Internal Consistency**   The third method of assessing reliability is **internal consistency.** This type of reliability assesses whether all the items on a test measure the same trait or ability; that is, whether the test's content is internally consistent. In the most common way of assessing internal consistency, a group of people are given a test. A coefficient is computed that represents the average correlation of each item on the test with each other item. This is called **coefficient alpha** and is the preferred measure of internal consistency in most situations.[7] Coefficient alpha will be high (.80 or above) if most of the items on the test measure the same thing.

Having reliable measures is critical. Reliability information can be obtained from several sources: (1) reliability studies conducted by the organization that will use the tests, (2) reliability information provided by commercial test publishers that sell the tests, (3) data from other companies that have used the same tests in their selection systems, or (4) data from individuals who have used the tests in research studies.

Reliability serves as the foundation for the validity of a test. If a test cannot measure people consistently, it cannot possibly be valid. The next section discusses the concept of test validity.

VALIDITY

When we "validate" a predictor test, we are not validating the test itself but rather the inferences and actions we take as a result of test scores.[8] In personnel selection, tests are used to measure some characteristic—for instance, mechanical ability—that is believed to relate to how well a person will be able to perform a job. In this situation, we are assuming that the test actually measures mechanical ability and that on the basis of how an applicant scores on the test, we can infer whether the individual will be able to perform the job. We then take action based on an applicant's test scores (we hire or do not hire the person). **Validity** deals with the issues of (1) whether the test is an adequate measure of the characteristic it supposedly measures and (2) whether inferences and actions based on test scores are appropriate.

Note that nothing in the law requires organizations to validate all selection tests. The organization would need validity evidence only if an applicant were to file a complaint and was able to establish a prima facie case of adverse impact. Then the employer might use validity data to show that the test was a good selection device that was necessary to improve the quality of hiring. However, techniques for validation were developed long before the passage of EEO laws. It makes sense to validate, even if a test has no adverse impact and the validity data will never be needed in court. This is so because no organization should want to spend time and money using a selection device that may not be useful. Validation shows the usefulness of a test in identifying applicants who will make good employees.

The EEOC's *Uniform Guidelines on Employee Selection Procedures* and the Society for Industrial and Organizational Psychology's *Principles for the Validation and Use of Personnel Selection Procedures* identify three types of validity: construct validity, content validity, and criterion-related validity.[9] We shall look at only two of these types of validity—content and criterion-related—because they are of the most significant practical concern to the HR specialist.

Content Validity

Content validity deals with whether or not a test is representative of some construct's "domain." Content validation is most appropriately done when the construct being measured consists of readily observable behaviors. Suppose, for instance, that an organization develops a technical math test for use in selecting engineering technicians. The test includes math problems in addition, subtraction, division, and multiplication. However, the job of an engineering technician in the organization requires an individual to work on advanced trigonometry, geometry, and calculus problems. Is the math test a representative sample of the types of math problems that are performed on the job? Content validity deals with this issue. In the preceding example, the math test is not content valid. Although it does measure some aspects of technical math, it does not adequately sample all aspects of the domain of technical math problems confronted on the job.

Determining the content validity of a test is primarily a judgmental process that should begin with a thorough job analysis.[10] Test items are evaluated on the degree to which they correspond to the skills and knowledge needed to perform critical job tasks. For instance, a typing test may be purchased or constructed for the job of secretary, and a test for knowledge of construction and electrical standards may be written for the job of building inspector. One approach to judging the content validity of such tests was developed by Charles Lawshe in 1975. Lawshe's approach uses a panel of experts to rate the items on a test as to whether or not each represents essential aspects of the same domain. The experts must be highly knowledgeable about the job.[11] These ratings yield a content validity score for each item. This allows the HR specialist to compare the content validity of one test item with that of another and to delete poor items. By averaging the content validity scores across all test items, an index of the content validity for the whole test can be obtained. This index can be used to compare several proposed tests to identify the test that most closely corresponds to the performance domain of a given job. Content validity indicates whether test items reflect critical aspects of job performance; it thus helps HR professionals determine whether inferences and actions (hire/not hire) based on test scores are warranted.

Criterion-Related Validity

In examining the **criterion-related validity** of a test, the HR specialist determines whether or not test scores are related to some important criterion variable. The criterion variable is simply whatever aspect of an individual's behavior the HR specialist is trying to predict, such as job performance, absenteeism, or turnover. Most frequently, the criterion variable is some measure of job performance (for the remainder of the discussion on validity, we will assume this is the case). In using a test in personnel selection, we are making an inference that applicants who score in a particular manner on the test will be better performers than those who score in some other way. Criterion-related validation procedures directly test the appropriateness of that inference. In some countries, however, the relationship between test scores and specific measures of job performance may be viewed as less important than other issues (see the International Perspective box).

In conducting a criterion-related study, the first step is to analyze the job. Information about the nature of the job helps the HR specialist choose one or more tests that seem likely to predict job performance. For instance, after analyzing the job of entry-level computer programmer, the HR specialist may choose tests of scheduling and planning, information processing, and problem solving.[12] Information from the job analysis is also used to develop a criterion measure of job performance. The criterion measure might be job-performance rating scales filled out by the supervisor or objective measures of the quality and quantity of output produced by individuals. A validity study is then conducted to determine whether or not the tests correlate with the job-performance criterion as expected.

Criterion-related validity is generally regarded as the preferred way of showing that a selection test is job related (see Chapter 5).[13] Two major procedures for determining the criterion-related validity of a test are concurrent validation and predictive validation. A comparison of the concurrent and predictive validation procedures is presented in Figure 7.4.

● **Concurrent Validation**   **Concurrent validation** involves the use of current employees. The procedure involves three steps:

1. Select a sample of current employees.
2. Give each employee the proposed selection test and simultaneously collect information on the criterion variable.
3. Compute the correlation between test scores and criterion scores.

The Validity of Educational Level for Selection: Some Different Perspectives

In *Griggs* v. *Duke Power Company* (1971), the Supreme Court ruled that requiring a high school diploma in selection was illegal because the company could provide no evidence that a high school education was a valid predictor of job performance. Elsewhere, however, the use of educational level as an important or even sole factor in selection is widespread. Japan, Taiwan, Korea, and Singapore see selection based on education level as a means of achieving broader organizational and national goals and show much less concern about whether education level is a valid predictor of performance on specific jobs.

In Japan, the "best" organizations recruit only students who have graduated from the top universities. Singapore provides another example in which the concern for job-specific validity often takes a back seat to the concern for broader (in this case, national) issues. In a study conducted by Morgan Guaranty Trust Company of New York, the economic success of Singapore, Korea, Taiwan, and Hong Kong was attributed partly to their success in increasing the education level of their populations. In line with government policy, organizations in Singapore place very high importance on educational level in their selection decisions. The importance of education continues beyond the selection stage; both the earnings and promotions of Singaporeans are substantially dependent on their education levels. Thus substantial incentives exist for obtaining and then furthering educational credentials.

For both Japan and Singapore, the use of education level as a primary selection tool has resulted in considerable national benefits. However, because the link between education and performance on specific jobs is often tenuous, there are dangers associated with this practice. These dangers lie primarily in the underutilization of available human resources. Individuals who, for whatever reason, do not achieve high levels of education may, through experience and/or natural ability, have skills of great value to organizations. In Japan and Singapore, these individuals often find it impossible to gain access to positions commensurate with their true abilities. Thus both the individuals and organizations lose.

K. F. Taylor (1987) cites other dangers of "credentialism":

- Performance appraisal, promotions, and compensation may be based on continued educational attainment rather than on actual contributions to the organization.
- When less educated employees see that their opportunities for advancement and increased pay are restricted, they may exhibit lower motivation and productivity.

Tony Buon and Bob Compton (1990) point out that credentialism also tends to perpetuate social inequality if access to more prestigious education is based partly on social class.

Sources: K. F. Taylor, "Interactions Between Human Resource Management and Governmental Education and Training Policies in Newly Industrialized Countries," paper presented at the International Conference on Human Resource Management, National University of Singapore, December 1987; S. S. Tan, "Asian NICs' Lessons for Debt-Ridden Countries," *The Straits Times,* March 18–19, 1987 (cited in K. F. Taylor, p. 4); and Tony Buon and Bob Compton, "Credentials, Credentialism, and Employee Selection," *Asia Pacific Human Resource Management,* November 1990, pp. 126–132.

● **FIGURE 7.4**

Concurrent and
Predictive Validation
Procedures

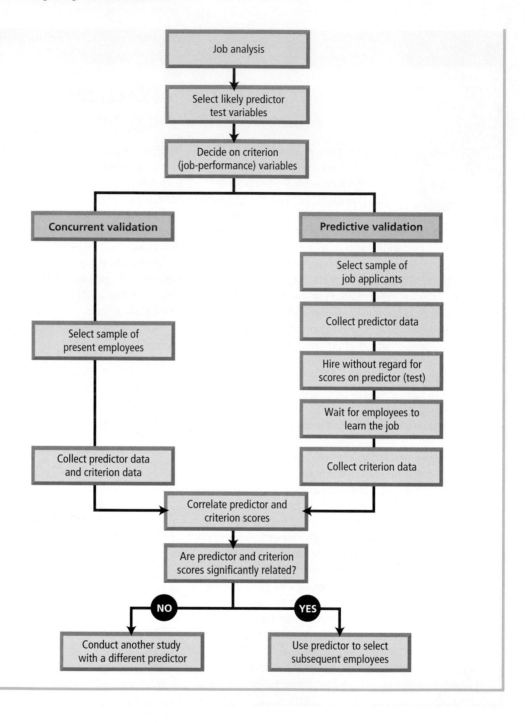

In the case of 200 currently employed computer programmers, for instance, this procedure might indicate a statistically significant correlation of .35 between scheduling-and-planning test scores and supervisory ratings of performance over the past month. This suggests that the scheduling-and-planning test perhaps can be used to select computer programmers who will be high performers.

Although concurrent validation seems relatively simple, it has two major problems. The first problem concerns the representativeness of the sample of employees. The question that arises is this: Does the relationship between test and performance scores for present employees apply equally well to job applicants (who might be very different from current employees in regard to age, gender, etc)?

The second major problem with concurrent validation is called **restriction of range.** Since present employees are used, it is unlikely that the sample will include individuals who are extremely poor performers (they would already have quit or been fired). The absence of very low performers results in a restriction of range on the performance scores found in the validation sample. If, in addition, the test is related to job performance, a restriction of range in the test scores also can occur because low performers, who would probably do poorly on the test, are absent from the sample. The effect of this double-edged restriction of range is to cause the correlation between the test scores and performance scores in the validation sample to appear lower than it should be.[14]

Restriction of range is a problem because it may cause the HR specialist to conclude that a test is not related to job performance when it really is. By selecting a representative sample to participate in the validation study, the HR specialist can reduce restriction of range, although not eliminate it entirely. Also, the HR specialist can use statistical methods developed specifically to estimate what the correlation between variables would be if no restriction of range were present. For example, normative test data from large national samples are usually available on many commercial tests, and these data can be used to estimate what an unrestricted sample would look like.[15]

● **Predictive Validation**   Another method of determining criterion-related validity is through **predictive validation,** a procedure that uses the scores of actual job applicants who are tested (time 1) and then hired. Their test scores are not used by HR specialists in deciding whom to hire, since the test has not yet been proved valid. Instead, the HR specialist measures the job performances of the new hires after a period of time (time 2) and then computes the correlation between time 1 test scores and time 2 performance scores.[16]

Problems associated with predictive validation are the sample size and time required to perform a typical predictive study. At one time, researchers thought that a predictive study could be conducted if thirty applicants were tested and hired for the same job. Later analyses, however, indicated that sample sizes of over 200 are actually needed to produce accurate information about test validity.[17] Obtaining sample sizes this large may be impossible for all but very large companies. If, for instance, an advertising firm hires about twenty new advertising designers a year, it would take the firm years to acquire data from the necessary number of individuals. However, depending on the overall size of the firm, a concurrent validation study *might* be feasible because all presently employed designers could be used.

Another problem with predictive validation relates to the time interval between collecting predictor scores and measuring the criterion. Some studies have found that predictive validity correlations tend to decline in magnitude as the time between predictor and criterion measurement increases. Thus a problem-solving test may correlate $r = .30$ with computer programmer performance ratings if the ratings of performance are collected no more than one month after the test is taken. If, instead, performance were measured six months after testing, the correlation may be only $r = .20$. There is some controversy about whether this problem exists, but it is certainly worth taking into account in designing and evaluating predictive validation studies.[18]

In the case of criterion-related validity, the HR specialist should be wary of the results of any validation study that has been done on just one sample of individuals—unless that sample is extremely large. The HR specialist should recheck the results of a validity study on another sample. This is necessary because the relationship between test scores and criterion measures may result from unique or chance factors in a particular sample. The hope is that a true relationship between test scores and criterion measures will occur in all samples. Only by checking this assumption, however, can the HR specialist confidently apply testing procedures to future samples of job applicants.

The HR specialist also should recheck the validity of tests after the selection system has been implemented. The need to recheck validity is due to two phenomena. The first is referred to as the **dynamic criterion**.[19] Over time, there may be systematic changes in the critical behaviors needed on a job. Likewise, the performance appraisal system used in the organization may change.[20] The second phenomenon is called **item parameter drift**.[21] This occurs when job applicants respond differently to individual items on a test due to educational, technological, cultural, or other changes that have occurred during the life of the test. Suppose, for example, that a test of "computer knowledge" was designed in 1995. On the test were several items dealing with use of the Internet. In 1995, it was found that these items tended to help differentiate between individuals with high versus low levels of computer knowledge. However, in 2001, given the increased familiarity with the Internet by most people in developed countries, these same items would probably not be as effective in distinguishing between job applicants with high versus low computer knowledge. As a result of both dynamic criteria and item parameter drift, tests that adequately predicted job performance in 1995 may not predict performance in 2001. Therefore, the HR specialist should recheck selection tests periodically to ensure that validity remains high over time.

Special Concerns in Validation

Showing that tests have good content and criterion-related validity is not the only task of the HR specialist. The legal context in which selection systems operate requires that any "valid" selection system must also be examined for potential unfairness or bias toward minority-group members.[22] Differential validity and differential prediction refer to whether or not a test makes equally accurate predictions of future performance for majority- and minority-group members. Measurement bias deals with the issue of whether or not minority- and majority-group members score differently on individual test items. A third issue, validity generalization, looks at whether tests that are valid for a job in one organization will also be valid predictors of performance in another job or organizational situation.

● **Differential Validity and Prediction**   Differential validity is presented graphically in Figure 7.5. In Figure 7.5a, it is clear that for majority employees, a strong

● **FIGURE 7.5**

Differential Validity and Differential Prediction

(a)

(b)

(c)

○ Majority

△ Minority

relationship exists between performance and scores on a problem-solving test. This is not the case for minority employees. **Differential validity** exists when the correlation between test scores and performance for one group is significantly lower than the correlation for another group.[23] In Figure 7.5b, no differential validity exists. The relationship between problem-solving test scores and performance for both groups is essentially equal, although minority-group members tend to score lower on the test. Also, if a regression equation were developed using all the employees, the predictions based on that equation would not systematically over- or underpredict for either group.

In Figure 7.5c, no differential validity exists. However, if a regression-line equation were developed using the total sample (line *T*), this equation would tend to systematically underpredict minority-group performance but overpredict majority-group performance. This is referred to as **differential prediction.** Although differential validity and differential prediction are issues that should be investigated in every criterion-related validation study, in reality, these problems occur infrequently.[24]

● **Measurement Bias**   Differential validity and prediction focus on whether overall test scores correlate with job performance at different levels (or result in different regression equations) for minority and majority groups. **Measurement bias** deals with whether minority- and majority-group members respond differently on individual test items. If this occurs, the differences in item scores would significantly affect overall test score and would make the development of valid selection tests very difficult. Luckily, studies indicate that this sort of test bias is probably of only moderate concern.[25] For example, in a 1999 study, potential measurement bias in the Armed Services Vocational Aptitude Battery was analyzed.[26] Specifically, the study looked at item responses of blacks and whites and of males and females across five time periods over sixteen years. The study found that although responses to items changed over time, the nature of the change did not differ significantly across the gender and racial groups, except for a very small number of items. The problem of measurement bias could be easily rectified by deleting those few items from the relevant tests. While the problem seems to occur infrequently, good test-development practice should include a check for item measurement bias.

● **Validity Generalization**   Measurement bias, differential validity, and differential prediction focus on whether the validity of selection tests changes depending on the types of people tested. There has also been a long-standing assumption that validity varies from one job to another and from one organization to another. This assumption is based on many studies that have found that a test that validly predicts performance in a job does not correlate significantly with performance in a different job in the same organization or in a similar job in a different organization. Over the past two decades, strong arguments have been made against this assumption of "situational specificity." The argument against situational specificity is called **validity generalization**—that is, that test validity is readily applicable across a variety of organizations and similar jobs. This approach suggests that most differences in the observed validity of tests across situations result from methodological and statistical problems rather than from true differences in the strength of relationships between predictor and criterion. Proponents of validity generalization submit that if these problems are controlled, tests found to be valid predictors of performance for a job will be useful for selecting for that job in all organizations.[27]

Proponents of validity generalization argue that tests of general cognitive ability are good predictors of job performance across a wide variety of jobs. General cognitive ability predicts whether or not an individual will be able to adequately learn a job; the level of competency then influences job performance.[28] There is considerable research support for the validity generalization view.[29] However, other researchers question both the statistical procedures used in validity generalization studies and the inferences drawn from them.[30] Studies have shown that test validities vary depending on the type of job-performance measures used and may be affected by the skills, experience, and job background of the researcher conducting the study.[31]

While HR specialists may draw on published validity generalization studies to identify potential selection tests, there are problems in using this approach. Perhaps the most obvious is that it seems to contradict EEOC guidelines for development of selection tests, since no job analysis is required and situational specificity is ignored. There are also certain advantages of doing one's own validation study. It allows the organization to look at the predictive power of unique combinations of tests and of tests predicting unique local measures of job performance. Validation studies also allow the organization to develop local norms and cutoff scores for the tests to use in hiring decisions.[32]

DECISION MAKING IN SELECTION

Generally, the HR specialist collects several types of information about job applicants before making a selection decision. In the process, the specialist uses reliable and valid selection procedures to collect this information. But managing the selection program does not end there. The HR specialist still has the problem of how to use these sources of information to make the best final hire/no-hire decision. At least four different methods exist for combining information and making a selection decision: additive models, multiple cutoff, multiple hurdle, and profile matching.

Additive Models

Additive models are a purely statistical approach to selection decision making.[33] When using additive models, the HR specialist simply converts test scores received by a job applicant to some common metric and then adds them up. The job applicants with the highest totals are hired. In some additive procedures, the test scores are weighted in some manner so that scoring high (or low) on one test may contribute more to an applicant's total than scoring high or low on another test. Multiple regression (mentioned earlier in this chapter) is a special form of additive procedure in which an equation is derived, using statistical procedures, that best represents the linear relationship between some criterion variable and a set of predictor variables that have been weighted so as to maximize their relationship with the criterion. Many other approaches to weighting tests in an additive model have been suggested.[34]

Suppose that an HR specialist developed an additive model in which performance = 2(problem-solving ability) + 3(scheduling and planning ability) + 1(interview rating). Three individuals apply for the job. They are given the problem-solving test and scheduling-and-planning test and then are interviewed by the HR manager, who rates each applicant on a 10-point scale. Their scores are as follows:

	Problem Solving Ability	Scheduling & Planning Ability	Interview Rating
Joe	20	5	9
Al	5	15	7
Sally	25	4	5

Joe's predicted performance score is 2(20) + 3(5) + 1(9) = 64. Al's and Sally's predicted scores are 62 and 67, respectively. If one job opening exists, Sally would be hired. In practice, the scores for each person would be "standardized," or converted to a common metric, before being added up. Any basic statistics text will explain this process of standardizing. Despite not being standardized, the preceding example gives you the basic idea of how additive models work.

Additive models are compensatory in that a high score on one characteristic can make up for a low score on another characteristic. Sally's high level of problem-solving ability compensated for her low levels of scheduling-and-planning and interview performance. The HR specialist must be certain that this assumption of compensatory characteristics is appropriate for the position being filled and that any weights assigned to particular test scores used in the model are appropriate.[35]

Multiple Cutoff

If the assumption of a compensatory relationship among predictor variables is inappropriate, other decision-making methods are needed. In the **multiple cutoff method,** job applicants are required to have some minimum level of each predictor variable. Multiple cutoff is a noncompensatory model of selection. In the preceding example with Joe, Al, and Sally, suppose that a multiple cutoff procedure is used. Cutoffs for each of the three predictor variables are set so that the minimum level of problem-solving ability needed is 10, a score of 5 on the scheduling-and-planning test is required, and an interview rating of 5 is necessary. Using this approach, Joe, not Sally, would be hired, because Sally does not meet the minimum standard for scheduling and planning. An advantage of the multiple cutoff method is that it is conceptually simple and easy to explain to managers. In operation, however, it is more difficult than it seems.[36]

If only a single predictor test is used, the cutoff score can be set using data on (1) how many job openings are likely to occur over a set time period, (2) how many job applicants are likely to apply during that period, and (3) the likely distribution of scores for applicants on that predictor test. The number of job openings and applicants can be obtained from company files on past openings and applicant flow. The likely distribution of test scores can be obtained from situations in which the test was given to other groups of job applicants. If twenty job openings will occur in the next year and 200 people are likely to apply for them, then the appropriate cutoff would be the 90th percentile score on the predictor—that is, the score that passes the top 10 percent of job applicants. Although this procedure, called the **predicted yield method,** is relatively easy when dealing with a single-predictor test, it becomes dramatically more difficult as the number of tests increases. When several tests are used, the setting of cutoffs tends to become a trial-and-error procedure. Another approach to setting cutoffs is the **regression-based method,** where cutoffs are set based on predicted levels of performance derived from regression equations. Other approaches, such as the **Anghoff method,** use experts to determine the test score that a *minimally competent person* would score on a test—minimally competent in the sense of minimally competent to do the job.[37]

An analysis of court cases involving the use of cutoff scores in selection has yielded some guidelines as to what the courts consider a "good" cutoff score.[38] Cutoff scores should enable the organization to select qualified candidates who are capable of learning the job and performing it in a safe, efficient manner; at the same time, these scores should allow the organization to meet any affirmative action goals it might have set.[39] Cutoff scores should be based on factors such as the validity and reliability of the predictor tests used as well as on the opinion of "experts." Luckily for HR specialists, the courts have accepted the fact that cutoff scores are somewhat imprecise. Thus the courts do not require evidence that a person who scores 1 point below the cutoff would be a poor performer whereas an individual who scores 1 point above the cutoff would perform well.

Multiple Hurdle

In both additive and multiple cutoff approaches, decision making is nonsequential. Each applicant takes all predictor tests, and the organization then makes the decision to hire or not hire. More often, however, selection is a sequential process, in which applicants pass through several selection stages (with individuals being rejected at each stage) before some are hired.[40] The **multiple hurdle method** can be described as a sequential multiple cutoff approach. Using the preceding example with Joe, Al, and Sally, suppose that all three applicants take the scheduling-and-planning test. This would be the first hurdle in the selection process. Sally would not pass this hurdle and would be excluded from further testing. Joe and Al both clear this first hurdle and move on to the second stage of selection. Joe and Al then take the problem-solving test. Joe successfully meets the minimum level of problem-solving ability required; Al does not. Al would be excluded from further testing. The HR specialist then interviews Joe and eventually hires him.

One advantage of the multiple hurdle approach is that it can be more cost-effective than either additive models or the multiple cutoff method. To illustrate, suppose that (for each applicant) the scheduling-and planning test costs $10, the problem-solving test costs $25, and the interview costs $50. Using an additive model or multiple cutoff method, the total cost of processing 100 applicants would be $85 × 100 = $8,500. Suppose, instead, that a multiple hurdle approach is used. Of the hundred applicants, only fifty pass the first hurdle (scheduling and planning) to go on to the second, problem solving. Of these fifty, only ten go on to the interview. The cost to the organization of this selection system would be $10(100) + $25(50) + $50(10) = $2,750. This method represents considerable savings over additive models and multiple cutoff.

One problem with the multiple hurdle approach is restriction of range. In the first step of the process, the sample of job applicants is relatively unrestricted. As the applicants move through the process, more and more are rejected. By the time the final group of applicants reaches the last hurdle, they represent a very select sample of people, making validation of the final hurdles very difficult. Selection procedures that are sufficiently sensitive to differentiate among the individuals in this final group are difficult to design.

Profile Matching

The three preceding methods of decision making assume that more is better. Given two people who meet the minimum cutoff on some predictor, the individual with the higher level of that predictor will be selected. In additive models, the person with the highest predicted score will be hired. **Profile matching** assumes that there is some ideal level of predictor variables that an applicant should have rather than some minimum level that must be met or exceeded. In profile matching, groups of good and of poor employees are identified. Individuals in these groups are measured on several likely predictor variables. If good performers score differently from poor performers on a characteristic, then the variable is useful in selecting good performers. Once several variables that differentiate between good and poor performers have been identified, an ideal profile of the successful employee is developed. For example, the ideal employee might have average intelligence, good social skills, a low need for dominance over others, and a high level of planning ability. In profile matching, the job applicants hired are those who most closely match the profile of a successful employee.

A comparison of the decisions made by profile matching, the additive model, and multiple cutoff is presented in Table 7.1. One common procedure for determining the degree of profile match is to sum the squared differences between an applicant's score on each predictor variable and the profile score for that variable. Thus Bill's profile-matching score would be $(16 - 20)^2 + (43 - 50)^2 + (6 - 5)^2 = 66$. If you calculate the match scores for George and Maria, you find that their scores are larger than Bill's. The smaller the score, the closer is the match; thus Bill would be hired if the profile-matching procedure is used.

The results reached by these decision-making procedures are quite different. In deciding which procedure to use, the HR specialist must take into account whether a compensatory or noncompensatory model is more appropriate. The number of applicants and the cost of testing are also important considerations. It may be possible to combine several of the methods within a single selection system. Applicants could be given several tests early in the hiring process. These test scores could be combined using an additive model to decide which applicants go on to the second phase of selection. In the second phase, several more tests could be given and a multiple cutoff procedure used. In the third phase, a profile-matching procedure could be employed to make the hire/no-hire decisions. All

● **TABLE 7.1**

Hiring Decisions Based on Three Decision-Making Methods

	Test 1	Test 2	Test 3
Weights	.6	.3	.1
Average score of successful job incumbents	20	50	5
Minimum cutoff score set by job experts	15	45	5
George's scores	70	44	65
Maria's scores	50	47	45
Bill's scores	16	43	6

If only one job opening is available:

• An additive model would select George because his predicted performance of 61.7 is greater than Maria's 48.6 or Bill's 23.1.

• Multiple cutoff would select Maria because George and Bill do not meet the minimum cutoff for test 2.

• Profile matching would select Bill because his pattern of scores most closely matches that of successful job incumbents.

three steps of this process, taken together, form a multiple hurdle approach to selection.

Adjusting Test Scores of Minority-Group Members

As noted earlier, no tests are completely reliable or valid. They are, to varying degrees, imprecise predictors of an applicant's potential job performance. Additionally, there is some evidence that the validity and predictive power of selection tests may vary for majority- and minority-group members. In the past, some HR practitioners adopted the practice of adjusting the scores of minority-group members before selection decisions are made. These adjustments were made to enhance the diversity of the work force, affirmatively correct past hiring discrimination, or alleviate specific test bias or other imperfections in the testing process that tend to primarily affect minority-group members.[41]

However, the adjustment of minority-group scores in most cases is probably illegal. Section 106 of the Civil Rights Act of 1991 prohibits the adjustment of test scores on the basis of race, color, religion, sex, or national origin. Thus adding bonus points to the scores of minority-group members, using separate cutoffs for different groups, or using top-down selection from separate lists to choose majority- and minority-group members are legally questionable procedures because they are directly based on the sex, race, color, or national origin of applicants. Rather than simply abandoning tests that have some level of bias, there are a number of things that practitioners may do to keep the tests in their selection battery.[42] Tests users can attempt to justify the use of a test based on "business necessity" (e.g., a test that measures an ability essential to safe performance of the job) or very obvious job relatedness. Practitioners may also modify a test in order to reduce its level of bias. For example, David Chan and Neal Schmitt found that black/white differences in performance on a situational judgment test was reduced by using a video-based method of testing rather than a paper-and-pencil format.[43] Others have found that highly structured interviews reduce differences in ratings between black and white applicants compared to less structured interview procedures.[44]

Another approach to rescuing tests with some level of bias that may be legally permissible is through the use of **banding**.[45] In a banding approach, people within a certain range of test scores are treated as if they had all scored exactly the same. The range of scores (band width) depends on the reliability of the test. If a test is highly reliable, then the band width is quite narrow; if the reliability is low, then the band is quite wide. There are basically two alternative banding methods. In **fixed banding** a band is set relative to the initial highest score observed and the bands are fixed from that point on. Individuals are selected until a band is depleted; then persons from the next lower band are selected. Alternatively, **sliding bands** can be used—a new band is established each time the highest-scoring person is hired or eliminated from the applicant pool. Sliding bands generally provide more opportunity for lower-scoring individuals to be hired. However, the proportion of minority-group members in the applicant pool, the mean difference between minority- and majority-group members, and the standard deviations of the two group distributions will determine the level of impact that banding has on minority-group selection.[46] From a legal perspective, the critical issue when using banding is to base the hiring of individuals *within a band* on factors other than sex, race, color, or national origin.

UTILITY OF A SELECTION SYSTEM

In evaluating a selection system, the HR specialist needs to know if the system has utility for the organization. **Utility** concerns the overall value of the selection system to the organization; it is analogous to cost-benefit analysis. Recent research also has incorporated concepts such as net present value into utility equations.[47] The economic benefit of a properly developed selection system can be impressive. For example, in a situation where there are twenty-five new hires a year for five years, one analysis calculated the increased value of a structured interview procedure (compared to a traditional unstructured interview) as $1,121,250! [48] The HR specialist should evaluate the potential utility of a selection system not only after it is ready to be implemented but also throughout its development. Asking the right questions at the right time can save time, effort, and money.

The traditional view of the utility of a selection system is that it is composed of three major factors: the efficiency of selection, the standard deviation of performance in dollars, and the costs associated with selection. These factors are discussed below. However, for an alternative view of of factors that contribute to utility see A Different Point of View.

Efficiency of Selection

Whenever an organization makes hiring decisions, some of those decisions are correct and some are not. The results of a selection process are presented graphically in Figure 7.6a. This scattergram represents the relationship between X, some predictor variable, and Y, the known future performance of a group of job applicants. All applicants above the horizontal line are successful performers, whereas those below the line are unsuccessful. The vertical line represents a cutoff score on the predictor variable set by the organization. Individuals who score to the right of the cutoff would be hired; those to the left would not. Four types of selection decisions are represented in Figure 7.6a:

- *Quadrant A:* **True-positive decisions,** in which the individuals who are hired turn out to be good performers

- *Quadrant B:* **False-negative decisions,** in which individuals are not hired but would have turned out to be good performers (e.g., a National Football League team does not draft a particular college player, and later this player becomes a star running back for another team)

- *Quadrant C:* **True-negative decisions,** in which individuals who would have been unable to perform the job are not selected

- *Quadrant D:* **False-positive decisions,** in which individuals who are hired turn out to be poor performers

If no selection system is used (ignore the cutoff line) and the organization simply hires people on a random basis, the proportion of successful performers hired to unsuccessful performers hired would equal $(A + B)/(A + B + C + D)$. If scores on the predictor variable are used to select employees, the proportion of successful to unsuccessful persons selected would equal $A/(A + D)$. The efficiency of the selection system can thus be defined as

There's More to Utility Than Meets the Eye

Many authors have criticized the traditional view of utility for being too narrow in its focus on what factors affect utility. They also suggest that the definition of "utility" primarily in terms of dollar costs versus dollar benefits may be too restricting. This new view can be called the *multi-attribute approach* to utility analysis. In addition to the traditional factors affecting utility, there are other, more strategic influences on selection-program value. Craig Russell and his associates argue that fully understanding utility requires HR practitioners to take into account the "strategic impact" of personnel selection systems. They cite an example of this problem in a retail chain store. A new selection system resulted in the hiring of managers who were approximately $3,000 per quarter "better" than those previously hired. Unfortunately, the average retail store was losing $3,660 per quarter. Even with the new, improved selection system, the stores would remain unprofitable. Did the new selection system meet the strategic needs of the firm (i.e., to make stores profitable)? Obviously not!

The labor market also influences utility. A selection procedure that hires high-performing employees has considerable utility. However, these employees may demand higher salaries, especially if such workers are scarce in the current labor market. The increased costs in salaries would reduce the overall utility of the hiring procedure. Another complicating factor is that employees hired using a selection procedure typically work for the firm for more than one year. Thus one selection procedure might result in hiring employees who are very productive early in their tenure with the firm but less so as time progresses. Another selection procedure might result in hiring employees who have less initial value to the firm but whose productivity increases the longer they stay. Which selection procedure has the highest utility?

A fourth strategic issue that complicates our view of utility relates to the distribution of performance across employees. Traditional views of utility assume that the ideal situation for a firm is to have an employee work force comprised exclusively of high performers. This may be an inappropriate assumption. A situation creating optimal value to the firm may re-

quire a "mix" of performance levels among employees. If we draw an analogy to American football teams, good teams have a mix of skill levels among players. Someone must be willing to sit on the bench while others serve as first-string players. A team filled with star athletes most likely would (1) cost the owners a horrendous amount in salaries and (2) be filled with such dissension and low morale that, in the end, the team probably would not be very good.

The final issue that has recently been included in the multi-attribute view of utility is that of adverse impact on minority-group members. In the traditional view of utility, the higher the validity of a selection test, the better its utility. Calvin Hoffman and George Thornton argue, however, that tests with high validity may also have high adverse impact on minority-group members. For example, a test with a correlation of .40 with job performance may be found to exclude 90 percent of minority-group members from selection. Another test may correlate .25 with job performance but exclude only 20 percent of minority-group members from the selection process. Which test has higher overall utility? Hoffman and Thornton suggest that, for many organizations, the test with lower validity but also lower adverse impact might be viewed as having higher overall value to an organization.

Sources: J. W. Boudreau, "Utility Analysis for Decisions in Human Resource Management," in *Handbook of Industrial and Organizational Psychology,* ed. M. D. Dunnette and L. M. Hough, 2d ed., Vol. 2, (Palo Alto, Calif.: Consulting Psychologists Press, 1991), pp. 621–745; John P. Campbell, "Modeling the Performance Prediction Problem in Industrial/Organizational Psychology," in *Handbook of Industrial and Organizational Psychology,* ed. M. D. Dunnette and L. M. Hough, 2d ed., Vol. 2, (Palo Alto, Calif.: Consulting Psychologists Press, 1990), pp. 687–732; Calvin Hoffman and George Thornton III, "Examining Selection Utility Where Competing Predictors Differ in Adverse Impact," *Personnel Psychology,* Vol. 50 (2), 1997, pp. 455–470; Philip Roth and Philip Bobko, "A Research Agenda for Multi-Attribute Utiity Analysis in Human Resource Management," *Human Resource Management Review,* Vol. 7 (3), 1997, pp. 341–368; Craig Russell, Adrienne Colella, and Philip Bobko, "Expanding the Context of Utility: The Strategic Impact of Personnel Selection," *Personnel Psychology,* Vol. 46 (4), 1993, pp. 781–801; and C. J. Russell and D. R. Domm, "On the Validity of Role Congruency–Based Assessment Center Procedures for Predicting Performance Appraisal Ratings, Sales Revenue, and Profit," paper presented at the fifty-fourth annual meeting of the Academy of Management, San Francisco, August 1990.

● **FIGURE 7.6**

Efficiency in Selection Decision Making

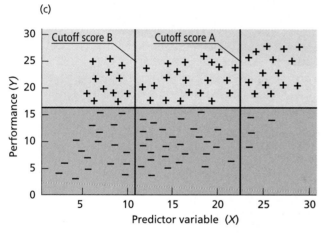

$$\text{Efficiency} = \frac{A}{(A + D)} - \frac{(A + D)}{(A + B + C + D)}$$

Efficiency of selection is the extent to which the system increases the proportion of successful selections. This definition assumes that no selection procedures are presently being used by the organization. If the organization is using some existing system, then the efficiency of the new system can be defined as

$$E = [A/(A + D)]_n - [A/(A + D)]_o$$

where n = new selection system
    o = old selection system

In this equation, the only goal of the organization is to maximize the number of true-positive decisions and minimize false-positive decisions. There is no concern for false-negative decisions. Three factors affect the efficiency of a selection system: validity, selection ratio, and base rate of success.

● **Validity**   The validity, or degree of relationship between the predictor variable and job performance (criterion) variable, affects the efficiency of the selection system.[49] The stronger the relationship, the more "valid" is the predictor and the greater is the accuracy of the selection decisions based on that predictor. Figure 7.6b presents graphically the relationship of validity to efficiency. (Figures 7.6a, b, and c use the same predictor cutoff and success points.) In Figure 7.6a, the correlation between X and Y is approximately .50; the efficiency of the predictor is about .17. That is, with random selection, 50 percent of the persons hired are successful, but with a predictor test as the basis for selection, 67 percent of the persons selected are successful ($E = .67 - .50 = .17$). In Figure 7.6b, the validity of the predictor is .75, and the efficiency increases to .27. In other words, random selection yields successful employees 50 percent of the time, but using the predictor test increases the percentage of successful employees hired to 77 percent. Thus, as validity increases, so does efficiency.

● **Selection Ratio**   A second factor that affects efficiency is the selection ratio.[50] The **selection ratio (SR)** is defined as the number of job openings divided by the number of job applicants. If the organization has to fill twenty job openings and a hundred people apply for them, SR = 20/100 = .20. Figure 7.6c illustrates the relationship between the selection ratio and efficiency. Assume that the correlation between X and Y is .50. If a hundred applicants apply for twenty jobs, then the cutoff score (A) on the predictor test is set so that the top twenty applicants are selected. Of those selected, nearly 80 percent will turn out to be successful employees, whereas if no selection test is used, only 50 percent of those hired will be good performers. If seventy job openings have to be filled from a hundred applicants, the cutoff score (B) is set to hire the top seventy applicants. In this case, only 55 percent of those selected will be successful performers. When SR = .20, $E = .80 - .50 = .30$. When SR = .70, $E = .55 - .50 = .05$. Thus, generally, as the selection ratio decreases, efficiency increases—if the validity of the test is constant. However, if SR is very small (e.g., 1 job and 1,000 applicants), the sheer cost of testing the applicants may outweigh any gain due to selecting the one right person for the available job.

● **Base Rate of Success**   The **base rate of success (BRS),** the third factor that affects efficiency, is the proportion of applicants who perform a job successfully when they are hired randomly, without the use of a selection system.[51] Suppose that Acme Paper Company decides to set up a selection system for the job of packer/stacker. The job requires an employee to place five-pound stacks of paper into boxes, seal the boxes with tape, and stack the boxes on top of other boxes. If Acme Paper hires people randomly, what proportion will be able to perform the job of packer/stacker? Nearly everyone. Acme Paper Company will gain very little from the use of a selection test. Suppose, instead, that Acme Paper Company is interested in developing a selection system for a job in which only 1 of 10,000 people performs successfully—that is, a job with a very low BRS. Although the efficiency of the system that could select this single person would be very great, Acme Paper faces a problem. It will probably be impossible to devise such a sensitive system.

Generally, midlevel BRSs (.40 to .60) have the highest potential for increased selection efficiency.

Taylor-Russell tables have been developed to show how efficiency varies as a function of validity, selection ratio, and base rate of success.[52] Table 7.2 contains a portion of these tables. The entries in the table represent the proportion of applicants selected who will be successful. Three different base rates of success are represented, along with four different levels of validity and selection ratios ranging from .05 to .95. Taylor-Russell tables can be used to determine the efficiency of a selection system compared with no selection system, or they can be used to compare one selection system with another. For each base rate of success, the row corresponding to $r = 0.00$ represents the use of no selection system, and each entry in this row equals the base rate. Suppose that Acme Paper Company has no present selection procedures and that BRS = .50. If the company develops a selection test (test A) where SR = .40 and where validity = .25, the proportion of successful employees selected will rise to .60, and the efficiency will be .10 ($E = .60 - .50$). If an alternative predictor test (test B) is available—where validity = .75, BRS = .50, and SR = .40—the proportion of successful employees selected will be .82. The increased efficiency of using test B instead of test A would be $E = .82 - .60 = .22$. Whether Acme Paper Company decides to use test A or test B might then depend on the cost of testing. If test A costs $0.50 per applicant to administer and test B costs $50 per applicant, the gain in efficiency might not be worth the additional cost of test B. Obviously, efficiency is not the only factor that determines the utility of a selection system.

Standard Deviation of Performance in Dollars

Utility models require another concept before utility can be calculated: the **standard deviation of performance in dollars (SDP$).** This variable is much more difficult to measure than the selection ratio or base rate. It assumes that an employer can put a dollar value on the performance of an employee. Many researchers have attempted to measure performance in terms of this dollar criterion.[53]

Proponents of the dollar criterion suggest that an organization should be able to measure the output of an employee and place a dollar value on that output (e.g., an employee produces 600 widgets that are each sold for a profit of $0.50). The organization also should be able to compute the cost of the employee to the company (e.g., salary, fringe benefits, etc.). The dollar value of the employee would be equal to the profits attributable to that employee minus the costs to the company of employing that person.

Unfortunately, few jobs allow for such an easy computation of costs versus profits. For example, how can an organization calculate the dollar value of a midlevel manager or of an assembly-line worker whose performance is directly affected by the actions of employees farther up the line? Sometimes cost-accounting procedures have been used to estimate the dollar value of employee performance. Other researchers have suggested that cost-accounting procedures are simply not appropriate. These researchers have developed more subjective procedures that assess SDP$ using ratings made by job experts.[54] One procedure has shown that the difference in dollar value of an employee performing at the 85th percentile level and an employee performing at the 50th percentile level is equal to about 40 percent of the salary of the job.[55]

● **TABLE 7.2**

Examples from the Taylor-Russell Tables

Base Rate of Success (BRS)	Level of Validity	Selection Ratio (SR)										
.30	r	.05	.10	.20	.30	.40	.50	.60	.70	.80	.90	.95
	.00	.30	.30	.30	.30	.30	.30	.30	.30	.30	.30	.30
	.25	.50	.47	.43	.41	.39	.37	.36	.34	.33	.32	.31
	.50	.72	.65	.58	.52	.48	.44	.41	.38	.35	.33	.31
	.75	.93	.86	.76	.67	.59	.52	.47	.42	.37	.33	.32
.50	r	.05	.10	.20	.30	.40	.50	.60	.70	.80	.90	.95
	.00	.50	.50	.50	.50	.50	.50	.50	.50	.50	.50	.50
	.25	.70	.67	.64	.62	.60	.58	.56	.55	.54	.52	.51
	.50	.88	.84	.78	.74	.70	.67	.63	.60	.57	.54	.52
	.75	.99	.97	.92	.87	.82	.77	.72	.66	.61	.55	.53
.70	r	.05	.10	.20	.30	.40	.50	.60	.70	.80	.90	.95
	.00	.70	.70	.70	.70	.70	.70	.70	.70	.70	.70	.70
	.25	.86	.84	.81	.80	.78	.77	.76	.75	.73	.72	.71
	.50	.96	.94	.91	.89	.87	.84	.82	.80	.77	.74	.72
	.75	1.00	1.00	.98	.97	.95	.92	.89	.86	.81	.76	.73

Source: Adapted from H. C. Taylor and J. T. Russell, "The Relationship of Validity Coefficients to the Practical Effectiveness of Tests in Selection," *Journal of Applied Psychology,* Vol. 23, 1939, pp. 565–578.

The greater the standard deviation of performance in dollars, the greater is the utility. A **standard deviation** is a statistic that measures the variability of a distribution of scores. A large standard deviation of performance in dollars means that the dollar value of a high performer is much greater than that of a low performer. A low standard deviation of performance in dollars indicates little difference in the value of high and low performers. Selection systems developed for jobs in which there is a low standard deviation of performance in dollars will be of less overall utility than for jobs where performance differences reflect very different levels of employee dollar value.

However, the total payoff to the organization also depends on the number of persons hired. For instance, a valid test for selecting mail clerks may produce less payoff per hire than another test of equal validity used to select vice presidents. This is so because the value to the organization of hiring a good versus a poor mail clerk is probably substantially less than the value of hiring a good versus a poor vice president. However, if fifty good mail clerks are hired using a valid test, their combined contribution to the organization may exceed the utility gained by hiring one good vice president.

To summarize the preceding discussion, a test is more likely to have utility if the following conditions are present:

- Validity is high.
- The selection ratio is reasonably low.
- The base rate of success is moderate.
- The job has a large standard deviation of performance in dollars.
- Many positions are to be filled.

Costs Associated with Selection

Several costs are associated with any selection system. One of the most obvious is the **cost of testing,** which includes the value of testing materials and the dollar value associated with the time of individuals involved in setting up and running the selection process. Among the setup costs are those associated with developing, monitoring, and analyzing validation studies conducted prior to implementing a new selection system. These validation costs would include the costs of consultants or internal staff to develop the validation procedures, monitor the study as it progresses, and then analyze the data collected in the study. In the case of a predictive validity study, all costs associated with hiring job applicants would need to be assessed. For concurrent validation studies, the value of the time expended by current employees in the validation process would need to be evaluated. For content validation, the value of the time given by job experts to assess the content validity of the selection test also would need to be costed.

Given two selection procedures of equal validity, the test that costs less will provide the organization with the greater value for its investment in selection. Furthermore, if either the selection ratio or base rate of success is extremely low, the organization is faced with the cost of testing many applicants when only a few of them will actually be hired. Another cost issue relevant to selection utility is the differential costs associated with making specific types of selection errors.[56] Consider the costs of making a false-positive hiring decision—that is, hiring someone who is not a successful performer. These costs are (1) recruiting and testing costs, (2) induction and orientation costs, (3) training costs, (4) employee relations costs when the employee is fired, and (5) costs associated with firing the employee (e.g., severance pay).[57]

Analogously, false-negative hiring decisions also entail certain costs. These include (1) competitive advantage costs (e.g., the football team that fails to draft a particular player later loses in the Super Bowl because that player scores the winning touchdown against them) and (2) legal costs. False-negative applicants are often minority-group members and/or women. If these individuals file suit against the company and are able to prove that they really were qualified for the job, both actual and reputation costs to the company can be high. These types of costs associated with false-negative decisions are often referred to as the "social consequences" of selection decisions.[58] A selection procedure that has high dollar utility to the firm but that results in a lot of false-negative errors may be less desirable to management than one that has lower dollar utility but that minimizes false-negative errors.

Traditionally, HR specialists have tried to avoid false-positive errors but have paid little attention to false-negative ones. Thus HR specialists have set selection-test cutoffs to minimize the number of false-positive errors. If the costs associated with both types of selection errors are taken into account, however, employers can achieve the greatest utility by setting cutoff scores that reduce the overall number of both false-positive and false-negative hiring decisions.[59]

Utility: A Critical Issue in Strategic HRM

In Chapter 2, one of the defining features of strategic HRM was that HR practices must "add value" to the organization. The concept of utility lies at the heart of this concept. In our discussion above, utility may seem a relatively easy aspect with which to deal. After all, in relation to selection systems, the concept of utility simply indicates that a selection system should:

- Make correct decisions about whom to hire and not hire
- Be developed only when there are enough applicants to warrant it
- Not be used for jobs that are really easy to do well
- Be used only for jobs where the level of performance is important from a financial perspective
- Not be too expensive to use.

These "simple" concepts are, however, more difficult to assess than they seem to be. If we add to this picture the types of other factors affecting the utility of a selection system that are discussed in A Different Point of View on page 303, utility becomes a devilishly complex aspect of SHRM. Nevertheless, HR practitioners must attempt to assess the utility of their HR activities as best they can to provide some measure of the "value added" by HR procedures.

Summary of Key Points

A personnel selection system requires effective measurement, decision-making, and evaluation methods. The first requirement of a selection instrument is that it be a reliable measure. Reliability can be assessed over time, between raters, or within the context of a single test. If an instrument does not measure something consistently (reliably), it cannot possibly predict a criterion—so it cannot be valid. Validity is usually established by using one of the criterion-related methods (predictive or concurrent) or by proving that the content of the selection device matches critical job content. Additional concerns about validation include whether the results of the validation study are stable and useful in subsequent samples of applicants and whether the test predicts the job performance of minority- and majority-group members with equal accuracy and fairness.

Given valid measures, HR specialists must choose a decision-making strategy that takes into account the nature of the job, the number of applicants and job openings, and the costs of testing. Strategies include additive models, multiple cutoff, multiple hurdle, and profile matching. Approaches such as banding may be used in selection decision making in an effort to adjust individual scores so that the imprecise nature of testing can be taken into account.

For any selection system, the organization must make an attempt to evaluate the utility of the system. The organization should not wait until after the selection system has been developed and implemented to judge its likely utility. The company should evaluate data on probable validities, selection ratios, previous base rates of success, the standard deviation of performance in dollars, and the cost of tests before the development procedure begins. In addition, there are a number of broader strategic issues that determine the value of a selection system to an organization. By analyzing these factors before spending the time, effort, and money to develop a selection system, HR specialists can more wisely develop and use selection procedures in their organizations.

The Manager's Vocabulary

additive models
Anghoff method
banding

base rate of success (BRS)
coefficient alpha
coefficient of stability
concurrent validation
content validity
correlation analysis
cost of testing
criterion-related validity
differential prediction
differential validity
dynamic criterion
efficiency of selection
false-negative decisions
false-positive decisions
fixed banding
item parameter shift
internal consistency
inter-rater reliability
item parameter drift
measurement bias
multiple cutoff method
multiple hurdle method
Pearson product moment correlation coefficient
predicted yield method
predictive validation
profile matching
random error
regression analysis
regression-based method
reliability
restriction of range
selection ratio (SR)
sliding bands
standard deviation
standard deviation of performance in dollars
    (SDP$)
systematic error
Taylor-Russell tables
test—retest method
true-negative decisions
true-positive decisions
utility
validity
validity generalization

Questions for Discussion

1. Why are the Pearson correlation coefficient and regression analyses important statistical devices in personnel selection?
2. The reliability of a test indicates the extent to which random error influences test scores. Why is this factor of concern to the HR specialist who is setting up a selection system?
3. What are the different ways of assessing reliability?
4. How are the predictive and concurrent methods for determining criterion-related validity similar to or different from one another?
5. What is content validity? How would you document content validity?
6. Why should the results of a validation study always be "rechecked" before the test is used on job applicants?
7. If the proponents of validity generalization are correct, what implications does this assumption have in developing selection systems in organizations?
8. HR specialists can take either a compensatory or a noncompensatory approach to combining information about a job applicant when making a final hire/no-hire decision. How do these two approaches to decision making differ from one another?
9. What is banding? Is it legal to adjust test scores using banding? Why?
10. If measurement bias exists in a selection test, what actions could an HR practitioner take to eliminate or reduce this bias so that the test could continue to be used in hiring employees?
11. What is the utility of a personnel selection system? What traditional and strategic factors influence the utility of a selection system?

● Case 7.1
The Delta Intelligence Test

For the past ten years, Eastern Amalgamated Paper Company (EAPCO) has used the Delta Intelligence Test (DIT) to select employees for its unskilled production jobs. There are approximately 1,000 employees in these jobs, and the average turnover rate in EAPCO plants is high—about 35 percent each year. Pay for employees in these jobs is around $20,000 per year. Job applicants have been considered for employment only if they score above the national average score of all employees taking the DIT. This national average score is published yearly by Selection Systems, Inc. (SSI), the developer of the DIT, and is based on the test scores of more than 100,000 job applicants. This year's national average score was 22. Test–retest reliability data are also available from SSI. Some regular users of the DIT are asked to give the DIT to a sample of their employees twice, with the second administration following the first by one week. Typical test–retest data reported by SSI indicate coefficients of stability of around .85.

In analyzing the hiring patterns of the company, Paul Hawke, the new manager of human resources for EAPCO, noticed that a large number of black applicants failed the test. Out of every hundred white applicants, eighty-five passed the DIT, and approximately fifty were hired for positions in the company. In contrast, out of every hundred black applicants, thirty passed the DIT, and only ten were hired. Hawke was concerned about the potential legal implications of this hiring system. He found no evidence that systematic job analyses had been conducted on the unskilled production jobs or that EAPCO had validated the DIT against any measure of job performance. Validity data on the DIT were available from SSI. These data typically consisted of the results of concurrent validation studies conducted by other organizations using the DIT. Hawke decided that it was time for an internal EAPCO validation study to be done.

Hawke contacted Validation Consulting, Inc. (VCI), a local firm, and hired it to conduct the study. One week later, Steven Peabody-Reynolds, a partner at VCI, arrived at Hawke's office. Peabody-Reynolds spent the morning discussing the current selection system with various managers and first-line supervisors. He returned one week later and

presented Hawke with a plan for validating the DIT. The study was designed as a concurrent validation procedure. Peabody-Reynolds recommended using just the Kentucky plant in the study to save money. There were a hundred unskilled production workers at the Kentucky plant—ninety whites and ten blacks. Most of the employees had been with the company for quite some time and had not taken the DIT since their initial hiring. Fifteen of the employees in the proposed study (all white) had been at the Kentucky plant for eighteen years or more. Hawke agreed to the plan, and one week later the study was conducted at the Kentucky plant. All employees in the study were given the DIT (time 1). One week later (to allow VCI to check the test–retest reliability of the DIT), the same employees were given the DIT again (time 2), and their supervisors were asked to rate their overall work performance using a 7-point scale where 1 = very unsatisfactory performer, 2 = unsatisfactory performer, 3 = satisfactory performer, 4 = good performer, 5 = very good performer, 6 = excellent performer, and 7 = truly exceptional performer. Performance ratings and DIT scores were returned to Peabody-Reynolds. He conducted statistical analyses on the data and reported to Hawke that he had found a significant correlation (.85) between DIT (time 2) scores and performance ratings. Hawke concluded that the DIT was related to job performance and was a valid test for use in screening employees to fill unskilled production jobs.

Six months after the study was completed, James Wilson, a black job applicant, took and failed the DIT. He then filed a charge of racial discrimination against EAPCO. The EEOC attempted to conciliate between Wilson and EAPCO, but the company refused to offer any sort of settlement that was acceptable to Wilson. The EEOC decided to file suit against EAPCO in federal court. Hiring data from EAPCO's personnel files clearly indicate a prima facia case of discrimination. However, the company is basing its case on the arguments that the use of the DIT is justifiable because DIT scores are related to job performance and that use of the DIT has substantial utility. With around 1,000 applications for unskilled production jobs each year,

EAPCO feels that the DIT is an important, inexpensive ($20 per applicant) screening device in the hiring process. The data from the validation study conducted by Steven Peabody-Reynolds are presented in the table that follows. In the table, ID = the employee ID number, Perf. = employee performance rating, DIT = Delta Intelligence Test score for the employee, and Group = an indication of whether the employee is white (codes 1 or 3) or black (code 2) and whether the employee has eighteen years' experience with EAPCO (code 3) or less than eighteen years' experience (codes 1 and 2).

Through various legal maneuvers, the case against EAPCO has been delayed several times. During this period, Paul Hawke has resigned as human resource manager director and Bronwyn Downer, a local HR consultant with significant HR experience in a variety of industries, has been hired as Hawke's replacement. The CEO of EAPCO has indicated some concern as to whether Paul Hawke was handling the Wilson case in the best interests of the company. The CEO has asked Ms. Downer to review the situation and make a recommendation as to whether EAPCO should seek to settle the discrimination case with Wilson. EAPCO's lawyers have indicated that they believe Wilson will accept a settlement of around $200,000. The CEO has asked Ms. Downer, in making her analysis of the situation, to consider all the important issues. These include the following:

- The reliability of the DIT
- The validity of the DIT (including differential validity)
- The adequacy of the validation study conducted by Peabody-Reynolds
- The efficiency and utility of the current selection system based on the DIT

The CEO wants Ms. Downer to make a recommendation, based on her analysis of these critical issues, as to how EAPCO should proceed in the case brought against them by Mr. Wilson.

Put yourself in the position of Ms. Downer. Conduct your analysis and make a recommendation, supported by sound arguments, to the CEO.

Option 1

Your instructor will provide you with the following information taken from the data collected by Steven Peabody-Reynolds:

1. The correlation (coefficient of stability) between DIT scores collected at time 1 and those collected at time 2
2. The correlation between DIT (time 2) and performance ratings for
   a. The total sample
   b. Black employees (group code 2)
   c. White employees (group codes 1 and 3)
   d. Employees with eighteen years' experience or more (group code 3)
3. The average DIT (time 2) score for each level of performance rating
4. The average performance of employees scoring above 22 on the DIT (time 2)
5. The average performance of employees scoring 22 or less on the DIT (time 2)
6. EAPCO's typical selection ratio
7. An estimate of the base rate of success for job applicants
8. An estimate of the standard deviation of performance in dollars (SDP$)

Option 2

Using the data provided in the following list, conduct your own statistical analyses. You will need to calculate all of the information listed in Option 1. Information necessary for estimating the selection ratio and SDP$ is given in the text of the case. Discuss with your instructor how you might use the performance rating data in the table to estimate the base rate of success. You can conduct your statistical analyses using any spreadsheet package such as Microsoft Excel or Lotus 1-2-3 or with a more advanced statistical analysis package such as SPSS for Windows. You also can do the necessary calculations on a hand calculator (it will take a while, though). Just look up the "computational formula" for a correlation in any standard statistics text. The rest is just averaging numbers for different groups.

ID	Perf	DIT1	DIT2	Group	ID	Perf	DIT1	DIT2	Group
143	2	21	20	2	250	3	17	18	3
144	6	24	20	1	251	6	29	19	1
145	7	22	23	1	252	3	20	20	1
146	5	21	20	1	253	4	22	24	1
147	4	25	19	3	254	6	27	18	1
148	4	16	22	1	255	6	36	38	3
149	5	19	23	3	256	4	24	26	1
150	6	22	20	1	257	4	24	24	1
151	6	27	34	3	258	4	20	21	3
152	5	29	26	1	259	3	24	23	1
153	5	20	27	1	260	6	23	25	1
154	4	27	20	1	261	3	18	23	1
155	3	19	19	3	262	5	18	20	1
156	2	23	22	2	263	3	21	23	1
157	3	17	20	1	264	6	24	27	1
158	5	20	23	1	265	3	24	23	1
159	5	25	22	1	266	6	24	24	1
160	2	18	19	3	267	3	27	27	1
161	6	20	23	1	268	2	21	21	2
162	6	20	30	1	269	5	20	22	1
163	3	27	25	1	270	5	22	21	1
164	5	17	19	1	271	6	25	24	1
165	2	27	25	1	272	1	19	25	2
166	6	26	25	1	273	1	17	18	2
167	5	21	20	1	274	6	19	20	1
210	6	22	24	1	275	5	24	19	1
211	6	22	22	1	276	5	20	20	1
212	5	27	24	1	277	6	18	23	1
213	6	19	25	1	280	3	22	22	2
214	5	20	25	1	282	4	22	20	1
215	7	38	35	3	283	5	15	22	1
216	6	20	27	1	285	5	21	27	1
217	3	20	21	2	286	3	25	19	2
218	4	31	24	1	289	5	24	28	1
219	6	17	30	1	290	5	22	26	1
220	3	20	22	2	297	3	17	20	2
221	4	23	23	1	300	4	20	21	1
222	5	20	22	1	430	3	40	44	1
223	7	27	33	3	432	6	12	10	1
224	6	26	29	3	433	6	24	28	1
225	6	45	42	1	434	5	19	29	1
226	3	20	25	1	435	6	26	30	3
227	5	18	24	3	436	4	32	30	1
228	3	31	23	1	437	5	35	34	1
229	6	26	22	1	439	5	28	34	3
248	3	20	20	1	440	5	30	29	1
249	3	20	21	1	441	5	26	25	3

ID	Perf	DIT1	DIT2	Group	ID	Perf	DIT1	DIT2	Group
442	6	35	21	1	445	4	26	33	1
443	6	31	34	1	446	6	18	10	1
444	4	29	30	1	447	5	26	28	1

● Exercise 7.1
Finding Test Information on the Internet

It is clear from Chapter 7 that an HR professional needs to collect a substantial amount of information about potential selection tests before actually using the tests in hiring decisions. There are many specialist consulting firms that have developed selection tests for use by organizations, and many of these firms advertise their test products on the Internet. The following exercise will give you an opportunity to use the Internet to locate some of these test publishers and examine the types of information they provide about their selection-test products.

Instructions

1. Decide on some general occupational group that will be your focus in this exercise. For example, you might focus on hospitality, general clerical, computer programming, or midlevel managerial jobs.
2. Using the key words of "employment test publishers," use one of the Web search engines to identify several firms that publish employment tests. You can use other key words to help expand your search (e.g., personnel tests or personnel testing).
3. Identify firms that publish tests that seem of potential relevance to hiring people into your focal occupational group.
4. Identify which kinds of information these firms provide on the Internet about their test products (e.g., reliability information, cost of the tests, or type of people for whom the tests are appropriate).
5. From what you have learned in Chapter 7, what other types of information would you need to obtain from these employment test publishers before making a rational decision about whether their test would be useful in hiring people into the occupational group?

● Exercise 7.2
Looking for Measurement Bias

Option 1

Course instructor brings copies of questions taken from several common cognitive ability, personality, or other typical selection tests to class.

Students work in groups of three or four and evaluate each of the test items for possible measurement bias. In evaluating the items students should ask themselves the following questions:

- Would different racial, gender, or socioeconomic groups be likely to respond to the items in a different way? Why? For example, on an intelligence test an eighteen-year-old white male from a prosperous suburb might be much more likely to know the answer to the question "Which is better, a par or a bogie?" than would an eighteen-year-old black male from the inner city.

- Suppose that these test items had been given to a group of people in 1985, 1990, 1995, and 2000. Would you expect some of the groups to be more (or less) likely to respond to the items correctly—or to respond differently at the different times. (For an example, see the discussion of the computer knowledge test discussed in the chapter.)

- If measurement bias did exist in some of the items, what effect would it likely have on the people taking the test? Would it advantage some and disadvantage others? Would the bias in the items likely "cancel each other out" so that overall test scores for all groups would be about the same?

Students then report their findings to the class.

Option 2

Rather than the instructor's bringing test items to class, students could, in conjunction with Exercise 7.1, bring to class examples of test questions they have found on the Internet. The same analysis of test items would then be conducted.

Notes and References

1. Richard Sisley, "The Recruitment Gamble: Improving the Odds," *Management*, Vol. 44 (4), 1997, pp. 22–24.

2. R. M. Guion, "Recruiting, Selection, and Job Placement," in *Handbook of Industrial and Organizational Psychology*, ed. M. D. Dunnette (Chicago: Rand-McNally, 1976), pp. 778–828.

3. For a more detailed description of correlation and regression analysis, see J. Cohen and P. Cohen, *Applied Multiple Regression/Correlation Analysis for the Behavioral Sciences* (Hillsdale, N.J.: Erlbaum, 1975), pp. 73–122.

4. R. M. Guion, *Personnel Testing* (New York: McGraw-Hill, 1965), chap. 2.

5. J. C. Nunnally, *Psychometric Theory* (New York: McGraw-Hill, 1967), p. 172.

6. American Psychological Association, *Standards for Educational and Psychological Testing* (Washington, D.C.: Author, 1999); and Robert Guion, *Assessment, Measurement, and Prediction for Personnel Decisions* (Mahwah, N.J.: Erlbaum, 1998).

7. L. J. Cronbach, "Coefficient Alpha and the Internal Structure of Tests," *Psychometrika*, Vol. 16, 1951, pp. 297–334.

8. Guion, *Assessment, Measurement, and Prediction for Personnel Decisions*.

9. *Uniform Guidelines on Employee Selection Procedures* (Washington, D.C.: Bureau of National Affairs, 1979); and Society for Industrial and Organizational Psychology, *Principles for the Validation and Use of Personnel Selection Procedures*, (Bowling Green, Ohio: SIOP Publications, 1987), 3d ed.

10. Guion, *Assessment, Measurement, and Prediction for Personnel Decisions*.

11. Charles Lawshe, "A Quantitative Approach to Content Validity," *Personnel Psychology*, Vol. 28, 1975, pp. 563–575; and *United States v. State of South Carolina*, 445 F. Supp. 1094, 15 FEP 1196 (1977).

12. This example is based on reports from a validation study of computer adaptive testing by Randall Overton, Harvey Harms, Rogers Taylor, and Michael Zickar, "Adapting to Adaptive Testing," *Personnel Psychology*, Vol. 50 (1), 1997, pp. 171–185.

13. For an example of the legal importance of this concept, see also *Griggs v. Duke Power Co.*, 401 U.S. 424, 3 FEP 175 (1971).

14. Norman Abrahams, Edward Alf, Jr., and Idell Neuman, "The Treatment of Failures in Validation Research," *Military Psychology*, Vol. 5 (4), 1993, pp. 235–249; and Jules Borack, "Estimating Predictive Validity When Range Restriction Due to Selection and Attrition Is Present," *Military Psychology*, Vol. 6 (3), 1994, pp. 193–204.

15. Calvin Hoffman, "Applying Range Restriction Corrections Using Published Norms: Three Case Studies," *Personnel Psychology*, Vol. 48 (4), 1995, pp. 913–923; and Paul Sackett and Daniel Ostgaard, "Job-Specific Applicant Pools and National Norms for Cognitive Ability Tests: Implications for Range Restriction Corrections in Validation Research," *Journal of Applied Psychology*, Vol. 79 (5), 1994, pp. 680–684.

16. For a description of several other versions of the basic predictive validity procedure, see R. M. Guion and C. J. Cranny, "A Note on Concurrent and Predictive Validity Designs: A Critical Reanalysis," *Journal of Applied Psychology*, Vol. 67, 1982, pp. 239–244.

17. F. L. Schmidt, J. E. Hunter, and V. W. Urry, "Statistical Power in Criterion-Related Validity Studies," *Journal of Applied Psychology*, Vol. 61, 1976, pp. 473–485.

18. Gerald Barrett, Ralph Alexander, and Dennis Doverspike, "The Implications for Personnel Selection of Apparent Declines in Predictive Validities over Time: A Critique of Hulin, Henry, and Noon," *Personnel Psychology*, Vol. 45 (3), 1992, pp. 601–617; and C. Hulin, R. Henry, and S. Noon, "Adding a Dimension: Time as a Factor in the Generalizability of Predictive Relationships," *Psychological Bulletin*, Vol. 107, 1990, pp. 328–340.

19. G. V. Barrett, M. S. Caldwell, and R. A. Alexander, "The Concept of Dynamic Criteria: A Critical Reanalysis," *Personnel Psychology*, Vol. 38, 1985, pp. 41–56.

20. D. L. Deadrick and R. M. Madigan, "Dynamic Criteria Revisited: A Longitudinal Study of Performance Stability and Predictive Validity," *Personnel Psychology*, Vol. 43, 1990, pp. 717–744.

21. Kim-Yin Chan, Fritz Drasgow, and Linda Swain, "What Is the Shelf Life of a Test? The Effect of Time on the Psychometrics of a Cognitive Ability Test Battery," *Journal of Applied Psychology*, Vol. 84 (4), 1999, pp. 610–619.

22. Guion, *Assessment, Measurement, and Prediction for Personnel Decisions*.

23. L. G. Humphreys, "Statistical Definitions of Test Validity for Minority Groups," *Journal of Applied Psychology*, Vol. 58, 1973, pp. 1–4.

24. Scott Maxwell and Richard Arvey, "The Search for Predictors with High Validity and Low Adverse Impact: Compatible or Incompatible Goals?" *Journal of Applied Psychology*, Vol. 78 (3), 1993, pp. 433–437.

25. For examples, see Chan, Drasgow, and Swain, "What Is the Shelf Life of a Test?"; Judith Collins and David Gleaves, "Race, Job Applicants, and the Five-Factor Model of Personality: Implications for Black Psychology, Industrial/Organizational

Psychology, and the Five Factor Theory," *Journal of Applied Psychology*, Vol. 83 (4), 1998, pp. 531–544; and David Whitney and Neal Schmitt, "Relationship Between Culture and Responses to Biodata Employment Items," *Journal of Applied Psychology*, Vol. 82 (1), 1997, pp. 113–129.

26. Chan, Dragsow, and Swain, "What Is the Shelf Life of a Test?"

27. Frank Schmidt, Kenneth Law, John Hunter, Hannah Rothstein, Kenneth Pearlman, and Michael McDaniel, "Refinements in Validity Generalization Methods: Implications for the Situational Specificity Hypothesis," *Journal of Applied Psychology*, Vol. 78 (1), 1993, pp. 3–12.

28. J. E. Hunter, "Cognitive Ability, Cognitive Aptitudes, Job Knowledge, and Job Performance," *Journal of Vocational Behavior,* Vol. 29, 1986, pp. 340–362.

29. H. R. Rothstein, F. L. Schmidt, F. W. Erwin, W. A. Owens, and C. P. Sparks, "Biographical Data in Employment Selection: Can Validities Be Made Generalizable?" *Journal of Applied Psychology*, Vol. 75, 1990, pp. 175–184; Calvin Hoffman, "Generalizing Physical Ability Test Validity: A Case Study Using Test Transportability, Validity Generalization, and Construct-Related Validation Evidence," *Personnel Psychology*, Vol. 52 (4), 1999, pp. 1019–1041; and L. L. Wise, J. McHenry, and J. P. Campbell, "Identifying Optimal Predictor Composites and Testing for Generalizability Across Jobs and Performance Factors," *Personnel Psychology*, Vol. 43, 1990, pp. 355–366.

30. Steven Ashworth, H. G. Osburn, John Callender, and Kristin Boyle, "The Effects of Unrepresented Studies on the Robustness of Validity Generalization Results," *Personnel Psychology*, Vol. 45 (2), 1992, pp. 341–361.

31. H. H. Meyer, "Predicting Supervisory Ratings Versus Promotional Progress in Test Validation Studies," *Journal of Applied Psychology*, Vol. 72, 1987, pp. 696–697; B. R. Nathan and R. A. Alexander, "A Comparison of Criteria for Test Validation: A Meta-Analytic Investigation," *Personnel Psychology*, Vol. 41, 1988, pp. 517–535; and Craig Russell, Randall Settoon, Robert McGrath, Elyssa Blanton, Roland Kidwell, Franz Lohrke, Elton Scifres, and George Danforth, "Investigator Characteristics as Moderators of Personnel Selection Research: A Meta-Analysis," *Journal of Applied Psychology*, Vol. 79 (2), 1994, pp. 163–170.

32. S. Messick, "Validity," in *Educational Measurement,* cd. R. L. Lim (New York: American Council on Education/ Macmillan, 1989), pp. 13–103.

33. Cohen and Cohen, *Applied Multiple Regression/Correlation Analysis for the Behavioral Sciences*, pp. 73–122.

34. Winfred Arthur, Dennis Doverspike, and Gerald Barrett, "Development of a Job Analysis–Based Procedure for Weighting and Combining Content-Related Tests into a Single Test Battery Score," *Personnel Psychology*, Vol. 49 (4), 1996, pp. 971–985; and Kevin Murphy and Ann Shiarella, "Implications of the Multidimensional Nature of Job Performance for the Validity of Selection Tests: Multivariate Frameworks for Studying Test Validity," *Personnel Psychology*, Vol. 50 (4), 1997, pp. 823–854.

35. W. F. Cascio, E. R. Valenzi, and V. Silbey, "Validation and Statistical Power: Implications for Applied Research," *Journal of Applied Psychology*, Vol. 63, 1978, pp. 589–595; W. F. Cascio, E. R. Valenzi, and V. Silbey, "More on Validation and Statistical Power," *Journal of Applied Psychology*, Vol. 65, 1980, pp. 135–138.

36. L. S. Buck, "Guide for Setting of Appropriate Cutting Scores for Written Tests," in *Manpower Planning and Programming*, ed. E. H. Burack and J. W. Walker (Boston: Allyn and Bacon, 1972).

37. Guion, *Assessment, Measurement, and Prediction for Personnel Decisions;* and T. J. Mauer, R. A. Alexander, C. M. Callahan, J. J. Bailey, and F. H. Dambrot, "Methodological and Psychometric Issues in Setting Cutting Scores Using the Angoff Method," *Personnel Psychology*, Vol. 44, 1991, pp. 235–262.

38. W. F. Cascio, R. A. Alexander, and G. V. Barrett, "Setting Cutoff Scores: Legal, Psychometric, and Professional Issues and Guidelines," *Personnel Psychology*, Vol. 41, 1988, pp. 1–24.

39. *Evans* v. *City of Evanston,* 881 F. 2d 382 (7th Cir. 1989); and *Richardson* v. *Lamar County Board of Education,* 51 FEP 1274 (N.D. Ala. 1989).

40. L. J. Cronbach and G. C. Gleser, *Psychological Tests and Personnel Decisions* (Champaign: University of Illinois Press, 1965).

41. Paul Sackett and Steffanie Wik, "Within-Group Norming and Other Forms of Score Adjustment in Preemployment Testing," *American Psychologist*, Vol. 49 (11), 1994, pp. 929–954.

42. Guion, *Assessment, Measurement, and Prediction for Personnel Decisions.*

43. David Chan and Neal Schmitt, "Video-Based Versus Paper-and-Pencil Method of Assessment in Situational Judgment Tests: Subgroup Differences in Test Performance and Face Validity Perceptions," *Journal of Applied Psychology*, Vol. 82 (1), 1997, pp. 143–159.

44. Allen Huffcutt and Philip Roth, "Racial Group Differences in Employment Interview Evaluations," *Journal of Applied Psychology*, Vol. 83 (2), 1998, pp. 179–189.

45. Sackett and Wik, "Within-Group Norming and Other Forms of Score Adjustment in Preemployment Testing."

46. Kevin Murphy, Kevin Osten, and Brett Myors, "Modeling the Effects of Banding in Personnel Selection," *Personnel Psychology*, Vol. 48 (1), 1995, pp. 61–84.

47. Wilfred De Corte, "Utility Analysis for the Probationary Selection Decision to Obtain a Fixed Quota of Successful Selectees," *Journal of Organizational Behavior*, Vol. 18, 1997, pp. 67–82; and Wilfred De Corte, "Recruitment and Retention Decisions That Maximize the Utility of a Probationary Selection to Obtain a Fixed Quota of Successful Selectees," *Personnel Psychology*, Vol. 49 (2), 1996, pp. 399–428.

48. Philip Roth and Philip Bobko, "A Research Agenda for Multi-Attribute Utility Analysis in Human Resource Management," *Human Resource Management Review*, Vol. 7 (3), 1997, pp. 341–368.

49. H. E. Brogden, "On the Interpretation of the Correlation Coefficient as a Measure of Predictive Efficiency," *Journal of Educational Psychology*, Vol. 37, 1946, pp. 64–76.

50. Cronbach and Gleser, *Psychological Tests and Personnel Decisions.*

51. P. E. Meehl and A. Rosen, "Antecedent Probability and the Efficiency of Psychometric Signs, Patterns, or Cutting Scores," *Psychological Bulletin*, Vol. 52, 1955, pp. 194–216.

52. H. C. Taylor and J. T. Russell, "The Relationship of Validity Coefficients to the Practical Effectiveness of Tests in Selection," *Journal of Applied Psychology*, Vol. 23, 1939, pp. 565–578.

53. H. E. Brogden and E. K. Taylor, "The Dollar Criterion—Applying the Cost Accounting Concept to Criterion Construction," *Personnel Psychology*, Vol. 3, 1950, pp. 133–154; and Victor

Catano and V. W. Johnston, "Estimating the Dollar Value of Performance for a Complex Military Occupation: The Influence of Supervisory Rank and Experience," *Military Psychology*, Vol. 5 (4), 1993, pp. 201–218.

54. W. F. Cascio and J. R. Morris, "A Critical Reanalysis of Hunter, Schmidt, and Coggin's 'Problems and Pitfalls in Using Capital Budgeting and Financial Accounting Techniques in Assessing the Utility of Personnel Programs,' " *Journal of Applied Psychology*, Vol. 75, 1990, pp. 410–417; W. F. Cascio and V. Silbey, "Utility of the Assessment Center as a Selection Device," *Journal of Applied Psychology*, Vol. 64, 1979, pp. 107–118; S. F. Cronshaw and R. A. Alexander, "Why Capital Budgeting Techniques Are Suited for Assessing the Utility of Personnel Programs: A Reply to Hunter, Schmidt, and Coggin," *Journal of Applied Psychology*, Vol. 76, 1991, pp. 454–457; and J. E. Hunter, F. L. Schmidt, and T. D. Coggin, "Problems and Pitfalls in Using Capital Budgeting and Financial Accounting Techniques in Assessing the Utility of Personnel Programs," *Journal of Applied Psychology*, Vol. 73, 1988, pp. 522–528.

55. F. L. Schmidt, J. E. Hunter, R. C. McKenzie, and T. W. Muldrow, "Impact of Valid Selection Procedures on Work Force Productivity," *Journal of Applied Psychology*, Vol. 64, 1979, pp. 609–626.

56. L. Siegel and I. M. Lane, *Personnel and Organizational Psychology* (Homewood, Ill.: Irwin, 1982).

57. M. D. Dunnette, *Personnel Selection and Placement* (Monterey, Calif.: Brooks/Cole, 1966), pp. 174–175.

58. Messick, "Validity," pp. 13–103.

59. E. E. Cureton, "A Recipe for a Cookbook," *Psychological Bulletin*, Vol. 54, 1957, pp. 494–497.

Assessing Job Candidates: Tools for Selection

HR Challenge

You are human resources director at Health Source, the drugstore chain mentioned at the beginning of Chapter 6 that is preparing to open new stores in Dallas and Houston. Each store will require about fifteen clerks. Your recruiting efforts have been successful, and each store has attracted about a hundred applicants for those fifteen jobs. You have performed a job analysis and concluded that the clerks must be able to learn to operate a cash register and make change accurately, take the initiative in providing friendly assistance to customers, and show up for work on time. In addition, because of the presence of controlled drugs on the premises, you want clerks who have no history of drug problems or theft.

How will you go about selecting clerks? What legal and ethical considerations will affect your decisions? How many selection devices will you use, and in what order? How much is each selection device likely to cost, and—on the basis of the literature—how valid might you expect it to be? What effect will your selection system have on both the hired and the rejected candidates' attitudes toward Health Source?

Selection follows the recruitment of a pool of job applicants. The selection process involves assessing the applicants to decide who will be hired. Ideally, the people who are hired will be better employees, on average, than those who are rejected. If the selection devices used to assess applicants have been chosen and validated properly, this goal should be realized. Chapter 8 discusses the benefits of proper selection, the selection process itself, and the range of selection devices available to human resource professionals.[1]

OVERVIEW OF THE SELECTION PROCESS

Benefits of Careful and Strategic Selection

Organizations vary in the complexity of their selection systems. Some merely skim application blanks and conduct brief, informal interviews, whereas others engage in testing, repeated interviewing, lengthy assessment centers, background checks, and so on. Although the latter course is more costly per applicant, many benefits are realized from careful, thorough selection. A prominent sociologist has pointed out that organizations need to have members who are both skilled and motivated to perform their organizational roles. Either such members can be identified by careful selection, or attempts can be made to develop them after hire by extensive training and socialization. Thus cursory selection may increase training and monitoring costs greatly, whereas spending more on the selection process will reduce these post-hire expenses by bringing well-qualified people into the organization to begin with.[2]

The cost of hiring the wrong person can be very large. Removing a bad hire from the organization can be fraught with legal difficulties, and during that person's tenure the organization can suffer from lost sales and missed opportunities, dissatisfied customers, and low morale among disenchanted coworkers, to say nothing of wasted managerial time, training expenditures, and the inept employee's salary and benefit costs. To replace the poor hire, costs are incurred in advertising, selection, relocation, and training of a successor. One estimate of the cost of replacing a poor hire in a job requiring a high school education is $14,000, while for a university graduate job the cost is closer to $66,000. Yet another study suggests that the cost of hiring a bad sales representative is three times the rep's annual compensation, including salary, commission, expenses, and benefits.[3]

On the other hand, the dollar savings (utility) of appropriate selection procedures can be very large. Researchers estimated that using cognitive ability tests for selection could yield the 5,000-member Philadelphia Police Department $18 million in savings from increased performance for each year's hires. Similarly, the U.S. government, by improving selection strategies for its work force of 3 million people, could save $15.6 billion annually.[4]

Selecting the right people is also critical to successful strategy implementation. The organization's strategy may affect job duties and design, and the job should drive selection. For instance, if a company plans to compete on the basis of

INTERNATIONAL PERSPECTIVE

Employee Selection in Korea

The basic idea underlying many HR practices in the West is that "people are different"—different in skills, aptitudes, and job performance. HR practices are based on measuring and responding to these differences throughout the employee's career via selection testing, differential assignment to training programs, individual performance appraisal, and performance-based pay. Implicit in these processes is the need to evaluate and judge others.

Soonmook Lee, a Korean HR scholar, points out that the basic assumption in many Asian countries is that people are the same, and it is in bad taste for one individual to notice or judge differences in others. This cultural tendency is called "collectivism," as opposed to the "individualism" that is prevalent in the West. Collectivism also means that group membership and group identities are very important to people. Korean organizations see themselves as family groups, with employees being given lifetime employment. Loyalty from employees (family members) is a prime expectation, even more than competence. As in a biological family, all family members remain such regardless of

how good or bad their behavior or performance might be, and other members do not judge them on their contribution to the family. A manifestation of this in Korean organizations is that performance-based pay is very seldom used. Korean companies usually recruit generalists at the entry level, whom they develop in-house through job rotation. This contrasts with the Western approach of hiring people with specific skills for specific jobs. Nearly all promotions in Korean companies are from within, because only family members who have proven their loyalty over time are trusted to take important roles in the company.

Because the family relationship of employment is lasting, it is very important to adopt the right people into the family. At the blue-collar level, much of recruiting is via the "back door." This refers to selecting people who are recommended by or related to a present employee and thus already have an indirect relationship with the organization. Whom you know is more important than what you know in getting a job. Coming from the same geographic region as other company members is also desirable, because it makes one already part of the extended family.

prompt, polite, personalized service, then service and communication skills should be featured in the job specification and selection devices that can identify these skills in front-line applicants should be chosen. This argument is based on the assumption that the organization's strategy is clear, well known, and stable enough that people who fit the strategy can be selected. However, some scholars have pointed out that in a rapidly changing, uncertain world, not all organizations are able to stick to a single strategy long enough for staffing practices to catch up and bear fruit.

Another approach to strategic staffing suggests that human resources come first and drive strategy rather than the reverse: "Companies are beginning to realize that the foundation of their competitive strategy is the quality of their human capital."[5] Having a top-notch, flexible, innovative staff may be a competitive advantage that is more sustainable than technological or marketing advantages. Such people will be able to generate and implement a wide range of new strategies to respond quickly to a changing environment. This suggests hiring the best individuals one can find rather than hiring those who fit a specific job or strategy that exists today but may be gone tomorrow. "Best" in this new context means best in

When recruiting university graduates, connections also matter. References from professors and other high-status people are very important in the "whom you know" sweepstakes. Which school a candidate attended is critical. Competition to get into the top schools is fierce, so having attended a highly ranked university is considered to guarantee a desirable level of mental ability and motivation. It is also an indicator of social status, and this is very important because someone of lower status probably will not be able to credibly manage subordinates of higher status. Other indicators of status depend on the region in which one was born, the prestige of the district in which one presently resides, and the occupations and affluence of one's parents and grandparents.

Most companies follow the approach of screening based on university and social status, followed by company-sponsored examinations in English and in one's major subject. A new economics graduate, for instance, would be asked to take an economics examination as part of the selection process. A graduate of a technical or vocational institute would need to present a certificate from the National Skill Testing Agency to document his or her knowledge. Testing is followed by interviews, often with top executives or even the company president. In large companies, many new graduates must be interviewed by the executive panel, so interviews tend to last about ten minutes.

Large Korean conglomerates (called *chaebols*) have recently responded to business pressure to hire high performers rather than merely people of good character. They have reduced reliance on educational credentials and tests similar to university examinations. Instead, they are focusing on assessment center–like activities, situational interviews, and evaluation of candidates during summer internships. However, biases based on university status are still so culturally pervasive that several companies circumvent them by conducting "blind interviews" in which interviewers are not informed of the university a student has attended.

Sources: B. De Mente, *Korean Etiquette and Ethics in Business* (Lincolnwood, Ill.: NTC Business Books, 1988); R. M. Steers, Y. K. Shin, and G. R. Ungson, *The Chaebol: Korea's New Industrial Might* (New York: Harper and Row, 1989); S. Lee and D. Lee, "Effectiveness of Multi-Stage Selection Strategies in Korean Organizations," paper presented at the 2nd Australian Industrial and Organizational Psychology Conference, Melbourne, June 1997; and Hak-Chong Lee, "Transformation of Employment Practices in Korean Businesses," *International Studies of Management and Organization*, Winter 1998, pp. 26–39.

intelligence, best in interpersonal skills, and best in motivation, since many jobs in rapidly changing organizations involve self-management, continuous learning, teamwork, negotiation, and relationship management. In Korean organizations, the hiring process has traditionally served a slightly different purpose, as explained in the International Perspective box.

The Process of Selection

Most organizations use more than one selection device to gather information about applicants. Often these devices are used sequentially, in a multiple hurdle decision-making scheme: Candidates must do well on an earlier selection device to remain in the running and be assessed by later devices. Figure 8.1 shows a fairly typical order in which selection devices might be used. Less expensive devices such as application blanks and some written tests tend to be used for the initial screening of large numbers of applicants. More costly procedures such as interviews and assessment centers are used later in the process for candidates that have passed the earlier assessments. Often the HR department takes responsibil-

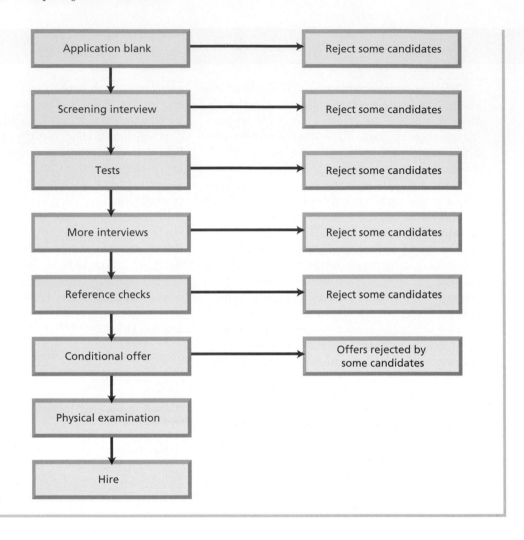

● **FIGURE 8.1**

Typical Order in Which
Selection Devices Are
Used

ity for the first few hurdles. Then one or more managers or supervisors interview the survivors of these hurdles and choose from among the short-listed candidates. Pending satisfactory reference checks, offers are made, medical examinations are completed, and hiring is finalized. The following sections will explore the use and benefits of a variety of selection devices.

APPLICATION BLANKS AND BIODATA

Effective and Legal Use of Application Blanks

The application blank and/or the résumé represents the first selection hurdle for most jobs. Application blanks typically request information about education, work history, and skills, as well as the names and contact details of the applicant and several references. Most of the information requested is factual and can be verified, such as degrees earned or dates of employment. Application blank or résumé fraud is not uncommon. Some studies have found that a significant proportion of candidates falsify or slightly inflate some of their credentials.[6] Thus, seeking outside confirmation of important credentials is a wise practice.

Most organizations use application blanks or résumés to screen out candidates who do not meet the minimum job specifications on education or experience. Beyond these basics, a manager or HR officer may evaluate the application informally to find the candidates who look most promising. The criteria applied in making this judgment may not be explicit, job-related, or consistent from one screener to the next and thus may pose a legal problem.

A second way that organizations can use application blank data is to apply a validated weighting scheme, in which only items known to relate to later job success are scored and utilized in decision making. **Weighted application blank (WAB)** procedures have been shown to produce scores that predict performance, tenure, and employee theft. Because the weights are valid and are applied consistently to all applicants, this method of using application blank data is more defensible than the above-mentioned informal evaluation.

● **Questions to Avoid on an Application Blank**   To comply with federal employment laws, a firm must not discriminate in hiring on the basis of age, race, color, sex, religion, or national origin. This does not mean that it is illegal for a recruiter to ask about age, religion, and so on in the selection process; it is just illegal for the recruiter or interviewer to act on this information in a discriminatory fashion. In the interests of playing it safe, however, interviewers should avoid questions about any of these subjects unless they are clearly job-related. Further, such questions may be illegal under state or city human rights laws. One study of application blanks from eighty-eight organizations found that each blank included at least two "inadvisable" items; on average, there were 7.2 inadvisable items per application blank.[7]

The Americans with Disabilities Act of 1990 specifically prohibits asking questions about disabilities or the present or prior health status of candidates before making a job offer. Inquiries can be made about the candidate's ability to perform essential functions of the job but not broadly in regard to disabilities.[8] For example, if lifting is an essential feature of the job, candidates may be asked whether they are able to perform this function, but they may not be asked in general about "back problems" or past workers' compensation claims.

In addition, application blanks and interviews should avoid questions that appear neutral but cause disparate impact if used as selection standards—for example, questions about height and weight. Examples of inquiries that tend to exclude a disproportionate share of minorities are those concerning arrest record, type of military discharge, credit rating, and home ownership.[9] Table 8.1 lists some permissible and inadvisable questions. Employers should bear in mind that they can and should ask any truly job-related questions. Accordingly, when interviewing candidates for the job of bank guard, the recruiter for the bank should ask about armed robbery convictions; when hiring for a job that involves control of money, the recruiter should ask about embezzlement convictions; and when selecting truck drivers, the recruiter should ask about traffic violations.

● **Constructing a Weighted Application Blank (WAB)**   There are several procedures for deriving valid application blank weighting schemes. In most of them, the first step is deciding which criterion to predict and defining high and low levels of this criterion. For instance, if tenure is the criterion of interest, "high" could be

● **TABLE 8.1**

Problematic and Acceptable Questions of Job Candidates

Topic	Problematic Questions	Acceptable Questions
Name	Do you prefer the title Mr., Ms., Miss, or Mrs. What is your maiden name?	Are your recent work records in another name?
Age	What are your age, birthdate, and year of high school graduation?	Are you age 18 (21) or over? (if legally required minimum age, such as to serve alcohol)
Marital/family status	What are your marital status, number and age of children, plans for having future children, child-care arrangements?	Only after hiring for insurance and tax purposes.
Birthplace/national origin	Where were you born, when were you naturalized, what is your mother tongue?	Do you have permission to live and work in the United States?
Organization membership	List all the clubs and organizations you belong to.	List memberships and offices held in relevant professional organizations.
Gender	What is your gender?	Only if bona fide occupational qualification.
Religion	What is your religion, what religious holidays do you observe? Please give pastor or rabbi's name as a reference.	Are you available to work the following required schedule?
Criminal record	List all arrests and convictions.	List job-related and recent convictions.
Physical characteristics	What are your height and weight? Please supply a photo.	Photo is permissible only after hire, height and weight only if bona fide occupational qualification.
Handicap	Do you have any handicaps? Provide full medical history. Have you received workers' compensation?	Explain job requirements and ask if candidate is able to perform them with or without reasonable accommodation.

defined as staying at least two years after hire and "low" as leaving before the end of one year. The steps involved in deriving weights are described in Figure 8.2 and Table 8.2. The aim is to identify which questions and answers reliably distinguish between the low and the high criterion groups. Before they are used to screen new applicants, the weights must be cross-validated to ensure that they are stable and generalizable to a different sample rather than merely the result of chance relationships in the development sample.

Relatively few organizations use WABs, even though WABs tend to be quite helpful in predicting performance. WAB development procedures can be quick and easy to apply, given a suitable sample size, though more complex biodata instruments require professional assistance for design and analysis.

Using Biodata, Experience, and Accomplishment Records for Selection

Biodata is a term used to refer to any type of personal history, experience, or education information. Some organizations use a biographical information questionnaire instead of, or in addition to, the usual application blank. Biodata question-

● **FIGURE 8.2**

Steps in Constructing a Weighted Application Blank

1
Define high and low criterion levels. (At least 125 people must meet each level.)

2
Randomly choose 75 high- and 75 low-criterion group members as a development sample. The rest are a holdout sample.

3
Using the development sample, calculate the percent of high- and low-criterion group members who selected each response.

4
Subtract the low-criterion group percent from the high-criterion group percent. Round and move the decimal point so that all weights are whole numbers between −10 and +10.

5
Compute a WAB score for each member of the development sample by summing the weights corresponding to each response.

6
Correlate the WAB score with criterion group membership (1=high-group member, 0=low-group member) to see how accurately the weights predict group membership.

7
Cross-validate by applying weights to the holdout sample and correlating their WAB scores with their group membership.

8
If the correlation in the holdout sample is significant, set a cutoff and begin using WAB scores to select new employees.

naires may be much more detailed than application blanks and may be scored with keys based on very sophisticated statistical analyses.[10] Sample questions might include, "Do you repair mechanical things in your home, such as appliances?" "As a child, did you collect stamps?" "How many times did your family move while you were growing up?" One such biodata question—"Did you ever build a model airplane that flew?"—was almost as powerful a predictor of success in flight training during World War II as the entire U.S. Air Force battery of selection tests.[11] The life insurance industry trade association, LIMRA, has been developing and validating biodata instruments since the 1930s. In 1997, 240,000 applicants in the United States and Canada completed their instrument, called the Career Profile. Biodata characteristics that have been found helpful in selecting life insurance agents include educational attainment, financial success and stability, and "natural

● **TABLE 8.2**

Application Blank Responses and Corresponding Weights

Items	Percent of Responses		Difference	Weight
	Criterion			
	Low	High		
1. Number of jobs held in last five years:				
1	10%	50%	40%	4
2	30	30	0	0
3 or more	60	20	−40	−4
2. Reason for leaving last job:				
Better opportunity	10	40	30	3
Dissatisfied	20	10	−10	−1
Laid off	40	40	0	0
Fired	30	10	−20	−2
3. Number of languages spoken:				
1	70	60	−10	−1
2	30	30	0	0
3	0	10	10	1

market"—that is, whether the candidate's friends and acquaintances are the type of people who tend to buy life insurance.[12]

● **Validity of Biodata**   In most studies that compare the validity of different types of predictors, empirically scored biodata are among the most effective predictors of subsequent job behavior.[13] Biodata have predicted success in occupations as diverse as U.S. Navy underwater demolitions expert, pilot, office worker, engineer, research scientist, salesperson, supervisor, and manager.[14] James Asher offers three theories for the high predictive power of biodata:

1. *Nonfiction theory:* Reporting on the verifiable aspects of one's past history reveals the truth about one's entire relevant past. A person's past history probably provides a sounder basis for predicting future behavior than does a short experience such as the interview, in which candidates are on their best behavior and can present an artificially positive picture of themselves.

2. *Relevant-item theory:* Weighted application blanks and biodata questionnaires are valid because the only items that receive weights are those that are individually valid. Thus every item is related to the criterion. In contrast, in most tests only the total score is validated against the criterion. If some individual items do not predict job success, they are still part of the total score and may depress the overall validity of the test.

3. *Point-to-point theory:* Biodata use past behavior to directly predict future behavior of the same type. There is no need to hypothesize or measure intervening constructs that may be imperfectly related to behavior, either past or fu-

ture. For instance, high school grade point average (GPA) is the best predictor of college GPA. There is no need to measure an abstract trait such as verbal ability or intelligence to predict college GPA.[15]

A fourth explanation for the success of biodata as a predictor of behavior on the job suggests that many biodata items serve as indicators of important personality traits such as "will to achieve" or conscientiousness.[16] These stable traits may both underlie past performance and contribute to future performance.

A fifth reason for the usefulness of biodata may be that biodata measures tap both cognitive and noncognitive abilities. That is, past activities and achievements reflect skill and intelligence as well as personal qualities such as motivation or leadership.[17]

● **Experience and Accomplishment Records**   When candidates have job-related experience, appropriate measures of that experience can be valid predictors of subsequent job performance.[18] Rather than relying on informal methods of evaluating job experience and accomplishments, some organizations use content-valid **job experience questionnaires** to screen candidates for technical and professional jobs. The usual procedure is to conduct a job analysis by the task inventory method to identify the most important or time-consuming tasks. The results of this job analysis are turned into questions about past work experience with each task or with each type of equipment used. Usually a content-evaluation panel of job experts verifies the job relatedness of each question.[19]

Applicants answer each question by selecting one of the following responses: "I have never done this task"; "I have done it under supervision"; "I have done it on my own"; or "I have supervised and/or taught this task." Some systems award additional points for more recent experiences. To discourage inflated self-ratings, the questionnaire may ask applicants to list the names and addresses of people who can verify their experience with each task.[20] The California State Personnel Board is using an Internet-delivered experience questionnaire as the first step in screening candidates for correctional officer, property appraiser, and the entry-level university graduate position of staff services analyst.[21] Visit their web site at http://exams.spb.ca.gov.

When selecting experienced professionals to hire or promote, a firm may find it helpful to use a structured, content-valid **accomplishment record** for soliciting information about candidates' past specific achievements. A federal regulatory agency demonstrated the feasibility of this approach by developing such a form for promoting attorneys. The procedure followed in developing the form had several steps. First, a job analysis was performed using the critical incident method. Incidents were sorted into eight job dimensions, including research, oral communication and assertive advocacy, independent work, and use of legal knowledge. Three hundred current attorneys then provided examples of their accomplishments on each dimension. Next, a group of job experts used these examples to generate keys and guidelines for scoring applicant accomplishments. The agency trained evaluators to use the keys reliably. Finally, the agency applied the system to assess the accomplishments of attorneys seeking promotion. Figure 8.3 shows one of the dimensions from the accomplishment record, guidelines for scoring that dimension, and a specific accomplishment submitted by a candidate for promotion.[22]

● FIGURE 8.3

Sample Dimension of an Accomplishment Record

Source: From Leaetta M. Hough, "Development and Evaluation of the 'Accomplishment Record' Method of Selecting and Promoting Professionals," *Journal of Applied Psychology,* February 1984, pp. 135–146. Copyright 1984 by the American Psychological Association. Reprinted by permission of the author.

Using Knowledge

General definition   Interpreting and synthesizing information to form legal strategies, approaches, lines of argument, etc.; developing new configurations of knowledge, innovative approaches, solutions, strategies, etc.; selecting the proper legal theory; using appropriate lines of argument, weighing alternatives, and drawing sound conclusions.

Guidelines for rating   In using knowledge, accomplishments at the lower levels are characterized by the resolution of legal issues that lack impact and importance or issues easily resolved by existing case law or precedent. At progressively higher levels, the accomplishments describe the formulation of increasingly complex legal strategies or the resolution of difficult legal issues that may be included in a case or procedures of substantial import. At the highest levels, accomplishments may refer to the assumption of significant personal responsibility in drafting major rules, regulations, proposed statutes, or like materials. Awards or commendations are likely.

Time period:

General statement of what you accomplished:

I was given the task of transferring our antitrust investigation of _____ into a coherent set of pleadings presentable to _____ and the Commission for review and approval within the context of the Commission's involvement in shopping centers nationwide.

Description of exactly what you did:

I drafted the complaint and proposed order and wrote the underlying legal memo justifying all charges and proposed remedies. I wrote the memo to the Commission recommending approval of the consent agreement. For the first time, we applied antitrust principles to this novel factual situation.

Awards or formal recognition:

none

The information verified by: _____

TESTS

A test is a means of obtaining a standardized sample of behavior. Tests are standardized in content, scoring, and administration. That is, every time the test is given, its questions are identical or, in the case of tests with more than one form, equivalent. The scoring rules are constant. The administration is also the same: All test takers get the same instructions, have the same length of time to work, and take the test under similar conditions. Because tests are standardized, they provide information about job candidates that is comparable for all applicants. Other aspects of competing candidates cannot be compared so readily. For instance, grade point averages could be compared, but if candidates went to different schools or took somewhat different courses, this measure would not mean exactly the same thing for all applicants. In 2000, about 60 percent of companies surveyed by the American Management Association used some form of testing for selection.[23]

Testing and EEO

Before Title VII of the Civil Rights Act became law, quite a number of firms tested applicants for blue-collar jobs. General intelligence and mechanical comprehension tests were especially popular, although they were seldom empirically validated for the jobs in question. As Title VII was interpreted by the courts over the years, the doctrine of disparate impact developed, along with the requirement to demonstrate the job relatedness (validity) of tests that excluded a disproportionate share of minority applicants. When the courts rejected some reasonably well-conducted validity studies as inadequate, many firms simply gave up testing to avoid the possibility of litigation and the cost of further validation. Instead, they used unscored and subjective procedures for hiring and promotion decisions. However, in 1988 the U.S. Supreme Court ruled that informal and subjective methods of making employment and advancement decisions were not immune from legal challenge if they created adverse impact.[24] This ruling opened the door for a return to testing, on the basis that a properly validated test would be more effective and stand up to legal challenge better than an informal decision-making procedure. Some organizations are still wary of tests, however, and choose less valid selection devices that are thought to be less likely to provoke objections.

In the late 1960s and early 1970s, there were many allegations that tests were culturally biased and thus unfair to minority applicants. Extensive research, however, indicates that properly constructed ability tests do measure people of different races with equal accuracy.[25] Differences in test performance most often mirror differences in ability rather than being a result of cultural bias.

Paper-and-Pencil Tests of Ability

Properly chosen **paper-and-pencil tests** of cognitive ability have been found to have high validity and utility in the selection process.[26] Such ability tests are usually developed by psychologists and are purchased by organizations from test publishers. Tests that are readily available cover such abilities as general intelligence, numerical ability, verbal ability, clerical ability, abstract reasoning, and mechanical aptitude.[27] Figure 8.4 shows sample items from two commercially available clerical skills tests. Some large organizations or industry associations employ psychologists to develop and validate tests suited to their particular needs, such as computer programming aptitude or stockbroker aptitude.

In the past, industrial psychologists have recommended the use of tests that measure very specific and visibly job-related abilities, such as mechanical aptitude for mechanical jobs and verbal aptitude for clerical jobs. There is substantial evidence, however, that general cognitive ability, or intelligence, underlies scores on a number of different specific ability tests and that general cognitive ability is a good predictor of success in nearly all jobs.[28] It is a particularly effective predictor in more complex jobs.[29] In sum, the data support a return to testing for general cognitive ability, at least for preliminary applicant screening, possibly with the use of more specific ability tests for placement or further selection within groups of similar general ability.[30] Whether or not society will approve of widespread mental ability testing for selection is a different matter.

● **Choosing Tests**   As discussed in Chapter 7, the procedure for empirical validation begins with job analysis, followed by selection of potential predictors, development of criteria, and collection and analysis of validity data. If validity is to be established nonempirically, via content validation or validity generalization, job analysis becomes even more important.

The selection of potential predictors is a critical step. Because so many published tests are available, a firm must collect information and consider it carefully before selecting several tests for a validation effort. The choice process should involve reading test reviews written by knowledgeable people and carefully reading the **test manual,** which details test content, purpose, administration, scoring, and developmental procedures.[31] Among the several characteristics to look for in a published test are the following:[32]

- *Specific ability assessed:* The test should measure aptitudes or abilities that make sense for the job in question. For instance, for the job of proofreader, a firm might try a test of spelling ability. Table 8.3 gives one test publisher's recommmendations of which of their basic skills tests to use for different types of clerical jobs.

- *Reliability:* The test should have high internal consistency reliability and reliability over time. Tests that are used to make important decisions about individuals, as in the selection process, must have high reliability (at least .80 but preferably much higher).

- *Proper test development procedures:* Developing a test entails much more than writing questions on a piece of paper. HR managers should check to be sure that thorough test-development procedures have been followed. These procedures include applying item and factor analysis, trying out successive versions of the test on large samples of people, developing evidence for the construct validity of the test, and compiling normative data on large samples of people.

- *Administrative ease:* HR professionals must consider whether the test can be given to a group of people at the same time or whether it must be administered individually; how much time and expertise are required to administer, score, and interpret the test; and how much the test materials will cost.

● **FIGURE 8.4**

Sample Items from Paper-and-Pencil Skills Tests

Source: Basic Skills Tests, available from Psychological
Services, Inc., Glendale, Calif. Reprinted by permission.

(a) Sample item from the
Coding Test of the Basic
Skills Tests battery. The
entire Coding Test
contains 72 items with
a time limit of 5 minutes.

*The examinee reads a table containing a list of items that are classified into three or four
categories; each item has a unique code. The examinee then reads a new set of information
and selects the correct code from five alternatives for each item in the set.*

Look at the sample table of codes. The sample table lists codes for Department,
Department Size, and Travel Budget. Below the tables are two sample problems.
In the problems, mark the circles below the codes that correspond to the
information found in the table.

Department	Department Size	Travel Budget
31 Marketing	1 1–9 employees	A $500–999
25 Operations	2 10–19 employees	B $1,000–2,499
42 Accounting	3 20–39 employees	C $2,500–5,999
11 Research & Dev.	4 40–59 employees	D $6,000–7,999
28 Personnel	5 60 or more employees	E $8,000–10,000

Accounting Dept., staff of 10, $3,000 Travel Budget

Department	Department Size	Travel Budget
11 25 28 31 42	1 2 3 4 5	A B C D E
○ ○ ○ ○ ○	○ ○ ○ ○ ○	○ ○ ○ ○ ○

Marketing Dept., staff of 45, $9,500 Travel Budget

Department	Department Size	Travel Budget
11 25 28 31 42	1 2 3 4 5	A B C D E
○ ○ ○ ○ ○	○ ○ ○ ○ ○	○ ○ ○ ○ ○

(b) Sample item from the
Following Written
Direction Test of the Basic
Skills Tests battery. The
entire Following Written
Directions Test includes
36 items with a time
limit of 5 minutes.

*The examinee reads a set of rules, determines what action to take in various situations
by applying the rules, and selects the correct answer.*

Read the sample set of rules below. Answer the problems by following the rules.

Rules for Determining Type of Mail Delivery
The three types of delivery used for mailing packages are regular, freight, and
express. Listed below are the rules for deciding which type of delivery to use.

☐ Regular or freight delivery should be used for packages that do not need to
be received urgently.
☐ Express delivery should be used for packages that need to be received urgently.
☐ Freight delivery should be used for large packages only.
☐ Regular delivery should be used for small packages only.
☐ Express delivery may be used for large or small packages.

	Regular	Freight	Express
Large crate, not urgent	○	○	○
Small package, urgent	○	○	○

● TABLE 8.3

Test Publisher's Recommendations for Combinations of Basic Skills Tests to Use for Various Types of Clerical Jobs

	General Clerk	Receptionist/ Information Clerk	Secretary/ Administrative Clerk	Figure Clerk	Typist Clerk	Bookkeeping Clerk	Machine Operator Clerk	Comprehensive Clerical Battery
BST 1 Language skills	✓	✓			✓			✓
BST 4 Computation			✓	✓	✓			✓
BST 5 Problem solving						✓		
BST 7 Following oral directions			✓					
BST 8 Following written directions							✓	✓
BST 9 Forms checking			✓		✓			
BST 11 Classifying	✓	✓						
BST 12 Coding						✓		✓
BST 15 Visual speed and accuracy				✓			✓	

Source: Brochure on the Basic Skills Tests, available from Psychological Services, Inc., Glendale, Calif. Reprinted by permission.

- *Past success:* HR specialists should find out whether past empirical validation studies of the test on similar jobs have been successful, the extent to which the test is being used in the industry, and the record (if any) of the test in EEO proceedings.

● **Computerized Testing**   We have been referring to the above-mentioned ability tests as paper-and-pencil tests to distinguish them from **performance tests** (work samples and trainability tests), which are discussed in the next section. However, some ability tests can be administered and scored by computer rather than on paper. This can speed up testing and scoring and reduce the need for a trained test administrator. Some companies are moving toward Internet-based at-home testing, though issues of test security and faking (having someone else take the test for you) are potential problems.[33] However, computerized tests can be easily administered at company testing centers to avoid these concerns.

Capital One, a $4 billion per year credit card and financial services company, is using computer-administered tests as the first step in hiring call-center operators. In addition to replacing employees who quit, the fast-growing company needed to hire 30 to 40 percent more customer service representatives each year. Their old selection system included three paper-and-pencil measures: a cognitive skills test, a math test, and a biodata questionnaire. It took far too long to administer and score these instruments by hand. During 1998 Capital One streamlined and revalidated their selection tests, and in late 1999 they rolled out an online testing system consisting of biodata, a math test, and a role-played phone call simulation. Candidates answer each question on the computer. For the simulation, they put on headphones, listen to seven calls, and answer multiple-choice questions about what they would say or do in each situation. Scores are available the next day. Hiring has become quicker, easier, and less expensive, freeing twenty-two HR employees for other duties in the company. Improvements to the system planned for the future are expected to generate savings of $3.7 million dollars per year.[34]

Computers can do more than simply administer the items in a test. It is also possible to have the computer create a customized test for each candidate by selecting items on the basis of the correctness of past answers. For instance, if a moderately difficult item is answered correctly, the computer will next present a more difficult item. If the test taker fails this item, the computer will next choose an item between the first and second in difficulty. Called **adaptive testing,** this method quickly zeros in on the person's true ability level by selecting the most diagnostic items for the person being tested. This method can provide an accurate test score in about half the number of items needed to produce an equally accurate score via nonadaptive methods in which everyone answers all questions.[35]

Work-Sample and Trainability Tests

Work-sample and trainability tests ask applicants to do a portion of the job to demonstrate that they have the skill and knowledge to perform or the ability to learn the job. Because these tests are developed directly from a thorough job analysis and are double-checked by one or more panels of job experts, they are said to have a "point-to-point correspondence" with the job and are considered content valid. Properly developed tests of this sort need not be validated empirically. Note that the work-sample test does not need to represent the entire job. Some skills may be better assessed by an interview or an ability test. Simple job skills or information that can be readily taught to new hires also should not be included on the test.

● **Work-Sample Tests**   **Work-sample tests** are used when the applicant is expected to possess one or more crucial job skills—skills that the organization does not intend to teach to new hires. After conducting a thorough job analysis to verify the level and need for these kinds of skills, the HR specialist can construct a carefully standardized work-sample test. For example, if 80 percent of the job of secretary requires typing manuscripts from handwritten copy, then the work-sample test should include typing from handwritten copy. The tester should give all candidates the same copy, equipment, instructions, and length of time to complete the test. Scoring standards that have been developed in advance should be applied consistently for all applicants.

In one application of work-sample testing, a company developed a set of four role-plays for selecting telemarketing representatives. Candidates for telephone sales jobs made two simulated "cold calls" and returned two calls to hypothetical clients who had already indicated interest in the product. The supervisor playing the role of the client was trained to follow each of the four scripts fairly closely. This supervisor and another trained supervisor who also listened to the calls rated the candidate on communication, social sensitivity, sales ability, and overall performance.[36] In a concurrent validation design, a composite of these ratings significantly predicted telephone sales performance. See Table 8.4 for further examples of work-sample tests.

● **TABLE 8.4**

Work Sample Tests

	Test of Skill	Definition
Construction superintendent	Blueprint reading	Locate errors in blueprints.
	Scrambled subcontractors' test	Correctly order the desired sequence of 30 building subcontractors needed to construct a building from start to finish.
	Construction-error recognition test	Locate errors (25 in all) built into a small test building.
	Planning and scheduling exercise	Matching employee skills to job and schedule demands in a written exercise.
	Structured interview	Questions focusing on security of tools and materials, site safety, relationships to building inspector and other regulators, and ethical issues in dealing with subcontractors.
Police emergency operator/dispatcher	Listening, recording, and spelling test	Listen to tape-recorded emergency calls and correctly record important information on forms provided.
	Memory test	Recall information on locations and activities of several patrol units after information has been presented orally.
	Phone call simulation	Role-play the handling of calls from distraught callers in simulated emergency situations. Callers are role-played with experienced operators trained to behave consistently with all applicants. Scores are based on skill and judgment in calming the caller and eliciting the most important information.

Sources: For first example (construction superintendent), David D. Robinson, "Content-Oriented Personnel Selection in a Small Business," *Personnel Psychology,* Spring 1981, pp. 77–87. For second example (police emergency operator/dispatcher), Neal Schmitt and Cheri Ostroff, "Operationalizing the 'Behavioral Consistency' Approach: Selection Test Development Based on a Content-Oriented Strategy," *Personnel Psychology,* Spring 1986, pp. 91–108.

Work-sample tests also may be paper-and-pencil tests of job knowledge. For instance, the HR specialist might develop a written test assessing knowledge of electrical standards to help select building inspectors. Some firms have used technical reading comprehension tests to assess candidates applying for jobs in which employees need to obtain critical information from manuals or other written sources.[37] Others have had very good results from what are called **situational judgment tests.** Using critical incidents from the job and a panel of subject matter experts, a set of questions is developed to assess whether candidates make good choices when faced with typical dilemmas on the job.[38] Two items from situational judgment tests are shown in Figure 8.5.

● **Trainability Tests**   **Trainability tests** are used for semiskilled jobs in which the candidate is not expected to know the skill when applying for the job. They are intended to assess the ease with which a candidate can learn the type of skill required by the job. The first part of a trainability test consists of a carefully stan-

● FIGURE 8.5

Items from Situational Judgment Tests

Source: J. A. Weekley and C. Jones, "Further Studies of Situational Tests," *Personnel Psychology*, Vol. 52, 1999, pp. 679–700.

For each question, applicants are to indicate which response they believe is best under the circumstances, and which response is worst. Points are gained for correctly identifying best and worst choices.

From a test for the job of retail clerk:

> A customer asks for a specific brand of merchandise the store doesn't carry. How would you respond to the customer?
> a) Tell the customer which stores carry that brand, but point out that your brand is similar.
> b) Ask the customer more questions so you can suggest something else.
> c) Tell the customer that the store carries the highest quality merchandise available.
> d) Ask another sales person to help.
> e) Tell the customer which stores carry that brand.

ANSWER: Best is (b), worst is (d)

For a job in a hotel:

> You are the only bellcap at the front of the hotel because your coworker just left for a short break. A guest asks you to get him some fresh towels. What would you do?
> a) Ask the guest to inform someone inside of the hotel of the request.
> b) Leave your door to get the towels for the guest.
> c) Wait until your coworker returns and then take care of the request.
> d) Explain to the guest that you are unable to leave your post.
> e) Get someone else to help the guest and follow-up.

ANSWER: Best is (e), worst is (a)

dardized period of instruction during which the trainer introduces a task, explains and demonstrates each step, and has the candidate perform the task once or twice while being coached. The second portion is the actual test, during which the candidate performs the task several times without coaching. The trainer observes and uses a checklist to record errors. At the conclusion of the performance period, the instructor rates the overall trainability of the candidate.

Figure 8.6 is an instructor's evaluation form used in trainability tests for overlock sewing machine operators who have been taught to sew a simple bag. Trainability tests have also been used successfully for electronic assemblers, bricklayers, carpenters, lathe operators, milling machine operators, and a variety of simple U.S. Navy jobs. In addition, they have been used to select current employees for advanced training on new digital equipment in the telephone industry.[39]

● FIGURE 8.6

Instructor's Scoring
Sheet for a Trainability
Test

Source: From I. T. Robertson
and R. M. Mindel, "A Study of
Trainability Testing," *Journal of
Occupational Psychology,* June
1980, pp. 131–138. Reprinted
by permission.

Overlock Trainability Assessment Form

Factory _____   Assessor _____

Name _____   Date _____

	Bag 1	Bag 2	Bag 3
Aligns wrong seam first			
Presents incorrect corner			
Forgets to position cloth correctly			
Forgets to align seam			
Puts thumb on top			
Does not use fingers of left hand correctly			
Does not use fingers of right hand correctly			
Seam not completed in one sew			
Does not remember cutting method on last seam			

Other errors (please describe)

Total errors

Overall ratings

Positioning of hands good	always	generally	sometimes	rarely
Positioning of feet good	always	generally	sometimes	rarely
Notices errors and subsequently corrects	always	generally	sometimes	rarely

Please circle appropriate letter.

A Extremely good. The assessor would expect him/her to become a very good machinist in a short time.

B Fairly good without being outstanding. The assessor would expect him/her to reach 100 performances in a reasonable time.

C Good enough for simple work. The assessor would expect him/her to become a steady worker on a simple machine or task.

D Would have difficulty in training. The assessor would expect him/her to take longer training and to perform a simple task.

E Would not be trainable. Even with a great deal of attention, he/she would not make the grade, even on an easy operation.

● **Advantages of Work-Sample and Trainability Tests**   Work-sample and trainability tests have many advantages. First, when empirical validation studies have been conducted, the predictive power of work-sample tests has been found to be quite high.[40] Trainability tests have shown moderate validities with job success, though the strength of the correlations sometimes diminishes over time, indicating that eventually even less trainable employees are able to learn the job. Second, work-sample and trainability tests can be developed and used even for very small samples, unlike tests requiring empirical validation. Third, these tests tend to have less adverse impact than cognitive ability tests. Fourth, they possess excellent face validity; thus applicants who do poorly can readily understand why they are being rejected and probably will not file complaints of unfair treatment. Finally, since work-sample and trainability tests embody important aspects of the job, they can serve as realistic job previews. Candidates who do not enjoy the work sample may choose to turn down a job offer, thus sparing the organization the expense of hiring, training, and then losing an employee to early turnover.[41]

Personality Tests

In 2000, about 15 percent of companies in an American Management Association survey reported using personality tests for selection.[42] Unlike the tests already described, personality tests do not have *correct* answers. The intent of these tests is to elicit *self-descriptive* answers. Measures of personality must be developed as carefully as measures of cognitive ability. In evaluating such measures, one would expect to see a complete test manual detailing extensive development work utilizing large samples, followed by evidence of validity against job-performance criteria. There are a number of personality tests on the market that amount to little more than quackery, so potential buyers must take care.

Personality inventories are sets of objectively scored questions or statements to which the test taker responds *yes* if the item is self-descriptive and *no* if it is not. Some personality inventories are long—up to 400 questions or more—and some ask extremely personal questions about religious beliefs, sexual fantasies, and other non-work-related issues that an interviewer would never even consider asking. Applicants may justifiably feel that their privacy has been invaded when asked to take some personality tests. In the case of *Soroka* v. *Dayton Hudson Corporation*, Target stores in California agreed to cease using a personality test for security guards because some of the questions seemed non-job-related, invasive, and potentially discriminatory.[43] Despite this decision and the apparent irrelevance of isolated questions on some tests, remember that well-developed personality tests sum up a large number of questions to produce reliable scores on well-defined dimensions of personality. Items that lack face validity for job performance may still be helpful in assessing important basic personality traits, and these traits may predict behavior on the job.

There are a number of well-developed personality inventories available. Most give scores on several traits, such as dominance, tolerance, extroversion, aggression, self-esteem, authoritarianism, neuroticism, and independence. Even though these inventories are scored objectively, their proper interpretation may require special training. Users should also be aware that tests that specifically diagnose mental illnesses rather than relative standing on normal personality traits may be illegal in preemployment screening under the Americans with Disabilities Act.[44]

Historically, predictive validities have been thought to be lower for personality measures than for other types of tests.[45] Low validities have been attributed to (1) the transparency of some personality inventories, which may invite efforts to "fake good" by applicants eager to be hired, (2) the "shotgun" approach of attempting to find relationships between many personality dimensions and job performance without giving much thought to the actual demands of the job, and (3) the fact that very few jobs require one and only one type of personality for success. There may be several ways to do the same job well, perhaps by being diligent or creative or persuasive. Thus for many years industrial psychologists recommended that personality tests not be used for employee selection. Since 1990, however, a number of studies have shown that appropriately chosen personality measures often do help predict interpersonal, noncognitive aspects of job success, although cognitive ability measures remain the best predictors of task performance.[46] Because personality measures are usually uncorrelated with ability measures, adding an appropriate personality test to a selection battery of ability tests may well increase the overall validity of the selection system. Some employers rely heavily on assessing the personality of applicants, believing that it is better to hire motivated, reliable, honest, sober, respectful, conscientious employees and then train them to do a specific job than to seek only smart, skilled people who may or may not be responsible and trustworthy.[47]

Recent advances in understanding the dimensions of personality are bearing fruit in the selection arena. Until about 1990, there was no clear consensus on the structure of personality, and various personality inventories assessed a differing number of traits, from one or two to sixteen or more. Factor analyses of large numbers of these inventories have now revealed that much of the variance is accounted for by the **"Big Five" personality dimensions** defined in Table 8.5. When past selection research is categorized into these five factors, there is evidence that some personality dimensions are consistently related to job success. For instance, conscientiousness is related to success in job training, to job performance, and to personnel data such as absenteeism and disciplinary actions in virtually all jobs. Openness to experience predicts success in training, while extraversion is positively related to success in management and sales.[48] There is also evidence that personality-type measures of "customer service orientation" can be useful in predicting the performance of service employees.[49] The correlations between personality and desirable behavior on the job tend to be small to moderate in size but are of use when combined with appropriate ability measures.

● **TABLE 8.5**

The Big Five Personality Dimensions

1. Extraversion ↔ Introversion
2. Friendliness, agreeableness ↔ Hostility, noncompliance
3. Neuroticism ↔ Emotional stability
4. High conscientiousness, high dependability, and high self-control ↔ Low conscientiousness, low dependability, and low self-control
5. High intellect, high openness to experience and new ideas ↔ Low intellect, low openness to experience and new ideas

Source: Table designed from material appearing in J. M. Digman, "Personality Structure: Emergence of the Five-factor Model", Figure 1, page 421, of the *Annual Review of Psychology,* Vol. 41, 1990.

An example of a particularly appropriate use of personality tests in selection is provided by a nuclear utility company. To meet a Nuclear Regulatory Commission requirement that reactor operators be emotionally stable, the company retained a psychological consulting firm to assess this personality trait in applicants. The psychologists first performed a job analysis and collected critical incidents of unreliability or emotional instability among nuclear plant operators. Then the consultants clearly defined the construct of "behavioral unreliability" and selected subscales from several existing personality inventories to assess the various aspects of unreliability. They also developed an interview procedure to assess these aspects. The company uses the test and interview procedures to screen candidates for high-risk jobs. It rejects the least stable ones and then bases further selections from the stable group on job-related ability rather than personality.[50]

An example of the inappropriate use of personality testing is found in two British companies that utilized personality tests to decide whom to lay off and whom to rehire after a layoff. A data-entry clerk was told that she would not be rehired because her test indicated that she was too low on innovation and conceptual thinking to do the job—yet she had been doing the job satisfactorily for years![51] In any case, it seems unlikely that innovation and conceptual thinking would be important in this type of routine job. When firsthand knowledge of employees' performance and work behavior is available, as in assessing present employees for layoff, it is unlikely that any test would provide additional useful information about their ability to perform their current jobs.

● **Integrity Tests**   Many employers today are interested in screening out job candidates who may be likely to steal from them. Estimates of the cost to American business of employee theft, pilferage, or unexplained inventory shrinkage range up to $200 billion per year.[52] Employers who subscribe to the "bad apple" theory believe that rejecting potential thieves and hiring only honest employees will greatly reduce losses. This view is only partly correct, since research has shown that post-hire factors such as pay equity, job satisfaction, and opportunity to steal also play a role in determining actual theft.[53]

Traditionally, two types of **integrity tests** have been used to identify potentially dishonest employees: polygraph examinations and paper-and-pencil tests. The **polygraph,** or lie detector, measures and graphs respiration, blood pressure, and perspiration while the person being tested answers questions. Doubts about the validity of the polygraph and horror stories of honest individuals who were discharged or denied employment because of erroneous polygraph results have led to legal restrictions on the use of polygraphs.

The Employee Polygraph Protection Act of 1988 prohibits private-sector employers from using polygraph tests on applicants or employees, with a few exceptions. Companies that provide security services or manufacture and distribute controlled drugs may continue to use polygraphs; polygraph tests may also be used for investigating specific crimes against the employer, such as theft or embezzlement. In no case, however, may a company discharge or discipline an employee solely on the basis of polygraph results.[54]

Since polygraph testing has been restricted, paper-and-pencil integrity tests have increased in popularity. There are two types of written integrity tests on the market: overt integrity tests that assess attitudes toward theft and ask about past dishonest behavior, and personality-oriented integrity tests that focus on broader traits such as dependability, rule-following, impulse control, and conscientiousness. Most available tests have satisfactory reliability and reasonable validity in identifying individuals who have been caught stealing in the past or who will be caught stealing in the future.[55] Nordstrom, Inc., uses the Reid Report, an overt integrity test, to select department store employees. This company finds that the test helps identify candidates who will cause problems or be likely to quit if hired.[56] Personality-oriented tests predict not only theft but also composite measures of other types of counterproductive behavior, such as abuse of sick leave, excessive grievance filing, drug use at work, and rule breaking.[57] These behaviors are more common than outright theft and can cost organizations a great deal of money and aggravation. Another behavior that these measures predict—violence—is discussed below.

● **Predicting Violence in the Workplace**   Violence (threats, verbal abuse, harassment, physical attacks, and homicide) is another problem that many organizations face. In fact, homicide is the leading cause of death among female employees. (See Chapter 14 for more on workplace violence.) Employers are increasingly interested in screening applicants for violent tendencies, both to reduce the incidence of violence and to reduce liability for negligent hiring. While preemployment screening with personality tests and background checks may be a partial answer, a complete solution must include education, recognition of early warning signs, effective supervision, and appropriate preventive action.[58]

Statistically, it is very difficult to accurately predict rare events such as workplace homicide, but it is possible to measure personality traits that tend to be associated with generally noncompliant, hostile, and impulsive behavior. Research on specially constructed violence scales as well as personality-type integrity scales has shown that these instruments do have validity for predicting violent and counterproductive behavior at work. The research has also shown that these scales tap the Big Five personality dimensions of (low) conscientiousness, (low) agreeableness, and neuroticism.[59]

THE INTERVIEW

Virtually all organizations use interviews as a selection device for most jobs. Most commonly, candidates are interviewed by at least two people before being offered a job. Typically, an HR specialist and the individual who will be the candidate's immediate supervisor conduct these interviews. For managerial and professional jobs, it is common for the candidate to have a third interview with one or more higher-level managers.

A recent trend in interviewing is to conduct preliminary interviews with distant candidates via videoconferencing or telephone. International executive search firm Korn/Ferry has been using videoconferencing for several years and finds that it speeds up searches by two to four weeks, as well as saving travel costs. Florida International University has used the technology to make its students available to recruiters who may not wish to visit the campus in person.[60] The Gallup Organization has developed and validated procedures for structured telephone interviewing for a number of jobs. Their procedures allow all screening interviews for large multisite organizations to be conducted centrally from a single office using highly trained interviewers and scorers.[61]

Because the interview is so popular, one might expect that it is a highly useful selection device. While interviews can be valid if done properly, this is not always the case. The next two sections consider the reliability and validity of the interview.

Reliability of the Interview

In the interview context, reliability is consensus, or agreement, between two interviewers on their assessments of the same candidates. This is called **inter-rater reliability.** Research shows that it is usually rather weak. Interviewers might agree fairly well on the overall assessment of a candidate (e.g., one is outstanding, another is a dismal prospect) and on factual issues (e.g., the candidate has or has not worked on a similar job in the past), but interviewers seem unable to agree on more subjective or future-oriented characteristics (e.g., whether the candidate is creative or will be able to work without close supervision).[62]

Validity of the Interview

Historically, the predictive validity of the interview has been thought to be quite low. Research in the 1970s and 1980s suggested that the average validity of the interview for predicting job performance was as low as .14.[63] However, recent research has suggested that some interview procedures can yield reasonable validity.[64] Interviews also tend to capture somewhat different aspects of a person than do cognitive ability tests, so that a properly conducted interview can add to the prediction of job performance over and above tests.[65]

Still, many interviews are relatively ineffective. What can go wrong in the typical interview to cause interviewers to make inaccurate predictions? It seems that interviewers often commit judgmental and perceptual errors that can compromise the validity of their assessments.[66]

● **Similarity Error**   Interviewers tend to be positively predisposed toward candidates who are similar to them (in hobbies, interests, or personal background). They tend to be negatively disposed toward candidates who are unlike them. When the dissimilarity or similarity is not job-related, it may still color the interviewer's judgment and introduce invalid variance into the interviewer's ratings.

● **Contrast Error**   When several candidates are interviewed in succession, raters tend to compare each candidate with the preceding candidates rather than with an absolute standard. Thus an average candidate might be rated as higher than average if he or she comes after one or two poor candidates and as lower than average if he or she follows an excellent interviewee.

● **Overweighting of Negative Information**   Interviewers tend to see their job as a search for negative or disqualifying information about candidates. Thus they may overreact to a single minor piece of negative information. Relatedly, they are more likely to change their initial opinion of a candidate from positive to negative than from negative to positive.[67]

● **Race, Sex, and Appearance Bias**   Interviewers may be more or less positive about a candidate on the basis of the candidate's race, sex, or age. In general, interviewers rate blacks more favorably than similarly qualified whites and females lower than comparable males. There is some evidence that sex interacts with the nature of the job. For example, interviewers assess men and women who are applying for jobs traditionally held by their sex positively but less positively when these same individuals are applying for jobs held predominantly by the opposite sex.[68] Finally, there is evidence of a "beautyism" bias—that is, attractive males receive a positive rating, whereas attractive females get less credit for their own success and are rated somewhat more negatively, especially when they are applying for responsible positions.[69] Overweight candidates are also viewed less favorably, particularly if they are female.[70]

● **First Impression Error**   Some interviewers tend to form a first impression of candidates rather quickly, based on a review of the application blank or on the first few moments of the interview. Thus this impression is based on relatively little information about the candidate. Nevertheless, the initial judgment may be resistant to change as more information or contradictory information is acquired. In addition, the interviewer may choose subsequent questions based on the first impression, in an attempt to confirm the positive or negative impression.[71] The result is **first impression error.**

● **Traits Rated and Halo Error**   **Halo error** occurs when either the interviewer's overall impression or strong impression of a single dimension spreads to influence his or her rating of other characteristics. For instance, if a candidate impresses the interviewer as being very enthusiastic, the interviewer might tend to rate the candidate high on other characteristics, such as job knowledge, loyalty, and dependability. This is especially likely to happen when the interviewer is asked to rate many traits or to rate traits that are difficult to observe in a short interview. Research has shown that only a few traits, such as intelligence and sociability, are accurately assessed in the typical interview. Preliminary evidence suggests that interviewers are not very good at assessing conscientiousness, the personality trait that is usually most useful in predicting job success.[72]

● **Nonverbal Factors**   Many studies have demonstrated that interviewers are influenced by nonverbal factors in the interview. Candidates who wear appropriate clothing, make eye contact, smile, show animation, speak fluently, and modulate their voices make more positive impressions on interviewers.[73] For jobs involving technical skill and low contact with others, this interviewer tendency probably weakens validity. On the other hand, it may contribute valid variance to the prediction of success in jobs involving a great deal of public contact.

● **Faulty Listening and Memory**   An interviewer may miss a substantial portion of what the interviewee says because of poor listening habits or preoccupation with what to ask next. Immediately after the interview, an interviewer who has not taken notes may have forgotten up to 75 percent of the information given by the candidate.[74]

● **Differences Between Interviewers**   There is evidence that interviewers selecting for the same job differ from one another in many ways, including the following:

- Different selection criteria and weights. They look for different qualities in applicants and disagree on which qualities are most important.
- Different definitions of what the ideal candidate looks like.
- Different recommended hire rates. Some recommend most of the candidates they see; others are very choosy.
- Different decision strategies. Some are analytical and consider many separate criteria in reaching a final decision; others are more intuitive and rely mainly on overall impressions.

- Different abilities to build rapport with the candidate. Those who build more rapport are able to elicit more information during the interview.[75]

These differences contribute to low inter-rater reliability and undoubtedly reduce the validity of the interview as a selection tool. Despite all the above problems, interviewers tend to believe that they are "good judges of character" and "can spot a winner at fifty paces." Managers like using interviews because they feel interviews allow them more flexibility and control over selection decisions compared with more rigid and quantitative methods such as ability tests and biodata questionnaires.[76]

Types of Interviews

Interviews can be classified by their degree of structure or the extent to which interviewers plan the questions in advance and ask the same questions of all the candidates for the job. Three types of interviews, based on three degrees of structure, can be defined: unstructured, semistructured, and structured interviews.

● **Unstructured Interviews** In the **unstructured interview,** questions are not planned in advance, and interviews with different candidates may cover quite different areas of past history, attitudes, or future plans. Unstructured interviews have low inter-rater reliability and overall have the lowest validity. Because questions are not planned, important job-related areas may remain unexplored, and illegal questions may be asked on the spur of the moment. Interviewers may also rely too much on single favorite questions of dubious validity, such as "If you were in a salad, what type of vegetable would you be?" Unstructured interviews generally should not be used for evaluating job candidates.

● **Semistructured Interviews** The **semistructured interview** involves some planning on the part of the interviewer but also allows flexibility in precisely what the interviewer asks candidates. This permits interviews to be customized to explore the differing backgrounds and aspirations of candidates. Semistructured interviews may be used for higher-level positions or for final interviews for short-listed candidates following more structured interviews. Semistructured interviews are likely to be more valid than unstructured ones but not as valid as highly structured interviews.

In an excellent book on semistructured interviewing techniques, Thomas Moffatt suggests that interviewers plan their objectives in terms of what they hope to learn about the candidate and then use a "cone" approach to elicit this information.[77] A cone is a mini-interview on a particular topic, such as the candidate's last job, feelings about working in groups, or military experience. Each cone is introduced by a very broad question, which is followed by more specific questions on aspects of the topic. These questions may vary from interviewee to interviewee, but all pertain to the topic of the cone. The interviewer might plan to include four to eight cones in an hour-long interview.

In the cone approach, most questions are designed to elicit a reasonably lengthy response. As in all types of interviews, leading questions are avoided. Leading questions are those that imply a correct answer, such as "You don't plan to remain a secretary for your whole life, do you?" Finally, yes–no and short-answer questions are used sparingly because they tend to turn the interview into an interrogation and do not provide as much useful information as longer answers. Figure 8.7 is a partial example of a cone on the candidate's last job.

● **Structured Interviews**   Research shows conclusively that the highest reliability and validity are realized in the structured interview.[78] In a **structured interview,** questions are planned in advance and are asked of each candidate in the same way. The only difference between interviews with different candidates might be in the probes, or follow-up questions, if a given candidate has not answered a question fully. Interviews that feature structured questions usually also provide structured rating scales on which to evaluate applicants after the interview. At least three types of structured interviews have been discussed in the research literature: the patterned interview, the situational interview, and the behavior description interview.

In the traditional **patterned interview,** questions tend to focus on past work activities, education, career goals, and so on. The questions may be job-related, or they simply may be questions that interviewers typically ask, such as "What are your strengths and weaknesses?" or "What do you plan to be doing five years from now?" This type of structure does increase inter-rater reliability and may prevent the interviewer from talking too much, but it does not necessarily result in high validity.

High predictive validity depends on eliciting from the candidate relevant information on the skills, abilities, and attitudes needed for job success. The **situa-**

● **FIGURE 8.7**

Cone Method of Semistructured Interviewing

Broad introductory question on topic	"Tell me about your last job."
Moderately specific questions	"What did you learn from that job?" "What were your major duties?" "What were your greatest accomplishments?" "How would you describe your boss on that job?"
Probes	"Could you tell me more about that?" "Elaborate on why you chose to do it that way."
Very specific and yes/no questions	"How many subordinates did you have?" "Were you paid on a commission basis?"

tional interview and the **behavior description interview** attempt to collect and properly evaluate job-relevant information. Both these structured approaches begin with a thorough job analysis. Interview questions are based directly on the job analysis and are double-checked by job experts so that the interview is demonstrably content-valid. In some cases, empirical validation work is also conducted, to identify interview questions and answers that best differentiate between successful and unsuccessful employees.[79] The situational interview focuses mainly on future-oriented questions about what the candidate *would do* if faced with a hypothetical job situation, whereas the behavior description interview asks about past behaviors—what the candidate actually *did do* in past situations similar to those likely to occur on the job. The evidence to date suggests that both approaches work, and there is no clear evidence favoring either past- or future-oriented questions.[80]

The situational interview, which was developed by Gary P. Latham and his colleagues, involves three types of interview questions.[81] The first type of question is situational, or hypothetical. The interviewer asks the candidate what he or she would do in a particular job situation. For instance, the interviewer might ask a candidate for camp counselor how he or she would respond to a child who was very homesick or who was disruptive. The second type of question involves job knowledge, such as defining a term, explaining a procedure, or demonstrating a skill. Job knowledge questions may be written rather than oral, depending on their number. The last type of interview question focuses on the employee's willingness to comply with job requirements such as different shifts, travel, or physically demanding work.

As the job experts develop the questions, they also write good, average, and poor sample responses. This answer key helps interviewers give more reliable ratings of candidates' answers. In the situational interview, a panel of three or more interviewers conducts all the interviews. The interviewers do not attempt to reach a consensus on each candidate. Instead, their independent ratings are averaged to produce an overall score for each candidate.

Tom Janz and his colleagues developed the behavior description interview. This approach to structured interviewing is based on the assumption that "the best predictor of future performance is past performance in similar circumstances."[82] Traditionally, interviewers often applied this principle by asking candidates about experience with tasks similar to those of the job for which they were applying. According to Janz, however, interviewers often fall into the "experience equals excellence fallacy" by assuming that if a candidate has performed a task at all, he or she has performed it well. Behavior description interviewing overcomes this problem by requiring candidates to give specific examples of how they performed job duties or handled job problems in the past.

Job experts derive behavior description interview questions from the critical incidents technique of job analysis. Suppose, for example, that the job expert, using this technique, identifies one dimension of a sales job as "establishing new client contacts." Then, based on this dimension, a behavior description item for experienced candidates might be, "Tell me about the most difficult new client contact you have made in the last six months." After the candidate has described a specific incident, the interviewer's next questions might be, "What was the obstacle you faced? What did you say when you were stumped? What did you do to overcome the difficulty?"[83] Research has shown that behavior description interviews are much more valid than unstructured interviews.[84] Behavior description interviewing has been widely adopted in organizations around the English-speaking world over the past fifteen years.

Improving the Interview

Clearly, the interview can be a useful selection device, though often its potential is not used properly. Ideally, the interview should (1) be based on a thorough job analysis, (2) be structured, (3) contain either situational or behavior description items, and (4) be conducted by a panel of interviewers who have been trained to avoid common errors. Validity seems to be enhanced if interviewers act more as information gatherers than as decision makers. Also, the statistical combination of interviewer item or dimension ratings often yields more valid predictions than overall subjective judgments of individual interviewers or panels.[85] To be effective, the interview should have the well-planned and reasonable objective of assessing important applicant characteristics that cannot be better evaluated by other selection methods.

PHYSICAL TESTING

The Physical Examination

One of the final steps in the selection process may be a physical examination or test. A survey in 2000 found that 52 percent of firms required medical examinations of all new hires, while an additional 15 percent required exams for some jobs.[86] The examination is required by law for jobs such as pilot, interstate truck driver, and any position that involves handling of food. Note that under the Americans with Disabilities Act, an employer may not require physical examinations (or other health-related information) until *after* the candidate receives a conditional offer of employment.

Information gained from physical examinations can serve several purposes:

1. To revoke conditional employment offers to persons who are found to be physically unable to perform the essential functions of the job
2. To place individuals in jobs that they are fit enough to handle—for instance, to place individuals with chronic bronchitis in jobs in which they will not be exposed to high concentrations of dust or irritating fumes
3. To prevent the spread of contagious diseases to current employees or customers
4. To document preexisting injuries and illnesses to prevent fraudulent group insurance or workers' compensation claims

As with all selection devices, reliability, validity, and utility are relevant in the evaluation of physical examinations. Reliability may not be extremely high. Physicians who are not knowledgeable about job demands may not be able to agree on whether a candidate is fit enough or can perform essential job functions. Moreover, some physiological measures, such as blood pressure, are not highly reliable over time. The validity of the physical examination for assessing strength or endurance is also questionable. When jobs require unusual strength or stamina, actual physical tests are likely to be more valid than a physician's opinion. In terms of utility, physical examinations are expensive because they must be administered individually by a costly tester. Thus physical examinations should be used only for good and sound reasons rather than as a routine procedure for all jobs.

Additional limitations are placed on the physical examination as a selection device by the Americans with Disabilities Act. This act states that individuals may not be rejected due to physical inability to perform a "marginal" job function. "Marginal" means infrequent and nonessential. Thus determinations of physical ability to do the job must be based on a clear understanding of which job duties are essential and which are marginal. An employer that uses a physical examination must give the examination to all candidates who have been offered the job, not just to those who appear to have disabilities.[87] Further, information generated from the examination must be treated confidentially and must be stored in a file separate from other employee records.

Strength and Fitness Testing

For physically demanding jobs, employers may be wise to directly measure applicant strength or fitness as part of the selection process. Research has shown that strength and fitness are positively related to the successful completion of training and negatively related to the incidence of lower back injuries for steelworkers, underwater demolition divers, and telephone and outdoor craftworkers. It has also been found that a person's maximum oxygen uptake (aerobic power) should be at least 2.5 times the level required on a continuing basis during an eight-hour shift.[88] Thus ability to perform a demanding job during a brief work sample does not necessarily mean that a person is fit enough to do the same job all day.

It is possible to put together a battery of physical tests that will be content-valid.[89] The procedure is based on a very thorough job analysis, and the process may also involve objective measures of the heart rates or oxygen uptakes of current employees.[90] Based on this information, appropriate tests of strength, endurance, or flexibility can be selected and cutoff points can be established. Employers should be aware that physical testing frequently has adverse impact on female candidates and, to a lesser extent, Hispanic candidates. Consequently, the validity of the tests and the appropriateness of the cutoff scores must be carefully established.[91]

Drug Testing

It has been estimated that in 1999, 9.4 million drug users were working full time. The nationwide cost of drug abuse at work is estimated at more than $30 billion per year in lost productivity and quality.[92] To cope with this situation, many employers have adopted drug and alcohol screening programs for both applicants and current employees. Initial and random testing of all individuals involved in operating commercial vehicles is required by law, but employers often test other categories of employees as well. Many employers routinely drug-test all applicants during the final states of hiring. It is estimated that companies spent half a billion dollars on drug testing of employees in 1996, with the average test costing $35.[93] Because use of illegal drugs is not considered a disability, drug testing is perfectly legal under the Americans with Disabilities Act.[94] Drug testing may also be conducted before a conditional offer of employment is made, unlike medical examinations.

There may be good reasons for avoiding hiring substance abusers. Some studies suggest that drug and alcohol abusers have higher rates of absenteeism and accidents. Furthermore, employers may be liable for negligent hiring if a drug-using employee causes an accident that harms others.

The U.S. Postal Service reported impressive results from an experimental drug-testing program in selected sites. More than 5,000 job candidates were tested, and 9 percent were found to be drug users. Second tests on some specimens showed virtually no errors—no nonusers were mistakenly declared users—suggesting that properly conducted testing is highly reliable and hence fair to applicants. Because this was a predictive validation study, results of the drug tests were kept confidential and not used in selection. When criterion data were collected fifteen months after hiring, drug users were found to have experienced 60 percent more absenteeism and were 47 percent more likely to have been involuntarily discharged. Utility analysis was applied to determine the net gain to the Postal Service if drug screening were to be widely implemented as a selection procedure. The cost of testing ($11 per applicant) was minimal compared with the cost of increased absenteeism and terminations for cause that occurred when drug users were hired. The researchers estimated that if all 180,000 applicants were tested in a given year, the return to the Postal Service over an average career of ten years for the 61,588 people hired in that year would be $52,750,000.[95]

Drug tests appear to be reasonably reliable, but usually a second, more sophisticated confirmatory test is performed when a sample gives an initial positive reading. In order to be fair to candidates, it is important to choose a properly certified laboratory to conduct drug tests. It is also necessary to have a step-by-step procedure to ensure that samples are labeled properly and actually have been provided by the person being tested.[96]

Overall, drug testing is a relatively expensive and invasive procedure. Whether or not it has utility (cost-effectiveness) in a given setting depends on the extent to which drug users are represented in the applicant pool and the extent to which drug use actually compromises job performance, attendance, or safety in the job in question.[97]

A number of researchers have evaluated job candidates' attitudes toward drug testing. They have found that drug users are more negative than nonusers to the idea of drug testing but that most job candidates say they are less likely to apply to an organization that requires drug testing than to one that does not. As might be expected, candidates give less approval to alcohol testing than to testing for illegal drugs. Attitudes toward testing also vary with the job involved. Testing is much more strongly approved for jobs involving danger to the incumbent or risk to others, such as airline pilot, surgeon, police officer or firefighter, air traffic controller, nuclear engineer, and truck driver, than for jobs less likely to put other people's lives in jeopardy, such as janitor, salesperson, or secretary. Finally, testing for candidates and incumbents is more acceptable when the system is seen as providing "procedural justice." This means that the system is perceived as fair and open, retesting is available, the reasons for testing are clearly explained, testing is announced and scheduled in advance rather than being random and unannounced, and current employees who test positive once are referred for treatment rather than immediately discharged.[98]

REFERENCE AND BACKGROUND CHECKS

Most organizations check candidates' references in varying degrees of detail as part of the selection process. In one survey, over 80 percent of firms said they regularly checked the references of executive, professional, administrative, and technical job candidates. Sixty-eight percent checked references for skilled laborers, 57 percent for part-time employees, and about 40 percent for temporary and seasonal workers.[99] The goal in reference checking is often to verify information that the candidate has already given the organization, such as academic degrees, dates of employment, job responsibilities, and salary. It has been estimated that between 10 and 30 percent of applicants falsify their résumés in some way, so such verification is a reasonable precaution. Reference and **background checks** are also used to discover new information on the history or past performance of the candidate, such as relevant criminal convictions or reasons for leaving a previous job. These investigations may be performed by the organization or by an investigative services firm hired by the employer. When an outside agency is hired to do the investigation, the Fair Credit Reporting Reform Act requires employers to disclose to applicants that credit or background checks may be performed, to obtain written authorization, and to inform applicants if the investigation influenced a decision not to hire them.[100] Figure 8.8 shows the percentage of employers who conduct different types of reference and background checks.

Obtaining Reference Information

Reference information is usually collected by HR specialists from a candidate's former employers or teachers or from other knowledgeable persons the candidate lists. Ideally, an organization should seek additional reference information from people other than those the candidate names. To get additional references, an employer should ask the listed references for the names of other people who might know the candidate well enough to comment on his or her qualifications. Background information may also be solicited from neighbors, credit agencies, and court or police records. A basic background check by an investigative services firm typically costs between $50 and $200.[101]

Information from references may be solicited in writing, in a phone interview, or in a face-to-face interview. Generally, letters are the least useful. Because writers have time to carefully censor what they say, their letters are nearly always positive and relatively unrevealing. Interviewing the references can be more helpful, since an interview allows the interviewer to establish a rapport with the reference, note voice tones that may convey doubts about the candidate, and probe more deeply into important issues.[102] Phone interviews are more common and more economical than face-to-face interviews with references. As with any interview, the reference interview should be planned carefully in advance and focus on job-related issues.[103]

Validity and Legality of Reference Information

Studies of the validity of reference information agree that predictive validity tends to be low but is sometimes significant.[104] The most informative references are former or current superiors who know the candidate's work well and who have observed the

● **FIGURE 8.8**

Percent of Companies Conducting Different Types of Reference and Background Checks

Source: Society for Human Resource Management, in *Personnel Journal*, December 1995, p. 88. Reprinted with permission.

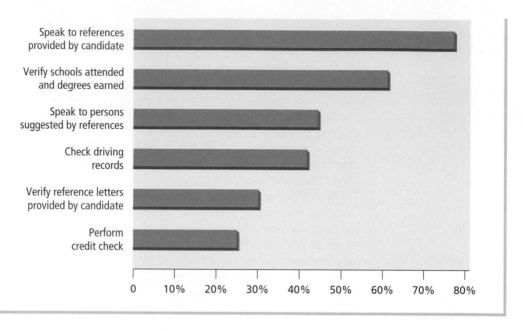

candidate perform in a similar job. In addition, reference information may be more accurate if (1) the reference knows that the candidate is being thoroughly assessed and (2) if the reference has no hidden motivations, such as to keep the candidate from leaving the present job or to unload a problem employee on an unsuspecting new employer. References may be more useful to screen out candidates who have falsified their credentials or who have had behavioral problems on several past jobs than to predict the job performance of reasonably qualified candidates.

There are several potential legal problems associated with references. The first involves the new employer. If an employer hires someone who subsequently causes injury to another—and the employer should have known, through appropriate reference and background checks, about the employee's propensity for committing injurious acts—then the employer is liable for **negligent hiring.** For instance, a company was found guilty of negligent hiring when its apartment manager used his passkey to enter the apartment of a resident and rape her. The organization should have discovered the manager's past conviction for rape and not hired him in a capacity that allowed this kind of access.[105]

There may also be legal problems for employers who give references. One involves possible lawsuits for defamation when an employer or former employer gives a negative reference. Thus many companies are discouraging candidates' superiors from giving any reference information at all. Instead, these firms are handling all requests for reference information centrally, from the personnel office, and they are limiting the information to facts such as dates of employment and job title.[106] Although this policy may appear wise for an employer or former employer, it complicates the task of the potential future employer who would like a frank assessment of a candidate, and it creates a second possible legal problem. By remaining silent about a problem employee, the former employer may be liable for negligent referral, or for violating a duty to warn, if the candidate is hired and subsequently causes harm to others.[107]

Because reference information can be helpful in identifying potential problem employees, moves have been made to reduce the risks of both giving and seeking references. By mid-2000, thirty-five states had passed "job reference immunity statutes" protecting employers who provide reference information in good faith.[108] Further, a large majority of organizations now require candidates to sign a release authorizing the company to contact referees and waiving the right to legal action against current or former employers who provide reference information.

SELECTING MANAGERS

The selection of managers for hire or promotion is a particularly important and difficult task. Estimates of the percentage of American managers who are incompetent range from 50 to 75 percent, while 30 to 50 percent of all appointments at the executive level end in firing or resignation.[109] Clearly, there is room for improvement in managerial selection practices. There are many different ways to be a successful manager, but one thing is certain: Managing requires a wide range of skills. Thus single-factor ability tests are seldom very useful in selecting managers. Nevertheless, some studies have found significant correlations between mental ability tests and managerial performance, and some personality characteristics such as extraversion, need for power, need for achievement, conscientiousness, emotional stability, or general activity have some predictive success.[110] Emotional intelligence is also thought to be important for managerial success. As a rule, the best predictors of managerial success tend to be relatively broad measures, such as supervisor ratings of promotion potential or assessment center ratings.

Assessment Centers

An **assessment center** is a content-valid work sample of the managerial job, most often used to select nonmanagerial employees for promotion to low-level management positions. Since these individuals are not currently performing managerial duties, an appraisal of their work performance is not likely to predict success in the job of manager or supervisor. Hence there is a need for a work-sample test for the managerial job. Assessment centers also have been used to select salespersons, higher-level managers, and supervisors who will succeed in a team environment.[111] One recent survey found that more than 500 U.S. organizations used assessment centers.[112] The technique is also popular in public-sector organizations that must select and promote on some form of merit. Assessment centers can last from one day to one week and have three characteristics: multiple means of assessment, multiple assessees, and multiple assessors.

● **Characteristics of Assessment Centers**   Multiple means of assessment or different situational exercises and tests cover a wide range of activities and skills that are performed by a manager. Assessment centers virtually always include an **in-basket test,** in which the candidate is given a stack of letters and messages to deal with. He or she must prioritize the problems and act on each by making a decision or an appointment, referring, delegating, or asking for more information.

Assessment centers also include some sort of **leaderless group discussion** exercise, because so much of a manager's time is spent in meetings or groups of some sort. Assessment centers may also include two-person role-playing (e.g., salesperson with customer, supervisor with problem subordinate), management games, interviews with assessors, written tests of intelligence or personality, and possibly preparing and delivering a speech. Throughout all these exercises, assessees are observed and evaluated on dimensions such as decision making, planning, leadership, persuasiveness, energy, interpersonal sensitivity, and communication. The choice of assessment dimensions and exercises is based on a careful job analysis of the type and level of managerial job for which candidates are being evaluated.

If group exercises are to be used, more than one candidate must be assessed at the same time. Typically, six to twelve candidates will form an assessment center class. Three to six assessors will be used to observe and evaluate the performance of the candidates. Assessors are usually managers two to three levels higher than the job for which they are assessing candidates.

Assessors undergo training on the exercises and assessment dimensions, observe candidates during the exercises, and then meet for one or two days after the candidates leave to determine ratings and to hammer out an assessment report on each candidate's managerial potential and development needs. There is some evidence that serving as an assessor has the side benefit of improving a manager's interviewing and communication skills.[113]

● **Validity and Utility of Assessment Centers**   Studies have shown that assessment center data do predict both short- and long-term success and advancement in management positions. Validities are often relatively high. Furthermore, assessment centers are equally valid for both sexes and all races and do not seem to produce adverse impact.[114] There are some questions about the construct validity of assessor ratings,[115] but despite these issues, well-designed centers do seem to be effective in identifying management potential. Assessment centers are probably the most expensive selection device in common use. However, the relatively high validity and the potential losses from hiring an incompetent manager seem more than enough to offset the cost, leading to the conclusion that assessment centers are likely to offer high utility.[116]

Other Selection Methods for Managers

When the use of an assessment center is not feasible, careful reference checking and behavior description interviewing by a panel probably hold the most promise as selection methods for managers. Following a careful job analysis, behavior description interview formats should be developed for both candidates and their references. A thorough investigation of candidates' past behavior in situations similar to those of the new job should provide the most useful information.

Some organizations hire a consulting clinical or organizational psychologist to provide **individual assessments** of candidates for middle- and upper-level management positions. The assessment process normally includes gathering information about the job and organization and then gathering information from the candidates by means of a personal history questionnaire, cognitive and personality tests, and a clinical interview. Finally, all this information is combined judgmentally, and the assessor writes a report detailing the candidate's strengths, weaknesses, and suitability for the job. There are no empirical data available on the validity of these judgments because sample sizes are very small. Unfortunately, however, there is evidence that inter-rater reliability is low when more than one expert assesses the same candidate.[117]

Finally, in selecting higher-level managers, an organization or subunit may find that its business strategy and environment are important in determining the type of managerial skills needed.[118] Table 8.6 lists some recommendations for candidate skills and attitudes that best match various business situations and strategies.

● **TABLE 8.6**

Suggestions for Selecting Executives Who Match Business Strategy

Situation	Major Job Thrusts	Specific Characteristics of Ideal Candidates
Start-up	Creating vision of business Establishing core technical and marketing expertise Building management team	Vision of finished business Hands-on orientation: a "doer" In-depth knowledge in critical technical areas Organizing ability Staffing skills Team-building capabilities High energy level and stamina Personal magnetism and charisma Broad knowledge of all key functions
Turnaround	Rapid, accurate problem diagnosis Fixing short-term and, ultimately, long-term problems	"Take charge" orientation: strong leader Strong analytical and diagnostic skills, especially financial Excellent business strategist High energy level Risk taker Handles pressure well Good crisis management skills Good negotiator
Liquidation/divestiture of poorly performing business	Cutting losses Making tough decisions Making the best deal	"Callousness": tough-minded, determined—willing to be the "bad guy" Highly analytical regarding costs/benefits—does not easily accept current ways of doing things Risk taker Low glory seeking; willing to do dirty jobs—does not want glamour Wants to be respected, not necessarily liked

Behavior description and situational interview questions might be used to assess these characteristics.

CRITERIA FOR CHOOSING SELECTION DEVICES

A large number of selection devices have been described in this chapter. Conscientious human resource managers are faced with the daunting task of choosing which measures to use. Some of the criteria that may be applied to this decision are discussed below.

● **Validity**   Traditionally, validity or job relatedness has been recommended as the most important single characteristic of a selection device. Validity is usually assessed against *individual performance on a specific job*. However, as organizations change, we may see some redefinition of what types of validity matter—predicting the single best individual performer or predicting who will fit best with an existing work team or with the organization's strategy, culture, and values. (See the A Different Point of View box for more information.)

● **Utility**   Utility models remind us that factors other than validity are also important in assessing the total contribution of a new selection device to the organization. Factors such as the costs of developing and using the device, the tenure of those selected, the base rate of success, the standard deviation of performance in dollars, and the selection ratio all affect the benefits obtained from an additional selection device. The devices discussed in this chapter vary widely in cost, from simple application blanks to days-long assessment centers. Some devices are costly to develop initially, such as empirically scored biodata questionnaires or custom-designed ability tests, but relatively inexpensive to use once developed. An additional consideration is **incremental validity.** This is the extent to which the new selection device contributes over and above those selection devices already in use. This may suggest that the greatest benefits come from adding a different type of selection device, such as a personality test or an in-depth background check, to a standard battery of ability tests and interviews.

● **Legality**   It goes without saying that selection devices must be legal, complying in their design, administration, and use with the relevant local, state, and federal laws.

● **Acceptability to Managers**   Credibility among managers is another criterion that appears to be used in choosing selection devices. Unfortunately, managers' views of the usefulness of selection devices often do not parallel the research findings about validity (witness the popularity of the unstructured interview). One study found a strong relationship between managers' and consultants' *beliefs* about the validity of various selection methods and their frequency of use. However, there was almost no correlation between the frequency of use of selection devices and their actual empirical validity. Another study found that organizations seemed to prefer selection methods that were traditional rather than new and that were nontechnical and hence easy to use.[119]

● **Applicant Reactions**   Applicants do not respond equally positively to all selection devices. Some devices that can be problematic are stress interviews, drug tests, background investigations, personality inventories, and honesty tests. These may be seen as violating privacy or not being job-related, even though in fact they may be valid. These devices may alienate very good applicants. The way applicants are treated before, during, and after selection devices are applied can also influence their reactions. The Ethical Perspective box on page 357 raises the issue of test takers' rights surrounding the testing event. The following are selection methods that applicants tend to like:

- Those with unmistakable face validity—such as work-sample tests, assessment centers, and ability tests containing job-related questions

Which Should We Hire for: The Job, the Team, or the Organization?

Traditionally, selection has been aimed at assessing individual skills to perform an individual job, with little consideration given to the team or organizational context in which the job is embedded. However, the notion of a static job with stable knowledge, skill, and ability requirements is becoming less realistic as the pace of change increases. While there are still specific job and technical competencies required for hire into most jobs, some organizations are also attempting to assess how well job candidates will fit with the organization's values and culture.

Hiring for cultural fit is not without liabilities. Some organizations don't have a distinctive culture that can be enunciated clearly enough to guide hiring. There are concerns that hiring for cultural fit will simply replicate the present work force and might negatively impact diversity and EEO goals. In addition, if employees are too much alike in their values and outlook, there may be some danger of groupthink and excessive conformity.

"High-involvement organizations" and those that rely heavily on self-directed work teams (see Chapter 10) have been experimenting with selection systems that assess both team skills and the "fit" between applicants' needs, values, and personalities and the organization's culture and work style. These new selection systems usually take longer and cost much more than the selection systems of typical manufacturers. For instance, Toyota (USA) screened 50,000 candidates to fill 3,000 factory jobs when it opened its plant in Georgetown, Kentucky. Finalists spent eighteen hours in assessments of various kinds before being hired. Mazda spent $13,000 per hire to find just the right people for its new plant in Michigan. A high-involvement float glass plant put candidates through four half-days of assessment and assigned them homework between days before making final hiring decisions.

Selection systems for these special circumstances still include traditional ability measures (job-related math and reading, trainability tests, etc.) but go well beyond ability to personality, values, and team skills. For instance, the float glass plant looked for employees who were high in the personality traits of affiliation and growth needs. These individuals were willing to work in teams, eager to learn new skills, and able to take responsibility. Team skills were further measured by assessment center–type group exercises and a panel interview with top management.

There has been an implicit assumption that hiring the best individual performers will result in the best group and organizational results. In a high-interdependence situation, however, this may not be true. Hiring individuals of homogeneous ability might be more important than mixing a few high-ability team members with average-ability members and expecting them to work together effectively. In addition to the appropriate ability mix, it is likely that teamwork skills—including conflict resolution, collaborative problem solving, communication, goal setting and performance management, and planning and task coordination—will be important.

In addition to these individual skills, new-hire personality, work style, and values probably should either match or complement those of other team members. Conscientiousness may become an increasingly important attribute as employees are empowered to manage themselves and hierarchical supervision and control is reduced. One way to ensure a good fit is to involve the members of existing teams in hiring their own new members. In a number of plants where self-managed teams are used, teams themselves interview and hire from among candidates who have passed extensive screening by the HR Department.

In sum, hiring against wider criteria, including fit with a team and fit with an organization's values and management style, seems to be the wave of the future.

Sources: Edward E. Lawler, *From the Ground Up: Six Principles for Building the New Logic Corporation* (San Francisco: Jossey-Bass, 1996); Michael J. Stevens and Michael A. Campion, "The Knowledge, Skill, and Ability Requirements for Teamwork: Implications for Human Resource Management," *Journal of Management,* Vol. 20, 1994, pp. 503–530; David E. Bowen, Gerald E. Ledford, Jr., and Barry R. Nathan, "Hiring for the Organization, Not the Job," *Academy of Management Executive,* November 1991, pp. 35–51; C. E. Montgomery, "Organizational Fit Is Key to Job Success," *HRMagazine,* January 1996, pp. 94–96; Greg L. Stewart and Kenneth P. Carson, "Moving Beyond the Mechanistic Model: An Alternative Approach to Staffing for Contemporary Organization," *Human Resource Management Review,* Vol. 7 (2), 1997, pp. 157–184; L. Grensing-Pophal, "Hiring to Fit Your Corporate Culture," *HR Magazine,* August 1999, pp. 50–54; and M. J. Stevens and M. A. Campion, "Staffing Work Teams: Development and Validation of a Selection Test for Teamwork Setting," *Journal of Management,* Vol. 25, 1999, pp. 207–228.

- Those that are seen as being "fair"
- Those that are so traditional that applicants expect to encounter them, like the interview or application blank
- Those on which applicants expect to perform well[120]

Table 8.7 provides a rundown on the validity, acceptability to managers, and applicant reactions associated with many of the selection devices discussed in this chapter.

● **Societal Impact**   Frank Schmidt points out the inherent conflict in what is good selection for the organization and what may be good for our multicultural society. The research clearly shows that using selection tests of general cognitive ability will improve the quality and performance of hires. To compete effectively in the tough international marketplace, firms need to hire the best performers they can find. However, cognitive ability tests produce unmistakable adverse impact on minority groups. The best statistical compromise involves top-down hiring within race groups (hiring the highest-scoring whites and the highest-scoring blacks, etc.), but this form of hiring, based on scores within race groups, is expressly forbidden by the Civil Rights Act of 1991. This is undoubtedly an issue that will receive more attention in the future.[121]

Benefits of Proper Selection Systems

While the preceding criteria can be applied to choosing individual selection devices, there is much to be gained from having a coherent selection system made up of several state-of-the-art devices. There is evidence that using a larger number of "good selection practices" is related to a firm's financial success. In one study, whether or not firms used five good selection practices was measured. The practices were assessment of recruiting source quality, validation of predictors, structured interviews, use of cognitive aptitude and ability tests, and use of biodata or weighted application blanks. The average number of good practices used by firms was only 1.36, so there is considerable room for improvement. There was a significant positive correlation between the number of practices used and the annual profit and profit growth of the companies. This relationship was especially strong for service and financial organizations. Clearly, where people deliver services directly, there is a substantial payoff from good selection processes.[122]

The most accurate selection should occur where several valid selection devices are used together to assess different aspects of candidates' abilities and/or motivation to do the job. An increasing amount of research has verified that different types of individually valid selection devices can complement each other to add unique information about applicants' likelihood of success. For instance, personality and biodata both explain variability in performance beyond that explained by general mental ability, and structured interviews add to the validity of a selection system beyond mental ability and conscientiousness.[123] One comprehensive review of selection devices suggests that the best prediction will normally be obtained from a combination of a test of general mental ability, a work sample, and an integrity test. For inexperienced employees for whom the work sample is not appropriate, a structured interview can be used instead.[124]

Test Takers' Rights

 We are used to focusing on the legal requirements of test use—demonstrable validity— when tests produce adverse impact, or on utility issues involving how much benefit a test will return to the organization using it. But are there ethical and moral issues involved in test use as well? Do test takers (and job applicants more generally) have rights in the selection process beyond those legally mandated? What if the selection process actively does harm to the candidate's self-esteem or well-being? Candidates are in a much lower power position than employers, suggesting that abuse of some sort could be possible.

The 1999 American Psychological Association Standards for Educational and Psychological Testing list some test taker rights, including the rights to:

- Be tested with measures that meet professional standards and are suitable to the purpose for which they are being used
- Be tested by a properly trained professional under conditions that do not unfairly disadvantage any test taker
- Be told in advance the purpose of the test, the testing procedures and rules, and whether or not taking the test is optional
- Receive a written or oral explanation of test results in understandable terms, unless such rights are waived (and they often are in employment testing)
- Have test results kept confidential and used only for their stated purpose
- Be informed of any accommodations available for testing those with disabilities or language problems.

The right to receive feedback on employment tests has become more accepted in recent times, but there is still quite a lot of variability in what, if anything, companies do in this area. Job candidates who have taken employment tests may simply find out whether or not they got a job offer. Some firms tell applicants specifically whether or not they passed various tests; others provide even more detailed feedback, such as percentile scores on each subtest. Some employers feel that (1) they don't have time to give everyone feedback, (2) releasing too much information may eventually compromise the usefulness or security of the test, and (3) the more information test takers have, the more likely unsuccessful applicants will be to file a complaint rather than quietly disappear. Other employers take a different perspective, believing that

providing honest feedback will reduce the number of complaints and encourage scarce applicants to reapply to the company for another job or try again when their test performance is likely to have improved.

Generally, the higher the job level and the more intensive the assessment, the more likely it is that feedback will be provided. For instance, a substantial majority of psychologists who perform individual assessment of managerial candidates (see page 352 for more on individual assessments) do offer to give candidates face-to-face feedback as part of the assessment process. Most often, this consists of suggestions for future development, a narrative summary of the strengths and weaknesses of the candidate, and some interpretation/explanation of test scores. Feedback is also more likely following assessment centers than simple paper-and-pencil tests. Firms whose testing program is overseen by qualified industrial psychologists are more likely to give useful feedback. Finally, detailed and developmental feedback is more likely to be provided to internal candidates for transfer or promotion than to external candidates.

In some countries, applicant rights to feedback are more strongly established. The British Psychological Society's Code of Good Practice for Occupational Testing now states that individuals who use psychological tests in occupational settings are expected to provide understandable feedback to test takers. A survey of 200 firms in the United Kingdom showed that by 1995, prior to the adoption of this guideline, 87 percent of HR managers believed that test takers should receive feedback on their performance, and 56 percent and 86 percent of firms provided such feedback to external and internal candidates, respectively. These percentages have probably risen considerably in the last few years. Feedback is also expected by employment test takers in France.

Sources: B. R. Baker and J. N. Cooper, "Fair Play or Foul? A Survey of Occupational Test Practices in the UK," *Personnel Review*, Vol. 24 (3), pp. 3–18; B. Barry Baker and John Cooper, "Occupational Testing and Psychometric Instruments: An Ethical Perspective," in *Ethical Issues in Contemporary Human Resource Management*, ed. Diana Winstanley and Jean Woodall (London: MacMillan Business, 2000) pp. 59–84; Ann Marie Ryan and Paul R. Sackett, "A Survey of Individual Assessment Practices by I/O Psychologists," *Personnel Psychology,* Autumn 1987, pp. 455–488; American Psychological Association, *Standards for Educational and Psychological Testing*, (Washington, DC: American Psychological Association, 1999); British Psychological Society, "Code of Good Practice for Occupational Testing," www.bps.org.uk/about/psychometric13.cfm; and personal communication, Nancy Tippins, June 6, 2001.

● **TABLE 8.7**

A Comparison of Selection Devices

Selection Device	Validity	Acceptability to Managers	Applicant Reactions	Cost
Application blank	Low to Medium	High	High	Very Low
Biodata questionnaire	Medium	?	Medium to high	High to develop, low to use
Accomplishment record/ experience	Medium	High	High	Low
Interview	Low to high, depending on structure	High	Medium to high	Medium
Ability test	High	Medium	Medium	Low to medium
Work-sample or trainability test	Medium to high	High	High	Medium
Personality or integrity test	Low to medium	Medium	Low to medium	Low to medium
Drug test	?	High	Low to medium	Medium
References	Low	High	Medium to high	Low to medium
Background check	Low to medium	Medium	Low to medium	Medium
Assessment center	Medium to high	High	High	High

Summary of Key Points

A wide variety of selection devices may be used to assess job applicants. One of the most common is the application blank. This device may be used informally for screening or systematically through the weighted application blank procedure. Biodata—whether obtained through application blanks, biodata questionnaires, or experience and accomplishment records—are often impressively valid predictors of job success. Properly chosen tests of cognitive ability are also excellent predictors, as are work-sample and trainability tests.

Personality tests are making a comeback and can have modest but consistent validity for some aspects of job success. The delineation of the Big Five dimensions of personality has helped clarify the underlying relationships between personality and some aspects of job performance. Honesty tests are being used increasingly to screen out employees who may steal from their employers or otherwise present behavioral problems, including violence.

Interviews are a widely used selection device. The traditional interview is not especially valid because interviewers make errors and may not ask job-related questions. More current interview techniques, such as situational and behavior description interviewing, are effective when interviewers are trained properly and are prepared to conduct a structured, content-valid interview.

The physical examination is often the final step in the hiring process. The Americans with Disabilities Act requires that a conditional job offer be made before a physical examination is given. A few companies use strength or fitness tests as predictors of success in physically demanding jobs. Many more use drug tests as screening devices.

Because résumé fraud is not uncommon, organizations find it a wise practice to verify important credentials before making job offers. In addition to verifying credentials, reference checks and background investigations may be used to discover additional information about job candidates.

Selecting managers is an especially difficult task because managerial jobs are highly complex and require many different skills. The assessment center, though expensive, can be a content-valid way to identify management talent. Other methods include interviews, tests, reference checks, and individual assessment by a psychologist.

A number of criteria might be considered in choosing a selection device. Among these are validity, utility, legality, acceptability to management, applicant reactions, effect on society, and incremental validity beyond devices already in use.

The Manager's Vocabulary

accomplishment record
adaptive testing
assessment center
background check
behavior description interview
Big Five personality dimensions
biodata
contrast error
first impression error
halo error
in-basket test
incremental validity
individual assessment
integrity test
inter-rater reliability
job experience questionnaires
leaderless group discussion
negligent hiring
paper-and-pencil test
patterned interview
performance test
personality inventory
polygraph
semistructured interview
similarity error
situational interview
situational judgment test
structured interview
test manual
trainability test
unstructured interview
weighted application blank (WAB)
work-sample test

Questions for Discussion

1. What are the steps in a typical selection process? Compare the selection process on your last job with that shown in Figure 8.1.
2. Describe how to construct a weighted application blank (WAB). Why do WABs tend to have high validity?
3. What are some questions that should not be included in an application blank? Why?
4. Explain how experience and accomplishment records can be used in selection. How would you construct these so as to ensure content validity?
5. What qualities would you look for in a test if you were picking one for a validation effort in your organization?
6. How would you go about designing a work-sample test for the job of pizza delivery driver?
7. How does a trainability test differ from a work-sample test? What are the advantages of each type of test? Can you think of any disadvantages?
8. What role do you think personality testing should play in selection for most jobs?
9. What types of integrity tests are available, and when might they be most useful?
10. What types of errors are committed by interviewers?
11. What is meant by the degree of structure in an interview? How does structure affect reliability and validity?
12. How do patterned, situational, and behavior description interviews differ from one another?
13. Why would an organization choose to use a physical examination as the last step in the selection process? In what ways must the organization be cautious in using the examination?
14. Debate both sides of this thesis: All job candidates should be screened for the use of illegal drugs.
15. How and why should reference information be collected about job candidates? What legal problems can arise with giving and collecting references?
16. What are the special problems and procedures involved in hiring managers?
17. Why might traditional hiring-for-the-job approaches be inadequate for high involvement or team-based organizations?

18. Consider the type of job you wish to obtain after graduation from your current course of study. How should incumbents for this type of job be selected in order to maximize their chances of being successful performers? How does your proposed selection system stack up against the criteria listed in the last section of this chapter?

● **Exercise 8.1**
How Should You Have Been Hired?

Working alone or in a group, do the following:

1. Pick a job that you or another member of your group has held.
2. Consider the knowledge, skills, abilities, and experience needed to perform that job. List the attributes that you believe an employer should look for in hiring a new employee for that job.
3. Determine how you would go about measuring these attributes.
4. Now, assume that you have decided to use an interview to assess some of the attributes.

5. Plan a cone-type semistructured interview for the job.
6. Write some situational and some behavior description questions that would be useful in selecting employees for that job.
7. Write questions for a reference interview with a candidate's former supervisor.

If you are working in a group, conduct one or more interviews with one another for the target job and one or more reference interviews.

● **Exercise 8.2**
Hiring at Health Source

Recommend a complete selection system for Health Source, as introduced in the HR Challenge at the beginning of this chapter. What characteristics are you looking for in drugstore clerks? How will you measure each?

Suppose that you have a strong preference for work-sample or trainability tests as a part of the selection system. How might you use work samples for this job? Lay out your system and its scoring key in as much detail as possible.

How would you handle the integrity/drug use portion of the selection system?

How do you expect applicants to react to the selection process at Health Source?

● **Exercise 8.3**
Preparing to Conduct an Interview

Your job responsibilities have just expanded to include interviewing job applicants. The first interviews will take place in about ten days. Fortunately, there are up-to-date job descriptions available for the jobs for which you will be conducting interviews. Still, you feel a bit uncertain of exactly how to proceed. You decide to check the Internet for advice on how to conduct interviews. You even find a couple of tutorial simulations that help you develop your questioning technique.

1. Locate resources that would be useful to you in learning how to conduct interviews.
2. Find and work through at least one interviewer training simulation.
3. Write a brief report of what you have learned about how to conduct an effective job interview.

Notes and References

1. See H. G. Heneman III, T. A. Judge, and R. L. Heneman. *Staffing Organizations,* 3d ed. (Middleton, Wis.: Mendota House/Irwin-McGraw-Hill, 2000), for more detail on employee selection.

2. A. Etzioni, *A Comparative Analysis of Complex Organizations* (New York: Free Press, 1975); C. L. Mulford, G. E. Klonglon, G. M. Beal, and J. M. Bohlen, "Selectivity, Socialization, and Role Performance," *Sociology and Social Research,* Vol. 53, 1968, pp. 68–77; Lawrence M. Rudner, "Pre-Employment Testing and Employee Productivity," *Public Personnel Management,* Summer 1992, pp. 133–150.

3. G. Cornick, "The Cost of a Poor Hire." (Available at: www. shrm.org/peoplewise/1099cornick.htm)

4. John E. Hunter and Frank L. Schmidt, "Ability Tests: Economic Benefits Versus the Issue of Fairness," *Industrial Relations,* Fall 1982, pp. 293–308.

5. Charles C. Snow and Scott A. Snell, "Staffing as Strategy," in *Personnel Selection in Organizations,* ed. N. Schmitt and W. C. Borman and Associates (San Francisco: Jossey-Bass, 1993), pp. 448–478.

6. "Recruiters Beware: Lying Is Common Among Applicants," *HRFocus,* October 1992, p. 5; Irwin L. Goldstein, "The Application Blank: How Honest Are the Responses?" *Journal of Applied Psychology,* October 1971, pp. 491–492; and Thomas E. Becker and Alan L. Colquitt, "Potential Versus Actual Faking of a Biodata Form: An Analysis Along Several Dimensions of Item Type," *Personnel Psychology,* Vol. 45, 1992, pp. 389–408.

7. Stephen J. Vodanovich and Rosemary H. Lowe, "They Ought to Know Better: The Incidence and Correlates of Inappropriate Application Blank Inquiries," *Public Personnel Management,* Fall 1992, pp. 363–370.

8. Adin C. Goldberg, "What You Can and Cannot Ask," *IIRFocus,* July 1992, p. 6; and *CCH's Explanation of the Americans with Disabilities Act of 1990* (Chicago: Commerce Clearing House, 1990).

9. For more information, see Clifford M. Koen, Jr., "Guide to Pre-Employment Inquiries Interview Questions: What You Can and Cannot Ask," *HRFocus,* June 1995, pp. 4–5; and W. E. Barlow, "Pre-Employment Interviews: What You Can and Can't Ask," *Personnel Journal,* January 1996, p. 99.

10. M. D. Mumford and Garnett S. Stokes, "Developmental Determinants of Individual Action: Theory and Practice in Applying Background Measures," in *Handbook of Industrial and Organizational Psychology,* Vol. 3, 2d ed., ed. M. D. Dunnette and L. M. Hough (Palo Alto, Calif.: Consulting Psychologists Press, 1992), pp. 61–138. See also Garnett S. Stokes, Michael D. Mumford, and William A. Owens (eds.), *Biodata Handbook,* (Palo Alto, Calif.: CPP Books, 1994).

11. James J. Asher, "The Biographical Item: Can It Be Improved?" *Personnel Psychology,* Summer 1972, pp. 251–269.

12. "Spotting a Winner in Insurance," *Business Week,* February 12, 1979, pp. 122, 127; M. A. McManus and M. L. Kelly "Personality Measures and Biodata: Evidence Regarding Their Incremental Predictive Value in the Life Insurance Industry," *Personnel Psychology,* Vol. 52, 1999, pp. 137–148.

13. R. R. Reilly and G. T. Chao, "Validity and Fairness of Some Alternative Employee Selection Procedures," *Personnel Psychol-*

ogy, Spring 1982, pp. 1–62; J. E. Hunter and R. F. Hunter, "Validity and Utility of Alternative Predictors of Job Performance," *Psychological Bulletin,* Spring 1984, pp. 72–98; and M. K. Mount, L. A. Witt, and M. R. Barrick, "Incremental Validity of Empirically Keyed Biodata Scales over GMA and the Five Factor Personality Constructs," *Personnel Psychology,* Vol. 53, 2000, pp. 299–323.

14. Robert Helmreich, Roger Bakeman, and Roland Radloff, "The Life History Questionnaire as a Predictor of Performance in Navy Diver Training," *Journal of Applied Psychology,* April 1973, pp. 148–153; Russell J. Drakely and Peter Herriot, "Biographical Data, Training Success, and Turnover," *Journal of Occupational Psychology,* Vol. 61, 1988, pp. 145–152; Hannah R. Rothstein, Frank L. Schmidt, Frank W. Erwin, William A. Owens, and C. Paul Sparks, "Biographical Data in Employment Selection: Can Validities Be Made Generalizable?" *Journal of Applied Psychology,* April 1990, pp. 175–184; and Craig J. Russell, Joyce Mattson, Steven E. Devlin, and David Atwater, "Predictive Validity of Biodata Items Generated from Retrospective Life Experience Essays," *Journal of Applied Psychology,* October 1990, pp. 569–580.

15. Asher, "The Biographical Item."

16. F. A. Mael and A. C. Hirsch, "Rainforest Empiricism and Quasi-Rationality: Two Approaches to Objective Biodata," *Personnel Psychology,* Winter 1993, pp. 719–738; Garnett S. Stokes and Sarita Reddy, "Use of Background Data in Organizational Decisions," in *International Review of Industrial and Organizational Psychology,* Vol. 7, ed. C. L. Cooper and I. T. Robertson (Chichester, England: Wiley, 1992); and M. D. Mumford, D. P. Costanza, M. S. Connelly, and J. F. Johnson, "Item Generation Procedures and Background Data Scales: Implications for Construct and Criterion-Related Validity," *Personnel Psychology,* Summer 1996, pp. 361–398.

17. B. K. Brown and M. A. Campion, "Biodata Phenomenology: Recruiters' Perceptions and Use of Biographical Information in Résumé Screening," *Journal of Applied Psychology,* Vol. 79 (6), 1994, pp. 897–908.

18. M. A. Quinones, J. K. Ford, and M. S. Teachout, "The Relationship Between Work Experience and Job Performance: A Conceptual and Meta-Analytic Review," *Personnel Psychology,* Vol. 48, 1995, pp. 887–910; and P. E. Tesluk and R. R. Jacobs, "Toward an Integrated Model of Work Experience," *Personnel Psychology,* Vol. 51, 1998, pp. 321–355.

19. For a detailed treatment of scoring systems for training and experience measures, see R. A. Ash, J. C. Johnson, E. L. Levine, and M. A. McDaniel, "Job Applicant Training and Work Experience Evaluation in Personnel Selection," *Research in Personnel and Human Resource Management,* Vol. 7, 1989, pp. 183–226.

20. Cathy D. Anderson, Jack Warner, and Cassie C. Spenser, "Inflation Bias in Self-Assessment Examinations: Implications for Valid Employee Selection," *Journal of Applied Psychology,* November 1984, pp. 574–580; David C. Myers and Sidney A. Fine, "Development of a Methodology to Obtain and Assess Applicant Experiences for Employment," *Public Personnel Management Journal,* Spring 1985, pp. 51–64; and Ronald D. Pannone, "Predicting Test Performance: A Content-Valid Approach to

Screening Applicants," *Personnel Psychology,* Autumn 1984, pp. 507–514. See also Michael A. McDaniel, Frank L. Schmidt, and John E. Hunter, "A Meta-Analysis of the Validity of Methods for Rating Training and Experience in Personnel Selection," *Personnel Psychology,* Vol. 41, 1988, pp. 283–309.

21. K. Coffee, J. Pearce, R. Nishimura, "State of California: Civil Service Testing Moves into Cyberspace," *Public Personnel Management,* Summer 1999, pp. 283–300.

22. Leaetta M. Hough, "Development and Evaluation of the 'Accomplishment Record' Method of Selecting and Promoting Professionals," *Journal of Applied Psychology,* February 1984, pp. 135–146.

23. American Management Association, *2000 AMA Survey on Workplace Testing: Basic Skills, Job Skills, and Psychological Measurement.* (Available at: www.amanet.org)

24. *Watson* v. *Fort Worth Bank and Trust* (1988), 47 FEP Cases 102, U.S. Sup. Ct., No. 86–6139, June 29.

25. J. E. Hunter, F. L. Schmidt, and R. Hunter, "Differential Validity of Employment Tests by Race: A Comprehensive Review and Analysis," *Psychological Bulletin,* July 1979, pp. 721–735; Alexandra K. Wigdor and Wendell Garner (eds.), *Ability Testing: Uses, Consequences, and Controversies,* Part I (Washington, D.C.: Committee on Ability Testing, National Research Council, National Academy Press, 1982), pp. 145–147. Subsequent reviews have reached similar conclusions—see J. A. Hartigan and A. K. Wigdor, *Fairness in Employment Testing* (Washington, DC: National Academy Press, 1989); U. Neisser, G. Boodoo, T. J. Bouchard, A. W. Boykin, N. Brody, S. Ceci, D. Halpern, J. Loehlin, R. Perloff, R. Sternberg, and S. Urbina, "Intelligence: Knowns and Unknowns" *American Psychologist,* Vol. 51, pp. 77–101; and D. Lubinski, "Scientific and Social Significance of Assessing Individual Differences," *Annual Review of Psychology,* Vol. 51, 2000, pp. 405–444.

26. See Keith Hattrup and Neal Schmitt, "Prediction of Trades Apprentices' Performance on Job Sample Criteria," *Personnel Psychology,* Autumn 1990, pp. 453–466; and Hunter and Hunter, "Validity and Utility of Alternative Predictors of Job Performance."

27. Joyce Hogan and Robert Hogan (eds.), *Business and Industry Testing: Current Practices and Test Reviews* (Austin, Tex.: Pro.ed, 1990).

28. John Hawk, "Real World Implications of g," *Journal of Vocational Behavior,* Vol. 29, 1986, pp. 411–414; John E. Hunter, "Cognitive Ability, Cognitive Aptitudes, Job Knowledge, and Job Performance," *Journal of Vocational Behavior,* Vol. 29, 1986, pp. 340–362; Hunter and Hunter, "Validity and Utility of Alternative Predictors of Job Performance"; Arthur R. Jensen, "g: Artifact or Reality?" *Journal of Vocational Behavior,* Vol. 29, 1986, pp. 301–331; M. J. Ree, J. A. Earles, and M. S. Teachout, "Predicting Job Performance: Not Much More than g," *Journal of Applied Psychology,* Vol. 79, 1994, pp. 518–524.

29. F. L. Schmidt and J. E. Hunter, "The Validity and Utility of Selection Methods in Personnel Psychology: Practical and Theoretical Implications of 85 Years of Research Findings," *Psychological Bulletin,* Vol. 124, 1998, pp. 262–274.

30. R. L. Thorndike, "The Role of General Ability in Prediction," *Journal of Vocational Behavior,* Vol. 29, 1986, pp. 332–339.

31. One source for finding out about tests is B. S. Plake and J. C. Impara (eds.), *The Fourteenth Mental Measurements Yearbook* (Lincoln, Nebraska: University of Nebraska Press, 2001).

32. C. Paul Sparks, "How to Read a Test Manual," in Hogan and Hogan (eds.), *Business and Industry Testing,* pp. 36–47.

33. J. M. Stanton, "Validity and Related Issues in Web-Based Hiring," *The Industrial Psychologist,* January 1999, pp. 69–77.

34. G. Nicholson, "Automated Assessment at a Large Company," *Workforce,* Vol. 79 (12), December 2000, pp. 102–104.

35. N. Schmitt, S. W. Gilliland, R. S. Landis, and D. Devine, "Computer-Based Testing Applied to Selection of Secretarial Applicants," *Personnel Psychology,* Vol. 46, 1993, pp. 149–165; F. Drasgow, J. B. Olson, P. A. Keenan, P. Moberg, and A. D. Mead, "Computerized Assessment," *Research in Personnel and Human Resource Management,* Vol. 11, 1993, pp. 163–206; and R. C. Overton, H. J. Harms, L. R. Taylor, and M. J. Zickar, "Adapting to Adaptive Testing," *Personnel Psychology,* Vol. 50, 1997, pp. 171–185.

36. Paul Squires, Steven J. Torkel, James W. Smither, and Margaret R. Ingate, "Validity and Generalizability of a Role-Play Test to Select Telemarketing Representatives," *Journal of Occupational Psychology,* Vol. 64, 1991, pp. 37–47.

37. Rosemarie J. Park, Rene V. Davis, Elizabeth K. Rengel, and Rebecca L. Storlie, "The Selection and Validation of a Reading Test to Be Used with Civil Service Employees," *Public Personnel Management,* Fall 1985, pp. 275–284; and Lyle F. Schoenfeldt, Barbara B. Schoenfeldt, Stanley R. Acker, and Michael R. Perlson, "Content Validation Revisited: The Development of a Content-Oriented Test of Industrial Reading," *Journal of Applied Psychology,* October 1976, pp. 581–588.

38. J. A. Weekley and C. Jones, "Further Studies of Situational Tests," *Personnel Psychology,* Vol. 52, 1999, pp. 679–700.

39. I. T. Robertson and R. M. Mindel, "A Study of Trainability Testing," *Journal of Occupational Psychology,* June 1980, pp. 131–138; Arthur I. Siegel, "The Miniature Job Training and Evaluation Approach: Additional Findings," *Personnel Psychology,* Spring 1983, pp. 41–56; and Richard R. Reilly and Edmund W. Israelski, "Development and Validation of Minicourses in the Telecommunication Industry," *Journal of Applied Psychology,* Vol. 73, 1988, pp. 721–726.

40. James J. Asher and James A. Sciarrino, "Realistic Work Sample Tests: A Review," *Personnel Psychology,* Winter 1974, pp. 519–533; Ivan Robertson and R. S. Kandola, "Work Sample Tests: Validity, Adverse Impact, and Applicant Reaction," *Journal of Occupational Psychology,* September 1982, pp. 171–183; and Schmidt and Hunter, "The Validity and Utility of Selection Methods in Personnel Psychology."

41. Wayne F. Cascio and Neil F. Phillips, "Performance Testing: A Rose Among Thorns?" *Personnel Psychology,* Winter 1979, pp. 751–766; J. L. Farr, B. S. O'Leary, and C. J. Bartlett, "Effect of a Work Sample Test upon Self-Selection and Turnover of Job Applicants," *Journal of Applied Psychology,* October 1973, pp. 283–285; Sylvia Downs, "Job Sample and Trainability Tests," in *Assessment and Selection in Organizations,* ed. Peter Herriot (Chichester, England: Wiley, 1989), pp. 391–399; and K. A. Hanisch and C. L. Hulin, "Two-Stage Sequential Selection Procedures Using Ability and Training Performance: Incremental Validity of Behavioral Consistency Measures," *Personnel Psychology,* Vol. 47, 1994, pp. 767–786.

42. American Management Association, *2000 AMA Survey on Workplace Testing.*

43. *Soroka* v. *Dayton Hudson Corp.,* 6 Ind. Empl. Rights Cas. (BNA) 1491 (Cal. Ct. App. 1991); see also Daniel P. O'Meara,

"Personality Tests Raise Questions of Legality and Effectiveness," *HRMagazine*, January 1994, pp. 97–100.

44. D. C. Brown, "EEOC Issues Revised Policy on Medical Examinations Under the ADA," *The Industrial and Organizational Psychologist,* January 1996, pp. 107–108.

45. Murray R. Barrick and Michael K. Mount, "The Big Five Personality Dimensions and Job Performance: A Meta-Analysis," *Personnel Psychology,* Spring 1991, pp. 1–26; M. K. Mount and M. R. Barrick, "The Big Five Personality Dimensions: Implications for Research and Practice in Human Resource Management," *Research in Personnel and Human Resource Management,* Vol. 13, 1995, pp. 153–200; Neal Schmitt, Richard Z. Gooding, Raymond A. Noe, and Michael Kirsch, "Meta-Analysis of Validity Studies Published Between 1964 and 1982 and the Investigation of Study Characteristics," *Personnel Psychology,* Autumn 1984, pp. 407–422.

46. David V. Day and Stanley B. Silverman, "Personality and Job Performance: Evidence of Incremental Validity," *Personnel Psychology,* Spring 1989, pp. 25–36; John R. Hollenbeck and Ellen M. Whitener, "Reclaiming Personality Traits for Personnel Selection: Self-Esteem as an Illustrative Case," *Journal of Management,* Vol. 14, 1988, pp. 81–91; Robert L. Helmreich, Linda L. Sawin, and Alan L. Carsrud, "The Honeymoon Effect in Job Performance: Temporal Increases in the Predictive Power of Achievement Motivation," *Journal of Applied Psychology,* Vol. 71, 1986, pp. 185–188; Leaetta M. Hough, Newell K. Eaton, Marvin D. Dunnette, John D. Kamp, and Rodney A. McCloy, "Criterion-Related Validities of Personality Constructs and the Effect of Response Distortion on Those Validities," *Journal of Applied Psychology,* October 1990, pp. 581–595; C. D. Fisher and G. J. Boyle, "Personality and Employee Selection: Credibility Regained," *Asia Pacific Journal of Human Resources,* Vol. 35 (2), 1997, pp. 26–40; McManus and Kelly, "Personality Measures and Biodata."

47. See O. Behling, "Employee Selection: Will Intelligence and Conscientiousness Do the Job?" *Academy of Management Executive*, February 1998, pp. 77–86, for an excellent discussion of when to hire mainly for conscientiousness and when to hire mainly for intelligence.

48. Barrick and Mount, "The Big Five Personality Dimensions and Job Performance"; Mount and Barrick, "The Big Five Personality Dimensions"; and D. S. Ones and C. Viswesvaran, "Bandwidth-Fidelity Dilemma in Personality Measurement for Selection," *Journal of Organizational Behavior,* Vol. 17, 1996, pp. 609–626. For dissenting opinions on the Big Five, see Leaetta M. Hough, "The 'Big Five' Personality Variables—Construct Confusion: Description Versus Prediction," *Human Performance,* Vol. 5, 1992, pp. 139–155; R. J. Schneider, L. M. Hough, and M. D. Dunnette, "Broadsided by Broad Traits: How to Sink Science in Five Dimensions or Less," *Journal of Organizational Behavior,* Vol. 17, 1996, pp. 639–655; and T. A. Judge, C. A. Higgins, C. J. Thoresen, and M. R. Barrick, "The Big Five Personality Traits, General Mental Ability, and Career Success Across the Life Span," *Personnel Psychology,* Vol. 52, 1999, pp. 621–652.

49. M. A. McDaniel and R. L. Frei, "Validity of Customer Service Measures in Personnel Selection: A Meta-Analysis," paper presented at the Ninth Annual Conference of the Society for Industrial and Organizational Psychology, Nashville, April 1994.

50. Sandra O. Davis, "The Design and Conduct of Individual Psychological Assessments in Industry," paper presented at the First Annual Conference of the Society for Industrial and Organizational Psychology, Chicago, April 1986.

51. D. C. Brown, "Test Misuse in the United Kingdom," *The Industrial and Organizational Psychologist,* April 1995, pp. 65–66.

52. S. Greengard, "Are You Well Armed to Screen Applicants?" *Personnel Journal,* December 1995, pp. 84–95; and B. P. Niehoff and R. J. Paul, "Causes of Employee Theft and Strategies the HR Managers Can Use for Prevention," *Human Resource Management*, Spring 2000, pp. 51–64.

53. Richard C. Hollinger and John P. Clark, *Theft by Employees* (Lexington, Mass.: Lexington Books, 1983).

54. "Congress Clears Lie-Detector Ban," *Congressional Quarterly Weekly Reports,* June 11, 1988, p. 1630.

55. Paul R. Sackett, Laura R. Burris, and Christine Callahan, "Integrity Testing for Personnel Selection: An Update," *Personnel Psychology,* Autumn 1989, pp. 491–529; D. S. Ones, C. Viswesvaran, and F. L. Schmidt, "Comprehensive Meta-Analysis of Integrity Test Validities: Findings and Implications for Personnel Selection and Theories of Job Performance," *Journal of Applied Psychology,* Vol. 78, 1993, pp. 679–703; H. J. Bernardin and D. K. Cooke, "Validity of an Honesty Test in Predicting Theft Among Convenience Store Employees," *Academy of Management Journal,* Vol. 36, 1993, pp. 1097–1108; K. R. Murphy, *Honesty in the Workplace* (Pacific Grove, Calif.: Brooks/Cole, 1993); and M. R. Cunningham, D. T. Wong, and A. P. Barbee, "Self-Presentation Dynamics on Overt Integrity Tests: Experimental Studies of the Reid Report," *Journal of Applied Psychology,* Vol. 79 (5), 1994, pp. 643–658.

56. S. Greengard, "Are You Well Armed to Screen Applicants?" *Personnel Journal,* December 1995, pp. 84–95.

57. Joyce Hogan and Robert Hogan, "How to Measure Employee Reliability," *Journal of Applied Psychology,* April 1989, pp. 273–279.

58. L. P. DiLorenzo and D. J. Carroll, "Screening Applicants for a Safer Workplace," *HRMagazine,* March 1995, pp. 55–58.

59. R. D. Arvey, "Violence in the Workplace," paper presented at the Annual Meeting of the Academy of Management, Dallas, August 1994; D. S. Ones, C. Viswesvaran, F. L. Schmidt, and A. D. Reiss, "The Validity of Honesty and Violence Scales of Integrity Tests in Predicting Violence at Work," *University of Houston CBA Working Paper Series,* 1994, p. 278.

60. "Solve the Long-Distance Hiring Dilemma," supplement to the August 1996 issue of *Personnel Journal,* pp. 18–20; and K. O. Magnusen and K. G. Kroeck, "Videoconferencing Maximizes Recruiting," *HRMagazine,* August 1995, pp. 70–72.

61. F. L. Schmidt and M. Rader, "Exploring the Boundary Conditions for Interview Validity: Meta-Analytic Validity Findings for a New Interview Type," *Personnel Psychology*, Vol. 52, 1999. pp. 445–464.

62. J. M. Conway, R. A. Jako, and D. F. Goodman, "A Meta-Analysis of Interrater and Internal Consistency Reliability of Selection Interviews," *Journal of Applied Psychology,* Vol. 80 (5), 1995, pp. 565–579; and Eugene C. Mayfield, Steven H. Brown, and Bruce W. Hamstra, "Selection Interviewing in the Life Insurance Industry: An Update of Research and Practice," *Personnel Psychology,* Winter 1980, pp. 725–740.

63. Tom Janz, Lowell Hellervik, and David C. Gilmore, *Behavior Description Interviewing* (Boston: Allyn and Bacon, 1986);

Hunter and Hunter, "Validity and Utility of Alternative Predictors of Job Performance."

64. George F. Dreher, Ronald A. Ash, and Priscilla Hancock, "The Role of Traditional Research Design in Underestimating the Validity of the Employment Interview," *Personnel Psychology,* Vol. 41, 1988, pp. 315–327; A. I. Huffcutt and W. Arthur, Jr., "Hunter and Hunter (1984) Revisited: Interview Validity for Entry-Level Jobs," *Journal of Applied Psychology,* Vol. 79, 1994, pp. 184–190; M. McDaniel, D. Whetzel, F. Schmidt, and T. Maurer, "The Validity of Employment Interviews: A Comprehensive Review and Meta-Analysis," *Journal of Applied Psychology,* August 1994, pp. 599–616; and E. D. Pulakos, N. Schmitt, D. Whitney, and M. Smith, "Individual Differences in Interviewer Ratings: The Impact of Standardization, Consensus Discussion, and Sampling Error on the Validity of a Structured Interview," *Personnel Psychology,* Vol. 49, 1996, pp. 85–102.

65. M. A. Campion, J. E. Campion, and J. P. Hudson, Jr., "Structured Interviewing: A Note on Incremental Validity and Alternative Question Types," *Journal of Applied Psychology,* Vol. 79 (6), 1994, pp. 998–1002; and E. D. Pulakos and N. Schmitt, "Experience-Based and Situational Interview Questions: Studies of Validity," *Personnel Psychology,* Vol. 48, 1995, pp. 289–308.

66. Richard Arvey and James Campion, "The Employment Interview: A Summary and Review of Recent Research," *Personnel Psychology,* Summer 1982, pp. 281–322; Neal Schmitt, "Social and Situational Determinants of Interview Decisions: Implications for the Employment Interview," *Personnel Psychology,* Spring 1976, pp. 79–101.

67. M. M. Okanes and H. Tschirgi, "Impact of the Face-to-Face Interview on Prior Judgments of a Candidate," *Perceptual and Motor Skills,* February 1978, pp. 46, 322.

68. Richard D. Arvey, "Unfair Discrimination in the Employment Interview: Legal and Psychological Aspects," *Psychological Bulletin,* July 1979, pp. 736–765.

69. Madeline E. Heilman and Melanie Stopeck, "Attractiveness and Corporate Success: Different Causal Attributions for Males and Females," *Journal of Applied Psychology,* May 1985, pp. 379–388.

70. R. Pingitore, B. L. Dugoni, R. S. Tindale, and B. Spring, "Bias Against Overweight Job Applicants in a Simulated Employment Interview," *Journal of Applied Psychology,* Vol. 79 (6), 1994, pp. 909–917.

71. John F. Binning, Mel A. Goldstein, Mario F. Garcia, and Julie H. Scattaregia, "Effects of Pre-Interview Impressions on Questioning Strategies in Same- and Opposite-Sex Employment," *Journal of Applied Psychology,* Vol. 73, 1988, pp. 30–37; Therese Hoff Macan and Robert L. Dipboye, "The Relationship of Interviewers' Preinterview Impressions to Selection and Recruiting Outcomes," *Personnel Psychology,* Winter 1990, pp. 745–768; and T. W. Dougherty, D. B. Turban, and J. C. Callender, "Confirming First Impressions in the Employment Interview: A Field Study of Interviewer Behavior," *Journal of Applied Psychology,* Vol. 79 (5), 1994, pp. 659–665.

72. M. R. Barrick, G. K. Patton, and S. N. Haugland, "Accuracy of Interviewer Judgments of Job Applicant Personality Traits," *Personnel Psychology,* Winter 2000, pp. 925–951.

73. See Sandra Forsythe, Mary Frances Drake, and Charles E. Cox, "Influence of Applicant's Dress on Interviewers' Selection Decisions," *Journal of Applied Psychology,* May 1985, pp. 374–378; Robert Gifford, Cheuk Fan Ng, and Margaret Wilkin-

son, "Nonverbal Cues in the Employment Interview: Links Between Applicant Qualities and Interviewer Judgments," *Journal of Applied Psychology,* November 1985, pp. 729–736; Thomas V. McGovern and Howard E. A. Tinsley, "Interviewer Evaluation of Interviewee Nonverbal Behavior," *Journal of Vocational Behavior,* October 1978, pp. 163–171; and T. DeGroot and S. J. Motowidlo "Why Visual and Vocal Interview Cues Can Affect Interviewers' Judgments and Predict Job Performance," *Journal of Applied Psychology,* Vol 84, 1999, pp. 986–993.

74. Though forcing interviewers to take notes may not be helpful, see J. R. Burnett, C. Fan, S. J. Motowidlo, and T. DeGroot, "Interview Notes and Validity," *Personnel Psychology,* Vol. 51, 1998, pp. 375–396.

75. L. M. Graves and R. J. Karren, "The Employee Selection Interview: A Fresh Look at an Old Problem," *Human Resource Management,* Vol. 35, Summer 1996, pp. 163–180.

76. A. H. Church, "From Both Sides Now: The Employee Interview—The Great Pretender," *The Industrial and Organizational Psychologist,* July 1996, pp. 108–117.

77. Thomas L. Moffatt, *Selection Interviewing for Managers* (New York: Harper and Row, 1979).

78. Huffcutt and Arthur, "Hunter and Hunter (1984) Revisited: Interview Validity for Entry-Level Jobs"; and McDaniel, Whetzel, Schmidt, and Maurer, "The Validity of Employment Interviews."

79. Schmidt and Rader, "Exploring the Boundary Conditions for Interview Validity."

80. McDaniel, Whetzel, Schmidt, and Maurer, "The Validity of Employment Interviews"; and Campion, Campion, and Hudson, "Structured Interviewing: A Note on Incremental Validity and Alternative Question Types."

81. Gary P. Latham, Lise M. Saari, Elliot D. Pursell, and Michael A. Campion, "The Situational Interview," *Journal of Applied Psychology,* August 1980, pp. 442–427; Elliott D. Pursell, Michael A. Campion, and Sarah R. Gaylord, "Structured Interviewing: Avoiding Selection Problems," *Personnel Journal,* November 1980, pp. 907–912; Michael A. Campion, Elliott D. Pursell, and Barbara K. Brown, "Structured Interviewing: Raising the Psychometric Properties of the Employment Interview," *Personnel Psychology,* Vol. 41, 1988, pp. 25–42; and Jeff A. Weekley and Joseph A. Gier, "Reliability and Validity of the Situational Interview for a Sales Position," *Journal of Applied Psychology,* Vol. 72, 1989, pp. 484–487.

82. Janz, Hellervik, and Gilmore, *Behavior Description Interviewing.*

83. Ibid., pp. 64–65.

84. Tom Janz, "Initial Comparisons of Patterned Behavior Description Interviews Versus Unstructured Interviews," *Journal of Applied Psychology,* October 1982, pp. 577–580; Janz, Hellervik, and Gilmore, *Behavior Description Interviewing;* Christopher Orpen, "Patterned Behavior Description Interviews Versus Unstructured Interviews: A Comparative Validity Study," *Journal of Applied Psychology,* November 1985, pp. 774–776; S. J. Motowidlo, G. W. Carter, M. D. Dunnette, N. Tippins, S. Werner, J. R. Burnett, and M. J. Vaughn, "Studies of the Structured Behavioral Interview," *Journal of Applied Psychology,* Vol. 77, 1992, pp. 571–587.

85. Frank Landy, "The Validity of the Interview in Police Officer Selection," *Journal of Applied Psychology,* April 1976, pp. 193–198; Dougherty, Ebert, and Callender, "Policy Capturing in the Employment Interview," *Journal of Applied Psychology,* Vol.

71, 1986, pp. 9–15; Y. Ganzach, A. N. Kluger, and N. Klayman, "Making Decisions from an Interview: Expert Measurement and Mechanical Combination," *Personnel Psychology*, Vol. 53, 2000. pp. 1–20.

86. American Management Association. *AMA Survey on Workplace Testing—Medical Testing*. (Available at: www.amanet.org)

87. Jonathan A. Segal, "Pre-Employment Physicals Under the ADA," *HRMagazine,* October 1992, pp. 103–107.

88. Michael A. Campion, "Personnel Selection for Physically Demanding Jobs: Review and Recommendations," *Personnel Psychology,* Autumn 1983, pp. 527–550; and B. R. Blakley, M. A. Quinones, M. S. Crawford, and I. A. Jago, "The Validity of Isometric Strength Tests," *Personnel Psychology,* Summer 1994, pp. 247–274.

89. R. D. Arvey, T. E. Landon, S. M. Nutting, and S. E. Maxwell, "Development of Physical Ability Tests for Police Officers: A Construct Validation Approach," *Journal of Applied Psychology,* Vol. 77, 1992, pp. 996–1009; Larry T. Hoover, "Trends in Police Physical Ability Selection Testing," *Public Personnel Management,* Spring 1992, pp. 29–40; Blakley, Quinones, Crawford, and Jago, "The Validity of Isometric Strength Tests."

90. Edwin A. Fleishman, "Evaluating Physical Abilities Required by Jobs," *Personnel Administration,* June 1979, pp. 82–90; J. C. Hogan, "Physical Abilities," in Dunnette and Hough (eds.), *Handbook of Industrial and Organizational Psychology.*

91. C. C. Hoffman, "Generalizing Physical Ability Test Validity: A Case Study Using Test Transportability, Validity Generalization, and Construct-Related Validation Evidence," *Personnel Psychology*, Vol. 52, 1999, pp. 1019–1041; and D. Biddle and N. S. Sill, "Protective Service Physical Ability Tests: Establishing Pass/Fail, Ranking, and Banding Procedures," *Public Personnel Management*, Summer 1999, pp. 217–225.

92. R.J. Sagall, "Drug Abuse Testing," *Workforce Week*, December 17–23, 2000. (Available at: www.workforce.com)

93. (Available at: www.scll-free.com/Rainbow/facts.html)

94. E. R. Greenberg, "Test-Positive Rates Drop as More Companies Screen Employees," *HRFocus,* June 1992, p. 7; S. MacDonald and P. Roman (eds.), *Drug Testing in the Workplace* (New York: Plenum Press, 1994); and T. D. Hartwell, P. D. Steele, M. T. French, and N. F. Rodman, "Prevalence of Drug Testing in the Workplace," *Monthly Labor Review,* November 1996, pp. 35–42.

95. Jacques Normand, Stephen D. Salyards, and John J. Mahoney, "An Evaluation of Preemployment Drug Testing," *Journal of Applied Psychology,* December 1990, pp. 629–639.

96. Mark D. Uhrich, "Are You Positive the Test Is Positive?" *HRMagazine,* April 1992, pp. 44–48; J. F. Atwood, "Applicant Drug Testing: An Intriguing Odyssey," *Public Personnel Management,* Summer 1992, pp. 119–132; and W. Arthur, Jr., and D. Doverspike, "Employment-Related Drug Testing: Idiosyncratic Characteristics and Issues," *Public Personnel Management,* Spring 1997, pp. 77–87.

97. Russell Cropanzano and Mary Konovsky, "Drug Use and Its Implications for Employee Drug Testing," *Research in Personnel and Human Resource Management,* Vol. 11, 1993, pp. 207–257.

98. Michael Crant and Thomas S. Bateman, "An Experimental Test of the Impact of Drug-Testing Programs on Potential Job Applicants' Attitudes and Intentions," *Journal of Applied Psychology,* April 1990, pp. 127–131; Mary A. Konovsky and Russell Cropanzano, "Perceived Fairness of Employee Drug Testing as a Predictor of Employee Attitudes and Job Performance," *Journal of Applied Psychology,* October 1991, pp. 698–707; Kevin R. Murphy, George C. Thornton III, and Kristin Prue, "Influence of Job Characteristics on the Acceptability of Employee Drug Testing," *Journal of Applied Psychology,* June 1991, pp. 447–453; Kevin R. Murphy, George C. Thornton III, and Douglas H. Reynolds, "College Students' Attitudes Toward Employee Drug Testing Programs," *Personnel Psychology,* Autumn 1990, pp. 615–631; and B. J. Tepper, "Investigation of General and Program-Specific Attitudes Toward Corporate Drug-Testing Policies," *Journal of Applied Psychology,* Vol. 79, 1994, pp. 392–401.

99. Report available from the "1998 SHRM Reference Checking Survey." Society for Human Resource Management, 1800 Duke St. Alexandria, VA, 22314.

100. For more information, see www.ftc.gov

101. For more on reference checking, see Greengard, "Are You Well Armed to Screen Applicants?"; and P. A. Dunn, "Pre-Employment Referencing Aids Your Bottom Line," *Personnel Journal,* February 1995, pp. 68–75.

102. Paul Dobson, "Reference Reports," in Herriot (ed.), *Assessment and Selection in Organizations,* pp. 455–468.

103. For detailed advice on conducting the references interview, see Susan J. Herman, *Hiring Right: A Practical Guide* (Thousand Oaks, Calif.: Sage, 1994).

104. James C. Baxter, Barbara Brock, Peter C. Hill, and Richard M. Rozelle, "Letters of Recommendation: A Question of Value," *Journal of Applied Psychology,* June 1981, pp. 296–301; Alan Jones and Elizabeth Harrison, "Prediction of Performance in Initial Officer Training Using Reference Reports," *Journal of Occupational Psychology,* March 1982, pp. 35–42; M. G. Aamodt, D. A. Bryan, and A. J. Whitcomb, "Predicting Performance with Letters of Recommendation," *Public Personnel Management,* Spring 1993, pp. 81–90; Schmidt and Hunter, "The Validity and Utility of Selection Methods in Personnel Psychology.

105. Ann Marie Ryan and Marja Kasek, "Negligent Hiring and Defamation: Areas of Liability Related to Pre-Employment Inquiries," *Personnel Psychology,* Summer 1991, pp. 293–319; and B. T. McMillan and M. Muraco, "Background Checks: Prudent Practice or Legal Requirement?" (Available at: www.shrm.org/peoplewise/0700mcmillan.htm)

106. Charles S. White and Lawrence S. Kleiman, "The Cost of Candid Comments," *HRMagazine,* August 1991, pp. 54–56; and Betty Southard Murphy, Wayne E. Barlow, and D. Diane Hatch, "Job Reference Liability of Employers," *Personnel Journal,* September 1991, pp. 22, 26.

107. Laren Matthes, "Staying Neutral Doesn't Mean You're Protected," *HRFocus,* April 1993, p. 3; J. Swerdlow, "Negligent Referral: A Potential Theory for Employer Liability," *California Law Review,* Vol. 64, 1991, p. 1645. See also D. C. Meinderstsma, "Implications of the 1996 Job Reference Immunity Statutes," Society for Human Resource Management white paper. (Available at: http://www.shrm.org/docs/whitepapers/61207.htm*)*

108. C. Hirschman, "The Whole Truth," *HR Magazine,* June 2000, pp. 87–92.

109. R. Hogan, G. J. Curphy, and J. Hogan, "What We Know About Leadership: Effectiveness and Personality," *American Psychologist,* June 1994, pp. 493–504; and C. Fernandez-Araoz, "Hiring Without Firing," *Harvard Business Review,* July–August 1999, pp. 109–120.

110. I. T. Robertson and P. A. Iles, "Approaches to Managerial Selection," in *International Review of Industrial and Organizational Psychology,* Vol. 3, ed. C. L. Cooper and I. Robertson (Chichester, England: Wiley, 1988), pp. 159–211; Glen Grimsley and Hilton F. Jarrett, "The Relationship of Past Managerial Achievement to Test Measures Obtained in the Employment Situation: Methodology and Results," *Personnel Psychology,* Spring 1973, pp. 31–48; and Michael J. Stahl, "Achievement, Power, and Managerial Motivation: Selecting Managerial Talent with the Job Choice Exercise," *Personnel Psychology,* Winter 1983, pp. 775–789.

111. A. Armstrong, "Using Assessment Centres to Select Team Leaders," *Asia Pacific Journal of Human Resources,* Vol. 35 (2), 1977, pp. 67–79.

112. A. C. Spyychalski, M. A. Quinones, B. B. Gaugler, and K. Pohley, "A Survey of Assessment Center Practices in Organizations in the United States," *Personnel Psychology,* Spring 1997, pp. 71–90.

113. Robert V. Lorenzo, "Effects of Assessorship on Managers' Proficiency in Acquiring, Evaluating, and Communicating Information About People," *Personnel Psychology,* Winter 1984, pp. 617–634.

114. Barbara B. Gaugler, Douglas B. Rosenthal, George C. Thornton III, and Cynthia Bentson, "Meta-Analyses of Assessment Center Validity," *Journal of Applied Psychology,* August 1987, pp. 493–511; Joel L. Moses and Virginia R. Boehm, "Relationship of Assessment Center Performance to Management Progress of Women," *Journal of Applied Psychology,* August 1975, pp. 527–529; J. R. Huck and D. W. Bray, "Management Assessment Center Evaluations and Subsequent Job Performance of White and Black Females," *Personnel Psychology,* Spring 1976, pp. 13–30; and Neal Schmitt, Jeffrey R. Schneider, and Scott A. Cohen, "Factors Affecting Validity of a Regionally Administered Assessment Center," *Personnel Psychology,* Spring 1990, pp. 1–12.

115. Michael T. Brannick, Charles E. Michaels, and David P. Baker, "Construct Validity of In-Basket Scores," *Journal of Applied Psychology,* December 1989, pp. 957–963; Ted H. Shore, George C. Thornton III, and Lynn McFarlane Shore, "Construct Validity of Two Categories of Assessment Center Dimension Ratings," *Personnel Psychology,* Spring 1990, pp. 101–116; and Richard Klimoski and Mary Brickner, "Why Do Assessment Centers Work? The Puzzle of Assessment Center Validity," *Personnel Psychology,* Vol. 40, 1987, pp. 243–260.

116. Wayne F. Cascio and V. Sibley, "Utility of the Assessment Center as a Selection Device," *Journal of Applied Psychology,* April 1979, pp. 107–118.

117. Ann Marie Ryan and Paul R. Sackett, "A Survey of Individual Assessment Practices by I/O Psychologists," *Personnel Psychology,* Autumn 1987, pp. 455–488; Ann Marie Ryan and Paul R. Sackett, "Exploratory Study of Individual Assessment Practices: Interrater Reliability and Judgments of Assessor Effectiveness," *Journal of Applied Psychology,* August 1989, pp. 568–579; and Ann Marie Ryan and Paul R. Sackett, "Relationships Between Graduate Training, Professional Affiliation, and Individual Psychological Assessment Practices for Personnel Decisions," *Personnel Psychology,* Vol. 45, 1992, pp. 363–387.

118. James P. Guthrie and Judy D. Olian, "Does Context Affect Staffing Decisions? The Case of General Managers," *Personnel Psychology,* Summer 1991, pp. 263–292; A. K. Gupta, "Executive Selection: A Strategic Perspective," *Human Resource Planning,* Vol. 15, 1992, pp. 47–61; and M. S. Van Clieaf, "Strategy and Structure Follow People: Improving Organizational Performance Through Effective Executive Search," *Human Resource Planning,* Vol. 15, 1992, pp. 33–46.

119. S. Dakin and J. A. Armstrong, "Predicting Job Performance: A Comparison of Expert Opinion and Research Findings," *International Journal of Forecasting,* Vol. 5, 1989, pp. 187–194; and Mike Smith and Morton Abrahamsen, "Patterns of Selection in Six Countries," *The Psychologist,* May 1992, pp. 205–207.

120. Sara L. Rynes, "Who's Selecting Whom? Effects of Selection Practices on Applicant Attitudes and Behavior," in Schmitt and Borman and Associates (eds.), *Personnel Selection in Organizations,* pp. 240–274; J. W. Smither, R. R. Reilly, R. E. Millsap, K. Pearlman, and R. W. Stoffey, "Applicant Reactions to Selection Procedures," *Personnel Psychology,* Vol. 46, 1993, pp. 49–76; A. N. Kluger and H. R. Rothstein, "The Influence of Selection Test Type on Applicant Reactions to Employment Testing," *Journal of Business and Psychology,* Fall 1993, pp. 3–25; T. H. Macan, M. J. Avedon, M. Paese, and D. E. Smith, "The Effects of Applicants' Reactions to Cognitive Ability Tests and an Assessment Center," *Personnel Psychology,* Vol. 47, 1994, pp. 715–738; S. L. Rynes and M. L. Connerley, "Applicant Reactions to Alternative Selection Procedures," *Journal of Business and Psychology,* Spring 1993, pp. 261–277; and D. D. Steiner and S. W. Gilliland, "Fairness Reactions to Personnel Selection Techniques in France and the United States," *Journal of Applied Psychology,* April 1996, pp. 134–141.

121. Frank. L. Schmidt, "Personnel Psychology at the Cutting Edge," in Schmitt and Borman and Associates (eds.), *Personnel Selection in Organizations,* pp. 497–515; and A. T. G. McArthur and M. J. Young, "Discriminatory Constraints and Personnel Selection," *Asia Pacific Journal of Human Resources,* Spring 1992, pp. 11–24.

122. D. E. Terpstra and E. J. Rozell, "The Relationship of Staffing Practices to Organizational Level Measures of Performance," *Personnel Psychology,* Vol. 46, 1993, pp. 27–48.

123. Judge, Higgins, Thoresen, and Barrick, "The Big Five Personality Traits, General Mental Ability, and Career Success Across the Life Span"; Mount, Witt, and Barrick, "Incremental Validity of Empirically Keyed Biodata Scales over GMA and the Five Factor Personality Constructs"; J. M. Cortina, N. B. Goldstein, S. C. Payne, H. K. Davison, and S. W. Gilliland, "The Incremental Validity of Interview Scores Over and Above Cognitive Ability and Conscientiousness Scores," *Personnel Psychology,* Vol. 53, 2000, pp. 325–351; and McManus and Kelly, "Personality Measures and Biodata."

124. Schmidt and Hunter, "The Validity and Utility of Selection Methods in Personnel Psychology."

PART FOUR

Building Individual and Organizational Performance

9

Human Resource Development

HR Challenge

Since their introduction a few years ago, e-tickets have taken off at Mach speed, to account for 60 percent of all tickets sold by United Airlines by mid 2000. E-tickets were first introduced on United shuttle flights on the West Coast in late 1994 and by the end of 1995 were available for all domestic flights. Overseas markets were added gradually, and by the end of 1999, e-tickets were available to every United destination in the world. Paperless tickets save the airlines 50 cents per ticket. They are easier for customers, who don't have to worry about losing their tickets or waiting for them to be delivered. Itinerary changes can be made quickly, twenty-four hours per day. At check-in, customers have only to produce identification such as a driver's license or passport to claim their boarding pass.[1]

The advent of e-tickets created a pressing training need for the airline. United's 10,000 customer service agents around the world needed to learn to issue, modify, and process the new tickets, as well as to deal with customers who were unfamiliar with the new ticketing system. Errors in ticket processing could causes delays at check-in, problems with collecting payment for flights, reuse of the same ticket more than once, and ultimately disgruntled customers. The training mission was complicated by the fact that two different reservation and check-in systems were in use while e-ticketing was being rolled out—some airports had shifted to a Windows-like interface, while others were still using a command-line format.[2]

How do you suppose United Airlines dealt with the need to quickly train large numbers of employees at many locations to use e-ticketing with high reliability?

The training function, now popularly called **human resource development (HRD),** coordinates the provision of training and development experiences in organizations. This chapter examines the training process, which begins with the diagnosis of training needs and the establishment of clear objectives for training programs. The next step is to design and deliver learning activities that use appropriate methods and procedures to maximize the learning and subsequent job performance of trainees. Finally, training efforts are evaluated to see whether they met their objectives and were cost-effective.

HUMAN RESOURCE DEVELOPMENT: AN INTRODUCTION

Scope and Cost of Human Resource Development

In recent years, the scope of HRD has broadened from simply providing training programs to facilitating learning throughout the organization in a wide variety of ways. There is increasing recognition that employees can and should learn continuously, and that they can learn from experience and from each other as well as from formally structured training programs. Nevertheless, formal training is still essential for most organizations. Employers provide training for many reasons: to orient new hires to the organization or teach them how to perform in their initial assignment, to improve the current performance of employees who may not be working as effectively as desired, to prepare employees for future promotions and increased responsibilities, or, like United Airlines, to enable employees to deal with changes in the design, processes, or technology of their present jobs. Table 9.1 summarizes the specific types of training that American organizations with more than 100 employees report having provided to their employees in 2000. Computer applications training and new employee orientation were the most popular training topics. Various management and supervisory skills such as leadership, performance appraisal, interviewing, and problem solving were also commonly taught. Note that many organizations train employees about sexual harassment and diversity to reinforce the organization's policies with respect to fair treatment. Seventy-four percent of organizations provide "train-the-trainer" courses for superiors or peers who will in turn provide on-the-job training to others. About a quarter to a third of organizations surveyed provide remedial training in reading, math, writing, English as a second language, or welfare-to-work for employees who lack basic skills on hire.

Besides being one of the most important HRM functions, HRD is also one of the most expensive. A survey of American organizations conducted by *Training*

● **TABLE 9.1**

Percentages of Firms Providing Each Type of Training to Employees in 2000

Training Topic	Percent of Firms Providing
Computer applications	99
New employee orientation	92
Customer service	88
Leadership	81
Sexual harassment	81
New equipment operation	80
Performance appraisal	80
Team building	77
Safety	77
Problem solving/decision making	76
Train-the-trainer	74
Product knowledge	72
Public speaking/presentation skills	70
Hiring/interviewing	70
Quality/process improvement	67
Managing change	64
Technical writing	64
Strategic planning	61
Diversity	60
Wellness	57
Sales	56
Creativity	52
Ethics	48
Remedial math	35
English as a second language	30
Foreign language	28
Welfare-to-work transition	25

magazine revealed that in 2000, these organizations spent $54 billion on formal training for their employees.[3] This does not include the cost of training equipment or facilities, employee salaries during training, or the hard-to-quantify costs of on-the-job training and informal coaching. Organizations with fewer than 100 employees were not included in the survey, so the actual amount spent on training was probably considerably higher than $54 billion. The majority of training expenditures ($34.7 billion) went to training staff salaries, whereas $19.3 billion was spent on outside vendors of training programs and materials. Further information about the HRD profession can be found on the home page of the American Society for Training and Development at http://www.astd.org.

Strategy and HRD

Training can help an organization succeed in a number of ways. Ultimately, it is employee knowledge and skill that produce the organization's product or service. Training facilitates the implementation of strategy by providing employees with the capability to perform their jobs in the manner dictated by the strategy. Training also assists in solving immediate business problems, such as when a team of managers in an action learning program studies a real problem (e.g., "Why isn't the marketing campaign working as well as expected in Europe?") and recommends a solution. Finally, to keep ahead in a highly competitive and turbulent environment, it has been suggested that the training function must foster a continuous learning culture and stimulate managers to reinvent their corporation.[4]

Recent changes in the environment of business have made the HRD function even more important in helping organizations maintain competitiveness and prepare for the future.[5] Technological innovations and the pressure of global competition have changed the ways organizations operate and the skills that their employees need. The tight labor market of the late 1990s and early 2000s has increased the importance of training in several ways. First, higher employee turnover means that more new employees need training. Second, it has been suggested that frequent and relevant development experiences are an effective way to gain employee loyalty and enhance retention of top-quality staff.[6]

Training must be tailored to fit the organization's strategy and structure. For instance, an organization whose strategy involves providing exceptional service through a committed, long-service cadre of extremely well-qualified employees will need more complex training and career development systems than an organization that competes on the basis of simple, low-cost services provided by transient, unskilled employees. The latter will need a highly efficient new employee orientation and basic training scheme. Team-based high-involvement organizations find that extensive training in team skills as well as in individual job skills is necessary to make innovative organizational structures function as intended. When strategy changes, training is often needed to equip employees with the skills to meet new demands. For instance, Xerox Corporation decided to become "the document company," providing not just machines but also assistance in designing document-handling systems from start to finish. This meant that Xerox sales staff needed substantial additional training, a need that prompted Xerox to spend $7 million to expand the company training center to accommodate this new training need.[7] Case Corp., a manufacturer of farm equipment in Wisconsin, changed the role of its sales representatives in Europe from just selling equipment to dealers to acting as business consultants who help advise dealers on how to succeed over the long run. Careful thinking about the competencies required in this new strategic role resulted in new selection standards as well as development activities for current employees.[8]

Training is seen as pivotal in implementing organization-wide culture-change efforts, such as developing a commitment to customer service, adopting total quality management, or making a transition to self-directed work teams.[9] Pace-setting HRD departments have moved from simply providing training on demand to solving organizational problems. Trainers see themselves as internal consultants or performance-improvement specialists rather than just instructional designers or classroom presenters. Training is only one of the remedies that may be applied by the new breed of HRD practitioners.[10]

In an age of network organizations, alliances, and long-term relationships with just-in-time suppliers, leading companies are finding that they need to train people other than their own employees. Some organizations offer quality training to their suppliers to ensure the quality of critical inputs. Organizations with a strong focus on customer service may provide training for purchasers of their product. For example, 61 percent of respondents in the training industry survey in 2000 said they provided some customer education. Xerox trained members of the National Association of Quick Printers in the hope that nurturing success among small printing companies would eventually increase the demand for the printing equipment sold by Xerox.

A Systems Model of the Training Cycle

Because the objective of HRD is to contribute to the organization's overall goals, training programs should be developed systematically and with the organization's true needs in mind. However, often they are not. Instead, training objectives may be undetermined or hazy, and the programs themselves may not be evaluated rigorously or at all. In fact, it sometimes seems that what is important is that the training program is "attention getting, dramatic, contemporary, or fun. Whether or not [the program] changes behavior becomes secondary."[11]

One solution to this haphazardness is to develop training programs following an **Instructional Systems Design (ISD)** model like that presented in Figure 9.1. The model shows four phases: (1) needs assessment, (2) design and development of training, (3) delivery of training, and (4) evaluation of training. If each step is carefully implemented, effective and relevant training is likely to be the results. The rest of this chapter focuses on these phases of the training cycle. (See A Different Point of View on page 379 for a counterargument to the ISD approach.)

Note that systematically planning and implementing a training program involves more than just trainers. Figure 9.2 gives an example of a breakdown of

● **FIGURE 9.1**

An Instructional Systems Design Model

ASSESS NEEDS	DESIGN AND DEVELOP	DELIVER	EVALUATE
Assess training needs • Organizational analysis • Job and task analysis • Person analysis Develop training objectives	Design and develop training, applying knowledge of learning principles • Select training methods • Develop detailed content • Develop training materials • Pilot test training program • Train trainers	Deliver training	Evaluate training: Were objectives met? • Reaction • Learning • Behavior • Results

Modify and improve program

● **FIGURE 9.2**

A Summary of the Training Cycle

Source: Adapted with permission from the January 1987 issue of *Training*, The Magazine of Human Resources Development. Copyright 1987, Lakewood Publications, Inc., Minneapolis, MN (612) 333-0471. All rights reserved.

Steps	Management Actions	Training Department Actions
Management goals	Management decides that it wants to reach certain target markets using telemarketing techniques.	No decision making. Should actively pursue up-to-date knowledge of management direction and key goals.
Identify training needs	Makes a decision that a segment of the new agent orientation program should cover target markets and how to use telemarketing techniques to reach those markets.	Suggests and recommends ways that training might best be used. May identify areas that could best be learned on the job, recommend ways for line managers to support desired performance, etc.
Determine audience and training content	Hires new agents. Determines training schedule. Provides key people for training department to interview to determine training content.	Conducts a content analysis using interview and observation data. Recommends training content. Makes suggestions on prerequisite skills.
Design and deliver training	Communicates expectations to trainees prior to program, including on-the-job application of skills to be learned.	Provides advice on how to conduct precourse discussions with trainees. Designs and delivers a program that enables students to use telemarketing techniques to reach certain target markets.
Apply skills on the job	Gives specific assignments for new agents to use telemarketing techniques to reach certain target markets. Gives rewards for effort and results in this area.	Provides suggestions on how to follow through on and support the skills learned in the program.
Evaluate training outcomes	Determines if new agents are using the telemarketing techniques and if their performance shows that the techniques are helping them reach target markets.	Gathers specific data on the application of new skills. Provides feedback to management on revisions to training content, audience, precourse preparation, and/or supervision for application on the job.

management and HRD department activities as one organization moved through the training cycle from beginning to end. There is often yet another party involved, as many organizations use consultants in the development and/or delivery of training. The in-house HRD specialist may participate with a consultant in conducting a needs analysis and designing a customized program, which may be delivered either by the consultants or by trainers from the organization. In other cases, the HRD specialist may select off-the-shelf programs from outside vendors to meet the training needs he or she has identified.

THE NEEDS ASSESSMENT PHASE

Successful training begins with a thorough **needs assessment** to determine *which employees* need to be trained and *what* they need to be trained to do. Allison Rossett and Joseph W. Arwady state: "The question is not *whether* you will solicit this kind of information through needs assessment. It's *how much* of it you will do and using which tools."[12] The culmination of the assessment phase is a set of objectives specifying the purpose of the training and the competencies required in trainees after they complete the program.

Needs assessment takes time and money. Unfortunately, a great many organizations undertake training without this necessary preliminary investment.[13] Often there is little effort to predict future training needs or to determine if perceived needs and problems really exist and can be addressed properly by training. Not infrequently, an organization undertakes training as a knee-jerk reaction to a perceived problem or as a response to a popular fad in training programs. Training that is undertaken without a careful analysis of whether or not it is needed is likely to be ineffective and a waste of money. Inappropriate training also can sour the attitudes of trainees toward all organizationally sponsored training and reduce their motivation to attend future and perhaps more useful programs.

Purposes and Methods of Needs Assessment

An organization can use many methods of gathering information and several sources of information for needs assessment, as shown in Table 9.2.[14] The choice of methods and sources depends partly on the purpose of the training. If the purpose is to improve employees' performance in their present job, then clearly the trainer must begin by looking at present performance and identifying performance deficiencies or areas where there seems to be room for improvement compared to desired levels. Sources of information on performance deficiencies include supervisors' and clients' complaints, performance appraisal data, objective measures of output or quality, and even special performance tests given to determine the current knowledge and skill level of employees. In addition, HRD specialists might collect critical incidents of poor job performance and look at accident reports to locate possible skill or knowledge problems.

Individual or group interviews with superiors, incumbents, or even clients are another means of gathering information on performance discrepancies and perceived training needs. Group techniques are especially helpful for anticipating future training needs, for prioritizing training demands, or for ambiguous situations. A group of executives, for instance, might work together to predict and prioritize

● **TABLE 9.2**

Methods and Sources of Information for Needs Assessment

Methods of Gathering Data for Needs Assessment	Sources of Information
Search of existing records	Existing records (e.g., output, quality, waste, downtime, complaints, accident reports, requests for training, exit interviews, performance appraisals, equipment operation manuals, procedures manuals, job descriptions, hiring criteria, personnel files, competency models and profiles)
Individual interviews	
Group interviews	
Questionnaires	
Performance tests	
Written tests	
Assessment centers	Incumbents
Observation	Superiors
Collection of critical incidents	Subordinates
Job analysis	Subject matter experts
Task analysis	Clients

the new skills that will be needed by top managers in the organization over the next decade.

When a large number of potential trainees are involved, or when they are geographically dispersed, a subsample may be selected for needs assessment interviews, or a questionnaire on needs assessment may be developed for wider distribution. Typically, existing data will be scrutinized and some interviews will be held prior to designing the questionnaire. An important advantage of methods that involve large numbers of superiors and potential trainees in the assessment phase is that such early participation may enhance acceptance and commitment to the eventual training product.

Once the organization has identified a performance deficiency, the next step is to determine whether the deficiency should be addressed by training. In some cases, motivation, constraints, or poor task design cause the deficiency. In such situations, training in job skills would not solve the performance problem.[15] For instance, if the employee used to be able to perform as desired, he or she may simply need practice, performance feedback to facilitate self-correction, or a job aid (such as a checklist of steps) rather than full-blown training. If the employee could do the job correctly if his or her life depended on it, then motivation rather than skills or knowledge may be the problem. Perhaps good performance is being ignored or even punished, while poor performance is accepted without criticism. In these cases, the solution is to act on the environmental and reward system rather than to train the employee.

If training is being planned for current employees destined for promotion or transfer, needs assessment is more complex. The training specialist must measure the demands of the future job and then attempt to assess the ability of the employees to meet those demands. Because the employees being assessed do not yet hold the future job, their current level of performance may or may not indicate their ability to do the future job. Therefore, the training specialist may have to use special techniques to assess the employees' level of skill and knowledge relative to the demands of the future job. Such techniques include assessment centers (for candidates under consideration for management jobs) and tests or supervisory ratings of relevant abilities. Organizations that have developed and applied competency models to their managerial jobs (see Figure 4.5) are finding that measuring the developmental needs of managers against the requirements of future jobs is becoming easier and more systematic.[16]

When training is being designed for new hires, the methods used must be slightly different. Training is designed on the basis of a careful analysis of job content and the assumed characteristics of the trainees. If the trainees are not yet hired, it is difficult to assess their current level of knowledge. Thus the training specialist must coordinate closely with the staffing manager as the latter sets hiring criteria and evaluates candidates. For instance, the training specialist can design a more advanced training program for entry-level drafters if the staffing manager includes completion of a high school mechanical drawing course as a requisite job qualification. Similarly, the training specialist could consider scores on a job knowledge selection test given to applicants for the job of welder when designing post-hire training for this group.

Three Levels of Needs Assessment

Regardless of the specific methods used to evaluate needs, any thorough assessment effort must address three key areas: the organization, the job and tasks, and the individual.

● **Organizational Analysis**   **Organizational analysis** looks at the proposed training within the context of the rest of the organization. Table 9.3 provides a list of issues that may be explored in the organizational analysis portion of the needs assessment. A prime consideration is whether or not the proposed training will be

● **TABLE 9.3**

Issues in Organizational Analysis

- What are the training implications of the organization's strategy?
- How does this training program fit in with the organization's future plans and goals?
- Where in the organization is training needed?
- How are various units performing compared with expectations or goals?
- In which units is training most likely to succeed?
- Which units should be trained first?
- Can the organization afford this training?
- Which training programs should have priority?
- Will this training adversely affect untrained people or units?
- Is this training consistent with the organization's culture?
- Will this training be accepted and reinforced by others in the organization, such as the trainees' superiors and subordinates?

compatible with the organization's strategy, goals, and culture and whether employees will be likely to transfer the skills they learn in training to their actual jobs. Corporate-culture compatibility is especially important for management training and executive development. Efforts to train managers to lead, make decisions, or communicate in ways that are not valued or expected by powerful others in the work environment are doomed to failure.

The impact that the training of one unit has on other related units must also be considered in an organizational analysis. For instance, if the accounting group is trained to produce different measures of financial performance, then the other groups that either provide input to the accounting group or use the reports produced by this group also may need some orientation.

If training is to be provided to a large number of employees throughout the organization, the organizational analysis may ask which units should receive the training first. The answer may be the units that need it most. Alternatively, one may decide to begin with units known to be especially receptive to training in order to develop a record of success and a positive image for the training program before extending it to other units in the organization. When a cultural or value change is the aim of the training, it is usually a good idea to train from the top down, so that each group of trainees is managed by individuals who have already learned about and accepted the change. Quite often, the higher-level managers who were trained first become the trainers as the change is cascaded down the organization.[17]

The organization's future plans must also be considered. For instance, a training specialist would not want to plan a massive training effort for a product or process that top management plans to discontinue in a year or two. Finally, the availability of trainers, facilities, and financial resources and the priorities of competing training programs must be considered as part of the organizational analysis.

● **Job and Task Analysis** The duties and responsibilities of the job, together with the knowledge, skills, and abilities needed to perform them, are the focus of the second stage of needs analysis. Several approaches for analyzing jobs are available (see Chapter 4). Although any of these methods could be used as inputs into training needs assessment, the task inventory and critical incident methods are especially helpful. Task inventories can pinpoint specific tasks performed on the job, and the critical incidents method helps identify tasks that are not being performed correctly.

Once the preceding methods have identified the duties or tasks for which training may be needed, the next step is to develop a detailed analysis of each task. The purpose of this step is to verify that the task is important and should be the object of training and to develop in-depth information about the task knowledge and procedures that should be taught. The trainer will need to call on **subject matter experts** such as superiors and high-performing employees to generate **task analysis** information. Some of the questions to ask the experts are shown in Table 9.4. Written documents such as equipment instruction manuals and procedures manuals are another source of detailed task information.

● **Individual Analysis** The final level of analysis looks at the individuals to be trained. The **individual analysis** attempts to determine which employees should receive training and what their current levels of skill and knowledge are. The trainer may single out individuals on the basis of their past performance or select

● **TABLE 9.4**

Some Task Analysis Questions

> - How hard is this task?
> - Can it be learned on the job, or should it be taught off the job?
> - How important is it that incumbents be able to do this task from the very first day on the job?
> - What are the consequences of performing this task incorrectly?
> - What knowledge, skills, information, equipment, materials, and work aids are needed to do this task?
> - What signals the need to perform this task?
> - Exactly what are the steps in performing this task?
> - How can the incumbent tell if the task has been performed correctly?

an entire work group or all incumbents with a specific job title. Then the trainer assesses, or at least estimates, the skill and knowledge levels of the chosen trainees so that the training is neither too simple nor too complex.

Attention must focus on prerequisite basic skills as well as on existing job-related skills and knowledge. For instance, Hewlett-Packard Company conducted a training program on statistical quality control for a number of its employees. Later the company found that the employees were unable to use the techniques they had been taught. Careful investigation revealed that many of the employees were unable to do basic mathematics but had been too embarrassed to make this known during the training. To resolve this problem, the company offered a remedial program in basic math to 500 employees.[18] If a better individual analysis had been conducted before the quality control program was initiated, the trainer could have included basic math at the start of the course, and the employees would have been better prepared to benefit from the training. United Airlines eventually turned to CD-ROM training for the e-ticketing training need described in the HR Challenge at the start of this chapter. During a pilot test of the program, they discovered that some employees did not know how to use a computer mouse and had no idea how to navigate, or "surf," the learning choices in the program. They added tutorials on these topics to this program and all their other introductory computer-based training programs.

If individual analysis indicates a wide range of trainee skills and knowledge, trainers may wish to group employees into remedial and advanced groups. Alternatively, trainers could choose a training method that allows for self-paced learning or individualized instruction. Whenever possible, this kind of variance should be recognized and planned for before the training begins so that all trainees can have an appropriate and satisfying learning experience.

Identifying Training Objectives

The final step in the assessment phase is to translate the needs identified by the organizational, task, and individual analyses into measurable objectives that can guide the training effort. Training can be evaluated at four levels: reaction, end-of-training

A DIFFERENT POINT OF VIEW

Is the Instructional Systems Design Approach Obsolete?

Generations of trainers have been taught to follow a systematic training model such as that shown in Figure 9.1. Many organizations have their own versions of the model, with detailed requirements for the conduct, documentation, and approval of each step in the process of creating a training program from needs assessment through design, development, and delivery. Following a systematic model has been thought to ensure that no important steps are overlooked and that an effective training experience is produced and delivered.

Recently, however, a number of experts on training have criticized the Instructional Systems Design (ISD) approach, calling it obsolete, inefficient, overly prescriptive, and too rigid. They contend that in rapidly changing jobs and organizations, training is out of date by the time an instructional design team has completed all the steps. Critics also point out that ISD assumes that there is one best way to do a task, which can be discovered by appropriate task analysis and then taught to all trainees. In fact, it is not uncommon to find that equally effective performers approach and execute the same task in different ways, so training that imposes homogeneity is not always helpful. ISD can help produce reliable clones but is less well adapted to producing a creative, flexible, thinking work force that can solve nonroutine problems as they arise. With an emphasis on behavioral objectives and observable actions, ISD is better suited to teaching physical skills than sophisticated problem solving and judgment tasks, emotional competencies, or attitudes and values.

Further, especially in the case of executive education, training content isn't necessarily out there to be found so that it can be taught. All-knowing subject matter experts may not exist in a turbulent world, and executive training may be more effective if learners invent some of the content themselves. Diane Gayeski, professor of instructional design and training consultant, says, "We [trainers] need to be more like air-traffic controllers for spontaneous and indigenous organizational learning, instead of playing the role of pilot and tour guide who takes people to a predetermined performance destination."

Because ISD prescribes detailed steps, there is a tendency to evaluate program quality on the basis of how well the steps have been followed in the design of the program. This emphasis on getting the process right can drive out attention to getting the results right. Trainers should instead focus first and foremost on understanding the business need that the training is meant to address. Programs should be judged on how well they achieve the desired business result in the time frame allowed.

ISD was invented to serve the needs of military and industrial trainers who were developing programs to teach routine skills to large numbers of unskilled people in a stable work environment. It serves this purpose reasonably well. However, ISD may not always be the best approach to designing training in fast-moving, turbulent, and unpredictable organizational settings.

Sources: "Is There a Learning Curve in This Business?" *Training,* February 1999, pp. 28–39, quote from p.33; J. Gordon and R. Zemke, "The Attack on ISD," *Training,* April 2000, pp. 43–53; R. J. Torraco, "Integrating Learning with Working: A Reconception of the Role of Workplace Learning," *Human Resource Development Quarterly,* Fall 1999, pp. 249–270.

learning, on-the-job behavior, and results. Analogously, objectives can be written for each of these levels.[19] For instance, "reaction" refers to how the trainees felt about the training—whether or not it was interesting and satisfying. A reaction objective might be to have an average rating of 4 on a 5-point scale of trainee satisfaction. The opposite end of the evaluation continuum is "results"—that is, measurable outcomes at the group or organizational level. A results objective might be to reduce by 20 percent the total number of products that fail inspection.

Reaction and results objectives are not very useful for specifying exactly what must go on in the training program or what individual trainees must master. **Behavioral objectives** specify these critical requirements—that is, what the trainee will learn and how that learning will be demonstrated after training. A behavioral objective states *what* the person will be able to do, *under what conditions*, and *how well the person will be able to do it*.[20]

The following examples are *inadequate* behavioral objectives:

- Be able to perform as a project supervisor after training.
- Develop an appreciation of statistical quality control techniques.

These objectives fail to specify what behaviors the trainee will display at the end of the training or when the individual is back on the job. They also do not specify how well or under what conditions the trainee will be able to perform and so are not helpful in designing the training program. On the other hand, the following examples meet all the requirements for *good* behavioral objectives:

- Within one minute, point to the seven emergency exits on a Boeing 747 airliner.
- Within five minutes, strip a bed and remake it with clean sheets to hotel standards (hospital corners, tucked in tautly all around, top sheet folded over blanket, spread centered and one inch above floor all around).

With these behavioral objectives in hand, the training specialist can begin to design the training and simultaneously to plan the evaluation phase of the training cycle.

THE DESIGN AND DEVELOPMENT PHASE

Once the training specialist has identified training needs and prepared objectives, the next step is to develop a training program that will achieve those objectives. This is accomplished by selecting training methods and developing training materials that convey the knowledge and skills identified in the behavioral objectives. The later stages may involve pilot testing the program and training the trainers who will be delivering the program. The evaluation of the training program must also be planned before the training is delivered. In order to design an effective training program, it is necessary to understand how people learn.

Learning Principles

Nearly 100 years of research on human and animal learning have led to the discovery of a number of principles that underlie and facilitate the learning process. This section briefly examines these principles.[21]

● **Process of Learning**   Research by J. R. Anderson and others suggests that individuals go through three stages in learning to perform consistent tasks. (A "consistent" task is one in which most of the rules remain constant—for instance, in the task of typing, the keys are always located in the same place.) At each stage of learning a consistent task, different abilities are important and different teaching methods may be needed. In the first stage, trainees acquire what is called **declar-**

ative knowledge, the factual information and concepts relevant to the task. This has been referred to as "knowing what" about the task. Intelligence is important at this stage of learning, since there are high demands on memory and attention while learning about the task. Performance at this stage is slow and halting, with the learner concentrating and planning each step in the task. Errors are common, as facts or rules are forgotten or not yet learned. An example might be the early stages of learning to type, in which learners have to remind themselves of the "home" position on the keyboard and remember to press the space bar between words. With additional practice, learners pass through the second stage, called knowledge compilation. Facts and behaviors that go together are "chunked" into a routine, and parts of the task become better integrated. Performance improves and smooths out. In the case of typing, short commonly used words may be typed without the need to think about each letter individually.

When this stage is finished, the learners are at the final stage of procedural knowledge, where they not only "know what" but also "know how." Facts are organized into well-learned "if–then" rules that allow performers to apply their knowledge to carrying out task procedures fluidly. Much of the task can be performed automatically, with little attention or conscious thought. This frees mental capacity to think about unusual or more demanding aspects of the task. Psychomotor skills such as hand-eye coordination are often the most important abilities needed for performance in this final stage, which is referred to by some theorists as automaticity. To return to the example of learning to type, the final stage is reached when trainees are touch-typing without having to look or think consciously about the location of the keys. The extra mental capacity available can now be used to compose sentences while typing them.[22]

● **Preconditions for Learning**   For training to be most successful, two preconditions for learning—readiness and motivation—should be cultivated. Trainee readiness means that trainees possess the background skills and knowledge necessary to learn the material that will be presented to them. For instance, knowing basic math is a prerequisite for learning statistical quality control techniques. Some top U.S. business schools feel that several years of work experience constitute a prerequisite that enhances readiness to learn in M.B.A. programs. The other precondition for learning is trainee motivation. Ideally, trainees should see a need for the new skills and understand how successful training will benefit them. Although some learning can occur without motivation, learning is much more efficient if trainees want to learn. There are several ways to increase trainee motivation.

Research has shown that the attitudes and expectations of trainees as they begin a training program can affect their reactions to the program and the amount they learn.[23] Individuals who freely choose to attend a training program learn more than those who are required to attend.[24] Moreover, individuals who are committed to their careers and have engaged in career planning seem to respond better to training.[25] Organizations can influence the attitudes of potential trainees by involving them in the needs assessment phase and/or by giving them a realistic training preview—a synopsis of what they can expect from the training program and how it fits into their career plans.

Two additional ways to increase motivation are goal setting and self-efficacy enhancement. A number of studies have shown that when individuals set specific goals for themselves, they perform better than when they have no goals or vague goals.[26] For a long training program, trainees should have a clear picture of their final desired goal but should also set intermediate goals, allowing them to get a feeling of success and progress as they increase their mastery of different components of the training program. Recent research suggests that setting end goals or speed goals early in the declarative knowledge stage is not a good idea. The high levels of concentration needed at this stage leave little spare attention for goals. In later stages, speed goals are more appropriate.[27]

Self-efficacy expectations are simply one's beliefs that one will be able to perform a task successfully. These beliefs are a strong determinant of persistence and eventual success in learning difficult tasks.[28] Thus it has been suggested that trainers attempt to increase the efficacy expectations of trainees by (1) *persuasion*—telling the trainees that they can do it, that there is a high rate of success in the program; (2) *modeling*—showing the trainees (in person or on videotape) others like themselves who have succeeded in training; or (3) *enactive mastery*—causing the trainees to experience success in the early stages of training.[29] Since mastery is usually the most potent method of increasing efficacy expectations, trainers should structure early success opportunities into the training program and provide positive feedback on initial performance improvements.

In addition to the two preconditions for learning—trainee readiness and motivation—several other important learning principles must be considered in the design of a training program. These learning principles involve:

- Conditions of practice
- Knowledge of results
- Overcoming of interference
- Transfer of training
- Adult learning principles

● **Conditions of Practice**   Actively practicing the skill or task is essential for efficient learning and movement through the stages toward automaticity. Lack of opportunity for active, hands-on practice is a critical downfall of many training programs, especially those conducted in a classroom setting. United Airlines initially developed a classroom training program on e-ticketing. Trainers would log in to the reservations system and show trainees how to create an e-ticket. The training was not very successful, partly because there was not enough opportunity for trainees to actively use the reservation system or to practice their new skills on a variety of customer problems. After the training, there was no provision for trainees to get further practice or review their skills, except on the still-rare occasions when a customer arrived with an e-ticket. United subsequently switched to CD-ROM–based training on e-ticketing. The CD contained a simulated reservations system that allowed unlimited practice with a variety of e-ticketing situations, and trainee performance improved considerably.

The training designer must always ask "How much practice is enough?" and be sure to include at least enough to move trainees to the performance level specified in the behavioral objectives. Sometimes, however, practicing even more is desirable. **Overlearning** is practicing far beyond the point at which the trainee has mastered and performed the task correctly several times. Overlearning is particularly useful for critical tasks that are performed infrequently or under stress, such as cardiopulmonary resuscitation (CPR) or an airline crew's activities during a flight emergency. Overlearning should be used in training when the trainee is learning a task in which the first reactions must be absolutely correct. Overlearning is important for several reasons:[30]

1. It increases retention over time.
2. It makes the behavior more automatic.
3. It increases the quality of performance under stress.
4. It helps trainees transfer what they have learned to the job setting.

Another aspect of practice is deciding whether to have the **whole** task taught and practiced as one unit or to break down the task into separately learned and practiced **parts.** If the task is simple, it can be learned and practiced as a whole. If the task is complex, it probably should be broken down into component parts that can be taught and practiced as separate elements. For instance, the various aspects of issuing, changing, and checking-in an e-ticket would probably have been introduced and practiced to proficiency one at a time in United's program.

Another condition of practice that the trainer must consider is whether the practice should be **distributed** (divided into spaced segments with time or some other activity in between) or **massed** (scheduled in one long session). Cramming the night before an examination is an example of massed practice. Research has shown that when information must be remembered over a long period of time, distributed practice is generally better than massed practice.[31] Classroom training is often massed, as trainees are trained for hours or days on end after being brought into the training center. It is possible that some of United's problems with classroom training on e-ticketing stemmed from the massed nature of the training, whereas the CD-ROM training could be undertaken in shorter segments spread over days or weeks with regular work in between study sessions.

● **Knowledge of Results**   For effective learning to take place, trainees need to receive **feedback,** or **knowledge of results,** on how they are performing. Feedback is critical for both learning and motivation.[32] If feedback is not provided, trainees may learn the technique incorrectly or lose the motivation to learn. Feedback, because it makes the learning process more interesting for trainees, maximizes trainees' willingness to learn. Feedback is also necessary if goals for maintaining or improving performance have been set.

The trainer should plan to give plenty of feedback and encouragement early in the training program. At first, the trainer should praise any improvement at all. Gradually, as trainees' skills increase, the trainer should raise the performance level required to receive positive feedback. Later in the program, the trainer should teach trainees how to evaluate their own performance, and trainees should move toward reliance on self-generated feedback rather than feedback from others. This increases the likelihood that trainees will be able to continue to perform correctly when back on the job.

● **Overcoming Interference**   **Interference** occurs when habits and/or learning acquired prior to training make it difficult for the trainee to absorb new material. Interference is most severe when the trainee has learned a strong stimulus–response connection in the past and now has to learn a totally different response to the same or similar stimulus. One of the authors of this book experienced a great deal of interference when attempting to learn to sail a boat. Many years of daily horseback riding had established a strong connection between the stimulus "sensation of excessive speed" and the response "pull back on the reins." When the sailboat picked up too much speed, she automatically pulled back on the rope attached to the boom. Unfortunately, this action can be counted on to make sailboats increase speed and tip over. Despite understanding the principles of sailing and knowing that the correct response was to slacken the rope, the old habit of pulling back was almost irresistible.

Interference can be a special problem when the new correct response must be performed reliably under stress. Under stress, individuals have a tendency to revert to their old habitual responses. Suppose, for example, that an individual who learned to drive in the United States visited England and began to drive on the left-hand side of the road. In an emergency situation, the driver's strong habit of keeping to the right would probably take over.

The trainer should try to anticipate any inappropriate habits that trainees might bring with them to the learning situation and explicitly address them in the training program. To overcome interference, the trainer should clearly teach the principles underlying the new correct response and provide a great deal of practice to increase the strength and automaticity of the new stimulus–response connection.

● **Transfer of Training**   If learning that has occurred in the training session is not transferred to the job, the training program has been a waste of company resources. Many training programs have been criticized for their lack of impact on trainees' actual behavior on the job.[33]

Traditional learning theory recommends a number of ways to maximize **transfer of training.** Dealing mainly with training content and methods, these recommendations include maximizing the similarity between training and work settings, teaching the principles that underlie the practice being taught, building in time for overlearning, using a variety of job-related examples so that trainees can see how to apply the skill in a wide range of situations, and making sure that the material really is relevant to trainees' on-the-job needs. Besides these guidelines for training content and methods, organizations can follow a number of additional procedures to enhance transfer. Some of these occur during training, whereas others have to do with the pre- and posttraining environment.

During the training, the trainer should work on building trainee self-efficacy, since it has been shown that self-efficacy at the end of training predicts the extent to which trainees attempt to use their new skills when back on the job.[34] In addition, as trainees learn skills, the trainer should ask them to develop an action plan, including measurable goals, for performing the new behaviors back on the job. After the training, trainees should be encouraged to assess themselves against these personal goals on a regular basis.[35]

A model borrowed from addiction research has been adapted to facilitate transfer of training back to the job. Called the **relapse-prevention model,** its goal is to help trainees avoid relapsing into their old behavior patterns. This model suggests that training time should be devoted both to anticipating situations that could cause relapse and to planning strategies for dealing with these situations in advance.[36] For instance, if managers who have just been taught to use a participative leadership style expect a relapse to the old autocratic style when working under a tight deadline, they can plan how to avoid the relapse.

Back on the job, a number of factors can affect transfer. One important factor is the opportunity to perform trained tasks. If one is taught how to use a new computer program but does not have on-the-job access to the program for several months after the training, clearly some benefits of the training will be lost. One study of Air Force jet mechanics found that, on average, trainees had performed only about half the trained tasks in the four months following training. Some had performed only four of thirty-four trained tasks during this period![37]

Another key factor is the extent of support for the new behavior in the workplace. If superiors and peers do not accept or reward new behaviors by trainees, the new behaviors will be given up quickly or may not be tried at all. If superiors do not themselves receive the training, they should be briefed on what their subordinates are learning and how they can support use of the new skills. To facilitate transfer, trainees should be counseled both before and after the training by their immediate superior and receive encouragement to follow through with what they have learned.[38]

Whenever possible, groups or teams that will be working together should be trained together so that they can learn both the training content and how to apply it in the unique mix of personalities and abilities found in their own team. Training intact groups should also facilitate the development of group norms that support the new behaviors.

If a training program is held in several sessions over the course of weeks or months, trainees can be given homework assignments that require them to apply what they are learning to an actual work problem and report back at the next session. Some training programs are structured to include an initial classroom component, followed by an on-the-job application project and then a presentation of project results to the rest of the class and to higher-ups. (When applied to training managers, this is called *action learning* and will be discussed in more detail later.) This sequence ensures serious efforts to learn and apply the new skills to solving real-world problems.

Another method of enhancing transfer is to provide reminders or job aids to cue and to support performance. If employees have been taught time-management techniques, a cue might be a screen message to each computer user first thing in the morning asking, "Have you made your to-do list today?" A wallet card listing the steps in a systematic decision-making process or a template to lead the performer through a task would be examples of performance-supporting job aids.

A program for teaching continuous improvement techniques at Cummins Engine Company is a model of ensuring transfer of training through relevance, similarity to the work setting, practice, and building self-efficacy. In a five-day program, improvement teams spend the first day learning and practicing principles and techniques in the classroom. The second day is spent on the factory floor, analyzing a real problem or bottleneck in the manufacturing process. On the third day, the teams plan improvements to the process, and on the fourth day, they implement and assess these improvements. The fifth day is spent finalizing the improvement and then preparing and delivering a report to management about what they have done. The applied practice and high probability of success built into this program make it much more likely that graduates will apply continuous improvement methods back on the job than if they had been limited to classroom study of the topic.[39]

Trainers should plan as carefully for transfer of training as they do for the formal portion of the training. The key concept is **embedding.** Recent research clearly shows that training programs are more effective when they are thoroughly embedded in the work setting. Programs must be consistent with the organization's culture and values; be understood, sold to, and supported by trainees' superiors beforehand; and be reinforced by peers, superiors, opportunities, and reward systems afterwards.[40]

● **Adult Learning Principles**   Most instructional techniques are based on the well-researched science of teaching children, which is called **pedagogy.** Some educators believe that different techniques are more effective with adult learners. The science of teaching adults has been labeled **andragogy.** Andragogy is based on assumptions about key differences between adult and child learners. Malcolm Knowles has enunciated several differences that adult educators consider important. First, adults already have a great deal of knowledge and experience that they can learn from and share with others. Second, adults want to take responsibility for themselves and their learning. Third, adults are problem-centered; they want to learn things that have immediate usefulness in solving current problems.[41] These characteristics mean that adults may resent being treated like children in a learning situation. That is, when a trainer assumes that adults know very little, that their experience is irrelevant, and that they should learn exactly and only what the trainer tells them to learn, adults do not learn effectively. One author suggests that the best and brightest employees often avoid organizational training programs because these pedagogically oriented programs insult their intelligence.[42]

Andragogy suggests that learning should be active and student-centered rather than passive and instructor-centered. Instructor-centered teaching occurs when teachers decide what students should learn, present that content as they think best, and then test the learners' mastery of it. A student-centered approach allows learners to be involved in diagnosing their own training needs, picking their own learning goals and objectives, and even structuring their own evaluation, thus ensuring that trainees consider the program relevant.[43] Andragogy also recommends that training focus on real-world problems, perhaps through techniques such as case studies, role-playing, and action learning. Finally, andragogy acknowledges and uses the experience and knowledge that adults bring with them. Group discussions can be very effective in getting learners to share relevant experiences and to explicitly discover principles that they already know on an intuitive level. According to one adult trainer, "Never teach an adult something he or she already knows, and never tell a group anything you can get from the group itself."[44] The trainer should take the role of facilitator and resource person rather than all-knowing expert, providing input and guidance as needed when the group falters in its self-directed learning.

In recent years, the principles of andragogy have been challenged.[45] There is no concrete evidence that the learning process is truly different for adults as compared with children; some children respond well to student-centered learning, and sometimes adults prefer direction and instructor-imposed structure to self-diagnosis and personal responsibility for learning. Thus a pure andragogical approach is not always appropriate just because the learners are adults. For instance, it does not apply when the program teaches completely unfamiliar technical or physical skills or when the trainees have chosen to attend in order to learn from an acknowledged expert in the field. However, andragogical principles can contribute much to the design of management development programs and can be used in varying degrees to increase the motivation and personal responsibility of trainees in many kinds of programs. Switching between instructor-centered methods such as lectures and student-centered methods such as group discussion can help ensure relevance and maintain learner interest over the course of a long training day.

● **TABLE 9.5**

Characteristics That May Affect Optimal Teaching Style

1. **Instrumentality** Degree to which the trainee is concerned with the immediate applicability of the concepts and skills being taught.
2. **Skepticism** Degree to which the trainee exhibits a questioning attitude and demands logic, evidence, and examples.
3. **Resistance to change** Degree to which the trainee fears the process of moving to the unknown or the personal effects of that process.
4. **Attention span** Length of time the trainee can focus attention before substantial attentiveness is diminished.
5. **Expectation level** Level of quality (process) and quantity (content) that the trainee requires from the trainer or the training.
6. **Dominant needs** Range of intrinsic and extrinsic individual needs that currently drive the trainee.
7. **Absorption level** Pace at which the trainee expects and can accept new information.
8. **Topical interest** Degree to which the trainee can be expected to have personal (job-relevant) interest in the topic.
9. **Self-confidence** Degree to which the trainee independently and postively views him- or herself and thus requires high or low levels of feedback, reinforcement, and success experiences.
10. **Locus of control** Degree to which the trainee perceives that she or he can implement the training successfully back on the job with or without organizational support.

John Newstrom and Mark Lengnick-Hall suggest that two learning models, pedagogy and andragogy, are too few to cover the diversity of training situations encountered in organizations. They propose a number of characteristics of learners aside from chronological age that may influence which learning approach is most successful (see Table 9.5). For instance, they suggest that learners with short attention spans should receive a wide range of different teaching methods, whereas those with low self-confidence should be exposed to new material more slowly and with a chance for early success in an easy application. Highly instrumental trainees should receive minimal theory and plenty of opportunity to practice clearly job-related skills; low-interest trainees should be started off with graphic examples of how the training content can help them.[46]

In conclusion, all the above-mentioned learning principles must be considered in the design of training programs. If these principles are ignored, an effective training program is much less likely to result.

Training Methods

This section considers the choice of methods for employee training. With training objectives defined and learning principles in mind, the trainer must choose appropriate training methods and design the sequence of events in the training program. Perhaps the first decision to be made is whether to conduct the training on the job or away from the job. In many cases, the decision is to do some of both. Figure 9.3 diagrams two training options. In each case, the right circle represents

● FIGURE 9.3

Deciding Where and How to Train

(a)

Job Requirements ⌐   Initial Trainee
                      Knowledge and Skills ⌐

Formal off-the-job training

On-the-job practice, informal coaching

Already known

└ Formal on-the-job training

(b)

Job Requirements ⌐   Initial Trainee
                      Knowledge and Skills ⌐

Formal off-the-job training

Already known

On-the-job practice, informal coaching ⌐

└ Formal on-the-job training

what an employee already knows when hired. The left circle is what he or she needs to know to be a fully effective employee. If the person was hired because he or she already possessed some relevant skill and knowledge, there will be overlap between the circles, and this content need not be trained. The remaining area of job skill is what the employee must learn. Some aspects of this can be learned informally by on-the-job practice and informal coaching, whereas some should be taught formally. The formal instruction could be structured on-the-job training, off-the-job classroom training, or a combination of both. Figure 9.3(a) diagrams a job that is largely learned on the job, perhaps waiting tables in a pizza restaurant. Figure 9.3(b) shows a job in which more off-the-job training is required—perhaps tax-return preparation. The final increment in speed, confidence, and dealing with unusual nuances always happens with on-the-job practice, but many principles and laws must first be learned in the classroom.

● **On-the-Job Training**   Formal **on-the-job training (OJT)** is conducted at the work site and in the context of the actual job. The vast majority of all industrial training is conducted on the job, often by the trainee's immediate superior or a nominated peer trainer. On-the-job training has several advantages:

1. Because the training setting is also the performance setting, the transfer of training to the job is maximized.

2. The costs of a separate training facility and a full-time trainer are avoided or reduced.

3. Trainee motivation remains high because it is obvious to trainees that what they are learning is relevant to the job.

4. Trainees generally find on-the-job training more valuable than classroom training.[47]

A formal OJT program should be constructed as carefully as a classroom training program. Ideally, the supervisor or peer who acts as the trainer will be taught how to introduce and explain new tasks. The trainer should consider carefully the order in which to introduce new tasks and should use a written checklist and objectives for each stage of the training process.[48] Periodically, the trainer should give the trainee performance tests to ensure that the material is being mastered and to maintain trainee motivation through feedback.[49] **Job Instruction Training,** a procedure developed to train new defense plant workers during World War II, is outlined in Table 9.6. This is a proven and systematic way to teach a new task.

On the negative side, OJT may suffer from frequent interruptions as the trainer or trainee is called away to perform other duties. Moreover, what many organizations call OJT is really very little training at all. Employees are abandoned on the job and expected to pick up necessary skills as best they can. Often these employees are not informed about important but infrequent events (such as emergency procedures or annual maintenance) and may learn bad habits and unsafe procedures from coworkers.

● **TABLE 9.6**

Job Instruction Training Procedure

How to Get Ready to Instruct
1. Have a timetable. —How much skill you expect and when. 2. Break down the job. —List the important steps. —Pick out the key points. 3. Have everything ready. —The right equipment, material, and supplies. 4. Have the workplace properly arranged. —As you would expect the worker to maintain it.

How to Instruct	
Step 1: *Prepare the Worker* a. Put the worker at ease. b. Find out what he or she knows. c. Arouse interest. d. Place the worker correctly.	Step 3: *Try Out Performance* a. Have the worker perform the operation. b. Have the worker explain the key points. c. Correct errors. d. Reinstruct as needed.
Step 2: *Present the Operation* a. Tell. b. Show. c. Explain. d. Demonstrate.	Step 4: *Follow-up* a. Put the worker on his own. b. Encourage questioning. c. Check frequently. d. Taper off assistance.

Source: K. Wexley/G. Latham, *Developing and Training Human Resources in Organizations,* 2nd Edition (Figure 6.2 from page 150). © 1991 Addison Wesley Longman Inc. Reprinted by permission of Addison Wesley Longman.

On-the-job training is taking on increased importance as more and more organizations move toward **multiskilling** or **cross-training**, often in a team context. In these systems, workers first learn their own jobs and then learn one or more of the other jobs performed by members of their team. This provides more interesting work variety, allows for more flexibility in getting work done when team members are absent, and enables workers to better understand the entire work process—all of which are beneficial for continuous improvement and quality efforts. The majority of such cross-training is accomplished on the job using peer coaching and prepared self-paced learning materials (manuals, audiotapes, self-tests, etc.).[50] Another reason for improving structured on-the-job training is to comply with the quality certification requirements of ISO 9000. Companies wishing to be certified must document their processes, including those for assuring that employees have the skills needed to perform their jobs.[51]

Researchers have recently begun to explore informal learning on the job and are finding that sometimes unstructured learning from peers can be more effective than formally specified classroom training programs (see A Different Point of View).

● **Apprenticeship Training**   **Apprenticeship training** is a combination of on- and off-the-job training. The Department of Labor regulates apprenticeship programs, and often management and a union jointly sponsor apprenticeship training. Apprenticeship programs require a minimum of 144 hours of classroom instruction each year, together with on-the-job experience working with a skilled worker. These programs can last from two to five years, depending on the complexity of the skill being taught. Skilled trades that are usually learned through apprenticeship training include the bricklaying, sheet metal, carpentry, plumbing, and electrical trades. In 2000, there were 37,000 registered apprenticeship programs in the United States, serving 440,000 apprentices.[52] The federal government is placing increased emphasis on apprenticeship training programs to facilitate the school-to-work transition of young Americans. However, the rate of participation in formal apprenticeships is still very low in the United States compared with other developed Western nations.[53]

● **Off-the-Job Training**   **Off-the-job training** is conducted in a location specifically designated for training. It may be near the workplace or away from work, at a special training center or a resort. Conducting the training away from the workplace minimizes distractions and allows trainees to devote their full attention to the material being taught. However, off-the-job training programs may not provide as much transfer of training to the actual job as do on-the-job programs.

Many people equate off-the-job training with the lecture method, but in fact, a very wide variety of methods can be used. Table 9.7 lists a number of potential training methods and activities.

● **Selecting a Training Method**   Figure 9.4 shows the most commonly used instructional methods, based on a 2000 survey of U.S. companies with more than 100 employees. Note that the data represent the percentage of companies using each method in at least some of their training, not the absolute frequency of use across all training programs. The vast majority of organizations use live classroom instruction, workbooks/manuals, and videotapes in at least some of their training programs.

Communities of Practice and On-the-Job Learning

In a study by the U.S. Bureau of Labor Statistics, employees kept diaries for ten working days, recording any times they were "taught a skill or provided with information to help you do your job better." The results showed that, on average, 70 percent of employees' training time was spent in informal on-the-job training, with only 30 percent of training being "planned in advance with a defined curriculum." The authors concluded that informal training—employees sharing their skills and insights with each other—should be encouraged.

From the organization's point of view, informal training can be worrisome because there's no official record of it, there's no certification of learning or mastery, it may or may not actually occur for any given employee, and it's often hard to tell whether employees are helping one another with their work or just wasting time chatting.

Traditional good practice in training would suggest that when employees need to learn complex new skills, training experts should analyze the job carefully and then design, deliver, and evaluate a detailed training program. For instance, when Xerox decided to integrate the work of three separate customer service departments so that a single operator could solve all of a caller's problems, the formal training plan called for up to fifty-two weeks of full-time classroom training to teach each employee the jobs of the other two departments. Trainees would be taught how to deal with every possible problem that could come up in any of the three jobs; then they'd begin work and try to remember their many hours of instruction.

Instead of following this expensive plan, Xerox chose to experiment with informal peer training. Groups of six or seven employees from the three departments worked together in a common office space, each taking customer calls from the very first day. They helped one another learn the ropes by providing advice as and when it was needed. They also organized and taught a few brief classroom sessions when they felt a more systematic approach to a topic was required. The employees were astonishingly successful at teaching one another and found the experience "exhilarating and challenging."

The key idea driving the Xerox experiment is that "learning is social." People working together create a shared view of the world, develop their own intuitive understanding of job tasks, and can pass these intuitions on to others. In some cases the knowledge is so subtle and tacit that it cannot be abstracted into general principles and taught in the classroom. The technical term for groups that share information and develop unusual skills through their interaction is a **community of practice.** Often these cut across formal organizational boundaries. Ralph Volpe, manager of education and learning at Xerox, says, "If you can recognize and leverage the idea of naturally existing communities of practice, training gets better because you're not fighting human nature. Learning becomes more efficient and less expensive, and people like it better."

Shell Oil Company has successfully implemented learning communities in its Deepwater Division in New Orleans. The organization is structured around multidisciplinary "asset teams," each responsible for exploring and developing a different deepwater oil field. While this structure facilitates project work on each asset, it tended to isolate technical specialists from one another. For instance, there might be only one petrophysicist in each team. Learning communities were established to bring these specialists back together and facilitate their sharing technical knowledge and advising one another on complex technical problems. Each community is responsible for managing knowledge in its area. Members discuss current problems and systematize and disseminate the knowledge they generate. Shell estimates that just one of the sixteen communities saved the company as much at $120 million per year by reducing testing and drilling in sites not likely to be productive.

Sources: D. Stamps, "Communities of Practice," *Training,* February 1997, pp. 34–42; G. Benson, "Informal Training Takes Off," *Training & Development,* May 1997, pp. 93–94; G. Chao, "Unstructured Training and Development: The Role of Organizational Socialization," in *Improving Training Effectiveness in Work Organizations,* eds. J. K. Ford, S. W. Kozlowski, K. Kraiger, E. Salas, and M. S. Teachout (Mahwah, N.J.: Erlbaum, 1997), pp. 129–151; K. Dobbs, "Simple Moments of Learning," *Training,* January 2000, pp. 52–58; R. McDermott and J. Kendrick, "Shell Oil Company: Building Knowledge Sharing Communities," in *Linkage Inc.'s Best Practices in Knowledge Management and Organizational Development Handbook,* ed. P. Harkins, L. Carter, and A. Timmons (Lexington, Mass.: Linkage Inc., 2000).

● **TABLE 9.7**

Some Off-the-Job Training Methods and Activities

Action planning Often a closing activity asking participants to specify or set goals about exactly what they will do differently back on the job.

Behavior-modeling training Use of a videotape to demonstrate the steps in a supervisory activity (such as conducting a disciplinary interview), followed by role-played skill practice and feedback.

Behavioral simulation Large-scale multiperson role-play, noncomputerized business game.

Brainstorming Creative idea-generation exercise in which no criticism is allowed.

Business game Computerized business simulation that requires participants to make decisions about strategy and investments and then provides financial results based on the decisions.

Buzz group Small-group discussion of several minutes' duration on an assigned topic.

Case study From a one-paragraph vignette to a fifty-page Harvard-style case.

Demonstration

Experiential exercise

Field trip

Group discussion

Guest speaker

Guided teaching Drawing from the group the points the lecturer otherwise would make him- or herself.

Ice breaker Get-acquainted exercise.

Information search Asking trainees to locate the answers to questions in the training materials or manuals provided.

Intergroup exchange Small groups share their ideas or findings with another group.

Learning game Competition between teams in a quiz show format.

Lecture

Mental imagery Asking participants to close their eyes and visualize or recall something or engage in mental rehearsal of a physical or interpersonal skill.

Outdoor leadership training Team activities that may include hiking, rope courses, or other physical challenges along with problem-solving activities.

Pair and trio discussion tasks

Panel discussion

Problem-solving activities

Role-play

Self-assessment instrument or quiz An example is a conflict resolution–style inventory.

Team building A series of group activities and sometimes surveys used to develop team skills and role clarity in a team of people who must work together closely on the job.

Videotapes Can be used alone but are most effective if embedded in discussion and practice.

Given a wide range of possible training methods, how does a trainer select the best methods for a particular course? Clearly, one must consider the cost of the method, the number of individuals to be trained, their location and availability, and the skill and preference of the trainer. It is also important to consider trainee preferences, expectations, and likely reactions. Reactions to training content and methods vary across cultures, so training that will be presented in overseas locations requires special consideration (see the International Perspective box). An-

● **FIGURE 9.4**

Percentage of Firms Using Different Instructional Methods for Employee Training

Source: Reprinted with permission from the October 2000 *Training* magazine Industry Report. Copyright 2000. Bill Communications, Minneapolis, MN. All rights reserved. Not for resale.

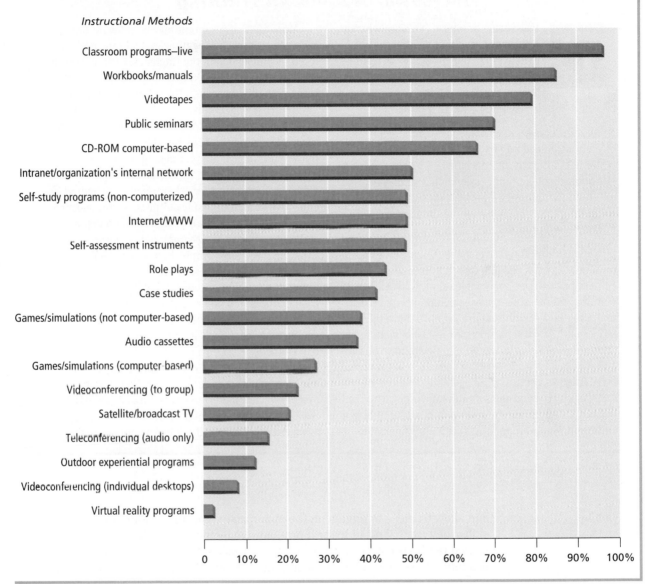

other decision is whether to deliver the training live and in person (about 73 percent of training in 2000), live via technology (as in videoconferencing, about 6 percent of training), entirely via computer (13 percent), or by other methods (9 percent) such as self-study using videos or workbooks.[54] Computer-delivered training will be discussed later.

Among the most important criteria in selecting a training method is its match with the training content. The methods chosen must convey needed information

INTERNATIONAL PERSPECTIVE

Intercultural Issues in Training

 Interesting problems can arise when a trainer or consultant goes on the road to deliver training programs to trainees overseas. Training programs that have been very successful in one country can be a disaster elsewhere for a number of reasons:

- Training content does not transfer across cultures.
- Content is acceptable, but the methods of delivery are not culturally appropriate.
- Norms about training session behavior may be different.
- Trainer's personal behavior may be inappropriate.
- Equipment problems may occur.

Especially in the case of management training, cultural assumptions and practices may mean that the content of a training program is simply wrong for that culture. For instance, it may be inappropriate to attempt to teach supervisors in a very high power distance country to use participative decision making. In these countries, the leader is supposed to have all the answers, and inviting subordinates to become involved is regarded as a sign of weakness and incompetence. Likewise, a program on how to give clear negative feedback in a disciplinary interview may be unsuitable in a culture in which saving face is critically important.

More often, the content may be relevant but the highly interactive and egalitarian training methods often recommended in the English-speaking West do not suit local learners. In high power distance cultures, subordinates generally will not speak out in a group with people of mixed levels or status—only the most senior person will speak. Trainers often like to stimulate vigorous debate, but this approach will fall flat when trainee status is unequal or in a culture that values harmony. Competitive games that pit one individual or team against another are also not suited to collective or high-harmony cultures. Active learning methods involving role-plays or other public practice methods can be very threatening in a culture sensitive to saving face. For example, behavior-modeling training is not well received in Hong Kong because of the substantial amount of role-playing involved. Learners from cultures that are sensitive to saving face and to power distinctions are often more comfortable with didactic methods such as lectures than with participative methods.

We have found that cultures seem to vary as to whether inductive or deductive methods are best for presenting new material. In the English-speaking West, we tend to present a theory first and then give some examples of how it might be applied (deduc-

and allow trainees to engage in the appropriate type and amount of practice for the skills they are trying to learn. For example, lectures, Web-based training, and assigned readings can be used to convey factual content, but they are inadequate for teaching physical or interpersonal skills. A group interaction method would be better suited for teaching interpersonal skills, whereas on-the-job training might be best to teach a physical skill.[55] Table 9.8 gives several examples of how training methods can be matched to training needs.

Often it is desirable to use different training methods at different points during the training process. For instance, the first step may require a method that is good for conveying information or an overview (lectures, videotapes), whereas later steps may require hands-on practice alternating with discussion of how one might apply the principles being taught on the job. Adult learners need variety and involvement, so methods should be as active as possible and change frequently over the course of a training day to maintain attention. Table 9.9 demonstrates how a tion). During a management development course in Brunei, it seemed that supervisors were confused when the theory was introduced first but caught on when several concrete examples preceded the presentation of a general principle (induction). A sensitive cross-cultural trainer should be prepared to switch strategies on noticing differences like these.

There are a variety of norms about training session behavior that differ across cultures. For instance, in Germany, training is *not* supposed to be fun; it is serious business. The trainer who opens a session with a joke and uses games as teaching aids quickly loses credibility. There are also norms about formality and punctuality. In much of Europe it would be impolite to call people one had just met by their first names. Titles are important, so name badges should show their wearer's company position as well as full name. In Germany, training sessions should begin and end on time and be clearly structured. In Spain, France, and Italy, time must be allowed for socializing and networking because relationships are very important in these cultures.

Trainers must behave in ways that are culturally appropriate. This may mean dressing more formally than they might for training sessions at home. Female trainers should dress very modestly in conservative countries (the Middle East, Asia). In Japan, teachers are very highly respected and must act in a way de-

serving of such respect rather than being casual and overly friendly. In cultures sensitive to saving face, the trainer should be careful not to put anyone on the spot by singling them out or asking for an answer before they have had time to prepare.

Finally, there can be equipment problems in cross-cultural training. Electrical systems differ, and high-tech training equipment may not be available or electrically compatible. We recall a training experience at a Chinese university in 1989. We thought our equipment needs were very modest but found that access to a copy machine was simply not possible and that obtaining an overhead projector was possible but not easy.

A clever international trainer will be prepared with back-up methods and activities in case the VCR does not work or the intended methods just do not seem to be getting through to the audience. The trainer will also do a lot of homework before traveling to learn as much as possible about the culture and organization in which he or she will be teaching.

Sources: P. S. Kirkbride and S. F. Y. Tang, "The Transferability of Management Training and Development: The Case of Hong Kong," *Asia Pacific Human Resource Management,* February 1989, pp. 7–19; G. Adler, "The Case of the Floundering Expatriate," *Harvard Business Review,* July–August 1995, pp. 24–40; and B. Filipczak, "Think Locally, Train Globally," *Training,* January 1997, pp. 41–48. See www.presentations.com for articles and tips on presenting in other cultures.

variety of methods might be used for different topics in a one-day training program on win–win negotiation.

● **Computer-Delivered Training**   As can be seen in Figure 9.4, a large share of firms are currently using computers in the training delivery process. **Computer-delivered training** has been developing rapidly since the earliest "teaching machines" of the 1960s. Programs range from text presentation to simple tutorials to sophisticated interactive programs that assess the trainee's initial level of competence and then provide a customized set of learning modules, exercises, and tests based on the trainee's performance.[56] **Multimedia** programs are now offered on CD-ROM, on company intranets, and on the Web. Multimedia training programs feature text, graphics, sound, pictures, and often videos and simulations. Hypertext links allow learners to move around the program at will to structure their own learning experience.[57] Computer-delivered training is used most often for

● **TABLE 9.8**

Matching Instructional Techniques to Training Needs

Situation/Requirement	Approach
Need to equip sales personnel with necessary product knowledge for the release of a major new product family two months from now.	Live instruction would appear to be the best choice. Experienced designers/instructors assigned full time can deliver the new program in the time frame available. (The really important question here is: Why was the training left until the last minute in the product development life cycle?)
FASBI098/99. New accounting regulations will require the controllers in each department in the organization to handle asset calculation and tracking in an involved new way. The new regulations go into effect in eleven months.	Complexity of topics prevents handling by means of a simple informational desk drop (as was done in support of the installation of new phone equipment last year). A majority of the controllers are on the corporate LAN, the requirement has almost a year of lead time, and this population has a track record of successful use of self-study approaches—the discipline is there. CBT (computer-based training) software running on the LAN will furnish satisfactory instruction in this case. A version of the CBT for stand-alone PCs will provide for those not on the LAN.
A continuing need to orient new hires to the culture of the organization, its vision of the future, its strategies, and geographic circumstances. Hire rate: 130 people per month, in seven different HR centers around the world.	The training job here is to design something that can be handed off for use in the seven HR centers as part of their new-hire intake process. The material may well include a videotape of the organization's president talking about the organization's culture and values. An advantage of this is that the tape can be dubbed in all the needed languages; the acculturation demands, however, preclude solely videotape. Live instruction will be necessary, including the involvement of local senior management as guests. Materials will have to include a full-scale Leader's Guide for the host facilitator, written to the lowest level of detail, in all the right languages, and thoroughly tested before release.
Incoming clerical staff in the Indianapolis Operations Center consistently need work on basic skills: math, writing, reading, keyboarding, word processing.	Needed programs can be bought off the shelf, both self-study materials and live instruction. No need to reinvent these wheels. A mix of programs will allow the Indianapolis Center to provide employees with the approach that best suits their learning styles and preferences. Self-study modules also may serve as prework or reinforcement for live programs where this makes sense.
New middle managers need to learn the core job requirements of being the managers of managers, particularly with regard to (a) policy demands concerning performance management, and (b) the value and use of employee attitude surveys.	Some of the need here may be simply informational and can perhaps be met by simple lecture, live or mediated. Learning about performance and appraisal, however, requires hands-on skill practices. Major portions of this learning requirement can be met only by live, interactive instruction, with people working in classroom groups where skills practice and peer/instructor feedback are possible.

Source: From *Training for Organizations*, 2nd edition, by B. N. O'Connor, M. Bronner, and C. Delaney © 1995. Reprinted with permission from South-Western Educational Publishing, a division of Thomson Learning. Fax 800-730-2215.

● **TABLE 9.9**

Outline for a Training Program on Win–Win Negotiating

Activity	Time (minutes)	Method
I. Opening activities		
A. Agenda review	5	Presentation
B. Things we have in common	30	Icebreaker
C. Interactive overview of conflict resolution	45	Intergroup exchange
II. What you bring to conflict situations		
A. Feelings about conflict	20	Physical continuum
B. Looking at your conflict style	20	Game
C. Assessing your conflict style	30	Questionnaire
D. Experiencing different approaches to conflict	30	Role play
E. Conflict behavior is situational	10	Checklist
F. Misunderstandings in conflict situations	15	Lecturette
G. Viewing others objectively	15	Writing task
III. Conflict-resolution effectiveness		
A. Stating complaints and requesting change	30	Skills practice
B. Anatomy of an argument	30	Information search
C. Dealing with difficult people	25	Mental imagery
D. Reframing conflict scenarios	20	Dyadic discussion
E. The steps of negotiation	45	Skills practice
F. Putting it all together	30	Role play
G. What to do when negotiation fails or never gets started	20	Intergroup exchange
IV. Closing activities		
A. Action planning	30	Writing task
B. Obstacle assessment	20	Mental imagery

Source: From M. Silberman's *Twenty Active Training Programs.* Copyright © 1992 Pfeiffer/Jossey-Bass. Reprinted by permission.

individual training in a self-paced format, although many organizations also apply the technology in learning labs with a tutor present.

There are many advantages to delivering training with computers, in terms of logistics, cost, and efficiency of learning (see Table 9.10). United's CD-ROM program for e-ticketing efficiently and quickly disseminated training to employees all over the world. Some of the keys to success were the simulated reservations system that allowed for active practice and the embedding of video clips on dealing with difficult customers in the body of the training. This equipped trainees to deal with both the human and the technical sides of e-tickets.

Rockwell Collins, a manufacturer of instruments and communication systems for aircraft, expects to realize similar benefits from a shift to high-tech training methods. The Cedar Rapids–based company has 14,000 employees in forty-two domestic locations and fifteen overseas offices. In 1998, it found that the half of its employees who worked in Cedar Rapids received the lion's share of the training and that many employees throughout the company reported that they had been

● **TABLE 9.10**

Advantages of Computer-Delivered Training

Logistical Advantages

- Training can be conducted at remote sites and on all shifts.
- Training can be fit into lulls in the work schedule that would otherwise be unproductive.
- Employees can be trained at their desks so they are available to handle urgent work problems if needed.
- Trainer costs are very low once the program is established.
- Trainee transportation and lodging costs are nonexistent.
- There is consistent quality of instruction over time and from group to group, unlike programs relying on several in-person trainers.
- Changes and updates can be distributed to all sites very quickly.
- Very large numbers of people can receive the training at the same time.
- Electronic systems for keeping records on who has commenced and/or completed which training programs can be automatically updated.

Learning Advantages

- It is self-paced, and the average time to complete a learning unit is up to 30% faster than when the same material is presented using traditional classroom methods.
- Some programs provide immediate assessment and feedback.
- Interactive programs can provide remedial and customized instruction according to each learner's needs.

Source: Based on Stephen Schwade, "Is It Time to Consider Computer-based Training?" *Personnel Administrator,* February 1985, pp. 25–35. Reprinted by permission of the author.

unable to attend or complete classroom training sessions due to the demands of their work. To improve the availability and convenience of training for employees at all locations, Rockwell Collins has made a commitment to deliver 70 percent of all training via technology by 2003. The company plans to use self-paced Web-based programs, CD-ROM programs in learning labs, and live training in online virtual classrooms. They anticipate that training offerings will be increased by 40 percent while delivery costs will decline by $14,000,000 over three years.[58]

It has been suggested that computer-delivered training is ideal for work forces with high diversity in age, learning speed, and skill, which could cause difficulty in a traditional classroom setting.[59] There is some evidence that training time can be reduced with computer-delivered training, as more knowledgeable trainees can skip sections they know and progress more quickly than they could in a classroom. In some ways, computer-delivered training in its advanced forms is consistent with the ideals of andragogy in that it is self-paced and tailored to the individual learner; in addition, employees can choose to view a training module when they feel the need for it in solving a current job problem. Training can be "just in time" rather than "just in case" and thus can be much more relevant. As more and more employees work on computers on a daily basis, days-long off-the-job training programs may be replaced by a large menu of short, on-demand tutorials or access to expert systems to help employees solve current problems or refresh skills needed at the moment. These systems are called **performance support systems** and are rapidly increasing in popularity.[60]

Will computers replace trainers? The demise of the traditional training room has been predicted (wrongly) since the first primitive teaching machine was developed decades ago. Experts, however, are once again confident that an increasing share of training will be delivered by sophisticated technology and that face-to-face training will decline.[61] The e-learning market is expected to quadruple between 2000 and 2005. KPMG has gone from 90 percent classroom to 70 percent electronic training in the past few years. The company says that classroom training is too expensive and too slow to keep their people worldwide up to date on the latest things they need to know.[62]

However, there are disadvantages to computer-delivered training. The start-up costs for equipment can be high. Custom-designed multimedia packages can be expensive and time-consuming to develop, though improved authoring programs are reducing these problems. Some commercially available online training programs are very good, but many are little more than text on a screen.[63] When employees are offered the opportunity to take commercial or university-based courses online, there are often problems with quality of instruction, choosing among the many programs available, and flagging learner motivation.[64] There are also concerns that employers may "require" employees to complete online training programs on their own time, without the compensation that may be legally due to them.[65]

Most experts agree that computer-delivered training is well suited to information dissemination but much less effective for teaching soft or interpersonal skills. For some types of content, a live instructor is essential, as is the opportunity to engage in role-played practice. For instance, Steelcase, a large office furniture manufacturer, decided that computer-delivered training did not meet its need for training salespeople because the skills needed were largely interpersonal.[66] Networking and learning from one's peers are also features of live training sessions that are unlikely to be duplicated by computers. In these cases, if computers are used at all, they may be part of a larger classroom experience, serve as prework for classroom training, or provide refresher training on demand following a live program.[67]

Management Development

Because managerial work is important, complex, and challenging, many organizations provide regular management training. Training for executives, managers, and supervisors accounted for 64 percent of training dollars spent in 2000, despite the fact that there are many more nonmanagerial employees than managers.[68] The results of all this training, however, are not always clear because management development programs are seldom evaluated rigorously. A comprehensive review of the evaluations that have been done concluded that many types of management development programs do have a beneficial impact on job behavior.[69] Among these programs, those that provide carefully designed training linked to a thorough needs assessment should be more effective than faddish programs purchased from vendors of canned, one-size-fits-all management development packages.

Figure 9.5 reflects research showing that managers learn their craft in a number of ways. Most say that they have learned the greatest amount not through studying for university degrees or from company-sponsored management training, but from actually doing the job and interacting with others in the work environment. Managers say that the most intense learning occurs from job assignments that are very difficult and challenging, such as building a new start-up operation or

● **FIGURE 9.5**

How Managers Learn

University Education

Work Role
- Regular job
- Special projects
- Job rotations
- Unusual job events or demands

MANAGERIAL LEARNING

Formal Training and Development
- In-house courses
- External short courses

Work Relationships
- Coach, mentor
- Role model
- Experts
- Networks

turning around a failing operation; from assignments that represent a major change or increase in responsibility, such as moving from a staff to a line position, moving to a different functional area, or moving to a job with greatly increased responsibilities for people, dollars, or units; and from hardships, such as a personal or business failure or dealing with very difficult individuals. Thus a complete program of management development should include a job assignment and succession system that continuously presents new challenges.[70]

Formal training of supervisors and junior managers is often done by in-house trainers or by training consultants. These employees may need basic skills in planning, leading, organizing, and controlling. Methods such as lectures, behavior modeling training, case studies, behavioral simulations, experiential exercises, and role-plays are commonly used. Table 9.11 shows a management development curriculum for four levels of managers in a large Australian banking organization. Mentoring is also important to new managers. Some mentorship relations develop informally, while other companies assign more senior managers to coach one or more junior managers on their job performance and advise them on career plans.[71]

Higher-level managers and executives usually have basic managerial skills already and need a qualitatively different type of development. Table 9.12 summarizes some recent trends in state-of-the-art executive development.[72] Mini-M.B.A. and similar programs that focus on teaching functional skills such as accounting and marketing have been on the decline for the past decade. In their place are customized in-house programs that are closely tied to important business needs, including managing change and strategic leadership. Many of the largest and most successful organizations have what amounts to their own "university," such as General Electric's Crotonville Management Development Institute in New York State.

Another trend over the past ten years is the use of **competency models**. Competency models are carefully derived organization-specific lists of the skills or

● **TABLE 9.11**

The Management Development Curriculum at Westpac Banking Corporation

Topic	Supervisor Level	Manager Level	Manager of Managers Level	Executive Level
Achieving results	Supervising for peak performance	Managing for performance	How to run a business	Strategic human resource management Strategic planning
Managing change	Thriving on change	Change management	Change management	Managing change
Leading and motivating	Supervision: the people factor	Leading the team HR practices for managers	Generating commitment	Tapping group energy
Evaluating performance	The appraisal equation	Investing in the appraisal interview	Evaluating team performance	Performance plus
Developing subordinates	Coaching: a partnership approach	Development planning	Identifying management potential Developing and selecting managers	Reviewing and developing executive talent
Communicating	The communicating manager	Communication: involving the team	Influencing others	Strategic management of communication
Promoting relationships	Working relationships one to one	Team building	Teamwork/conflict resolution	Teamwork, cooperation, and conflict resolution
Negotiating		Negotiate to win	Advanced negotiate to win	Negotiations for executives

Source: Westpac Banking Corporation, in *Training Australians: A Better Way of Working* (Melbourne: Business Council of Australia, 1990), pp. 30–31. Reprinted by permission of the Business Council of Australia.

competencies needed to manage effectively in that organization. The models are used to integrate HR practices, so that selection, performance appraisal, 360-degree feedback instruments, and training programs are all aimed at building the same essential skills. Managers understand the competencies valued by their organization, receive appraisal and 360-degree feedback on their possession of these competencies, attend formal training programs aimed at improving key competencies, and can engage in self-directed learning or receive individual coaching to build their standing on specific competencies.[73]

● **Action Learning**   An increasingly common method of middle- and upper-management development combines on- and off-the-job learning in innovative ways. The term **action learning** was coined by Reg Revans in Great Britain over thirty years ago, and his approach has become increasingly popular in the United States over the past decade. The underlying idea is that formal training is good at conveying **programmed knowledge** (facts) but poor at teaching **questioning insight** (the ability to seek out and use knowledge to solve complex problems in

● **TABLE 9.12**

Trends in State of the Art Executive Development

There is less:

Use of university-based programs and mini-M.B.A.'s

Focus on functional knowledge (marketing, accounting, finance)

There is more:

Use of personal coaches

Emphasis on customized, in-house programs and corporate universities

Emphasis on strategic leadership and change management

Use of 360-degree feedback programs to motivate learning and build learning experiences customized to individuals

Use of action learning

Training driven by strategic and business needs

Training of entire top management teams

Use of executives as trainers rather than professors or training specialists

Cascading of training from top down

Use of multicompany consortia for developing top talent

Use of competency models to drive an integrated program of selection, appraisal, and training

innovative ways), yet it is the latter that is most crucial for managerial success. Action learning programs usually feature some classroom instruction together with an applied project tackled by a team of trainees. They investigate and solve a real organizational problem that is outside their area of expertise and very complex. They struggle to analyze the problem—learning from fellow trainees and tutors, collecting data, and reading from the literature as necessary—to discover a solution. In the process, they develop specific managerial competencies along with learning how to learn.[74]

A typical action learning program begins with a week of classroom instruction followed by a two-week to three-month period during which the action learning project is undertaken (full or part time). Additional classroom work may be interspersed if trainees discover they have a need for a certain kind of formal input. The final classroom segment involves trainees' presentations of their project work, usually to an audience of senior executives.[75]

New Employee Orientation

A very common type of training is new employee orientation. All employees, whether managerial or nonmanagerial, should be provided with a systematic orientation when they first join an organization. Newcomers have much to learn about their supervisors and coworkers, the demands of their job, company rules and procedures, and the organization's culture and assumptions. Until employees learn enough to feel comfortable in these areas, they can experience uncertainty and stress.[76]

A thorough introduction to the organization's culture and mission is especially important when employees must convey the culture to clients through their actions. For example, new hires ("cast members") at Walt Disney World in Orlando, Florida, spend their first day and a half at Disney University taking a course called Traditions 1. They learn about the history of the company, the special language used, and the importance of cheerful and informative interactions with guests.[77]

Employees usually say that their best source of information about the organization is coworkers. Thus, if at all possible, newcomers should be assigned a "buddy" or be given a position in which they have plenty of access to friendly coworkers.[78] In addition, the organization should provide one or more orientation sessions. Some organizations simply give a presentation on employee benefits. Such material is often confusing, however, and it is seldom of immediate value to the employee. Newcomers are much more interested in learning the formal and informal rules that govern daily behavior on the job than in learning how to fill out insurance claim forms. Thus organizations would do better to save benefits presentations until after new employees feel comfortable in their jobs and have attention to spare.

A more relevant new employee orientation might feature two parts: (1) an introduction to the specific job and department, provided by the supervisor, and (2) one or more sessions of general orientation to the company, coordinated by the HRM department. Supervisors should be trained to orient new employees and should use a checklist to be sure that they cover all important points. Table 9.13 lists sample contents for both parts of the orientation process.[79]

●TABLE 9.13

Content of a Two-Phase New-Employee Orientation System

Administered by the Supervisor	Administered by a Trainer, with Guest Appearances by Company Leaders
About the department: 　Relationships to other units 　Mission and goals 　Procedures 　Work flow 　Facilities 　Schedule 　Introduction to coworkers About the job: 　Workstation 　Duties 　Goals/performance standards 　Tools and equipment 　Where to go, whom to ask for help 　On-the-job training Human resource issues: 　Performance appraisal process 　Promotion criteria 　Salary increase schedule and criteria 　Training plans	About the organization: 　History 　Products 　Goals 　Organization structure 　Who's who in the organization 　Culture, ethical principles Rules and procedures: 　Employee handbook 　Work hours 　Vacation and leave 　Provision of pay and benefits 　Discipline system 　Complaint/suggestion systems

Source: Based on G. Dessler, *Personnel Management* (Reston Va.: Reston Publishing Company, 1984), pp. 223–277.

A good orientation program can help employees feel comfortable and become competent in their jobs quickly. It may also help to increase loyalty and reduce turnover among newcomers.[80] Another important aim of an orientation program is to teach newcomers the ethical norms, beliefs, and attitudes that prevail in the organization. The organization's values and guiding principles can be communicated explicitly through formal presentations and implicitly through organizational stories and myths. For example, telling a story about an organizational hero who defied authority to do what was "right" can send a powerful message. The goal is to convince new employees that the values they are being taught are not just window dressing but represent the values and beliefs of the organization's leadership—the tone at the top of the organization.

THE EVALUATION PHASE

The third step in the Instructional Systems Design model (see Figure 9.1) is to deliver the training that has been designed in the second step to meet the needs identified in the first step. We will not discuss delivery specifically in this chapter but will proceed to the final step in the training cycle, which is **evaluation.**[81] Evaluation is the determination of the extent to which the training activities have met their goals. Unfortunately, the evaluation is often done poorly or ignored altogether. One reason for this is that managers simply tend to assume that training will work. Another is that a manager who champions a training program may feel threatened by the prospect of an objective evaluation of the program's effectiveness.[82]

The basic approach to evaluation should be to determine the extent to which the training program has met the objectives identified prior to the training. Planning for the evaluation should start at the same time that planning for the training program begins. If the goals of the program are clearly stated as specific objectives, the appropriate evaluation method can be implemented at the same time as the program.

Evaluation Levels and Purposes

Donald Kirkpatrick developed the best-known and most widely used framework for the evaluation of training programs.[83] **Kirkpatrick** identified the **four levels of evaluation** shown in Figure 9.6. Each level answers a very important but different question about the effectiveness of the program.

● **Reaction** The first level involves **reaction measures,** or the participants' feelings about the program. Reaction information is usually gathered by questionnaire during or immediately after the program. At least two aspects of reaction should be assessed: Did the trainees *enjoy* the program, and do they think the program will be *useful* to them. Figure 9.7 shows the training evaluation questionnaire used by Black & Decker in their Eastern Hemisphere locations.

● **Learning** The second level of evaluation has to do with learning. **Learning measures** assess the degree to which trainees have mastered the concepts, information, and skills that the training tried to impart. Learning is assessed during

● **FIGURE 9.6**

Kirkpatrick's Four Levels of Training Evaluation

Source: Reprinted with permission from the November 1983 issue of *Personnel Administrator*, copyright, 1983, the Society for Human Resource Management, Alexandria, VA.

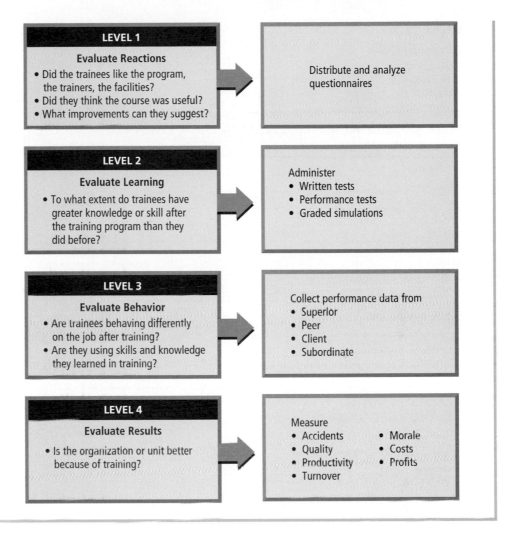

LEVEL 1

Evaluate Reactions
- Did the trainees like the program, the trainers, the facilities?
- Did they think the course was useful?
- What improvements can they suggest?

Distribute and analyze questionnaires

LEVEL 2

Evaluate Learning
- To what extent do trainees have greater knowledge or skill after the training program than they did before?

Administer
- Written tests
- Performance tests
- Graded simulations

LEVEL 3

Evaluate Behavior
- Are trainees behaving differently on the job after training?
- Are they using skills and knowledge they learned in training?

Collect performance data from
- Superior
- Peer
- Client
- Subordinate

LEVEL 4

Evaluate Results
- Is the organization or unit better because of training?

Measure
- Accidents
- Quality
- Productivity
- Turnover
- Morale
- Costs
- Profits

and/or at the end of the training program with paper-and-pencil tests, performance tests, and graded simulation exercises.

● **Behavior**   On-the-job behavior is the third level of evaluation in Kirkpatrick's approach. **Behavior measures** ask whether employees are doing things differently on the job after training, whether they are visibly using what they have been taught. In essence, this is transfer of training. On-the-job behavior can be assessed by any of the performance evaluation techniques discussed in Chapter 11. Behavior ratings can be collected from the superior, peers, subordinates, or clients of the trained employees.

● **Results**   The final level of evaluation involves **results measures.** At this level, the impact of the training program on the work group or organization as a whole is assessed objectively. The appropriate objective measures to use depend on the content and objectives of the training. Sample measures of results include cost savings, profit, productivity, quality, accidents, turnover, and employee attitudes.

● **FIGURE 9.7**

Training Evaluation Form

Source: Reprinted with the permission of The Black & Decker Corporation.

BLACK & DECKER	TRAINING EVALUATION FORM
EASTERN HEMISPHERE	

NAME OF PARTICIPANT :	(OPTIONAL)	Scale	1 Poor
COURSE TITLE :			2 Fair
COURSE PROVIDER :			3 Meet Expectations
INSTRUCTOR (S) :			4 Exceed Expectations
COURSE DURATION : _____ TO _____			5 Outstanding

1. CONTENT   *Please circle your response*

To what extent did this course meet your learning objectives?   1   2   3   4   5

Remarks: _____

2. TRAINING METHODOLOGY

a) lectures/exercises were comprehensive & appropriate   1   2   3   4   5

b) visual aids reinforced the learning   1   2   3   4   5

c) handouts/manual were well written & will be a useful reference   1   2   3   4   5

Remarks: _____

3. INSTRUCTOR EFFECTIVENESS

a) was well prepared and organised   1   2   3   4   5

b) able to communicate the concepts & impart skills effectively   1   2   3   4   5

c) encourages participation and learning in class   1   2   3   4   5

Remarks: _____

4. OVERALL RATING OF THE COURSE   1   2   3   4   5

5. Would you recommend this course to others in the organisation?   (   )Yes   (   ) No   (   )Maybe

Remarks : _____
(Please suggest names/designation where appropriate)

6. COMMENTS

Which three(3) aspects of the course were most helpful? In what way was it most helpful?

_____
_____
_____

Which three(3) aspects of the course could be improved? Please elaborate.

_____
_____
_____

Additional Comments

_____
_____

To be filled in by the Immediate Supervisor(for external programs)

7. SHARING OF LEARNINGS   [   ] not applicable

[   ] will share his/her learnings with at least one colleague

[   ] will share his/her learnings in the department meeting

SIGNATURE OF IMMEDIATE SUPERVISOR   DATE

Kirkpatrick suggests that the last three levels of evaluation may form a hierarchy. Change farther up the hierarchy of outcomes is unlikely unless change has occurred lower in the hierarchy. That is, if no learning has occurred, it is unlikely that on-the-job behavior will change. If behavior does not change, it is unlikely that measurable improvements in results will be observed. However, a favorable reaction is not necessarily a prerequisite to learning—a fun program may or may not be a useful one.[84]

A thorough evaluation would include measurements at all four of these levels. Such a thorough evaluation should be undertaken for expensive or strategically important training programs where there is an opportunity to use the data to improve the program in the future. However, for an inexpensive program offered only once to a small group of employees, a simple reaction questionnaire may provide all the evaluation needed.[85]

Evaluation Designs

Designing a good evaluation effort involves knowing when to collect evaluation measures and which groups to collect them from.[86] Together these factors define the experimental design used to assess the impact of the training.

Because reaction measures assess whether or not participants like the training and think it will be useful, these measures are collected during or immediately after the training. Ideally, an additional reaction questionnaire should be sent to participants several months after the training to see if they still believe that the training has been of use in their jobs.

The purpose of learning, behavior, and results measures is quite different from that of reaction measures, in that the trainer is trying to discover whether or not a *change* has occurred in the variable being measured—that is, do trainees know more, behave differently, or produce better results after than before the training? If there has been a change, the trainer will want to know whether or not it can be attributed to the training program—that is, did the training program bring about the change?

There are two basic strategies for determining whether a change has occurred. The first is to compare the trainees after the training to the way they were before the training. At the very least, this comparison involves the collection of evaluation measures at two points in time. The second strategy is to compare the learning, behavior, or results of the trained group to the learning, behavior, or results of a group that has not been trained but is otherwise as similar as possible to the trained group. The strongest evaluation designs draw on both these strategies. There are many complex and highly effective designs for evaluating training. This section covers only a few of the more straightforward ones (see Figure 9.8).

● **One-Shot Posttest-Only Design**   In the **one-shot posttest-only design,** training evaluation measures are collected only from the trained group, after the training has been conducted. Because there is no pretraining measure and no untrained group for purposes of comparison, there is no way to determine whether or not a change has occurred or whether any change has been caused by the training. However, if the aim is to determine whether a desired standard of performance has been reached, this simple design might produce some useful data. For instance, one might be able to verify that 90 percent of the trainees passed the

● FIGURE 9.8

Designs for Evaluating Training

(a) Simple designs

One-shot
posttest-only design

| Train | → | Measure |

One-group pretest–
posttest design

| Measure | → | Train | → | Measure |

(b) Stronger designs for training evaluation

Multiple-baseline
design

| Measure | → | Measure | → | Measure | → | Train | → | Measure | → | Measure | → | Measure |

Pretest–posttest
control-group design

| Measure | → | Train | → | Measure |

Group 1

| Measure | → | No training | → | Measure |

Group 2

learning test at the end of training or that after the training program customer complaints averaged one per thousand.

● **One-Group Pretest–Posttest Design**   Another very simple design is the **one-group pretest–posttest design,** in which the training group is assessed both before and after the training. For instance, the productivity of the trained group might be found to be 5 percent higher after training than it was before training. Although this design does allow a trainer to determine if there has been a change, it does not enable the trainer to conclude with absolute certainty that the training brought about the change. A change from one time period to another can be caused by anything that occurs between measurements, not just by the training. For instance, there might be a new supervisor, revised work methods, a change in the quality of raw materials, an increase in workload, employee turnover, a change in the pay system, or union activity. Any of these or similar factors could affect behavior or results measures and cause the training evaluation to be misleading. If nontraining concurrent events seem unlikely to account for a change from before to after training, then the trainer can gain some useful information about the effectiveness of the training from this simple design.

● **Multiple-Baseline Design** An improved evaluation design that avoids some of the above-mentioned problems is the **multiple-baseline design.** In this design, the trainer measures the group several times both before and after the training. The trainer probably should not use an obtrusive measure, such as a questionnaire or learning test, or trainees could improve over time just because they are gaining practice with the measure. Objective measures of behavior or results (such as sales volume, profit, or customer complaints) are less obtrusive, and they are easy to collect repeatedly.

The multiple-baseline design allows the trainer to observe trends in performance and to see if there is a change in the trend immediately after the training. For instance, a trainer may find that employees are slowly improving with experience over time but that a big jump in performance occurs after the training. This design is the best one to use if all employees are to be trained simultaneously, leaving none to serve as a control group.

● **Pretest–Posttest Control-Group Design** An even better design uses a control group of employees who are very similar to the training group except that they do not receive the training (at least not yet). In the **pretest–posttest control-group design,** both the group to receive the training and the control group are measured at least once before and once after the training. This design allows the trainer to draw quite firm conclusions about (1) whether any change has occurred and (2) if it has, whether the change was due to the training.

The trainer might normally expect to find that the trained group improves from pretest to posttest, whereas the control group stays the same. However, other patterns of results also can be interpreted under this design. For instance, if the training group is the same after the training as before, but the control group is worse on the posttest than on the pretest, then the training probably was effective in preventing a decline in performance that would otherwise have occurred.

Using the Evaluation to Improve Training

Information from the training evaluation can be used in making decisions about whether to continue the training program or how to improve it. Modifying the training based on reaction measures is fairly straightforward. A boring speaker can be replaced, a film rated as irrelevant dropped, or a caterer changed, depending on the feedback received. If a sound evaluation design was used, additional modifications of the training might be suggested by scores on the learning, behavior, or results measures.

If insufficient learning occurred, the training presentation itself may have been at fault. Information may have been presented unclearly, or inadequate time and practice may have been allowed for trainees to absorb the material. Alternatively, trainee readiness or motivation may have been deficient so that an otherwise well-designed training experience had no real impact on the trainees.

If behavior on the job did not improve despite gains in learning, the fault could lie in the needs assessment, the training program itself, or the work environment. If the initial needs assessment was not performed correctly, trainees might have mastered material that was not relevant to the demands of their jobs. Thus, while they might have learned something from the training, what they learned is not something that they can use. Another possibility is that the training content might have been appropriate, but there was insufficient emphasis either on transfer of training to the job or on relapse prevention. Finally, the fault could lie in the work environment if supervisors or the environment do not facilitate the use of new skills.

When learning and behavior change, but results do not improve, the appropriateness of the training or validity of the results measures should be scrutinized. If people are behaving differently, but the behavior has no impact on the bottom line, then the training may be teaching the wrong things. This problem could stem from a poor needs assessment. If, on the other hand, the trained behaviors are better and more effective than the behaviors used previously, then the problem may be simply that the results measures are too coarse or contaminated to register their beneficial effect. Results measures like profit and turnover are affected by many factors outside the organization, such as general economic and labor-market conditions. Perhaps a training program does have a beneficial impact, but the impact is simply not visible against larger trends in global results measures.

Utility of Training Programs

In Chapter 7, the concept of utility, or cost-benefit analysis, was applied to selection systems. **Utility** is the net dollar gain realized by an organization as a result of adopting a given HRM practice, and it can be calculated for training programs as well as for selection systems.[87] Jack Phillips has championed adding a fifth level to Kirkpatrick's training evaluation hierarchy, return on investment.[88] Phillips believes that the benefits of training should be carefully quantified and compared to the cost of delivering the training in order to justify training expenditures and evaluate the relative worth of different training programs. For instance, one study estimated that the net return to a bank (over a five-year period) of a four-day training program for sixty-five supervisors would be $148,400.[89]

Calculating utility or return on investment requires both assessing the costs of the training and putting a dollar value on the benefits of the training. Some cost categories associated with training are shown in Table 9.14. They include one-time costs incurred in developing the program initially, costs that are incurred each time the program is repeated, and costs incurred for each person trained. It is harder to put a dollar value on the benefits of training than it is to assess the costs. First, one must estimate how much better a trained employee will perform than an untrained employee. The dollar payback of a certain percentage of improvement in performance depends on the importance of the job. It is probably worth more to an organization to increase an executive's performance by 10 percent than to increase a secretary's performance by 10 percent. The amount gained per trainee per year is multiplied by the number of persons trained.

Next, the duration of the training's impact must be estimated. Because the benefit of training an employee is lost when that employee quits, turnover rates are often built into utility calculations. However, even if an employee stays with the organization, the effects of some kinds of training gradually wear off as trainees forget what they have learned or the knowledge becomes obsolete. Thus an estimate of the "half-life" of the training intervention also must be factored in.[90]

● **TABLE 9.14**

Costs of Training

One-Time Costs
- Needs assessment costs
- Salaries of training designers or consultants
- Purchase of reusable training equipment and materials
- Full-scale evaluation of the program when first offered

Per-Session Costs
- Trainer salaries, travel, and lodging
- Facilities rental

Per-Trainee Costs
- Trainee wages or salary during training
- Transportation, food, and lodging for trainees during training
- Nonreusable training materials, handouts, etc.

The final step in calculating utility is to subtract the total costs from the total benefits of a particular training program given to a specified number of people. Estimating the necessary parameters and calculating utility can be extremely complex, but by doing so, an employer can build a solid justification for a training program on purely economic grounds.

Properly conceived and implemented training programs can have definite effects on organizational performance and profits.[91] A recent extensive study of the utility of several training programs in a large pharmaceutical company found that training programs varied widely in their impact. Managerial training programs had an average return on investment of 45 percent, whereas sales and technical training had an average return on investment of 156 percent. Information of this sort can be used to decide where to direct training resources to produce the largest impact.[92]

Benchmarking HRD

In addition to evaluating the impact of individual programs, training departments often wish to assess themselves against the best practice in the industry or the field. Figure 9.9 shows some measures that might be used to benchmark HRD activities across companies or divisions or from year to year in the same unit. These metrics fall into three classes: training activities (percentage of employees trained, hours of training per employee, etc.), training results in terms of Kirkpatrick's four outcome levels, and training efficiency measures, such as cost per student hour. These measures were developed by the manager of HRD at Magnavox Electronic Systems Company, who used them to compare his training function with those of three Malcolm Baldrige National Quality Award winners.[93] An additional measure of increasing importance is cycle time—days from becoming aware of a training need to delivering an effective program to address the need.

● **FIGURE 9.9**

HRD Metrics

Metric Name	Metric Type	How to Calculate	Example
Percent of payroll spent on training	Training activity	Total training expenditures ÷ total payroll	U.S. average = 1.4 percent of payroll spent on training per year.
Training dollars spent per employee	Training activity	Total training expenditures ÷ employees served	Three Baldrige winners spent $1,100 per employee on training in 1990.
Average training hours per employee	Training activity	Total number of training hours (hours x participants) ÷ total employees served	U.S. average for large firms (100+ employees) = 33 hours per employee in 1990.
Percent of employees trained per year	Training activity	Total number of employees receiving training ÷ total employee population	Three Baldrige winners trained an average of 92.5 percent of their work forces in 1990.
HRD staff per 1,000 employees	Training activity	Number of HRD staff ÷ total employee population x 1,000	Three Baldrige winners had an average of 4.1 HRD staff members per 1,000 employees.
Average percent of positive participant ratings per year	Training results: reactions	Total number of employees rating courses "good" or "effective" ÷ total number of employees who completed course surveys per year	Three Baldrige winners averaged 93 percent positive participant course ratings in 1990.
Average percent of satisfied HRD customers	Training results: reactions	Total number of customers rating HRD services "good" or "effective" ÷ total number of customers who completed customer satisfaction survey	Three Baldrige winners averaged 84 percent positive HRD customer-service ratings in 1990.
Average percent gain in learning per course	Training results: learning	Average percent of learning gain (difference between pre- and post-test) for each class, averaged over all classes tested	Three Baldrige winners averaged 70 percent learning gain in more than 50 technical classes in 1990.
Average percent of improvement in on-the-job performance after training, per course	Training results: behavior	Average job performance gain (difference between pre- and post-training behavior) for each class, averaged over all classes measured	An electronics firm reported 49 percent improvement in management ratings after supervisor training in 1990.
Cost savings as a ratio of training expenses	Training results: bottom-line	Total savings in scrap or waste ÷ dollars invested in training	A Baldrige winner reported saving $30 for every $2 spent on TQM training
Revenues per employee per year	Training results: bottom-line	Total yearly revenues or sales ÷ total number of employees	Two Baldrige winners reported average revenues per employee of $94,000 in 1990.
Profits per employee per year	Training results: bottom-line	Total yearly gross profits ÷ total number of employees	An electronics firm earned average profits per employee of $21,000 in 1990.
Training costs per student hour	Training efficiency	Total costs of training ÷ total number of hours training	Three Baldrige winners reported $27 in average training costs per hour of training in 1990.
Billable rate (time on task)	Training efficiency	HRD staff time spent on billable or key tasks ÷ total HRD staff time	An electronics firm reported an HRD billable rate of .82 in 1991 (82 percent of staff time spent on billable tasks).

Source: Donald J. Ford "Benchmarking HRD," *Training & Development,* June 1993, p. 39. Copyright June 1993, *Training & Development,* American Society for Training and Development. Reprinted with permission. All rights reserved.

The American Society for Training and Development manages a benchmarking survey that includes training departments from 750 organizations. A small number of these have been identified as using "leading-edge" training practices. The leading-edge companies spent an average of 4.4 percent of payroll on training activities and trained 86 percent of their employees every year.[94] Other organizations in the survey spent less than 2 percent of payroll on training 74 percent of their employees, while it has been estimated that the nationwide average training expenditure is 0.9 percent of payroll.[95] As with any benchmarking, it is important to be sure that measures are relevant. The focus in evaluating HRD at present seems to be away from benchmarking activities (number of courses offered, number of hours of training provided) or expenditures and toward direct measures of results or effectiveness (was the problem solved?).[96]

HUMAN RESOURCE DEVELOPMENT IN THE FUTURE

Experts seem to agree that HRD in the future may be significantly different from the way it is practiced at present. These changes will derive in part from the revolution in technology (e.g., performance support systems, increasing reliance on computer-delivered training) and in part from changes in organizational structure and the increasing demands to be quick, innovative, and flexible in order to remain competitive. Changes will occur both in training content and in delivery. Training will become more responsive and individualized, and more of it will be conducted electronically or by managers or peers rather than by professional in-house trainers. Training seems to be becoming integrated into organizational strategy to a greater extent, with some training and career management systems being adopted to assist in attracting and retaining valuable employees as well as to assure current job performance. Executive education is becoming more practical and tightly linked to business needs. Finally, there is an increasing emphasis on learning for both individuals and for organizations, and an appreciation that learning can take place quite apart from formal training. HRD specialists in the future will be charged with creating and maintaining learning environments and communities of practice, managing and coordinating a portfolio of custom and commercial e-training options, and, to a decreasing extent, designing and delivering face-to-face training.[97]

Summary of Key Points

Training is a planned effort by an organization to facilitate employees' learning of job-related knowledge and skills for the purpose of improving performance. The Instructional Systems Design approach to training involves four phases: needs assessment, design and development of training programs, delivery of programs, and evaluation. The assessment phase determines who needs to be trained and what they need to be trained to do. Assessment involves organizational analysis, task analysis, individual analysis, and the identification of clear and measurable training objectives.

The design and development phase includes choosing appropriate training methods and developing training materials. The design of a training program must consider issues such as conditions of practice, knowledge of results, interference, transfer of training, and adult learning principles. A large number of training methods are available, and training can be delivered on or off the job. Methods should be chosen to assure that content is delivered clearly, appropriate opportunities for practice occur, and sufficient variety is provided to the trainee.

Management development is intended to improve the present and future performance of managers. Many millions of dollars are spent on formal management training each year, although managers probably do most of their learning from on-the-job experiences. This suggests that a complete management development system should include both training courses and challenging job assignments. Action learning programs combine on- and off-the-job learning for managers.

In the evaluation phase, the training is evaluated (1) to determine whether it has achieved its objectives and (2) to make improvements in the training program. Four levels of evaluation measures should be collected for a thorough evaluation: reaction, learning, behavior, and results. A sound experimental design should be used to assess the impact of the training. Finally, the utility of a training program can be calculated by assessing its costs and putting a dollar value on its benefits to the organization.

The Manager's Vocabulary

action learning
adult learning principles
andragogy
apprenticeship training
automaticity
behavior measure
behavioral objectives
community of practice
competency model
computer-delivered training
cross-training
declarative knowledge
distributed practice
embedding
evaluation
feedback/knowledge of results
human resource development (HRD)
individual analysis
Instructional Systems Design (ISD)
interference
Job Instruction Training
Kirkpatrick's four levels of evaluation

knowledge compilation
learning measure
massed practice
multimedia
multiple-baseline design
multiskilling
needs assessment
off-the-job training
on-the-job training (OJT)
one-group pretest–posttest design
one-shot posttest-only design
organizational analysis
overlearning
part learning
pedagogy
performance support systems
preconditions for learning
pretest–posttest control-group design
procedural knowledge
programmed knowledge
questioning insight
reaction measure
relapse-prevention model
results measure
self-efficacy expectations
subject matter experts
task analysis
trainee motivation
trainee readiness
transfer of training
utility
whole learning

Questions for Discussion

1. In what ways does the HRD function relate to the organization's strategy?
2. What methods might you use in analyzing the needs of present employees in their present jobs?
3. What are some possible causes of performance deficiencies other than a need for training?
4. What concerns are addressed at the organizational analysis phase of training needs assessment?
5. How would you conduct the task analysis phase of training needs assessment for the job of movie theater ticket seller?

6. What are the characteristics of a good behavioral objective? What purpose do training objectives serve?
7. Explain Anderson's three-step learning process. Explain how it might apply to the task of learning to drive a car.
8. What can a trainer do to build trainee motivation before and during a training course?
9. What is self-efficacy, why is it important in training, and how can trainers influence it?
10. What is massed practice? What effect does massed practice have on retention?
11. What is overlearning? When and why should it be used?
12. Suppose you are planning a training course on customer service for front-line staff. How would you go about embedding this course in the organization to maximize its effectiveness and transfer?
13. Redesign this class using the principles of adult learning. Would you prefer the course to be run along adult learning lines or in a more traditional teacher-centered fashion? Why?
14. What are the advantages and disadvantages of on-the-job training? Discuss your personal experiences being trained on the job. Was it done well or poorly? What improvements would you suggest?
15. Suppose that you were being sent overseas to deliver a training program for your company. What factors would you want to consider as you prepared for this training assignment?
16. What are the advantages and disadvantages of computer-delivered training?
17. How would you go about selecting and sequencing training methods for a day-long training program on the topic of "conducting the employment interview"?
18. Suppose that you were asked to teach a group of somewhat experienced but not formally trained supervisors how to conduct a disciplinary interview with a subordinate who has performed badly or broken a rule. Come up with ten different methods or activities you could use to do this. Which method do you think would be most effective? How might you combine several methods for the best effect?
19. What is action learning?
20. Develop the outline for an orientation program for a new secretarial employee at your college or business school.
21. Explain four levels at which training can be evaluated.
22. The career center at you university is preparing to offer a one-day course for graduating students on how to find a job. They have asked you to plan an evaluation of the effectiveness of this training program. Which of Kirkpatrick's levels of evaluation would you use? Which specific measures would you collect? Which research design would you use?
23. Explain how utility concepts can be used to estimate the net dollar value of a training program.

● **Case 9.1**
Management Development Systems at Resort Wear of California

You are part of a consulting group that has been hired by Resort Wear of California, a chain of twelve upscale women's clothing shops located between San Diego and San Francisco. The owner of the business is worried about the quality of store managers. Some are good, some are promising but inexperienced, and some do not seem to be very effective. The owner plans to double the number of stores starting next year and would like to build up the skills of store managers and assistant managers to support this expansion.

The owner is willing to commit a reasonable amount of money to develop managers, but you do not have a blank check (you can't afford to send them all to a university or even bring them together physically more than once or twice). It is also necessary to keep all stores running while management training is occurring.

Your team has been retained to design a management development strategy to be implemented over the next two years. Using what you know about both on- and off-the-job management develop- ment, decide how you should proceed and what you might recommend to the owner. Consider training content as well as methods.

● Case 9.2
Training New Employees at Health Source

Health Source, the drugstore chain mentioned in earlier chapters, is in need of training for the staff of the two new stores that will soon be opening in Dallas and Houston. Approximately fifty new employees will need to be oriented, and the thirty of them who are clerks need to learn how to operate a cash register, stock shelves, and provide quality customer service "The Health Source Way." Being a small firm, Health Source does not have a full-time training officer. However, it does have an HR director (you) and a number of experienced Houston-based supervisors and employees. Plan how you will accomplish the necessary training for the clerks at the two locations. How will you determine exactly what content must be taught? Which skills will be taught on the job? Which should be taught in the classroom? What must be taught prior to opening, and what can be taught later? Which training methods are likely to be most successful with the clerks? Who will the trainers be?

Health Source has never had a formal employee orientation program before, but it also has never needed to orient so many people at the same time. If expansion continues beyond these two stores, a formal orientation program will be useful again and again. What material should go into the orientation program for all new employees? Who should deliver the program, and how?

● Exercise 9.1
Applying Learning Principles

You are designing a two-day workshop to teach intact teams of managers to use systematic group problem-solving methods. The managers include several state managers and their three to five immediate subordinates, each of whom manages an area within a state. These individuals are required to attend the training program. The content of the program includes several steps in the problem-solving process (defining the problem and generating decision criteria, generating alternatives, choosing an alternative, action planning for implementation, and evaluating success) and several types of skills (listening, consensus seeking, brainstorming, cause-and-effect analysis, force-field analysis, action planning).

How will your training program incorporate or deal with each of the following learning principles or conditions? Are there any that will not concern you? Which may be most crucial in this situation?

1. Readiness
2. Motivation
3. Interference
4. Feedback
5. Overlearning
6. Distributed versus massed practice
7. Whole versus part learning
8. Transfer of training

● **Exercise 9.2**
Planning a Needs Assessment

You are director of education at a 400-bed hospital. Authorization has just been received to create a new job title, "Nurse Aide," and to hire thirty individuals over the next year. None of the other hospitals in your area have a similar job title, and there are no vocational training programs producing nurse aides in your state. You have been requested to develop a combined classroom and on-the-job training program for the new job. You have a staff of one secretary and two trainers (who are degreed nurses) to help you. Recruiting will begin in three months, and the first "class" of fifteen nurse aides will begin training in four months.

Develop a complete plan and timetable for needs assessment for this project. What sources of information will you use? What methods will you use to gather information? What kinds of information do you need to get?

● **Exercise 9.3**
Training Resources on the Internet

You have just realized that your career opportunities would be stronger if you took a course to build your sales skills. You decide to see what's available by checking the Web. We have been hearing a lot about "learning portals" lately. These are "one stop shops" providing access to information about a wide variety of commercial training programs.

1. Check out some learning portals to see what they can offer in the way of e-training on sales skills. What do you think of the portals? What do you think of the courses? Can you find enough information to assess the quality of the offerings? Would you prefer an e-course to a live classroom course? Why or why not?

2. Visit America's Learning Exchange (www.alx.org) to see if you can find a live course on sales skills within a reasonable distance of where you live. Note that you can search available courses by topic, location, and mode of delivery (classroom, CD-ROM, correspondence, conference, Web-based, etc.).

● **Exercise 9.4**
Training Method Choice at Bob Brown Ford

Suppose you are planning a four-day training program for six newly hired, inexperienced automobile salespersons. These people need to learn about (1) car models, features, and prices for the vehicles sold at the dealership; (2) personal selling techniques; and (3) the dealership's rules and procedures for salesperson conduct and closing deals. Your training budget is reasonably generous but not unlimited. What training methods/techniques might you use to teach each type of content, and why did you choose these? Be thorough, be inventive, and consider the desirability of variety in methods over the course of a program.

Notes and References

1. http://www.united.com

2. K. Kiser, "E-Learning Takes Off at United Airlines," *Training*, December 1999, pp. 66–72.

3. "Industry Report 2000," *Training,* October 2000 pp. 51–55.

4. J. J. Martocchio and T. T. Baldwin, "The Evolution of Strategic Organizational Training," *Research in Personnel and Human Resources Management*, Vol. 15, 1997, pp. 1–46.

5. Irwin L. Goldstein and Patrice Gilliam, "Training System Issues in the Year 2000," *American Psychologist,* February 1990, pp. 134–143; L. J. Bassi and D. P. McMurrer, "Training Investment Can Mean Financial Performance," *Training & Development,* May 1998, pp. 40-42.

6. R. L. Cardy and J. S. Miller, "A Customer-Based Approach to Managing the Two R's" *Human Resource Division News*, Fall 2000, pp. 10-11; and R. Elsdon and S. Iyer, "Creating Value and Enhancing Retention Through Employee Development: The Sun Microsystems Experience," *Human Resource Planning*, Vol. 22 (2), 1999, pp. 39–47.

7. Linda Thornburg, "Training in a Changing World," *HRMagazine,* August 1992, pp. 44–47.

8. R. Zemke and S. Zemke, "Putting Competencies to Work," *Training*, January 1999, pp. 70-76.

9. John K. Berry, "Linking Management Development to Business Strategies," *Training and Development Journal,* August 1990, pp. 20–22; Richard Wellins and Jill George, "The Key to Self-Directed Teams," *Training and Development Journal,* April 1991, pp. 26–31; G. M. McEvoy, J. R. Cragun, and M. Appleby, "Using Outdoor Training to Develop and Accomplish Organizational Vision," *Human Resource Planning*, Vol. 20 (3), 1997, pp. 20–28; and J. A. Conger and K. Xin, "Executive Education in the 21st Century," *Journal of Management Education*, Vol. 24, 2000, pp. 73–101.

10. K. V. Linde, N. Horney, and R. Koonce, "Seven Ways to Make Your Training Department One of the Best," *Training & Development*, August 1997, pp. 20–28; and P. A. Galagan, "Reinventing the Profession," *Training & Development*, December 1994, pp. 20–27.

11. J. R. Hinrichs, "Personnel Training," in *Handbook of Industrial and Organizational Psychology,* ed. M. D. Dunnette (Chicago: Rand McNally, 1976), p. 830.

12. Allison Rossett and Joseph W. Arwady, *Training Needs Assessment* (Englewood Cliffs, N.J.: Educational Technology Publications, 1987), p. 68.

13. L. A. Digman, "Determining Management Development Needs," *Human Resource Management,* Winter 1980, pp. 12–17; and Lise M. Saari, Terry R. Johnson, Steven D. McLaughlin, and Denise M. Zimmerle, "A Survey of Management Training and Education Practices in U.S. Companies," *Personnel Psychology,* Winter 1988, pp. 731–743.

14. For a detailed treatment of needs analysis methods, see Irwin L. Goldstein (ed.), *Training and Development in Organizations,* 3d ed. (Pacific Grove, Calif.: Brooks/Cole, 1993), chap. 3. See also C. E. Schneier, J. P. Guthrie, and J. D. Olian, "A Practical Approach to Conducting and Using the Training Needs Assessment," *Public Personnel Management,* Summer 1988, pp. 191–205; and P. J. Taylor, M. P. O'Driscoll, and J. F. Binning, "A

New Integrated Framework for Training Needs Analysis," *Human Resource Management Journal*, Vol. 8 (2), 1998, pp. 29–50.

15. Robert F. Mager and Peter Pipe, *Analyzing Performance Problems,* 3d ed. (Atlanta, Ga.: Center for Effective Performance, 1997).

16. R. Zemke and S. Zemke, "Putting Competencies to Work," *Training*, January 1999, pp. 70–76. For more on competency models, see J. S. Shippmann, R. A. Ash, M. Battista, L. Carr, L. D. Eyde, B. Hesketh, J. Kehoe, K. Pearlman, E. P. Prien, and J. I. Sanchez, "The Practice of Competency Modeling," *Personnel Psychology*, Autumn 2000, pp. 703–740.

17. Conger and Xin, "Executive Education in the 21st Century."

18. V. S. Kaman and J. P. Mohr, "Training Needs Assessment in the 80's: Five Guideposts," *Personnel Administrator,* October 1984, pp. 47–53.

19. F. O. Hoffman, "The Hierarchy of Training Objectives," *Personnel,* August 1985, pp. 12–16.

20. Robert F. Mager, *Preparing Instructional Objectives* (Belmont, Calif.: Lake Publishing, 1975).

21. For more on recent advances in learning theory, see Howard M. Weiss, "Learning Theory and Industrial and Organizational Psychology," in *Handbook of Industrial and Organizational Psychology,* 2d ed., ed. Marvin D. Dunnette and Leaetta M. Hough (Palo Alto, Calif.: Consulting Psychologists Press, 1990), pp. 171–221; for a good chapter on applying learning principles to training design, see K. N. Wexley and G. P. Latham, *Developing and Training Human Resources in Organizations* (New York: HarperCollins, 1991), chap. 4; for a nontechnical summary of Gagne's significant contributions to learning theory, see R. Zemke, "Toward a Science of Training," *Training*, July 1999, pp. 32–36.

22. J. R. Anderson, "Skill Acquisition: Compilation of Weak-Method Problem Solutions," *Psychological Review,* Vol. 94, 1987, pp. 192–210; Phillip L. Ackerman, "Predicting Individual Differences in Complex Skill Acquisition: Dynamics of Ability Determinants," *Journal of Applied Psychology,* Vol. 77, 1992, pp. 598–614; and William C. Howell and Nancy Jawarski Cooke, "Training the Human Information Processor: A Review of Cognitive Models," in Goldstein (ed.), *Training and Development in Organizations,* pp. 121–182.

23. R. A. Noe, "Trainees' Attributes and Attitudes: Neglected Influences on Training Effectiveness," *Academy of Management Review,* October 1986, pp. 736–749; for more on trainee motivation and pretraining influences of training effectiveness, see T. T. Baldwin and R. J. Magjuka, "Training as an Organizational Episode: Pretraining Influences on Trainee Motivation," pp. 99–127, and J. E. Mathieu and M. W. Martineau, "Individual and Situational Influences on Training Motivation," pp. 193–221, both in *Improving Training Effectiveness in Work Organizations,* ed. J. K. Ford (Mahwah, N.J.: Erlbaum, 1997).

24. W. D. Hicks and R. J. Klimoski, "Entry into Training Programs and Its Effects on Training Outcomes: A Field Experiment," *Academy of Management Journal,* September 1987, pp. 542–552; and Timothy T. Baldwin, Richard J. Magjuka, and Brian T. Loher, "The Perils of Participation: Effects of Choice of

Training on Trainee Motivation and Learning," *Personnel Psychology,* Vol. 44 (1), Spring 1991, pp. 51–65.

25. R. A. Noe and N. Schmitt, "The Influence of Trainee Attitudes on Training Effectiveness: Test of a Model," *Personnel Psychology,* Autumn 1986, pp. 497–523.

26. Edwin A. Locke and Gary P. Latham, *A Theory of Goal Setting and Task Performance* (Englewood Cliffs, N.J.: Prentice-Hall, 1990).

27. Ruth Kanfer and Phillip L. Ackerman, "Motivation and Cognitive Abilities: An Integrative/Aptitude-Treatment Interaction Approach to Skill Acquisition," *Journal of Applied Psychology,* Vol. 74, 1989, pp. 657–690.

28. A. Bandura, "Self-Efficacy: Toward a Unifying Theory of Behavioral Change," *Psychological Review,* Vol. 84, 1977, pp. 191–215.

29. Marilyn E. Gist, Catherine Schwoerer, and Benson Rosen, "Effects of Alternative Training Methods on Self-Efficacy and Performance in Computer Software Training," *Journal of Applied Psychology,* December 1989, pp. 884–891; John E. Mathieu, Jennifer W. Martineau, and Scott I. Tannenbaum, "Individual and Situational Influences on the Development of Self-Efficacy: Implications for Training Effectiveness," *Personnel Psychology,* Vol. 46, 1993, pp. 125–147; and Marilyn E. Gist and Terence R. Mitchell, "Self-Efficacy: A Theoretical Analysis of Its Determinants and Malleability," *Academy of Management Review,* Vol. 17, 1992, pp. 183–211.

30. James E. Driskell, Ruth P. Willis, and Carolyn Copper, "Effect of Overlearning on Retention," *Journal of Applied Psychology,* Vol. 77, 1992, pp. 615–622.

31. Frank N. Dempster, "The Spacing Effect: A Case Study in the Failure to Apply the Results of Psychological Research," *American Psychologist,* August 1988, pp. 627–634; and J. J. Donovan and D. J. Radosevich, "A Meta-Analytic Review of the Distribution of Practice Effect: Now You See It, Now You Don't," *Journal of Applied Psychology,* Vol. 84, 1999, pp. 795–805.

32. D. R. Ilgen, C. D. Fisher, and M. S. Taylor, "Motivational Consequences of Individual Feedback on Behavior in Organizations," *Journal of Applied Psychology,* August 1979, pp. 349–371, and Joseph J. Martocchio and Jane Webster, "Effects of Feedback and Cognitive Playfulness on Performance in Microcomputer Software Training," *Personnel Psychology,* Vol. 45, 1992, pp. 553–578.

33. For more detail on transfer of training, see S. W. Kozlowski and E. Salas, "A Multilevel Organizational Systems Approach for the Implementation and Transfer of Training," in Ford (ed.), *Improving Training Effectiveness in Work Organizations;* and M. L. Broad and J. W. Newstrom, *Transfer of Training* (Reading, Mass.: Addison-Wesley, 1992).

34. Thomas Hill, Nancy D. Smith, and Millard F. Mann, "Role of Efficacy Expectations in Predicting the Decision to Use Advanced Technologies: The Case of Computers," *Journal of Applied Psychology,* Vol. 72, 1987, pp. 307–313.

35. K. N. Wexley and T. T. Baldwin, "Posttraining Strategies for Facilitating Positive Transfer: An Empirical Exploration," *Academy of Management Journal,* September 1986, pp. 503–520; Timothy T. Baldwin and J. Kevin Ford, "Transfer of Training: A Review and Directions for Future Research," *Personnel Psychology,* Spring 1988, pp. 63–105; and Paul L. Garavaglia, "How to Ensure Transfer of Training," *Training & Development,* October 1993, pp. 63–68.

36. R. D. Marx, "Relapse Prevention for Managerial Training: A Model for Maintenance of Behavior Changes," *Academy of Management Review,* Vol. 7, 1982, pp. 433–441; Marilyn E. Gist, Anna G. Bavetta, and Cynthia Kay Stevens, "Transfer Training Method: Its Influence on Skill Generalization, Skill Repetition, and Performance Level," *Personnel Psychology,* Autumn 1990, pp. 501–523; and L. A. Burke and T. T. Baldwin, "Workforce Training Transfer: A Study of the Effect of Relapse Prevention Training and Transfer Climate," *Human Resource Management,* Fall 1999, pp. 227–242.

37. J. Kevin Ford, Miguel A. Quinones, Douglas J. Sego, and Joann Speer Sorra, "Factors Affecting the Opportunity to Perform Trained Tasks on the Job," *Personnel Psychology,* Vol. 45, 1992, pp. 511–527.

38. J. B. Tracey, C. I. Tannenbaum, and M.J. Kavanagh, "Applying Trained Skills on the Job: The Importance of the Work Environment," *Journal of Applied Psychology,* April 1995, pp. 239–252; for more on transfer of training, see S.W.J. Kozlowski and E. Salas, "A Multilevel Organizational Systems Approach for the Implementation and Transfer of Training'" in Ford (ed.) *Improving Training Effectiveness in Work Organizations.*

39. David L. Taylor and Ruth Karin Ramsey, "Empowering Employees to 'Just Do It,' " *Training & Development,* May 1993, pp. 71–76.

40. "Support Systems for Training," in *Designing Training Programs,* ed. L. Nadler and Z. Nadler (Houston: Gulf Publishing, 1994), pp. 212–233; S. Rynes and B. Rosen, "A Field Survey of Factors Affecting the Adoption and Perceived Success of Diversity Training," *Personnel Psychology,* Vol. 48, 1995, pp. 247–270; J. D. Facteau, G. H. Dobbins, J. E. A. Russell, R. T. Ladd, and J. D. Kudisch, "The Influence of General Perceptions of the Training Environment on Pretraining Motivation and Perceived Transfer," *Journal of Management,* Vol. 21, 1995, pp. 1–25; Tracey, Tannenbaum, and Kavanagh, "Applying Trained Skills on the Job."

41. Malcolm Knowles, *The Adult Learner: A Neglected Species* (Houston: Gulf Publishing, 1978); for more on adult learning, see Robert Burns, *The Adult Learner at Work* (Sydney, Australia: Business and Professional Publishing, 1995).

42. R. F. Crapo, "It's Time to Stop Training . . . And Start Facilitating," *Public Personnel Management,* Winter 1986, pp. 443–449.

43. For more on managing student-centered learning experiences, see Jill Baldwin and Hank Williams, *Active Learning: A Trainer's Guide* (Oxford, England: Blackwell, 1988).

44. Crapo, "It's Time to Stop Training," p. 446.

45. D. Feuer and B. Geber, "Uh-oh . . . Second Thoughts About Adult Learning Theory," *Training,* December 1988, pp. 31–39; Sharon B. Merriam, "Adult Learning and Theory Building: A Review," *Adult Education Quarterly,* Summer 1987, pp. 187–198; and R. Zemke and S. Zemke, "Adult Learning: What Do We Know For Sure?" *Training,* June 1995, pp. 31–40.

46. John W. Newstrom and Mark L. Lengnick-Hall, "One Size Does Not Fit All," *Training and Development Journal,* June 1991, pp. 43–48.

47. D. Schaff, "What Workers Really Think About Training," *Training,* September 1998, pp. 59–66.

48. Alice Bird McCord, "Job Training," in *Training and Development Handbook,* 3d ed., ed. Robert L. Craig (New York: McGraw-Hill, 1987), pp. 363–382.

49. W. J. Rothwell and H. C. Kazanas, *Improving On-the-Job Training: How to Establish and Operate a Comprehensive OJT*

Program (San Francisco: Jossey-Bass, 1994); and R. L. Jacobs and M. J. Jones, *Structured On-the-Job Training: Unleashing Employee Expertise in the Workplace* (San Francisco: Berrett-Koehler, 1995).

50. Margaret Kaeter, "Cross-Training: The Tactical View," *Training,* March 1993, pp. 35–39; and Bob Filipczak, "Frick Teaches Frack," *Training,* June 1993, pp. 30–34.

51. B. Filipczak, "Who Owns Your OJT?" *Training,* December 1996, pp. 44-49.

52. Wexley and Latham, *Developing and Training Human Resources in Organizations,* pp. 111–114. For more on apprenticeship training, see the Department of Labor Employment and Training Administration Web site http://www.doleta.gov/atels_bat/reg-apprentice.asp#apprenticeship.

53. Larry Reynolds, "Apprenticeship Program Raises Many Questions," *HRFocus,* July 1993, pp. 1, 4; and Robert J. Gitter, "Apprenticeship-Trained Workers: United States and Great Britain," *Monthly Labor Review,* April 1994, pp. 38–43.

54. "Industry Report 2000," *Training,* October 2000, pp. 57–64.

55. Carol Rocklin Kay, Sue Kruse Peyton, and Robert Pike, "Diagnosing the Training Situation: Matching Instructional Techniques with Learning Outcomes," *The 1987 Annual: Developing Human Resources* (San Diego: University Associates, 1987), pp. 203–212.

56. S. Schwade, "Is It Time to Consider Computer-Based Training?" *Personnel Administrator,* February 1985, pp. 25–35.

57. M. L. Hillinger, "What's Really New About Multimedia," *Training & Development*, August 1997, pp. 47–55.

58. S. Fister, "Reinventing Training at Rockwell Collins," *Training,* April 2000, pp. 64–70.

59. Chris Lee, "Who Gets Trained in What," *Training,* October 1991, pp. 47–59.

60. Carolyn Ladd, "Should Performance Support Be in Your Computer?" *Training & Development,* August 1993, pp. 22–26; and Beverly Geber, "HELP! The Rise of Performance Support Systems," *Training,* December 1991, pp. 23–29.

61. L. J. Bassi and S. Cheney, "Changes in Benchmarked Training," *Training & Development*, December 1996, pp. 29–33.

62. K. Dobbs, "Who's in Charge of E-Learning?" *Training*, June 2000, pp. 55–58.

63. For some do's and don'ts on Web-based trainings, see K. Kiser, "10 Things We Know So Far About Online Training," *Training,* November 1999, pp. 66–74.

64. D. Zielinski, "Can You Keep Learners on Line?" *Training,* March 2000, pp. 64–75; and S. Boehle, "My Exasperating Life as an Online Learner," *Training,* June 2000, pp. 64–68.

65. D. Zielinski, "The Lie of Online Learning," *Training,* February 2000, pp. 38–40.

66. Schwade, "Is It Time to Consider Computer-Based Training?" pp. 25–35; and Nina Adams, "CBT or Not CBT?" *Training,* May 1993, pp. 73–75.

67. L. Keegan and S. Rose, "The Good News About Desktop Learning," *Training & Development*, June 1997, pp. 24–27; and J. Gordon and M. Hequet, "Live and in Person," *Training,* March 1997, pp. 24–31.

68. "Industry Report 2000."

69. M. J. Burke and R. R. Day, "A Cumulative Study of the Effectiveness of Managerial Training," *Journal of Applied Psychology,* May 1986, pp. 232–245; for a recent nonempirical review, see

Timothy T. Baldwin and Margaret Y. Padgett, "Management Development: A Review and Commentary," in *International Review of Industrial and Organizational Psychology,* Vol. 8, ed. C. L. Cooper and I. T. Robertson (Chichester, England: Wiley, 1993), pp. 35–85.

70. Morgan W. McCall, Jr., M. M. Lombardo, and A. M. Morrison, *The Lessons of Experience: How Successful Executives Develop on the Job* (Lexington, Mass.: Lexington Books, 1988); G. Cattegno and R. Millwood, "Work-Based Learning for Managers," in *Enterprising Nation*, Research Report Vol. 1 (Commonwealth of Australia, 1995), pp. 75–114; Jean M. Bartunek and Meryl Reis Louis, "The Design of Work Environments to Stretch Managers' Capacities for Complex Thinking," *Human Resource Planning,* Vol. 11 (1), 1988, pp. 13–22; and Gail S. Robinson and Calhoun W. Wick, "Executive Development That Makes a Business Difference," *Human Resource Planning,* Vol. 15, 1992, pp. 63–75.

71. B. R. Ragins and J. L. Cotton, "Mentor Functions and Outcomes: A Comparison of Men and Women in Formal and Informal Mentoring Relationships." *Journal of Applied Psychology*, August 1999, pp. 529–550.

72. For more on trends in executive development, see Conger and Xin, "Executive Education in the 21st Century"; J. Zenger, D. Ulrich, and N. Smallwood, "The New Leadership Development," *Training & Development*, March 2000, pp. 22-27; L. Baird, J. Briscoe, L. Tuden, and L. M. H. Rosansky, "World Class Executive Development," *Human Resource Planning,* Vol. 17 (1), 1994, pp. 1–15; W. Lawler, "The Consortium Approach to Grooming Future Leaders," *Training & Development*, March 2000, pp. 53–57; and J. D. Olian, C. C. Durham, A. L. Kristof, K. G. Brown, R. M. Pierce, and L. Kunder, "Designing Management Training and Development for Competitive Advantage: Lessons from the Best," *Human Resource Planning,* Vol 21 (1), 1998, pp. 20–31.

73. R. J Mirabile, "Competency-Based Strategies," *Handbook of Business Strategy* (New York: Faulkner & Gray, 1997), pp. 297–305; D. Giber, L. Carter, and M. Goldsmith (eds.), *Linkage, Inc.'s Best Practices in Leadership Development Handbook* (Lexington, Mass.: Linkage Inc. 2000); and Olian, Durham, Kristof, Brown, Pierce, and Kunder, "Designing Management Training and Development for Competitive Advantage."

74. D. L. Dotlich and J. L. Noel, *Action Learning* (San Francisco: Jossey-Bass, 1998).

75. Joseph A. Raelin and Michele LeBien, "Learning by Doing," *HRMagazine,* February 1993, pp. 61–70; V. Marsick, "Experience-Based Learning: Executive Learning Outside the Classroom," *Journal of Management Development,* Vol. 9, 1990, pp. 50–60; J. L. Noel and R. Charan, "Leadership Development at GE's Crotonville." *Human Resource Management,* Vol. 27, 1988, pp. 433–447; P. Froiland, "Action Learning: Taming Real Problems in Real Time," *Training*, January 1994, pp. 27–34; and J. A. Raelin, "The Design of the Action Project in Work-Based Learning." *Human Resource Planning,* Vol. 22 (3), 1999, pp. 12–28.

76. C. D. Fisher, "Organizational Socialization: An Integrative Review," *Research in Personnel and Human Resources Management,* Vol. 4, 1986, pp. 101–145.

77. Michelle Neely Martinez, "Disney Training Works Magic," *HRMagazine,* May 1992, pp. 53–57.

78. M. R. Louis, B. Z. Posner, and G. N. Powell, "The Availability and Helpfulness of Socialization Practices," *Personnel Psychology,* Winter 1983, pp. 857–866.

79. For more advice on planning an orientation program, see Mary F. Cook (ed.), *The AMA Handbook for Employee Recruitment and Retention* (New York: AMACOM, 1992), chap. 7.

80. Daniel C. Feldman and Jeanne M. Brett, "Coping with New Jobs: A Comparative Study of New Hires and Job Changers," *Academy of Management Journal,* June 1983, pp. 258–272; and H. J. Klein and N. A. Weaver, "The Effectiveness of an Organizational-Level Orientation Training Program in the Socialization of New Hires," *Personnel Psychology*, Spring 2000, pp. 47–66.

81. Good sources on training delivery skills are J. E. Eitington, *The Winning Trainer* (Houston: Gulf Publishing, 1996); and B. L. Delahaye and B. J. Smith, *How to Be an Effective Trainer* (New York: Wiley, 1998).

82. For recent thinking on training evaluation, see S. M. Brown and C. J. Seidner (eds), *Evaluating Corporate Training: Models and Issues* (Boston: Kluwer Academic Publishers, 1998).

83. Kirkpatrick, "Four Steps to Measuring Training Effectiveness," *The Personnel Administrator,* Vol. 28, 1983, pp. 19–25; D. L. Kirkpatrick, *Evaluating Training Programs: The Four Levels* (San Francisco: Berrett-Koehler, 1994).

84. G. M. Alliger, S. I. Tannenbaum, W. Bennett, Jr., H. Traver, and A. Shotland, "A Meta-Analysis of the Relations Among Training Criteria," *Personnel Psychology,* Vol. 50, 1997, pp. 341–358.

85. S. I. Tannenbaum and S. B. Woods, "Determining a Strategy for Evaluating Training: Operating Within Organizational Constraints," *Human Resource Planning*, Vol. 15 (2), pp. 63–81

86. This section is based on C. D. Fisher, "Laboratory Research," in *Method and Analysis in Organizational Research,* ed. T. S. Bateman and J. R. Ferris (Reston, Va.: Reston Publishing Co., 1984), pp. 169–185; T. D. Cook and D. T. Campbell, "The Design and Conduct of Quasi-Experiments and True Experiments in Field Setting," in M. D. Dunnette (ed.), Handbook *of Industrial and Organizational Psychology.*

87. Richard A. Swanson and Deane B. Gradous, *Forecasting Financial Benefits of Human Resource Development* (San Francisco: Jossey-Bass, 1988); and Wayne F. Cascio, "Using Utility Analysis to Assess Training Outcomes," in I. L. Goldstein (ed.) *Training and Development in Organizations* (San Francisco: Jossey-Bass, 1989), pp. 63–117.

88. Jack J. Phillips, *Handbook of Training Evaluation and Measurement Methods* (Houston: Gulf Publishing, 1991).

89. J. E. Mathieu and R. L. Leonard, Jr., "Applying Utility Concepts to a Training Program in Supervisory Skills: A Time-Based Approach," *Academy of Management Journal,* June 1987, pp. 316–335.

90. F. L. Schmidt, J. E. Hunter, and K. Pearlman, "Assessing the Economic Impact of Personnel Programs on Work Force Productivity," *Personnel Psychology,* Summer 1982, pp. 333–347.

91. J. S. Russell, J. R. Terborg, and M. L. Powers, "Organizational Performance and Organizational Level Training and Support," *Personnel Psychology,* Winter 1985, pp. 849–863.

92. C. C. Morrow, M. Q. Jarrett, and M. T. Rupinski, "An Investigation of the Effect and Economic Utility of Corporate-Wide Training," *Personnel Psychology,* Spring 1997, pp. 91–119.

93. Donald J. Ford, "Benchmarking HRD," *Training & Development,* June 1993, pp. 36–41.

94. A full report on the most recent benchmarking survey can be found on the American Society for Training and Development Web site www.astd.org.

95. L. J. Bassi and S. Cheney, "Changes in Benchmarked Training," *Training & Development,* December 1996, pp. 29–33.

96. K. A. Willyerd, "Balancing Your Evaluation Act," *Training*, March 1997, pp. 52–56.

97. "Trends That Will Influence Workplace Learning and Performance in the Next Five Years," *Training & Development,* May 1994, pp. S28–S31; and M. London and J. W. Smither "Empowered Self-Development and Continuous Learning," *Human Resource Management*, Spring 1999, pp. 3–15.

Human Resource Approaches to Improving Competitiveness

HR Challenge

The Midtown News Courier, *the daily newspaper for a medium-sized city in the U.S. Midwest, is in the process of implementing a formal quality program aimed at making it more competitive against alternative news sources, primarily cable news networks and the Internet. The quality program represents a paradigm change from former management practices. It is envisioned that employees will play a much larger role in controlling their individual processes and in making operational decisions.*

In the newspaper business the daily 10 P.M. print deadline is critical, and some recent delays have been traced to problems in the Prepress Department. (Prepress formats advertisements and does the layout and pagination of news stories with ads.) Apparently, the Prepress Department does not always release copy to Platemaking on schedule. Suppose you have recently been hired as quality coordinator by the Midtown News Courier. You have a number of initiatives underway, but one of your first assignments is to develop a plan for getting the Prepress problem identified and on the road toward resolution. You have decided that in keeping with the new participative approach, an employee involvement team (quality circle) should be formed to look into the issue and make recommendations. Where would you begin? Who should be on the team, and how should they be trained, tasked, and supported? What are the fundamental human resource and general management principles that will be essential if the new quality circle is to be effective? This is the first quality circle in the company, and you are acutely aware that its success (or otherwise) will be a powerful influence on your credibility and that of the entire quality program.[1]

"Competitiveness is a constantly moving target, and marketplace agility—the organizational capacity to influence or anticipate changes in customer needs and to develop products and services to meet these needs better, faster, and smarter than current or potential competitors—becomes critical."[2] The job of any manager entails contributing to the organization's competitiveness through better productivity, quality, cycle time, customer service, and innovation. Many approaches to improving competitiveness involve significant changes in the structure, technology, and work processes of organizations. As will be clear by the end of this chapter, corresponding changes are also required in human behavior, organizational culture, and human resource management practices. As experts on people, attitudes, and effective communication, HR managers have an especially important role in facilitating the success of performance-enhancing changes.

THE COMPETITIVE IMPERATIVES: PRODUCTIVITY, QUALITY, CUSTOMER SERVICE, SPEED, INNOVATION, LEARNING

Increased competition, both globally and domestically, has seen heightened concern first for productivity (in the 1970s) and then for quality (1980s to present). Concern for quality is not restricted to manufacturing industries but has taken root in the service sector as well.[3] It can be argued that quality is even more important in services, since services are rendered to clients in real time. There is no chance to inspect and correct errors before the product reaches the client; the service produced is either good or not good, and it is consumed the moment it is produced.

Quality demands are imposed not just by end consumers of goods or products, but by intermediate consumers as well. Employees are encouraged to provide excellent service to their "internal customers," those to whom they provide service or product, whether that be another department in the company that might consume their work output or the next person on the assembly line. Some organizations also demand that their suppliers have a sound quality process for ensuring that quality is a high priority, that it is built into products, and that it is continuously improved.[4] Vendor certification requirements for quality are increasingly common. A movement toward quality systems certification by the International Organization for Standardization, now represented in the **ISO9001:2000** standard, also has influenced many companies. Being certified as meeting ISO standards is seen as a substantial competitive advantage and is required by some purchasers.[5]

In addition to ISO standards, a series of awards reflect the increasing concern for quality. The **Malcolm Baldrige National Quality Awards** program was begun in the United States in 1987, with the first award made in 1988. The first European Quality Award was given in 1992, and the first British Quality Award was given in 1994. However, the first Deming Prize for quality was awarded in Japan in 1951!

Many American companies have used the Baldrige award criteria as guidelines for their own improvement efforts. There are now three Baldrige awards given each year—in health care, in education, and in business. The criteria for business are listed in Table 10.1. Full details can be found at www.quality.nist.gov. The underlying philosophy for the award is that all aspects of leadership, strategy, systems, people, and values must be aligned around goals of satisfying customers. This can only happen when information is collected and used to monitor performance and customer wishes as well as to benchmark best practice. Further detail on category five of the criteria, Human Resource Focus, can be found later in the chapter in Table 10.14. Note that 165 out of 1,000 points are directly based on human resource practices and results. Arguably, effective performance in many of

● **TABLE 10.1**

Malcolm Baldrige National Quality Award: 2001 Criteria for Performance Excellence in Business

2001 Categories/Items		Point Values
1. Leadership		**120**
1.1 Organizational leadership	80	
1.2 Public responsibility and citizenship	40	
2. Strategic planning		**85**
2.1 Strategy development	40	
2.2 Strategy deployment	45	
3. Customer and market focus		**85**
3.1 Customer and market knowledge	40	
3.2 Customer relationships and satisfaction	45	
4. Information and analysis		**90**
4.1 Measurement and analysis of organizational performance	50	
4.2 Information management	40	
5. Human resource focus		**85**
5.1 Work systems	35	
5.2 Employee education, training, and development	25	
5.3 Employee well-being and satisfaction	25	
6. Process management		**85**
6.1 Product and service processes	45	
6.2 Business processes	25	
6.3 Support processes	15	
7. Business results		**450**
7.1 Customer-focused results	125	
7.2 Financial and market results	125	
7.3 Human resource results	80	
7.4 Organizational effectiveness results	120	
TOTAL POINTS		**1000**

Source: "Baldrige National Quality Program 2001, Criteria for Performance Excellence," p. 9. (Available at: www.quality.nist.gov/2001_Criteria.pdf.htm#BUSINESS)

the other categories can be achieved only through the actions of appropriately se-lected, trained, and motivated employees.

While quality remains an important imperative, in the 1990s there was addi-tional concern with reengineering work processes to remove steps that did not add value. Rather than just doing things with high quality, the aim was to examine and streamline work processes to do only those things that really need to be done. A related concern is speed. In many industries, the most competitive businesses are those that are fast and flexible, and reengineering should increase the speed of most processes. Other aspects of speed include quickly perceiving or anticipating customer needs and then designing and bringing to market—much faster than ever before—new products that meet these needs. The life cycles of many prod-ucts, especially high-tech products, are becoming shorter, requiring organizations to respond much more quickly.[6] Organization must be better than the competition both at product innovation and in adopting new organizational structures to sup-port changing demands and processes.[7]

All this means that organizations must be better at learning—recognizing, cod-ifying, and disseminating the lessons of experience from one part of the organiza-tion to another. The organizations that will survive are those that learn most quickly and effectively so that they can change and improve at a faster rate than their competitors.[8]

In the past few decades, American businesses have experimented with a variety of approaches to improve competitiveness. Some of the approaches rely heavily on computer-controlled manufacturing, statistical methods, and new arrangements with suppliers, such as just-in-time delivery systems. However, many approaches to improving competitiveness emphasize the human role, either alone or in conjunc-tion with some of the preceding methods. Any major change targeted at productiv-ity, quality, or process has a major impact on employees' jobs and is critically depen-dent on employees for success. This chapter introduces a number of approaches to improving organizational competitiveness and performance through people.

PLANNING FOR IMPROVED COMPETITIVENESS

Each organization needs to tailor its own approach to improving competitiveness, focusing on the criteria of most importance to success in its industry and in its par-ticular strategic niche. Some organizations will find that speed is most important, whereas others will need to strive for zero defects, breakthrough innovations, or extreme efficiency, though the most successful firms are good at several of these criteria. The literature offers a number of approaches,[9] but the most successful or-ganizations create a customized blend that best fills their needs.[10] Any plan for im-proving performance requires careful diagnosis of the problem and then attention to the issue of getting the approach accepted and fully implemented in the organi-zation.

Diagnosis and Benchmarking

Prior to undertaking any approach to improving productivity, processes, or quality, the organization must develop a thorough understanding of the current state of af-fairs so that it can choose appropriately targeted methods and monitor progress.

● **TABLE 10.2**

Steps in Benchmarking

Define business issue of importance

Decide what to benchmark and what specific measures to use

Determine whom (which firms) to benchmark

Collect measures from benchmark firms (by questionnaire and some site visits)

Analyze data, compare performance of company to benchmark information, locate gaps

Plan actions to close gaps

Implement plans

Monitor results

Frequently, when managers are faced with poor productivity or quality, they attribute the difficulty to low employee effort or carelessness. However, programs to improve employee motivation will have minimal impact if productivity problems are due to defective raw materials, poorly conceived manufacturing processes, or inappropriate organizational structures. Clearly, careful diagnosis must precede any efforts to improve productivity and quality. Diagnosis starts with a study of the organization itself and usually should include reactions from the organization's clients. An additional popular tool for providing a frame of reference for interpreting internal measures is **benchmarking,** studying the performance and practices of world leaders in the industry or function being assessed.[11] Table 10.2 shows the steps involved in the benchmarking process.

The United States Air Force adopted benchmarking on a large scale in 1993. Benchmarking champions were appointed to drive the process at each of its thirty-five commands and field operating agencies. A benchmarking effort was the stimulus for substantial changes in the basic recruit training program at Lackland Air Force Base in San Antonio. This program trains 35,000 to 40,000 recruits per year. Fourteen major issues were identified, comprising items such as physical conditioning, training technology, academic curricula, and facilities. These were examined in a tour of six other basic training organizations in the United States (Navy, Marine Corps, Army) and the United Kingdom. As a result of seeing how these other organizations managed their recruit training activities, the Air Force implemented a number of changes. These included smaller class sizes, physical training based on preexisting fitness levels, and a redesign of the layout and purpose of the obstacle course. All Air Force recruits are now benefiting from these changes. Benchmarking champion Lieutenant Colonel Bruce Jaeger says, "When we change one hour of basic training, we get 35,000 hours of improvement per year."[12]

Obtaining Commitment

No improvement plan, no matter how well it is suited to the situation, will succeed without the understanding and commitment of employees. All stages of planning and implementation should include getting more people on board and overcoming or minimizing resistance to change. The assessment and benchmarking process just described is often very powerful in gaining top management's commitment to a change.[13] Others who have been involved in the surveys or the benchmarking study are also likely to see a need for change and increase their level of commitment. In general, wider employee participation at early stages will pave the way for wider acceptance in later stages. Many of the approaches that have recently become popular place great emphasis on employee participation and empowerment. HR managers can provide a valuable service to other managers by emphasizing these points and developing mechanisms for employee input.

It seems to be critical that top management commit to and support major organizational change efforts.[14] Turning all responsibility for the program over to the HR department, the quality department, or hired consultants is a likely recipe for failure. Given ongoing and visible commitment at the top, a number of steps are needed to convert the rest of the organization. These almost always include extensive educational efforts and may also include pilot projects that demonstrate the utility of the change being proposed. A rule of thumb for organizations attempting major changes is that such changes will be at least three times as difficult and take twice as long to implement as expected; miracles do not happen overnight, and sometimes they do not happen at all.[15] Nevertheless, more and more organizations are managing to make the transition to a high-quality or high-performance mentality.

Organizations can choose from a large number of possible methods to improve productivity or quality. Some of these methods focus on the entire organization and entail changes in the organization's culture, values, structure, and relationships between and within work units. Other interventions are on a somewhat smaller scale and may be put in place with less cultural change; they range from individual goal setting and financial incentives to job enrichment.

MAJOR ORGANIZATIONAL APPROACHES TO COMPETITIVENESS

Although it is beyond the scope of this book to explore organizational-level productivity and quality-enhancing strategies in great depth, we will discuss several major thrusts in this area before turning to a consideration of some more specific techniques. The first is business process improvement or reengineering. The second is total quality management. The third is a comprehensive form of employee involvement called the high-involvement organization (HIO).

Business Process Improvement (Reengineering)

Generally attributed to IBM, **business process improvement** is a set of practices for regularly examining and improving the processes that go on in an organization. A "process" is a repeated set of activities, often carried out in sequence by several departments, that adds value and produces measurable outputs. Examples include billing, distribution, materials management, and procurement.[16] In a traditional approach to quality, each department involved in a process would try to do its portion of the activity more quickly and accurately, but the entire process from start to finish is unlikely to be critically evaluated or redesigned. Thus very dated, inefficient systems might be tweaked into becoming faster—but still dated and inefficient—systems.

Business process improvement became extremely popular during the 1990s and is often called **reengineering.**[17] Reengineering is defined as "the fundamental rethinking and *radical redesign* of business *processes* to bring about *dramatic* improvements in performance."[18] The focus is on a major change that greatly streamlines an entire work process rather than making minor incremental changes. An example of a process is order fulfillment. The several steps in receiving and filling an order (such as order taking, verifying the customer's ability to pay, selecting goods from a warehouse, packing them, and shipping them) are often split across several departments (sales, accounts, warehouse). As work is handed from one group to the other, delays and errors occur and unnecessary paperwork is required. Reengineering cuts out unnecessary steps and breaks down barriers between departments.

In reengineering, someone is assigned responsibility for the whole process. This manager works with a cross-functional team to assess the state of the process and develop new ways to perform it better. Statistical quality measurement and analysis techniques may be used, and small-scale experiments with new processes may be tried. The process is then redesigned and further improvements made on the basis of experience. The steps in business process improvement used at IBM are shown in Table 10.3. One example of a successful implementation of this approach involved accounts payable at Ford Motor Company. After benchmarking its accounts payable function against Mazda Motor Corporation, Ford realized that its employee head-

●**TABLE 10.3**

Business Process Analysis Methodology Steps

1. Assign ownership.
   —Charge key managers to improve process.
2. Perform activity analysis at task level.
   —Establish measurements, true cost of quality.
3. Document current procedures.
   —Iterate with key employees until accuracy is achieved.
4. Document the process.
   —Functional/cross-functional relationships.
5. Determine process requirements and secure customer concurrence.
6. Assess impact of any mismatch.
   —Prioritize problems based on requirements vs. existing process.
7. Analyze potential solutions to bring process into conformance.
   —Eliminate failure cost and improve control through:
      a. Process simplification by elimination of redundant tasks, combining like tasks, adding missing tasks.
      b. Restructure and automate where appropriate.
   —Review additional resources, retraining requirement, new capital equipment, etc.
   —Pilot test process changes with specific pass/fail criteria to ensure fix is permanent and complete.
8. Select and implement best alternatives.
9. Update target and measurement criteria for new process.
10. Establish regular next level management review plan vs. actual.
11. Feedback new management control activity requirements.
12. Update managers' performance plan to be quality specific for the new process.

Source: H. James Harrington, *The Quality/Profit Connection* (Milwaukee, Wis.: ASQC Quality Press, 1989). Reprinted with the permission of ASQC Quality Press.

count in this function was probably five times what it should have been. By helping employees to perform the same tasks faster, only a 20 percent reduction in staff would be possible. But by redesigning the entire system for keeping track of orders, deliveries, and invoices, the company dramatically simplified the process. Before the changes, clerks had to check and match fourteen items on three forms before paying an invoice; they spent much of their time trying to unravel mismatches. Now only three items have to be matched, and a computer system does the matching automatically and prepares the check. The function requires 75 percent fewer people, and errors have been reduced substantially.[19]

Some companies in both the United States and Europe have received enormous benefits from well-executed reengineering efforts. American Express saved over $1 billion per year, while Progressive Insurance greatly reduced claims processing time, increased customer satisfaction, and increased revenue per employee by more than 70 percent. However, for every success story, there is also a failure—probably due to misunderstanding what reengineering is all about, poor leadership, or resistance to change.[20] In some cases, the rhetoric of reengineering has been used as a pretext to greatly reduce employee headcount. If processes have not really been streamlined, fewer employees are left to struggle with a still-inefficient process.

Total Quality Management

Total quality management (TQM) ideas began to gain increasing acceptance in the United States in the mid-1980s. By 1993, 76 percent of *Fortune* 1000 firms had adopted total quality management for at least part of their work force. By 1997, 57 percent of a representative sample of establishments in the United States said they had adopted TQM for at least half of their work force. TQM first became popular in manufacturing organizations, but it has also been widely adopted in service settings.[21] While the phrase TQM is starting to go out of vogue, its fundamental principles have become routine and widely accepted business essentials.

TQM ideas have been most clearly enunciated by experts such as Philip Crosby, Joseph Juran, W. Edwards Deming, Armand J. Feigenbaum, and Genichi Taguchi.[22] These ideas were adopted and mastered by the Japanese and only later spread to American companies. While there are many variations on the TQM theme, the characteristics described below and listed in Table 10.4 seem to be typical of the approach.[23]

Quality is the most important focus of attention in TQM. Doing high-quality work the first time improves productivity and reduces the costs of inspection and rework. Employees are encouraged, both individually and in quality circle teams, to make frequent suggestions on how the work process or quality can be improved. Great leaps forward are viewed as resulting from many small steps toward continuous improvement. The term **kaizen** (Japanese for "continuous small improvements") is widely used in American organizations.

TQM organizations try to be strongly customer-focused. Typically, employees are trained to identify their customers—the people who depend on the employees' output. These can be either internal customers or external purchasers of the organization's product or service. The needs of these customers are assessed; then employees make an effort to meet their customers' needs fully, the first time, every time. TQM organizations may also work closely with suppliers to ensure high-quality input and perhaps to allow for just-in-time delivery of materials.

● **TABLE 10.4**

Common Principles Underlying Most Approaches to TQM

- Customer-first orientation
- Top management leadership of the quality improvement process
- Focus on continuous improvement
- Respect for employees and their knowledge (Employees are actively involved in the improvement process.)
- Reduction of product and process variation
- Provision of ongoing education and training to employees
- Familiarity with a statistical way of thinking and the use of statistical methods throughout the organization
- Emphasis on prevention rather than detection
- View of vendors as long-term partners
- Performance measures that are consistent with the goals of the organization
- Standardization—the development of and adherence to the best known ways to perform a given task
- Product or service quality begins with its definition and design
- Cooperation and involvement of all functions within an organization
- Awareness of the needs of internal customers
- Substantial cultural change

Source: Ronald M. Fortuna, "The Quality Imperative," in *Total Quality: An Executive's Guide for the 1990s,* ed. by Ernst & Young Improvement Consulting Group (Homewood, Ill.: Dow Jones–Irwin, 1990), p. 110.

Statistical process control methods are used to detect variances from the desired standard, allowing for prompt correction and prevention of further defects from the same cause. There is heavy emphasis on measurement, and many employees in TQM organizations are trained in statistical methods. Most workplaces feature charts, which are updated daily, showing trends in quality indicators.

Many organizations have had good results from implementing TQM.[24] Others have found that adopting the tools, techniques, and meetings without gaining employee acceptance and internalization of quality goals is fairly ineffective. Critical to the success of TQM is the adoption of a quality culture in the organization.[25] When the culture remains unchanged, TQM may produce fewer positive results than promised. See A Different Point of View for more on this issue.

High-Involvement/High-Performance Human Resource Systems

As long ago as 1985, a shift in the basic paradigm of managing employees was foreshadowed by R. E. Walton in the *Harvard Business Review.*[26] He forecasted, correctly, that organizations would increasingly turn from a supervision- and control-oriented strategy for managing employees to one based on self-control and employee commitment. Table 10.5 details these changes. Edward Lawler points out that a control-oriented approach, in which employees add limited value to a product by applying simple and standardized skills, is only feasible in a low-wage environment. In developed countries, where wages are higher, employees can only cover their costs by adding value with their heads as well as their hands, so work systems and human resource practices must be designed to enable and motivate this greater contribution.[27]

A DIFFERENT POINT OF VIEW

Does TQM Really Work?

 Although TQM has been very popular and has been adopted by a large number of organizations, it does not always "work." Research in America, Europe, and Australia suggests that TQM produces measurable improvement in only 20 to 30 percent of companies that say they have adopted it. The most vocal critics seem to agree that a related set of problems can plague TQM efforts:

1. TQM is seen as a "quick fix," a set of techniques to be adopted for instantaneous results. Unless other changes in corporate culture and structure are undertaken to gain widespread commitment, reduce bureaucracy to get closer to the customer, redesign incentive systems for top managers so that rewards are tied to improving customer satisfaction, and enter into new types of relationships with suppliers, TQM techniques will have little impact. Some feel that TQM allows managers to "hide" from these very difficult bigger problems yet still be viewed as doing something.

2. TQM tends to be focused largely on improving internal processes, to the exclusion of concern for external results such as satisfying customers. Short-term internal measures such as waste, productivity, and conformity to standards receive great attention, but often there is little concern about the long-term effects of these improvements on customers. Do customers want a zero-defects buggy whip, or do they want something entirely different? Efficiency may go up as the work is done better, but effectiveness may not increase if the firm is doing the wrong kind of work.

3. TQM tends to be activity-based, not results-based. The firm feels it is making progress because 85 percent of employees have been to quality training, twenty quality circles are operating, and every department displays quality progress charts on the wall. One author refers to this as "excessive activity syndrome" and feels that it takes managers' focus off the results that really matter: actually improving quality and customer satisfaction.

4. TQM may stifle innovation and creativity. It has been accused of being rigid and sterile, tied to standardized measures and processes. An overemphasis on "doing it right the first time" may slow down responses to change, while a willingness to tolerate less-than-perfect efficiency may be more useful in quickly responding to new opportunities or customer needs.

5. While TQM is supposed to make everyone responsible for quality, it often creates its own bureaucracy and localizes responsibility for quality in the quality department, quality experts, and consultants.

TQM advocates have responded strongly to these criticisms. They deny that the problem is in the TQM concept but agree that it may reside in how TQM is implemented in particular organizations. One has gone so far as to say that if a supposed TQM program actually causes the preceding problems, then it is not a TQM program but a haphazard adoption of some TQM techniques without the underlying TQM philosophy. Another describes the latter as "partial quality management."

Sources: Oren Harari, "Ten Reasons Why TQM Doesn't Work," *Management Review,* January 1993, pp. 33–38; Selwyn W. Becker, "TQM Does Work: Ten Reasons Why Misguided Attempts Fail," *Management Review,* May 1993, pp. 30–33; Oren Harari, "The Eleventh Reason Why TQM Doesn't Work," *Management Review,* May 1993, pp. 31–37; John A. Goodman, Gary F. Bargatze, and Cynthia Grimm, "The Key Problem with TQM," *Quality Progress,* January 1994, pp. 45–48; B. M. Staw and L. D. Epstein, "What Bandwagons Bring: Effects of Popular Management Techniques on Corporate Performance, Reputation, and CEO Pay," *Administrative Science Quarterly*, September 2000, pp. 523–556; and J. Yong and A. Wilkinson, "The State of Total Quality Management: A Review," *International Journal of Human Resource Management*, February 1999, pp. 137–161.

● **TABLE 10.5**

The Evolution from Control to Commitment-Oriented Workforce Strategies

	Control	Transitional	Commitment
Job design principles	Individual attention limited to performing individual job.	Scope of individual responsibility extended to upgrading system performance, via participative problem-solving groups in quality of work life (QWL), employee involvement (EI), and quality circle programs.	Individual responsibility extended to upgrading system performance.
	Job design deskills and fragments work and separates doing and thinking.	No change in traditional job design or accountability.	Job design enhances content of work, emphasizes whole task, and combines doing and thinking.
	Accountability focused on individual.		Frequent use of teams as basic accountable unit.
	Fixed job definition.		Flexible definition of duties, contingent on changing conditions.
Performance expectations	Measured standards define minimum performance. Stability seen as desirable.		Emphasis placed on higher, "stretch objectives," which tend to be dynamic and oriented to the marketplace.
Management organization: structure, systems, and style	Structure tends to be layered, with top-down controls.	No basic changes in approaches to structure, control, or authority.	Flat organization structure with mutual influence systems.
	Coordination and control rely on rules and procedures.		Coordination and control based more on shared goals, values, and traditions.
	More emphasis on prerogatives and positional authority.		Management emphasis on problem solving and relevant information and expertise.
	Status symbols distributed to reinforce hierarchy.	A few visible symbols change.	Minimum status differentials to de-emphasize inherent hierarchy.
Compensation policies	Variable pay where feasible to provide individual incentive.	Typically no basic changes in compensation concepts.	Variable rewards to create equity and to reinforce group achievements: gain sharing, profit sharing.
	Individual pay geared to job evaluation.		Individual pay linked to skills and mastery.
	In downturn, cuts concentrated on hourly payroll.	Equality of sacrifice among employee groups.	Equality of sacrifice.

(continued)

● TABLE 10.5 (continued)

	Control	Transitional	Commitment
Employment assurances	Employees regarded as variable costs.	Assurances that participation will not result in loss of job. Extra effort to avoid layoffs.	Assurances that participation will not result in loss of job. High commitment to avoid or assist in reemployment. Priority for training and retaining existing work force.
Employee voice policies	Employee input allowed on relatively narrow agenda. Attendant risks emphasized. Methods include open-door policy, attitude surveys, grievance procedures, and collective bargaining in some organizations.	Addition of limited, ad hoc consultation mechanisms. No change in corporate governance.	Employee participation encouraged on wide range of issues. Attendant benefits emphasized. New concepts of corporate governance.
	Business information distributed on strictly defined "need to know" basis.	Additional sharing of information.	Business data shared widely.
Labor-management relations	Adversarial labor relations: emphasis on interest conflict.	Thawing of adversarial attitudes; joint sponsorship of QWL or EI; emphasis on common fate.	Mutuality in labor relations; joint planning and problem solving on expanded agenda. Unions, management, and workers redefine their respective roles.

The terms **high-involvement organization (HIO)** and **high-performance work systems** have been used to describe a bundle of human resource practices designed to produce superior outcomes in terms of organizational learning, customer satisfaction, flexibility, quality, morale, and overall effectiveness. Typical practices of high-involvement organizations are listed in Table 10.6. High involvement organizations share power, information, knowledge, and rewards with employees.[28]

Power is shared downward by various mechanisms for obtaining employee input into decisions. These may include quality circles or other forms of work-improvement teams, suggestion systems, job enrichment that gives employees more responsibility for broader work tasks, and self-directed work teams. (Self-directed work teams will be discussed in more detail later in this chapter.) Decision making is often decentralized and delegated to the lowest level possible, with employees and teams taking responsibility for decisions that would ordinarily be the province of management. Another manifestation of shared power is "symbolic egalitarianism." This means reducing visible power and status differences between levels of employees and management. All employees may be called "associates" or "members," everyone may dress in the same way, and there are no perquisites like reserved parking places or executive dining rooms.[29]

● **TABLE 10.6**

Practices Often Found in High-Involvement Organizations

- Employment security
- Selective hiring of new personnel
- Self-managed teams and decentralization of decision making as the basic principles of organizational design
- Comparatively high compensation contingent of organizational performance
- Extensive training
- Reduced status distinctions and barriers, including dress, language, office arrangements, and wage differences across levels
- Extensive sharing of financial and performance information throughout the organization.

Source: Reprinted by permission of Harvard Business School Press. From *The Human Equation: Building Profits by Putting People First* by Jeffrey Pfeiffer. Boston, MA, 1998, pp. 64–65. Copyright © 1998 by Harvard Business School Publishing Corporation. All rights reserved.

Information about the business is widely shared with employees so that they have the understanding and background to contribute to decision making in the organization. For instance, employees at all levels may be given information about the overall performance of the firm, the performance of their work units, technological changes likely to affect the organization, financial results, and information about the company's strategy and competitors.

Knowledge is enhanced by frequent job skills training, cross-training on related jobs, and teamwork training to equip employees for more complex jobs, decision-making responsibilities, and team-oriented work.

Financial *rewards* from superior organizational performance are also shared with employees. While base pay may be low, bonuses based on organizational or unit performance bring take-home pay to levels well beyond average for the industry, in recognition of the greater skills and responsibilities employees possess.[30] Profit sharing, gain sharing, and/or employee stock ownership programs are used to enhance employee identification with the organization. Some HIOs use pay-for-skills systems to determine base pay. These systems reward learning additional jobs within the team and encourage multiskilling and flexibility. Generally, however, pay differences between individuals and jobs in HIOs are downplayed so that everyone can focus on organizational performance rather than competing against one another.

HIOs spend a great deal of time and effort in selecting employees in order to obtain those with the skills and values needed both for teamwork and for more complex tasks and responsibilities. They may start with a large candidate pool, then assess applicants intensively on learning ability, team skills, and attitude as well as current skills. To retain their heavy investment in human resource selection and development, HIOs often provide greater assurance of employment security than do typical organizations.

There is convincing evidence that the adoption of high-performance work systems can bring benefits in terms of organizational performance.[31] Correctly implemented, HIO practices create a unique culture that is difficult for competitors to imitate and can provide a sustained competitive advantage.[32] Adopting one or two practices is unlikely to be nearly as effective.[33] Table 10.7 contains a questionnaire for assessing how far along an organization is in adopting a range of HIO practices.

● **TABLE 10.7**

The High-Involvement Human Resource Practices Scale

Extent to which this question describes your organization's practices:	Not at all or a little	Some	A great extent
Training and development			
1. Does your organization provide training in teamwork?	1	2	3
2. Does your organization provide experience on multiple jobs through job rotation?	1	2	3
3. Are employees certified on certain skills once they demonstrate their proficiency?	1	2	3
4. Does your company provide training in areas not directly related to one's line of work?	1	2	3
5. Do supervisors attend the training programs in which their subordinates participate?	1	2	3
6. Are employees taught how to do other people's jobs?	1	2	3
7. Are employees trained on new skills, regardless of whether these are part of their primary responsibilities?	1	2	3
Selection and promotion			
8. Does applicants' selection depend on how they will fit into the team?	1	2	3
9. Is the ability to learn multiple jobs more important in selecting applicants than proficiency in one specific skill?	1	2	3
10. When screening applicants, is the possession of skills that are in accordance with the company's strategy a factor taken into account?	1	2	3
11. Do coworkers interview applicants to assess their ability to work effectively with others?	1	2	3
12. When selecting new employees, are current employees asked for their input?	1	2	3
13. Is how well the employee works with others more important than the employee's technical qualifications when deciding who gets promoted?	1	2	3
Performance evaluation			
14. Are teams as opposed to individuals the focus of performance evaluations?	1	2	3
15. Is anyone other than direct supervisors asked for input in the employee performance evaluation?	1	2	3
16. Do performance evaluations promote employee cooperation?	1	2	3
17. Is how well employees serve internal and external customers one of the most important factors in performance evaluation?	1	2	3
18. Are team achievements an important factor in evaluating employee performance?	1	2	3
19. Are suppliers questioned about the performance of those employees who come in contact with them?	1	2	3
20. Is the ability to work in teams one of the most important components of the performance evaluation?	1	2	3

(continued)

● **TABLE 10.7** (continued)

Extent to which this question describes your organization's practices:	Not at all or a little	Some	A great extent
Job redesign			
21. Are employees given opportunities to participate in tasks outside their normal job duties?	1	2	3
22. Are job descriptions broad rather than specific?	1	2	3
23. In most jobs, is only minimal interaction with other employees needed?	3	2	1
24. Do employees frequently rotate throughout different jobs?	1	2	3
25. Are job boundaries clearly defined?	3	2	1
26. In most jobs, are job responsibilities constantly changing?	1	2	3
27. Is job redesign carried out solely by management?	3	2	1
Compensation	1	2	3
28. Is employee compensation dependent on overall team or departmental performance?	1	2	3
29. Are team efforts unrewarded for the most part?	3	2	1
30. Do employees receive a salary raise when they demonstrate mastery of a new skill?	1	2	3
31. Does the company compensate employees on the basis of team or group performance?	1	2	3
32. Does the company compensate according to the extent to which employees master particular skills?	1	2	3
33. Are a majority of employees compensated hourly (rather than salaried?)	3	2	1

Source: J. I. Sanchez, E. Kraus, S. White, and M. Williams, *Group & Organization Management,* December 1999, pp. 461–478, copyright © 1999 by Sage Publications, Inc. Reprinted by permission of Sage Publications, Inc.

The HIO approach may not be feasible for every organization. If the work itself is extremely routine and cannot be redesigned so that employees can contribute more value through enhanced skills and responsibility, the approach will fail. Research has shown that high-performance work practices enhance performance more in automobile plants that have also implemented lean and flexible manufacturing processes. In flexible manufacturing, low buffer stocks between processes increase interdependence and require employees to take initiative in troubleshooting and remedying problems on the spot. The flexible manufacturing design is complemented by a series of multiple, overlapping, and mutually reinforcing human resource practices that assure that employees have needed skills and motivation to cope with these task demands. For instance, high selectivity, formal training for both new and experienced employees, cross-training within teams, and job rotation act together to enhance skill and knowledge.[34]

In the service sector, evidence is emerging that the adoption of an integrated set of high-performance work practices can create loyal, satisfied, high-tenure, capable employees who enjoy providing superior service to customers. Recruiting costs decline, employee skills grow with experience, and investments in training pay off over longer periods of time when employee turnover is low. Good service means that customers are retained—and it is much less expensive to retain an

● **FIGURE 10.1**

The Service–Profit Chain

Source: Reprinted by permission of *Harvard Business Review,* Exhibit from "Putting the Service–Profit Chain to Work" by J. L. Heskett, T. O. Jones, G. W. Loveman, W. E. Sasser, Jr., and L. A. Schlesinger, March/April 1994. Copyright © 1994 by the Harvard Business School Publishing Corporation. All rights reserved.

existing customer than to attract a new one. Further, satisfied customers tell their friends, thus increasing business volume.[35] Figure 10.1 demonstrates the **"service–profit chain"** established by researchers over the past decade. Clearly, effective human resource management through high-involvement practices can pay off for service organizations as well as for manufacturing organizations.

SPECIFIC INTERVENTIONS

This section addresses some specific changes that organizations may adopt to improve productivity, quality, or other aspects of competitiveness. Some of these might be used as part of a large-scale TQM or HIO effort, whereas others can be adopted as relatively freestanding programs. Some of the methods rely on groups, whereas others are aimed more at employees as individuals.

Group-focused interventions are based on the belief that employees at all levels in the organization desire to contribute to the effective functioning of the organization, that everyone has useful insights to contribute, and that groups are a good forum for generating and refining ideas. Thus the objective of group participative programs is to empower groups of employees to identify and solve performance problems in their own areas of expertise.[36] Group programs include part-time or "off-line" work improvement teams, also known as quality circles (QCs), in which members get together for a few hours each week to solve problems, and full-time self-directed work teams in which most of the responsibility for ongoing production is delegated to the work group itself.[37]

Work-Improvement Teams (Quality Circles)

Work-improvement teams or **quality circles (QCs)** became extremely popular in the 1980s, particularly in the aerospace, automobile, steel, and consumer goods industries. Although the term "quality circle" has declined in popularity, the incidence of such groups has grown. A recent survey found that 27 percent of responding firms had quality circles in 1992, while 58 percent of a similar sample had them in 1997.[38] Quality circles are almost always featured in TQM programs.[39] A quality circle consists of a small number of volunteers, typically eight to ten employees from the same department, who meet for a few hours each week to examine productivity and quality problems. Initially, these circles may be led by a supervisor, but they usually evolve to nonmanagement leadership. QC members identify a problem, study it, and present their recommendations for change and improvement to a committee of higher management.[40]

Quality circles are not limited to manufacturing work. At Velcro USA, half the teams are in administrative units.[41] Potentially large gains can result when quality circles made up of managers analyze their process of holding meetings and figure out how to make that activity more efficient.[42] Furthermore, it is not always true that QC members come from the same department. Cross-functional QCs are sometimes assembled to work on larger problems that transcend departmental boundaries.

At the *Midtown News Courier*, the Prepress quality circle was successful. The team was formed of employees in the Prepress Department, plus a representative from Platemaking, the downstream customer of the Prepress Department. Formal team training was not undertaken, but the quality coordinator and a consultant attended most team meetings and provided just-in-time input in the form of teaching the group about cause-and-effect analysis and similar quality tools. The team brainstormed to generate a large list of reasons that their material could be late to Platemaking. Some of these reasons were deemed to be under their control, and others were not. The latter included late receipt of material from other units and delays in feedback from advertisers on draft layouts. The team worked diligently to modify processes and improve timeliness for issues under their own control and internal to the Prepress Department. The quality coordinator took the list of reasons for lateness not under Prepress's control and formed another quality circle upstream of Prepress to address these issues. Anecdotally, members of the Prepress quality circle seemed to have become more interested in their work, developed higher morale, understood the entire process surrounding their specific job more thoroughly, and become more sympathetic when problems in other departments created "unreasonable" deadlines in Prepress.

● **Effectiveness of Work-Improvement Teams**   As at *Midtown News Courier*, quality circles can be quite effective. Some organizations have reported a return on investment ranging from 200 to 800 percent. Experts have also suggested that since the technique is a participative one, improved employee morale should be an additional result. However, this is not always the case.[43] In one review of research, about half the studies of QC implementations reported uniformly positive results—that is, improvement in all variables measured in the study (such as productivity, quality, absenteeism, or job attitudes). One-quarter of the studies found that QCs had some beneficial effects, and the other quarter reported no beneficial changes.[44] Other reviews are less positive, particularly about the effects of quality circles on productivity and quality.[45] Part-time teams that provide suggestions, like QCs, are generally less effective than full-time teams that collaborate to actually do the work.[46] Further, the success (or otherwise) of QCs may depend partly on national culture issues. See the International Perspective box for a discussion of why quality circles largely failed in Hong Kong.

Work-improvement teams are often part of organizational-level changes toward a total quality management culture. In this context, they seem likely to succeed, since they will be embedded in a supportive environment and will be consistent with other changes taking place at the same time. If QCs are adopted as a stand-alone program that is inconsistent with other systems in the organization, the prospects for success diminish. However, quality circles have been suggested as a bridge between a nonparticipative approach to management and more far-reaching changes in the work structure, such as self-directed work teams.[47]

● **Problems in Implementing Work-Improvement Teams**   When implementing work-improvement teams, companies must address several possible problems. Often managers and workers are skeptical of the program because they view it as simply a fad that is being imposed on them. Supervisors may also tend to be nervous about such a program, viewing it as a threat to their authority. Moreover, employees who volunteer for QCs may wish to air complaints against management or discuss issues such as wages and benefits. These issues are usually explicitly off-limits for quality circles, but when employees find that they must comply with this ban, they may become disillusioned about the depth of management's commitment to participation.

Another typical problem with QCs, especially early in the program, is that they stretch the volunteerism concept. When circles are just being formed, they require much time and effort, something workers might be unprepared for.[48] Most quality circles begin with a great deal of training in identifying work problems, applying statistics to track and evaluate quality, and working together in a group. This stage can be frustrating for employees who want to get right to work on a problem. For circles to succeed over the longer term, management needs to show its commitment by implementing some of the groups' suggestions and providing prompt feedback on the disposition of all suggestions. It seems that QCs have a definite life cycle of from one to three years. Few circles continue to operate beyond this period of time because they run out of either motivation or easily solved problems.

Full-Time Work Teams

It has become increasingly common to put workers into full-time teams, with a recent survey suggesting that 80 percent of *Fortune* 500 companies had half or more of their work forces in teams.[49] Some supervisor-led teams are only slight

INTERNATIONAL PERSPECTIVE

Why Quality Circles Fail in Hong Kong

 Paul Kirkbride and Sara Tang have written an interesting article both exposing and explaining the difficulties that the quality circle concept encountered in Hong Kong. At first, one might assume that the concept would transfer relatively well from its birthplace in Japan to Hong Kong because of their shared cultural roots in Confucianism and their dynamic business environments, but this has not been the case. Quality circles have found advocates in Hong Kong, and a number of companies have tried to adopt the practice. However, surveys suggest that relatively few have been successful. The reasons underlying this lack of success appear to stem from both business and cultural factors.

Several aspects of Hong Kong's business environment make quality circles less likely to function well. One is labor instability. Turnover is high and employees generally are not strongly committed to a single employer, so they are less motivated to become involved in extra (especially unpaid) workplace activities. Many Chinese businesses operate in highly competitive markets with large fluctuations in demand or short production runs. These situations do not lend themselves to careful study and improvement because of the instability of work processes. In addition, Hong Kong has a very large number of small family businesses. One survey found that the average manufacturing business had only seventeen employees. In operations this small, the owner/manager is close enough to the work to notice any needed changes personally. Another factor may be the low education level of many staff and the unwillingness of owners, particularly of small businesses, to spend money on training employees for quality circles.

Cultural factors that mitigate against the success of quality circles include high power distance, meaning that superiors tend to act in an autocratic rather than a participative way toward their subordinates. Managers often feel threatened by the power that quality circles give blue-collar workers. Subordinates are relatively untrusting of management but also unwilling to cause a superior's loss of face by making suggestions that could be seen as indirect criticism.

Hong Kong has a highly collectivist culture, suggesting that working in groups and for the good of the group should come naturally. However, the collectivism tends to be strongly family-oriented—unlike Japan's collectivism, which extends to the workplace family. In collectivist cultures, great loyalty is shown to the in group, but very little interest, charity, or commitment is extended to outgroups. In Hong Kong, this means that workplace quality circle groups are met with resounding apathy.

Japanese culture is different from Hong Kong's in that the former places much more emphasis on achievement, recognition, challenge, and the importance of work. Hong Kong's culture places more emphasis on making money. Since quality circles seldom involve tangible rewards, their lukewarm reception should not be surprising.

It is worth noting that there are success stories of quality circles in Hong Kong. As one might expect, they are found primarily among larger organizations (e.g., Cathay Pacific Airways, Hong Kong Bank, the Mass Transit Railway Corporation) and among foreign-owned organizations whose home-country culture more strongly supports participative management.

Sources: Paul S. Kirkbride and Sara F. Y. Tang, "From Kyoto to Kowloon: Cultural Barriers to the Transference of Quality Circles from Japan to Hong Kong," *Asia Pacific Journal of Human Resources,* Winter 1994, pp. 100–111; Ka-kui Tse, "Will Quality Circles Work in Hong Kong?" *The Hong Kong Manager,* Vol. 17 (11), 1981, pp. 16–24; Geert Hofstede, *Culture's Consequences* (Beverly Hills: Sage, 1984); and J. Kivela and F. Go, "Total Quality Management Transfer: A Case of Hong Kong Hotels," *Asia Pacific Journal of Human Resources,* Vol. 34 (1), 1996, pp. 63–76.

variations on traditional work structures, but self-directed work teams are truly innovative and are becoming increasingly common.

The **self-directed (or self-managed) work team,** also called the **autonomous work group,** is given near-total responsibility for a defined area of work on a product or service. These full-time teams make most of their own production decisions, such as scheduling, assigning work, deciding on methods, and even selecting new members, doing performance evaluations, training one another, and allocating pay raises. There is no supervisor, but there is often an elected team leader or coordinator. Management is responsible for providing information to the group on costs, quality, output requirements, and any technical assistance that is requested.[50] This concept is widely used in high-involvement organizations.

Companies that have been integrating self-directed work teams into their plants include Procter & Gamble, Cummins Engine Company, General Motors, Westinghouse Electric Corporation, TRW, Inc., GTE, Sherwin-Williams Company, AT&T, Boeing, Unisys, and IBM. These companies claim that the teams can increase productivity by 30 to 50 percent. Studies of self-directed work teams verify that sometimes, but not always, autonomous work teams result in increased quality and productivity.[51] Some dips in productivity would be expected in the early stages as the teams struggle to adapt to new ways of working, and it can take up to three years for teams to reach their full potential.

Self-managed work teams do not fit all situations. Teams only make sense when the work tasks within a team are interdependent, when the company's culture is consistent with participation and empowerment, and when the company is willing to make a long-term commitment to the team concept. For self-directed work teams to succeed, the company must loosen control systems, remove bureaucratic procedures, and provide a great deal of team training. It must also assure that near-continuous information is available on targets and relevant current performance (output, quality, cost, waste, etc.). Teams use this information to regulate their actions from moment to moment. Where unions exist, the company must convince the union to loosen its restrictive demands, especially concerning narrow job classifications. Often one of the most difficult problems can be finding appropriate roles for former supervisors. Some work as team leaders during the transition to self-management (which usually takes several years), but many do not seem to possess the skills needed for this job.[52] As a rule, it is easier to implement self-managed teams at a new facility when a new work force is hired. Converting existing plants and work forces is more difficult but has been done successfully.

Self-directed work teams are usually implemented gradually, with increasing responsibility being given to the team as it develops the capability to handle it. Table 10.8 is a list of tasks that could reside with either teams or a supervisor or higher level of management. It is essential that all participants be very clear on who has responsibility for each type of task and when a responsibility is transferred.

An example of the autonomous group method is provided by a confectionery factory in England, where a new plant was designed specifically for autonomous groups. Each group of eight to twelve employees was responsible for a single product line; all group members were expected to learn to perform the eight different jobs involved in making their product. There were no supervisors. Groups made their own decisions about job allocation and scheduling at weekly meetings.

● **TABLE 10.8**

Decisions About Responsibilities in the Design of Self-Managed Teams

	Team	Management
1. Assign individuals to work activities	_____	_____
2. Set relief and break schedules	_____	_____
3. Perform housekeeping in own work area	_____	_____
4. Select work team leader	_____	_____
5. Dismiss work team leader	_____	_____
6. Make minor equipment design changes	_____	_____
7. Make major equipment design changes	_____	_____
8. Discipline late/tardy work team members	_____	_____
9. Train new work team members	_____	_____
10. Keep timekeeping records	_____	_____
11. Maintain spare parts inventory	_____	_____
12. Make quality inspections	_____	_____
13. Keep quality service records	_____	_____
14. Prepare labor budgets	_____	_____
15. Prepare material budgets	_____	_____
16. Keep daily logs of work-in-progress	_____	_____
17. Make changes in work practices	_____	_____
18. Select new work team members	_____	_____
19. Dismiss work team members	_____	_____
20. Evaluate team members	_____	_____
21. Determine pay rates for team members	_____	_____
22. Conduct monthly safety meetings	_____	_____
23. Conduct weekly team meetings	_____	_____
24. Reject work performed if it does not meet quality standards	_____	_____
25. Review monthly team performance	_____	_____

Source: Peter Lorenzi, Henry P. Sims, Jr., and Charles C. Manz, "Management Without Supervision: How Self-Managing Teams Create Competitive Advantage," in P. C. Flood, M. J. Gannon, and J. Paauwe, *Managing Without Traditional Methods* (Wokingham, England: Addison-Wesley, 1996), p. 244. Reprinted by permission of Henry P. Sims, Jr.

The groups had some input in selecting new group members, and they had full responsibility for meeting production, hygiene, and quality standards; recording output; ordering raw materials; calling for engineering support when needed; and even delivering finished goods to stores. This innovation raised the intrinsic job satisfaction of employees and saved the company money by eliminating supervisory positions.[53]

Closer to home, a service-sector example is provided by the Aid Association for Lutherans, one of the largest life insurance companies and fraternal benefit societies in the country. This organization adopted self-directed work teams at its headquarters in Wisconsin. Each team is able to provide full support services to a specified set of field agents, who are their "clients." People in the teams are cross-trained, with the result being that agents get up to 75 percent faster "one-stop" service. At the same time, the management structure has been reduced from eight levels to three, headquarters staff has dropped 15 percent, and the volume of business being handled is up 50 percent.[54]

Financial Mechanisms for Aligning Employee Efforts with Organizational Needs

● **Pay Incentive Systems**   One of the most common methods that organizations use to increase productivity is some form of performance-based pay. For such systems to succeed, employees must desire more pay, believe that they will receive more pay if they improve their performance, be physically able to improve their performance, and trust that the organization will administer the pay-for-performance system fairly.[55] There are many systems available for linking pay to individual, group, or organizational productivity. It is essential that the pay system chosen be consistent with other initiatives in place in the firm. Adopting individual pay incentives in conjunction with teamwork structures, for example, would obviously be counterproductive.

Individual incentive systems and commission plans directly tie the size of each individual's paycheck to output. A great deal of research has shown that individual incentives are effective in increasing output. One study tracked changes in productivity at an iron foundry for 114 months. At the forty-fifth month, the company introduced an incentive system to replace the previous hourly rate pay system. As shown in Figure 10.2, productivity jumped sharply. This jump is attributed to the fact that the workers quickly learned that greater output would result in greater rewards. Note, however, that productivity continued on an upward trend for years after the incentive system was first introduced. The researchers believe that this

● **FIGURE 10.2**

Trend in Monthly Productivity Before and After Incentive Intervention

Source: John A. Wagner III, Paul A. Rubin, and Thomas J. Callahan, "Incentive Payment and Nonmanagerial Productivity: An Interrupted Time Series Analysis of Magnitude and Trend," *Organizational Behavior and Human Decision Processes*, Vol. 42, August 1988, p. 59. Reprinted by permission.

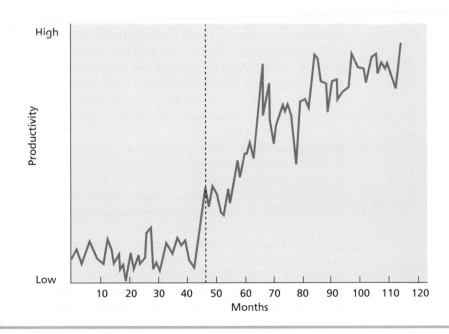

trend was caused by employees' gradually devising and implementing more and more efficient ways to do their jobs. Without the incentives, employees would probably not have been motivated to come up with these strategies for improving performance. Note that labor cost per ton and grievances did not increase as a result of the incentive system.[56]

Alternatives to individual incentives include various plans for rewarding employees on the basis of group or company performance. For instance, plantwide gain-sharing plans return to employees 50 to 75 percent of the dollars saved when productivity increases beyond an agreed-on standard.[57] These plans, discussed in detail in Chapter 13, can be quite effective in motivating employees to work both "smarter" and harder. At the Saturn assembly plant, workers receive three kinds of pay: base pay, which is below the market rate; risk pay, which is the difference between the base and a normal market rate and is paid if team goals are met; and reward pay, which is earned for above-goal performance.[58]

Any time that incentives are implemented, it is important to assure that the right performance measures are being used and that providing incentives for one type of desirable behavior does not undermine another type of desirable behavior that may not be measured and rewarded as directly.[59] At the *Midtown News Courier*, a bonus for reducing paper waste in the pressroom had some unintended side effects on quality. A device, called a flying paster, automatically attaches a new paper roll when the existing roll is nearly spent, creating a pasted seam and a thirty- to sixty-second drop in web tension throughout the entire press. Print quality immediately deteriorates as clarity and resolution disappear. A ringing bell and flashing light alert the operators, who are supposed to pull off and discard as defective all newspapers printed during this time. When reducing waste was emphasized and rewarded, employees became reluctant to discard even those papers that were of unreadable quality, for fear of missing their waste target and its associated bonus.

● **Pay for Skills**   A newer type of pay system, often used in self-directed work teams, is **skill-based pay** (see Chapter 13). New employees start at a base wage and earn increases by mastering additional skills needed for the tasks performed by their group. This method not only encourages employees to learn all the jobs of their group but also provides greater variety and more interesting work. Problem solving regarding quality also should improve when employees understand the entire process and all the jobs involved. Management realizes additional benefits in greater flexibility in covering jobs when employees are absent.

● **Employee Share Ownership Scheme**   Systems for encouraging employee ownership of company shares have increased greatly in popularity over the past few decades, with about 20 percent of U.S. adults owning stock in the company for which they work.[60] **Employee share ownership schemes** of various sorts have long been offered to top management, but increasingly they are being offered to all or nearly all employees. The idea is that if employees are part owners of the company, they will become much more interested in company performance and more committed to improving its long-term success through their own efforts on the job. Somewhat indirectly, improved company performance converts to financial rewards for employees. Some systems, such as employee stock ownership plans (ESOPs; see Chapter 13 for more information) purchase company stock within employee retirement programs. Other systems award shares to employees as a performance bonus or allow employees the option to purchase shares at a guaranteed price for a period of time. Employers such as Pepsico, Starbucks, Travelers Group, Bank of America, Merck, and The Gap offer stock options to most employees. Ninety-seven percent of the top e-commerce companies offer stock options to all or most of their employees. In total it is estimated that about 10 million employees receive stock options in the United States.[61]

Research suggests that share ownership and option programs often—but not always—have positive effects on company performance.[62] The best results seem to occur when ownership is combined with some form of meaningful participation or empowerment that creates an "ownership culture" and allows employees to contribute meaningfully to corporate performance.[63] Further advice on employee ownership can be found at http://www.nceo.org/index.html, the homepage of the National Center for Employee Ownership.

● **Open-Book Management**   A promising new approach to engaging employee interest, motivation, and loyalty is represented by **open-book management (OBM).**[64] Open-book management means sharing a great deal of financial and operating information with employees at all levels, including sensitive information normally restricted to top management. Used in combination with some form of employee ownership or profit sharing, OBM allows employees to appreciate *how* the company makes money and become motivated to contribute effectively to that end. Business literacy training is always part of the adoption of OBM—employees need to understand what the operating and financial measures mean and how they are influenced by shopfloor activities. This understanding, together with the ready availability of information for goal setting and frequent performance feedback (usually in weekly meetings), enables employees to produce improved business results. OBM seems to work best in smaller, newer businesses or smaller divisions or profit centers, where employees can see the direct effects of their daily behavior on company performance indicators, then share in the rewards that follow from improved company performance. Table 10.9 lists the principles of OBM.

● **TABLE 10.9**

Principles of Open-Book Management

1. Turn the management of a business into a game that employees can win.
2. Open the books and share financial and operating information with employees.
3. Teach employees to understand the company's financial statements.
4. Show employees how their work influences financial results.
5. Link nonfinancial measures to financial results.
6. Target priority areas and empower employees to make improvements.
7. Review results together and keep employees accountable.
8. Post results and celebrate success.
9. Distribute bonus award based on employee contributions to financial outcomes.
10. Share the ownership of the company with employees.

Source: Reprinted from *Organizational Dynamics*, Winter 1997, T. R. V. Davis. "Open-Book Management: Its Promise and Pitfalls," p. 12. Copyright 1997, with permission from Elsevier Science.

Evidence to date suggests that OBM can be effective. Companies that have had OBM in place for three or more years experienced annual sales growth of 1 to 2 percent more than matched companies without such systems.[65]

Suggestion Systems

Suggestion systems were first introduced in the late 1800s and have been in use in U.S. organizations even since. They have received renewed attention of late because of their compatibility with the employee involvement or TQM philosophy that everyone has valuable ideas to contribute. Employees are encouraged to submit written suggestions for how the work in their area can be improved. Suggestions are evaluated, and some form of reward is given to employees for suggestions that are implemented. Rewards range from a simple "thank you" or coffee cup, to points that can be exchanged for gifts, to cash awards. It has been estimated that U.S. firms pay out over $150 million per year to employees for suggestions and that these suggestions generate savings for employers worth more than $2 billion.[66] According to the *kaizen* philosophy, it is precisely these suggestions, no matter how minor, that multiply over time to produce big improvements.[67]

Bank of America has had a suggestion system since 1928, when the CEO's chauffeur suggested the idea that led to traveler's checks. He received a $1 bonus for the idea. Recently, a manager made a suggestion that saved the bank $363,520 per year. She received a cash award of 10 percent of the first-year savings, or over $36,000.[68] Japan originally borrowed the idea of suggestion systems from the U.S. Air Force, but the Japanese have made it a much bigger part of their success than have most American organizations. Matsushita reported the largest number of employee suggestions in one year in Japan —more than 6 million. The most suggestions made by a single individual in that year was a mind-boggling 16,821.[69]

United Electric Controls Company provides an example of an effective suggestion system. The company places emphasis on making suggestions rather than on determining their exact value and pays a $100 bonus for every suggestion that is implemented. Everyone who submits a suggestion in a given month receives a chance in a monthly prize drawing, and people whose suggestions are implemented receive two chances. The process of submitting a suggestion has been streamlined to a one-page form. The employee submits the form to the immediate superior, who can implement the suggestion at once if it is straightforward. More complex ideas go to a volunteer committee of workers for evaluation. Feedback is provided on the percentage of the work force involved in suggestions in a given year, and the company has set a goal of 100 percent participation. Although tangible rewards are part of the system, participants say that recognition and the fact that management is listening to them are at least as satisfying as the prizes.[70] Table 10.10 shows ten tips for implementing a successful suggestion system.

Award Programs

Organizations have long used various types of awards to recognize and motivate employee performance. Relatively infrequent awards that most people have no chance of winning (e.g., salesperson of the year, teacher of the year) may help signal what the organization values yet have little motivating effect on the bulk of employees. Some organizations have developed very innovative **award programs** in

● **TABLE 10.10**

Ten Tips for Successful Suggestion Systems

1. Enlist the support of top management.
2. Determine the objectives top management hopes to achieve through the program.
3. Provide an environment in which managers and supervisors are receptive to ideas from others.
4. Designate an individual to administer the program—not to accept or reject suggestions but to act as a liaison between employees and management.
5. Determine an awards schedule and be prepared to follow through with it.
6. Inform employees about the plan with a written announcement explaining how the system works, how they can turn in suggestions, and how they will benefit from the program.
7. Publicize the program on a regular basis.
8. Respond promptly to each suggestion, whether it is adopted or not.
9. Keep complete and accurate records of all transactions relating to the suggestion system.
10. Have a company officer make the presentation of major awards whenever possible.

Source: Employee Involvement Association, formerly National Association of Suggestion Systems, Chicago, IL.

which rewards quickly follow behavior, and everyone who performs can earn them. For instance, Diamond Fiber Products, which makes cardboard egg cartons, has instituted an award system called the 100 Club. Employees earn points by achieving perfect attendance, working safely, making suggestions, meeting performance targets, and participating in community service. Upon achieving 100 points, they get a company jacket. Subsequent points can be traded for small gifts from a catalog. Most employees hold on to their points until they reach 600 (after three to four years of excellent work) and then trade them in for a gift with a value of less than $125. The system keeps everyone in the plant focused on relevant performance targets, and, of course, plenty of feedback occurs along with the points.[71]

Triad Systems Corporation, a computer company that specializes in systems for retailers, gives 700 awards per year to its 1,500 employees. Some walk away from the annual awards banquet with four or five awards. There are quarterly and annual awards for sales, innovation, cross-departmental cooperation, customer service, effort, success in training, and anything else the company values.[72]

Continental Cablevision in Florida has a reward system called Conopoly, similar to the board game Monopoly. Supervisors and managers receive books of play money to dispense to employees who exceed expectations in customer service, cooperation, leadership, and the like. Each month employees can exchange their Conopoly money for "properties" or purchase upgrades such as improved cable TV service, movie channels, or digital cable radio for properties purchased earlier. There is also the possibility of winning small prizes. The company feels that this system not only makes employees more aware of the services the company offers but also encourages behaviors that result in better service to internal and external customers.[73]

Goal Setting

Goal setting is a proven technique that is often quite successful in improving motivation and job performance.[74] Goal setting is effective with employees as diverse as managers and professionals, salespersons, and hourly workers such as tree planters and truck drivers.

● **Four Characteristics of Effective Goals**   Decades of research have shown that to be effective, goals must have four characteristics:

1. The goals must be difficult but not impossible to accomplish. Consequently, employees can feel challenged and also experience a sense of achievement when they meet their goals successfully.

2. The goals must be specific and measurable. Vague goals, such as "do your best" or "try to improve," are not nearly as effective as specific goals, such as "try to sell $100,000 of product."

3. The goals must be accepted by the employee, who then must strive to meet them. One way to ensure acceptance is to allow participation in goal setting. Either the subordinate can set the goal or the subordinate and superior can decide jointly on what the goal will be. However, reasonable goals assigned by the superior without the subordinate's participation are often accepted just as well.

4. Feedback is necessary for goal setting to be effective over time. Feedback can be intrinsic to the task so that the employees themselves can tell how close they are to meeting their goal, it can be delivered impersonally by production reports or progress graphs, or it can be delivered face to face by a superior.[75]

● **Why Goal Setting Works**   There are several possible reasons for the success of goal-setting programs. First, setting a specific goal clarifies which behaviors are desired. Many people suffer from role ambiguity—that is, they are not really sure what they are supposed to be doing—and thus expend effort on unnecessary tasks. As a result, their productivity may be low. Specific goals should remedy this problem. Second, specific and difficult goals combined with feedback allow people to receive motivational rewards for meeting their goals. The rewards may be praise or more tangible rewards from a superior or just the good feeling of having succeeded in a challenging endeavor. Finally, having a goal may motivate people to think more strategically about their job duties. Someone with a challenging goal may devise a more efficient way to get the job done when otherwise he or she would not have given it any thought.[76]

Increased competitive pressure in the 1990s led companies such as Boeing, 3M, CSX, and General Electric to adopt **stretch targets.** These companies found that ordinary goals, such as to improve by 2 percent, obtained just that—a rather ordinary 2 percent achievement. But outrageous and seemingly impossible goals, such as to improve by 20 or 30 percent, tended to produce extraordinary results.[77] United Aluminum in Connecticut had been working on improving the productivity of its rolling mills for years but had been improving at the paltry rate of 0.5 percent for each of the previous six years. Suddenly management decided to call the work force together and ask for a quantum leap in productivity. Employees decided to aim for a 15 percent improvement in a period of just eight weeks. A team made up of management, supervisors, and operators developed a list of barriers to productivity, then worked to dismantle as many barriers as possible. Astonishingly, the plan achieved a 17 percent increase in productivity, with no major expenditures on new equipment. The company then turned its attention to timeliness of deliveries—and in three weeks improved the on-time rate from 80 to 100 percent. Over the next year, they achieved an on-time delivery rate above 95 percent.[78]

The secrets to successful stretch goals seems to be acceptance by employees (United Aluminum employees chose their own goal), empowerment of employees to question or try almost anything that might work without waiting for layers of management to approve, immunity from punishment if innovative ideas fail, and, of course, constant feedback on progress. Benchmarking to show that outstanding performance is possible can also help motivate employees to try.

Behavior Modification

Behavior modification is a technique for improving employee productivity using reinforcement theory (also known an operant conditioning). Its most common application would be to relatively simple blue-collar jobs with easily measurable results. Behavior modification seeks to change the frequency, duration, or intensity of a behavior by manipulating the consequences of the behavior.[79] Behavior modification techniques are solidly grounded in decades of research on human and animal learning and motivation rather than in opinion or fad. Behavior modification requires managers to think clearly about what behaviors they really want from employees and to assure that desirable behaviors are reliably followed by desirable consequences.

● **Consequences of Behaviors**   Controlling the consequences of performance is the key to modifying employee behavior. Several kinds of consequences can be used: positive reinforcement, punishment, and no consequences (extinction). In practice, positive reinforcement is by far the most commonly used type of consequence.

Positive Reinforcement   **Positive reinforcement** is giving some kind of reward to an employee as soon as possible after he or she has performed in a desirable way. Rewards need not be tangible. While financial rewards are often used in organizational behavior modification, social recognition and feedback are also very commonly used.[80] Table 10.11 identifies several types of positive reinforcers.

In an ideal positive reinforcement system, **rewards** are **positive, immediate, and certain (PIC)** rather than **positive, future, and uncertain (PFU).** A feedback system, or a pay-by-commission system, is PIC—everyone who performs is sure to get the reward, and the reward is delivered almost immediately. Merit pay raises, on the other hand, are PFU and therefore not effective reinforcers. Often there is a long delay between performance and receiving the raise, performers may not be sure exactly which behaviors are being rewarded, and there is no certainty that good performance will in fact earn a merit raise. Even employee-of-the-month award systems have been criticized by organizational behaviorists because the reward is given in the future and is uncertain. Many employees may perform well, yet only one gets the reward.[81]

Punishment   Another consequence, **punishment,** is the administration of an aversive stimulus to reduce the frequency of undesirable behaviors. Punishment can be effective if employees clearly understand which behaviors are unacceptable

● **TABLE 10.11**

Possible On-the-Job Reinforcers

Social	Special Privileges
Verbal praise	Own parking space
Special job title	No-punch lunch
Recognition in front of coworkers	Birthday off
Notes of thanks	Longer coffee breaks
Picture in company paper	Flexible work schedule
Pats on the back	Training for better job
Greetings from boss	Earned time off
Material	**Tokens**
Awards/plaques	Telephone credit cards
Fringe benefits	Points backed by prizes
Special badges or insignias	Coupons redeemable at local stores
Raises/bonuses	Chances to win a prize (lottery)
Large office	
Performance appraisal ratings	
Free tickets to sporting events	

Source: Rodney R. Nordstrom and R. Vance Hall, "The Platinum Rule." Copyright 1986, *Training and Development Journal,* American Society for Training and Development. Reprinted with permission. All rights reserved.

and are warned in advance that punishment may be administered. It is very important that punishment (discipline) be administered fairly and impartially and that it occur as soon as possible after the undesired behavior. Chapter 16 contains more information on punishment and discipline systems in organizations.

Punishment has some potential drawbacks. It may tend to alienate employees and/or lead to the filing of grievances alleging unfair discipline. However, punishment can be a reasonable way to deal with persistent undesired behaviors. For example, suppose that an employee continually makes long-distance personal calls from work and all of the manager's attempts to change this behavior have failed. Finally, the manager decides to dock the employee's pay for the cost of past calls and suggests that suspension or termination will follow continued abuse of the phone system.

Extinction **Extinction,** or providing no consequences at all, is sometimes the preferred alternative to punishment. It is simply ignoring an undesirable behavior. For instance, a team may ignore a member's disruptive interjections in a team meeting. Eventually, such behavior should lessen in frequency. If the team goes out of its way to reward appropriate behavior from that team member as well as ignore disruptive behavior, desirable change will occur quickly. Unfortunately, many undesirable organizational behaviors are inherently rewarding, so ignoring them is not an effective way to get rid of them. For instance, suppose that workers violate safety rules by not wearing their hardhats because the hats are uncomfortable. The manager's ignoring the violation certainly does not solve the problem in this case because employees' violation of the rule is positively reinforced by the natural consequence of comfort.

The ideas of reinforcement, punishment, and extinction can also be used to diagnose performance problems and reward systems. If reward systems are not designed carefully, they may be rewarding the wrong behaviors or unintentionally punishing desired behaviors. Reinforcement theory points out very clearly that managers will get the behaviors they reward, whether or not these are the behaviors they actually intend to elicit from their employees. If an employee is doing something management does not want, ask "What's in it for the employee?" If some sort of reward is occurring for undesirable behavior, perhaps this reward can be removed. For instance, a supervisor might accidentally reward poor performance by lightening the workload of an employee who cannot be trusted to do anything correctly, and that same supervisor might inadvertently punish top performers by loading extra work on them because they do it well.[82]

● **The Behavior Modification Process**   The behavior modification process relies on careful, objective measurement of clearly defined behaviors, followed by the application of consequences for those behaviors. The process for applying behavior modification is illustrated in Figure 10.3. The process begins when the manager determines which behaviors are desired and which are not. In the second step, the manager measures current levels of performance on the selected behaviors.

In the third step of the behavior modification process, the intervention strategy is developed. This third step is a three-part process: (1) Powerful and durable reinforcers are selected, (2) employees are told which behaviors are to be rewarded, and (3) the work situation is designed so that subordinates are able to perform the desired behavior and receive the reward.

The fourth step is the critical one in a successful behavior modification program. In this step, the manager must faithfully measure the desired behaviors and administer the appropriate rewards in a timely fashion. In the fifth and sixth steps, current performance is compared with that at preintervention levels to determine whether or not behaviors have changed as intended. If they have, then the manager simply keeps reinforcing the behaviors to maintain them. If behaviors have not improved, the organization should reevaluate what it is using as reinforcers. Perhaps a different reward will work better.

Often the most effective way to change behavior is to use several types of consequences at the same time to reduce an undesired behavior and replace it with a desired behavior. In the case of a widespread tardiness problem, a firm might institute a system of increasingly severe penalties for repeated instances of tardiness, use feedback charts to graphically display changes in tardiness behavior over time for the work group as a whole, reward individuals for each week of perfect on-time attendance with a ticket in a monthly prize lottery, and offer complimentary doughnuts and coffee to employees who arrive ten minutes before the start of their shift.

A hotel in Texas used behavior analysis and modification to improve the accuracy and timeliness of catering setups for banquets from a preintervention baseline of 69 percent correct.[83] The analysis showed that feedback was nonexistent, some employees were unaware of desired setup standards (for instance, were salt and pepper shakers supposed to be on each table for breakfast buffets?), and some

● **FIGURE 10.3**

Behavior Modification Process

Source: Rodney R. Nordstrom and Vance Hall, "The Platinum Rule." Copyright 1986, *Training and Development Journal,* American Society for Training and Development. Reprinted with permission. All rights reserved.

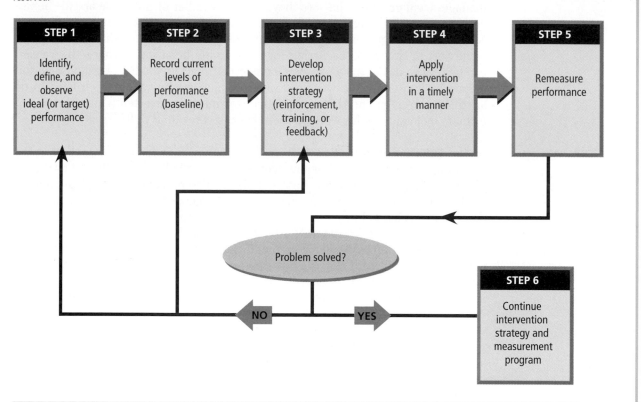

frequently needed supplies were inconveniently located and so sometimes forgotten. A comprehensive intervention was undertaken that included some rearrangement of storage areas for greater convenience, the provision of training and checklists for different types of setups (e.g., breakfast buffet, plated lunch), daily feedback in the form of a chart showing setup completion percentages, goal setting, and a small financial reward for sustained high performance for a month. During the intervention, setup performance jumped quickly to over 99 percent accuracy and remained there for four months. In the fifth month, a new banqueting manager halted the program, and performance fell to 82 percent accuracy. Several months later the intervention was reintroduced, and performance returned to over 99 percent accuracy almost immediately.

Behavior modification has been very successful in a wide variety of situations.[84] A recent review of 125 behavior modification projects revealed an average increase in performance of 17 percent. The technique was slightly more effective in manufacturing than service organizations, and the best results were obtained when a combination of financial (money and prizes), nonfinancial (feedback), and social (recognition and attention) rewards were used.

Behavior modification techniques were developed decades ago and used in organizations quite successfully starting in the early 1970s. In today's more open and participative organizational cultures, behavior modification may sound too manipulative and unilateral to be attractive; it is often presented as something managers do to workers in order to control them. However, this need not be the case. Individuals and groups certainly can be involved in designing their own measurement and reward system, from identifying critical behaviors and developing feedback measures to selecting desirable rewards and devising a system for dispensing them when performance warrants.

● **Behavioral Self-Regulation**   A new twist to behavior modification is **behavioral self-regulation.** In using this technique, people identify behaviors that they wish to perform and then promise themselves rewards for performing the desired behaviors. This technique can be used by anyone who wishes to work more effectively, though it is most often recommended for managers and professionals who are assumed to be well motivated at the outset. For instance, a lawyer might promise himself the reward of a cup of coffee as soon as he finishes the next two pages of the brief he is working on. Or a manager could promise herself that she will work on a task she enjoys if she finishes a disliked activity first.

Another part of this technique is (1) to analyze the environmental cues that lead to the performance of desired and undesired behaviors and (2) to modify the environment so that it triggers desired behaviors rather than undesired ones. For instance, if making a priority list of tasks to accomplish each day is desired behavior, a manager could hang a sign in front of her desk reminding herself of this time-management principle. Or if a supervisor feels that he is too easily and frequently distracted from productive activity by the delivery of mail and messages, he could ask his assistant to hold all nonurgent mail and messages until late in the day.[85]

Job Redesign

A technique that is sometimes applied to productivity and quality problems is redesigning a job in order to increase its motivating potential. This technique is known as **job redesign** or **job enrichment.** It is based on the premise that altering certain aspects of the job to satisfy employees' psychological needs will motivate workers to try harder to do a good job. Job enrichment is often found as part of a high-involvement organization's approach.

Job redesign attempts to correct the "mistakes" of previous job design methods. In the past, jobs were designed with the principles of simplification, standardization, and specialization. This led to the removal of many sources of satisfaction and motivation from the job.[86] Contemporary theory, illustrated in Figure 10.4, attempts to expand the scope of the job to increase its variety, significance, identity, autonomy, and feedback. These dimensions satisfy the individual's psychological needs for personal control, knowledge of results, and meaningfulness of work. Because the job satisfies psychological needs, the employee enjoys the job more and may strive to do higher-quality work of which he or she can be proud. Redesigning a job to be more interesting and satisfying, however, does not guarantee that

● FIGURE 10.4

Job Characteristics Theory

Source: J. R. Hackman and G. R. Oldham, "Motivation Through the Design of Work: Test of a Theory," *Organizational Behavior and Human Performance,* Vol. 16, 1976, pp. 250–279. Reprinted by permission of Academic Press and the authors.

* "Task identity" means doing a whole identifiable piece of work, such as assembling an entire television set.

productivity will improve. The interesting way to do the job isn't always the most streamlined and efficient way. The research results are mixed, with some job re-design efforts resulting in increased performance and others not having this ef-fect.[87] Nevertheless, under the right conditions, job enrichment can pay off.[88]

One of these conditions is the level of "growth need strength" among employ-ees. It seems that some employees respond to enriched work better than others. Individuals who are high on the personality characteristic of "growth need strength" are most likely to enjoy the challenges provided by an expanded job. In-dividuals low on this trait are not particularly attuned to receiving this kind of satis-faction from their work. They may agree that the redesigned jobs are more interesting but also tend to feel that they should be paid more for taking on added responsibilities.

A number of specific changes may be made in the way a job is performed in order to increase the job's motivating potential. The following kinds of changes are typical:

1. *Combining tasks:* This involves giving a single employee a set of interrelated tasks that might previously have been performed by several workers in an assembly-line fashion. This larger unit of work results in an identifiable product for which the employee can feel personally responsible. In one early job enrichment experiment, the twenty-one separate tasks involved in compiling a phone directory were combined and given to a single employee, so that each employee became responsible for putting together an entire phone book.

2. *Establishing client relationships:* This involves empowering the employee to go directly to his or her "client," whether inside or outside the organization, to clarify questions regarding the work. Prior to enrichment, typically only the supervisor would contact clients, so employees had no direct sense of whom they were working for, why the work was important to the client, or exactly what the client needed or wanted. Modifying a "typing pool" system so that each typist is permanently assigned to a few specific managers would be an example of establishing client relationships.

3. *Opening feedback channels:* This can be accomplished by direct client contact, increased feedback from the superior, or increased self-generated feedback. Some job enrichment programs make employees their own quality control inspectors, thus allowing them to generate instant feedback on performance.

4. *Forming natural work units:* Work teams are established to be responsible for a meaningful unit of work. For instance, a team of ten autoworkers may assemble an entire engine.

5. *Vertical loading:* This approach involves increasing the amount of responsibility and decision-making authority granted to employees. It may include decisions about how to make the product, when to stop machines for repair, whether or not a given part is acceptable, and so on.[89]

A success story demonstrates how job enrichment helped obtain the best results from automated manufacturing technology. When robot operators were given increased power, knowledge, and control to maintain and repair rather than just monitor their machines, downtime was reduced and employee satisfaction increased. Researchers attributed this gain in performance to (1) increased motivation, (2) less time spent waiting for a specialist to come to deal with machine problems, and (3) better anticipation of problems and, therefore, fault prevention by knowledgeable and responsible operators.[90]

Job redesign first began in the 1960s, with a few organizations undertaking job redesign with the primary goal of making work more interesting and fulfilling to employees. Such purely humanistic motives are less common now. Job redesign is more likely to be part of a movement toward an HIO culture from which an organization would expect to reap many tangible benefits, such as improved quality and flexibility and reduced employee turnover. Further, many organizations have enriched jobs almost by accident. Those that have adopted TQM or reengineering usually find that one by-product is jobs with increased responsibility, empowerment, feedback, and complexity.

Relative Effectiveness of Specific Interventions

Even when programs are chosen and implemented appropriately, not all programs are equally powerful. Two reviews have compared the effectiveness of different interventions. The results of the earlier review by Edwin A. Locke appear in Table 10.12. Locke concluded that financial incentives are the most effective way to increase productivity. Goal setting is also quite effective, whereas participative decision-making systems and job redesign are relatively less certain to produce significant improvements.

A review by Richard A. Guzzo and his colleagues at New York University suggests that employee training and goal setting are most likely to improve productivity, followed closely by sociotechnical system innovations (including autonomous work groups) and carefully designed financial incentives. On the whole, job redesign is less powerful but still has a significant impact on productivity.[91] Employee ownership alone and participation alone may have negligible impacts, but when they are implemented together, very good results can be achieved. Opening the books only works when business literacy training and some form of sharing the resulting wealth with employees are in place. In sum, combined interventions that reinforce one another are more effective than single-method programs. The success of TQM and high-involvement techniques probably rests partly on the fact that both require an integrated set of changes tied together by a strong corporate culture.

An Example of a Successful Intervention

Robert D. Pritchard and his colleagues have reported a highly successful group-focused productivity intervention conducted in five support units at a U.S. Air Force base.[92] This intervention used group participation in designing productivity and quality measures and then group-focused feedback, goal setting, and rewards to motivate improvement. The unique aspect of this intervention was probably the development of the unit effectiveness measure. Supervisors and employees worked together, with guidance from the researchers, to define and construct indices of performance in their units. A multistep procedure was followed.

● TABLE 10.12

Summary of Studies Comparing Four Motivational Techniques

Technique	Number of Studies	Median Improvement	Percentage Showing Some Improvement	Percentage Showing 10% or More Improvement	Range
Money	10[a]	+30%	100%	90%	+3% to +49%
Goal setting	17	+16%	100%	94%	+2% to +57.5%
Participation	16	+0.5%	50%	25%	−24% to +47%
Job enrichment	10[b]	+8.75%[b]	90%[b]	50%[b]	−1 to +61%[b]

[a]Individual piece rate studies only.
[b]Excluding three questionable studies.
Source: Edwin A. Locke, "Employee Motivation: A Discussion," *Journal of Contemporary Business,* Vol. 11, 1982, p. 75. Reprinted by permission of the author.

FIGURE 10.5

Relationship of One
Quality Indicator to
Effectiveness

Source: Robert D. Pritchard,
Steven D. Jones, Philip L. Roth,
Karla K. Stuebing, and Steven
K. Ekeberg, "Effects of Group
Feedback, Goal Setting, and
Incentives on Organizational
Productivity," *Journal of
Applied Psychology*, Vol. 73
(2), 1988, p. 342. Copyright
1988 by the American
Psychological Association.
Adapted with permission.

First, unit members agreed on what their primary products or services were. For instance, a communication and navigation equipment repair unit decided that two of its "products" were (1) meeting repair demand and (2) producing high-quality repairs. In the next step, measures of each product were devised. Meeting repair demand was operationalized as the number of units repaired divided by the number brought in for repair in a given month. Quality of repairs was assessed by the percentage of units that failed again immediately after having been reinstalled in planes. The third step was to agree on how effective the maximum, minimum, and intervening levels of performance were on each indicator. For instance, the group decided that a 2 percent failure rate after reinstallation was the lowest that could be attained, given the unreliable nature of electronic components. It decided that a 20 percent failure rate was the worst that could realistically occur. A mid-point, representing neither good nor poor unit performance, was pegged at a 10 percent failure rate. Levels in between also were rated for effectiveness, with the results shown in Figure 10.5.

Note that the same-sized improvement in performance has a different meaning at different points in Figure 10.5. Improving from a 12 to an 8 percent failure rate represents a bigger gain in effectiveness (from below expectations to above) than jumping from 6 to 2 percent (from very good to excellent). This reflects the fact that not all productivity gains have the same value to an organization. The slopes of the curve for an indicator also suggest when energy might be spent more profitably elsewhere. Once the failure rate is reduced to 6 percent, a greater payoff in total effectiveness may be realized by concentrating on improving a different indicator (such as percentage of repairs completed on time) than by focusing on becoming perfect on the first indicator.

After indicators were developed, baseline data on effectiveness were gathered in all units for eight months. Starting in the ninth month, the feedback intervention began. Each unit received a monthly report of its effectiveness on each indicator; the report was posted in the work area and discussed in a monthly meeting. Feedback was given for five months, and then units were trained to set their own goals.

Goal setting plus feedback continued for an additional five months. Then the tangible reward of time off with pay for meeting various effectiveness levels was added for the final five months of the study.

Gains in effectiveness were calculated as a percentage of the maximum possible gain. The maximum possible gain was defined as moving from the baseline level on an indicator to the maximum possible level (i.e., 2 percent failures for the quality-of-repair indicator). Summing across indicators, the units in the study achieved 50 percent of the maximum possible gain during the months when only feedback was given. When goal setting was added, performance increased to 75 percent of the maximum possible gain. The time-off incentive caused only a 1 percent additional rise, to 76 percent. However, this does not necessarily mean that the incentive was ineffective. Perhaps the units had already improved as much as was humanly possible. One also might expect that a tangible reward would help maintain long-term interest in the effectiveness feedback and goals.

THE ROLE OF HRM IN THE NEW WORKPLACE

A Gallup survey of senior executives found that quality and productivity were seen as the most important competitive issues facing American business, yet relatively few organizations have made the jump to full-on high-performance work systems. It appears to be very difficult to do so successfully—and is certainly not possible without expert assistance in the HR area.[93] When asked about the effectiveness of various methods of improving quality, the executives first listed employee motivation, then organizational culture change, then employee education—all human resource issues. Of much less importance were control systems, inspections, and new equipment.[94] (For an alternate opinion, see A Different Point of View.)

Clearly, HR managers have important and varied roles to play in quality and productivity improvement efforts. The first may be to apply quality principles to improve their own operations and better satisfy their internal clients. Administrative work is often a fertile site for quality circle improvement ideas. HRM systems also may be prime candidates for reengineering. For instance, it may be possible to substantially streamline an internal job posting and promotion system, such as that shown in Figure 6.3, or to improve or simplify forms and record-keeping practices to save time and reduce errors. Many HRM departments are benchmarking by comparing their operations in selected areas with recognized best-practice HRM departments in other organizations.

Second, HR professionals may serve a role in spotting and resolving inconsistencies between policies that are sending mixed messages to employees or otherwise derailing quality efforts. For instance, an organization may have detailed step-by-step procedures for providing customer service. What happens if these procedures are left in place when management suddenly decides to "empower" employees to "do whatever it takes" to make customers happy?[95] Researchers describe "deadly combinations"—practices that may make sense in isolation but interact destructively with other policies. An example of a deadly combination would be a decision to promote largely from within when the organization does not practice careful selection, does not provide training, and does not use systems to retain talented employees. On the other hand, a "powerful connection" may result when the same decision to promote from within is paired with systems to attract, keep, and develop highly talented people.[96]

Productivity and Quality—
Motivation Versus Systems and Knowledge

Many of the interventions suggested in this chapter focus on motivating employees by reward or recognition systems, goals, or interesting work. But how important is motivation for productivity and quality? We seem to have a stereotype that performance problems are due largely to lazy or careless employees, but this may be wrong. Quality guru W. Edwards Deming suggests that 85 percent of quality problems are due to faulty design or systems rather than lack of employee effort. In other words, the problems are ultimately management's fault for creating poor systems. To the extent that this is true, solutions aimed at employee motivation will not be very effective unless accompanied by the authority and information needed to allow employees themselves to redesign faulty systems. TQM and reengineering are approaches that focus more on systems than on the motivation of individual employees.

A new approach to increasing organizational effectiveness is based on culture and systems that support organizational learning. There is some evidence that the most effective organizations are **learning organizations**—they notice problems, investigate them, and modify systems to prevent the same mistakes from happening again. They learn from examining their own experiences and from contact with suppliers and customers. Learning organizations encourage risk taking and experimentation as a means of learning and have systems to codify and disseminate the knowledge that results.

Increasingly, theorists feel that the key to long-term success in the marketplace is not physical or financial resources but **intellectual capital**—the

knowledge and skills of employees that allow them to provide quicker innovation or better service than competitors. Intellectual capital resides in employees' heads, in patents owned by the organization, and also in organizational systems for capturing and perpetuating the knowledge of organization members. These systems can range from informal "communities of practice" (see Chapter 9) to extremely sophisticated computer networks.

Some of the most encouraging performance-enhancing innovations on the horizon are knowledge-sharing networks. Properly designed, these can vastly enhance the productivity of professionals. Among the leading examples are the systems established by major international management consulting firms: Accenture's Knowledge Xchange, Booz Allen & Hamilton's Knowledge On-Line, KPMG Peat Marwick's Knowledge Manager, and the like. These systems make it possible for a consultant operating anywhere in the world to log on and immediately find out who the company's experts in a particular area are, locate documents and prior projects relevant to the current project, or post a query to colleagues. This greatly increases the ability of consultants to provide expert advice to their clients without having to reinvent the wheel each time a problem is encountered that has been solved before elsewhere in the organization.

Sources: J. B. Quinn, P. Anderson, and S. Finkelstein, "Leveraging Intellect," *Academy of Management Executive,* November 1996, pp. 7–27; Thomas A. Stewart, *Intellectual Capital: The New Wealth of Organizations* (New York: Doubleday, 1997); and W. E. Deming, *Out of the Crisis* (Cambridge, Mass.: MIT Center for Advanced Engineering Study, 1982).

The third role for the HR professional is to facilitate the implementation of quality or productivity interventions in the rest of the organization through HR activities such as staffing, training, appraisal and compensation, and labor relations. Each of these may require attention to make it optimally fit the organization's new goals, work methods, and culture.[97] HR staff may also be the source of expertise on "change management" needed to successfully introduce any new program. Table 10.13 gives suggestions as to how the role of the HR department might change when an organization moves from a traditional bureaucratic structure to self-managed work teams. Table 10.14 shows the standards expected of Baldrige Quality Award applicants in terms of their human resource practices. Examples of fitting specific HR activities to productivity and quality initiatives are discussed further below.[98]

● **TABLE 10.13**

Changes in HRM for Self-Managing Work Teams

HRM Functions	Traditional HRM	HRM for Self-Managing Work Teams (SMWT)
Role of HRM department	Centralized/functional/staff auditor	Decentralized/coach/counsellor/adviser
Recruitment and selection	Recruiting/testing, screening done by HRM development; selection by management	HRM department screening SMWT involvement in recruiting and selection of team members
Training and development	HRM department administers training program	HRM department trains the trainers in SMWT
Job descriptions	HRM department reviews job descriptions	HRM department assists in job/skill descriptions. SMWT members' jobs are defined by overlapping skill areas
Wage and salary	Wage system based on skill levels, step increases, seniority, and performance	Wage system includes learn to earn and some gain-sharing
Performance appraisal	Appraisals done by management using HRM department guidelines	SMWT members appraise member performance and are responsible for some discipline and rewards
Benefits administration	HRM department administers fringe benefits, insurance	HRM department administers fringe benefits and insurance
	Management schedules vacations and work times	SMWTs determine vacation and work times
Employment law/EEOC/wrongful discharge	HRM department administers and reviews HRM process including recruitment, selection, interviewing, and termination to ensure legal compliance	SMWT members follow HRM department guidelines
Industrial relations	Union as adversary	Cooperative union/management relations
HR planning	HRM department plans based on business strategy including manpower and career planning	HRM department plans based on business strategy SMWT involved in succession, downsizing, and growth plans

Source: David K. Banner, W. Anthony Kulisch, and Newman S. Peery, "Self-Managing Work Teams (SMWT) and the Human Resource Function," *Management Decision,* Vol. 30 (3), 1992, p. 44. Reprinted by permission.

● **TABLE 10.14**

Detailed Questions for Baldrige Quality Award Applicants Related to Human Resource Systems

---

5.1 Work Systems (35 pts.)

Describe how your organization's work and jobs, compensation, career progression, and related workforce practices motivate and enable employees and the organization to achieve high performance.

Within your response, include answers to the following questions:

a. Work Systems

(1) How do you organize and manage work and jobs to promote cooperation, initiative/innovation, your organizational culture, and the flexibility to keep current with business needs? How do you achieve effective communication and knowledge/skill sharing across work units, jobs, and locations, as appropriate?

(2) How do you motivate employees to develop and utilize their full potential? Include formal and/or informal mechanisms you use to help employees attain job- and career-related development/learning objectives and the role of managers and supervisors in helping employees attain these objectives.

(3) How does your employee performance management system, including feedback to employees, support high performance and a customer and business focus? How do your compensation, recognition, and related reward/incentive practices reinforce these objectives?

(4) How do you accomplish effective succession planning for senior leadership and throughout the organization?

(5) How do you identify characteristics and skills needed by potential employees? How do you recruit, hire, and retain new employees? How do your work systems capitalize on the diverse ideas, cultures, and thinking of the communities with which you interact (your employee hiring and customer communities)?

5.2 Employee Education, Training, and Development (25 pts.)

Describe how your organization's education and training support the achievement of your overall objectives, including building employee knowledge, skills, and capabilities and contributing to high performance.

Within your response, include answers to the following questions:

a. Employee Education, Training, and Development

(1) How do education and training contribute to the achievement of your action plans? How does your education and training approach balance short- and longer-term organizational objectives and employee needs, including development, learning, and career progression?

(2) How do you seek and use input from employees and their supervisors/managers on education and training needs and delivery options?

(3) How do you address in your employee education, training, and development your key organizational needs associated with technological change, management/leadership development, new employee orientation, safety, performance measurement/improvement, and diversity?

(4) How do you deliver education and training? Include formal and informal delivery, including mentoring and other approaches, as appropriate. How do you evaluate the effectiveness of education and training, taking into account individual and organizational performance?

(5) How do you reinforce the use of knowledge and skills on the job?

(continued)

Source: Malcolm Baldrige National Quality Award. Additional information can be obtained by contacting the Baldrige Award Office at 301-975-2036 or visiting the Baldrige web site at www.quality.gov.

● **T A B L E 1 0 . 1 4** (continued)

5.3 Employee Well-Being and Satisfaction (25 pts.)

Describe how your organization maintains a work environment and an employee support climate that contribute to the well-being, satisfaction, and motivation of all employees.

Within your response, include answers to the following questions:

a. Work Environment

How do you improve workplace health, safety, and ergonomics? How do employees take part in improving them? Include performance measures and/or targets for each key environmental factor. Also include significant differences, if any, based on varying work environments for employee groups and/or work units.

b. Employee Support and Satisfaction

(1) How do you determine the key factors that affect employee well-being, satisfaction, and motivation? How are these factors segmented for a diverse workforce and for varying categories and types of employees, as appropriate?

(2) How do you support your employees via services, benefits, and policies? How are these tailored to the needs of a diverse workforce and different categories and types of employees, as appropriate?

(3) What formal and/or informal assessment methods and measures do you use to determine employee well-being, satisfaction, and motivation? How do you tailor these methods and measures to a diverse workforce and to different categories and types of employees, as appropriate? How do you use other indicators, such as employee retention, absenteeism, grievances, safety, and productivity, to assess and improve employee well-being, satisfaction, and motivation?

(4) How do you relate assessment findings to key business results to identify priorities for improving the work environment and employee support climate?

Human Resource Planning

The demands of high-performance, quality-oriented workplaces require extra attention to some aspects of human resource planning. Successful reengineering often means that the same amount of work can be done by fewer people, necessitating planning for reductions in force or redeployment of employees to other jobs or facilities. High-involvement work systems often feature lateral career tracks to encourage multiskilling. While there will be fewer managers and supervisors, they may be more likely to be promoted from within. Thus career movement systems will require modification in organizations seriously focused on quality. The management of voluntary employee turnover is also a concern in high-involvement work settings. A great deal is invested in training employees so that they can add as much value as possible. Those who leave represent a substantial loss to the organization, so programs to control turnover at low levels may be needed. Finally, the staffing mix between permanent full-time employees and contingent workers must be thought out carefully. Permanents are likely to be very well trained, active in quality circles, able to self-manage, and generally committed to the organization's quality processes. Contingent workers may lack quality-related knowledge, skills, and commitment. On the other hand, judicious use of contingent workers may be necessary to allow promises of job security to be made to permanent employees.[99]

Job Analysis

Traditional job analysis may be somewhat less relevant in a high-involvement organization. This is so because the work is less specialized and less static. Consider the job of operator at a team-oriented plant in Canada, described as follows in a recruiting brochure: "An operator is someone who performs the tasks necessary to run the production line. This includes ordering materials and ensuring quality, as well as running production. Operators are responsible for routine machine and equipment maintenance. In addition, an operator rotates jobs on a regular basis and takes turns acting as the coordinator of team activities."[100]

Job analysis usually considers the requirements of the immediate job and the human skills required to perform that job. In high-involvement organizations, successful employees need not only to fit their job but also to fit the organization's somewhat unusual culture. It has been suggested that job analysis for high-involvement organizations should focus to a greater extent on worker attributes (attitudes, personality, skills, and knowledge) than on specific tasks per se.[101] An example of a job description and specification for a team member is given in Table 10.15.

In team-based organizations, the appropriate unit for job analysis may not be the individual job but rather the team job. Teams may have a great deal of input into the way their "jobs" are broken down and defined. Individual responsibilities within the team will be flexible and vary from day to day. On the other hand, pay-for-skills systems do require some systematic way of breaking down the team's work into jobs or skill units that employees can master one by one.[102]

⬤ **TABLE 10.15**

Job Description and Attribute Specification for Self-Managed Team Member

Tasks or Duties Associated with Being a Team Member	Attributes Associated with Success of Team Members
Carry out day-to-day work tasks and assignments	Flexibility/adaptability (openness to change)
Learn a number of tasks and skills	Teamwork orientation (group identification involvement)
Improve work processes and procedures	
Troubleshoot problems	Skill in relating to others (listening to others, developing cooperative relationships, and dealing with conflict)
Develop work schedules and assignments	
Train other team members	
Select new team members	Conscientiousness (thorough, responsible, hard-working)
Provide performance feedback information	Openness to learning, development, and retraining
Meet scheduling and work demands	Skill in problem solving
Interact with others outside the group (suppliers, internal and external customers, other functions or units)	Planning and organizing
	Oral communication
	Reading comprehension
	Technical/professional proficiency
	Judgment

Source: R. B. Morgan and J. E. Smith, *Staffing the New Workplace: Selecting and Promoting for Quality Improvement* (ASQ Quality Press, 1996), p. 459.

Staffing

Major changes in job responsibilities, such as those occasioned by a shift to total quality management or self-directed work teams, require substantial changes in the type of people recruited and selected. In addition to looking for core job skills, one also would like to see basic mathematical skills (to learn statistical process control techniques), interpersonal skills (to work effectively in groups), and a high level of motivation to take responsibility. Japanese firms building plants in the United States are using a great deal of cognitive testing to ensure that employees have the mental capability to participate fully in a high-quality work environment. Interpersonal skills and the motivation to take responsibility may be assessed in interviews and by group exercises or mini–assessment centers. Some personality tests assessing conscientiousness or service orientation also may be useful. In sum, organizations with a philosophy emphasizing high quality need to attract a special kind of applicant and then be much more selective than usual. Figure 10.6 shows a recruitment ad for a new manufacturing plant belonging to 3M Canada. Note the emphasis on quality, service, and team skills even at this early stage of the selection process.

Fortunately, modern new plants featuring high-involvement work designs tend to attract a large number of applicants, so a favorable selection ratio permits more careful selection. In preparing to open its plant in Georgetown, Kentucky, Toyota screened 50,000 applicants for 3,000 factory jobs. Finalists underwent eighteen hours of assessment, including knowledge and attitude tests, an assessment center focusing on interpersonal skills, a long interview, and a manufacturing exercise that provided a realistic job preview.[103] One study verified that organizations using advanced manufacturing technology or total quality management were in fact more selective than nonusers in hiring operators.[104]

Some organizations allow team members substantial input when new team members are being chosen. Typically, the HR department advertises and screens candidates extensively and then refers finalists to be interviewed by teams with vacancies. This means that team members need to be trained in interviewing skills and made aware of equal opportunity laws. The practice of allowing teams to select new members who "fit" with existing members may create EEO problems if not monitored carefully.

An additional staffing issue in implementing self-directed work teams and other highly participative systems is that some old-style supervisors have a hard time changing their management approach in the required way. If training and coaching are ineffective in helping them to make the transition to a more participative workplace, enhanced retirement or outplacement and replacement may become the only alternatives.

Training

As mentioned earlier, many interventions rely heavily on training. The need for business literacy training in open book management firms has also been noted. In TQM firms, virtually everyone would be trained in quality appreciation, and a majority of people would be trained in specific quality monitoring and control techniques.[105] Table 10.16 shows recommendations for training content for various groups when TQM is implemented. If teams are used, whether as part-time quality circles or as

● **FIGURE 10.6**

Quality-Oriented Ad from 3M Canada

Source: Reprinted with the permission of 3M Canada Company.

PROCESS OPERATORS

At 3M Canada Co. we believe that success comes through commitment to customer satisfaction and the continuous improvement of our products, quality and services. If you share this vision, we may have a challenging opportunity available for you.

3M Canada has several openings in its new Brockville plant for process operators. Successful candidates will become members of a high-performance, self-managed work team in our state-of-the-art tape making facility.

We are looking for candidates who:

- Have a minimum of Grade 12 education or equivalent
- Are willing to work rotating shifts on a 24-hour, 7-day basis.
- Enjoy working in a diverse team environment
- Are capable of learning and performing all operator job functions in the plant
- Have excellent interpersonal and communication skills

3M offers competitive compensation and a full benefits package. We offer interesting and challenging work in a friendly, safe, supportive atmosphere. Applicants may be asked to complete a number of tests and group exercises, as well as interviews before being offered a position.

All qualified applicants are invited to complete an application at the 3M Brockville site, 60 California Ave., Brockville. We will be receiving applications from March 1–March 6, 1993 only, from 8:30 am–8:00 pm Monday–Friday and from 8:30 am–4:00 pm on Saturday. In order to keep this process as smooth as possible, we ask that people use the following schedule:

Surnames beginning with:

Monday	A–C	
Tuesday	D–J	
Wednesday	K–M	*Please note that NO special consideration*
Thursday	N–S	*will be given to those candidates showing*
Friday	T–Z	*up early to complete applications. Also, no*
Saturday	Open	*phone calls, please!*

 Employment and
Immigration Canada

3M gratefully acknowledges the support and assistance of the Canada Employment Centre in our hiring process.

3M Canada Co.
P.O. Box 755
Brockville, Ontario
K6V 5W1

3M

3M Canada Co. encourages applications from women, men, members of visible minorities, aboriginal peoples and persons with disabilities.

● **TABLE 10.16**

The Quality Education Matrix

	Executives	Middle Managers	Engineers	Supervisors	Workers
Quality improvement overview	X	X	X	X	X
Employee involvement	X	X	X	X	X
Leadership/facilitator workshop	X	X	X	X	
Team building	X	X	X	X	X
Creative thinking	X	X	X	X	X
Supplier management	X	X	X		
Setup reduction and cellular processes		X	X	X	X
Problem solving—basic	X	X	X	X	X
Problem solving—advanced statistical process control	X	X	X	X	X
Problem solving—train the trainer		X		X	X
Design of experiments		X	X	X	X
Total quality control audit	X	X			
Competitive benchmarking	X	X	X		
Statistical thinking (how to understand variability and the correct approach to reducing it)	X	X	X	X	X
Quality function deployment	X	X	X	X	
Total productive maintenance	X	X	X	X	X
General business perspective				X	X
Parameter design using Taguchi methods			X		
Policy deployment	X	X	X	X	

Source: David L. Muthler and Lucy L. Lytle, "Quality Education Requirements," in *Total Quality: An Executive's Guide for the 1990s,* ed. by Ernst & Young Improvement Consulting Group (Homewood, Ill., Dow Jones–Irwin, 1990).

full-time work teams, additional training is required on teamwork, communication, problem solving, and so on. When teams are empowered to manage themselves, nonsupervisory employees need to be trained in supervisory skills such as budgeting and scheduling. If self-directed teams take on HR responsibilities such as performance appraisal and selection, even more skills are needed.

Self-directed work teams and pay-for-skills systems often require a high level of cross-training across a set of related jobs. Most typically, this training will be on the job and self-paced. This means that HR training experts may need to provide workbooks and other materials for self-paced learning, train team members to serve as on-the-job trainers, and develop certification tests to verify that competency in each new skill has been achieved.

Appraisal and Reward Systems

It is very important that appraisal and reward systems support the types of behaviors the organization desires from employees. Often, reward systems that were developed before TQM or employee involvement were adopted will be inconsistent with the new culture and behaviors. For instance, appraisal systems that penalize risk taking and mistakes, demand individual results at all costs, and provide for individual incentives or merit pay may be a hindrance in implementing group-based systems intended to foster innovative experimentation and cooperation. Similarly, top-down appraisal by management of subordinates may violate the spirit of empowerment. In some organizations, self-directed work teams take responsibility for appraising, rewarding, and—if necessary—disciplining their own members. In addition, 360-degree feedback (assessment of managers by their superiors, peers, and subordinates) is in keeping with a high-involvement approach that involves the sharing of power.

It has been said that "quality is a team sport."[106] This suggests that appraisal systems that assess cooperation and team skills, as well as technical skills, should be used. Hard measures of performance should be collected at the team level rather than at the individual level if tasks are highly interdependent. Constant feedback of team results may replace an emphasis on annual formal appraisals, and when the latter occur, they should be future- and development-focused rather than past- and judgment-focused. Quality guru W. Edwards Deming is opposed to performance appraisal in almost any form, believing that it creates an unhealthy atmosphere of fear and blame placing.

Rewards must motivate the behaviors most necessary to making the quality initiative succeed. For systems that rely on cross-training and flexibility within teams, pay-for-skills systems are a good way to reward individuals without stimulating dysfunctional competition among team members. Pay-for-skills systems can coexist with other reward systems that pay off for team, site, or corporate performance. Group-based incentives, gain sharing, and profit sharing are often recommended for high-involvement organizations.

Organizations seriously committed to employee empowerment and involvement also tend to change pay and benefits systems so as to minimize differences between management and workers. This may mean shifting to an all-salaried work force and doing away with time clocks, reducing some executive perquisites such as reserved parking or a special dining room, and even adopting more homogeneous dress standards at the plant. As an example of the latter, suits and ties may be banned for executives, and all employees may wear similar uniform jackets.

Changing the appraisal and reward system can be a crucial part of successful culture change in an organization. The HR manager's role is to assess the fit of existing systems to the intervention and consider recommending a change. In truly participative systems, groups of employees might become involved in designing any changes to these systems.

Labor Relations

Systems involving widespread employee involvement require close cooperation with the employees' union. This is so because job duties may change, expanding across traditional craft boundaries, and employees may take on decision-making responsibilities formerly reserved for supervisory staff. A cooperative labor relations climate makes implementing these changes much easier.[107] Cooperation removes overt organized resistance and provides another credible channel of communication to employees about the need for changes and the likely benefits of improved performance for all concerned. In some participative interventions, the most time-consuming activity has been to get traditionally adversarial managers and union leaders to jointly design the program prior to its implementation. But once cooperation is forthcoming, the rest of the process is fairly smooth. Employee involvement systems and team production approaches seem to work well in a collaborative unionized environment.[108]

The Saturn plant provides a graphic example of union–management cooperation in implementing work teams in a new facility. The United Auto Workers (UAW) union was involved with General Motors managers from the first stages of plant design. Union–management teams traveled more than 2 million miles to visit the world's best small-car manufacturing plants and devise a cooperative work system that would work for GM. The UAW signed a pathbreaking labor agreement designed to increase cooperation and the spreading of responsibility from management to line workers. Each manager is "paired" with a similarly ranked union official, with whom he or she consults daily on virtually all decisions. Supporting this system is a massive amount of training to enable employees to take on the new responsibilities being urged on them by both management and union leaders.[109]

In some cases, programs to improve competitiveness can benefit union–management relationships. In the city of Seattle, joint labor–management work improvement teams have been successful in improving the efficiency of service delivery and in repairing an adversarial union–management climate. Several years ago the city considered improving the effectiveness of service delivery by contracting out some city services to private companies. Unions of city workers objected and threatened to strike. Joint work-improvement teams were subsequently put in place to explore other means of increasing efficiency of service. Ultimately, service was improved without the subcontracting of services. Further, the next round of union contract negotiation was accomplished very much more quickly and easily than in the past because of the trust and working relationships developed through the joint work-improvement teams.[110]

Summary of Key Points

Pressures on businesses to improve productivity, quality, service, speed, and organizational learning have been mounting over the past three decades. A number of methods for improving productivity and quality are available, from organizationally based culture changes and group-oriented approaches to individual motivational methods. For any type of program to be effective, it must be preceded by an appropriate diagnosis, and careful thought must be given to building commitment to the new system.

Business process improvement (reengineering) is an approach to analyzing and radically streamlining work processes by deleting steps that waste time and do not add value. Reorganized work processes may be substantially faster and require fewer people. Total quality management is a philosophy and culture change that uses a variety of techniques to make everyone in the organization responsible for supplying products and services that must meet customers' needs 100 percent of the time.

High-involvement organizations use an integrated set of high-performance work practices that share power, information, knowledge, and rewards with all employees. High-involvement organizations use self-directed work teams, job enrichment, ownership and group financial incentives, symbolic egalitarianism, job security, and careful selection and training to develop multiskilled and highly flexible and motivated work forces.

Group-oriented participative methods increase the amount of responsibility and decision-making power that line employees have in productivity and quality issues. Work-improvement teams (quality circles) allow groups of employees to spend company time preparing suggestions on how to improve the work process. Self-directed work teams are a more radical innovation, usually replacing the supervisor role with group decision making about daily work practices.

Increasing employee effort is a common approach for improving productivity. One way to do this is by performance-based pay systems. Employee ownership methods and open-book management can also attract greater employee commitment and effort. Suggestion and award systems are used to increase productivity and quality and to reward employees who contribute to these goals. Goal setting can be a very effective way to improve performance. Specific and challenging goals, with feedback on goal attainment, can both motivate high performance and clarify the organization's expectations of employees. Stretch goals are a recent innovation.

Another technique to enhance individual performance is behavior modification, in which the consequences of behavior are manipulated to get results. Positive reinforcement increases desired behaviors, whereas punishment and extinction are used to eliminate undesirable ones. Clear specification and measurement of desired behaviors are essential components of behavior modification.

Job redesign, or job enrichment, attempts to improve motivation by restructuring the work so that it provides more feedback and intrinsic rewards for the employees. Tasks are rearranged so that employees use a variety of skills to complete meaningful units of work for an identifiable client.

In sum, increased demands for quality and productivity have challenged many organizations in the last few decades. In response, major changes have occurred in organizational culture and practices. The success of these changes depends on enthusiastic and educated participation by all employees. HR managers have a large role to play in supplying and cultivating these employees, mainly by redesigning HR systems so that the behaviors required of employees are (1) possible (via selection and training) and (2) motivated (via appraisal and reward systems).

The Manager's Vocabulary

autonomous work group
award program
behavior modification
behavioral self-regulation
benchmarking
business process improvement
employee share ownership scheme
extinction
goal setting
high-involvement organization (HIO)
high-performance work systems
intellectual capital
ISO9001:2000
job enrichment
job redesign
kaizen
learning organization
Malcolm Baldrige National Quality Award
open-book management (OBM)
positive, future, and uncertain rewards (PFU)
positive, immediate, and certain rewards (PIC)
positive reinforcement
punishment
quality circles (QCs)
reengineering
self-directed (or self-managed) work teams
service–profit chain

skill-based pay
stretch target
suggestion systems
total quality management (TQM)
work-improvement teams

Questions for Discussion

1. Companies are having to improve their competitiveness to stay in business. In what ways might they improve?
2. What is benchmarking, and how can it be useful to an organization seeking to become more competitive?
3. What is business process improvement? Name a process with which you are familiar that could benefit from the application of this approach.
4. What common principles appear in most versions of TQM?
5. What is *kaizen*?
6. Describe an organization that has implemented TQM successfully. What kinds of ideas are central to this organization? What kinds of systems might you see in place for monitoring and improving quality? Pick an organization you are familiar with and brainstorm about how it would be changed by a true commitment to TQM.
7. What is a high-involvement organization? Would you like to work in one? Why or why not?
8. Describe the service–profit chain. What are the implications of this model for a service organization?
9. Describe quality circles. What are some of the positive results of quality circles? What are some potential problems?

10. What kinds of functions might be performed by a self-directed work team?
11. Have you ever held a job for which financial incentives for performance were in place? How well did they work to motivate desired employee behavior?
12. Think about your current or most recent job. How much did you know (and care) about the company's financial performance? How would things have changed if this organization had adopted open book management?
13. Design a suggestion system for a job you have held (or for this class). In what ways will you apply/implement the ten tips shown in Table 10.10?
14. Explain how and why goal setting works.
15. Explain how behavior modification can be used to change employee behavior.
16. Prepare a plan for yourself to self-regulate your study behavior.
17. What is job redesign? Why would an organization use it? Pick a job you are familiar with and redesign it, following the principles given in the chapter and in Figure 10.4.
18. Debate: "The best way to solve quality, productivity, and service problems is to motivate employees to work as hard and conscientiously as possible."
19. You are in charge of recruiting and staffing systems at a company that is planning to switch to a high-involvement approach. How will your job change?
20. You are a training manager at a company that is about to implement TQM. How will your job change?

● Case 10.1
Customcraft Marine Interiors, Inc. (contributed by Hal Aikens)

Customcraft manufactures the interiors for powerboats ranging from modest 15 footers to luxury 40-foot-and-over yachts. Customcraft interiors are used by some of the top boat-builders in the indus-try. The production process is low-tech and involves operations such as woodworking, pattern-making, cut-and-sew, finishing, and final assembly. The jobs are semiskilled and skilled (carpentry, upholstery, drapery making, etc.), with Customcraft providing skill training for new hires.

For two decades the company has been located in Fayetteville, Arkansas, and has recruited its factory workers mainly from the local community. In the past few years, it has become increasingly difficult to attract and retain good personnel. Turnover has been very high (over 200 percent), and the company has had difficulty replacing those leaving from its usual labor market. Efforts to fill vacancies have increased the ethnic diversity of the workplace, with a nearby Lithuanian community supplying a number of recruits. When vacancies still remained, a number of Mexican workers were hired and relocated from Texas. Unfortunately, Customcraft did not pay attention to language skills in selection, and many of the new employees have at best rudimentary English skills. This has had a devastating effect on the work environment. Morale is at an all-time low, turnover remains high, an environment of mistrust and misunderstanding exists between coworkers, supervisors have great difficulty in communicating with their employees, training has become almost impossible because of language problems, and quality and productivity have plummeted. A highly directive work atmosphere prevails. Given these chronic problems, Customcraft is thinking about abandoning the Fayetteville plant altogether.

With the help of federal and state economic development grants, Customcraft was able to raise the capital to build a new manufacturing plant in Lincoln, a small town seventy miles west of Fayetteville. This was to be a "fresh start" for the company, with the intent that the Fayetteville plant would eventually be closed. High unemployment in Lincoln and the surrounding county meant that unskilled trainees could be found readily. Core personnel, including both supervisors and skilled workers, were transferred from Fayetteville to Lincoln to train new employees and work in the new facility.

Don Brighton was hired as the first plant manager for the Lincoln plant. Don had previously been the production superintendent of a large multinational consumer goods manufacturer, where he had experience with state-of-the-art plants. Customcraft gave Don a five-year contract with an attractive compensation package, including annual productivity bonuses and profit sharing. The CEO of Customcraft, John Weatherall, made it very clear that Don would be accountable for getting the new plant op-

erational within a four-month time frame and for demonstrating a 20 percent productivity improvement (compared to Fayetteville) within one year of start-up. Additionally, further annual improvements of 10 percent were expected for each of the following four years.

Don had big plans for the Lincoln facility. He hoped that starting up a new facility would allow him to integrate progressive ideas into the work design from day one. He planned to build an empowered teamwork culture and inculcate shared values and high-performance goals throughout the work force. Don's previous company had been successful in organizing the shop floor into manufacturing cells, managed by the workers themselves. Teams were empowered to make decisions concerning scheduling and quality and could even approve annual leave and personal time off within the team. Training needs were also a team responsibility, and those needs that could not be met within the team were requisitioned from and formally arranged by the HR Department. With empowerment came accountability, and Don had observed firsthand the phenomenon of psychological ownership shifting from management to the workers themselves. With this transition came a sense of pride and self-esteem that had positive impacts on quality, productivity, and morale. Once the transition was complete, management agreed that the results were well worth the costs, trials, and tribulations. The work environment was happier and more productive, and quality was measurably better. There really was no discernible downside. When the work force is motivated, Don had learned, the game is not zero-sum—hence his desire to install a similar system at the new Customcraft plant.

Unfortunately, Don was the only person with an understanding of team-oriented work systems at Customcraft. His local supervisors, transferred from the Fayetteville plant, were good at giving orders but had neither the skills nor the patience to function as team advisors. Further, Customcraft did not possess the sophisticated human resources and training support for team approaches that he had enjoyed at his previous employer. In the interest of getting the plant productive, Don decided to start with a traditional system in which supervisors trained employees and ran functional departments. He hoped to begin a gradual transition to teams and cellular manufacturing by the end of the first year, once employees had begun to master their initial job assignments. He also planned to hire a few experienced supervisors who could assist in implementing teams.

When the Lincoln facility had been operational for about six months, Don made some personnel changes in an attempt to boost productivity. One of the reassignments was to move Charlie Banks, who had been the woodshop superintendent, into a material expediter role and to assign Bernie Fleegle, the QC manager for the past few months, to the woodshop supervisory position. Don had recruited Bernie straight out of college with an M.B.A. degree on top of an engineering undergraduate degree, and he hoped that Bernie would become a central part of the "new management team." On the morning after this change was announced, as Don arrived at the plant, he encountered the entire woodshop crew putting down their tools and walking out the door. Some of the senior members of the crew were quite vocal in their refusal to work for "that wet-behind-the-ears college kid!" Angrily, Don told them that if they walked out the gate, they need not return as there would be no jobs for them. The woodshop employees kept walking. Fearing reprisals by outraged former employees, the plant security chief called the local sheriff to protect the plant against possible vandalism. Lincoln is a small town in which "everyone knows everyone and everything," and the mass firing became common news throughout the town within the hour.

Don is facing a dilemma. His authority has been challenged, but more importantly, his entire strategy for the future is in serious jeopardy. He knows that how he handles the current situation will be carefully scrutinized not only by his work force but also by the entire town. He cannot afford to lose on public relations points.

1. What should Don do right now, as sacked employees protest outside the gate?
2. If he could roll back the clock several days, what should Don have done to prevent this situation from arising in the first place?
3. What could he have done as he arrived at work and encountered the unhappy woodshop employees?
4. Assuming Don can defuse the current crisis, how and when should he begin to introduce a team-oriented manufacturing philosophy to Customcraft? What hurdles will he need to overcome?
5. Turning to the troubled Fayetteville plant, what advice would you give to management? Should they close the Fayetteville facility or should they keep trying to turn the plant around? How would you address the language problem? the morale problem? the recruitment problem? the productivity and quality problems?
6. If the Fayetteville facility remains open and continues under its present work system, do you think it will be possible to operate that plant and the Lincoln plant under two different manufacturing philosophies?
7. How might human resource practices have to differ at the two plants to support their respective systems?
8. What might the Fayetteville plant do within a traditional work structure to assure that quality and productivity are acceptable?

Source: Contributed by Dr. C. H. (Hal) Aikens, Professor of Industrial Engineering, University of Tennessee and reprinted with his permission.

● Case 10.2
Reducing the Crime Rate in New York City

In 1994 William Bratton was appointed police commissioner for New York City. Crime was unacceptably high and Bratton was charged with doing something about it, using his staff of seventy-six precinct commanders and 38,000 police officers. Two years later, crime was down by 27 percent overall, an astonishing accomplishment that drew admiring attention from police around the globe. How did Bratton do it?

First, he implemented a computerized crime statistics information system, Comstat, which produced up-to-the-minute data on precinct-by-precinct crime rates in categories such as rapes, murders, robberies, assaults, burglaries, and car thefts. Then he made precinct captains accountable for results on these measures. They received frequent feedback and each month were grilled by Bratton and his top managers on trends in their precinct. There was always pressure for more improvement, and they were expected to have specific action plans for improving any numbers that were creeping in the wrong direction.

Bratton also used goal setting. A stretch target of reducing the citywide crime rate by 10 percent in the first year was set. The actual reduction at the end of the year was 12 percent. The second year, the target was a further 15 percent reduction, which was surpassed at 17 percent. This very difficult goal also produced some changes in strategy. Police changed tactics by interrogating suspects not only about the crime they may have committed but also about other gun and drug dealers they knew. They adopted a zero-tolerance policy on minor offenses such as public drunkenness, urinating on the street, graffiti, and vandalism. This had two effects: Some wanted individuals were apprehended when their IDs were checked for very minor offenses, and the general tenor of the street was cleaned up, increasing civic pride and law-abiding behavior across the board.

Along with changes in policing strategy, enhanced computer programs were installed to provide faster processing of crime data. In some cases this allowed police to identify and stop repeat offend ers after just a few incidents of crime rather than after the thirty or more they might have chalked up before coming to the attention of police in the past.

While the program was wildly successful in improving police performance defined in terms of the crime rate, there were some side effects. Half of the precinct commanders quit or were replaced when they couldn't fulfill the new demands. Bratton and his managers could be brutal in their "perform-or-else" style. Some captains are reputed to have fudged the definitions of crimes to produce the numbers they needed. For instance, one way to reduce the assault figures is to redefine an assault as requiring the victim to have a broken bone, not just a black eye or fat lip, following the attack. Civil libertarians contend that cops became more aggressive and more often violated suspects' rights. Nevertheless, most city residents were very happy with the improvement in public safety.[111]

1. Why did Bratton's policing performance improvement program work? Describe what he did using concepts from this chapter.
2. Can you think of anything else Bratton could have done, based on ideas in this chapter?
3. This was very much a top-down program imposed by upper management. What do you think of this approach compared to a more participative style? Consider the situation, existing organizational culture, and so forth.

● Exercise 10.1
Diagnose Your Organization

Use the High-Involvement Human Resource Practices Scale in Table 10.7 to describe human resource practices at the organization where you currently work or previously worked. Calculate a score for the total scale by averaging your responses to all questions. Create subscale scores for different classes of practices by averaging your responses to the items in that category.

Compare your organization to others using the normative data provided below. These scores are based on a survey of 107 U.S. organizations.[112] A company that scores one standard deviation above the mean is at the eighty-fourth percentile, while one that scores one standard deviation below the mean is at the sixteenth percentile. An organization with an overall score of 2.13 (mean of 1.84 + 1 SD of .29) would be at the eighty-fourth percentile, while an organization two standard deviations above the mean (about 2.42, or mean of 1.84 + .29 + .29) would be in the top 2 percent in terms of the overall adoption of HIO practices.

1. How does your organization compare to these norms?

2. How would you describe the productivity, quality, flexibility, innovation, customer satisfaction, employee satisfaction, and employee turnover rate at your organization?
3. Do you think your organization could benefit from moving further toward a high-involvement approach? Why? Consider the type of work and the organization's strategy as well as its current performance and practices in your answer.
4. What practices would you recommend changing first?
5. Compare notes with other students. Do you see any relationship between extent of adoption of

HIO practices and the outcomes mentioned in item 2 across the organizations that you have rated?

Scale	Mean	Standard Deviation
Training and development	1.91	.45
Selection and promotion	1.85	.42
Performance evaluation	1.79	.49
Job redesign	1.93	.49
Compensation	1.72	.38
Overall (average of all items)	1.84	.29

● **Exercise 10.2**
To Team or Not to Team?

Form discussion groups of five. Consider jobs you each presently hold or have held in the past. To what extent is or was each job accomplished in a team setting?

For one job at a time, discuss the following questions:

1. To what extent might it be feasible to change to a team approach for the job?
2. Would full-time teams be effective, or would a part-time work-improvement team make more sense?
3. If you believe that full-time teams are feasible, how would they be organized?

4. What changes and training would be necessary for present team members?
5. What changes in HR practices might be required to support a team approach?
6. Could this team be self-managing, or would it require a hierarchical leader?
7. What benefits might the organization receive from adopting a team approach to this type of work?

Following the discussion of several jobs, draw your own conclusions about which types of jobs tend to lend themselves to a team approach and which do not.

Notes and References

1. This HR Challenge is based on the experience of an actual newspaper. The case was written by Dr. Hal Aikens, Professor of Industrial Engineering, University of Tennessee.
2. P. M. Wright, L. Dyer, and M. G. Takla, "What's Next? Key Findings from the 1999 State-of-the-Art & Practice Study," *Human Resource Planning,* Vol. 22 (4), 1999, pp. 12–20; quote, p. 14.
3. Ron Zemke and Dick Schaaf, *The Service Edge* (New York: New American Library, 1989).
4. K. Theodor Krantz, "How Velcro Got Hooked on Quality," *Harvard Business Review,* September–October 1989, pp. 34–40.

5. For more information, see Frequently Asked Questions About the ISO9000 Series, http://www.asq.org/standcert. iso.html.
6. Cited in Warren Brown and Necmi Karagozoglu, "Leading the Way to Faster New Product Development," *Academy of Management Executive,* February 1993, pp. 36–47.
7. Edward E. Lawler III, *From the Ground Up: Six Principles for Building the New Logic Corporation* (San Francisco: Jossey-Bass, 1996).
8. Richard M. Hodgetts, Fred Luthans, and Sang M. Lee, "New Paradigm Organizations: From Total Quality to Learning

to World-Class," *Organizational Dynamics,* Winter 1994, pp. 4–19; and K. E. Watkins and V. J. Marsick, *Sculpting the Learning Organization: Lessons in the Art and Science of Systemic Change* (San Francisco: Jossey-Bass, 1993).

9. For several approaches to quality improvement, see Arthur R. Tenner and Irving J. DeToro, *Total Quality Management: Three Steps to Continuous Improvement* (Reading, Mass.: Addison-Wesley, 1992), or John Beckford, *Quality: A Critical Introduction* (London: Routledge, 1998).

10. E. E. Lawler, S. A. Mohrman, and G. E. Ledford, *Employee Involvement and Total Quality Management: Practices and Results in Fortune 1000 Companies* (San Francisco: Jossey-Bass, 1992).

11. Robert Camp, *Benchmarking: The Search for Industry Best Practices That Lead to Superior Performance* (Milwaukee, Wis.: ASQC Quality Press, 1989); and Robert C. Camp, *Business Process Benchmarking* (Milwaukee, Wis.: ASQC Quality Press, 1995). The American Productivity and Quality Center Web site at www.apqc.org contains a great deal of information on benchmarking.

12. Cited in Vicki J. Powers, "United States Air Force: A Benchmarking Success Story," American Productivity and Quality Center, 1995. (Available at: http://www.apqc.org/free/ articles/dispArticle.cfm?ProductID=649)

13. For an excellent example of how to get people on board for a change, see R. Cooper and M. L. Markus, "Human Reengineering," *Sloan Management Review,* Summer 1995, pp. 39–50.

14. T. Y. Choi and O. C. Behling, "Top Management and TQM Success: One More Look after All These Years," *Academy of Management Executive,* Feburary 1997, pp. 37–47.

15. B. W. Hennestad, "Implementing Participative Management: Transition Issues from the Field," *Journal of Applied Behavioral Science,* September 2000, pp. 314–335; and R. Forrester, "Empowerment: Rejuvenating a Potent Idea," *Academy of Management Executive*, August 2000, pp. 67–80.

16. Edward J. Kane, "IBM's Quality Focus on the Business Process," *Quality Progress,* April 1986, pp. 24–33. See also C. E. Schneier, D. G. Shaw, and R. W. Beatty, "Companies' Attempts to Improve Performance While Containing Costs: Quick Fix Versus Lasting Change," *Human Resource Planning*, Vol. 15 (3), 1992, pp. 1–25; and Daniel Morris and Joel Brandon, *Re-Engineering Your Business* (New York: McGraw-Hill, 1993).

17. M. Hammer and J. Champy, *Reengineering the Corporation* (New York: HarperBusiness, 1993).

18. M. Hammer and S. A. Stanton, *The Reengineering Revolution* (New York: HarperBusiness, 1995), p. 3.

19. Michael Hammer, "Reengineering Work: Don't Automate, Obliterate," *Harvard Business Review,* July–August 1990, pp. 104–112.

20. Hammer and Stanton, *The Reengineering Revolution;* and Joseph J. Gufreda, Larry A. Maynard, and Lucy N. Lytle, "Employee Involvement in the Quality Process," in *Total Quality: An Executive's Guide for the 1990s,* ed. Ernst & Young Improvement Consulting Group (Homewood, Ill.: Dow Jones–Irwin, 1990), pp. 162–176.

21. Edward E. Lawler III, S. A. Mohrman, and G. E. Ledford, Jr., *Creating High Performance Organizations* (San Francisco: Jossey-Bass, 1995); and C. G. Partlow, "Human-Resources Practices of TQM Hotels," *Cornell Hotel and Restaurant Administration Quarterly*, October 1996, pp. 67–77.

22. Tenner and DeToro, *Total Quality Management;* and Beckford, *Quality: A Critical Introduction.*

23. For more information on how TQM differs from traditional management, see Robert M. Grant, Rami Shani, and R. Krishnan, "TQM's Challenge to Management Theory and Practice," *Sloan Management Review,* Winter 1994, pp. 25–35.

24. T. J. Douglas and W. Q. Judge, Jr., "TQM Implementation and Competitive Advantage: The Role of Structural Control and Exploration," *Academy of Management Journal*, February 2001, pp. 158–169.

25. D. Dow, D. Samson, and S. Ford, "Exploding the Myth: Do all Quality Management Practices Contribute to Superior Quality Performance?" *Production and Operations Management*, Spring 1999, pp. 1–27.

26. R. E. Walton, "From Control to Commitment in the Workplace," *Harvard Business Review*, March–April 1985, pp. 77–84.

27. Lawler, *From the Ground Up*; and Edward E. Lawler III, *The Ultimate Advantage: Creating the High-Involvement Organization* (San Francisco: Jossey-Bass, 1992).

28. Lawler, *The Ultimate Advantage.*

29. J. Pfeffer, *Competitive Advantage Through People: Unleashing the Power of the Work Force* (Boston: Harvard Business School Press, 1994); J. Pfeffer, *The Human Equation: Building Profits by Putting People First* (Boston: Harvard Business School Press, 1998); and C. A. O'Reilly III and J. Pfeffer, *Hidden Value: How Great Companies Achieve Extraordinary Results with Ordinary People* (Boston: Harvard Business School Press, 2000).

30. Lawler, Mohrman, and Ledford, *Employee Involvement and Total Quality Management;* Lawler, *From the Ground Up*; and J. Pfeffer and J. F. Veiga, "Putting People First for Organizational Success," *Academy of Management Executive*, May 1999, pp. 37–48.

31. M. Patterson, M. West, and T. Wall, "HRM and Company Performance: A Critique and Some UK Evidence," paper presented at the Annual Meeting of the Academy of Management, Toronto, 2000; A. Varma, R. W. Beatty, C. E. Schneier, and D. O. Ulrich, "High Performance Work Systems: Exciting Discovery or Passing Fad?" *Human Resource Planning,* Vol. 22 (1), 1999, pp. 26–37; J. P. Guthrie, "High Involvement Work Practices, Turnover, and Productivity: Evidence from New Zealand," *Academy of Management Journal*, February 2001, pp. 180–190; and R. J. Vandenberg, H. A. Richardson, L. J. Eastman, "The Impact of High Involvement Work Processes on Organizational Effectiveness: A Second-Order Latent Variable Approach," *Group and Organization Management*, September 1999, pp. 300–339.

32. Pfeffer, *Competitive Advantage Through People.*

33. C. Ichniowski and K. Shaw, "The Effects of Human Resource Management Systems on Economic Performance: An International Comparison of U.S. and Japanese Plants," *Management Science*, May 1999, pp. 704–721.

34. J. P. MacDuffie, "Human Resource Bundles and Manufacturing Performance: Organizational Logic and Flexible Production Systems in the World Auto Industry," *Industrial and Labor Relations Review*, January 1995, pp. 197–222.

35. J. L. Heskett, T. O. Jones, G. W. Loveman, W. E. Sasser, Jr., and L. A. Schlesinger, "Putting the Service-Profit Chain to Work," *Harvard Business Review*, March–April 1994, pp. 164–174; and J. L. Heskett, W. E. Sasser, Jr., and L.A. Schlesinger, *The Service Profit Chain* (New York: The Free Press, 1997). Note that the authors do *not* contend that a

satisfied employee will be more productive than a dissatisfied employee. They merely point out that a generally satisfied work force will have longer tenure and hence higher skills, stronger relationships with repeat customers, and so forth. Further, in a well-structured workplace, being empowered to provide good service is itself satisfying to employees.

36. Gufreda, Maynard, and Lytle, "Employee Involvement in the Quality Process."

37. Eric Sundstrom, Kenneth P. De Meuse, and David Futrell, "Work Teams: Applications and Effectiveness," *Psychological Bulletin,* February 1990, pp. 120–133.

38. Paul Osterman, "Work Reorganization in an Era of Restructuring: Trends in Diffusion and Effects of Employee Welfare," *Industrial and Labor Relations Review,* January 2000, pp. 179–196.

39. Gerald E. Ledford, Jr., Edward E. Lawler III, and Susan A. Mohrman, "The Quality Circle and Its Variations," in *Productivity in Organizations: New Perspectives from Industrial and Organizational Psychology,* ed. John P. Campbell, Richard J. Campbell, et al. (San Francisco: Jossey-Bass, 1988), pp. 255–294.

40. Edward E. Lawler and Susan A. Mohrman, "Quality Circles: After the Honeymoon," *Organizational Dynamics,* Spring 1987, pp. 42–55.

41. Krantz, "How Velcro Got Hooked on Quality."

42. Gufreda, Maynard, and Lytle, "Employee Involvement in the Quality Process."

43. Thomas C. Head, Julie L. Molleston, Peter F. Sorensen, and Joseph Cargano, "The Impact of Implementing a Quality Circles Intervention on Employee Task Perceptions," *Group and Organizational Studies,* December 1986, pp. 360–373.

44. Murray R. Barrick and Ralph A. Alexander, "A Review of Quality Circle Efficacy and the Existence of a Positive-Finding Bias," *Personnel Psychology,* Autumn 1987, pp. 579–592.

45. Ledford, Lawler, and Mohrman, "The Quality Circle and Its Variations."

46. S. G. Cohen and D. E. Bailey, "What Makes Teams Work: Group Effectiveness Research from the Shop Floor to the Executive Suite," *Journal of Management,* Vol. 23, 1997, pp. 239–290; and Rosemary Batt, "Work Organization, Technology, and Performance in Customer Service and Sales," *Industrial and Labor Relations Review,* July 1999, pp. 539–564.

47. Ricky W. Griffin, "Consequences of Quality Circles in an Industrial Setting: A Longitudinal Assessment," *Academy of Management Journal,* June 1988, pp. 338–358.

48. Gordon W. Meyer and Randall G. Stott, "Quality Circles: Panacea or Pandora's Box?" *Organizational Dynamics,* Spring 1985, pp. 35–50.

49. C. Joinson, "Teams at Work," *HR Magazine,* May 1999, pp. 30–36.

50. Thomas M. Rohman, "Bosses—Who Needs 'Em?" *Industry Week,* February 23, 1987, pp. 15–16; and John Case, "What the Experts Forgot to Mention," *Inc.,* September 1993, pp. 66–77.

51. Paul S. Goodman, Rukmini Devadas, and Terri L. Griffith Hughson, "Groups and Productivity: Analyzing the Effectiveness of Self-Managing Teams," in Campbell, Campbell, et al. (eds.), *Productivity in Organizations,* pp. 295–327; R. D. Banker, J. M. Field, R. G. Schroeder, and K. K. Sinha, "Impact of Work Teams on Manufacturing Performance: A Longitudinal Study," *Academy of Management Journal,* Vol. 39 (4), 1996, pp. 867–890; J. L. Cordery, "Work Redesign: Rhetoric vs. Reality," *Asia Pacific*

Journal of Human Resources, Winter 1995, pp. 3–19; Cohen and Bailey, "What Makes Teams Work"; R. Batt and E. Applebaum, "Worker Participation in Diverse Settings: Does the Form Affect the Outcomes?" *British Journal of Industrial Relations,* Vol. 33, 1995, pp. 353–378; and B. Macy and H. Izumi, "Organizational Change, Design, and Work Innovation: A Meta-Analysis of 131 North American Field Studies," *Research in Organizational Change and Development,* Vol. 7, 1993, pp. 235–313.

52. T. A. Williams, "The End of Supervision? A Case Study and Critique of the Attempted Conversion of Supervisors into Team Leaders," *Asia Pacific Journal of Human Resources,* Vol. 35 (3), 1997, pp. 62–79.

53. Toby D. Wall, Nigel J. Kemp, Paul R. Jackson, and Chris W. Clegg, "Outcomes of Autonomous Work Groups: A Long-Term Field Experiment," *Academy of Management Journal,* June 1986, pp. 280–304.

54. Fred Luthans, "A Conversation with Charles Dull," *Organizational Dynamics,* Summer 1993, pp. 57–70.

55. C. C. Durham and K. M. Bartol, "Pay for Performance," in *Principles of Organizational Behavior,* ed. E. A. Locke (Oxford, England: Blackwell, 2000), pp. 150–165.

56. John A. Wagner III, Paul A. Rubin, and Thomas J. Callahan, "Incentive Payment and Nonmanagerial Productivity: An Interrupted Time Series Analysis of Magnitude and Trend," *Organizational Behavior and Human Decision Processes,* August 1988, pp. 47–74.

57. T. M. Welbourne and L. R. Gomez-Mejia, "Gainsharing: A Critical Review and a Future Research Agenda," *Journal of Management,* Vol. 21, 1999, pp. 559–609.

58. Stephanie Overman, "Saturn Teams Working and Profiting," *HRMagazine,* March 1995, pp. 72–74.

59. F. Luthans and A.D. Stajkovic, "Reinforce for Performance: The Need to Go Beyond Pay and Even Rewards," *Academy of Management Executive,* May 1999, pp. 49–57.

60. M. M. Blair and D. L. Kruse, "Worker Capitalists?" *The Brookings Review,* Fall 1999, pp. 23–26.

61. "Employee Stock Options Fact Sheet." (Available at: http://www.nceo.org/library/optionfact.html)

62. Theresa M Welbourne and Linda A. Cyr, "Using Ownership as an Incentive," *Group & Organization Management,* December 1999, pp. 438–460; Zahid Iqbal and Shaikh Abdul Hamid, "Stock Price and Operating Performance of ESOP Firms: A Time-Series Analysis," *Quarterly Journal of Business and Economics,* Summer 2000, pp. 25–48; and William N. Pugh, Sharon L. Oswald, and John S. Jahera, Jr., "The Effect of ESOP Adoptions on Corporate Performance: Are There Really Performance Changes?" *Managerial and Decision Economics,* July–August 2000, pp. 167–180.

63. "Employee Ownership and Corporate Performance." (Available at: http://www.nceo.org/library/corpperf.html)

64. T. R. V. Davis, "Open-Book Management: Its Promise and Pitfalls," *Organizational Dynamics,* Winter 1997, pp. 7–20; J. Strack, *The Great Game of Business* (New York: Doubleday, 1992); J. Case, *Open Book Management: The Coming Business Revolution* (New York: HarperBusiness, 1995); and J. P. Schuster, J. Carpenter, and M. P. Kane, *The Power of Open-Book Management: Releasing the True Potential of People's Minds, Hearts, and Hands* (New York: Wiley, 1996).

65. "Open-Book Management and Corporate Performance." (Available at: http://www.nceo.org/library/obm_nceostudy.html)

66. "Employee Suggestion Programs." *BNA Human Resources Library.* (Available at: http://www.bna.com/prodhome/hrl/hrcd)

67. Masaaki Imai, *Kaizen: The Key to Japan's Competitive Success* (New York: McGraw-Hill, 1986).

68. Michael E. Trunko, "Open to Suggestions," *HRMagazine,* February 1993, pp. 85–89.

69. Imai, *Kaizen,* p. 112.

70. Dawn Gunsch, "Award Programs at Work," *Personnel Journal,* September 1991, pp. 85–89.

71. Daniel C. Boyle, "The 100 Club," *Harvard Business Review,* March–April 1987, pp. 26–27.

72. Michael Ramundo, "Service Awards Build Culture of Success," *HRMagazine,* August 1992, pp. 61–66.

73. Karen L. Webb and Sandra L. O'Neil, "Creative Game Rewards Managers," *HRMagazine,* November 1993, pp. 55–56.

74. M. L. Ambrose and C. T. Kulik, "Old Friends, New Faces: Motivation Research in the 1990s," *Journal of Management,* Vol. 25 (3), 1999, pp. 231–292.

75. Edwin A. Locke and Gary P. Latham, *A Theory of Goals Setting and Task Performance* (Englewood Cliffs, N.J.: Prentice-Hall, 1990).

76. Gary P. Latham and Thomas W. Lee, "Goal Setting," in *Generalizing from Laboratory to Field Settings,* ed. E. A. Locke (Lexington, Mass.: Lexington Books, 1986), pp. 101–117.

77. Shawn Tully, "Why to Go for Stretch Targets," *Fortune,* November 14, 1994, pp. 145–158.

78. Richard Denton, Brian Davies, and James Reed, "Making the Most of Things." BBC Education and Training, 1993 (videotape).

79. W. Clay Hamner and Ellen P. Hamner, "Behavior Modification and the Bottom Line," *Organizational Dynamics,* Spring 1975, pp. 2–21.

80. A. D. Stajkovic and F. Luthans, "Differential Effects of Incentive Motivators on Work Performance," *Academy of Management Journal,* June 2001, pp. 580–590.

81. Aubrey C. Daniels, *Bringing Out the Best in People* (New York: McGraw-Hill, 1994).

82. Steven Kerr, "On the Folly of Rewarding A While Hoping for B," *Academy of Management Journal,* December 1975, pp. 766–783.

83. T. LaFleur and C. Hyten, "Improving the Quality of Hotel Banquet Staff Performance," *Journal of Organizational Behavior Management,* Vol. 15, 1995, pp. 69–93.

84. Aubrey C. Daniels, "Performance Management: The Behavior Approach to Productivity Improvement," *National Productivity Review,* Summer 1985, pp. 225–236; and J. Austin, M. L. Kessler, J. E. Riccobono, and J. S. Bailey, "Using Feedback and Reinforcement to Improve the Performance and Safety of a Roofing Crew," *Journal of Organizational Behavior Management,* Vol. 16, 1996, pp. 49–75.

85. Charles C. Manz, *The Art of Self-Leadership* (Englewood Cliffs, N.J.: Prentice-Hall, 1983).

86. J. Richard Hackman and Greg R. Oldham, *Working Redesign* (Reading, Mass.: Addison-Wesley, 1980).

87. Lisa R. Berlinger, William H. Glick, and Robert C. Rodgers, "Job Enrichment and Performance Improvement," in Campbell, Campbell, et al. (eds.), *Productivity in Organizations,* pp. 219–254; and R. W. Griffin, "Effects of Work Redesign on Employee Perceptions, Attitudes, and Behaviors: A Long-Term In-vestigation," *Academy of Management Journal,* Vol. 34, 1991, pp. 425–435.

88. Richard A. Guzzo, Richard D. Jette, and Raymond A. Katzell, "The Effects of Psychologically Based Intervention Programs on Worker Productivity: A Meta-Analysis," *Personnel Psychology,* Summer 1985, pp. 275–291.

89. Richard E. Kopelman, *Managing Productivity in Organizations* (New York: McGraw-Hill, 1986), pp. 211–243.

90. Toby D. Wall, J. Martin Corbett, Robin Martin, Chris W. Clegg, and Paul R. Jackson, "Advanced Manufacturing Technology, Work Design, and Performance: A Change Study," *Journal of Applied Psychology,* December 1990, pp. 691–697; and Toby D. Wall, Paul R. Jackson, and Keith Davids, "Operator Work Design and Robotics System Performance: A Serendipitous Field Study," *Journal of Applied Psychology,* Vol. 77, 1992, pp. 353–362.

91. Guzzo, Jette, and Katzell, "The Effects of Psychologically Based Intervention Programs on Worker Productivity."

92. Robert D. Pritchard, Steven D. Jones, Philip L. Roth, Karla K. Stuebing, and Steven E. Ekeberg, "Effects of Group Feedback, Goal-Setting, and Incentives on Organizational Productivity," *Journal of Applied Psychology,* Vol. 73, 1988, pp. 337–358.

93. J. Pfeffer, "Why Do Smart Organizations Occasionally Do Dumb Things?" *Organizational Dynamics,* Summer 1996, pp. 33–44.

94. Poll results cited in David E. Bowen and Edward E. Lawler III, "Total Quality-Oriented Human Resources Management," *Organizational Dynamics,* Spring 1992, pp. 29–41.

95. Mick Marchington, Adrian Wilkinson, and Peter Ackers, "Waving or Drowning in Participation?" *Personnel Management,* March 1993, pp. 46–50.

96. B. E. Becker, M. A. Huselid, P. S. Pickus, and M. F. Spratt, "HR as a Source of Shareholder Value: Research and Recommendation," *Human Resource Management,* Spring 1997, pp. 39–47.

97. For more detail on how HR can support the shift to a quality mentality, see Randall S. Schuler and Drew L. Harris, "Deming Quality Improvement: Implications for Human Resource Management as Illustrated in a Small Company," *Human Resource Planning,* Vol. 14, 1991, pp. 191–207.

98. For several articles on aligning HR practices with TQM, see the *Journal of Quality Management,* Vol. 1 (1), 1996.

99. R. B. Morgan and J. E. Smith, *Staffing the New Workplace: Selecting and Promoting for Quality Improvement* (Chicago: CCH Incorporated, 1996).

100. Cited in ibid., p. 48.

101. Ibid.

102. David K. Banner, W. Anthony Kulisch, and Newman S. Peery, "Self-Managing Work Teams (SMWT) and the Human Resource Function," *Management Decision,* Vol. 30 (3), 1992, pp. 40–45.

103. "Japan's Gung-Ho U.S. Car Plants," *Fortune,* January 30, 1989, pp. 78–85.

104. Scott A. Snell and James W. Dean, Jr., "Integrated Manufacturing and Human Resource Management: A Human Capital Perspective," *Academy of Management Journal,* Vol. 32 (3), 1992, pp. 467–504.

105. M. V. Gee and P. C. Nystrom, "Strategic Fit Between Skills Training and Levels of Quality Management: An Empirical Study of American Manufacturing Plants," *Human Resource Planning,* Vol. 22 (2), 1999, pp. 12–23.

106. Patricia K. Zingheim and Jay R. Schuster, "Linking Quality and Pay," *HRMagazine,* December 1992, pp. 55–59.

107. Y. Reshef and H. Lam, "Union Response to Quality Improvement Initiatives: Factors Shaping Support and Resistance," *Journal of Labor Research*, Winter 1999, pp. 111–131.

108. E. Applebaum and R. Batt, *The New American Workplace.* (Ithaca, NY: ILR Press, 1994).

109. Charlene Marmer Solomon, "Behind the Wheel at Saturn," *Personnel Journal,* June 1991, pp. 72–74.

110. L. Lyons and A. D. Vivenzio, "Employee Involvement in Seattle: Reengineering Government in a City Lacking a Financial Crisis," *Public Personnel Management*, Spring 1998, pp. 93–101.

111. Eric Pooley, "One Good Apple," *Time*, January 15, 1996, pp. 48–50.

112. Subscale scores were provided in a personal communication from Juan Sanchez, June 29, 2001.

PART FIVE

Rewarding Employees

11

Performance Assessment and Management

HR Challenge

Ford Motor, "the company, widely regarded as the strongest and best-run U.S. auto maker, is suddenly on the defensive."[1] There are several causes for Ford's recent troubles, not the least of which is the performance management process used to evaluate about 18,000 managers and supervisors, about 5 percent of Ford's work force.

This employee evaluation system, instituted in 2000, requires supervisors to rank employees from best to worst along a curve: 10 percent get As, 80 percent get Bs, and 10 percent get Cs. Getting a C means no bonus. Two Cs in a row is grounds for demotion or dismissal. "Instead of measuring an employee's performance against a set of objectives, the employee is measured against others with similar jobs."[2] Using this system, a supervisor with twenty subordinates is required to rate two as A, sixteen as B, and two as C. This is similar to grading students on a curve with a specified proportion being assigned particular letter grades.

480

The impetus for forced-distribution (also called forced-ranking) appraisal systems that require supervisors to grade subordinates along a curve is the common reluctance to accurately assess the performance of subordinates. David Murphy, Ford's vice president of human resources, said Ford was doing a reasonable job of identifying top-notch employees, but "we weren't getting the differentiation that we needed between great performers, the very good performances and the poor performers."[3] Leniency in performance ratings is a widespread phenomenon with the result that everybody gets favorable ratings. Forced-distribution systems require supervisors to use the specified percentages for assigning grades to subordinates.

Of course, the downside is that the supervisor with twenty employees may have three or four that deserve As and none that deserve Cs. Alternately, in a subpar work group, it may be that no employees deserve As. No matter—the supervisor is required to adhere strictly to the distribution requirements of 10 percent As, 80 percent Bs, and 10 percent Cs. Another negative of the forced-ranking system is its inconsistency with the team atmosphere Ford is trying to engender.[4]

Ford's CEO, Jacques Nasser, defended the performance management process. Nasser believes that it is important for management to be candid with employees about their performance. "A system that doesn't encourage that dialog in a positive way is a very cruel system, because you end up with employees who are not motivated, and maybe in the wrong positions. Then, when reality dawns, it may be too late."[5] Still, Nasser has heard the complaints and changed the system. The first revision was that only the bottom 5 percent of performers will get C grades. Then Nasser announced that the letter system was being replaced by three designations: top achiever, achiever, and improvement required. Further, there would be no fixed percentages for the "improvement required" category. The decision would be at the discretion of the supervisor.[6]

The complaints have been voiced in another way—at least six discrimination lawsuits have been filed as a result of the performance management process. About sixty Ford middle managers filed suit in Wayne County state court in May 2001, charging that Ford's performance management process was being used to sweep out older workers.[7] The workers bringing the suit argued that the ranking system favors some groups of employees over others.

What do you think? Is leniency a widespread problem? Does leniency undermine important objectives that appraisal is intended to serve? Is the forced-ranking system the way to solve problems of excessive leniency in ratings? Does it lead to candid discussions among managers and subordinates? What does forced-ranking do to the team concept Ford is trying to promote?

A critical factor related to an organization's long-term success is its ability to measure how well employees perform and then use that information to ensure that performance meets present standards and improves over time. This process is referred to as performance management, the handy umbrella term for all of the organizational activities involved in managing people on the job.[8] The measurement portion of the system is called *performance assessment, performance appraisal,* or *performance evaluation.* It is a complex task that is difficult to do, and it is not done well by most organizations.[9]

This chapter explains some of the ways that sound assessment information can be collected and used to improve performance; it also explores the difficulties of developing a **performance assessment and management** system. Several different methods of assessing performance are examined. Another part of the chapter focuses on one particularly important part of an assessment system: the process by which performance feedback is provided to employees.

THE PERFORMANCE ASSESSMENT AND MANAGEMENT PROCESS

Performance Management

Performance management is the integration of performance appraisal systems with broader human resource systems as a means of aligning employees' work behaviors with the organization's goals. Performance management should be an ongoing, interactive process that is designed to enhance employee capability and facilitate productivity. The performance management cycle is illustrated in Figure 11.1.

There is no one way to manage performance. Whatever system is adopted needs to be congruent with the culture and principles that pervade the organization.[10] However, most systems of performance management have several parts:

1. *Defining performance:* It is desirable to carefully define performance so that it supports the organization's strategic goals. The setting of clear goals for individual employees is a critical component of performance management.

● **FIGURE 11.1**

Performance Management Cycle

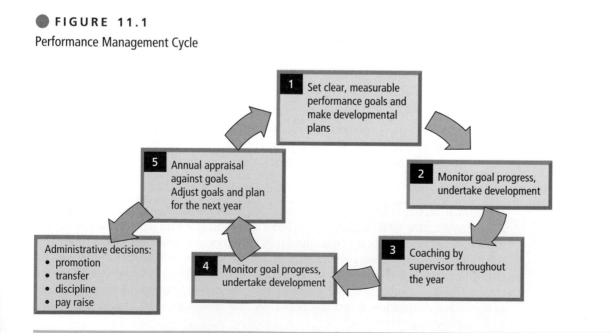

2. *Appraisal process:* It is important to conceptualize an appraisal process that will be steady across the organization and consistent with the culture of the organization. The are many ways to conceive of appraising employee performance, and the system adopted has to be one that will work in the context of the particular organization involved.

3. *Measuring performance:* Measuring performance does not need to be narrowly conceived but can bring together multiple types of performance measured in various ways. The key is to measure often and use the information for midcourse corrections.

4. *Feedback and coaching:* In order to improve performance, employees need information (feedback) about their performance, along with guidance in reaching the next level of results. Without frequent feedback, employees are unlikely to know that behavior is out of synchronization with relevant goals or what to do about it.[11]

The purpose of performance management is to make sure that employee goals, employee behaviors used to achieve those goals, and feedback of information about performance are all linked to the corporate strategy. However, as illustrated by the example of Ford Motor in the HR Challenge, frequently performance management is not done particularly well. While an effective process can benefit an organization, creating, implementing, and maintaining a system is no easy task. For instance, less than 20 percent of businesses accomplish their performance management goals and less than 10 percent judge their systems to be effective.[12]

Performance Appraisal

Performance appraisal is that part of the performance assessment and management process in which an employee's contribution to the organization during a specified period of time is assessed. Performance feedback lets employees know how well they have performed in comparison with the standards of the organization. Delivering and receiving **performance feedback** can be an emotionally laden process that dramatically affects employees' attitudes toward the organization and themselves. If used effectively, performance assessment and management can improve employee motivation and performance. If used inappropriately, it can have disastrous effects. (See A Different Point of View for more on possible negative consequences of assessment.) An anonymous quote published by James Bowman provides a humorous definition of the process: "Personnel Appraisal (pers'-n-el a-pra'-zel) *n*: given by someone who does not want to give it to someone who does not want to get it."[13]

Assessment and feedback can occur informally, as when a supervisor notices and comments on a good or poor performance incident. A more formal method is the structured annual performance review, in which a supervisor assesses each employee's performance using some official assessment procedure. Larger organizations tend to use both formal and informal methods, whereas many smaller organizations use only informal supervisory feedback.

Over the years, a great deal of research has been devoted to performance assessment systems. This research has looked at who should do the assessment, what methods of appraising are best, when and how often assessments should be done, and for what purposes assessment information should be used.

A DIFFERENT POINT OF VIEW

Does the Downside of Performance Appraisal Outweigh the Benefits?

In the last fifty years, performance appraisal has been accepted as a vital and widely used tool of effective management. However, appraisal systems remain controversial, with a few scholars believing they do more harm than good.

As long ago as 1957, Douglas McGregor (creator of the famous concepts of Theory X and Theory Y) expressed his uneasiness with the use of appraisal systems. Conventional performance appraisal, "unless handled with consummate skill and delicacy, constitutes something dangerously close to a violation of the integrity of the personality. Managers are uncomfortable when they are put in the position of playing God."*

Perhaps the most vocal critic of appraisals was quality guru W. Edwards Deming, who claimed that they are devastating to individuals and destructive to organizations. An annual appraisal rating system "nourishes short-term performance, annihilates long-term planning, builds fear, demolishes teamwork, nourishes rivalry and politics. It leaves people bitter, crushed, bruised, battered, desolate, despondent, dejected, feeling inferior, some even depressed, all unfit for work for weeks after receipt of rating, unable to comprehend why they are inferior."† Other effects may be that appraisals "discourage risk taking and pit people against each other for the same rewards. . . . The result is a company composed of prima donnas, of sparring fiefdoms. People work for themselves, not the company."‡ There is evidence that appraisals that are perceived as unfair can contribute to stress and job burnout.

Researchers at American Cyanamid Company asked employees for reactions to their forced-distribution appraisal system. Employees expressed largely negative reactions: "Until it is my turn, I can't get a better rating no matter what I do," said one of the employees. Another didn't take performance appraisal seriously: "It's a Mickey Mouse numbers game. My superior and I just laugh at it, we get through it as soon as we can."§ Other criticisms are that those who get low ratings become discouraged rather than motivated. Further, they may lose so much confidence in their abilities that they stay in the organization for years as substandard performers, rather than braving the labor market in search of a job that might fit them better.

Opponents of performance appraisal attack it on a variety of grounds. Some seem to feel that the idea of appraisal is sound, but the execution weak (the wrong things are rated, the forced distribution is inappropriate for the group in question, supervisors aren't trained to prepare accurate appraisals or give feedback effectively, etc.). Others feel that the very concept is flawed.

STRATEGIC IMPORTANCE OF PERFORMANCE ASSESSMENT

Strategically, it is hard to imagine a more important HR system than performance assessment and management. As shown in Chapter 1 (Figure 1.2) and clarified in subsequent chapters, organizations strive to do the following at all levels:

- Design jobs and work systems to accomplish organizational goals.
- Hire individuals with the abilities and desire to perform effectively.
- Train, motivate, and reward employees for performance and productivity.

It is this sequence that allows organizations to disperse their strategic goals throughout the organization. Within this context, the evaluation of performance is

For instance, Deming believes that much of performance variability is due to system factors rather than individual effort or ability. If this is true, then appraisal systems that hold individuals accountable for results that actually are beyond their control would certainly be seen as unfair and demotivational.

A number of organizations have revamped their appraisal systems in a bid to reduce possible negative outcomes. In some cases this has involved dropping numerical rating systems that required raters to make very fine (and potentially divisive) distinctions among people in favor of more qualitative, narrative approaches. American Cyanamid has abandoned its forced-distribution, ten-grade, system and now uses only three grades: unacceptable (rarely used), good (for the vast majority of employees), and exceptional (for astonishingly good performance). For employees rated as good, pay raises are based on seniority and position in the pay range rather than on merit. Bonuses are available to those rated as exceptional.

On the other hand, forced-ranking systems have also become more popular, with 20 percent of companies estimated to be using them. Employees call them "rank and yank" systems, because people at the bottom are targeted for retrenchment. Employees may feel that their placement depends partly on how persuasive their manager is in ranking meeting or that horse trading in these meetings determines their future. ("OK, I'll accept Fred moving down to the satisfactory category if you'll agree to Janet moving into the excellent category.") At Enron, employees were classi-

fied as superior (5 percent), excellent (30 percent), strong (30 percent), satisfactory (20 percent), and needs improvement (15 percent), with ranking done every six months. Those in the lowest category received coaching and drafted an improvement plan—if their performance wasn't up to standard in six months, they were terminated. While the system produces some tension and grumbling, many of the companies using it (e.g., GE and Microsoft) are top performers.

Appraisal is a complex issue, and it is clear that to be effective, a system must be designed and implemented with great care. It is also clear that in some situations, a poorly conceived appraisal system will create more problems than it solves.

*Douglas McGregor, "An Uneasy Look at Performance Appraisal," *Harvard Business Review,* September–October 1972, pp. 133–138; quote: p. 134.
†W. E. Deming, *Out of the Crisis* (Cambridge, Mass.: MIT Press, 1986), p. 37.
‡Mary Walton, *The Deming Management Method* (London: Mercury Books, 1989), pp. 88–89.
§Tom Peters, *Thriving on Chaos* (London: Pan Books, 1989), p. 495; and Saul W. Gellerman and William G. Hodgson, "Cyanamid's New Take on Performance Appraisal," *Harvard Business Review,* May–June 1988, pp. 36–37, quote: p. 37.
Sources: Clinton O. Longenecker and Steven J. Goff, "Performance Appraisal Effectiveness: A Matter of Perspective," *SAM Advanced Management Journal,* Spring 1992, pp. 17–23; Gerald T. Gabris and Douglas M. Ihrke, "Does Performance Appraisal Contribute to Heightened Levels of Employee Burnout?: The Results of One Study," *Public Personnel Management,* Summer 2001, pp. 157–172; and John Greenwald, "Rank and Fire," *Time,* June 18, 2001, pp. 46–48.

the control mechanism that provides not only feedback to individuals but also an organizational assessment of how things are progressing. Without performance information, managers and employees can only guess as to whether they are working toward the right goals, in the correct way, and to the desired standard.[14]

Consistency Between Organizational Strategy and Job Behavior

Performance assessment plays another important role in organizational strategy, that of ensuring strategy-consistent behavior.[15] A truism of organizational life is that people engage in the behaviors that they perceive will be rewarded.[16] Employees want to be rewarded and will try to do those things that the organization is emphasizing. For example, if the focus is on service, employees will behave in ways that gain the rewards associated with service delivery. If the focus is on cost control, employees will seek ways to control cost and thus be recognized and rewarded. If the focus is on rewarding productivity, employees will strive for productivity. Performance assessment becomes a means of knowing whether employee behavior is consistent with the overall strategic focus and a way for bringing to the fore any negative consequences of the strategy–behavior link. For example, a single-minded productivity focus may include potential negative consequences, such as decreased quality and cooperation. Performance assessment is an important organizational mechanism to elicit feedback as to the consistency of the strategy–behavior link.

Consistency Between Organizational Values and Job Behavior

Performance assessment is also a mechanism to reinforce the values and culture of the organization (see Figure 11.1). For example, how is an organization that articulates the value of developing its people to know whether managers throughout the organization share this value? A history of developing people or communication from the highest executives is not enough. Managers typically have more to do than time to get it done and will let slide what is not reinforced. If managers are held accountable for developing their people by being judged on this task in their own performance assessment, they will be likely to spend more time developing subordinates.

A further element in the strategic importance of performance assessment is in the alignment of the assessment with the organizational culture. For example, many organizations have adopted a more team-oriented focus; in such a culture, the stress is on team management, teamwork, and more open and trusting relationships among all employees. In a team-oriented system, the traditional assessment that rates one employee in comparison with others may be counterproductive.[17] Such a system will engender competition rather than teamwork among employees. In such a setting, an assessment system that emphasizes coaching and development, and involves feedback from coworkers, may be more appropriate than the traditional supervisor-based rating.

FUNCTIONS OF PERFORMANCE ASSESSMENT

One survey delineated a large number of purposes, divided into four major categories, for which formal performance assessment or appraisal can be used. These multiple uses are illustrated in Table 11.1. Goal setting and **developmental uses** of assessment focus on setting goals and improving employees' capability to reach these goals, whereas **administrative uses** of assessment include decision making about merit raises and promotions. Assessment information is also used to contribute to organizational well-being (e.g., to anticipate HR needs) and for documentation (e.g., to provide criteria for validation research).[18] Each of these applications of performance assessment and assessment information is explored in this section.

Performance Assessment as a Goal-Setting and Employee Development Tool

Performance assessment can be used in several ways to help employees set goals, to assess the congruence of their efforts toward these goals, and then to assess

● **TABLE 11.1**

Multiple Organizational Uses for Performance Information

General Applications	Specific Purposes
Goal setting and developmental uses	Setting of clear, measurable performance goals
	Monitoring of goal progress
	Identification of individual training needs
	Performance feedback and coaching
	Determining of transfers and job assignments for developmental purposes
	Identification of individual strengths and developmental needs
Administrative uses/decisions	Salary
	Promotion
	Retention or termination
	Recognition of individual performance
	Layoffs
	Identification of poor performers
	Discipline
Organizational maintenance/objectives	Human resource planning
	Determining of organization training needs
	Evaluation of organizational goal achievement
	Information for goal identification
	Evaluation of human resource systems
	Reinforcement of organizational development needs
Documentation	Documentation of human resource decisions
	Helping to meet legal requirements

Source: J. N. Cleveland, K. R. Murphy, and R. E. Williams, "Multiple Uses of Performance Appraisal: Prevalence and Correlates," *Journal of Applied Psychology*, Vol. 74, 1989, pp. 130–135. Copyright © 1989 by the American Psychological Association. Adapted with permission.

tools needed to achieve these targets. It plays a role in reinforcing and improving performance and in determining career paths and training needs.

● **Goal Setting**   The managers work with employees and agree on a set of goals to achieve during a specified period of time. Goals should be quantifiable and should include an agreed-upon target. It is important that employees then be empowered to achieve these goals. For example, a retail manager's goal might be to reduce customer returns to no more than 3 percent of the dollar amount of sales; that is, no more than $300 in returns for every $10,000 in sales. Consistent with company policy, the manager then should be empowered in specific methods of achieving this goal. Extensive research suggests that when employees have a voice in the appraisal process, as in setting performance goals, they are more satisfied with the appraisal results.[19]

● **Reinforcing and Sustaining Performance**   Using performance assessment as an employee development tool can place supervisors in the role of reinforcing and sustaining performance. By providing feedback on past performance, supervisors can encourage employees to continue on a positive trajectory. Praise can augment any financial rewards that the employee may receive. In our Western culture, virtually all employees like to be told when they are doing a good job.

● **Improving Performance**   The supervisor can use performance assessment data to suggest ways in which employees might perform better in the future. The supervisor can point out strengths and weaknesses and help employees identify more effective ways to accomplish important tasks. Additionally, the supervisor can discuss work goals with the employee and agree on a timetable for achieving these goals. A more detailed discussion of how to use performance feedback to improve employee performance is provided later in this chapter.

● **Determining Career Progression Goals**   The performance assessment session gives supervisors and employees an opportunity to discuss employees' long-term career goals and plans. The supervisors can advise employees on the steps to take to reach these goals. On the basis of past skills, supervisors can give employees short-term, specific suggestions on how to improve performance in ways that will help employees achieve longer-term career goals. As a result, employees may become more highly motivated to perform well in their present positions because it is seen as a necessary step toward an ultimate goal.

● **Determining Training Needs**   Performance assessment can determine the training needs of individual employees. If particular employees are not performing up to expectations, a training program may enable them to correct any skills or knowledge deficiencies. Employees who are performing above the requirements of the position can be placed in a development program that will prepare them for promotion to a higher-level job. Performance assessment also supplies information useful in developing training programs that will fit the needs of most employees. For example, if employees' communication skills are rated uniformly low, the company can develop a program to address this need.

Performance Assessment as an Administrative Tool

Besides their use in employee development, performance assessments also play a role in administrative decision making. Performance assessments are used to link rewards to performance and to evaluate the effectiveness of HR policies and practices.

It is worth noting that performance assessments used for administrative purposes are, on average, scored considerably higher than those used for development. In a review and summary (meta-analysis) of twenty-two studies and a total sample of more than 57,000 ratings, it was found that evaluations were much more lenient when those ratings were "for keeps."[20] These results are an indication of the discomfort raters experience when rewards hang in the balance. Of course, it

Performance Appraisal
and Performance-Based Rewards in China

 Performance appraisal and performance-based pay have been a feature of U.S. HR systems for many decades, consistent with American individualistic values that people should be rewarded on the basis of their contribution. However, neither performance appraisal nor performance-based pay are universal practices. China provides a case in point.

Until fairly recently, employment practices in the People's Republic of China were described as "the iron rice-bowl." Labor was not regarded as a commodity, so there could be no labor market. There was no unemployment, as all workers were assigned by the state to an employer. Employers could not fire employees, and employees could not choose their workplace. An employer provided a job for life and cradle-to-grave welfare (housing, education, medical care, pension) for employees and their families. All employees "ate out of one big pot," meaning they received pay and benefits on an egalitarian basis, regardless of their contribution. Wage differentials were based on position and age rather than performance. Further, wage structures were flat, with top managers in state-owned enterprises making only two or three times as much as junior technical workers. Managerial advancement was based more on proper political beliefs than on performance on the job. In a system like this, Western-style performance appraisal was simply unnecessary, as there was no possibility of differential treatment on the basis of merit.

Since reforms began in the late 1970s, Chinese HR practices have been changing gradually. Foreign-invested joint ventures are leading the changes, but state-owned enterprises are updating their HR practices as well. Central Committee recommendations for managerial performance appraisal were issued in late 1979; throughout the 1990s the government endorsed movement toward fixed-term labor contracts, rather than lifetime employment, and also encouraged more widespread adoption of performance-based rewards at all levels.

The recommended appraisal system for white-collar employees ("cadres") includes ratings on a 4-point scale of the following dimensions:

- "Good moral practice" (appropriate political beliefs, extent of complying with government directives)
- "Adequate competence" (educational qualifications, leadership and management skills, and physical status including age)
- "Positive working attitude" (diligence, attendance, initiative, sense of responsibility)
- "Strong performance record" (actual results including quantity and quality of output)

In addition, some employees are assessed against annual goals and objectives set for their position.

Blue-collar workers are also assessed following a scheme set down by the government. Correct ideological and political beliefs are part of the appraisal system (and their weighting was increased after the Tiananmen Square incident in 1989), but work achievements are also emphasized.

Compensation rates used to be set by the central government and did not take account of either individual or organizational performance. Since the mid-1980s, state-owned enterprises have been made more accountable and wages can now vary with the performance of the enterprise. The payment of bonuses based on individual performance is also encouraged, though a legacy of egalitarianism means that nearly identical bonuses are sometimes given to everyone at the same level to prevent jealousy. Foreign-invested enterprises, which have more leeway in compensation rates and methods, have been more successful in implementing pay-for-performance systems.

Sources: K. Goodall and M. Warner, "Human Resources in Sino–Foreign Joint Ventures: Selected Case Studies in Shanghai, Compared with Beijing." *International Journal of Human Resource Management*, Vol. 8, 1997, pp. 569–594; J. Child and Y. Lu (eds.) *Management Issues in China*, Vol. 2 (New York: Routledge, 1996); C. J. Zhu and P. J. Dowling, "Managing People During Economic Transition: The Development of HR Practices in China," *Asia Pacific Journal of Human Resources*, Vol. 28 (2), 2000, pp. 84–106; and D. Z Ding, K. Goodall, and M. Warner, "The End of the 'Iron Rice-Bowl': Whither Chinese Human Resource Management?" *International Journal of Human Resource Management*, April 2000, pp. 217–236.

is to the advantage of both the organization and individual that ratings be honest and accurate, topics addressed in the following sections.

● **Linking Rewards to Performance**   Performance assessments are part of the reward and punishment system of an organization. Employees who receive favorable evaluations tend to receive organizational rewards, such as merit pay increases and bonuses, whereas those with unfavorable evaluations receive organizational sanctions, including demotions or discharge. Other personnel decisions commonly linked to performance assessments include promotions, layoffs, transfers, and discipline decisions.

The goal in linking pay to performance and to other personnel decisions is to motivate employees to perform better. Unfortunately, matching performance and reward is much easier said than done. The performance of individuals must be assessed accurately, the rewards provided must truly be of value to employees, and the organization must develop a performance-based reward system that employees perceive as being administered fairly. The system will fail if employees believe managers and supervisors distribute rewards on the basis of favoritism or political considerations.

● **Evaluating HRM Policies and Programs**   Performance assessment data can also be used to evaluate the effectiveness of HRM programs. Assessments can be performed before and after an intervention to measure the amount of change that has occurred. Interventions that might be evaluated with performance assessment data include training programs, job enrichment or redesign, quality circles, and the like. Recall from Chapter 7 that the empirical validation of selection devices requires scores on a job performance criterion. This information is usually collected by some method of performance assessment.

Of course, in some cultures, performance assessment and the applications illustrated are either shunned or take on a different role. Performance appraisal in China is a case in point. (See the International Perspective box for more on performance appraisal and performance-based rewards in China).

CRITERIA FOR A GOOD ASSESSMENT SYSTEM

As mentioned previously, surveys find that the overwhelming majority of both private- and public-sector organizations use some type of performance assessment.[21] At the same time, "in almost every major survey most employees who get . . . evaluations and most supervisors who give them rate the process a resounding failure."[22] Another survey, conducted in 2000 on behalf of the Society for Human Resource Management, found that only one in three respondents were satisfied with their system of performance assessment.[23] Sadly, many assessment systems are poorly designed and poorly implemented. The Ethical Perspective box gives some advice for designing assessment systems that employees perceive as fair and just.

The fundamental decisions about what type of performance to assess and how to measure that performance should be shaped by four desirable criteria: validity, reliability, freedom from bias, and practicality, including user acceptance.

Developing a Procedurally Just Performance Appraisal Process

When organizations make decisions about people—such as whom to hire or promote, what appraisal ratings or merit raise to give, or how to discipline a particular infraction—it is very important that the decisions be seen as fair and just. Research has shown that at least two aspects of justice influence employees' job satisfaction and organizational commitment, and both must be considered in organizational decisions.

The first type is "distributive justice," or the perceived fairness of particular outcomes. It has to do with the distribution of rewards and punishments across people. Distributive justice would exist if employees agreed that the best person had been chosen for a promotion, that the punishment fit the crime in a discipline case, or that the size of merit raises accurately reflected true differences in performance across the people involved. Distributive justice is specific to a particular decision—we might agree that one promotion decision was fair, but that is no guarantee that we will think the next one is fair. This is because distributive justice doesn't include evaluation of the fairness of the method or process by which the decision was made. The latter is called "procedural justice." Presumably, a just policy or procedure should help assure equitable outcomes every time, whereas a single instance of distributive justice could occur by chance, favoritism, or some other unfair process.

What makes an allocation procedure just? Following are six rules for procedural justice:*

- *Consistency rule:* Allocation procedures should be consistent across persons and over time.
- *Bias suppression rule:* Personal self-interest in the allocation process should be prevented.
- *Accuracy rule:* Decisions must be based on accurate information.

- *Correctability rule:* Opportunities must exist to enable decisions to be modified.
- *Representativeness rule:* The allocation process must represent the concerns of all recipients.
- *Ethicality rule:* Allocations must be based on prevailing moral and ethical standards.

Performance appraisal is a situation in which decisions are made about individuals (allocation of ratings or rankings and associated rewards), and the potential for misunderstandings and feelings of injustice are great. This means that a very fair and clear process should be adopted.

Research has shown that appraisals are seen as more fair when consistent standards are applied to all ratees; there is a system by which the ratee can appeal or rebut the evaluation; and raters are familiar with the ratee's work, solicit employee input before assigning ratings, provide prompt feedback, and allow two-way communication in the appraisal interview. In addition, procedures are more likely to be perceived as fair if employees understand the rating dimensions and the superior's expectations well before the rating takes place. Ideally, ratees should also have input into determining the rating criteria.

These appraisal procedures meet most of the six rules given above and should help assure that the emotionally laden process of performance appraisal is seen as fair, insofar as is humanly possible.

*Folger and Greenberg, p. 146.
Sources: Robert Folger and Jerald Greenberg, "Procedural Justice: An Interpretive Analysis of Personnel Systems," *Research in Personnel and Human Resource Management,* Vol. 3, 1985, pp. 141–183; and Robert Folger and Russell Cropanzano, *Organizational Justice and Human Resource Management* (Thousand Oaks, Calif.: Sage, 1998).

Validity

A good measure of performance should measure important job characteristics (relevancy) and be free from extraneous or contaminating influences; it also should encompass the whole job (not be deficient).[24] As discussed in Chapter 7, a measure is content-valid if it measures important parts of a job and does so in a representative way. A measure is construct-valid if it measures what it claims to measure—in this case, job performance. The relationship between these two types of validity and the concepts of relevance, contamination, and deficiency is quite clear. A relevant measure assesses aspects of performance that are truly important in determining job effectiveness. For example, a relevant measure for assessing the performance of a college professor would include teaching performance. A measure is not deficient if it measures all-important aspects of performance. In the case of the college professor, the measure of performance would be deficient unless it assessed such factors as service and intellectual contributions (research and publications) as well as teaching performance. A measure is free of contamination if it avoids assessing other constructs besides performance. If the professor's performance rating included an assessment of how well the professor's shoes were shined, the measure would be contaminated by this irrelevant content. The relationships between relevance, deficiency, and contamination are presented graphically in Figure 11.2.

A performance assessment system must be valid. It is essential that a good job analysis be conducted before developing the performance measure so that all rele-

● FIGURE 11.2

The Relationships Among Relevance, Deficiency, and Contamination

Perfect Measure of Performance

Actual Measure of Performance

Deficiency

Relevance

Contamination

Important aspects of a perfect measure of performance that are not included in the actual measure the organization is using

The overlap between the perfect measure of performance and an actual measure

Aspects unrelated to performance that are somehow included within the actual measure vant aspects of performance are covered and irrelevant factors do not contaminate the assessment measure.

Reliability

Inter-rater reliability is the most relevant type of reliability for performance assessment. Reliability is high when two or more raters agree on the performance of an employee and low when they do not. Inter-rater reliability is usually quite good when performance raters come from the same level of the organization, such as two superiors or two peers of the person being rated. However, there is often legitimate disagreement between raters at different levels, such as a peer and a superior or a superior and a subordinate. Thus high inter-rater reliability is expected only among raters at the same organizational level.

In a study of almost 10,000 employees from seventy-nine organizations, Hannah Rothstein found that inter-rater reliabilities—that is, the correlation (see Chapter 7) between two raters observing the same employee—typically ranged from 0.65 to 0.73, a high enough level to lend confidence to the stability of the rating process.[25] Another study observed lower values (from 0.45 to 0.63), with the lowest ratings being of communication and interpersonal skills (0.45 and 0.47, respectively).[26] Ratings for the dimensions of productivity, quality, and administrative skill were all in the high 0.50s or low 0.60s, again at a high enough level to know that there is a consistency in observation. In the latter study, agreement among peers was notably lower, generally ranging between 0.33 and 0.42, suggesting that any system involving peers needs to incorporate extensive training.[27]

Internally consistent reliability and reliability over time are not especially important in performance assessment because performance itself may not be internally consistent or stable over time. A person may be very good at certain aspects of a job but quite weak at others, so a measure that accurately gauged these different aspects of performance would not show high internal consistency. Similarly, because performance may improve with experience or training and fluctuate with effort or luck, strong stability over time is not necessarily expected.[28]

For more objective measures of performance, another aspect of reliability is important. Suppose absenteeism from work is used as one measure of an employee's performance. If the supervisor sometimes records when the employee is absent and sometimes does not, then this measure of performance is unreliable. Thus, when evaluating the reliability of performance assessments, it is very important to know exactly what type of measure was used and, in the case of subjective ratings of performance, who was making the ratings.

Freedom from Bias

In performance assessment, the criterion of freedom from bias has two components. The first concerns legal issues of fairness to employees; the second has to do with the subjectivity of one person's judgments about the performance of others.

● **Legal Issues of Fairness** In one sense, an assessment is free from bias if it is fair to all employees regardless of their race, sex, national origin, disability status, and so on. Employment legislation permits employers to use a bona fide assessment system but not one that has an unjustifiably adverse impact on minorities, women, older employees, or other protected groups of people.[29] In *Brito* v. *Zia Company* (1973), the court ruled that the *Uniform Guidelines* (see Chapter 5) were applicable and must be followed in evaluating the adequacy of a performance assessment instrument.[30] In other words, a performance assessment is a "test" and can be evaluated by the same standards. Spanish-surnamed workers were reinstated with back pay because the company had used a performance assessment instrument of questionable validity to make layoff decisions. In addition, Spanish-surnamed employees had been promoted significantly less frequently than were other employees. The court was critical of Zia's subjective assessment process, noting that some supervisors making ratings had never directly observed the employees' performance. Zia Company failed to present evidence of the validity of its assessment procedure.

In June 1989, the Supreme Court reaffirmed the importance of objective standards in performance assessment in the case of *Price Waterhouse* v. *Hopkins*.[31] Ann B. Hopkins filed charges of sex discrimination against the accounting firm of Price Waterhouse after being turned down for promotion to partner despite high performance. Hopkins charged that gender stereotyping was involved in the decision; she had been told she would have "to walk more femininely, talk more femininely, dress more femininely, wear makeup, have her hair styled, and wear jewelry" to be considered for promotion.[32] The Court ruled in Hopkins's favor, stating that her obligation to show that gender was a factor in the employment decision had been satisfied, whereas Price Waterhouse had failed to show that the same decision would have been made in the absence of gender as a factor. The Court's decision dealt with the effect of gender stereotyping in the workplace and the need for objectivity in performance evaluation.[33]

Although there is no legal mandate for an organization to have and use an assessment system that meets some state-of-the-art requirement for soundness, the methods of assessment that an organization employs should not have an adverse impact on groups protected by the law. If challenged, the organization will seek to defend itself on the basis of the soundness, objectivity, and validity of its assessment system.[34] Most performance assessment systems currently in use probably would not fare too well if they were subjected to legal challenge. A system can be discriminatory for any of the following reasons:

1. The rating content is not job-related or valid.
2. The content of the ratings is not developed from a thorough job analysis.
3. The raters do not observe ratees performing their work.
4. Ratings are based on raters' evaluations of subjective or vague factors.
5. Ratings are not collected and scored under standardized conditions.[35]

An employer can reduce the probability of a legal challenge in several ways. A primary rule is to use only assessment systems that are based on a thorough job analysis. The assessment process should incorporate only those duties or characteristics that are important for job performance. Supervisors must be trained to use the rating instrument properly, and the results and rationale for all evaluations must be carefully documented.[36] If possible, formal appeal mechanisms should be established, and upper-level or human resource managers should review ratings.[37] Finally, some form of counseling should be offered to help poor performers improve.

Race Differences There has been a long-standing interest in the effects of rater and ratee race on performance ratings. Recently, several large-scale studies[38] have examined this issue, with one of the larger studies finding that black raters (whether peers, subordinates, or supervisors) assigned more favorable ratings to ratees of their own race.[39] Results for white raters differed according to the particular rating source. White supervisors assigned more favorable ratings to ratees of their own race, but white subordinates and peers did not. White and black managers received higher ratings from black raters than from white raters.[40] Through training and other procedures, employers should take special care to ensure that race bias is understood and then eliminated from performance ratings.

Age Differences It is worth noting that cases brought under the federal Age Discrimination in Employment Act (ADEA; see Chapter 5) have not scrutinized defendant organizations' assessment systems. The intent of the ADEA is to protect those aged forty or over from discriminatory employment decisions. A study of more than fifty-three age discrimination cases found that in contrast to Title VII cases, the outcome of ADEA cases was not influenced by the soundness of the performance assessment system.[41] Formal performance evaluation procedures were not required by the courts for an employer to mount a successful defense; instead, less reliable sources of employee performance information have been accepted as conclusive evidence substantiating an employer's claim of nondiscrimination in employment decisions. However, employers would be wise to have a sound, objective, and valid assessment system to defend ADEA charges should they arise. It should be added, too, that research generally has shown that there is no relationship between age and performance, despite the prevalence of a stereotype of older workers being less effective.[42]

● **Freedom from Rating Errors** When an assessment system requires individuals to make subjective judgments about the performance of others, the second component of freedom from bias becomes important. Ratings may be biased, either intentionally or unintentionally. Common rating errors are described below and shown graphically in Figure 11.3. Some of these errors also occur in interviewing—another situation in which one person judges and evaluates another.

Leniency Errors Sometimes raters give employees more positive performance ratings than they deserve. For example, an analysis of U.S. Marine Corps officer fitness reports showed that on a 9-point scale, with 9 representing "outstanding performance," the average performance ratings for a sample of more than 2,000 officers was 8.2.[43] Although officers are well trained and devoted to their service, it is difficult to believe that almost all of them are truly outstanding. For the military in general and Marines in particular, leniency is part of the assessment organizational culture.

With a large number of employees, one would expect the true distribution of performance ratings to approximate a bell-shaped curve (see the curve indicating true distribution of performance in Figure 11.3a). Of course, assuming modestly successful recruiting (see Chapter 6), selection (see Chapters 7 and 8), and development (see Chapter 9), the true distribution of performance may be negatively skewed. When **leniency errors** occur, most employees receive very high performance ratings (see the curve indicating leniency error in Figure 11.3a). Leniency is a very common type of rating bias, although recent research suggests that it is a

● **FIGURE 11.3**

Leniency, Severity, Central Tendency, and Halo Errors

(a) Leniency and severity errors

True distribution of performance
Distribution resulting from leniency error
Distribution resulting from severity error

(b) Central tendency error

True distribution of performance
Distribution resulting from central tendency error

(c) Halo error

stable characteristic of raters that could be predicted using measures of individual differences.[44]

Severity Errors   Sometimes raters evaluate employees more unfavorably than their performance warrants. When such **severity errors** occur, as shown in Figure 11.3a, the distribution of performance ratings shifts dramatically to the left of the true distribution of performance. Severity error is the reverse of leniency error.

Central Tendency Errors   Sometimes a supervisor rates all employees near the midpoint of a performance scale. Few if any employees receive very high or very low ratings. As Figure 11.3b shows, such **central tendency errors** result in a rating distribution that is highly compressed around the middle. Central tendency errors are often caused by the rater's failure to observe or ambiguity caused by poor descriptions of the performance dimensions.

When central tendency, leniency, or severity errors are frequent, an assessment system cannot accomplish its purpose of differentiating between good and poor workers. When one of these errors occurs, nearly everyone receives the same rating—a high, low, or average score, depending on the type of error.

Halo Errors   Whereas leniency, severity, and central tendency errors occur when several employees are appraised, **halo errors** involve the rating of a single individual on several aspects of performance. This pervasive form of rating error has been long recognized yet is not well understood.[45] Jack M. Feldman defines halo error as a very high correlation among ratings across several performance areas or, more simply put, the tendency of raters to color performance judgments by general feelings toward the individual.[46] For example, a supervisor may be asked to rate an employee on quality and quantity of performance, working with coworkers, leadership, and finishing projects on time. In general, one would expect an employee to be good at some tasks, average at others, and perhaps weak in some performance areas. The individual would receive some high ratings, some low, and some average, depending on the performance area. The correlation among those ratings would be moderate to low. When halo error occurs, an employee receives nearly identical performance ratings on all performance areas, and the resulting correlation among the ratings is very high.[47] An example of halo error is given in Figure 11.3c.

● **Why Do Rating Errors Occur?**   Rating errors occur through both unintentional and intentional processes.

Unintentional Errors   One way to examine why rating errors occur is to use the approach called **cognitive information processing (CIP).** Proponents of CIP argue that performance assessment is best viewed as a complex memory task in which the assessors must do the following:

- Acquire performance information about an employee.
- Encode and store that information in their memory.
- Retrieve that information at a later date when asked to assess the employee's performance.
- Weight and combine the information into an overall performance judgment.[48]

The amount of performance information available about an employee is enormous. Raters can notice and recall only a limited amount of information on each employee, and research has shown that they use a variety of methods to condense the information they do receive.[49] This can result in a variety of memory and judgment errors in assessment. One cognitive shortcut that people use in processing information about others is the schema. **Schemas** are simply mental categories that an individual uses to organize information and classify people.[50] For example, a supervisor might use two schemas in classifying employees: the good worker schema and the bad worker schema. Associated with each schema is a set of attributes, called a **prototype,** that represents the essential characteristics associated with that schema.[51] Thus the prototype for the supervisor's good worker schema might include the following: never absent, writes well, always gets projects done on time, and gets along well with coworkers. A ratee need not exhibit all the prototype characteristics to be classified into the schema. For instance, noticing that an employee is never absent from work, the supervisor might categorize that person as a good worker, even without direct evidence that the employee writes well, hands in projects on time, or gets along well with coworkers. It should be added that this is an example of failure to observe all categories of employee behavior as well as of preexisting category construction.

When asked to assess the performance of an employee, a supervisor searches his or her memory to determine into which schema the employee has been placed. The supervisor recalls information about the employee, *including the schema prototype.* The supervisor's judgment of the employee is based not only on the precise behaviors observed but also on the prototype associated with the schema. This recollection of behavior that never actually occurred (but that fits a particular schema) is the source of halo error. Often an employee rated high on work attendance will also receive positive ratings on all other aspects of performance *even though he or she may not have actually performed well in these areas.* Similarly, an employee originally categorized as a poor worker may be rated low on all criteria even though the supervisor may not really have observed poor performance in some areas. This process is shown in Figure 11.4.

Leniency and severity errors may also be influenced by the nature of schema prototypes. If a supervisor's prototype characteristics for the good worker are so extreme that few employees will ever exhibit behavior that allows them to be classified as good workers, severity error may occur. If some of the prototype charac-

● **FIGURE 11.4**

How Cognitive Information Processing Causes Rating Errors

Prototype of a "Good Worker"	Never absent	Writes well	Always finishes projects on time	Gets along well with coworkers
Employee's Actual Behavior Observed by Supervisor	Never absent			
Supervisor's Later Appraisal of Employee (applies prototype)	Never absent	Writes well	Always finishes projects on time	Gets along well with coworkers

teristics of a good worker are very easy for most employees to exhibit, leniency error may occur.

Intentional Errors   Sometimes supervisors intentionally rate employees inaccurately for political or other reasons. A company vice president summarized one common view of the politics of assessment:

> As a manager, I will use the review process to do what is best for my people and the division. . . . I've got a lot of leeway—call it discretion—to use this process in that manner. . . . I've used it to get my people better raises in lean years, to kick a guy in the pants if he really needed it, to pick up a guy when he was down or even to tell him that he was no longer welcome here. It is a tool that the manager should use to help him do what it takes to get the job done. I believe most of us here operate this way regarding appraisals. . . . Accurately describing an employee's performance is really not as important as generating ratings that keep things cooking.[52]

A term for the approach exhibited by this VP is *backfilling*—that is, deciding on the end evaluation result and then rigging the numbers to achieve the predetermined end. As stated by one researcher, "It would be naïve to think of performance appraisal as anything other than a political process. Rating accurately is not always the goal of appraisers and there are many situations where providing inaccurate appraisal data is sound management."[53] While many would find this reprehensible, such actions are probably more common than is admitted.

The preceding approach to performance assessment can lead to cynicism on the part of employees. One employee's view is expressed as follows:

> In the end it still comes down to this: My boss can give me any rating he wants and there isn't a lot I can do about it. I can hit my numbers, but he might think I should have exceeded them. . . . Perhaps he didn't like my style or the way I handled a certain deal. In the end I'll get what he wants me to have.[54]

Recent work has begun to shed some light on how political factors affect performance assessments.[55] For example, intentional leniency error can occur for several reasons. Supervisors may feel that having subordinates with high performance ratings will make them look good to their own superiors, or they may fear that their working relationship with employees will be ruined by an unfavorable assessment.[56] Also, supervisors simply may find it difficult to give negative feedback to their employees and may inflate ratings to avoid this unpleasant task.[57] For these reasons, intentional leniency error is far more prevalent than severity error, although some intentional severity error can occur. The common reasons that supervisors give for inflating or deflating performance ratings are summarized in Table 11.2.

Practicality

It takes time, effort, and money to develop, implement, and use a performance assessment system. The benefits to the organization of using the system must outweigh its costs. The assessment system should also be relatively easy to use and should have a high degree of employee and managerial acceptance. Even the best-developed assessment system is futile if it is not used.[58]

● **TABLE 11.2**

Why Supervisors Inflate and Deflate Ratings

Reasons for Inflating

To maximize the merit raise an employee is eligible to receive, particularly when the merit raise ceiling is low.

To protect or encourage an employee whose performance has suffered because of personal problems. The supervisor feels sorry for the employee.

To avoid "hanging out dirty laundry" that would reflect badly on the supervisor or unit.

To avoid creating a written record of an employee's poor performance that becomes part of the employee's permanent record.

To avoid a confrontation with an employee.

To reward an employee who has shown improvement in performance, even though performance is still not high.

To increase the likelihood that an employee whom the supervisor does not like will be promoted out of the supervisor's work unit.

Reasons for Deflating

To shock an employee back onto a higher performance track.

To teach a rebellious employee a lesson about who is in charge.

To send a message to an employee that he or she should consider leaving the organization.

To build a strongly documented, written record of poor performance so that an employee can be fired.

Source: Based on C. O. Longenecker, H. P. Sims, and D. A. Gioia, "Behind the Mask: The Politics of Employee Appraisal," *Academy of Management Executive,* Vol. 1, 1987, pp. 183–193.

The development and use of an assessment system can be an expensive undertaking. Table 11.3 shows the estimated costs of developing a performance assessment system that were reported in a study by M. A. Jones. The costs required to develop the system were distinguished from those needed to implement and run it within the organization. In all, the assessment system that Jones analyzed would cost more than $600,000 (1997 dollars) to develop and implement.

Since dollar costs are high, an important practical criterion on which to judge an assessment system is the savings it might bring to the organization.[59] The process of measuring dollar return to an organization, called *utility analysis,* was discussed earlier in connection with both selection and training. Feedback, like training and careful selection, can improve employee performance. Estimates of performance improvement following feedback range from 8 percent to as much as 26 percent. The dollar value of improvements can be calculated using an estimate of the standard deviation of performance in dollars.[60] In one study, the cost of developing and implementing an assessment system was estimated at $700 per employee. Subtracting the costs of conducting assessments and giving feedback from the estimated dollar value of performance improvements, analysts estimated that an organization in which 500 managers were appraised and provided with feedback could realize benefits of $5.3 million in the first year.[61] Thus, even though assessment systems are expensive to develop and implement, they offer great potential benefits.

● **TABLE 11.3**

Costs of Developing and Implementing an Appraisal System

Item	Development	Implementation
Operating Costs		
Production and development	$105,500	$35,400
Data-entry hardware	N/A	$800
Paper	$3,300	$1,600
Mailing/distribution	$1,000	$13,000
Training	N/A	$46,000
Human Resource Costs		
Job analysis/experts	$72,400	N/A
Clerical	$21,900	$21,700
Professional coordinator	N/A	$14,100
Consultant	$49,900	$2,900
Rater time	N/A	$157,900
Ratee time	N/A	$58,300
Total	$254,000	$351,700
Grand total		$605,700

Source: Adapted from M. A. Jones, "Estimating Costs in the Development and Implementation of a Performance Appraisal System," paper presented at the First Annual Scientist-Practitioner Conference in Industrial-Organizational Psychology, Old Dominion University, Norfolk, Virginia, 1980. Reprinted by permission. Dollar figures (1997) have been rounded to the nearest $100.

DECIDING WHAT TYPES OF PERFORMANCE TO MEASURE

The criteria for evaluating performance assessment systems described earlier provide the basis for making important decisions when developing an assessment system. One crucial choice is simply what type of performance to assess. There are three basic categories of performance information.

1. *Trait-based* assessment systems assesses the abilities or other personal characteristics of an employee. For example, in a performance management system, it might be important that a service employee have a pleasant personality.

2. *Behavior-based* systems measures the extent to which an employee engages in specific, relatively well-defined behaviors while on the job. For example, in a performance management system, it might be important that an employee be a positive contributor to a team.

3. *Results-based* systems measures the "bottom line" associated with an employee's work: Did the job get done? Were the financial results positive?[62] For example, in a performance management system, a store manager's goal might be to reduce returns to 3 percent of sales.

● **FIGURE 11.5**

Examples of Trait-,
Behavior-, and Results-
Based Performance
Appraisal Systems

A. Trait-based appraisal

Rate the employee on each of the following traits:

1. Loyalty to company   very low   low   average   high   very high

2. Communication ability   very low   low   average   high   very high

3. Cooperativeness   very low   low   average   high   very high

B. Behavior-based appraisal

Using the scale below, rate the frequency with which
the employee exhibits the following behaviors:

1 = never   3 = sometimes   5 = almost always
2 = rarely   4 = frequently

_____ 1. Greets customers in a pleasant and friendly manner.

_____ 2. Is unable to explain technical aspects of a product
       to a customer.

_____ 3. Fills out charge card slips correctly, getting approval
       from supervisor for all charges above $300.

C. Results-based appraisal

From your production and employee files, please provide the
following information for this employee:

1. Number of units produced this month: _____

2. Number of units produced that were rejected and scrapped by
quality control: _____

3. Number of units produced that were rejected and returned for
repair by quality control: _____

4. Days this month the employee was absent without certified
medical cause: _____

Each type of assessment system has some advantages and disadvantages. Figure 11.5 illustrates the three types of systems.

Trait-Based Appraisals

Trait-based appraisals are used to assess the personality or personal characteristics of employees, such as their ability to make decisions, loyalty to the company, communication skills, or level of initiative. This type of assessment asks a lot about what a person is but relatively little about what he or she actually *does* and, as such, concerns "who" performs the job. While trait-based assessment are easy to construct, the disadvantages of focusing on traits are significant.

Trait-based approaches have questionable validity. Traits assessed in this type of approach often do not relate well to how employees really behave on the job because job behavior is strongly influenced by situational and environmental factors. An employee who is usually boisterous and aggressive with coworkers may act in a restrained, considerate manner when dealing with clients. Since the link between personal traits and actual job behavior is weak, trait-based systems are potentially more susceptible to charges of unfairness by minorities, women, and other protected groups. Trait-based systems are not as likely to be accepted by the courts. As noted earlier, court decisions such as *Price Waterhouse* v. *Hopkins* have made it very clear that what is assessed in a performance assessment system should have a clear link to effectiveness on the job.[63]

A further problem is that the inter-rater reliability of trait-based ratings is often low. The traits are difficult to define accurately, and the different frames of reference used by different raters make agreement among raters unlikely. A final disadvantage is that trait-based assessments are not helpful for providing feedback to employees. For example, telling an employee that he or she is too shy is not very useful. The information does not indicate how the employee can be less shy. Also, the basic personality traits of individuals are relatively well fixed by the time they are hired by an organization and are very difficult to alter.

Behavior-Based Appraisals

Assessment can consider the behavior of employees rather than their personal traits or "how" the job is done. Behavior measures are appropriate when the process used to accomplish the job is very important, and thus behavior measures are used to emphasize how a job is done. For example, a salesperson should greet customers as they enter the store, help them find what they are looking for, take their payment promptly, and thank them for their business. It is possible that a salesperson who did not greet or assist customers might complete sales, but this individual would not be representing the store in the way managers preferred. A sound behavior-based assessment would note the salesperson's failure to follow the preferred process.

In **behavior-based appraisals,** employees are assessed on how they do their job. Such assessments are more acceptable to the courts than trait-based assessments. Behavior measures can be very useful for feedback purposes because they indicate exactly what an employee should do differently. For instance, although a shy employee may always be shy, a behavior-based assessment might point out particular things that the person could do differently, such as contributing ideas at regularly scheduled staff meetings.

Deficiency may be a problem with some behavior-based assessments because they often will not include all behaviors that could lead to job effectiveness. For some jobs, effective performance can be achieved using a variety of different behaviors. For example, one salesperson may sell twenty cars a month using an aggressive, "pushy" style. Another salesperson may sell just as many cars using a reserved, considerate, fact-oriented approach. An assessment system that assumes that an aggressive sales style is best would unfairly assess the performance of the second salesperson. Of course, if the aggressive style is most consistent with the dealer's organizational approach, the salesperson with the reserved manner may want to find an employer with a culture more consistent with this style, for example, a Saturn dealership.

While behavior-based measures would usually be custom designed for each organization or job class, there has been some research on generic behavior dimensions. An example of this approach in the case of retail sales jobs is illustrated by a study of more than 18,000 employees from thirty-six different companies. The results were eight generic work behaviors organized into five minimum performance behaviors and three organizational citizenship behaviors.[64] The eight dimensions, along with example behaviors of each, are shown in Figure 11.6.

● **FIGURE 11.6**

Generic Work Behaviors for Retail Sales

Source: Adapted from Steven T. Hunt, "Generic Work Behavior: An Investigation into the Dimensions of Entry-Level, Hourly Job Performance," *Personnel Psychology,* Vol. 49, 1996, pp. 51–83.

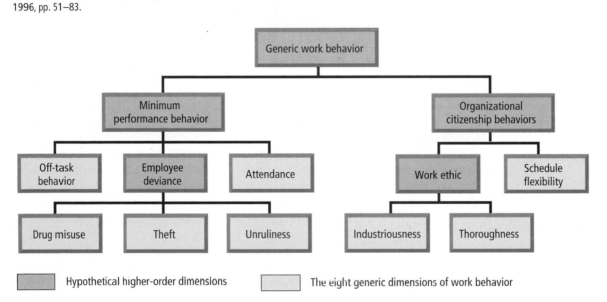

Generic Work Behavior	Example
Industriousness	Takes the initiative to find another task when finished with regular work.
Thoroughness	Notices merchandise out of place and returns it to the proper area.
Schedule flexibility	Works flexible hours by accepting schedule changes when necessary.
Attendance	Skips work without calling in.
Off-task behavior	Uses store phones to make unauthorized personal calls.
Unruliness	Refuses to take routine orders from supervisors.
Theft	Advises friends how to steal merchandise.
Drug misuse	Comes to work under the influence of alcohol or drugs.

Results-Based Appraisals

Another approach to performance assessment measures the results of work behavior. This approach deals with bottom-line issues such as how many cars an employee sold or how much profit the employee brought into the organization during the month. When it is not important how results are achieved, or when there are many different ways to succeed, a **results-based appraisal** would be appropriate. Under this approach, both the car salespersons described earlier would receive the same evaluation, even though they achieved their results using very different means.

Despite their intuitive appeal, results-based assessments pose questions of practicality, contamination, and deficiency. Results-based measures may be difficult to obtain for some jobs. What are the performance results of a high school teacher's behavior? Furthermore, results are not always under the control of an individual employee. Equipment breakdowns, a change in the economy, bad luck, inadequate budgetary or staff support, or other factors not directly controlled by an employee may greatly affect the job results.[65] Results measures are therefore contaminated by these external factors. Another problem is that results-based assessments may foster a "results at all cost" mentality among employees.[66] For example, in an organization that evaluated its telephone order takers on the basis of sales, employees on the telephone bank learned to hang up on customers calling to cancel orders or arrange returns because these counted against sales. Obviously, such a practice was not what the organization intended and would hurt customer satisfaction and repeat sales.

Teamwork among employees may suffer if individuals are preoccupied with their own *personal* results and will not take the time to help coworkers. Results-based measures are deficient in that they may not tap such aspects of performance as cooperation, which may have important benefits for the organization. A final disadvantage is that results-based assessments are less helpful for employee development. Although they may indicate that results are below acceptable levels, they do not always provide clear information on how to improve work performance.

Care must be taken in deciding what type of performance is appropriate to assess for a specific job. Unless a clear link between traits and job effectiveness can be shown, trait-based assessments should be avoided; in general, fewer legal problems are associated with behavior- and results-based systems. A carefully constructed combination of behavior-based and results-based approaches may be most appropriate for many jobs. The next section of this chapter describes some specific methods of assessing performance. Some of these techniques are, by their nature, suited to assessing only one type of performance information. Others, particularly those involving subjective ratings, may be used to assess more than one performance type.

METHODS OF APPRAISING PERFORMANCE

Performance can be measured in many different ways. Most of the performance measures currently in use can be characterized as either objective or subjective. Objective measures are typically results-based measures of physical output, whereas subjective measures can be used to assess traits, behaviors, or results.

Objective Measures

Objective measures assess performance in terms of numbers, such as the amount of a product an employee produces or sells, the number of defective products produced, the number of times an employee is absent or late to work, or some other direct numerical index of how well or quickly an employee can perform certain tasks. While some job measures are more objective than others, nothing is truly objective. For example, the number of defective products produced may be the result of a machine defect or the quality of raw materials received from the supplier. Most workers are quick to report that many of the "objective" measures of job performance really relate to job elements beyond their control.

There are five major types of objective measures: production measures, dollar sales, personnel data, performance tests, and business unit measures.

● **Production Measures**   The manufacturing industry has used production measures for at least the last 100 years. These measures simply involve counting the number of items produced by an employee or the number of defective units made or obtaining some other quantitative index of production. Production measures can be used appropriately when an employee produces a measurable, physical product. As with any results-based assessment, production measures may not be available for many of the jobs in an organization or they may be influenced by factors beyond an employee's control. For example, if a coworker is habitually late in getting raw materials to an employee, that employee's production rate could be slowed down. Or a worker may be assigned to an older piece of equipment or a machine that is prone to break down. For a production measure to be a valid measure of performance, three conditions must be met: (1) Production should be on a repetitive basis, (2) the amount of product should be measurable, and (3) the employee should be primarily responsible for the amount produced; that is, production needs to be sensitive to the employee's ability and effort, not system-driven.

● **Dollar Sales**   Sales performance is usually measured by the dollar amount of sales made in a given period of time. Typically, some minimum acceptable level of sales is defined, and performance beyond that quota is rewarded more highly. Sales measures are also results-based and suffer from many of the same shortcomings as production measures. For example, a salesperson assigned to a rural territory may have to spend many hours traveling from town to town, whereas a salesperson assigned to a large city can devote more time to actual client contact. The salesperson in the city will probably sell more than the salesperson in the rural area, even if both work equally hard and are equally skilled. The sales measure is contaminated by this difference in sales territory, which creates a so-called **opportunity bias.**[67] Thus it is appropriate to use dollar sales as an index of performance only when individuals have substantial control over their sales performance or when it is possible to adjust for contaminants such as differences in sales territory.

● **Personnel Data**   Information from an employee's personnel file is sometimes used in performance assessment. **Personnel measures** would include such particulars as the number of times an employee has been absent or late to work and the number of reprimands or disciplinary actions taken against the individual.

Serious problems arise in the use of personnel data. One is **contamination.** If an employee is absent from work because of illness or is late to work because of a flat tire, does this mean that this employee is a poor performer? Personnel data are of questionable relevance. If an employee is habitually late to work but consistently produces more and better-quality products than coworkers, is the employee a poor performer? Personnel measures may also be unreliable because some supervisors record absenteeism or tardiness more carefully than others. Personnel data should be used as a measure of performance only when a clear link can be made between the measure (e.g., tardiness) and actual job effectiveness, such as the delay of the start of business as a result of an employee's tardiness.

● **Performance Tests**   Performance tests are work samples or simulations under standardized conditions. For example, telephone operators may all receive the same set of scripted calls and be evaluated on speed, accuracy, and courtesy of service. Pilots fly periodic "check rides" in flight simulators to assess their ability to handle both routine and emergency procedures. Performance tests are useful when it is difficult to collect comparable or uncontaminated performance data in any other way, but they suffer from three major problems. First, they tend to be deficient because only some aspects of a job can be realistically simulated. Second, if employees know that they are being tested on their job effectiveness, they are likely to work very hard to perform the test well. Performance tests then become a measure not of typical performance but of maximum employee capability. For example, whereas pilot inattentiveness is a cause of many air emergencies, how many pilots will be inattentive while being observed in a simulator? The final problem is that of practicality. Many jobs simply do not lend themselves to this kind of assessment, and for those that do, performance tests are generally expensive and time-consuming to develop and implement.

● **Business Unit Performance Measures**   The preceding objective measures are seldom useful for managers. However, the performance of upper-level managers and executives is sometimes assessed by objective measures of the performance of the business unit that they head. Measures might include stock price, return on equity, profit, or market share. Clearly, these measures can be contaminated by economic factors beyond the manager's control, but they can often be valuable when benchmarked against the industry.

● **Overall Value of Objective Measures**   Each type of objective measure has its own strengths and weaknesses. For instance, objective measures have the advantages of being free from the types of errors and biases that plague subjective measures. However, objective measures seldom capture the individual's total contribution to the organization. Measures of quantity, quality, attendance, and even profit may represent important dimensions of performance but are **deficient** in that they ignore dimensions such as cooperation or willingness to contribute in ways that go beyond the job description. Most organizations believe that subjective assessments are more complete in their representation of performance and thus use subjective measures of performance either to supplement or to replace objective measures in the assessment system.

Subjective Measures

Because they rely on human judgment, **subjective measures** are prone to the rating errors discussed earlier. Most performance assessment systems place heavy emphasis on subjective ratings of performance. One study reported that among ninety-six police departments in major cities, nearly 90 percent used supervisory ratings as their primary performance assessment tool.[68] Anyone who has the opportunity to observe an employee's performance—including superiors, peers, subordinates, clients, and the employees themselves—can make subjective ratings. For the vast majority of organizations, however, it is the immediate supervisor who judges performance. Advantages and disadvantages of using other sources of performance judgments are considered later in this section.

Unlike objective measures, subjective judgments can be used even when the employee does not produce a measurable physical product. Subjective ratings can be used to measure the behavior or personal traits of employees as well as results. The major problem with subjective measures of performance is that the raters have to observe and evaluate job-related behavior. Raters may not have the chance to observe relevant behavior, and even if they do, their ratings may be biased. Several different types of subjective measures can be used. Generally, they can be classified as either comparative procedures (ranking) or assessments against absolute standards (rating).

● **Comparative Procedures** Subjective comparison of the overall work performance of individual employees can yield a rank ordering of employees from best to worst. Three kinds of **comparative procedures** are used in performance assessments: ranking, paired comparisons, and forced distributions.

Ranking When **ranking** is used, employees are compared directly against one another. Ranking is easy to explain, understand, and use. It is generally not time-consuming and is less expensive than other evaluation techniques. The simplest ranking procedure is **straight ranking,** in which the evaluator arranges employees in order from best to worst on the basis of their overall performance. First, the best employee is identified, then the second best, and so on until the worst employee is assigned the lowest rank. A variation is called **alternate ranking.** In this procedure, the evaluator first ranks the best employee, next the worst employee, then the second best, then the second worst, and so on until all employees are ranked.

In **paired-comparison ranking,** all possible pairs of employees are formed. The evaluator indicates which individual in each pair is the better performer. An employee's rank is determined by the number of times that he or she is chosen as the better performer in a pair. The person chosen most often is ranked first. Use of this method requires the comparison of many pairs even when the total number of employees is not large. The formula for the number of possible pairs of employees is $n(n-1)/2$, where n = the number of employees. For example, if there are 10 employees in a work group, $10(9)/2 = 45$ judgments must be made. In the case of 20 employees, 190 pairs must be compared. Paired-comparison ranking is more complicated than straight ranking, but the process is believed to result in more consistent, reliable ranks than the straight-ranking approach.

A variation of this approach is to present pairs of statements, allowing the rater to chose the statement that best describes the employee's performance. In a recent study a group of researchers modified this form of paired-comparison rating of performance to a computerized adaptive rating scale (CARS).[69] The computer presents pairs of statements, but then moves on to the next employee when a stable estimate of performance is obtained. The advantage of the procedure is that it is interactive and adaptive. In this way, superior rating accuracy can be achieved with fewer comparisons.

Forced Distribution   When using a **forced-distribution method,** also called **forced-ranking method,** the evaluator has to place a certain percentage of employees into each of several performance categories. An example of such a system is that used by Ford Motor and described in the HR Challenge. Ford's performance management process required that 10 percent of its employees receive As, 80 percent Bs, and 10 percent Cs (the lowest grade). Ford is not the only company relying on forced rankings to differentiate employees. For example, recently Enron, Hewlett-Packard, General Electric, and Microsoft have also adopted such systems, either as a part of work-force reduction programs or as indicative of the competitive cultures they sought to engender—the latter being a fact mentioned in many articles on Enron's bankruptcy filing.[70]

Forced-distribution judgments are usually based on an overall assessment of the employees' performance. Examples of performance levels and distribution targets in a forced-distribution procedure are presented in Table 11.4.

Advantages and Disadvantages of Comparative Procedures   Comparative procedures are easy to explain and use; help in making layoff, promotion, and merit raise decisions; and serve as controls for leniency, severity, and central tendency errors. They have a number of disadvantages, however.

- Employees are evaluated according to their overall performance rather than on a number of distinct aspects of performance. Comparative procedures provide no clue as to the absolute difference in performance among employees. It is impossible to tell whether the top-ranked employee in a group is a lot or just a little better than the second-ranked person.
- It is not possible to compare across work groups. The person ranked third in a good group may be better than the person ranked first in a weaker group.
- Comparative methods also require that one evaluator know the performance of every employee in a unit. In large groups, this may not be possible.

● **TABLE 11.4**

Forced-Distribution Appraisal Method

Performance Level	Distribution Target
Level 1: Employee is below acceptable performance standards.	5% of unit
Level 2: Employee meets acceptable performance standard but has room for improvement.	15% of unit
Level 3: Employee shows a uniformly good level of performance.	50% of unit
Level 4: Employee shows a very high level of performance.	20% of unit
Level 5: Employee consistently shows outstanding performance.	10% of unit
Each of the employees in a work unit is allocated to one of the performance levels shown in the table. Associated with each peformance level is a "distribution target" that should be used in allocating employees to the various levels.	

Because comparative procedures generally do not focus on specific job-related behaviors, they risk legal challenge. The courts have ruled against companies when comparative methods have had an adverse impact on minorities or women. Another problem is that comparative methods are not useful for employee development. An employee learns how he or she compares with other employees, but this feedback does not indicate how to improve performance. Comparative procedures may foster competition and resentment among employees. After all, only one person can receive the top ranking.

A major problem with forced distributions is that a group of employees may not conform to the predefined distribution used in the procedure; in highly selected groups, a majority of employees truly may be outstanding. Furthermore, performance may not be distributed normally if the organization has made successful efforts to reward and retain high-rated employees while encouraging poor performers to leave. Employees are often unhappy with forced-distribution systems because most employees believe that they are above average.[71] A forced-distribution system allows only a few to receive the ratings that most think they deserve. Supervisors generally dislike forced-distribution systems because they limit the rater's discretion. Of course, in most cases, it was the inappropriate use of this rater "discretion" in the form of excessive leniency that caused the organization to institute the forced-distribution system in the first place.

Finally, many companies, including those that recently adopted forced-distribution systems, are trying to emphasize team-oriented work. Forced-distribution systems are generally not consistent with the team concept, leading a spokesperson for a company that previously used the system to state, "My recollection is it created 10 problems for every one it solved." Others view the system as a Band-Aid approach to dealing with work force performance issues.[72]

Despite their drawbacks, comparative methods can be a useful component of an overall performance assessment system. They are useful in forcing evaluators to make distinctions between employees when differential rewards are to be distributed. In most situations, it may be best to combine comparative methods with other forms of performance assessment, such as the absolute standard approaches discussed below. A recent research article described how the type of global assessments resulting from comparative methods can be improved through a process of priming; that is, using the global assessment as a lead-in to more specific job ratings.[73] In this way, one may have the advantages of both an accurate global assessment and meaningful assessments of specific job behaviors.

● **Absolute Standards**   Instead of comparing an employee's performance with that of fellow employees, an assessment system can be based on absolute performance standards for the job. Each employee is evaluated against the standards. **Absolute standards** facilitate comparison of employees from different departments. Performance is measured on a number of specific dimensions so that employees can be given more helpful feedback than is generated by comparative procedures. Variations of the absolute standards technique include graphic rating scales, weighted checklists, the critical incidents technique, behaviorally anchored rating scales, and behavioral observation scales.

Graphic Rating Scales   **Graphic rating scales** are the most widely used evaluation technique. The rater evaluates an employee on each of several performance dimensions using a continuum made up of clearly defined scale points. Figure 11.7

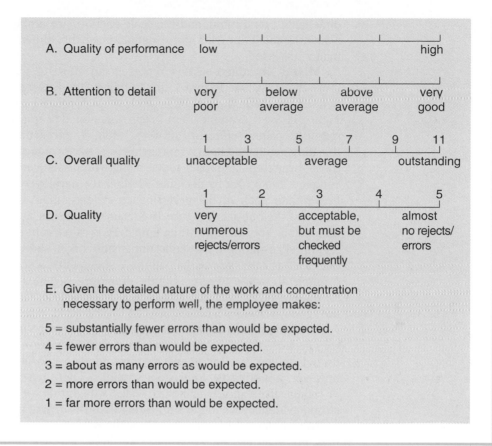

FIGURE 11.7

Examples of Typical Graphic Rating Scales

gives some examples of graphic rating scales for measuring performance along the dimension of quality. The rating dimensions should be based on a careful job analysis.

In the graphic rating scale method, the rater describes an employee as falling at some point on a performance continuum—such as unsatisfactory, average, or outstanding—on each dimension. The scale points can be assigned scores (e.g., ranging from 5 points for outstanding to 0 points for unsatisfactory), and a total score for an employee can be computed by summing the ratings across all dimensions rated. If some characteristics are more important than others, the rating on these dimensions can be multiplied by an appropriate weight before the total is calculated.

Graphic rating scales have several advantages. They are relatively easy to develop and use, more than one performance dimension can be included, employees' scores can be compared, and the method is well accepted by raters. If properly developed for relevance and clarity, graphic rating scales can be just as reliable and valid as more complicated techniques. On the other hand, this method offers little protection from rating errors, such as leniency, severity, central tendency, and halo errors. Graphic rating scales are often criticized because the performance dimensions on which the employee is rated and the scale anchors used in making the rating may be ill defined and vague. In Figure 11.7, scale A does not define the dimension being rated, and the scale anchors are ambiguous and uninformative. Scales D and E provide more definition of the dimension and levels of performance assessed.

Mixed standard scales represent an effort to make graphic rating scales more effective (see Figure 11.8). In this method, three statements are written to define low, medium, and high levels of performance along each dimension.[74] In Figure 11.8, for example, item 7 represents good performance on a dimension that might be called "efficiency of work"; item 5 represents average performance on this dimension, and item 2 represents poor performance. The rating form presents these three items in mixed order, along with items from other dimensions. Raters complete the scales by deciding whether the employee is worse than, equal to, or better than each of the performance statements. A special scoring procedure, shown at the bottom of Figure 11.8, is used to assign a performance score for each dimension. For example, if the employee is rated better than all three of the statements representing a particular dimension, he or she receives a score of 7. If the employee is rated worse than all three statements, a score of 1 is assigned. In the example shown in Figure 11.8, the employee is better than the "poor" statement for dimension 2, equal to the "average" statement for dimension 2, and worse than the "good" statement, for a score of 4.

Mixed standard scales are supposed to reduce halo, leniency, and severity errors because the scale items are mixed randomly throughout the rating form and do not present a clear hierarchy from good to bad performance. Unfortunately, however, it is still easy to bias one's ratings. There have been several comparisons of ratings from mixed standard scales with ratings from other formats, and no strong evidence was found suggesting that this format is superior to others.[75]

Mixed standard scales also allow the detection of careless or inconsistent ratings. For example, suppose that a rater indicated that an employee was worse than the statement representing a low level of work efficiency but also rated the employee equal to the statement representing average efficiency. Under the mixed standard procedure, this inconsistent evaluation of the employee could be identified and verified with the rater.

● **Weighted Checklists**   In another approach to assessment, a rater is given a list of job-related characteristics or behaviors and is asked to check the items that are typical of a particular employee. When such a **weighted checklist** is developed, job experts indicate how good or poor each behavior is. These goodness weights are then used in summing ratings to determine the overall performance of an employee. The rater, however, is asked to be a "reporter" and is not made aware of the weights associated with each item. An example of a weighted checklist is given in Figure 11.9.

A variant of this technique is the **forced-choice system,** a procedure developed specifically to reduce leniency error. It is often easy for a rater using a standard weighted checklist to identify the most favorable items. Raters who wish to be lenient can check the items that make an employee look good, whether or not they represent the behavior of the employee. In the forced-choice procedure, items are assembled in pairs; in each pair, the rater must choose the item that is more characteristic of the employee. The pairs are designed so that both items *appear* equally good or bad to the rater, but only one is related to actual job performance. Here is a forced-choice item pair for the job of college professor:

● **FIGURE 11.8**

A Mixed Standard Scale
and Scoring Key with
Example Ratings for One
Employee

Source: Adapted from F. Blanz
and E. E. Ghiselli, "The Mixed
Standard Scale: A New Rating
System," *Personnel
Psychology,* Vol. 25, 1972, pp.
185–199. Reprinted by
permission.

Dimension Represented[a]	Item	Employee Rating[b]
2 (A)	1. Has normal self-confidence, with only occasional uncertainty. Usually open and self-assured.	0
1 (P)	2. Some lack of efficiency. May take too much time to complete assignments, and sometimes does not really finish them.	+
3 (G)	3. Written and oral reports are well formulated and thorough. They rarely need explanation.	+
2 (P)	4. He/she is shy and uncertain. Avoids situations that require the taking of a strong position.	+
1 (A)	5. He/she is efficient enough, usually gets through assignments in reasonable time.	+
3 (P)	6. Sometimes reports are so incomplete and poorly organized they are of little value and must be done over.	+
1 (G)	7. He/she is quick and efficient, able to keep work on schedule. Really gets going on a new task.	0
2 (G)	8. Behaves confidently. Reacts in all situations without hesitation.	−
3 (A)	9. Reports are useful and meaningful, but often require additional explanation.	+

Scoring key:

	Statements			Score
	Good	Average	Poor	
	+	+	+	7
	0	+	+	6
Ratings	−	+	+	5
	−	0	+	4
	−	−	+	3
	−	−	0	2
	−	−	−	1

Ratings by dimension for employee:

	G	A	P	Score
Dimension 1	0	+	+	6
Dimension 2	−	0	+	4
Dimension 3	+	+	+	7

[a]Numbers 1–3 indicate dimension that the statement represents. Letters in parentheses characterize statement: G = good performance, A = average performance, and P = poor performance. This information would not be provided on the actual rating form.
[b]Ratings are such that + = employee better than the statement, 0 = employee same as the statement, and − = employee worse than the statement.

FIGURE 11.9

Weighted Checklist for Supervisory Job, with Example Evaluation of One Supervisor

Source: James B. Shaw, Abdul Jalil bin Ismail, and Cynthia D. Fisher, "A Cognitive Categorization Approach to Managerial Performance Appraisal: Analysis of the Singapore Manager," paper presented at the First International Conference on Personnel/Human Resource Management, National University of Singapore, December 1987. Reprinted by permission.

Instructions:

Check those statements that represent the typical actions of the employee.

	Statement	Value[a]
✓	Acts decisively when encountering problems	4.9
___	Is fair to all subordinates in his/her promotion decisions	5.0
___	Provides temporary solutions to problems that keep appearing	3.0
✓	Assesses the mood of subordinates before pursuing a subject that would damage relationships	3.9
✓	Evaluates performance once or twice a year	4.1
✓	Is unwilling to point out subordinates' poor work performance	2.2
___	Conducts detailed discussions with worker to solve problems	4.6
___	Checks subordinates' work thoroughly and is sharp at finding errors	4.2
✓	Gives merit increment to a poor performer	2.0
___	Carries out the policies of the company without regard to individual welfare or circumstances	2.3
✓	Signs subordinates' work without carefully checking it	2.0
___	Is unable to provide guidelines for making decisions when faced with a problem	2.3
✓	Maintains very good relations with other supervisors in the division	5.0
___	Shows concern for employee welfare but does not act on it	2.7

Performance

Score for employee = (4.9 + 3.9 + 4.1 + 2.2 + 2.0 + 2.0 + 5.0) = 24.1

[a]High values indicate that the statement represents good performance. These values would not be included on the actual rating form.

1. Lectures with confidence.
2. Keeps the interest and attention of the class.[76]

Only items that are important for job performance are scored in determining the performance level of the employee. In the preceding example, item 1 is socially desirable but has little to do with how effectively a professor actually teaches, whereas item 2 is truly diagnostic of good teaching.

Forced-choice items help control intentional leniency because the rater does not know which item to check to make the employee look good. Drawbacks are that the items are difficult to develop and raters dislike the approach. Frustrated that they are not free to describe the employee as they want to, they may feel that they have been "tricked" into doing a proper evaluation. Finally, the results of the forced-choice approach allow only overall ("excellent," "average," "below average") feedback to employees. Because the rater is unaware of the key, he or she cannot tell employees what behavior led to the overall rating or how they might change their behavior to improve performance.

Critical Incidents Technique When performance assessment is to be based on critical incidents, the evaluator keeps a log for each employee, recording behaviors and performance incidents that are particularly effective or ineffective. Incidents are recorded for each employee as soon as possible after they occur. At the end of the evaluation period, this log is used to evaluate the performance of the employee. The **critical incidents technique** is time-consuming for the evaluators, and it may be hard to quantify or structure the incidents into a final narrative evaluation. However, since most evaluators have trouble remembering the full range of employee behavior over the rating period, a critical incidents log can be very useful in supporting any of the more structured subjective methods described in this chapter. Recent research has shown that structured diaries of specific incidents produced ratings with less leniency and more fine-grained distinctions.[77] The log also helps the supervisor provide specific examples when explaining ratings to subordinates.

Behaviorally Anchored Rating Scales Some assessment systems use graphic rating scales on which anchor points are defined in considerable detail, using examples of behavior that represent particular levels of performance. Such a **behaviorally anchored rating scale (BARS)** is developed for each of several important performance dimensions. Raters are asked to mark the scale point that best represents the performance of an employee. Figure 11.10 illustrates a BARS developed for the performance dimension "problem solving/decision making" for the job of midlevel manager.

The development of a BARS is a time-consuming and costly process that involves the efforts of many people. The steps are as follows:

1. A group of knowledgeable employees (perhaps including both workers and supervisors) identifies the important dimensions that make up effective performance. This group writes a clear definition for each dimension.

2. A second group comes up with as many critical incidents as it can to illustrate effective, average, and ineffective performance for each dimension.

3. A third group is given the list of dimensions and a stack of cards, each containing one of the critical incidents. The task of each member of this group is to assign each critical incident to the dimension it seems to characterize. This is called "retranslation." Critical incidents that are not placed in the same dimension by a majority of the retranslation group are discarded as unclear.

4. A fourth group rates the level of performance each remaining incident represents. For example, suppose that the incident "smiles and greets customers" has been reliably sorted into the "customer service" dimension of performance. Members of the fourth group then rate this incident as to whether it represents outstanding, above-average, average, or below-average performance. The mean and standard deviation of these ratings are computed for each critical incident. Items are discarded if group members are unable to agree on the performance level represented. From the remaining items, incidents are chosen to anchor each point along the BARS. Each anchor is

● **FIGURE 11.10**

Example of Behaviorally Anchored Rating Scale for the Performance Dimension of Problem Solving/Decision Making

Source: James B. Shaw, Abdul Jalil bin Ismail, and Cynthia D. Fisher, "A Cognitive Categorization Approach to Managerial Performance Appraisal: Analysis of the Singapore Manager," paper presented at the First International Conference on Personnel/Human Resource Management, National University of Singapore, December 1987. Reprinted by permission.

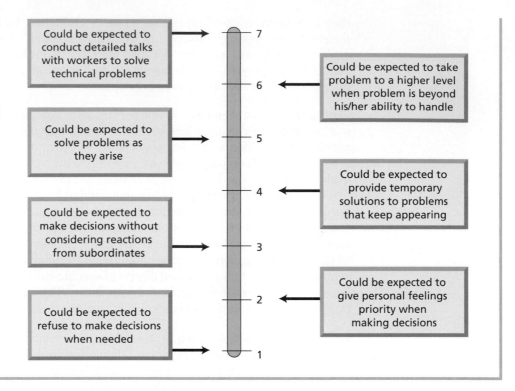

worded "Could be expected to . . ." so that it can be selected by a rater who has observed similar, but not precisely identical, behavior in an employee.

5. As a final step, the rating scale is pilot tested in the organization.

Note that a BARS can be developed with only two groups rather than four. In this case, the first group carries out steps 1 and 2, and the second group completes steps 3 and 4.

A BARS is time-consuming to develop because the development process involves so many people. Interestingly, this potential weakness is also the method's major advantage. The employees who are to be rated with the scales may have helped develop them. Their involvement increases the chance that the BARS will be a valid measure of performance and that the employees will accept its use. Since a BARS is necessarily job-related, it is less vulnerable to legal challenges than many other assessment methods. Use of this method may not be practical, however. Each job category requires its own BARS, which may not be possible in many organizations either because of economic reasons or because there are too few employees in a particular job to make the development technique feasible.

It would seem that a BARS should be superior to other assessment techniques. However, some research has concluded that the use of a BARS does not always reduce rating errors and in some cases introduces a new form of bias not found in other forms of rating.[78] Even so, a BARS still has the advantage of increasing employee involvement in the assessment development process. In constructing a BARS, employees and supervisors may clarify their understanding about the nature of the job and how it should be performed.

● **FIGURE 11.11**

Example of Behavior
Observation Scale for the
Performance Dimension
Communicating with
Subordinates

Source: James B. Shaw, Abdul
Jalil bin Ismail, and Cynthia D.
Fisher, "A Cognitive
Categorization Approach to
Managerial Performance
Appraisal: Analysis of the
Singapore Manager," paper
presented at the First
International Conference on
Personnel/Human Resource
Management, National
University of Singapore,
December 1987. Reprinted by
permission.

	Almost never				Almost always
Puts up notices on bulletin board when new policies or procedures are implemented	1	2	3	4	5
Maintains eye contact when talking to employees	1	2	3	4	5
Uses both written memos and verbal discussions when giving instructions	1	2	3	4	5
Discusses changes in policies or procedures with employees before implementing them	1	2	3	4	5
Writes memos that are clear, concise, and easy to understand	1	2	3	4	5

Total Performance Level

Below adequate	5–9
Adequate	10–14
Good	15–19
Excellent	20 +

Behavioral Observation Scales   Raters who use a BARS may find it difficult to select a single scale point to represent the performance of an employee who sometimes engages in some very positive behaviors but at other times performs poorly.
Behavioral observation scales (BOSs) were developed partly in response to
this problem (see Figure 11.11).

To develop BOSs, job experts first identify groups of similar behavioral incidents and form them into performance dimensions. In Figure 11.11, several behavioral incidents have been grouped to form a performance dimension called "communicating with subordinates." Job experts evaluate the behavioral incidents to
make sure that they are relevant to the dimension and important for distinguishing
between successful and unsuccessful employees. If experts cannot agree about an
incident's relevance, it is discarded. A 5-point frequency-of-occurrence scale is attached to each incident, which raters use to indicate how frequently each employee engages in the behavior.[79]

Behavioral observation scales have many advantages. They are based on a careful analysis of the job. The content validity of BOS incidents is evaluated directly, and
BOSs are likely to be found acceptable to the courts. BOSs can also be helpful in providing performance feedback to employees. Because they use frequency scales

rather than simply indicating the one behavior that best represents an employee's performance, BOSs may provide a greater depth of performance information than a BARS. Research, however, has not shown BOSs to be clearly superior.[80]

Management by Objectives

A previously popular individualized method of evaluating the performance of managers and professionals was **management by objectives (MBO).** The MBO process involves three steps:

1. The employee meets with his or her superior and agrees on a set of goals to achieve during a specified period of time. Goals should be quantifiable and should include an agreed-upon target.

2. Throughout this period, progress toward the goals is monitored, though the employee is generally left free to determine how to go about meeting them.

3. At the end of the period, the employee and superior again meet to evaluate whether the goals were achieved and to decide together on a new set of goals.

Of course, if this sounds like performance management it is because much of MBO has been subsumed under performance management as described previously.

MBO has several advantages similar to those of the broader approach, performance management. Observable, results-oriented goals replace the difficult-to-observe, subjective traits that are sometimes used in other measures of performance. MBO can encourage innovation and creativity, since employees are free to determine how they will meet their goals. Such a process can be valuable in gaining the commitment of employees, since they are actively involved in setting goals. It can also empower employees, since they have a degree of latitude in deciding how to meet their goals.

Management by objectives can lead to performance improvement, particularly if goals are specific, moderately difficult, and accepted by the employees—and if the procedure has top management committment. A summary of seventy studies of MBO programs found that when the commitment of top management was high, the average gain in productivity was 56 percent. When commitment was low, the average gain in productivity was only 6 percent.[81] When properly established and supported by top managers, MBO can lead to positive results.

RATERS OF EMPLOYEE PERFORMANCE

In most organizations, supervisors provide subjective ratings of employee performance. However, there are several other potential sources for performance ratings, including employees themselves; peers; subordinates; and customers, both internal (e.g., the customers of HRM) or external to the organization. Each of these sources has its own advantages and disadvantages.

A consistent finding in the performance assessment literature is that ratings obtained from different rating sources have only partial agreement.[82] Self-ratings tend to be most dissimilar from those of other sources, probably the result of individuals rating themselves higher (leniency error) than other comparison groups (supervisor, subordinate, or peer).[83] In one study, peer ratings correlated 0.62 with those of supervisors[84] while in another the correlation was 0.79,[85] both very substantial degrees of relationship. Finally, a further study involved a single instrument containing forty-eight behaviorally oriented items representing ten dimensions of managerial performance. The items were presented separately rather than as scales. The study found no difference in the way self, peer, supervisor, and subordinate groups organized the item to the scales. In other words, the ten scales were seen as analogous irrespective of the group doing the rating.[86]

Self-Evaluation

Employees are sometimes asked to evaluate themselves. It seems logical that individuals would be the best judges of their own performance, particularly if supervisors cannot observe them on a regular basis. If employees are asked to evaluate themselves, they may respond by becoming more motivated and involved in the evaluation process.

Self-ratings tend to show more leniency error than supervisor ratings, although halo errors are lower.[87] **Self-evaluations** have become popular as a part of the management by objectives process, when the supervisor and the subordinate jointly evaluate goal attainment. Self-evaluation seems most appropriate when it is used as an employee development tool rather than to make administrative decisions.[88] It also may serve as an important input into a supervisory assessment. An employee's self-assessment may provide important information of which the supervisor was not aware. The supervisor can then factor this information into his or her performance ratings of the employee.

Peer Evaluation

Compared with supervisory ratings, peer or coworker evaluations are more stable over time, can tap more dimensions of performance, are better able to distinguish effort from performance, and can focus more on task-relevant abilities. One study has concluded that peer ratings may be the most accurate evaluations of employee performance.[89] **Peer evaluations** can be particularly useful when supervisors do not have the opportunity to observe an individual's performance but fellow employees do.

Peers sometimes resist evaluating one another. An individual may not want to give a fellow employee a favorable evaluation for fear of looking inferior in comparison. On the other hand, an individual may not want to jeopardize a good working relationship by giving an unfavorable rating to a colleague. Friendship bias may lead an employee to rate his or her friends higher than other employees. Finally, if resources are finite, as for salary increases, workers in a unit may see peer evaluation as a win–lose scenario.

A survey of 218 industrial employees who had used a peer evaluation system for more than a year found a high degree of user acceptance.[90] It seems, however, that peer evaluations, like self-evaluations, are best used for employee development rather than for administrative decisions. The same survey found that users were more favorable in their attitudes toward peer assessments that were used for developmental rather than for evaluative purposes.

When teamwork, participation, and cohesiveness are part of the organization's culture, peer evaluations can work well. In organizations that are competitive and have a low level of trust among employees, peer evaluations may be little more than a way for employees to enhance themselves by belittling their fellow employees.

Subordinate Evaluation

Evaluation by subordinates may provide valuable information. Subordinates know how well a supervisor performs with respect to leading, organizing, planning, delegating, and communicating. In fact, evaluating the boss is becoming a popular mechanism in many organizations.[91]

Subordinates, however, may inflate their rating of a supervisor, especially if they think that the supervisor will be able to discern who has given a particular rating. Complete anonymity is essential if this technique is to provide valid ratings.[92] However, some systems of subordinate evaluation tend to compromise anonymity. For example, in one organization, supervisor evaluations by employees on a series of open-ended performance questions go to the supervisor's manager. The manager's secretary word processes the comments of each person in order. In other words, the comments of employees 1 through 15 are given for the first item, for the second item in the same order, and so forth. The supervisors and manager can then read all the comments of employee 1 for each item, all the comments of employee 2, and in this way have a good idea as to the identity of each of the fifteen employees. Of course, this could be easily remedied by having the secretary scramble the employee responses so that they are in a different order for each item, but as it turned out, both the supervisor and manager appreciated the semblance of anonymity (rather than real anonymity) in reviewing the comments.

Open channels of communication and an abundance of trust between supervisors and subordinates are also needed if this type of evaluation is to be worthwhile. Like self- and peer evaluations, **subordinate evaluation** is useful for development but historically has not been used widely for making administrative decisions. In fact, one study looked at subordinate ratings and found that managers whose initial level of performance was moderate or low improve over time, thus showing that upward feedback has the desired effect.[93]

Customer Evaluation

Another source of assessment information comes from customers or clients. Such assessments are popular in the context of service delivery, where there is a high degree of client involvement and when the service employee is relatively removed from other employees or supervisors.[94] Customers can be internal or external to the organization. For example, the "customer set" for human resource professionals includes the employees of the organization.

As an example of external customers, it would be difficult for the owner or manager of a carpet-cleaning company to know whether the service was performed to the company's standards and to customer's satisfaction in the absence of feedback from the customer. This feedback could be obtained through a phone interview with the customer or a formal survey. Alternately, customer feedback can be through "shoppers," individuals who appear to be regular customers but who are actually hired to carefully observe and rate the service using a predefined protocol.

360-Degree Assessment

A new approach to performance assessment is that of simultaneously using many or all of the sources of feedback described in this section. As a contemporary innovation, 360-degree assessments are described in the next section of this chapter.

CONTEMPORARY ASSESSMENT CHALLENGES

360-Degree Appraisal

An estimated 90 percent of *Fortune* 1000 firms use some form of **360-degree assessment,** where performance ratings are collected simultaneously from subordinates, peers, supervisors, and employees themselves.[95] Introduced as a popular method of assessing performance in the early 1990s, the 360-degree method is reminiscent of Walt Disney's *Snow White and the Seven Dwarfs*. In that story the wicked queen self-confidently demands of her magic mirror, "Mirror, mirror on the wall, who's the fairest of them all?" When done well, 360-degree feedback is like that truth-telling magic mirror in that it gives us information we did not expect and possibly did not want to hear, but information that can help us grow and be more effective.[96]

Although we generally view enough snapshots of ourselves that there are few surprises, a profile or the view from the back may show us some features about ourselves we had not expected. In one study, those appraised using the 360-degree approach reported that 25 percent of the feedback was expected positive feedback, 30 percent was unexpected positive feedback, 20 to 30 percent was expected negative feedback, and 15 to 20 percent was unexpected negative feedback.[97] For most of those appraised, the varying perspectives will ensure surprises as well as useful learning.

Such assessments can be used for any of the purposes described in Table 11.1, although many researchers[98] and practitioners[99] maintain that it is best for development and feedback purposes rather than for salary or other administrative uses. The focus on development assures those participating—groups such as subordinates, peers, and customers—that the 360-degree assessment is being done to improve all involved and is not part of the competitive win–lose scenario that so often accompanies salary and promotion decisions. The focus is on evaluation of skills and competencies that are relevant for job performance in useful behavioral terms. Information can be collected through rating forms, open-ended comments, or some combination of both. The 360-degree approach works best when results are filtered through a coach and combined with self-evaluation. Although many firms are using 360-degree assessments, they are most successful in organizations that offer open and participative climates as well as active career development systems.[100]

Studies have reported improvement in performance following 360-degree feedback, with the most notable results for those who initially rated themselves higher than the ratings they received from others.[101] The assumption of the 360-degree feedback process is that negative or discrepant feedback—that is, ratings that are lower than one's self-ratings—can create an awareness of the need to improve in specific ways. Although this is certainly the desired result, other studies have shown that it is not always the case. Some researchers have found that in approximately one-third of the cases negative feedback caused those who received it to be discouraged or to see the results as less accurate, particularly when the feedback concerned personal characteristics rather than task behaviors.[102]

The 360-degree system is believed to have a number of advantages over traditional assessment systems. Supervisors, peers, subordinates, and employees themselves typically differ in their ability to appraise various dimensions of performance. These raters observe different behaviors and may interpret them with divergent standards. Thus each source has access to unique information about performance.[103] Perhaps the best approach is to use as many different sources as possible to maximize the breadth of information and cancel out biases unique to a particular source. Multiple sources can be used regardless of which specific subjective method of measuring performance is adopted.

● **360-Degree Assessment at Lloyd Investment**[104]   In the early 1990s, Lloyd Investment implemented a 360-degree assessment system for 2,000 professional employees on a worldwide basis. The development and implementation of the system cost more than $1.5 million. The system involved feedback from superiors, peers, subordinates, internal clients, and the professionals themselves through a self-evaluation.

The 360-degree procedure began with the professional being evaluated selecting an evaluation director (ED), typically the person's manager or supervisor, to coordinate all aspects of the process. The evaluee then worked with the ED to identify those people within the firm with whom they regularly interacted and who would be in a position to provide substantive feedback on their performance.

Four broad categories were evaluated, although each was tailored to the particular job, tasks, and divisions involved: (1) market/professional skills, (2) management and leadership, (3) commercial orientation, and (4) teamwork, including cooperation with all Lloyd Investment units and employees. The list of evaluators, called the evaluation request form, was submitted to the Office of Development, which undertook the following series of steps:

1. First, the appropriate evaluation form was structured for each evaluator.
2. The evaluators were then directed to the intranet address where they were to provide their evaluative feedback to the professional undertaking the 360-degree assessment.[105] (The Office of Development used the computer to make sure evaluators were not overloaded with assessments. If a professional sought the rating of someone who had already done ten ratings, he or she received a notice that the individual was not available.)
3. The system then audited responses as they were submitted and checked to see that they fell within predefined limits, in this way preventing invalid input from being submitted.
4. A computer program was then used to create a ten- to twenty-page book of results for each professional from the evaluative feedback received.
5. Finally, this anonymous raw data was sent to the evaluation director to be interpreted and synthesized before being reviewed with the professional being evaluated.

Lloyd Investment clearly believed in the value of multiple perspectives in developing its professionals. Lloyd Investment's commitment to the process and results included the following:

1. The initial cost of developing and implementing the system
2. The creation of an Office of Development to coordinate all administrative aspects of each 360-degree evaluation
3. The time and effort of employees throughout the firm in participating in the 360-degree evaluation of others
4. The commitment of the 2,000 professionals and their managers or supervisors (in serving as EDs)

There is little doubt that 360-degree assessment has received much attention in the past decade. A growing number of U.S. firms have implemented 360-degree programs. Lloyd Investment is exemplary of an organization that is committed to 360-degree feedback and is willing to do what is necessary to assure the integrity of the process.

A variety of individual and organization improvement goals have been attributed to these assessment processes. However, despite the attention given to 360-degree assessment, there has been much more discussion about how to implement such programs than about why organizations have rushed to jump on the bandwagon or even what they expect to accomplish.[106] There has been little critical evaluation of the outcomes of 360-degree appraisal or the changes desired.[107] For example, Lloyd Investment provided a window into the type of commitment necessary to implement and sustain a 360-degree appraisal system. One might ask how many of the business firms rushing to adopt 360-degree assessment have the commitment to the system to assure its success.

Self-Managed Teams

More and more companies are looking to self-managed teams as the productivity and quality-of-work-life breakthrough of the twenty-first century.[108] The use of teams—groups of individuals organized to work together—for productivity improvement was discussed in Chapter 10. A survey showed that teams of various types are in use in nearly all of the *Fortune* 1000 companies.[109] Teams come in many forms. They may vary on the following characteristics:

- Temporary versus permanent
- Parallel to the existing organizational structure (most often used for temporary teams) versus incorporated into it
- Autonomous, semiautonomous, or working under the direction of a supervisor versus working independently
- Cross-functional—that is, made up of workers from several functional areas (e.g., product design, manufacturing, and marketing)—versus functionally homogeneous workers
- Full time versus part time (e.g., committees, quality circles)

Self-managed teams create special challenges for performance assessment. When teams perform highly interdependent activities, evaluating them using an assessment system that focuses only on individual results may be inappropriate as well as discouraging to the teamwork necessary to get results. In addition, when teams are working effectively, they manage themselves. There is no supervisor, yet historically it is the supervisor who has made performance assessment

● **TABLE 11.5**

A Partnership Approach to Team Appraisals

The performance appraisal team consists of the

- Team member being evaluated, the **evaluee.**
- Performance appraisal **chairperson,** the evaluee's advocate. The chairperson is selected by the evaluee.
- **Committee members,** two individuals selected by the chairperson from a list of all team members.
- **Management consultant** to both provide input into the evaluee's performance and facilitate the process.

Steps in the performance appraisal process include:

1. Evaluee selects the performance appraisal chairperson.
2. PA chairperson selects two committee members.
3. Evaluee provides chair, committee members, and consultant with a list of accomplishments and training for the previous year.
4. The PA team members provide feedback on the evaluee's accomplishments and training to the chair and the evaluee.
5. The evaluee writes his or her own performance appraisal document from the input received and sends a copy of the PA document to the committee for their review.
6. Following the committee's review of the PA document, the committee and evaluee meet. A final rating is determined, and the committee jointly sets goals for the evaluee for the next year.
7. The PA chairperson writes a summary of the meeting, including the ratings and recommendations. The completed document is signed by the committee members (including the management consultant) and forwarded to human resources.

Source: Adapted from Carol A. Norman and Robert A. Zawacki, "Team Appraisals—Team Approach," *Personnel Journal,* September 1991, pp. 101–104.

judgments about employees. For example, one company reorganized from a traditional structure of a supervisor for each group of fifteen to twenty hourly employees to semiautonomous teams with one division manager responsible for 150 workers.[110] There is no way a division manager can have sufficiently detailed knowledge of 150 employees to accomplish the specific goals of performance assessment illustrated in Table 11.1. Consequently, teams must assume responsibility either for developing a performance assessment system for their members or for applying an existing system to suit the purposes of the team.

As an example, one team-oriented organization uses a partnership approach to performance assessments, including self-assessments and ratings from peers.[111] The process, described in Table 11.5, is initiated when the team member, the evaluee, chooses an advocate of his or her work to lead the performance assessment. The advocate then assembles a committee to participate with the evaluee in completing the performance review and setting goals for the coming year.

It is important that both team and individual performance be measured. Understanding the team's objectives and each member's responsibility toward those objectives is one of the keys to successful team evaluation.[112] The team must begin by understanding its customers and the work process that will be followed to satisfy customer needs. Otherwise, processes for team performance evaluation are not that different than those for individual assessment. Methods used to appraise performance should be free from (system and personal) bias and should be designed to enhance performance. Finally, team members must be trained to collect and act on the information: feeding it back to other team members, addressing performance issues, setting goals, and so forth.

ENHANCING THE MEASUREMENT OF EMPLOYEE PERFORMANCE

In developing a performance assessment system, particularly one that involves subjective evaluations of performance, a number of serious problems must be overcome. Training evaluators and giving them feedback are ways to improve raters' ability to make accurate assessments.

Training Evaluators

Several rater training programs have been developed that aim to help evaluators produce reliable and accurate performance ratings. Programs can generally be classified into three types: rater-error training, frame-of-reference training, and information-processing training.

● **Rater-Error Training**   People can be taught how to reduce rating errors, such as leniency, severity, central tendency, and halo errors.[113] In **rater-error training (RET),** evaluators view examples of the common errors and receive suggestions on how to avoid them. RET has been found effective in reducing common rating errors. Several critics, however, have argued that error reduction often comes at the expense of rating accuracy.[114] For example, if a supervisor has many high-performing employees, all of them should be rated high. If the supervisor decides to avoid the appearance of leniency error by lowering the ratings of some employees, the evaluations become less accurate. In this manner, a risk of training is replacing one response set (leniency) with another (reduced accuracy).

● **Frame-of-Reference Training**   Attempts have been made to reduce errors by developing a common frame of reference among raters for evaluating performance.[115] Examples of actual employee behavior in the organization are used to develop norms for good and poor performance. Raters are then trained to observe these behaviors and use them as the standard against which to judge the performance of employees. The goal is the development of a common appraisal language, including agreed-upon labels and a shared nomenclature.

In a review of the effectiveness of rater training programs, four of seven studies using **frame-of-reference (FOR) training** were reported to have reduced leniency error. Only three of ten studies using FOR training to reduce halo error reported positive results.[116] Another study focused on implementation problems associated with FOR training, including procedures to identify incidents and then to understand differences between supervisors and subordinates with respect to appropriate frames of reference.[117] It appears that many of the implementation issues associated with FOR training can be overcome but that FOR training is most useful in improving rating accuracy when combined with other methods.[118]

● **Information-Processing Approaches**   Some training efforts focus on how performance raters observe, store, recall, and use information. In a 1980 study, raters were trained to avoid eight different "errors of observation."[119] Their accuracy in observing and remembering behavior improved, but no measures of rating error or rating accuracy were taken. Another study introduced two information-processing methods of rater training that did increase rater accuracy.[120] **Observation training** (similar to the approach used in the 1980 study) focused on helping raters to improve the way they observed the behavior of employees and to identify important performance activities. **Decision-making training** introduced raters to good strategies for use in decision making and helped them identify mistakes in inference that supervisors often make when appraising performance. (Given several accurate pieces of information, a supervisor may make inappropriate inferences about them and their relation to one another and end up making a bad decision.)

● **Which Training Method Is Best?**   Since rater error training and frame-of-reference training have had limited success, information-processing approaches may be the most promising methods for improving rating accuracy. However, regardless of which training method is used, raters who are actively involved in their training programs are more likely to learn to reduce rating errors. Involvement may be in the form of group discussions or of practice rating an employee whose performance has been videotaped. Practice rating is followed by feedback on what the most accurate rating would have been. Both practice and feedback seem to be essential for effective training. Neither discussion nor lecture without practice and feedback has been shown to reduce rating errors.[121] Ultimately, it comes down to rater motivation to rate accurately, and, as discussed previously (see the section on intentional errors), accurate ratings frequently lead to more challenges for already-overworked managers.[122]

Feedback to Evaluators

Since feedback is an important component of successful training programs, rating the raters may be a good way to reduce systematic bias.[123] One approach is to structure an evaluator's own performance assessment so that it pays attention to how well and accurately he or she rates the performance of others; that is, supervisors should be assessed on how well they appraise their subordinates. This approach should enhance motivation for the rating process and let raters know what others think of their evaluations. Another possibility is to require that their own superiors endorse supervisors' assessment ratings. Called a one-over-one review to connote the two levels of evaluation, this is a common method of achieving additional accountability and the accuracy associated with it.[124] In this manner the person doing the rating of subordinates has to defend them to at least one other person. The superiors provide quality control by helping prevent extreme leniency, severity, or central tendency errors in the ratings. The second level of review also assures a degree of consistency in evaluations across departments within an organization.

FEEDBACK OF RESULTS: THE PERFORMANCE ASSESSMENT INTERVIEW

One of the potentially most important aspects of performance management is providing performance feedback to employees. In order to improve performance, employees need information (feedback) about their performance, along with guidance in reaching the next level of results. Most theories of work motivation point out that before employees can improve their performance, they must know how well they are currently doing.

In the usual situation, neither the supervisor nor the employee looks forward to the assessment interview. It can be an uncomfortable and anxiety-provoking experience for both parties. One would expect a supervisor to be apprehensive about discussing a negative evaluation with an employee, but most managers see little or no practical value in conducting performance assessment interviews, no matter what the evaluation.[125] Conducting a good interview requires a great deal of effort and skill on the part of the supervisor. This section considers several types of feedback interviews, problems that can occur in giving feedback, and ways to improve the process.

Types of Feedback Interviews

The feedback interview is a discussion between the supervisor and the employee concerning the employee's past performance and how that performance can be improved in the future. The three main approaches to feedback discussion are often referred to as "tell and sell," "tell and listen," and "problem solving."

● **Tell and Sell** In a **tell-and-sell feedback interview,** the supervisor tells the employee how good or bad the employee's performance has been and then attempts to persuade the employee to accept this judgment. The employee has no input into the evaluation. Because it is very directive and one-sided, the tell-and-sell interview can lead to defensiveness, resentment, and frustration on the part of the subordinate. It fails to recognize the possibility that the employee may have information pertinent to the evaluation—information of which the supervisor is unaware. The employee may not accept the results of the interview and may not be committed to achieving the goals that are set. This may lead to poor performance in the future.

For new employees or those who have little desire for participation, the tell-and-sell interview can be effective in providing feedback and improving performance. New employees often feel unqualified to judge their own performance and prefer to be told how they are doing and what is expected of them.[126]

● **Tell and Listen** In the **tell-and-listen approach** to the feedback interview, the supervisor tells the employee what has been right and wrong with the employee's past performance but then gives the employee a chance to react. The extent of the subordinate's participation in the interview can vary widely. The subordinate may simply be given an opportunity to react to the supervisor's statements or may be permitted to offer a full self-assessment, challenging the supervisor's assessment. There is evidence that subordinates prefer even very limited participation to none at all.[127]

● **Problem Solving** The employee has much more control over the **problem-solving interview.** Employees evaluate their own performance and set their own goals for future performance. The supervisor is primarily a helper and colleague rather than a judge and proffers observations and advice in a noncritical manner. An active and open dialogue ensues, in which goals for improvement are established mutually. The problem-solving interview is more difficult for the supervisor than the other types of interviews, but it is more likely to result in employee acceptance and commitment to the established goals. Training can help supervisors learn to conduct such interviews effectively. A drawback of problem-solving interviews is that some employees may prefer a more direct approach. Some may be hesitant to discuss poor performance with their supervisor, particularly if personnel decisions such as salary increases will be based on the interview.

The problem-solving approach is most consistent with the goals of performance management; that is, an ongoing, interactive process that is designed to enable a employee to develop to his or her full potential. For those employees uncomfortable in taking the lead, a tell-and-listen approach will get the discussion going before transitioning into a problem-solving approach for discussing employee development issues and planning for future performance.

Problems with the Feedback Interview

Two major problems complicate the process of giving feedback to subordinates. The first has to do with disagreement about the rated level of performance and the second with the use of the feedback interview for multiple purposes.

● **Disagreement and Defensiveness**   Supervisors and subordinates often disagree about how well the subordinate has performed. One review of studies found that the average correlation between subordinate and supervisor ratings was only 0.22.[128] Subordinates in the United States usually rate their performance higher than do supervisors. In only one of the eighteen studies reviewed were supervisors' ratings of subordinate performance higher than the subordinates' ratings of their own performance.

Even when supervisor and subordinate agree on the level of performance, they often disagree about its causes. Supervisors tend to feel that subordinates are personally responsible for their performance, especially poor performance. On the other hand, subordinates often (sometimes legitimately) blame poor performance on situational factors such as bad luck, lack of resources, or insufficient cooperation from others.[129]

Disagreement on either level of performance or cause sets the stage for subordinate defensiveness. The subordinate makes excuses for past performance and argues with the supervisor's rating. The subordinate becomes unable to listen and learn from any legitimate points the supervisor may have. Note that defensiveness is not restricted to employees who receive a low performance rating. One study found that subordinates who were judged "satisfactory" had lower satisfaction and commitment because they had expected higher ratings.[130]

Another author maintains that the traditional manager-to-subordinate performance assessment feedback is an authoritarian procedure—a parent–child type of exchange. It is suggested that as organizations move toward involvement-oriented working, a performance discussion based on the subordinate's self-review may be more appropriate.[131] Further, such a review has the advantage of forcing the manager into a counseling and coaching mode rather than a largely judicial one.[132]

● **Multiple Purposes**   Assessment interviews are often used to review past performance, convey administrative decisions, plan for future work goals, and discuss the employee's career goals and development needs.[133] This is a great deal to accomplish in a single meeting. In addition, supervisors must play two incompatible roles, judge and coach, in a multipurpose interview. For merit raise decisions to have credibility, they must be clearly linked to past performance. Thus it is wise to couple these two purposes in the assessment interview. However, conventional wisdom holds that it is counterproductive to discuss future goals and development in that same interview. Criticism of past work or announcement of a smaller-than-expected raise may make the subordinate defensive and unwilling to address performance-improvement issues seriously. Thus a separate interview a few weeks later has been recommended for developmental issues. This recommendation, however, which is accepted as gospel by many HR practitioners, is based on only a single study conducted in 1965.[134]

More recent research has challenged this view.[135] Two studies in field settings found that discussing salary issues did not hurt the developmental aspects of a feedback interview and, in fact, had some positive effects. Including salary discussion in the assessment interview may force the supervisor to give more specific feedback in order to back up the decision. Salary discussion can also energize the interview and elicit more subordinate participation. Perhaps, with sufficient skill and tact on the part of the supervisor, both administrative and developmental purposes can be served in the same assessment interview. A compromise position may be wisest: The supervisor can plan to talk about past performance, merit pay decisions, future performance goals, and development in a single interview; if the subordinate becomes defensive or upset after discussing past performance and salary, the supervisor can postpone the discussion of the future.

● **Impression Management in the Feedback Process**   Recent research has emphasized the role of impression management in the feedback process.[136] **Impression management** refers to behaviors by an employee designed to control how he or she appears to the supervisor. For example, impression management tactics could include (1) taking sole credit for positive events even when credit should be shared, (2) making the supervisor aware of one's accomplishments, (3) arriving early or staying late to give the impression of being a hard worker, or (4) taking an interest in the supervisor's personal life and perhaps doing personal favors.[137]

Poorly performing employees use impression management strategies to minimize the amount of negative feedback they receive. For the employee, the goal is one of maintaining positive self-esteem. At the same time, such strategies on the part of the employee meet the needs of the supervisor, who generally has an underlying reluctance to give negative performance feedback. In any case, impression management tends to skew the assessment and feedback interaction.[138] Several researchers have examined procedures for minimizing impression management in the appraisal process.[139] Suggestions to control the effects of politics and impression management are given in Table 11.6.

Improving the Performance Assessment Interview

Feedback is most effective in improving performance when it is specific, when the employee accepts it, and when it helps define clear goals for future performance.[140]

● **Feedback Specificity**   Feedback is particularly helpful if it comes from a behaviorally based assessment instrument and if the performance rating is backed up with specific examples of good or poor performance. A critical incidents log can be useful in providing this type of specific feedback. **Specific feedback** helps

TABLE 11.6

Recommended Steps to Control Impression Management in Performance Appraisal

Steps to Minimize Dysfunctional Politics and Impression Management
- Make sure appraisal has a single clear purpose—multiple purposes create potential conflicts.
- Make sure the appraisal criteria are well defined, specific, and relevant to the job—generic measures create more opportunities for distortion.
- Train raters on use of the appraisal and sensitize raters to impression management and its effects.
- Use developmental appraisals—they are less prone to politics.
- Use more than one rater and make raters accountable to upper-level review.
- Conduct appraisals in a climate of mutual trust and respect.
- Build top management support for appraisal system integrity.

Steps to Maximize Impression Management That Supports Organizational Goals
- Clearly communicate the goals of the appraisal process.
- Create consensus on the goals of the appraisal process.
- Make sure that appraisal processes are perceived to be uniform across the organization—perceptions that other units are more lenient or less lenient lead to dysfunctional politics.
- Build an organizational culture and climate that promotes integrity and consistency with organizational goals, e.g., the motivation of employees.
- Foster a climate of openness to encourage employees to be honest about weaknesses so as to promote self-improvement.
- Recognize employee accomplishments that are not self-promoted.
- Consider a separate rating process for appraisals that are linked to important outcomes.
- Give raters some flexibility to recognize ratees for value-added contributions that are not well-defined performance criteria.

Source: Adapted from Steve W. J. Kozlowski, Georgia T. Chao, and Robert F. Morrison, "Games Raters Play: Politics, Strategies, and Impression Management in Performance Appraisal," in *Performance Appraisal: State of the Art in Practice,* ed. James W. Smither (San Francisco: Jossey-Bass, 1998).

employees determine exactly what they should do differently to improve performance. Research has shown that subordinates prefer specific feedback in the assessment interview, even if it concerns poor performance, to assessments that contain only vague performance information.[141]

● **Subordinate Acceptance**   For feedback to be accepted by a subordinate, it must come from a credible, trustworthy source. Credibility is enhanced when the evaluator is seen as being knowledgeable about the subordinate's job, has had adequate opportunity to observe the behavior of the subordinate, and has clearly taken the time to prepare carefully for the assessment interview. Research has shown that feedback is more likely to affect subsequent performance when it comes from a believable source.[142] In addition, feedback should be given often and as soon as possible after both good and bad performance events so that employees always know where they stand and can quickly take any necessary corrective action. The formal interview should be the culmination of the ongoing, continual process of informal performance feedback. Nothing in the annual assessment interview should come as a surprise to the subordinate.

It may be particularly difficult for the subordinate to accept negative feedback. Destructive criticism and threats to the subordinate are ineffective and may cause subsequent performance to deteriorate.[143] Thus the supervisor should discuss specific incidents of poor performance in a considerate, constructive way. Two studies have shown that when the supervisor attributes poor performance to situational causes, the subordinate is better able to accept negative feedback.[144] For example, a supervisor may note that a salesperson fell far below sales goals but also acknowledge that the economy was in a downturn (a possible external cause of poor performance). The supervisor can then proceed to discuss what the subordinate might do differently to improve performance even when economic conditions are poor. This approach will help to minimize defensiveness on the part of the salesperson.

A number of studies support the notion that satisfaction with and acceptance of assessment feedback are a function of the subordinate's degree of contribution and participation in the assessment discussion.[145] Anything that moves the interview from an authoritarian boss–subordinate interaction to a discussion among two knowledgeable and committed individuals will enhance acceptance of the results.

● **Setting Clear Goals**   The process of goal setting has already been discussed in the context of performance management and MBO and as a productivity-enhancing technique. Whatever assessment system has been used, assessment discussions should culminate in specific goals that focus the subordinate's attention on performance improvement. Later the supervisor should follow up on goal progress and give additional feedback when necessary to help the subordinate achieve the desired level of performance.

Summary of Key Points

Performance management can serve a strategic function by focusing employee efforts on the types of behaviors required to successfully attain organizational goals. Performance management should be an ongoing, interactive process that is designed to enhance employee capability and facilitate productivity. The measurement portion of the system is called performance appraisal. Appraisals are also used (1) to make administrative decisions about employees, (2) to provide feedback for employee development, and (3) to evaluate HR policies and programs.

A good appraisal system should measure important job characteristics (relevancy), be free from extraneous or contaminating influences, and encompass all important aspects of the job (not be deficient). It should be reliable and avoid rating errors. Appraisal systems must be fair to minorities, women, and other protected groups. Appraisals must also be practical. Meeting all these criteria in an appraisal system is a challenge.

Performance measures can be characterized as objective or subjective. Objective and subjective measures can be used in combination. Subjective measures can compare employees with each other (ranking), or they can judge performance against absolute standards for the job (rating). A number of types of rating procedures can be used, including graphic rating scales, mixed standard rating scales, behaviorally anchored rating scales (BARSs), and behavioral observation scales (BOSs). Ratings may be obtained from subordinates, peers, or the employee being assessed, although most commonly the only rater is the employee's supervisor. An additional assessment system, management by objectives (MBO), features joint superior and subordinate goal setting and performance assessment against these individualized standards.

Traditionally, when one thinks of performance appraisal, it is in terms of supervisors evaluating subordinates. In addition to supervisors, raters of employee performance include the employees themselves, peers, subordinates, and customers, including "customers" internal to the organization. A new approach to performance assessment is 360-degree assessment, using many or all of the sources of feedback described.

Performance assessment is an important tool for motivating and improving employee performance. Unfortunately, its potential is seldom fully realized. Assessments can be improved by careful development of an appropriate assessment instrument, by training raters to use the system properly, and by providing feedback to raters as to how well they are performing their assessment and development functions with their own subordinates. The annual performance assessment interview is a valuable opportunity for the supervisor and subordinate to communicate about past performance, current concerns, and goals for the future. This meeting does not have to be an unpleasant confrontation and can enhance the relationship between the supervisor and the subordinate. When giving performance feedback to subordinates, supervisors must ensure that the feedback is credible, specific, constructive, and accompanied by concrete examples of poor or good performance. They should also allow an appropriate degree of participation and ensure that goals for future performance are set.

The Manager's Vocabulary

360-degree assessments
absolute standards
administrative uses of performance assessment
alternate ranking
behavior-based appraisals
behavioral observation scales (BOSs)
behaviorally anchored rating scale (BARS)
central tendency errors
cognitive information processing (CIP)

comparative procedures
contamination
critical incidents technique
decision-making training
deficient
developmental uses of performance assessment
forced-distribution method
forced-choice system
forced-ranking method
frame-of-reference (FOR) training
graphic rating scales
halo errors
impression management
leniency errors
management by objectives (MBO)
mixed standard scales
objective measures
observation training
opportunity bias
paired-comparison ranking
peer evaluations
performance appraisal
performance assessment and management
performance feedback
performance management
personnel measures
problem-solving interview
prototype
ranking
rater-error training (RET)
results-based appraisals
schemas
self-evaluations
severity errors
specific feedback
straight ranking
subjective measures
subordinate evaluation
tell-and-listen approach
tell-and-sell feedback interview
trait-based appraisals
weighted checklist

Questions for Discussion

1. In what ways can performance assessment and management assist an organization in ensuring congruence between strategic goals and the behavior of employees?

2. What strategic goals of Ford Motor were served by adopting the forced-ranking system? In what ways was the forced-ranking system counterproductive?

3. What purposes can be served by performance assessment and management?

4. How can an organization design a performance assessment or change one already in use to make it more consistent with legal mandates?

5. What types of errors characterize the performance assessment process?

6. If you were an employee, would you want to be evaluated by traits, behavior, or results? Why?

7. Why would a supervisor intentionally distort performance ratings of a subordinate? What can be done to prevent intentional distortion of performance ratings?

8. What are some of the advantages and disadvantages of using trait-based, behavior-based, and results-based types of assessment?

9. Compare and contrast ranking versus rating systems of assessment and management in terms of their advantages and disadvantages.

10. What are mixed standard scales, how do they work, and what special purposes do they serve?

11. What is the difference between a BARS and a BOS? Which do you think is better and why?

12. What does the cognitive information-processing approach to performance assessment say about how to improve assessment?

13. What is 360-degree assessment? In what types of organizations will it work best?

14. What are some of the impressive aspects of 360-degree as used by Lloyd Investment?

15. Who should rate the performance of employees? Explain your answer.

16. Why is the performance assessment interview important?

17. What is the range of styles in which a performance assessment interview might be conducted? For which situations might each style be best?

18. Is it possible for a supervisor to include discussions of past performance, merit raise, and future performance goals in the same assessment interview?

19. How can superiors increase the effectiveness of the feedback they give to subordinates?

20. How does the evaluation of teams differ from the evaluation of individuals? What evaluation challenges do teams create?

● Case 11.1
Performance Management at Jet Food Services

It is now the end of Teresa Ross's first year as regional manager for Jet Food Services. As regional manager, Teresa supervises a total of ten districts, each of which has a manager responsible for sales and service to customers in that area.

Jet Food provides contract food services for hospitals, schools, colleges, business firms, and other institutions that need meals prepared on site but that do not wish to be responsible for operating such services. Jet Food Services hires all necessary kitchen employees, purchases all supplies, and prepares meals in accordance with specifications agreed on with customers. The district manager is responsible for coordinating all customer activities. This includes planning, budgeting, hiring and supervising Jet's on-site representative (customer ser-

vice manager), customer satisfaction, and contract renegotiations.

Teresa was recruited after years of experience as director of food services for a multicampus university. In that job, she had oversight responsibility for the food services at several campuses. The Jet Food position offered an opportunity for continued growth and advancement.

In her first year, Teresa has concentrated on getting to know the district managers and the customers with whom they work. She spent more than a week with each district manager and visited each customer with him or her. At this point, she feels comfortable with her job and the knowledge she has gained of both operations and personnel, and it is time to appraise the performance of the district managers and to schedule review meetings with these employees.

Teresa's Assessment of Blake Mack Blake Mack is the longest-term district manager in Teresa's region. He completed less than one year of college, held several short-term jobs, and then joined Jet as a shift supervisor of the company's services at a large college. At present, he is completing twelve years of employment with Jet. He has been a district manager for three years.

In working with Blake, Teresa has observed his strengths, along with some problems. Blake has a talent for working with people, Jet employees and customers alike. In fact, in his years with Jet, no customer he worked with has ever switched to a competitor. Many on-site supervisors recruited, trained, and supervised by Blake have gone on to become managers of other districts.

On the other hand, Blake's unhealthful eating habits—despite doctors' warnings—have contributed to some serious medical difficulties. During the past year, Blake was out of work for three months with gallbladder and heart problems, attributable in part to obesity. And Blake's behavior toward others can be overbearing. Teresa kept track of her phone calls from district managers during the year, and there were more calls (or messages) from Blake than from the other nine district managers taken together—calls to promote or advertise his own efforts.

Although Blake can be charming, he has started to be loud and rude with regional personnel whom he perceives as excessively rule-oriented. All in all, Blake's style and appearance have become entirely different from what Teresa is accustomed to in colleagues and employees.

Further, it has been announced that Teresa's region is going to be expanded and that a new position, that of assistant regional manager, will be created. Blake has made it clear that as Jet's longest-tenured district manager in the region, he feels entitled to this promotion. However, Teresa does not feel she could work with Blake as the assistant regional manager. She feels that their management styles are too different and that Blake's behavior might irritate regional and corporate personnel.

As Teresa looks over Jet's performance assessment and management instrument, she realizes that her honest assessment of Blake's performance in his current job is generally excellent. She glances at the last page of the assessment and management form and the overall ratings from which she will have to choose. Jet's overall rating system is on a 1–10 scale, with 10 as outstanding; 7–9, different degrees of excellent performance; 5–6, satisfactory; 3–4, below average; and 1–2, unacceptable. Teresa is uncertain as to what overall rating to assign. If she gives Blake too high a rating, he will expect to be promoted. If the rating is too low, Blake will doubtless be angry, feeling that an injustice has been done.

Blake Mack's Self-Assessment and Management Blake sees himself as different from the other district managers. An outgoing, gregarious type, he loves to visit his customer locations and work with his company's personnel. His idea of a successful day is one spent teaching a customer service manager a new operating procedure or management technique. In fact, Blake is known to roll up his sleeves and teach Jet employees a new recipe or how to improve an existing dish.

Blake has worked for several district managers and has always liked to keep them informed about his activities, sometimes phoning two or three times each day. From discussions with Teresa, he is aware that she thinks many of these calls are not necessary, but he wants her to know how things are going with his employees and customers. He is also aware of Teresa's views regarding his ignoring medical advice.

Blake is proud of his career and of what he has been able to do without much higher education. He feels he is qualified to become a regional manager, and he looks forward to the possibility of promotion to the new assistant regional manager position as a step toward this ultimate goal.

Blake's Assessment Rating In reviewing the situation, Teresa decides to give Blake an overall rating of 6. She feels justified, given that Blake did miss months of work as a result of neglecting his health. She knows that Blake will expect a higher overall rating, but she is prepared to stand behind her evaluation. Teresa then goes back to considering the separate ratings she will assign and to making plans for their feedback review.

1. How would you describe Teresa Ross's approach to the assessment and management of Blake's performance?

2. Are Teresa's concerns with Blake's performance legitimate? Will Blake have justifiable reasons for feeling dissatisfied with the assessment and management results?

3. How could Jet Food's system of performance assessment and management be improved? If you were Jet's vice president of human resources, what changes would you suggest?

● Exercise 11.1
Assessing a Performance Assessment and Management Measure

This exercise is designed to give you hands-on experience in evaluating measures of performance that are actually being used by organizations.

Step 1. Two or three weeks before doing the exercise, obtain from an organization in your local area a copy of the assessment and management instrument that is used in assessing employee performance. If possible, find out something about how the instrument was developed. Also find out for which jobs the assessment and management instrument is used. Be sure that the name of the company is removed from all materials to ensure confidentiality. At least one week before the exercise, bring to class the assessment and management instrument, a description of how it was developed (if possible), and a list of jobs for which it is used.

Step 2. In class, break into groups of three or four. The instructor will have reviewed the assessment and management instruments and made an overhead transparency of each instrument. Each group will be given one instrument, the description of the development process, and the list of jobs for which it is used.

Step 3. Each group will assess its assessment and management instrument and prepare a brief analysis of it for the class. Among the issues that should be addressed in the analysis are the following:

- What type of performance information is being obtained—traits, behaviors, results, a combination?
- To what extent did supervisors, subordinates, and other job experts participate in the development process?
- Are the performance dimensions measured reasonable for the jobs involved?
- Are there any apparent deficiencies, irrelevant dimensions, or possible contaminants?
- Are the performance dimensions and rating anchors defined clearly enough so that raters will understand exactly what they are rating?
- Who should make the ratings—supervisor, peers, subordinates?
- Do any of the performance dimensions lend themselves to a more accurate rating by a particular type of rater or to more objective assessment?
- How would your group members feel if their performance were assessed using the instrument?
- How can the instrument be improved?

● Exercise 11.2
Developing a Measure of Performance

In this exercise, you are given brief descriptions of three jobs. In doing the exercise you may wish to fill in information about a job from your own knowledge or experience. Keep a record of any information you add to the description provided.

Step 1. Divide into groups of three to five. Your instructor will assign one of the jobs to your group. Read the description of the job assigned to you.

Step 2. Your group's task is to develop a system for appraising the performance of employees on this job. Prepare a brief presentation to give to your fellow students. In this presentation, you must specify the following:

- The types of performance information you will collect—traits, behaviors, results.
- The exact method by which you will collect the information and, in the case of subjective ratings, who will make those ratings.
- The steps you will take to ensure that the information collected is reliable and valid.
- How often the measure(s) of performance will be obtained.

Job Descriptions

Post Office Clerk. Receives letters and parcels and sells postage stamps and money orders. Weighs packages to determine charges. Computes cost of insuring and registering mail. Answers questions concerning postal regulations and procedures. Places mail into slots after sorting by mail code or destination. Takes complaints regarding lost mail or mail theft, fills out forms, and submits for investigation.

Emergency Dispatcher/Operator. Answers telephone calls from the public regarding emergency situations that require police, fire, or medical assistance. Gathers pertinent information from callers using oral questionnaire and records data on a computer. Communicates with police, fire, or medical units in the field, dispatching them to appropriate locations. Monitors location and activities of all field units continuously. On request from field units, checks warrants for arrest, stolen-vehicle reports, runaway reports, and so forth using computer.

Animal Keeper (Zoological Garden). Cleans animal enclosures by hosing, sweeping, raking, scrubbing, and removing manure, soiled bedding, and unused food. Maintains enclosure materials such as nest boxes, plants, decorative materials, and bedding. Feeds and waters animals, preparing diet as instructed by the animal manager. Inspects and monitors animals and reports injuries, illnesses, or unusual behavior. Assists veterinarian in capturing and immobilizing animals when necessary.

● Exercise 11.3
Performance Assessment and Management Update

The president of your company would like an update on business articles being written on performance assessment and management. Proceed with the following steps:

1. Find the Pathfinder homepage at http://www.pathfinder.com/

2. Search using the following: performance <and> assessment and management.
3. Read and summarize an article on employee performance assessment and management.

● Exercise 11.4
Computers in Performance Evaluation

Your organization is considering ways to use computers to streamline performance evaluation. Proceed with the following steps:

1. Find the SuccessFactors product page at http://www.successfactors.com/sf/products/index.shtml

2. Of the several computer-based products for employee performance evaluation, which do you think would work best?
3. Summarize the features of the product you have chosen, and explain why you think it is best.

Notes and References

1. Joann Muller, "Ford: Why It's Worse Than You Think," *Business Week,* June 25, 2001, pp. 80–89.

2. Ibid.

3. Cited in Mark Truby, "Forced Rankings Stirs Fierce Debate," *Detroit News,* April 29, 2001. (Available at http://detnews.com/2001/autos/0104/29/a10-218163.htm)

4. "On The Team" available at http://www.mycareer.ford.com/OnTheTeam.asp

5. Cited in Muller, "Ford: Why It's Worse Than You Think."

6. Barry Meier, "Ford Is Changing the Way it Rates Work of Managers," *New York Times,* July 12, 2001. (Available at: http://www.nytimes.com/2001/07/12/business/companies/12FORD.html?searchpv=nytToday)

7. Mark Truby, "AARP Joins Ford Age Bias Suit," *Detroit News,* July 8, 2001. (Available at: http://detnews.com/2001/autos/0107/08/c01-244536.htm)

8. Dick Grote, "Public Sector Organizations: Today's Innovative Leaders in Performance Management," *Public Personnel Management,* Spring 2000, pp. 1–20.

9. "Taming the Performance-Management Monster," *Training & Development,* June 1994, pp. 9–10; and Donald J. McNerney, "Improved Performance Appraisals: Process of Elimination," *HR Focus,* July 1995, pp. 1, 4–5.

10. Jai Ghorpade and Milton M. Chen, "Creating Quality-Driven Performance Appraisal Systems," *Academy of Management Executive,* Vol. 9, 1995, pp. 32–39.

11. Robert L. Cardy and Gregory H. Dobbins, "Performance Management," in *The Backwell Encyclopedic Dictionary of Human Resource Management,* ed. Lawrence H. Peters, Charles R. Greer, and Stuart A. Youngblood (Malden, Mass.: Blackwell, 1997).

12. James S. Bowman, "Performance Appraisal: Verisimilitude Trumps Veracity," *Public Personnel Management,* Vol. 28, 1999, pp. 557–576.

13. Ibid, p. 557.

14. Martha Gephart, "The Road to High Performance," *Training & Development,* June 1995, pp. 30–38.

15. Allan M. Mohrman, Jr., Susan M. Resnick-West, and Edward E. Lawler III, *Designing Performance Appraisal Systems—Aligning Appraisals and Organizational Realities* (San Francisco: Jossey-Bass, 1989).

16. Steve Kerr, "On the Folly of Rewarding A, While Hoping for B," *Academy of Management Journal,* Vol. 18, 1975, pp. 766–783.

17. Douglas G. Shaw and Craig Eric Schneier, "Team Measurement and Rewards: How Some Companies Are Getting It Right," *Human Resource Planning,* Vol. 18, 1995, pp. 34–49.

18. Nancy M. Somerick, "Strategies for Improving Employee Relations by Using Performance Appraisals More Effectively," *Public Relations Quarterly,* Vol. 38 (3), Fall 1993, pp. 537–539.

19. Brian D. Cawley, Lisa M. Keeping, and Paul E. Levy, "Participation in the Performance Appraisal Process and Employee Reactions: A Meta-Analytic Review of Field Investigations," *Journal of Applied Psychology,* Vol. 83, 1998, pp. 615–633.

20. I. M. Jawahar and Charles R. Williams, "Where All the Children Are Above Average: The Performance Appraisal Purpose Effect," *Personnel Psychology,* Vol. 50, 1997, pp. 905–925.

21. Alan H. Locher and Kenneth S. Teel, "Appraisal Trends," *Personnel Journal,* Vol. 67 (9), 1988, p. 139.

22. Timothy D. Schellhardt, "It's time to Evaluate Your Work and All Involved Are Groaning," *Wall Street Journal,* November 19, 1996, p. A1.

23. Society for Human Resource Management (SHRM), "Development Components Lacking in Performance Management Systems," December 15, 2000. (Available at: http://my.shrm.org/press/releases/default.asp?page=001215.htm)

24. See H. E. Brogden and E. K. Taylor, "A Theory and Classification of Criterion Bias," *Educational and Psychological Measurement,* Vol. 10, 1950, pp. 159–186; see also Jeffrey S. Kane and Edward E. Lawler III, "Performance Appraisal Effectiveness: Its Assessment and Determinants," in *Research in Organizational Behavior,* ed. Barry M. Staw (Greenwich, Conn.: JAI Press, 1979), pp. 425–478.

25. Hannah R. Rothstein, "Interrater Reliability of Job Performance Ratings: Growth to Asymptote Level with Increasing Opportunity to Observe," *Journal of Applied Psychology,* Vol. 75, 1990, pp. 322–327.

26. Chockaliangam Viswesvarar, Deniz S. Ones, and Frank L. Schmidt, "Comparative Analysis of the Reliability of Job Performance Ratings," *Journal of Applied Psychology,* Vol. 81, 1996, pp. 557–574.

27. Ibid.

28. David A. Hofmann, Rick Jacobs, and Steve J. Gerras, "Mapping Individual Performance Over Time," *Journal of Applied Psychology,* Vol. 77, 1992, pp. 185–195.

29. Hubert S. Feild and William H. Holley, "The Relationship of Performance Appraisal Characteristics to Verdicts in Selected Employment Discrimination Cases," *Academy of Management Journal,* Vol. 25, 1982, pp. 392–406.

30. *Brito* v. *Zia Company,* 478 F. 2d 1200 (10th Cir. 1973); and Gerald V. Barrett and Mary C. Kernan, "Performance Appraisal and Terminations: A Review of Court Decisions since *Brito* v. *Zia* with Implications for Personnel Practices," *Personnel Psychology,* Vol. 40, 1987, pp. 489–503.

31. *Price Waterhouse* v. *Hopkins,* 109 S.Ct 1775 (1989); and Bill Shaw, "Employee Appraisal Discrimination Cases, and Objective Evidence," *Business Horizons,* September–October 1990, pp. 61–65.

32. *Price Waterhouse* v. *Hopkins.*

33. Paul R. Sackett, Cathy L. Z. DuBois, and Ann Wiggins Noe, "Tokenism in Performance Evaluation: The Effects of Work Group Representation on Male–Female and White–Black Differences in Performance Ratings," *Journal of Applied Psychology,* Vol. 76, 1991, pp. 263–267.

34. Jon M. Werner and Mark C. Bolino, "Explaining U.S. Courts of Appeals Decisions Involving Performance Appraisal: Accuracy, Fairness, and Validation," *Personnel Psychology,* Vol. 50, 1997, pp. 1–24.

35. W. H. Holley and H. S. Feild, "Performance Appraisal and the Law," *Labor Law Journal,* Vol. 26, 1975, pp. 423–430.

36. J. T. Austin, P. Villanova, and H. Hindman, "Legal Requirements and Technical Guidelines Involved in Implementing Performance Appraisal Systems," in *Human Resource Management: Perspectives and Issues,* 3d ed., ed. G. R. Ferris,

K. R. Rowland. and M. R. Buckley (Boston: Allyn and Bacon, 1995).

37. Werner and Bolino, "Explaining U.S. Courts of Appeals Decisions."

38. K. Kraiger and J. K. Ford, "A Meta-Analysis of Ratee Race Effects in Performance Ratings," *Journal of Applied Psychology,* Vol. 70, 1985, pp. 56–65; and P. R. Sackett and C. L. Dubois, "Rater–Ratee Race Effects on Performance Evaluation: Challenging Meta-Analytic Conclusions," *Journal of Applied Psychology,* Vol. 76, 1991, pp. 873–877.

39. Michael K. Mount, Marcia R. Sytsma, Joy Fisher Hazucha, and Katherine E. Holt, "Rater–Ratee Race Effects in Developmental Performance Ratings of Managers," *Personnel Psychology,* Vol. 50, 1997, pp. 51–69.

40. Ibid.

41. Christopher S. Miller, Joan A. Kaspin, and Michael H. Schuster, "The Impact of Performance Appraisal Methods on Age Discrimination in Employment Act Cases," *Personnel Psychology,* Vol. 43, 1990, pp. 555–578.

42. Glenn M. McEvoy and Wayne F. Cascio, "Cumulative Evidence of the Relationship Between Employee Age and Job Performance," *Journal of Applied Psychology,* Vol. 74, 1989, pp. 11–17; and Bruce J. Avolio, David A. Waldman, and Michael A. McDaniel, "Age and Work Performance in Nonmanagerial Jobs: The Effects of Experience and Occupational Type," *Academy of Management Journal,* Vol. 33, 1990, pp. 407–422.

43. Cynthia D. Fisher and James B. Shaw, "Analysis of Officer Fitness Reports," prepared for U.S. Marine Corps as part of an Office of Naval Research research grant, unpublished.

44. Jeffrey S. Kane, H. John Bernardin, Peter Villanova, and Joseph Peyrefitte, "Stability of Rater Leniency: Three Studies," *Academy of Management Journal,* Vol. 38, 1995, pp. 1036–1051; and Peter Villanova, John Bernardin, S. A. Dahmus, and R. Sims, "Rater Leniency and Performance Appraisal Discomfort," *Educational and Psychological Measurement,* Vol. 53, 1993, pp. 789–799.

45. Brian E. Becker and Robert L. Cardy, "Influence of Halo Error on Appraisal Effectiveness: A Conceptual and Empirical Reconsideration," *Journal of Applied Psychology,* Vol. 71, 1986, pp. 662–671; R. Jacobs and S. Kozlowski, "A Closer Look at Halo Error in Performance Ratings," *Academy of Management Journal,* Vol. 28, 1985, pp. 201–212; and Barry R. Nathan and Nancy Tippins, "The Consequences of Halo 'Error' in Performance Ratings: A Field Study of the Moderating Effect of Halo on Test Validation Results," *Journal of Applied Psychology,* Vol. 75, 1990, pp. 290–296.

46. Jack M. Feldman, "A Note on the Statistical Correction of Halo Error," *Journal of Applied Psychology,* Vol. 71, 1986, pp. 173–176.

47. Nathan and Tippins, "The Consequences of Halo 'Error' in Performance Ratings"; William K. Balzer and Lorne M. Sulsky, "Halo and Performance Appraisal Research: A Critical Examination," *Journal of Applied Psychology,* Vol. 77, 1992, pp. 975–985; and Andrew L. Solomonson and Charles E. Lance, "Examination of the Relationship Between True Halo and Halo Error in Performance Ratings," *Journal of Applied Psychology,* Vol. 82, 1997, pp. 665–674.

48. For examples, see Kevin J. Williams, Angelo S. DeNisi, Bruce M. Meglino, and Thomas P. Cafferty, "Initial Decisions and Subsequent Performance Ratings," *Journal of Applied Psy-*

chology, Vol. 71, 1986, pp. 189–195; and Cynthia Lee, "Increasing Performance Appraisal Effectiveness: Matching Task Types, Appraisal Process, and Rater Training," *Academy of Management Review,* Vol. 10, 1985, pp. 322–331.

49. Daniel R. Ilgen, Janet L. Barnes-Farrell, and David B. McKellin, "Performance Appraisal Process Research in the 1980s: What Has It Contributed to Appraisals in Use?" *Organizational Behavior and Human Decision Processes,* Vol. 54, 1993, pp. 321–368.

50. S. T. Fiske and S. E. Taylor, *Social Cognition* (New York: Random House, 1984).

51. J. Crocker, S. T. Fiske, and S. E. Taylor, "Schematic Bases of Belief Change," in *Attitudinal Judgment,* ed. R. Eiser (New York: Springer-Verlag, 1984), pp. 197–226.

52. Cited in C. O. Longenecker, H. P. Sims, and D. A. Gioia, "Behind the Mask: The Politics of Employee Appraisal," *Academy of Management Executive,* Vol. 1, 1987, pp. 183–193.

53. Neil M. A. Hauenstein, "Training Raters to Increase the Accuracy and Usefulness of Appraisals," in *Performance Appraisal: State of the Art in Practice,* ed. James W. Smither (San Francisco: Jossey-Bass, 1998).

54. Cited in Dennis S. Gioia and Clinton O. Longenecker, "Delving into the Dark Side: The Politics of Executive Appraisal," *Organizational Dynamics,* Vol. 22 (3), 1994, pp. 47–57.

55. Beverly Geber, "The Hidden Agenda of Performance Appraisals," *Training,* June 1988, pp. 142–146.

56. Peter Villanova and John Bernardin, "Impression Management in the Context of Performance Appraisal," in *Impression Management in the Organization,* ed. R. Giacalone and P. Rosenfeldt (Hillsdale, N.J.: Erlbaum,1989).

57. Cynthia D. Fisher, "Transmission of Positive and Negative Feedback to Subordinates: A Laboratory Investigation," *Journal of Applied Psychology,* Vol. 64, 1979, pp. 533–540.

58. Gary P. Latham, Daniel Skarlicki, Diane Irvine, and Jacob P. Siegel, "The Increasing Importance of Performance Appraisals to Employee Effectiveness in Organizational Settings in North America," *International Review of Industrial and Organizational Psychology,* Vol. 8, 1993, pp. 87–132.

59. Frank J. Landy, James L. Farr, and Rick R. Jacobs, "Utility Concepts in Performance Measurement," *Organizational Behavior and Human Performance,* Vol. 30, 1982, pp. 15–40.

60. Ibid.

61. Ibid.

62. Gary P. Latham and Kenneth N. Wexley, *Increasing Productivity Through Performance Appraisal* (Reading, Mass.: Addison-Wesley, 1982).

63. *Brito* v. *Zia Company.*

64. Steven T. Hunt, "Generic Work Behavior: An Investigation into the Dimensions of Entry-Level, Hourly Job Performance," *Personnel Psychology,* Vol. 49, 1996, p. 51–83.

65. Larry H. Peters and Edward J. O'Connor, "Situational Constraints and Work Outcomes: The Influence of a Frequently Overlooked Construct," *Academy of Management Review,* Vol. 5, 1980, pp. 391–397; Peter Villanova and Marie A. Roman, "A Meta-Analytic Review of Situational Constraints and Work-Related Outcomes: Alternative Approaches to Conceptualization," *Human Resource Management Review,* Vol. 3 (2), 1993, pp. 147–175; and Peter Villanova, "Predictive Validity of Situational Constraints in General Versus Specific Performance Domains," *Journal of Applied Psychology,* Vol. 81 (5), 1996, pp. 532–547.

66. Latham and Wexley, *Increasing Productivity Through Performance Appraisal.*

67. H. John Bernardin and Richard W. Beatty, *Performance Appraisal: Assessing Human Behavior at Work* (Boston: Kent Publishing, 1984).

68. Frank J. Landy and James L. Farr, "Police Performance Appraisal," *JSAS Catalog of Selected Documents in Psychology,* Vol. 6, 1976, p. 83.

69. Walter C. Borman, Daren E. Buck, Mary Ann Hanson, Stephan J. Motowidlo, Stephen Stark, and Fritz Drasgow, "An Examination of the Comparative Reliability, Validity, and Accuracy of Performance Ratings Made Using Computerized Adaptive Rating Scales," *Journal of Applied Psychology,* Vol. 86, 2001, pp. 965–973.

70. John Greenwald, "Rank and Fire," *Time,* June 18, 2001, pp. 46–48; and Wendy Zellner and Stephanie Anderson Forest, "The Fall of Enron," *Business Week,* December 17, 2001, pp. 30–36.

71. Herbert H. Meyer, "Self-Appraisal of Job Performance," *Personnel Psychology,* Vol. 33, 1980, pp. 291–296.

72. Cited in Truby, "Force Ranking Stirs Fierce Debate."

73. R. Blake Jelley and Richard D. Goffin, "Can Performance-Feedback Accuracy Be Improved? Effects of Rater Priming and Rating-Scale Format on Rating Accuracy," *Journal of Applied Psychology,* Vol. 86 (1), 2001, pp. 134–144.

74. Garry L. Hughes and Erich P. Prien, "An Evaluation of Alternate Scoring Methods for the Mixed Standard Scale," *Personnel Psychology,* Vol. 39, 1986, pp. 839–847.

75. F. E. Saal and F. J. Landy, "The Mixed Standard Scale: An Evaluation," *Organizational Behavior and Human Performance,* Vol. 18, 1977, pp. 19–35.

76. Bernardin and Beatty, *Performance Appraisal,* p. 98.

77. Angelo S. DeNisi and Lawrence H. Peters, "Organization of Information in Memory and the Performance Appraisal Process: Evidence from the Field," *Journal of Applied Psychology,* Vol. 81, 1996, pp. 717–737.

78. T. A. DeCotiis, "An Analysis of the External Validity and Applied Relevance of Three Rating Formats," *Organizational Behavior and Human Performance,* Vol. 19, 1977, pp. 247–266; Kevin R. Murphy and J. I. Constans, "Behavioral Anchors as a Source of Bias in Rating," *Journal of Applied Psychology,* Vol. 72, 1987, pp. 573–577; and Michael J. Piotrowski, Janet L. Barnes-Farrell, and Francine H. Esrig, "Behaviorally Anchored Bias: A Replication and Extension of Murphy and Constans," *Journal of Applied Psychology,* Vol. 74, 1989, pp. 823–826.

79. Latham and Wexley, *Increasing Productivity Through Performance Appraisal.*

80. Ibid.

81. Robert Rodgers and John E. Hunter, "Impact of Management by Objectives on Organizational Productivity," *Journal of Applied Psychology,* Vol. 76, 1991, pp. 322–336.

82. Michael K. Mount, Timothy A. Judge, Steven E. Scullen, Marcia R. Sytsma, and Sarah A. Hezlett, "Trait, Rater and Level Effects in 360-Degree Performance Ratings," *Personnel Psychology,* Vol. 51, 1998, pp. 557–576.

83. G. C. Thornton III, "Psychometric Properties of Self-Appraisals of Job Performance," *Personnel Psychology,* Vol. 33, 1980, pp. 263–271; and M. K. Mount, "Psychometric Properties of Subordinate Ratings of Managerial Performance," *Personnel Psychology,* Vol. 37, 1984, pp. 687–702.

84. M. M. Harris and J. Schaubroeck, "A Meta-Analysis of Self–Supervisor, Self–Peer, and Peer–Supervisor Ratings," *Personnel Psychology,* Vol. 41, 1988, p. 43–62.

85. J. M. Conway and A. I. Huffcutt, "Psychometric Properties of Multisource Performance Ratings: A Meta-Analysis of Subordinate, Supervisor, Peer, and Self-Ratings. *Human Performance,* Vol. 10, 1997, pp. 331–360.

86. Jeffrey D. Facteau and S. Bartholomew Craig, "Are Performance Appraisal Ratings from Different Rating Sources Comparable?" *Journal of Applied Psychology,* Vol. 86, 2001, pp. 215–227.

87. George C. Thornton III, "Psychometric Properties of Self-Appraisals of Performance," *Personnel Psychology,* Vol. 33, 1980, pp. 263–271; Harris and Schaubroeck, "A Meta-Analysis of Self–Supervisor, Self–Peer, and Peer–Supervisor Ratings"; and Brian W. Schrader and Dirk D. Steiner, "Common Comparison Standards: An Approach to Improving Agreement Between Self and Supervisory Performance Ratings," *Journal of Applied Psychology,* Vol. 81, 1996, pp. 813–820.

88. Donald J. Campbell and Cynthia Lee, "Self-Appraisal in Performance Evaluation: Development Versus Education," *Academy of Management Review,* Vol. 13, 1988, pp. 302–314.

89. Kenneth N. Wexley and Richard Klimoski, "Performance Appraisal: An Update," in *Research in Personnel and Human Resources Management,* Vol. 2, ed. Kendrith M. Rowland and Gerald R. Ferris (Greenwich, Conn.: JAI Press, 1984), pp. 35–80.

90. Glenn M. McEvoy and Paul F. Buller, "User Acceptance of Peer Appraisals in an Industrial Setting," *Personnel Psychology,* Vol. 40, 1987, pp. 785–797.

91. Joann S. Lublin, "Turning the Tables: Underlings Evaluate Bosses," *Wall Street Journal,* October 4, 1994, pp. B1, B14; Sue Shellenbarger, "Reviews from Peers Instruct and Sting," *Wall Street Journal,* October 4, 1994, pp. B1, B4; "Companies Where Employees Rate Executives," *Fortune,* December 17, 1993, p. 128; Joyce E. Santora, "Rating the Boss at Chrysler," *Personnel Journal,* May 1992, pp. 41–45; and Oren Harari, "How Am I Doing?" *Management Review,* November 1992, pp. 55–57.

92. David Antonioni, "The Effects of Feedback Accountability on Upward Appraisal Ratings," *Personnel Psychology,* Vol. 47, 1994, pp. 349–356.

93. James W. Smither, Manuel London, Nicholas L. Vasilopoulos, Richard R. Reilly, Roger E. Millsap, and Nat Salvemini, "An Examination of the Effects of an Upward Feedback Program over Time," *Personnel Psychology,* Vol. 48, 1995, pp. 1–34.

94. Leonard L. Berry and A. Parasuraman, *Marketing Services: Competing Through Quality* (New York: Free Press, 1991).

95. Leanne Atwater and David Waldman, "Accountability in 360 Degree Feedback," *HRMagazine,* May 1998, pp. 96–104.

96. Richard Lepsinger and Anntoinette D. Lucia, *The Art and Science of 360° Feedback* (San Francisco: Pfeiffer, 1997).

97. David Antonioni, "Designing an Effective 360-Degree Appraisal Feedback Process," *Organizational Dynamics,* Vol. 25, Autumn 1996, pp. 24–38.

98. David W. Bracken, Maxine A. Dalton, Robert A. Jako, Cynthia D. McCauley, and Victoria Pollman, *Should 360-Degree Feedback Be Used Only for Developmental Purposes?* (Greensboro, N.C.: Center for Creative Leadership, 1997); Ellen Van Velsor, Jean Brittain Leslie, and John W. Fleenor. *Choosing 360: A Guide to Evaluating Multi-Rater Feedback Instruments for Management Development* (Greensboro, NC: Center for Creative

Leadership, 1997); and Walter W. Tornow and Manuel London (eds.), *Maximizing the Value of 360-Degree Feedback* (San Francisco: Jossey-Bass, 1998).

99. Brian O' Reilly, "360-Degree Feedback Can Change Your Life," *Fortune,* October 17, 1994, pp. 93–100; Peter Ward, *360-Degree Feedback* (London, Institute of Personnel and Development, 1997); Atwater and Waldman, "Accountability in 360 Degree Feedback"; and Susan J. Wells, "A New Road: Traveling Beyond 360-Degree Evaluation," *HR Magazine,* September 1999, pp. 83–91.

100. Bob Cardy and Greg Dobbins, "The Changing Face of Performance Appraisal: Customer Evaluations and 360° Appraisals," *Human Resources Division News,* Vol. 16, Spring 1993, pp. 17–18; and David A. Waldman, Leanne E. Atwater, and David Antonioni, "Has 360-Degree Feedback Gone Amok?" *Academy of Management Executive,* Vol. 12 (2), 1998, pp. 86–94.

101. L. E. Atwater, P. Roush, and A. Fischthal, "The Influence of Upward Feedback on Self- and Follower Ratings of Leadership," *Personnel Psychology,* Vol. 48, 1995, pp. 35–60; J. W. Johnson and K. L. Ferstl, "The Effects of Interrater and Self-Other Agreement on Performance Improvement Following Upward Feedback," *Personnel Psychology,* Vol. 52, 1999, pp. 271–303; and R. R. Reilly, J. W. Smither, and N. L. Vasilopoulos, "A Longitudinal Study of Upward Feedback," *Personnel Psychology,* Vol. 49, 1996, pp. 599–612.

102. A. N. Kluger and A. DeNisi, "The Effects of Feedback Interventions on Performance: A Historical Review, a Meta-Analysis, and a Preliminary Feedback Intervention Theory," *Psychological Bulletin,* Vol. 119, 1996, pp. 254–284; and Joan F. Brett and Leanne E. Atwater, "360° Feedback: Accuracy, Reactions, and Perceptions of Usefulness," *Journal of Applied Psychology,* Vol. 86, 2001, pp. 930–942.

103. Kane and Lawler, "Performance Appraisal Effectiveness"; David W. Bracken, "Straight Talk About Multirater Feedback," *Training & Development,* September 1994, pp. 44–51.

104. Fictitious company as example of 360-degree appraisal.

105. Jim Meade, "Visual 360: A Performance Appraisal System That's 'Fun'," *HRMagazine,* July 1999, pp. 118–122; G. Douglas Huet-Cox, Tjai M. Nielsen, and Eric Sundstrom, "Get the Most from 360-Degree Feedback: Put It on the Internet," *HRMagazine,* May 1999, pp. 92–103; David W. Bracken, Lynn Summers, and John Fleenor, "High-Tech 360," *Training & Development,* August 1998, pp. 42–45.

106. Waldman, Atwater, and Antonioni, "Has 360 Degree Feedback Gone Amok?"

107. A. S. DeNisi and A. N. Kluger, "Feedback Effectiveness: Can 360-Degree Appraisals Be Improved?" *Academy of Management Executive,* Vol. 14, 2000, pp. 129–139; and J. Ghorpade, "Managing Five Paradoxes of 360-Degree Feedback," *Academy of Management Executive,* Vol. 14, 2000, pp. 140–150.

108. S. Jay Liebowitz and Kevin T. Holden, "Are Self-Managing Teams Worthwhile? A Tale of Two Companies," *SAM Advanced Management Journal,* Spring 1995, pp. 11–17.

109. Edward Lawler and Susan Cohen, *American Compensation Journal,* Vol. 1, 1992, pp. 16–19.

110. Shaw and Schneier, "Team Measurement and Rewards."

111. Carol A. Norman and Robert A. Zawacki, "Team Appraisals—Team Approach," *Personnel Journal,* September 1991, pp. 101–104.

112. Susanne G. Scott and Walter O. Einstein, "Strategic Performance Appraisal in Team-Based Organizations: One Size Does Not Fit All," *Academy of Management Executive,* Vol. 15, 2001, pp. 107–116.

113. H. John Bernardin, "Effects of Rater Training on Halo Errors in Student Ratings of Instructors," *Journal of Applied Psychology,* Vol. 63, 1978, pp. 301–308.

114. H. John Bernardin and M. R. Buckley, "Strategies in Rater Training," *Academy of Management Review,* Vol. 6, 1984, pp. 205–212; Jerry W. Hedge and Michael J. Kavanagh, "Improving the Accuracy of Performance Evaluations: Comparison of Three Methods of Performance Appraiser Training," *Journal of Applied Psychology,* Vol. 73, 1988, pp. 68–73; and Kevin R. Murphy and William K. Balzer, "Rater Errors and Rating Accuracy," *Journal of Applied Psychology,* Vol. 74, 1989, pp. 619–624.

115. H. John Bernardin, "Rater Training: A Critique and Reconceptualization," *Proceedings of the Academy of Management,* August 1979, pp. 131–135; Bernardin and Buckley, "Strategies in Rater Training."

116. David E. Smith, "Training Programs for Performance Appraisal: A Review," *Academy of Management Review,* Vol. 11, 1986, pp. 22–40.

117. Neil M. A. Hauenstein and Roseanne J. Foti, "From Laboratory to Practice: Neglected Issues in Implementing Frame-of-Reference Rater Training," *Personnel Psychology,* Vol. 42, 1989, pp. 359–378.

118. Lorne M. Sulsky and David V. Day, "Frame-of-Reference Training and Cognitive Categorization: An Empirical Investigation of Rater Memory Issues," *Journal of Applied Psychology,* Vol. 77, 1992, pp. 501–510; David V. Day and Lorne M. Sulsky, "Effects of Frame-of-Reference Training and Information Configuration on Memory Organization and Rating Accuracy," *Journal of Applied Psychology,* Vol. 80, 1995, pp. 158–167; and David J. Woehr and Allen I. Huffcutt, "Rater Training for Performance Appraisal: A Quantitative Review," *Journal of Occupational and Organizational Psychology,* Vol. 67, 1994, pp. 189–205.

119. George C. Thornton and S. Zorich, "Training to Improve Observer Accuracy," *Personnel Psychology,* Vol. 29, 1980, pp. 351–354.

120. Hedge and Kavanagh, "Improving the Accuracy of Performance Evaluations."

121. Bernardin, "Effects of Rater Training"; Robert D. Bretz, Jr., George T. Milkovich, and Walter Read, "The Current State of Performance Appraisal Research and Practice: Concerns, Directions, and Implications," *Journal of Management,* Vol. 18, 1992, pp. 321–352.

122. Michael M. Harris, "Rater Motivation in the Performance Appraisal Context: A Theoretical Framework," *Journal of Management,* Vol. 20, 1994, pp. 737–756.

123. R. R. Sims, J. G. Veres, and S. M. Heninger, "Training Appraisers: An Orientation Program for Improving Supervisory Performance Ratings," *Public Personnel Management,* Vol. 16, 1987, pp. 37–46.

124. Neal P. Mero and Stephan J. Motowidlo, "Effects of Rater Accountability on the Accuracy and the Favorability of Performance Ratings," *Journal of Applied Psychology,* Vol. 80, 1995, pp. 517–524.

125. N. K. Napier and G. P. Latham, "Outcome Expectancies of People Who Conduct Performance Appraisals," *Personnel Psy-*

chology, Vol. 39, 1986, pp. 827–837; Yitzhak Fried, Robert B. Tiegs, and Alphonso R. Bellamy, "Personal and Interpersonal Predictors of Supervisors' Avoidance of Evaluating Subordinates," *Journal of Applied Psychology,* Vol. 77, 1992, pp. 462–468; and Manuel London, "Giving Feedback: Source-Centered Antecedents and Consequences of Constructive and Destructive Feedback," *Human Resource Management Review,* Vol. 5, 1995, pp. 159–188.

126. J. M. Hillery and K. N. Wexley, "Participation in Appraisal Interviews Conducted in a Training Situation," *Journal of Applied Psychology,* Vol. 59, 1974, pp. 168–171.

127. Mary Beth DeGregorio and Cynthia D. Fisher, "Providing Performance Feedback: Reactions to Alternate Methods," *Journal of Management,* Vol. 14, 1988, pp. 605–616.

128. Harris and Schaubroeck, "A Meta-Analysis of Self–Supervisor, Self–Peer, and Peer–Supervisor Ratings."

129. T. R. Mitchell and L. S. Kalb, "Effects of Job Experience on Supervisor Attributions for Subordinate's Poor Performance," *Journal of Applied Psychology,* Vol. 67, 1982, pp. 81–188.

130. Joan L. Pearce and Lyman W. Porter, "Employee Responses to Formal Performance Appraisal Feedback," *Journal of Applied Psychology,* Vol. 71, 1986, pp. 211–218.

131. Herbert H. Meyer, "A Solution to the Performance Appraisal Feedback Enigma," *Academy of Management Executive,* Vol. 5, 1991, pp. 68–76.

132. Donald L. Kirkpatrick, *How to Improve Performance Through Appraisal and Coaching.* (New York: American Management Association, 1982).

133. M. W. McCall, Jr., and D. L. DeVries, "Appraisal in Context: Clashing with Organizational Realities," technical report prepared for the Center for Creative Leadership, 1977.

134. Herbert H. Meyer, E. Kay, and J. French, "Split Roles in Performance Appraisal," *Harvard Business Review,* Vol. 43, 1965, pp. 123–129.

135. J. B. Prince and Edward E. Lawler III, "Does Salary Discussion Hurt the Developmental Performance Appraisal?" *Organizational Behavior and Human Decision Processes,* Vol. 37, 1986, pp. 357–375.

136. James R. Larson, Jr., "The Dynamic Interplay Between Employees' Feedback Seeking Strategies and Supervisors' Delivery of Performance Feedback," *Academy of Management Review,* Vol. 14, 1989, pp. 408–422; Gerald R. Ferris, Timothy A. Judge, Kendrith M. Rowland, and Dale E. Fitzgibbons, "Subordinate Influence and the Performance Evaluation Process: Test of a Model," *Organizational Behavior and Human Decision Process,* Vol. 58, 1994, pp. 101–135; Sandy J. Wayne and Robert C. Liden, "Effects of Impression Management on Performance Ratings: A

Longitudinal Study," *Academy of Management Journal,* Vol. 38, 1995, pp. 232–260; Sandy J. Wayne, Robert C. Liden, Isabel K. Graf, and Gerald R. Ferris, "The Role of Upward Influence Tactics in Human Resource Decisions," *Personnel Psychology,* Vol. 50, 1997, pp. 979–1006; and Thomas E. Becker and Scott L. Martin, "Trying to Look Bad at Work: Methods and Motives for Managing Poor Impressions in Organizations," *Academy of Management Journal,* Vol. 38, 1995, pp. 174–199.

137. S. J. Wayne and K. M. Kacmar, "The Effects of Impression Management on the Performance Appraisal Process," *Organizational Behavior and Human Decision Processes,* Vol. 48, 1991, pp. 70–88.

138. Elizabeth Wolfe Morrison and Robert J. Bies, "Impression Management in the Feedback-Seeking Process: A Literature Review and Research Agenda," *Academy of Management Review,* Vol. 16, 1991, pp. 522–541.

139. Steve W. J. Kozlowski, Georgia T. Chao, and Robert F. Morrison, "Games Raters Play: Politics, Strategies, and Impression Management in Performance Appraisal," in *Performance Appraisal: State of the Art in Practice,* ed. James W. Smither (San Francisco: Jossey-Bass, 1998).

140. Barry R. Nathan, Allan M. Mohrman, Jr., and John Milliman, "Interpersonal Relations as a Context for the Effects of Appraisal Interviews on Performance and Satisfaction: A Longitudinal Study," *Academy of Management Journal,* Vol. 34, 1991, pp. 352–369; and Daniel R. Ilgen, Cynthia D. Fisher, and M. Susan Taylor, "Consequences of Individual Feedback on Behavior in Organizations," *Journal of Applied Psychology,* Vol. 64, 1979, pp. 349–371.

141. Meyer, "A Solution to the Performance Appraisal Feedback Enigma"; Daniel R. Ilgen, Terence R. Mitchell, and J. W. Frederickson, "Poor Performers: Supervisors and Subordinates' Response," *Organizational Behavior and Human Performance,* Vol. 27, 1981, pp. 386–410.

142. P. Christopher Earley, "Trust, Perceived Importance of Praise and Criticism, and Work Performance: An Examination of Feedback in the United States and England," *Journal of Management,* Vol. 12, 1986, pp. 457–473.

143. Robert A. Baron, "Negative Effects of Destructive Criticism: Impact on Conflict, Self-Efficacy, and Task Performance," *Journal of Applied Psychology,* Vol. 73, 1988, pp. 199–207.

144. Brendan D. Bannister, "Performance Outcome Feedback and Attributional Feedback: Interactive Effects on Recipient Responses," *Journal of Applied Psychology,* Vol. 71, 1986, pp. 203–210.

145. Campbell and Lee, "Self-Appraisal in Performance Evaluation."

Compensation System Development

HR Challenge

As compensation manager of Electro Tech, you have followed state-of-the-art practices in establishing internal and external fairness or equity. To establish internal equity, you undertook a traditional point-factor plan to evaluate the 160 different jobs in the organization. In fact, the plan you developed—several years ago—was commended in the industry trade journal as an innovative approach to job evaluation. As a result, other companies have adopted the plan.

External equity has been established through annual surveys of a nationwide sample of competitor companies. These competitors include companies in your industry as well as those in related industries, companies that represent potential employers of Electro Tech's technical talent.

It has now been several years since jobs were analyzed and evaluated. In response to your request for an additional assistant to coordinate efforts to bring the job evaluations up to date, the executive committee has expressed the view that such procedures are too bureaucratic and should be abandoned. Several of the executives have heard that many companies are rethinking the need to evaluate jobs, and these individuals feel that simply matching Electro Tech's pay ranges to those of competitors should be sufficient. The CEO has asked you to comment on these concerns before any decisions are finalized.

Although you too had heard of organizations' bypassing formal job evaluation, you had thought those were smaller companies. The notion of having no formal process to establish internal equity runs counter to your professional training and beliefs. There are benefits to job evaluation, so you are not sure how to respond. Can the procedures for establishing internal equity, procedures that companies have found valuable for over fifty years, simply be set aside? What effects would such a decision have on employee perceptions of the compensation system at Electro Tech?

An organization exists to accomplish specific goals and objectives. The individuals hired by the organization have their own needs. One is for money, which enables them to purchase a wide variety of goods and services available in the marketplace. Hence there is a basis for an exchange: The employee offers specific behaviors desired by the organization to meet its goals and objectives in return for money, goods, and/or services. Taken together, the money, goods, and/or services the employer provides employees constitute the employer's compensation system.[1]

The system that an organization uses to reward employees can play an important role in the organization's efforts to gain a competitive advantage and to achieve its major objectives. Compensation systems should do the following:

- Signal to employees (and others) the major objectives of the organization—such things as quality, customer focus, teamwork, and other goals—by emphasizing these through compensation.
- Attract and retain the talent an organization needs.
- Encourage employees to develop the skills and abilities they need.
- Motivate employees to perform effectively.
- Support the type of culture (e.g., entrepreneurial) the company seeks to engender.[2]

Ideally, a reward system should align individual objectives with important strategic goals of the organization, but for most organizations, the reality falls far short of this ideal. The design and implementation of a compensation system constitute one of the most complex activities for which human resource managers are responsible. The intricacy of compensation inspired the observation by one researcher that "reward systems are one of the most prominent and frequently discussed features of organizations."[3] The following are some of the factors that contribute to this complexity:

- While other aspects of human resource systems (e.g., training, career management, appraisal systems, and quality-of-work-life programs) are important to some employees, compensation is considered crucial by virtually everyone.
- One goal of a compensation system is to motivate employees, yet there is tremendous variation in the value different individuals attach to a specific

A DIFFERENT POINT OF VIEW

Some Myths About Pay

 Jeffrey Pfeffer has written an article claiming that managers often believe things about pay that are incorrect and, consequently, make ineffective decisions about how much to pay people and on what basis to pay them.

The first myth is: "Labor rates and labor costs are the same." That is, managers assume that they will save money by paying a lower hourly labor rate—that paying $17 per hour is bound to cost less than paying $21 per hour. This is not necessarily true. Total labor costs depend on productivity and the number of employees being paid as well as the hourly pay rate. If the employees a firm can attract for $21 are much more skilled and efficient than those it can get for $17, it may take fewer of them and fewer labor hours to produce the same amount of output. The labor cost per unit of output may actually be less at the higher wage rate! Hence myth number two—"You can lower your labor costs by cutting labor rates." As we have seen, hiring the cheapest labor available is not always a good strategy. These individuals may lack skills and motivation; the organization may incur costs due to high employee turnover (see Chapter 16); and customer service, quality, and productivity may be compromised.

Myth number three is: "Labor costs constitute a significant proportion of total costs." While this is true in some industries (like consulting, accounting, and legal services), in many others raw materials, plant, equipment, and distribution are much more expensive than labor. Trying to realize large overall savings by cutting labor costs is bound to fail if labor is a relatively small portion of total cost. Another reason to avoid just targeting labor costs in an effort to become more competitive is myth number four— "Low labor costs are a potent and sustainable competitive weapon." Anyone can offer low rates of pay. It is better in the long run to compete on a basis that cannot be so readily copied, such as innovation in design, high quality, or outstanding service. None of these three, by the way, are likely to be achieved by firms paying bottom dollar for talent.

Myth five is: "Individual incentive pay improves performance." While individual incentives certainly can motivate performance, there can also be some negative side effects from poorly designed incentive systems. This issue is addressed in more detail in A Different Point of View in the next chapter.

The final myth is: "People work for money." While it is certainly true that very few people will work without being paid at all, Pfeffer points out that individuals desire a lot more from work than just a paycheck. Firms that assume that money is the only motivator may fail to provide other outcomes that are actually very important in attracting, keeping, and motivating high-quality employees. For example, the SAS Institute has a very low turnover rate of sales and information technology staff. While SAS pays competitive rates, it does not offer stock options and the chance to become an overnight millionaire that are common in other IT companies. Instead, SAS focuses on providing meaningful work in a family-friendly atmosphere with stimulating colleagues and the latest high-tech equipment. The organizational culture and the satisfying day-to-day work activities and challenges keep people loyal, not the paycheck.

Source: Jeffrey Pfeffer, "Six Dangerous Myths About Pay," *Harvard Business Review*, May–June 1998, pp. 108–119.

reward or package of rewards. Further, an individual's values also may change over time.

- The jobs in most organizations involve an almost endless variety of knowledge, skills, and abilities and are performed in situations with a wide range of demands.
- Compensation systems consist of many elements in addition to pay for time worked; these components must be coordinated to work together.

- Employee compensation is a major cost of doing business—up to 80 percent for service firms—and can determine the competitiveness of a firm's products or services.
- A number of federal and state regulations affect compensation systems.
- Employees, either directly or through collective bargaining arrangements, may desire to participate in the determination of compensation.
- The cost of living varies tremendously in different geographic areas, an important consideration for firms with multiple locations.

All of the above lead to many myths about pay. The ideas of a leading researcher, Jeffrey Pfeffer, concerning the myths about pay are discussed in A Different Point of View.

In most organizations, the compensation system involves a multifaceted package, not just pay for work and performance. The components of the compensation system can be roughly divided into direct (wages) and indirect (benefits) forms of compensation (see Figure 12.1). This chapter discusses procedures for designing and administering a compensation system. Chapter 13 examines the special

● **FIGURE 12.1**

Components of the Compensation System

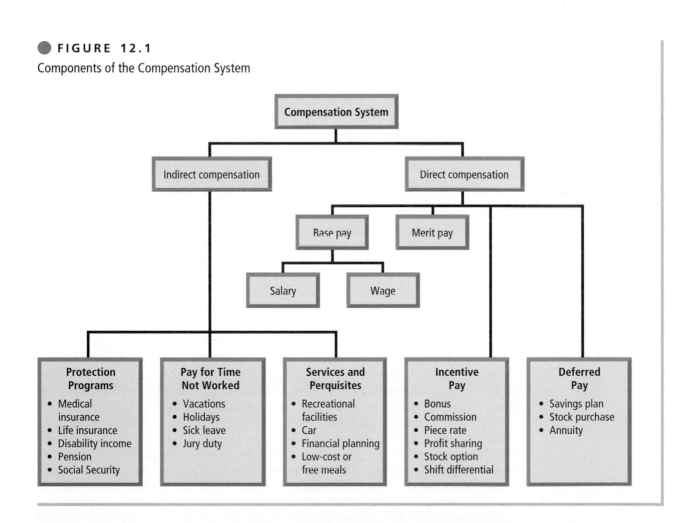

aspects of pay-for-performance systems, as well as indirect compensation. Taken together, direct compensation and benefits define **total compensation.**

EMPLOYEE SATISFACTION AND MOTIVATION ISSUES IN COMPENSATION DESIGN

People have no basic or instinctive need for money, a commodity that is important only if it can satisfy other needs. Organizations frequently overestimate the value workers place on monetary reward.[4] For example, if money were the primary motivation for working, why would hourly employees object to overtime, given the premium rate of pay associated with it?[5] Yet this is just what we see happening, as workers at several companies have strenuously objected to the amount of overtime they have been asked to put in.[6] In fact, when surveyed, just over half of Americans said they would rather have more free time even if it meant less money.[7]

Many supervisors become frustrated and disillusioned when pay increases do not produce a corresponding rise in productivity. Still more troublesome is the fact that the rewards that effectively motivate some workers do not succeed with others. The equity and expectancy theories (see Chapter 13) can help explain employees' reactions to compensation systems.

Equity Theory

Employees want to be treated fairly. *Equity* is the balance between the inputs an individual brings to a job and the outcomes he or she receives from it. Employee inputs include experience, education, special skills, effort, and time worked. Outcomes include pay, benefits, achievement, recognition, and any other rewards.

Individuals use a complex process to determine what is fair. Inputs are continually compared with outcomes—the individual's special skills and efforts are weighed against the pay and recognition given by the organization. However, inputs and outcomes are in different units and are hard to compare with each other directly. Thus **equity theory** suggests that individuals determine whether they are being treated fairly by comparing their own outcomes/inputs ratio with the outcomes/inputs ratio of someone else. This other person (or group of people) may be in the same job or in other jobs, in the company or outside the company, in the same industry or outside the industry. A sense of inequity arises when the comparison process uncovers an imbalance between inputs and outcomes of the employee compared with others.

Equity theory suggests that individuals will usually make some attempt to relieve the tension created by any perceived inequity.[8] An employee may perceive the ratio of his or her rewards and contributions to be less favorable than the ratio prevailing for others (see Figure 12.2). For example, a police officer may believe that he or she expends more effort at greater risk than is required of firefighters in the same community who receive the same pay. The police officer may seek to redress the inequity in several ways, perhaps by (1) reducing effort (e.g., writing fewer citations, spending more time in the doughnut shop), (2) working with colleagues to lobby the city council for higher pay for police officers, or (3) seeking employment in a community where police officers are paid more than firefighters. The desire to achieve equity even extends to the point of employee theft as a reaction to underpayment. A study measured employee theft rates before, during, and after a period in which pay was temporarily reduced

● FIGURE 12.2

Equity Theory

Person		Comparison Other

$$\frac{\text{My rewards (outcomes)}}{\text{My contributions (inputs)}} = \frac{\text{Other's rewards}}{\text{Other's contributions}}$$

Equity

$$\frac{\text{My rewards}}{\text{My contributions}} < \frac{\text{Other's rewards}}{\text{Other's contributions}}$$

Inequity (under-reward)

$$\frac{\text{My rewards}}{\text{My contributions}} > \frac{\text{Other's rewards}}{\text{Other's contributions}}$$

Inequity (over-reward)

Actions to Restore Equity from Underreward Inequity

Person could:
- Ask for a raise
- Reduce contributions (work less hard)
- Try to get other to increase contribution (work harder)
- As a last resort, quit the job or choose another comparison other

Actions to Restore Equity from Overreward Inequity

Person could:
- Increase contributions (work harder or longer, cultivate additional skills)
- Ask for a pay cut
- Attempt to get other a raise
- Attempt to get other to reduce his or her contribution
- As a last resort, quit the job or choose another comparison other

by 15 percent. Theft increased markedly in plants where pay was reduced; it returned to prior levels when normal pay was resumed.[9]

People also notice when they are overrewarded in relation to others. In such a case, the individual might work harder than he or she did previously or volunteer for an extra assignment to eliminate the perceived inequity. Research has also shown that motivation from being overcompensated is relatively short-lived. Most individuals quickly decide that they deserve whatever pay rate they receive and do not try to sustain a higher level of performance.[10]

Satisfaction with Pay

Survey data regularly show compensation to be one of the areas of employment with which employees are least satisfied.[11] For example, a recent study involving more than 50,000 employees from U.S. manufacturing and service organizations asked whether workers felt that they were paid fairly compared to others performing similar work for different employers. Nearly 60 percent of those surveyed reported that they were dissatisfied with their pay.[12] It is not unusual to find that individuals who are otherwise satisfied with their career and the organization for which they work believe that their compensation leaves something to be desired. Sometimes it seems that employees are never satisfied with their compensation.

One reason for the reduced degree of satisfaction with compensation has to do with the number of possible comparisons.[13] Individuals seem to seek comparison information from a wide variety of sources, both internal and external to the organization, and then hold to the least favorable comparison. If there are not unfavorable comparisons with those in their line of work, individuals may compare themselves to those in a related line of work. For example, a police officer may compare his or her pay favorably with other police officers working for the same city and other cities but feel underrewarded in comparison with the pay, benefits, and work expectations of federal marshals. Highly paid executives frequently attempt to justify their compensation by comparing it with that of top-level entertainers, who earn even more.

A successful compensation system needs to incorporate the equity concerns of all participants in the employment relationship. This is achieved by establishing a system that includes both external and internal comparisons in setting pay levels. In addition, it is more important to focus on the specific employees who are dissatisfied with compensation than on the overall level of satisfaction. If poor performers are dissatisfied, this may be the intended result.

Designing Equitable Compensation Systems

Three elements of equity can be distinguished: internal, external, and individual. **Internal equity** refers to the relationship among jobs within a single organization. Employees expect the president of a company to earn more than the executive vice president, who in turn earns more than the plant manager, and so on. Among other things, compensation is presumed to be correlated with the level of knowledge, skill, and experience required to do the job successfully. Thus no one is surprised that people high in the organizational structure earn more than lower-level employees do. Internal equity exists when the pay differentials between different jobs within the organization are perceived as fair—neither too large nor too small.

External equity refers to comparisons of similar jobs in different organizations (e.g., the pay received by presidents of various electrical manufacturing firms). It would be no surprise to learn that the president of a firm with annual sales of $1 billion earns more than the president of a $500 million firm. Presumably a doubling of company size requires more knowledge, skill, and experience on the part of its leader. Location matters, as well as industry and company size. When the administrative assistant working for an electrical manufacturing plant manager worries about external equity, the comparison is likely to be with administrative assistants at the automobile plant across town rather than with electrical manufacturers nationwide.

The final element, **individual equity,** refers to comparisons among individuals in the same job with the same organization. In many ways this is the most critical question. If it is not answered satisfactorily, attention to internal and external equity will have been wasted. For example, suppose the human resource manager establishes, through internal and external comparisons, that all administrative assistants in the organization should receive between $2,000 and $2,500 per month.

Achieving Distributive Justice:
Alternate Bases for Reward Allocation

The Ethical Perspective box in Chapter 11 distinguishes between procedural and distributive justice and emphasizes the importance of clear, fair, and open decision-making processes for attaining procedural justice. Although procedural and distributive justice are intertwined, this discussion focuses primarily on distributive justice.

Recall that distributive justice involves a fair result in the distribution of any type of outcome across people. Here we concentrate on the outcomes of base salary and pay increases and how they are allocated across individuals in the organization.

Whether or not a given pay decision (and the rules and procedures generating it) is seen as fair and just depends very much on the value basis chosen to underlie the decision. There are a number of bases on which pay allocation decisions can be made:

- *Equality:* Because all humans have equal value and dignity, all should be rewarded equally, regardless of ability, effort, performance, or any other factor.
- *Need:* Each individual should be rewarded according to his or her needs, with greater rewards flowing to those with greater needs, regardless of contribution.
- *Equity:* Each person should be rewarded in direct proportion to his or her individual contribution.

Socialist countries tend to emphasize the equality and need bases for reward distribution, and this is reflected in quite low pay differentials across levels. For instance, before China's reforms allowing small-scale entrepreneurship, the highest-paid people made only six times what the lowest-paid people did.

Reward allocation partly on the basis of need does occur in some situations in the United States, such as the housing allowances received by military personnel, which are keyed to the number of dependents as well as rank. Labor organizations often lean toward equality as the basis of compensation, at least within a single job category. However, Western work organizations and managers generally favor equity as the basis for reward distribution, with those who make greater contributions seen as deserving more compensation. Note that there is still ample room for disagreement on which contributions should carry the most weight in pay allocation decisions. The choices include education, experience, effort, quality of output, amount of output, job importance, length of service, and so on.

Research has shown that individuals will choose different bases for reward allocation depending on the situation. When the primary goal is to preserve group harmony, avoid conflict, facilitate cooperation, or prevent turnover, decision makers favor an equality basis for compensation decisions. When the decision is cast in terms of friendship rather than formal organizational roles, decision makers tend to distribute rewards on the basis of need, as one would do in a family situation. When the purpose is to weed out low performers, equity is chosen so that large pay differentials between high and low performers send an unmistakable message.

Thus there is no single basis for compensation decisions that will always be seen as fair. Justice seems most likely to be attained when the parties agree on the most appropriate basis for reward distribution, but such agreement cannot be assumed to occur without discussion.

Sources: Jerald Greenberg, "A Taxonomy of Organizational Justice Theories," *Academy of Management Review,* January 1987, pp. 9–22; Sara M. Freedman and John R. Montanari, "An Integrative Model of Managerial Reward Allocation," *Academy of Management Review,* July 1980, pp. 381–390; C. C. Chen, "New Trends in Reward Allocation Preferences: A Sino–U.S. Comparison," *Academy of Management Journal,* April 1995, pp. 408-428; Robert Folger and Russell Cropanzano, *Organizational Justice and Human Resource Management* (Thousand Oaks, Calif.: Sage, 1998); and Barbara F. Meeker, "Need as a Basis for Reward Allocation," *Advances in Group Processes,* Vol. 15, 1998, pp. 81–102.

The problem now is to determine the pay rate of each administrative assistant. Should long-service administrative assistants be paid more than those who have just been hired? If yes, what is the value of each additional year of service? Should pay differences be based on job performance? If so, how will performance be measured? How will the differences in performance be translated into pay differences? Employees must perceive that these questions are answered fairly in order for individual equity to exist (see the Ethical Perspective box).

There are accepted procedures for establishing internal, external, and individual equity within an organization. These procedures will be reviewed in the following sections.

ESTABLISHING INTERNAL EQUITY: JOB EVALUATION METHODS

The major purpose of job evaluation is to determine the relative worth of the jobs within an organization. A systematic comparison can define an internal job hierarchy that ranks jobs in terms of their relative contribution to the organizational objectives.

Fulfillment of a company's objectives depends more on the job done by its president than that done by its plant manager. But how much is the differential worth? Since there is no direct way to measure the value of jobs in relation to organizational objectives, rewards are usually based on important components generally agreed to make one job worth more than another is. These aspects, called *compensable factors,* may include such things as skills, effort, and education required; amount of responsibility involved; and working conditions.

Approximately 75 percent of all companies employ some form of job evaluation.[14] To be most effective, the process needs to involve the employees whose jobs are affected. The following questions need to be considered:

- Which of several possible evaluation procedures is to be used?
- Will one evaluation procedure be used throughout the organization, or will different procedures be used for broad classes of jobs (e.g., exempt versus nonexempt)?
- If the procedure that is selected takes into account several compensable factors, which of these factors are to be included, and how are they to be weighted?

The five most frequently used job evaluation methods are (1) job ranking, (2) job grading or classification, (3) the point method, (4) the Hay plan, and (5) factor comparison. As shown in Figure 12.3, these methods can be classified on the basis of the approach taken. Along one dimension are job ranking and factor comparison, which compare one job with another, versus the other methods that compare the job with one or more rating scales. The other dimension considers the quantitative sophistication of the procedures.

Job Ranking

Job ranking, the simplest way to evaluate jobs, is used primarily in small organizations. Normally, a committee of managers reviews all the job descriptions and ranks them in order of their relative worth or importance to the organization. The ranking method is simple, inexpensive, fast, and easy to understand. However, it is nonquantitative and rather subjective, for although jobs are compared with one an-

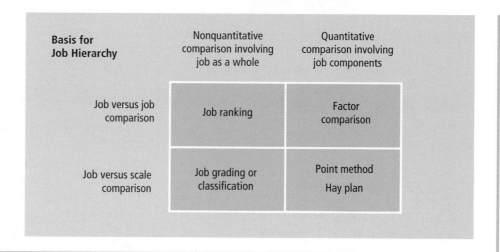

FIGURE 12.3

Job Evaluation
Procedures

Source: John M. Ivancevich,
"Job Evaluation Procedures,"
from *Foundations of Personnel.*
Copyright © 1992 by Richard
D. Irwin. Reprinted by
permission.

Basis for Job Hierarchy	Nonquantitative comparison involving job as a whole	Quantitative comparison involving job components
Job versus job comparison	Job ranking	Factor comparison
Job versus scale comparison	Job grading or classification	Point method / Hay plan

other, there is no explicit set of compensable factors used in this comparison. Additionally, simple ranking gives no information about the distances between jobs, making it difficult to assign salary levels. Even though there may be agreement that job A is more valuable than job B, the magnitude of the difference is not known. A final difficulty is purely practical. Except in a very small organization, there may be no one who is knowledgeable about every single job in the organization, as would be necessary for meaningful ranking.

A special method of ranking is the paired-comparison technique. This method was discussed in Chapter 11 as a means of comparing employees with one another on the basis of overall performance. In the job evaluation context, the content and importance of different jobs, not the performance of incumbents, is the object of comparison. In this approach, each job is compared directly against every other job, using a matrix of the type shown in Table 12.1. Reading across each row, an X is marked each time the job is ranked more highly than the job in that column. (For example, the executive secretary job is ranked higher than computer operator but not higher than systems analyst.) The totals column records the number of comparisons in which the job is ranked higher. This total determines the job's overall rank. Although this technique is somewhat more systematic than simple ranking, the number of comparisons increases quite rapidly as the number of jobs increases. Some evidence suggests that the paired-comparison approach is more reliable than simple ranking.[15]

Job Grading or Classification

The **job grading** or **job classification** method is a nonquantitative job evaluation technique that compares the whole job with a predetermined standard. In this approach, jobs are assigned to predefined grades or classes. Job grading is common in the public sector. The federal government's General Schedule (GS) has eighteen grades: fifteen grades into which most jobs are classified and three top "supergrades" that cover senior executives. GS 11 through GS 15 include general management and highly specialized jobs, GS 5 through GS 10 are for management trainees and lower-level managers, and GS 1 through GS 4 are for clerical and nonsupervisory personnel. Table 12.2 contains representative examples of the type of

● **TABLE 12.1**
Paired-Comparison Ranking Table

	Messenger	Data-Processing Manager	Data-Entry Operator	Executive Secretary	Computer Operator	Systems Analyst	Control Clerk	Programmer	File Clerk	Assistant Director	Total
Messenger	—										0
Data-processing manager	X	—	X	X	X	X	X	X	X	X	9
Data-entry operator	X		—						X		2
Executive secretary	X		X	—	X		X	X	X		6
Computer operator	X		X		—		X		X		4
Systems analyst	X		X	X	X	—	X	X	X		7
Control clerk	X		X				—		X		3
Programmer	X		X		X		X	—	X		5
File clerk	X								—		1
Assistant director	X		X	X	X	X	X	X	X	—	8

Instructions: Place X in space where job in row is more important than job ir column.
Source: Richard Henderson, *Compensation Management: Rewarding Performance,* 5th ed., © 1989, p. 199. Adapted by permission of Prentice-Hall, Inc., Englewood Cliffs, New Jersey.

● **TABLE 12.2**

Grade Descriptions and Representative Job Titles from the Classification System Used by the Federal Government

Grade Level	Grade Description	Jobs Included in Grade
GS 1	Includes those classes of positions the duties of which are to perform, under immediate supervision, with little or no latitude for the exercise of independent judgment: —the simplest routine work in office, business, or fiscal operations; or —elementary work of a subordinate technical character in a professional, scientific, or technical field.	Typist, messenger
GS 2	Includes those classes of positions the duties of which are —to perform, under immediate supervision, with limited latitude for the exercise of independent judgment, routine work in office, business, or fiscal operations, or comparable subordinate technical work of limited scope in a professional, scientific, or technical field, requiring some training or experience; or —to perform other work of equal importance, difficulty, and responsibility, and requiring comparable qualifications.	Engineering aide
GS 5	Includes those classes of positions the duties of which are —to perform, under general supervision, difficult and responsible work in office, business, or fiscal administration, or comparable subordinate technical work in a professional, scientific, or technical field, requiring in either case —considerable training and supervisory or other experience; —broad working knowledge of a special subject matter or of office, laboratory, engineering, scientific, or other procedure and practice; and —the exercise of independent judgment in a limited field; —to perform other work of equal importance, difficulty, and responsibility, and requiring comparable qualifications.	Chemist, accountant, engineer (civil), statistical clerk

Source: From *The Management of Compensation* by Alan N. Nash and Stephen J. Carroll (Copyright © 1976 by Wadsworth, Inc.) Reprinted by permission of the author.

grade descriptions used by the federal government. In the private sector, job classification is commonly used in managerial and scientific or engineering jobs.[16]

It is usually fairly easy for organizations to group jobs and for employees to accept the classifications. Flexibility is another advantage of the job classification method. It can be applied to a large number and wide variety of jobs. As the number of jobs in the organization grows, these new jobs can easily be assigned to the grades that already exist.

The job classification method has been criticized because subjective judgments are used to place jobs into the grades (e.g., when a job seems to fall between two grades). A related disadvantage is that the job classification method relies heavily on the use of job titles rather than on a more detailed examination of job content.

Point Method

As seen in Figure 12.3, unlike job ranking or classification, the **point method** breaks the job into components and evaluates each of these job elements against specially constructed scales. A quantitative approach, the point method is rather complex to design but relatively simple to understand and administer once it is in place. It is the most widely used method of job evaluation; well over half the organizations that use job evaluation use the point method.[17]

Four steps are followed in applying the point method: selection of compensable factors, establishment of factor scales, assignment of points to degrees, and application to organizational jobs.

● **Compensable Factors**   **Compensable factors** are those job dimensions or job requirements that will be the basis for paying employees. Organizations select three to twenty-five compensable factors, with the typical point method using about ten factors. The plan developed by the National Electrical Manufacturers Association (NEMA) involves eleven factors that are grouped into the following four dimensions: (1) skill (education, experience, knowledge), (2) effort (physical demand, mental or visual demand), (3) responsibility (equipment or process, material or product, safety of others, work of others), and (4) job conditions (working conditions, hazards).

● **Factor Scales**   Once the compensable factors have been chosen, scales reflecting different degrees within each factor are constructed. Examples of the scales for the knowledge factor are defined in some detail in Table 12.3. As much as possible, each degree is defined to be equidistant from the adjacent degrees.

● **Assigning Points to Degrees**   The next step is to assign points to degrees. First, however, the job evaluation committee decides on the relative importance of the different factors. For instance, in the system in Table 12.4, the committee has decided that experience is the most important factor and has awarded it the largest

● **TABLE 12.3**

Defining a Compensable Factor and Associated Degrees: An Illustration

Knowledge
This factor measures the knowledge or equivalent training required to perform the job duties.
1st Degree: Use of reading and writing, adding and subtracting of whole numbers; following of instructions; use of fixed gauges, direct reading of instruments, and similar devices; where interpretation is not required.
2nd Degree: Use of addition, subtraction, multiplication, and division of numbers including decimals and fractions; simple use of formulas, charts, tables, drawings, specifications, schedules, wiring diagrams; use of adjustable measuring instruments; checking of reports, forms, records, and comparable data; where interpretation is required.
3rd Degree: Use of mathematics with the use of complicated drawings, specifications, charts, tables; various types of precision measuring instruments. Equivalent to one to three years' applied trades training in a particular or specialized occupation.
4th Degree: Use of advanced trades mathematics, together with the use of complicated drawings, specifications, charts, tables, handbook formulas; all varieties of precision measuring instruments. Equivalent to complete accredited apprenticeship in a recognized trade, craft, or occupation; or equivalent to a two-year technical college education.
5th Degree: Use of higher mathematics involved in the application of engineering principles and the performance of related practical operations, together with a comprehensive knowledge of the theories and practices of mechanical, electrical, chemical, civil, or like engineering field. Equivalent to complete four years of technical college or university education.

Source: Adapted from *Compensation,* 3rd ed. by George T. Milkovich and Jerry M. Newman. Copyright © 1990 by Richard D. Irwin. Reproduced with permission of The McGraw-Hill Companies.

● **TABLE 12.4**

A Typical Point Plan

Factors	Degrees	Points				
		1st	2nd	3rd	4th	5th
Skill						
1. Education		14	28	42	56	70
2. Experience		22	44	66	88	110
3. Knowledge		14	28	42	56	70
Effort						
4. Physical demand		10	20	30	40	50
5. Mental demand		5	10	15	20	25
Responsibility						
6. Equipment/process		5	10	15	20	25
7. Material/product		5	10	15	20	25
8. Safety of others		5	10	15	20	25
9. Work of others		5	10	15	20	25
Job conditions						
10. Working conditions		10	20	30	40	50
11. Hazards		5	10	15	20	25

Source: Richard Henderson, *Compensation Management: Rewarding Performance,* 5th ed., © 1989, p. 204. Adapted by permission of Prentice-Hall, Inc., Englewood Cliffs, New Jersey.

number of points (110 for the highest degree). Education and knowledge are next in importance, followed by physical demand and working conditions, and then the remaining factors. Once the highest degree of each factor is given a point allocation reflecting its importance, the lower degrees are assigned proportionately lesser point values in accord with factor importance.

Note that the determination of factors and the assignment of points to these factors become an important mechanism for communicating to employees what is valued in the organization. The typical plan illustrated in Table 12.4 tells employees that experience, education, and knowledge are equal to all the other factors taken together. For example, an employee wanting to know what it takes to progress from the loading dock to more responsible and rewarding positions might think about evening courses at the community college.

● **Application to Jobs**   Once the compensable factors have been identified, defined, and assigned points, jobs can be evaluated and "scored." In this process, the job evaluation committee will thoroughly review job analysis data and perhaps observe the job or speak with incumbents. Then it will determine which degree of each factor best describes that job. The points associated with these degrees are summed for each job. An example of this procedure is given in Table 12.5.

Note that the points assigned to a job do not need to exactly match those of the plan (see knowledge factor in Table 12.5). In this example, the level of knowledge required by loading dock workers is between the first and second degrees (see

● **TABLE 12.5**

Application of a Point System to Two Jobs

Compensable Factors	Loading Dock Workers		Forklift Repair Mechanics	
	Degree	Points	Degree	Points
Education	1	14	2	28
Experience	1	22	3	66
Knowledge	1–2	21	3	42
Physical demand	4	40	2	20
Mental demand	1	5	3	15
Responsibility for equipment/process	2	10	3	15
Responsibility for material/product	2	10	1	5
Responsibility for safety of others	1	5	1	5
Responsibility for work of others	1	5	1	5
Working conditions	3	30	2	20
Hazards	4	20	3	15
Total points		182		236

Table 12.3), resulting in 21 points. Often jobs with similar point totals are later grouped together for administrative convenience. For instance, all jobs with 150 to 180 points may form a single pay grade.

In principle, the point method could be used to develop a single set of factors and weights for all the jobs in the organization. In practice, however, organizations tend to use several different point plans. There may be one plan for office and clerical employees, another for production workers, and a third for managerial staff. Rarely do the same compensable factors apply to jobs at widely different levels. For example, the job condition factors shown in Table 12.4 are not equally applicable to office/clerical, production, and managerial workers. In such a case, it may make sense to replace factors that do not apply with those more meaningful to the jobs involved. Physical demands and hazards, for instance, seldom appear in point systems for managerial jobs.

The Hay Plan

Hay Associates, one of the largest compensation consulting firms in the world, developed a well-known version of the point method. The **Hay plan** is used for evaluating managerial and executive positions by a large number of organizations worldwide.[18]

The universal factors used by the Hay plan are know-how, problem solving, and accountability. These factors, along with the associated subfactors, are described in Table 12.6. *Know-how* is the total of all the knowledge and skills required to do the job; it includes the subfactors of technical knowledge, manage-

● **TABLE 12.6**

The Factors of the Hay Plan

Know-How	Problem Solving (Mental Activity)	Accountability
The sum total of all knowledge and skills, however acquired, needed for satisfactory job performance (evaluates the job, not the person).	The amount of original, self-starting thought required by the job for analysis, evaluation, creation, reasoning, and arriving at conclusions:	The measured effect of the job on company goals.
Know-how has three dimensions:	Problem solving has two dimensions:	Accountability has three dimensions:
• The amount of practical, specialized, or technical knowledge required	• The degree of freedom with which the thinking process is used to achieve job objectives without the guidance of standards, precedents, or direction from others	• Freedom to act, or relative presence of personal or procedural control and guidance; determined by answering the question, "How much freedom has the job holder to act independently?"; for example, a plant manager has more freedom than a supervisor under his or her control.
• Breadth of management, or the ability to make many activities and functions work well together; the job of company president, for example, has greater breadth than that of a department supervisor	• The type of mental activity involved; the complexity, abstractness, or originality of thought required	• Dollar magnitude, a measure of the sales, budget, dollar value of purchases, value added, or any other significant annual dollar figure related to the job.
• Requirement for skill in motivating people	Problem solving is expressed as a percentage of know-how for the obvious reason that people think with what they know. The percentage judged to be correct for a job is applied to the know-how point value; the result is the point value given to problem solving.	• Impact of the job on dollar magnitude, a determination of whether the job has a primary effect on end results or has instead a sharing, contributory, or remote effect.
Using a chart, a number can be assigned to the level of know-how needed in a job. This number—or point value—indicated the relative importance of know-how in the job being evaluated.		Accountability is given a point value independent of the other two factors.

Note: The total evaluation of any job is arrived at by adding the points for know-how, problem solving, and accountability. The points are not shown here.
Source: From *Effective Personnel Management,* 3rd ed., by Schuler, Buetell, and Youngblood © 1989. Reprinted by permission of South-Western College Publishing, a division of Thomson Learning. Fax 800-730-2215.

ment responsibility, and responsibility for motivating others. *Problem solving* is the amount of original thinking required by the job for arriving at decisions; it includes the subfactors of degree of freedom and type of mental activity. *Accountability* is defined as being answerable for actions taken on the job; its three subfactors are freedom to act, dollar magnitude, and impact. The Hay guide chart allows the evaluator to assign a point value for each factor. The total of the points across all factors is the value of the job.[19]

Factor Comparison

The **factor-comparison method** is a method of quantifying the job versus job comparison (see Figure 12.3). It is the least commonly used method of job evaluation.[20] The first step is to select key jobs to help anchor the system. Key jobs are those that are found in many organizations and have relatively stable job content;

●**TABLE 12.7**

A Factor Comparison Scale

Rate	Skill	Effort	Responsibility	Working Conditions
$.50				Job 3
.75			Job 1	Job 4
1.00				Job 2
1.25	Job 1	Job 1		
1.50	Job 2	Job 3	Job 3	(Job X)
1.75		Job 2		
2.00		Job 4		
2.25			Job 2	
2.50		(Job X)		Job 1
2.75				
3.00	Job 4			
3.25			Job 4 (Job X)	
3.50				
3.75	Job 3 (Job X)			
4.00				
4.25				
4.50				
4.75				
5.00				

Hourly rates: job 1, $5.75; job 2, $6.50; job 3, $7.25; job 4, $9.00.

they also have to be jobs for which the prevailing wage rates are known.[21] The second step is to rank the key jobs on a few compensable factors, such as skill, effort, responsibility, and job conditions. In Table 12.7, job 1 has lower skill requirements than all other jobs but is ranked highest on working conditions. The third step is to determine for each key job the amount of the present pay rate that is attributable to each of the factors. Of job 1's total rate of $5.75, $1.25 is allocated for its level of skill, $1.25 for effort, $0.75 for responsibility, and $2.50 for working conditions.

The factor-comparison method can be applied to other jobs by comparing their standings on each factor with that of the key jobs and summing the associated dollar values to arrive at an hourly rate. For example, suppose that a new job, job X, is being evaluated. Job X is determined to have the same level of skill requirements as job 3 ($3.75), the same level of responsibility as job 4 ($3.25), somewhat more hazardous working conditions than job 2 ($1.50), and somewhat greater effort requirements than job 4 ($2.50). Thus the appropriate hourly pay for job X would be $11.00.

The procedure is rather cumbersome and requires constant updating; hence the relative infrequency of its use. Organizations interested in a quantitative approach to job evaluation are more likely to rely on a point system, which tends to be more straightforward and to result in greater flexibility.

Computerized Job Evaluation

The most popular job evaluation procedures were developed at a time when greater value was placed on having accurate narrative job descriptions. The most frequent means of collecting job data was by having analysts interview incumbents and/or observe work performed and then write job descriptions. This process is labor-intensive, generates a tremendous amount of qualitative data, and must be updated frequently.

A recent trend is the computerization of job evaluation.[22] Typically, after some training, incumbents complete structured questionnaires, such as the Position Analysis Questionnaire (see Chapter 4) or a task-oriented questionnaire (see Figure 12.4), which are then checked by supervisors. Supervisors also may complete the questionnaires for the jobs they supervise. Responses about time spent on and importance of various tasks are then incorporated into a statistical (regression) technique to calculate job points and the appropriate location of a job in the salary structure. Services that score the Position Analysis Questionnaire also provide job evaluation information.

Other computer-based procedures operate in similar fashions. That is, they facilitate a survey of jobs, evaluation of jobs, and the aggregation of market data for comparisons (see the next section, on external equity).[23] More and more, computers are playing an important role in removing the drudgery from salary determination.

Results of Job Evaluation

To some, job evaluation is exemplary of all that is wrong with a traditional approach to human resources. Perhaps this is the point of view of Electro Tech's CEO and executive committee (see HR Challenge at the beginning of this chapter). To its critics, job evaluation is seen as the following:

- Being an overly bureaucratic procedure that allows jobs to be placed in hierarchical boxes[24]

- Encouraging employees to focus on how to advance in the organization at a time when there may be only limited opportunity for advancement as the result of downsizing[25]

- Promoting an internal focus instead of focusing on how best to serve the customer

- Being unsuitable for a forward-thinking organization that has reorganized twenty job titles as, say, three broad jobs (see discussion of broadbanding later in this chapter)

Many ask: Why not simply establish the going rate through wage surveys (see next section) and use this information to guide salary decisions? In other words, why not bypass the process of evaluating jobs?

In fact, this is frequently done and is termed **ranking to market.**[26] Salaries are based on a survey of salaries paid by competitors. Although expedient—and useful for many jobs, especially managerial and professional jobs—the method has disadvantages. First, such an approach allows competitors, not strategic decisions within the organization, to dictate salaries. Second, not all jobs can be compared across firms. Comparisons can be made for key jobs and then pay established for

● **FIGURE 12.4**

Sample Segment of Structured Job Evaluation Questionnaire

Source: Reprinted with permission of Panel Publishers, Inc., 36 West 44th St., New York, NY 10036, from *Topics in Total Compensation,* Vol. 3: *Computerizing Job Evaluation for Greater Efficiency and Effectiveness,* p. 248. Copyright 1989.

Relative Time Scale

1	2	3	4	5	6	7

very small
(<5% of time)   moderate
                       (15–20% of time)   substantial
                                                 (>30% of time)

Relative Importance Scale

1	2	3	4	5	6	7

Insignificant compared
with all other tasks   Important compared
                              with all other tasks   Critical compared
                                                            with all other tasks

	Relative Time Spent		Relative
	Performing	Supervising	Importance
89. Allocates acquired work resources.	☐	☐	☐
90. Interfaces with vendors on work resources.	☐	☐	☐
91. Coordinates work resources maintenance and replacement.	☐	☐	☐
92. Addresses usefulness and usage of work resources.	☐	☐	☐
93. Arbitrates differences of opinion on work-related decisions.	☐	☐	☐
94. Sets direction on work-related subjects and makes appropriate assignments.	☐	☐	☐
95. Establishes appropriate work environment such as productive, creative, or team oriented.	☐	☐	☐
96. Determines desired work action after assessing alternatives.	☐	☐	☐
97. Determines policy and procedure needs using company handbook and other sources.	☐	☐	☐

similar jobs, but this slotting of similar jobs is best accomplished by means of job evaluation.

Ranking to market is useful for some jobs, but for large organizations with many and varied jobs, the only way to construct a sound basis for the wage structure is through job evaluation. At the same time, methods such as broadbanding (discussed later in this chapter) and skill-based pay (covered in Chapter 13) have been seen as making job evaluation relevant to restructured organizations.

Once decisions about the relative value of jobs are made, the next step is assigning actual dollar amounts to the points, ranks, or grades produced by the job evaluation. The concept of external equity is very important in this process; pay levels must be set that consider the "going rate" for that type of job and employee in the relevant labor market.

ESTABLISHING EXTERNAL EQUITY

Just as there is no given price for a pound of apples, there is no absolute rate of pay for a job. You expect to pay less for apples at a farmers' market than at a supermarket and less at a supermarket than at a convenience store. Since orchards produce more small apples than large ones, you expect small apples to cost less per pound than large ones. You expect to pay more for apples in some seasons than in others and more in New York City than in Albany, New York. And if the price for apples seems too high, there is always the possibility of buying other, less expensive, fruit.

Pay to employees reflects the same dynamics that underlie the price of apples and consumers' reactions to these price differences. Just as you probably would not consistently shop at a store that charges higher prices, unless there is some special reason, you probably would not work for a company that offers less pay than you could receive at a nearby organization (again, unless there is some special reason). Employers need to compete for the skills and knowledge they require to operate their businesses—in order to attract workers with needed skills and to motivate and retain those already employed. They use wage and salary surveys to find out what other organizations are paying for particular skills. Then, in setting pay rates, they seek to integrate the external information with what they have learned through the internal evaluation of jobs. This process is called **pricing the wage structure.**

Wage and Salary Surveys

To establish a competitively priced wage structure, organizations typically rely on wage and salary survey data collected from other organizations. The survey process involves identifying the jobs to be included, selecting the organizations to be surveyed, and then actually collecting the data. The data must then be interpreted so that wage rates can be set within the context of the organization's pay policy. Well over 90 percent of all companies regularly use wage and salary survey data in setting their own pay standards.

● **Identifying Key Jobs**   In practice, employers do not seek market data on all jobs. Instead, they gather survey information only for key jobs, which generally have the following characteristics:

1. The job content is relatively stable over time.
2. The jobs occur frequently both in the organization and in the surveyed organizations.
3. The jobs can be defined quite precisely.
4. The jobs are performed in a similar manner in most organizations.

Key jobs should span the range of positions to be included in the wage structure. For example, it would not be desirable to identify only entry-level positions as key jobs. Jobs at the middle and upper levels also need to be included. Moreover, jobs need to be carefully defined. For example, the job of secretary would seem to meet all the characteristics of a key job. However, in today's computer age, the secretarial job has been transformed. It is necessary to be specific as to the skills and responsibilities involved. Data may be collected on several clearly defined types or levels of secretaries.

● **Selecting Organizations to Survey**   Identifying organizations to survey can be important. In considering how to price its apples, a supermarket in New York City is not particularly concerned about supermarket prices in Albany because it will not lose any business to an Albany competitor. In the same way, organizations tend to be most interested in rewards offered by their competitors in the same labor market.

Organizations to be covered in a wage survey typically include those that (1) employ workers with the same skills, (2) are within geographic distances that would make employees willing to commute or relocate, and (3) are in the same or similar industry. However, the considerations that go into selecting a set of organizations to be surveyed vary for different jobs. For example, it is far less important that these organizations be in the same industry when the survey focuses on wages of common jobs like secretary or truck driver. However, industry is crucial in establishing competitive pay for industry-specific jobs, for instance, petroleum engineers. The geographic area to be surveyed also depends on the job. For secretaries, all the relevant organizations competing for the skills are likely to be in the local area. For more complex jobs requiring sophisticated qualifications, however, the geographic area increases. Competition for managerial, professional, and technical jobs tends to be carried out at the regional, national, or—in some instances—international level.[27]

Other special considerations also may arise in selecting a sample of organizations to survey. For instance, suppose an organization makes wheel covers for General Motors Corporation at a plant in rural West Virginia. A local wage survey may show that wages for blue-collar workers in the area are generally quite low. However, because of intermittent activism by employees interested in being organized by the United Auto Workers, the management of this plant also needs to collect information on the pay and benefits of UAW members in plants elsewhere in the country. The wage level actually chosen may reflect both area and industry considerations.

● **Collecting Data**   Rather than running their own wage survey, many organizations obtain the results of surveys undertaken by industry associations (e.g., the American Assembly of Collegiate Schools of Business), professional associations (e.g., the American Chemical Society, American Management Association), government agencies (e.g., the Bureau of Labor Statistics), or consulting firms (e.g.,

Hay Associates, Hewitt Associates, Towers, Perrin, Foster and Crosby). Numerous annual surveys cover a wide choice of job families and industries. At local levels, chapters of the Society for Human Resource Management or Chambers of Commerce often undertake surveys for their membership.

Self-Surveys   For a company that wants to collect and analyze its own data, it is important to obtain information on the characteristics of the responding organization, as well as on both direct and indirect compensation (see Figure 12.1). The organizational information (e.g., total number of employees, sales, return on investment, product lines) is needed to judge the comparability of the competitor in terms of size, products, and financial condition. It is also crucial to know the types and amounts of benefits offered (e.g., fully covered medical plan versus plan supported in part by employee contributions), as well as incentives and hourly pay. Hourly pay rates or salaries may be misleading if bonuses for which employees are likely to qualify are not taken into account.

Government Surveys   A salary survey report can take several forms. Table 12.8 illustrates a report published by the U.S. Bureau of Labor Statistics as part of its ongoing program of wage surveys in major geographic areas. The table gives information on a sample of jobs in metropolitan Charlotte, North Carolina, and is based on establishments employing fifty workers or more in the white- and blue-collar occupations shown. The Bureau of Labor Statistics also provides information on compensation rates in other countries (see the International Perspective box).

Interpreting the Data   The report shows a detailed frequency distribution of hourly wage rates for each job, along with the median wage. If the workers were ordered from highest earnings to lowest earnings, the earnings of the person in the middle would represent the median. The mean is also possible, although it is not given in Table 12.8. The mean is computed by adding up the earnings of all workers and dividing the total by the number of workers surveyed.

Of the two summary measures, the median is the most useful in setting wage ranges. The mean can easily become distorted if a few workers are paid at extreme rates. The median is not subject to such distortion. For an employer hiring a secretary (see Administrative support), such information can be of value in suggesting that wages of close to $14 per hour would be required to be competitive. A wage between $18 and $19 per hour would assure the employer that top applicants would seek the job with a good chance that they would accept it if offered.

Avoiding Antitrust   Recently, the U.S. Department of Justice and the Federal Trade Commission have questioned the legality of salary surveys under antitrust laws. The fear is that employers that compete for the same labor pool may use the results to collectively fix the wages of employees. For example, the hospitals in a metropolitan area could share wage information through a salary survey in an effort to avoid competing with one another for available talent.

As a result of investigations, federal antitrust agencies have indicated that they will not scrutinize compensation surveys that are consistent with four guidelines:[28]

1. Survey data need to be collected by an independent third party, such as a consultant, not by the competing employers themselves. (Employers would be wise to avoid undertaking their own salary surveys or relying on surveys of local trade groups, such as the local hospital board.)

● **TABLE 12.8**

Hourly Wages for Selected Occupations, Full-Time Workers, Charlotte-Gastonia, North Carolina, June 2000

Occupation[3]	10	25	Median 50	75	90
All	$8.43	$9.99	$13.71	$19.82	$27.65
All excluding sales	8.53	10.09	13.77	19.85	27.44
White collar	9.20	11.60	17.35	23.71	34.62
White collar excluding sales	9.60	12.00	17.90	23.75	34.90
Professional specialty and technical	14.39	18.80	21.50	25.72	34.61
Professional specialty	16.90	19.35	21.84	26.84	34.36
Engineers, architects, and surveyors	15.00	23.80	32.78	34.83	36.13
Electrical and electronic engineers	23.56	26.84	34.83	36.13	43.54
Mechanical engineers	23.80	25.42	32.37	34.61	34.61
Engineers, n.e.c.	15.00	15.00	15.00	32.78	37.50
Mathematical and computer scientists	20.19	20.68	31.35	33.81	39.96
Computer systems analysts and scientists	20.19	20.68	31.35	33.81	39.96
Natural scientists	—	—	—	—	—
Health related	18.10	19.31	19.35	20.16	35.71
Registered nurses	18.61	19.31	19.35	19.65	24.08
Teachers, college and university	19.98	23.20	27.92	32.20	40.95
Teachers, except college and university	20.01	21.16	21.95	23.71	28.05
Elementary school teachers	20.01	20.44	21.91	23.07	24.54
Secondary school teachers	20.27	21.16	21.50	23.50	24.76
Teachers, special education	21.07	21.60	28.07	28.16	28.16
Librarians, archivists, and curators	—	—	—	—	—
Social scientists and urban planners	—	—	—	—	—
Social, recreation, and religious workers	13.46	14.39	16.90	19.33	21.00
Social workers	13.50	14.39	16.90	19.33	21.00
Lawyers and judges	—	—	—	—	—
Writers, authors, entertainers, athletes, and professionals, n.e.c.	11.58	12.71	18.03	23.79	27.07
Technical	11.66	14.10	19.23	25.38	44.99
Clinical laboratory technologists and technicians	9.84	10.10	17.96	17.96	25.38
Licensed practical nurses	13.00	13.76	13.99	15.54	18.17
Health technologists and technicians, n.e.c.	9.43	9.97	12.37	13.10	22.44
Electrical and electronic technicians	11.66	21.75	24.52	24.79	25.48
Engineering technicians, n.e.c.	15.41	18.02	21.08	29.06	34.90
Executive, administrative, and managerial	18.97	21.82	30.84	42.63	51.38
Executives, administrators, and managers	20.91	25.88	32.63	46.31	58.60
Administrators and officials, public administration	17.99	25.13	28.65	46.07	58.65
Financial managers	21.96	46.31	48.43	50.65	58.60
Managers, marketing, advertising, and public relations	21.82	29.29	34.62	55.03	84.10
Administrators, education and related fields	25.88	25.88	28.59	29.83	33.81
Managers and administrators, n.e.c.	18.97	23.00	34.20	43.59	65.38
Management related	15.69	19.14	21.57	34.12	38.73
Accountants and auditors	14.10	19.14	19.14	21.06	21.06
Other financial officers	21.98	21.98	36.66	44.62	44.62
Personnel, training, and labor relations specialists	13.25	19.18	19.18	19.18	22.50
Purchasing agents and buyers, n.e.c.	16.54	19.11	28.42	33.41	44.18
Sales	7.39	7.86	11.15	19.23	29.59
Supervisors, sales	7.45	10.50	13.73	28.39	31.25
Cashiers	6.80	7.03	7.88	9.25	11.15

(continued)

● **TABLE 12.8** (continued)

Occupation[3]	10	25	Median 50	75	90
White collar (continued)					
Administrative support, including clerical	9.00	9.95	11.94	14.12	17.50
Supervisors, distribution, scheduling, and adjusting clerks	12.50	12.50	17.56	18.93	19.92
Computer operators	14.13	14.13	19.14	20.16	20.16
Secretaries	10.57	13.03	13.77	15.89	18.24
Receptionists	8.50	9.39	10.00	10.50	11.87
Order clerks	10.33	11.60	11.82	12.56	12.60
Library clerks	9.03	10.09	10.25	10.66	11.56
Records clerks, n.e.c.	10.77	10.77	10.78	14.12	15.88
Bookkeepers, accounting and auditing clerks	9.46	11.88	12.59	13.47	14.33
Dispatchers	9.68	10.35	11.75	12.01	18.26
Traffic, shipping and receiving clerks	9.54	10.59	10.88	11.28	11.30
Stock and inventory clerks	8.80	9.60	11.39	17.50	17.50
Material recording, scheduling, and distribution clerks, n.e.c.	15.02	15.02	16.12	19.79	19.79
Bill and account collectors	11.18	11.53	18.05	18.05	18.05
General office clerks	9.00	9.50	11.45	12.55	13.00
Teachers' aides	8.68	9.00	9.10	9.41	9.82
Administrative support, n.e.c.	9.02	9.02	10.30	11.89	18.78
Blue collar	8.12	9.66	12.92	16.67	21.14
Precision production, craft, and repair	10.18	12.96	15.55	19.23	24.24
Supervisors, mechanics and repairers	24.68	27.31	30.07	30.22	47.89
Automobile mechanics	15.26	16.67	17.85	17.85	21.08
Bus, truck, and stationary engine mechanics	12.96	14.20	15.77	16.50	17.55
Industrial machinery repairers	11.59	13.03	14.00	15.41	18.36
Mechanics and repairers, n.e.c.	12.89	21.15	21.51	25.24	27.81
Electricians	13.00	13.00	13.16	17.73	18.36
Electrical power installers and repairers	14.69	17.13	17.58	22.25	22.25
Construction trades, n.e.c.	8.90	10.68	10.68	10.87	13.93
Supervisors, production	15.24	17.46	20.13	23.13	24.24
Butchers and meat cutters	7.90	8.15	8.70	10.53	14.00
Inspectors, testers, and graders	8.45	13.38	16.60	20.17	20.17
Machine operators, assemblers, and inspectors	7.25	8.96	10.67	14.23	18.29
Winding and twisting machine operators	7.25	8.96	9.10	10.31	10.75
Knitting, looping, taping, and weaving machine operators	8.91	8.91	11.86	11.89	11.89
Mixing and blending machine operators	8.35	9.64	11.22	13.74	17.41
Miscellaneous machine operators, n.e.c.	8.37	9.75	13.18	17.71	23.36
Assemblers	6.76	8.42	9.50	13.65	18.22
Production inspectors, checkers and examiners	7.70	9.38	11.20	16.99	20.09
Transportation and material moving	9.96	11.94	14.28	17.11	21.22
Truck drivers	10.67	12.43	14.58	18.39	22.38
Industrial truck and tractor equipment operators	8.00	9.96	12.75	16.98	19.10
Miscellaneous material moving equipment operators, n.e.c.	13.13	13.13	15.92	17.11	24.15
Handlers, equipment cleaners, helpers, and laborers	7.37	8.57	10.15	12.78	17.78
Helpers, construction trades	9.23	9.23	11.00	12.92	12.92

(continued)

● **TABLE 12.8** (continued)

Occupation[3]	10	25	Median 50	75	90
Blue collar (continued)					
Handlers, equipment cleaners, helpers, and laborers (continued)					
Production helpers	8.70	9.40	10.37	13.35	16.24
Stock handlers and baggers	7.91	8.40	10.90	21.42	21.57
Machine feeders and offbearers	7.37	7.37	8.21	10.25	13.21
Freight, stock, and material handlers, n.e.c.	6.95	7.25	10.80	13.55	17.99
Hand packers and packagers	8.30	9.32	9.44	9.97	10.94
Laborers, except construction, n.e.c.	6.90	8.01	8.70	10.84	11.79
Service	6.91	8.29	9.12	15.25	22.73
Protective service	11.78	13.90	15.62	20.33	23.41
Supervisors, police and detectives	17.07	19.33	22.02	27.44	29.70
Police and detectives, public service	13.69	15.38	15.62	16.25	19.92
Correctional institution officers	11.78	11.78	11.78	13.18	14.05
Food service	6.00	6.73	7.85	8.60	9.05
Waiters, waitresses, and bartenders	—	—	—	—	—
Other food service	7.00	7.81	8.49	8.88	9.56
Cooks	7.00	7.81	8.23	8.63	9.00
Food preparation, n.e.c.	6.73	7.60	7.85	8.60	8.60
Health service	7.46	8.41	9.28	10.12	10.44
Health aides, except nursing	7.39	7.52	9.32	10.44	10.44
Nursing aides, orderlies and attendants	8.15	8.72	9.28	10.12	10.18
Cleaning and building service	7.79	8.24	8.57	8.83	9.20
Janitors and cleaners	7.91	8.24	8.57	8.83	9.12
Personal service	—	—	—	—	—

Source: "Charlotte-Gastonia-Rock Hill, NC-SC National Compenation Survey June 2000," U.S. Department of Labor, Bureau of Labor Statistics, Bulletin 3105-49, April 2001, Table 6-4. (Available at: http://www.bls.gov/compub.htm#NC)

2. Salary information provided by survey participants needs to be more than three months old.

3. For each job on which statistics are provided (e.g., x-ray technician, nurse), data need to be contributed by at least five employers.

4. Any information disseminated must be sufficiently aggregated so that recipients cannot attribute specific data to a particular employer.

Fortunately, these guidelines are consistent with sound practice in developing salary survey data for market comparisons.

Pay-Level Policy

Once an organization has completed an internal job evaluation and obtained wage survey data, it needs to translate this information into pay rates for each class of job. This process involves interpretation of survey results, the merging of the job evaluation with the survey data, and consideration of the organization's pay-level policy.

INTERNATIONAL PERSPECTIVE

International Compensation Comparisons

Substantial variation in compensation rates can be seen around the world; costs tend to be lower in developing economies compared with those that are more developed. Pay is higher in many European countries than in the United States. The U.S. Bureau of Labor Statistics has developed comparative measures of manufacturing compensation costs, allowing for international comparisons. These statistics provide a general indication of the relative total compensation cost in each country. Total compensation cost is made up of payment for time worked, holiday pay, and the cost of providing required benefits such as health insurance, pensions, workers' compensation, and unemployment insurance. In order to make a direct comparison, the United States is used as the benchmark country with defined costs at 100. The rest of the countries are reported relative to this standard. Note that fluctuations in the strength of each nation's currency against the U.S. dollar affect these data. The table illustrates how other countries compare with the United States in terms of manufacturing compensation for the years 1990 and 1999.

In 1999, U.S. manufacturing costs averaged $19.20 per hour. Germany had the highest compensation costs, at 140 percent of the U.S. level. Second was Norway, followed by Switzerland. Taken together, the newly industrializing Asian economies came in at about one-third of U.S. labor costs.

There are differences in compensation structures among the countries, such as variations in levels of paid leave and bonuses. For example, holiday pay and bonuses accounted for approximately 30 percent of total compensation costs in Japan, compared with some European countries, where it accounts for 15 to 20 percent of costs, and the United States, where it accounts for 6 percent. In Japan an annual bonus of three months' pay is typical, whereas in Europe an annual bonus of one to two months' pay is common.

Mexico is often seen as a low-wage country, and since the passage of the North American Free Trade Agreement, many companies have tried to take advantage of this by opening facilities in Mexico. Some of them have found that actual wage costs are greater than anticipated. While the official minimum wage is low, very few people actually work for the minimum wage. In addition, there are legally required cash allowances: fifteen days' pay for a Christmas bonus (though most employers pay a full month), a vacation premium of 25 percent beyond regular pay, and required sharing of 10 percent of pretax profits. Overtime must be paid at twice the normal rate. A number of additional bonuses, such as fifteen to twenty days' pay as a reward for perfect attendance over one year, are not mandatory but are widely used and hence necessary to attract and keep good employees.

Hourly Compensation Costs for Production Workers in the Manufacturing Sector

Country	1990	1999
Australia	88	83
Austria	119	114
Belgium	129	119
Canada	107	81
Denmark	121	120
Finland	141	110
France	102	94
Germany	147	140
Hong Kong	21	28
Italy	117	86
Japan	86	109
Korea	25	35
Mexico	11	11
Norway	144	125
Singapore	25	37
Spain	76	63
Sweden	140	112
Switzerland	140	123
Taiwan	26	29
United Kingdom	85	86
United States	100	100

Sources: Fay Hansen, "An Update on International Labor Costs," *Compensation and Benefits Review*, November–December 2000, pp. 14–19; and Gillian Flynn, "HR in Mexico: What You Should Know," *Personnel Journal*, August 1994, pp. 34–44.

The first step in merging the internal and external data is a strategic decision on the organization's positioning in terms of the competition. The three fundamental options are to match, lead, or lag behind the market.

By setting its pay levels at the market rate, or **matching the competition,** an organization tries to keep its labor costs comparable with those of competitors. Such an approach tends to neutralize pay as a factor in attracting, retaining, and motivating employees while ensuring that labor costs are competitive.[29]

In adapting a **lead policy**—that is, paying a higher wage rate than its competitors—a firm hopes to attract and retain higher-quality employees while maximizing satisfaction of its current employees. Firms with a lead policy want to be the preferred employer so that they can select the best applicants while making it costly for competitors to persuade current employees to leave.[30] Frequently, such organizations have labor costs that represent a small proportion of the cost of production or have higher levels of productivity—making such a policy affordable.

Some organizations follow a **lag approach,** setting their pay rates below those of their competitors. On the surface, it might seem that such a policy would inevitably lead to difficulties in attracting, motivating, and retaining qualified employees. Some companies, however, have other ways to attract applicants, such as employment security (as with government jobs), superior benefits (e.g., holidays, vacation time, tuition reimbursement), or an enjoyable environment. Some organizations—because of the nature of the business (e.g., entertainment, airlines), social or business philosophy (e.g., Ben and Jerry's),[31] or excellent reputation—will attract well-qualified applicants even at below-market wages. Still other organizations may adopt a lag approach because they simply cannot afford to pay competitive salaries.[32] Research has shown that pay policy decisions often involve a complex mixture of factors.[33]

Figure 12.5 diagrams how the three policies might be put into practice. The diagonal market line illustrates the gradual increase of market wage rates as different organizations implement changes at various times. At the beginning of the planning cycle (a year in this case), a firm with a lead policy sets its wage rates at the level that the market will reach only at the end of the year. A typical lag policy, by contrast, begins the year at a level equal to the market and is well below it by the end of the year. An organization with a match policy is actually paying wages equivalent to competition only at midyear. As can be seen, the match rate is above the market level at the start of the year and below it at the end.

Finally, an organization need not have one policy for all jobs. For example, an organization that can count on a steady supply of clerical and trade employees might adopt a policy of lagging behind the competition for these groups. However, to attract the top professional talent, the same firm might adopt a lead policy in compensation for these groups.

Because wages paid by competitors are constantly changing, survey results are inevitably out of date when they reach the organization. For example, a survey initiated in mid-2001 might be compiled and ready for distribution by the end of the year. An organization that intended to use these data to set pay for mid-2002 would need to make adjustments to reflect changes between the time of data collection and the plan period (mid-2001 to mid-2002 in the example discussed). The adjustment is based on historical trends from previous years, economic forecasts (e.g., productivity trends, cost-of-living changes), and judgment as to any special circumstances. In the example, figures from mid-2001 will need to be projected twelve months ahead to obtain the market level as of mid-2002, the start of the 2002–2003

● **FIGURE 12.5**

Pay Policies over Time: Lag, Match, and Lead Pay Structures

Source: Richard Henderson, *Compensation Management: Rewarding Performance,* 5th ed., Copyright © 1989, p. 477. Reprinted by permission of Prentice-Hall, Inc., Englewood Cliffs, N.J.

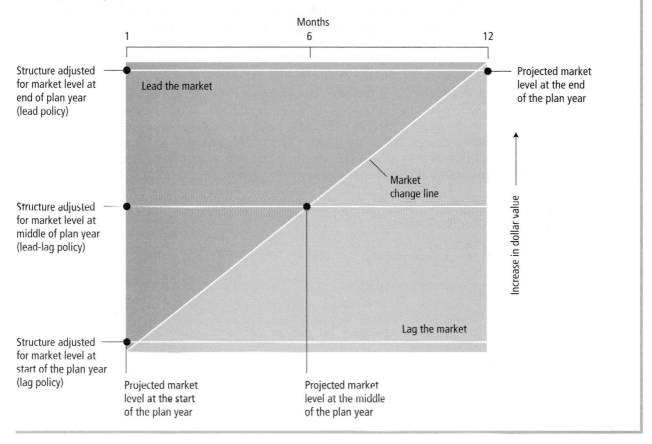

plan. Assuming that inflation and other factors will increase the market wage level at an annual rate of 4.5 percent, survey data should be multiplied by 1.045 to obtain the market rates for July 1, 2002, the beginning of the 2002–2003 plan year.

ESTABLISHING INDIVIDUAL EQUITY

As mentioned earlier, jobs evaluated as having nearly the same value are usually combined into a single wage grade. It would be cumbersome to have fifty different wage rates for fifty different job titles or a slightly higher rate for a job evaluated at 205 points versus one at 200 points. Thus wage grades are established (e.g., all jobs with between 200 and 225 points would be a grade), and all jobs within the grade are paid identically. A single wage may be selected for each grade and paid to every person whose job falls in that grade. More commonly, however, a range of pay rates is set for each grade. When a range is set, the issue of individual equity becomes salient, and the organization must have a system for determining where in the range the compensation of each employee should be.

Designing Pay Ranges

The range associated with a pay grade sets the upper and lower bounds of possible compensation for individuals whose jobs fall in the grade. There is no optimal number of pay grades for a wage structure, although most organizations define ten to sixteen pay grades.[34]

● **Establishing Pay Ranges** The first step is to define the pay policy line linking pay to job evaluation points. Think of a graph with wage grades along the horizontal axis and pay (dollars) along the vertical axis. (See Figure 12.6.) The policy line is based on salary survey data, appropriately adjusted and taking into consideration the firm's policy (lead, match, or lag). The points on the line will represent the midpoints of the **wage ranges,** which are calculated next.

● **FIGURE 12.6**

Pay Ranges

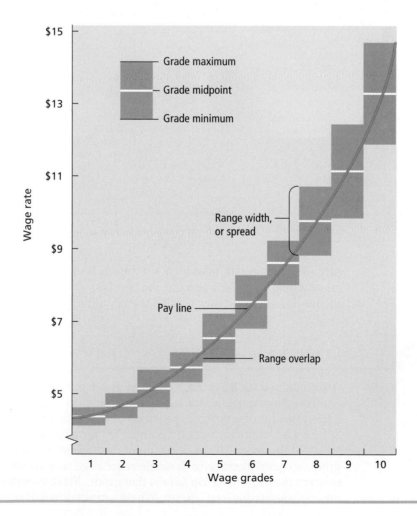

Each grade has a minimum, a maximum, and a midpoint. The spread around the midpoint may vary, with 10 to 20 percent on either side being typical, as shown in Figure 12.6.[35] The percentage spread is frequently greater for higher-level positions, on the assumption that there is more leeway to make an outstanding or very poor contribution in these more important jobs.

It is important that adjacent grades overlap, as shown in Figure 12.6, since an experienced employee in a lower grade may make a greater contribution than a relatively new employee in the next higher grade. Well over half of a given pay range may overlap the adjacent pay grade.

Although each range has a maximum, the structure is dynamic. Ordinarily, the pay policy line and all the ranges are adjusted upward each year as inflationary and competitive pressures push wages upward. At some point, the top-performing employees will eventually reach the maximum within a range. They should then be considered for promotion to a higher grade. If the overlap between grades is too large, even a promotion may not bring a large enough salary increase to have incentive value.

● **Broadbanding**   The concept of **broadbanding** was developed in an effort to make job evaluation more compatible with the downsizing and delayering that characterize many restructured organizations. An increasing number of companies are using broadbands or are considering applying this concept as a way to remove the artificial barriers created by job grades.[36] An advantage of broadbanding is in the flexibility it provides and the signals it sends to employees. For example, an employee may be interested in a job but be reluctant to explore moving into it if it is not at a higher grade. With broadbanding, the position may be in the same band, so the employee can focus on the content of the job, its challenges, and its developmental opportunities rather than on its grade level. In this way the employee can learn new skills and better contribute to the team without the possible stigma of a demotion or reduction in pay.[37]

In the example shown in Figure 12.7, four wage grades have been combined into one broad grouping of jobs. In this way, career growth would be defined in terms of responsibilities rather than through upward advancement.[38] Individuals would be expected to perform several of the activities, previously defined as jobs, that now fall within the same band. Instead of the 25 percent (50 percent range) on either side of the midpoint defining the minimum and maximum of a range, the spread from minimum to maximum would be 110 percent.

Broadbanding is not right for all companies. Managers must be trained to deal with banding's broader salary ranges and fewer control points. Workers may resist the absence of frequent, if small, symbols of their increased value through movement to higher grades.[39]

● **Above- and Below-Range Employees**   When the wage structure is formed initially, it is not unusual to find employees who are currently being paid above the maximum for a range or below the minimum. Those below the minimum are "green-circled," and increased to be within the range. If for some reason the gap is large between the employee's current rate and the minimum rate of the range, this increase may be over a period of time rather than all at once.

If employees earning more than the maximum qualify for promotion, they can be moved to a job in a higher range commensurate with their existing pay. If promotion is not possible, the employee is "red-circled"; that is, his or her pay is

● **FIGURE 12.7**

Illustration of a Typical Broadband

frozen at its present level until the range moves up, through annual increases, to include the individual. It is generally regarded as less than ideal to cut an employee's pay as a result of job evaluation. That said, cutting pay is not unheard of, although one needs to be aware of what such cuts are communicating to the employee. Ideally no one's pay is cut as a result of job evaluation.

Setting Individual Pay

Individual equity requires that rewards to employees be allocated fairly across individuals performing the same job. The two commonly used approaches to determine how workers are placed and progress through the pay ranges are seniority and merit. A newer method bases increments on the number of skills mastered.

● **Seniority**   When based on seniority, pay increases depend solely on the employee's experience or length of service on the job. Individuals all start out with equal pay and then progress through steps with each year of service. In addition to the step increases, the entire range (i.e., the entry rate and each of the steps) is adjusted to reflect the results of salary surveys and economic trends.

The **seniority-based pay** system rewards a stable, experienced work force. Seniority systems are often used when employees are unionized, when employees do not accept or trust the concept of merit pay, when differences in performance are difficult to measure accurately, or when jobs call for very similar work performance or output. Assembly-line jobs, for example, typically require similar work performance and output from all workers.

● **Merit Pay**   Many organizations try to link compensation to actual job performance through **merit pay**.[40] Merit increases are given, usually on an annual basis, with better-performing employees receiving larger raises. In theory, merit increases allow management to use pay to motivate employees to higher levels of performance. However, considerable data suggest that merit pay may not be as desirable, as easy to implement, or as widely used as is commonly believed. The next chapter discusses in more detail the theory and practice of using incentives, including merit pay.

Many workers distrust merit reward systems because they do not feel that their pay is related to their performance level. After comparing notes with their peers, employees may feel that they have not been treated fairly, usually because they perceive their own performance as being relatively high. In one study across all occupational groups, more than 95 percent of employees rated themselves as above average.[41]

One prescription for a successful merit system defines the following requirements:

1. A high level of trust and belief in management
2. A correct and current job evaluation system and wage structure (alleviating the tendency to use supposed merit money to correct distortions caused by a wage structure that is incorrect or out of touch with the market)
3. Performance criteria agreed to by all levels of employees
4. Job-specific, results-based criteria to reduce subjective bias
5. Accurate performance appraisals (Since no single performance appraisal format is appropriate in all situations, alternate formats should be adopted for different situations.)
6. Appropriate administrative practices, such as minimizing the time between the performance appraisal and pay increase, to maximize the reinforcement principle
7. Skillfully administered feedback during the performance appraisal session to ensure that employees are aware of expected performance
8. Managers trained in the correct use of the compensation system[42]

● **Skill-Based Pay**   Still another basis for establishing individual pay rates has to do with the knowledge one has mastered on the job.[43] **Skill-based pay** plans analyze the job knowledge an employee will need to progress. All employees begin at an entry-level rate. As they learn additional skills, and as the learning is verified through demonstration or tests, they qualify for increments in pay. Skill-based pay is especially compatible with broadbanding because employees can be rewarded for gaining additional skills within a broader array of job activities. Skill-based pay, along with the incentives it engenders for employees, is described further in the next chapter.

LEGAL REGULATION OF COMPENSATION SYSTEMS

The major factors influencing an organization's reward system include job content (assessed by job evaluation), market forces (e.g., supply of labor, competition for labor, prevailing wages, and employer's ability to pay), and the pay policy of the organization. Certain legal constraints also influence all compensation systems. In fact, the recent increase in government regulations has made legal constraints a major factor in planning and administering a compensation system.

Legal issues related to direct compensation (e.g., pay rates, hours, and so forth) are considered in this chapter. Legislation that affects indirect compensation (e.g., pensions, Social Security, and so on) is discussed in the next chapter.

The Fair Labor Standards Act

The **Fair Labor Standards Act (FLSA)** of 1938 is the major law affecting direct compensation. Its provisions on the minimum wage, hours of work, and equal pay directly affect the design of compensation systems. Sections of the FLSA dealing with child labor and record-keeping requirements are also important but have fewer direct consequences and are not considered in this chapter.

The terms "exempt" and "nonexempt" are crucial for understanding and complying with the FLSA. **Exempt employees** include executive, administrative, and professional employees who are exempt from the minimum wage, work hours, and overtime provisions of the FLSA. **Nonexempt employees** are subject to the provisions of the FLSA.

To be exempt as an executive, an employee must supervise two or more employees, have the authority to hire and fire, and otherwise exercise independent judgment. Administrators need not supervise other employees but do need to exercise independent judgment in carrying out top management policies. Professionals are exempt under the definition of the FLSA if they perform unstandardized artistic or intellectual work of a varied nature that requires independent judgment.

Correctly determining the exempt or nonexempt status of a job is important, although not always easy.[44] For instance, we tend to think of accountants and engineers as professionals, but in some cases they are not professionals under the FLSA guidelines. A lower-level accountant who applies accounting principles with little independent judgment or a newly hired engineer who does setup work for other engineers would not be exempt. Under the law, their employer is liable for overtime pay for these individuals.

A final class of individuals who are exempt from the FLSA is outside salespersons. An outside salesperson must spend 80 percent or more of the workweek away from the employer's place of business, making visits to customers. Outside salespersons need not be paid overtime, and they are often paid only by commission.[45]

Because the Constitution empowers Congress and the federal government to regulate interstate commerce, almost all employers are covered by the FLSA. The act applies to all employers producing goods for interstate commerce or having employees who handle, sell, or otherwise work on such goods or materials. This means that any organization that uses a product produced in another state (e.g., a day-care facility using disposable diapers made in another state) is covered.

● **Minimum Wage** The **minimum wage** provisions of the FLSA establish the lowest pay an employer can offer an employee. The minimum wage was first set at $0.25 in 1938 to prevent the exploitation of workers and establish a "level playing field" for all employers. The law establishing the federal minimum wage called for a balancing act that is relived each time there is a discussion of increasing the minimum wage. The legislation stipulated that workers be paid at least enough to maintain a "minimum standard of living necessary for health, efficiency and general wellbeing." At the same time, though, it sought to do this "without substantially curtailing employment."[46]

After many years with the minimum wage set at $3.35 per hour, President George Bush signed a bill raising the minimum wage to $3.80 in 1990 and then to $4.25 in 1991. In 1996, President Bill Clinton signed legislation authorizing two $0.45 increases, the first in October 1996 and the second in September 1997, bringing the minimum wage to $5.15 per hour. Although the minimum wage increased $1.80 in nominal dollars during the 1990s, the increase (to 1999) was actually $0.27 when adjusted for inflation.[47] The economic growth and tight labor conditions of the 1990s thinned the ranks of minimum wage workers to only about 1 percent of hourly employees earning exactly $5.15 per hour, down from 9 percent in 1980.[48] At the same time, more than 11 million Americans still hover around the pay floor, earning from $5.15 to $6.64 an hour. Each year Congress and/or the president discuss proposed increases in the minimum wage, but so far there have been no increases since 1996.[49]

Despite the wide coverage of the minimum wage provisions, it does not apply to all nonexempt workers. Employers need not pay the minimum wage to apprentices or agricultural workers. If employees receive more than $30 per month in tips, employers may reduce the hourly wage below the minimum by a specified amount.

● **Hours of Work**   The overtime provisions of the FLSA require payment of one and one-half the regular hourly rate for work over forty hours per week. Union contracts may specify greater amounts (e.g., twice the regular hourly rate) or lower thresholds (e.g., overtime after thirty-five hours per week) that supersede the FLSA provisions.

Employers may pay overtime to exempt employees (e.g., executives and professionals) but are not obligated to do so. Salaried nonexempt employees are covered; to calculate appropriate overtime pay, their salary is converted into an hourly rate. Employers of nonexempt employees are required to keep thorough records of the hours worked to be sure that employees receive overtime payment when it is due.[50]

The Wage and Hour Division of the Department of Labor has responsibility for enforcing the FLSA. Most inspections are triggered by an employee complaint, but once the inspection begins, all records for all employees may be scrutinized and back pay for all affected workers can be ordered. In addition, the Wage and Hour Division targets certain industries for scrutiny, including garment manufacturing, nursing homes, and agricultural processing. These industries have had repeated violations in the past. For example, in the first quarter of FY 2001 (October–December, 2000) the Department of Labor recovered almost $600,000 in back wages for 712 garment workers. A total of 37 contractors and 144 facilities were found in violation of the FLSA. In addition to the back pay, $70,000 in civil penalties were assessed.[51] Therefore, it is wise for employers to know the provisions of the FLSA and to follow them carefully.

Equal Pay Act

Passed as an amendment to the FLSA, the Equal Pay Act (EPA) of 1963 requires an organization to offer equal pay for equal work, regardless of the sex of the employee. The Equal Pay Act defines equal work as (1) requiring equal skill, (2) requiring equal effort, (3) requiring equal responsibility, and (4) being performed under similar working conditions. Thus men and women performing the same job in the same location for the same employer must be offered the same pay, all other things being equal. The use of two job titles for what is essentially the same job as a pretext for paying one group less than the other is not permitted (e.g., calling men "office managers" and women "senior secretaries" when their duties are identical).

Equal pay is not required if differences in the average pay of men and women arise because of a seniority system, a merit system, or a system that measures earnings by quantity or quality of production. In other words, the customary approaches used to establish individual pay are acceptable even if they create unequal pay between men and women. Such discrepancies would arise, for example, if an organization based individual pay on seniority and most of its female employees were more recently hired.

The Equal Pay Act would seem to be a natural basis for pursuing the issue of comparable worth, a topic discussed later in this chapter. In fact, the rather strict requirements of identical skill, effort, responsibility, and working conditions have made it difficult to use this legislation as the basis for insisting on equal pay for work of comparable worth.

Other Laws Affecting Compensation

Other legal regulations that affect reward systems have to do with discrimination, wages paid by contractors who work for the U.S. government, and wage garnishment. In addition, some states have their own wage and hour laws.

Title VII of the Civil Rights Act prohibits discrimination on the basis of race, color, sex, national origin, and religion in all aspects of employment, including compensation. Thus it would be illegal to pay minority employees less than similarly qualified nonminority employees for doing the same job in the same location.

Several laws (Davis–Bacon Act of 1931, Walsh–Healy Public Contracts Act of 1936, and McNamara–O'Hara Service Contract Act of 1965) require that suppliers of goods or services to the federal government pay at least the "prevailing wage" to their employees. In practice, the prevailing wage usually has been set by the Department of Labor as the average wage of unionized workers in an area or industry. The intent of these laws is to prevent the government from buying "sweatshop" goods and thus indirectly exploiting workers. Some argue that this causes wages to be artificially raised and costs the government more than it would have to pay without this law[52]

A final law, the Consumer Credit Protection Act of 1968, covers wage garnishment, the procedure by which a creditor can get a court order compelling the employer to pay over a portion of an indebted employee's earnings. The act limits the amount that can be ordered withheld from each paycheck and prohibits an employer from firing an employee for the first incident of garnishment.

The regulatory context has a powerful influence on organizational reward systems. The human resource manager must carefully obey the law in many aspects of establishing and administering a compensation system. Regulatory constraints are equally significant with respect to benefits, a topic covered in the next chapter.

ADMINISTERING COMPENSATION SYSTEMS

Even the best-designed compensation system will be ineffective if it does not gain employee acceptance, and this acceptance is often determined by the way the reward system is administered. This section discusses several of the major issues associated with the administration of compensation systems.

Pay Secrecy

The process by which a compensation system is formulated and administered is critical to the organization. One important administrative issue concerns the availability of compensation information to employees. Unfortunately, in most organizations, the tendency is toward secrecy. **Pay secrecy** is an administrative strategy that may increase the manageability of the system in that less information has to be communicated and fewer challenges to fairness may have to be heard.

Studies by Edward E. Lawler have shown that employees regularly misperceive the pay of others, including subordinates, peers, and superiors.[53] For example, superiors were perceived as receiving less than their actual salary, while subordinates and peers were thought to receive more than they actually did. Another study showed that managers make different pay allocation decisions when pay is secret than when it is open.[54] Secrecy makes it easier for allocators to use whatever criteria they wish, since their decisions are less likely to be known by others.

Just how much and what types of information about pay should be provided to employees are questions that are troubling to compensation professionals. These are not simple questions to answer. Much has been written about the effects of secrecy on the behavior and attitudes of employees.

On one end of the spectrum is a policy of full, or open, disclosure; that is, information regarding individual salaries is available on request. When the government is the employer, full disclosure is the norm, because pay policies and even individual salaries are a matter of public record. Similarly, most union contracts spell out wages on the basis of job title and time in grade.

Most other employees are provided very little information about pay. In a survey conducted by the Bureau of National Affairs, only 18 percent of responding companies said that managers had knowledge of the salaries of their superiors or peers.[55] Open systems with regard to pay are the exception, not the rule. In fact, in some organizations, as a condition of employment, employees are asked to sign a contract stating that salary is to be regarded as confidential and that violation of this condition can lead to discharge.

The goals of achieving equity and, to the extent possible, participant satisfaction would seem to call for telling employees about pay policies and levels. For merit systems to have a motivating effect, employees need to know how effort translates into rewards. Information about the maximum and the average raise should be made available each year. Each employee should be told what the midpoint is for his or her job, as well as the pay range. In addition, the organization should explain how it arrived at the pay structure. Allowing employees to see where their jobs are located in the wage structure should not create significant problems for an employer that has a well-designed job evaluation plan.

Employee Participation

People tend to be more committed to programs they had a hand in developing. When employees help create compensation plans, there is generally less resistance, and the plan is much more likely to be a successful motivator than would a plan imposed by management.[56]

It is appropriate to involve employees in many phases of a reward system. For example, a wide variety of employees should serve on job evaluation committees. If a point plan is adopted, it is reasonable to involve employees in identifying the compensable factors to be used and the weight to be assigned to each factor.

Employees are also likely to have good insight into which competitor firms should be included in a wage survey.

There are several mechanisms for employee involvement. At the broadest level, employees can be surveyed to learn their preferences. Employee task forces can help integrate these preferences into a system. Such groups are usually an excellent way to involve employees in the decisions associated with a reward system.

The decision to involve employees in designing or administering a compensation system should not be made without deliberation, however. This approach is unlikely to work well unless the organization has already established an overall philosophy of participative management, as well as a reasonable climate of organizational trust. Participation takes considerable time, so if time and trust are limited, a more traditional, top-down approach might be more appropriate.

Wage Compression

Wage compression results when wages for new hires are increasing faster than the wages of people already on the payroll.[57] As a result, the pay differentials between individuals becomes very small or nonexistent. For example, a business school may find that to be competitive it needs to offer inexperienced assistant professors $70,000 for nine months. At the same time, assistant professors with two or three years' experience are earning between $66,000 and $68,000, and several associate professors with as much as ten years' experience are earning only $77,000. Constrained by a limited budget, the dean chose to use the limited available funds primarily to recruit new faculty, who were getting attractive offers from other schools. This meant that the traditional wage differentials between ranks could not be maintained. The dean elected to create internal inequities in the interest of external competitiveness for new faculty.

Although wage compression often must be accepted in the short run, it can be extremely counterproductive if allowed to continue. In the business school example, senior faculty became dissatisfied and searched for new jobs at other universities. Since the best qualified could most easily secure new positions, the average quality of the school's remaining faculty was at risk.

Much of employers' resistance to increases in the minimum wage is not directly related to additional costs for entry-level jobs but to the threat of wage compression and the cost of preventing it. Similarly, managers frequently experience wage increases indirectly as a result of union negotiations. As wages of union members increase, the company raises salaries of lower- and middle-level managers to prevent wage compression.[58]

Impact of Inflation

Even well-designed compensation systems can have major problems in inflationary or deflationary times. In the late 1970s, many firms were limited to giving 10 percent merit raises to their best people even though the inflation rate was 13 to 14 percent. Employees felt that they were losing purchasing power. At a minimum, they hoped to keep even with inflation.

In the early 1980s, firms began catching up, giving raises in the 12 and 13 percent range. Then, once inflation had been checked, salary increases soon fell back to 7 percent. In the 1990s and thus far in the twenty-first century, merit budgets have averaged 4 percent or less. Under these circumstances, it has been difficult to convince employees that current salary increase levels are sufficient when expectations had adjusted to higher levels.[59] In order to maximize the perception of fairness, it is essential to have good communication with employees about their compensation package and salary increases.

All-Salaried Work Force

As part of the move to increase employee participation at all organizational levels, many firms have moved to an all-salaried work force. All employees, even the blue-collar workers, receive the agreed-upon salary each pay period, and the size of their checks does not depend primarily on the number of hours worked. That is, employees are not docked for lateness or other absences. This policy is meant to eliminate the feeling of hourly employees that they are second-class citizens.

The employer remains responsible for enforcing the Fair Labor Standards Act, however, and from this perspective, nonexempt salaried employees are still paid by the hour. Employers must keep a record of hours worked (presumably by less obtrusive means than a time clock) and pay overtime to all nonexempt employees who work more than forty hours in any one week, whether or not they are otherwise treated as salaried employees by the employer.

Wage Concessions

It is not unusual to read about a strike resulting from an impasse in collective bargaining. Typically, the contract has expired, and the union and management cannot agree on wages. Perhaps the union is asking for a 14 percent increase over the three years of the contract period, while the final management offer is 10 percent. But difficult economic times bring a new twist to this scenario. In one strike, management was asking the workers to take a 20 percent wage reduction. The employees, cabin attendants for TWA, were willing to accept a cut of only 15 percent, the result being a strike over the magnitude of the concession.[60]

Until the 1980s it was almost inconceivable that a well-entrenched union would agree to concessions (or reductions) in wages and benefits. Yet this is exactly what happened in the decade between the mid-1980s and mid-1990s. In the automobile, steel, and other manufacturing industries, less expensive foreign labor forced American manufacturers to bring their costs in line. Wage concessions were one part of the strategy. In other industries, such as transportation, deregulation opened routes and activities to new competition. Low-cost, nonunionized airlines were flying many of the same routes, forcing the established unionized carriers to slash labor costs.[61]

One solution adopted by some companies and unions was the two-tier wage contract. In this type of agreement, current employees continue to receive their existing wage rates, but any new hires after a specified date are paid at a much lower rate. This has proven to be a shortsighted solution because it creates substantial internal inequity, and individuals hired at the lower rate do not feel fairly treated by either the union or the company. The problems intensify the longer the system is in effect, as the lower-paid workers increase in number and in seniority.

THE ISSUE OF COMPARABLE WORTH

A policy of equal pay for equal work was mandated by the Equal Pay Act of 1963. The notion of comparable worth goes further, calling for equal pay for jobs of comparable work. **Comparable worth** is based on the idea that traditionally female-dominated jobs are underpaid relative to traditionally male-dominated jobs that require the same level of (although perhaps a different) skill and make an equally valuable contribution to the employer. At times, the ideological and political debate surrounding comparable worth has been fierce. This section examines the elements of this controversy.

The Earnings Gap

The comparable worth debate centers on what has come to be known as the **earnings gap.** Each year, the Bureau of the Census reports on the difference between women's and men's median incomes. As shown in Table 12.9, in 2000 women employees earned about $0.83 per hour for each dollar men earned.[62] Despite the gap between men and women, the 2000 figure is quite an improvement from 1979, when women earned $0.64 per hour for each dollar men earned. Questions about the earnings gap include the following: (1) Does the earnings gap represent discrimination against women by a male-dominated economic system? (2) Does it reflect the voluntary choices that women make regarding education and occupation, as filtered through the elements of supply and demand in the labor market? Although there is no complete answer to these questions, there are relevant data.[63]

There can be no doubt that women have made progress. Figure 12.8 shows that between 1964 and 1999 women's jobs doubled in nine of ten industry groups (every industry except nondurable manufacturing) while men's jobs doubled in only three of ten groups (services, retail trade, and finance). This indicates that opportunities for women have increased rather dramatically in the past four decades.

Even with the expanded opportunity for women, part of the reason for the wage gap is that women tend to hold different jobs from men, even within an occupational category. For instance, women are more likely to be nurses than physicians, both of which are part of the services industry, specifically professional health occupations. Table 12.10 shows that twenty occupations (of 427 census-defined occupations) account for almost half the women employed full time. Further, the twenty occupations employing half of all working women are among the lowest-paying occupations.[64] More recent reports reaffirm that men and women gravitate toward different kinds of jobs.[65] Further, jobs dominated by females traditionally pay less because supply exceeds demand.[66] For example, over 45 percent of today's women are in the service sector (many of the occupation categories from Table 12.10 plus others), where wages are frequently below average.[67]

Women in their late twenties or early thirties earn as much as men in the same occupation and with similar qualifications.[68] The discrepancy in earnings comes when women have children, for it is then that they cut back on work time and make different choices within career options. Overall, when occupation is included as a variable, up to 90 percent of the earnings gap between men and women can be explained.[69] This means that males and females in the same occupation with com-

● **TABLE 12.9**

Women's Earnings as a Percent of Men's: 1979–2000

Year	Hourly	Weekly	Annual
1979	64.1	62.5	59.7
1980	64.8	64.4	60.2
1981	65.1	64.6	59.2
1982	67.3	65.4	61.7
1983	69.4	66.7	63.6
1984	69.8	67.8	63.7
1985	70.0	58.2	64.6
1986	70.2	69.2	64.3
1987	72.1	70.0	65.2
1988	73.8	70.2	66.0
1989	75.4	70.1	68.7
1990	77.9	71.9	71.6
1991	78.6	74.2	69.9
1992	80.3	75.8	70.8
1993	80.4	77.1	71.5
1994	80.6	76.4	72.0
1995	80.8	75.5	71.4
1996	81.2	75.0	73.8
1997	80.8	74.4	74.2
1998	81.8	76.3	73.2
1999	83.8	76.5	72.2
2000	83.2	76.0	

Source: Department of Labor Women's Bureau, February 2001. (Available at http://www.dol.gov/dol/wb/public/wb_ubs/2000.htm)

parable seniority are closer in income, whether as word processors, assembly-line workers, or physicians.

This does not mean that there are no differences within occupations. Within occupations, women and minorities tend to hold the lower-status jobs rather than being paid less for doing the same job.[70] Women also tend to hold nonunion jobs, which are often paid less than the unionized jobs held more commonly by men. One study found that regardless of field of occupation, women had different standards for fair pay than men and expected to earn less than men.[71]

Still another explanation could have to do with types of employers preferred by men and by women. It could be that more men than women are employed by organizations with greater ability to pay. For instance, female lawyers may tend to seek jobs with public or legal aid organizations rather than with private law firms. Finally, differences reflect possible discriminatory promotion practices and related factors.

● FIGURE 12.8

Changes in Employment for Men and Women by Occupation: 1964–1999

Source: "Women's Jobs 1964–1999: More Than 30 Years of Progress," U.S. Department of Labor, Women's Bureau. (Available at: http://www.dol.gov/dol/wb/public/jobs6497.htm)

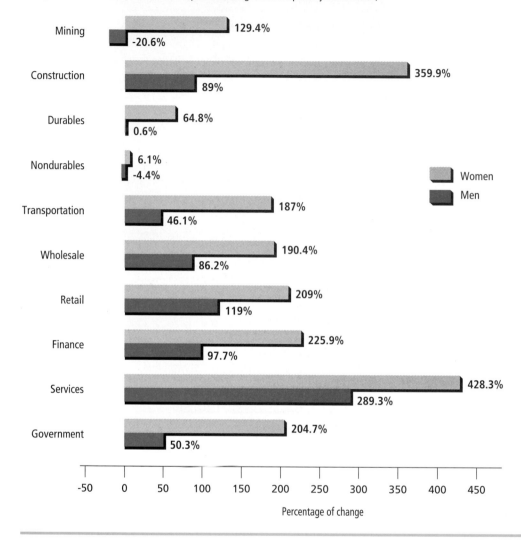

Two examples illustrate why the comparable worth debate has aroused such passion. In the city of San Jose, California, the positions of senior legal secretary (predominantly female) and senior carpenter (predominantly male) were both assigned 226 job evaluation points, yet the secretaries earned $665 per month, whereas the carpenters earned $1,040 per month. In other words, the senior secretaries' earnings were only 64 percent of the senior carpenters'—despite equivalent job evaluation points.[72] The same San Jose study found that librarians (a predominantly female job) and street sweeper operators (predominantly male) received equivalent pay of $750 per month, even though librarians were assigned many more job evaluation points than sweeper operators were.

● **TABLE 12.10**

20 Leading Occupations of Employed Women in 2000

Occupations	Women Employed (in thousands)	Total Employed (Men and Women)	Percent Women
Total, 16 yrs and over (full-time)	62,915	135,208	46.5
Sales, retail, & personal services	4,306	6,782	63.5
Secretaries	2,594	2,623	98.9
Managers and administrators	2,418	7,797	31.0
Cashiers	2,277	2,939	77.5
Sales supervisors and proprietors	1,989	4,937	40.3
Registered nurses	1,959	2,111	97.8
Elementary school teachers	1,814	2,177	83.3
Nursing aides, orderlies, and attendants	1,784	1,983	90.0
Bookkeepers, accounting, & auditing clerks	1,584	1,719	92.1
Receptionists	984	1,017	96.8
Sales workers	949	1,428	66.5
Accountants and auditors	903	1,592	56.7
Cooks	899	2,076	43.3
Investigators and adjusters (excluding insurance)	833	1,097	75.9
Janitors and cleaners	811	2,233	36.3
Secondary school teachers	764	1,319	57.9
Hairdressers and cosmetologists	748	820	91.2
General office clerks	722	864	83.6
Mgrs, food service and lodging	677	1,446	46.8
Teachers' aides	646	710	91.0

Source: "20 Leading Occupations of Employed Women 2000 Annual Averages," Department of Labor, Women's Bureau. (Available at: http://www.dol.gov/dol/wb/public/wb_pubs/20lead2000.htm)

Legal and Judicial Developments

The Equal Pay Act has not been conducive to redressing issues of comparable worth. Instead, most court cases have relied on Title VII of the Civil Rights Act. Courts generally have held that Title VII incorporates the equal pay for equal work standard (skill, effort, responsibility), along with the four affirmative defenses for pay differentials (seniority, merit, quality or quantity of work, or any condition other than sex), and allows a broader inquiry into compensation practices of defendants. The argument has been that workers in predominantly female jobs are paid less than workers in predominantly male jobs and that this is discriminatory because the jobs, although different in content, are of comparable worth to the employer.

The early pay discrimination cases showed clearly that employers had to pay workers at the same rate if those jobs required substantially the same work performed, knowledge, and skill as jobs filled predominantly by men. In *Schultz* v.

Wheaton Glass Co.,[73] men and women inspected and boxed empty bottles, yet men received 10 percent more for occasionally stacking boxes and performing other duties. The difference was ruled to be sex biased. In *Hodgson* v. *Brookhaven General Hospital*,[74] female aides claimed that their jobs were equal to those performed by more highly paid male orderlies. However, the hospital presented evidence that the duties performed by men were different, and the pay discrepancy was found to be legal.

Christensen v. *State of Iowa* was a major comparable worth case. Clerical workers (predominantly female) at the University of Northern Iowa argued that their jobs were equivalent to those of physical plant workers (predominantly male) in terms of job evaluation points, yet physical plant workers were paid at a higher rate. The university's defense was that conditions in the local labor market required it to pay physical plant workers more in order to be competitive. The court sided with the university, noting:

> The value of the job to the employer [job evaluation] represents but one factor affecting wages. Other factors may include the supply of workers willing to do the job. . . . We find nothing in the text and history of Title VII suggesting that Congress intended to abrogate the law of supply and demand or other economic principles that determine wages for various kinds of work. We do not interpret Title VII as requiring an employer to ignore the market in setting wage rates for genuinely different work classifications.[75]

The courts have consistently rejected comparable worth claims. The specific reasons for final rulings have varied but seem to reflect a sense that comparable worth is not a viable legal theory under Title VII.

Even though the courts have not been sympathetic to comparable worth, twenty states have specifically enacted legislation or adopted policies implementing comparable worth standards in the state civil service.[76] Minnesota's law is among the most stringent, requiring all public employers (state, county, school district, and so on) to establish equitable compensation relationships between female- and male-dominated jobs.[77]

Comparable Worth and Job Evaluation

Job evaluation provides one possible means of equating jobs that are different in content but equal in value. However, even the values assigned to different compensable factors may tend to discriminate against traditionally female jobs. For instance, the level of skill required to operate a word processor or teach children may be underestimated, or the value of physical work performed in nonoffice settings may be overweighted.

To clarify the role of job evaluation in pay decisions, the Equal Employment Opportunity Commission (EEOC) initiated a study of pay-related job measurement by the National Academy of Science (NAS), an independent research institute. The NAS report acknowledged the difficulty of determining comparable worth and suggested that each employer equally compensate jobs of comparable value to the organization, whether or not the work content is substantially equal.[78]

However, there are legitimate criticisms of the use of job evaluation as a vehicle to establish comparable worth.[79] Clearly, the skill, effort, and responsibility framework of job evaluation does not cover all job factors important to working individuals. For example, the positions of senior legal secretary and senior carpenter in San Jose may have been equal in job evaluation points, but few would consider them equivalent alternatives in terms of the type of work done, types of colleagues, potential for flexibility in schedule, variety, work locations, and so forth.[80]

Alternatives

One argument against comparable worth is that it would be a threat to the labor-market process of establishing wages based on supply and demand. Many contend that market rates accurately reflect job worth. The 1981 National Academy of Science report mentioned earlier noted that the market wage disparity between positions filled primarily by women and those filled primarily by men tends to reflect past practices. The report adds, "one of the features of wage differentials between jobs held by men and by women is that they become customarily accepted as the standard rates for the jobs."[81] Thus market forces do not always operate efficiently.

Market forces create many kinds of pay differences, not just between men and women. For example, college teachers in the liberal arts are paid less than engineering faculty, even though both jobs require similar skill, effort, and responsibility. The market forces that affect the two groups are quite different. Universities are locked in fairly high-level competition with private-sector firms to attract doctoral engineers to join their faculties, whereas competition for doctoral philosophers is far less acute, primarily because there are fewer nonacademic opportunities.

Further, it would be financially and motivationally ineffective for a university to equalize salaries of the engineering and liberal arts faculty. Running counter to market trends would create its own set of perceived inequities. For example, chemical engineering faculty members would see that liberal arts faculty members were being given an above-market premium while they were not. As a result, the engineers would become more likely to seek higher-paying industry positions, whereas liberal arts faculty members may not have such opportunities. In turn, academic institutions would need to raise salaries of chemical engineers to attract faculty, and the cycle would continue.

Ultimately, no job or group of jobs has an intrinsic economic worth. In the energy boom of the mid-1980s, one oil company found that accountants, attorneys, and petroleum engineers were similar in terms of job complexity, education required, and other job evaluation factors. However, the company found that it could hire all the accountants and attorneys it wanted for $22,000 to $24,000 a year but could not hire a petroleum engineer for less than $32,000. A few years later, when the energy slump hit, thousands of petroleum engineers were out of work. The company could then hire engineers for less than accountants.

Prospects for the Future

We still have not explained why jobs held predominantly by women, almost without exception, are paid less than those held predominantly by men. Are women's jobs fairly valued using existing procedures? Even though the courts and the federal legislation process have not implemented the notion of comparable worth, a number of states have proceeded in that direction.

The most aggressive approach has been in the province of Ontario, Canada. The Pay Equity Act of 1987, passed by the Ontario Legislative Assembly, was designed to redress systemic gender discrimination in compensation for female jobs.[82] The law covers every company with more than ten employees. Most organizations, especially larger organizations, are reevaluating jobs, using the point method or a computer-based evaluation procedure, to bring salaries of those in predominantly female jobs to the level of those males in equivalent jobs. One organization with 15,000 employees in 580 jobs expects the cost to be a few million dollars annually in equity adjustments.[83] Other results have been mixed. For example, almost one-third of the female-dominated jobs had no comparable-value male job. Fifty percent of the workers in female-dominated job categories at large private-sector firms were already earning the same or more than workers in comparable-value male jobs. Over 40 percent of clerical jobs received pay equity increases as compared with 19 percent in the manual/blue-collar trades and 12 percent of managerial jobs.[84]

Comparable worth is the subject of several legislative proposals at the federal level, namely the "Paycheck Fairness Act" introduced in 2001 by Senator Tom Daschle (D-SD) and Representative Rosa DeLauro (D-CT). The Paycheck Fairness Act encourages employers to develop comparable worth pay systems as a means of raising women's wages. Specifically, the bill would allow the secretary of labor to establish voluntary job evaluation guidelines. Employers would be encouraged to compare the wages paid to similarly rated jobs and identify pay disparities between those occupations dominated by women and those dominated by men.[85]

The experience of the U.S. public sector in twenty states, along with the results in Ontario, suggests that comparable worth may yet become a significant issue. As a result, many major organizations are quietly working to reduce the gap between the pay of men and women.[86]

Summary of Key Points

Compensation is an important human resource function. Pay issues are of concern to managers because of the high cost of labor to the company. Managers are also concerned about developing pay policies and methods that will help them attract, retain, and motivate employees.

The main problems in designing a direct compensation system revolve around internal, external, and individual equity. Internal equity is based on paying jobs of equal value the same amount and paying jobs of different value an acceptable set of differentials. Internal equity is established through job evaluation.

Four general approaches to job evaluation have been discussed. The two nonquantitative methods that evaluate jobs as a whole are job ranking and job classification. The other two job evaluation methods break jobs down into compensable factors to evaluate their worth. These methods are the point and factor-comparison methods. The Hay plan and computerized job evaluation procedures are variations of the point method. Job evaluation results in a wage structure or hierarchy of jobs.

The next step is to price the wage structure, being aware of external equity, or how the organization's wage rates compare with those of other employers in the labor market. Wage surveys are used to find out what other employers are paying for various jobs and to set equitable midpoints and ranges for each wage grade.

The final equity concern centers on setting the pay of individuals within a wage grade. Typical bases for this decision include seniority, merit, and skill. Merit pay systems have the potential to motivate high performance, but they are difficult to administer in a way that employees perceive as fair.

There are numerous legal constraints on compensation practices. The most important of these concern minimum wage and overtime pay and are found in the Fair Labor Standards Act and its many amendments. Additional issues in compensation include the secrecy or openness of pay systems, employee involvement in compensation decisions, and the concept of comparable worth.

The Manager's Vocabulary

broadbanding
comparable worth
compensable factors
earnings gap
equity theory
exempt employees
external equity
factor-comparison method
Fair Labor Standards Act (FLSA)
Hay plan
individual equity
internal equity
job grading (or job classification)
job ranking
lag approach
lead policy
matching the competition
merit pay
minimum wage
nonexempt employees
pay secrecy
point method
pricing the wage structure
ranking to market
seniority-based pay
skill-based pay
total compensation
wage ranges

Questions for Discussion

1. Identify at least four reasons why designing and implementing reward systems constitute one of the most complex HRM activities.
2. What is total compensation, and what are its components?
3. What does equity theory say about the way individuals evaluate and respond to their pay level?
4. What are the three elements of compensation equity? Why is each important?
5. What are the purposes of job evaluation? Why do organizations use job evaluation?

6. What are the major methods of job evaluation? Which is the most popular? Explain how each works.
7. For what types of jobs would the Hay method of job evaluation most likely be used?
8. Recommend a job evaluation system for a small family-owned business with six job titles and thirty incumbents. Recommend a system for an oil refinery with 800 employees in managerial, technical, and blue-collar jobs. Why do your recommendations differ?
9. Why do some believe job evaluation is not necessary, and even counterproductive, to the operation of a modern organization?
10. How would you go about designing a survey for setting the pay of trade employees (e.g., plumbers, electricians, welders, etc.) on your campus?
11. How would you go about designing a survey for setting the pay of faculty members on your campus? In what ways would the survey for faculty members differ from that for trade employees?
12. Define the term "pay-level policy," and discuss the three types of policies. Under what circumstances would each pay-level policy be used?
13. Which pay policy for trade employees would you recommend to your university? What circumstances faced by your university influenced your recommendation?
14. Identify three major reasons why employees doing the same job in an organization might receive different compensation.
15. What is the major purpose of the Equal Pay Act? What does it require of employers?
16. What are the advantages and disadvantages of a policy of pay openness versus pay secrecy?
17. What is wage compression? How does wage compression relate to the impact of inflation?
18. Why might two people disagree about whether or not a given pay system is fair? What are three factors on which distributive justice can be based?
19. What is meant by comparable worth, and how does this issue affect the design of a compensation system?
20. To what extent are there differences in the level of pay of men and women? Identify four possible reasons for these differences.

● Case 12.1
A Dilemma for Magnolia State Bank

Magnolia State Bank, serving a small community, has successfully bid to take over the insolvent City Bank and Trust in a large city fifty miles away. The president of Magnolia State is anxious to examine the comparability of the wage plan of the newly acquired branch with that of the Magnolia headquarters location.

Tellers and clerks, the majority of the work force at Magnolia State Bank, receive a starting wage of $250 a week ($13,000 per year), which can increase to $315 ($16,380 per year) with experience. The cost of living in Magnolia is low, and Magnolia State Bank stands virtually alone as a prestigious employer with good working conditions. In fact, the low-wage structure at Magnolia State Bank is part of the competitive strategy that has allowed the bank to maintain its position as the sole bank in the community.

City Bank and Trust is one of many banks in the large, nearby city. The cost of living is higher, and there are numerous reputable employers competing for available talent. As a result, City Bank and Trust has found that it must start clerks and tellers at $340 ($17,680), with ranges up to $425 ($22,100), to attract and retain employees with needed skills.

1. Could Magnolia State Bank justify continuing the approximate 35 percent wage differences that exist between Magnolia and the newly acquired branch?
2. If yes, how would you, as president of Magnolia State Bank, explain the differences to employees in Magnolia? Given what you know about equity theory, how would employees be likely to respond? How would you address employee concerns?
3. If no, how would you proceed to merge the systems? What effect would wage reductions have on attracting and retaining employees at the city branch? What effect would wage increases have on the competitive position of the bank in Magnolia?

● Case 12.2
The Case of Frontier Steel

Marvin Smith took pride in the company he founded, Frontier Steel, a small steel fabricator in the St. Louis area. He developed the company to its current 125 employees and considered each employee as a friend. In the early 1980s, he decided that having some employees paid by the hour and others as salaried employees created an unnecessary division within his "family." As a result, he sought help from a consultant and followed the recommendation to create an all-salaried work force at Frontier Steel. The time clock used by hourly employees was removed, and all employees were paid a fixed monthly salary.

Recently, Mary Jones, a long-time employee, was dismissed as a result of differences with her supervisor. Smith was surprised to learn that Jones had filed a federal wage-and-hour claim seeking back pay for the overtime she had worked over a five-year period. More specifically, approximately five years before Jones was dismissed, she asked and was granted permission to arrive at work thirty minutes early every day so that she could ride to the plant with her husband. Jones was now claiming that these approximately 600 extra hours worked over the five years were overtime, a potential cost of $7,200. More troubling to Smith was the fact that many employees had been given permission to vary their schedules in the same way that Jones had done.

1. What are the rules governing an all-salaried work force?
2. Would Frontier Steel be liable for back overtime pay for all employees who worked extra hours? If yes, why? If no, what would determine liability?
3. What should Frontier Steel have done to avoid the type of claim Mary Jones filed?

Source: Adapted from Kent Banning, "Know the Rules on Pay and Hours." Reprinted by permission, *Nation's Business,* April 1991. Copyright 1991, U.S. Chamber of Commerce.

Exercise 12.1
Yates Manufacturing Company

Job Evaluation at Yates   Yates Manufacturing is in the process of installing a job evaluation program in the machine shop. The program is an attempt to establish more consistent relationships between the hourly rates for the various occupations and generally to improve the company's overall wage structure.

As a machine shop supervisor, you have been assigned to the Evaluation Committee. The Evaluation Committee consists of supervisors and employees from the machine shop plus the head of human resources. As its first task, the Evaluation Committee prepared job descriptions for the different jobs in the machine shop. The committee then assigned job evaluation points to the jobs on the basis of a widely published point-rating plan.

Of the jobs evaluated, the actual hourly rates for fourteen were believed by the committee to represent current competitive rates. Therefore, it was decided to base the intraplant wage survey on these fourteen key jobs and to establish the policy line

linking pay to job evaluation points. After this policy line was established, the hourly rates for the balance of jobs could be determined from the various point values assigned by the committee. As a result of the survey, Table 1 was constructed with the job names, point ratings assigned by the Evaluation Committee, and actual hourly rates.

Spreadsheet Instructions for Determining the Policy Line   These instructions presume student access to spreadsheet software such as Lotus, Quattro Pro, or Excel.

1. Enter the point ratings in rows A1–A14 of the spreadsheet. The value 275 should be entered in cell A1 (automatic screw machine operator) and 150 in cell A14 (custodian/runner).
2. Enter hourly pay in rows B1–B14 of the spreadsheet. The value $8.50 should be entered in cell B1 and $5.25 in cell B14.
3. Enter the job titles in rows C1–C14 of the spreadsheet. (Optional.)

●**TABLE 1**

Point Ratings and Hourly Rates

Job No.	Job	Point Rating	Hourly Rate
1	Automatic screw machine operator	275	$9.35
2	Bench lathe operator	241	$8.89
3	Bench worker A	164	$6.97
4	Casting grinder and polisher	209	$9.09
5	Drill press operator	224	$7.61
6	Milling machine operator	311	$9.64
7	Machine operator (tool room)	311	$10.87
8	Punch press operator	271	$9.28
9	Soldering	216	$7.37
10	Stores clerk	205	$7.33
11	Tool crib attendant	246	$8.89
12	Toolmaker	381	$10.80
13	Turret lathe operator	331	$10.21
14	Custodian/runner	150	$5.78

4. Double-check all entries against the values in Table 1.
5. Use the correlation function, specifying A1–A14 as the first sequence and B1–B14 as the second sequence.
6. Use the chart function to plot the fourteen jobs in Table 1 in a scatterplot. The hourly rates should be specified as the Y (vertical) axis and the point ratings as the X (horizontal) axis. Each of the points represents the intersection of rating points and hourly rates for a job. The toolmaker should be in the upper right (with 381 points and an hourly rate of $9.82) and the custodian/runner in the lower left (with 150 points and an hourly rate of $1.50).
7. Print the scatterchart produced in step 6.
8. Using the forecast (or equivalent) function, predict the hourly rate (Y) for a job with 100 rating points. Then predict the hourly rate (Y) for a job with 300 rating points. Plot the two points on the chart printed in step 7. Connect the two points with a line. The result is the "line of best fit," or regression line.

9. Finally, using the instructions in the text and Figure 12.6, construct pay ranges for Yates Manufacturing's machine shop jobs.

Calculator Instructions for Determining the Policy Line   A calculator and grid-lined paper are needed for the following instructions:

1. On regular grid-lined paper ($8\frac{1}{2} \times 11$), plot the point ratings as the (X) variable along the 11-inch side of the paper and the corresponding hourly rates as the (Y) variable along the $8\frac{1}{2}$-inch side of the paper. Start both scales from zero in the lower left corner, and allow one-half inch for each 25 points and each $1.
2. Fill in the required calculations in Table 2. The calculations include the square of each point rating value (X^2), the square of each hourly rate (Y^2), and the cross-products of the point rating times the hourly rate $(X \times Y)$.
3. Sum the values in each of the five columns to obtain ΣX, ΣX^2, ΣY, ΣY^2, and ΣXY.
4. Double-check all calculations.

● **TABLE 2**

Calculation Sheet

Job No.	(X) Point Rating	(X²)	(Y) Hourly Rate	(Y²)	(X × Y)
1	275		$9.35		
2	241		$8.89		
3	164		$6.97		
4	209		$9.09		
5	224		$7.61		
6	311		$9.64		
7	311		$10.87		
8	271		$9.28		
9	216		$7.37		
10	205		$7.33		
11	246		$8.89		
12	381		$10.80		
13	331		$10.21		
14	150		$5.78		
Totals					
N = 14	(ΣX)	(ΣX^2)	(ΣY)	(ΣY^2)	(ΣXY)

● **TABLE 3**

Warehouse Department Positions

Job	Point Rating	Actual Hourly Rate	Predicted Hourly Rate
Assistant superintendent	400	$11.55	
Lift truck operator	206	$9.57	
Shipping clerk	315	$7.92	
Stockperson	246	$6.82	
Loader	175	$6.16	

5. Calculate the correlation coefficient (r) using the following formula:

$$r = \frac{N\Sigma\, XY - \Sigma\, X\Sigma\, Y}{\sqrt{[N\Sigma\, X^2 - (\Sigma\, X)^2][N\Sigma\, Y^2 - (\Sigma\, Y)^2]}}$$

6. Calculate the linear regression to predict hourly rate (Y) from job evaluation points (X) using the following formula:

$$Y = b_{yx}\, X + a_{yx} \quad \text{where}$$

$$b_{yx} = \frac{\Sigma\, XY - (\Sigma\, X\Sigma\, Y/N)}{\Sigma\, X^2 - [(\Sigma\, X)^2/N]}$$

$$a_{yx} = \frac{\Sigma\, Y - b_{yx}\, \Sigma X}{N}$$

7. Using the formula developed in step 6, predict the hourly rate (Y) for a job with 100 rating points. Then predict the hourly rate (Y) for a job with 300 rating points. Plot the two points, on the chart drawn in step 1. Connect the two points with a line. The result is the "line of best fit," or regression line.

8. Finally, using the instructions in the text and Figure 12.6, construct pay ranges for Yates Manufacturing's machine shop jobs.

The Warehouse at Yates   Soon after the job evaluation was completed for the Yates machine shop, the warehouse superintendent asked the Evaluation Committee if the results suggested salary adjustments in the warehouse. The Evaluation Commit-

tee evaluated the warehouse jobs and used the point values to predict hourly rates. These predicted hourly rates were then compared to actual rates. The warehouse positions, point values, and hourly rates are shown on Table 3.

Instructions for Determining Warehouse Wages   Instructions are the same for calculator or spreadsheet.

1. Using a different-colored ink from that used previously, plot the job evaluation points and hourly wages from Table 3 on the chart prepared previously.
2. Using the information from Table 3 and the instructions in step 8 (spreadsheet) or step 7 (calculator), determine the predicted hourly wages for each warehouse job.
3. Enter the predicted hourly wages on Table 3.

Questions

1. How many ranges did you construct?
2. Were any of the machine shop jobs outside the ranges? If so, what are your pay recommendations for these jobs?
3. Did any of the warehouse jobs fall outside the ranges? If so, what are your recommendations to the warehouse superintendent regarding the pay for warehouse jobs?

Source: Adapted from Raymond L. Hilgert, Sterling H. Schoen, and Cyril C. Ling, *Cases and Experiential Exercises in Human Resource Management* (Boston: Allyn and Bacon, 1990).

● Exercise 12.2
Standard-of-Living Adjustment

Your company is transferring an employee from Atlanta, Georgia, to open a new office in Los Angeles, California. The employee owns a home in Atlanta, is currently making $55,000 in Atlanta, and is concerned about how far that salary will go in Los Angeles. What income will the employee need in Los Angeles to own a home and have an income equivalent to the current Atlanta income? To answer this question, proceed as follows:

1. Locate the following web site: HYPERLINK http://www.homefair.com/
2. On the tools bar, click the "salary calculator."

3. On the state screen, enter the respective states of Georgia and California. Then click "show cities."
4. On the cities screen, enter the salary, $55,000, and the respective cities, Atlanta and Los Angeles. For housing preference, select "own."
5. At the bottom of the cities screen, click "calculate" and note the Los Angeles income needed for a standard of living equivalent to the standard of living in Atlanta.

Source: Adapted from Georganna Hall and Gemmy Allen, *The Internet Guide for Human Resources* (Cincinnati, Ohio: South-Western College Publishing, 1997).

● Exercise 12.3
External Equity

Your instructor will provide you with average weekly earnings for two positions at your college:

1. Entry-level secretary
2. Entry-level computer systems analyst

Using the web site http://stats.bls.gov:80/ocsntl93.htm, answer the following questions:

1. Using the geographic areas where your campus is located, how do the earnings for these two entry-level positions compare with the region?
2. How do the entry-level earnings for these two positions compare with the U.S. average?

Notes and References

1. Greg Cornish and Garry Adams, "Trends in Remuneration: The Concept of Total Quality Pay," *Asia Pacific Human Resources*, Vol. 31, 1993, pp. 75–86.

2. Elizabeth J. Hawk, "Culture and Rewards: A Balancing Act," *Personnel Journal*, April 1995, p. 37.

3. Edward E. Lawler, "The Design of Effective Reward Systems," in *Handbook of Organizational Behavior,* ed. J. W. Lorsch (Englewood Cliffs, N.J.: Prentice-Hall, 1987), p. 255.

4. F. A. Heller and L. Porter, "Perceptions of Managerial Needs and Skills in Two National Samples," *Occupational Psychology*, Vol. 40, 1966, pp. 1–13.

5. "The High Price of Overtime," *Los Angeles Times*, January 16, 1990, pp. A1, A20–A21.

6. Douglas Lavin and Gabriella Stern, "GM-UAW End 3-Day Strike at Parts Plant," *Wall Street Journal*, January 23, 1995, p. A2; and Sunil Babbar and David J. Aspelin, "The Overtime Rebellion: Symptom of a Bigger Problem?" *Academy of Management Executive*, Vol. 12, 1998, pp. 68–76.

7. John Marks, "Time Out," *U.S. News & World Report*, December 11, 1995, pp. 85–96.

8. J. Stacy Adams, "Toward an Understanding of Inequity," *Journal of Abnormal and Social Psychology*, October 1963, pp. 422–436.

9. Jerald Greenberg, "Employee Theft as a Reaction to Underpayment Inequity: The Hidden Cost of Pay Cuts," *Journal of Applied Psychology*, Vol. 75, 1990, pp. 561–568.

10. Edward E. Lawler, *Motivation in Work Organizations* (Pacific Grove, Calif.: Brooks/Cole, 1973).

11. Edward E. Lawler, *Strategic Pay* (San Francisco: Jossey-Bass, 1990).

12. "Majority of Workers Are Dissatisfied with Pay," *HR Magazine*, June 2001, pp. 35, 37.

13. Robert W. Rice, Suzanne M. Phillips, and Dean B. McFarlin, "Multiple Discrepancies and Pay Satisfaction," *Journal of Applied Psychology*, Vol. 75, 1990, pp. 386–393.

14. Bureau of National Affairs, *Wage and Salary Administration* (Washington, D.C.: U.S. Government Printing Office, 1990), p. 6.

15. L. Dyer, D. P. Schwab, and R. D. Theriault, "Managerial Perceptions Regarding Salary Increase Criteria," *Personnel Psychology*, Vol. 29, 1976, pp. 233–242.

16. Robert B. Pursell, "R&D Job Evaluation and Compensation," *Compensation Review*, Vol. 2, 1972, pp. 21–31; and T. Atchinson and W. French, "Pay Systems for Scientists and Engineers," *Industrial Relations*, Vol. 7, 1967, pp. 44–56.

17. Bureau of National Affairs, *Wage and Salary Administration,* p. 6.

18. Pursell, "R&D Job Evaluation and Compensation."

19. Edward N. Hay and Dale Purves, "The Profile Method of High Level Job Evaluation," *Personnel*, September 1951, pp. 162–170.

20. Hewitt Associates, *Total Compensation DataBase CompBook 1989–1990* (Lincolnshire, Ill.: Author, 1990).

21. Donald P. Schwab, "Job Evaluation and Pay Setting: Concepts and Practices," in *Comparable Worth: Issues and Alternatives,* ed. E. Robert Livernash (Washington: Equal Employment Advisory Council, 1980).

22. N. Fredric Crandall, "Computerizing Job Evaluation for Greater Efficiency and Effectiveness," *Topics in Total Compensation*, Vol. 3, 1989, pp. 241–250.

23. Denise Barry and Kara McLaughlin, "A S.M.A.R.T. Method for Comp Analysis," *HRMagazine*, May 1996, pp. 80–83.

24. Lawler, *Strategic Pay.*

25. Jay R. Schuster and Patricia K. Zingheim, *The New Pay: Linking Employee and Organizational Performance* (Lexington, Mass.: Lexington Books, 1992).

26. Ibid.

27. Emily Pavlovic, "Choosing the Best Salary Surveys," *HRMagazine*, April 1994, pp. 44–48.

28. Anthony J. Dennis, "Avoiding the Antitrust Traps," *HRFocus*, September 1995, p. 11.

29. Lester C. Thurow, *Generating Inequity: Mechanisms of Distribution in the U.S. Economy* (New York: Basic Books, 1975); Caroline L. Weber and Sara L. Rynes, "Effects of Compensation Strategy on Job Pay Decisions," *Academy of Management Journal*, Vol. 34, 1991, pp. 86–109; and Brian S. Klaas and John A. McClendon, "To Lead, Lag, or Match: Estimating the Financial Impact of Pay Level Policies," *Personnel Psychology*, Vol. 46, 1996, pp. 121–141.

30. Daniel J. B. Mitchell, "How to Find Wage Spillovers (Where None Exist)," *Industrial Relations*, Fall 1982, pp. 392–398; and H. Gregg Lewis, "Union Relative Wage Effects: A Survey of Macro Estimates," *Journal of Labor Economics*, January 1983, pp. 1–27.

31. See http://www.benjerry.com.

32. Thomas A. Mahoney, *Compensation and Reward Perspectives* (Homewood, Ill.: Irwin, 1979).

33. Chockalingam Viswesvaran and Murray R. Barrick, "Decision-Making Effects on Compensation Surveys: Implications for Market Wages," *Journal of Applied Psychology*, Vol. 77, 1992, pp. 588–597.

34. Kenneth S. Law and James R. Carlopio, "Two Statistical Aids for Determining the Optimal Number and Width of Pay Grades," *Asia Pacific Human Resources*, Vol. 30, 1992, pp. 60–71.

35. Ibid.

36. Larry Reissman, "Nine Common Myths about Broadbands," *HRMagazine,* 1995, Vol. 40(8), pp. 79–86.

37. Peter V. LeBlanc and Michael McInerney, "Need a Change? Jump on the Banding Wagon," *Personnel Journal,* January 1994, pp. 72–78.

38. Frank H. Wagner, "Broadbanding in Practice: Hard Facts and Real Data," *Journal of Compensation and Benefits*, Vol. 10, July–August 1994, pp. 27–34.

39. Karen Jacobs, "A New Approach to Pay Scales Gives Employers Flexibility," *Wall Street Journal*, April 10, 1997, p. A10.

40. W. A. Evans, "Pay for Performance: Fact or Fable," *Personnel Journal*, September 1970, pp. 726–729.

41. Herbert H. Meyer, "The Pay-for-Performance Dilemma," *Organizational Dynamics*, Winter 1975, pp. 71–78.

42. Nathan B. Winstanley, "Are Merit Increases Really Effective?" *Personnel Administrator*, Vol. 4, 1982, pp. 23–31; regarding requirement 5, see also Michael Keeley, "A Contingency Framework for Performance Evaluation," *Academy of Management Review*, July 1978, pp. 428–438.

43. H. Tosi and L. Tosi, "What Managers Need to Know About Knowledge-Based Pay," *Organizational Dynamics*, Vol. 14 (3), 1986, pp. 52–64.

44. Michelle Conlin, "Revenge of the 'Managers,'" *Business Week*, March 12, 2001, pp. 60–61.

45. Larry M. Wolf and Kevin C. McCormick, "Highlights of Wage and Hour Law," paper presented at the Whiteford, Taylor, and Preston 1989 Employment Law Update, Baltimore, May 24, 1989.

46. Rick Wartzman, "Devalued: How Minimum Wage Lost Its Status as a Tool of Social Progress," *Wall Street Journal*, July 19, 2001, pp. A1, A10–A11.

47. "Nominal and Real Federal Hourly Minimum Wage Rates, 1980-99." (Available at: http://www.dol.gov/dol/ilab/public/media/reports/oiea/wagestudy/FS-UnitedStates.htm)

48. Wartzman, "Devalued."

49. Richard S. Dunham, "The GOP Squabbles, and Business Suffers," *Business Week*, March 2, 1998, pp. 38–39; and Wartzman, "Devalued."

50. Gillian Flynn, "Overtime Compensation Isn't as Simple as It Seems," *Personnel Journal*, December 1995, p. 104.

51. "Garment Enforcement Report October 2000–December 2000," U.S. Department of Labor. (Available at: http://www.dol.gov/dol/esa/public/nosweat/garment21.htm)

52. Marc J. Wallace, Jr., and Charles H. Fay, *Compensation Theory and Practice* (Boston: PWS-Kent, 1988), pp. 136–138.

53. Edward E. Lawler, "Managers' Perception of Their Subordinates' Pay and of Their Superiors' Pay," *Personnel Psychology*, Vol. 18, 1965, pp. 413–422.

54. L. H. Kidder, G. Bellettirie, and E. S. Cohn, "Secret Ambitions and Public Performances," *Journal of Experimental Social Psychology*, Vol. 13, 1977, pp. 70–80; and Kathryn M. Bartol and David C. Martin, "Effects of Dependence, Dependency Threats, and Pay Secrecy on Managerial Pay Allocations," *Journal of Applied Psychology*, Vol. 74, 1989, pp. 105–113.

55. Bureau of National Affairs, *Wage and Salary Administration*, p. 21.

56. E. E. Lawler III and J. R. Hackman, "The Impact of Employee Participation in the Development of Pay Incentive Plans: A Field Experiment," *Journal of Applied Psychology*, Vol. 53, 1969, pp. 467–471.

57. Thomas J. Bergmann, Frederick S. Hills, and Laurel Priefert, "Pay Compression: Causes, Results, and Possible Solutions," *Compensation Review*, Vol. 15, 2nd Qtr., 1983, pp. 17–26.

58. R. Kemp, Salary Compression Workshop, Regional Conference Proceedings, American Compensation Association, 1978.

59. Labor Letter, "A Special Report on People and Their Jobs in Offices, Fields, and Factories: Top Officers' Pay Slowed in 1982, but Fringes Abound," *Wall Street Journal*, April 26, 1983, p. 1

60. Carol J. Loomis, "The Comeuppance of Carl Icahn," *Fortune*, February 17, 1986, pp. 18–25.

61. Frank Swoboda and Don Phillips, "US Airways Chief Tells Employees He Will Begin 'Operational Changes,'" *Washington Post*, May 6, 1997, p. C3.

62. Department of Labor Women's Bureau, February 2001. (Available at: http://www.dol.gov/dol/wb/public/wb_ubs/2000.htm)

63. Edwin G. Dolan, *Economics of Public Policy*, 5th ed. (St. Paul, Minn.: West/Wadsworth, 1995).

64. Mary V. Moore and Yohannan T. Abraham, "Comparable Worth: Is It a Moot Issue?" *Public Personnel Management*, Vol. 21, 1992, pp. 455–472.

65. Kathleen Schalch, "Ending Male/Female Income Inequality," National Public Radio, April 2, 1998> (Available at: http://www.npr.org/programs/ morning/archives/1998/980402.me.html)

66. Marlene Kim, "Women Paid Low Wages: Who They Are and Where They Work," *Monthly Labor Review*, September 2000, pp. 26–30.

67. Ibid.

68. Schalch, "Ending Male/Female Income Inequality."

69. Dolan, *Economics of Public Policy*; Erica L. Groshen, "The Structure of the Female/Male Wage Differential: Is It Who You Are, What You Do, or Where You Work?" *Journal of Human Resources*, Vol. 26, 1991, pp. 457–472; and Schalch, "Ending Male/Female Income Inequality."

70. G. Johnson and G. Solon, *Pay Differences Between Women's and Men's Jobs* (Cambridge, Mass.: National Bureau of Economic Research, 1984).

71. Linda A. Jackson, Philip D. Gardner, and Linda A. Sullivan, "Explaining Gender Differences in Self-Pay Expectations: Social Comparison Standards and Perceptions of Fair Pay," *Journal of Applied Psychology*, Vol. 77, 1992, pp. 651–663.

72. Ronnie J. Steinberg, "Identifying Wage Discrimination and Implementing Pay Equity Adjustments," in *Comparable Worth: Issue for the 80's* (Washington: U.S. Commission on Civil Rights, 1985), Vol. I.

73. *Schultz* v. *Wheaton Glass Co.*, 421 F. 2d 259 (1970).

74. *Hodgson* v. *Brookhaven General Hospital*, 436 F. 2d 719 (5th Cir. 1970).

75. *Christensen* v. *State of Iowa*, 16 FEP Cases 232 (1977).

76. Thomas J. Patten, *Fair Pay* (San Francisco: Jossey-Bass, 1988).

77. Richard D. Arvey and Katherine Holt, "The Cost of Alternative Comparable Worth Strategies," *Compensation and Benefits*, Vol. 20, 1988, pp. 37–46.

78. Donald J. Treiman and Heidi I. Hartman (eds.), *Women, Work, and Wages: Equal Pay for Jobs of Equal Value* (Washington, D.C.: National Academy Press, 1981).

79. Thurow, *Generating Inequity;* and Peter B. Olney, Jr., "Meeting the Challenge of Comparable Worth," Part 1, *Compensation and Benefits*, Vol. 19, 1987, pp. 34–44.

80. *American Nurses Association* v. *State of Illinois*, 37 FEP Cases 495 (1985).

81. Cited in Treiman and Hartman, *Women, Work, and Wages.*

82. Kenneth A. Kovach and Peter E. Millspaugh, "Comparable Worth: Canada Legislates Pay Equity," *Academy of Management Executive*, Vol. 4, 1990, pp. 92–101; and Lynne Kilpatrick, "In Ontario, 'Equal Pay for Equal Work' Becomes a Reality, but Not Very Easily," *Wall Street Journal*, March 9, 1990, p. B1.

83. Kovach and Millspaugh, "Comparable Worth."

84. Brian P. Smeenk, "Canada's Pay Equity Experiments," *HRMagazine*, Vol. 38, 1993, pp. 58–61.

85. Society for Human Resource Management (SHRM) Governmental Affairs Department, "Equal Pay," Legislative Fact Sheets, March 2001.

86. Aaron Bernstein, "Comparable Worth: It's Already Happening," *Business Week,* April 28, 1986, pp. 52, 56.

Incentive Compensation and Benefits

HR Challenge

You are manager of compensation at Charisma Tubing Company, a medium-sized manufacturer of metal and plastic pipes, tubes, and conduits. The company has three manufacturing plants in the Midwest. The HR group has just conducted an employee attitude survey, and you are looking at the responses to questions concerning Charisma's merit pay system. This merit system has been in place since the early 1970s. It features annual performance reviews culminating in a merit pay recommendation for each employee. In some years the top merit increase has been as high as 12 percent, whereas more recently the top raise has been only 2 or 3 percent. Employees apparently feel that the system is quite unfair, with top performers during the belt-tightening years earning less than those who excelled in earlier years when generous increases were more common. Some employees feel that there is a great deal of favoritism in recommendations for merit increases. Few employees think that the system has any positive motivational impact, and you are convinced that it has out-lived its usefulness.

You would like to install an entirely new system for rewarding high perfor-mance. Such a system should be tied to Charisma Tubing's ability to pay; should mo-tivate high performance by individuals, groups, and entire plants; should be as ob-jective as possible; and should encourage innovation and ongoing improvement. You mull over the variety of plans available, including individual or group bonuses, pay-for-skills plans, profit sharing, gain sharing, and so on. Which will best suit the needs of Charisma Tubing?

Global competition has posed a difficult challenge for organizations in general and for human resource specialists in particular.[1] HR managers must try to de-velop human resource programs that improve productivity and enhance organiza-tional effectiveness. Attaining these goals will help ensure that American busi-nesses will be competitive in national and world arenas.

One popular approach to enhancing productivity has been the linking of re-wards to performance through various forms of **incentive pay.**[2] In fact, the idea of incentive pay is so widely accepted that most organizations say that they pay for performance. A survey by Hewitt Associates, the compensation and benefits con-sulting firm, found that in 2001, 81 percent of the almost 1,000 companies surveyed were using incentive pay for nonexecutive employees based on some measure of performance.[3] This was an increase from 70 percent in 1999. According to the Hewitt survey, the most common types of incentive pay were the following:

- *Special recognition* to acknowledge outstanding individual or group achieve-ments with small cash awards or merchandise (e.g., gift certificates)
- *Individual performance* rewards based on specific employee performance crite-ria
- *Business incentives,* which are awards to employees for a combination of finan-cial and operational measures for company, business unit, department, plant and/or individual peformance
- *Stock ownership* rewards to professionals who meet specific goals

Incentive pay went from 4 percent of total compensation (for salaried workers) to almost 11 percent in the 1990s.[4] Most managers and many workers believe that performance should be the most important factor in determining salary increases.[5] Besides, studies indicate that linking pay to performance can lead to better em-ployee performance.[6]

The goal of performance-based reward systems is to reward participants in di-rect relation to their individual performance and contribution to organizational suc-cess. In the past, compensation practice was dominated by traditional (fixed) pay plans, in which pay increases were given across the board or based on the cost of living or seniority.

The preceding chapter defined *organizational rewards* as the money, goods, and/or services provided by an employer to its employees. Thus the reward sys-tem includes more than just direct compensation, and direct compensation may include more than just base pay (salary or wage). This chapter covers some of the additional components that, taken together, make up the reward system. The first part of this chapter explores the elements of direct compensation that go beyond fixed salary and wages—specifically, various types of individual and group incentive systems. (The Ethical Perspective box provides a cautionary note for managers attempting to use reward systems to motivate appropriate employee behavior.) In the second part of this chapter, the discussion focuses on indirect compensation, particularly legislatively mandated benefits (such as Social Security and workers' compensation) and optional benefits (such as insurance, pensions, vacations, and sick leave). The implementation and administration challenges associated with both incentives and benefits are examined.

STRATEGIC IMPORTANCE OF VARIABLE PAY

E. E. Lawler gave the name **new pay** to reward programs that seek to align compensation with organizational goals, values, and culture, as well as with the challenges of the global economy.[7] New pay goes beyond individual or group incentive pay and seeks to provide a mechanism for an organization to use all elements of compensation, direct (cash compensation) and indirect (benefits), to help forge a partnership between the organization and its employees. The aim is employees who exhibit the following qualities:

- Understand the goals of the organization
- Know their role in accomplishing these goals
- Become appropriately involved in decisions of the organization
- Accept that their rewards are related to their contribution to the goal attainment of the organization[8]

Having determined their goals, objectives, and values, how do organizations signal these elements to their employees? Assuming that an organization has selected the right individuals, has trained these individuals, and has established appropriate work systems, it is still a challenge to have these employees understand what needs to be done. A major mechanism for indicating the organizational goals and objectives is the compensation system. This can best be understood from examples of misalignment:

- What is being signaled to coworkers when well-intentioned but ineffective employees are given above-average merit increases?
- What is being signaled to employees when executives are given large bonuses after the organization has had a below-average year, and only small increases are given to other workers?
- What is being signaled if high commissions and other incentives are paid to field sales representatives, but there is no monitoring of sales practices?
- What is being signaled if an organization has an established bonus system, does not attain the profits necessary to trigger the bonuses in a given year, but decides to pay them anyway "because it was a tough year"?

Basic to the effective functioning of any organization is the way it uses its system of total compensation to communicate to employees both what needs to be done and their role in accomplishing these objectives. The preceding examples of misalignment are frequently well-intentioned actions on the part of managers but obviously are not consistent with the desired alignment between rewards and or-

Reward Systems and Unethical Behavior

When individuals are caught in organizational wrongdoing, there is a tendency to blame the individual for some sort of character weakness and to suggest that the appropriate remedy is to hire more ethical employees. However, in many cases the organizational reward system is at least partly at fault. Some reward systems "lead employees into temptation"* in subtle ways, whereas others actively threaten employees with severe punishment if they fail to go along with organizational wrongdoing. Steven Kerr, in a classic article entitled "On the Folly of Rewarding A While Hoping for B," points out that employees are very good at figuring out what really gets rewarded and doing (or appearing to do) those things, regardless of what the organization officially says it wants employees to do.

Erik Jansen and Mary Ann Von Glinow describe a common situation faced by employees called "ethical ambivalence." This occurs when the openly espoused norms or desires of the organization or some of its constituents (clients, regulatory agencies) are in conflict with the workings of the reward system and the norms generated by that system. Examples include the following contradictory pairs of norms:[†]

Follow the rules	Get the job done any way you can
Take responsibility	Avoid committing yourself; pass the buck
Teamwork	Individual visibility, grandstanding
Develop and mentor subordinates	Look out for number one
Cooperate and help others	Look good compared to others

If the reward system pays off for cutthroat behavior, this is what the organization will get, despite protestations by upper management that teamwork and cooperation should be the order of the day. If the organization wants high-quality work but measures only attendance and tardiness, it will get prompt attendance but probably not high-quality work. If the organization says that it wants good customer service but pays only for net sales, it will have salespersons who push unneeded merchandise onto customers and

are very reluctant to take returns. There are cases in which sales employees made large purchases on their own credit cards to get their department over its quota for the month and then returned the merchandise to another branch of the store. Clearly, this is not what the organization wants, but the reward system allows and even pays off for such behavior. And once any person figures out how to outsmart the system, there is pressure on others to do likewise or fall behind.

Another point (from expectancy theory) is that people act on the basis of what they think will be rewarded or punished. A subordinate who is uncomfortable with an order received from a superior or some other company action may envision negative consequences for speaking up and may feel pressure to comply whether or not the consequences would actually follow. This subtle or imagined pressure is probably behind a lot of the ethical conflicts experienced by employees in organizations.

Finally, there certainly are cases in which organizations intentionally threaten and pressure individuals to do the wrong thing—for example, to falsify data to get a government contract or to cover up a problem with product safety.

The HR practitioner must remember that the appraisal and reward system is very potent. It can be harnessed to assess and encourage responsible and ethical behavior. However, it also can (either intentionally or unintentionally) motivate behavior that is interpersonally, organizationally, or socially dysfunctional. Careful attention to the design of appraisal and reward systems is necessary to ensure that they do in fact elicit the type of behavior the organization wants from its employees.

Sources: Erik Jansen and Mary Ann Von Glinow, "Ethical Ambivalence and Organizational Reward Systems," *Academy of Management Review,* October 1985, pp. 814–822; Steven Kerr, "On the Folly of Rewarding A While Hoping for B," *Academy of Management Journal,* December 1975, pp. 769–783; Saul W. Gellerman, "Why 'Good' Managers Make Bad Ethical Choices," in *Ethics in Practice: Managing the Moral Corporation,* ed. Kenneth R. Andrews and Donald K. David (Boston: Harvard Business School Press, 1989), pp. 18–25; and Andre H. J. Nijhof and Marius M. Rietdijk, "An ABC-Analysis of Ethical Organizational Behavior," *Journal of Business Ethics,* May 1999, pp. 39–50.

*Jansen and Glinow, "Ethical Ambivalence and Organizational Reward Systems," p. 821.

†Ibid., slightly modified.

ganizational objectives. Any system of compensation is highly visible and becomes central to the very fabric of the organization.

LINKING PAY TO PERFORMANCE

Employers believe that reward systems in general and incentive systems in particular influence performance. Among respondents to an American Productivity and Quality Center survey of employers, for example, the vast majority believed that various incentive pay systems have a very positive effect on performance (see Table 13.1). In addition, many workers prefer that pay be linked to performance, reinforcing the motivation to use such reward systems.

Reasons to Link Pay to Performance

● **Motivation**   Several studies, including research based on free agency and final-offer arbitration in major league baseball,[9] have indicated that when pay is contingent on performance, individual and group performances are consistently higher than when this contingency is not present.[10] Vroom's **expectancy theory** suggests that a pay–performance link is essential for motivating performance.[11] Among approaches to understanding work motivation, expectancy theory is widely accepted and has fairly strong empirical support in applied and theoretical

● **TABLE 13.1**

Ratings of the Overall Performance Impact of Reward Systems

Reward System	(N)	Percent[a]
Pay for knowledge[b]	70	89%
Earned time off	99	85
Gain sharing	170	81
Small group incentives	185	75
Profit sharing	507	74
Individual incentives[c]	192	73
All salaried[b]	169	67
Lump-sum bonus[b]	163	66
Recognition[c]	487	30

[a]Percent reporting "positive" or "very positive" on a scale of 1 to 5:
1 = very negative impact on performance
2 = negative
3 = no impact
4 = positive
5 = very positive impact on performance
[b]Only includes firms using plans with production and/or service workers.
[c]Percent reporting "effective" or "very effective" on scale of 1 to 5 from (1) not effective at all to (5) very effective.
Source: People, Performance, and Pay, American Productivity and Quality Center, 1987. Reprinted by permission.

settings.[12] As shown in Figure 13.1, the expectancy model has three major components, each of which is based on a series of fairly straightforward observations.

1. **Expectancy:** The individual's perceptions of the probability that effort will lead to task accomplishment or performance
2. **Instrumentality:** Perceptions of the probability that performance will result in receiving rewards (such as pay or recognition)
3. **Valence:** The subjective value or desirability that the individual places on the attainment of a certain reward

The expectancy model can be summarized as

$$M = E \Sigma(IV)$$

Where M = motivation, E = expectancy, I = instrumentality, and V = valence.

As an example of how expectancy theory works, consider the case of an organization sponsoring a contest to motivate its salespersons. A trip around the world will be awarded to the salesperson with the greatest dollar volume of sales for the calendar year. According to expectancy theory, the motivational impact of this contest would depend on individual salespersons' expectancy (perceived chance of being the top salesperson), instrumentality (belief that the company will actually award the prize), and valence (desirability of the round-the-world trip). A salesperson who thinks she has a decent chance to win, believes the trip will be awarded, and has a strong desire to travel should be highly motivated by this contest. A second salesperson who believes that she has absolutely no chance of being the top seller (zero expectancy) probably will make little effort to win, even if she would greatly enjoy the trip. A third salesperson may have a very low instrumentality, believing that the company will not really award such an expensive prize. Mistrustful of the offered bargain, he will not be motivated by the contest. Also unresponsive will be a salesperson who feels that the reward is not positively valent (e.g., if he hates to travel and is terrified of airplanes).

To produce maximum motivation, all three components of the expectancy model must be high. Incentive compensation systems are designed to raise two of the three components. Instrumentality beliefs should be strengthened by making rewards contingent on good performance, and valence should be high because more money is a reward that most people find highly attractive.[13]

Expectancy theory offers useful guidelines to diagnose possible problems in incentive systems. First, one must ask whether employees believe that they can be good performers if they try. Are they properly selected, trained, and equipped to do the job? Do they get feedback so that they know where they stand and can take corrective action as necessary? Second, one must be sure that employees perceive a link between their performance and their rewards (instrumentality). Do they truly believe that better performance will make more money, or does a higher salary seem to be more a function of luck or politics? Finally, the offered reward must be of value (valence) to employees. They must be able to earn something they strongly desire, such as a promotion or a sizable raise. The prospect of a small merit raise may not be enough to motivate superior performance over an extended period of time. The International Perspective box points out that the valence of rewards differs not only from one employee to the next, but also across countries and cultures.

● **Retention**   Linking pay to performance is likely to help improve work force composition. High performers will tend to gain a larger share of compensation resources and thus be motivated to stay with the organization. Below-average performers will become discouraged and will tend to leave the organization. Reward systems that are not linked to performance tend to have the opposite effect and thus result in the worst of both possibilities. Well-paid poor performers may stay with the organization: They are well rewarded and will not be sought by other organizations. By contrast, top performers feel underrewarded and are likely to be sought by organizations that appropriately value their contributions.

Some organizations link rewards to performance by using commissions as the primary or exclusive basis for compensation. Top performers in real estate, insurance agencies, and stock brokerage houses, for example, may earn ten times more than poor performers. It is not surprising that the top performers desire to continue earning several hundred thousand dollars each year, whereas the poor performers leave the profession quickly.

● **Productivity**   When performance is linked to rewards, those capable of doing what will lead to top productivity are motivated to do so. In the real estate, insurance, and stock brokerage organizations mentioned earlier, nobody becomes productive by waiting for business to come along. The top performers make the extra effort that will result in productivity when they know they will share in the rewards of their productivity. In the financial services business, the "extras" that result in productivity frequently involve working evenings, entertaining clients, soliciting business, and volunteering in community activities, to name a few. Technical competence is important, but as one top performer was heard to say, "Not 1 in 500 makes it to the top ranks on technical skills alone." This may be an overestimate.

International Benefits—Comparisons and Complications

Countries differ greatly in the benefits typically offered to employees. These differences may be due to cultural preferences, values, and traditions; local law and tax codes; economic conditions; and many other factors. In some cases, particular levels of benefits are mandated by law; in other cases they are simply common practice. Paid vacation is a good example. There are no legal minimum standards for paid vacation in the United States, though new permanent full-time employees typically earn two weeks of paid vacation after one year of service. Employees may need to work for the same employer for five or ten years to become entitled to three weeks of vacation, and fifteen to twenty years to obtain four weeks of paid vacation per year. In the European Economic Community, the legally mandated minimum paid vacation is four weeks. France requires more—a minimum of twenty-five days. However, many employers give more than the required minimum. Although Germany requires twenty days of paid holiday, most employers give thirty days (six weeks). In Europe, all employees are eligible for the full amount of paid vacation, from the very first year of employment. Since vacation time does not increase with seniority, its administration is more straightforward for HR staff.

In China, a very desirable benefit is employer-subsidized housing. In the United Kingdom, company cars are still a benefit offered to a relatively large share of managers. The popularity of cars remains high even though the tax benefits of this item have declined. In particularly high tax regions, such as Scandinavia, perquisites that are tax-effective are often more attractive than increases in cash payments, and this must be kept in mind when designing performance incentive systems.

Some countries, such as China and Russia, prohibit individuals from owning securities in foreign companies, creating barriers to the use of employee ownership or stock-option plans. Cisco Systems overcame this barrier by creating a system of same-day cashless buy-and-sell transactions when shares were granted. In India, Cisco Systems discovered that its normal stock-option plan created individuals who were so wealthy (relative to the local cost of living) that they retired at a very early age, depriving the company of their services. The usual formula for the award of options was halved to reduce this problem. In the Netherlands, stock options are taxed up front, not when they are exercised, creating a penalty for employees who do not use their options. In nearby France, a heavy tax is imposed if options are exercised within five years of receipt. Clearly, the advice of an expert local lawyer is required to design equitable and motivational incentive and benefits programs in each country.

Another complication in administering pay and benefits multinationally is the issue of "acquired rights." In some countries in Europe and Latin America, any extra incentive, benefit, or perquisite that is offered for a period of time (two years in Brazil) becomes an acquired right and cannot be unilaterally discontinued by the employer.

With many companies having employees all over the world, issues of local practice and expectation versus fairness and equality of treatment can become an issue, especially when employees around the world communicate daily by e-mail and have many opportunities to notice discrepancies in pay and benefits. How, for example, does a company justify giving software engineers in India fewer stock options and one-quarter the pay of their colleagues in the United States for exactly the same effort and skill?

Sources: Jennifer Laabs, "Time-Starved Workers Rebel," *Workforce*, October 2000, pp. 26–28; C. D. Fisher and A. Yuan, "What Motivates Employees? A Comparison of U.S. and Chinese Responses," *International Journal of Human Resource Management*, Vol. 9, 1998. pp. 516–528; Calvin Reynolds, "Global Compensation and Benefits in Transition," *Compensation and Benefits Review*, January–February 2000, pp. 28–38; and Steven E. Gross and Per L. Wingerup, "Global Pay? Maybe Not Yet!" *Compensation and Benefits Review*, July–August 1999, pp. 25–34.

A DIFFERENT POINT OF VIEW

Do Rewards Motivate Performance?

Author Alfie Kohn has been making waves by claiming that rewards and pay-for-performance systems are fundamentally flawed and incapable of motivating improved performance. In a controversial *Harvard Business Review* article, "Why Incentive Plans Cannot Work," Kohn summarized his book, *Punished by Rewards: The Trouble with Gold Stars, Incentive Plans, A's, Praise, and Other Bribes.*

Kohn claims that rewards elicit temporary compliance at best and do not motivate sustained changes in attitude or commitment. He calls rewards as manipulative and controlling as the threat of punishment, stating that "Do this and you'll get that" is not really very different from "Do this or here's what will happen to you." He cites laboratory research showing that people become less interested in performing inherently interesting tasks after being paid contingently than when paid at an hourly rate or not paid at all.

Agreeing with W. Edwards Deming, Kohn believes that individual incentives breed unhealthy competition among coworkers; reduce teamwork, risk taking, and creativity; and lead to political behavior, short-term fixes, and cover-ups of errors. He claims that managers use incentives as a cheap and easy way to increase employee effort when they should be concentrating instead on deeper causes of performance problems, such as poor job design, lack of feedback, and ineffective leadership.

These arguments seem to be of two kinds: (1) asserting that the concept of using rewards to motivate performance is simply wrong and (2) asserting that some individual incentive plans are badly designed and reward the wrong thing. Let us consider the first type of argument—that rewards simply cannot work, no matter how well designed. It is true that most people resent being closely controlled by others and that some reward systems, especially piece-rate incentives or systems that rely on subjective judgments by high-handed superiors, can be seen as very controlling. However, there is also research showing that performance-contingent pay actually can increase employees' feelings of control, by giving them the ability to determine how much they earn. Further, most pay-for-performance systems provide more than just the extrinsic reward of dollars. Earning more money under

● **Cost Savings**   An obvious benefit of pay for performance is the capability to link compensation costs with productivity results. By basing pay on performance, employers can ensure that compensation costs, typically a major cost of doing business, will be tied to organizational results. When the results are poor and the organization is less able to pay, compensation costs are lower. With a salaried and/or hourly work force, compensation costs are not related to business results and, even worse, continue to grow each year as cost-of-living and merit increases are added.

● **Organizational Objectives**   It is always a challenge to make sure that all employees understand organizational objectives. Because of their important influence on motivation and satisfaction, reward systems have the ability to communicate organizational objectives.[14] By linking pay to organizationally defined performance, it is also possible to ensure that individual objectives are in line with organizational objectives. Employees whose efforts are not synchronized with organizational objectives will not enjoy an equal share of the rewards.

these systems also conveys feedback and recognition that a job was done well and is appreciated. Research shows that when the information/feedback value of a reward is seen as more salient than its controlling aspects, intrinsic motivation is enhanced.

Much of the research that shows intrinsic motivation being undermined by payment has explored the effect of monetary incentives on enjoyable leisure-time activities for which people would not normally expect to be paid. In this case, the novelty of payment seems to make people stop and think about why they are engaging in the activity and conclude that since they are being paid to engage in it, it must not be much fun or very interesting. Other research shows that when pay is a normal, expected part of a setting, it does not harm and may even increase intrinsic motivation. For instance, poker and casino games are much more fun when the possibility of monetary gain is present. Certainly people expect to be paid for their performance at work, so money need not reduce intrinsic motivation in that context. Thus it seems that the concept of rewards for performance is not flawed.

However, the execution of reward systems can leave much to be desired, and sometimes negative consequences do flow from poorly designed incentive systems. A few companies have dropped commission systems for salespersons because they found that sales staff were becoming too aggressive in their approach and the hard-sell tactics were driving away customers. When managers focus too much attention on installing the perfect incentive system, they may neglect to explore other causes of, and solutions for, performance problems. A balanced approach is needed, bearing in mind that it is possible to design incentive systems to reward teamwork and creativity and that group-oriented profit-sharing or gain-sharing systems can increase commitment and interest in business performance among employees.

Sources: Alfie Kohn, "Why Incentive Plans Cannot Work," *Harvard Business Review,* September–October 1993, pp. 54–63; "Rethinking Rewards," *Harvard Business Review,* November–December 1993, pp. 37–49; Edward L. Deci and Richard M. Ryan, *Intrinsic Motivation and Self-Determination in Human Behavior* (New York: Plenum Press, 1985); Alfie Kohn, *Punished by Rewards: The Trouble with Gold Stars, Incentive Plans, A's, Praise, and Other Bribes* (Boston: Houghton Mifflin, 1993); Cynthia D. Fisher, "The Effects of Personal Control, Competence, and Extrinsic Reward Systems on Intrinsic Motivation," *Organizational Behavior and Human Performance,* Vol. 21, 1978, pp. 273–288; and Jeffrey Pfeffer, "Six Dangerous Myths About Pay," *Harvard Business Review,* May–June 1993, pp. 108–119.

Reasons Not to Link Pay to Performance

Linking pay to performance is not always possible or successful. As noted in A Different Point of View, pay-for-performance systems can be misguided. An example of performance-based pay gone awry occurred when Sears Auto Centers in California acknowledged having made unnecessary repairs on customers' cars. The compensation system used by Sears Auto Centers based rewards on services and parts sold. As a result, California investigators charged Sears with defrauding its customers by selling unnecessary parts and services. Sears subsequently settled for approximately $15 million, an expensive lesson on the double-edged nature of performance-based pay.[15]

Pay-for-performance systems also take more time to administer successfully than do traditional reward systems. With fixed compensation (salary or wage), it is often a case of "set it and forget it." With pay for performance, one needs to reevaluate the motivation, retention, productivity, and organizational objectives continually, with the idea of fine-tuning the system to make sure that rewards are aligned with desired performance.

A union's position on this type of reward system may also influence the feasibility of instituting a pay-for-performance system in a particular organization. Historically, unions have opposed performance-based pay systems. Although some unions are willing to back this type of compensation, most see no need to differentiate the pay of union workers who are doing the same job. Unions believe that pay differences based on subjective supervisor assessments of employee performance may foster discrimination or favoritism. Unions favor objective methods of determining pay increases, such as across-the-board increases or seniority increases. Unions also believe that merit pay plans may weaken solidarity, since employees compete against their fellow union members to receive the highest rewards. Unions may be more receptive to group incentive plans because they tend to result in cooperation rather than competition. Thus a union would more likely favor a bonus plan for all employees based on a company's profitability.

Factors Affecting the Design of Incentive Systems

There are numerous ways of linking pay to performance, each with its own advantages and drawbacks. One consideration is the level of aggregation of the incentive pay: Will the incentive be based on the performance of the individual em-

● **TABLE 13.2**

Ratings of Pay Incentive Plans[a]

	Basis for Reward	Tie Pay to Performance	Produce Negative Side Effects	Encourage Cooperation	Employee Acceptance
Salary reward					
Individual plan	Productivity	4	1	1	4
	Cost-effectiveness	3	1	1	4
	Superiors' rating	3	1	1	3
Group plan	Productivity	3	1	2	4
	Cost-effectiveness	3	1	2	4
	Superiors' rating	2	1	2	3
Organizational plan	Productivity	2	1	3	4
	Cost-effectiveness	2	1	2	4
Bonus					
Individual plan	Productivity	5	3	1	2
	Cost-effectiveness	4	2	1	2
	Superiors' rating	4	2	1	2
Group plan	Productivity	4	1	3	3
	Cost-effectiveness	3	1	3	3
	Superiors' rating	3	1	3	3
Organizational plan	Productivity	3	1	3	4
	Cost-effectiveness	3	1	3	4
	Profit	2	1	3	3

[a]On a scale of 1 to 5, 1 = low and 5 = high.

Source: E.E. Lawler, *Pay and Organization Development,* © 1981 Addison Wesley Longman, Inc. Reprinted by permission of Addison Wesley Longman.

ployee, the work group, the division, or the entire organization? Another consideration is the degree of objectivity involved in measuring performance. Qualifying to receive the incentive may be based on a subjective supervisory rating of performance or on purely objective measures such as sales, production, or profit. A further complication is the fact that it is not unusual for companies to have several incentive systems; for example, one system based on work group performance and another as a function of organizational performance.

Other considerations in the design of an incentive system relate to the strength of the performance–pay linkage, the potential for negative side effects, whether the system encourages cooperation, and employee acceptance. The results of Edward E. Lawler's analysis of incentive plans with respect to these criteria are shown in Table 13.2. Objective measures of performance (productivity and cost savings) tend to have greater employee acceptance and credibility. Individual incentive programs are often reported to yield higher productivity than group incentives. One explanation is that linking individuals' pay to the group's performance diffuses the connection between pay and each person's effort. Some individuals may have a tendency to "free-ride" (let others in the group do the work for them).[16] Research has shown that group members are especially likely to free-ride if their contribution to group performance is not readily identifiable and their loafing is unlikely to be noticed.[17]

On the other hand, group plans have some advantages not generally attainable with an individual incentive system. Group systems often result in more cooperation and coordination. They are better suited for organizations in which performance is difficult to measure at the individual level and success depends on effective teamwork.

INDIVIDUAL INCENTIVES

When individual productivity is measurable, individual incentives are most successful in boosting performance through a fairly direct link between performance and rewards. The adoption of individual incentives has accelerated in recent years. Popular individual incentive plans discussed in this section include piece-rate incentive, commissions, and bonuses. Skill-based pay—a highly acclaimed recent innovation in individual incentives—and merit raises are also discussed.

Piece-Rate Incentive

Piece-rate incentive is the most common form of individual enticement for production workers. Employees are paid a fixed rate for each unit of output produced. The amount to pay per unit of output is determined as follows: First, the typical pay rate for the job is determined, probably by a wage survey. Then, the typical output per day is measured. A time and motion study by industrial engineers may also provide information on the number of units that an employee should be able to make per day. The average daily wage is divided by average units per day to produce the price paid per piece. For example, if the average daily rate is $48 and each employee ought to be able to produce 96 units per day, the rate paid for each piece will be $0.50.

Some piece-rate systems pay only on the basis of units produced, so an employee who made only 70 units would receive $35 for that day. Many piece-rate systems, however, guarantee a base wage equal to the standard output level, so that all employees making 96 or fewer units receive $48. (Of course, employees who are consistently below the standard may not continue on the job.) The incentive is paid for all units in excess of the standard. Thus an employee who made 110 units would receive $48 plus $7 (14 extra units × $0.50), or $55.

The major shortcoming of the typical piece-rate incentive is in the signal it sends. Instead of suggesting a partnership between the goals of the individual and those of the organization, it implies that the organization actually distrusts the individual. As a result, a piece-rate system is likely to encourage behaviors opposite to those sought. Workers may restrict output because of the possible adverse consequences associated with high productivity.[18] For example, workers may fear layoffs if all employees dramatically increase their output. Other workers may fear being ostracized by colleagues if they try to produce at a higher-than-normal level. Finally, workers may fear that if they consistently produce at a high rate—say, 150 units per day—the time and motion study will be redone, thereby increasing the production standards and reducing the rate paid per piece. They would then have to work harder to earn the same pay.

As suggested previously, these negative views of the piece-rate incentive can be traced to the adversarial nature of management–worker relations that it signals. On the other hand, Lincoln Electric in Cleveland, Ohio, represents a long-standing example of a successful piece-rate incentive system, a plan first introduced in 1934. Lincoln pays factory workers for each acceptable piece that is produced. In addition, each employee receives a year-end bonus based on a yearly merit rating of his or her dependability, ideas, productivity, and product quality. Lincoln's success is related to the partnership it signals. The pay of every employee from the CEO on down is at risk—contingent on individual and corporate performance.

An incentive system sometimes can lead to overemphasis on one dimension of a job and neglect of other important job elements. For instance, a piece-rate system may increase output but also increase the number of units that fail to pass inspection. Other aspects of the job that do not directly convert into units of output, such as machine maintenance, housekeeping activities, or training of new employees, may be ignored under a piece-rate system.

● **The Taylor Plan**   A variation of the piece-rate system was developed by Frederick W. Taylor around the turn of the century. Unlike the straight piece-rate plan, the **Taylor plan** offers differential piecework rates. In the preceding example, the Taylor plan might specify $0.50 per unit up to 96 units per day but reward workers producing 125 percent of standard or more (120 units) with the higher rate of $0.65 for each unit over 96.

● **Standard Hour Plan**   The **standard hour plan** is similar to the straight piecework plan except that the standard is set in time units. Automobile repair shops often use such systems. If the customer wants to know the cost of replacing an engine timing belt, for example, he or she will be given an estimate based on the mechanic's hourly rate multiplied by the average time needed to replace the component on cars of that type. If the charge is $40 per hour and the replacement of the timing belt requires six hours on average, the expected labor cost would be $240. This is the labor cost quoted to the customer before work begins. An experienced mechanic may complete the job in five hours. The customer is still charged $240, and the mechanic is paid for six hours' work (the standard time allotted for the job). If complications arise and the job takes longer than estimated (e.g., the mechanic strips a bolt and has to repair the error), charges to the customer and payment to the mechanic are still based on six hours' work. In this case, auto repair shops have manuals with the standard hours for each type of repair. Standard hour plans are generally used with longer-cycle operations that are nonrepetitive.

Commissions

Commission reward systems, which are usually found in sales jobs, allow the salesperson to receive a percentage of his or her gross receipts (e.g., 5 percent of all sales). About two-thirds of all salespersons are paid on **commission** basis—either straight commission or a base salary plus commission.

Commission payments offer a very clear link between pay and worker performance and therefore are an effective financial incentive. Commission plans are easy to administer and justify because there is no subjective element, and rewards are purely a function of performance. Because of this clear link, department stores are converting thousands of hourly sales employees to straight commission.[19] The retailers hope that the potential for higher rewards to those with strong sales skills will motivate current staff and attract better salespersons in the future.

As has been illustrated by the earlier discussion of the double edged nature of incentives, commissions, more than most other incentive systems, require active control on the part of management. For example, commission payment may reduce cooperative teamwork. Employees may compete with one another for individual sales or for the most lucrative sales territory. The result is that several salespersons besiege customers as soon as they enter the area.

In the case of department stores shifting to straight commission, sales staff may give customers a hard time on refunds or exchanges. If an employee's pay is based strictly on sales, all other coworker- and company-related considerations may be secondary. For example, the salesperson who works hard to sell the customer a computer may not want to take the time to instruct him or her in its use. After the sale, service may not be what is expected or needed, resulting in a dissatisfied customer.

In the case of financial services, incentive-based pay has frequently led to churning of customer accounts to generate commissions or to the emphasis of products not in the best interest of the customer. The need for management controls with commission rewards was illustrated in the instance of Baring Brothers and Company, a British bank. A quest by a Baring Brothers and Company's employee to maximize his rewards led to losses of almost $1 billion—and the failure of the bank.[20]

From the employee's point of view, a disadvantage of commission-based compensation is the unpredictable amount of take-home pay from week to week. Any number of things outside the employee's control—such as weather, economic conditions, or the amount spent on advertising—may influence the number of sales and therefore the amount of reward. However, assuming that the salesperson can tolerate this kind of risk, commission plans offer considerable advantage to the organization by directly linking performance to rewards and keeping labor costs in line. Furthermore, for the employees who are effective, the rewards are far greater than they would otherwise be—perhaps even several times the amount that the employees could have expected if compensated by salary or wage. As an example, successful Nordstrom sales employees typically earn several times more than their counterparts with other department stores.

Bonuses

One of the most popular trends in compensation is the use of **bonuses:** one-time lump-sum payments given for meeting a performance goal. Bonuses can be based on objective goal attainment or a subjective rating. In some organizations all employees share in the bonus awards if organizational goals are met, whereas in others the size of the bonus is tied to each individual's performance. An example of the former approach is Ford Motor Company. In a plan agreed to by the United Auto Workers and Ford in the early 1980s, all hourly and salaried employees receive profit-sharing bonuses when Ford achieves its projected goals. In the early 1990s workers did not receive profit-sharing checks as a result of decreased organizational performance. However, as a result of increased profits, bonus payments ranged from $1,350 (1992) to $4,400 (1998) later in the decade. As we start a new decade. things have come full circle for Ford. Executives did not even wait until the end of the year to announce that there would be no bonuses paid in 2001, given that the company lost more than $500 million in the first half of the year.[21] Another example of a bonus based on individual performance is the clause in some baseball players' contracts that specifies that they will receive a bonus (usually several thousand dollars) if voted onto the all-star team or if they reach some other performance standard.

Table 13.3 shows a sample award distribution chart for lump-sum bonuses based on both organizational and employee performance. Plans such as this also might assign different bonus ceilings to levels within the organization. For in-

● **TABLE 13.3**

Lump-Sum Award Determination Matrix

The Employee's Performance (Weight = 50)	The Organization's Performance (Weight = .50)				
	Outstanding (1.00)	Excellent (.80)	Commendable (.60)	Acceptable (.40)	Marginal or Unacceptable (0)
Outstanding (1.00)	1.00	.90	.80	.70	.50
Excellent (.80)	.90	.80	.70	.60	.40
Commendable (.60)	.80	.70	.60	.50	.30
Acceptable (.00)	–0–	–0–	–0–	–0–	–0–
Unacceptable (.00)	–0–	–0–	–0–	–0–	–0–

Instructions: To determine the dollar value of each employee's incentive award, (a) multiply the employee's annual, straight time wage or salary times his or her maximum incentive award and (b) multiply the resulting product times the appropriate percentage figure from this table. For example, if an employee had an annual salary of $20,000 and a maximum incentive award of 10%, and if her performance and the organization's performance were both "excellent," the employee's award would be $1,600 ($20,000 × .10 × .80 = $1,600).

Source: Republished with permission of American Management Association, from "The Future of Merit Pay Programs" by John F. Sullivan, *Compensation and Benefits* Review, May/June 1988. Permission conveyed through Copyright Clearance Center, Inc.

stance, top managers might be eligible to earn up to 50 percent more than their salary, middle managers 25 percent, and lower-level employees 10 percent.

Bonuses not only help the employer control costs but appear to improve employee satisfaction. A company that gives a raise to an employee is making a permanent change that improves his or her pay now, in the future, and also in retirement, through a pension. This is a more costly commitment than a one-time bonus payment. Because bonuses arrive in one lump sum, they may feel to the employees like more money than a comparable-sized raise. Suppose an employee earning $20,000 is given a $1,000 bonus. The sizable bonus check is equal to 5 percent of the salary. If a raise of the same size were given, the $1,000 would be distributed across 52 weeks, and the employee would see only about $20 more per week in his or her paycheck. Bonus plans are easy to maintain because they do not require much documentation and are quite flexible.[22] A major advantage of a bonus plan is that it is based partly on organizational performance; in a bad year, when corporate performance is down and resources are strained, bonuses will be much smaller or even nonexistent. Of course, on the other hand, when bonuses cannot be paid, as with Ford, it tends to hurt morale, especially in light of the strength of the economy and the stock market in recent years and the expectations of extra income in the form of bonus payments.[23]

Skill-Based Pay

Skill-based pay (or **pay for knowledge**) is a reward system that pays employees on the basis of the work-related skills they possess rather than associating rewards with performance levels or seniority.[24] Under a typical skill-based pay plan, an employee is hired and receives initial training on one job. He or she then joins a work group at the entry-level rate of pay and has the opportunity to learn new job-related skills through on-the-job experience and further training. As the employee demonstrates mastery of different jobs performed by other group members, his or her pay is increased.[25] Typically, a minimum of four to five years is required for employees to top out—that is, master all the skills.[26] Skill-based pay frequently is used in conjunction with autonomous work groups or other job enrichment programs.[27]

Several models are used to design skill-based pay plans. The *stair-step model* is applicable when the learning progression is fairly logical. Successive skill levels are defined, and pay is increased as the learning of additional skills is verified. The *job-point accrual model* is used when there is a wide variety of jobs. The varied jobs are given a relative point rating based on value added or learning difficulty, and the points for each job mastered then determine the employee's pay grade. The *cross-department model* places a premium (in terms of rewards) on employees who learn the skills required to fill in at another department as needed.[28]

The single biggest advantage of skill-based pay is increased flexibility. Because workers know more than one job, they can move to provide expertise when and where needed.[29] Tying pay increases to skill acquisition creates an incentive for learning, self-improvement, and performance.[30]

The success of such plans depends on the needs of the organization and the employee. Skill-based pay should be implemented only if the organization has a commitment to employee training and development and has something to gain from increased flexibility. This system also rests on the assumption that employees want to grow and to improve their job skills.

Although a creative approach to compensation, skill-based pay is not for every-one.[31] For those companies that do use skill-based pay, part of the reason for the popularity of skill-based pay lies in what it indicates to employees. For example, skill-based pay has the following qualities:

- It is associated with work teams or self-managed work groups.
- It is prevalent in organizations committed to egalitarian principles—high-involvement or all-salaried work forces.
- It is embraced by reorganized organizations that have adopted a broadened conceptualization of the job.
- It is associated with organizations seeking employee involvement through total quality, continuous improvement, and similar initiatives.[32]

Merit Pay

Merit pay, because it is the standard procedure for attempting to tie pay increases to individual performance, is a major motivational device for employees at all levels—managerial, professional, and hourly.[33] **Merit pay** is an annual increment tied to the employee's performance during the preceding year. For example, during periods of low inflation and competitive pressures on corporations' costs, a top performer may receive a 5 percent increase, whereas an average performer receives 3 percent and a below-average performer receives no increase.

Even though merit pay continues to be used widely, it has come under major criticism.[34] Merit raises represent a permanent commitment to an increased salary (pay is virtually never reduced if performance falls), thereby creating an annuity that can be an expensive fixed cost to an organization during economic downturns. Suppose a top-performing employee with a salary of $40,000 receives an increase of 2 percent more than that of an average employee. If paid biweekly, this employee would see about $31 more in each pay packet than the average employee would. This amount is so small that the top employee is likely to feel that his or her performance has not been rewarded, yet the organization has made a fairly expensive commitment. The commitment is in the form of continuing this increase for as long as the employee remains, no matter what the future performance. For example, assuming no further increases in future years, the organization will pay $20,000 more over ten years. Compounding by future pay increases magnifies the value. Assume in this example that if for each of the next ten years the top employee meets expectations and receives a 4 percent base pay increase, the organization will be paying an additional $24,012 (in today's dollars). Finally, if benefits directly related to base pay are 30 percent of base, the compounded increase will be $31,216 for the ten-year period. The result is a lose–lose situation—an expensive annuity for the organization and a top-performing employee who does not feel rewarded.

In practice, the size of merit raises usually depends on both performance and the employee's current position in the salary range established for that job. If all top performers were given large raises, within a few years outstanding employees might be making more than the allowable maximum for their jobs—more than the jobs are worth, no matter how well they are performed. Thus merit increase guidelines, like those shown in Table 13.4, are often used. Among employees in the same part of the pay range, better performers receive a larger percentage in-

● **TABLE 13.4**

Merit Increase Guidelines

| | Performance Level | | | |
Current Position in Range	Excellent	Good	Average	Poor
Top quarter	5%	3%	1%	0
Third quarter	6%	4%	2%	0
Second quarter	7%	5%	3%	0
Lowest quarter	8%	6%	4%	0

crease. However, an excellent performer near the maximum of the range allowed for the job will receive a smaller percentage increase than an excellent performer earning below the midpoint of the range.

There are several important difficulties involved in using merit increases to link pay to performance. First, merit increases are almost always based on the supervisor's subjective evaluation, so employees may perceive a weak link between performance and pay. Many employees like the idea of a merit system but feel that the system in their organization is not implemented in a completely fair, unbiased manner. Recall from Chapter 11 that supervisors can make a number of intentional and unintentional errors in judging performance. These errors may lead to perceived inequities in the way merit money is distributed. Second, merit increases are usually awarded annually, so they do not immediately follow the specific instances of good performance that the organization wishes to reinforce. Third, variations in the size of merit raises are generally not large enough to be highly motivating. For example, using the guidelines illustrated in Table 13.4, an excellent performer would receive a 5 to 8 percent raise, whereas a poor performer would receive nothing. Yet the excellent performer certainly makes more than an 8 percent difference, possibly even a 100 percent difference, in terms of contribution to the organization. Fourth, the size of the total merit budget may vary substantially from year to year so that the same performance level does not always earn the same reward. As a result of a smaller merit pool, this year's top performer may receive a 6 percent increase, whereas last year's was awarded 9 percent.

Edward E. Lawler aptly stated the bottom line with respect to merit pay:

> The combined effect of year-to-year differences in salary-increase budgets and the annuity feature of merit raises almost always creates a situation in which the total compensation of individuals is unrelated to their performance at any point in time.[35]

According to Lawler, the best-paid individuals are likely to be those employees who are among the most senior and who have performed adequately over a period of time.

Despite the problems with merit pay, it is likely to remain a staple of compensation systems. At the same time, it is likely that in the future merit programs will be supplemented with other types of individual or group incentives. Organizations will rely on merit pay for the broad range of adjustments but will reward top performers with individual bonuses or all employees with a group incentive based on company performance.[36]

GROUP INCENTIVES

Group incentives are designed to accomplish the same objectives as individual incentives—that is, to link rewards to performance. The difference is that performance is measured on the level of an organizational unit and is viewed as resulting from the combined efforts of a group rather than from individual effort. As illustrated by the Lincoln Electric example described previously, individual and group incentives are not mutually exclusive but can be combined to emphasize the desired mix of individual and group linkage of rewards to performance. Lincoln Electric successfully uses a piece-rate system (individual bonus) as well as an annual profit-sharing bonus (group incentive).

A group incentive system was developed and evaluated by the Navy Personnel Research and Development Center for the Pearl Harbor Naval Shipyard.[37] Shipyard production workers typically work together in gangs of ten to twenty employees. Thus it seemed reasonable that the work gang be the basis for assessing productivity. Work gangs were studied to develop a baseline measure of person-hours needed to complete various assignments. Performance efficiency was then calculated by dividing the hours expected by the actual hours needed. The shipyard paid out half the cost savings associated with performance efficiency to gang members as incentive awards. In addition to performance improvement and cost savings, the project produced other positive benefits, including more sophisticated labor cost accounting and improved allocation of people. Surveys of participants revealed that 80 percent of the workers had a favorable opinion of the system.

In another study, production workers on a series of tightly interconnected assembly lines in a unionized iron foundry participated in a group incentive program.[38] Productivity standards were established for each assembly line, and credit was given for output above the established standard. The researchers found a sustained trend of increasing productivity over several years following implementation of the incentive system. Sharp early increases in output were due to increased effort, whereas continued small increases over the years were attributed to employee innovations. The presence of the incentive encouraged employees to continuously develop new and more efficient ways to complete their group tasks.

Group incentives, like those for individuals, have possible negative aspects. If the group is too large, employees may feel that their efforts will have little effect on total performance. Group members may also become concerned about overproduction and thus restrict output.

Profit Sharing

Profit sharing is an incentive system in which designated employees share the business profits. Profit-sharing plans differ from gain-sharing plans (to be discussed next) in two respects:

1. They are often implemented corporation-wide, whereas gain sharing is often at the unit level.

2. They use a formula based on profit rather than on productivity improvement.

The usual profit-sharing program establishes a base-level profit target. After this target is achieved, a percentage of additional profits is set aside in a bonus pool to be distributed to participants. Sometimes the bonus pool is distributed in equal dollar shares to all employees. At other times the distribution is made according to organizational level or salary/wages.

There are three broad types of profit-sharing plans:

1. *Current distribution plans* (or cash plans), which pay a share of the company's profits in cash or in company shares

2. *Deferred payout plans*, in which an employee's share of the company's profits is placed in a trust fund to be distributed at a later date (usually on retirement, disability, death, or termination)

3. *Combination plans*, which provide both cash payments and deferred payments[39]

Some features of profit-sharing plans are very attractive. First, when there are no profits, the company bears no costs for this type of reward system. These plans also make employees more aware of the organization's competitive position in its industry and facilitate a cooperative atmosphere. Although profit sharing may be best suited to smaller companies, where the line of sight from individual performance to corporate profits is more evident, such plans are easy to administer in larger companies as well. The profit-sharing deferment plan allows employees to postpone taxation and therefore increase rewards.

One disadvantage of profit-sharing plans is the fact that when companies have had a bad year, even good employees may go unrewarded. Low profits may be due to factors beyond the employees' control, such as economic conditions. Another drawback is that deferred payout plans may have less incentive value because of the long time lapse between the good performance and the eventual payment. Also, employees' shares of the profits are seldom tied to individual performance. Most commonly, all employees share in the profits, either equally or in proportion to their base pay. Thus there is virtually no line of sight between how hard individuals work and the size of their profit-sharing payoffs, especially if the organization is large. For all these reasons, the link between pay and performance is very weak.

Assumptions about management practices, employee participation, and productivity targets, as they relate to profit-sharing plans, are summarized in Table 13.5.

Gain-Sharing Plans

Gain sharing is a type of group incentive in which a portion of the *gains* the organization realizes from group effort is *shared* with the group. The concept also implies an organizational philosophy that engenders the kind of cooperativeness and trust needed to facilitate group efforts.[40]

As Figure 13.2 shows, many organizations are seeking productivity and quality improvement through gain-sharing plans. Other important reasons for adopting gain-sharing plans have to do with employee relations, labor costs, and a desire to link pay to performance.[41]

● **Scanlon Plan** One very popular and widely used form of gain sharing is the **Scanlon plan,** which was first implemented in the late 1920s. Its developer, Joseph Scanlon, was a union leader who was trained in cost accounting and had a

● **TABLE 13.5**

Principal Features of Gain-Sharing and Profit-Sharing Programs

	Scanlon	Rucker	Improshare	Profit Sharing	Winsharing
Management practices	Participative system highly stressed	Participative system recommended	Reduction in conflict between labor and management recommended	Better education and communications recommended	Successful participative management
Employee participation	Suggestion committees or work teams	Rucker committees	Good ideas used when they occur	None specified	Recommendations and improvements solicited and used in each unit
Productivity target	Reduction in cost and/or labor	Cost reduction with emphasis on labor	Reduction in labor time, direct and indirect	Improved profit	Business goals, including productivity levels, are established
Bonus basis	Ratio of costs to sales value of production	Labor: percentage of value added	Hours saved compared with standard	Share of profit	Financial results in excess of business goals
Bonus frequency	Monthly to quarterly	Monthly to quarterly	Weekly	Annually— usually deferred	Quarterly, semiannually, or annually
Participants	All employees	Hourly employees— others optional	Hourly employees only	All employees	All employees

Sources: Robert Doyle, *Gainsharing and Productivity: A Guide to Planning, Implementation, and Development.* Copyright © 1983 by AMACOM, a division of American Management Association. Sections adapted from Jay R. Schuster and Patricia K. Zingheim, *The New Pay: Linking Employees and Organizational Performance* (Lexington, Mass.: Lexington Books, 1992).

strong concern for management–labor cooperation. Scanlon believed that the average worker was a great reservoir of untapped information concerning labor-saving methods. Workers needed a mechanism permitting them to "work smarter, not harder."[42]

The Scanlon plan involves employee participation in reducing labor costs. The two main features are a system of departmental and plantwide screening committees to evaluate and implement employee cost-saving suggestions and the sharing of labor cost savings with employees as an incentive. Savings are determined as the ratio of payroll to sales value of production and are usually calculated monthly and compared with baseline months to determine the bonus to be shared.[43] A typical distribution of savings would be 50 percent to employees, 25 percent to the employer, and 25 percent retained for an emergency fund to reimburse the company

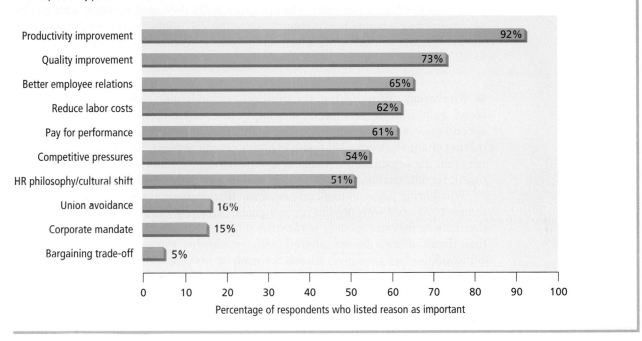

● **FIGURE 13.2**

Reasons for Adopting Gain Sharing

Source: People, Performance, and Pay,
American Productivity & Quality Center,
1987. Reprinted by permission.

for any months when the actual wage bill is larger than the baseline. Remaining emergency funds are distributed to workers at the end of each year.

● **Rucker Plan**   The **Rucker plan** is similar to the Scanlon plan, but the bonus formula includes the dollar value of all materials, supplies, and services that are used to make the product. The resulting formula is

$$\frac{\$ \text{ value of personnel costs}}{\$ \text{ value of production} - \$ \text{ value of material, etc.}}$$

The resulting bonus formula is the value added to a product per labor dollar. The Rucker plan provides an incentive to save on all inputs, both human and material.

● **Improshare**   Another noteworthy approach to gain sharing is the **Improshare** (*Im*proved *Pro*ductivity through *Shar*ing) **plan** developed by Mitchell Fein and first used in 1974.[44] Whereas the Scanlon and Rucker plans are first-generation gain-sharing plans, Improshare is considered second generation as a result of its expanded scope.

Improshare is similar to the previously discussed plan at the navy shipyard, but at an organization level. A standard of the number of person-hours required to produce an expected level of output is developed. This standard could be determined from a base period (as with the Scanlon plan) or through time and motion studies. For example, the base may be established as 5,000 hours of labor (direct and indirect) to produce 1,000 units each week, or 5 hours per unit. If in a given week 5,000 hours are used to produce 1,300 units, 1,500 hours have been saved (300 units at 5 hours per unit). The company splits the gains fifty-fifty with its employees, giving a bonus for 750 hours. Since the 750 hours represent 15 percent of the 5,000 hours worked (750/5,000), employees receive a 15 percent bonus for the week.

● **Winsharing**   **Winsharing,** the third generation in gain sharing, is an attempt to blend gain sharing and profit sharing.[45] One of the problems with first- and second-generation gain-sharing plans is that they cannot respond to economic and market changes. A possible result is highly productive employees producing products that the organization cannot sell. Winsharing expands the set of objectives to include profit, quality, customer value, and productivity performance.

Winsharing pays out to all employees in the group on the basis of group performance compared with predetermined goals. Business goals are established, goals that may or may not include performance improvements. The plan is designed so that financial awards are shared with employees once the organization has achieved the business goal. Above the goal, 50 percent of the financial results are shared with employees, and 50 percent reverts to the organization. Quality comes into play in that the cost of poor quality (i.e., cost of rework, rejects, and warranty expense as a percentage of volume) over a budgeted amount is subtracted from the winsharing fund.

Winsharing is different from profit sharing in that winsharing has group measures that determine funding in addition to profit. The goal is to use a broader range of business goals as the basis of plan funding and award determination.

● **Summary**   Except for winsharing, the gain-sharing plans seem much the same. The Scanlon, Rucker, and Improshare plans all base the bonus paid on the savings resulting from productivity improvement. However, as shown in Table 13.5, there are differences. For example, with the Scanlon plan, the sales value of production (i.e., the amount received for the produced products) is part of the bonus calculation. With the Improshare plan, the standard is the number of hours required to produce an expected level of output. With all three plans, it is possible that sales or price fluctuations will overshadow productivity improvements. Winsharing is designed to incorporate business and profit goals with productivity targets.

Gain-sharing plans generally work best with smaller firms or units (e.g., divisions or plants) that have fairly stable production processes, good labor–management relations, and a culture emphasizing employee participation.[46] In smaller firms or units there is a **"line of sight"** from individual performance to firm or unit improvement. Individual employees can see that their efforts make a difference. A stable production process is necessary because any cost-savings plan that involves comparisons with a base period will be misleading if technology is continually changing or if production varies for reasons beyond the employees' control.

Employee Stock Ownership Plans (ESOPs)

In many companies, employees at all levels own stock in the organization for which they work. Changes in the federal tax laws since the late 1970s have made **employee stock ownership plans (ESOPs)** a common vehicle for profit sharing and the funding of pension plans. ESOPs also have been used by employees to buy out firms that might otherwise have been sold or closed.

Typically, a public company borrows money to buy its own stock, either from the company treasury or on the market, and places the shares in its ESOP. As the loan is paid down, a trustee allocates stock to individual employees, usually in the form of a deferred pension benefit.[47] According to the National Center for Employee Ownership (NCEO), as of 2000, there were approximately 11,400 ESOPs in force involving 8.5 million employees.[48] ESOPs are popular in both publicly and privately held companies. The top ten companies that are over 50 percent employee-owned through an ESOP, stock purchase plan, or other broad-based ownership plan are shown in Table 13.6 and include several well-know names, such as United Parcel Service, Publix Supermarkets, and United Airlines.

The popularity of ESOPs has less to do with employee participation than with tax breaks, restructuring, and pension paring. The more stock a company's ESOP holds, the better the company can fend off a raider, proceed with a leveraged buy-out, or undertake other forms of reorganization. Some companies use an ESOP to reduce or replace benefits, such as pension benefits, thus leading to considerable savings.

There is some evidence that employee ownership may increase employee commitment, loyalty, and motivation, but such benefits are by no means preordained.[49]

● **TABLE 13.6**

America's Largest Companies That Are over 50% Employee-Owned

Company	Location	Plan	Industry	No. of Emp's
United Parcel Service	Atlanta, Ga.	401(k)	Package delivery	344,000
Publix Supermarkets	Lakeland, Fla.	ESOP, stock purchase	Supermarkets	109,000
United Airlines	Chicago, Ill.	ESOP	Airline	95,000
Hy-Vee	W. Des Moines, Iowa	ESOP	Supermarkets	46,000
Science Applications International	San Diego, Calif.	ESOP, others	Computer systems	41,000
Tharaldson Motels	Fargo, N.D.	ESOP	Motel management	18,000
Dyncorp	Reston, Va.	ESOP	Technical services	17,000
Parsons Corp.	Pasadena, Calif.	ESOP	Engineering and construction	12,000
CH2M Hill, Inc.	Denver, Colo.	Stock purchase	Engineering and construction	12,000
Lifetouch	Minneapolis, Minn.	ESOP	Photography studios	12,000

Source: Adapted from "The Employee Ownership 100," National Center for Employee Ownership, May 2001. (Available at: http://www.nceo.org/library/eo100.html)

A study of the performance of public companies with more than 10 percent broad employee ownership showed that they returned 106 percent between 1992 and 1997.[50] This is compared with 83 percent growth in the Dow and 70 percent growth in the S&P 500 during this same period.

The key to gaining the benefits is to combine ownership with the line-of-sight link between individual and organizational performance.[51] As was seen with profit sharing, especially deferred profits, the link between employee effort and company results is frequently weak. [52] With ESOPs, this relationship is further diminished because success is a function not only of profits but also of the whims of Wall Street with respect to the valuation the financial markets put on companies—a factor employees find difficult to control. Burlington Industries, the textile giant, is an example of an ESOP gone wrong as employees watched the price of the stock go from $38 at the time of the employee buyout to $15 and then to near zero as Burlington filed for bankruptcy, thus greatly devaluing retirement nest eggs for individual employees.[53]

BARRIERS TO PAY-FOR-PERFORMANCE SUCCESS

There is tremendous disparity between theory and reality when organizations try to use pay to motivate performance. The anticipated benefits of pay-for-performance systems, in terms of motivation and satisfaction, are extremely elusive. Success may be made difficult by the nature of the task, performance measurement, the amount of payout, and the failure to achieve a credible link between pay and performance.

Nature of the Task

The design of a pay-for-performance system requires consideration of the employee's task. If the purpose is to engender motivation, the employee needs to feel that he or she can influence results—that is, control the performance that is being measured.[54] This simple principle can be a major stumbling block in practice. For example, imagine twenty-five data-entry specialists, each working at a terminal and paid on the basis of the number of characters entered per hour (piece rate). Is some of the data entry more challenging than others, for example, from handwritten data sheets versus printed material? Are the twenty-five terminals equivalent—the same make and model? Do some of the terminals work better than others? Are some areas of the work location better than others in terms of lighting, ventilation, and freedom from glare or distractions? Are there variations in the comfort of the workstations? The point is that whereas data entry is a good example of a job where effort is tied to results (performance), there still exists some level of opportunity bias—unevenness in opportunity of the data-entry operators to produce at their respective maximum levels as a result of situational differences.

Very few employees have total control over their own performance. Direct pay-for-performance incentives should be adopted only when employee skill and effort have a substantial impact on output. Skill-based pay and bonus or profit-sharing approaches are more appropriate if employees are less able to control performance.

Performance Measurement

Any pay-for-performance system presumes accurate and fair measurement of performance. Subjective measures of performance are notorious for their lack of validity. As a result, individuals are likely to feel that their rewards are not related to their effort but instead are a function of the judgments of their particular supervisor. Objective measures are not always better, as suggested by the example of the data-entry specialists. Almost any individual whose pay is a function of "objective" performance, such as sales, can point to numerous inequities or contaminants in the measurement procedures.

Amount of Payout

To be effective, the incentive reward for successful performance needs to be significant. Studies show that to truly motivate employees, one needs to offer them an award for outstanding performance that is at least 15 to 20 percent above their base salary.[55] Although improving, incentive compensation—including bonuses, stock options, and profit sharing—on average accounts for only 10 percent of base compensation; thus the size of the payout is frequently a barrier to the successful linkage of pay and performance. For example, recent merit pay increases have about equaled the rate of inflation, between 4 and 5 percent during the past few years. A company fortunate enough to be able to offer 6 percent average increases during this period, almost a best-case scenario, typically would have 75 percent of its employees receive increases between 3 and 9 percent. How many employees will go all out all year long for a 9 percent increase when they could receive 3 or 4 percent for minimal effort and 6 percent for average effort?

The amount of payout and frequency of payout are linked. Although motivational theory argues for frequent reward opportunities, it is generally true that the more frequent the rewards, the smaller each reward will be. For this reason, it is often better to pay lump-sum rewards over a longer period of time, such as quarterly or annually. In this way, rewards will be larger and will have a greater impact on behavior.

Frailty of the Linkage

Pay-for-performance systems tend to focus attention on monetary rewards to the exclusion of other potential rewards. In fact, managers have the opportunity to influence employees in more ways than they may realize. Depending on the position and organization, the manager may be able to manipulate a large number of job elements to link tangible and intangible rewards with performance. There may be twenty-five to thirty "rewards" or job features at stake, each of which can make an employee's life easier and more enjoyable or, alternately, more difficult. Table 13.7 lists the job elements that a university department head might use to influence or motivate a faculty member. A similar list could be developed for other types of organizations, and most supervisors would be surprised at the length of the list.

To have the maximum motivational impact, both money and these other rewards should be closely tied to performance. Unfortunately, managers who do not understand all the rewards they control may unintentionally send mixed signals to

● **TABLE 13.7**

Rewards for University Faculty

1. Base salary/salary increases	17. Supplies
2. Number of courses assigned to teach	18. Telephone access (including long distance)
3. Types of courses assigned to teach	19. Photocopy access
4. Schedule of courses assigned to teach	20. Access to equipment '
5. Location of courses assigned to teach	21. Funds to attend workshops
6. Amount of secretarial support	22. Parking location
7. Technical capability of secretarial support	23. Availability of department head and dean for meetings
8. Amount of student assistant support	24. Committee assignments within department and college
9. Level of qualification of student assistant support	25. Contact with distinguished visitors to department
10. Office location/size	26. Invitations to social events
11. Furniture for office	27. Nominations for awards/honors
12. Permission to travel	28. Support for promotion
13. Resources to travel (professional conventions, etc.)	29. Involvement in activities of department
14. Consulting referrals	30. Praise
15. Permission to consult	
16. Funds to use mainframe computer	

their subordinates. Thus an employee who is evaluated as a below-average performer and is given a low merit increase may later be granted a request to attend a prestigious conference. The manager believes the low annual merit increase has successfully linked performance to rewards. Understandably, the employee is not so sure.

The situation is no different for top-performing employees. A good employee who is given an undesirable office, the worst secretary, or the greatest number of extraneous assignments may well wonder about the value of his or her contribution, whatever the size of the annual merit increase. The manager is then shocked to find that the employee who received the top merit increase has decided to quit and join a competitor. These situations are all too typical. Most of the week-to-week activities of the manager convey to the employee the absence of a link between performance and rewards.

SUMMARY: MAKING VARIABLE PAY SUCCESSFUL

Pay-for-performance systems are problematic. In some organizations, the forces tending to weaken and negate the links outweigh the factors that enhance and strengthen the relationship between pay and performance. Some of the characteristics of successful incentive systems are as follows:[56]

- *Employee–organization partnerships* designed to ensure that the organization achieves measurable financial gain when the employees receive awards

- *Employee empowerment* to make decisions that influence how work is performed
- *Relevant, simple measures* that are meaningful to the organization and clear enough for employees to understand quickly
- *Effective communication* about the variable pay program and progress toward goals
- *Balance between short- and long-term performance factors* so that the organization does not sacrifice the future for the present
- *Line-of-sight considerations* through focusing as much as possible on performance measures that are within the direct control of plan participants

The typical pay-for-performance system, whether individual incentive or organization-wide bonus, is perceived positively as long as payouts are forthcoming. When individual and/or organizational performance decreases and payouts are reduced or eliminated, employee commitment and trust in the system begin to wane. At this point, the motivational capacity of the pay-for-performance link is greatly diminished. Variable pay plans are not "everlasting." Even in the conceptualization of an incentive pay plan, it is important to envision that circumstances are going to change and that the plan will need to be adapted to the new circumstances.

Despite the problems, the idea of pay for performance remains popular in the United States. New pay organizations find a way to have some pay of all employees at risk. Typically, this translates to competitive base pay (as described in Chapter 12) plus individual and/or group incentives. For these organizations, the attempt to link pay and performance represents an important competitive quest, an effort to attract, motivate, and retain talented individuals in the work force.

EXECUTIVE COMPENSATION

For more than fifty years, a spring issue of *Business Week* has reported on executive pay at publicly held companies, a total of 365 in the 2001 report (for the year 2000). In addition to reporting executive pay, *Business Week* also rates the performance of these companies for the most recent three years and the often-tenuous links between company performance and chief executive officer (CEO) pay. For some forty years of this survey, most readers (and others) were not overly concerned with executive pay. Until recently, people were interested and even envious, but most understood that these executives represented a special resource to organizations because of their potential to influence results and hence deserved quite high pay.

All of this changed in the 1990s when executive pay became a highly charged topic. The reason for the intense interest can be summed up in two words, "equity" and "excess," as evidenced by these statistics:[57]

- CEO cash compensation increases averaged 18 percent in 2000, whereas salaried- worker pay increased 4.3 percent.[58]
- In 1993, the average CEO earned $3,841,273. In 1997, just four years later, CEO pay more than doubled to an average $7.8 million. In 2000, despite weakening returns, U.S. CEOs earned on average a princely $13.1 million. All of this occurred at a time when inflation was about 4 percent.[59]

- Apple's Steve Jobs received the year 2000's mightiest pay package, $381 million. This is more than the fourteen highest-paid CEOs combined received in 1992, just nine years earlier, and a figure slightly larger than the gross domestic product (GDP) of the country of Grenada.[60]

- In 1980, CEO pay was 42 times the pay of the ordinary factory worker; by 1991, this ratio had increased to 104; by 1993, to 149; and in 1997, the CEO earned 326 times as much as a factory worker.

- Michael Eisner, chairman and CEO of Disney, averaged $233 million in the years 1998–2000, while shareholders' return decreased by 10 percent (1999–2000).[61]

Extremely high executive compensation compared with the wages being earned by lower-level participants in organizations have led to perceptions of unfairness and low distributive justice.

Goals of Executive Compensation

The theory of compensating the top people in an organization is straightforward: What is in the best interest of the shareholders also should be what brings the greatest reward to the executives. In most organizations, executive pay is not supposed to be based on individual performance measures but rather on unit or organizational performance. The reason is that an executive's own performance is assumed to be directly reflected in measures of unit or corporate performance. Of course, situations differ, but shareholders want the executives to take the organization forward, that is, to improve things, both in the short and the long term. This wish translates into executive compensation being based on both short-term incentives (e.g., annual bonuses) and long-term ones (e.g., stock options). Consideration must be given to the structure of the incentive arrangements and the performance measures on which incentive compensation will be based.

In practice, incentives are important in determining executive compensation. Although various performance measures are used to determine payouts, most management incentive plans are "formula-driven" plans based on financial measures such as return on equity, profit before or after taxes, and return on invested capital. However, these attempts to tie executive compensation to organizational performance have not proved as effective as intended.[62] A number of studies have found no correlation between a company's stock performance and its compensation of executives.[63] The proliferation of stock-option grants, combined with the rise of unbelievable retirement deals, sign-on bonuses, and ironclad severance packages for CEOs, has made a mockery out of attempts to truly link pay to performance.[64] The result, irrespective of talent or lack thereof, is that virtually all CEOs have seen their net worth rise by at least several million dollars.

Several special considerations complicate the process of determining executive compensation. For example, because executives generally enjoy a high base salary, compensation arrangements seek to minimize their income tax liability. Attention to tax considerations can make a large difference in the after-tax income of an executive. Another consideration has to do with nonfinancial incentives—the perquisites associated with the executive position.

Executive Bonus Plans

Bonuses play an important role in today's competitive executive payment programs. One study found that 92 percent of manufacturing companies in the United States have annual incentive bonus plans for their managers and executives (varying from an average 57 percent of salary for CEOs to about 20 to 25 percent for lower-level executives).[65] This type of incentive is usually a short-term one (annual) and is based on performance. Consequently, the definition of performance is especially critical.

There are almost as many bonus systems as there are companies using this form of executive compensation. In some systems, the annual bonus is tied by formulas to objective measures, such as gross or net profits, earnings, share price, or return on investment. Other executive bonus plans are based on the subjective judgment of the board of directors and CEO. More complex systems establish certain targets—for example, a 10 percent increase in corporate earnings from the previous year—and generate a bonus pool after the target is attained. The bonus is then distributed, either in accordance with a preset formula or on the basis of subjective judgments. For example, at Coca-Cola, CEO Douglas Daft stands to gain $87.2 million, but only if he manages to increase earning per share by 20 percent a year for five years, a task that may be difficult, if not impossible.[66]

Long-Term Incentives

Publicly held organizations in the United States have been criticized for their focus on the short term. To encourage a longer perspective, many boards of directors are adopting programs of **long-term incentives** for executives. In the six years from 1985 to 1991, the proportion of executive pay related to long-term incentives increased fourfold, from 8 to 31 percent of total compensation.[67] In recent years, stock options accounted for more than 50 percent of a CEO's average pay package. Salary and bonus mean less and less, with options being the significant factor. As an example, Dennis Kozlowski, CEO or Tyco International, needs to beat tough earning goals to exercise 900,000 stock options. Kozlowski was quoted as suggesting that he has "all my eggs in this basket, but I'm watching [it] real closely."[68]

The most popular approach is to give stock or stock options to executives. The options are valuable as long as the price of the stock keeps increasing. However, the stock purchased (or the right to buy stock) can decrease in value and even become worthless if the company goes bankrupt. Executives of many large companies have suffered this fate in recent years.

Stock options are also attractive to shareholders. First, an option is not a bonus. Executives must use their own resources to exercise their right to purchase the stock. Second, the executives are assuming the same risk as all other shareholders, namely, that the price could move in either direction. Options are a form of profit sharing that links the executive's financial success to that of the shareholders. Finally, stock options are one of the few ways to offer large rewards to executives without the embarrassment of "millions of dollars of obvious money changing hands."[69] Nevertheless, the risk factor in this type of incentive may be too great for it to be attractive to executives.

Perquisites

Perquisites, better known as **"perks,"** are the extras that frequently go with executive status. Used to supplement the basic benefit package, perks range from such amenities as special parking and plush offices to pay for vacation travel, automobile expenses, and company-paid memberships in clubs. More personal perks, such as low-cost loans and personal use of company facilities (e.g., airplanes), have been slowly disappearing over the last ten years as various tax and regulatory agencies have ruled that their value must be included in the executive's taxable income. However, the list of perks offered is long and will remain an expected feature of the upper levels of the executive ladder. Speaking of perks, in 2000, Apple Computer's CEO, Steve Jobs, received the ultimate nonfinancial incentive—a $90 million Gulfstream V jet of his own.[70]

Determining Executive Compensation

Who determines the pay of the top people in a publicly held organization? Obviously, it would be a conflict of interest to have the CEO determine the reward structure for the top executives, including him- or herself. Most publicly held companies in the United States have a compensation committee composed of members of the board of directors who are not officers of the firm. The compensation committee makes recommendations to the board on overall organizational pay policies, including salaries, incentives, and perquisites for top officers. Frequently, the compensation committee seeks advice from consultants who specialize in salary and rewards for executives.

Reforming Executive Compensation

To quote one author, "We are entering a new era in executive compensation, in which companies increasingly will have to sell their executive-pay programs to stockholders."[71] Having a committee of shareholders develop a plan that combines salary, annual bonus for short-term performance, and longer-term stock options sounds like a good way to align executive interests with those of critical constituencies, including shareholders, the investment community, and employees. In the recent past, however, there have been several reasons that this approach has not worked as envisioned.[72]

Frequently, the members of the board of directors, including those serving on the compensation committee, are not independent. This lack of independence can have several causes. For instance, members of the board may be appointed by the chairman and CEO. Or the members of the board may be attorneys or investment bankers who receive fees from the company. It is not unusual for a CEO to have the CEO of another company on the board and, in turn, serve on the other CEO's board. All this leads to potential conflicts of interest.[73]

Research on the role of the board of directors and CEO salary is mixed. One study showed that the longer the tenure of the CEO, the less of a link there is between compensation and company performance—a result of the CEO's ability to build influence within the board and use this influence to weaken incentive alignment mechanisms.[74] More recent research found no evidence that director independence (or lack thereof) led to greater levels of, or changes in, CEO compensation.[75] The latter researchers argue that directors, regardless of their level of independence, are ever mindful of their obligations to shareholders. Perhaps this is reinforced by a third study that showed that CEO compensation in companies whose stock is popular with institutional investors (e.g., large mutual or pension funds) tends to be more in line with shareholder preferences.[76] As extremely large investors or shareholders, institutional investors pressure the board of directors to do what is right with respect to CEO compensation.

Incentives are frequently not what they seem. Whereas shareholders have something at risk—namely, their investment in purchasing the shares—many of the forms of long-term incentives and options offered to executives have only upside potential. For example, stock appreciation rights and restricted stock require no investment or risk.[77] In other cases, boards have been known to reprice stock options to allow executives to reap benefits even though performance targets were not realized.[78] For example, options are issued to an executive when the stock is at $50, but then it falls to $30. Instead of allowing the executive to be out of the money, as should be the case, the board may cancel the $50 options and issue new ones at $30.

While options are great, many think they are out of control in today's environment. For example, the ten CEOs with the most stock options that have yet to be exercised each have more than $1 billion in options.[79] The total unexercised dollar value of the options for these ten CEOs is more than $10.29 billion. One CEO, Lawrence Ellison of Oracle, is sitting on more than $3.4 billion of unexercised options. Wealth of this magnitude is already leading to a degree of outrage among shareholders.[80]

Several important executive compensation reforms have been implemented:

1. The Securities and Exchange Commission now requires the disclosing of executive pay and trends in executive pay in proxy statements and allows shareholders a nonbinding vote on corporate pay policies.[81] Pay of top executives is now reported annually in a prescribed and relatively straightforward manner. As a result, all aspects of executive compensation are now clearly disclosed.

2. Legislation now imposes a $1 million cap on the amount of executive pay that is deductible (by the corporation). The idea behind the legislation is that any payment beyond this amount must be earned by stock options and bonus arrangements linked to performance standards. Some have argued that this has not slowed the growth in executive pay but has instead created a minimum wage for executives.[82]

All the signs point to heightened sensitivity to executive pay on the part of executives, board members, and shareholders. For example, many board of directors compensation committees now keep a closer eye on compensation and use the opinions of independent experts when designing executive compensation systems. Several organizations hold the CEO's base salary to a multiple of the average worker's salary. (For instance, CEO salary and bonus at Herman Miller is limited to twenty times the average paycheck.)[83]

THE ROLE OF BENEFITS IN REWARD SYSTEMS

Once a largely neglected issue, the topic of benefits has become front-page news in the past decade. Child care, health care costs and coverage, flexible benefits, and changes in pension benefits are among the most dynamic compensation

● **FIGURE 13.3**

Employment Cost Index for Civilian Workers, 1982–2001: Changes in Wages and Salaries and Benefit Costs

Source: Bureau of Labor Statistics, Employment Cost Index. (Available at: http://www.bls.gov/wh/ectbrief.htm)

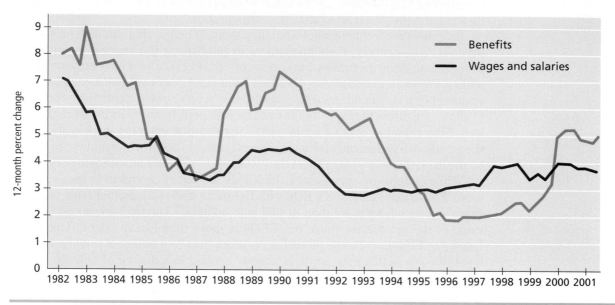

topics today. Whereas the issue of executive compensation has receded from the front page over time, issues related to benefits continue as news of the day.

A major reason for the increased attention to benefits is costs.[84] Fifty years ago, indirect compensation cost less than 5 percent of the direct compensation offered to most employees. As shown in Figure 13.3, increases in wages and salaries have averaged between 3 percent and 4 percent over the last 10 years. The cost of benefits has increased at a faster rate, averaging 5 percent in recent years.

At the present time, benefits equal 30 percent of the cost of direct compensation for companies with 500 or more employees.[85] Most of the increase does not reflect new benefits but rather the higher costs of legally required payments (e.g., the employer's share of Social Security) and optional benefits (especially health insurance); the costs for both doubled over a twenty-year period. The breakdown of the cost of benefits is shown in Table 13.8. Of course, the 30 percent figure (benefits as a percent of direct compensation) is an average. It is much higher for some major companies. For example, for Ford Motor Company, benefits have averaged 46 percent of direct compensation—almost half of the total compensation package.[86]

The increased cost of benefits has created something of a value gap—while the cost has gone up, employee satisfaction with benefits has gone down, and the value of benefits in meeting strategic organizational goals has diminished.[87] Because benefits are contingent on membership in the organization, they help a company attract and retain employees. Benefit programs do not directly motivate increased employee performance, for the link between performance level and

● **TABLE 13.8**

Benefits in Relation to Total Compensation

	All Companies		Small Companies (1–99 workers)		Large Companies (500+ workers)	
	$	%	$	%	$	%
Total compensation	$20.81		$17.86		$28.17	
Wages and salaries	$15.18		$13.41		$19.67	
Total benefits	$5.63	27.1	$4.45	24.9	$8.50	30.2
Mandated Benefits[a]	$1.73	8.3	$1.59	8.9	$2.09	7.4
Pay for time not worked[b]	$1.37	6.6	$1.02	5.7	$2.27	8.1
Health benefits	$1.28	6.2	$0.94	5.3	$2.00	7.1
Pensions	$0.62	3.0	$0.42	2.4	$1.12	4.0
Other benefits	$0.61	2.9	$0.47	2.6	$0.95	3.4

[a]Mainly Social Security and workers' compensation.
[b]Includes vacation and other paid leave.
Source: Employer Costs for Employee Compensation, Bureau of Labor Statistics, March 2001. (Available at: htt://www.bls.gov/news.release/ecec.t14.htm)

benefit level is virtually zero. All employees receive similar benefit coverage, regardless of their performance levels.

Employees gain several advantages by receiving part of their compensation in this indirect form. For example, even though employees may contribute to or even pay the entire cost of benefits such as insurance, the cost associated with the group coverage of all employees is likely to be considerably lower than equivalent insurance purchased individually. In addition, some benefits are given favorable tax treatment; the employee need not pay tax on the value of health insurance, for example. The following section reviews many of the common benefit plans currently in use and discusses related issues such as cost containment and legal considerations.

TYPES OF BENEFITS

The major categories of benefits include mandatory protection programs, pay for time not worked, optional protection programs, private retirement plans, and a wide variety of other services.

Mandatory Protection Programs

Several benefits are provided to employees because either the federal or the state government legislatively mandates them. The most notable required protection program is specified by the Federal Insurance Contribution Act (FICA) of 1935, better known as the Social Security Act. Social Security is designed to protect employees and their dependents by providing retirement income, disability income, health care (Medicare), and survivor benefits. Other mandated protection programs include workers' compensation and unemployment compensation.

● **Social Security**   For many employers and employees, **Social Security** is the most expensive benefit purchased. Two-thirds of the workers in the United States pay more toward Social Security/Medicare than they pay in income tax.

As of 2001, both employee and employer contribute 7.65 percent, 15.3 percent in all, of earnings up to a maximum of $80,400, for a combined total of as much as $12,301. A total of 6.2 percent of the tax rate is for Social Security; 1.45 percent is for Medicare. Employees who earn more than $80,400 must continue to pay the Medicare portion, with matching employer contributions. Beginning with 1994, there is no limit on the amount of wages that are subject to Medicare tax.

Social Security is not funded on an actuarial basis, as are most pension or insurance programs. In other words, the contributions are not invested in such a way as to grow and thereby cover the promised pension. Instead, money collected from currently employed individuals is used to meet the program's monthly obligations to those who are now retired or disabled. In the late 1970s, it was realized that changing demographics (a rapid increase in the elderly population) would mean too few workers to support those entitled to payments. Accordingly, Social Security has undergone major changes, the most significant being the 1983 amendments to the Social Security Act. These changes increased both the percentage of earnings contributed and the maximum earnings base. At the same time, some benefits were eliminated, and future benefits were scaled back. For example, an earnings test was added such that Social Security beneficiaries aged sixty-five to seventy could earn $10,200 a year without penalty; benefits are then cut $1 for every $3 earned above that amount. As of January 2000, the Retirement Earnings Test has been eliminated for individuals aged sixty-five to sixty-nine. It remains in effect for those aged sixty-two through sixty-four. A modified test applies for the year an individual reaches age sixty-five.

The future of Social Security is now the subject of increasing and vocal controversy. The problem is that Social Security was designed for a world that no longer exists. Some of the issues are as follows:

- *Income redistribution:* Baby boomers and young people are paying much more than they are getting. Someone born in 1955 will, if he or she is married, the sole provider of the couple, and a high earner ($60,000 in 1993 dollars), receive $750,000 less than he or she paid in. Even an average earner ($24,444 in 1993 dollars), if the sole worker in the couple, loses $268,000. If both spouses work, and one earns $60,000 while the other makes $24,444, they lose more than $1.2 million.

- *Longevity:* In 1940, only 54 percent of American men and 61 percent of American women could expect to celebrate their sixty-fifth birthday. By 1990, 72 percent of men and 84 percent of women could count on reaching age sixty-five. Further, the 1990 percentages are of a much larger population, the result being that the number of retirees increased from less than 10 million in 1955 to more than 40 million by 1995.

- *Retirement age:* Currently, those retiring at age sixty-five qualify for full Social Security benefits. In the future, that age will shift upward, to sixty-seven years in 2027. Many think the retirement age should be adjusted to seventy years of age.

- *Ratio of workers to retirees:* In 1950 there were sixteen workers paying taxes for every retiree collecting benefits. Now three workers support each retiree. By 2030, there will be only two workers to support each retiree.

- *Means testing:* At present, many well-off retirees receive more benefits than they need, whereas many poor ones receive fewer benefits than they require.[88]

Although a long way from approval, there is much discussion about a system whereby people would buy their retirement income coverage privately and tax subsidies would be used exclusively to boost the retirement incomes of low-income people. This could be achieved through a two-tiered system, where the first tier provides a flat or means-tested benefit for the elderly and the second tier involves something like a mandated income retirement account (IRA).[89] One thing is certain: The Social Security system will continue to be debated and analyzed.

● **Unemployment Compensation**   The Social Security Act of 1935 also established a system of **unemployment compensation insurance (UCI)** in the United States. UCI provides benefits, at the rate of 50 to 80 percent of normal pay, to out-of-work employees who have been laid off and who are actively looking for work. Those seeking benefits must be registered with the state employment office in their area and are expected to accept work commensurate with their skills. The benefit period is a function of the length of prior employment, up to a maximum of twenty-six weeks of benefits. Workers who are fired for misconduct, quit voluntarily, or do not actively seek employment generally are not eligible for UCI benefits.

Unlike Social Security, which is managed by the federal government, UCI is handled by the states in accordance with federal guidelines. As a result, the exact details of employer contributions, employee eligibility for coverage, and amount of benefits vary considerably. In most states, employers finance this benefit by paying a small tax on the first $7,000 of an employee's wages. The size of the employer's contribution varies on the basis of past claims against that employer, thus providing an incentive to employers to avoid frequent layoffs. The experience-based tax rate also provides an inducement for employers to keep careful records of the reasons that employees leave and to document all discharges due to misconduct.

In periods of an extended economic downturn, it is not unusual for the twenty-six-week limit on benefits to be extended. In 2002, just such an extension was enacted by Congress and signed by the president as part of the economic stimulus for unemployed workers in the aftermath of the September 11, 2001, terrorist attack.

● **Workers' Compensation**   As the United States became increasingly industrialized in the late 1800s and early 1900s, disabling worker injuries and worker deaths became more common. Most workers had no avenue of redress and no employee benefits if they were injured on the job. Injured workers and their families simply went without compensation, and employers were not accountable for workplace hazards, which were often very great.

The first **workers' compensation,** a type of no-fault insurance for occupational disabilities and death, was initiated in the early 1900s, and most states have had such a program since 1920. Currently, all states have some form of workers' compensation, which offers reasonable and prompt benefits when workers are injured or killed on the job, regardless of fault. Workers do not need to bear the expense of time-consuming court action against their employers.

As with most insurance, the cost to employers is based on injury experience. The costs of medical treatment, rehabilitation programs, and disability income can be high, especially in cases of serious injuries. As a result, employers have an incentive to encourage employee safety. Unlike other mandated protection programs, workers' compensation is handled entirely by the state, with no federal standards or involvement. Consequently, the specific benefit provisions vary from state to state.

Many organizations and states are experiencing problems with workers' compensation. As presently conceived, there is substantial discontent with workers' compensation—discontent on the part of workers with job-related injuries, the organizations they work for, and insurers.[90] Workers' compensation incidents inevitably involve medical treatment; thus the organizational and insurer discontent is related to rapidly escalating medical costs.[91] Employee discontent is related to concerns over possible loss of income, since workers' compensation benefits are generally less than actual income. Additional worker concerns have to do with job security as well as possible medical and legal hassles.

States have been forced to deal with issues relating to workers' compensation because it is an important factor in business decisions to locate or expand in a particular area. Several years ago, one state, Texas, had so many workers' compensation problems that the governor called a special session of the legislature to deal with the issues. The legislature devoted a one-month session exclusively to workers' compensation.

Compensation for Time Not Worked

Almost all employers provide full-time employees with some payments for time not worked. Figure 13.4 illustrates a wide range of such benefits.

● FIGURE 13.4

Payment for Time Not Worked

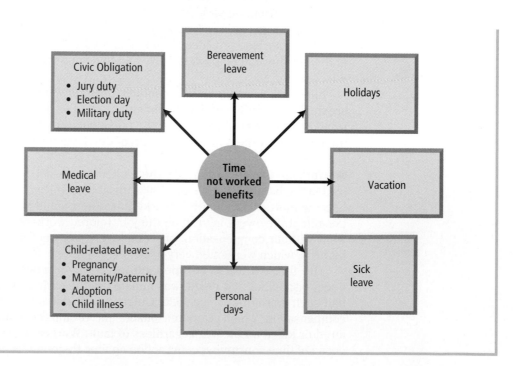

● **Holidays** Virtually all employers pay employees for major national holidays. Some employers have additional holidays, such as Presidents' Day (February), Columbus Day (October), or Veterans' Day (November), whereas others observe religious holidays such as Good Friday and Rosh Hashanah. Employers that must operate on holidays (e.g., hospitals or police departments) generally provide overtime pay to employees who work on holidays.

● **Vacation** Most employers offer paid vacations to their permanent employees, the amount depending on length of service. A majority of employers stagger vacation schedules to remain well staffed throughout the year, whereas some schedule a plant shutdown and have all employees take vacation at that time.

● **Sick Leave** A usual pay-for-time-not-worked benefit is sick leave. Many employees accrue sick leave in proportion to days worked. For instance, one half-day of paid sick leave may be given for each fifteen days worked. Some firms allow unused sick leave to accumulate over the years, to be used in case of extended illness. Another popular alternative is to pay employees for unused sick leave as an incentive to come to work regularly and to use sick leave only when it is really needed.

● **Personal Days** Some employers offer one or two personal holidays each year. Employees can decide when to use these days off—for instance, to celebrate a birthday. Personal days off are sometimes called "mental health days"—for the occasional times when one has to get away from work or "go crazy."

● **Other Leaves** In 1993, the Family and Medical Leave Act became law. This act mandates unpaid leave of up to twelve weeks, with benefits and reinstatement rights, in the event of the birth or adoption of a child or serious illness in the immediate family, including parents. Health benefits must be maintained for employees on this type of leave. Leave is available to employees who have worked at least 1,250 hours in the previous twelve months of employment with the same employer. The importance of leave and other child-care benefits was highlighted in September 1992, when a consortium of 137 companies and nonprofit groups, including 11 major corporations, announced that they had formed the American Business Collaboration for Quality Dependent Care. The goal of the consortium is to raise $25 million to fund a variety of child- and elder-care projects across the United States.[92]

As indicated in Figure 13.4, additional leave benefits can include medical, civic, and bereavement leave. Medical leave allows employees extended time off for major medical reasons. Frequently, such leave is unpaid and takes effect when all sick leave days have been exhausted. Leave for civic obligations includes time off for jury duty, part (or all) of the day off to vote in national elections, and leave for military duty, such as National Guard or reserve military service. Bereavement leave allows the employee time off for a death in the immediate family.

Optional Protection Programs—Health Insurance

Optional protection programs are not mandated by law but are offered to make the employer more competitive in the labor market and to improve employee satisfaction and quality of life. Medical or health insurance is a major optional protection benefit offered by most employers. The goal of **health insurance** is to provide partial or complete coverage of medical expenses incurred by the employee and the employee's family. In practice, this means either paying directly or reimbursing the employee for hospital charges, surgery, and other personal or family medical expenses. Many plans also pay for dental care.

Health plans vary in their comprehensiveness of coverage and specifics of funding, but rapidly rising costs have made health insurance a major concern in most organizations. As shown in Figure 13.5, health care expenditures will continue to rise at a faster rate than either the gross domestic product or the consumer price index.[93] For example, in 2000 health insurance increased by 10 percent, a rate that is faster than it has ever been in relation to the overall rate of inflation. For a decade, premiums increased at twice the rate of inflation but are now rising at four times the rate of inflation.[94] The simple fact is that most organizations cannot afford to provide as much coverage as they have done in the past. Cost-containment strategies have included the redesign of medical plans, a search for funding alternatives, and other approaches aimed at slowing the increase in health care costs.

● **Health Plan Redesign**   In the past, health care insurance was typically regarded as a total package shielding employees from all health care costs. Increasingly, however, the goal is shifting to protection of employees against major and catastrophic costs. Instead of reimbursing employees for all medical bills, many employers have begun using deductibles, copayments, and coordinated coverage as ways of containing costs.

Many medical plans have a **deductible** of $100 to $400 or more for each family member each year. Only expenses over this amount will be reimbursed by the insurance fund. Thus a person in good health, who makes only one or two medical or dental visits in a year, may receive no reimbursement.

● **FIGURE 13.5**

Percent Change in Health Spending and Consumer Prices, 1987–2002

Source: Adapted from Joel E. Miller, *Déjà Vu All Over Again: The Soaring Cost of Private Health Insurance and Its Impact on Consumers and Employers* (Washington, D.C.: National Coalition on Health Care, May 2000).

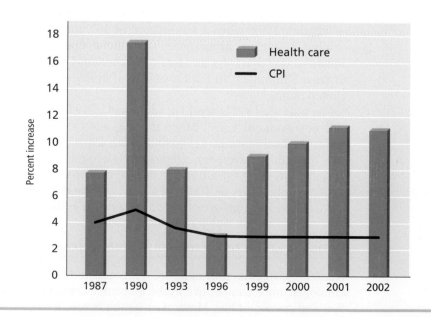

Coinsurance means that expenses beyond the deductible are shared, usually in a ratio between 50:50 and 80:20. Thus an employee submitting a bill of $500 for simple surgery in the doctor's office would receive reimbursement for $400, assuming an 80:20 split and no deductible. To take care of catastrophic expenses, costs beyond a maximum of several thousand dollars are then reimbursed 100 percent under most coinsurance plans. For example, an individual with bills of $75,000 for heart surgery might pay 20 percent of the first $5,000 (or $1,000), with insurance covering the remaining $74,000. Copayment plans have the advantage of making employees more aware of health care costs. Also, because the employee pays some of each expense, copayments tend to discourage unnecessary use of health insurance benefits.

The hospitalization segment of IBM's health plan is an example of carefully identified cost sharing. IBM's health plan provides fifty-two weeks of hospitalization for plan participants. Analysis of hospitalization showed that 31 percent of the hospitalizations were for only two days. The cost-sharing change required an employee to pay 40 percent of the cost of the first day of hospitalization. As a result, the number of admissions decreased by 36 percent, saving IBM approximately $100 million a year.[95]

Another common alternative is to require employees to contribute some of the costs of health insurance. For employees accustomed to having their entire health care costs paid by employers, the shifting of costs has become an emotional issue that has, in some cases, triggered employee work stoppages (strikes). Thus employers must be very careful if they switch from noncontributory, no-deductible, full-coverage plans to systems in which employees become responsible for a share of health costs. Employees tend to regard existing benefits as rights rather than privileges and strongly resent any reductions in benefit levels. It may help to appoint a benefits-cost task force, including employees from various organizational levels, to study the problem and to communicate the reasons for a cost-reduction move.

Employers are increasingly concerned with **coordinating benefits** as a way of containing costs. The objective is to prevent duplicate payment for the same health care service. For instance, an employee may be covered both by his or her employer's plan and by a working spouse's benefits. Careful checking is necessary to ensure that reimbursement is made only once.

● **Health Funding Alternatives**   Another approach to cost containment has been to seek funding alternatives. Instead of relying on insurance companies such as Blue Cross/Blue Shield, some employers have begun to self-insure or to use preferred provider organizations or health maintenance organizations. By self-insuring, an employer sets aside funds to pay health claims in lieu of insurance coverage. If the base of employees is large enough to spread the risk, the employer can achieve significant savings.[96]

A **preferred provider organization (PPO)** is a limited group of physicians and hospitals that agree to provide services in accordance with competitive fee schedules negotiated in advance. The physicians and hospitals benefit from knowing that they have a guaranteed customer base. Employees are free to use any physician or hospital that is part of the PPO or another provider if they are willing to pay any difference. Many employers have organized PPOs in communities located near their facilities.[97]

A **health maintenance organization (HMO)** provides complete medical care for employees and their families at a fixed annual fee. Supplemental policies typically cover hospitalization for those HMOs not associated with hospitals. Since doctor visits are not charged on a per-visit basis, individuals are more likely to seek preventive care, thus reducing the incidence and costs of more serious illness.

● **Legal Requirements for Health Care**   Health benefits programs have been relatively free from government regulation, although health care and the public role in its delivery have been the topic of widespread public debate in the last several years. The Health Maintenance Organization Act of 1973 requires that companies with at least twenty-five employees living in an area served by an HMO offer HMO membership as an alternative to regular group health coverage. Consequently, the number of HMOs and their participants has increased dramatically. Further, a more recent trend has been a merging of HMOs to form giant managed care facilities serving millions of people in multistate territories.[98]

In 1985, the Consolidated Omnibus Budget Reconciliation Act (COBRA) was passed to prevent gaps in health care coverage. It requires employers with twenty or more employees to provide extended health care coverage for up to eighteen months to employees who are terminated and up to thirty-six months for widowed or divorced spouses and dependent children of former or current employees. The employer may pass along the full cost of the premium to the employee or employee's family, along with a 2 percent administrative fee.

● **Health Benefits for Retirees**   Companies that provide health coverage for employees typically provide continuing coverage for retirees. Such continuing coverage is coordinated with Medicare, which provides certain benefits beginning at age sixty-five. Companies try to cover the costs—and there are many—not paid by Medicare.

In an effort to clarify the potential costs of retiree medical coverage, in 1992 the Financial Accounting Standards Board (FASB) adopted Financial Accounting Standard 106, which requires organizations to subtract a portion of their obligations from their annual earnings reports. Organizations were required to (1) set up a huge "catch-up" reserve for current and retired employees and (2) accrue, or set aside, a reserve each year for postretirement medical benefits for employees currently working. The cost was staggering for many organizations. For example, General Motors had a one-time charge of $16 billion to $24 billion, an amount equal to between 60 and 88 percent of GM's equity or total value. In addition, GM will have a continuing charge of $2 billion to $2.3 billion—a 22 to 33 percent reduction in pretax profits.[99] The impact is not as large for other companies, and some organizations have "prefunded" retiree medical costs. For most organizations, however, the one-time and continuing charges can be measured in millions of dollars, with double-digit reductions in pretax profits being common.

Retiree medical benefits have gone from a long-accepted and little-noticed element of a benefit package to a front-burner issue in terms of impact on profits. The strategic, legal, accounting, and financial constraints will be weighed against general HR practices of doing nice things for retirees as organizations reevaluate the level of medical benefits they will provide for retired workers.

● **Health Benefits for Nonfamily Members**   Given the general trend to control and cut back on the expense of health care, why would organizations offer to extend coverage to other people besides employees and their legal dependents? Recently many companies have moved to provide what are called domestic-partner benefits; that is, the same benefits for the long-term partners of homosexual employees as it provides for the spouses of heterosexual employees. More than 145 (29 percent) of *Fortune* 500 companies now offer domestic-partner benefits, more than quadruple the number that offered them in 1997.[100] Of the 100 best companies to work for, nearly half (forty-seven) offer domestic-partner benefits.[101]

The rationale for domestic-partner benefits is simple: Studies showed that committed homosexual couples are at no greater risk of illness, including the catastrophic illness of AIDS, than are married heterosexual pairs. A survey of companies offering domestic-partner benefits found that the cost was less than 1 percent of the total benefit costs. On a cost-benefit basis, those companies offering such benefits feel that the value in terms of attracting and retaining employees outweighs the cost of the coverage.

Optional Protection Programs—Life and Disability Insurance

Many companies offer life insurance as a benefit, providing support for the employee's family in the case of the death of the wage earner.[102] By purchasing a group package, the employer can obtain coverage at far lower rates than would be available to individuals. Coverage is generally based on annual earnings, and for many employees, coverage is offered for twice annual earnings. Some organizations allow employees to purchase additional life insurance at the group rate.

Many employers provide long-term disability insurance to guarantee income for employees who become disabled and are unable to work—an event far more likely than death of the wage earner. Disabled employees and their families are entitled to payments from Social Security, but most need additional income to approach replacement of prior earnings. Long-term disability payments typically do not begin until the employee has been unable to work for a specified period, usually three to six months.

Private Retirement/Pension Plans

A very important benefit to most employees is a private pension plan. In some cases, pensions are funded entirely by employer contributions, but most involve both employer and employee contributions. A **pension** is essentially an investment to which contributions are added at regular intervals. Invested funds, along with interest, dividends, and/or capital gains, grow and accumulate to provide income during retirement. Under some plans, an account identified as belonging to the employee is established. With other pensions, funds are pooled, with a known share reserved for the employee on retirement. Pensions are subject to intricate financial, legal, and tax rules and considerations.

Virtually all pensions are "qualified"—that is, they conform to stringent Internal Revenue Service requirements. Both employer and individual contributions to qualified plans are exempt from income tax, and interest, dividends, and gains are allowed to accumulate tax-free. Retired employees must pay income tax on the pension payments they receive, but often their tax rate is lower than when they were working and had a larger income. Thus employee contributions are a valuable means of deferring tax on income. In this context, pensions are deferred wages: rewards for long service. However, if an employer wishes to implement a pension plan for a select group of employees, such as key executives, the plan must be nonqualified.[103] This approach is frequently used to provide supplemental retirement benefits for executives.

Retirement plans are expensive, costing the employer an estimated 10 percent of payroll (see Table 13.8), including the company contribution to Social Security and pensions. The amount that the employee will receive on retirement is usually based on length of service with the company and salary level. Benefits average between 20 and 30 percent of preretirement salary for most plans. (Remember that the retired employee also will qualify for Social Security.) The pension plans in use today can be categorized into three broad types: defined benefit plans, defined contribution plans, and capital accumulation plans.[104]

● **Defined Benefit Plans**   The **defined benefit plan** is the most prevalent type, comprising 91 percent of all plans in American industry.[105] Under a defined benefit plan, retirement benefits depend on a formula that includes length of service and average earnings in the final years of employment. Such plans have the advantage that employees know the amount of their retirement benefits ahead of time. Employer and employee contributions are determined by actuarial calculations.

● **Defined Contribution Plans**   A less expensive—and less widely used—type of pension is the **defined contribution plan,** also termed a **money purchase plan.** Contributions are made at a fixed rate to an account established for the employee. Benefits are a function of contributions plus gains (or losses) as a result of interest, dividends, or capital gains. Profit-sharing plans and ESOPs fall into this category. Defined contribution plans offer less security and predictability of retirement benefits because the employee, not the company, assumes the risk of investment performance.

● **Capital Accumulation Plans**   Through **capital accumulation plans,** employees have the opportunity to establish individual retirement accounts. The principal capital accumulation vehicles are thrift plans and 401(k) plans. Employees may make tax-deferred contributions, which, under thrift plans, may be matched by the organization. A common matching rate would be $1 of employer contribution for each $2 contributed by the employee.

Thrift plans were popular in some industries for many years and then became the basis for 401(k) plans as a part of the Internal Revenue Act of 1978.[106] Although they involve no employer match, 401(k) plans allow employees to set aside salary and participate in tax-deferred earnings. In 2001, employee contributions to 401(k) plans were limited to 20 percent of salary, up to a maximum of approximately $10,500 a year, a figure that is adjusted annually for inflation.

Regulations Governing Retirement Plans

Private employer retirement plans were subject to little government regulation before 1974. Employers had great latitude in establishing and administering pension plans for their employees. As it turned out, many of the pension plans were not sound because of either poor actuarial planning or company economic reversals. Thus many employees believed that they were accruing pension rights when in fact they were not. In response to these problems, during the last twenty years a wide array of legislation has been enacted and IRS regulations formulated with respect to pensions.

● **ERISA**   The initial legislation setting standards in pensions was the **Employee Retirement Income Security Act of 1974 (ERISA),** which established reporting requirements and fiduciary standards, along with rules regarding plan participation, vesting, funding, and pension plan termination. Favorable tax treatment of employer contributions is available only for plans that meet ERISA guidelines. (Note that employers are not required to offer private pensions.)

In terms of participation, ERISA requires that employees who are at least twenty-one years old and have completed one year with the company be eligible to participate in the pension plan. Another important concept is **vesting,** the right to receive pension benefits contributed on the employee's behalf by the company even if the employee leaves the company before retirement. ERISA established complex alternate rules regarding vesting but basically ensured that any employee would have rights to at least 50 percent of the employer's contributions after ten years of service and would be 100 percent vested after fifteen years. Thus employees can be assured of certain pension levels if they have worked a minimum number of years, even if they leave the company before retirement. Vesting rules also prevent company abuses, such as firing long-service employees shortly before retirement in order to avoid paying them a pension. Vesting applies only to employer contributions. Employees retain rights to any contributions they make and can withdraw them or roll them over into another private pension plan if they leave the company.

Before ERISA, many private pension plans were not protected if the company went bankrupt. To protect employees and retired employees, ERISA created a system of **pension plan termination insurance** and a government agency, the Pension Benefit Guaranty Corporation (PBGC), to administer the program. The insurance is funded through premiums paid by employers.

The long-range goals of ERISA are to make private pensions equitable and to put them on a firm financial footing. The burden imposed on employers or pension trustees is substantial. As a result, in the initial years of ERISA, many employers terminated their pension plans rather than comply with the law.

● **Single-Sex Pension Benefits**   A final legal issue concerning pensions involves sex bias. Before 1978, it was common to use actuarial tables in planning pension contributions and payouts. Women as a group live longer than men; as a result, under most pension plans, they were required to make greater contributions to receive retirement benefits equal to those of men. Alternately, women were forced to accept lower monthly benefits after retirement than men, again because statistically they can expect to collect benefits for more years.

In 1978, the U.S. Supreme Court found this practice illegal.[107] The Court extended this concept in 1983, forcing pension plan administrators to eliminate sex distinctions in mortality tables used to determine pension benefits.[108] The Retirement Equity Act of 1984 was passed to bring legislation in line with these Court decisions. As a result, there is now no distinction in the benefits received by men and women.

● **GATT Treaty (1994)**   When Congress agreed to liberalize world trade by passing the General Agreement on Tariffs and Trade (GATT), little noticed were 129 pages of pension legislation added at the end. Many believe this bill constitutes "the most significant pension funding changes in twenty years."[109] Companies with underfunded pension plans will have to contribute more, and faster, or pay higher insurance premiums to the PBGC. For example, General Motors must now speed up plans for narrowing a $20 billion underfunding of its pension obligations. There were other changes as well.

Why was this pension legislation a provision of GATT? The liberalized trade legislation, GATT, meant less income for the United States through tariff cuts. Budget rules required that this diminished income be offset—hence pension revisions that promised $1 billion in new income.

Other Benefits

Many organizations offer additional benefits, some of which provide innovative opportunities for employees. Included are such benefits as vision care, prescription drugs, concierge services (e.g., dry-cleaning pickup/delivery), legal counseling, and financial counseling.[110] Many organizations have established employee assistance programs (EAPs), offering short-term counseling for employees under stress as a result of work or nonwork problems.[111] EAPs are discussed in more detail in Chapter 14. Other important benefits include those described in the sections that follow.

● **Wellness Programs**   In an effort to stimulate wellness, many employers provide exercise or recreational facilities for employees or reimburse employees for health club memberships. Other companies provide incentives in the form of monthly stipends or similar payments for employees to participate in exercise programs, quit smoking, lower blood pressure or cholesterol, or take similar steps toward good health.[112]

● **Educational Assistance**   Another important benefit is **educational assistance.** Typically, employees are reimbursed for tuition and possibly for books or other associated costs. In general, educational assistance is limited to courses or degree programs that are job-related.

● **Child-Care Assistance**   It is likely that every major company will soon consider offering child-care assistance as an employee benefit. Such assistance can take the form of on-site child care, financial assistance, or information and referral. The number of women in the labor market has increased dramatically. As of 1999, 70 percent of all mothers with children three to five years of age and 61 percent with children under three years of age were in the workforce.[113] Furthermore, satisfaction with child-care arrangements has been found to be related to less work–family conflict and to lower levels of absenteeism but unrelated to performance.[114]

Twenty-six of the 100 Best Companies to Work For offer on-site day care—many more offer assistance and/or referral.[115] Even though the total number of companies providing such assistance is unknown, the number will be growing, partly as a part of a little-known tax credit included in the Bush administration's mammoth tax cut bill of May 2001. Included in the bill is a 25 percent tax credit for employer-related expenses for child-care activities, such as a company-sponsored day-care center and direct company subsidization of day care.[116]

Direct corporate involvement was stimulated by what has been called the "child-care crisis"—the finding that over 70 percent of day care is mediocre and 12 percent is poor. The economics of day care are such that even mediocre care is expensive—almost $5,000 per year to provide services for one child. This $5,000 represents 8 percent of the median U.S. family pretax income for a dual-career family and 23 percent of earnings for families headed by a single working parent.[117]

Another avenue of corporate involvement has been through corporate–community partnerships. As part of the American Business Collaboration for Quality Dependent Care, eleven corporations have enlisted the help of some 145 entities and raised $27 million to fund dependent-care projects in forty-five communities.[118]

Because child-care needs and preferences are extremely diverse, multifaceted, and changing, employers are advised to undertake a systematic needs assessment of employees before developing specific programs.[119] Many employers find that the best method of assisting a diverse work force is through referral services. Such services allow employees to more readily find the type of child care best suited to their needs.

Of the companies with some type of child-care benefit, approximately half provide financial assistance, typically through a dependent-care option in a flexible benefits plan. Organizations can help employees pay for dependent care through pretax salary deductions. The Internal Revenue Code specifies that up to $5,000 of employee payments for dependent-care expenses may be excluded from an employee's annual taxable income. For example, if the proper administrative arrangements are established, an employee needing dependent care could agree to have the employer reduce his or her salary by $300 per month ($3,600 per year), with this amount then being directed to an account to pay for dependent care. Although there are administrative costs, there is no direct cost to the employer, and the employee is, in effect, paying for dependent care with pretax dollars. Without this type of plan, $3,600 worth of dependent care would cost a family earning $40,000 a total of $5,000—$3,600 for care and about $1,400 for federal income tax. Thus the savings involved can be significant. The only drawback is that any balance in a dependent-care account cannot be refunded directly or carried forward at the end of the plan year. Also, to take advantage of the tax savings, care providers need to have a Social Security number or an employer identification number. Thus the dependent care provided by the student wife from Spain cannot be paid for with before-tax contributions to a dependent-care account.

Note that such plans can be used for any qualified dependents, not just children. Many families need to arrange day care for elderly parents. Elder care was clearly one of the new benefits issues of the 1990s, and its importance is expected to increase in the twenty-first century as the population ages.[120]

Finally, some research suggests that offering child-care benefits can cause resentment among childless workers and/or workers with children who do not take advantage of the benefits.[121] A recent study found that current, past, and anticipated future use of child-care programs was related to more positive attitudes to child-care programs, but not to more general attitudes or behaviors. The so-called family-friendly backlash was not a serious problem.[122]

ISSUES IN INDIRECT COMPENSATION

Cost Containment

Because of the rapidly increasing costs of health care, pensions, and other benefits, employers must focus on strategic **cost containment** if they are to survive. A recent *Wall Street Journal* article related the story of the impact on hospital and insurance costs of a single patient who spent thirty-four days in the hospital, with a resulting bill of $5.2 million.[123] Even though dramatic, benefit packages can add up to more than 40 percent above the cost of direct compensation. A tradeoff analysis can help in evaluating benefit possibilities. In one case, a firm with 5,000 employees had high productivity, but rising health insurance costs were eroding profits.[124] Premiums had increased 75 percent, and a 20 percent increase—to $8.5 million—was projected. The executives were determined to reduce costs by 10 percent while identifying potential improvements in the system.

After the initial analysis, a decision was made to limit tradeoffs to health benefits. Employee satisfaction with alternative tradeoffs was solicited by inviting a 15 percent sample from all levels of the organization to participate in half-hour discussion meetings. Employees rated how much less satisfied they would be with their benefits if each alternative were implemented. The "satisfaction loss" (expressed as a percentage) for each of the potential reductions is shown in Table 13.9. Similarly, satisfaction gains were identified for suggested improvements to the plan. The satisfaction losses and gains were then divided by the percentage of premium saved (or spent) for each change. The resulting column "Satisfaction Loss per Dollar Saved" of Table 13.9 provided guidance as to changes in medical coverage that could yield the needed savings with minimal dissatisfaction from employees. As can be seen, the first choice was to add the requirement of precertification prior to hospitalization as a means of eliminating unneeded hospital days. With regard to the deductible for hospitalization, the satisfaction loss doubled in going from $100 to $200, but the loss per dollar saved was equivalent for these two alternatives. The organization decided to select the $200 deductible. The clear preference, in terms

●TABLE 13.9

Example of Tradeoff Analysis to Evaluate Potential Health Care Savings

Plan Reductions					
Benefit	**Change (from/to)**	**Satisfaction Loss**	**Employer Savings (% of Prem.)**	**Satisfaction Loss per Dollar Saved**	**Cumulative Savings (% of Prem.)**
Precertification	Not. Req./ Req.	11.4%	4%	2.85	4.0%
Hospital deductible	None/$100 None/$200	5.7% 11.4%	1.7% 3.4%	3.35 3.35	7.4%
Major medical deductible	$100/$150 $100/$200	11.4% 32.9%	2.5% 5.0%	4.56 6.58	9.9%
Dependent coverage	$5/$10 $6/$15	14.3% 31.4%	2.4% 4.7%	5.96 6.68	12.3%
Hospital coinsurance	100%/95% 100%/90%	18.6% 41.4%	3.0% 6.0%	6.20 6.90	
Surgical coinsurance	100%/90% 100%/80%	27.1% 50.0%	1.0% 2.0%	27.10 25.00	

of both satisfaction loss and loss per dollar saved, was for a $150 major medical deductible. The same was true with dependent coverage options; a charge of $10 had the least satisfaction loss per dollar saved. The result was a 13.3 percent reduction in cost, with 1.4 percent then being allocated to three new plan improvements with high satisfaction gain per dollar spent. The net result was four plan reductions with a projected 1986 savings of just over $1 million, along with an added premium of $119,000 for plan improvements for a total savings of 10.9 percent in benefit costs. The tradeoff analysis guided the effort in selecting health plan changes that would produce the savings with minimal employee dissatisfaction.

Two methods of reducing costs of benefits are through copayments and self-insurance. Both alternatives have already been discussed as funding alternatives for health insurance, but they apply more broadly. Plans with copayment require that the employee contribute to the benefit costs. This technique is cost-effective and also an indirect way of communicating the high cost of benefit packages to employees. When copayment makes employees aware of the costs of medical care, a reduction in unnecessary or abusive uses of the available benefits may result. There is some evidence that employees view benefits as part of their employment rather than as a privilege. For this reason, care must be taken when switching over to a copayment plan to ensure that employees do not see this as a reduction in the compensation package.

Larger organizations can establish a fund to cover some benefit costs and thus avoid the premium expenses. In addition to the potential savings, self-insurance allows organizations to become familiar with the benefit program through in-depth knowledge of day-to-day claims and other issues related to use. In this way, still further areas of potential savings may be discovered.

Partial self-insurance can be incorporated into health plans for small businesses. For example, one small business provides health insurance to three key employees. When premiums were slated for a 20 percent increase, $200 per month, the company increased the deductible for large claims (serious illnesses, not routine treatment) from $500 to $2,000, with a commitment to pay the difference ($1,500).[125] The maximum liability would be $4,500 if all three employees had major claims, as from surgery or serious illness. So far, in two years, there have been no such claims, saving the company $4,800.

Flexible Benefit Options

One way to increase employee satisfaction with benefits and overall job satisfaction without increasing the cost of the compensation package is by offering a **flexible benefit package,** also termed a **cafeteria-style benefit plan.**[126] Under this plan, employees are automatically given a core plan with minimum coverage in medical insurance and retirement benefits. In addition, they receive benefit credits each year, which they can "spend" on additional benefits of their choice (e.g., more vacation time, more life insurance, more dental insurance, etc.).

Flexible benefit plans are very effective and popular because they recognize that employees of different ages and life situations have differing personal needs. Flexible benefits allow individual employees to choose the benefits they want. Most companies provide a request form annually, allowing employees to modify their package.

A flexible benefit program involves several additional costs. First, communication of benefit options is more difficult. As many organizations can attest, it is extremely difficult to get the word out on a single benefit package. When there are multiple packages, as with flexible benefits, the communication problem is far more difficult. Administrative costs also increase with the number of options.

For companies willing to invest the extra effort to ensure that flexible benefit programs will work, the advantages outweigh the disadvantages. Flexible benefit programs enhance an organization's reputation for progressive treatment of its employees.

Communicating About Benefits

The main goal of both direct and indirect compensation should be to achieve company goals by providing rewards that are valued by employees. Employers must weigh both the costs of implementing benefit packages and the employee reaction to such plans, which may include behaviors such as turnover. Communication is critical for the successful administration of benefits. Organizations that do not invest effort in communicating a specific benefit might be better off not offering the benefit in the first place.

If the employer's intention is to attract entry-level employees, marketing immediate benefits such as a longer vacation or educational incentives may be more effective than advertising the pension plan, a benefit that will be more likely to reduce midcareer turnover. Also, if employees are to be satisfied with their benefit package, they must first be able to appreciate what goes into it. Although benefits may equal 40 percent or more of direct compensation, employees often grossly underestimate their cost and value.[127]

Organizations have at least two ways to correct the undervaluing of benefits. The first is to explain clearly to employees the objective costs of these benefits, pointing out why particular benefits may be of greater value than direct payment (e.g., because of tax considerations and favorable group insurance rates). Second, one study reported that employees know the value of their specific benefits almost to the penny when they make contributions to the fund.[128] Thus contributing and copayment systems not only reduce the organization's costs but have communication and educational advantages as well.

Communicating about benefits is not an easy task. Plans and options can be quite complex, and employees tend to have little interest in benefits until they need to use them. There are several ways to improve communication about benefits. First, written communication should be in plain language, not insurance jargon. Second, communication should be frequent and timed to occur when employees are likely to listen. Describing benefits when employees first begin work is unlikely to be effective because new employees have many more pressing issues to attend to in the first few weeks on the job. Finally, communication should be directed not just to the employee but also to other consumers of the benefit—most commonly, the spouse.

Work–Family Issues

More companies, especially larger firms, are trying to help their employees balance work and family demands. Studies have shown that work conflict leads to family conflict and that family conflict has a significant negative influence on an individual's attendance and quality of work.[129] These research findings, confirmed by organizational observations, have resulted in many employers' sensitivity to the well-being of their employees.[130] There can be little doubt that job and life satisfaction are related.[131]

While the greatest increase in organizational response has been through child-care benefits, there are other work–family benefits that also are popular. Table 13.10 presents the results of a survey of just over 2,600 HR professionals regarding the most popular family–workplace initiatives.[132] Clearly, larger organizations are leading the way, but work–family benefits are on the rise among all organizations.

Work and family issues have gained a great deal of attention. For example, *Business Week* has now had two surveys of family-friendly corporate policies, the most recent being September 1997.[133] As part of the survey, companies were graded on their programs and strategies as well as employee response. The grading criteria and results are shown in Table 13.11. Work–family issues are the problem of the twenty-first century. We can expect that more and more companies will take up the issues identified in the survey as they attempt to become more family-friendly.

● **TABLE 13.10**

Most Popular Family–Workplace Initiatives

	All Companies	Company Size (No. of Employees)				
		<100	101–500	501–2,500	2,501–5,000	>5,000
Dependent care flexible spending account	69%	55%	68%	79%	77%	88%
Flextime	58%	64%	51%	60%	71%	75%
Telecommuting	37%	41%	30%	43%	45%	50%
Compressed workweek	31%	21%	30%	36%	45%	53%
Paid family leave (other than FLMA)	26%	25%	23%	33%	29%	25%
Job sharing	25%	19%	20%	33%	55%	38%
Domestic-partner benefits (opposite-sex partners)	25%	28%	27%	22%	23%	19%
Ability to bring child to work in emergency	24%	39%	25%	12%	19%	9%
Child-care referral service	20%	13%	18%	26%	39%	34%
Scholarships for employees' families	20%	10%	16%	31%	32%	41%
Elder-care referral service	19%	13%	18%	17%	39%	31%
Adoption assistance	16%	10%	14%	19%	32%	34%
Domestic-partner benefits (same-sex partners)	16%	14%	17%	15%	19%	28%
Location program/designated area	16%	11%	16%	18%	29%	28%
Emergency sick child care	13%	11%	11%	14%	42%	25%

Source: Adapted from Society for Human Resource Management, "2001 Benefits Survey," April 2000. (Available at: http://www.shrm.org/surveys/results/default.asp?page=01benefits.asp)

● **TABLE 13.11**

The Family-Friendly Grades of Top-Scoring Companies

Top 10 S&P and Non-S&P Companies					
S&P 500 Companies	**Programs & Strategies**	**Employee Response**	**Non-S&P 500 Companies**	**Programs & Strategies**	**Employee Response**
1. MBNA America	A	A	First Tenn. Bank	A–	A
2. Motorola	A–	A–	Sequent Computer Syst.	A–	A–
3. Barnett Banks	A–	A–	Calvert Group	A–	A
4. Hewlett-Packard	B+	A–	SAS Institute	B–	A
5. UNUM	B	B+	Eddie Bauer	B	A
6. Lincoln National	B+	B+	Edward D. Jones	B–	A–
7. Merrill Lynch	B+	B+	Commercial Finl. Svces.	C+	A
8. Dupont	A–	B	BE&K	B	B+
9. TRW	B	B+	Lancaster Labs	B	B
10. Cigna	B	B	KPMG Peat Marwick	B	B

Scoring Criteria			
Programs & Strategies		**Employee Response**	
Programs	**Percent**	**Employee Assessment**	**Percent**
Flexible work arrangements	25%	Quality of work life	30%
Family and dependent care	20%	Job flexibility	30%
Other programs	15%	Family-friendly culture	30%
Work-family organizational infrastructure	10%	Overall family friendliness	10%
Availability of programs to hourly and part-time workers	10%		
Strategic and business rationale	20%		

Source: Reprinted from September 15, 1997, issue of *Business Week* by special permission, copyright © 1997 by The McGraw-Hill Companies, Inc.

Summary of Key Points

Performance-based rewards are an attempt to link compensation to performance. It is hard to underestimate the strategic importance of using variable pay to align compensation with organizational goals and to signal to employees what the major organizational values are.

Other reasons for seeking such a linkage are employee preferences and the motivational aspects of tying pay to performance. Linking pay to performance also provides an increased incentive for top performers to remain with the organization, a means of reinforcing organizational objectives, and a method of keeping labor costs in line with productivity.

As has been illustrated in A Different Point of View, there also are reasons to carefully consider the approach to linking rewards to performance. In some instances, programs linking rewards to performance are a "quick and dirty" substitute for good management. Furthermore, some programs attempting to link pay to performance have potential negative consequences, such as an emphasis on quantity over quality.

Pay can be linked to performance at the individual, group, or organizational levels. Individual plans can be used only where individual performance is measurable. Group systems are important where worker cooperation and coordination are necessary.

Individual plans include piecework, commission, individual bonus, and merit salary increases. In addition, an increasing number of organizations are basing pay on the number of different skills or jobs mastered, as a way of motivating continued learning and flexibility.

Group incentives may be piece rates based on group output, gain-sharing plans, or profit-sharing plans. Profit sharing is an incentive system in which designated employees share the business profits. Gain-sharing plans include the Scanlon plan, Improshare, and the Rucker plan, all of which seek employee suggestions to cut costs and then share the savings with the employees. These plans work best in small to medium-sized organizations. Winsharing is a gain-sharing program that attempts to incorporate profits in addition to motivating productivity improvements.

Though linking pay to performance has its advantages, a number of factors may hinder its successful implementation. First, linking pay to performance is not going to work if employees have only limited control over performance, as is often the case. Second, performance is frequently difficult to measure. Third, many incentive rewards are not large enough to be motivational. Finally, many managers think incentive systems alone will provide the necessary linkage between pay and performance, and they may ignore many other aspects of the work or work-related environment that can reinforce the association between performance and rewards.

Executives are especially important to organizations and thus usually operate with a somewhat different system of compensation and incentives. Frequently, executive reward packages include bonus plans based on organizational performance and long-term incentives in the form of stock options. Executives may have perks such as company-paid automobiles, club memberships, and other considerations associated with their role. Executive pay has been criticized as being excessive in amount and inequitable when compared with organizational performance. Furthermore, executive pay has increased much faster than the pay of the average worker or than inflation.

Issues related to employee benefits have become a major topic not only in most organizations but also at the national level. Greater interest in benefits stems from the overall cost, forty cents for every dollar in payroll in many cases; the rapid increases in the expense of some programs; the effectiveness of various programs; and an increase in legislation associated with benefit programs. Employee benefits include mandatory protection programs, compensation for time not worked, optional protection programs, and private retirement (pension) plans.

Mandatory protection programs include Social Security, unemployment compensation, and workers' compensation. Unemployment compensation provides benefits to out-of-work employees who are actively looking for work. Workers' compensation is a type of no-fault insurance for occupational injuries, disabilities, and death. Both unemployment compensation and workers' compensation systems are operated by the states, whereas Social Security is a federal program.

Many employees receive pay for holidays and vacations. Pay for time not worked may also include sick leave, personal days, and leaves for maternity and infant or elder care. Other protection programs include health insurance, life insurance, and disability insurance. As a result of the skyrocketing costs of health care, employers have been forced to redesign plans by increasing deductibles, splitting some costs with employees (coinsurance), and exploring alternatives such as preferred provider and health maintenance organizations.

Pension plans are funds established by employers to provide income to employees after retirement. Some plans require contributions by employees in addition to those of employers. Plans vary, with most providing defined benefits. Others define contributions, with benefits being a function of investment growth. In addition, many employers provide other types of capital accumulation plans, such as thrift plans or 401(k) plans that allow employees to invest pretax dollars toward retirement.

In the last twenty years, there have been a variety of federal laws and regulations regarding benefits. ERISA specifies vesting and fiduciary standards to which private pension plans must adhere. COBRA requires the extension of group medical benefits to terminated employees, at the employees' expense.

Benefits raise several important issues, including cost containment, flexible benefit options, and work–family issues. As benefit costs have increased more rapidly than inflation, employers have had to resort to innovative ways of containing costs. Some companies have resorted to self-insurance by establishing funds to cover benefit costs and thus eliminating the segment of premiums that goes to insurance companies. Flexible benefits provide an important means of tailoring benefits to employee needs. Such programs have additional administrative costs and are difficult to communicate to employees, but if used effectively, they can enhance the organization's reputation as a progressive, employee-oriented firm. Finally, work–family benefits are also achieving increased prominence as employers realize that work issues affect families, and vice versa.

The Manager's Vocabulary

bonus
capital accumulation plans
coinsurance
commission
coordinating benefits
cost containment
deductible
defined benefit plan
defined contribution plan
educational assistance
Employee Retirement Income Security Act of 1974 (ERISA)
employee stock ownership plans (ESOPs)
expectancy
expectancy theory

flexible benefit package (or cafeteria-style benefit plan)
gain sharing
health insurance
health maintenance organization (HMO)
Improshare plan
incentive pay
instrumentality
line of sight
long-term incentives
merit pay
money purchase plan
new pay
pension
pension plan termination insurance
perquisites (or "perks")
piece-rate incentive
preferred provider organization (PPO)
profit sharing
Rucker plan
Scanlon plan
skill-based pay (or pay for knowledge)
Social Security
standard hour plan
stock options
Taylor plan
unemployment compensation insurance (UCI)
valence
vesting
winsharing
workers' compensation

Questions for Discussion

1. What is new pay? Why is it important?
2. In what ways can the expectancy theory of motivation be used to improve compensation systems?
3. What are the advantages of linking pay to performance? The disadvantages?
4. What are some of the reasons that employees tend to resist piece-rate incentive systems?
5. What are the five major individual incentives described? How would each be best matched with the following groups of employees: (a) production workers, (b) sales employees, (c) professional employees, (d) electronics assem-

bly workers, (e) managers, (f) scientists/engineers?

6. What is line of sight? How do individual and group incentives differ in line of sight?

7. What are some of the considerations involved in using individual versus group incentives?

8. Describe the advantages and disadvantages of the various gain-sharing plans.

9. What are the major barriers to successfully linking pay to performance? Which barriers are most associated with each type of incentive?

10. What are the advantages of skill-based pay?

11. Why does E. E. Lawler believe that merit pay, after a period of several years, will end up creating differences in employee pay that are unrelated to performance?

12. What is an ESOP? How would an ESOP improve employee motivation?

13. What are stock options? Why have they had minimal impact on linking CEO pay to performance?

14. What are some of the reasons that employee benefits as a proportion of total labor costs have increased substantially in the past several years?

15. Why is Social Security controversial? What are some of the ideas for solving problems with Social Security?

16. What is the federal government's role in regulating benefits?

17. What are the differences between unemployment compensation and workers' compensation, both as to the purpose of the programs and as to how they are administered?

18. Define each of the following medical insurance terms.
    i. Deductible
    ii. Coinsurance
    iii. Coordinated benefits
    iv. Self-insurance
    v. PPO
    vi. HMO

19. What are domestic-partner benefits, and why do so many companies offer them?

20. What is the difference between defined benefit and defined contribution pension plans?

21. What is a 401(k), and what advantages does it offer?

22. What is ERISA, and what impact does it have on private pension plans?

23. What are the advantages and disadvantages of flexible benefits over standard benefit packages?

24. What are the key elements of communicating benefits to employees? Why is communication so important?

25. What are some of the reasons for increased interest in family-friendly corporate policies? Is this interest a fad or the start of a trend, and why?

● **Case 13.1**
The Gyro Chemical Corporation

The Gyro Chemical Corporation produces and sells a broad line of more than 400 high-quality industrial cleaning and custodial products to companies throughout the United States. Sales are made through a network of 1,500 sales representatives. The sales representatives are compensated entirely by commission.

An effective sales force is the key factor in Gyro's profitability. It is important that each of the sales territories be fully staffed with trained, effective sales representatives. A number of sales representatives are extremely successful and earn between $100,000 and $300,000 each year in commissions. At the same time, the firm has recruited, hired, and trained many others (at a cost of $10,000 each), only to find that they are not suited to commission sales.

About 100 sales managers, each assigned to a district, are responsible for recruiting, hiring, supervising, and field-training approximately fifteen sales representatives each. Initial training of sales representatives is through a ten-day program at

Gyro headquarters. The sales managers find that they spend so much time recruiting and hiring that the daily supervision and field training of current salespeople are neglected.

In an effort to remedy this situation, Gyro's top management has decided to hire twelve professional recruiters, one for each of the sales regions. The recruiters will be responsible for finding job candidates, performing initial screening, and proposing final candidates to sales managers. Hiring decisions will continue to be the responsibility of the sales managers.

The commission system that underlies the compensation of sales representatives provides the impetus for various incentive plans that pervade all levels of the organization. Even though the recruiters have a limited role, they represent an important component in assisting the sales managers. Naturally, Gyro wants the compensation of the recruiters to have an incentive component of some type.

1. What are the individual incentive alternatives for compensating the recruiters, along with the advantages and disadvantages of each? Pay particular attention to possible dysfunctional aspects of each alternative.
2. Should incentive payments to recruiters be based on (a) the number of candidates interviewed, (b) the number of candidates recommended to sales managers, (c) candidates recommended and hired, (d) candidates hired and successful? What are the advantages and disadvantages of each possibility?
3. What compensation arrangement, including combination of base and incentive pay, would you recommend for the recruiters?
4. How might sales managers be compensated in order to motivate them to choose and nurture highly effective salespeople?

● **Case 13.2**
Incentive Pay for Fox Geomapping

Fifteen years ago, when John Fox started Fox Geomapping, the idea of using computers in planning school, election, and other political districts was in its infancy. Fox's idea was to store residential information about a city or county in a computer and then use mathematical models to optimize the boundaries desired in government planning (e.g., schools, election districts, etc.). The challenge was to incorporate the entire scope of census information—streets, dwellings, numbers of residents, occupations, and incomes—into a computer and then manipulate the information to satisfy the multiple goals of planning officials. The software was complex and needed to recognize logical division points, such as major highways, rivers, and political boundaries, in developing solutions.

At first, the procedures Fox used were rudimentary and ad hoc. Information was collected and stored and then processed by a series of programs adapted from other applications. One program tracked numbers and distances. Another program placed this information on computer representations

of city maps. Programs adapted from operations research employed optimization routines to develop solutions. The work was tedious and cumbersome.

Over the years, hardware and software developments streamlined the process, but still the sequence was complex. At first Fox lined up the projects and then did the work. However, as the demand for the services grew, Fox Geomapping needed employees for all phases of the business. At the present time, Fox Geomapping has ten young professionals from various backgrounds involved in the many projects underway.

As Fox began to hire employees, he realized that virtually no one had the range of skills needed to run the many projects that were waiting to be done. Workers needed specialized skills in computers, understanding of mathematical modeling, knowledge of census procedures, as well as expertise in city planning. Mr. Fox was hiring college graduates, but whatever the major of those hired, two to three years of training were needed before an employee could understand the entire scope of the effort and be productive at even a minimal level. Fox was hiring talented people, was paying above-market salaries for their majors, and was then hoping they would learn enough in the first two or three years to become a valued contributor to Fox Geomapping.

The problem was that many of the most talented employees left for better jobs within the first two years. Fox became convinced that he needed some type of incentive system that increased an employee's commitment to Fox Geomapping, particularly in the first several years of employment.

1. What types of incentive systems would be possible for Fox Geomapping?

2. What would be the advantages of each system Fox might consider? What would be the disadvantages?
3. Fox Geomapping has a benefit package, but Fox wonders what role increased benefits might have in gaining employee commitment. What role might benefits play in retaining professional employees?
4. Given the facts, what recommendations would you offer Fox? What incentive compensation system would you recommend for Fox Geomapping, and why?

● Exercise 13.1
Controlling Medical Benefit Costs

A company finds that the cost of its medical benefits has increased far beyond what was expected, and further increases are projected.

1. List the alternatives available to bring medical costs under control.
2. Compare and contrast the advantages and disadvantages of each alternative for controlling costs.

3. What input, if any, should employees have in evaluating various alternatives to contain health care costs?
4. How can employee input best be solicited? How can decisions, once reached, best be communicated to employees?

● Exercise 13.2
Flexible Benefit Decisions

You have just been hired by Pico Electronics. In addition to salary or wages, Pico Electronics has a flexible benefit arrangement for each employee. Employees have a benefit account and can draw from this account to fund various benefits.

Your salary and position entitle you to $1,000 per month in benefit dollars to allocate among the various choices. If your total benefit cost is less than $1,000 per month, you will keep half the difference as a monthly cash bonus. If your total is over

$1,000 per month, the difference is deducted from your salary. Under normal circumstances, benefit options, once selected, cannot be altered for five years.

Go through the benefit choices listed in the table below and indicate how much of your $1,000 in monthly benefit dollars you will allocate to each benefit. Place a 0 for benefits you do not wish to purchase. Then total the allocated amounts and place the total in the last row.

Benefit	Cost	Amount Allocated
Pension plan	Up to $500/month, matched 50:50 by Pico	_____
Paid vacations	$50/month for 2 weeks/yr	_____
Paid holidays	$50/month for 10 days/yr	_____
Paid sick leave	$50/month for 10 days/yr	_____
Medical insurance	$250/employee, $350/family/month	_____
Health maintenance organization	$200/employee, $250/family/month	_____
Legal insurance	$50/month for 100% legal needs	_____
Vision care	$50/month	_____
Subsidized child care	$60/month per child for on-site care	_____
Credit union	$25/month	_____
Subsidized company cafeteria	$50/month for free lunches	_____
Tuition reimbursement	$50/month for 100% of tuition	_____
Funeral leave	$50/month for 3 days/year	_____
Life insurance	$50/month for $100,000	_____
Disability insurance	$75/month to cover salary if disabled	_____
Dental insurance	$50/month for all checkups and required care	_____
Parking	$50/month (local lots charge $75/month)	_____
Total		_____

1. What assumptions did you make about your situation now and for the immediate future? (For example: Married? Children? Further education?) How were these assumptions reflected in your choices?
2. Was your goal to use all of the $1,000 (and possibly more) to purchase options needed and desired or to maximize the amount left over each month?
3. What three benefit options are worth the most to you? Why?
4. What three benefit options are worth the least to you? Why?
5. Do you perceive any of the options as "too good to pass up"? Why or why not?

Source: From *Personnel/Human Resource Management* 3/e by Michael E. Carrell, Frank E. Kuzmis, and Norbert F. Elbert. Merrill, MacMillan Publishing Company. © 1989. Adapted by permission of the authors.

● **Exercise 13.3**
Executive Pay Update

As a compensation specialist with a major pharmaceutical company, you are interested in executive pay. The vice president of human resources asks you for an update of the industry. Using the following web site, provide the information sought: http://www.paywatch.org.

Notes and References

1. Wayne Brockbank, "HR's Future on the Way to a Presence," *Human Resource Management,* Vol. 36 (1), 1997, pp. 65–69.

2. Thomas B. Wilson, *Innovative Reward Systems for the Changing Workplace* (New York: McGraw-Hill, 1995).

3. Hewitt Associates, "Salary Increases 2001 and 2002." (Available at http://was.hewitt.com/ebusiness/ compensationcenter/library/pp_libr_index.jsp#); and Bureau of National Affairs, *Non-Traditional Incentive Pay Programs* (Personnel Policies Forum Survey No. 148) (Washington, D.C.: Bureau of National Affairs, 1991).

4. Hewitt Associates, "Salary Increases 2001 and 2002."

5. L. Dyer, D. P. Schwab, and R. D. Theriault, "Managerial Perceptions Regarding Salary Increase Criteria," *Personnel Psychology,* Vol. 29, 1976, pp. 233–242.

6. George Graen, "Instrumentality Theory of Work Motivation," *Journal of Applied Psychology,* Vol. 53, 1965, pp. 1–25; R. D. Prichard, D. W. Leonard, C. W. Von Bergen, Jr., and R. J. Kirk, "The Effects of Varying Schedules of Reinforcement on Human Task Performance," *Organizational Behavior and Human Performance,* Vol. 16, 1976, pp. 205–230; and Hewitt Associates, "Salary Increases 2001 and 2002."

7. E. E. Lawler III, *The New Pay* [CEO Publication G84-7(55)] (Los Angeles: Center for Effective Organizations, University of Southern California, 1986).

8. Edward E. Lawler III and G. Douglas Jenkins, Jr., "Strategic Reward Systems," in *Handbook of Industrial and Organizational Psychology,* 2d ed., Vol. 3, ed. Marvin D. Dunnette and Leaetta M. Hough (Palo Alto, Calif.: Consulting Psychologists Press, 1992).

9. Joseph W. Harder, "Equity Theory Versus Expectancy Theory: The Case of Major League Baseball Free Agents," *Journal of Applied Psychology,* Vol. 76, 1991, pp. 458–464; and Robert D. Bretz, Jr. and Steven L. Thomas, "Perceived Equity, Motivation, and Final-Offer Arbitration in Major League Baseball," *Journal of Applied Psychology,* Vol. 77, 1992, pp. 280–287.

10. Deborah A. Mohr, James A. Riedel, and Kent S. Crawford, "A Group Wage Incentive System Can Boost Performance and Cut Costs," *Defense Management Journal,* second quarter 1986, pp. 13–17; B. S. Georgopolous, G. M. Mahoney, and M. W. Jones, "A Path Goal Approach to Productivity," *Journal of Applied Psychology,* Vol. 41, 1957, pp. 345–353; and D. P. Schwab and L. Dyer, "The Motivational Impact of a Compensation System on Employee Performance," *Organizational Behavior and Human Performance,* Vol. 9, 1973, pp. 215–225.

11. V. H. Vroom, *Work Motivation* (New York: Wiley, 1964).

12. T. R. Mitchell, Mabmoub A. Wabba, and Robert J. House, "Expectancy Theory in Work Motivation: Some Logical and Methodological Issues," *Human Relations,* Vol. 27 (2), 1974, pp. 121–147.

13. Donald P. Schwab, "Impact of Alternative Compensation Systems on Pay Valence and Instrumentality Perceptions," *Journal of Applied Psychology,* Vol. 58 (3), 1973, pp. 308–312.

14. J. L. Kerr and J. W. Slocum, "Managing Corporate Culture Through Reward Systems," *Academy of Management Executive,* Vol. 1, 1987, pp. 99–108.

15. F. Filipczak, "Why No One Likes Your Incentive Program," *Training,* August 1993, p. 21.

16. N. L. Kerr and S. E. Bruun, "Dispensability of Member Effort and Group Motivation Losses: Free-Rider Effects," *Journal of Personality and Social Psychology,* Vol. 44 (1), 1983, pp. 78–94.

17. B. Latané, K. Williams, and S. Harkins, "Many Hands Make Light the Work: The Causes and Consequences of Social Loafing," *Journal of Personality and Social Psychology,* Vol. 37 (6), 1979, pp. 822–833.

18. Edward E. Lawler, *Pay and Organizational Effectiveness* (New York: McGraw-Hill, 1971).

19. Amy Dunkin and Kathleen Kerwin, "Now Salespeople Really Must Sell for Their Supper," *Business Week,* July 31, 1989, pp. 50, 52.

20. "The Bank That Disappeared," *The Economist,* March 4, 1995, pp. 11–12.

21. Micheline Maynard, "Ford Motor Will Not Pay Annual Bonuses to Managers," *New York Times,* August 30, 2001, p. C1, Reed Abelson, "Market Fallout: Year-End Bonuses Are No Longer Routine," *New York Times,* September 4, 2001, p. C9.

22. Daniel C. Rowland, "Incentive Pay: Productivity's Own Reward," *Personnel Journal,* March 1987, pp. 48–57.

23. Abelson, "Market Fallout."

24. Dale Feuer, "Paying for Knowledge," *Training,* May 1987, pp. 57–66; and Richard L. Bunning, "Skill-Based Pay: Restoring Incentives to the Workplace," *Personnel Administrator,* June 1989, pp. 65–70.

25. Edward E. Lawler and Gerald E. Ledford, Jr., "Skill-Based Pay: A Concept That's Catching On," *Compensation and Benefits Review,* January–February 1986, pp. 54–61.

26. Gerald E. Ledford, Jr., "Three Case Studies on Skill-Based Pay: An Overview," *Compensation and Benefits Review,* March–April 1991, pp. 11–22.

27. N. Gupta, G. D. Jenkins, Jr., and W. P. Curington, "Paying for Knowledge: Myths and Realities," *National Productivity Review,* Spring 1986, pp. 107–123.

28. Richard L. Bunning, "Models for Skill-Based Pay Plans," *HRMagazine,* February 1992, pp. 62–64.

29. Lawler and Jenkins, "Strategic Reward Systems."

30. Edward E. Lawler, "The New Plant Revolution Revisited," *Organizational Dynamics,* Autumn 1990, pp. 4–14; and Edward E. Lawler, "The New Plant Approach: A Second Generation Approach," *Organizational Dynamics,* Summer 1991, pp. 4–14.

31. Robert S. Nadel, "Compensation Alternatives: Changes in Business Strategy, Plans and Expectations," July 2001. (Available at http://www.shrm.org/whitepapers/ documents/ default.asp?page=61440.asp)

32. John Dantico, "Skill Based Pay," Society for Human Resource Management White Paper, July 2001. (Available at: http://www/shrm.org)

33. Edward E. Lawler, G. E. Ledford, and S. A. Mohrman, *Employee Involvement in America* (Houston: American Productivity and Quality Center, 1989).

34. Edward E. Lawler, *Strategic Pay* (San Francisco: Jossey-Bass, 1990), pp. 71–85.

35. Ibid., p. 73.

36. John F. Sullivan, "The Future of Merit Pay Programs," *Compensation and Benefits Review,* Vol. 20, May–June 1988, pp. 22–30.

37. Mohr, Riedel, and Crawford, "A Group Wage Incentive System," pp. 13–17.

38. John A. Wagner III, Paul A. Rubin, and Thomas J. Callahan, "Incentive Payment and Nonmanagerial Productivity: An Interrupted Time Series Analysis of Magnitude and Trend," *Organizational Behavior and Human Decision Processes,* Vol. 42, 1988, pp. 47–74.

39. Don Nightingale, "Profit Sharing: New Nectar for the Worker Bees," *Canadian Business Review,* Spring 1984, pp. 11–14.

40. Brian E. Graham-Moore and Timothy L. Ross, *Gainsharing: Plans for Improving Performance* (Washington, D.C.: Bureau of National Affairs, 1990).

41. Susan C. Hanlon, David C. Meyer, and Robert R. Taylor, "Consequences of Gainsharing: A Field Experiment Revisited," *Group and Organizational Management,* Vol. 19 (1), 1994, pp. 87–111.

42. Brian E. Graham-Moore and Timothy L. Ross, *Productivity Gainsharing* (Englewood Cliffs, N.J.: Prentice-Hall, 1983).

43. A. J. Geare, "Productivity from Scanlon Type Plans," *Academy of Management Review,* Vol. 1 (3), 1976, pp. 99–108.

44. W. C. Freund and E. Epstein, *People and Productivity* (Homewood, Ill.: Dow Jones–Irwin, 1984).

45. Jay R. Schuster and Patricia K. Zingheim, *The New Pay: Linking Employee and Organizational Performance* (Lexington, Mass.: Lexington Books, 1992).

46. Charles R. Gowen and Sandra Jennings, "The Effects of Changes in Participation and Group Size on Gainsharing Success: A Case Study," *Journal of Organizational Behavior and Management,* Vol. 11, 1990, pp. 147–169; Denis Collins, Larry Hatcher, and Timothy L. Ross, "The Decision to Implement Gainsharing: The Role of Work Climate, Expected Outcomes, and Union Status," *Personnel Psychology,* Vol. 46, 1993, pp. 77–104; Woodruff Imberman, "Gainsharing: A Lemon or Lemonade?" *Business Horizons,* January–February 1996, pp. 36–40; and Darlene O'Neill, "Blending the Best of Profit Sharing and Gainsharing," *HRMagazine,* March 1994, pp. 66–70.

47. "ESOPs: Are They Good for You?" *Business Week,* May 15, 1989, pp. 116–123.

48. "A Statistical Profile of Employee Ownership," April 2001. (Available at: http://www.nceo.org/library/eo_stat.html)

49. "ESOPs Broaden Employee Stock Ownership," *Wall Street Journal,* January 7, 1987, p. 1; and J. L. French, "Employee Perspectives on Stock Ownership: Financial Investment or Mechanism of Control?" *Academy of Management Review,* July 1987, pp. 427–435.

50. "A Statistical Profile of Employee Ownership."

51. Lawler, *Strategic Pay,* pp. 26–27.

52. "ESOPs: Are They Good for You?"

53. "This Is Some Way to Build Employee Loyalty," *Business Week,* March 2, 1992, p. 84.

54. Gene Milbourne, Jr., "The Relationship of Money and Motivation," *Compensation Review,* second quarter 1980, pp. 33–44.

55. Thomas J. Hackett, "Seven Steps to Successful Performance-Based Rewards," *HR Focus,* September 1999, p. 11–13.

56. Schuster and Zingheim, *The New Pay.*

57. A. Farnham, "The Trust Gap," *Fortune,* December 4, 1989, pp. 76–78; "What, Me Overpaid? CEOs Fight Back," *Business Week,* May 4, 1992, pp. 142–148; "That Eye-Popping Executive Pay," *Business Week,* April 25, 1994, pp. 52–58; and "CEO Pay: Ready for Takeoff," *Business Week,* April 24, 1995, pp. 88–94.

58. Louis Lavelle, "Executive Pay," *Business Week,* April 16, 2001, pp. 76–80.

59. Ibid.

60. Geoffrey Colvin, "The Great CEO Pay Heist," *Fortune,* June 25, 2001, pp. 64–70.

61. "Pay for Performance: Both Ends of the Scale," *Business Week,* April 16, 2001, p. 78.

62. Jennifer Reingold, "The Folly of Jumbo Stock Options," *Business Week,* December 22, 1997, pp. 36–37.

63. Jeffery Kerr and Richard A. Bettis, "Boards of Directors, Top Management Compensation and Shareholder Returns," *Academy of Management Review,* December 1987, pp. 645–664; C. J. Loomis, "The Madness of Executive Compensation," *Fortune,* Vol. 106 (1), 1982, pp. 42–52; M. Haire, E. E. Ghiselli, and M. E. Gordon, "A Psychological Study of Pay," *Journal of Applied Psychology Monograph,* Vol. 51, 1967 ; and John L. Pearce, William B. Stevenson, and James L. Perry, "Managerial Compensation Based on Organizational Performance: A Time Series Analysis of the Effects of Merit Pay," *Academy of Management Journal,* Vol. 28, 1985, pp. 261–278.

64. "Executive Pay."

65. Charles Tharp, "Linking Annual Incentives and Individual Performance," *Personnel Administrator,* January 1986, pp. 85–90.

66. "Executive Pay."

67. Geoffrey Colvin, "How to Pay the CEO Right," *Fortune,* April 6, 1992, pp. 60–69.

68. Cited in "Executive Pay."

69. Jane Bryant Quinn, "Slow Profits, Slow Pay," *Newsweek,* December 22, 1986, p. 52.

70. Colvin, "The Great Pay Heist."

71. John D. McMillan, "Executive Pay a New Way," *HRMagazine,* June 1992, pp. 46–48.

72. Colvin, "The Great Pay Heist."

73. "Comp Committees, or Back-Scratchers-in-Waiting?" *Business Week,* May 4, 1992, pp. 146–147.

74. Charles W. L. Hill and Phillip Phan, "CEO Tenure as a Determinant of CEO Pay," *Academy of Management Journal,* Vol. 34, 1991, pp. 707–717.

75. Catherine M. Daily, Jonathan L. Johnson, Alan E. Ellstrand, and Dan R. Dalton, "Compensation Committee Composition as a Determinant of CEO Compensation," *Academy of Management Journal,* Vol. 41, 1998, pp. 209–220.

76. David Parthiban, Rahul Kochhar, and Edward Levitas, "The Effect of Institutional Investors on the Level and Mix of CEO Compensation," *Academy of Management Journal,* Vol. 41, 1998, pp. 200–208.

77. Graef S. Crystal, "Incentive Pay That Doesn't Work," *Fortune,* August 28, 1989, pp. 101, 104.

78. Shaifali Puri, "Pay for Underperformance," *Fortune,* December 8, 1997.

79. "Fortunes in the Future," *Business Week,* April 16, 2001, p. 79.

80. Carol J. Loomis, "This Stuff Is Wrong," *Fortune,* June 25, 2001.

81. Kevin G. Salwen, "SEC Unveils New Rules on Disclosures of Corporate Executives' Pay Packages," *Wall Street Journal,* February 14, 1992, p. A4.

82. "That's Some Pay Cap, Bill," *Business Week,* April 25, 1994, p. 57.

83. "Herman Miller Links Worker–CEO Pay," *Wall Street Journal,* May 7, 1992, pp. B1, B8.

84. Robert J. Greene and Russel G. Roberts, "Strategic Integration of Compensation and Benefits," *Personnel Administrator,* May 1983, pp. 79–81.

85. *Employer Costs for Employee Compensation.* Bureau of Labor Statistics, June 2001.(Available at: http://www.bls.gov/news.release/ecec.t14.htm)

86. 2000 Annual Report. Ford Motor Company, 2001. (Available at: http://www.ford.com/2000annualreport/printable.html)

87. Emmett Seaborn, "Strengthen Links Between Benefits and Strategy," *HR Focus,* June 1999, pp. 11–14.

88. David R. Henderson, "The Bleak Future of Social Security," *Fortune,* September 30, 1996, pp. 34–48; Rob Norton, "The Evils of Social Security," *Fortune,* April 15, 1996, p. 65.; and "Social Security: Invaluable or Outmoded?" *Modern Maturity,* Vol. 35, April–May 1992, pp. 34–46, 84–85.

89. Franco Modigliani, "A Way Out of the Social Security Squeeze," *Business Week,* October 11, 2001 (Available at: http://www.businessweek.com/bwdaily/dnflash/oct2001/nf20011011_2902.htm?$sc); and David R. Henderson, "Fix Social Security? Why Not Abolish It?" *Fortune,* September 8, 1997, pp. 15–22.

90. "First Aid for Workers' Comp," *Business Week,* March 18, 1996, p. 6; and Karen Roberts and Sandra E. Gleason, "What Employees Want from Workers' Comp," *HRMagazine,* December 1991, pp. 49–53.

91. James A. Swanke, Jr., "Ways to Tame Workers' Comp Premiums," *HRMagazine,* February 1992, pp. 39–41.

92. "Family Care: Tips for Companies That Are Trying to Help," *Business Week,* September 28, 1992, p. 36.

93. Kenneth E. Thorpe, "Changes in the Growth in Health Care Spending: Implications for Consumers." The National Coalition on Health Care, April 1997. (Available at: http://www.nchc.org/implication/implications.html)

94. Joel E. Miller, *Déjà Vu All Over Again: The Soaring Cost of Private Health Insurance and Its Impact on Consumers and Employers* (Washington, D.C.: National Coalition on Health Care, 2000).

95. Anthony J. Rucci and John J. Sinnott, "Health Care," *Human Resource Management,* Vol. 31, Spring–Summer 1992, pp. 69–79.

96. Ronald Bryan, "A Primer on Self-Funding Health Care Benefits," *Personnel Administrator,* April 1983, pp. 61–64.

97. William E. Wymer, George Faulkner, and Joseph A. Parente, "Achieving Benefit Program Objectives," *HRMagazine,* Vol. 37, March 1992, pp. 55–62.

98. George Anders and Ron Winslow, "The HMO Trend: Big, Bigger, Biggest," *Wall Street Journal,* March 30, 1995, pp. B1, B4.

99. New Medical-Benefits Accounting Rule Seen Wounding Profits, Hurting Shares," *Wall Street Journal,* April 22, 1992, pp. C1–C2.

100. "Domestic Partner Benefits: Overview," National Lesbian and Gay Journalists Association. (Available at: http://www.nlgja.org/pubs/DP/Dpovrvw.html)

101. Robert Levering and Milton Moskowitz, "America's Top Employers," *Fortune,* January 8, 2001, pp. 148–168.

102. Jerry S. Rosenbloom and G. Victor Hallman, *Employee Benefit Planning,* 2d ed. (Englewood Cliffs, N.J.: Prentice-Hall, 1986).

103. James W. Herlihy, Jr., and Jamie D. Owens, "Methods to Implement a Nonqualified 401(k) Plan," *HRMagazine,* January 1992, pp. 52–56.

104. Allen Stiteler, "Finally, Pension Plans Defined," *Personnel Journal,* February 1987, pp. 44–53.

105. Ibid.

106. Barbara Rudolph, "Shelter from April Showers," *Time,* February 22, 1988, p. 51.

107. *Los Angeles* v. *Manhart,* 435 U.S. 702 (1978).

108. *Arizona Governing Committee* v. *Norris,* 103 U.S. 3492 (1983).

109. Albert R. Karr and Ellen E. Schultz, "Pension Rules Tacked Quietly on Trade Bill Portend Vast Changes," *Wall Street Journal,* March 15, 1995, pp. A1, A8.

110. Alarice Huang, "Concierge Services Free Employees from Distractions," *HR Focus,* July 1999, p. 6; "50 Benefits and Perks That Make Employees Want to Stay Forever," *HR Focus,* July 2000, pp. S2-S3; and "What Benefits Are Companies Offering Now?," *HR Focus,* June 2000, pp. 5–7.

111. Commerce Clearing House, *Employee Assistance Programs: Drug, Alcohol, and Other Problems* (Chicago: Commerce Clearing House, 1986).

112. "Paying Workers for Good Health Habits Catches on as a Way to Cut Medical Costs," *Wall Street Journal,* November 26, 1991, p. B1.

113. Department of Labor, "Work-Related Child Care Statistics," 2000. (Available at: http://www.dol.gov/dol/wb/childcare/ccstats.htm)

114. Pamela Mendels, "Kiddie Care Doesn't Have to Break the Bank," *Business Week,* September 1, 1997. (Available at: http://www.businessweek.com/1997/35/b3542039.htm); Stephen J. Goff, Michael K. Mount, and Rosemary L. Jamison, "Employer Supported Child Care, Work/Family Conflict, and Absenteeism: A Field Study," *Personnel Psychology,* Vol. 43, 1990, pp. 793–809; Ellen Ernst Kossek and Victor Nichol, "The Effects of On-Site Child Care on Employee Attitudes and Performance," *Personnel Psychology,* Vol. 45, 1992, pp. 485–509; and Judith G. Gonyea and Bradley K. Googins, "Linking the Worlds of Work and Family: Beyond the Productivity Trap," *Human Resource Management,* Vol. 31, 1992, pp. 209–226.

115. Levering and Moskowitz, "America's Top Employers."

116. Karyn-Siobhan Robinson, "Child Care Tax Credit: Boone for Employers," Society for Human Resource Management, October 28, 2001. (Available at: http://www.shrm.org/hrnews/articles/default.asp?page=061201a.htm)

117. "Honey, We're Cheating the Kids."

118. "Financing Child Care in the Private Sector," The American Business Collaboration for Quality Dependent Care. (Available at: http://www.nccic.org/pubs/financing-cc/child037.html)

119. Shirley Hand and Robert A. Zawacki, "Family-Friendly Benefits: More Than a Frill," *HRMagazine,* October 1994, pp.

79–84; and Ellen Ernst Kossek, "Diversity in Child Care Assistance Needs: Employee Problems, Preferences, and Work-Related Outcomes," *Personnel Psychology,* Vol. 43, 1990, pp. 769–791.

120. "The 'Baby Boomers' Triple Whammy," *Business Week,* May 4, 1992, pp. 178–179; Neville Tompkins, "Child Care and Elder Care Assistance," *HR Horizons,* Winter 1991, pp. 53–55; Bette Ann Stead, "Eldercare: Personal Triumph! Professional Downfall?" *Business Horizons,* May–June 1991, pp. 72–76; and Jeff L. Lefkovich, "Business Responds to Elder-Care Needs," *HRMagazine,* June 1992, pp. 103–108.

121. D. Harris, "The Fairness Furor," *Working Mother,* September 1997, pp. 28–32; and L. Jenner, "Family-Friendly Backlash," *Management Review,* May 1994, p. 83.

122. Teresa J. Rothausen, Jorge A. Gonzalez, Nicole E. Clarke, and Lisa L. O'Dell, "Family-Friendly Backlash—Fact or Fiction? The Case of Organizations' On-Site Child Care Centers," *Personnel Psychology,* Vol. 51, 1998, pp. 685–706.

123. Ron Winslow, "A $5.2 Million Bill for 34 Days in the Hospital," *Wall Street Journal,* August 2, 2001, p. A1.

124. Jesse A. Sherman and Michael Carter, "Benefits: Profiting from Trade-Off Analysis," *Personnel Journal,* August 1987, pp. 120–122.

125. Alison Stein Wellner with Joshua Kendall, "The Health Care Crisis: Why Small Companies Are Getting Hit So Hard and What You Can Do About It," *Business Week,* July 10, 2000. (Available at: http://www.businessweek.com/2000/00_28/b3689040.htm?$se)

126. Alison E. Barber, Randall B. Dunham, and Roger A. Formisano, "The Impact of Flexible Benefits on Employee Satisfaction: A Field Study," *Personnel Psychology,* Vol. 45, 1992, pp. 55–75.

127. Marie Wilson, George B. Northcraft, and Margaret A. Neale, "The Perceived Value of Fringe Benefits," *Personnel Psychology,* Vol. 38, 1985, pp. 209–320.

128. Ibid.

129. Christopher Alan Higgins, Linda Elizabeth Duxbury, and Richard Harold Irving, "Work–Family Conflict in the Dual-Career Family," *Organizational Behavior and Human Decision Processes,* Vol. 51, 1992, pp. 51–75; and "Link Absenteeism & Benefits and Help Cut Costs," *HR Focus,* April 2000, pp. 5–6.

130. Hal Morgan and Frances J. Milliken, "Keys to Action: Understanding Differences in Organizations' Responsiveness to Work-and-Family Issues," *Human Resource Management,* Vol. 31, 1992, pp. 227–248.

131. M. Tait, M. Y. Padgett, and T. T. Baldwin, "Job and Life Satisfaction: A Reevaluation of the Strength of the Relationship and Gender Effects as a Function of the Date of the Study," *Journal of Applied Psychology,* Vol. 74, 1989, pp. 502–507; and Teresa J. Rothausen, "Job Satisfaction and the Parent Worker: The Role of Flexibility and Rewards," *Journal of Vocational Behavior,* Vol. 44, 1994, pp. 317–366.

132. Society for Human Resource Management 2001 Benefits Survey, April 2001. (Available at: http://www.shrm.org/surveys/results/default.asp?page=01benefits.asp)

133. "Work and Family," *Business Week,* September 15, 1997, pp. 96–99.

PART SIX

Maintaining Human Resources

14

Safety and Health: A Proactive Appoach

HR Challenge

As the HR manager of Russell Enterprises, a chemical processing company with 400 employees, you are distressed to learn of an accident during the day shift. An employee mistakenly opened the incorrect valve and released high-pressure gas. The gas ignited, and the resulting fire killed the employee and damaged equipment nearby.

The plant manager has asked you to gather the necessary facts for the Occupational Safety and Health Administration investigators on their way to the plant. In the process of talking with your staff and with other employees, and in examining company records, you find a number of troublesome facts:

- *The victim was a long-time employee who was unable to read.*
- *Because of years of service, he and other senior operators had been "passed through" the extensive safety training program put in place several years previously.*

- *A buddy system had been established whereby some of the more skilled opera-tors were covering for those who lacked certain fundamental abilities.*

- *In lieu of required monthly employee safety meetings, many supervisors were submitting minutes for sessions that never took place.*

- *The required written safety procedures were not at the operating sites.*

These facts cause you great concern. Carl Russell, the owner of Russell Enter-prises, has always insisted on safety first. Until now, Russell's record has been good. You wonder what could have gone wrong, what could account for such divergence from the ideals Russell has always sought to attain.

A total of 3.8 million American workers in private industries suffered from dis-abling injuries on the job during 1998. There were 5,100 workplace fatalities. This means that there was a fatal injury every 103 minutes and a disabling injury every 8 seconds. Highway traffic incidents, homicides, falls, and being struck by an object were the four leading causes of fatalities. Although workplace homicides fell to their lowest level in seven years, they remained the second-leading cause of death on the job, with a total of 709 workplace homicides reported in 1998. For women workers, homicides were the leading cause of death on the job.[1] (See the International Perspective box for an international comparison of job-related deaths and injuries.)

Most organizations are very much concerned about providing a safe and healthy workplace. Part of this concern is simple humanitarianism. Few firms would knowingly send unprotected employees into a dangerous situation. Aside from altruism, there are two other reasons for corporate concern about safety and health in the work environment.

First, there are definite bottom-line performance consequences of workplace injuries and illness. It is estimated that production time lost in U.S. private in-dustries due to on-the-job injuries totaled about 80 million days in 1998. Produc-tion time lost in future years due to on-the-job injuries in 1998 will total an esti-mated 60 million days. Analyses of 1998 data indicate that work injuries cost Americans a total of around $125.1 billion. This amount is equivalent to almost three times the combined profits reported by the top five *Fortune* 500 companies in 1998.

Many organizations have reported significant savings from actively promoting safety in the workplace. For instance, Horizon Steel Erectors adopted a 100 per-cent fall protection program to prevent all falls by steelworkers during construc-tion. The company also changed to a program that holds supervisors accountable for safety. These changes resulted in a 96 percent reduction in accident costs, down to $0.18 per man-hour from the previous level of $4.25 per man-hour. New Balance Athletic Shoe, Inc., in Maine has seen its workdays lost due to injury and illness drop from 11,190 to 549 per year over a four year period. Workers' compen-sation claims dropped from $1,213,176 to $89,154 over the same period, resulting in a savings of over $1 million per year from improved safety.[2]

In addition to bottom-line results, the other major incentive for companies to be concerned with employee safety and health is to avoid the penalties for violating occupational safety laws.[3] Before 1970, a company that was a dangerous place to work might have had higher insurance rates. Since then, however, the penalties

INTERNATIONAL PERSPECTIVE

Job Safety: The International Picture

In a 1999 report, Jukka Takala of the International Labour Office, Occupational Safety and Health Branch described the status of occupational injuries and illness around the world. Mr. Takala opened the report by stating that:

The 1948 Universal Declaration of Human Rights recognizes the right of all people to just and favorable conditions of work. Yet, it is estimated that workers suffer 250 million accidents every year, with 330,000 fatalities. 160 million cases of occupational diseases and an even higher number of threats to workers' physical and mental well-being cause further suffering. The economic losses are equivalent to 4 per cent of the world's gross national product; in terms of shattered families and communities, the damage is incalculable." (p. 1)

Comparing rates of occupational accidents and injuries across countries is quite difficult. Nations follow different reporting standards regarding what constitutes an injury and whether it must be reported. Even for workplace fatalities, which should be less ambiguously reported than injuries, variation in methods makes cross-national comparisons difficult. For instance, some countries include deaths that occur when a person is traveling to or from work; some do not count deaths from occupational disease. The International Labour Office, however, publishes data that

provide a picture of safety and health around the world. A sample of data on occupational fatalities from the Takala 1999 ILO report is shown below.

Fatal Occupational Accidents in the World—Estimates

Region*	Fatality Rate (F_r) (per 100,000)	Employment (E) (in millions)	Fatalities $(F_r \times E)$
EME	5.3	366.437	19,662
FSE	11.1	140.282	15,563
IND	11.0	334.000	36,740
CHN	11.1	614.690	68,231
OAI	23.1	339.840	80,586
SSA	21.0	218.400	45,864
LAC	13.5	195.000	26,374
MEC	22.5	186.000	41.850
WORLD	14.0	2,394.667	334,870

*EME: established market economies
FSE: formerly socialist economies of Europe
IND: India
CHN: China
OAI: Other Asia and Islands
SSA: Sub-Saharan Africa
LAC: Latin America and the Caribbean
MEC: Middle Eastern Crescent

have become more severe. In addition to insurance costs, fines are common, and top managers can be sent to prison for criminal negligence when unsafe conditions cause the death of a worker.[4]

In this chapter we provide an overview of occupational health and safety legislation and the role of the Occupational Safety and Health Administration in enforcing that legislation. In addition, we will look at the role of managers and employees in making sure that their workplace is a safe one. We will examine the types of safety issues that organizations face in the twenty-first century and provide examples of how some firms are meeting these safety challenges by proactively promoting employee physical and mental health.

As can be seen in the table, fatality rates in different regions can vary widely. This is the case for a number of reasons, including the mix of industries present in each country. Some industries are inherently more dangerous than others. For instance, the mining and quarrying industries tend to have the highest fatality rate in most countries, while construction, transportation, utilities, and agriculture have moderately high rates. The retail trade, banking, and social service industries generally have many fewer fatalities.

A country's occupational safety and health laws and enforcement procedures may also influence fatality rates. For example, in Sweden, union-run safety committees may order production stopped if they believe that a hazard exists and keep it stopped until the hazard is remedied. These committees also have a great deal of control over the hiring and firing of industrial physicians and safety engineers.

In general, unions and the philosophy of industrial democracy are stronger in Europe than in the United States. These factors have led to the passage of laws giving European employees or their elected worker representatives a stronger role in monitoring and enforcing workplace safety. Legally mandated works councils or workers' safety committees in the Netherlands, Luxembourg, France, Belgium, and Denmark give workers substantially more control over occupational safety than U.S. workers have.

At the opposite end of the spectrum, the state of occupational safety remains deplorable in many developing countries. Occupational safety laws are often rudimentary, and few funds for enforcing such laws are provided by local governments. Furthermore, efforts to attract foreign investment are likely to be more successful if the country offers a business environment relatively free from government regulation. Because unions are weak or are preoccupied with more basic issues such as politics, wages, and fair treatment, they provide little impetus toward improved workplace safety. Labor-intensive industries, dated equipment, pressure for production, and lack of safety training also contribute to the poor safety record in many developing nations.

This is a situation of grave concern to international organizations such as the ILO. Given the enormous cost of accidents and illnesses, it is a situation that should be of concern to governments, organizations, and the public around the world.

Sources: Jukka Takala, "Introductory Report of the International Labour Office," International Labour Office, Occupational Safety and Health Branch, May 1999. (Available at http://www.ilo.org/public/ english/protection/safework/cis/oshworld/xvwc/intrep.htm); Ray H. Elling, *The Struggle for Workers' Health: A Study of Six Industrialized Countries* (Farmingdale, N.Y.: Baywood Publishing, 1986), pp. 427–450; J. K. M. Grevers, "Worker Participation in Health and Safety in the EEC: The Role of Representative Institutions," *International Labour Review,* July–August 1983, pp. 411–428; David C. E. Chew, "Effective Occupational Safety Activities: Findings in Three Asian Developing Countries," *International Labour Review,* Vol. 127 (1) 1998, pp. 111–124; and Michael B. Bixby, "Emerging Occupational Safety Issues in the United States, Europe, and Japan," in *Proceedings of the Third Conference on International Personnel and Human Management,* Vol. 1 (Berkhamsted, England, International Human Resource Conference, 1992).

OCCUPATIONAL SAFETY AND HEALTH LEGISLATION

Worker health and safety have been the subject of much state and federal legislation. Between 1911 and 1948, states passed workers' compensation laws requiring businesses to compensate employees injured on the job, and all states still have such laws in effect. Compensation includes some replacement of lost income while injured, medical and rehabilitation expenses, payments (lump sums) for certain permanent disabilities, and death benefits for survivors. Most employers participate in an insurance plan to cover these expenses. Because premiums go up if there are many injury claims, workers' compensation laws provide some incentive for employers to maintain a safe work environment. However, workers' compensation laws also limit employers' liability for injuries and deaths to the amounts specified by state law. Employees who accept workers' compensation benefits give up their right to sue the employer. Thus, workers' compensation laws somewhat reduce an organization's need to be concerned with workplace safety. This fact provided part of the impetus to pass a variety of federal workplace safety laws.[5]

By far the dominant piece of Federal safety and health legislation is the **Occupational Safety and Health Act of 1970.** The purpose of this act was to centralize the regulation of workplace safety and to expand coverage to include all organizations in the United States. In passing the act, Congress declared its purpose to be "to assure so far as possible every working man and woman in the nation safe and healthful working conditions and to preserve our human resources."[6]

Who Is Covered by the Occupational Safety and Health Act?

The Occupational Safety and Health Act of 1970 covers all employers and their employees in the fifty states and in all territories and jurisdictions under federal authority. Thus, employers and employees in the District of Columbia, Puerto Rico, the Virgin Islands, American Samoa, and Johnston Island are covered, as well as those operatoring on the Outer Continental Shelf Lands as defined in the Outer Continental Shelf Lands Act. *As defined by the Occupational Safety and Health Act, an employer is any "person engaged in a business affecting commerce who has employees, but does not include the United States or any State or political subdivision of a State."*[7] If religious groups employ workers for "secular purposes," the act applies. The act does not cover the self-employed or immediate members of farming families who do not employ outside workers. It does not cover employees whose working conditions are regulated by other federal agencies under other federal statutes, such as mine workers, certain truckers and railroad workers, and atomic energy workers. Public employees in state and local governments also are not covered.[8]

Three Agencies Created by the Occupational Safety and Health Act

The Occupational Safety and Health Act created three autonomous but related agencies to ensure occupational safety and health: the Occupational Safety and Health Review Commission, the National Institute for Occupational Safety and Health, and the Occupational Safety and Health Administration.[9] The basic activities of these three agencies are shown in Figure 14.1 and discussed below.

The **Occupational Safety and Health Review Commission (OSHRC)** is based in the Department of Labor. This commission plays a judicial role in administering workplace safety and health. Organizations can appeal a safety or health citation by requesting a review by OSHRC. If dissatisfied with an OSHRC ruling, an employer may appeal through the federal court system.

The **National Institute for Occupational Safety and Health (NIOSH)** has primary responsibility for conducting and coordinating research on workplace safety and health. This research could be to determine safe levels of particular chemicals in the atmosphere, for example, or what decibel level of machine noise

● FIGURE 14.1

Development of the Occupational Safety and Health Act

Source: Reproduced from James Ledvinka and Vida G. Scarpello, *Federal Regulation of Pesonnel and Human Resource Management,* 2d ed., with the permission of South-Western College Publishing Company, a division of International Thomson Publishing, Inc. Copyright © 1991 PWS-Kent Publishing Company. All rights reserved.

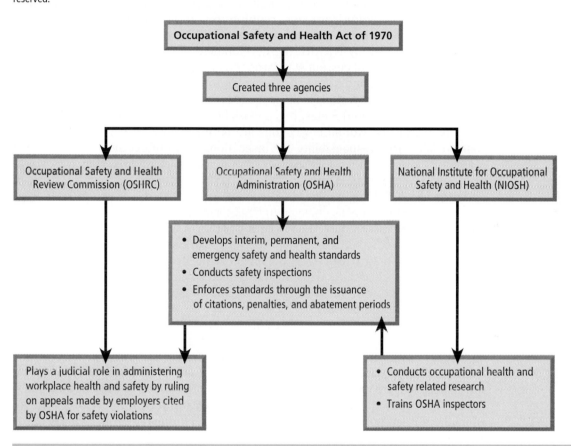

requires ear protection to prevent injury. NIOSH's research provides the basis for making recommendations to the Occupational Safety and Health Administration concerning possible regulations. The NIOSH homepage can be found at http:// www.cdc.gov/niosh.

The **Occupational Safety and Health Administration (OSHA)** was established as a branch of the Department of Labor. It is by far the most visible of the three agencies because it is responsible for formulating and enforcing the regulations for on-the-job safety and health. In the past few years, OSHA has been reinventing itself as a customer service and results-oriented organization, with a view to becoming more of a partner with business to improve safety than a heavy-handed enforcer of sometimes trivial regulations.[10] OSHA's web site can be visited at http://www.osha.gov.

OSHA's Primary Tasks

Immediately after OSHA was established, its first task was to develop health and safety standards and regulations. In its early days, OSHA formulated regulations under a policy of creating a **no-risk environment.** That is, OSHA's standards held employers responsible for eliminating any possible threat in the workplace, regardless of the costs involved, even if the risk to workers was very slight. [11] After the Supreme Court made several judgments against OSHA, the no-risk standard was replaced with **significant-risk regulations,** an orientation recognizing that the law requires safety but not necessarily a risk-free environment. [12] With the help of research provided by NIOSH, the development of new safety and health standards and the review of current standards remains a major OSHA activity today.

Enforcing health and safety regulations is the second responsibility of OSHA. The agency conducts workplace inspections for this purpose. Given the millions of workplaces in the United States, it is impossible for one government agency to inspect all employers. Not all inspections are performed by OSHA. OSHA allows a state to take over responsibility for inspections and enforcement of workplace safety if its laws are at least as stringent as the federal standards. However, workplace inspections remain a primary task that OSHA performs.

Originally, OSHA was allowed to inspect any work area at any "reasonable" time. Once again, business objected to OSHA's liberal interpretation of the legislation, and the Supreme Court ruled to curb OSHA's freedom. [13] Employers may now deny OSHA inspectors access to all or part of a work site. Additionally, employers are not required to turn over every document requested by an OSHA inspector. To gain access to work areas and documents denied by an employer, OSHA has to obtain a legal search warrant (assuming a negotiated agreement cannot be reached with the employer for access). [14]

There are two basic types of OSHA inspections. Before 1996, **programmed inspections** were based on national scheduling programs that targeted employers or industries with the highest injury and illness rates. However, in 1996 OSHA began gathering data on workplace and injury rates itself and now focuses on workplaces that are among the 2, 200 most dangerous places to work in the United States. The second type of inspection, **unprogrammed inspections,** occurs when there is a report to OSHA of imminent dangers or fatalities in a workplace or when OSHA receives specific complaints about safety or health hazards from employees or others. [15]

Either type of **OSHA inspection** involves a very complete examination of the workplace (see Table 14.1 for an "anatomy" of an OSHA inspection along with some tips for employers in handling the inspections). As indicated above, an employer is not required by law to allow an OSHA inspector onto a work site. However, the advice from most experts on OSHA procedures is for employers to be cooperative but also to exert their rights relating to OSHA inspection procedures. [16] In an inspection, the OSHA inspector looks for unsafe conditions and violations of OSHA standards. Typically, the inspector is accompanied by representatives of both management and labor. If a violation is discovered, the OSHA inspector will issue a citation, identifying the specific violation and stating a time by which the employer must correct the situation. [17] If a violation is not corrected in the allotted time, OSHA will levy a fine against the employer. The types of citations issued and related penalties are shown in Table 14.2. However, for some situations, OSHA has recently implemented an **Expedited Informal Settlement Agreement** program

● **TABLE 14.1**

Anatomy of an OSHA Inspection

Inspection Stage	What Happens	What Management Should Do
Initial contact	• Inspectors arrive, present their credentials. • If management is not on site, the inspector is responsible for attempting to contact management. • If management is not available within an hour, the inspector may begin an inspection without management there.	• Refer inspector to your OSHA coordinator. • Check inspector's credentials. • Ask why inspector is inspecting your workplace. • If there is a complaint, you are entitled to know if the complainant is a current employee—but not his/her name. • Notify your lawyer, who should review all OSHA requests for documents, interviews, and anything you provide to OSHA. • Employer may decide to deny inspector access.
Opening conference	• Inspector explains purpose of inspection and may provide copies of complaints; the conference is open to designated employee representatives. • Inspector outlines the scope of the inspection (which physical facilities and which employees will be involved). • Employees may also appoint a representative to accompany the inspector.	• Designate at least one representative to accompany the inspector. • Discuss the procedure for protecting trade secrets, conducting employee interviews, and producing documents. • Show the inspector that you have safety programs in place.
Walk-around inspection	• Accompany the inspector and take notes. • If inspector takes a photo or video, you should, too. • Ask the inspector for copies of physical samples and all test results. • Be helpful and cooperative, but don't volunteer information. • If possible, immediately correct any violations identified.	• Inspectors can view things that are "in plain view" but cannot walk over to things that are "not in plain view" without the consent of management. • Request another conference if you feel that the inspector is expanding the inspection beyond that already discussed.
Closing conference & after inspection	• This can occur immediately after the inspection or later over the telephone. • Inspector describes violations observed. • If citations are issued for safety violations, OSHA specifies a period during which corrections must be made. • OSHA may schedule follow-up inspections.	• Notify OSHA when the corrections are complete. • Ask for an extension of the time period for corrections if necessary (describe reasons for extension and actions already taken). • Appeal the citation if appropriate.

Sources: Adapted from information in William Atkinson, "When OSHA Comes Knocking," *HRMagazine,* Vol. 44 (10), 1999, pp. 35–38; and Robert Grossman, "Handling Inspections: Tips from Insiders," *HRMagazine,* Vol. 44 (10), 1999, pp. 41–45.

in which paperwork for violations is reduced and penalties can drop by 30 percent if the employer remedies the unsafe situation quickly.[18]

OSHA has increasingly taken on a third responsibility—to work cooperatively with business to improve safety outside the inspection/penalty system. OSHA offers no-cost consulting to organizations who ask for assistance in improving workplace safety and health systems. OSHA also runs the **Voluntary Protection Program (VPP)** to encourage and recognize organizations that do an outstanding job with

● **TABLE 14.2**

Types of OSHA Violations

Type of Violation	Minimum Penalty per Violation	Maximum Penalty per Violation
Nonserious		$7,000
Serious	$100	$7,000
Posting		$7,000
Willful	$5,000	$70,000
Willful with fatality, **first** conviction		**$250,000/500,000 or 6 months in prison or both**
Willful, with fatality, **second** conviction		**$250,000/$500,000 or 1 year in prison or both**
Repeated	$5,000	$70,000
Failure to abate cited violation beyond the prescribed abatement date		$7,000 per day

1. Willful—"Willfulness" is established by a conscious, intentional, deliberate decision and also may be characterized by a careless disregard of the requirements of the act or an indifference to employee safety.
2. Repeated violations—a prior violation of the same standard constitutes a "repeated violation."
3. Serious—a violation where there is a substantial likelihood that serious physical harm or death could result. Proposed penalties of up to $1,000 are mandatory.
4. Nonserious—a violation that has an immediate relationship to job safety but that probably would not cause serious physical harm or death.

Sources: Adapted from David P. Twomey, *A Concise Guide to Employment Law* (Dallas, Tex.: South-Western Publishing Company, 1986), p. 131. Reprinted by permission; and U.S. Department of Labor, Occupational Safety and Health Administration, "All About OSHA," OSHA 2056, 2000 (Revised), p. 32. (Available at: http://www.osha.gov/Publications/osha2056.pdf)

safety. In a VPP, OSHA and an employer create a formal agreement to operate a safety and health program that includes elements such as worksite analysis, hazard prevention and control, and safety and health training. OSHA verifies the program, then removes the site from its list of routine scheduled inspections.[19] With programs like VPP, the "new" OSHA has put businesses on notice that they have a clear choice: Become a partner with OSHA in proactively improving workplace health and safety through voluntary consultation and reap the benefits of less frequent inspections and lower fines, or ignore safety and regard OSHA as an adversary and experience traditional inspections and rigorous enforcement.[20]

The federal agencies set up as part of the Occupational Safety and Health Act of 1970 represent only one side of the equation in determining employee health and safety in the workplace. Obviously, management plays a critical role in determining the health and safety of workers. In the next section of this chapter we will examine that role.

MANAGEMENT'S ROLE IN SAFETY AND HEALTH

In meeting the health and safety needs of its employees, management may take either a minimalist or more proactive stance. In the **minimalist approach to safety and health,** management complies with the legal requirements placed upon it by the Occupational Safety and Health Act and other state and federal regulations. For example, the Occupational Safety and Health Act of 1970 outlines a set of employer responsibilities for the health and safety of employees. In general, these responsibilities fall within three areas: (a) providing a safe workplace for employees, (b) informing and training employees about health and safety issues, and (c) complying with specific regulations or directives of OSHA. A more detailed list of these employer responsibilities is found in Table 14.3.

Obviously, to meet OSHA requirements, all employers must have some safety rules. However, many organizations go well beyond these minimal requirements with a more **proactive approach to safety and health.** In these firms, health and safety programs are based on a strategic human resource philosophy; that is, that workers represent a valued asset of the organization and a signficant source of

●**TABLE 14.3**

Some Responsibilities of an Employer Under the Occupational Safety and Health Act of 1970

Providing a safe work environment

- Meet general duty to provide a workplace free from recognized hazards.
- Evaluate workplace conditions.
- Make sure employees have and use safe, properly maintained tools and equipment (including appropriate personal protective equipment).
- Establish or update operating procedures and communicate them to employees.
- Minimize or eliminate potential hazards.

Informing and training employees about safety and health issues

- Keep workers informed about OSHA and safety and health matters with which they are involved.
- Communicate operating procedures to employees.
- Make copies of safety and health standards available to employees for review upon request.
- Warn employees of potential hazards.
- Provide training required by OSHA standards.
- Post a copy of the *OSHA 200— Log and Summary of Occupational Injuries and Illnesses* for the prior year each year during the entire month of February unless otherwise specified.
- Post, at a prominent location within the workplace, specific OSHA information that informs employees of their rights and responsibilities.

Complying with specific safety and health regulations and directives

- Be familiar with mandatory OSHA standards.
- Comply in a responsible manner with standards, rules, and regulations issued under the Occupational Safety and Health Act.
- Report within eight hours any accident that results in a fatality or the hospitalization of three or more employees.
- Keep OSHA-required records of work-related injuries and illnesses, unless otherwise specified.
- Provide access to employee medical records and exposure records.
- Cooperate with OSHA compliance officers.
- Do not discriminate against employees who properly exercise their rights under the Occupational Safety and Health Act.
- Post OSHA citations and abatement verification notices at or near the worksite involved.
- Abate (i.e., correct) cited violations within the prescribed period.

Source: Adapted from U.S. Department of Labor, Occupational Safety and Health Administration, "All About OSHA," OSHA 2056, 2000 (Revised), p. 10. (Available at: http://www.osha-slc.gov/SLTC/smallbusiness/sec1.html)

the firm's competitive advantage. As a result, safety and health issues and programs designed to deal effectively with them become a way for organizations to protect one of the firm's most valuable competitive assets—its people.

There are a number of characteristics that seem to distinguish between successful, proactive programs and all the rest. To make sure that these characteristics exist in their safety and health programs, management must play five key roles.

Leading from the Front

One of the most important roles for management is that of leading from the front. Managers must take the initiative in safety and health issues. Employees must see managers as proactive rather than reactive. If top management pays only lip service to safety, workers will follow this lead and regard safety policies as unimportant. As part of management's leadership role, managers must accept accountability for the results of safety and health programs.

Involving Employees

Involving employees in the development of safety and health programs is the second key role of management. Doing so will improve the overall quality of safety and health programs because employees who work "at the coal face" are most likely to understand the nature of work hazards and their possible solutions.[21] One of the most common and effective strategies for involving employees is the use of company **safety committees** consisting of management and nonmanagement employees.[22] These committees identify safety hazards through self-inspections, statistical analyses, and employee input. Typically, they also attempt to find solutions to hazards that have been identified or suggest that experts be hired to resolve a problem. Figure 14.2 is part of a **hazard analysis** for the task of grinding castings. Table 14.4 gives a detailed example of potential hazards in grinding castings, the causes of those hazards, and possible remedies to reduce or remove the hazards. Safety committees also arrange for training seminars and other activities to increase employee awareness of safety.

Analyzing Data

The third major role of management is to ensure that a thorough analysis of the health and safety environment in the workplace is undertaken. Not doing this may lead a firm to "solve the wrong problem." For example, a midwestern firm developed a wellness program for employees to help reduce health care costs and absenteeism. The centerpiece of the program was a new fitness center. Unfortunately, the new program did little to reduce employee health problems or absenteeism. After surveying employees, the firm found that most employees were already physically active and that the majority of workers were women of childbearing age. Many employees smoked. What the firm needed was a smoking-cessation program and programs that focused on the health issues of women—not a gymnasium.[23] This is a good example of the negative results that may occur from not analyzing the work environment *and* not encouraging employee participation early enough in the process.

Job Hazard Analysis

Source: Job Hazard Analysis, Occupational Health and Safety Administration Publication No. 3071, 1998 (revised).
(Available at: http://www.osha.gov/Publications/osha3071.pdf)

a. Grinding castings: Job steps

1. Reach into metal box to right of machine, grasp casting, and carry to wheel.

2. Push casting against wheel to grind off burr.

3. Place finished casting in box to left of machine.

b. Grinding castings: Hazards

1. Strike hand on edge of metal box or casting; cut hand on burr; drop casting on toes.

2. Strike hand against wheel; flying sparks, dust or chips, wheel breakage; wheel not guarded; no dust removal; sleeves could get caught in machinery.

3. Strike hand against metal box or castings.

c. Grinding castings: New procedure or protection

1. Provide gloves and safety shoes.

2. Provide larger guard over wheel and safety goggles; install local exhaust system; instruct worker to wear short or tight-fitting sleeves.

3. Provide for removal of completed stock.

● **TABLE 14.4**

Sample Job Hazard Analysis: Grinding Castings

Step	Hazard	Cause	Preventive Measure
1. Reach into right box and select casting	Strike hand on wheel	Box is located beneath wheel	Relocate box to side of wheel
	Tear hand on corner of casters	Corners of casters are sharp	Require wearing of leather gloves
2. Grasp casting, lift and position	Strain shoulder/elbow by lifting with elbow extended	Box too low	Place box on pallet
	Drop casting on toe during positioning	Slips from hand	Require wearing of safety shoes
3. Push casting against wheel, and grind burr	Strike hand against wheel	Wheel guard is too small	Provide larger guard
	Wheel explodes	Incorrect wheel installed	Check rpm rating of wheel
		Cracked wheel	Inspect wheel for cracks
	Flying sparks/chips	Wheel friction with caster	Require wearing of eye goggles
	Respirable dust	Dust from caster metal and wheel material	Provide local exhaust system
	Sleeves caught in machinery	Loose sleeves	Provide bands to retain sleeves
4. Place finished casting into box	Strike hand on castings	Buildup of completed stock	Remove completed stock routinely

Source: Job Hazard Analysis, Occupational Health and Safety Administration Publication No. 3071, 1998 (revised), p. 9.

Motivating Safe Behavior

Most employees know how to use safety devices and protective equipment properly. However, a significant problem for an organization is to motivate employees to follow safety rules on a daily basis. As illustrated by the Russell Enterprises example (see the HR Challenge), because doing things in a less safe way may be faster and require less effort, safety precautions tend to be ignored, even though most employees know about them. Thus, the fourth role of mangement in developing effective safety and health programs is to motivate safe work behavior in employees. At least five different approaches are being used by organizations to motivate employees to work safely:[24]

1. *Programs that reward results:* These programs provide employees with cash or other tangible incentives for reaching certain safety goals.

2. *Programs that recognize results:* These programs have the same basic approach as rewarding results; however, meeting safety goals leads only to forms of "social recognition" through dinner events, "safe-employee-of-the-month" certificates, and the like.

3. *Programs that reward behaviors:* These programs provide employees with cash or other tangible incentives for engaging in behaviors that have been shown to reduce or prevent accidents and injuries (e.g., wearing hardhats and safety belts) or that promote safety and health in the workplace (e.g., participating in specific safety training programs).

4. *Programs that recognize behaviors:* These programs have the same basic approach as those rewarding behaviors, but programs that merely recognize safe behaviors have the same limitations as those that merely recognize results (see item 2 above).

5. *Programs that focus on expecting behavior:* In these programs employees are shown the value of working safely: They are taught how to work safely, how to observe coworkers to see if they are working safely, and how to discuss safety observations with coworkers. No formal rewards are given.

There is no definitive evidence that one type of program is superior to the others. One of the major problems with rewarding or recognizing results is that this may lead employees to hide or underreport health and safety problems. Programs that focus on behavior rather than results should avoid this problem. Proponents of the "expecting-behaviors" approach to motivating safety in the workplace argue that external rewards or recognition should not be necessary because safety and health have intrinsic value to employees. There are obviously financial and administrative advantages to these programs relative to systems in which results or behaviors have to be closely monitored and rewarded or recognized.[25]

Although the arguments of the behavior-versus-results and expecting-versus-rewarding/recognizing proponents seem well founded, effective results on safety have been achieved through all of these types of programs. For example, Vitler Manufacturing Corporation in Cudahy, Wisconsin, introduced a results-oriented program in 1998. Employees were divided into five teams, and monthly targets were set for the number of recordable injuries. If the company, as a whole, beat the targets, then each employee in the team with the lowest injury rate received $5. With this program, Vitler slashed recordable injuries by 70 percent and accidents resulting in lost time by 90 percent. It also earned a $210,000 refund from its workers' compensation insurance and an $85,000 reduction in its workers' compensation premiums.[26] Vitler's program was based on a fairly traditional *rewarding-results* approach, with a few interesting twists, such as the focus on team performance and the fact that the entire organization had to beat its safety targets before rewards to any team were handed out. Given such results, the key role for management is to work with employees to identify methods that work in their organization to motivate safety in the workplace.

Innovating

With management leadership, employee participation, careful data analysis, and motivation, any firm is well on its way to achieving successful programs in safety and health. However, one last management role needs to be mentioned—innovating. A key role for management is to be creative in its approach to safety and health programs. Such innovation is likely to be enhanced when management and employees work together on common problems. For example, Steelcase, a major manufacturer of office furnishings, has developed a program considered to be the model for emergency medical services (EMS) systems.[27] First, the company developed its own on-site medical center, staffed by physicians and nurses. Company security guards were then replaced with protection services officers who, in addition to their typical security duties, were also responsible for administering first aid to accident victims. All the officers had had college training in emergency medical assistance, including the use of advanced technological devices such as defibrillators. A telephone hotline was created to serve as an in-house 911 emergency number.

In addition to this system, the Steelcase medical center installed an automatic telephone link with a local ambulance service. The entire system is computerized, making information on the location and nature of any incident instantly obtainable by both the medical staff and the ambulance service. Having trained its employees in how to use the service, through its emphasis on innovative program design, Steelcase can now respond quickly to workplace accidents and has saved lives through fast, efficient treatment.

The roles that are described above will help ensure that programs designed to enhance workplace safety and health will be successful. Firms in which management takes on these five roles in relation to occupational safety and health will receive numerous benefits. As is evidenced in some of the examples provided so far, good safety and health programs can have significant bottom-line benefits. Firms implementing such programs are also more likely to create a cooperative working relationship with OSHA officials. Cooperation between management and OSHA will reduce the likelihood that the firm will be inspected by OSHA, and if inspections occur, the probability of citations or fines will be reduced. All of this, in turn, should result in a safer, healthier, and more productive workplace—and thus enhance the overall competitive advantage of a firm in the marketplace.

Thus far this chapter has described the legislative environment related to occupational safety and health in which organizations must operate. The roles that both federal agencies and an organization's management and employees play in safety and health programs have also been discussed. The remainder of this chapter identifies specific safety and health issues that are the focus of OSHA standards and regulations.

SAFETY AND HEALTH ISSUES IN THE WORKPLACE

The Occupational Safety and Health Administration focuses on several aspects of workplace safety and health. Among the most prominent of OSHA's concerns are on-the-job injuries, exposure to hazardous chemicals, injuries or death due to workplace violence, and a broad range of occupational diseases. This section of the chapter discusses the nature of these safety issues.

On-the-Job Injuries

The reduction of on-the-job injuries is one of the main goals of the Occupational Safety and Health Act of 1970. Although injury rates over the past decade have been decreasing, far too many accidents and injuries still occur. Table 14.5 presents data on the number and some of the common types of injuries that resulted in lost work time during the period 1992–1998. While there were various causes for these accidents, an estimated 88 percent of them resulted directly from em-

● **TABLE 14.5**

Number of Occupational Injuries and Illnesses (in thousands) Involving Time Away from Work by Selected Nature of Injury and Illness, 1992 to 1998

	1992	1994	1996	1998
Sprains, strains, tears	1,022.7	963.5	819.7	760.0
Bruises, contusions	222.7	212.0	174.9	153.1
Cuts, lacerations	173.6	164.6	133.2	137.6
Fractures	143.6	138.5	120.5	115.4
Heat burns, scalds	41.0	37.3	29.0	28.4
Chemical burns	15.7	16.5	11.6	11.7
Amputations	12.4	12.2	10.2	10.2

Source: Department of Labor, Bureau of Labor Statistics. "Lost-Worktime Injuries and Illnesses: Characteristics and Resulting Time Away from Work," USDL 00-115,1998, (Available at: http://stats.bls.gov/oshhome.htm)

ployees performing unsafe acts, often in direct violation of company policies.[28] Research indicates that over 80 percent of accidents involving employee error result from misjudging the degree of hazard.[29] Regardless of whether an employee violates a safety regulation knowingly or unknowingly, if an accident occurs, it is legally the responsibility of the employer.

Figure 14.3 shows factors that have been statistically related to worksite accidents. Aside from employee disregard for safety regulations, accidents are related to several other employee factors. New workers show a higher incidence of accidents than senior employees, perhaps because they do not have enough training or experience to fully comprehend workplace dangers. Workers under severe stress also appear to have more accidents on the job. More dangerous yet are practices in which employees either remove or bypass safety devices, such as taping

● **FIGURE 14.3**

Factors Related to Accidents at Work

Source: Robin C. Ballau and Roy M. Buchen, "Study Shows That Gender Is Not a Major Factor in Accident Etiology," *Occupational Health and Safety,* September 1978, pp. 54–58.

Individual Factors	**Task-related Factors**	**Organizational Factors**
• Worker inexperience • Worker stress • Worker carelessness • Use of improper techniques • Underestimation of risks • Use of inappropriate tools • Disregard for safety rules	• Night-shift work • Early in shift • Rotating shift	• Medium-sized organization • Specific dangerous industries

back the guards on saw blades or disconnecting automatic cutoff switches. All these factors can be controlled to some degree by the employer through increased awareness and proper employee training.

Task-related factors also appear to contribute to workplace accidents. For example, there is a much higher incidence of accidents on night shifts than on day shifts. This discrepancy may be attributable to the typically smaller supervisory staff on night shifts, as well as to employee drowsiness and inattentiveness. Accidents also tend to occur early in shifts rather than after breaks or toward the end of shifts. Also, employees on rotating shifts have more accidents.[30]

The size of the firm is an organizational factor that is related to on-the-job accidents. Moderate-sized organizations—with 50 to 100 employees—have higher accident rates than do smaller or larger companies. This statistic may reflect the fact that smaller companies supervise their employees closely and personally and that larger organizations can afford comparatively elaborate safety programs.

Finally, because of their work processes, certain industries experience more risks than others. For example, banks and insurance companies are usually safer than construction sites or industrial plants. The tools used, the environments in which they are operated, and the tasks that need to be performed contribute to this difference.

Although a company may be in a dangerous industry, it does not have to be a dangerous place to work. DuPont, through massive safety programs, has an accident record that is many times lower than its industry's average. Thus a corporate commitment to safety—through training, increasing safety awareness, and developing safe practices for employees—may go a long way toward reducing accidents, even in an inherently dangerous industry.

Hazardous Substances

Hazardous substances represent a special category of agents that can inflict injuries on the job. The **Hazard Communication Standard (HCS)** of OSHA, implemented in the mid-1980s, requires a hazard communication program to train employees in the dangers of the chemicals with which they work. Hazardous substances may be those that cause an immediate injury through burning or poisoning or those that may have insidious longer-term effects through occupational disease. The HCS gives employees the right to know the hazards of chemicals in the workplace, along with precautions to take in working with those chemicals. OSHA also outlines special and extensive inspection procedures for identifying hazardous substances in the work environment.[31] Employers are required to provide **Materials Safety Data Sheets (MSDSs)** for each potentially dangerous chemical used, label containers appropriately, and conduct training. This can be a big job. Battelle-Pantex does contract work for the Department of Energy's nuclear weapons disassembly facility in Amarillo, Texas. Four employees are needed to manage 11,000 MSDSs for the plant, which employs 3,500 people.[32]

Violence in the Workplace

In the Midwest, a postal employee opened fire in one of the deadliest workplace shootings in history. Fourteen people died and seven were wounded. Coworkers had expressed concern about this individual for several years.[33]

Unfortunately, violence in the workplace has become an increasingly important safety and health issue in the United States. A 1997 report by the National Institute for Occupational Safety and Health found that an average of twenty workers were murdered each week. An additional 18,000 employees *per week* were victims of nonfatal assaults.[34] Consistent with these NIOSH findings, the Department of Justice's National Crime Victimization Survey (NCVS) published in 1998 found that assaults and threats of violence against Americans at work numbered almost 2 million a year. There were an average of 1.5 million simple assaults, 396,000 aggravated assaults, 51,000 rapes and sexual assaults, 84,000 robberies, and 1,000 homicides a year in the period 1992–1996.[35]

● **Who Commits Acts of Violence?**   Violence in the workplace does not always involve one employee assaulting another. In fact, there are at least four sources of violence in work settings. **Violence by strangers** occurs when the individual who assaults a person in the workplace has no legitimate relationship to the worker or workplace. They have often entered the workplace on the pretense of being a customer, perhaps with the intention of committing a robbery. Workplace violence by strangers may also occur when an employee is not physically located at the worksite but is conducting work-related activities elsewhere, for example, delivering goods to a client. **Violence by customers/clients** occurs when violence is committed by someone who receives a service provided by a business, such as a current or former customer, client or patient, or passenger. In the case of an employee working in the criminal justice system, the customer may be a criminal suspect or a prisoner. Violence by customer/clients is usually divided into two subcategories. Some customers, such as prison inmates or mental health service recipients, may be known to be of an inherently violent nature. The other type involves people who are not normally violent but become so when something in a situation sets them off. Many employees in the complaints department of firms face customers of this type all too frequently. In incidents of **violence by coworkers,** perpetrators have an employment connection with the workplace. They could be a current or former employee, a prospective employee, or a current or former supervisor or manager. This type of violence is also often divided into two types—violence between managers/supervisors and subordinates or violence between two employees of equal level in the firm. The final source of violence is **violence by personal relations.** Here acts of violence are committed by someone who has a personal relationship with the worker, such as a current or former spouse or partner, a relative, or a friend. These types of incidents often involve the nonemployee entering the workplace with the intention of harming the worker with whom he or she has the personal relationship.[36]

● **Job Factors Associated with Violence**   The risk of being a victim of workplace violence depends significantly on the occupation in which one is employed. Figures from the recent National Crime Victimization Survey presented in Table 14.6 show that, not surprisingly, being a police officer carries a much higher risk of assault (306 assaults per 1,000 employees) than does being an elementary school teacher (16 assaults per 1,000 employees). In addition to occupation, a number of other factors have been identified as increasing the likelihood that someone will become a victim of workplace violence. Among these are the following:[37]

●TABLE 14.6

Crime Victimization Risk Rates by Occupation

Occupation	Rate per 1,000
Police officers	306
Private security guards	218
Taxi drivers	184
Prison guards	117
Bartenders	91
Mental health professionals	80
Gas station attendants	79
Convenience, liquor store clerks	68
Mental health custodial workers	63
Junior high/middle school teachers	57
Bus drivers	45
Special education teachers	41
High school teachers	29
Elementary school teachers	16
College teachers	3

Source: Occupational Safety and Health Administration, "Workplace Violence," August 19, 1999. (Available at: http://www.osha.gov/oshinfo/priorities/violence.html)

- Having contact with the public
- Being involved in the exchange of money
- Delivering passengers, goods, or services
- Having a mobile workplace, such as a taxicab or police cruiser
- Working with unstable or volatile persons in health care, social services, or criminal justice
- Working alone or in small numbers
- Working late at night or during the early morning hours
- Guarding valuable property or possessions
- Working in community-based settings

● **Organizational Factors Associated with Violence**   In addition to these job-related factors, several organizational factors may increase the probability that a violent incident will occur.[38] Poorly trained supervisors who exhibit aggressive behavior and/or reinforce such behavior in their subordinates may enhance the likelihood of violence. Highly authoritarian company cultures that tend to deprive employees of dignity and respect may also increase violence in the workplace. Organizations undergoing downsizing or in which employees are frequently fired are more likely to experience violent acts. Finally, violence is more likely to occur in firms that do not have clear policies about what types of behavior are acceptable and unacceptable and systems that guide the behavior of employees who find themselves harassed by others.

● **The Cost of Workplace Violence** The cost of this violence for employers is enormous. One estimate indicated that each act of violence committed resulted in an average of 3.5 days of lost work time, worth approximately $55 million in wages alone. This estimate did not include other costs such as legal expenses, property damage, damage to a firm's public image, and expenses incurred for increased security measures. Other potential costs that may be borne by employers include liability for death or injuries suffered by employees if the employer is found to have been negligent in providing a safe work environment. Nonemployees who have been assaulted and seriously injured while visiting a workplace have also won significant awards in suits against businesses. With these other costs taken into account, the financial impact of workplace violence can probably be measured in the billions of dollars.[39]

The **general duty clause,** Section 5(a)(1) of the Occupational Safety and Health Act of 1970, requires employers to provide employees with a place of employment that "is free from recognizable hazards that are causing or likely to cause death or serious harm to employees." Within the general interpretation of this clause, an employer that has experienced acts of workplace violence, or has become aware of threats, intimidation, or indicators of potential violence in the workplace, would need to take actions to reduce the likelihood that employees would become the victims of violent acts. Given this legal requirement, along with the staggering financial cost of workplace violence, many employers are developing **workplace violence prevention programs (WVPPs)** within their firms (see Table 14.7 for examples of workplace violence prevention strategies.). The basic components of these programs should include a written violence prevention statement; the establishment of a threat assessment team; a process for hazard assessment, control, and prevention; programs for employee training and education; a system for reporting, investigating, and following up on incidents; and some means of evaluating the overall effectiveness of the violence prevention program.[40]

In a **workplace violence prevention policy statement,** an organization should make it clear that adequate authority and budgetary resources will be assigned to the WVPP and those in charge of it. The statement should encourage employee participation in the design and conduct of the program. The policy should state that the organizations will not tolerate violence in the workplace and that workplace violence prevention policies will be applied consistently and fairly to all employees, including supervisors and managers. The policy should also include statements about the need for prompt and accurate reporting of violent incidents. A strong, clear statement that the firm will not discriminate against victims of workplace violence is a critical part of the policy document.[41] An example of a workplace violence prevention policy statement is given in Figure 14.4.

A **threat assessment team** should be formed to assess the vulnerability of the workplace to violence. This team should be comprised of both management and employee representatives and include individuals from key functions within the organization, such as security, human resources, finance, and legal affairs. Typical activities of the assessment team would be to review current records relating to violent incidents that have occurred, to conduct a workplace security analysis of the organization, and to survey employees in an attempt to identify potential security problems. This function might be performed by an organization's general safety committee, but given the special and complex nature of workplace violence, a special team to examine this issue might be warranted.

TABLE 14.7

Examples of Workplace Violence Prevention Strategies

Redesigning the work environment
- Physically separating employees from customers, clients
- Using locked drop safes
- Posting signs that indicate limited amount of cash is available
- Carrying small amounts of cash only
- Enhancing visibility and lighting
- Limiting access and egress from the workplace (e.g., number of entry doors)
- Security devices such as cameras, alarms, two-way mirrors, card-key access, etc.

Administrative controls and practices
- Escorting clients within the work area
- Prohibiting unsupervised movement within the work area
- Increasing the number of staff in some areas
- Making more secure such practices as money drops and pickups by employees performing tasks outside the workplace building
- Training employees about workplace violence issues
- Having police check on employees regularly
- Closing the establishment during high-risk periods (late night or early morning)
- Developing a reasonable grievance procedure
- Developing specific procedures for dealing with high-risk individuals, e.g., safeguards against dismissed employees

Behavioral strategies
- Enhancing employee skills in nonviolent response and conflict resolution
- Ensuring that employees do not resist during robberies
- Training employees in methods to address hazards associated with specific tasks and relevant prevention strategies
- Training employees on appropriate use and maintenance of protective equipment and increasing their awareness of workplace risks

---

Sources: Gregory Moffatt, "Subjective Fear: Preventing Workplace Homicide," *HR Focus,* Vol. 75 (8), 1998, pp. 11–12; National Institute for Occupational Safety and Health, *Current Intelligence Bulletin 57: Violence in the Workplace: Risk Factors and Prevention Strategies* (DHHS [NIOSH], 1996, Publication No. 96-100) (Available at: http://www.cdc.gov/niosh/violrisk.htm); and National Institute for Occupational Safety and Health, "Preventing Homicide in the Workplace," NIOSH Alert, May 1995, DHHS [NIOSH] Publication No. 93-109. (Available at: http://www.cdc.gov.niosh/homicide.htm)

Once an assessment of security risks has been made, the threat assessment team's next function is to recommend actions to control and prevent workplace violence. The National Institute for Occupational Safety and Health has identified three major categories of actions that firms typically take to control or prevent workplace violence. Firms may alter the environmental design of the workplace, institute specific administrative controls, or train employees in a variety of behavioral strategies to enhance their safety in the workplace.[42] Table 14.7 provides some more detailed examples of violence prevention strategies that are commonly taken.

As seen in Table 14.7, employee training is an important part of any violence prevention program. Training should be focused on at least three groups of em-

ABC Company's WVPP Policy Statement

Our establishment, ABC COMPANY, is concerned and committed to our employees' safety and health. We refuse to tolerate violence in the workplace and will make every effort to prevent violent incidents from occurring by implementing a workplace violence prevention program (WVPP). We will provide adequate authority and budgetary resources to responsible parties so that our goals and responsibilities can be met.

All managers and supervisors are responsible for implementing and maintaining our WVPP. We encourage employee participation in designing and implementing our program. We require prompt and accurate reporting of all violent incidents whether or not physical injury has occurred. We will not discriminate against victims of workplace violence.

A copy of this Policy Statement and our WVPP is readily available to all employees from each manager and supervisor.

Our program ensures that all employees, including supervisors and managers, adhere to work practices that are designed to make the workplace more secure and do not engage in verbal threats or physical actions which create a security hazard for others in the workplace.

All employees, including managers and supervisors, are responsible for using safe work practices; for following all directives, policies, and procedures; and for assisting in maintaining a safe and secure work environment.

The management of our establishment is responsible for ensuring that all safety and health policies and procedures involving workplace security are clearly communicated and understood by all employees. Managers and supervisors are expected to enforce the rules fairly and uniformly.

Our program will be reviewed and updated annually.

ployees. First, workers in job tasks or locations with a high risk for violent incidents should be provided specialized training to deal with this risk. Second, managers and supervisors should be trained to recognize a potentially hazardous situation and take corrective actions to eliminate or reduce the hazard. Managers and supervisors should also be trained to prevent employees from being placed in dangerous situations in the first place. Managers and supervisors may also need training in special interpersonal skills needed to effectively deal with employees who have been victims of violence. Obviously managers and supervisors should be totally familiar with all aspects of the policies and procedures associated with the firm's workplace violence prevention policy. Finally, security personnel need to be trained in their specific job duties, the facility layout in which they work, the proper use of security equipment on premises, and any actions they may need to take to prevent violence from occurring in specific high-risk jobs.[43]

As part of a WVPP, an organization must develop specific procedures for reporting incidents. The procedures should focus not only on violent acts in which physical injury has occurred but also on situations involving verbal abuse, threats, or other menacing acts. Incident reports should be in writing, and employees making these reports should be assured of confidentiality. Management must do all it can to encourage employees to bring their concerns to management without fear of reprisal. If a violent incident is reported, a thorough investigation should be conducted to identify the causes of the incident and recommend corrective actions to be taken. Follow-up of the incident investigation should occur to make sure that any actions recommended have indeed been taken. Follow-up of an incident may also involve providing medical and psychological help to employees affected by the violence. Careful records of all incidents should be kept so that a historical picture of violence in the workplace can be obtained and this information used by threat assessment teams to improve workplace safety in the future. An overall evaluation of the WVPP should take place periodically to ensure that the program is having a desirable effect.[44]

● **The Americans with Disabilities Act (ADA) and Violent Employees**   In dealing with employees who appear to pose a threat to other workers, an employer may run into a conflict between protecting employees from a violent coworker and the possibility of discriminating against violent employees who have a legitimate mental illness (and are thus protected by the ADA). Employers have the right to fire mentally ill employees for work-related reasons. However, dealing with employees who are on medication for their illness becomes somewhat complex. It may be that an employee functions effectively while on medication but becomes a danger to other workers without medication. In this case, employers may need to take a somewhat cautious approach. If an employee fails to take needed medication in an initial instance, the employer should attempt to make reasonable accommodation. If a second failure to take medication occurs, then the employer probably has grounds for dismissal, assuming that a serious work-related problem occurs as a result.[45]

In *Palmer* v. *Circuit Court of Cook County, Ilinois,* a federal circuit court of appeals supported the idea that a worker with a mental illness could be fired for threats made to other employees and that such firing was not "because of their illness."[46] According to the court, the ADA does not require employers to retain potentially violent employees. Employers, however, should attempt to resolve the behavioural problem and obtain treatment for the employee. Otherwise, upon firing, the employee may resort to violence against others.

Occupational Diseases

The prevention of occupational diseases is the second dimension of the regulations concerning safe and healthful working conditions. "Occupational diseases" are long-term health problems caused by substances that are absorbed through the skin, inhaled from the atmosphere, taken internally through the mouth, or that affect one of the five senses.[47] Table 14.8 provides some examples of conditions caused by workplace exposure to hazardous substances and some typical symptoms. It has been estimated that of the 63,000 chemicals manufactured and used in American workplaces, about 160 are proven carcinogens and another 2,000 are potential carcinogens.[48]

● **TABLE 14.8**

Some Occupational Diseases and Their Causes

Condition and Some Typical Symptoms	Example Industries or Occupations	Agent
Silicon tuberculosis: Decrease in maximum breathing capacity; bloodstained sputum; attacks of bronchopneumonia; malaise; disturbed sleep; anorexia; chest pains.	Quarrymen, sandblasters, silica processors, mining, metal foundries, ceramic industry	SiO_2, silica
Anthrax: *Cutaneous form:* Red-brown papule skin eruption which enlarges with red patches of variable size and shape; pus-like pimples; and hardening of tissue; muscle pain; headache; fever; nausea; and vomiting. *Pulmonary form:* Symptoms are insidious, suggesting an influenza-like illness. Increased fever is followed in 1–3 days by severe respiratory distress with bluish-purplish discoloration of mucous membranes and skin; shock; and coma.	Shepherds, farmers, butchers, veterinarians, weavers	Bacillus anthracis
Malignant neoplasm of nasal cavities: Malignant tumor; headache; pain; paralysis of the lateral rectus muscle of the eye.	Woodworkers, cabinet and furniture makers; boot and shoe industry; radium chemists and processors; dial painters; chromium producers, processors, users; nickel-smelting and refining	Possibly hardwood dusts; radium; nickel; chromates
Lymphoid leukemia, acute: Abrupt onset of fever with secondary infection of mouth, throat, or lungs; joint pains; minute rounded spots of hemorrhage on skin, mucous membrane, or organ, and discoloration of skin due to blood vessel rupture, plus bleeding from mouth, nose, kidneys, and bowel.	Rubber industry, radiologists	Unknown; ionizing radiation
Parkinson's disease: Listlessness and sleepiness by day but insomnia by night; muscular pains, including cramps in the calves; unsteady gate; weakness and stiffness of the limbs; involuntary movement of the arms, legs, trunk, jaw, and head which may be severe enough to shake the bed; occasionally uncontrollable laughter or crying.	Manganese processing, battery makers, welders, internal combustion engine industries	Manganese fumes, carbon monoxide

Source: Occupational Health and Safety Administration, *OSHA Record Keeping Guidelines, Appendix C. Selected Illnesses Which May Result from Exposure in the Work Environment,* March 1999.

● **Detecting Occupational Disease**   The major problem with reducing the occurrence of occupational diseases is the difficulty of detecting them and then pinpointing their cause. Typically, the disease is linked to the workplace through statistics. Researchers compare the percentage of employees who have the disease with the percentage of people in the general population who have the disease. If the percentage is significantly greater for the employees than for the general population, researchers suggest that something at the workplace may have caused the disease.

Such detective work is not simple.[49] The disease may surface only after many years of exposure or years after the employee is exposed. Thus the organization and the workers may not know that a problem exists because the causal agent has not been around long enough for people to show symptoms of the disease. Sometimes symptoms do not appear until long after a worker's retirement. Another difficulty is that most individuals work in different jobs at several organizations throughout their careers. Thus, to determine which organization and which job caused the disease, researchers must perform analyses that consider all the jobs and all the employees who have held the jobs in the previous years.

Even if an organization is able to determine that its employees are suffering from an illness related to their occupation, the difficulties are not over. Next, the company must determine exactly what aspect of the work environment and/or the job caused the illness. Statistics and medical research help in this process, but the detective work may have to be done up to forty years after the exposure.

Of course, the detection of occupational diseases is not always difficult. Medical science aids the process through studies of the impact of various environmental factors on health, and sometimes the cause is apparent, as in the case of hearing loss from sustained exposure to loud noises. When an illness is determined to be caused by something in the work environment, the organization is just as responsible in cases where the cause is not readily apparent as it is in more obvious cases.

● **Smoking in the Workplace**   A workplace contaminant that has been receiving much attention in the last several years is **environmental tobacco smoke (ETS).** ETS contains more than 4,000 chemicals, at least 43 of which are known or suspected to be carcinogens. Exposure to ETS has been associated with many adverse health effects in nonsmokers, including lung cancer, heart disease, asthma, reproductive effects, and mucous membrane irritation. OSHA estimates that 21 million individuals are exposed to ETS at work. Among nonsmoking workers, OSHA estimates that there will be up to 700 cases of lung cancer per year and from 2,000 to 13,000 deaths from heart disease per year attributable to exposure to ETS.[50]

Given such evidence, the Environmental Protection Agency now classifies secondhand smoke as a life-threatening carcinogen.[51] In the United States, workplace costs associated with smoking may be as high as $72 billion per year.[52]

In reaction to scientific evidence showing the potentially harmful effects of ETS, OSHA proposed indoor air quality (IAQ) standards in 1994 that would largely ban smoking in the 6 million workplaces it covers. The draft standards provoked more comments from the public than any other OSHA document ever had. As the assistant secretary for occupational safety and health explained to the Senate Committe on Labor and Human Resources in February 1998:

> The Agency has been reviewing and analyzing the more than 115,000 comments received, identifying and addressing issues that need to be resolved. . . . Several steps remain before a final IAQ standard can be published. OSHA must complete the preamble to the final rule, finish the final economic impact analysis, respond to comments in the record, prepare compliance assistance materials, obtain legal and policy review within the Department, work with the Small Business Administration to minimize any potentially significant small business impacts identified, and obtain OMB review. . . . OSHA must ensure that it has complied with all applicable laws related to the rulemaking process.[53]

In 2000, these final ETS rules remained in development. Despite this, many states have developed regulations placing smoke-free indoor air restrictions on private worksites. For example, California, Montana, Utah, Nebraska, Minnesota, Wisconsin, Michigan, Illinois, Missouri, Louisiana, and most of the states in the Northeast require firms to have some sort of designated smoking area. In some of these states, the designated smoking area must have a separate ventilation system.[54] Nevertheless, many organizations have developed programs to combat ETS effects. In 1991, the Bureau of National Affairs developed a model policy in regard to smoking in the workplace. The policy had as its purpose the health and accommodation of all employees and provided nine guidelines. These guidelines specified smoking areas, locations where smoking was prohibited, departmental options to formulate smoking policies, and procedures for resolving disputes.[55] The model program also offered employees free smoking-cessation programs and provided a one-time $50 bonus for any employee who successfully quit smoking for one year. In a 1998 study by the National Cancer Institute, of 80,661 employees responding to a survey, 65 percent said that they worked in places where smoking was banned in either the office or in other common areas. That compares with only 47 percent in 1993.[56]

A common practice is for firms to phase in antismoking policies over a period of time.CDW Computer Center, Inc., in Vernon, Illinois, at one time allowed employees to smoke at their desks. This was changed to smoking only in the lunchroom, then to smoking only outside the building. In conjunction with the Great American Smokeout in 1994, CDW banned smoking anywhere on its premises, including the parking lots.[57] Some employers have gone so far as to refusing to hire people who smoke, although this is a contentious legal issue, with some arguing that tobacco addiction is a type of disability that may be covered by the Americans with Disabilities Act.[58] There is little doubt that smoking in the workplace will remain an important issue for HR managers for some time to come.

● **Musculoskeletal Disorders**   Each year work-related musculoskeletal disorders (MSDs) account for one-third of all occupational injuries and illnesses reported to the Bureau of Labor Statistics. In 1997 it was estimated that employers paid $15–20 billion dollars in workers' compensation costs related to MSDs, with additional injury-related expenses increasing the total cost to $45–54 billion dollars.[59] In 1998, employers reported 592, 500 incidents of MSDs, with the median time away from work as a result of the injury being seven days.[60] Among these musculoskeletal injuries, **cumulative trauma disorders (CTDs)**—also called **repetitive strain injury (RSIs)**—are the fastest-growing workplace injury in the United States, having increased more than 770 percent from 1988 to 1998.[61]

CTDs seem to be caused by repeating the same movement many times without a break. Low-back problems are common among employees who repeatedly lift objects. Butchers in meatpacking plants frequently suffer CTDs of the hands and arms, while word-processing and data-entry operators also report the problem fairly often. Automation seems to be a culprit—it simplifies the motions needed and removes the chance to take breaks. For instance, word-processing operators enter keystrokes constantly for hours on end. In past years, these employees would have alternated their activities by inserting paper into a typewriter, manually erasing errors, and returning the typewriter carriage. Carpal tunnel syndrome is the CTD that occurs most commonly in people working with computer keyboards. It results in pain and loss of grip strength in the hands and arms due to swelling of tissues and subsequent pressure on nerves that run through the carpal bones of the wrist.

CTDs have reached epidemic proportions in some areas and, as a result, have attracted a great deal of research interest. It has been found that nontask factors such as previous personal injury or illness, hobbies, job satisfaction, and physical condition are just as important as work-related conditions.[62] For example, one study found that the prevalence of CTDs was more than seven times greater among morbidly obese as compared with slender individuals. At the same time, the prevalence of CTDs was six times higher among those who exercise minimally or lightly as compared with those who exercise vigorously.[63] Undoubtedly, some apparent cases of CTD are not due to the workplace at all but may be an expression of mental distress or an attempt to malinger by employees.

OSHA has recognized CTDs as a legitimate problem and levied fines of $5.7 million against IBP, the nation's largest meatpacker. The fines subsequently were reduced because IBP implemented a $1–2 million program to research and correct the problem. In the mid-1980s, U.S. West Communications spent about $1 million on redesigned workstations for telephone operators after a large number of CTD claims were filed.[64] Besides redesigning workstations, some employers are rotating workers among jobs or incorporating active rest periods so that workers have a chance to engage in other movements with the affected tendons and muscles.[65]

The science of **ergonomics** investigates the interactions between humans and mechanical systems. Ergonomically designed tools and work processes can greatly reduce the incidence of CTDs. Something as simple as a curved handle on a knife—so that the wrist does not have to be bent at an angle for long periods—can reduce the incidence of CTD in butchers. In 1995, OSHA proposed specific standards on the ergonomic design of work but was unable to get them accepted. Ergonomics is still a young science, and there was deemed to be insufficient proof that those particular standards were necessary, correct, or sufficient to prevent CTD.[66] Although this 1995 attempt failed, in 1999 OSHA proposed new ergonomic workplace regulations, which were adopted in final form in November 2000.[67]

Ergonomics does have a great deal to contribute to the effective design of equipment and workplaces. Figure 14.5 shows how to properly position computing equipment to minimize strain on the back, neck, shoulders, wrists, and eyes. Consideration of ergonomic work design may help prevent workplace accidents as well as occupational disease. The human errors that cause so many accidents may themselves be due to poorly designed equipment. For instance, injuries may occur when trying to repair or service equipment that is mounted too high or too close to other equipment. Poorly designed switches or gauges may violate intuitive expectations and thus cause errors in the confusion of an emergency situation. In the United States and Canada, the "up" position on switches is generally expected to mean "on" or "open" or "start," whereas "down" means "off." The opposite is true in Europe[68]

The impact of ergonomics programs can be quite dramatic. For example, after the first year of a new ergonomics program, Mitsubishi in Normal, Illinois, saw cumulative trauma disorders drop 25 percent.[69] As part of its ergonomic program, the *Sacramento Bee* newspaper gave employees a choice of chairs for their workstations. Computer tables were fitted with adjustable monitor arms and keyboard

● **FIGURE 14.5**

Minimizing
Musculoskeletal Strain at
the Keyboard

*Source: Working Safely with
Video Display Terminals,*
Occupational Safety and Health
Administration, Department of
Labor, OSHA Publication No.
3092, 1996 (revised), p. 8.
(Available at: http://www.osha.
gov/oshpubs/osha3092.pdf)

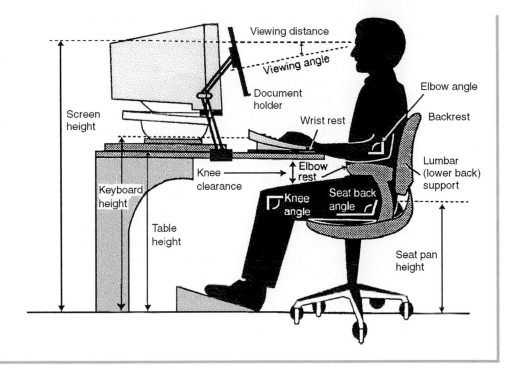

platforms. Employees were also supplied with foot rests, wrist rests, and antiglare screens. Reports of CTDs dropped about 60 percent.[70] The reduction in CTD incidents has a significant financial impact. However, saving money is not the only benefit of ergonomic programs. In "Sit Up Straight," Kathryn Tyler reports a conversation with Hank Austin, the manager of safety and environmental affairs at USAA, an insurance and financial services company in San Antonio, Texas. Austin said, "After we started our ergonomics training program, a lady came up and hugged me. . . . She said her life is completely changed because she doesn't hurt at the end of the day anymore."[71] Given such positive reactions from workers, it is not surprising that 3M found that employees provided ergonomically designed workstations had a 13 percent better attendance rate than employees without the new workstations.[72]

OTHER WORKPLACE-RELATED HEALTH ISSUES

In addition to on-the-job injuries, workplace violence, and occupational diseases, there are a variety of other health and safety issues in the workplace that are worthy of discussion. These include acquired immune deficiency syndrome (AIDS) and other bloodborne pathogens, fetal protection policies, drugs, and a variety of issues that fall within the general topic of employee psychological health. Many pages would be needed to address each of these issues adequately. The next few pages of this chapter provide only a general overview of key aspects of these other health issues.

AIDS and Other Bloodborne Pathogens

In the past two decades, employers have had to learn to deal with issues of AIDS in the workplace. As was noted in Chapter 5, AIDS is a handicap covered by legal statutes. Employees who have AIDS or who test positive for the HIV virus that causes AIDS must be considered handicapped and must be accommodated.[73] Despite the legal statutes and the fact that there is no evidence that AIDS can be spread through casual contact in the workplace, people greatly fear the disease. For this reason, employers are put in the role of educating their employees about AIDS, its transmission, and the fair treatment of coworkers with AIDS.

Partly in response to the danger of AIDS, in 1992 OSHA issued a set of **Bloodborne Pathogen Standards.** The standards cover "all employees who can be 'reasonably anticipated' as the result of performing their job duties to face contact with blood and other potentially infectious materials." Employers are required to identify, in writing, job duties that may expose employees to blood or other bodily fluids. The standards also outline procedures for evaluating incidents when exposure to potentially harmful bodily fluids occurs. The plan must be accessible to employees and must be reviewed annually. The standards describe procedures for handling and shipping infectious materials . Employers must provide employees, at no cost, with personal protective equipment. The standards also require employers to make available to employees appropriate vaccinations for hepatitis B within ten working days of assignment. Procedures for evaluating and following up on employees who have been exposed to infectious materials are set out. The standards require specific warning labels to be placed on hazardous waste containers and mandate training of employees to reduce the likelihood of exposure. The standards also include record-keeping requirements.[74]

Fetal Protection from Occupational Hazards

While OSHA tries mainly to protect current workers, some workplace hazards may influence the unborn children of employees. In the past, some companies excluded women of childbearing age from jobs in which exposure to chemicals or radiation could pose a health hazard to their reproductive systems. In a landmark 1991 decision (*UAW* v. *Johnson Controls, Inc.),* the Supreme Court ruled that **fetal protection policies** are a form of illegal sex discrimination prohibited by Title VII.[75] Among other things, Johnson Controls manufactures automotive batteries, which contain lead, a known danger to a developing fetus. In an effort to protect employees from this danger and to avoid potential liability, Johnson Controls excluded women employees capable of bearing children from jobs—many of which were highly paid—involving lead exposure. The Court ruled that risk and childbearing decisions are best left to employees, but this ruling has resulted in companies being caught between Title VII of the Civil Rights Act and OSHA requirements to provide a workplace free from recognized hazards. Companies must provide information to female employees about fetal health risk and allow them to make their own decisions.

Drugs in the Workplace

According to the Institute for a Drug Free Workplace, illegal drug use costs U.S. companies $60-$110 billion a year. Eleven percent of employed adults are currently illegal drug users and 42 percent of employees in a Gallop survey indicated that illegal drug use "greatly affects" safety at their workplace. A survey by the U.S. Postal Service found that drug-using employees were one-third less productive, more likely to use sick leave, twice as likely to be disciplined, and 47 percent more likely to be involuntarily terminated than non–drug users.[76]

More and more employers are concerned about drugs in the workplace and the potential for serious accidents caused by drug-impaired employees. Under the 1988 Federal Drug-Free Workplace Act, federal contractors must certify that they will maintain a drug-free workplace.[77] Among other things, this certification includes enforcing a drug-free policy, providing awareness programs, and making absence of substance abuse a condition of employment.

Many employers are testing applicants or current employees for drug abuse. It is important that organizations have appropriate policies for testing either applicants or current employees. Such policies need to involve (1) informed consent, (2) scheduling, (3) assurance of test validity, and (4) confidentiality. Such screening is likely to increase because drug use continues to be a problem for the larger society and the liability associated with having an employee under the influence of drugs is a cost companies are expected to bear.

There are several controversial approaches to drug testing, one of which is hair-strand analysis.[78] Proponents of this method claim that the test can detect drug use from three to ninety days previously. Critics argue that false-positive errors can frequently occur, since the test may identify someone as a drug user even though the person had only been in a room where marijuana was smoked. A potential legal complication with this method is that under the Americans with Disabilities Act, someone who is a *current* drug user can be terminated or not hired. However, hair analysis can detect drug use three months earlier. If the person only used drugs three months ago, is it appropriate to classify him or her as a current user? It would be possible that the person had gone through a drug rehabilitation program in the last three months and is no longer using illegal drugs. Despite this, only a few states prohibit hair testing.

Psychological Health

We have seen that employers have clear responsibilities regarding employees' physical health. But what about their mental health? The employer's responsibility for the psychological well-being of employees has been addressed mainly by case law rather than by formal regulation. Employers are sometimes held responsible for mental and psychological distress that is work related, just as they are for on-the-job physical injury.[79] One company was sued for $6 million by the widow of an executive who committed suicide. Constantly overworked, he had been persuaded not to take early retirement and promised additional assistants to relieve some of his stress. The additional help was never allocated, however, and the executive suffered from severe anxiety, which led to his suicide. The widow claimed that the company was negligent because of its "callous and conscious disregard" for its employee's mental health.[80]

The psychological health of employees may be affected by many work-related circumstances. Being a victim of workplace violence is certainly one of the most drastic examples of intense psychological strain. There are, however, many less dramatic forms of psychological stress that employees face in their workplace.

The courts have established four categories of on-the-job stress for which individuals may be allowed to file for workers' compensation.[81] The first category involves mental stimuli from the job that result in a physical illness—for example, when consistent stress causes a heart attack. The second category consists of physical stimuli on the job that result in a psychological illness—for example, a work injury that causes anxiety so severe that the employee cannot go back to work. The third category covers situations in which a mental stimulus on the job causes a psychological illness. One example would be a person who suffers from depression and loss of self-esteem because of on-the-job stress and consequently is unable to perform his or her job.

The final category relates to a slightly different pattern of circumstances. The courts have maintained that individuals may obtain damage awards when they experience distress due to intentional or reckless acts of the employer that degrade or humiliate the employee. This principle may cover a wide range of possible actions, including sexual harassment.[82]

Employers should be aware of their potential liabilities for stress-related illnesses, as well as the loss in employee productivity that can occur when workers are overstressed for a long period. Hewlett-Packard is an excellent example of an organization that puts considerable effort into *de-stressing* the workplace. In a 1999 article, Joanne Cole wrote:

> Hewlett-Packard takes its leisure goals seriously, requiring employees to meet personal goals as defined. If they fall short, supervisors are held accountable. Here's how it works: At monthly meetings, team members are asked to list three business goals and three personal ones. When a staff member achieves a milestone, such as leaving at 2 p.m. to take a daughter roller-blading, co-workers are encouraged to applaud with the same enthusiasm they would applaud someone landing a sales order.[83]

Hewlett-Packard also encourages its management to reduce employee stress by making sure they take the stress out of their own jobs. Managers are asked to examine the quantitative workload of their employees and redistribute work where needed. Managers also engage in open and regular communication with employees about job stress. As part of an overall approach, HP employees are encouraged to take minivacations, for example, going to an aerobics class at 3:00 P.M. as a means of reducing stress on the job.[84] Some companies have recognized that something as simple as encouraging employees to eat lunch away from their desks can help reduce job stress. One way to do this is for companies to provide a desirable place for employees to have lunch. Highland Cellular's 100 employees are offered an indoor kitchen with microwave, stove, sink, and dining area, as well as an outdoor dining area with benches and a gazebo.[85] Conscientious employers try to keep workplace stressors such as overwork, harassment, conflict, and bad supervision at bay. An increasing number of employers use more formal programs to mitigate employee stress and health problems in the form of employee assistance plans and employee wellness programs.

EMPLOYEE ASSISTANCE PROGRAMS

Concern for workplace health and safety is critical in creating a productive work environment. There is more to an employee's life, however, than the job. Organizations are beginning to realize that the quality of employees' nonwork lives can have a dramatic effect on their job performance. Problems outside the organization can interfere with a worker's concentration, endurance, and motivation.

Many employers offer **employee assistance programs (EAPs)** in an attempt to improve performance and retention by helping employees solve personal problems.[86] In 1980, about 12 percent of American workers had access to EAPs. In 1991, this figure exceeded 36 percent, while in 1998 over 50 percent of workers were covered by EAPs.[87] More than three-fourths of all *Fortune* 500 companies have EAPs. One major oil company, for example, offers counseling and referral for stress, marital and family problems, drug and alcohol dependence, and similar difficulties. Their EAP coordinator pointed out that EAP usage increased as a declining economy and threat of retrenchment magnified other problems employees were experiencing in the early 1990s.[88] Nationwide, usage of EAP counseling services jumped sharply just after the September 11 terrorist atacks. The types of counseling offered in EAPS in 2000 is shown in Figure 14.6. Generally, larger firms are more likely to offer a complete range of counseling services through their EAP.

● **FIGURE 14.6**

Employee Assistance Programs: Percentage of Employers Offering Counseling in Specified Areas[a]

[a]Graph represents figures for exempt (administrative, professional, executive) employees only. Similar findings were noted for nonexempt office and plant employees.

Source: 1994 Survey of Employee Benefits, Business & Legal Reports, Inc. Reprinted by permission.

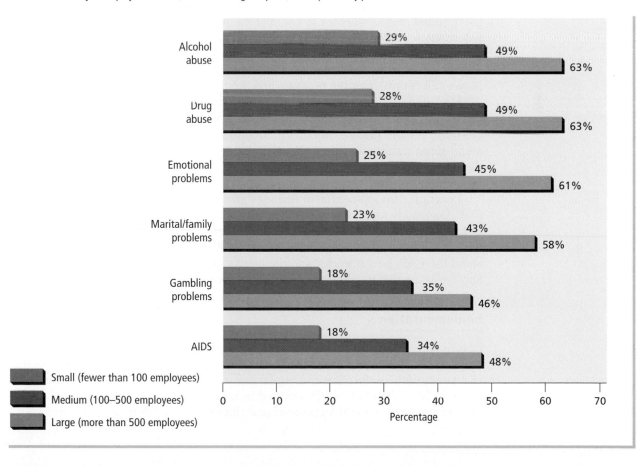

To set up an EAP, a company should follow a four-stage process of problem identification, program development, implementation, and evaluation.[89]

Problem Identification

The first stage in developing an EAP is to determine what problems are afflicting employees. Among the most common problems employees bring to EAPs are those involving marital and family relationships.[90] Substance abuse also ranks high on the list and generally costs more to treat. Interestingly, demographics and geography play a role in determining the type of EAP a company adopts. Companies near Atlantic City, New Jersey, home of many gambling casinos, tend to see problems related to such activities. The EAP for the Association of Flight Attendants, which represents 30,000 individuals from nineteen airlines, has an unusual number of people seeking help for weight loss.

Two important considerations at this stage are whether the problem is significantly affecting employee performance and whether enough employees suffer from the problem to make an EAP cost-effective. Even if productivity improvement is not a major motivation for the program, it is important to determine how widespread the problem is in the work force. A relatively isolated problem may be best handled by referring affected employees to private counseling, paid for through insurance.

Program Development

The second stage involves developing specific appropriate programs. The employer must decide whether to conduct the program on the premises or at an outside agency. An in-house program could be more expensive and might raise questions about confidentiality but would also offer some major advantages.[91] A workplace location illustrates management's commitment and also gives the employer full control over the program and the philosophy of treatment.

Management also must decide whether the counseling will be conducted during regular hours or after work. Employers prefer not to disrupt work, but employees may be more likely to attend the therapy if it is offered on company time. Decisions about publicizing the EAP must also be made. Emphasizing the success of the program and the personal benefits gained through participation will help to ensure employee commitment.[92]

Program development also includes communication to employees about the EAP. One study found that the willingness of employees to use an EAP was related to familiarity with the program, perceptions of its trustworthiness, and opportunities for personal attention.[93] For this reason, it is important that employees understand the EAP, how it works, and the benefits that might accrue. Confidentiality is another issue that must be addressed, as discussed in the Ethical Perspective box.

Implementation

The third stage is the delivery of the various programs. Most often it is the employer who initiates treatment. After realizing that an employee has a problem that is affecting job performance, a supervisor recommends the employee for treatment. (The problems typically covered in EAPs need much more than homespun advice; managers should let professionals handle the problem once it is detected.)

ETHICAL PERSPECTIVE

Confidentiality of Employee Medical and EAP Records

 Employers are increasingly involved in providing physical and mental health benefits to their employees. This occurs when employers are self-insured and thus handle medical claims and prescription reimbursements in-house or when they sponsor employee assistance programs that provide counseling for a variety of personal and work-related problems. While these services are valuable to employees, they result in the employer's having potential access to information that normally would be considered very private.

In some cases, this has caused an ethical dilemma for employers. For instance, medical or prescription records might suggest that an employee has a problem that could harm the organization, other employees, or the public—but at what point is it legitimate, or even mandatory, for the organization to act on this information? Bill Leonard raises two examples:

1. A heavy-equipment operator seems to have kicked a drug addiction with the continued use of prescription medication. One day the health plan administrator notices that the employee is no longer submitting reimbursement requests for this medication. Should he worry that the employee may be back on illegal drugs that could make him a danger to others? Whom should he notify of his suspicions?

2. A senior executive in charge of a very important project begins to submit reimbursement requests for an antidepressant drug. Does top management have a right to know that this individual may be suffering from psychological problems?

A more disturbing situation surrounds company access to EAP records. Troubled employees may have spoken freely to counselors about serious personal problems after being guaranteed confidentiality. Most EAP program administrators and counselors regard client records as strictly confidential, but organizations sometimes apply pressure to find out their content. In cases where employees later sue their employers (for discrimination, breach of contract, unlawful discharge, etc.) or even file for workers' compensation, EAP records can be subpoenaed as evidence by the company. There are reports of these records being used to virtually blackmail employees into dropping claims rather than risk public disclosure of personal peccadilloes.

Employers have a duty to protect their employees and the public and a duty to their shareholders to control costs and avoid payouts in frivolous or fraudulent lawsuits or workers' compensation claims. At what point do these duties come into conflict with employees' legitimate expectations of privacy when they use a company-sponsored employee assistance or medical plan?

Sources: Bill Leonard, "The Tough Decision to Use Confidential Information," *HRMagazine,* July 1993, pp. 72–75; and Ellen E. Schultz, "If You Use Firm's Counselors, Remember Your Secrets Could Be Used Against You," *Wall Street Journal,* May 26, 1994, p. C1.

Thus it is essential that supervisors be trained in how to recognize various problem symptoms and how to approach a troubled employee.[94] For example, Table 14.9 shows some of the symptoms that supervisors should notice as warnings of possible alcohol abuse by a subordinate.

Supervisors must also be careful in how they approach employees about participating in an EAP, given the *Houlihan* v. *Lucky Stores, Inc.* court decision.[95] The facts of this case were as follows. Lucky Stores management received numerous employee complaints about a store manager's abusive behavior. Company representatives met with the manager and offered assistance. The manager denied there were any problems. The company transferred him to another store. After

● **TABLE 14.9**

Workplace Symptoms of Alcohol Abuse

- Excessive absenteeism, especially on Mondays and Fridays
- Unexcused and frequent absences
- Tardiness and early departures
- Altercations with fellow employees
- Causing other employees injuries through negligence
- Poor judgment and bad decisions
- Unusual on-the-job accidents
- Deteriorating personal appearance

Source: Reprinted with permission from the June 1979 issue of *Personnel Administrator,* copyright 1979, The Society for Human Resource Management, Alexandria, Va.

fifty-one complaints at the new store, company representatives met with him and offered him the choice of suspension pending an investigation or a leave of absence if he contacted the company's EAP. Psychologists at the EAP found that the manager was experiencing stress-related problems, and a doctor diagnosed him as being mentally ill. After six months of leave, the company fired him. He sued under provisions of the Americans with Disabilities Act. A district court found that the manager was not disabled, since he had been working eighty hours per week as a real estate agent while on leave. The manager appealed the decision. The Ninth Circuit Court of Appeals found that Lucky Stores may have regarded the manager as having a disabling mental condition, as evidenced by a company representative asking him if he had any "problems" and encouraging him to seek counseling; the circuit court remanded the decision back to the district court. There was an out of court settlement.

One of the main implications of this case is that supervisors must be careful in how they approach employees whom they feel may benefit from the services of an EAP. For example, rather than saying "You seem to have a drinking problem," a supervisor should focus on specific job-related problems, saying, for example, "You've been late to work three times in two weeks, your performance is slipping, and I've smelled alcohol on your breath." Rather than saying "We'd like you to get therapy for your problems," a supervisor should suggest that "We'd like you to try the EAP for assistance with these concerns." [96]

Evaluation

The final stage in an EAP program is evaluation. One approach is simply to count the number of employees who make use of the program and ascertain their reactions to it. Additionally, a utility approach can be used to assess the dollar benefits realized (the gains from improved employee performance and tenure minus the costs of offering the program). One study proposed that EAP evaluation focus on five performance standards: effort, outcomes (for employees seeking EAP services), adequacy (relative to the need that the EAP is intended to serve), efficiency, and process.[97]

A simple utility approach was developed by the city of Phoenix to estimate the value of its EAP. Using this procedure, a company would first determine its average annual wage costs and then multiply this figure by the estimated percentage of troubled employees (17 percent at the time the utility study was done). Twenty-five percent of the resulting figure represents the company's losses due to employees' problems, if it is assumed that personal problems degrade performance by one-quarter. EAP intervention can be expected to recover 50 percent of those losses, reflecting the fact that 100 percent rehabilitation is not possible in all cases. To determine the net benefit of the program, its costs are subtracted from the estimated savings.[98] Using this method, the city of Phoenix calculated that it saved $2.5 million by adopting an EAP.

Other studies have shown similar results. McDonnell Douglas Corporation tracked 25,000 employees over a four-year period and showed that the company's EAP saved $4 in health claims and absence for every $1 spent. In another study, General Motors was able to attribute an annual saving of $37 million to its EAP, which provides services to 10,000 employees each year.[99] Of course, not all EAP benefits can be measured in dollar terms. Just knowing that the company provides the resources for employees to resolve problems, whether they be work-related or a family matter, is important to individuals.

EMPLOYEE FITNESS AND WELLNESS PROGRAMS

Fitness programs involve employees in some form of controlled exercise or recreation activities. Fitness programs range from subsidized membership in a local health club to company softball teams to very sophisticated company-owned facilities. As an example of the latter, Kimberly-Clark Corporation constructed its own $2.5 million fitness center and staffed it with fifteen full-time professional employees. By the mid-1980s, Xerox had seven facilities, one of which cost $3.5 million and included putting greens, soccer fields, a swimming pool, two gyms, tennis and racquetball courts, a weight room, and 2,300 acres of wooded land with running trails.[100] While these programs are impressive, employers should conduct a careful analysis of employee health problems and needs before deciding that fancy gyms and swimming pools are the solution. Wellness programs may represent more effective means of enhancing employee health.

Wellness programs promote employee health by providing education on health issues, encouraging lifestyle changes (weight loss, smoking cessation) designed to reduce the risk of illness, or providing early warning of developing health problems through screening for high blood pressure, high cholesterol, and the like. A 1997 survey of American companies found that 89 percent had some form of fitness or wellness program in place, compared with 64 percent in 1992.[101]

Benefits of Fitness and Wellness Programs

Organizations can benefit in several ways from sponsoring employee fitness and wellness programs. The more elaborate the programs, the greater the potential benefits. One of the basic gains is in employee morale. Employees view the activities as fun, and they feel better about themselves. The employees also may be healthier, and so insurance rates may decrease. There is some evidence that employee job satisfaction can increase. Besides enhancing group spirit and corporate identification, fitness programs can help the organization attract high-quality job applicants.

Employers may receive some direct benefits from having healthier employees. Absenteeism due to illness may decrease, for example, and employee productivity may increase. Finally, employee fitness programs have a positive effect on the corporate image and visibility in the community and the industry.[102]

A review of the evaluative studies of fitness programs concluded that the benefits in reduced absenteeism, injuries, and health care costs have been satisfactorily demonstrated.[103] At the same time, these benefits have been realized far more by white-collar than by blue-collar employees. Another study compared four experimental wellness program models over a three-year period. The four models were implemented at different but similar sites. The interventions and respective per-employee costs were (1) health education only ($17.68), (2) physical fitness only ($39.28), (3) health education and follow-up counseling ($30.96), and (4) health education, follow-up counseling, and plantwide organization to encourage and support employees ($38.57). Intervention 2, for physical fitness only, showed the lowest percentage of employees exercising regularly at the end of the three-year period. In contrast, interventions 3 and 4 used systematic outreach and follow-up counseling, and they were more cost-effective in terms of both engaging employees at risk and reducing their risks.[104] This is consistent with findings from another study that just offering fitness programs is not enough. Intervention must reach out by working to reduce the perceived work- and health-related barriers to participation.[105]

One author pointed out a potential drawback of fitness plans, one that may become visible in years to come. If employees live longer after retirement because of company-sponsored wellness and fitness programs during the working years, companies' pension liabilities may increase significantly.[106]

Summary of Key Points

There are three reasons why organizations try to create a safe and healthy work environment for their employees. The first reason is altruism; that is, the organization genuinely cares for its members. The second is the financial and nonfinancial benefits for the company: lower absenteeism and turnover, higher productivity, reduced insurance rates, improved employee morale, and enhanced appeal to job applicants. The third reason is compliance with federal, state, and local regulations. Violations of health and safety laws can mean large fines, bad publicity, and even jail sentences for top managers.

A century of social awareness preceded passage of the Occupational Safety and Health Act of 1970. This act covers all employers in the fifty states and several federal territories and jurisdictions. The Occupational Safety and Health Act of 1970 created three separate federal agencies for administering the law. The Occupational Safety and Health Administration (OSHA) is responsible for developing and enforcing regulations. OSHA enforces its regulations by inspecting workplaces and issuing citations for violations. The Occupational Safety and Health Review Commission (OSHRC) holds hearings on employers' appeals of citations and penalties. The third agency, the National Institute of Occupational Safety and Health (NIOSH), conducts research on workplace safety and health.

OSHA is the lead agency for formulating workplace safety and health regulations and enforcing those regulations on the job. OSHA conducts two types of safety inspections. Unprogrammed inspections are in response to accident reports and complaints. Programmed inspections are part of regular enforcement activities that target high-risk employers. OSHA also provides free assistance to employers and works with them in voluntary cooperative programs.

In meeting the health and safety needs of its employees, management may take either a minimalist or more proactive stance. Proactive approaches to safety and health require management to lead from the front, involve employees in program design and implementation, carefully analyze data related to safety and health problems, motivate workers to behave safely, and be innovative in its approach to workplace safety and health.

The Occupational Safety and Health Administration focuses on several aspects of workplace safety and health. Among the most prominent of these are on-the-job injuries, exposure to hazardous chemicals, injuries or death due to workplace violence, and a broad range of occupational diseases.

Most worksite accidents are caused by employee errors, but the organization remains responsible nevertheless. Employee factors that contribute to accidents include lack of experience, high stress, and poor judgment. Shift work, organizational size, and industry are organizational factors that have been found to be related to accidents.

Hazardous substances represent a special category of agents that can inflict injuries on the job. OSHA has issued special standards to ensure that firms manage these substances carefully. These standards include procedures for inspecting workplaces and identifying the hazardous chemicals that are present. Standards also help protect workers from the effects of these substances through regulation of protective equipment and procedures for handling and disposing of the materials.

Workplace violence is an increasingly important issue in safety and health on the job. Violence against an employee can be perpetrated by a stranger, a customer or client, another employee, or a person who has some personal relationship to the employee. Workplace violence can also affect nonemployees, such as customers visiting a workplace. Workplace violence prevention programs are an important aspect of providing a safe work environment for many organizations.

Occupational diseases are health problems caused by long-term exposure to something at the worksite, such as chemicals that cause cancer or loud noises that may lead to hearing loss. Smoking in the workplace can affect both those who smoke and those who must breathe the tobacco smoke exhaled by others. Musculoskeletal disorders make up about one-third of all occupational injuries. Cumulative trauma disorder is the most commonly occuring type of occupational disease. This is an umbrella term for musculoskeletal problems such as tendonitis, carpal tunnel syndrome, and low-back problems caused by repeating the same series of motions again and again in a way that eventually stresses the body.

Employers also bear responsibility for a variety of other issues related to employees' health on the job. AIDS, fetal protection from occupational hazards, drug use on the job, and employee psychological health are among the issues that concern management in modern organizations. Some organizations offer employee assistance programs to help counsel workers with personal problems that affect job performance. Employee fitness and wellness programs are also aimed at improving employee well-being.

The Manager's Vocabulary

Bloodborne Pathogen Standards
cumulative trauma disorder (CTD)
employee assistance programs (EAPs)
environmental tobacco smoke (ETS)
ergonomics
Expedited Informal Settlement Agreement
fetal protection policy
fitness programs
general duty clause
hazard analysis
Hazard Communication Standard (HCS)
Materials Safety Data Sheets (MSDSs)
minimalist approach to safety and health
National Institute for Occupational Safety and
    Health (NIOSH)
no-risk environment
Occupational Safety and Health Act of 1970
Occupational Safety and Health Administration
    (OSHA)
Occupational Safety and Health Review Commission (OSHRC)
OSHA inspection
proactive approach to safety and health
programmed inspections
repetitive strain injury (RSI)

safety committee
significant-risk regulations
threat assessment team
unprogrammed inspections
violence by coworkers
violence by customers/clients
violence by personal relations
violence by strangers
Voluntary Protection Program (VPP)
wellness program
workplace violence prevention policy statement
workplace violence prevention programs (WVPPs)

Questions for Discussion

1. Why should organizations be concerned about health and safety in the workplace?
2. Broadly, what are the requirements of the Occupational Safety and Health Act of 1970?
3. What are the major activities of the Occupational Safety and Health Adminstration?
4. How does OSHA enforce workplace safety?
5. What roles must management play in developing effective safety and health programs in an organization?

6. What factors tend to cause on-the-job injuries?
7. Think of a job you have held, and list the specific aspects of that job and work setting that could contribute to injuries. What actions, if any, did the employer take to minimize the risk of accidents and injuries?
8. What factors contribute to an employee's risk of becoming a victim of workplace violence?
9. What are the main components of a workplace violence prevention program?
10. What advice would you give to a firm thinking about developing a "smoking in the workplace" policy?
11. What is a cumulative trauma disorder? How can the incidence of CTDs be reduced?
12. What are the bloodborne pathogens standards and to whom do they apply?
13. What is an EAP, why do some organizations have them, and what are the steps in developing such a program?
14. How might the Americans with Disabilities Act influence how supervisors treat employees with possible mental health problems?
15. Why do some organizations offer employee fitness and wellness programs? What features do these programs usually offer?

● Case 14.1
Refusing to Work in "Unsafe" Conditions

The Occupational Safety and Health Act states that employers have a specific duty to comply with safety regulations and standards promulgated under the act, as well as a "general duty" to provide a workplace free of recognized hazards that are likely to harm employees. The act further prohibits employers from discriminating against employees who exercise their rights under the law. Rights include notifying OSHA of unsafe conditions and talking with inspectors. An additional regulation issued by the secretary of labor states that an employee may refuse to perform a task that he or she reasonably believes would pose a serious threat to safety or life if he or she is unable to notify OSHA of the problem immediately. Of course, under the general duty clause, an employer should not ask any employee to perform a highly dangerous task. However, people may differ in their perceptions of

whether a task is dangerous, and employers do have a right to assign work and discipline employees for insubordination.

Discuss the following two situations. In each case, do you think the employee has the right to refuse the work, or is the employer justified in imposing discipline? Why?

Situation 1 Bambi Clark had been a secretary for Central States Manufacturing for six months. One morning she appeared at work in a very agitated state. She told her office manager, Diane Holmes, that she and her husband were trying to start a family and that she had just read in the *National Inquirer* that prolonged exposure to video-display terminals causes mutations and birth defects. Clark was quite upset, worried that she might already have conceived a monster. She flatly refused to turn on her computer and begin work. Holmes called the chief safety engineer, who assured Clark that the terminals did not give off harmful radiation. In his professional opinion, there was absolutely no danger to her or to her potential offspring in working with a video screen. Clark still refused to operate the computer or even to perform other duties in the office where other secretaries worked on computers. Holmes gave her one last chance to change her mind and then suspended her without pay for the rest of the day.

Situation 2 An overhead conveyor belt delivered materials throughout a manufacturing plant. A wire mesh screen had been installed just below the conveyor belt to catch items that rolled off the belt. The screen was about twenty feet above the floor. Every week employees would climb up and stand on the iron braces supporting the screen while removing items from the screen. It was sometimes necessary to step out onto the wire mesh itself to recover an object. Several employees had fallen partway through the screen when they stepped on it, and in June an employee had stepped on the old mesh and fallen to his death. The company recognized this safety hazard and was in the process of replacing the old mesh with stronger mesh. In the meantime, employees were told to step only on the iron braces, not on the mesh.

On July 9, two employees complained to the plant safety director about the screen and requested the phone number of the regional OSHA office so that they could report what they saw as a serious problem. The next night the same two employees were ordered to service an older section of the screen. They refused, stating that there seemed to be a very real probability of injury or death associated with working on the screen. The employees were suspended without pay and later received written reprimands for failing to obey orders.

Source: Abstracted from *Whirlpool Corporation* v. *Marshall*, Supreme Court of the United States, 445 U.S. 1 1980.

● Exercise 14.1
Restaurant Safety

Divide into groups of no more than four or five students per group. Each group should do the following:

1. Develop a list of the types of hazards and accidents that can happen to restaurant employees. Consider such causes as
   a. Overexertion in lifting, bending, or climbing
   b. Bumping into or against equipment
   c. Falling
   d. Exposure to harmful substances such as cleaning agents
   e. Slipping or tripping
   f. Burns
2. Visit a restaurant in the community. At each restaurant, the group should seek information about the extent of employee hazards and accidents and steps the restaurant takes to reduce incidents. How does each restaurant handle safety training, accident reports, and other aspects of maintaining a safe work environment?
3. Report to the class and compare results.

● Exercise 14.2
Safety and Health Programs

Divide into seven groups. Each group should investigate and report on one of the following programs in the college or university. Specifically, what is your college or university doing in each of the following areas?

1. *Smoking in the workplace:* Does your college or university have a formal policy? When was it developed? What problems or issues led to the development of the policy? Are there plans to review or alter the current policy? How do employees feel about the policy?

2. *Workplace injuries:* What does your college or university do to prevent workplace injuries? Is there a safety specialist? What is this individual's training? What responsibilities does this individual have? Who is reponsible for first aid in the event of an injury?

3. *AIDS in the workplace:* Does your college or university have a formal policy concerning employees or students with AIDS? When was the policy developed? What problems led to its development? How has it worked?

4. *Hazardous chemicals:* What hazardous chemicals are used in your college or university? Who is responsible for maintaining and distributing Materials Safety Data Sheets? Obtain several of these sheets and note their contents.

5. *Occupational disease:* Have there been instances of repetitive strain injuries among employees at your college or university? What has been done to reduce problems associated with repetitive strain? Have there been concerns with any other occupational diseases?

6. *Employee assistance programs:* Does your college or university have an EAP? What types of problems is it designed to address? Is the program offered on campus or given off-campus by community professionals (or some combination of the two)? How do employees know of the program? What is the level of participation? Has the effectiveness of the program been evaluated relative to its costs?

7. *Employee fitness programs:* Does your college or university have an employee fitness program? What level of commitment by the institution is involved? What is the level of participation?

● Exercise 14.3
Preventing Violence on the Job

Option 1:

1. Divide into groups of four or five.
2. Each group is to visit a different site on campus where staff or faculty work.
3. Identify aspects of those worksites that either reduce or increase the likelihood that employees may become victims of violence.
4. Among the issues that will be of relevance in their analysis are:

   • Does the physical design of the facilities ensure safe and secure conditions for employees; for example, are they designed so that employees can communicate with other staff in emergency situations via clear partitions, video cameras, speakers or alarms, and so forth, as appropriate to the workplace situation?

   • Are work areas designed and furniture arranged to prevent entrapment of the employees and/or minimize potential for assault incidents?

   • Is access to employee work areas controlled through the use of locked doors, buzzers, card access, and the like?

   • Is adequate lighting provided for all indoor and outdoor facilities?

   • What electronic or other security systems are used?

   • Is there evidence that these systems are properly maintained?

   • Are there written policies evident that instruct employees how to deal with emergency situations?

- In talking with employees, is it clear that they have been trained to be aware of, avoid, and take actions to take to prevent mugging, robbery, rape, and other assaults?

Option 2:

Do this same analysis but in cooperation with local businesses with which you have contacts.

● Exercise 14.4
Safety on the Web

1. Rumor has it that the job of elephant keeper has the highest rate of occupational fatalities. However, there are so few elephant keepers that national statistics are not kept on the job as a separate entity. Find out which occupations and which industries are the most dangerous in terms of (1) the number of accidents and (2) the number of fatalities per year. Hint: Data are available at OSHA sites, Bureau of Labor Statistics sites, and National Safety Council sites.

2. Your small company is about to develop its first written safety policy. Locate some safety policies from other companies and assess their likely usefulness for your organization.

3. Your firm is thinking about joining OSHA's Voluntary Protection Program. Find out about the requirements and procedures for membership.

Notes and References

1. National Safety Council, *Injury Facts™* (5th ed.), 1999. (Available at: http://www.nsc.org); and Department of Labor, Bureau of Labor Statistics, "Census of Fatal Occupational Injuries," August 4, 1999. (Available at: http://stats.bls.gov/oshhome.htm)

2. "OSHA Success Stories," http://www.osha.gov/oshinfo/success.html.

3. Based in part on D. S. Thelan, D. Ledgerwood, and C. F. Walters, "Health and Safety in the Workplace: A New Challenge for Business Schools," *Personnel Administrator,* October 1985, pp. 37–46.

4. Jonathan Tusini, "A Death at Work Can Put the Boss in Jail," *Business Week,* March 2, 1987, pp. 37–38; and "Company, Supervisor Assessed Criminal Fines," *Occupational Hazards,* Vol. 53, August 1991, p. 9.

5. James Ledvinka and Vida Gulbinas Scarpello, *Federal Regulation of Personnel and Human Resource Management* (Boston: PWS-Kent, 1991).

6. Occupational Safety and Health Act of 1970, Public Law 91–596, 91st Congress, S.2193, December 29, 1970.

7. U.S. Department of Labor, Occupational Safety and Health Administration, "All About OSHA," OSHA Document No. 2056, (Washington, D.C.: U.S. Department of Labor, 2000, rev.), p. 6.

8. U.S. Department of Labor, Occupational Safety and Health Administration, "All About OSHA."

9. Occupational Safety and Health Act of 1970, Public Law 91–596, 91st Congress, S.2193, December 29, 1970.

10. "The New OSHA: Reinventing Worker Safety and Health." (Available at: http://www.osha.gov.oshinfo/reinvent/)

11. "The Cost of Safety," *Wall Street Journal,* July 10, 1980, p. 18.

12. *Industrial Union Department, AFL-CIO* v. *American Petroleum Institute,* 448 U.S. 607 (1980); *American Textile Institute* v. *Donovan,* 452 U.S. 490 (1981); and Ledvinka and Scarpello, *Federal Regulations.*

13. *Marshall* v. *Barlow's, Inc.,* 436 U.S. 307 (1978).

14. William Atkinson, "When OSHA Comes Knocking," *HRMagazine,* Vol. 44 (10), 1999, pp. 35–38.

15. Ibid.

16. Ibid.; and Robert Grossman, "Handling Inspections: Tips from Insiders," *HRMagazine,* Vol. 44 (10), 1999, pp. 41–45.

17. U.S. Department of Labor, Occupational Safety and Health Administration, "All About OSHA."

18. Grossman, "Handling Inspections."

19. William Atkinson, "Welcome OSHA as a Partner," *HRMagazine,* Vol. 44 (10), 1999, pp. 47–50.

20. U.S. Department of Labor, Occupational Safety and Health Administration, "All About OSHA."

21. Occupational Safety and Health Administration, "Ergonomics: Special Assistance for Small Business." (Available at: http://www.osha-slc.gov/sltc/ergonomics; last revision, November 20, 1999); and Peter Richardson and James Larsen, "Repetitive Strain Injuries in the Information Age Workplace," *Human Resource Management,* Vol. 36 (4), 1997, pp. 377–384.

22. For a complete discussion of company safety committees, see G. R. Carnehan, "Using Safety Committees Effectively," *Personnel Administrator,* Vol. 19, 1974, pp. 46–49.

23. Michelle Martinez, "Using Data to Create Wellness Programs That Work," *HRMagazine,* Vol. 44 (2), 1999, pp. 106–113.

24. William Atkinson, "Safety—At a Price," *HRMagazine,* Vol. 44 (11), 1999, pp. 52–59. .

25. Ibid.

26. Ibid.

27. Sharon Nelton, "Planning That Saves Lives," *Nation's Business,* May 1986, pp. 41–42.

28. Albert Opdyke and Jan Thayer, "The Work Environment: A Social and Technical Response to Injury and Illness Losses," *Personnel Journal,* February 1987, pp. 37–42.

29. Robert F. Scherer, James D. Brodzinski, and Elaine A. Crable, "The Human Factor,"*HRMagazine,* Vol. 38 (4), 1993, p. 93.

30. "Rotating Shift Work Causes Many Problems," *Occupational Health and Safety,* September 1978, p. 21.

31. OSHA Directives CPL 2-2.38D—Inspection Procedures for the Hazard Communication Standard, 29 CFR. (Available at: http://www.osha-slc.gov/OshDoc/Directive_data/CPL_2-2_38D.html)

32. J. M. Patterson, "VPP Companies' Best Practices," *Occupational Health and Safety,* January 1997, pp. 60–61.

33. Gregory Moffatt, "Subjective Fear: Preventing Workplace Homicide," *HR Focus,* Vol. 75 (8), 1998, pp. 11–12.

34. National Institute for Occupational Safety and Health, "Violence in the Workplace: Risk Factors and Prevention Strategies." (Available at: http://www.cdc.gov/niosh/violrisk.htm)

35. Greg Warchol, *Workplace Violence, 1992–96: National Crime Victimization Survey.* (Report No. NCJ-168634) (Washington, D.C.: Department of Justice/Bureau of Justice Statistics, 1998).

36. Long Island Coalition for Workplace Violence Awareness and Prevention, *Workplace Violence Awareness & Prevention: An Information and Instructional Package for Use by Employers and Employees* (New York: U.S. Department of Labor–OSHA, 1996).

37. National Institute for Occupational Safety and Health, "Violence in the Workplace."

38. Moffatt, "Subjective Fear."

39. Ronet Bachman, *National Crime Victimization Survey: Violence and Theft in the Workplace* (Washington, D.C.: Bureau of Justice Statistics, U. S. Department of Justice, 1994).

40. Long Island Coalition for Workplace Violence Awareness and Prevention, *Workplace Violence Awareness & Prevention.*

41. Ibid.

42. National Institute for Occupational Safety and Health, "Violence in the Workplace."

43. Long Island Coalition for Workplace Violence Awareness and Prevention, *Workplace Violence Awareness & Prevention.*

44. Ibid.

45. Dominic Bencivenga, "Dealing with the Dark Side," *HRMagazine,* Vol. 44 (1), 1999, pp. 50–58.

46. *Palmer* v. *Circuit Court of Cook County, Ilinois,* U.S. 7th Circuit Court of Appeals, No. 95-3659.

47. N. A. Ashford, "The Nature and Dimension of Occupational Health and Safety Problems," *Personnel Administrator,* August 1977, p. 45.

48. R. Lewy, "The Healthy Workplace," in *The Columbia University College of Physicians & Surgeons Complete Home Medical Guide,* 3d ed., (New York: Crown Publishers, 1997).

49. H. M. Sandler, "The Challenge of Low-Level Workplace Exposures," *Occupational Hazards,* January 1997, pp. 83–85.

50. Statement of Charles N. Jeffress, assistant secretary for occupational safety and health, U.S. Department of Labor, before the Senate Committe on Labor and Human Resources, February 24, 1998. (Available at: http://www.osha-slc.gov/OshDoc/ Testimony_data/T19980224.html)

51. Jeffrey S. Harris, "Clearing the Air," *HRMagazine,* Vol. 38, February 1993, pp. 72–79; and Robert D. Ramsey, "It's Time to Settle the Smoking Issue Once and for All," *Supervision,* November 1994, pp. 14–16, 23.

52. Lin Grensing-Pophal, "Smokin' in the Workplace," *HRMagazine,* Vol. 44 (5), 1999, pp. 58–66.

53. Statement of Charles N. Jeffress, assistant secretary for occupational safety and health, U.S. Department of Labor, before the Senate Committee on Labor and Human Resources.

54. Grensing-Pophal, "Smokin' in the Workplace."

55. Bureau of National Affairs, *Employment Guide* (Washington, D.C.: Author, 1991).

56. Grensing-Pophal, "Smokin' in the Workplace."

57. Ibid.

58. Ibid.

59. Department of Labor, Occupational Safety and Health Administration, "Ergonomics—Introduction," 29 CFR Part 1910 [Docket No. S-777] RIN No. 1218-AB36, Federal Register #: 64:65768-66078. (Available at: http://www.osha-slc.gov/ FedReg_osha_data/FED19991123.html)

60. Department of Labor, Bureau of Labor Statistics. "Lost-Worktime Injuries and Illnesses: Characteristics and Resulting Time Away from Work," USDL 00-115, 1998. (Available at: http://stats.bls.gov/oshhome.htm)

61. Kathryn Tyler, "Sit Up Straight," *HRMagazine*, Vol. 43 (10), 1998, pp. 122–128.

62. Sara Kiesler and Tom Finholt, "The Mystery of RSI," *American Psychologist,* Vol. 43, December 1988, pp. 1004–1015; P. Harber, L. Pena, G. Bland, and J. Beck, "Upper Extremity Symptoms in Supermarket Workers," *American Journal of Industrial Medicine,* Vol. 22, 1992, pp. 873–884; and E. F. Pascarelli and J. J. Kella, "Soft-Tissue Injuries Related to Use of the Computer Keyboard," *Journal of Occupational Medicine,* Vol. 35, 1993, pp. 522–532.

63. P. A. Nathan and R. C. Keniston, "Carpal Tunnel Syndrome and Its Relation to General Physical Condition," *Hand Clinics,* Vol. 9, 1993, pp. 253–261.

64. Mallory and Bradford, "An Invisible Workplace Hazard," *Business Week,* January 30, 1989, No. 3089, pp. 92–93.

65. Peter A. Stori, "Getting a Grasp on Carpal Tunnel Syndrome," *Risk Management,* Vol. 37, March 1990, pp. 40–48; Larry Reynolds, "OSHA Asks Can You Repeat That?" *Personnel,* Vol. 68 (2), February 1991, p. 19; and Michelle Neely Martinez and Joe Lamoglia, "Hands-On Answers to Hidden Health Costs," *HRMagazine,* March 1992, pp. 48–53.

66. N. C. Tompkins, "Office Ergonomics: Focusing on the Problem," *Occupational Health and Safety,* May 1996, pp. 93–97.

67. Department of Labor, Occupational Safety and Health Administration, "Ergonomics Program," (29 CFR 1910. 900, November 14, 2000).

68. G. LaBar, "Can Ergonomics Cure 'Human Error'?" *Occupational Hazards,* April 1996, pp. 48–51.

69. Tyler, "Sit Up Straight."

70. Richardson and Larsen, "Repetitive Strain Injuries in the Information Age Workplace."

71. Cited in Tyler, "Sit Up Straight."

72. Ibid.

73. Linda C. Kramer, "Legal and Ethical Issues Affecting Conduct Toward AIDS Sufferers," *Occupational Health and Safety,* Vol. 59, January 1990, pp. 49–50, 57.

74. U.S. Department of Labor, Occupational Safety and Health Administration, "Bloodborne Pathogens Final Standards: Summary of Key Provisions," OSHA Fact Sheet No. OSHA 92-46. (Available at: http://www.osha-slc.gov/OshDoc/Fact_data/ FSNO92-46.html)

75. "Justices Bar 'Fetal Protection' Policies," *Wall Street Journal,* March 21, 1991, pp. B1, B8; and *United Automobile Workers* v. *Johnson Controls, Inc.,* U.S. Sup.Ct., No. 89–1215 (1991).

76. Stephanie Overman, "Splitting Hairs," *HRMagazine,* Vol. 44 (8), 1999, pp. 42–48.

77. Janet Deming, "Drug-Free Workplace Is Good Business," *HRMagazine,* Vol. 35, April 1990, pp. 61–62.

78. Overman, "Splitting Hairs."

79. M. S. Novit, "Mental Distress: Possible Implications for the Future," *Personnel Administrator,* August 1982, pp. 47–53.

80. B. Berkeley Rice, "Can Companies Kill?" *Psychology Today,* June 1981, pp. 78–85.

81. "The Cost of Safety."

82. For a complete discussion of sexual harassment on the job, see R. H. Faley, "Sexual Harassment: A Critical Review of Legal Cases with General Principles and Practice Measures," *Personnel Psychology,* December 1982, pp. 583–600.

83. Joanne Cole, "Destressing the Workplace: Hewlett-Packard Pushes the Envelope," *HR Focus,* Vol. 76 (10), 1999, p. 10.

84. Ibid.

85. Susan McCulloch, "Take the Bite Out of the Lunch Crunch," *HRMagazine,* Vol. 43 (8), 1998, pp. 55–62.

86. Robert W. Hollman, "Beyond Contemporary Employee Assistance Programs," *Personnel Administrator,* September 1981, pp. 37–41.

87. Stuart Feldman, "Today's EAPs Make the Grade," *Personnel,* Vol. 68, February 1991, p. 3.

88. Jim Spangler, "Assistance Available for Those Under Stress," *Amoco Torch,* June 29, 1992, pp. 1–2.

89. Andrew J. Brennan, "Worksite Health Promotion Can Be Cost-Effective," *Personnel Administrator,* April 1983, pp. 39–42.

90. Feldman, "Today's EAPs Make the Grade."

91. Art Durity, "Can You Keep a Secret?" *Personnel,* Vol. 68, February 1991, p. 1.

92. William G. Wagner, "Assisting Employees with Personal Problems," *Personnel Administrator,* November 1982, pp. 59–64.

93. Michael M. Harris and Mary L. Fennell, "Perceptions of an Employee Assistance Program and Employees' Willingness to Participate," *Journal of Applied Behavioral Science,* Vol. 24, 1988, pp. 423–438.

94. Jane Easter Bahls, "Handle with Care," *HRMagazine,* Vol. 44 (3), 1999, pp. 60–66.

95. *Houlihan* v. *Lucky Stores Inc* (CA 9, 95-55409, 1996).

96. Bahls, "Handle with Care."

97. Ronald W. Perry and N. Joseph Cayer, "Evaluating Employee Assistance Programs: Concerns and Strategies for Public Employees," *Public Personnel Management,* Vol. 21, Fall 1992, pp. 323–333.

98. Mary F. Davis, "Worksite Health Promotion," *Personnel Administrator,* December 1984, pp. 45–50.

99. Feldman, "Today's EAPs Make the Grade."

100. Jack N. Kondrasuk, "Corporate Physical Fitness Programs: The Role of the Personnel Department," *Personnel Administrator,* December 1984, pp. 75–80.

101. "An Apple a Day," *HR Focus,* October 1997, p. 7.

102. Russell W. Driver and R. A. Ratcliff, "Employers' Perceptions of Benefits Accrued from Physical Fitness Programs," *Personnel Administrator,* August 1982, pp. 21–24.

103. Deborah L. Gebhardt and Carolyn E. Crump, "Employee Fitness and Wellness Programs in the Workplace," *American Psychologist,* Vol. 45, 1990, pp. 262–272.

104. John C. Erfurt, Andrea Foote, and Max A. Heirich, "The Cost-Effectiveness of Worksite Wellness Programs for Hypertension Control, Weight Loss, Smoking Cessation, and Exercise," *Personnel Psychology,* Vol. 45, 1992, pp. 5–27.

105. David A. Harrison and Laurie Z. Liska, "Promoting Regular Exercise in Organizational Fitness Programs: Health-Related Differences in Motivational Building Blocks," *Personnel Psychology,* Vol. 47, 1994, pp. 47–71.

106. M. T. Matteson and J. M. Ivancevich, "Health Promotion at Work," in *International Review of Industrial and Organizational Psychology,* ed. C. L. Cooper and I. R. Robertson (New York: Wiley, 1988), pp. 279–306.

Labor Relations and Collective Bargaining

HR Challenge

You are the HR director of Southern Poultry, a large nonunion poultry producer in the southeastern United States. Your company operates six major growout complexes, each with its own processing plant, feed mill, and array of contract growers. Altogether Southern Poultry directly employs more than 15,000 workers and indirectly employs another 6,000 to 8,000 grower-contractors. The vast majority of the workers are in the processing plants. Currently they are paid at or above average wages and they have a small health benefits package.

Just as happens every few years, you are facing union organizing campaigns at two of your processing plants. This year, however, the plants in question seem more vulnerable than in the past to a pro-union vote. A combination of relentless competition and economic recession has brought major changes in work force composition. While wages remain at or above area averages, they haven't grown substantially in recent years. Under the best circumstances poultry processing is hard work and the plants have had difficulty attracting workers. A decade ago, nearly all of the workers were drawn from communities surrounding the plant. Today, 60 percent of the workers have migrated to the area from communities in Mexico and Guatemala. So many workers have arrived from Central America that, in a few locations, the company opened mobile-home parks to provide housing. While overtly hostile acts have been rare, there is clearly an underlying tension in the relationship between native and immigrant workers. It is not entirely clear, but it appears to you that the union has at least some support among both groups.

Your CEO would like you to put together a report on the unionization challenge. He really wants you to let him know what can be done to keep the union out. But there are some unresolved issues in your mind. What will be your campaign strategy? What is in the best long-term interest of the company? What are the issues that made employees feel a need to unionize? Could their needs have been addressed without resorting to a union? Is it too late? What are the ethical issues at stake? Will race and ethnicity be a factor in the campaign? Can you use it to your advantage? Should you? Why are your CEO and other senior managers so adamantly opposed to the union?

COLLECTIVE BARGAINING AND LABOR RELATIONS IN CONTEXT

This chapter begins with an overview of the labor relations context in the United States. This includes some history of unionization and a discussion of the legal system that protects certain union activities in the private and public sectors. In addition, there is a discussion of the increasingly global context of labor–management relations. From there, the chapter goes on to describe consecutive phases of the **labor relations process.** These include the process of forming a union, collective bargaining after the union has been formed, and the various dispute-resolution processes used when agreement cannot be reached.

Employees have the right to form organizations for the purpose of seeking to influence their working conditions, wages, hours, and benefits. These employee-created organizations, called unions, seek to manage their working environment primarily through a process called **collective bargaining.** When unions are not present, employers usually set employment terms and conditions unilaterally (i.e., without consulting employees), within constraints imposed by market conditions and the Fair Labor Standards Act. Collective bargaining allows employees to participate in setting terms and conditions of employment through their unions. Although this process puts additional constraints on employers, it also creates a more participative system of employee involvement.

Historical Context

Developments that have affected organized labor are closely related to changes in the political, social, and economic environments. Organized labor has in turn affected the development of society at large and is responsible for securing many of the workplace protections and privileges that Americans now enjoy.

The first unions, formed in the 1700s, were primarily craft guilds in occupations such as shoemaking and carpentry. Their goal was to control the price of the skilled labor they provided by limiting apprenticeships, demanding uniform rates, and controlling output.[1] Later, in the 1850s and 1860s, the Industrial Revolution saw the rise of new unions in industries such as railroads and printing. The **American Federation of Labor (AFL)** was organized in 1886 by the leaders of a group of craft unions. **Craft unions,** sometimes called trade unions, are those that organize workers on the basis of skill, trade, or occupation. Examples of early craft unions were the cigar makers, printers, and carpenters. The AFL emphasized collective bargaining about bread-and-butter issues as a means of improving working conditions for skilled workers.[2] The AFL set the stage for contemporary unionism.

The continued expansion of mass production created entirely new industries that employed large numbers of workers in large industrial facilities. The AFL found it difficult to organize the skilled workers in these facilities and was opposed to organizing the masses because doing so violated the principles of craft unionism. The **Congress of Industrial Organizations (CIO)** was formed in 1935 to fill this void. **Industrial unions** organize on the basis of industry, regardless of skill. The CIO sought to create one major union for each major industry and to include all workers, from the most highly skilled to the unskilled. Within a couple of years the CIO helped create the United Auto Workers, the United Steel Workers, and several other major unions.[3]

Unions grew dramatically alongside the economic expansion associated with World War II and its aftermath. Membership swelled to 35 percent of the labor force in 1946 and remained at roughly that level through 1955. Unions helped establish the basic contours of the American social compact. A forty-hour week became the norm, child labor was abolished, employers became liable for work-related accidents and injuries, minimum wages were enacted into law, and workers were insured against the risk of lost income because of unemployment or old age. More subtly, through contract negotiations, unions created pensions, health insurance, and grievance and grievance-arbitration procedures, as well as establishing the principle that wages should move as a function of (1) inflation (to keep purchasing power whole) and (2) productivity (a gain-sharing program). In combination, these and other factors helped the United States create the largest, wealthiest middle-class the world has ever known.

The American labor movement was united under the leadership umbrella of the **AFL-CIO** (http://www.aflcio.org*)* when the AFL and the CIO merged in 1955.[4] Unions were at the height of their strength in the American economy, with one-third of the nation's nonagricultural work force belonging to them. As a percentage of the labor force, union membership began declining slowly but steadily thereafter. In 1965, only 28.4 percent of the nonagricultural work force belonged to unions (see Figure 15.1). In absolute numbers, union membership continued to grow, reaching a peak in the late 1970s at around 24 million members. But absolute membership declined through the 1980s and 1990s, accelerating the decline in membership as a proportion of the work force. By 2000, only 13.5 percent of the nonagricultural work force was unionized. However, a reasonable share of the work force belong to professional associations that are developing some similarities to unions (see the A Different Point of View box).

In contrast to the private sector, which has experienced a half-century of declining unionization, the public sector experienced a dramatic surge in the 1960s and 1970s. By the 1980s, public-sector unionization had grown to 35 to 40 percent

● **FIGURE 15.1**

Union Membership as a Percentage of the Nonagricultural Labor Force,
1940–2000.

Sources: Data points 1980 and earlier compiled from Bureau of Labor Statistics, *Handbook of Labor Statistics,* 1980, Table 165. Data points for 1985 and later compiled from Bureau of Labor Statistics, *Employment and Earnings,* January 1986, 1991, 1996, and 2001.

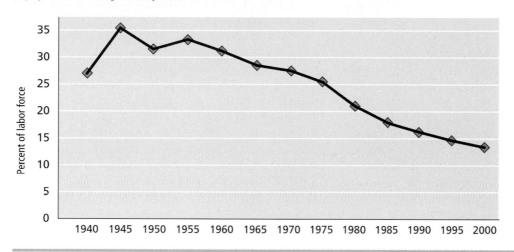

and has remained in that range ever since.[5] (See Table 15.1.) The National Education Association, the American Federation of State, County, and Municipal Employees, and the American Federation of Teachers represent some of the largest and most powerful employee organizations in the country.

Union membership rates vary significantly across industries (see Table 15.1). Membership is relatively high in the transportation, communications, and public utilities industries, as well as in the public sector. It is quite low in the services, finance, insurance, and real estate industries. Although unions now constitute less than 15 percent of the nonagricultural work force, their impact on workers remains quite powerful. Many wholly or partially nonunionized employers copy the practices of unionized firms with regard to wages and benefits, both to discourage the further unionization of their work forces and to continue to be able to attract top employees. Unions also have taught management important lessons about the value of employee participation, and many progressive companies have tried to adopt participative management environments. Furthermore, unions have made employers realize the importance of workplace justice, leading many employers to incorporate extensive employee grievance systems into their operations.[6]

The Legal Context

Union–management relations in the United States are highly regulated, with the federal government playing a very active part. This section considers the role of the federal government in regulating the labor–management relationship. Congress establishes the rules of conduct for unions and employers. The executive branch, through such agencies as the **National Labor Relations Board (NLRB)** (http://www.nlrb.gov/) and the Department of Labor (http://www.dol.gov/),

A DIFFERENT POINT OF VIEW

Professional Associations—Future Unions?

 Here's a surprise! Professional employees are now more heavily unionized than manufacturing employees. Actually, they have been for some years now. This is largely due to the heavy concentration of professional employees (including teachers, social workers, nurses, lawyers, engineers, university professors, and others) in the public sector.

But professional employees also have alternatives to unions. They have their professional associations. The number of labor unions in the United States is in the hundreds, but the number of professional associations runs into the thousands. There are associations for doctors, lawyers, engineers, accountants, therapists, social workers, scientists, teachers, nurses—just about every distinctive occupational group has its professional association.

The traditional distinction between unions and professional associations is that unions engage in collective bargaining while professional associations do not. That is, associations do not typically negotiate formal collective-bargaining agreements with employers. If professional associations do not bargain, what do they do? The range of services varies greatly but tends to center around principles of mutual aid and political action. Services may include legislative lobbying, establishing standards of practice and ethical codes of conduct, setting entrance and continuing education requirements, providing continuing education programs, offering low-cost group insurance, running job placement services, conducting salary surveys, and other functions.

Some associations, such as the American Medical Association and the American Bar Association, are extremely powerful, exerting a much more profound influence over the conditions of work than most unions are able to achieve. Most associations are not so influential, but their services are valuable enough to attract and maintain a substantial membership base.

Professional associations might play an important role in the future of unions and unionization in two ways. First, professional associations may become unions in the future. That is, they may transform themselves into bargaining organizations. There is ample precedent for this in the past. In fact, much of the tremendous growth in public-sector unionization is attributable more to the transformation of preexisting employee associations into unions than to the creation of entirely new public employee unions. The American Medical Association's recent endorsement of collective bargaining for physicians who work as employees of health maintenance organizations and the existence of several hybrid organizations—such as the National Education Association and the American Association of University Professors—that bargain in some locations and act as professional associations in others suggest that, under the right conditions, professional associations can readily embrace collective bargaining and, in effect, become unions.

Second, professional associations might be the future of unionism in the sense that their organizational form provides the model for unions of the future. Professor Charles Heckscher of MIT coined the term "associational unionism" to convey the idea that many of the most successful unions today are acting more and more like associations at the same time that numerous professional associations are acting more and more like unions.

Sources: Charles C. Heckscher, *The New Unionism: Employee Involvement in the Changing Corporation* (New York: Basic Books, 1989); and Sar A. Levitan and Frank Gallo, "Collective Bargaining and Private Sector Professionals," *Monthly Labor Review,* Vol. 112 (9), 1989, pp. 24–33.

● **TABLE 15.1**

Demographics of Union Membership

	Percentage of Work Force Unionized			
	1985	**1990**	**1995**	**2000**
Total work force	18.0	16.1	14.9	13.5
Industry				
manufacturing	24.8	20.6	17.6	14.8
mining	17.3	18.0	13.8	10.9
construction	22.3	21.0	17.7	18.3
transportation, communication,				
and utilities	37.0	30.5	27.0	24.0
trade	7.2	6.3	6.1	4.7
finance, insurance, and real estate	2.9	2.5	2.1	1.6
government	35.8	36.5	37.8	37.5
Other characteristics				
Race				
Black	24.3	21.1	19.9	17.1
Hispanic	18.9	14.8	13.0	11.4
White	17.3	15.5	14.2	13.0
Sex				
Female	13.2	12.6	12.3	11.5
Male	22.1	19.3	17.2	15.2

Source: U.S. Department of Labor, Bureau of Labor Statistics, *Employment and Earnings,* January issues, 1986, 1991, 1996, and 2001.

assure implementation of the rules. And the federal courts interpret the rules. Some states and municipalities have also enacted legislation affecting labor relations issues.

This highly regulated framework has not always been in place. For many years unions and union members had few or no legal rights and were actively persecuted by employers and the courts. This began to change about eighty years ago. (See Table 15.2 for a listing of major labor laws.) At present, the two main laws that regulate the relationships between unions and employers are the **Railway Labor Act** and the **National Labor Relations Act.** In turn, the National Labor Relations Act is comprised of two main laws, the **Wagner Act of 1935** and the **Taft-Hartley Act of 1947** (also known as the **Labor-Management Relations Act**). The Railway Labor Act regulates labor–management relations in the railroad and airlines industries; the National Labor Relations Act regulates labor–management relations in the rest of the private sector. While there are important differences between the Railway Labor Act and the National Labor Relations Act, they are similar in their basic features. Both laws recognize worker rights to organize into unions, to bargain collectively with employers, and, under appropriate circumstances, to strike.

The Railway Labor Act came about first, in 1926. The railroads comprised a large industry themselves, but they were also critically important to the rest of industry. There was also a long history of labor strife in the railroads, so it is no surprise that it was the first industry to be regulated. In 1935, the Wagner Act, the first major portion of the National Labor Relations Act, extended the principles of the Railway Labor Act to most of the rest of the private sector. Since the National

●**TABLE 15.2**

Major Labor Laws

1926	Railway Labor Act	Railway workers are permitted to organize and bargain collectively. Airline workers were added in 1934.
1935	National Labor Relations Act (Wagner Act)	Establishes rights to organize, to bargain collectively, and to engage in concerted activities; creates the National Labor Relations Board to implement and enforce the act.
1947	Labor Management Relations Act (Taft-Hartley Act)	Amends the NLRA. Adds union unfair labor practices (Section 8b). Weakens rights of workers and unions.
1962	Executive Order 10988	Encourages bargaining in federal sector. Followed by state laws encouraging bargaining by state and local government employees.
1970	Postal Re-organization Act	Places the U.S. Postal Service under the NLRA.
1974	Health Care Amendments	Places the private sector of the health care industry under the NLRA.
1978	Civil Service Reform Act	Establishes the current system for regulating labor–management relationships in the federal government.

Source: Thomas A. Kochan and Harry C. Katz, *Collective Bargaining and Industrial Relations* (Homewood, Ill.: Irwin, 1988), pp. 74–75. Reprinted by permission.

Labor Relations Act covers more of the economy, and since it is viewed as the bedrock of American labor policy, its provisions are summarized here.

The Wagner Act of 1935 reaffirms the principle that employees have the right to join, form, or assist unions free from the interference, restraint, or coercion of employers, to bargain collectively, and to engage in concerted activities in support of their aims (e.g., to strike). "It is hereby declared to be the policy of the United States," said Congress in Section 1 of the Wagner Act, to encourage unionization by "encouraging the practice and procedure of collective bargaining and by protecting the exercise by workers of full freedom of association, self-organization, and designation of representatives of their own choosing." But the Wagner Act went beyond a mere declaration of rights; it also created important implementation and enforcement mechanisms that were not included in the earlier laws. The Wagner Act was clearly a pro-employee and pro-union statute.[7]

In contrast to the Wagner Act, the Taft-Hartley Act of 1947 was clearly a pro-employer law intended to weaken many of the employee and union rights established by the Wagner Act. Early sections of the National Labor Relations Act sketch the broad contours of American labor policy; later sections specify the details of implementation and enforcement:

- Section 2 defines various terms, such as "employers" and "employees," and spells out who is covered under the law and who is not. Basically, the National

Labor Relations Act covers nearly all employees in the private sector. It does not cover very small firms that do not engage in interstate commerce; employees covered under the Railway Labor Act; public employees in federal, state, or local government; or agricultural workers. The Taft-Hartley Act excluded managerial and supervisory employees from coverage.

- Section 3 establishes the National Labor Relations Board (NLRB) to administer the act.

- Section 7 is the heart of the act, articulating employee rights. "Employees shall have the right to self-organization, to join, form or assist labor organizations, to bargain collectively through representatives of their own choosing, and to engage in other concerted activities for the purpose of collective bargaining or other mutual aid or protection."

- The new rights given to employees in Section 7 implied that there were certain management behaviors that could no longer be considered acceptable. Section 8 of the Wagner Act establishes a set of employer **unfair labor practices.** Taft-Hartley establishes a set of union unfair labor practices. Compare these lists of unfair labor practices in Table 15.3.

Most of the remaining sections of the act specify in detail the administrative processes of the National Labor Relations Board. The NLRB has two basic functions: an implementation function, whereby **questions concerning repre-**

● **TABLE 15.3**
Unfair Labor Practices

Management Unfair Labor Practices Wagner Act—Section 8a	Union Unfair Labor Practices Taft-Hartley Act—Section 8b
• Interfere with, restrain, or coerce employees in the exercise of their rights to organize, bargain collectively, or engage in other concerted activities for mutual aid or protection.	• Interfere with, restrain, or coerce employees in the exercise of their rights under the act.
• Dominate, interfere with, or contribute financial assistance to a labor organization.	• Cause or attempt to cause an employer to discriminate on the basis of union activities or sentiments.
• Discriminate against employees on the basis of their union activities or sentiments.	• Refuse to bargain (in good faith) with the employer.
• Discriminate or retaliate for filing charges or giving testimony under the act.	• Induce or encourage a work stoppage for the object of forcing an employer to stop doing business with another employer (secondary boycott) or forcing an employer to assign work to members of a particular union (jurisdictional strike).
• Refuse to bargain (in good faith) with the exclusive representative of the employees.	• Charging excessive dues or discriminatory initiation fees.
	• Cause or attempt to cause an employer to pay for work not performed or not to be performed (featherbedding).
	• Engaging in organizational or recognition picketing.

Source: Adapted with permission from *Primer of Labor Relations,* 24th ed., by John J. Kenny and Linda G. Kahn, p. 1–3. Copyright 1989 by The Bureau of National Affairs, Inc. Washington, D.C.

sentation are resolved, and an enforcement function, whereby unfair labor practice charges are adjudicated. Questions concerning representation are most commonly settled by holding secret-ballot elections. These are discussed more fully in the portion of the chapter devoted to union organizing. Adjudication of unfair labor practices involves a process for receiving and investigating complaints. It also involves, when necessary, attempting conciliation, holding formal hearings, issuing rulings, determining remedies for wrongdoing, and handling appeals.

In contrast to the private sector, public employees were exempted from the National Labor Relations Act and did not participate in the growth of unionization following its passage. Labor–management relations in the public sector remained largely unregulated, though strikes were strictly prohibited, into the 1960s. Beginning in the 1960s and continuing through the 1970s, many states, along with the federal government, passed laws creating a statutory framework for regulating labor–management relations between governments and their employees. Forty states have enacted laws regulating at least some aspect of labor–management relations in state and local governments.[8] Many of these state laws contain union certification provisions modeled after the National Labor Relations Act whereby a union that wins an election majority is certified as the exclusive bargaining representative, which, in turn, triggers the employer's duty to bargain with the union. Twenty-one states now permit strikes by some public employees, but no state permits strikes by its safety forces (e.g., police and firefighters). In an effort to balance a policy encouraging collective bargaining against a desire to avoid disruption of public services by strikes, states have experimented with and developed an elaborate array of advanced dispute-resolution techniques combining mediation, fact finding, and various forms of interest arbitration.

In the federal government, a series of executive orders issued by Presidents Kennedy, Nixon, and Ford expanded the rights of federal employees to organize and bargain. These rights and others were codified into law in the Civil Service Reform Act of 1978 that created the **Federal Labor Relations Authority (FLRA)** (http://www.flra.gov), which is responsible for overseeing certification elections and investigating charges of unfair labor practices. Federal employees now have the right to unionize and bargain collectively, but the scope of issues over which bargaining occurs is dramatically narrower in the federal sector. Most significantly, collective bargaining does not occur over wages and most benefits, as these are set by Congress. Strikes by federal employees remain illegal, and negotiation impasses are resolved with the aid of the **Federal Mediation and Conciliation Service,** by arbitration, or by the Federal Services Impasse Panel.

Global Context: Labor Relations Around the World

As national economies merge with the global economy, multinational enterprises and their workers are increasingly participating in operations around the world in countries and regions that may have very different labor policies and practices from their own. Reconciling labor policy and practice of the home country with that of the host country is not always easy. The labor problems a multinational enterprise will have to address may be very different depending on whether it is doing business in an advanced economy or a developing economy.

There are a number of important contrasts between the United States and other advanced economic democracies. The first, and most dramatic, contrast is in level of unionization. As Table 15.4 indicates, the United States is, and has been, among the most lightly unionized of the advanced economies. American firms operating in Europe or Japan are more likely to deal with unions there than here. European and Japanese firms operating on American soil are pleasantly surprised to learn that remaining union-free is an option. Even if the American firm is able to avoid direct dealing with unions in Europe and Japan, the unions have other ways to exert their influence. For example, bargaining tends to be more centralized, often on an industry-by-industry basis. Firms are expected and sometimes required by law to adopt the industry bargain. Unions are often more deeply involved in politics than they are in the United States. As a result, protective legislation is far more prevalent in many of the advanced economies than it is in the United States. For example, the United States is the only advanced economy that still recognizes employment-at-will (see Chapter 16) and the only one without universal health insurance. Finally, there are a greater variety of employee representation schemes in many economically advanced nations. Two are worth mentioning—works councils and codetermination.

Works councils are mandated by law in most European countries. Each workplace has its own council of elected workers that participates in the shared

● **TABLE 15.4**

Union Membership as a Percentage of the Labor Force in Advanced Economies, 1950–1990.

	1950	1960	1970	1980	1990
Finland	29	39	62	82	71
Sweden	68	73	73	88	84
Norway	50	63	51	57	57
Denmark	52	63	64	86	88
Germany	35	38	38	41	33
Austria	62	66	64	59	58
Switzerland	39	36	30	33	31
Belgium	49	58	57	46	53
Netherlands	42	39	37	32	33
France	38	21	22	17	11
Italy	50	35	38	54	47
Ireland	46	54	53	57	42
UK	44	44	47	51	38
USA	28	26	27	22	16
Canada	33	35	35	31	36
Australia	59	58	50	49	41
New Zealand	44	44	39	48	40
Japan	56	32	35	31	25

Source: James C. Docherty, *Historical Dictionary of Organized Labor* (London: Scarecrow Press, 1996), p. 264. Reprinted by permission.

governance of the workplace. These councils are often linked together by an elaborate network of corporate, industrial, or geographic councils. While the specific role and authority of councils varies from country to country, they generally participate with management in local governance of the workplace. They provide advice and consultation on a wide array of issues. On some issues, such as safety and health, they may have investigatory authority.

Codetermination is the European term for worker representation on the company's board of directors. Worker representation is required in some European countries (e.g., Germany). Even where it is not required by law, it tends to be more common than in the United States. Worker representation on the corporate board means that worker interests must be considered at the strategic level of the firm (e.g., which plant will be closed? where will the new plant be built?). In the United States, there is no comparable system of employee representation at the strategic level of the firm, though union representatives have sometimes been placed on the boards of financially distressed companies.

When corporations from economically advanced nations set up operations in other such nations, they typically have little difficulty adapting and conforming to the new legal and cultural norms. For example, when IBM, a staunchly nonunion American firm, operates in Germany, it readily adapts to dealing with industry-wide bargaining, works councils, and codetermination processes. On the other hand, when firms from other economically advanced nations operate in America, such as Honda in Ohio or BMW in South Carolina, they often adopt an anti-union posture that would not be considered acceptable in their home countries.

When corporations from economically advanced nations operate in less developed nations, however, they often find labor conditions and standards that are well below those of the economically advanced nations. Numerous scholars and policymakers have commented on the **global division of labor** that has developed in recent decades, whereby design, financing, and marketing are managed in economically advanced nations, but production and assembly are increasingly shifted to poorer economies where unskilled labor can be bought cheaply. Long hours for poverty-level wages, primitive health and safety precautions, prevalent use of child labor, even outright slavery—all occur in parts of the developing world. In these cultures unions are more likely to operate as part of a broader social reform movement, but in many countries they may be illegal or severely legally constrained. Some countries continue to persecute labor leaders through official political channels.

For many years, corporations from economically advanced nations operating in developing nations adopted one of two approaches for dealing with the local labor problem. First, those corporations that relied on skilled labor to produce and assemble complex products, such as automobiles or petroleum refineries, simply set up operations based largely on the American model. Plants were either owned by the home corporation or operated as joint ventures with prominent local firms. Because they relied on skilled labor, firms found it necessary to invest heavily in worker training and therefore found it beneficial to put in place practices that would reduce labor turnover. As a result, local-country employees of these firms, while poorly paid by American standards, often had higher standards of living and greater income security than many of their neighbors. The second approach, more commonly used by firms that rely on less skilled labor, was to subcontract production or assembly work to independent firms located in the host country. This has been a common arrangement in agricultural commodities, such as coffee and

Universal Human Rights in Employment

 Employment is more than a contractual relationship involving contractual rights. It is more than a legal relationship involving statutory and, perhaps, constitutional rights. Employment is a fundamental human relationship and, therefore, necessarily implicates fundamental human rights. But just what human rights are at stake in employment?

The International Labour Organization (ILO) has been struggling with this question since it was founded in 1919. The ILO came about as part of the Treaty of Versailles that brought World War I to a close and remains the only surviving agency of the ill-fated League of Nations. Today the ILO is part of the United Nations.

The ILO seeks to advance worker rights and conditions of work around the globe. Its aims and purposes are grounded in three core principles:

1. Labour is not a commodity.
2. Freedom of expression and of association are essential to sustained progress.
3. Poverty anywhere constitutes a danger to prosperity everywhere.

A major milestone in the movement for global human rights occurred just after World War II with the founding of the United Nations and the adoption of the Declaration of Universal Human Rights in 1948. The declaration was followed by other seminal United Nations human rights accords, including the International Covenant on Civil and Political Rights and the International Covenant on Economic, Social and Cultural Rights of 1966, and the 1989 Convention on the Rights of the Child. All of these documents recognize the concept of worker rights as a subset of human rights. Human rights are deemed acquired by virtue of one's humanity and ought not be dependent on, or comprised by, any act of government or anyone else. In turn, employment rights are those acquired by virtue of employment and ought to exist independently of employer whim, government effectiveness, or stage of political or economic development.

Within the UN framework for human rights, the ILO has adopted nearly 200 conventions addressing standards for employment rights. Over the years, eight of these conventions have come to be seen as fundamental. They are:

- Forced Labour Convention (#29)
- Freedom of Association and Protection of the Right to Organize (#87)
- Right to Organize and Collective Bargaining Convention (#98)
- Equal Remuneration Convention (#100)
- Abolition of Forced Labour Convention (#105)
- Discrimination (Employment and Occupation) Convention (#111)
- Minimum Age Convention (#138)
- Convention on Elimination of the Worst Forms of Child Labour (#182)

In turn, these eight conventions have come to be seen as embracing four fundamental human rights in employment. In 1998 the ILO adopted a Declaration on Fundamental Principles and Rights at Work that

> declares that all Members, even if they have not ratified the Conventions in question, have an obligation arising from the very fact of membership in the Organization to respect, to promote and to realize, in good faith and in accordance with the Constitution, the principles concerning the fundamental rights which are the subject of those Conventions, namely:
>
> a) freedom of association and the effective recognition of the right to collective bargaining;
> b) the elimination of all forms of forced or compulsory labour;
> c) the effective elimination of child labour; and
> d) the elimination of discrimination in respect of employment and occupation.

Ironically, the United States, which considers itself a bastion of human rights, has one of the worst records in the world in terms of ratification of the fundamental worker rights conventions. The United States has ratified only two of the eight. Only 3 of 175 member nations have ratified fewer. The United States has ratified only conventions 105 (on forced labour) and 182 (on elimination of worst forms of child labour—and this will require amending the Fair Labor Standards Act to bring it into compliance in agriculture).

sugar, and remains prevalent in many of the garment and needle trades, from clothing and footwear to carpeting and soccer balls. One factor in the prevalence of subcontracting for unskilled labor is that the disparities between home- and host-country labor standards and practices were just too great to be reconciled. The low-wage, low-skill sectors of developing nations often resembled throwbacks to a bygone era from which modern multinational corporations wished to distance themselves. By subcontracting production to host-country or even third-country firms, they could maintain the flow of goods without accepting responsibility for local labor conditions.

In recent years, it has become increasingly clear that multinational corporations can no longer divorce themselves from the labor conditions under which their products are made. Recall the International Perspective box from Chapter 3. When consumers are made aware that their favorite products are produced by forced labor, child labor, or otherwise under sweatshop conditions, they react in ways that can affect bottom-line considerations such as market share and stock prices. Companies including Nike, Reebok, Adidas, the Gap, Levi-Strauss, Disney, Philips-Van Heusen, Liz Claiborne, General Electric, Starbucks, Sears, Wal-Mart, and many others have been so embarrassed (and some of these have a strong reputation for better-than-average labor standards).

Under traditional subcontracting arrangements, there was little role for the human resource management function. But now that companies are realizing they must assume responsibility for the labor conditions of their contractors, human resource management comes back into the picture. Many firms are adopting codes of conduct and incorporating these codes into their contracts with Third World suppliers. The codes often require adherence to international employment rights standards as well as compliance with local laws. Some companies, but not all, have established monitoring programs to assure contractor compliance with the codes. And a few companies have incorporated social provisions, including employment rights concerns, into their auditing programs. (See the Ethical Perspective box.)

HOW UNIONS ARE FORMED: ORGANIZING

Why Employees Want Unions

A substantial body of theory and research has been devoted to discovering why employees join, form, and support unions. There have been sociological, political, economic, institutional, psychological, religious, and even sociobiological theories advanced as to why unions develop. An understanding of a number of these perspectives is helpful if one is to comprehend the many complex reasons behind the impulse toward unionism.

Unions have been viewed by a number of theorists as part of a larger process of economic and political activity. Karl Marx saw the formation of unions as the first step in the political struggle of the working class. To Marx, the formation of unions was an inevitable function of the disparity between capital and labor.[9] The union as agent of social change was not confined to Marxist theorists; many other theorists have indicated that unions are a critical contributor to social change leading to a social order with a fairer distribution of material goods and opportunity. Preeminent among these theorists were Sidney and Beatrice Webb, who coined the term "collective bargaining." The Webbs believed that unions presented the first real opportunity for working people to participate meaningfully in the operation and direction of industry. They referred to this participation as "industrial democracy," in that through the election and representation of the union, the employee had a representative voice.[10]

The possibility that unionization is influenced by psychological and even sociobiological processes is an idea of more recent origin. Some theorists see unions as conservative groups gathered together to ensure that, in a world of change, their jobs and lifestyle will remain intact.[11] Others go even further, believing that the tendency to collectivize in the face of threat (e.g., job loss, change affecting one's work, loss of income level) is an innate human characteristic.[12] Both the psychological and the sociobiological views of union formation have in common the notion that employees respond to threat and uncertainty by finding others of similar feelings and forming a collective response.

In contrast, economic models of union formation emphasize a weighing of the anticipated costs of unionization against the benefits. In this rational calculus, employees evaluate the likelihood of material gains in pay, benefits, and job security, but also less tangible potential gains including voice, control, respect, and health and safety. Employees must weigh not only how much they expect to benefit from the presence of a union but also what a union may cost them. Some costs are economic. Unions collect dues from their members to cover the costs of representation. A typical union member's dues might amount to the equivalent of two hours' pay per month.[13] Other perceived economic costs might include the potential loss of income because of a strike. Noneconomic costs might include concern about how the employer will react to the presence of a union. Employees may fear retaliation against individual union supporters, or a general deterioration in conditions at the workplace, or even the possibility that the workplace might close as a result of the union's coming in.

The NLRB and the Organizing Process

The amended National Labor Relations Act establishes procedures by which employees may organize. The procedures dictate the process through which a union may be formally recognized as the **exclusive bargaining representative** of the employees for the purpose of collective bargaining. While the process is conceptually simple—do a majority of the employees want a union?—it has become highly legalistic and is usually hotly contested. Figure 15.2 provides a simple overview of the process.

The process starts when either a union representative contacts a potential target group of employees or the employees themselves contact the union and inquire about the possibility of organizing their workplace. At this point the union has to analyze the target plant, assess the possibility of success in organizing the workers, and, if it decides to proceed, start the initial advances to reach the employees. Usually an **organizing committee** is formed among the workers early in the process.

At some point, **authorization cards** are distributed and employees are asked to sign them if they support the formation of a union. Under NLRB rules, at least 30 percent of the employees in a proposed bargaining unit must sign the cards for the board to proceed. However, most union organizers insist on having signatures

● **FIGURE 15.2**

The Organizing Process

of at least 50 percent of the employees before petitioning the NLRB. They reason that, during the election campaign, employer opposition is likely to erode union support somewhat. Thus, if the union is not able to gain 50 percent of employee support, it may drop the organizing effort or start a new authorization card campaign later.

If support for the union during the authorization card campaign exceeds 50 percent, the union can approach management and request **voluntary recognition** as the exclusive bargaining agent. Since, if management grants such a request, it will be legally required to bargain in good faith over the terms and conditions of employment, voluntary recognition occurs only rarely. If management rebuffs the request, it triggers the NLRB election process that potentially leads to union **certification** as the exclusive representative.

The National Labor Relations Board must make several administrative determinations before it will hold a recognition election. When it receives a petition, its first step is to determine whether it has jurisdiction over the matter (i.e., whether the employees and employer are covered by the National Labor Relations Act). Second, the NLRB will investigate whether at least 30 percent of the employees in the unit have expressed interest in joining a specific union.

Perhaps the most difficult and important set of determinations involves the appropriateness of the proposed **bargaining unit.** The bargaining unit is made up of all employees who will be eligible to join the union and who will be covered by the union contract. The NLRB will first approach the parties (the union and employer) and seek an informal agreement on the proposed bargaining unit. If the parties cannot agree on the bargaining unit, then the NLRB will conduct a formal investigation and make the unit determination itself. In making unit determinations, the NLRB looks for a **community of interests** among employees with respect to wages, hours, skills, and working conditions. It may also consider history and traditions within the industry and the organization of the human resource management function within the firm.

Elections

Recognition elections are conducted by secret ballot by agents of the NLRB. The ballot will offer the voter at least two choices. One choice is always labeled "no representative." The other choice will be the name of the proposed union. In order to win, the union must obtain a majority of the valid votes cast. Sometimes there may be two or more unions listed on the ballot. In these cases, if no choice receives a majority on the first ballot, a runoff election is held between the two highest vote getters. Table 15.5 shows the percentage of union victories in certification elections.

The amended National Labor Relations Act also provides for the decertification of union representatives. Employees who are dissatisfied with their union may petition the NLRB to hold a **decertification election.** While decertification elections are held much less frequently than certification elections, unions tend to lose most of them. In 1996, for example, a total of 485 decertification elections were held, and unions lost in 69 percent of them.[14]

Employer and Union Conduct During Organizing Campaigns

As noted previously, it is considered an unfair labor practice for either unions or employers to violate Section 7 of the National Labor Relations Act, which gives employees the right to form unions and to engage in collective activities. In numerous decisions, the National Labor Relations Board and federal courts have interpreted the meaning of these provisions with respect to the behavior of the parties during an organizing campaign. In simple terms, the employer may not *threaten* or *intimidate* employees in an attempt to convince them to vote against the union. The employer may not *promise* benefits to employees if the union is defeated or

● **TABLE 15.5**

Results of Representation Elections, 1973–1995

Year	Total Elections	Union Victories	Percent Union Victories
1973	9,389	4,786	51.1%
1974	8,958	4,425	50.0%
1975	8,577	4,138	49.2%
1976	8,638	4,159	48.1%
1977	9,484	4,363	46.0%
1978	8,240	3,791	46.0%
1979	8,043	3,623	45.0%
1980	8,198	3,744	45.7%
1981	7,512	3,234	43.1%
1982	5,116	2,064	40.3%
1983	4,405	1,895	43.0%
1984	4,436	1,861	42.0%
1985	4,614	1,956	42.4%
1986	4,520	1,951	43.2%
1987	4,069	1,788	43.9%
1988	4,153	1,921	46.3%
1989	4,413	2,059	46.7%
1990	4,210	1,965	46.7%
1991	3,752	1,663	44.3%
1992	3,599	1,673	46.5%
1993	3,586	1,706	47.6%
1994	3,752	1,665	46.6%
1995	3,399	1,611	47.4%

Source: Adapted from the *Sixtieth Annual Report of the National Labor Relations Board for the Fiscal Year Ended September 30, 1995* (Washington, D.C.: U.S. Government Printing Office, 1996).

preemptively improve wages or conditions during an organizing campaign. Finally, an employer may not spy on employees at unionization meetings.

To what extent does someone arguing for unionization have the right to obtain access to employees to deliver that message? The answer depends on the employment status of the messenger. The Supreme Court has ruled that employers have the right to severely restrict nonemployees' access to employees. In other words, employers may bar nonemployees (such as professional union organizers) from their premises, provided two conditions are met. First, nonemployees must have reasonable access to the employees through some other means, such as print or electronic media or social functions away from the workplace. In addition, the employer must enforce a general ban on nonemployee solicitation of employees at the work site, a ban that is not selectively applied to unions. For instance, a company that permits nonemployees into the workplace to solicit for charities or political causes would have a hard time denying union organizers similar access to employees. Pro-union employees, however, have much more extensive rights to approach their peers at work. They may carry the union message to employees during nonworking periods in nonworking areas—for instance, during lunchtime in the cafeteria.

To what extent are employers free to express their views regarding unionization during the course of a campaign to unionize? Section 8(c) of the amended National Labor Relations Act establishes a general principle that "the expressing of views, argument, or opinion, or the dissemination thereof, whether in written, printed, graphic, or visual form, shall not constitute or be evidence of an unfair labor practice . . . if such expression contains no threat of reprisal or force or promise of benefit." Management may hold meetings and speak out against the union, as well as explain why they think employees do not need a union, so long as the meetings are held more than twenty-four hours prior to the election.[15] (See Table 15.6)

●TABLE 15.6

Issues in Pre-Election Campaigns

Management Issues	Percent of Campaigns	Union Issues	Percent of Campaigns
Improvements not dependent on unionization	85	Union will prevent unfairness, set up grievance procedure/seniority system	82
Wages good, equal to/better than under union contract	82	Union will improve unsatisfactory wages	79
Financial costs of union dues outweigh gains	79	Union strength will provide employees with voice in wages, working conditions	79
Union is outsider	79	Union, not outsider, bargains for what employees want	73
Get facts before deciding, employer will provide facts and accept employee decision	76	Union has obtained gains elsewhere	70
If union wins, strike may follow	70	Union will improve unsatisfactory sick leave/insurance	61
Loss of benefits may follow union win	67	Dues/initiation fees are reasonable	64
Strikers will lose wages, lose more than gain	67	Union will improve unsatisfactory vacations/holidays/pensions	61
Unions not concerned with employee welfare	67	Employer promises/good treatment may not be continued without union	61
Strike may lead to loss of jobs	64	Employees choose union leaders	55
Employer has treated employees fairly/well	60	Employer will seek to persuade/frighten employees to vote against union	55
Employees should be certain to vote	54	No strike without vote by members	55
		Union will improve unsatisfactory working conditions	52
		Employees have legal right to engage in union activity	52

Source: From *Labor Relations: Development, Structure and Process,* 6th ed., pp. 158, 160 by John A. Fossum. Copyright © 1995 by Richard D. Irwin, Inc., Burr Ridge, Ill. Reproduced with the permission of The McGraw-Hill Companies.

WHAT UNIONS DO WHEN THEY ARE FORMED: COLLECTIVE BARGAINING

The certification of a union as an exclusive bargaining representative simultaneously triggers the employees' right, and the employer's duty, to bargain collectively over "rates of pay, wages, hours of employment, or other conditions of employment." Employers and unions have a mutual obligation to bargain in **good faith** toward the settlement of a collective-bargaining contract. In the United States there are tens of thousands of agreements in place. With so many different employers and unions involved across the country, bargaining relationships are understandably highly varied. There are, however, some distinctive structures and types of bargaining that help to provide a frame of reference for understanding these diverse relationships. This section discusses the basic types of bargaining structures, the characteristics of the negotiation process, the types of bargaining that arise between and within parties, and the types of issues over which the parties typically negotiate.

Structure of Bargaining

The **bargaining structure** refers to the range of persons covered or affected by a current or planned collective-bargaining agreement. The formal structure consists of those employers and employees who are legally tied to the contract under negotiation. The informal structure includes those who may be materially affected by the negotiations. Often a settlement between two parties sets a pattern for subsequent settlements among many of the employers and unions in that industry.[16] For instance, **pattern bargaining** occurs in the automobile-manufacturing industry, where the United Auto Workers (UAW) typically focus on negotiating a settlement with one of the large domestic manufacturers, calling a strike against the target company if necessary. After a settlement is reached with the target company, the UAW expects and usually receives very similar agreements with the other large automakers. Historically, pattern bargaining has had the effect of taking such factors as wages out of the competitive matrix for employers in the same industry. Firms in an industry where all their competitors were unionized and under similar contracts did not have to consider the relative cost of labor in developing competitive strategies. With increasing globalization, pattern bargaining is now much less acceptable to U.S. firms because the "pattern" does not extend to primary competitors in Asia and Europe.

Another aspect of bargaining structure has to do with centralization within and among employers. A decentralized structure of bargaining is typified by a single-employer, single-plant arrangement, in which an employer negotiates with a union on a plant-by-plant basis. In a more centralized approach, an employer may negotiate on a multiplant basis, bargaining with the same union for employees in multiple plants. A higher level of centralization occurs when several employers combine to negotiate a common agreement with a union. This is **multiemployer bargaining.**

Multiemployer bargaining is often conducted in a geographically defined region or a single labor market. For instance, most of the builders in a metropolitan area might form an employer association to negotiate master agreements with the unions representing carpenters, electricians, plumbers, and bricklayers. However, some multiemployer bargaining covers an entire industry. For example, a number of interstate trucking companies have formed an association to negotiate the National Master Freight Agreement with the Teamsters Union. Often the major **economic issues** (such as wages and benefits) are decided in the organization-wide multiplant contract or industry-wide master contract. Further bargaining on **noneconomic issues** (such as work rules) is conducted at the plant level.

Contract Negotiations

Before contract negotiations begin, both the union and management typically engage in considerable planning and research. Both sides assess the financial condition of the company and research patterns in competitor firms and among comparable workers. If there is an existing contract, it will be reviewed for areas where changes are needed. Both sides must select their bargaining teams and identify their chief negotiators. Finally, both sides need to develop a prioritized agenda of issues they intend to pursue. For the union, setting the bargaining agenda usually involves canvassing the membership in some way.

In the early stages of bargaining, important issues to be decided are the agenda and the ground rules for the remainder of the sessions. Decisions concerning these issues set the atmosphere for the bargaining process. For example, negotiating easy-to-resolve issues at the beginning of the session could create an atmosphere of trust and build good rapport between the parties, leading to a smoother resolution of difficult issues later on. Initial demands may have a strategic dimension. A seemingly unreasonable demand could provide future room for negotiation or serve as a tradeoff in return for concessions on other issues. After the initial demands are presented, more reasonable demands are expected to follow. Proposals and counterproposals are exchanged. Sometime thereafter, concessions are likely to follow. Concessions should be timed carefully. A hastily offered concession could convey a message of weakness or unpreparedness to the other side. More significant, however, is the possibility of having failed to consider all the ramifications of a concession. This mistake could have serious economic consequences for the conceding party. In this regard, costs estimates must be made on every proposal.

As negotiations approach their deadline, usually the expiration date of the existing contract, pressure builds. In addition to resolving the remaining substantive issues—and these are often the most difficult issues—the parties have several other important matters to address. What is the likelihood of reaching a settlement? Can a work stoppage be avoided? Is intervention by a third-party mediator needed? If a work stoppage appears likely, how will it be managed?

Types of Bargaining

Labor–management relations in the United States are commonly perceived as being highly adversarial in character. Press coverage of unions focuses attention on strikes, which, although rare, do represent an obvious manifestation of conflict. In practice, the negotiating parties can take a position anywhere along a broad spectrum of conflict to cooperation. Distributive bargaining and integrative bargaining differ with respect to the degree of conflict exhibited. A third type of bargaining is intraorganizational bargaining.[17]

Distributive bargaining, the most common type, has been defined as "the complex system of activities instrumental to the attainment of one party's goals when they are in basic conflict with those of another party."[18] This is zero-sum negotiation, in which one party's gain is the other party's loss. Wage issues typify distributive bargaining—every additional dollar paid to employees means a dollar less in profit for management.

Integrative bargaining, on the other hand, refers to activities "instrumental to the attainment of objectives which are not in fundamental conflict with those of the other party. Such objectives are said to define an area of common concern, a problem."[19] In this situation, one party's gain need not translate into another party's loss. Integrative bargaining can result in collaborative problem solving in which both parties come out ahead. Examples include gain-sharing programs or joint labor–management programs to improve the quality of work life, provide retraining for employees with obsolete skills, or improve plant safety.

Both the distributive and the integrative types of bargaining involve negotiations between two parties—labor and management. In contrast, **intraorganizational bargaining** is the process of resolving differences among members of the same party. Participants on each side have to make a number of decisions among themselves before and during bargaining. Union negotiators, for instance, must decide on their priorities and secure a ratification vote of a tentatively negotiated agreement from the rank and file. Hence they might have to "sell" the settlement to their own constituents.

Scope of Bargaining

The **scope of bargaining** is defined as the range of items over which the parties negotiate. Over time, the law has come to recognize three distinct categories of bargaining items—mandatory subjects, permissive subjects, and illegal subjects. These distinctions are not trivial, for they affect the rights of the parties in other areas, such as strikes. After examining these important legal distinctions, we will explore a more familiar dichotomy used to categorize the subject matter of collective bargaining. This is the distinction between economic and noneconomic issues.

Both parties have an obligation to negotiate over **mandatory subjects** in good faith if either party insists. This does not mean the parties are required to reach agreement; it only means they must try. **Permissive subjects** are matters over which the parties may negotiate if they both agree to, but neither is required to do so. Neither party may engage in a strike or lockout over a permissive issue or pursue a permissive issue to the point of impasse. Finally, neither party can legitimately bring **illegal subjects** to the bargaining table. Table 15.7 provides some examples to illustrate the distinctions among mandatory, permissive, and illegal subjects of bargaining.

Economic Issues

The economic matters commonly discussed in negotiations may be divided into two subgroups: wages and benefits. Several aspects of the wage system may be discussed. First, unions seek to raise the average wage level within the establishment in order to improve the standard of living among bargaining unit members. Unions typically raise pay by 10 to15 percent over comparable nonunion jobs (the raise is somewhat less in the public sector and highly competitive sectors). Unions also attempt to influence how pay is structured. Unions tend to prefer more egalitarian pay structures and equal pay for equal work. As a result, unionized firms tend toward flatter pay structures from top to bottom and smaller differentials be-

● TABLE 15.7

Subjects of Bargaining with Examples

Mandatory Subjects	Permissive Subjects	Illegal Subjects
Wages	Retiree benefits (changes in)	Featherbedding
Benefits	Product pricing and labeling	Discrimination in hiring
Incentive pay	Contract ratification procedures	Closed shop agreements
Overtime	Performance bonds	
Layoff and recall	Corporate investment policy	
Union security clause		
Management rights clause		
Grievance procedures		
Seniority rights		
Safety		

Source: Adapted from R. Allen and T. Keaveny, *Contemporary Labor Relations* © 1988 by Addison Wesley Publishing Company. Reprinted with permission of the publisher.

tween jobs.[20] Competition may emerge within the union between highly skilled craft workers who would prefer sharp skilled-based differentials and less-skilled workers who would prefer more egalitarian structures. Where there are pay differences among persons doing the same work, unions typically favor **seniority** as the basis rather than more subjective, management-controlled criteria, such as performance appraisal ratings.

If unions exert a substantial impact on wages, their impact on benefits is even greater. Union members receive 25 to 30 percent more in benefits than comparable nonunion workers.[21] The range of benefits negotiated in union contracts may include supplemental unemployment benefits, severance pay, death and disability insurance, legal aid, wellness programs, employee assistance programs, paid holidays, paid vacations, and sick days. Often where employer-provided benefits cannot be negotiated, the union provides the benefit itself. The union advantage is especially evident in two benefits of particular importance to many workers: health insurance and pensions.

Traditionally, two major concerns have exerted a profound influence on wage and benefits bargaining between labor and management: inflation and productivity. Many contracts specify a cost-of-living allowance, which provides for pay raises and benefit increases during the life of a contract, based on changes in some index of inflation. The basic purpose is to preserve whatever real wage gains the union secured in the original settlement. Second, unions have generally expected that their members would share in whatever productivity gains they produced. Productivity gain-sharing bonus plans were once popular, but once productivity gains became permanent, unions sought to incorporate them into the base pay. This combination of inflation and productivity as the basic factors governing wage movement dominated in the post–World War II era up to the mid-1970s.

Since then two additional factors have assumed the dominant role: ability to pay and comparability. Ability to pay refers to the financial condition of the firm and suggests that wages should be closely tied to profitability. Through the 1980s, many unions granted wage and benefit concessions as corporate profits were squeezed. While unions strive to get back the give-backs when better times return, concessions remain a common theme where companies can demonstrate a bona fide financial crisis. Comparability represents the ghost of pattern bargaining. No longer able to maintain strict industry patterns, both unions and management base their arguments on maintaining comparability with similarly situated others. For unions, this means maintaining a standard of living comparable to workers who have traditionally shared socioeconomic status. For companies, this means not being put at a cost disadvantage relative to competitors.

Noneconomic Issues

A number of issues may arise in the noneconomic area, including work rules, job security, quality of work life, management rights, and union security. The concept of *work rules* covers a great deal of ground, from crew size and the types of work that can (and cannot) be performed by members of various crafts to rest periods and dress codes. *Job security* refers to the protections from discharge or layoff afforded to employees. Unions typically attempt to negotiate just-cause provisions, which limit an employer's right to discharge or discipline employees to situations where there is *just cause* for such an action (e.g., incompetence, excessive absenteeism, or insubordination). Other provisions to enhance job security may specify that layoffs will be based on seniority and regulate the conditions under which more senior employees whose jobs are ending may "bump" (or displace) less senior employees out of their positions. Finally, unions usually negotiate a grievance procedure through which employees can protest managerial decisions involving contract administration. The *quality of work life* (QWL) area includes a host of issues ranging from occupational safety and health, job training or retraining, and educational opportunities to social and recreational facilities and child care.

A noneconomic issue that has become increasingly significant in recent decades concerns the ability of the firm to subcontract union work. *Subcontracting* refers to the employer's decision to reassign bargaining unit work to outside firms. Restraints on subcontracting are sought by the union as a means of protecting members' job security. Employers, on the other hand, prefer as few restrictions as possible on their ability to contract out bargaining unit jobs. Under current labor law, subcontracting is usually considered a mandatory subject of bargaining.[22] A duty to bargain over subcontracting arises when the managerial decision to subcontract is based on labor costs.[23]

In negotiating a contract, both parties are understandably mindful of their institutional position and needs. In this context, management typically seeks a **management rights clause,** which explicitly reserves to management certain decision-making prerogatives. For instance, this clause may give management alone the right to decide on the types of products to produce or services to deliver, to supervise employees, to control production processes, and to control the introduction of new technologies into the production process.[24] Table 15.8 shows two sample management rights clauses. The top one reserves to management all rights not specifically shared with the union in other provisions of the contract. The second clause enumerates the rights kept by management.

Unions also have an institutional status to protect. As recognized exclusive representatives, they have the obligation to negotiate for *all* members of the bargain-

●TABLE 15.8

Examples of Management Rights Clauses

> The Company retains the exclusive right to manage the business and direct the work force. In the exercise of its rights, the Company shall obey the provisions of this Agreement.
>
> The right to hire, promote, discipline or discharge for cause, transfer, and lay off due to lack of work remain the sole responsibility of the Company. The Company also has the exclusive right to control the products to be manufactured, the subcontracting of work, plant locations and plant closings, and the introduction of new technology.

ing unit, whether or not they have joined the union. Thus nonmembers who work in the bargaining unit will benefit from union representation as much as union members, even though they do not have to bear any costs, such as dues. To prevent employees in these units from "free-riding," unions negotiate **union security clauses** of various kinds. These arrangements ensure that nonunion members of bargaining units will assume at least part of the cost of union representation. The union shop and the agency shop are two common union security arrangements. The **union shop** requires nonmembers to join the union within a certain time period (such as sixty days after hire) as a condition of continued employment. The **agency shop** requires that nonmembers in represented bargaining units pay a representational fee (usually equal to the dues paid by members) as a condition of continued employment. Both union and agency shop provisions are legal under the amended National Labor Relations Act. However, the act allows states to pass "right-to-work" laws that disallow these union security arrangements. As of 2001, twenty-two states had enacted such laws. Table 15.9 lists the states that currently have right-to-work statutes in force.

●TABLE 15.9

Right-to-Work States

Alabama	Nevada
Arizona	North Carolina
Arkansas	North Dakota
Florida	Oklahoma
Georgia	South Carolina
Idaho	South Dakota
Iowa	Tennessee
Kansas	Texas
Louisiana	Utah
Mississippi	Virginia
Nebraska	Wyoming

Source: Adapted from *Labor Management Relations in a Changing World,* First ed., p. 69 by Michael Ballot. Copyright © 1992 by John Wiley & Sons, New York, N.Y. Reprinted by permission of John Wiley & Sons, Inc.

WHEN COLLECTIVE BARGAINING BREAKS DOWN: IMPASSE

Level of Strike Activity

Thousands of contract negotiations take place each year. Historically, most contract negotiations have resulted in a settlement without a strike. The estimate is that strikes occur in less than 2 or 3 percent of negotiations.[25] Strikes are more likely to occur in larger bargaining units.[26] Table 15.10 summarizes strike activity

● **TABLE 15.10**

Major Work Stoppages in the United States—1948–2000

Year	Number of Work Stoppages	Workers Involved (in thousands)	% of Work Time Lost
1948	245	1,435	.22
1950	424	1,698	.26
1952	470	2,746	.38
1954	265	1,075	.13
1956	287	1,370	.20
1958	332	1,587	.13
1960	222	896	.09
1962	211	793	.08
1964	246	1,183	.11
1966	321	1,300	.10
1968	392	1,855	.20
1970	381	2,468	.29
1972	250	975	.09
1974	424	1,796	.16
1976	231	1,519	.12
1978	219	1,006	.11
1980	187	795	.09
1982	96	656	.04
1984	62	376	.04
1986	69	533	.05
1988	40	118	.02
1990	44	185	.02
1992	35	364	.01
1994	45	322	.02
1996	37	273	.02
1998	34	387	.02
1999	17	73	.01
2000	39	394	.06

Source: U.S. Department of Labor, Bureau of Labor Statistics, *Monthly Labor Review,* various issues. A major work stoppage is one involving at least 1,000 workers and lasting for at least a full shift.

in the United States in the period 1948–2000. Several points can be made from an inspection of these data. The total percentage of work time lost to strikes has never been particularly large. In terms of lost work time, the economic impact of the common cold is far larger than that of strikes. Second, the level of strike activity declined sharply and persistently in the 1980s. Some of the decline is attributable to the decline in union strength, but a large part is associated with a particular management practice—**permanent replacement of strikers**—that became prominent after a particular watershed event: President Reagan's firing of the air traffic controllers in 1981 (see the Ethical Perspective box).

Before 1980, management attempted to continue operations during strikes through a variety of means. Managers and supervisors could often maintain some level of production, or production could be shifted to nonstruck facilities or temporarily contracted out. Some employers could stockpile prior to an anticipated strike and sell out of inventory. In some industries, employers created mutual-protection strike pacts with their competitors to insure each other against permanent economic loss caused by strikes. Finally, management could hire temporary replacements who would do the work as best they could during the strike but would be let go when the strike was over. While it was probably legal to hire permanent replacements, it was just not done.[27]

When the Professional Air Traffic Controllers Organization (PATCO) struck in 1981, The Federal Labor Relations Authority ordered the union decertified, and, much to PATCO's surprise, President Reagan fired all the striking controllers and permanently replaced them. Reagan's example emboldened private employers to confront strikes more aggressively. The use of permanent replacements has since become fairly common in U.S. labor relations,[28] and the threat of permanent replacements plays a more frequent role in negotiations. It is important to remember that because the air traffic controllers were federal employees, their strike was illegal. In contrast, most private-sector workers who have been permanently replaced were engaged in a perfectly legal strike.

Types of Strikes and Rights of Strikers

There are many different types of strikes, and the rights of strikers and employers depend on the type. Three types discussed here are the economic strike, the unfair labor practice strike, and the wildcat strike.

● **Economic Strikes**   If the parties have negotiated in good faith but fail to reach an agreement, any strike that follows is called an **economic strike**.[29] This is the most common type of strike, and it is fully protected by Section 7 of the NLRA. In theory, economic strikers cannot be fired for engaging in protected concerted activity, and discrimination against employees for supporting a strike would be illegal. But economic strikers can still lose their jobs if they are permanently replaced. They retain a right to return to their jobs after the strike only so long as the jobs still exist and the employer has not hired permanent replacements.[30]

● **Unfair Labor Practice Strikes**   As mentioned earlier, employers and unions have a duty to negotiate in good faith. Good faith may be breached by such actions as refusing to respond to a party's request to bargain, refusing to send bargaining representatives with sufficient authority to the negotiations, continually shifting bargaining positions in a clearly obstructionist manner, delaying and hampering

ETHICAL PERSPECTIVE

Permanent Replacement of Strikers

 There is no management action that evokes greater condemnation by unions today than permanent replacement of strikers. Section 7 of the NLRA grants workers a legal right to strike, "to engage in other concerted activities for the purpose of collective bargaining or other mutual aid or protection." Unions claim the permanent replacement doctrine nullifies that right. As Professor James Atleson points out:

> Section 8(a)(1) protects concerted activity such as strikes against "interferences," and Sections 7 and 13 make doubly clear the critical role of the strike in the congressional scheme. One can conceive of few interferences greater than permanent replacement for striking. The replaced striker has joined the ranks of the unemployed because of the exercise of the statutory right to strike and the situation may well serve to deter protected activity by other employees. . . . Moreover, when the employer favors a replacement over a striker seeking reinstatement at the end of a strike, the employer literally "discriminates" on the basis of the exercise of protected activity, a seemingly clear violation of Section 8(a)(3).

Workers may be justifiably confused over the fine legal distinction between having been fired and having been merely permanently replaced. In either case they have lost their jobs for engaging in a perfectly legal and protected strike. Under a threat of permanent replacement, striking can become the equivalent of committing mass occupational suicide. Therefore, strikes have become far less common since employers have begun to resort to the permanent replacement strategy. Some employers have become so emboldened as to deploy the "strike-decertification scenario," where the employer deliberately provokes a strike and then recruits a replacement work force that will vote the union out. In this way the employer is able to get rid of not only the strikers but also the union itself.

Can meaningful collective bargaining occur if workers are effectively barred from striking? What pressure can the union bring to bear to force management to take its concerns seriously? Trade unionists believe the permanent replacement doctrine not only nullifies the right to strike but is also inherently destructive of the bargaining process. The International Labour Organization agrees and has found that the permanent replacement doctrine violates ILO Convention #98 on collective bargaining.

But, while a key source of their power may have been nullified, unions are not taking the matter lying down. Changing the law to outlaw permanent replacements is one of organized labor's highest political priorities. But the unions are doing more than that. They are devising new strategies that enable them to put pressure on employers in ways that better protect worker jobs. Instead of the large, protracted, all-or-nothing strike, they may engage in intermittent strikes, rolling strikes, or demonstration and publicity strikes. These activities may be coordinated with campaigns directed at the consuming public, the corporation's board of directors, or other community organizations. Or the union might strike on the job. Instead of vacating the workplace and making it easier for the employer to bring in replacements, workers remain on the job (and continue collecting their pay) but put pressure on employers through slowdowns, work-to-rule campaigns, mass grievance filings, and any number of other creative and innovative tactics. Some of these tactics are controversial, and many are not considered protected concerted activities under the National Labor Relations Act, but unions often find them the only way to effectively pressure the employer while protecting worker jobs.

Sources: James B. Atleson, *Values and Assumptions in American Labor Law* (Amherst: University of Massachusetts Press, 1983); Lance Compa, *Unfair Advantage: Workers' Freedom of Association in the United States Under International Human Rights Standards* (Washington, D.C.: Human Rights Watch, 2000); Ken Gegala, *Union Organizing and Staying Organized* (Reston, Va.: Reston Publishing Company, 1983); and AFL-CIO, *The Inside Game: Winning with Workplace Strategies* (Washington, D.C.: Industrial Union Department, 1986).

negotiations, and refusing to make any counterproposals at all. If a strike is provoked or prolonged by an employer's unfair labor practice, such as the failure to bargain in good faith, the NLRA forbids the permanent replacement of strikers. Employers found guilty of causing an **unfair labor practice strike** have a legal obligation to reinstate the strikers, even if they have hired permanent replacements in the interim.[31]

● **Wildcat Strikes** Despite binding commitments to the contrary, some strikes occur in direct violation of a collective-bargaining agreement, usually without the official approval of union leaders. Contracts almost always contain no-strike clauses, through which the union pledges not to strike during the life of the contract but instead to use the grievance procedure to resolve any disagreements about the way the contract is applied. Employees who strike in defiance of such a clause are said to be on **wildcat strikes.** Generally, wildcat strikes lose the protection of Section 7 of the NLRA. Injunctions can be issued against the union, with damages or fines levied directly against union funds. In addition, striking employees may be discharged and have no right to return to their jobs. In practice, however, few employers find it feasible to terminate and replace their entire work force because of a wildcat strike.

Preventing Strikes

While strikes and lockouts have little impact on the economy as a whole, they can have a dramatic impact on the parties involved. Workers go without pay, and this affects them, their families, and the merchants and banks with whom they trade. Companies experience diminished revenues, which may adversely affect shareholders, other workers, and the company's trading partners. So, while strikes and lockouts may sometimes be necessary, considerable resources have been invested in developing **alternative dispute resolution (ADR)** procedures to reduce the likelihood of strikes.

Mediation is a widely used alternative dispute resolution procedure. It occurs when a neutral third party who has no binding authority assists union and management in reaching agreement. Mediators help by scheduling meetings, keeping the parties engaged in negotiations, carrying messages between the parties, and making suggestions. This task is often performed by federal mediators who are full-time employees of the Federal Mediation and Conciliation Service (http://www.fmcs.gov/). While mediation is credited with reducing the frequency of strikes, it cannot guarantee that disputes will be resolved because the mediator lacks binding authority.

Interest arbitration is an alternative dispute resolution procedure that can guarantee resolution of disputes and can therefore eliminate strikes altogether. Interest arbitrators are third-party neutrals authorized to make binding decisions to resolve interest disputes. Interest arbitration is rarely used in the private sector, but it is widely used in the public sector, where it is designed to compensate for the fact that public employees have no right to strike. Figure 15.3 traces the development of interest arbitration techniques.

The first forms of interest arbitration adopted in state laws were typically non-binding forms of arbitration, sometimes called advisory arbitration or fact finding. Nonbinding arbitration, like mediation, may have reduced the frequency of strikes, but it could not eliminate them altogether. To eliminate strikes, states

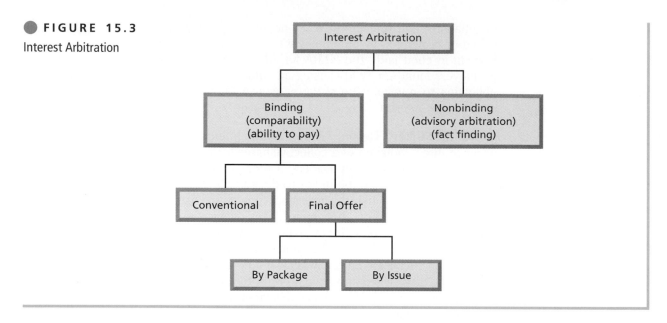

found they had to enact binding arbitration laws. To assure that arbitrators stayed within reasonable bounds, law required that arbitrators base their awards on factors such as ability to pay and comparability.

The first form of binding arbitration that was tried is called **conventional interest arbitration.** As with other forms of interest arbitration, the arbitrator is briefed on the positions of the parties, hears evidence from each side, and renders a decision. In conventional arbitration, the arbitrator is free to impose whatever settlement he or she deems reasonable. As a result, the tendency is to "split the difference" between the positions of the parties. Conventional interest arbitration solved the problem of strikes, but it had some unfortunate effects on the bargaining process. First, it produces a "chilling effect" on bargaining.[32] That is, parties introduce unrealistic initial offers and engage in surface bargaining until the arbitrator is called in to split the difference. It reduces the incentives to make meaningful concessions or engage in the give-and-take that is essential to real negotiations. Second, conventional interest arbitration produces a related "narcotic effect" whereby the parties become dependent on arbitration and unable to resolve conflicts on their own.[33]

To overcome some of the problems associated with conventional arbitration, more modern laws call for **final-offer arbitration.** In this approach, the arbitrator must choose between the final position of one party or the other. There is no opportunity to split the difference. This raises the risk to parties that fail to reach an agreement on their own. Final-offer arbitration forces labor and management to compete for the middle ground in negotiations. In other words, this approach encourages the parties to move toward reasonable final offers that will be attractive to the arbitrator; as a result, they may reach a settlement without resorting to arbitration at all.[34] Final-offer arbitration takes two forms. The first is final offer by issue, in which the arbitrator accepts one or the other final offer on each item remaining to be resolved. This form remains popular in many state laws. The second is final offer by package, in which the arbitrator accepts the final position of one party or the other on all issues submitted to arbitration. This is the state-of-the-art in arbitration techniques. It eliminates strikes but does so in a way that maximizes the incentives on the parties to resolve their own disputes in a mutually satisfactory way. Ironically, where final offer by package arbitration is required by law, it is seldom used.

National Emergency Dispute Procedures

The Taft-Hartley Act provides a set of procedures to help resolve strikes that constitute a national emergency because they threaten the health or safety of the general public. The act allows the president to seek an injunction to prohibit the strike for eighty days. During this so-called **cooling-off period,** the parties continue to bargain with the aid of the Federal Mediation and Conciliation Service. Meanwhile, fact finding and the force of public opinion are brought to bear on the parties. If no settlement is reached within the cooling-off period, the union is free to resume the strike. Since the late 1940s, these procedures have been invoked only forty times, most frequently in the coal mining, atomic energy, maritime, and long-shoring industries.[35]

WHEN THE MEANING OF THE CONTRACT IS IN DISPUTE: THE GRIEVANCE PROCEDURE

Administering the Contract

Once a collective-bargaining agreement is in place, it is a legally binding contract. In the normal course of events, there may be very little conflict in the day-to-day administration of the agreement. In fact, most union contracts are printed as shirt-pocket-sized booklets so that minor disputes over "what the contract says" can be resolved on the spot. However, over time, difficult disputes over the meaning of the contract are bound to arise. These are referred to as **rights disputes** (as distinct from interest disputes) because they involve legally enforceable rights under the contract. Although both parties have agreed to live by the provisions of the contract, there is always room for disagreement about how the agreement should be interpreted and applied in specific cases. An employee who believes that his or her rights under the contract have been violated may file a **grievance.** Virtually all contracts provide a grievance procedure for resolving disagreements about contract administration.[36] Since the overwhelming majority of grievance procedures culminate in arbitration, they are particularly important in maintaining workplace justice.

Steps in the Grievance Procedure

A typical grievance procedure clause is shown in Table 15.11. The procedure starts when an employee believes that he or she has been treated unfairly with respect to some right spelled out in the contract. For instance, the contract may specify that the "most senior qualified employee" be chosen for promotion. If someone else is promoted, the most senior employee may then file a grievance claiming that he or she was qualified and should have been selected. In the first

● **TABLE 15.11**

A Grievance Procedure Clause

Step 1	The employee and the department steward, if the employee desires, shall take the matter up with his [or her] foreman. If no settlement is reached in Step 1 within two working days, the grievance shall be reduced to writing on the form provided for that purpose.
Step 2	The written grievance shall be presented to the foreman or the general foreman and a copy sent to the personnel office. Within two working days after receipt of the grievance, the general foreman shall hold a meeting, unless mutually agreed otherwise, with the foreman, the employee, and the departmental steward and the chief steward.
Step 3	If no settlement is reached in Step 2, the written grievance shall be presented to the departmental superintendent, who shall hold a meeting within five working days of the original receipt of the grievance in Step 2 unless mutually agreed otherwise. Those in attendance shall normally be the departmental superintendent, the general foreman, the foreman, the employee, the chief steward, departmental steward, a member of the personnel department, the president of the UNION or his representative and the divisional committeeman.
Step 4	If no settlement is reached in Step 3, the UNION COMMITTEE and an international representative of the UNION shall meet with the MANAGEMENT COMMITTEE for the purpose of settling the matter.
Step 5	If no settlement is reached in Step 4, the matter shall be referred to an arbitrator. A representative of the UNION shall meet within five working days with a representative of the COMPANY for the purpose of selecting an arbitrator. If an arbitrator cannot be agreed upon within five working days after Step 4, a request for a list of arbitrators shall be sent to the Federal Mediation and Conciliation Service. Upon obtaining the list, an arbitrator shall be selected within five working days. Prior to arbitration, a representative of the UNION shall meet with a representative of the COMPANY to reduce to writing wherever possible the actual issue to be arbitrated. The decision of the arbitrator shall be final and binding on all parties. The salary, if any, of the arbitrator and any necessary expense incident to the arbitration shall be paid jointly by the COMPANY and the UNION.

Source: From *Labor Relations: Development, Structure and Process,* 6th ed., p. 430 by John A. Fossum. Copyright © 1995 by Richard D. Irwin. Reproduced with permission of The McGraw-Hill Companies.

step of a typical grievance procedure, the employee and/or his or her shop steward presents the complaint, usually orally, to the grievant's immediate superior. The superior must respond within a fixed time period, either agreeing that the employee has a valid point and suggesting a remedy or denying that the grievance has merit. If the answer received does not satisfy the grievant, the union puts the grievance in writing and appeals to the next level of management—perhaps to the foreman or a representative of the human resource management department. If the decision received at this level is not satisfactory, the grievance may be appealed yet again, to upper management. At this point, a representative from the national union may be present to help represent the grievant.

Grievance Arbitration

Most grievances are settled through the early steps, but when no mutually acceptable resolution is reached between the parties themselves, 96 percent of contracts specify binding **grievance arbitration** as the final step.[37] Nearly all contracts limit the arbitrator to interpreting the existing contract. The arbitrator is not allowed to change or amend the contract in any way but merely to clarify and apply its provisions.

Costing Grievances

Like most HR activities, grievance processing can be costed. It is a useful exercise to do so because costs that one is unaware of are unlikely to be effectively controlled. Costs incurred in processing a grievance include the time of the aggrieved employee, the union steward, the supervisor, foreman, local and then divisional or corporate HR staff, and ultimately lawyers and arbitrators if the grievance is not resolved at an earlier step. Table 15.12 is an example of likely grievance costs. Clearly, it is much more efficient to prevent a grievance or resolve it in the early stages than later on. An additional cost not accounted for in the example is sustained ill will during the weeks that a grievance remains unresolved. Both the affected employee and his or her workmates are likely to feel increasingly disenchanted with the organization if they believe that fair treatment is not forthcoming. These feelings may indirectly cause costly employee turnover, an increase in the filing of grievances, and an adversarial climate in future labor relations within the unit.

THE ROLE OF LABOR RELATIONS IN HUMAN RESOURCE MANAGEMENT

Clearly, there is a great deal to know about labor law and labor relations. While unions today have a smaller role in many organizations, every HR manager needs to be conversant with labor law and highly attuned to preventing employee discontent that could grow into active conflict with a union. NLRB and court decisions interpreting relevant acts frequently fine-tune the requirements of management. Unionized firms need someone with expertise in this area to guide their practices. In most organizations, the HR function provides labor relations expertise. Larger establishments will have industrial or labor relations specialists within the HR department, whereas in smaller firms the HR generalist may do most of the work.

When a union is present, HR and labor relations (LR) experts are responsible for educating management and supervisors on the details of the contract and how to comply with it. They also liaise with the union if changes in work procedures are envisioned, such as reengineering or implementing joint employee–management committees. Prior to contract negotiations, HR/LR experts will have a large role in helping to develop the bargaining position of the company. This may involve holding meetings with supervisors to discover problems of working under the present contract and suggestions for modifying work rules. It will also include research and meetings with top management to develop a position on pay and other expensive benefits. HR/LR experts are also often involved in face-to-face negotiations and in advising management on proposed settlements.

In firms without unions, the HR function of managing the relationship between managers and workers is often called **employee relations.** Firms in which only some of the employees are unionized may have both employee relations and labor relations functions for dealing with the two types of employees. When operating without a union, HR experts and all other managers need to be aware of the law so that they do not accidentally commit an unfair labor practice such as threatening or firing an employee who starts to discuss the possibility of unionizing. HR experts also need to ensure that wages are fairly administered and competitive with other employers. In all areas, employer practices should be scrupulously fair and

● **TABLE 15.12**

Costing a Grievance

What Happens?	Who Is Involved?	How Long? (hours)	Cost per Hour	Cost per Item	Cost per Step	Total Cost
1. Worker complains to foreman	Worker	.25	$ 25	$ 6.25		
	Foreman	.25	$ 32	$ 8.00	$ 14.25	$ 14.25
2. Worker complains to steward	Worker	.5	$ 25	$ 12.50		
	Steward	.5	$ 25	$ 12.50	$ 25.00	$ 39.25
3. Local union officer tells worker how to write up grievance	Worker	.5	$ 25	$ 12.50		
	Union officer	.5	$ 25	$ 12.50	$ 25.00	$ 64.25
4. Worker writes up grievance	Worker	.5	$ 25	$ 12.50	$ 12.50	
						$ 76.75
5. Union–plant meeting	Plant HR director	.75	$ 50	$ 37.50		
	Worker	.75	$ 25	$ 18.75		
	Local union president	.75	$ 29	$ 21.75	$ 78.00	$ 154.75
6. Division HR person travels to national union headquarters to meet with international union rep.	Division HR representative	16	$ 75	$1,200.00		
	Cost of trip			$ 500.00	$1,700.00	$1,854.75
7. Legal preparation for arbitration	Division HR representative	6	$ 70	$ 420.00		
	Plant HR director	4	$ 50	$ 200.00		
	Corporate staff lawyer	16	$ 90	$1,440.00		
	Labor lawyer	4	$200	$ 800.00	$2,860.00	$4,714.75
8. Arbitration	Division HR representative	4	$ 70	$ 280.00		
	Plant HR director	4	$ 50	$ 200.00		
	Corporate staff lawyer	4	$ 90	$ 360.00		
	Labor lawyer	4	$200	$ 800.00		
	Arbitration fee	$2,000	Half paid by company	$1,000.00		
	Arbitrator travel	$350		$ 175.00	$2,815.00	$7,529.75

Source: Adapted from Lyle M. Spencer, Jr., *Calculating Human Resource Costs and Benefits* (New York: Wiley-Interscience, 1986), pp. 144–146.

consistent and in line with written policies. Employees should have "voice mechanisms" to bring their complaints forward. These mechanisms should include a nonunion grievance procedure that can be modeled after the traditional union grievance procedure, with or without binding arbitration as the final step. Alternatively, a nonunion grievance procedure can use panels of peers (coworkers) to make recommendations to management on disposition of grievances, or it can use an HR ombudsman to respond to employee concerns. These voice mechanisms can be supplemented by a management open-door policy, regular employee question-and-answer sessions with management, employee surveys, and the like.

It has been said that organizations "get the union they deserve." This means that good, fair, conscientious human resource management can either prevent employees from feeling the need for a union to protect them or result in smooth and cooperative relations with an exisiting union because there are few issues on which employees feel mistreated. Employment practices seen as arbitrary, unfair, or exploitative are likely to lead to the formation of a more militant union.

Summary of Key Points

Unions have had a long and uneven history in the United States. Craft unions were formed first, and later workers began to organize by industry. Union membership as a percentage of the work force peaked in the late 1940s and has been declining since the late 1950s, despite a rise in unionization among public-sector employees.

In 1935, the Wagner Act opened the door to widespread unionization by establishing election procedures for unions to become certified bargaining agents for groups of employees, requiring management to bargain in good faith with a properly certified representative of its employees, and preventing discrimination against employees regarding their right to unionize. In 1947, the Taft-Hartley Act placed some limits on union behavior, shifting the balance of power back toward management. In the 1960s and 1970s, federal, state, and local governments began to extend limited collective-bargaining rights to public-sector employees.

Once a union has been certified as representing a group of employees, it can begin negotiations with management in an attempt to secure a contract. Bargaining can be conducted in several different structural arrangements. Mandatory bargaining issues include wages, hours, and conditions of employment. Permissive items may be discussed, but neither party may insist on them to the point of impasse, and illegal items may not be bargained over. If an impasse is reached, private-sector employees may choose to strike. Economic strikers have some

right to return to their jobs after a strike, whereas unfair labor practice strikers have unconditional rights and wildcat or illegal strikers have no rights to return to their jobs. As an alternative to strikes, mediation or various forms of arbitration may be used. To settle disagreements over contract administration during the life of a contract, the grievance system is used.

The Manager's Vocabulary

AFL-CIO
agency shop
alternative dispute resolution (ADR)
American Federation of Labor (AFL)
authorization card
bargaining structure
bargaining unit
certification
codetermination
collective bargaining
community of interests
Congress of Industrial Organizations (CIO)
conventional interest arbitration
cooling-off period
craft unions
decertification election
distributive bargaining
economic issues
economic strike

employee relations
exclusive bargaining representative
Federal Labor Relations Authority (FLRA)
Federal Mediation and Conciliation Service
final-offer arbitration
global division of labor
good faith
grievance
grievance arbitration
illegal subjects of bargaining
industrial union
integrative bargaining
interest arbitration
intraorganizational bargaining
Labor-Management Relations Act (Taft-Hartley Act) of 1947
labor relations process
management rights clause
mandatory subjects of bargaining
mediation
multiemployer bargaining
National Labor Relations Act (Wagner Act) of 1935
National Labor Relations Board (NLRB)
noneconomic issues
organizing committee
pattern bargaining
permanent replacement of strikers
permissive subjects of bargaining
question concerning representation
Railway Labor Act of 1926
rights dispute
scope of bargaining
seniority
Taft-Hartley Act of 1947
unfair labor practices
unfair labor practice strike
union security clauses
union shop
voluntary recognition
Wagner Act of 1935
wildcat strike
works council

Questions for Discussion

1. Why study unions and collective bargaining?
2. Compare and contrast craft unions and industrial unions.
3. How do multinational companies adapt to the different labor conditions they encounter in other parts of the world?
4. What are the major provisions of the Wagner Act? the Taft-Hartley Act?
5. What factors explain the high unionization rate among public-sector workers as compared with private-sector workers? What problems might be associated with a highly unionized public sector?
6. What factors explain the decline in unionization for the last half-century? Have unions outlived their usefulness to society? Will they die out? Should they?
7. What factors do individuals consider in choosing whether or not to support a union? What arguments does management commonly use in trying to persuade employees not to support a union?
8. Describe the certification process by which a union can become recognized as the sole bargaining agent for a group of employees. Does the process seem overly cumbersome to you? What can management do to discourage union activity?
9. What is a bargaining unit? Does the collective-bargaining contract apply to employees in the bargaining unit who have chosen not to join the union?
10. Scholars and practitioners continue to debate whether the Taft-Hartley Act restored a balance of power between labor and management that had been distorted by the Wagner Act, or whether it tilted the balance of power back in management's favor. Examine the list of union unfair labor practices created by Taft-Hartley and compare them to the employer unfair labor practices from the Wagner Act (Table 15.3). Which ones seem to reflect a balancing of power? Which ones seem designed to tilt the balance of power toward management?
11. How can procedural issues during negotiations be used strategically by the parties?
12. What is meant by the term "bargaining structure"? What might be the advantages and disadvantages to management of joining a multiemployer association for the purpose of negotiating a master agreement?
13. Compare and contrast distributive and integrative bargaining. Which of the two is preferred?

Even though preferred, why might it be difficult to achieve?

14. What is meant by the phrase "bargaining in good faith"?

15. Suppose the union wants a cost-of-living adjustment in the pensions being paid to current retirees. May the union press this issue to the point of impasse and then strike because of it? Why or why not?

16. Distinguish between three major classes of strikes. Describe what rights (if any) strikers have to return to their jobs after each type of strike.

17. What methods may be used to resolve a bargaining impasse short of a strike?

18. Explain how the grievance procedure is used to enforce a contract.

● **Case 15.1**
Contract Negotiations at Southerly's Stores

Southerly's Stores, a retail grocery chain, was unionized in most of its operations in Maryland and Virginia, but stores in the Carolinas and Georgia were union-free. Beginning in the 1980s, American grocery stores endured a substantial shift in the structure of their markets. Large grocery chains, among them several unionized chains, were challenged by new discount grocery stores that were largely nonunion. The discount grocery stores competed with the traditional stores solely on cost; the discount stores did not stock the variety of goods that the traditional stores did, but they sold their limited stock at lower prices. The discount stores also kept labor costs to a minimum by hiring a largely part-time work force at near–minimum wage. The effect on traditional stores was profound. A number of large chains, including Southerly's, experienced millions of dollars in losses, and many chains began closing their more marginal stores. In collective bargaining, traditional stores sought wage give-backs and other labor cost–reduction measures to counter the low-cost operations. The traditional retail food industry was organized by the United Food and Commercial Workers Union (UFCW), which found itself negotiating increasingly concessionary contracts to try to keep its members' jobs.

At Southerly's, the company racked up over $500 million in debt by 1988 that it sought to repay through wage concessions. From the mid-1980s on, each contract with the union had been a concessionary contract. Three successive contracts included wage cuts totaling a third of worker wages. In addition, each contract included increased employee costs for pension and health insurance benefits. The most recent contract was basically a freeze—no real gain, but also no real loss. As Southerly's sat down to negotiate a new contract with the UFCW, circumstances had improved dramatically. The company's debt had been paid down and restructured to the point that the board had recently increased shareholder dividends and industry analysts were once again promoting its stock. In 1998, for the first time since the mid-1980s, the company began opening new stores. Per-store profit/loss and revenue/cost ratios had experienced sustained gains since 1996, especially in their traditional markets.

Rebecca, the local union president for the Northern Virginia region, realized that the time was ripe for a substantial wage and benefit increase. In her view, the union had funded Southerly's return to profitability through its concessions. She could show that the total wage and benefit concessions could have purchased every outstanding share of company stock. If pain were to be shared, as it was in the recent past, gain should be shared today. Furthermore, she could show that her region, which includes the rapidly growing suburban Washington, D.C. area, was responsible for a disproportionately large share of the company's profit and growth. She proposed a 25 percent wage increase spread over the life of a three-year contract, 50 percent of dependent health insurance covered by the company (currently, full-time employees are covered under the health insurance plan, but employees must pay the full cost to cover their dependents), and a modest improvement in the pension.

Southerly's balked. Yes, the company was doing well. But, more than anything else, management did not want to jeopardize their current competitive position. They were still being menaced, now by the warehouse stores that were, again, mostly nonunion and competed on the basis of low cost. Now was not the time to create a competitive disadvantage in labor costs.

So, the lines were drawn in negotiations. The union wanted paybacks for its earlier concessions. The company wanted to maintain its competitive position in the market. As negotiations approached their deadline, neither party had altered its fundamental position. While insisting that she wished to avoid it at all costs, Rebecca raised the prospect of a strike. Management responded by expressing its intention to hire permanent replacements in the event of a strike (in a later session, management showed Rebecca the newspaper ads it was purchasing to recruit replacements).

Southerly's knows that, if a strike occurrs, it will be costly. But it would be more costly to give in to the union's demands. Its aim is to limit the costs to the short term. It feels it could count on the loyalty of the management team in most stores. Southerly's also has among the best training programs in the industry. If replacing the entire work force might produce some temporary disruptions, replacement workers could be brought up to speed fairly quickly. Even though the unemployment rate is low, there are always workers looking for entry-level jobs. Again, while there might be temporary disruptions, eventually it could recruit a replacement work force. In managing the strike, the company knows that it can legally keep picketing workers out of the parking lots and away from the doors of the stores. They will be restricted to the entrances to the lots from public roadways, and so their contact with either customers or replacement workers will be limited. If Southerly's strategy works, it may even mean the decertification of the union. Getting rid of the union was not the principle motivation for resisting the union's wage and benefit demands. But now that a strike appears imminent, getting rid of the union has become a part of the strike strategy.

Outwardly, Rebecca remains defiant. She knows, in her heart, that her position is both economically correct and socially just. She also knows that discontent among workers in the stores is high and that she can count on strong support for a strike. She thinks many among the store management group will also be sympathetic—she has worked with many of them for years. In sum, she could claim the moral and rhetorical high ground and lead a strong, effective strike. It would be the culminating and defining event of her career as a labor leader. Inwardly, however, Rebecca is deeply troubled. She is one of the few remaining hourly employees at Southerly's who had personally endured the lean years (most of those who remained had, by now, been promoted to management, and this is why Rebecca thinks many managers would be sympathetic to a strike). Most of her membership has been with Southerly's only a few years. While they seemed itching for a strike, their reasons were different from hers (their concerns centered around issues like abusive managers, little control over their hours, the stress of intrusive accountability and performance measurement systems, and deteriorating safety conditions). Most of all, Rebecca worries that she is leading lambs to the slaughter. That is, she fears that management may ultimately be able to make good on its threat to permanently replace her membership. She has no idea how to stop management, and the UFCW, while pledging full support for the strike, seems to have only vague ideas about how to counter the permanent replacement strategy. So what if she is right? Does she have the right to put all of her members' jobs in jeopardy?

1. If Rebecca is convinced the company can replace her members, should she put their jobs in jeopardy by leading them out on strike?
2. Should Rebecca cave in and accept the best offer she can get to avoid a strike?
3. Are there alternative bargaining strategies that Rebecca and Southerly's could have pursued?
4. What are Rebecca's alternatives in leading a strike? What about other job actions short of a total strike?
5. At what point should concessionary contracting end? Do these workers deserve the wage and benefit increases Rebecca is demanding?
6. What are the risks associated with Southerly's strategy?

Case 15.2
The Arbitration Process

Mike is a forklift operator at a large industrial warehouse. During a particularly busy shift, Mike tipped over a very large load of television sets. Although no one was injured in the accident, about $10,000 worth of merchandise was damaged. Mike's supervisor (who had said on several occasions that Mike was a poor worker) insisted that Mike be given drug and alcohol tests. Mike tested positive for marijuana and was dismissed. He immediately filed a grievance, claiming that he had smoked the marijuana the previous weekend, that he was not incapacitated at the time of the accident, and that he had never been high at work. The company refused to reverse its decision, and the matter will now be brought before an arbitrator.

Company policy regarding drug testing reads as follows: "Employees may be tested at the discretion of the supervisor following any accident in which another employee is injured or where there is significant damage to the employer's property." No employee had ever been tested in a property-damage accident before, although accidents involving many thousands of dollars of merchandise had occurred. Regarding the outcome of drug and alcohol testing, the company manual states, "Employees found to be incapacitated shall be summarily dismissed."

1. What strategy would you follow if you were preparing Mike's grievance? What kind of information would you want the arbitrator to be aware of?
2. Given what you have read here, how would you rule in this case if you were arbitrating it? What factors would lead you to your conclusion?
3. Do you think that the language of the company policy is properly worded? Would you have decided the case differently if Mike had passed a preemployment urinalysis and then tested positive after the accident?

Case 15.3
Firing the Organizer

Dunlop Associates is a major third-party administrator in both workers' compensation and employee health insurance, handling claims processing for a number of large, self-insured employers and even a few insurance companies. It was now facing an unusual problem—a union organizing campaign in its major claims-processing center. Dunlop had never encountered a union organizing drive before and was caught by surprise. To management's chagrin, it looked as though the union might have a good chance of success. None of Dunlop's competitors in the industry were unionized and Dunlop did not relish the idea of becoming the first.

Kay Harrison was leading the charge for the union in the claims-processing center. In addition to distributing union information pamphlets and talking up the union to her coworkers, she began to wear "Say Union Yes" T-shirts, hats, and buttons regularly to work. Supervisors began to notice that Kay was frequently away from her work area and seemed to be involved in animated conversations with other workers. Upon being questioned by the supervisors, some of the employees who had been seen talking with Kay at their work stations verified that she was trying to "sell them" on the union. After three weeks of this activity, Kay was called into her supervisor's office and advised that her behavior was disruptive and that she must refrain from any activity that interfered with other employees' work. She was also told that her own work had been observed to be below the acceptable standard for the past three weeks, and she was warned that she would be dismissed if it did not return to standard and remain there for at least three consecutive weeks.

Kay continued to wear the union paraphernalia, although she confined her conversations with other workers to break rooms and the cafeteria. Her work barely met the acceptable standard the following week. When it dropped below standard the week after that, Kay's employment was terminated. Immediately following the termination, Kay filed a complaint with the National Labor Relations Board, claiming that her dismissal was an unfair labor practice under Section 8 of the NLRA. At the board hearing on the matter, Dunlop insisted that it had terminated Kay because of her failure to meet performance standards.

1. How do you think this case should be resolved? Was Kay protected under the NLRA? What factors will the NLRB weigh in deciding the case?

2. What effect do you think Kay's dismissal will have on the union organizing attempt?
3. If the NLRB ordered that Kay be reinstated to her job, what effect do you think that would have on the union organizing effort?
4. Why did Dunlop fire Kay, really? Was it her performance? Or was it her union activities? Would they have fired her for her performance if she had not also been engaged in pro-union activities?

● Exercise 15.1
Unions on the Web

Visit the AFL-CIO site: http://www.aflcio.org/

1. What is the general "feel" of the site? How does organized labor seem to view itself? Is this different from your personal view of unions and their role in society?
2. What seem to be hot issues for organized labor today?
3. Suppose you are the HR manager of a small city. You have heard that the American Federation of

State, County, and Municipal Workers is likely to start an organizing drive among city employees. Find out as much information about this union as you can. What are their current interests? What kinds of issues do you think they are likely to raise in an organizing campaign? How can you counter these arguments?

Notes and References

1. John R. Commons et al., *History of Labour in the United States,* 2 Vols. (New York: Macmillan, 1918).
2. Foster Rhea Dulles and Melvyn Dubofsky, *Labor in America: A History of the International Workers of the World* (Arlington Heights, Ill.: Harlan Davidson, 1984), chap. 9.
3. Ibid., chap. 16.
4. Ibid., chap. 19.
5. Hugh D. Hindman and David B. Patton, "Unionism in State and Local Governments: Ohio and Illinois, 1982–1987," *Industrial Relations,* Vol. 33, 1994, pp. 106–120; and Statistical Abstract of the United States, 2000. Table No. 713 "Union members by selected characteristics: 1999," U.S. Census Bureau. (Available at: www.census.gov/prod.www/statistical-abstract-us.html)
6. Richard Freeman and James Medoff, *What Do Unions Do?* (New York: Basic Books, 1984).
7. *NLRB* v. *Jones & Laughlin Steel Corp.,* 301 U.S. 1 (1937).
8. This section on public employee unionization is based on Benjamin J. Taylor and Fred Whitney, *Labor Relations Law* (Englewood Cliffs, N.J.: Pretice-Hall, 1987), chap. 21.
9. Karl Marx and Friedrich Engels, *Manifesto of the Communist Party* (Moscow: Foreign Languages Publishing House, 1948).
10. Sidney Webb and Beatrice Webb, *Industrial Democracy* (London: Longmans, 1897).
11. Frank Tannenbaum, *A Philosophy of Labor* (New York: Knopf, 1951).
12. Hoyt N. Wheeler, *Industrial Conflict: An Integrative Theory* (Columbia: University of South Carolina Press, 1985).
13. Arthur A. Sloane and Fred Witney, *Labor Relations,* 8th ed. (Englewood Cliffs, N.J.: Prentice-Hall, 1993), pp. 190–193.
14. Sixty-First Annual Report of the National Labor Relations Board for the Fiscal Year Ended September 30, 1996 (Washington, D.C.: U.S. Government Printing Office, 1997).
15. Bureau of National Affairs, *Primer of Labor Relations,* 25th ed. (Washington, D.C.: Author, 1994), chap. 4.
16. Thomas A. Kochan and Harry C. Katz, *Collective Bargaining and Industrial Relations,* 2nd ed. (Chicago: Irwin, 1988), pp. 136–140.
17. Ibid, chap. 1.
18. Ibid, chap. 4.
19. Ibid, chap. 5. See also Edward Cohen-Rosenthal and Cynthia E. Burton, *Mutual Gains: A Guide to Union-Management Cooperation* (New York: Praeger, 1987).

20. Freeman and Medoff, *What Do Unions Do?* chaps. 3, 5.

21. Ibid, chap. 4.

22. *Fibreboard Paper Products Corp.* v. *NLRB,* 379 U.S. 203 (1964).

23. *Otis Elevator Company,* 269 NLRB No. 62 (1984).

24. Commerce Clearing House, *Labor Law Course,* 26th ed. (Chicago: Author,1987), p. 3351.

25. Kochan and Katz, *Collective Bargaining and Industrial Relations,* chap. 8.

26. Cynthia L. Gramm, "The Determinants of Strike Incidence and Severity," *Industrial and Labor Relations Review,* April 1986, pp. 361–376.

27. *NLRB* v. *MacKay Radio & Telegraph Co.*, 304 U.S. 333 (1938).

28. *Replacement Workers: Evidence from the Popular and Labor Press, 1989 and 1990* (Washington, D.C.: Bureau of National Affairs, 1991).

29. Taylor and Whitney, *Labor Relations Law,* pp. 396–399.

30. Bureau of National Affairs, *Primer of Labor Relations,* chap. 7.

31. Taylor and Whitney, *Labor Relations Law,* pp. 467–470.

32. Carl M. Stevens, "Is Compulsory Arbitration Compatible with Bargaining?" *Industrial Relations,* Vol. 5, 1966, pp. 38–50.

33. Hoyt N. Wheeler, "Compulsory Arbitration: A Narcotic Effect?" *Industrial Relations,* Vol. 14, 1975, pp. 117–120.

34. Peter Feuille, *Final Offer Arbitration* (Chicago: International Personnel Management Association, 1975), pp. 35–48.

35. Taylor and Whitney, *Labor Relations Law,* chap. 19.

36. Bureau of National Affairs, *Collective Bargaining Negotiations and Contracts,* (Washington, DC: 1989) pp. 51.5–51.8.

37. Ibid., p. 51.6.

Employment Transitions

HR Challenge

It is estimated that 3 to 5 percent of the U.S. labor force now works in call centers. Employee turnover in call centers has always been high. The industry average was about 15 percent in 1996, and quit rates rose steadily to over 23 percent in 2000. To help attract and keep employees, wages rose quickly as well, with average agent salaries increasing from $14,826 in 1996 to $23,859 in 2000.[1] It is hard for companies to deliver high-quality customer service with such high turnover of front-line staff, and even harder to service growth. Capital One's call centers serve more than 30 million credit card holders around the world, and the company adds 25,000 new customers each day. Replacing agents who leave in addition to hiring for growth is a contant battle fought by most call-center managers.

While some call-center positions require advanced technical expertise and strong troubleshooting ability, such as providing telephone assis-

tance from a computer help desk, most feature much simpler transaction-process-ing, order-taking, sales, or information-giving activities. Jobs in call centers are often seen as just jobs, not as stepping stones to a career, and very few people aspire to become call-center agents. Call centers are sometimes less than ideal working envi-ronments; in fact, they have been likened to sweatshops and called "the factories of the future." Some work is highly routinized, with agents following precise scripts, having little leeway to respond to unusual customer needs, and being closely moni-tored by both electronic systems and supervisors. Shiftwork is common, with some centers operating on a 24/7 schedule. The work is often considered stressful, and burnout is common after several months or a year of work. Employees may feel caught between conflicting demands. On the one hand, they are required to appear polite and helpful to customers; on the other, to handle calls very quickly and con-tinuously in a highly controlling and almost dehumanized environment.[2]

The Royal Automobile Club (RAC) Customer Service Center in Bristol, England, provides an example of issues and potential solutions in managing employee turnover in a call center. In late 1996, the RAC began to consolidate seventeen sepa-rate units that took calls from existing and potential customers into a single call cen-ter. The new center was located in Bristol. This location may have been a poor choice for a labor-intensive operation, because the area has traditionally had low unemployment and a number of other large call centers had recently moved in. Competition to attract and retain agents was fierce. In the three years leading up to the consolidation, employee turnover in the RAC's call-center units had averaged 27 to 35 percent annually. Each unit had specialized in one type of transaction, such as membership renewals, telesales, travel insurance, and so forth, meaning that cus-tomers often had to be tranfered from agent to agent to have a range of issues ad-dressed. Because agents had to master only one type of work, training was very lim-ited and the work was highly repetitive. Two wage systems were in place—an hourly salary plus overtime for those who answered customer questions and recorded sim-ple information, and a commission-based system for agents selling products or memberships. On the whole, pay was below the market average. There were no progression routes between jobs.

Shortly after the consolidation, a number of innovative HR policies were devel-oped to simultaneously improve customer service and employee retention. They were successful, with employee turnover reduced to 8 percent in 1997 and an aston-ishing 2 percent in 1998.[3] *How did RAC do it? Where would you start if you wished to attract, retain, and motivate call-center staff in a competitive environment?*

This chapter is about transitions made by employees after they enter an organiza-tion. Individuals may transition from one job or location to another within the organization. These moves may be relatively unplanned and ad hoc, or the result of careful career planning and preparation with a long time horizon. Movements can be upward (promotion), lateral (to a different set of responsibilities or different function at the same level), or even downward (demotion). Many organizations recognize the importance of careers to their employees and provide career plan-ning to encourage employees to stay and continuously upgrade their skills in antic-ipation of future opportunities. Such planning also assures that suitably skilled em-ployees will be available to meet the organization's future human resource needs.

Another type of transition is exit from the organization. Departures from the organization can be classified as voluntary, in which the employee makes a decision to leave, or involuntary, in which the employer terminates the employee. Voluntary turnover has been an increasing concern for many organizations in the tight labor markets of the turn-of-the-century boom. Average tenure has declined sharply, especially in industries such as information technology. When the basis for competition is intellectual capital and skilled employees, organizations with a high rate of employee turnover are severely handicapped. Another form of (usually) voluntary turnover is retirement. With the aging of the large baby-boom cohort, this is an increasingly important issue for organizations to plan and manage.

Involuntary exit may occur when employees are discharged for inappropriate behavior or substandard performance. There are legal issues to be considered in disciplining and discharging employees for cause, and employers must assure that their processes minimize the risk of litigation as well as nurture the perception of fair treatment among all employees. Another form of involuntary exit occurs when employees are retrenched or laid off because the employer no longer needs their services. While this can happen at any time when a business reorganizes or experiences a setback, it is a widespread concern in periods of slower economic growth. The high rate of mergers over the past decade has also been accompanied by large-scale retrenchments of surplus employees.

Distinctions among the different types of organizational exit have important practical implications. For example, a common concern of HR managers is whether or not a departing employee is eligible for unemployment compensation. When an employee voluntarily leaves a job or is fired for some good reason, he or she is not eligible to receive unemployment benefits. Only when employees lose their jobs through no fault of their own (as in layoffs) are they entitled to unemployment compensation in most states.[4]

CAREER PATHS AND CAREER PLANNING

Most employees make a number of transitions between jobs during their working lives. These may include both job changes within a single employer and quitting one firm to take a job at another firm. In either case, there is usually the intention to grow and increase in skills, responsibility, and remuneration, and/or improve the "fit" between employee skills and desires and job requirements. A sequence of jobs that build on one another is called a career path, and a career path is likely to be more satisfying and successful if both the individual and the organization spend some time planning and preparing for these future transitions. The section that follows will first explore trends and options in career paths, then consider how individuals and employers might engage in career planning to maximize outcomes for both parties.

New Organizational Structures and Changing Career Patterns

A number of economic and demographic trends have affected career patterns and expectations in the past two decades. A strong trend since the mid-1980s has been called **restructuring, downsizing,** or, more euphemistically, **rightsizing.** Organizations cut their labor costs by reducing the size of their permanent full-time staff. Some organizations abolished multiple levels of management to become "flatter," quicker to respond, and closer to the customer. To meet varying labor needs, rightsized firms may hire temporary workers or outsource work to smaller firms and consultants.[5] There was a rise in part-time employment during the 1990s both because part-timers are less expensive and receive fewer fringe benefits, and because they provide greater flexibility in scheduling employees for peak demand periods.[6] In general, it is safe to say that for many employees, the "psychological contract" they have with their employer has changed from "If you do your job well, we'll employ you until you retire" to "We'll employ you as long as we need your contribution to help us succeed in business."[7]

Consequently, career patterns for individual employees are changing. The left side of Figure 16.1 shows a traditional **linear career path,** in which one enters an organization near the bottom, works in the same firm for many years, and gradually and predictably moves up, retiring from a fairly high-level position in the same firm. Research suggests that this career pattern may become the exception rather than the rule over the next few decades.[8] The bulge of baby boomers has made climbing the hierarchy much more competitive, the flattening of organizational structures has reduced the number of management positions just as the number of candidates has increased, and massive layoffs have destroyed faith in the employer as a long-term source of security. These changes have caused a great deal of frustration as middle-aged employees fail to advance as they had expected.[9] Even greater frustration and career blocking are afflicting baby busters as boomers monopolize middle- and upper-management positions.[10]

Organizations are trying to maintain the motivation and creativity of **career-plateaued** employees by developing alternatives to the traditional linear career success model. To some extent, the meaning of career success is changing. Some feel that career success now has more to do with self-actualization, skill growth, and self-satisfaction than climbing a fixed ladder of jobs. Balancing family and life commitments with work also seems to be taking on more importance for many employees.[11] Table 16.1 shows four possible career paths that an employee could follow. An **expert, or professional, career ladder** rewards growing expertise in a single technical speciality without the need to move into management. Professional ladders allow for career advancement within a single employer, even a "flat"

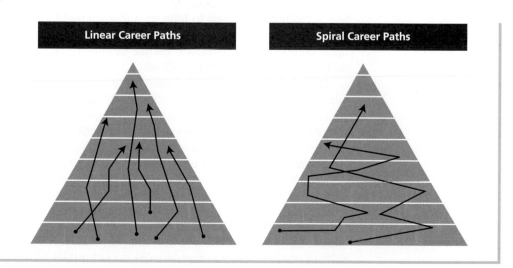

● **FIGURE 16.1**

Career Patterns

● **T A B L E   16 . 1**

Characteristics of Four Career Paths

	Linear	Expert	Spiral	Transitory
Direction of movement	Upward	Little movement	Lateral	Lateral
Duration of stay in one field	Variable	Life	7–10 years	3–5 years
Incumbent motives	Power Achievement	Expertise Security	Personal growth Creativity	Variety Independence
Organizational structure	Tall pyramid	Flat Strong functional departments	Matrix Self-directed interdisciplinary teams	Loose, flexible structure Temporary teams
Organizationally valued performance factors	Leadership Efficiency Logistics management	Quality Reliability Stability Technical competence	Creativity Teamwork People development	Speed Adaptability Innovation
Organizational rewards	Promotions Management perquisites Executive bonuses	Fringe benefits Recognition awards Continuing technical training	Lateral assignments Cross-training Creative latitude	Immediate cash bonuses Independence and autonomy Special temporary assignments Job rotation

Source: Adapted from K. R. Brousseau, M. J. Driver, K. Eneroth, and R. Larsson, "Career Pandemonium: Realigning Organizations and Individuals," *Academy of Management Executive,* November 1996, Table 1 (p. 56) and Table 3 (p. 59).

one. In academics, an example is the move from assistant to associate to full professor, without the need to take on a management role such as department head or dean. Scientists and engineers also can follow similar ladders of increasing technical competence and status (junior engineer, engineer, senior engineer, etc.) without managerial responsibilities.

RAC found that part of the solution to high turnover in the perceived dead-end job of call-center agent was to build a career progression system. First, the job was retitled "customer adviser" and incumbents were trained to provide a much wider range of services to customers, including both providing information and selling. They were empowered and encouraged to solve problems and remedy complaints rather than passing them on to another agent or supervisor. An expert career ladder with five steps was installed for customer advisers. Each level has higher performance requirements and, when achieved, provides a higher wage rate as well as the possiblity of greater bonuses for above-target performance.[12] Though not used at RAC, there is a movement in the United States toward certifying call-center staff in basic skills such as "controlling the call, showing empathy, identifying and solving problems, and acting on sales opportunities." This is another effort to raise the status of the occupation, and thus perhaps attract more people to enter and re-main in the field.[13]

Another widely touted alternative career structure is the **spiral career path** (right side of Figure 16.1), which involves a number of lateral moves between functional areas within the same organization. This combines broadening experi-ence and the continuous challenge of new tasks with slower hierarchical progress.[14] As an example, one might begin a career in sales, move to operations after several years, move to a different operations job, and then move into the fi-nance area by midcareer. To make these complex spiral career paths work, organi-zations need to design sophisticated career planning and career information sys-tems to generate and disseminate information about lateral career opportunities throughout the organization.[15]

Organizational pay and job structures are changing to accommodate new forms of career movement. **Broad banding** is the increasingly common practice of combining many previously discrete job titles, ranks, and pay grades into much wider categories. Northern Telecom has collapsed 19,000 job titles and more than thirty-two salary grades into just 200 titles and thirteen salary bands. This system encourages lateral job movement by deemphasizing progress through a myriad of vertical job grades and by rewarding both performance excellence and in-band job changes.[16]

Another increasingly common path is the **transitory career path.** In this ap-proach, the career occurs virtually independent of any single organization. The in-dividual may move into and out of organizations and even occupations on a regular basis, either in search of better jobs and more satisfying challenges or because there is little choice when secure permanent jobs are rare. Some or even most of a transitory career may be spent as a consultant or independent contractor, short-term contract employee, part-timer, or entrepreneur. Individuals on this career path think of themselves as possessing and maintaining a portfolio of competen-cies that give them security and employability rather than assuming that security and employment are provided by a single organization. Career and development planning is critical for individuals on a transitory career path, but they are more likely to become their own career strategists than to rely on input from formal employer-provided career-planning systems.[17]

Spiral or transitory career paths may offer another attraction to today's em-ployees: the possibility of staying in one location much longer. With the increas-ing number of dual-career couples, individuals may prefer to remain in the same community for a longer period, moving between different types of jobs within the same establishment or moving within the same specialty across local employers.

Unfortunately, HR specialists are finding that it is difficult to change the pre-vailing "up-or-out" culture of most organizations, which defines lack of upward progress as failure. Traditional linear careers are less feasible than before, and employer-initiated creative career planning is even more important to effectively utilize talent and provide satisfying careers for today's employees. It has been sug-gested that the most effective organizations of the future will provide all four types of career paths (linear, expert, spiral, and transitory) in varying proportions to meet the needs of their work force and provide the combination of stable and flexi-ble staffing necessary to carry out their business plans.[18] The lower two rows of Table 16.1 suggest the way in which performance appraisal criteria and reward systems might need to be tailored to meet the needs of employees on different types of career paths.

Career Planning

Ultimately, individuals are responsible for their own careers, though many organizations provide assistance with career planning. Organizational efforts to plan career moves for top managers were discussed in Chapter 3 under the rubrics of replacement charting and succession planning, but top management candidates are not the only employees in need of career-planning attention from the organization. Lower-level managers, professionals, and nonexempt employees also desire satisfying careers and may leave organizations that are not seen as offering appropriate opportunities. Having defined career goals and being aware of other job opportunities within the firm also may motivate employees to work harder at developing their skills because they understand how effort now will pay off later. Career and development planning also helps ensure that skilled employees will be available internally when they are needed. Realizing this, many organizations engage in for-

●**TABLE 16.2**

Organizational Career Planning and Development Tools

A. Self-assessment tools
   1. Career-planning workshops
   2. Career workbooks
   3. Preretirement workshops

B. Individual counseling
   1. Personnel staff
   2. Professional counselor
      a. Internal
      b. External
   3. Outplacement
   4. Supervisor or line manager

C. Internal labor-market information/placement exchanges
   1. Job posting
   2. Skills inventories
   3. Career ladders/career path planning
   4. Career resource center
   5. Other career communication formats

D. Organizational potential assessment processes
   1. Assessment centers
   2. Promotability forecasts
   3. Replacement/succession planning
   4. Psychological testing

E. Developmental programs
   1. Job rotation
   2. In-house human resource development programs
   3. External seminars/workshops
   4. Tuition reimbursement/educational assistance
   5. Supervisor training in career counseling
   6. Dual-career programs
   7. Mentoring systems

Source: Thomas G. Gutteridge, "Organizational Career Development Systems: The State of the Practice." In D. T. Hall and associates, *Career Development in Organizations,* Table 1, p. 61. Copyright 1986 by Jossey-Bass Inc., Publishers. Reprinted by permission.

mal career-planning activities with their employees.[19] Table 16.2 lists some of the tools that organizations may use to facilitate employee career planning.

Career planning typically involves several steps. The first is self-assessment by the employee—that is, coming to understand who one is, what one values, what one is good at and enjoys, and what one wants to accomplish over the longer term. Recent research suggests that individuals in business careers tend to be motivated by one to three of the eight deeply held "life interests" shown in Table 16.3. Jobs in which these skills and interests can be exercised will be much more interesting and satisfying over the long term. Sometimes these interests have minimal overlap with an employee's technical skills. For instance, a computer programmer may have deep-seated interests in counseling and mentoring, or a lawyer in enterprise control. If the organization can match or adapt job responsibilities to interests, retention should improve.[20] For instance, the computer programmer may take responsibility for user education, or the lawyer may move into managing a law office rather than prosecuting cases.

Individuals are not always aware of what they are good at or what they most enjoy doing.[21] The process of self-assessment should include structured thinking about oneself in terms of skills, values, and life interests. Sometimes testing is helpful in this regard. After completing a self-assessment, employees should solicit feedback from others who know them well or who have worked with them or supervised them. At the end of this process, employees should have formed a clear picture of what they need or want and what they can offer to an employer.

The second step is gathering information about different job opportunities and potential career paths either inside or outside the present organization. This is

● **TABLE 16.3**

Eight Life Interests

> **Application of technology.** Intrigued by the inner working of things. Curious about finding better ways to use technology to solve problems. Enjoy analyzing and redesigning systems and processes. Excited by new technology.
>
> **Quantitative analysis.** Excel at and enjoy using numbers and analysis to solve problems. Like to build mathematical models and do forecasts.
>
> **Theory development and conceptual thinking.** Like to think about the big picture, strategy, and abstract concepts; are academically oriented.
>
> **Creative production.** Imaginative, out-of-the-box thinkers, thrive on initiating new and original projects. May be entrepreneurs, research and development scientists, advertisers, entertainers. Bored by established practices and products.
>
> **Counseling and mentoring.** Enjoy teaching, coaching, and guiding others. When the job doesn't allow this, may satisfy this interest in volunteer activities.
>
> **Managing people and relationships.** Enjoy dealing with people on a day-to-day basis. Enjoy accomplishing things through others, may enjoy sales and negotiation activities.
>
> **Enterprise control.** Like to be in control and make decisions.
>
> **Influence through language and ideas.** Feel most fulfilled when writing or speaking, love to communicate with and persuade others.

Source: Adapted from Timothy Butler and James Waldroop, "Job Sculpting: The Art of Retaining Your Best People," *Harvard Business Review,* September–October 1999, pp. 144–152.

● **FIGURE 16.2**

Aligning Personal Needs and Offers with Employer Needs and Offers
Source: Mike Broscio and Jay Scherer, Scherer Schneider Paulick, Chicago, www.sspcorp.net, "Taking Charge: Charting Your Way to Career Success," *Healthcare Executive,* Nov./Dec. 2000, pp. 18–22 © Scherer Schneider Paulick 2001.

Understanding My Needs

- What are my values?
- What is my life purpose?
- What are my interests?
- What motivates me?
- What demotivates me?
- What do I need to keep my life in balance?

Understanding My Organization's Offers

- What are the growth opportunities in my organization?
- What benefits does my employer offer?
- What would improve my likelihood of staying with my current employer?
- What can my employer offer me to assist me in being more effective?

CAREER PLAN

Understanding My Offers

- What are my strengths?
- How can my strengths benefit an employer?
- What are my accomplishments and experiences?
- What is my competitive advantage?
- What attributes differentiate me from others with a similar background?
- What are the unique services I can make available to my employer at this stage of my career?

Understanding My Organization's Needs

- What are the goals and the mission of my organization?
- What do my employer's customers want?
- What knowledge and skill sets do I need to help my employer and effectively perform my job?
- What changes in the industry are affecting my organization and my performance expectations?

information on what employers need and want from incumbents and what they can offer to employees. Figure 16.2 shows these two sets of needs and offers, and points out that both employer and employee must get a good exchange for the relationship to work over the long run. Individuals can engage in this step in career planning on their own, with little assistance from their employer. However, employer involvement is desirable because better information on internal career paths can be made available, a larger percentage of employees can be induced to consider options within the organization, and plans can be more realistic in view of future organizational needs and development opportunities. Employers may offer to help employees learn about career opportunities and job requirements elsewhere in the organization through a variety of means. These include individual meetings with a career counselor in the organization, discussions with superiors, videos, computer programs, booklets detailing job requirements and competencies throughout the organization, job rotations, and so on.

The third step is formulating career goals and a plan for achieving them. Plans may include on- or off-the-job training; special assignments; and changes in job, occupation, or employer. A discussion of the plan at least annually with one's supervisor is recommended.

First USA Bank has recently implemented a program of career planning and management for its nonexempt employees. Job satisfaction surveys showed that these employees were unhappy and unclear about their future prospects within the organization. The company responded by developing a careers program designed to increase job satisfaction, reduce voluntary turnover, and increase the rate of internal promotions. The idea was for employees to be more proactive in planning their own careers and to consider lateral as well as vertical movements. A consulting firm was hired to run a series of workshops on career planning. These first helped employees to assess themselves; then to seek feedback and confirmation of their self-assessment; then to understand more about the company, industry, and likely future needs in their profession; then to explore job alternatives and paths within the organization; and finally to create a blueprint for personal growth and job movement. The workshops were so eagerly received by employees that First USA Bank added two more components to the program, which was eventually called "Opportunity Knocks." The second component was career resource centers at each worksite. Employees can sign up to spend paid time in the room reading about careers, researching opportunities, and writing résumés. The third component was the hiring of "employment development advisers" to work with employees on their plans following the workshops. After pilot testing, the program was rolled out to multiple sites. In the first year, the rate of internal job changes increased by 50 percent and employee satisfaction with career development increased by 25 percent. Further, participants in the program were much more likely to stay with the organization than were nonparticipants. First USA estimates that it saved $2.2 million in replacement costs as a consequence of better career development of employees.[22]

Dual-Career and Family Issues in Career Planning

Career planning historically has targeted one employee at a time. Now, however, an increasing number of employees have spouses who are active in the work force and whose career and employment prospects must also be factored into career decisions. Some authors distinguish **dual-income families** from **dual-career families.** In the former, one or both spouses work at a non-career-oriented job, perhaps a less skilled position in retail, health care, food services, and so forth. The non-career-oriented partner's flexibility as to employer makes career planning relatively straightforward. This partner can seek employment wherever the other partner's career takes them. In dual-career families, each partner has a strong commitment to building a continuing and challenging career, and the needs of each must be carefully balanced in career-planning activities. It has been estimated that more than half of married couples are dual-income families and that up to 20 percent of dual-income families feature dual careers.

The need to consider a spouse's employment prospects has made many employees less willing to accept relocation offers from their employers, and it has necessitated changes in the way that organizations deploy and develop human resources. Organizations are paying more attention to the career needs of spouses employed by other firms when geographic transfers are necessary, and they are becoming more open to employing both partners in a dual-career marriage. DuPont has 3,500 dual-career couples in a work force of 100,000, and the U.S. Army has 36,000 soldiers registered in its Married Army Couples Program.[23] Attempts are made to transfer both parties to the same location at the same time whenever possible. Paying attention to spousal career issues is one way to retain valued professionals.

A related trend is for mothers to work.[24] The needs of working parents are somewhat different from those of the traditional (but increasingly scarce) husband-employee, mother-homemaker family. Working parents of either sex usually appreciate "family friendly" organizational policies, including some form of assistance with child care, flexible working hours, job sharing, part-time options, and generous family leave.[25] In terms of career planning, one or both parents may wish to cease work temporarily or enter a slower, lower-pressure career track while family responsibilities are at their peak. Innovative career systems that allow these arrangements without permanently stereotyping such employees as low-commitment, low-potential are needed.[26]

RETIREMENT

The last transition in most employees' careers is retirement. Daniel Feldman defines **retirement** as "the exit from an organizational position or career path of considerable duration, taken by individuals after middle age, and with the intention of reduced psychological commitment to work thereafter."[27] As Feldman's definition indicates, retirement is not a homogeneous phenomenon, and it is useful to recognize differences in voluntariness, completeness, and timing. While the Age Discrimination in Employment Act has essentially eliminated mandatory retirement, other forms of involuntary retirement exist, such as when health problems force an employee to stop working. Retirement may or may not take place at the age considered "normal" and may be either complete (the individual withdraws from all forms of employment) or partial (he or she continues to work part time for the same or a different employer).

For many years, retirement was seen as a relatively unimportant but quite predictable aspect of organizational functioning. As workers neared the mandatory retirement age, retirement-planning workshops may have been held, and, on reaching the magical age of sixty-five, employees were presented with a gold watch and shown the door. With the abolition of a mandatory retirement age, predictability decreased and employees now have many more choices. Because some benefit plans allow for partial benefits to be paid before age sixty-five, a larger share of employees are taking early retirement now than in the past. For instance, in 1963, 76 percent of males were in the work force between ages sixty-two and sixty-four. By 1997, that number had fallen to 46 percent. At the same time, others are choosing to work well beyond the traditional retirement age.[28] Many individuals retire from a career-oriented job and then accept a **bridge job**—possibly part time, possibly in another field, and probably with another employer.[29] Some interesting facts relevant to retirement are shown in Table 16.4.

Retirement is expected to become an increasingly important issue as the large baby-boom generation begins to leave the labor force. The leading edge of the baby boom reached age fifty-five in 2001. There are concerns about how the relatively smaller generations behind them will support such a potentially large num-

● **TABLE 16.4**

Some Facts Relevant to Retirement

- A child born today can be expected to live until age seventy-six.
- Someone who turns age sixty-five today can expect to live until age eighty-three.
- The fastest-growing segment of the population is those aged eighty-five and older.
- The age at which full Social Security retirement benefits can be received has been increasing gradually to age sixty-seven.
- Many defined benefit pension plans allow retirement with full benefits at age sixty or sixty-two.
- Most defined benefit pension plans allow early retirement at age fifty-five or earlier.
- The fastest-growing types of retirement plans allow participants to leave their employer and take their benefits at any time, regardless of age.
- Certain retirement accounts can be accessed without penalty once an individual reaches age fifty-nine and a half.
- Some accounts require distributions beginning no later than age seventy and a half.
- There is no longer a mandatory retirement age for most workers, and federal law protects older workers against discrimination regardless of their age.

Source: William J. Wiatrowski, "Changing Retirement Age: Ups and Downs," *Monthly Labor Review,* April 2001, p. 3.

ber of retirees. In an era of very low unemployment, there is concern among employers about how they will replace large numbers of highly skilled and experienced employees. Employees may worry about what they will do with themselves if they retire completely, given a life expectancy of eighteen years beyond the traditional retirement age of sixty-five. Another concern to many older employees is health insurance—they may be more willing to retire or retire early if their employer provides retiree medical benefits.[30]

Phased retirement is getting a lot of attention lately, with 16 percent of respondents in a 1999 survey saying their organization offers such programs.[31] Phased retirement means remaining in some sort of employment relationship with the same employer after retiring. This can include being rehired as a consultant, part-timer, or seasonal employee. For instance, Avaya Technologies has about 1,500 "variable" technicians who work on an as-needed basis as part of their phased-retirement program. Phased retirement can also include gradually reducing hours worked or allowing extended leaves of absence between periods of full-time work. Job sharing is another possibility, as is a transfer to a job that is less demanding and perhaps less time consuming. Phased-retirement programs benefit the organization by retaining access to valuable skills, usually a lower cost than having a full-time permanent employee. Phased retirement allows retirees a chance to augment their income, stay active and feel useful, and gradually become accustomed to not working (or working less). There are presently some legal disincentives to widespread phased-retirement programs, but forecasters expect these to be addressed in the near future. Changes that allow employees to continue part-time work without loss of pension and Social Security benefits would make early phased retirement more attractive.[32]

Impact of Retirement on the Organization

From the organization's perspective, retirement can be a very positive process. It allows new employees with up-to-date skills to enter the organization and replace older workers whose skills may have become obsolete. This process encourages innovation and new thinking in the organization. Retirement also motivates employees, since older workers tend to be higher in the organizational hierarchy and their departure provides opportunities for promotion. New employees also typically cost less than older workers because their salaries are lower. When head count must be reduced, providing incentives for early retirement is among the less painful alternatives.

Not all effects of retirement are positive, however. The loss of older workers may increase the level of uncertainty with which the organization must contend. In an increasing number of cases, well-qualified replacements for retiring workers are extremely difficult to find. When older workers leave, they take with them a wealth of knowledge about the organization's environment; the contacts and influence they have built up in dealing with the environment are also lost. The climate within the organization may become more unstable, since older workers are often a main source of internal knowledge about "who's who" and how to get things done, as well as about the organization's norms and traditions. If organizations have failed to anticipate or plan for the loss of staff through retirement, further disruptions can result.

For instance, the Defense Department is very worried about the impact of retirement on its Acquisitions work force. People in Acquisitions play a pivotal role in the development and purchase of new weapons systems. Acquisitions had about 124,000 civilian employees in 2000, and it is estimated that 60,000 of them will be eligible to retire by 2005. Funding cuts after the end of the Cold War meant that no new staff had been hired for eleven years, pushing up the average age of the work force. A major program to deal with the predicted shortfall is being put in place. This includes encouraging phased rather than complete retirements, increased recruitment, easier transfer of employees from other arms of government and from the defense industry, rehiring of retirees without financial penalties, and higher wages for high-demand occupations.[33]

The next sections of this chapter will consider earlier departures from the organization, initiated by employees themselves in the form of voluntary turnover.

VOLUNTARY TURNOVER

After a decade and a half of downsizing, employers are now frantically scrambling to keep employees rather than get rid of them. Rates of **voluntary turnover** are up nationwide and are especially severe in high-demand occupations such as information technology and in traditionally low-commitment work in retail and food services. For example, the average annual turnover rate of hourly staff in fast-food restaurants averaged 123 percent in 1999, while the turnover of salaried staff in the same sector was 100 percent.[34] Turnover in high-tech industries is estimated at 30 percent per year. The next section of this chapter explores the reasons that employees stay in or leave jobs and the processes by which they make the decision to depart. Then a strategic approach to thinking about turnover is described. Finally, retention management programs for reducing turnover are discussed.

Causes of Voluntary Turnover

Turnover has been intensively studied for decades, and there are literally hundreds of studies of variables that help predict quitting. Traditionally, most research on why employees quit has considered two classes of variables: those external to the organization and those internal to the organization. External factors include the unemployment rate and employee's perceptions of the external job opportunities available to them. Turnover is higher when unemployment in the labor market is low, so that alternative employment appears readily available to job leavers. Clearly, RAC employees in Bristol felt they could readily find employment in another call center or one of the new office parks that had recently sprung up nearby. Even in a poor labor market, if an employee believes that he or she can easily find superior alternative employment, the propensity to turnover will be higher.[35]

Internal factors are usually based on the employee's attitudes or perceptions with respect to the current job. The attitudes of job satisfaction and organizational commitment are usually significant predictors of a decision to quit, with leavers being less satisfied and less committed than stayers. Employees are also more likely to leave if they believe that the organization treats them unfairly; if they have a poor relationship with their manager; if job requirements are conflicting, unclear, or stressful; or if opportunities for growth, skill development, and promotion are lacking.[36] This sounds like a description of a typical call-center environment—perhaps it is not surprising that turnover in this sector tends to be high.

A great deal of research has confirmed that these attitudes and perceptions are correlated with turnover, but the relationships are not especially strong. Recently, a new predictor of staying versus quitting has been proposed that shows some promise—the **embeddedness** of the employee in the job setting. This approach considers that employees have a web of links and relationships between their family lives, work lives, and community. When these links are numerous and tight, employees are less likely to quit. Leaving a job means leaving the work itself, work friends, employer-provided development programs, and other work-related activities such as a company softball team. Further, leaving a job often means moving out of the community—leaving a spouse's job, a house, a school district, a church, hobby clubs, and nonwork friends. If the individual fits the job and community well and has developed many links, it is a substantial sacrifice to sever these links by quitting the job. Other sacrifices may occur if the employee must forgo unvested pension benefits, a company car, or other benefits based on seniority such as eligibility for sabbaticals. Research has shown that embeddedness contributes to the prediction of turnover above and beyond measures such as job satisfaction, organizational commitment, and the perception of viable employment alternatives.[37]

How Do Employees Decide to Quit?

In addition to identifying predictors of turnover, some researchers have investigated the *process* of deciding to quit a job. It turns out that the decision to quit can be made in different ways and in response to different stimuli. The **traditional model of turnover,** exemplified in a book published by Bill Mobley in 1982, suggests that the decision to quit is made in a logical and step-by-step fashion, largely

● **FIGURE 16.3**

Traditional Model of Deciding to Quit

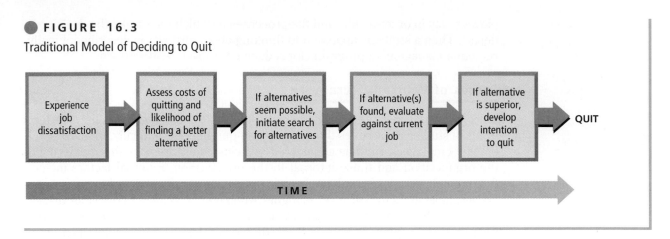

in response to dissatisfaction with the present job (see Figure 16.3). Individuals begin by evaluating the current job and level of satisfaction or dissatisfaction. If they are dissatisfied, they may begin to think of quitting, then assess the costs of quitting and the costs and likely success of searching for an alternative job. If they believe they have a reasonable chance of finding another job, they may begin a search. After the search, they compare the job alternatives they have discovered to the present job and decide whether it is better to quit or stay.[38] This model suggests that the process of deciding to quit is gradual and that an alternative job is located before the current job is left.

Other research finds that sometimes—about 25 percent of the time—individuals leave one job before beginning to search for another job. This may occur because they are suddenly and extremely unhappy in the old job or because they are highly confident of locating a new job with ease. Further, many people leave jobs not because of growing dissatisfaction but because of a single precipitating incident or "shock to the system." The incident can be negative and job related, such as being passed over for a promotion, receiving a bad performance review, or having a fight with a boss or peer. These negative work events can be relatively minor but still serve as "the last straw" that causes a sudden decision to leave. Not all shocks are negative events on the current job. A shock can also be positive and external, such as receiving an unsolicited job offer or being approached by a headhunter. Finally, the shock that initiates quitting could be an off-the-job event such as becoming pregnant, a spouse being transferred, or being accepted to graduate school.[39]

The Strategic Management of Voluntary Turnover

Research has provided information on why and how individuals choose to quit. The next question is how organizations should respond. Is all voluntary turnover bad, and should achieving a low turnover rate be a priority for all organizations for all their employees? As with so many decisions in strategic human resource management, it depends. Organizations must consider the costs and benefits of turnover in a particular situation and balance these against the costs of retention, as explained below.

● **Costs and Benefits of Turnover to the Organization**   The departure of an employee can have considerable costs, as outlined in the left side of Table 16.5.[40] It is

● **TABLE 16.5**

Costs and Benefits of Voluntary Turnover

Costs of Turnover	Benefits of Turnover
Exit costs Exit interviews Farewell parties on work time Administrative time to process final pay, close retirement accounts, etc.	Poor performers may choose to leave and can be replaced with better employees. Leavers are replaced with more junior employees who cost less. Morale improves following departure of problematic employees. Leavers are replaced with people with more up-to-date technical skill. Vacancies are created to allow for internal promotions of other employees, thus increasing their career satisfaction and motivation. Receptiveness to innovation and change may increase. Voluntary turnover is less painful than retrenchments.
Replacement costs Recruitment advertising Selection testing, interviewing, reference checking Hiring bonuses, relocation costs New employee orientation Administrative costs to add to payroll, enroll in benefits, etc. Formal training Informal mentoring and coaching of new employees by supervisors	
Other costs Lost business due to client loyalty to departing employees Lost business or poor quality due to short staffing before replacement, or lower skills before new hires are up to speed Expenses of hiring temporaries or paying overtime while awaiting replacements Reduced morale of those remaining, increased stress on those remaining while short staffed or breaking in replacements Reduction in company's reputation as an employer when many staff choose to leave; reduced ability to recruit in the labor market Inability to pursue growth or other business opportunities due to lack of staff Loss of training dollars invested in departing employee	

possible, though not easy, to put figures on these costs to estimate the actual dollar loss from the departure of an employee.[41] A shorthand estimate is 50 to 60 percent of annual salary, though the costs of replacing a software engineer or New York law firm associate are estimated at $200,000.[42] Even on a fairly simple job, costs can be high. The average cost of replacing a call-center operator in the United States is more than $6,500.[43] In the tight labor market of the early 2000s, employers are clearly being hurt by the departure of valued staff and have begun to act more aggressively to retain their employees.

This situation might lead one to believe that all turnover is dysfunctional and that the lowest possible rate of voluntary turnover would be the best. However, this is not necessarily true. Turnover also has benefits, as shown in the right side of Table 16.5. An organization with a turnover rate that is too low may become stagnant and hidebound, lack opportunities for employees to move up, and retain poor performers it would be better off without.

Current thinking suggests that organizations should aim for an **optimal rate of turnover** rather than the lowest possible rate. One scholar suggests that the optimal rate occurs where the curve of **turnover costs** crosses the curve of **retention costs,** as shown in Figure 16.4. As the turnover rate increases, so do the costs of replacement and lost productivity. The organization can reduce turnover, but only by incurring retention costs, such as higher wages, better benefits, quality-of-work-life and development programs, and so on. The point at which these two curves cross represents the lowest total cost and thus the optimal turnover rate for the organization. This type of analysis suggests that a relatively high turnover rate may sometimes be less costly than a lower one. Consider the case of fast-food preparation employees. Turnover tends to be quite high, and wages are quite low. If wages were doubled or tripled, turnover would surely drop, but this strategy would not be cost-effective since replacing fast-food workers is fairly inexpensive.

Looking at the overall turnover rate may be misleading. It is important to consider what types of employees are choosing to leave. Whether a given turnover

● **FIGURE 16.4**

Optimal Organizational Turnover

Source: Adapted from Michael A. Abelson and Barry D. Baysinger, "Optimal and Dysfunctional Turnover: Toward an Organizational Level Model," *Academy of Management Review,* Vol. 9, 1984, p. 333. Reprinted by permission.

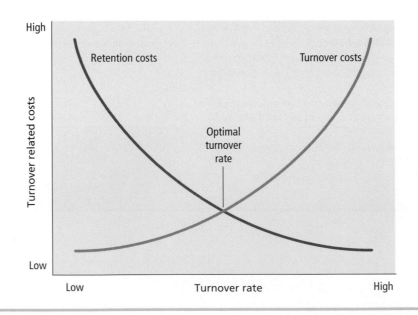

event hurts or helps the organization depends in part on the performance of the person leaving: Is he or she someone the organization would prefer to retain? A number of studies have explored the relationship between performance and turnover, and there appears to be a tendency for poor performers to be more likely to quit than good performers.[44] However, this may not be true for all organizations or at the extremes of the performance continuum. For instance, the very worst performers may not leave because no one else will hire them, and the very best may be repeatedly approached by other firms intent on luring them away.[45] Thus, it is not safe to assume that the organization is better off without the people who choose to leave.

A more sophisticated model for evaluating turnover functionality is shown in Figure 16.5. This model suggests that it is necessary to distinguish among turnover events in terms of both employee performance level (high, acceptable, and low) and replaceability (easy, difficult). To maximize benefits to the organization, quite different techniques should be applied in each cell of the matrix in Figure 16.5 to discourage or encourage turnover.

In cell A, turnover is highly dysfunctional because incumbents are excellent performers who are difficult to replace, either because the skill is in short supply in the marketplace or the position requires a great deal of organization-specific skill, experience, or relationship building with clients that takes time to develop. Employers whose competitive strategy relies heavily on personal relationships between employees and customers, such as some high-service brokerage houses, law firms, or medical practices, might find that they have a large percentage of employees in this cell. Employers should make every effort to retain high performers who are difficult to replace, both by providing an excellent work environment and by meeting their unique needs. An example of the latter is provided by the second

● **FIGURE 16.5**

Performance
Replaceability Strategy
Matrix

Source: D. C. Martin and K. M. Bartol, "Managing Turnover Strategically." Reprinted with permission from the November 1985 issue of *Personnel Administrator,* copyright 1985, The American Society for Personnel Administration, Alexandria, Va.

author of this textbook, who owns a rural resort. When his talented young chef got married and then couldn't find a place to rent because of their family dogs, Schoenfeldt bought a house of their mutual choice and contracted to rent it to the chef at a very modest rate in exchange for assurances that the chef would stay for at least two more years! When feasible, employers may also wish to identify and begin to develop successors in case staff members in this cell do leave.

Cell B is populated by high performers who are easier to replace. Turnover in this cell is dysfunctional but not disastrous. Efforts to retain these employees should be made, but extremely costly retention strategies are probably inappropriate. Sophisticated succession planning systems will also be unnecessary in this cell, as vacancies can be filled fairly easily.

Cell C contains acceptable performers who are hard to replace. Because of the disruption caused by their departure, turnover in this cell is considered dysfunctional. Efforts should be made to retain these employees and plan for replacement in case turnover occurs, Further, organizations should attempt to move cell C employees to higher levels of performance through training, goal setting, and performance-contingent rewards.

Cell D consists of acceptable performers who are easy to replace. Whether turnover in this cell is functional depends on the cost of finding and training a replacement and on the probability that the replacement will perform better than the current incumbent. If replacements are inexpensive and likely to possess better or more current skills than present employees, then special efforts to retain cell D employees will not be needed. However, any acceptable performers with potential should be trained, coached, and given incentives to improve their performance. In the case of some call centers, if the work is sufficiently simple and routine that training costs are low, new employees are easily found, and incumbents burn out after a year or so, it may make sense to tolerate a high turnover rate because new hires are likely to be more motivated and enthusiastic than their longer-tenure peers.

The final two cells contain poor performers. The organization's appraisal and reward system should encourage these employees to improve their performance to acceptable levels. If this effort fails, then turnover will probably be functional. Employees in cell F, who are easily replaced, may be discharged following a fair disciplinary procedure (discussed later in this chapter) or encouraged to leave with accurate negative feedback on performance and minimal rewards under a merit or bonus system. Hard-to-replace employees (cell E) whose performance does not improve to acceptable levels should be retained only until replacements can be located or developed, then encouraged to seek more suitable employment elsewhere.

Retention Management Programs

Having identified employees or job categories where turnover would be especially dysfunctional, organizations should be proactive in working to retain these people. An increasing percentage of employers, 60 percent in a 1997 survey, claimed to have strategies for promoting retention and a further 11 percent were developing a strategy. Twenty-seven percent of survey respondents said their organization had a formal retention program in place—but, not surprisingly, 100 percent of companies in the computer industry had such a program.[46] In some larger companies, positions such as "Manager of Recruiting and Retention" have been created to emphasize the importance of getting and then keeping high-quality staff.

A comprehensive **retention management program** must be built on accurate information about why people are leaving a particular organization. In the absence of such information, wrong conclusions may be drawn about the causes of departure and ineffective means to combat it adopted. Table 16.6 shows the opinions of 1,148 employees in twenty companies and 273 human resource managers about the relative importance of some external and internal causes for turnover. Clearly, the perceptions of the HR managers differ in some important ways from those of the employees who may actually do the quitting. Employees say that the least important factor in motivating them to quit is the availability of jobs that pay more. HR managers believe that this external factor, which is largely beyond their control, is the most important driver of turnover. In fact, employees say the most important reason they leave is because their work is underappreciated and not recognized. Clearly, any organization can improve in this area, regardless of the external labor market. Opportunities to move up and develop skills are also important to employees, and with proper career planning, innovative career ladders, mentoring, and employer-provided training or tuition reimbursement programs, much can be done in these areas as well.

The RAC call center used a number of approaches to reducing turnover. Because pay was substandard, it increased the amount by 10 to 30 percent, but it also made some of it contingent upon performance. This focused employee attention on doing the job well, made performance feedback more meaningful, and provided recognition of high-quality work as well as bringing total compensation for

● **TABLE 16.6**

Employee and HR Manager Beliefs About Why Employees Leave

Importance of Reasons for Leaving a Job	Employee Ranks	HR Manager Ranks
Reasons internal to firm		
Work goes unrecognized/unappreciated	1	7
Little chance to move ahead	3	4
Unhappiness with job demands/requirements	5	3
Friction with supervisor or coworker	6	6
Disliked management or supervisory style	7	8
Dissatisfaction with company policies	8	10
Attractions outside firm		
Availability of better training/career opportunities	2	5
Easy availability of more interesting work	4	2
Desire to return to school	9	9
Easy availability of equal or better paying jobs	10	1

Source: Data are reported in D. J. Campbell and K. M. Campbell, "Why Individuals Voluntarily Leave: Perceptions of Human Resource Managers Versus Employees," *Asia Pacific Journal of Human Resources*, Vol. 39, (1), 2001, pp. 23–41.

employees into the top quartile in the local labor market. Employee training was greatly increased to prepare agents to handle a much wider range of customer needs. A buddy system was adopted for new hires after their formal training finished. Teams were created, and the team leader's role was changed from supervision to motivating and coaching employees and figuring out how to make the workplace "fun." A number of employee involvement programs were implemented. The "Bright Ideas" suggestion program generated 2,400 ideas on how to improve business in 1998, each rewarded with a raffle ticket in the monthly prize drawing. Daily team meetings were conducted with plenty of feedback on performance measures. Social events were held frequently, teams had special themed dress-up days, and prizes like chocolates and wine were given spontanteously for especially noteworthy performance. Special cash bonuses were sometimes given to a team for surpassing performance standards. Taken together, these measures made the work more enjoyable, challenging, and rewarding.[47] The additional friendship bonds built with teammates increased embeddedness and made employees reluctant to leave.

Information about why employees quit or would think about quitting should be collected regularly by organizations. There are two methods for accessing this information: **exit interviews** and **organizational surveys.** Well over 90 percent of major organizations conduct exit interviews with employees who quit. The exit interview is generally conducted by a human resource professional, not by the employee's immediate superior. Several major topic areas should be discussed (see Table 16.7). Tactful probing may be needed to determine the real reason for quitting. A small percentage of organizations use a consultant rather than an organization member as the interviewer, to encourage the employee to speak more freely. Some conduct the interview by phone several weeks or months after the employee has left, again in the hope of gaining accurate information about the true cause of departure.[48]

About three-fourths of medium-sized and large companies use employee opinion surveys.[49] Anonymous employee surveys can be used for many purposes, depending on what questions are asked. For instance, many organizations now use surveys to track employee acceptance of culture-change efforts such as team-based work systems or total quality management. Another common use is to monitor employee satisfaction with such aspects of their jobs as pay, training and development, and supervision. Decreases in satisfaction may predict subsequent increases in turnover. If retention is a particular concern, surveys can be designed as written "pre-exit interviews," asking questions about why employees would consider leaving, what parts of their job are most frustrating or disappointing, or, more positively, why they stay.[50] Table 16.8 shows the results of one survey of why employees stay.

Accurate information about why employees stay or leave and how satisfied they are is useful in designing specific features of a retention program. Recall, however, that satisfaction is only part of the picture in terms of the decision to quit. While programs aimed at improving job satisfaction may be helpful, some turnover events are precipitated by single incidents like a mishandled appraisal or a reasonable request denied. One expert says, "People do not leave companies. They leave bosses." A software developer said, "I've worked at six different companies in the six years since college, and every time I left, the last straw had something to do with my boss being completely oblivious to the problems his people were having."[51] Clearly, an effective retention program must enlist the aid and understanding of every supervisor in the organization.

TABLE 16.7

Useful Exit Interview Questions

Resources, job information, and training

How adequate was the help and equipment to get the job done?

How clearly were job responsibilities defined?

How adequate and timely was job information?

How helpful and competent was supervision and management?

What suggestions could you provide relative to resources and job information?

How well trained were you for the job? Suggestions?

Job challenge and opportunity for advancement

How would you rate your job in terms of interesting work?

How adequate was your authority to do the job?

How much of an opportunity did you have to develop your special abilities?

How much freedom did you have to do your work?

What was most difficult to learn on your job?

How do you feel about advancement opportunities here?

Relations with supervisors, coworkers, and other departments

How well did you get along with your supervisor?

How would you evaluate the way your supervisor handled his or her employees? made work assignments? acted on complaints?

How well did you get along with your coworkers? friendly? helpful?

What is your evaluation of how well the various departments work together?

Comfort and working conditions

How did you feel about the physical surroundings?

How did you feel about the level of job stress?

How did you feel about the workload?

How much flexibility was there in working hours?

How convenient was travel to and from work?

Financial

How did you feel about your salary?

How about job security?

How about the fringe benefits?

Company policies

What comments can you make about our company policies? Are there any changes you would suggest?

Overall Questions

What do you think were some of the good features of your job?

What do you think were some of the good features of this organization?

What were some of the less desirable features of your job?

What were some of the less desirable features of working for this organization?

What overall improvements could you suggest?

What was the main factor in your decision to leave?

Source: Reprinted with permission of Science Research Associates, an imprint of Macmillan Publishing Company from *Interviewing: Key to Effective Management* by Joseph P. Zima. Copyright © 1983 by Science Research Associates.

●**TABLE 16.8**

Why Employees Stay

---

1. Career growth, learning and development
2. Exciting work and challenge
3. Meaningful work, making a difference and a contribution
4. Great people
5. Being part of a team
6. Good boss
7. Recognition for work well done
8. Fun on the job
9. Autonomy, sense of control over my work
10. Flexibility – for example, in work hours and dress code
11. Fair pay and benefits
12. Inspiring leadership
13. Pride in organization, its mission and quality of product
14. Great work environment
15. Location
16. Job security
17. Family-friendly
18. Cutting-edge technology

Source: Reprinted with permission of the publisher. From *Love 'Em or Lose 'Em: Getting Good People to Stay,* copyright © 1999 by Kaye and Jordan-Evans, Berrett-Kochler Publishers, Inc., San Francisco, CA. All rights reserved. www.bkconnection.com.

The following are some essential generic features of retention programs:

- Benchmark data on retention performance, retention programs, and other HR practices in the organization and successful firms in the same industry or labor market.

- Goal setting for retention – what is the target rate for each job or department? Remember that not all departures are preventable by the organization. Some flow from external events such as the transfer of a spouse, illness, an opportunity too good to pass up, or a decision to change lifestyle.

- A means of holding managers accountable for the retention of their staff. In addition to goals, this may include adding retention measures to their performance appraisal criteria and bonus formula.

Specific components in the race to keep talent might include the following:

- Many opportunities for challenging work, learning, and growth. These can be provided through job rotation, secondments, special projects, lateral transfers, mentoring, career planning, promotions, and so forth.

- Effective performance-contingent rewards and recognition and frequent and honest performance feedback to satisfy employees' desire for information and appreciation.

● **FIGURE 16.6**

Are You Flexible Enough for Today's Employees?

Source: Kaye and Jordan-Evans, "Retention: Tag, You're It!" *Training and Development*, April 2000, p. 34. Reprinted by permission.

Read the following scenarios, imagining that you are the boss of this person. Think about your responses to the requests. Decide when you would say yes *or* no *and why. Use the scoring box below.*

1. I want to adjust my work schedule (for personal reasons) three days a week, to come in half an hour earlier and leave half an hour earlier.
2. I want to get this task done in a brand-new way, not like you have ever seen it done before.
3. I want to complete the first five steps of this project before I have you review it with me.
4. I want to try a new technique, one that I'm more comfortable with, to increase sales.
5. Instead of taking that class you recommended, I found a mentor from whom I want to learn that skill.
6. I just took some great pictures on my vacation and want to put them on my cubicle walls.
7. I want to work from home two days a week.
8. I plan to work on Saturdays for a few weeks in order to get a project done on time, and I want to bring my well-trained dog to work with me.
9. I want to wear casual clothes to work rather than a business suit. I'm more comfortable and creative in my jeans and tennis shoes.
10. I know we've always done these projects solo, but I want to put together a team this time because I believe we will do a better job, more quickly.
11. I want six weeks off without pay to begin building my new home.
12. I want to bring my new baby to work for the first six weeks.

SCORING												
Your response	1	2	3	4	5	6	7	8	9	10	10	12
"Sure, no problem."												
"No way."												
"Let me see what I can do."												

Count your scores across the columns, then think over those that fall in the "No way" box. How could you be more creative and give more space?

- An innovative and competitive compensation system. Both fairness and amount of pay are important, though bear in mind that pay is not usually the only reason people leave.
- Flexibility in addressing special employee requests for job characteristics as well as work time and mode. See Figure 16.6 for examples of how some organizations might be flexible or inflexible to employee requests.
- Family-friendly policies such as emergency child care, flextime, leaves of absence, and so on if family responsibilities are a salient cause of departures.[52]

It is also helpful to *tell* particularly valuable employees that the firm is eager to keep them and ask what can be done to further this end. Some employees only find out after resigning that the firm really did value their work.[53] Following on from the embeddedness concept, it may also be helpful for firms to enhance the number of formal and informal links among the employee, the firm, and the community. This might be done by encouraging teamwork and mentoring, enrolling employees in long-term education/development programs, using employee share ownership plans, cultivating company volunteer or sporting activities, considering hiring spouses when qualified, providing child care, and perhaps providing home-purchase assistance.[54] As mentioned in Chapter 6, employees sometimes quit jobs that fail to meet the expectations they had when first hired. Both realistic job previews and a career-planning session in the first few months after hiring may help to cultivate realistic expectations that the company can meet.

The chapter has thus far focused on largely employee-initiated transitions such as retirement and quitting a job, or on reassignments involving promotions or transfers. Reassignments may be initiated by the organization to meet its needs and/or be requested by employees as part of a career development strategy. The next sections will consider **involuntary turnover**—instances in which individuals are forced to leave because the organization no longer wants or needs them.

INVOLUNTARY TURNOVER

Involuntary turnover has important strategic implications for the organization. First, it affects the perception of the organization by the community, the media, and current and former employees. For example, a firm that effectively and humanely manages a reduction in its work force may maintain or even enhance its image among employees and the public, which could result in a variety of long-term benefits. In contrast, one that develops a reputation for treating employees badly, either through frequent layoffs or arbitrary and unfair firing, will have a harder time drawing a qualified applicant pool in the future.

Second, involuntary turnover helps the organization achieve its strategic goals. Poor performers are terminated, and the productivity of a firm can be improved. Layoffs may allow an organization to reduce costs when market demand slumps. As an example, in a turnaround effort, the appliance maker Sunbeam Corporation closed eighteen of its twenty-six factories and reduced its work force by 6,000 employees.[55] Less than a year later, Sunbeam reported sales up 13 percent, an income increase of over 360 percent, and a price per share of $40, up from $12.[56] Clearly, a reduction of facilities and work force was an integral part of Sunbeam's turnaround strategy.

Third, organizational exit also aids coordination and integration within the organization by helping remove employees who cannot get along well with others and therefore disrupt the smooth operation of the firm. Finally, organizational exit serves as a strategic influence on the culture of the organization. Removal of key executives can allow an organization to change its strategic focus. Why people are selected out can send messages to other employees about important cultural norms and values, for example, a "no-exceptions" rule for using drugs while working or for violating safety rules.[57]

The sections that follow will first consider the discharge of individuals, usually for reasons of poor performance on unacceptable behavior, then turn to larger-scale layoffs usually motivated by economic or strategic concerns rather than the behavior of the workers themselves.

EMPLOYMENT-AT-WILL

Can employers fire any employee at any time, for any reason at all? The concept of **employment-at-will** says they can. In recent years, this issue has generated considerable debate. This section presents a definition and brief history of the concept of employment-at-will and discusses the factors that limit an employer's ability to terminate employees. Finally, some suggestions for how management should deal with the employment-at-will controversy are given.

What Is Employment-at-Will?

The employment-at-will doctrine stems from a nineteenth-century view that an employment contract is a private matter between free agents. A person is hired for an indefinite duration, and either employer or employee may end the relationship for any reason and at any time. In 1884, this doctrine found support in the case of *Payne* v. *Western and Atlantic RA Company*, when the court confirmed the right of an employer to hire or fire any individual for good cause, bad cause, or no cause at all.[58] Discussion of the employment-at-will issue has generally centered on the employer's right to fire a worker rather than on the employee's right to leave a job. With the Wagner Act of 1935, unions were able, through collective bargaining, to introduce the idea that employees should be fired only for just cause. Many public employees have also received statutory protection from arbitrary termination. The tenure system among university teachers, for example, protects teachers from arbitrary firing. More recently, managerial and professional employees have, in some instances, been able to negotiate employment contracts that protect them from at-will termination. However, between 70 and 75 percent of employees in the United States have no such explicit protection.[59] Nevertheless, an employer's right to fire employees at will is limited by several factors, including civil rights legislation, union contracts, whistleblower statutes, and employees' limited right to sue on the grounds of wrongful discharge.[60]

Civil Rights Legislation

Federal civil rights legislation has provided protection against employment discrimination for minority-group members, women, handicapped persons, older workers, and other protected groups. Organizations have learned to be careful about the fairness of their selection systems but frequently neglect to apply the same safeguards to their organizational exit procedures. The dismissal without cause of employees who are members of a protected class can be a dangerous affair, even when termination is part of a legitimate company-wide layoff. A worker who is discharged for *any* reason might claim that age, sex, or race was the *real* cause of the termination. If prima facie evidence of discrimination is found, the organization must spend considerable time, effort, and money to defend itself against the charge, or it must make a settlement with the plaintiff (possibly including back pay or reinstatement of the employee).

The issues of employment-at-will and employment discrimination have become closely linked in the matter of firing older employees. Chapter 5 describes the Age Discrimination in Employment Act, which prohibits employers from using age as a basis for hiring or firing people aged forty or above. Age discrimination suits are an increasingly common type of workplace bias charge. The typical litigant is a white male supervisor or professional between the ages of fifty and fifty-nine, discharged during corporate layoffs. Such employees have no unions to represent them but are sufficiently aware of the law to challenge their dismissal. As is shown in *Murphy* v. *American Home Products Corporation,* age discrimination can be used successfully to challenge at-will terminations when other, more traditional means of challenge are unsuccessful.[61] Even firing someone for having a "bad attitude" can be problematic—if that person can claim that his or her erratic or lethargic behavior is due to mental illness that is protected under the Americans with Disabilities Act.[62]

Union Contracts

Collective-bargaining agreements also limit an organization's application of the employment-at-will doctrine. Typically, these agreements between unions and management specify the reasons for which an employee may be discharged and the procedures that should be followed in such a discharge. Unions often negotiate seniority provisions that determine who is to be discharged in the event of a company-wide layoff. If an organization takes care to follow the terms of the contract and appropriately documents all cases of termination for cause or layoffs, the constraints imposed by unionization should not be a major difficulty. However, if proper discharge processes are not followed, a grievance may be filed by the employee. A formal grievance procedure then begins. The complaint is discussed at a series of meetings between representatives of the union and management at successively higher levels if agreement cannot be reached at lower levels. If the grievance procedure does not resolve the complaint, arbitration may follow. Arbitration avoids the expense and delay involved in an external judicial solution to an employee's claim, and arbitration judgments are almost always considered to be legally binding on both parties involved in the labor contract.[63]

The Concept of Wrongful Discharge

Many employees cannot rely on federal or state legislation, labor contracts, or individually negotiated contracts in dealing with employment discharge situations. For most U.S. workers, a lawsuit claiming **wrongful discharge** is the only protection against wholesale application of the employment-at-will doctrine.[64] The number and payouts of such lawsuits have increased greatly in recent years.[65] Court decisions associated with the wrongful discharge concept have delineated five types of situations under which the employment-at-will doctrine does not apply: (1) violations of public policy, (2) whistleblowing, (3) an expressed or implied guarantee of continued employment, (4) employer conduct that violates the concepts of "good faith and fair dealing," and (5) other tortious conduct by the employer.[66] These exceptions are summarized in Table 16.9.

● **Violations of Public Policy**   Employees may not be fired for exercising rights protected by law—for instance, filing workers' compensation claims, refusing to

● **TABLE 16.9**

Exceptions to Employment-at-Will

Exception	Example	Important Cases/Laws
Employment discrimination	Termination based on sex or age	Title VII, Civil Rights Act Age Discrimination in Employment Act
Union contracts	Seniority-based terminations	Wagner Act
Public policy violations	Whistleblowers	*Palmateer* v. *International Harvester Sheets* v. *Teddy's Frosted Foods*
Expressed or implied guarantee of employment	Verbal contracts Written policies in employee manuals	*Touissant* v. *Blue Cross & Blue Shield*
Good faith and fair dealing	Firing to prevent receiving benefits	*Fortune* v. *National Cash Register Co.*
Tortious conduct	Interfere with legitimate contract	*Monge* v. *Beebe Rubber Co.*

commit perjury, or taking time off to serve on a jury. Employees are also protected when they exercise the "rights of shareholders." Employees who are shareholders in a company may, for example, exercise their rights by voting for or against a merger or stock float without fear of firing by management opposed to that particular course of action.[67] Forty-three states have accepted the concept of wrongful discharge as a result of violations of public policy, though the situation is usually defined very narrowly. The critical issue is not whether the employee's behavior is of *benefit* to the public but whether a *clear and legal mandate* of public policy is involved.[68]

● **Whistleblowing** Various forms of **whistleblowing** are also protected (see the Ethical Perspective box). For example, in *Palmateer* v. *International Harvester,* an employee was subjected to wrongful discharge after he reported coworkers who were involved in criminal activity. In *Sheets* v. *Teddy's Frosted Foods,* an employee who insisted that the company comply with the Food, Drug, and Cosmetic Act was found to have been wrongfully discharged.[69]

● **Expressed or Implied Guarantee of Continued Employment** While violation of public policy is the most recognized exception to the employment-at-will doctrine, an **expressed or implied contract** between the employer and the employee is also held to limit arbitrary firing in thirty-eight states.[70] Implied contracts are created in several ways. In one case—*Touissant* v. *Blue Cross and Blue Shield of Michigan*—employees had been fired for no apparent reason, even though there had been statements by the employer to the effect that "you can have your job as long as you do your job." These statements were deemed to form a contract between employee and employer.[71] In the same case, there were also written personnel policies stating that good cause was required before any nonprobationary employee would be fired and that employees could be fired only after receiving a series of warnings and a disciplinary hearing. The employees had been fired without benefit of these procedures. They filed suit against the company and won the case.

Whistleblowing in Organizations

What should an employee do when he or she learns of ethically questionable behavior on the part of peers, superiors, or others in the organization? Historically, most organizations have taken the view that the employee should keep quiet and do nothing. Speaking up in an effort to get the situation remedied is much less acceptable.

Speaking up in the context of suspected organizational wrongdoing is called "whistleblowing." *Internal whistleblowing* is making one's suspicions known to a responsible person in the organization, in the hope that the problem will be corrected. *External whistleblowing* is making the wrongdoing known to someone outside the organization, such as the press, a law enforcement agency, or a regulatory agency. Either can be done anonymously or openly.

Whistleblowing is relatively rare in many organizations. Individuals often fear the consequences of speaking up, of possible retaliation ranging from ostracism by peers to demotion, discharge, blacklisting, loss of professional reputation, and, in some cases, even physical assault or murder. Estimates are that

65 percent of whistleblowers experience retaliation: Many are fired and few get their jobs back, and a good number are never able to work in their field again. While sacked whistleblowers have legal recourse in most states if the issue they raised concerns a violation of public policy by their employer, few can afford to pursue their case while unemployed, and most such suits are unsuccessful. One former federal employee tells the story of how he told the truth to investigators from the Inspector General's Office, despite being told to lie by his superior. He was fired, was unsuccessful in finding another job, lost his house, spent his life savings on lawyers, was divorced by his wife, and was still waiting for his case to be heard by the Merit Systems Protection Board six years later. When asked if he'd do it again, he said, "Are you crazy? Of course I wouldn't. I'd lie in a minute. It ruined my life and it didn't do any good anyway. The investigators didn't really want to know. They were just going through the motions."*

As ethical issues in business have become more salient over the recent years, some organizations have modified their view of whistleblowing. Instead of see-

● **Good Faith and Fair Dealing**   Judicial tradition also holds that a contract contains an implied promise of **good faith and fair dealing.** A violation of good faith on the employer's part may provide the basis for a suit claiming an exception to the employment-at-will doctrine. In *Fortune* v. *National Cash Register Company,* Fortune, a salesman, had worked for the company for twenty-five years under a contract that specifically stated that he had been hired on an at-will basis.[72] He was fired after having made a large sale—because, he charged, the company wanted to avoid paying him the commission it owed him. Although his contract included an at-will clause, the court ruled that National Cash Register had not acted in good faith and thus had violated the employment contract. Only eleven states recognize the covenant-of-good-faith exception to the employment-at-will doctrine.[73]

● **Tortious Conduct**   Some discharged employees have argued successfully that they were victims of **tortious conduct.** In law, a *tort* is the violation of a duty owed another person (aside from breach of specific contracts). "A termination by the employer of a contract of employment at will which is motivated by bad faith or malice or is based on retaliation is not in the best interest of the economic system ing it as disloyalty or boat-rocking to be punished, they are trying to harness it as an early warning that problems are occurring that need to be addressed. By making internal whistleblowing easier and safer, these firms hope to discover and correct wrongdoing before public damage is done. In one survey, 70 percent of responding organizations said that they had a formal procedure for employees to bring legal and ethical concerns to the attention of management.

An effective whistleblowing policy should do the following:

- Be written
- Be well communicated to employees
- Allow employees to go to someone other than their immediate supervisors with complaints (because a supervisor is often the one committing or condoning the problematic act)
- Allow for anonymous reporting
- Specify a formal investigation procedure, with feedback to the employee on the outcome of the investigation
- Forbid any form of retaliation against whistleblowers
- Provide an appeal process if an employee is still not satisfied

Human resource managers are often involved in whistleblowing cases. In the survey mentioned above, 77 percent of formal policies specified the HR department as one outlet for employees who wished to make a complaint. HR managers may also be involved in educating supervisors about the policy and in ensuring that whistleblowers do not experience retaliation.

If an employer does not have a whistleblowing procedure employees trust, there is also the option to report suspected wrongdoing via www.etheft.com, the Web site of Employee Theft Anonymous. This site will take anonymous employee complaints of wrongdoing such as theft, embezzlement, bribery, sexual harassment, or sabotage and pass them on to the organization member designated by the person doing the reporting.

*Cited in C. F. Alford, "Whistle-Blowers: How Much We Can Learn from Them Depends on How Much We Can Give Up," *The American Behavioral Scientist*, October 1999, pp. 264–277.
Sources: Kevin M. Smith, and John M. Oseth, "The Whistleblowing Era: A Management Perspective," *Employee Relations Law Journal*, Autumn 1993, pp. 179–192; Marcia P. Miceli and Janet P. Near, "Whistleblowing: Reaping the Benefits," *Academy of Management Executive*, August 1994, pp. 65–72; J. P. Near and M. P. Miceli, "Effective Whistle-Blowing," *Academy of Management Review*, Vol. 20 (3), 1995, pp. 679–708; and T. D. Miethe, *Whistleblowing at Work. Tough Choices in Exposing Fraud, Waste, and Abuse on the Job* (Boulder, Co.: Westview Press, 1999).

or the public good and constitutes a breach of the employment contract."[74] An employer who acts with malicious intent in terminating employees, intentionally inflicting emotional distress on them or defaming their character, can be found guilty of wrongful discharge.[75] In addition, an organization can be found guilty of tortious conduct if it interferes with an employment contract between other parties, resulting in an employee's discharge. For example, in a 1985 Minnesota case, a bus terminal company was found guilty of wrongful interference in an employment contract. The terminal had told a bus company that unless it "got rid of " a certain employee, it could no longer use the terminal.[76]

Management's Response

Dealing effectively with the issue of employment-at-will and avoiding charges of wrongful discharge are important practical considerations for organizations. For example, the average award for a successful wrongful discharge suit was $205,794 in 1997, up from $120,736 just four years earlier.[77] Organizations may approach the issue of employment-at-will in several ways. Many companies have taken actions

Can You Have It Both Ways? High- and Low-Involvement Trends

Employers today are facing conflicting models for the strategic management of human resources. A popular Australian business magazine unwittingly ran in the same issue two articles that seemed to represent diametrically opposing views of how organizations should treat employees. One article, entitled "How to Avoid Hiring a Dud," concluded that because firing a bad employee is so difficult, the best course is to avoid hiring any permanent employees in the first place. Instead, fixed-term contracts, leasing, and temporary staff are recommended to keep potential problem employees (and all others) at arm's length. Later in the same issue, Tom Peters discussed the key role played by "a growing web of trust" among management and employees in an increasingly competitive and fast-moving environment. He commented that "there is no such thing as half trusting an employee, any more than one can half fly an airplane." But if employees feel they may be here today and gone tomorrow, there seems to be little basis for trust.

These articles represent two extreme strategies that are becoming more common. On the one hand is the move to a more contingent work force with less job security: More than 20 percent of American workers are part time, temporary, contract, or leased. Some retailers now hire permanent full-time employees only in management positions, and all other staff are part time. Hiring for these part-time positions may be casual, training cursory, jobs simple, wages low, advancement impossible, layoffs common, and voluntary turnover high. Even among more traditional employers with reasonable pay and benefits, waves of downsizing and subsequent overwork for those still employed have soured employee commitment and trust. On top of this, companies wishing to avoid creating an implicit contract of employment repeatedly remind employees that they are employed at will. A 1999 survey found that only 45 percent of employees felt a strong personal attachment to their organization and only 42 percent believed their company deserved their loyalty.

The opposite strategy is adopted by other organizations. Firms in high-tech and other areas where retaining skilled and scarce employees is especially important are bending over backward to accommodate employee desires for challenging and flexible work as well as exotic benefits (sabbaticals, in-office massage, dry-cleaning service, etc.). High-involvement organizations (see Chapter 10) use a variety of methods, such as extensive training and multiskilling, teamwork, empowerment, employee share ownership, open book management, and high job security to build and retain a skilled and loyal work force.

Some experts worry that these opposing trends will increase the gap between the privileged few with satisfying, permanent jobs and the less fortunate, whose temporary or part-time jobs require few skills and return minimal rewards. So which is it to be? Bring employees in closer to the organization so that loyalty, trust, communication, and commitment can develop in a secure atmosphere that promotes high employee retention? Or treat employees like replaceable, unimportant hired hands who can be fired at will? It is possible that either system can be successful in the right situation, if all parts of the human resource system are consistent with the strategy and if the strategy promotes the type of behavior needed by the organization. What does not work is a mixed system—needing loyalty, involvement, and organization-specific skills based on long tenure from employees but using HR practices that produce marginalized employees with a high rate of turnover.

Sources: A. S. Tsui, J. L. Pearce, L. W. Porter, and J. P. Hite, "Choice of Employee–Organization Relationship," *Research in Personnel and Human Resource Management,* Vol. 13, 1995, pp. 117–151; J. M. Parks and D. L. Kidder, "Till Death Us Do Part . . . Changing Work Relationships in the 1990s," *Trends in Organizational Behavior,* Vol. 1, 1994, pp. 111–136; Adele Ferguson, "How to Avoid Hiring a Dud," *Business Review Weekly,* July 11, 1994, pp. 42–47; David James, "Tom Peters Sets the Record Straight," *Business Review Weekly,* July 11, 1994, pp. 80–81; Sinclair E. Hugh, "Employment at Will, an Idea Whose Time Has Come—And Gone," May 25, 2000 (Available at: www.workforce.com/archive/feature/00/17/17/); and "1999 Employee Relationship Report Benchmark" (Available at: www.walkerinfo.com).

such as including explicit at-will statements on job application forms and in employee handbooks.[78] Some require employees to sign statements acknowledging that they can be fired at any time for any reason. Firms also carefully train recruiters and supervisors to avoid making any promises of job security that might be construed as an implicit contract. While these actions may not completely protect firms from wrongful discharge litigation, they may reduce the likelihood of being taken to court.[79] A potential downside of repeating the at-will message frequently in employee communications is that it sends a very negative message to employees. See A Different Point of View for more on this issue.

Another approach has been to encourage specific labor contracts.[80] In the case of union contracts, discharge cases are handled within the framework of a collectively bargained grievance and arbitration procedure rather than in the courts. Individual employment contracts are commonly used with executive, professional, and sales employees. As well as specifying an at-will discharge policy, these contracts may include noncompete agreements and protect the employer's trade secrets or proprietary information should an employee leave or be fired. Some contracts also include a compulsory arbitration clause should the application of the contract be in dispute. Arbitration is likely to be much quicker and less costly than court procedings for both the employee and the employer.[81]

Firms also take measures to reduce the need for discharges.[82] Management can improve employee selection procedures. Companies can provide realistic orientation programs, where employees both learn what level of performance is expected and receive the training that can help them achieve this level. Firms can also avoid establishing promotion policies focused on the use of seniority as the basis for promotion. When fired, employees who have been promoted due to seniority (despite low performance) would have a substantial case for arguing wrongful discharge in the courts. Management may also develop accurate performance appraisal, performance feedback, and disciplinary systems, in which sanctions for poor performance are clearly specified and a paper trail of performance is maintained. Performance feedback provided by the system may help employees avoid termination. If termination is necessary, everyone understands why. The next section examines the situation in which employees are fired for "just cause," such as poor performance or violation of important organizational rules.

DISCIPLINE SYSTEMS AND TERMINATION FOR CAUSE

For most managers, dealing with problem employees and firing an employee are very difficult and unpleasant things to do and more often than not are done awkwardly.[83] Managers are afraid they may jeopardize friendships or make the situation worse. Taking disciplinary action or firing a member of a work group may also damage the image of the manager with other employees.[84] As a result, many managers try to avoid dealing with problem employees. They are often unsure about how to deal effectively with the situation and assume that "if you ignore it, it will go away." They confront problem employees only after the situation becomes so bad that they have no other choice.[85] Even when a just cause for termination exists, it is important that actions leading to termination be effective and well documented so as to avoid wrongful discharge litigation or even more serious consequences. For example, FBI data indicate that the incidence of employees' killing their supervisors or coworkers, often after having been fired, has escalated in recent years.[86]

In one organization, the U.S. Postal Service, there have been more than a dozen major incidents of disgruntled postal employees murdering colleagues in a fifteen-year period—enough to add the phrase "going postal" to the vernacular. The next section focuses on the use of discipline in organizations and the development of disciplinary systems, which should form an important part of the overall process leading to employees' **termination for cause.**

The Use of Discipline in Organizations

Considerable attention has been paid to whether disciplinary punishment is an appropriate part of organizational life. On the one hand, discipline helps provide cues or signals as to what behavior is or is not acceptable. It serves as a form of role clarification and identifies important organizational norms and values for the employee. Even if punishment does not change the behavior of the offender, other members of the work group may be deterred from engaging in inappropriate behavior. Arguments against the use of disciplinary punishment are that it is unethical or inhumane and that it never really eliminates the undesired behavior. Undesirable behavior is suppressed only until the threat of punishment is gone or the behavior "goes underground," where the possibility of detection is reduced.[87] Gail Ball, Linda Trevino, and Henry Sims describe the potentially negative effects of a punishment cycle in which the manager observes an employee commit an undesirable act and therefore categorizes the person as a "bad employee." The manager then takes punitive action against the employee, which causes the employee to label the manager a "bad (or unfair) manager." The employee reacts negatively to the manager and engages in more undesirable acts, which starts the cycle again, with both manager and employee developing increasingly negative attitudes toward one another.[88]

Organizations can take any of several different approaches to discipline.[89] One is largely punitive, imposing punishments as retribution to get even for past wrongdoings. Supervisors are seen as police, and employees committing violations are treated like children who must be spanked with increasing vigor for each additional infraction. At the opposite end of the scale is a future-oriented developmental approach that treats the employee as an adult. The latter approach is called **positive discipline** or **discipline without punishment.**[90] In this model, oral and written coaching for the first few violations is followed by a one-day suspension *with pay.* During the day off, the employee is to think about whether he or she is willing and able to abide by the company's rules. The next day, the employee tells the supervisor that he or she has decided to comply, or voluntarily resigns. The onus of controlling subsequent behavior falls squarely on the employee. A further similar violation results in discharge because the employee has chosen not to honour his or her pledge to the employer.

Research on the effective use of disciplinary punishment in organizations suggests that punishment must do the following:

- Be in proportion to the nature of the undesirable behavior exhibited
- Be applied before the undesired behavior has time to become a habit or a typical behavior pattern of the employee
- Focus on a specific behavior, not a general pattern of behavior
- Be applied consistently across people and time

- Not be followed by positive, noncontingent rewards that a manager gives to lessen his or her feeling of guilt about punishing the employee
- Be administered by someone whom the employee trusts and respects[91]

The goal of fair and effective discipline is more likely to be achieved when there is a detailed written discipline policy that is clearly communicated to all employees. Often such policies specify a **progressive discipline system.** Such a system is shown in Table 16.10, although the nature of offenses should be defined in more detail than is shown in the table. For instance, "excessive or habitual absenteeism" might be defined as missing more than four days of work, without a medical excuse or approval by the supervisor, during any sixty-day period.[92] While a few offenses—such as bringing a gun to work or striking a superior—warrant discharge the first time they are committed, others attract a graduated

● **TABLE 16.10**

An Example of a Progressive Disciplinary System

Key to symbols: V = verbal warning; W = written warning; 3, 5 = suspension days; D = discharge

Nature of Offense	Number of Offenses				
	1st	**2nd**	**3rd**	**4th**	**5th**
Excessive or habitual absenteeism	V	W	5	D	
Absence from overtime assignment	W	5	D		
Excessive or habitual tardiness	V	W	3	5	D
Leaving without permission	W	5	D		
Loafing, loitering, etc.	W	5	D		
Disorderly conduct	5	D			
Acts intending to harm persons or property	D				
Possessing alcohol at work	5	D			
Gambling	5	D			
Possession of narcotics	D				
Appearing for work under the influence of narcotics	D				
Possession of firearms at work	D				
Violating clearly marked safety rules	W	3	5	D	
Negligent acts during work that cause harm or damage to persons or property	5	D			
Stealing	D				
Unauthorized possession of company property	D				
Refusal to accept work or perform work in accordance with instructions	D				
Threats to or intimidation of management	D				
Slowdown, willful holding back of work	W	D			

Source: Adapted from Louis Imundo, *Employee Discipline: How to Do It Right* (Belmont, Calif.: Wadsworth, 1985), pp. 34–41.

(progressive) series of penalties. For minor offenses, an oral warning is the first step. This assures that the employee understands that a rule or expectation has been violated, that he or she should not do it again, and that more severe consequences will follow for persisting in the violation. A second similar offense attracts a written warning and starts to lay the paper trail documenting the organization's efforts to reform the employee. Further offenses may result in suspension without pay, and a further repetition of the same offense results in discharge. Table 16.11 shows the frequency with which each of these penalties was imposed on its employees by the Internal Revenue Service in one year.

While the process of discharging individuals for violation of rules, excessive absenteeism, or other discrete behaviors is fairly clear-cut, termination for poor work performance is often more difficult and sometimes more subjective. Superiors may tolerate poor performance for a long period of time before deciding to take action. They may write acceptable performance appraisals for poor performers to avoid unpleasantness or in the hope that the employee will improve with time. These actions may come back to haunt them if there is a subsequent attempt to discharge the employee for sustained poor performance. When there is a problem with poor job performance, employees need to be told very clearly (orally and in writing) exactly what the problem is, what they must do to fix the problem, how much their performance has to improve, by what date, and what will happen to them if improvement is not forthcoming.[93] Coaching during the designated period is helpful in showing that the employer has made a genuine effort to remedy the problem. At Sun Microsystems, employees in the bottom 10 percent on performance rankings are "loved to death." Following this intensive rehabilitation effort, those who do not reach performance goals are offered a "prompt exit" severance payment. If they refuse to take it, further poor performance results in termination without compensation.[94]

As part of an overall disciplinary procedure, the organization may want to develop personal counseling programs for problem employees. Like appraisal and feedback systems, these programs give the employee additional opportunities to correct behavior that will otherwise lead to termination. These **employee assistance programs** help employees with personal problems that affect performance,

● **TABLE 16.11**

Number of Each Type of Disciplinary Action Imposed by the IRS in One Year

Type of Penalty	Number
Oral admonishment confirmed in writing	776
Written reprimand	784
Suspension of 14 days or less	308
Suspension of more than 14 days	50
Demotion	45
Removal from job	257
Total	2,220

Source: C. J. Guffey and M. M. Helms, "Effective Employee Discipline: A Case of the Internal Revenue Service," *Public Personnel Management*, Spring 2001, pp. 111–127.

such as drug or alcohol abuse. These programs may help keep an employee from being fired.[95] Even if termination does occur, employees may feel less hostile if they recognize that the organization has done its best to help them stay employed. Supervisors may also feel less troubled about firing employees who have been given ample opportunity to correct their behavior.

Managing Termination for Cause

The effective use of performance appraisal and feedback, accompanied by employee assistance programs and progressive disciplinary actions, should reduce the need for terminating employees. However, firing is sometimes necessary, and a combination of actions taken both before termination and when termination occurs can make the firing easier on everyone involved and reduce the possibility of legal action against the organization by the employee. In the case of repeated violations, it is important to document the occurrence of each act and the feedback that was subsequently given to the employee. When a severe violation is suspected, a thorough investigation should be conducted to ascertain the guilt or innocence of the employee. One employee won a multimillion-dollar lawsuit against Penzoil because of an inadequate investigation. Penzoil had received an anonymous letter charging the employee with sexual harassment, illegal conduct, and mismanagement. Penzoil undertook an investigation, determined that there was sufficient evidence of sexual harassment, and terminated the individual. He sued on the grounds that the investigator's summary of evidence gave as much weight to hearsay evidence as it did to firsthand knowledge of his activities. The court found that the investigator had made no attempt to evaluate the credibility of those giving evidence. The employee won, and the Supreme Court later upheld the decision.[96] Guidelines for ensuring that investigations will meet court scrutiny include the following:

- Take notes during interviews with the employee and any witnesses.
- Emphasize confidentiality, and proceed discreetly throughout the investigation.
- Maintain a file of information resources, including a time line of occurrences, interview notes, and so forth.
- Conduct interviews in a private place under relaxed, nonintimidating circumstances.
- Do not conduct group interviews.
- Avoid accusatory questions and police-style tactics.
- Do not question the employee for an unreasonable amount of time.
- Avoid any appearance of force or the suggestion that an employee may not leave the room.
- Explain that the investigation is for the purpose of having employees tell what they know, explain their behavior, and provide a factual basis for any disciplinary action.
- Allow the person being interviewed to review any written statements and make changes in them.
- Tell those being interviewed that some of the information may become public (e.g., in a lawsuit or disciplinary action).

- Also tell them that they may be disciplined if they were guilty of wrongdoing.
- Consider having a witness present during the interview.
- Be aware that written sworn statements may be useful.
- Interview only people who have reason to know about the actions under investigation.[97]

Regardless of how thorough the investigation, a single person should rarely make the decision to terminate an employee. The decision should either be reviewed by a higher-level manager or made by a group of several managers.[98] This will help to prevent biased or spur-of-the-moment terminations.

The trauma associated with the firing of an employee can be lessened if the supervisor has been adequately trained in how to conduct the **termination interview.** Effective management of the termination process is a key to reducing the workplace violence that might occur when an individual is fired.[99] The purpose of this meeting is to inform the employee of the decision to terminate his or her employment and to explain why. Given the emotionally charged nature of the encounter, the supervisor must plan for it carefully. He or she must know all the important facts of the case and must be able to explain the reasons for the termination and give specific examples of the employee's inappropriate behavior. These examples help justify the termination decision and make it easier for the supervisor to respond to a challenge from a defensive or hostile employee. If an effective and systematic feedback system has been used, nothing in the termination interview should come as a surprise to the terminated employee.

Additional actions to smooth termination include having the final paycheck ready at the time of the interview. The check should include all payments due to the employee, such as salary and compensation for acrued leave. Some organizations offer "transition counseling" to terminated employees. This might include advice on how to register for unemployment compensation (if it is due) and some advice on beginning the job search process. If an employee has several years of service, a small severance package can ease the transition and reduce ill will, even if the payment is not contractually required. When there is a choice, it is recommended that the termination interview be conducted early in the week rather than on a Friday. This allows the employee to immediately begin searching for another job if he or she so desires. Finally, it is recommended that a witness be present at the termination interview.[100]

In the preceding sections on termination for cause, the focus has been on the termination of an individual employee. Another form of termination is layoff, whereby employees are terminated due to their jobs having become redundant or because of the need to reduce operating costs. The next section examines the issue of layoffs.

RETRENCHMENT AND LAYOFF

The term **retrenchment** is usually used to refer to permanently discharging an employee because he or she will not be needed for the foreseeable future. **Layoff** is sometimes used as a synonym for retrenchment, but it may also mean that an employee is temporarily put off work with the likelihood of being recalled once business picks up. American automobile manufacturers used to regularly lay off employees when the demand for cars dropped, then recall them a few months later when demand picked up.

The need for firms to become leaner, more efficient, and more productive in order to meet the challenge of international competition has been one stimulus to reducing employee head count in recent times. Economic downturns are another, and over the past two decades many American businesses have cut costs by reducing their work forces. Although a boom in the late 1990s reduced retrenchments for a while, a downturn in 2001 increased numbers again. The terrorist attacks of September 11, 2001 triggeed further job cuts. In the ten weeks following September 11, mass layoffs at 350 establishments affecting 103,781 employees were attributed to the attacks. Over 70 percent of these job losses were in the air transport and hotel and motel industries.[101] Although retrenching employees (also called a **reduction in force**) is not a new idea, historically it happened mainly to blue-collar workers. In contrast, layoffs during the 1980s and 1990s were felt throughout the hierarchy and among professional ranks in an unprecedented number of organizations.[102] With high-tech firms and dot.coms hit particularly hard in the most recent downturn, highly skilled information technology workers have found themselves suddenly jobless.

How Effective Have Mass Layoffs Been?

Proponents of layoffs claim that reducing the number of employees in a firm will result in a variety of positive outcomes, including those shown in Table 16.12. The table shows the percentage of firms that have actually realized these supposed benefits of layoff. These data indicate that the positive benefits expected from downsizing do not materialize for many organizations. As many as two-thirds of the firms that laid off employees ended up having to lay off more workers the next year.[103] In another study, more than 70 percent of companies surveyed reported grappling with serious problems of low morale and mistrust of management caused by multiple efforts to restructure.[104] Wayne Cascio suggests that the cost savings expected from work force reductions often do not occur because of the following reasons:

- Functions of those laid off are replaced by those of expensive outside consultants.
- Subsidiary units end up having to re-create the functions once carried out by corporate headquarters staff who have been laid off and so end up hiring new employees.
- When line staff are asked to perform duties formerly done by headquarters staff, the training needed to enable the line personnel to perform the functions is expensive and reduces the cost savings associated with the layoffs.[105]

In addition to employers not receiving the benefits associated with layoffs, there are numerous other negative results of work force reductions. Many organizations find that laid-off employees are needed later when market demand improves. For example, NYNEX cut 9,000 of its 25,000 staff, only to be forced to "backfill" 4,000 of those positions.[106] Employee morale often plummets, resulting in lower organizational commitment, lower job satisfaction, increased anxiety and feelings of job insecurity, increased job stress, voluntary turnover of high performers (who can find work elsewhere), and lower overall productivity. There is also

● **TABLE 16.12**

Outcomes of Using Layoffs to Increase Organizational Competitiveness

Outcome	Percentage of Firms Reporting the Outcome After Layoffs
Reduced expenses	46
Increased profits	32
Improved cash flow	24
Increased productivity	22
Increased return on investment	21
Increased competitive advantage	19
Reduced bureaucracy	17
Improved decision making	14
Increased customer satisfaction	14
Increased sales	13
Increased market share	12
Improved product quality	9
Technological advances	9
Increased innovation	7
Avoidance of takeover	6

Sources: A. Bennett, "Downsizing Doesn't Necessarily Bring an Upswing in Corporate Profitability," *Wall Street Journal,* June 6, 1991, p. B1; Kim S. Cameron, "Guest Editor's Note: Investigating Organizational Downsizing—Fundamental Issues," *Human Resource Management,* Vol. 33 (2), 1994, pp. 183–186.

research that indicates a negative effect of layoffs on a firm's stock price (at least in the short term).[107] In addition, a firm may face legal problems if layoffs are not handled properly—and sometimes even when they are. For example, Houston Power and Light (HP&L) laid off 1,000 workers with average severance benefits of $40,000. Employees were laid off on the basis of their performance as measured by the firm's performance appraisal system. Six months after the layoffs, HP&L faced a $516 million lawsuit filed by laid-off workers who argued that the layoffs had made it difficult for them to find work because they had been labeled as low-performing workers by the firm.[108]

Given the lack of positive outcomes from many layoff situations, along with the prevalence of negative outcomes, the question becomes how and when to use layoffs effectively. "Golden rules for effectively managing layoffs" are presented in Table 16.13 and discussed below.

Planning

Planning is a crucial element in managing layoffs. It is essential that the organization develop plans for coping with a labor oversupply *before* a crisis occurs. During the planning phase, it is important for human resources to be viewed as assets rather than liabilities. As a result of this view, planners should assess skills,

● **TABLE 16.13**

The Golden Rules for Effectively Managing Layoffs

Plan

- Prepare ahead of time for downsizing.
- View human resources as assets rather than liabilities.
- Assess skills, abilities, and knowledge of all employees to help improve HR decisions.
- Identify the firm's future strategy and strategic imperatives; treat downsizing as providing clear vision for the future, not just an escape from the past.
- Use HR planning practices that consider alternatives to layoffs.
- Set targets, deadlines, and objectives for downsizing.
- Implement downsizing by starting with small wins; i.e., things that can be changed quickly and easily and that achieve the desired results.

Focus on productivity improvement

- Approach downsizing as an opportunity for overall improvement.
- Focus on attacking sources of organizational fat.
- Map and analyze all processes in the organization to eliminate inefficiencies, redundancies, and non value added activities.
- Measure all activities and processes, not just output, to identify how improvements can be made.
- Institute a variety of cost-cutting procedures, not just head-count reduction.

Involve

- Involve employees, which includes the use of cross-level and cross-functional teams, to identify what needs to change and how.
- Hold everyone, not just top management, responsible for achieving targets and goals.
- Involve customers and suppliers.

Communicate

- Ensure that leaders are visible, accessible, and interactive.
- Project positive energy and initiative from leaders.
- Ensure that every employee is informed about what is happening.
- Make clear, direct, and emphatic announcements of layoff decisions.
- Explain why retrenchments must occur; if a clearly visible scapegoat exists that does not implicate management and is easy to understand, use it.
- Overcommunicate as layoffs proceed.

Take care of those laid off

- Give advance notification of layoffs.
- Provide safety nets for those who must leave, including severance pay, extended benefits, and outplacement assistance.
- Arrange collaboration between private- and public-sector organizations in providing services for those laid off.

(continued)

● **TABLE 16.13** (continued)

Take care of survivors
• Implement layoffs in a fair and humane manner.
• Develop trust between management and surviving employees.
• Manage the rumor mill effectively.
• Provide training, cross-training, and retraining in advance for survivors, so that they will be able to handle the new demands.
• Do everything possible to maximize the retention of high performers.
• Change appraisal, reward, and pay systems to match new goals and objectives.

Sources: Kim S. Cameron, "Strategies for Successful Organizational Downsizing," *Human Resource Management,* Vol. 33 (2), 1994, pp. 189–211; Daniel Feldman and Carrie Leana, "Better Practices in Managing Layoffs," *Human Resource Management,* Vol. 33 (2), 1994, pp. 239–260; Cynthia Hardy, *Strategies for Retrenchment and Turnaround: The Politics of Survival* (Berlin: Walter de Gruyter, 1990); and Mark Mone, "Relationships Between Self-Concepts, Aspirations, Emotional Responses, Intent to Leave a Downsizing Organization," *Human Resource Management,* Vol. 33 (2), 1994, pp. 281–298.

abilities, and knowledge of all employees to help improve HR-related decisions. Also essential is an understanding of the firm's strategy and future strategic imperatives. A reduction in the work force should be treated as involving a clear vision of the future, not just as an escape from past mistakes.

Management should seriously consider options that do not include outright dismissal.[109] Many organizations have developed innovative alternatives for reducing the number of employees. Aside from natural attrition, some offer enhanced early retirement packages or attractive severance agreements to those who voluntarily resign. They also reduce wage costs while keeping valuable employees by cutting working hours or salaries, shifting employees to part-time status, or encouraging job sharing. Because the downturn in the first half of 2001 was expected to be shortlived, firms invented new ways of retaining skilled staff who were not needed at the moment. Motorola gave some of its workers the opportunity to take the summer off without pay, while Accenture asked 800 consultants to take sabbaticals of up to a year on 20 percent pay and covered tuition if they wished to upgrade their skills during this time. Cisco Systems paid a finance professional one-third of her regular salary plus full benefits to keep the books at a group of women's shelters for a year until the company needed her again.[110]

Once economic conditions allow for work force growth, these organizations will not be forced to recruit in the open labor market for new employees but can simply recall these employees or increase reduced workloads. Such an approach represents a far more strategic way of dealing with an oversupply of labor, and the organization can avoid the cost of recruiting, orienting, and training new employees. Unfortunately, too few firms investigate alternative approaches to dealing with needed work force reductions. A study cited by Wayne Cascio and conducted by Right Associates indicated that while firms usually said that they used layoffs as a "last resort," only 6 percent of 909 firms that had reduced staff had tried cutting pay rather than firing, only 9 percent had shortened workweeks or used vacation without pay, and only 14 percent had developed job-sharing plans.[111]

Focusing on Productivity Improvement

Scholars have argued that the lack of positive effects of work force reductions is often due to a firm's ignoring the real nature of its productivity problems. Such firms become caught in a "vicious cycle of downsizing."[112] Stated simply, pressures to cut costs (1) lead to work force reductions, which (2) leave behind inefficient business practices and fewer workers to conduct that business, which (3) in turn causes lower quality and lower customer satisfaction, with fewer production innovations and improvements, which (4) leads to poorer organizational performance and reduced market share, resulting in more pressure to cut costs and reduce staff. Experts suggest that pressures to cut costs should be viewed by firms as an opportunity for overall improvement in the way they do business. Organizations should focus on attacking sources of organizational fat. They should map out and analyze all processes in the organization to eliminate inefficiencies, redundancies, and non-value-added activities and measure all activities and processes, not just output, to identify how improvements can be made. Rather than focusing simply on reducing head count, organizations should institute a variety of procedures that not only cut costs but also improve the essential way in which the firm makes its products or serves its customers.

Involving People in the Process

Research suggests that a key to successfully managing layoffs requires management to involve employees and others in the process. This may include the use of cross-level and cross-functional teams to identify what needs to change and how. When layoffs seemed necessary at the Pittsfield, Massachusetts plant of General Electric, a task force of HR staff and union officials was formed to manage the process. Teams of employees were formed to help design layoff procedures. These teams were allowed to go onto the plant floor to solicit information and encourage workers to take part in programs designed to lessen the negative effects of the layoffs.[113] In his analysis of best practices for downsizing, Kim Cameron noted that firms that had reduced staff successfully made specific efforts to hold everyone, not just top management, responsible for achieving targets and goals. Important organizational stakeholders such as customers and suppliers also were involved in the process.[114]

Communicating

Cameron and his colleagues also point to the important role communication plays in determining the success of layoff procedures.[115] They found that firms that downsized successfully had ensured that leaders would be visible, accessible, and interactive. Top leaders projected a positive energy and made sure that every employee was informed about what was taking place and why the layoffs were necessary. Announcements regarding layoff decisions were clear, direct, and emphatic.[116] Perceptions of fairness are important. Research has shown that layoffs are seen as more fair if they are caused by technological change or reduced market demand than if they are caused by improved productivity due to employee suggestions. Longer notice and more generous treatment of those laid off also contributes to perceptions of fairness, as does top management's "sharing the pain" by taking a pay cut or refusing a bonus payment.[117]

Taking Care of Those Laid Off

Deciding which employees are to be laid off is often a difficult matter. In some cases, union contracts specify a "last hired, first fired" approach. When such contractual procedures do not exist, management must decide on some fair and appropriate way of selecting those who will be laid off. In a few cases, where attractive early retirement or enhanced severance pay is offered, there may be enough volunteers to preclude the need for nonvoluntary layoffs. In most situations, however, employees may be eliminated on the basis of the functions they perform or as a result of their individual level of performance in those functions.[118]

Regardless of how individuals are selected, there are some actions that management should take. When the organization has decided to implement layoffs, affected personnel should be informed as quickly as possible. Face-to-face, individual discussions between the employees and their immediate supervisors are best. The supervisor should tell employees why the layoffs are being made and should discuss the severance package in detail. When possible, it is a good idea to offer extended benefits to laid-off employees—for example, to increase severance pay somewhat or to pay for the employee to remain on the firm's health insurance plan for several months after the layoff. Where possible, firms should collaborate with public-sector organizations in providing services for those laid off.[119] The employee should sign a detailed agreement that includes a description of the severance pay that he or she will receive, along with any noncash benefits and outplacement services that the organization may provide. In the case of employees who possess knowledge of the company's trade secrets, the severance agreement also may prohibit disclosure of proprietary information to the organization's competitors. In all cases, laid-off workers should be treated in as fair and courteous a manner as possible.[120]

Outplacement

Many organizations provide **outplacement** assistance to help laid-off employees find new jobs. Outplacement serves several functions. First, if an organization helps discharged employees find new jobs, reductions in force are likely to be less stressful and traumatic. Second, as noted earlier, knowing that an organization is willing to look after its departing employees enhances the morale of those who remain behind. Third, outplacement seems to help employees find new jobs faster than would otherwise be possible. Over the long run, helping people become reemployed reduces the organization's unemployment insurance benefit costs. Fourth, some experts feel that outplacement tends to reduce the threat of litigation about the discharge.[121] As Chuck Albrecht, an executive vice president of Drake Beam Morin, a large outplacement firm, said, "If people are talking to an outplacement counselor, they're not talking to a lawyer."[122] Finally, more and more business organizations are simply recognizing that they have a moral and ethical responsibility toward their employees. Some 90 percent of all major companies now provide outplacement services for employees being laid off.[123]

Outplacement can be provided by an organization's own human resource staff or by an external consultant. An in-house approach is less expensive, as outplacement consultants themselves agree, but the organization's human resource staff may not be credible to employees and may not have the resources needed to assist laid-off employees in their career transitions. Some organizations choose external outplacement consultants in the belief that employees will be more open to suggestions from and willing to work with a third party.[124] The extent of demand for outplacement services should also be considered. If a company is facing large-scale layoffs at all organizational levels, external outplacement or a mix of external and internal services might be appropriate. Small-scale layoffs of primarily lower-level employees might be better served by in-house sources.

Outplacement Activities

Outplacement services may include personal counseling, career assessment and counseling, advice and aid in job search activities, and assistance with résumé preparation.[125] Specific activities should be tailored to the type of employees involved. Top executives have different outplacement needs than do middle managers or factory floor workers.[126] There is evidence that outplacement assistance does pay off for employees in terms of faster reemployment.[127]

Both General Motors and Stroh Brewery initiated extensive and varied outplacement programs during major layoffs. A summary of the activities in each of these programs is presented in Table 16.14. Training in job search skills is a central outplacement activity. It generally involves helping the employee set goals for the job search, as well as develop a personal marketing strategy and good interview skills.[128] Employees who are laid off after working for many years in the same organization will have had little recent experience in looking for jobs. Psychological research has made a connection between confidence in job search skills and reemployment rates. A study of thirty-five laid-off hospital employees showed that those who found new jobs had been more confident about their job search skills than were the people who remained unemployed. The confident, reemployed persons also had engaged in more job search behaviors.[129] Outplacement services can build people's confidence by training them in relevant job search skills such as those emphasized in the GM and Stroh programs. Although small firms may be unable to offer such extensive outplacement services, they can provide on-site services to help with job search, such as telephones (with long-distance capability), an office, postage, good stationery, photocopiers, fax, and some career counseling.[130]

Taking Care of Survivors

Often those who remain after a reduction in force are considered the lucky ones and are ignored by management. However, research has shown that survivors of a layoff suffer significant problems, which may have a dramatic impact on the organization. Survivors frequently show decreased productivity and satisfaction. They lose their motivation to work, and they worry about the future of their own jobs. After a reduction in force, many survivors seek new jobs elsewhere.[131]

Dealing effectively with survivors is essential for the long-term health of the organization. Practitioners and researchers have suggested several ways to minimize the negative effects of layoffs on survivors. When organizations provide generous outplacement and severance benefits, survivors feel more positive toward

● **TABLE 16.14**

Outplacement Programs at General Motors and Stroh Brewery

General Motors	Stroh Brewery Company
• An internal marketing campaign made employees aware of the services.	• An orientation program was conducted to explain the outplacement programs.
• Streamlined procedures were devised for getting employees into the programs.	• Assessment exercises were used to look at skills and abilities.
• Employees were given skills assessment, development of job search skills, and assistance in networking.	• Assistance was given to individuals to improve job search skills.
• There were one-week workshops for employees on how to write résumés, market their skills effectively, and develop good interview skills.	• Job search assistance such as referrals and access to a computerized job bank was provided.
• A job developer met with each employee to tell him or her about a local employer looking for people with his or her skills.	• Individualized job search counseling was provided. • Job search skills workshops were conducted.
• Ten toll-free telephones were made available.	• Counseling sessions were conducted on financial planning, retirement planning, relocation, and entrepreneurship.
• Videotape equipment was made available for improving interview skills.	• Psychological counseling was provided if requested.
• GM provided a job-search-related reference library.	• A research library, free phones, and secretarial facilities were made available.
• Seminars on financial planning, stress management, family problems, and so forth, were offered.	• Extended health and severance benefits were given.

Source: Daniel Feldman and Carrie Leana, "Better Practices in Managing Layoffs," *Human Resource Management,* Vol. 33 (2), 1994, pp. 239–260.

the firm, more comfortable, and less stressed by the layoffs.[132] Survivors should be told why the terminations are occurring and who will be affected. It is critical that the same information be given to survivors as to the employees being laid off. Trust between management and employees during layoff episodes is very important. Any discrepancies will be discovered as employees compare notes, reducing the organization's ability to inspire confidence and commitment in its remaining employees.[133] Above all, survivors must perceive the layoff process as having been conducted fairly. If layoff procedures are not seen as fair, survivors react negatively toward the organization, particularly when those laid off are friends or close associates.[134] It is also important to inform survivors when layoff goals have been met, to relieve their anxiety that they might be next in line for termination. Managing the "rumor mill" in the organization after layoffs have occurred is critically important. For example, one manager set up a "rumor board" outside his office. Employees could write on the board any rumor they had heard, and within twenty-four hours, the manager would investigate the rumor and write the real facts on the rumor board.[135]

Increased training for survivors may also be essential. Survivors may be asked to add new tasks to their job duties—tasks that they may not have done before. Without adequate training, survivors may not only feel guilty about those laid off but also experience a sense of inadequacy and even failure in their newly defined jobs. A survey of HR executives indicated that at 80 percent of firms, employees experienced significant stress in trying to manage their post-layoff workload.[136]

The importance that should be placed on the management of layoff survivors cannot be understated. Survivors represent an essential resource for the organization's future survival. Duracell, Inc., offers a good example of how one company successfully managed its surviving employees after a 50 percent reduction in staff at its Waterbury, Connecticut, facility. Particularly concerned with its ability to keep high-performing workers from leaving, Duracell lost only two employees during the transition, and productivity levels were maintained. The procedures used to manage survivors included the following:

- Key managers attended group sessions in order to understand the nature of the restructuring.

- Each continuing employee was provided with career assessment to identify how the restructuring would affect him or her.

- Each of these employees was asked individually to stay on at Duracell and told about assistance that would be provided.

- Survivors were told of the support services provided to employees who had been laid off.

- Two days after the layoffs occurred, senior management met in groups with survivors to discuss their feelings and their anxieties about the future of the company.

- Issues raised at these first meetings became the focus of future meetings centered around more work-related issues.

- Top managers increased their personal contact with individual employees.

- HR managers increased their efforts to provide counseling to survivors.

- Outside counseling and assistance programs were made available (confidentially) to employees who requested extra help.

- Two months after the layoffs, a meeting was held to discuss unresolved issues and assess the progress of the transition procedures and of the firm itself.[137]

Legal Constraints on Layoffs

In planning layoffs, organizations must consider legal constraints as well as their own needs and those of employees. The current trend is for the courts to support management decisions in which seniority is used as the basis for layoffs. In a 1984 case, *Firefighters Local Union 1784* v. *Stotts,* the Supreme Court ruled that it was illegal to lay off white employees with greater seniority to protect black workers who had less seniority but had been hired as part of an affirmative action plan.[138] Another Supreme Court ruling underscores the need to consider state regulations on layoffs. The Court ruled that a Maine law requiring workers laid off in a plant closing to be given one week of severance pay for each year of employment did not conflict with federal law on employee benefits.[139]

The **Worker Adjustment and Retraining Notification Act (WARN),** commonly known as the "Plant Closing Bill," requires employers covered by the law to give affected employees sixty days' written notice of anticipated plant closings or other mass layoffs.[140] WARN, which went into effect in 1989, covers employers that have 100 or more full-time employees.[141] WARN covers nonprofit organizations but not federal, state, or local government.[142]

WARN defines **affected employees** as all workers, including managerial and supervisory personnel, who may suffer some employment loss as the result of a plant closing or mass layoff. Individuals who work less than twenty hours per week or who have been employed for less than six out of the twelve months immediately preceding the layoff are not covered. An **employment loss** means a layoff exceeding six months or a reduction in work hours of 50 percent or more for a period of six months.

According to WARN, a **plant closing** is any temporary or permanent shutdown of an entire facility or significant part of a facility if the closing results in employment loss during a thirty-day period for fifty or more employees. A **mass layoff** occurs when a facility is not closed but there is a reduction in force affecting at least 500 employees, or as few as fifty employees if these fifty employees constitute at least one-third of the work force. Employers violating the law may be required to provide back pay and benefits for up to sixty days to workers laid off without proper notification. In some cases, employers may be required to pay fines of $500 per day, up to $30,000.

There are some exceptions to WARN. A "faltering company" is exempt if it was actively seeking capital to prevent the plant closing or layoff and reasonably believed that giving notice to employees would have prevented the company from receiving financing. An "unforeseeable business circumstance" may also exempt a company, such as when employees at a major supplier suddenly and unexpectedly go on strike and the company cannot operate without the supplies. Closings due to natural disasters such as floods and earthquakes likewise exempt a company from the sixty-day-notice requirement. A final exemption covers closings of plants that were originally established as "temporary facilities" if employees were hired with the understanding that their employment was not permanent.[143]

Summary of Key Points

Much attention has been given to selecting, training, and motivating employees. Equally important however, is understanding the circumstances in which employees transition within organizations or leave them altogether. Most employees want to have a feeling of growth and progress through a series of jobs. Although career paths that take employees from one organization to the next fairly quickly seem to be increasingly common, organizations can and should assist employees to explore options and plot potential progress through a sequence of jobs within the firm. Lateral job moves across functions are becoming more common as a means of developing breadth of skills, particularily since opportunities for hierarchical movement have declined. Career planning involves self-assessment of skills, values, and interests; exploration of alternative job movements; and planning for future development to enable desired transitions.

Another transition eventually made by most employees is retirement. Retirement has become an important issue as the population grows older. In most occupations, employees may no longer be forced to retire upon reaching a designated age. Some employers offer enhanced retirement packages to reduce head count in a company with too many employees. Others offer incentives for older employees to continue working, either full or part time, to retain valued skills or enhance work force flexibility. Phased retirement seems to be the wave of the future.

Voluntary turnover occurs when employees quit their jobs. Turnover has increased as the economy has strengthened, and many employers are working hard to retain valued employees. Employees are more likely to quit if they believe they have good alternatives and if they are dissatisfied with their jobs. When employees are embedded in their jobs with a multitude of links among family, employer, and community, they are less likely to quit. Employees may comtemplate quitting for a long period of time as their job satisfaction gradually falls, or they may decide to quit suddenly on the basis of a single event. Retention management programs attempt to discover why employees quit or stay, then act to keep the most valuable employees by addressing their concerns.

Effectively managing nonvoluntary turnover is important. State legislation and court decisions have restricted the right of organizations to terminate employees at will. Workers may challenge their firing, using legal arguments relating to such concepts as violation of public policy, whistleblowing, implied contracts, good faith and fair dealing, or tortious acts. Organizations must have proper written documentation that supports their reasons for terminating an employee. When terminating an individual for cause, organizations must work within the limitations placed on them by employment discrimination laws and union contracts. In dealing with poor performers, it is important to use performance appraisal and corrective feedback, accompanied by an escalating series of punishments for employees who are unable or unwilling to improve their behavior. The actual termination of an employee must be dealt with in a humane fashion. A thorough investigation of the reasons for firing must be conducted before termination occurs.

Organizations may also need to carry out large scale layoffs or retenchments. Thorough advance planning for reducing the work force is critical. Organizations should focus on productivity improvement rather than on simply laying off employees. Firms should involve employees, unions, and other relevant stakeholders in the process and communicate early and often with employees about the reasons for and the exact nature of the reductions. It is vital to treat employees who are laid off humanely and to provide sufficient "outplacement" assistance. It is equally important for the organization to manage the survivors of a company-wide layoff. Proper counseling and training for survivors can help ensure a motivated and stable work force afterward.

The Manager's Vocabulary

affected employees (as defined by WARN)
bridge job
broad banding
career planning
career-plateaued
discipline without punishment
downsizing
dual-career family
dual-income family
embeddedness
employee assistance program
employment loss (as defined by WARN)
employment-at-will
exit interview
expert, or professional, career ladder
expressed or implied contract
good faith and fair dealing
involuntary turnover
layoff
linear career path
mass layoff (as defined by WARN)
optimal rate of turnover
organizational survey
outplacement
phased retirement
plant closing (as defined by WARN)
positive discipline
progressive disciplinary system
reduction in force
restructuring
retention costs
retention management program
retirement
retrenchment
rightsizing
spiral career path
termination for cause
termination interview
tortious conduct
traditional model of turnover
transitory career path
turnover costs
voluntary turnover
whistleblowing
Worker Adjustment and Retraining Notification Act (WARN)
wrongful discharge

Questions for Discussion

1. How are traditional career paths changing, and why? Do your career aspirations fit in with the changes that are occurring? Which type of career pattern appeals to you most?
2. Why should organizations become involved in career planning with their employees? What components might a career-planning system have?
3. Why is retirement an increasingly important issue, and how can it affect organizations?
4. When and how would you like to retire?
5. Why and how do individuals decide to quit a job?
6. What can organizations do to strategically manage voluntary turnover?
7. What is the difference between voluntary and involuntary turnover? between termination for cause and layoff?
8. What is employment-at-will? How does civil rights legislation restrict a company's ability to terminate employees at will?
9. Describe the difference between wrongful discharge as the result of an implied contract and as the result of a tortious act.
10. What is whistleblowing and how can companies benefit from it?
11. What are potential problems in the use of punishment in organizations?
12. Why is a progressive disciplinary system important when an organization is terminating an employee for cause? What should such a system involve?
13. How would you manage a disciplinary investigation into an employee you suspect may have been stealing from the company?
14. What are the "golden rules" of managing layoffs effectively?
15. Managing the survivors of layoffs is important. How would you help survivors deal with not having been laid off?
16. Why is the Worker Adjustment and Retraining Act important for organizations planning a reduction in force? Who is covered by the law, and what does it require organizations to do?
17. Defend or refute the following statement: "Organizations should routinely provide outplacement programs for workers laid off in a work force reduction."

● Case 16.1
A Messy Situation—Conducting a Disciplinary Investigation

Bronwyn Bocuse sits nervously at your desk, glancing around the room like a cat that has suddenly found herself in the middle of an attack dog kennel. You are director of human resources for Amalgamated All-Terrain Bikes, Inc., a manufacturer of rugged trail bikes. Bronwyn indicates that she has something very important to tell you and then says nothing. You encourage her to talk, telling her that as director of human resources, you are interested in the welfare of all employees and that if something important is going on, you need to know about it.

Finally, the story begins to come out. Bronwyn works on the 3:00 to 11:00 P.M. shift in the welding area. Several of the male employees who work with her have been giving her quite a bad time lately. As Bronwyn describes it, "They constantly tease me about my—ya know, my, uh, shape. They make weird gestures with their hands and laugh like someone has told them the funniest joke they've ever heard. I thought it was just sort of silly at first, but things seem to be getting a bit out of hand. I'm starting to dread coming to work. The guys just don't know when to let something drop—ya know, stop it."

She continues telling her story, with even more disturbing revelations, and states, "I'm really getting sick of it. They bug me all the time. Tease me. Give me all kinds of trouble. They've started pulling some pretty nasty practical jokes on me. Last night I found a balloon filled with silicone in my locker. It really made me mad. I'm particularly upset because I know these guys have been doing some other weird things at work, and I've kept my mouth shut.

. . . Let's just say that by the time they leave this job, they'll have had enough experience with drugs to start their own pharmacy! They should all be fired!"

You thank Bronwyn for her information and assure her that you will try to deal with this situation in as effective a manner as possible. As Bronwyn thanks you for listening and leaves, you wonder, "Now, just how do I deal with this?" What would you do first? Explain the steps you would take in trying to manage this difficult situation.

● **Exercise 16.1**
Planning Your Career: A Consideration of Alternate Paths

Divide into groups of three to five students with the same major.

1. Each individual should fill in the ideal job column of the accompanying grid, indicating his or her ideal job situation at intervals in the future. If you have difficulty with this assignment, perhaps you should spend more time in the self-analysis stage: What kinds of activities and tasks do you enjoy most? What do you want out of your life and career? What are your strengths and weaknesses? It also might be wise to spend more time in gathering data about career options and patterns within your occupation. One starting point is the Department of Labor's web site. Check the Occupational Outlook Handbook (http://www.bls.gov/oco) and the Career Guide to Industries (http://www.bls.gov/oco/cg/home.htm).

2. Discuss the various career paths outlined by each individual. What accounts for differences in preferences? Have you considered which of the eight life interests in Table 16.3 are most important to you in your choice of career activities? How likely is it that each career path will be achievable? How likely is it that your preferences will change with time and varying non-work responsibilities? Have you included additional formal education in your plan? To what extent are you relying on a single stable employer to provide your career? How important are variety and geographic location to you? Do you expect your spouse to have a career?

3. With advice from the group, each person should use the right column of the table to sketch out an alternative career path that might be equally satisfying.

Years Since Graduation	*Ideal Job Situation*	*Alternative Job Situation*
1		
2		
5		
10		
15		
20		
30		
40		

● Exercise 16.2
Conducting Exit Interviews

In class: Form into groups of four, with each group including at least two experiences of quitting a job. (A single person may have quit more than one job.) *Out of class:* Each individual or group is to locate and interview people who have quit at least four full-time jobs between them.

1. Prepare to conduct a structured exit interview. Table 16.7 may give you some ideas about questions to ask, but do not be limited to just these.

2. Interview each person about his or her decision to leave the job.
3. How did they make the decision to leave? Does the process resemble the transitional model, or was it more of a sudden decision based on a specific event?
4. Was this turnover functional or dysfunctional for the employer? Why?
5. Could the employer have prevented this turnover from occuring? How? Why didn't it?

● Exercise 16.3
Whom Would You Lay Off?

The class should divide into groups of three to five. Each group member should read the following scenario and then discuss his or her individual recommendations with the other group members. Each group may also present its suggestions to the class as a whole following this part of the exercise.

The Scenario   Because of severe economic conditions, your company is undergoing major layoffs. You have recently been assigned to the "execution committee," which must decide who will be laid off and who will be retained. So far the committee's decisions have been made without the benefit of any set policy for determining layoffs. The company is not unionized. The committee's decisions have resulted in the following distribution of layoffs among age groups of employees:

Ages (years)	Work Force Percentage before Layoffs	Percentage of Persons Terminated in Group
<40	50	5
40–44	10	5
45–49	10	7
50–54	10	9
55–59	10	12
60–64	10	25

The committee must decide whom to lay off, Sam or Fred. Some information about these two employees is provided in the following list. What would you do? What thoughts do you have about the decisions of the committee so far?

	Sam	*Fred*
Age (years)	45	59
Children	Still in college	On their own
House	Large mortgage	Owns home clear
Retirement benefits	Not vested	Vested
Hobbies	Workaholic	Golf
Results if terminated	Try to find job (difficult)	Retire
Past performance	Very good	Very good

Source: Adapted from Schlie and Grossman, *Employment Discrimination Law,* 2d ed. Reprinted by permission of the Bureau of National Affairs.

Notes and References

1. Data on call-center turnover and salaries are from Purdue University's Center for Customer Driven Quality.

2. J. Purcell and N. Kinnie, "Employment Regimes for the Factories of the Future: Human Resource Management in Telephone Call Centres," Paper presented at the Annual Meeting of the Academy of Management, Toronto, August 2000; A. Throne, "Capital One's Call Center Soars to New Heights," *Call Center Magazine*, March 2001, pp. 84–86; and B. R. Read, "Recipes for Effective Staffing," *Call Center Magazine*, April 2001, pp. 58–63.

3. S. Hutchinson, J. Purcell, and N. Kinnie, "Evolving High Commitment Management and the Experience of the RAC Call Centre," *Human Resource Management Journal*, Vol. 10 (1), 2000, pp. 63–78.

4. George T. Milkovich, Jerry M. Newman, and Carolyn Milkovich, *Compensation*, 5th ed. (Chicago: Irwin, 1995).

5. Joel R. DeLuca, "Strategic Career Management in Non-Growing Volatile Business Environments," *Human Resource Planning*, Vol. 11 (1), 1988, pp. 49–61; and Amanda Bennett, "Growing Small: As Big Firms Continue to Trim Their Staffs, 2-Tier Setup Emerges," *Wall Street Journal*, May 4, 1987, pp. 1, 20.

6. Chris Tilly, "Reasons for the Continuing Growth of Part-Time Employment," *Monthly Labor Review*, March 1991, pp. 10–18; and S. Hipple, "Contingent Work: Results from the Second Survey," *Monthly Labor Review*, November 1998, pp. 22–35.

7. W. R. Wilhelm, "Guest Editor's Note: The Employment Contract," *Human Resource Management*, Fall 1994, pp. 323–324. This entire issue is devoted to a discussion of the changing psychological contract between employees and employers. See also Denise M. Rousseau, *Psychological Contracts in Organizations: Understanding Written and Unwritten Agreements* (New York: Sage Publications, 1995).

8. The entire *Academy of Management Executive* issue for November 1996 and much of the issue for February 1997 are devoted to articles about careers in the twenty-first century. See also Michael B. Arthur and Denise M. Rousseau (eds.), *The Boundaryless Career: A New Employment Principle for a New Organizational Era* (Oxford: Oxford University Press, 1997).

9. Douglas T. Hall and Judith Richter, "Career Gridlock: Baby Boomers Hit the Wall," *The Executive*, August 1990, pp. 7–22.

10. Laura Zinn, "Move Over, Boomers: The Busters are Here—And They're Angry," *Business Week*, December 14, 1992, pp. 34–40.

11. F. L. Otte and W. M. Kahnweiler, "Long-Range Career Planning During Turbulent Times," *Business Horizons*, January–February 1995, pp. 2–7; and E. H. Schein, "Career Anchors Revisited: Implications for Career Develoment in the 21st Century," *Academy of Management Executive*, November 1996, pp. 80–88.

12. Hutchinson, Purcell, and Kinnie, "Evolving High Commitment Management and the Experience of the RAC Call Centre,"

13. B. B. Read, "Certifying Your Call Center Staff," *Call Center Magazine*, April 2001, pp. 30–49.

14. DeLuca, "Strategic Career Management in Non-Growing Volatile Business Environments."

15. R. H. Vaughn and M. C. Wilson, "Career Management Using Job Trees: Charting a Path Through the Changing Organization," *Human Resource Planning*, Vol. 17 (4), 1994, pp. 43–55.

16. Kate Donnelly, Peter V. LeBlanc, R. Dale Torrence, and Margaret A. Lyon, "Career Banding," *Human Resource Management*, Spring–Summer 1992, pp. 35–43.

17. K. R. Brousseau, M. J. Driver, K. Eneroth, and R. Larsson, "Career Pandemonium: Realigning Organizations and Individuals," *Academy of Management Executive*, November 1996, pp. 52–66; M. Peiperl and Y. Baruch, "The Post-Corporate Career," *Organizational Dynamics*, Spring 1997, pp. 7–22; and R. Barner, "The New Career Strategist," *The Futurist*, September–October 1994, pp. 8–14.

18. Brousseau, Driver, Eneroth, and Larsson, "Career Pandemonium: Realigning Organizations and Individuals."

19. Zandy B. Leibowitz, Caela Farren, and Beverly L. Kaye, *Designing Career Development Systems* (San Francisco: Jossey-Bass, 1988).

20. Timothy Butler and James Waldroop, "Job Sculpting: The Art of Retaining Your Best People," *Harvard Business Review*, September–October 1999, pp. 144–152.

21. Peter F. Drucker, "Managing Oneself," *Harvard Business Review*, March–April 1999, pp. 65–74.

22. Patrick J. Kiger, "At First USA Bank, Promotions and Job Satisfaction Are Up," *Workforce*, February 28, 2001. (Available at: www.workforce.com/archive/article/001/45/36.xci)

23. Christine M. Read and Willa M. Bruce, "Dual-Career Couples in the Public Sector: A Survey of Personnel Policies and Practices," *Public Personnel Management*, Summer 1993, pp. 187–199.

24. Howard V. Hayghe and Suzanne M. Bianchi, "Married Mothers' Work Patterns: The Job–Family Compromise," *Monthly Labor Review*, June 1994, pp. 24–30.

25. S. L. Grover and K. J. Crooker, "Who Appreciates Family-Responsive Human Resource Policies: The Impact of Family-Friendly Policies on the Organizational Attachment of Parents and Non Parents," *Personnel Psychology*, Vol. 48, 1995, pp. 271–288.

26. Catherine R. Smith, "Dual Careers, Dual Loyalties: Management Implications of the Work/Home Interface," *Asia Pacific Journal of Human Resources*, Summer 1992, pp. 19–29.

27. Daniel Feldman, "The Decision to Retire Early: A Review and Conceptualization," *Academy of Management Review*, Vol. 19, 1994, pp. 285–311; quote from p. 287.

28. William J. Wiatrowski, "Changing Retirement Age: Ups and Downs," *Monthly Labor Review*, April 2001, pp. 3–12.

29. D.C. Feldman and S. Kim, "Bridge Employment During Retirement: A Field Study of Individual and Organizational Experiences with Post-Retirement Employment," *Human Resource Planning*, Vol. 23 (1), 2000, pp. 14–25.

30. A. M. Rappaport, "Postemployment Benefits," *Compensation and Benefits Management*, Autumn 2000, pp. 59–62.

31. Judy Greenwald, "Phased Retirement Begins to Catch On," *Business Insurance*, May 28, 2001, pp. 10–12.

32. Patrick J. Purcell, "Older Workers: Employment and Retirement Trends," *Monthly Labor Review*, October 2000, pp. 19–30.

33. S. I. Erwin, "Pentagon Lays Out Game Plan to Address Workforce Losses," *National Defense*, January 2001, pp. 16–17.

34. Amy Zuber, "Career in Foodservice—Cons: High Turnover," *Nation's Restaurant News*, May 21, 2001, pp. 147–148.

35. Barry Gerhart, "Voluntary Turnover and Alternate Job Opportunities," *Journal of Applied Psychology*, Vol. 75 (5), 1990, pp. 467–476; and R. W. Griffith, P. W. Hom, and S. Gaertner, "A Meta-Analysis of Antecedents and Correlates of Employee Turnover: Update, Moderator Tests, and Research Implications for the Next Millennium," *Journal of Management*, Vol. 26 (3), 2000, pp. 463–488; and P. W. Hom and R. W. Griffeth, *Employee Turnover* (Cincinnati, Ohio: South-Western College Publishing, 1995).

36. Griffith, Hom, and Gaertner, "A Meta-Analysis of Antecedents and Correlates of Employee Turnover."

37. T. R. Mitchell, B. C. Holtom, T. W. Lee, C. J. Sablynski, and M. Erez, "Why People Stay: Using Job Embeddedness to Predict Voluntary Turnover," *Academy of Management Journal*, Vol. 44(6), 2001, pp. 1102–1121; and T. R. Mitchell, B. C. Holtom, and T. W. Lee, "How to Keep Your Best Employees: The Development of an Effective Retention Policy," *Academy of Management Executive*, Vol. 15(4), 2001, p. 96.

38. P. W. Hom, F. Caranikas-Walker, G. E. Prussia, and R. W. Griffeth, "A Meta-Analytical Structural Equations Analysis of a Model of Employee Turnover," *Journal of Applied Psychology*, Vol. 77, 1992, pp. 890–909; W. H. Mobley, "Intermediate Linkages in the Relationship Between Job Satisfaction and Employee Turnover," *Journal of Applied Psychology*, Vol. 62, 1977, pp. 237–240; and W. H. Mobley, *Employee Turnover: Causes, Consequences, and Control* (Reading, Mass.: Addison-Wesley, 1982).

39. Mitchell, Holtom, and Lee, "How to Keep Your Best Employees"; T. W. Lee and T. R. Mitchell, "An Alternative Approach: The Unfolding Model of Voluntary Turnover." *Academy of Management Review*, Vol. 19, 1994, pp. 51–89; and J. E. Sheridan, "A Catastrophe Model of Employee Withdrawal Leading to Low Job Performance, High Absenteeism, and Job Turnover During the First Year of Employment," *Academy of Management Journal*, Vol. 28, 1985, pp. 88–109.

40. Beverly Kaye and Sharon Jordan-Evans, "Retention: Tag, You're It!" *Training and Development*, April 2000, pp. 29–34; and Suzanne Dibble, *Keeping Your Valuable Employees* (New York: Wiley, 1999).

41. For more detail on costing turnover, see W. F. Cascio, *Costing Human Resources: The Financial Impact of Behavior in Organizations* (Boston: PWS-Kent, 1991).

42. Mitchell, Holtom, and Lee, "How to Keep Your Best Employees."

43. Data on call-center replacement costs are from Purdue University's Center for Customer Driven Quality.

44. Griffith, Hom, and Gaertner, "A Meta-Analysis of Antecedents and Correlates of Employee Turnover"; C. Williams and L. Livingstone, "Another Look at the Relationship Between Performance and Voluntary Turnover," *Academy of Management Journal*, Vol. 37, 1994, pp. 269–298; and D. Schwab, "Contextual Variables in Employee Performance-Turnover Relationships," *Academy of Management Journal*, Vol. 34, 1991, pp. 966–975.

45. C. Trevor, B. Gerhart, and J. Boudreau, "Voluntary Turnover and Job Performance: Curvilinearity and the Moderating Influences of Salary Growth and Promotions," *Journal of Applied Psychology*, Vol. 82, 1997, pp. 44–61.

46. Saratoga Institute, *Retention Management: Strategies, Practices, Trends* (New York: American Management Association, 1997).

47. Hutchinson, Purcell, and Kinnie, "Evolving High Commitment Management and the Experience of the RAC Call Centre."

48. Saratoga Institute, *Retention Management*.

49. A. I. Kraut and L. M. Saari, "Organizational Surveys: Coming of Age in a New Era," in *Evolving Practices in Human Resource Management*, ed. A. I. Kraut and A. K. Korman (San Francisco: Jossey-Bass, 1999), pp. 302–327.

50. Beverly Kaye and Sharon Jordan-Evans, *Love 'Em or Lose 'Em: Getting Good People to Stay* (San Francisco: Berrett-Koehler, 1999).

51. Kevin Dobbs, "Knowing How to Keep Your Best and Brightest," *Workforce*, April 2001, pp. 57-60. (Available at: www.workforce.com/feature/00/06/95)

52. Saratoga Institute, *Retention Management*.

53. Dick Sethi and Beverly Pinzon, "A Seven-Step Strategy to Help Retain Your Company's High-Impact Performers," *Human Resource Planning*, Vol. 21 (4), 1998, p. 16.

54. Mitchell, Holtom, and Lee, "How to Keep Your Best Employees."

55. "Al Dunlap Revs His Chain Saw," *Business Week,* November 25, 1996 p. 37.

56. "Sunbeam Shines Under 'Chainsaw Al,'" *Business Week,* August 4, 1997 p. 42.

57. Stephen Collarelli and Terry Beehr, "Organizational Exit: Firings, Layoffs, and Retirement," in *Personnel Selection in Organizations*, ed. Neal Schmitt, Walter Borman, et al. (San Francisco: Jossey-Bass, 1993), p. 343.

58. *Payne* v. *Western and Atlantic RA Company* (82 Tenn 507, 1884).

59. D. P. Twomey, *Equal Employment Opportunity*, 2d ed. (Cincinnati, Ohio: South-Western, 1990), p. 132.

60. Stuart Youngblood and Leonard Bierman, "Due Process and Employment-at-Will: A Legal and Behavioral Analysis," in *Research in Personnel and Human Resources Management*, Vol. 3, ed. Kendrith Rowland and Gerald Ferris (Greenwich, Conn.: JAI Press, 1985), pp. 185–230; Charles J. Muhl, "The Employment-at-Will Doctrine: Three Major Exceptions," *Monthly Labor Review*, January 2001, pp. 3–11; and D. A. Ballam, "Employment-at-Will: The Impending Death of a Doctrine," *American Business Law Journal*, Summer 2000, pp. 653–687.

61. *Murphy* v. *American Home Products Corporation* (461 N.Y.2d 232 N.Y. State Ct. of Appeals, 1983).

62. A. Fisher, "Dumping Troublemakers, and Exiting Gracefully," *Fortune*, February 15, 1999, p. 174.

63. Robert Coulson, *Labor Arbitration: What You Need to Know* (New York: American Arbitration Association, 1981).

64. Daniel Koys, Steven Briggs, and Jay Grenig, "State Court Disparity on Employment-at-Will," *Personnel Psychology*, Vol. 40, 1987, pp. 565–576; Youngblood and Bierman, "Due Process and Employment-at-Will."

65. Susan Gardner, Glenn M. Gomes, and James F. Morgan, "Wrongful Termination and the Expanding Public Policy Exception: Implications and Advice," *S.A.M. Advanced Management Journal*, Winter 2000, pp. 38–44.

66. William Fulmer and Ann W. Casey, "Employment at Will: Options for Managers," *Academy of Management Executive,*

Vol. 4 (2), 1990, pp. 102–107; and Benjamin W. Wolkinson and Richard N. Block, *Employment Law: The Workplace Rights of Employees and Employers* (Cambridge, Mass.: Blackwell, 1996).

67. Fulmer and Casey, "Employment at Will."

68. A recent precedent in California suggests a broader interpretation of public policy. See Gardner, Gomes, and Morgan, "Wrongful Termination and the Expanding Public Policy Exception."

69. *Palmateer* v. *International Harvester* (85 Ill.2d 124, 421 N.E.2d 876, 1981); *Sheets* v. *Teddy's Frosted Foods, Inc.* (179 Conn. 471 A. 2d 385,1980).

70. Muhl, "The Employment-at-Will Doctrine."

71. *Touissant* v. *Blue Cross and Blue Shield of Michigan* (408 Mich. 579, 292 N.W.2d 880, 1980).

72. *Fortune* v. *National Cash Register Company* (373 Mass. 96, 36 N.E.2d 1251, 1977).

73. Muhl, "The Employment-at-Will Doctrine."

74. *Monge* v. *Beebe Rubber Company* (114 N.H. 130, 316, A.2d 549, 1974).

75. This exception to the employment-at-will doctrine is sometimes referred to as "abusive discharge." The court case most closely linked to this concept is *Monge* v. *Beebe Rubber Co.* (114 N.H. 130, 316 A.2d 549, 1974), in which a female employee was fired for not agreeing to date her supervisor. This was deemed abusive discharge. A case like *Monge* v. *Beebe Rubber* would, today, most likely be handled as a case of sex discrimination; however, other instances of abusive discharge may occur that would be considered a tortious act.

76. Koys, Briggs, and Grenig, "State Court Disparity on Employment-at-Will," p. 573.

77. A.C. Goldberg, "Top 8 Legal Issues Affecting HR," *HR Focus*, December 1997, pp. 51–53.

78. Twomey, *Equal Employment Opportunity*, pp. 133–134.

79. Raymond Hilgert, "Employers Protected by at-Will Statements," *HRMagazine*, March 1991, pp. 57–60; and Sydney P. Freedberg, "Forced Exits? Companies Confront Wave of Age Discrimination Suits," *Wall Street Journal*, November 13, 1987.

80. Walt Baer, "Most U.S. Workers Still May Be Fired Under the Employment-at-Will Doctrine," *Supervision*, December 1987, p. 6.

81. C. M. Koen Jr. and W. H. Reinhardt Jr., "Employment Contracts: Preventative Medicine for Post-Termination Disputes," *Supervision*, July 2000, pp. 5–9.

82. Fulmer and Casey, "Employment at Will."

83. Kenneth Labich, "How to Fire People and Still Sleep at Night," *Fortune*, June 10, 1996, pp. 64–72.

84. Beth Tognetti, "How to Fire Someone Without Destroying Your Self-Esteem," *Supervision*, August 1987, p. 6.

85. Steven Brown, "The Case of the Incompetent Employee," *Supervisory Management*, Vol. 37 (1), 1992, pp. 1–2; Dave Day, "Training 101: Help for Discipline Dodgers," *Training & Development*, May 1993, pp. 19–21; and John Veiga, "Face Your Problem Employee Now!" *Academy of Management Executive*, Vol. 2 (2), 1988, pp. 145–152.

86. James Fox and Jack Levin, "The Workplace: Termination Can Be Murder," *Boston Globe*, May 2, 1993, p. 71.

87. Richard Arvey and Allen Jones, "The Use of Discipline in Organizational Settings: A Framework for Future Research," in *Research in Organizational Behavior*, Vol. 7, ed. L. Cummings

and B. Staw (Greenwich, Conn.: JAI Press, 1985), pp. 367–408; Linda Trevino, "The Social Effects of Punishment in Organizations: A Justice Perspective," *Academy of Management Review*, Vol. 17 (4), 1992, pp. 647–676; and Gail Ball, Linda Trevino, and Henry Sims Jr., "Just and Unjust Punishment: Influence on Subordinate Performance and Citizenship," *Academy of Management Journal*, Vol. 37 (2), 1994, pp. 299–322.

88. Ball, Trevino, and Sims, "Just and Unjust Punishment."

89. Louis Imundo, *Employee Discipline: How to Do It Right* (Belmont, Calif.: Wadsworth, 1985); Brian Klaas and Daniel Feldman, "The Evaluation of Disciplinary Appeals in Non-Union Organizations," *Human Resource Management Review*, Vol. 3 (1), 1993, pp. 49–81; and Jonathan Segal, "Firing Without Fear," *HRMagazine*, June, 1992, pp. 125–130.

90. C. J. Guffey and M. M. Helms, "Effective Employee Discipline: A Case of the Internal Revenue Service," *Public Personnel Management*, Spring 2001, pp. 111–127; and C. Osigweh and W. Hutchinson, "Positive Discipline," *Human Resource Management*, Vol. 28, 1991, pp. 367–383.

91. Arvey and Jones, "The Use of Discipline in Organizational Settings"; W. C. Hamner and D. W. Organ, *Organizational Behavior: An Applied Psychological Approach* (Dallas: BPI, 1978); and Terence Mitchell and Charles O'Reilly III, "Managing Poor Performance and Productivity in Organizations," *Research in Organizational Behavior*, 1983, Vol. 1, pp. 201–234.

92. Imundo, *Employee Discipline*.

93. Paul Falcone, "A Blueprint for Progressive Discipline and Terminations," *HR Focus*, August 2000, pp. 3–5.

94. John Greenwald, "Rank and Fire," *TIME*, June 18, 2001, pp. 46–48.

95. D. W. Myers, *Employee Assistance Programs* (Chicago: Commerce Clearing House, 1986).

96. This example is described in Cecily Waterman and Teresa Maginn, "Investigating Suspect Employees," *HRMagazine*, January 1993, pp. 85–87.

97. Adapted from CCH Business Law Editors, *Employee Termination Manual for Managers and Supervisors* (Chicago: Commerce Clearing House, 1991); and Waterman and Maginn, "Investigating Suspect Employees."

98. Kristin Kane, "Best Practices for Employee Termination." (Available at: www.wetfeet.com/employer/articles/article.asp?aid=389)

99. Bob Smith, "Cease Fire: Preventing Workplace Violence," *HR Focus*, February 1994, pp. 1, 6–7.

100. Kane, "Best Practice for Employee Termination."

101. Kim Clark, "You're Laid Off! Kind of. Firms Look Beyond Pink Slips," *U.S. News & World Report*, July 2, 2001, pp. 50–53; Bureau of Labor Statistics, "Mass Layoffs in November 2001," December 28, 2001. (Available at: http://www.bls.gov/news.release/pdf/mmls.pdf.)

102. Pascal Zachary and Bob Ortega, "Workplace Revolution Boosts Productivity at Cost of Job Security," *Wall Street Journal*, March 10, 1993, pp. A1, A11.

103. S. Pearlstein, "Corporate Cutbacks Yet to Pay Off," *Washington Post*, January 1994, p. B6.

104. Gene Koretz, "The Downside of Downsizing," *Business Week*, April 28, 1997, p. 26.

105. Wayne Cascio, "Downsizing: What Do We Know? What Have We Learned?" *Academy of Management Executive*, Vol. 7 (1), 1993, pp. 95–104.

106. Samuel Greengard, "Don't Rush Downsizing: Plan, Plan, Plan," *Personnel Journal,* November 1993, pp. 64–76.

107. Mark Mone, "Relationships Between Self-Concepts, Aspirations, Emotional Responses, and Intent to Leave a Downsizing Organization," *Human Resource Management,* Vol. 33 (2), 1994, pp. 281–298; and Dan Worrell, Wallace Davidson III, and Varinder Sharma, "Layoff Announcements and Stockholder Wealth," *Academy of Management Journal,* Vol. 34 (3), 1991, pp. 662–678.

108. Greengard, "Don't Rush Downsizing."

109. Linda Laarman, "Cut Compensation Costs to Avoid Layoffs," *Employment Relations Today,* Vol. 18 (2), 1991, pp. 137–142; and Gloria M. Protela and Rory K. Zaks, "Reductions in Force: A Practical Approach," *Employment Relations Today,* Vol. 16 (3), 1989, pp. 219–225.

110. Clark, "You're Laid Off! Kind of."

111. Cascio, "Downsizing: What Do We Know?"

112. Craig Schneier, Douglas Shaw, and Richard Beatty, "Companies' Attempts to Improve Performance While Containing Costs: Quick Fix Versus Lasting Change," *Human Resource Planning,* Vol. 15 (3), 1992, pp. 1–25.

113. Daniel Feldman and Carrie Leana, "Better Practices in Managing Layoffs," *Human Resource Management,* Vol. 33 (2), 1994, pp. 239–260.

114. Kim S. Cameron, "Guest Editor's Note: Investigating Organizational Downsizing—Fundamental Issues," *Human Resource Management,* Vol. 33 (2), 1994, pp. 183–186.

115. Ibid.; and K. Cameron, S. J. Freeman, and A. K. Mishra, "Best Practices in White-Collar Downsizing: Managing Contradictions," *Academy of Management Executive,* Vol. 5 (3), 1991, pp. 57–73.

116. Cynthia Hardy, *Strategies for Retrenchment and Turnaround: The Politics of Survival* (Berlin: Walter de Gruyter, 1990).

117. Gary Charness and David I. Levine, "When Are Layoffs Acceptable? Evidence from a Quasi-Experiment," *Industrial and Labor Relations Review,* April 2000, pp. 381-400.

118. Xiong Xiaoge, "How to Minimize the Effects of Downsizing," *Electronic Business,* Vol. 17 (7), 1991, pp. 51–54.

119. Feldman and Leana, "Better Practices in Managing Layoffs."

120. Daniel Feldman and Carrie Leana, "Managing Layoffs: Experiences at the Challenger Disaster Site and the Pittsburgh Steel Mills," *Organizational Dynamics,* Summer 1989, pp. 52–64.

121. Kenneth Dawson and Sheryl Dawson, "Immediate Outplacement Can Help Everyone Through the Transition," *HR Focus,* Vol. 71 (2), 1994, p. 4; and Robert J. Nobile, "Outplacement Counseling: Minimizing Legal Liability," *Personnel,* Vol. 68 (10), 1991, p. 10.

122. Cited in Chris Lee, "Outplacement: Throwing Them Life Preservers," *Training,* July 1987, p. 43.

123. R. J. Lee, "Outplacement Counseling for the Terminated Manager," in *Applying Psychology in Business: The Handbook for Managers and Human Resource Professionals,* ed. J. W. Jones, B. D. Steffy, and D. W. Bray (Lexington, Mass.: Lexington Books, 1991).

124. Lee, "Outplacement: Throwing Them Life Preservers."

125. Mark L. Lengnick-Hall, "Outplacement," in *The Blackwell Encyclopedic Dictionary of Human Resource Management,* ed.

Lawrence H. Peters, Charles R. Greer, and Stuart A. Youngblood (Malden, Mass.: Blackwell, 1997).

126. Peter Cowden, "Outplacement Services Assessment," *HRMagazine,* September 1992, pp. 69–70; and Jeanne C. Hill and William R. Fannin, "Developing an Effective Outplacement Program," *Business Forum,* Vol. 16 (1), 1991, pp. 14–17.

127. Lawrence J. Stybel, "How Managers React to Their Own Dismissal: Implications for Intervention Theory and Practice." Paper presented at the Academy of Management Conference, San Diego, August 1981.

128. Frank Strasbourg, "Corporate Outplacement," *Business and Economic Review,* Vol. 38 (1), 1991, pp. 11–13.

129. Ruth Kanfer and Charles L. Hulin, "Individual Differences in Successful Job Searches Following Lay-Off," *Personnel Psychology,* Vol. 30, 1985, pp. 835–847.

130. Jeanne C. Hill and Earl R. Thomas, "Outplacement: Considerations for the Small Firm," *SAM Advanced Management Journal,* Vol. 56 (2), 1991, pp. 10–15.

131. Joel Brockner, "Layoffs, Self-Esteem and Survivor Guilt: Motivational, Affective and Attitudinal Consequences," *Organizational Behavior and Human Decision Processes,* Vol. 36, June 1985, pp. 229–244; and Joel Brockner, Steven L. Grover, and Mauritz D. Blonder, "Predictors of Job Survivors' Job Involvement Following Layoffs: A Field Study," *Journal of Applied Psychology,* Vol. 73 (3), 1988, pp. 436–442.

132. Joel Brockner, "The Effects of Work Layoffs on Survivors: Research, Theory, and Practice," *Research in Organizational Behavior,* Vol. 10, 1988, pp. 213–255; and Strasbourg, "Corporate Outplacement."

133. Aneil Mishra and Karen Mishra, "The Role of Mutual Trust in Effective Downsizing Strategies," *Human Resource Management,* Vol. 33 (2), 1994, pp. 261–279.

134. Joel Brockner, Steven Grover, Thomas Reed, and Rocki Dewitt, "Layoffs, Job Insecurity, and Survivor's Work Effort: Evidence of an Inverted-U Relationship," *Academy of Management Journal,* Vol. 35 (2), 1992, pp. 413–425.

135. Dan Rice and Craig Dreilinger, "After the Downsizing," *Training and Development,* May 1991, pp. 41–44.

136. Jolene Sugarman, "The Survivor Syndrome," *Human Resource Executive,* January 1993, pp. 45–46.

137. Feldman and Leana, "Better Practices in Managing Layoffs."

138. *Firefighters Local Union 1784* v. *Stotts* (U.S. Sup.Ct. 34 FEP 1702, 1984).

139. Stephan Wermiel, "High Court Rules States May Require Companies to Pay Severance in Layoffs," *Wall Street Journal,* June 2, 1987, p. 10.

140. David Israel and Stephen Beiser, "Plant Closings and Layoffs Follow Special Rules," *HRMagazine,* July 1991, pp. 71–72.

141. Vida Scarpello, "Worker Adjustment and Retraining Notification Act, 1988," in Peters, Greer, and Youngbood (eds.), *The Backwell Encyclopedic Dictionary of Human Resource Management.*

142. For more detail on WARN, see www.doleta.gov/programs/factsht/warn.htm

143. Scarpello, "Worker Adjustment and Retraining Notification Act, 1988."

PART SEVEN

Multinational Human Resource Management

17. Managing Human Resources in Multinational Organizations

Managing Human Resources in Multinational Organizations

HR Challenge

La Bonne Mare is a Marseille-based French firm that custom-manufactures luxury yachts for clients in France, Italy, and various countries in the Middle East. Recently, La Bonne Mare has been considering exporting its products to Taiwan and Hong Kong. The idea of a possible move to an international exporting strategy was stimulated by the success of a small firm in Australia that custom-manufactures yachts. Aussie Yachts moved into the luxury yacht business in Japan in 1990 and has increased its sales by nearly 100 percent per annum since that time. Aussie Yachts has not entered the Taiwan or Hong Kong markets, and recent market analyses have suggested that considerable opportunities exist for La Bonne Mare in these two dynamic economies.

La Bonne Mare Yachts intends to set up two sales offices—one in Hong Kong and the other in Taipei—to sell and service its products. The problem facing La Bonne Mare is how to staff these offices. It is vitally important that the managers of the offices have extensive knowledge about La Bonne Mare custom yachts, including the technical manufacturing aspects. These managers must also be able to "mix, mingle, and network" with wealthy political and business figures in the two locations. La Bonne Mare yachts sell for an average of $1.5 million each, so potential buyers are relatively limited in number. While all of La Bonne Mare's current sales managers are experts in the technical and performance features of the yachts, none of them have ever worked in a foreign assignment, and none speak any foreign language. Many of the managers have spouses and many of those spouses have jobs—the typical dual-career situation of couples in the twenty-first century.

The senior management team of La Bonne Mare Yachts is meeting to discuss the new export venture. Giscard d'Avignon, the CEO, outlines the basic problem to his management team and then asks a straightforward question: "So what do we do about staffing the Taipei and Hong Kong offices?"

In 1978, Arvind Phatak defined a *multinational corporation* as "an enterprise that has an interlocking network of subsidiaries in several countries, whose executives view the whole world as its theater of operations, and who therefore obtain and allocate financial, material, technical, and managerial resources in a manner conducive to the achievement of total enterprise objectives."[1] Today, organizations that fit Phatak's definition are more likely referred to as global or transnational corporations, with their key feature being that executives see all operations within the corporation as part of a *highly integrated* set of business activities that must be managed collectively to ensure global competitiveness. In this chapter, the term **multinational corporation (MNC)** will be used to describe *any* organization that has international operations and attempts to achieve some moderate level of integration among its foreign units. The term **global corporation** will be reserved for firms that fit Phatak's definition of organizations with highly integrated operations across several foreign locations.

In the 1950s and 1960s, most large multinational companies were American and operated in a world economy relatively safe from competition. In the 1970s and particularly in the 1980s, the world of international business became far more complex and competitive. In the 1990s, MNCs were competing in a truly global marketplace, with it being possible for a French firm to manufacture a product in Germany in a plant partially staffed by U.S. and Belgian expatriates and sell most of its product in Britain. In the twenty-first century, the trends of the 1990s will continue, but added to that will be the competitive forces of the World Wide Web and e-commerce. MNCs will be competing not only with other MNCs but also with e-commerce firms that can penetrate international markets by using electronic means alone. The competition will become increasingly fierce and the stakes will get higher. For example, in January of 1999, the United States, Japan, Germany, France, and Britain alone imported goods and services worth $187,470 million from other countries![2] As we indicated in Chapter 2 of this text, an important source of competitive advantage for an organization is its human resources. The competitive value of effective human resource management in multinational firms is certainly as great as, if not greater than, its value in purely domestic organizations. In *The New Expatriates: Managing Human Resources Abroad*, Rosalie Tung states that "human resource planning is pivotal to the successful operation of a multinational corporation (MNC) because technology, capital, and know-how cannot be effectively and efficiently utilized nor transferred from corporate headquarters without using human power."[3] Although many factors contribute to or detract from international competitiveness, the efficient use of human resources is essential and will remain so for the foreseeable future.

This chapter examines issues involved in managing human resources in multinational corporations. The process is referred to as *international human resource management (IHRM)*. We begin with a discussion of the differences between human resource management in domestic and international environments and then look at the approaches to international human resource management that MNCs can take and the factors that affect the choice of approach. In the rest of the chapter we consider specific HR functions within an MNC, such as staffing, training, performance appraisal, and compensation, examining them from two perspectives. The first perspective is that of the HR manager operating within a foreign subsidiary, and the second, that of an HR manager based in the MNC's headquarters.

WHAT IS IHRM?

It is not easy to provide a precise definition of international human resource management. What an HR manager does in a multinational corporation varies from firm to firm. It also depends on whether the manager is located in a global corporation's headquarters or on-site in a foreign subsidiary.

A Definition

Broadly defined, **international human resource management (IHRM)** is the process of procuring, allocating, and effectively utilizing human resources in a multinational corporation. If the MNC is simply exporting its products, with only a few small sales offices in foreign locations, then the task of the international HR manager is relatively simple. However, in global firms, human resource managers must achieve two somewhat conflicting strategic objectives. First, they must integrate human resource policies and practices across a number of subsidiaries in different countries so that overall corporate objectives can be achieved. At the same time, the approach to HRM must be sufficiently flexible to allow for significant differences in the types of HR policies and practices that are most effective in different business and cultural settings. This problem of balancing **integration** (control and coordination from HQ) and **differentiation** (flexibility in policies and practices at the local subsidiary level) has long been acknowledged as a common dilemma facing HR and other functional managers in global corporations.[4] Although some argue that IHRM is not unlike HRM in domestic settings, others point out that there are significant differences. Specifically, compared with domestic HRM, IHRM (1) encompasses more functions, (2) has more heterogeneous functions, (3) involves constantly changing perspectives, (4) requires more involvement in employees' personal lives, (5) is influenced by more external sources, and (6) involves a greater level of risk than typical domestic HRM.[5]

When compared with domestic human resource management, IHRM requires a much broader perspective on even the most common HR activities. This is particularly so for HR managers operating from an MNC's headquarters (HQ) location. The number and variety of IHRM activities are daunting. International HR managers must deal with issues as varied as international taxation; international relocation and orientation; various other administrative services for expatriates; selecting, training, and appraising local and international employees; and managing host-government relations in a number of countries around the world. Even when dealing with one particular HR functional area such as compensation, the international HR manager is faced with a great variety of national and international pay issues. For example, when dealing with pay issues, the HQ-based HR manager must coordinate pay systems in different countries with different currencies that may change in relative value to one another over time. An American expatriate in Tokyo who receives a salary of U.S.$100,000 may suddenly find the buying power of that salary dramatically diminished if the Japanese yen strengthens in value relative to the U.S. dollar. A U.S. dollar purchased 248 yen in 1985 but less than 110 yen in 2000. In the case of fringe benefits provided to host-country employees, some interesting complications might arise. For example, it is common in the United States for companies to provide health insurance benefits to the employee and the employee's family, which usually means spouse and children. In some countries, however, the term "family" may encompass a more extended group of relatives—multiple spouses, aunts, uncles, grandparents, nephews, and nieces. How does the firm's benefit plan deal with these different definitions of family?[6]

A final aspect of the broader scope of IHRM is that HQ-based managers deal with employee groups that have very different cultural backgrounds. The HQ manager must coordinate policies and procedures to manage expatriates from the firm's home country **(parent-country nationals, PCNs), host-country nationals (HCNs),** as well as **third-country nationals (TCNs,** e.g., a French manager working for an American MNC in the firm's Nigerian subsidiary) in subsidiaries around the world. Although such issues are important for the HQ-based manager, they are also relevant to the HR manager located in a subsidiary. This manager must develop HR systems that are not only acceptable in the host country but also compatible with the company-wide systems being developed by his or her HQ-based counterpart. These policies and practices must effectively balance the needs and desires of local employees, PCNs, and TCNs.

It is at the subsidiary level that the increased involvement of IHRM in the personal lives of employees becomes particularly apparent. It is not unusual for subsidiary HR managers to be involved in arranging housing, health care, transportation, education, and recreational activities for expatriate and local staff. For example, foreign firms operating in Taiwan often provide dormitory housing for local assembly workers; this housing is managed by the MNC's local HR staff. Subsidiary managers may even find themselves dealing with expatriates who have marital and/or alcohol problems, acting as counselor and legal adviser.[7]

IHRM activities are also influenced by a greater number of external forces than are domestic HRM activities. The HQ-based manager may have to set equal employment opportunity (EEO) policies that meet the legal requirements of both the home country and a number of host countries. Because of the visibility that foreign firms tend to have in host countries (especially in developing countries), subsidiary HR managers may have to deal with government ministers, other political figures, and a greater variety of social and economic interest groups than would normally be encountered in purely domestic HRM.

The final difference between domestic and international HRM relates to the level of risks and consequences associated with HR decisions. There certainly are major risks associated with HRM in domestic situations. Unfair hiring practices may result in a firm's being charged with violation of EEO laws and subjected to financial penalties. The failure to establish constructive relationships with domestic unions can lead to strikes and other forms of labor actions. However, international HR managers face these same risks, as well as some additional ones that are unique and more threatening. Depending on the countries where the MNC operates, HQ and subsidiary HR managers may have to worry about the physical safety of employees. A colleague of the authors related his experience during a coup attempt in a South American country. As HR manager for the local subsidiary of a foreign firm, he found himself arranging transport for his expatriate employees and their families to the safety of the subsidiary's manufacturing plant. The process involved death threats, wild rides through the jungle, and standoffs at gunpoint. This is not the sort of problem usually confronted by domestic HR managers. In all too many countries, kidnapping and terrorism are of concern to international HR managers, although less than 50 percent of MNCs in a recent survey had formal programs for dealing with these threats.[8]

Besides these risks, it has been estimated that an average expatriate manager, with family, costs between U.S.$300,000 and $1 million per year to maintain overseas. Over the past decade in studies of 750 firms, Stewart Black and Hal Gregersen have found that between 10 and 20 percent of U.S. expatriates return early from foreign assignments.[9] If managers do not perform well and must be recalled to the home country, their failure represents a huge financial loss for the firm.

A final risk is that of expropriation or seizure of the MNC's assets by a host country's government. If HR policies antagonize host-country unions or important political groups, the MNC may be asked to leave the country, have its assets seized, or find the local government taking majority control of its operation. Again, this is not the sort of risk that most domestic HR managers face.

Approaches to IHRM

MNCs can approach the management of international human resources in a number of ways. Four of these are presented in Table 17.1. In the **ethnocentric approach,** the MNC simply exports HR practices and policies used in the home country to subsidiaries in foreign locations. Expatriates from the MNC's home country manage the foreign subsidiaries, and the MNC's headquarters maintains tight control over the subsidiaries' policies. In the **polycentric approach,** the subsidiaries are basically independent from headquarters. HR policies are adapted to meet the circumstances in each foreign location. Local managers in the foreign sites are hired to manage HRM activities. Allan Bird and his colleagues have identified a variation of the polycentric approach, which they refer to as the **closed hybrid model.** In this approach to HR, a subsidiary uses a parent-country "template" for HR but adapts practices within the template to local conditions.[10] The **regiocentric approach** represents a regional grouping of subsidiaries. HR policies are coordinated within the region to as great an extent as possible. Subsidiaries may be staffed by managers from any of the countries within the region. Coordination and communication within the region are high, but they are quite limited between the region and the MNC's headquarters. In the **geocentric approach,** HR policies are developed to meet the goals of the global network of home-country locations

● **TABLE 17.1**

Four Approaches to IHRM

Aspect of the Enterprise	Orientation			
	Ethnocentric	**Polycentric**	**Regiocentric**	**Geocentric**
HR strategy	Uniform strategy across units	Diverse strategies across units	Regional integration of strategy, but differentiation across regions	Global overarching strategy on key corporate issues but differentiated policies on more local issues
Performance criteria evaluation and control	By home-country HQ	By local subsidiary management	Coordination across countries in the region	Global as well as local standards and control
Information and resource flows	Mainly from HQ to local subsidiary	Little among subsidiaries, little between subsidiary and HQ	Little between subsidiary and HQ, medium to high among subsidiaries in region	Inflows and outflows between and among HQ and subsidiaries
Staffing mix	Home-country managers	Host-country managers	Host-country and third-country nationals from within the region	Best people where they can be best used
Career development	Home-country managers developed to work anywhere	Totally within subsidiary career paths and development	Regional career paths and development	Managers anywhere developed to work anywhere
Purpose of socialization processes	Gain loyalty, commitment, and understanding of HQ	Gain loyalty and commitment to the subsidiary	Gain loyalty and commitment to the region	Gain loyalty, commitment, and understanding of the total firm and its diverse units

Sources: Adapted from D. A. Heenan and Howard V. Perlmutter, *Multinational Organization Development* (Reading, Mass.: Addison-Wesley, 1979), pp. 18–19; Ken Kamoche, "The Integration-Differentiation Puzzle: A Resource-Capability Perspective in International Human Resource Management," *The International Journal of Human Resource Management,* Vol. 7 (1), 1996, pp. 230–244.

and foreign subsidiaries. This may include policies that are applied across all subsidiaries as well as policies adapted to the needs of individual locations—depending on what is best to maximize global results. Bird and his colleagues refer to this approach as an **open hybrid model** because subsidiary practices are a hybrid of activities to meet both global and local demands, with extensive sharing among subsidiaries of effective practices.[11] An attempt is made to identify the best HR practices from both the home and host countries and apply them in an integrative manner where most appropriate around the world. The firm is viewed as a single international business entity rather than a collection of individual home-country and foreign business units. HRM and other activities throughout the MNC are managed by individuals who are most appropriate for the job regardless of their nationality.[12] Thus you might find a British manager handling HRM activities in the New York office of a Dutch MNC.

Factors Affecting the Approach to IHRM

A number of factors may influence the IHRM approach taken by an MNC. Included among these are a number of external factors such as the political policies and legal regulations within the host countries; the state of managerial, educational, and technological development in the host countries; and the national cultures of both the home and host countries. There are also factors internal to the firm that affect the IHRM approach. These include the level of international experience in the firm, the method by which worldwide subsidiaries are founded, the technology and nature of the product or products of the MNC, the MNC's internal organizational culture, and the life cycle of the organization.[13]

● **Political Policies and Legal Regulations**   The nature of IHRM may be restricted by government policies and legal regulations in the host country. For example, policies limiting the number of expatriates and requiring extensive employment of host-country nationals may be in place to encourage MNCs to hire, train, and develop local employees, particularly managerial and technical staff. This is especially likely in developing countries, where management and technical training within the host country's educational system is rudimentary and the local government views the presence of MNCs in the country as a means of developing local expertise.

● **Managerial, Educational, and Technological Development in the Host Country**   An MNC opening subsidiaries in Europe faces a much different IHRM challenge than one opening subsidiaries in a country in, say, western Africa. In Europe, the available work force is likely to be well educated and have considerable technical and management experience. Therefore, the opportunity to develop polycentric, regiocentric, or geocentric IHRM strategies is available. In western African countries, management and technical education is likely to be limited, and the bulk of the work force may lack basic skills needed to deal with modern production processes or service activities. A more centralized IHRM strategy is necessary, with careful on-site monitoring by home-country personnel.

● **Home- and Host-Country Cultures**   Culture, particularly national culture at the headquarters level, plays a role in determining IHRM practices.[14] Culture may affect HQ decisions in at least two ways.

First, some cultures are simply more comfortable than others in taking an ethnocentric approach to management. For example, data indicate that Japanese MNCs more frequently staff management positions in their foreign subsidiaries with home-country managers than do American or European MNCs. There are, of course, exceptions to this, but worldwide this tendency toward ethnocentric staffing is greater in Japanese MNCs than in American or European firms.[15]

Second, the mix of cultures in the subsidiaries of an MNC and the level of cultural difference among the subsidiaries will restrict the IHRM approach taken. As the number and level of cultural differences among subsidiaries increase, it becomes much more difficult for HR staff at the MNC's headquarters to formulate and implement consistent HR practices worldwide. Thus, even though an MNC might prefer an ethnocentric approach to managing human resources, the policies and practices formulated at HQ may be totally inappropriate and unacceptable in particular subsidiary locations. A more polycentric or regiocentric approach may be necessary. (See the International Perspective box for more on within-region differences in HR practices.)

● **International Experience of the Firm**   Firms with extensive international experience have had the opportunity to develop more diverse methods of maintaining coordination and control over their foreign operation. Thus they may focus less on centralized control of HR functions than firms with little international experience. Newcomers to the global marketplace may view the international business environment as more unpredictable, higher in ambiguity and uncertainty, and perhaps more threatening than more experienced global players. Constriction of control—that is, a tendency toward centralizing decision making and coordination functions—is common in ambiguous, uncertain, and threatening situations.[16]

● **Method of Subsidiary Founding**   The method used to establish operations in foreign locations may also affect HR policies. At new sites, it may be more likely that HR practices and policies from the home country will be implemented. In the case of foreign operations that are acquired by merger or acquisition, the presence of existing HR practices in the acquired/merged operation likely will reduce the wholesale exportation of home-country HR systems into the subsidiary.

● **Technology and the Nature of the Product**   For technologically sophisticated products or services, the need to maintain specific production standards and quality control necessitates a greater degree of centralization of IHRM functions at the MNC's headquarters location and the use of home-country managers and technical personnel to monitor these standards. This is the case particularly when the subsidiaries involved are located in host countries with low levels of technological and managerial expertise. On the other hand, some products must be adapted to host-country tastes in order to succeed in the local market. For example, some food items that are highly popular in the United States would be viewed as quite repulsive in other countries. In this case, the reliance on local talent to adapt the product to suit the host-country market may require a very different approach to managing the subsidiary's recruiting activities.

● **Organizational Culture**   Regardless of the national culture of a firm, each organization develops its own internal work culture. While national culture has an impact on organizational culture, there is considerable room for variation across firms within the same country. Competitive orientation and profit focus, the level of employee involvement in decision making, and basic assumptions about employee proactivity, malleability, and responsibility seeking will affect how an MNC's headquarters approaches human resource management in foreign subsidiaries. Ethnocentric approaches to IHRM would be more likely in firms where employees are generally viewed as malleable, not very proactive, and not likely to desire and seek responsibility. In such organizational cultures, the more controlling nature of ethnocentric IHRM would likely seem most appropriate for HQ managers.[17]

INTERNATIONAL PERSPECTIVE

Managing Human Resources in a Foreign Country: How Well Would You Do?

You are really interested in a career in international human resource management. You want to work with a big global corporation, travel the world working with people from many different cultures—and make a nice fat salary while you are at it. You are sure you have the "right stuff." You took French in high school. You traveled for three weeks in Europe last summer. You even spent a week in Japan three years ago when your mother went there on a business trip and you tagged along. You are sure you have the right kind of "international perspective" to do well as an international HRM specialist.

Well, here is your chance to show your innate cross-cultural management skills. Below are twelve questions that deal with meeting, motivating, training, and appraising people from several cultures. Answer each question, then check at the end of the chapter on pages 852–853 to see how well you have done.

1. In talking with Americans, you should:
   (a) keep two arm's lengths away.
   (b) keep half an arm's length away.
   (c) keep one arm's length away.
   (d) put your left hand in your pocket.
2. At the end of a discussion with a Japanese colleague, you ask him if the sales proposal you have offered is acceptable. He answers "yes, yes"—meaning that:
   (a) he is confirming his acceptance of your price.
   (b) he has heard and understood your offer.
   (c) you should give a deeper discount.
   (d) he is politely saying no.
3. You are conducting an HR planning meeting with ten Arab managers and workers. Everyone is participating except one manager. What will you do?
   (a) Don't worry about him.

(b) Ask who has any more comments before the meeting ends.
(c) Look at that particular manager and ask if he has something to say.
(d) Tell him this is his last chance to talk.

4. You are HR director in a manufacturing facility in China. One of the expatriate managers from Australia approaches you one day and asks your advice on how to best motivate his production supervisor. The expatriate manager asks, "What should I tell Lee Chow Hou to really get him motivated to meet or exceed our production quotas?" Your advice is to tell him:
   (a) "If our department increases output by 10 percent, you will get a 1 percent bonus next month."
   (b) "I'm planning to reorganize the department, and I am thinking of promoting you if production increases."
   (c) "If your team does not meet the production quotas we have set for next month, you are fired."
   (d) "Why don't you put in some overtime to finish the production quotas for next month?"
5. Your Japanese team has just finished putting on a management development program for top executives in your firm. The CEO has told you that the program was exceptionally well done and of great value. Your team did a fantastic job. How should you acknowledge your team's achievements?
   (a) Treat the group to a sushi dinner, where you give special recognition to the group leader.
   (b) Don't mention it, because doing a good job is what they are supposed to do.
   (c) Call the oldest person in the group aside and thank him.

(d) Thank the group at your next meeting and ask them to increase their efforts toward excellence in the future.

6. The plan for a new compensation system for your local work force in Saudi Arabia is due in two days. The CEO, an English expatriate manager, is waiting eagerly to see what the plan will look like. You are behind schedule and may not be able to meet the CEO's deadline. You approach one of your Arab colleagues and ask them to help you finish the project. You are most likely to get her to help you by saying:
   (a) "In the name of God, please help me."
   (b) "If you help me, I'll buy you dinner."
   (c) "My friend, I need your help."
   (d) "Let's try to finish this project ahead of schedule."

7. Betty Hu, in Taiwan, is new on the assembly line and is having difficulty putting the units together properly. You want to train her. You should:
   (a) say, "Betty, you should pay closer attention to what you are doing!"
   (b) shout across the room, "Betty, do you need help?"
   (c) tell her, "Betty Hu, you are learning very fast," then show her how to put the units together.
   (d) take her aside and show her how to put the units together.

8. After completing your training program for a Japanese operations team, you want to hear their views. You should:
   (a) ask the senior person first.
   (b) ask for volunteers.
   (c) go around the room by seating order starting from the right.
   (d) ask the junior person first.

9. You are planning a training session in an Arab factory on the latest modifications to a piece of machinery. Whom should you invite to the training session?

(a) the president of the division
(b) everyone using the machine
(c) the section engineers
(d) the section technician in charge of preparing the machine

10. You are conducting a performance appraisal with a Vietnamese employee. You ask, "Where would you like to be in two years?" He looks surprised. The reason may be that:
    (a) he thinks you, the manager, should know that.
    (b) he thinks you are suggesting he should leave the firm.
    (c) he thinks you want him to change jobs in the firm.
    (d) he thinks you are not giving him a good evaluation.

11. How often do most Japanese managers conduct formal performance reviews of subordinates?
    (a) once a year
    (b) twice a year
    (c) never
    (d) whenever required

12. During a performance appraisal with her boss (a Singaporean manager), an American employee would probably:
    (a) agree with the manager because he is the boss.
    (b) point out how the company stock is rising and ask for a share in the profits.
    (c) openly discuss and defend her point of view.
    (d) point out her good relationship with other employees.

Source: Questions are adapted from tests of intercultural skills found in Farid Elashmawi and Philip Harris, *Multicultural Management: New Skills for Global Success* (Houston: Gulf Publishing Company, 1993), pp. 98–160.

● **Organizational Life Cycle**   Some researchers argue that the appropriate IHRM approach will depend on the life cycle of the organization and the life cycle of the firm's products within various international markets.[18] During the initiation stage, the organization is concentrating on getting itself started and establishing itself within domestic and limited foreign markets. International involvement may be restricted to exporting or very limited international sales operations. During this phase, the organization tends toward an ethnocentric approach to IHRM. In the functional growth stage, international operations become a significant part of this growth, with foreign product divisions established within the firm. The firm views foreign operations as "add-ons" to its organizational growth but not necessarily integral parts of its overall strategic development. A polycentric approach to IHRM is likely, with the firm's headquarters relying on local management to run each foreign location.[19] During controlled growth, the firm attempts to increase productivity and control costs. Ways are examined to find economies of scale and functional integration across major overseas and domestic units. A more regiocentric approach to IHRM may evolve, and trends toward a geocentric approach may develop. Finally, in the strategic growth stage, domestic and international competition forces the firm to view its operations as a truly global unit. Global networks, alliances, and joint ventures are formed. Functional areas within the organization (both domestic and international) must be integrated to maximize competitive advantage. A global, geocentric approach to IHRM is needed to match the integration of research and development, marketing, production, and distribution worldwide.

MANAGING HUMAN RESOURCES IN A FOREIGN SUBSIDIARY

Culture not only influences an MNC's overall approach to IHRM but also plays a critical role in determining the activities of HR managers within foreign subsidiaries. In fact, culture has a potential impact on every HR function.

Culture and HR Functions in a Foreign Subsidiary

The role of a subsidiary HR manager is to develop HR practices that are (1) acceptable within the local culture and (2) acceptable to management at the MNC's headquarters. The dual nature of the HR role is expressed by McDonald's Robert Wilner, home office director for international HR, and Rita Johnson, staff director in international HR in central Europe. Johnson and Wilner state:

> One of our guiding principles is that our restaurants should always be a reflection of the communities they serve—not only the individuals we employ and the culture and ethnicity of those communities, but also the employment practices. . . . While there may be some specific differences worldwide in local labor laws or employment practices, our philosophy is the same whether we're in Beijing or Budapest. . . . Our global perspective is that whatever market or country we're going into, we always employ the most positive people practices and exceed the expectations of our employees.[20]

The balancing of these two requirements is a difficult task. Whether subsidiary HR managers are home-, host-, or third-country nationals, they bring their own "cultural baggage," which may affect their ability to accommodate cultural differences in the host work force. Employees in a subsidiary may consist of a mixture of home-, host-, and third-country nationals—all with their own distinct cultural backgrounds and preferences. The subsidiary's HR manager must help all employees adapt to the HR practices operating in the subsidiary, even though these practices may be derived from cultures very different from their own. (See the Ethical Perspective box for more on this issue.)

Numerous studies indicate that cultural differences do affect how managers manage and how subordinates react to different management styles.[21] In order to relate differences in culture to differences in IHRM practices, it is first necessary to identify the aspects, or dimensions, of culture that vary from one culture to another. In 1961, F. Kluckhohn and F. L. Strodtbeck suggested that cultures vary from one another in how they view some very basic issues; these dimensions and a brief definition of each are presented in Table 17.2. In addition, any discussion of the effect of culture on organizations would be incomplete without mentioning the

● **TABLE 17.2**

Kluckhohn and Strodtbeck's Dimensions of Culture

Dimension	Orientation	Definition
Basic nature of human beings	Good	Left to their own devices, people are basically good and will act in a reasonable and responsible manner.
	Evil	People are basically evil and cannot be trusted.
	Mixed	People are a mixture of good and evil.
Relationships among people	Individualistic	The primary responsibility of an individual is to him/herself. Individual characteristics and abilities are of most concern.
	Group	Responsibility to family and group is most important. Ability to fit into the group, rather than individual ability, is paramount.
	Hierarchical	Basically the same orientation as for group, with the addition that distinct differences in status are expected and respected.
Activity orientation	Being	The point of life is to live and understand. Activity, in and of itself, is not important.
	Doing	The point of life is to do things, be involved in activities, and accomplish objective goals.
Relation to nature	Subjugation	Human activities are determined by nature and the environment.
	Harmony	Humans should live in harmony with their environment.
	Domination	Humans can control their destiny and can exert domination over their environment.
Time orientation	Past	History is important in determining our present actions.
	Present	Our actions should focus on the present, and the current situation should determine what we do.
	Future	Our actions should focus on the future and the attainment of future goals.

Source: F. Kluckhohn and F. L. Strodtbeck, *Variations in Value Orientations* (Evanston, Ill.: Row, Peterson, 1961).

Ethical Relativity Versus Ethical Absolutism: HR Decision Making in Overseas Operations

 What should an international human resource manager do when an employment practice that is illegal and morally repugnant in the home country is commonplace and legal in the host country? Examples might include blatant sex discrimination or racist practices in hiring, job assignment, or compensation; use of child labor; or provision of unsafe working conditions.

Ethicists discuss two opposite approaches to questions of this type. One approach is *ethical relativism,* which suggests that what is good is what a society defines as good. If a society says that virgins shall be sacrificed at every full moon or that women shall not be paid the same as men for the same work, those rules are right for that society at that point in time. There can be no external frame of reference for judging that one society's set of rules is "better" than another's. The IHR manager who attempts to impose his or her values on personnel practices in the host country is guilty of ethical imperialism. Under the doctrine of ethical relativism, it is entirely appropriate to follow local practices relating to the treatment of employees. While appearing on the surface to be a liberal, open-minded approach, this view may result in actions that most home-country constituencies would find entirely unacceptable, such as child labor or slavery.

The opposite position is called *ethical absolutism.* This is the view that there is a single set of universal ethical principles that apply at all times and to all cultures. This approach would be very useful, since it would suggest which local practices, while different from those of the home country, are morally acceptable because they do not violate universal principles and which ones are not morally acceptable and must not be followed. The problem with this view is in specifying what the universal principles are and developing a logical case for why these, and only these, principles are truly universal. Adopting the values of a single culture or religion as universal again runs the risk of ethical imperialism.

Ethicists can marshal impressive arguments against both the preceding views. So where does an expatriate decision maker turn for guidance? Thomas Donaldson has attempted to provide a framework for multinational decision making involving an ethical dimension. He states that the task is to "tolerate cultural diversity while drawing the line at moral recklessness."* In some ways his approach is absolutist because it relies on a statement of ten fundamental international rights: freedom of physical movement; the right to own property; freedom from torture; the right to a fair trial, nondiscriminatory treatment, physical security, and freedom of speech and association; and the right to minimal education, political participation, and subsistence. Organizations, wherever they may do business, need to avoid depriving individuals of these rights.

works of Gerte Hofstede and Fons Trompenaars. Their dimensions, along with definitions, are presented in Table 17.3.

Differences in culture based on Kluckhohn and Strodtbeck's, Hofstede's, or Trompenaars's dimensions may significantly affect HR practices. The following subsections on subsidiary HR planning, staffing, training, performance appraisal, and compensation describe the difficulties faced by the subsidiary HR manager in developing effective HR systems. Many of these difficulties stem from cultural differences. They are discussed along with other problems facing the HR manager that are not exclusively cultural in nature.

However, these rights alone are not sufficient guidelines. When IHR managers are attempting to decide whether a practice is permissible for a multinational corporation, when it is not legal or morally acceptable in the home country but is legal and acceptable in the host country, Donaldson suggests that they ask themselves a series of questions. First, ask why the practice is acceptable in the host country but not at home. Answers to this question fall into two categories: (1) because of the host country's relative level of economic development or (2) for reasons unrelated to economic development. If the answer is (1), the next question is whether the home country would have accepted the practice when it was or if it were at the same level of economic development. If it would have, the practice is permissible. An example would be building a fertilizer plant that provides a product absolutely crucial to feeding the starving population of a nation despite the fact that there is some slight risk of occupational disease for individuals working in the plant. If the home country itself were starving, it would accept the risk to workers in the interest of the greater good.

The second answer—that the difference is not based on economic considerations—requires a more complicated decision process. The manager must ask two additional questions: "Is it possible to conduct business successfully in the host country without undertaking the practice?" and "Is the practice a clear violation of a fundamental international right?"[†] The practice is permissible only if the answer to both questions is no. That is, the practice is acceptable if it is critical to doing business in the country and does not violate a fundamental right. Otherwise, the organization should refuse to follow the local practice.

A less structured decision model is suggested by Kohls and Buller. They recommend considering how important the ethical conflict is. It is important if it revolves around a core value (similar to Donaldson's fundamental rights) rather than a peripheral value, and if the home culture has a strong consensus about the value (so that most would disapprove its violation). In this case, one should probably hold out for home-country values. Other factors to consider are how much control one has over the situation (i.e., the power to force core home-country values on the situation) and the urgency of the decision (whether there is time to find a mutually agreeable solution). A consideration of these factors in a particular case might lead one to avoid surfacing the potential ethical conflict, accommodate to local practice, insist on home-country practice, or attempt to find a middle ground by means of negotiation, persuasion, education, or subtle infiltration of home-country values.

*Donaldson, *The Ethics of International Business,* p. 103.
†Donaldson, *The Ethics of International Business,* p. 104.
Sources: Walter T. Stace, "Ethical Relativity and Ethical Absolutism," in *Ethical Issues in Business,* ed. Thomas Donaldson and Patricia H. Werhane (Englewood Cliffs, N.J.: Prentice-Hall, 1988), pp. 27–34; William Shaw and Vincent Barry, *Moral Issues in Business* (Belmont, Calif.: Wadsworth, 1989), pp. 11–13; Thomas Donaldson, *The Ethics of International Business* (New York: Oxford University Press, 1989); and John Kohls and Paul Buller, "Resolving Cross-Cultural Ethical Conflict: Exploring Alternative Strategies," *Journal of Business Ethics,* Vol. 13, 1994, pp. 31–38.

HR Planning

The importance of HR planning has received considerable attention of late. Particularly in MNCs with strategic global objectives, planning for the efficient use of human resources is essential if the MNCs are to meet their goals.[22] However, the implementation of HR planning procedures may be more difficult in some subsidiaries than in others. In cultures where people are viewed as basically subjugated to nature, there is very little need for HR planning. After all, why plan when people are unable to determine what happens? The implementation of extensive

● **TABLE 17.3**

Dimensions of Culture

Dimension	Definition
Hofstede's Dimensions	
Power distance	The degree to which power is unequally distributed in a society or organization
Uncertainty avoidance	The degree to which a society considers itself threatened by uncertain events and ambiguous situations and tends to avoid these types of situations or tries to control them through formal means
Individualism– collectivism	The extent to which society emphasizes the importance of the individual versus the group
Masculinity– femininity	The extent to which society values masculine characteristics of aggressiveness, assertiveness, and not caring for others; also, the extent to which male and female roles are clearly defined
Trompenaars' Dimensions	
Universalism vs.	Rules are more important than relationships; legal contracts are drawn up, and to be seen as trustworthy you must honor them; a deal is a deal
Particularism	Whether a rule applies "depends"; attention is given to the particular relationships, obligations, and unique circumstances involved; relationships evolve
Individualism vs. Communitarianism	Essentially identical to Hofstede's individualism vs. collectivism dimension
Neutral vs.	Thoughts and feelings are hidden; there is a cool self-control; don't touch; monotone expression
Affective	People express their thought openly; there is a heated vitality to discussions; people touch, use gestures, and can be dramatic in their expressions
Specific vs.	Direct and to the point; precise, blunt, clear; looks at the facts, not the person involved
Diffuse	Indirect and tactful; ambiguous; considers the situation
Achieved status vs.	Little focus on titles; titles used only when they reflect competence; judged on what you do and know
Ascribed status	Many titles; the boss is boss; generally older male authority
Past vs. Present vs. Future	Essentially the same as Kluckhorn and Strodtbeck's time orientation dimension
Sequential	One thing at a time; schedule is more important than relationships; follow original plan
Synchronic	Many things at once; appointments are flexible; relationships are more important than schedules; like to "see what happens" to determine actions
Internal vs. External control	Essentially the same as Kluckhorn and Strodtbeck's subjugation and domination concepts in the sense of being able or not being able to control what happens

Source: Summarized from Richard M. Hodgetts and Fred Luthans, *International Management: Culture, Strategy, and Behavior,* 4 ed. (Boston: Irwin-McGraw Hill, 2000), pp. 116–117, 124–131.

HR planning systems in such cultures would be met with bemusement at best and significant resistance at worst. Likewise, cultures that are oriented toward the present would not view long-term planning as valuable. In cultures oriented toward the past, planning would tend to focus on purely historical data and the use of these data in predicting future HR needs. Such an approach might be appropriate for firms that operate in relatively stable environments but would not work well for firms operating in highly variable environments, where the past has little to do with the future.

Staffing in the Subsidiary

A subsidiary HR manager ought to use a hiring process that fits the local labor market. For example, an MNC may need the services of a local personnel selection agency to identify the sources of skilled employees. Local employment laws must be adhered to, and premium salaries may have to be offered to lure highly qualified individuals away from local firms. In Japan, the collective nature of Japanese society traditionally has made it difficult for foreign companies to hire qualified Japanese employees. These individuals tend to "stay in the family" and work for Japanese, not foreign, employers. Although during the downturn in the Japanese economy during the early 1990s this attitude became less prevalent, it still remains a problem.

In some countries, hiring may require using a government-controlled labor bureau. This may be particularly prevalent in hierarchical cultures with high power distance (see Table 17.3). In Vietnam, for example, local labor bureaus are heavily involved in the hiring process. Sometimes the local bureaus may supply a foreign subsidiary with employees who are not adequately skilled for the job, and it may be difficult for the subsidiary to refuse employment. Important staffing issues may have to be approved by very high government officials.[23]

In particularistic cultures, nepotism may be a problem in hiring. As defined in Table 17.3, personal relationships are important in particularistic cultures. Pressure may come from local managers or other employees to hire an individual because this person is a close personal friend or relative who is having financial problems and desparately needs a job. This person may not be the best individual to hire in terms of technical competency, however. If the HR manager hires the individual, then a potentially unqualified employee has been placed into the work setting. If the HR manager does not hire the individual, then important cultural values have been violated and the HR manager may be viewed as cold and unfeeling by local employees.

The development of a selection system may be complicated by the fact that selection tests used in the home country of the MNC may be culturally biased and inappropriate elsewhere. For example, many personality tests were developed using Western samples. Assertive individuals who take initiative and stand out from the crowd may appear well adjusted according to the norms of Western personality tests. However, a Japanese job applicant with a similar score might be a disaster if hired to work in the MNC's subsidiary in Tokyo because "standing out" as an individual is inconsistent with the more collectivist Japanese culture. Even if the concepts measured by the tests are applicable, there are difficulties in getting many tests adequately translated into the host-country language. Issues of race, age, and sex discrimination can cause considerable difficulties for the subsidiary HR manager. In some countries it is acceptable and legal to place job advertisements that specifically state the race, age range, and sex of employees being sought. This would blatantly violate American EEO laws. An American working as an HR manager in one of those countries could experience a moral dilemma in following practices that are in line with local laws and culture but conflict with home-country laws and home-country organizational culture.

There also can be unexpected disadvantages associated with hiring particular types of local employees. For example, in a multicultural society, the use of an employee from one ethnic group in a managerial position may not be acceptable to members of other ethnic groups. In India, the caste system, which historically has played a prominent role in Indian society, could make it inappropriate to hire someone from a lower caste to supervise employees of a higher caste. In some countries (Japan, for example), it may be inappropriate to hire a younger person for a job that has supervisory responsibilities over older employees.

Training in the Subsidiary

One of the major problems associated with hiring in less developed countries is that the skill level of individuals may be less than desired. In such circumstances, it is important to invest considerable time and effort in the selection process and to provide increased training to local employees when they arrive on the job.[24] However, much like the problem of transferring HQ-based selection procedures to subsidiaries, training programs designed in the home country to teach employees the skills needed to perform their jobs may be inappropriate for use in other cultures. Translating training materials may be difficult. In addition, how people learn and the methods of training with which they are comfortable vary across cultures. For example, the Chinese, whose culture is very hierarchical, are taught respect and deference for teachers. As a result, Chinese students see themselves as the "receivers" and the teachers as the "givers" of knowledge.[25] Chinese students rarely ask questions or challenge a teacher's statements. To do so would be disrespectful. Consequently, Chinese students take a passive role in learning, and the very active, high-participation methods often used in Western training programs would perhaps be inappropriate for them.

An alternative to training local employees in the subsidiary's foreign location is to train them in the MNC's home headquarters or in a training facility in some other country. This may be appropriate when good trainers and training facilities are unavailable in the host location or as a result of the special nature of the job for which the local employee must be trained. For example, McDonald's believes that local managers who operate foreign franchises need to receive their training on-site in an operational outlet. When McDonald's first moves into a country, obviously no such operational outlets exist. As a result, training is done in a nearby country in which McDonald's has functioning outlets. When ANZ Bank prepared to open operations in Vietnam, it needed twenty-eight people to staff its facility. No one was available locally with the appropriate financial expertise, so ANZ could not simply hire fully qualified Vietnamese bankers. Instead, it looked for locals with English-language ability and the ability to be trained. Once selected, these employees were trained in Australia for three months by Australian financial experts.[26] While this approach to training host-country employees has many advantages, it is not without its difficulties. MNCs must get visas and work permits for their employees to allow them to enter the home country for such training. Immigration laws and quotas placed on immigration by certain nations may make it difficult or even impossible to obtain the necessary visas and permits. Special agreements between the MNC and its home (or third-country) government may be needed.

Appraising the Performance of Subsidiary Staff

Culture helps determine the *importance* of performance appraisal, *what* aspects of performance should be appraised, and *how* that appraisal should be conducted. In cultures that value ascribed status, such as Austria or Saudi Arabia, your rank, title, family or social background may be more important than what you do. In such cultures, HR decisions about individuals may be influenced more heavily by who you are rather than how you perform. Thus, less importance is given to performance appraisal information than in achieved-status cultures like the United States, Ireland, or Norway.

Many of the performance appraisal methods discussed earlier in this text were developed in the United States—a very individualistic culture—and therefore tend to focus on the assessment of individual performance (e.g., behaviorally anchored rating scales, behavioral observation scales). By contrast, in collective cultures like Japan or China, group performance is critical, and appraisals that focus on individual performance are highly threatening. In Japan, behaviors directed toward maintaining group harmony and cohesiveness (e.g., helping resolve conflicts among group members) may be valued as much as, if not more than, behaviors focused on more objective performance activities (e.g., producing more widgets). A similar situation may exist in feminine cultures, in which maintenance of good personal relationships is valued. Managers who maintain good personal networks and develop warm, trusting relationships with their subordinates may be viewed as better managers than those with higher levels of objective task performance. Mark Easterby-Smith and his colleagues found marked differences in the criteria used by British and Chinese firms in determining whether employees were ready for promotion. In British firms, the focus was on bottom-line delivery, evidence of experience in more than one business area, and experience in another country. In Chinese firms, criteria included loyalty to the Communist party, good quality of relationships, evidence of being a hard worker, and good "moral" practices.[27]

In addition to *what* aspects of performance are measured, organizations vary in *how* they assess employee performance. Management by objectives (MBO) or other forms of goal setting are widely accepted in managing and appraising performance. In MBO, subordinates and supervisors agree on moderately difficult and challenging goals that the subordinates must achieve. There are at least four assumptions that underly the use of MBO programs. First, subordinates are assumed to be capable and have the right to negotiate with their boss about performance objectives. Second, managers accept the need to allocate responsibility and delegate authority to the subordinates. Third, both supervisors and employees accept the risk associated with employee involvement in setting and achieving objectives. Finally, performance is seen as important by both parties.

These assumptions are significantly violated in France, where there is a large power distance between the leaders and the led. Hierarchy and the chain of command are very important to both supervisors and subordinates. The role of managers in French firms is to eliminate risk and uncertainty and plan the methods to achieve the firm's objectives. The manager is assumed to be qualified for this role; otherwise, he or she would not have been made a manager. One role of an average French employee is to reduce risk—for himself or herself. MBO increases personal risk. MBO does not work in France.[28]

Another example of culture affecting *how* appraisals should be done relates to Trompenaars's neutral/affective and diffuse/direct cultural dimensions. Japan is a very neutral and diffuse culture. Thoughts and feelings are hidden, and communication is indirect and tactful in nature. While Americans and Australians might appreciate a direct and "to the point" discussion with a supervisor about their performance, a Japanese employee would likely see such a session as aggressive and harsh. The difficulties of transferring appraisal criteria and methods from the United States to France or Japan are not unique. Similar problems may be encountered elsewhere and make the development of effective performance appraisal systems in MNCs an extremely complex and arduous task.

Subsidiary Compensation Systems

The task facing the international compensation manager is pictured in Figure 17.1. Compensation policies within each subsidiary must be consistent with the local wage market, wage legislation and regulations (e.g., minimum wage), union influences, other legal restrictions (e.g., prohibitions against sex-based wage discrimination), and cultural preferences. At the same time, the subsidiary's compensation system must provide an adequate level of strategic consistency within the MNC's overall business strategy. Besides dealing with a pay system developed for host-country employees, the subsidiary HR manager must also deal with a separate system applicable to home-country expatriates and third-country nationals working for the subsidiary. Expatriate pay systems, which are discussed later in this chapter, are often very different from those used for host-country employees within a subsidiary. In some cases, expatriate employees make more money than host-country nationals who have jobs of equal or greater importance and complexity. These differences can often result in host-country employees feeling that they are being treated unfairly.

Factors Affecting Compensation Systems

There are a variety of factors that affect compensation systems within MNCs. MNC compensation systems are influenced by internal business factors such as varying wage costs, levels of job security, and differing business strategies. Compensation is affected by differences in prosperity and spending power related to the strength of

● **FIGURE 17.1**

Multinational
Compensation Systems

Expatriate and third-country national compensation system

- Attract and retain
- Facilitate movements
- Consistent and reasonable when compared with subsidiaries

Subsidiary 1
- Wage market
- Wage legislation
- Other legal restrictions
- Union influences
- Subsidiary's economic standing
- Cultural preferences

Subsidiary 2
- Wage market
- Wage legislation
- Other legal restrictions
- Union influences
- Subsidiary's economic standing
- Cultural preferences

national economies and currencies. Social factors—such as the extent to which pay differences are considered acceptable, the appreciation of different forms of pay, and the acceptance of different forms of compensation and appraisal (e.g., stock options, incentive pay based on performance)—also affect MNC compensation systems in a particular country. Wage and other legislation, along with the influence of unions, has an impact on compensation systems as well.

It is beyond the limits of this chapter to discuss the myriad influences on MNC compensation practices around the world. Suffice it to say that the subsidiary HR manager must know or have access to information about these issues. Regulations concerning pensions, medical insurance, and other benefits are critically important and vary greatly. In some countries, benefits such as housing, transportation, and year-end bonuses are common; in others, they are not.

Issues relating to sex-based or racially based wage differentials are of particular concern for subsidiaries of U.S. firms. Even though such differentials may be acceptable in countries where American MNCs operate, they are certainly not consistent with U.S. HR philosophies. An American HR manager in a foreign subsidiary must make decisions as to whether it is ethical to have discrimination in one part of the MNC but not in another. Union influences may play an important role in determining wage policies in some countries but not in others. For example, Australia has had for some years now a national wage-setting system in which the government and unions negotiate pay rates for workers that apply country-wide. In Hong Kong, by contrast, labor unions are extremely weak and wage rates are determined by the free market.

One aspect of compensation that varies from country to country and has important implications for both subsidiary HR managers and HQ-based managers is the issue of what happens if the MNC decides to leave a foreign country. When such a decision is made, termination liabilities may result in significant payouts to employees.[29] By tradition, law, or union contract, MNCs may be required to pay up to two years' salary to employees who are involuntarily terminated. In some countries, firms intending to close down operations may be required to develop a systematic plan to deal with severance payments, relocation expenses, retraining, and other services for employees who are laid off.

As with performance appraisal systems, cultural preferences may influence the type of compensation system that is appropriate. For example, Lincoln Electric, one of the first companies to successfully implement a productivity-based incentive system in the United States, has attempted to transfer that system of piecework, end-of-year bonus, and continuous employment to its operations in other countries. While the entire incentive package was implemented in its Australian operation, only part of the package operated in Mexico, and its European operations were highly resistant to the incentive plan.[30] If we relate specific cultural dimensions to pay systems, in high power distance cultures, compensation systems should reflect hierarchical divisions within the firm. Pay should reflect job and status differences, with large differences in the pay levels of the highest- and lowest-level workers. In contrast, compensation systems in low power distance cultures should be more egalitarian, with relatively small differences between the top and bottom earners. In individualistic cultures, compensation systems should reward individual achievement, and in collective cultures, pay should be group based or seniority based.[31] The highly individualistic incentive system of Lincoln Electric works wonderfully well in the United States, but it was less well received in more collectivist Europe.

The job of the HR manager in a foreign subsidiary is a difficult one. The procedures and policies developed must be consistent with the host country's legal requirements and cultural traditions. Overlaying this HR system are the policies and procedures of the home-country MNC. If the overall HR approach of the MNC is polycentric, then the HR manager's job is much simpler because subsidiaries are given substantial autonomy in developing their own HR policies. Where the MNC takes a more ethnocentric approach, inevitable conflict occurs as the subsidiary HR manager attempts to work within HQ's guidelines while providing procedures that are acceptable to the host country's work force. With regiocentric or geocentric IHRM approaches, the subsidiary HR manager's job becomes a delicate balancing act of local adaptation and strategic consistency to ensure that HR policies and procedures result in efficient use of subsidiary human resources to the maximum benefit of both the subsidiary and global MNC.

IHRM: THE VIEW FROM HEADQUARTERS

MNCs are increasingly faced with the problem of how to allocate limited resources among multiple subsidiaries around the world. The development of global markets and the existence of global competitors have made it necessary for MNCs to exert centralized, strategic control over their worldwide operations. At the same time, intensified competition in local markets, specific cultural conditions, and unique regulatory systems put pressure on MNCs to be locally responsive. To be competitive, an MNC cannot afford to sacrifice global competitiveness for local subsidiary performance. Neither can it sacrifice local performance and expect to survive globally. An MNC and its subsidiaries therefore must carefully balance the demands of strategic global control and local adaptability. For most MNCs, the person assigned to carry out this balancing act between global and local demands has been the expatriate manager. Vladimir Pucik and Tania Saba have defined an **expatriate manager** as "an executive who is able to assume a leadership position fulfilling international assignments across countries and cultures." [32] Traditionally, expatriates were employees from the home country of the MNC. However, during the 1980s and 1990s, as MNC operations became more diverse, managers from any country in which the MNC operated were selected to manage its foreign subsidiaries around the world. These third-country nationals are also considered as expatriate managers for the purposes of our discussions in this chapter. More recently, the selection and effective utilization of *inpatriates* (foreign-country managers brought to an MNC's home country) has become an important issue for many multinational firms.[33]

Much of what has been written about IHRM has focused on the problems of selecting and training managers for international assignments and then successfully repatriating them when their foreign tours of duty end. However, the task faced by HR specialists in the MNC's home headquarters in effectively managing expatriate assignments is an extremely complex one. For example, Reyer Swaak identified twenty-one separate and important aspects of an effective expatriate management system. These range from identifying employees with international assignment potential, to selecting employees for specific assignments, to managing relocation and immigration issues, to repatriating employees once their foreign assignments end. Issues such as dealing with dual-career couples and providing counseling and support for expatriates and their familes are also part of an overall expatriate management system.

The remaining sections of this chapter examine many of these important processes involved in effectively managing expatriates.

EXPATRIATE MANAGERS

Before examining the various aspects of effectively managing expatriates, two issues must be addressed. The first is "What is an expatriate assignment?" The second is "Why is it so important to manage expatriates effectively?"

Types of Expatriate Assignments

Reyer Swaak has identified several types of expatriate assignments.[34] **Developmental assignments** occur when managers are sent to work in foreign locations primarily to develop specific "global competencies" that are believed of long-term value to the firm. **Project assignments** occur when project work specialists develop and implement plans in a foreign location and then return home or go on to other expatriate assignments. These assignments may involve any type of project activity. **Technology transfer assignments** may be either short or long in duration and are carried out by technical specialists who aid the process of transferring specific technologies from one part of the organization to another. Technology transfer assignments are, for the most part, simply a special class of project assignment. In **management oversight assignments** senior executives are sent to a foreign subsidiary to manage and monitor the subsidiary's activities. The focus of these assignments is to provide a high level of management expertise to the operation as well as a significant level of coordination and control from the MNC's home headquarters. In **regional coordination assignments** managers who excel in managing local operations are given the task of connecting operations among countries in a particular geographic region, for example, South America. **Worldwide oversight assignments** occur when global career executives oversee worldwide activities in an attempt to connect and integrate the activities of the MNC's subsidiaries in several geographic regions.

Although these expatriate assignments cover a wide range of activities, Denise and Lawrence Welch argue that other, often more short-term assignments are also "expatriate" in nature and may have positive or negative consequences for the MNC. For example, employees in exporting firms often make brief visits to various foreign markets to check on distributors and customers or provide information about the nature and use of their product. The establishment of foreign franchises also involves important "expatriate assigments" that may require an initial lengthy setup stay and then multiple short-term follow-up visits for monitoring and control. Similarly, the establishment of joint ventures often requires a combination of brief visits for "flag waving," extended visits for, perhaps, training purposes, and then full, more traditional expatriate assignments as well. The Welches point out that most of the research on expatriation has focused on situations in which individuals go and live for an extended period of time in a foreign country. They suggest that while the depth of the expatriate experience may be greater in these traditional assignments, many of the problems of cultural adaptation, communication, and adjustment to a foreign business environment are also present in assignments of far shorter duration. Furthermore, short-term assignments, such as might be given to a sales representative of an exporting firm, can have significant negative consequences for the firm if they are not handled effectively.[35] The following brief story illustrates their point quite well:

> Once upon a time there came a Texan to Shanghai to do some business. In his first meeting with his Chinese hosts, he put his feet up on a table. Then he used his business card to pick his teeth. The Chinese hosts abruptly left the room. Meeting adjourned.[36]

The Cost of Expatriate Failures

The failure of an expatriate can have disastrous results. As mentioned earlier in this chapter, there are substantial monetary costs associated with sending expatriates abroad, bringing them back to the home country, and finding replacements (between $300,000 and $1 million per expatriate per year). One estimate is that U.S. companies lose $2 billion a year as a result of expatriate failure.[37] Furthermore, the poor performance of an expatriate may damage the firm's image in the host country. There are also the personal tragedies of employees who fail even though they had been viewed as competent managers within the domestic organization. These individuals may have sold their homes, left jobs they liked, and uprooted their families to take a foreign assignment—only to find themselves back in the home country branded as failures. Their early return may also affect their future career prospects in the firm.[38]

The common definition of an expatriate failure is when an expatriate is forced to return to his or her home organization before the expected duration of a foreign assignment is complete. These "early returns," however, are only one type of expatriate failure. Those expatriates who perform poorly but remain in their foreign assignment must also be considered failures. According to Rita Bennett, managing partner of Bennett Associates:

> The obvious failures—the visible mistakes—represent a small number of the assignments, yet these are the ones that corporate personnel still refer to when they talk about failed international assignments. . . . As long as companies focus on that, they're not recognizing where the real failures are, and they're in danger of neglecting the real problem. Those early returns may be costly, but we're more concerned about the people who stay on assignment and do damage, disrupting relationships with local nationals and other co-workers.[39]

While damage to the firm's reputation, loss of employee morale, and disrupted relationships with local nationals may be difficult to measure in dollar terms, these losses to an MNC are very real. That they occur all too regularly in many multinational firms simply increases the importance of effectively managing all types of expatriate assignments, thus decreasing both the monetary and nonmonetary costs of poorly performing expatriates.

Managing an Expatriate

A model of the life cycle of an expatriate assignment is given in Figure 17.2. It involves a process of determining the need for an expatriate assignment, identifying

The Expatriate Assignment Life Cycle

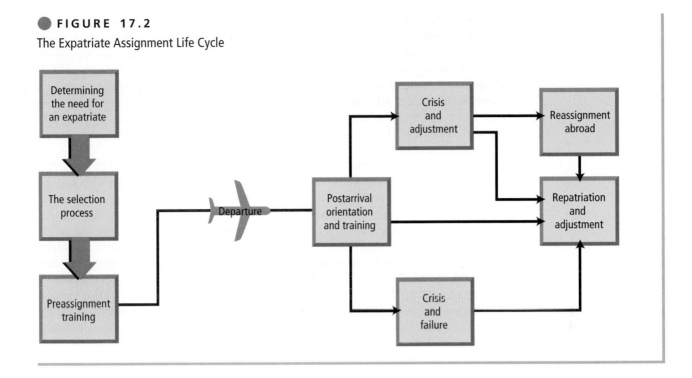

and then selecting likely candidates, preassignment training, departure, postarrival orientation and training, crisis and adjustment or crisis and failure, reassignment abroad, and/or repatriation and adjustment.

Determining the Need for an Expatriate

Although cost considerations and improvements in communication technology persuaded many companies to reduce their use of expatriate managers in the past decade, recent surveys indicate that expatriate assignments are now on the increase. In 1998, the National Foreign Trade Council estimated that 300,000 U.S. expatriates are on assignment at any given time. One 1998 survey found that 66 percent of a sample of thirty-two HR directors indicated that international assignments in their firms would be increasing. Another survey of companies in four different regions of the world found similar results, with 57.9 percent of the Australians, 84 percent of the Canadians, 51.2 percent of the Europeans, and 73.4 percent of the Americans responding to the survey indicating that the number of expatriate assignments in their companies would be increasing. However, the 1999 Global Relocation Trends Survey found that only 23 percent of expatriate assignments were for periods of three years or more—down from 32 percent in 1996. Thus, while the number of expatriate assignments may be increasing, the duration of those assignments is decreasing.[40]

As already noted, the decision as to whether a particular foreign assignment is filled with a home-country national, host-country national, or third-country national may derive partly from the overall IHRM approach taken by the MNC. However, other factors are also taken into account.

The level of the position in the foreign subsidiary is one such factor. One survey of U.S., European, and Japanese MNCs has indicated that expatriates are more likely to be found at the senior management level than at the middle- or lower-management level. On average, home-country expatriates filled 53 percent of top management positions but less than 30 percent of lower-management positions. There were national differences, however, with Japanese firms filling 74 percent of their top foreign subsidiary management positions with PCNs, while European and U.S. firms used PCNs to fill only 48 and 31 percent of their top management positions, respectively.[41]

The degree of interaction between host-country nationals and the person in the position is also an important issue in deciding whether an expatriate should be used. If the position requires a high level of interaction, which in turn requires a high level of knowledge about the local culture, then it may be best to use a host-country national. Such individuals often have political connections and influence networks that are of great value to the firm, and these connections and networks would be very difficult for an expatriate to develop. The similarity of the home and host cultures must be considered as well. If the cultures are very different, it may be difficult to identify an expatriate able to adapt and perform well in the foreign subsidiary. The MNC must then weigh any advantages associated with using an expatriate against the increased probability of the expatriate's failing to adjust and perform well in the assignment. The cost of the training needed to prepare the expatriate for the assignment in a very different culture also must be taken into account in this cost-benefit analysis.

Political factors, too, may determine whether an expatriate should be used to fill a foreign position. As noted earlier, there may be policies or regulations limiting the number of expatriates that can be used to fill positions in a foreign subsidiary. In situations where no such policies exist, it still may be good public relations to fill a large number of positions in a subsidiary with host-country nationals. In other cases, local people may have political or social disadvantages that would warrant the use of an expatriate. For example, in a country with many ethnic groups, giving a local person a prominent position in the subsidiary may alienate local employees from other ethnic groups. The perceived neutrality of an expatriate might be extremely important in such instances.

Firms such as Mitsui & Co. USA and 3M, make international assignments part of a managers' overall career development plans. Whirlpool, Westinghouse Electric, 3M, and Arthur Andersen make foreign assignments a prerequisite for promotion to senior management positions.[42] Thus, even though local nationals could do the job, some positions may be filled by expatriates because the positions give home-country managers the opportunity to develop skills in international dealings.

There are also very practical issues that may affect the use of PCN or TCN expatriates. The level of personal risk in the host country may make it difficult to send home- or third-country personnel to a particular location. Imagine the dangers involved in an American MNC sending a U.S. citizen to work in an operation opening in Palestinian-controlled Gaza or areas of the West Bank in the Middle East! The availability of appropriate job applicant pools both inside the firm and in the host country will determine what type of person is selected. This is often a problem for firms that are new to international business and would like to send a PCN to manage a foreign operation but simply do not have anyone in the home firm who has the experience, expertise, or willingness to manage its foreign activities.[43]

Factors Associated with Expatriate Success and Adjustment

Several studies conducted in the early and middle 1990s have examined the characteristics that are commonly considered by multinational firms when selecting expatriate managers. Taken collectively, a very clear picture of selection criteria emerges from these data. MNCs choose expatriates for international assignments primarily on the basis of their technical competence and past job performance or experience. While European firms seem to pay more attention to culturally oriented skills such as language and liaison skills, as well as to family issues, the primary focus remains on technical competence and past job performance/experience.[44] The question, then, is whether these criteria are the most important for determining whether an employee will be successful in an international assignment.

A number of studies conducted since the early 1980s have identified factors associated with expatriate success and adjustment. Two of the most significant early studies were conducted by Rosalie Tung in 1981 and by Mark Mendenhall and Gary Oddou in 1985.[45]

Tung identified eighteen variables that affected success and grouped them into four general categories: job competence, personality traits and relational abilities, environmental variables, and family variables. In particular, Tung highlighted the importance of family considerations, such as the stability of expatriate marriages and circumstances related to the interest and willingness of the spouse and children to move to a foreign location.

From an extensive review of the literature, Mendenhall and Oddou also identified four major dimensions that influenced whether an expatriate could adapt successfully to a foreign assignment. The first, **self-oriented dimension,** concerns activities that contribute to the expatriate's self-esteem and self-confidence. There are three subfactors in this dimension: (1) **reinforcement substitution,** (2) **stress reduction,** and (3) **technical competence.** Expatriates who are high on the reinforcement substitution factor are able to readily substitute activities in the new culture for those that they liked to do in their home culture. For example, an American manager in Australia would find it difficult to attend American football games. Instead, the manager might develop an interest in rugby, thus substituting a local sport for one that he or she enjoyed in the United States. Expatriate managers also tend to acculturate more readily if they engage in activities that help them reduce stress. To say that an expatriate's job is stressful is an understatement. Expatriates must adapt to a foreign environment and, in most instances, adjust to having greater responsibility than they did in their home country. Yet they are expected to perform at a higher level almost immediately on arriving in the new assignment. Individuals who can reduce stress by reading, jogging, sailing, watching television, meditating, or whatever tend to acculturate more readily than those without such means of relief. Technical competence also has a strong bearing on the acculturation process. Expatriates who are technically competent and feel confident in their ability to handle their international assignments acculturate more easily than those who are less qualified.

The second major dimension of acculturation, the **others-oriented dimension,** consists of two subfactors: (1) **relationship development** and (2) **willingness to communicate.** Expatriates who are able to develop lasting friendships and close relationships with people different from themselves acculturate more easily in overseas assignments. Additionally, individuals who are willing to communicate in the host country's language also adapt more readily. It is interesting to note that this second subfactor suggests that simply being able to speak a host country's language is unimportant unless one is willing to do so. A person who is less proficient in the host language but willing to use it even at the risk of making mistakes and looking foolish may adapt more easily than someone with excellent knowledge of the language but a reluctance to try it out in daily conversation.

The third dimension of acculturation, the **perceptual dimension,** concerns the ability of expatriates to understand why foreign nationals behave the way they do. Expatriates who do not jump to conclusions about the causes of a local employee's behavior have an easier time of adjusting than those who make judgments more quickly. There is a large body of research in social psychology indicating that people are motivated to attribute causes to other people's behavior. Thus, if an employee is performing poorly or acts in a dour, uncommunicative manner, the typical manager will attribute some cause to those actions—the employee is lazy or stupid or has a sullen personality. Social psychological research indicates that we are not very good at accurately assessing the causes of the behavior of people from our own culture. Imagine how poorly we do in explaining the behavior of persons from cultures very different from our own. Mendenhall and Oddou suggest that expatriates who are able to reserve judgment and gather more facts before assigning causes to behavior are able to adjust more readily to foreign assignments.

The final dimension discussed by Mendenhall and Oddou characterizes situations rather than people and is called **cultural toughness.** Some foreign assignments are tougher than others. American expatriates sent to a small village of yak herders in Mongolia would have a much harder time adjusting than if they had been assigned to Sydney, Australia—a modern city with friendly people and the same basic language.

A number of more recent studies have largely confirmed the basic findings of Tung and of Mendenhall and Oddou. For example, Simcha Ronen found that various job factors, relational traits, and motivational factors, along with the family situation and language skills, contributed to the success or failure of expatriates.[46] Issues identified by Ronen that were not so clearly delineated in earlier research are the importance of expatriate career path issues (i.e., the impact of the foreign assignment on the person's career) and the expatriates' overall belief in the mission that they would be carrying out in the foreign location.

In the 1990s, a number of studies identified specific competencies needed by international managers to perform successfully in a foreign assignment.[47] Taken collectively, these studies indicate that persons selected for an international assignment must meet six criteria: (1) They must be willing and motivated to go overseas, (2) they must be technically able to do the job, including having relevant managerial, administrative, and strategic skills, (3) they must be adaptable, (4) they must have good interpersonal and team-building skills and be able to form relationships, (5) they must have good communication ability, and (6) they must have a supportive family situation. An overall model of the factors important in selecting the right person for an expatriate assignment is presented in Figure 17.3.

Procedures for Selecting Expatriates

Since there is a good deal of knowledge about the factors linked to the success or failure of individuals in foreign assignments, and since expatriate failures are expensive, one might assume that MNCs spend considerable time and effort in

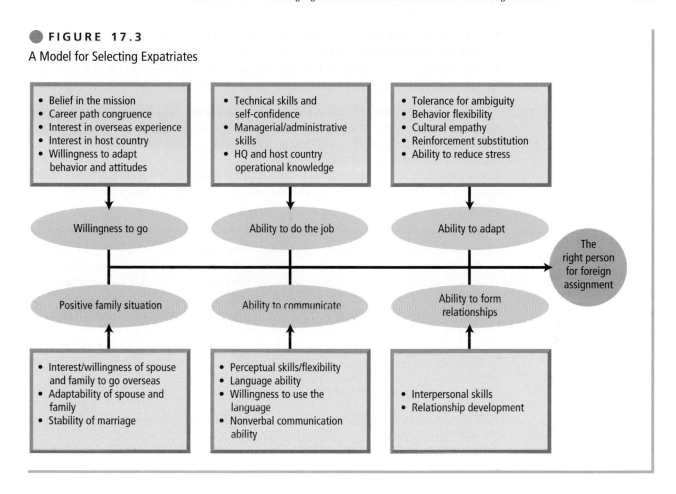

● **FIGURE 17.3**

A Model for Selecting Expatriates

screening employees and their families before sending them abroad. A 1995 survey by the National Foreign Trade Council and Survey Research International shed some light on common practices in expatriate selection.[48] Among the survey's findings were the following:

- Just over 50 percent of the firms had identified technical, managerial, and interpersonal skills that contribute to international success.

- Thirty-two percent had linked these international competencies criteria to the development of personnel and succession planning systems.

- Ninety-four percent held line management responsible for assessing the suitability of international assignees.

- Seventy-six percent said possible expatriates were interviewed by HR staff as well.

- Eighteen percent used structured interviews to assess expatriate candidates.

- Twelve percent used candidate/spouse self-assessment.

- Six percent used psychological and cognitive testing.

- Two percent had a formal assessment center.

- Fifty-six percent said that managers relied heavily on their own judgment when making final expatriate selection decisions.
- Ninety-six percent rated the technical requirements of the job as the most important selection criterion for international assignments.

These results indicate that many firms do not use sophisticated procedures to measure such attributes as relational skills and adaptability. However, this does not mean that they lack interest in the issues. Rather, they often assess such characteristics using less formal methods. For example, Stewart Black and Hal Gregersen describe a method used by Jon Huntsman of the Huntsman Corporation in Salt Lake City, Utah—a private chemical company with $4.75 billion in sales:

> [Huntsman] asks employees he believes have global leadership potential to accompany him on international trips, even if immediate business needs don't justify the expense. During such trips, he takes the managers to local restaurants, shopping areas, and side streets and observes their behavior. Do they approach the strange and unusual sights, sounds, smells, and tastes with curiosity or do they look for the nearest Pizza Hut? Do they try to communicate with local shopkeepers or do they hustle back to the Hilton? Huntsman also observes how managers act among foreigners at home. In social settings, he watches to see if they seek out the foreign guests or talk only with people they already know. During negotiations with foreigners, he gauges his managers' ability to take a collaborative rather than a combative approach. [49]

Whether informal approaches such as Jon Huntsman's or more formal means are used to assess foreign assignment capabilities, it is important to develop selection procedures specifically for international assignments. An organization should not rely on selection methods used for domestic hiring or on information about candidates that was collected with purely domestic purposes in mind. It is possible, for example, that an individual who is an excellent manager in a domestic situation does not have the ability to take on the additional responsibilities usually attached to international assignments. An American manager who is considered an excellent communicator by his U.S. colleagues because of his direct, face-to-face, to-the-point style may be a total disaster when required to communicate with Chinese or Japanese subordinates who value subtle, indirect forms of communication. Examples of methods that might be used to identify individuals with the important attributes for international success are given in Table 17.4.

Additionally, Noel Kreicker, founder of International Orientation Resources, has identified a number of "yellow flags" and "red flags" that firms should be aware of in determining who might not make good expatriates. Among Kreicker's yellow flags (i.e., things that might indicate possible difficulties in adjusting to a foreign assignment) are overblown expectations of career or financial rewards from the assignment, a resentful spouse, aging parents for whom the expatriate is mainly responsible, teenagers who must remain behind to finish school, imminent birth of a child, health problems, special schooling requirements, and denial by the expatriate and his or her family that any concerns or potential problems exist. None of these yellow flag issues will necessarily cause an expatriate to fail in an assignment. What they do indicate, however, is the need for careful thought and preparation by the expatriate, his or her family, and the company as to how these issues will be dealt with effectively. Among Kreicker's red flags (i.e., things that research and past experience

Some Methods for Selecting Successful Expatriates

Willingness to go
- Interview questions to assess the person's understanding of the mission and why the person thinks that he or she has the characteristics that will help accomplish that mission.
- Discussion of the career implications of the foreign assignment. What skills and experiences, in the individual's view, will the foreign position provide for advancement in the chosen career path? What position would the individual expect to receive upon return from the foreign assignment?
- Biodata that might indicate the level of the individual's interest in and knowledge of the host country—for example, history of holiday trips overseas, family connections to the country, and so forth.

Ability to do the job
- For individuals who may have made short-term (one to two weeks) troubleshooting trips overseas, assessments of their performance during those assignments collected from individuals with whom they worked.
- Technical knowledge tests related to particularly important or unusual aspects of the job that will occur in the foreign assignment, for example, technical standards required by the host country, knowledge of labor relations laws relevant to operation in the host country. Obviously, what is tested is determined by the exact nature of the foreign job assignment and what can be learned readily on the job.
- Assessment by domestic colleagues of the individual's managerial and administrative abilities. Current performance appraisals.
- Situational exercises, role-plays, or simulations in which the individual must deal with situations likely to arise in the foreign location. For example, the candidate might have to explain a relatively complicated technical procedure to a host-country national and also might be asked to role-play a performance feedback session with the person.

Ability to adapt
- Situational exercises characterized by high levels of ambiguity and time pressure to examine how well the candidate performs under such conditions.
- Behavior description interviews focused on previous examples of behavioral flexibility.
- Biodata concerning the nature and breadth of hobbies and other leisure activities and a check of the availability of those activities in the foreign location. For example, an individual whose sole hobby is horse jumping may have a difficult time finding an adequate substitute for that hobby in a country where practically no one has ever seen a horse and the few horses that do exist are used for food or as pack animals.

Ability to form relationships
- Psychological tests of traits typically associated with relationship development.
- Assessment of how the individual typically deals with conflict and how that compares with the conflict management norms in the host country.
- Situational exercises where the individual must meet, greet, and establish initial positive social interactions with people from different cultures.
- Biodata relating to the person's ability to establish friendships with people from other cultures.

Ability to communicate
- Traditional written and oral tests of language ability.
- Situational exercises in which the language ability must be used, e.g., explaining a technical procedure to individuals from the host culture using the host language.
- Videos of host-country nationals in which the candidate is asked to interpret the nonverbal communication taking place in the situation on the video.
- "Diplomacy exercises"—asking that the candidate, without saying "Your performance is lousy and I am going to have to fire you if you do not improve," express this same sentiment tactfully to a Japanese subordinate.

Family situation
- Interviews with spouse and family members to determine interest and willingness to go overseas.
- Family biodata to identify possible predictors of adjustment, for example, previous experiences abroad.
- In addition, most of the preceding selection procedures also may be used to assess the spouse's ability to adapt and communicate in a foreign environment.

have shown to make expatriate failure likely) are alcohol or drug dependency, obvious marital discord, evidence of marginal social functioning (e.g., excessive shyness, inability to interact with people in common social situations), serious health problems, mental illness, and obvious racism/ethnocentrism.[50]

Selecting Global Versus Expatriate Managers

As noted earlier, one of the types of assignments that an expatriate manager may be given is that of *worldwide oversight*. This type of assignment requires the manager to integrate the activities of the MNC's subsidiaries in several geographic regions. Vladimir Pucik and Tania Saba have suggested that this role requires something more than what one normally expects of an expatriate. Pucik and Saba have differentiated between an expatriate manager and a global manager. A **global manager** "refers to an executive assigned to a position with a cross-border responsibility, who has a flexible and open mind, with a well-rounded understanding of international business and an ability to work across cross-cultural and cross-functional boundaries, who perceives global competition as an opportunity, and who is able to balance the simultaneous demand of global integration and national responsiveness." [51] The key differences between expatriate and global managers are presented in Table 17.5, along with the different skills that Pucik and Saba believe are required of the two types of managers.

Factors Associated with Willingness to Accept a Foreign Assignment

Once a firm has identified an employee with the necessary skills to take on an expatriate assignment, there remains the issue of whether the employee will be willing to relocate. A survey by Shell Oil of approximately 11,000 employees and their family members who were or had been involved in foreign assignments found that family issues were critical in whether an employee was willing to accept a foreign assignment. The Shell survey found that the two biggest blocks to international mobility were (1) the fact that many spouses had their own careers and were reluctant to move overseas and (2) concern about children's education.[52]

Two Other Special Expatriate Selection Issues

● **Female Expatriates**   As noted above, the widespread existence of dual-career couples has reduced the attractiveness of foreign assignments to many male employees. One result of this has been to increase the likelihood that female employees will be needed to fill foreign assignments.[53] An important question is whether female expatriates have a more difficult time handling international assignments. After all, some Middle Eastern countries will not provide work permits for female employees, even if they are appointed to the foreign assignments by their firms.[54]

In one study conducted in the late 1980s, fifty-two female expatriates were interviewed during their assignments in Asia or shortly after their return from an Asian assignment. Ninety-seven percent of these women described their assignments as successful, and many of the women suggested that the most difficult part of their assignment had been getting their firm to send them abroad. Others suggested that they were discriminated against more by Western expatriates than by

●**TABLE 17.5**

Expatriate Versus Global Managers

	Expatriate Manager	Global Manager
Global perspective	• Focuses on a single foreign country and on managing relationships between headquarters and that country	• Understands worldwide business environment from a global perspective
Local responsiveness	• Becomes an expert on one culture	• Must learn about many foreign cultures' perspectives, tastes, trends, technologies, and approaches to conducting business
Synergistic learning	• Works with and coaches people in each foreign culture separately or sequentially	• Works with and learns from people from many cultures simultaneously
	• Integrates foreigners into the headquarters' national organizational culture	• Creates a culturally synergistic organizational environment
Transition and adaptation	• Adapts to living in a foreign culture	• Adapts to living in many foreign cultures
Cross-cultural interaction	• Uses cross-cultural interaction skills primarily on foreign assignments	• Uses cross-cultural skills on a daily basis throughout career
Collaboration	• Interacts with colleagues from within clearly defined hierarchies of structural and cultural dominance and subordination	• Interacts with foreign colleagues as equals
Foreign experience	• Expatriation or inpatriation primarily to get the job done	• Transpatriation for career and organizational development

Sources: N. J. Adler and S. Bartholomew, "Managing Globally Competent People," *Academy of Management Executive,* Vol. 6 (3), 1992, pp. 52–65; and Vladimir Pucik and Tania Saba, "Selecting and Developing the Global vs the Expatriate Manager: A Review of the State-of-the-Art," *Human Resource Planning,* Vol. 21 (4), 1998, p. 44.

local Asian businessmen. A 1992–1993 survey of foreign executive women in Toyko has supported these earlier findings. The women in this study indicated that they had adjusted very successfully to their work environment and that their performance had been very high.[55] In both studies many of the women cited their sex as an advantage. Their distinctiveness caused their clients and associates to remember them more readily—an asset in any sales position. Many of their male clients found it easier to talk with a woman, particularly in cultures where the aggressive American male approach is overly threatening. In the 1980s study, a common theme appeared: Female expatriates were regarded, first and foremost, as foreigners, and the normal rules associated with the behavior of local females were not applied to them. Women in the 1992–1993 study also indicated that having often been discriminated against in their home country because of their gender, they had developed skills that allowed them to deal effectively with any discrimination they encountered in their foreign assignments.

To summarize, what these research studies imply is that even in very masculine societies like Japan and Korea, female expatriates provide important skills and competitive advantages. In selecting individuals for foreign positions, it seems most rational to look for the kinds of attributes associated with success in foreign assignments, regardless of the gender of the candidate. Given the impact of dual careers on the willingness of many male managers to accept foreign assignments, such findings are good news for MNCs.

● **Inpatriates**   Like female expatriates, inpatriates are an increasingly frequent phenomenon in global organizations. **Inpatriates** are foreign nationals who are hired by an MNC and stationed for some length of time (often one to three years) in the MNC's home operations. Michael Harvey and his colleagues have identified five trends that are likely to see the use of inpatriates rising and that of expatriates declining:

- Expatriates' cost/failure/performance record is questionable.

- Expatriation will become more complex due to the increased number of dual-career couples.

- Future emerging markets will be more difficult to serve in, and these countries will present greater adjustment problems due to differences in culture and level of economic development.

- Inpatriate managers have the cultural/economic background to more effectively address the problems in emerging markets.

- Global competitors have adopted and will continue to adopt a multicultural perspective on global operations. [56]

Of late, Japanese firms have been involved in hiring inpatriates, usually fresh from university. Typically, the inpatriates spend two to three years in the firm's headquarters in Japan before returning to their home country. Japanese firms have found a number of advantages associated with the use of inpatriates. They are uncontaminated by their home-country work practices because they usually come fresh from university. They are young and willing to work in the Japanese system of slow promotions but high job security. They typically are very interested in international assignments as part of their careers. They are fluent in their home-country language when assigned back home, thus avoiding a common problem with typical expatriates. While the considerable cultural and social knowledge and understanding of inpatriates will prove to be an asset to any organization and they will provide a diversity of perspectives to corporate management and add contextual understanding of how to globalize yet act locally, there are some disadvantages associated with inpatriates. They often have less formal business education, do not have language or written communication skills as good as those of native speakers, and are more likely to be plagued by social class and status problems. They may also have different motivation and reward orientations, as well as different time perspectives on how long it should take to get things done. Inpatriates may sometimes be lost to the firm due to slow promotion practices. There may be legal restrictions that complicate the use of inpatriates in the home country. Jealousy may be felt by the inpatriate's home-country staff when he or she returns home but is treated by the firm as if he or she is an expatriate manager in terms of pay and other working conditions.

For the most part, the criteria for effective selection and management of inpatriates are similar to those for any expatriate manager. International competencies are important. Family issues must be dealt with effectively. Inpatriates may need assistance in dealing with basic aspects of life such as housing, transportation, or establishing a line of credit in the new home. Perhaps the greatest difference between inpatriates and expatriates is that expatriate assignments are often high in visibility, power, and responsibility, whereas inpatriates are brought to the MNC's home operations as "learners" rather than primarily as managers and controllers. Despite this difference, most of the issues we will discuss concerning expatriate training, appraisal, and compensation apply to inpatriates as well.[57]

TRAINING EXPATRIATES

The goal of good expatriate selection procedures is to identify individuals who will have the skills necessary to adjust to and perform well in an international assignment. However, Stewart Black and his colleagues point out that selection is only one of many factors that determine adjustment to an international assignment.[58] Among the other important factors affecting adjustment is the degree of training, both predeparture and postarrival, that the expatriate receives. Despite this, 70 percent of U.S. expatriates and 90 percent of their families are sent abroad without any training. Among the reasons given for this state of affairs are that training is not seen as effective, the time between selection for an assignment and departure is so short that there is no time to train, what training is needed is not clear, and there is a belief that technical skills are sufficient for success.[59] The following example of the lack of training given to expatriates is not uncommon:

> An employee of a small Australian firm was sent to Bangkok to start up the firm's new Thai operations. The employee was given two weeks notice, had very little international experience and even less international business experience, and received no training prior to leaving for Thailand.[60]

Is Training Effective?

The lack of adequate predeparture training for individuals assigned abroad is unfortunate, given the evidence that training enhances cross-cultural skills, subsequent adjustment to the assignment, and performance. There is support from anecdotal evidence of the importance of adequate cross-cultural training. For example, the HR manager at Johnson Wax reported that the firm's expatriate failure rate was less than 2 percent thanks largely to effective cross-cultural training. Shell Oil provided cross-cultural training to 800 employees in Saudi Arabia. Among this group of 800 employees, the company had only three failures.[61] A study of managers assigned to expatriate positions in South Korea found that managers who had received predeparture training adjusted more readily than those without such training. The same study also indicated that training had a positive effect on performance in the assignment. Managers who had been trained perceived their assignment as less difficult to adjust to and reported higher levels of performance than those who had received no training.[62] Given the benefits of predeparture training, it is vital to examine some of the methods available for use in such training and to consider when the various types of training are most appropriate.

Training Approaches

Two convenient ways to categorize the varied approaches to training expatriates are by the content of the program and by the specific technique used. Within the content category, some programs focus primarily on the job or organization, whereas others concentrate on aspects of the culture in the foreign location. Job training may stress the new operational or supervisory skills that will be needed in the foreign assignment. Another form of job training can be referred to as "strategic training," where expatriates are given the "big picture" of the global business strategy of the MNC, with emphasis placed both on the global strategy and on how the particular subsidiary to which the expatriate will be assigned fits into that strategy. Strategic training also might include the enhancement of strategic skills, such as the development and use of global information management systems or interpersonal communication skills that could aid in the transmission of critical information to and from headquarters and units around the world. Cultural training may offer basic information on topics such as geography, politics, cost of living, and social and business customs. Other types of cultural training may aim at increasing the expatriate's attributional and perceptual skills—that is, helping the expatriate accurately perceive and understand the behavior of persons from a foreign culture. Special issues like partners and families abroad, daily living issues, and repatriation issues should be covered prior to departure.[63]

Cultural and job training can be accomplished through a variety of techniques. Lectures, briefings, and assigned readings can convey factual information to trainees. Role-playing, case analyses, and simulations constitute more active learning methods. In **cultural assimilator** training, the employee must consider 75 to 100 cultural incidents selected by a panel of experts as representative of situations that the person may confront in the host culture. The trainee has to analyze what is happening in the situation and why it is happening; then the trainee receives feedback on the correctness of the analysis. Trainees may undergo field experiences as well, by visiting either the host country or enclaves of the host culture within the home country (e.g., they may visit a predominantly Chinese part of a city within the home country).[64]

Training programs may also be differentiated according to how long and rigorous they are. Stewart Black and his colleagues have identified three basic levels of training "rigor" on the basis of the amount of time spent in training and the mental involvement and effort required of both trainer and trainee. A program of low training rigor would last from 4 to 20 hours and involve such methods as lectures, films, books, and simple area briefings. Programs of moderate rigor would take 20 to 60 hours and include all the methods involved in low-rigor programs plus role-plays, cases, cultural assimilators, and "survival-level" language training. High-rigor programs would last from 60 to 180 hours, include all the previous methods, and also include assessment center activities, simulations, field trips, and in-depth language training.[65]

A Contingency Approach to Expatriate Training

The international HR manager faces a difficult task in deciding which of the various approaches to training should be used. Obviously, some are more expensive to conduct than others. To maximize efficiency, the international HR manager should select and develop training programs that best fit the particular assignment and individual. A number of authors have identified factors that can be used in making these decisions.[66]

Four factors are important in selecting the type of training program needed: (1) business strategy, (2) job toughness, (3) cultural toughness, and (4) communication toughness. The first factor is important only for training expatriates in managerial and control-level positions, but the remaining three apply to the training for any type of expatriate position (e.g., an expatriate on assignment to fix specific technical problems in manufacturing).

● **Business Strategy**   Business strategy partly determines the nature of training needed. The international involvement of some MNCs is limited primarily to a group of international sales offices or subsidiaries in various countries. Foreign profits and activities are simply add-ons to the activities and profits of the domestic organization. The manager of these overseas units may be given a great amount of discretion as to how the units operate. In such cases, the expatriate manager may need only a very basic understanding of overall business strategy. The primary focus would be on operational and cultural aspects of the subsidiary and the expectations that the domestic organization has of this particular foreign business unit. In other situations, the MNC may not have an integrated strategy for its overseas operations but may retain more central control over the activities within each unit because of product quality standards, legal requirements, or whatever. In these cases, the expatriate manager needs even less knowledge of the overall strategic plan of the organization.

In contrast to these first two scenarios, some MNCs are truly global businesses that have developed a worldwide business strategy. Their markets are global. Their competitors are global, and each foreign unit's activities and profits (or losses) have implications for other units around the world. As a result, strategic training becomes an essential part of preparation for the expatriate. However, as in MNCs without a global strategy, the level of central control maintained over individual foreign business units may temper the need for strategic training. For example, McDonald's is an MNC with a highly integrated global strategy. In this corporation, standard procedures related to product quality are strictly maintained by the headquarters organization. This limits the discretion of foreign subsidiary managers and thus reduces their need for extensive strategic training.

Another effect that a global business strategy will have on training is that it requires a more holistic approach to training rather than simply training programs focused on specific foreign assignments. This is consistent with the competencies needed by global managers described earlier.[67] Because of the complexity of this type of training, some researchers have suggested that such training requires a staged approach. For example, Kerstin Baumgarten suggests a cumulative, three-stage approach.[68] Stage 1 focuses on general skills needed for an international career. This training would focus on competencies such as general interpersonal skills or team-building skills that are useful in either domestic or international situations. This general skill training would begin immediately following selection into a firm. Stage 2 training would take place after a manager has been selected for an international career and would focus on all specific skills needed to function well in an international assignment. These might include general cross-cultural skills, training on the international legal environment, or training on issues associated with technology transfer. Stage 3 would occur after a manager has been selected for a specific assignment and would focus on location/job-specific skills that will be needed in that particular foreign assignment. This training would include aspects such as language training, information about the specific nature of the organization and operation in the foreign location, or information about the business culture and negotiation styles in the country to which the individual is being assigned.

● **Job Toughness**   "Job toughness" refers to whether the job in the foreign location is similar to other jobs that the expatriate has held. Although the basic functions of the domestic and foreign jobs may seem alike, often the scope and responsibility levels associated with the expatriate position are considerably greater. For example, an individual may be transferred to a foreign assignment from a managerial position in the domestic organization that involved supervising fifty employees. In that position, when issues involving equal employment opportunity, government regulations, or labor relations arose, the manager had specialist staff within the organization to call on for advice. In the foreign assignment, the manager may once again be supervising fifty employees carrying out the same basic task as in the domestic situation—for example, selling insurance to local businesses. However, in the foreign location the manager may have to deal with all the issues that other departmental specialists took care of at the home office. Differences in performance standards, material resources, technology, bureaucratic procedures, and legal restrictions will affect the "toughness" of the foreign job assignment.

To the extent that the foreign assignment requires new and different job skills compared with the domestic position, job content training becomes a more critical component of predeparture training. As noted in the section on expatriate selection, MNCs tend to choose individuals for foreign assignments on the basis of their competence in a domestic position. This approach often means that a person who has been an effective performer is assumed to have all the skills needed in the new assignment. The failure of many expatriates may stem from this assumption. Good international HR managers do not make such assumptions but instead carefully evaluate the novelty of the foreign position relative to the person's job history.

● **Cultural Toughness**   Expatriates may find themselves transferred from a domestic culture that is high on individualism, low on power distance, and moderately feminine to a foreign culture that is highly collective, has high power distance, and is extremely masculine. The values, attitudes, and behaviors in these two cultures would be quite different. In such a situation—for instance, in moving from the United States to China—cross-cultural training to help the expatriate understand the attitudes and values of the new culture and learn appropriate behavior patterns becomes more important. When the home- and host-country cultures are relatively similar (e.g., the United States and Australia), the need for cross-cultural training decreases but does not disappear.

● **Communication Toughness**   The difficulty and degree of communication with local nationals must also be considered in deciding the necessary level of cross-cultural training. Aspects of communication toughness include the following:

- Differences in the norms and rules for communication
- Frequency of communication
- Difficulty in learning the host language
- Length of the foreign assignment
- Mode of communication—face to face or by phone or memo only
- Formality of communication required [69]

Determining the level and nature of communication is critical. Even though the home and host cultures are quite different, if the expatriate is not expected to interact with local nationals to any great extent or if the interactions are of little importance, then limited cross-cultural training in the form of general cultural information might suffice. For example, some American expatriates in Jakarta, Indonesia, hold positions that require them to interact mainly with other expatriates from MNCs in the region—not local Indonesians. These Americans live in expensive expatriate neighborhoods outside the city. Houses are surrounded by high walls, protected by security personnel, and represent little replicas of Western society in an Asian land. Interaction with local nationals is confined to a few key Indonesian government officials and businessmen (who may have been educated in the West, possibly in the United States) and servants hired to clean, cook, wash, take care of the children, and drive the expatriates to work.

Even when the cultures are relatively similar, if extensive interaction and communication with local nationals are required, cross-cultural training becomes vital. An American sent to Australia to set up a new subsidiary would have to interact with many different types of local Australians: union leaders, managers, government officials, and so on. Even though Australia and the United States are relatively similar in culture, there are differences. The American expatriate who arrives to establish a new business in Australia and exhibits inappropriate behavior and attitudes would probably return home a failure because establishing the new business would require the American to gain acceptance by local Aussies. Some moderate level of cross-cultural training in this situation would be warranted.

The contingency model of cross-cultural training suggests that the content and rigor of cross-cultural training are contingent on the four factors just discussed. As job, cultural, and communication toughness increase, the training rigor needed to prepare an expatriate for an assignment increases. The content of the training will also depend on the relative toughness of the three areas as well as the overall business strategy of the firm. Thus, if communication toughness is very high, while job toughness is only moderate, training should focus more on communication issues than on job issues. To the extent that the firm's business strategy is moving toward a truly global enterprise, the content of training programs must stress strategic issues such as global production and efficiency systems, corporate culture, international strategy, and multicultural business systems.[70]

Postarrival Training and Training for the Expatriate Family

The training of expatriates involves two additional issues: (1) postarrival training and support and (2) training and support for the expatriate family. In a sense, the term **postarrival training** is somewhat inappropriate. What it actually refers to is the initial socialization of the expatriate into the work setting and practical assistance in getting settled into a new home and environment.

● **Postarrival Training and Support**   While predeparture training may have accomplished what has been called "anticipatory adjustment," the shock of arriving at the foreign assignment may warrant additional fine-tuning of cross-cultural or job skills.[71] As with any training program, the problem of transferring the training from the training site to the job is always present. Thus resources need to be available to help expatriates use what they learned before departure. For example, if knowing the host country's language is important in the expatriate's position, additional language training once the individual has arrived in the foreign location would be helpful. Providing a more experienced expatriate mentor or a reliable local contact is also a good idea. For instance, in every country of operation, Unilever assigns a manager who is a local expert to meet all expatriates as they arrive in the country.[72] Large MNCs with significant numbers of expatriates in any one location also have informal networks of expatriates who help new arrivals adjust and learn the lay of the land. Support from others is especially crucial during the first few months, when everything is unfamiliar and many questions need answers. Jan Selmer and his colleagues refer to this aspect of postarrival training as the **culture shock phase of training,** in which help should be provided in developing specific methods to cope with the wide range of new experiences and impressions that the expatriate has been experiencing.[73]

Training and Support for the Spouse and Family

In many ways, the adjustment of the spouse and family to an expatriate assignment may be more difficult than that of the expatriate. After all, the expatriate arrives at the foreign assignment with an already structured environment (the job) that has many similarities to the old environment. The expatriate is still working for the same company and using many of the same work procedures and practices. The expatriate's work helps insulate him or her from the foreign world outside the office, and there is a readily available source of friends and colleagues at work. The job provides structure and consistency—a sense of familiarity and comfort.

This is not the case for the spouse and family. Many of the adjustments required to accommodate to daily life in a foreign country fall more heavily on the children and spouse than on the expatriate. The children find themselves in a strange school and must cope with all the social traumas that this can cause. The spouse must cope with local tradespersons and shopping in an unfamiliar language, make new friends, and may be prohibited from seeking employment. In many cases, the expatriate family is a **dual-career couple** in which the spouse has left a good job in the home country.

This increased prevalence of dual-career couples has required MNCs to broaden their view of what the expatriation process must involve. For dual-career couples, that broader view must include adequate consideration and management of the **trailing spouse,** that is, the spouse who follows the partner to the foreign location, often having to quit his or her own job in the process. In addition to reducing the likelihood that a foreign assignment will be accepted, research indicates that dual-career couples in foreign assignments tend to take longer to adjust, often suffer decreases in overall family income, have heightened dysfunctional family consequences (e.g., drastically changed roles of the spouses within the marriage), and experience greater problems in repatriating to the home country.[74]

To combat these problems, Hewlett-Packard (HP) has developed specific training programs to help dual-career couples in foreign assignments. HP's program includes a one-day training session for the spouse that is either career-related or interest-related. There is a three-day cross-cultural counseling and orientation session for the whole family, as well as additional language training. In addition to training, HP has instituted a variety of other policies to aid dual-career couples. For example, if the spouse is an HP employee in the home country, then leave of absence for the duration of the spouse's assignment is granted with a guaranteed job back home once they return.[75] Some examples of other innovative dual-career programs are shown in Table 17.6.

● **TABLE 17.6**

Innovative Dual-Career Expatriation Programs

Firms	Nature of Programs
Motorola, Monsanto, Hewlett-Packard, Royal Dutch Shell, and GE	Allowances provided for accompanying spouses for career-enhancing activities such as education, attending conferences and seminars, purchasing computers, subscribing to trade publications, and paying attorney's fees for obtaining work permits.
Royal Dutch Shell	Full-time career counselors available at HQ and unmarried partners included in its spousal services.
Shell Oil	Created "Outpost," a network of forty-four information network centers around the world that creates and identifies employment opportunities for spouses abroad.
Deloitte & Touche	Established a Lotus Notes web-based data system that helps expatriate spouses to find work.
Eastman Chemicals	Spouses provided with a dislocation allowance while unemployed overseas, and this can last for three years.
Sara Lee and Quaker Oats	"Lifestyle assistance" policies established along with services for single-parent families on expatriate assignments, or expatriates with elder-care requirements, or those caring for the disabled.
Colgate Palmolive	Reimbursement program for spouses during the assignment as well as help in finding employment, career counseling, trips home to meet business contacts, seed money for setting up businesses, and tuition reimbursement for career- and non-career-related courses.
Ingersoll Rand	Mentoring/matching program established between former expatriate couples and new arrivals.

Reprinted with permission from Ruth Thaler-Carter, "Vowing to Go Abroad," *HRMagazine*, Vol. 44, No. 12, 1999, pp. 91–96 published by the Society for Human Resource Management, Alexandria, VA. Permission conveyed through Copyright Clearance Center, Inc.

Leveraging Internet and International Travel for Training Expatriates

The Internet is fast emerging as a tool for training/self-education of expatriates. In additon to consulting firms offering their services for a fee on the Internet, there are many free web sites that contain useful information for expatriates. The web sites constructed by expatriates themselves are particularly useful. Some examples: www.hostetler.net (an American family living in Italy), www.erols.com/stevehall (an American family living in Germany), www.geocities.com/The Tropics/Island/4509/index.html (a web site maintained by a British couple that contains very useful links for expatriates wherever they may be). Some other web sites that contain links that might be of benefit to expatriates are: Australians International (www.interstellar.com.au/ausint/ai_home.htm), CIA World Fact Book (www.ocdi.gov/cia/publications/factbook/), The Expat Forum (www.expatforum.com), and Relocation Journal (www.relojournal.com). [76]

As has been discussed earlier, there is a school of thought that recommends that short-term international assignments also be treated as expatriate assignments. Gary Oddou and his colleagues in fact suggest that short-term international assignments should be used as opportunities for development, not merely task accomplishment. Unfortunately, the travel policies of most organizations emphasize time and cost efficiency and aim at getting the executive in and out as quickly as possible, thus missing out on an opportunity to give on-the-job training to their managers.[77]

APPRAISING THE PERFORMANCE OF EXPATRIATES

Along with problems common to the development of any appraisal method, there are significant environmental and task factors that affect how MNCs appraise expatriate performance in foreign subsidiaries.[78] The physical distance that usually separates expatriate managers and their HQ superiors makes it difficult for HQ-based personnel to adequately observe and record expatriates' behavior. Environmental conditions vary considerably across different countries. Political upheavals may reduce the capacity of expatriates to perform. The conditions in some countries may be so difficult that expatriates and third-country nationals must expend considerable effort simply adapting to daily living. The education and skill level of the local work force may also affect performance. Managers of relatively unskilled employees may spend much of their time training workers and supervising the most basic activities in their subsidiary. Objective indicators of subsidiary performance may be low, even though the manager is doing a great job given what he or she has to work with.

The nature of an expatriate's specific task affects the performance dimensions that are appropriate for use in appraisal. For example, consider the criteria that would be used to assess the success of a developmental assignment. In addition to measures of typical job performance, success criteria would focus on the acquisition by the expatriate manager of skills and abilities needed by international managers and then the use of those skills in subsequent management positions. In contrast, for an expatriate in a technology transfer assignment, criteria of success would focus more on the speed and technical efficiency of the transfer as well as the transfer of skills to host-country employees who will use the technology.[79]

For managers in managerial oversight assignments, performance in terms of both the operational performance of the subsidiary and its strategic performance level must be assessed.[80] **Operational performance** is the performance of a subsidiary as a single business unit within the MNC. **Strategic performance** refers to how the performance of the subsidiary fits into the overall strategic objectives of the MNC. A subsidiary may perform well at an operational level yet not contribute significantly to strategic performance. For example, a subsidiary may have done well because of a large infusion of capital from the MNC parent organization. However, this capital might have contributed more to the overall strategic objectives of the MNC if it had been used in another subsidiary. A number of factors must be considered in developing operational and strategic measures of subsidiary performance; they are summarized in Table 17.7.

The development of performance appraisal systems for use with expatriates requires extreme care. The active involvement of the expatriate, home-country supervisor, and host-country supervisor is often important. For example, Monsanto has developed a performance appraisal plan for expatriates that includes the following steps:

- Employees going overseas talk with their home-country and host-country managers to produce an action plan.

● **TABLE 17.7**

Factors Affecting Operational and Strategic Appraisal

Factor	Implication
Currency conversions	A 10 percent profit of the subsidiary may be wiped out if the local currency is suddenly devalued relative to the home-country's currency. This lack of results is not under the control of the subsidiary management.
Accounting methods	Different countries have different accounting practices, which makes it difficult to compare results across subsidiaries.
Ethical and legal issues	Many MNCs assess performance using results-oriented measures. It may be important, however, to assess how the subsidiary management is achieving the results. For example, the Foreign Corrupt Practices Act makes it illegal for U.S. managers operating overseas to use bribes and payoffs to achieve business advantages.
Strategic role	A subsidiary may be opened in a market primarily to counter a competitor that has a dominant position in that market. Subsidiary performance may be limited, but the existence of the subsidiary has a strategic benefit.
Time and distance	Time and distance make it difficult for headquarters to understand the problems and situation of subsidiaries. Higher-level managers may have little real opportunity to observe the performance of subsidiary managers unless considerable time, effort, and money are expended in traveling to visit at subsidiary locations.
International volatility	Economic, social, and political changes may occur very rapidly in the world. These changes may directly affect subsidiary performance yet are often very difficult to monitor and predict.
HQ–subsidiary interdependence	How the subsidiary performs depends, to some extent, on how well the MNC as a whole performs.
Market maturity	Some markets are simply less well developed than others. Subsidiaries in these markets may perform much less well in terms of sales volume than subsidiaries in more established markets. This makes any purely bottom-line assessment of performance inappropriate.

Source: Based on information from Peter J. Dowling and Randall S. Schuler, *International Dimensions of Human Resource Management* (Boston: PWS-Kent, 1990), pp. 83–88.

- The employee writes a job description and a description of what he or she is supposed to do while on the assignment.
- Cross-cultural training then occurs to help achieve these bottom-line results.
- When the employee arrives at the foreign location, he or she sits down with the host-country manager and reconfirms agreement on the action plan.
- This action plan then serves as the basis for judging the expatriate's performance during the assignment.[81]

In addition to the question of what the performance criteria should be, the question of who should assess the expatriate's performance is also complex. As in the Monsanto approach just described, it is common for an employee's immediate superior to serve as the primary rater of that individual's performance. However, in the case of expatriate managers, the direct superior is often someone at the company's home office—several thousand miles away. Since the immediate superior may have little opportunity to observe the expatriate's performance, information about the expatriate must be provided by those in a position to evaluate his or her activities. As with performance evaluations handled in domestic situations, many different individuals may be able to provide useful information about the performance of a particular employee.

PAYING EXPATRIATES

Most expatriate compensation plans are designed to achieve four major objectives: (1) attract employees who are qualified and interested in international assignments, (2) facilitate the movement of expatriates from one subsidiary to another, from home to subsidiaries, and from subsidiaries back home, (3) provide a consistent and reasonable relationship between the pay levels of employees at headquarters, domestic affiliates, and foreign subsidiaries, and (4) be cost-effective by reducing unnecessary expenses. Specific policies vary across companies. Carolyn Gould reported the results of four surveys of expatriate compensation approaches in Australia, Canada, Europe, and the U.S.[82] Four basic approaches to compensation were identified:

- **HQ-based model:** Expatriates are paid according to the headquarters compensation structure.
- **Modified home-country model:** Expatriates are paid according to their home-country salary structures, and their living standard is protected so as to be comparable to the home country or some other chosen standard.
- **Better of home or host model:** Expatriates receive the higher of the home-country system or the host-country system.
- **Host-country/local-market package:** Expatriates are paid according to the host-country compensation structure.

By far the most widely used compensation method is the modified home-country approach—perhaps more widely known as the *balance sheet approach*.

Balance Sheet Approach

The **balance sheet approach** ensures that an expatriate has enough money to buy exactly the same basket of goods in the host country that he or she could buy in the home country. A **standard index** is derived for this basket of goods by calculating the total price of these goods in both the home and host countries. The difference between the two prices then serves as an index for adjusting the expatriate's compensation package. The expatriate's compensation package would include a group of allowances provided to cover differences between the home and host countries in the price of the goods included in the standard index and to cover additional expenses associated with setting up home in a new location. For example, since public schools in a foreign location are sometimes not suitable for the children of expatriates, companies may provide funds to allow expatriates to send their children to private schools. Shipping and storage costs are paid by the firm, and there is usually some allowance for home visits by all members of the expatriate's family at least once a year.[83] An example of how a balance sheet compensation might work is given in Table 17.8.

In addition to these components of a balance sheet–based compensation package, there may be a number of premiums paid to encourage and reward employees for going abroad and to compensate them for any hardships that may exist in the new assignment. These premiums may be paid in several ways. In some cases,

● **TABLE 17.8**

Example of the Balance Sheet Approach to Expatriate Compensation

Home country: the Netherlands Expatriate assignment is in Denmark Currency exchange rate is 27 Dutch florins (DFL) = 1 Danish krone (DK)	
Gross income in the Netherlands	DFL 90,000
• Less pension payments	3,200
• Less social security payments	18,800
• Less income tax	22,200
• Less health insurance premiums	2,500
• Less housing costs	9,000
• Less car expenses	12,000
Net income in the Netherlands	DFL 22,300
Net income in the Netherlands = DK 99,100	
Net income in Denmark	DK 99,100
• Add car expenses	44,000
• Add housing costs	28,000
• Add health insurance payments	8,500
• Add income tax	142,000
• Add social security payments	2,100
• Add pension payments	12,000
Gross income in Denmark	DK 336,600
Compensation package to the expatriate would = DK 336,600	

Source: Adapted from example on pp. 257–258 in Ed Logger and Rob Vinke, "Compensation and Appraisal of International Staff," in *International Human Resource Management: An Integrated Approach*, eds. Anne-Wil Harzing and Joris Van Ruysseveldt, (London: Sage, 1995), pp. 252–269.

a one-time payment of 10 to 20 percent of salary is made to encourage the employee to move abroad. In other cases, a constant premium is paid each year while the employee is on a foreign assignment. A final variation is a "phase-out" method; a premium is paid in decreasing amounts until it is phased out after a certain number of years. Continuous premiums encourage the expatriate to remain abroad, whereas phased-out payments tend to encourage the person to return home or move to another foreign location, where the premiums will start again.

When an employee takes an assignment in an undesirable location, a **hardship premium** is often paid, with the amount varying according to the level of hardship. Determining this level is not easy. Factors used in determining the level of hardship might include distance from the home country, difficulty of learning the host-country language, climate, quality of medical facilities, and risks such as terrorism or crime. Hardship premiums may be given in the form of direct cash payments or in more innovative forms such as company-paid holidays or additional annual trips home.

International Citizen's Approach

Recent alternatives to the balance sheet have been suggested, including the **international citizen's approach.**[84] In this approach to expatriate compensation, an international basket of goods is used for all expatriates regardless of country of origin. The basket of goods includes food, clothing, housing, and so forth. However, expatriates are not provided pay adjustments that would allow them to purchase exactly the same item in the host country as in the home country. Rather, they receive adjustments that would allow them to purchase a comparable local product of the same nature; for example, rather than a Mercedes (which they had in the home country), they could buy a local luxury car. Kimberly Freeman and Jeffrey Kane suggest that there are a number of advantages to using the international citizen's (IC) approach.[85]

In terms of its cost-effectiveness, an IC approach is about 30 percent lower than a standard index based on the balance sheet approach. The IC approach may also have advantages in terms of its consistency and fairness. Traditionally, cost-of-living allowances (COLAs) were determined through a comparison of a specific pair of countries (home–host for each expatriate). Such pairing could result in situations wherein an American might get a 60 percent bonus for going to Brazil, but a Brazilian might get only a 20 percent bonus for going to the United States. The international citizen's basket of goods is the same for all expatriates, and so the comparison is between the international basket and the host country for everyone. The IC approach might also aid in attracting and retaining good international managers. The traditional balance sheet approach has tended to result in favorite assignment locations due to the high COLAs given for those sites. The IC approach reduces the luxury aspects of most foreign assignments and these favorite sites in particular. This makes it easier for MNCs to move staff from one location to another. The reduction of luxury compensation packages also helps reduce repatriation problems that occur when expatriates are reluctant to return home due to reduced compensation packages in the home location relative to their foreign assignment. The IC approach also may be more in keeping with the desire of global firms to have managers take a global view of the firm's operations. The IC approach promotes this global view by its very nature as an international (rather than bilateral) basket of goods. This international basket is also more likely to require expatriates to interact with locals in order to purchase local substitutes for desired home items, thus increasing their cross-cultural skills and adaptability. Finally, the IC approach may have positive motivational effects. Traditional balance sheet packages have resulted in large expenses going simply to the upkeep of the expatriate. The international citizen's approach reduces these costs and allows more funds to be used for performance incentives.

Issues Common to Most Compensation Packages

Because of the potential for their having a highly negative impact on expatriates, most compensation packages, regardless of the particular approach taken, must deal effectively with tax and social security issues. There are many ways in which companies provide tax protection or equalization so that the employees do not incur a tax liability (or at least are taxed at a low rate) in foreign countries. A perquisite, such as the use of a company car, might not be taxable, whereas an increase in salary sufficient for buying or leasing a car would be. Companies usually deduct income taxes from the employee's pay at the rate that would be paid in the home country. The company then pays any additional tax owed because of higher tax rates in the foreign location. For U.S. expatriates, the taxation problems are particularly troublesome, for they are taxed by both the foreign country where they earn their salary and by the U.S. government. U.S. expatriates can shelter from U.S. taxes up to U.S.$70,000 of their salary earned abroad. Income above this level is taxed at applicable U.S. rates.

Social security systems also require attention within any expatriate's pay package. This is a complex issue. Reciprocal agreements between some countries may allow an expatriate to remain in the home country system, at least for a while, before having to pay the host country's social security tax. This may simplify the problem if the assignment is of a duration that falls within this grace period. However, if the expatriate is required to pay host-country social security taxes, then a variety of difficulties can arise. The pension earned in a host country may be significantly less than that in the home country (which may be important if the host-country assignment is for a substantial number of years). The host-country pension may be payable in host-country currency, which might fluctuate dramatically or decrease in value relative to the home country's currency over the years. Finally, it may be difficult for an expatriate to collect the social security benefits to which he or she is entitled from the host country. This is particularly so if many years pass between the assignment and retirement.[86]

Clearly, developing and monitoring an expatriate pay system constitute a complex task. Expatriates may work in a number of different countries, each with a pay system based on its own cultural preferences, traditions, and legal precedents. Expatriate compensation systems must be flexible enough to take into account this variability and not create unacceptable levels of perceived inequity on the part of local employees when they compare their wages and benefits with those of their expatriate colleagues.

EXPATRIATE REENTRY

One aspect of the HQ-based HR manager's job that often gets overlooked is the task of effectively repatriating employees after their foreign assignments. All too often the story of the returning expatriate is similar to this one reported by Stewart Black and Hal Gregersen:

> The man was sent to Saudi Arabia on a four-year assignment at a cost to his employers of about $4 million. During those four years he learned fluent Arabic, gained new technical skills, and made friends with important business people in the Saudi community. But upon returning home, the man was shocked to find himself frequently scolded that "the way things were done in Saudi Arabia had nothing to do with the way we do things at headquarters.' Worse, he was kept waiting almost nine months for a permanent assignment which, when it came, gave him less authority than he had had abroad. Not surprisingly, the engineer left to join a direct competitor a few months later and ended up using the knowledge and skills he had acquired in Saudi Arabia against his former employer.[87]

The Problems and Impact of Reentry

Twenty to forty-eight percent of expatriates intend to leave their firm within a year after they return home, and many returnees suggest that returning home results in a greater "culture shock" than moving abroad. Unfortunately, it seems that U.S. organizations do not do a particularly good job of helping expatriates return home, even though some estimates of the cost of losing a repatriated manager may be as high as $1.2 million dollars.[88]

The process of readjustment for a returning expatriate must occur at two levels, general cultural readjustment and readjustment to the job.

● **General Cultural Readjustment**   There is often a cultural and social loss associated with reentry into the home culture. The international assignment may have been an exciting, interesting, and fulfilling experience. The lifestyles of many expatriates may have been of a considerably higher standard (servants to take care of the cooking, cleaning, and children) abroad than it can be on return to the home culture. Children may have a difficult time readjusting to school. Marital problems may develop as each spouse faces the problems of returning to the domestic lifestyle, and there may be unexpected financial pressures as salaries revert to domestic levels and allowances disappear.[89]

● **Job Readjustment**   In summarizing the findings of several studies on repatriation, Patricia Borstorff and her colleagues note that less that 15 percent of returning expatriates receive a promotion when they get home. In fact, over 75 percent report receiving a demotion and 70 percent indicate that they did not know their specific job assignment when they returned.[90] No wonder so many expatriates leave their firms within the first year back from a foreign assignment.

Douglas Allen and Sharon Alvarez cite several reasons that returning expatriates face relatively bleak job prospects.[91] First, employees who are sent overseas have too often been mediocre performers because overseas assignments are given secondary importance. In many companies overseas assignments are seen as a career risk, so high-potential employees avoid them. These high-potential employees stay home and occupy the best jobs—thus limiting the positions available to returning expatriates. Foreign assignments often result in an "out of sight, out of mind" situation for expatriates due to the foreign assignment's physical remoteness from HQ. Job opportunities are further limited for repatriates because of an organization's short-term planning horizons and/or organizational restrictions such as requiring expatriates to return to the same division they were in when they left. Going overseas may also cause a "burnt bridges" situation between the expatriate and his or her potential future bosses since while in the foreign assignment, the expatriate may come into conflict with home-country managers as a result of the traditional home HQ–foreign subsidiary relationship. When the expatriate returns home, none of these managers want the expatriate in their division. Finally, returning expatriates often receive a hostile reception from their home-country colleagues simply due to a "fear of anything foreign."

Even if returning expatriates find a reasonable position within the firm, technology may present problems for them. Those who have been abroad for a relatively long period of time may be technologically obsolete when they return home. Technology levels in foreign subsidiaries may be less advanced than those in the home country. As a result, returnees may find themselves asked to deal with technological systems with which they are unfamiliar. It may take a considerable amount of time for an expatriate to get "up to speed" on the new technology.

Another significant problem arises when supposedly equivalent positions in the domestic organization have a level of responsibility and authority much lower than the expatriate had in the foreign assignment. Expatriates often have considerable autonomy and decision-making power abroad, but much of that disappears once they are back in the home office. This transition is very difficult to make.

Enhancing the Likelihood of Reentry Adjustment

A study found that 77 percent of international transferees received no career counseling from their employers on their return from abroad and only 6 percent were offered reentry training.[92] Poor repatriation often results in managers being unwilling to take foreign assignments. Given the increased use of expatriate assignments reported by many firms, this presents a major problem for firms attempting to compete effectively in the global marketplace. Put simply, having a good repatriation program is important. Building a good program, however, requires effort not only by the company but also by the expatriate manager. Several key components of organizational and individual strategies for effective repatriation have been suggested and are described below.[93]

● **Organizational Strategies for Effective Repatriation**   As suggested earlier, it is advisable to discuss repatriation issues during predeparture training. Good repatriation requires an organization to select highly qualified employees for foreign assignments. This improves the probability that the expatriate will be successful overseas and subsequently seen as a valuable human resource upon returning home. Firms should assign a formal sponsor for each expatriate to prevent the "out of sight, out of mind" phenomenon—and train the sponsor in that role. The sponsor should have had personal international experience and have sufficient clout in the organization to provide support for the expatriate while overseas and after returning. The organization should create a repatriate directory so that newly repatriated employees can seek advice from "old hands" as well as their sponsor. Companies should also leverage technology. Sending periodic e-mails about changes and career opportunities, having a special Web site, and publishing quarterly newsletters can help companies remain in constant touch with expatriates.[94]

It is also suggested that expatriates be retained in the home-country HR planning system. Overseas assignments must be linked to long-term career plans. For example, as we noted earlier, Whirlpool, Westinghouse Electric, 3M, and Arthur Andersen make foreign assignments a prerequisite for promotion to senior management positions.[95] The length and flexibility of the time period during which an expatriate can return home may need to be increased. This provides a greater likelihood of having the person come into a job where they are needed. Divisional boundaries must also be transcended, that is, an expatriate should be able to return to any division within the firm, not just the one he or she left. If absolutely necessary, a *meaningful* holding pattern should be created for the returnee. That is, the repatriate should be employed as an internal consultant until a permanent job is found—*and* this job should involve important projects. One of the main reasons repatriated employees grow dissatisfied with their jobs after they return is that they feel their new skills and experience are not being put to use.[96] One possible use for repatriates is as trainers for managers who are getting ready to take on an expatriate position. This provides a very direct way of making use of the skills gained by repatriates while in their own foreign assignments. It is also important for top managers to foster an appreciation in the home-country environment of the value of international assignments. This may mean sending home-country managers overseas for short-term projects. These sorts of actions, if undertaken by an organization, should significantly enhance the probability that returning expatriates will adapt well and become valuable human assets to the firm.

Although many firms do a poor job of managing repatriation, there are notable exceptions. For example, at the Monsanto head office, planning starts three to six months in advance of an expatriate's return. An HR manager and the expatriate's senior line officer look at the skills gained by the expatriate during the foreign assignment. The HR manager and senior line officer review potential job openings within Monsanto for the expatriate upon his or her return. At the same time, the expatriate writes a report that self-assesses skills and identifies career goals. The expatriate, HR manager, and senior line officer meet and decide which of the available jobs best fits. As a result of this process, turnover rates among repatriates has dropped significantly.[97]

● **Individual Strategies for Effective Repatriation**   In addition to actions taken by the organization, the expatriate manager must play a critical role in ensuring that the repatriation process is effective. Among the actions that the expatriate should take are the following:

1. Remain in close contact with the sponsor at home.
2. In addition to the formal sponsor, develop close relationships with several informal sponsors at home to gain a broader view of the home environment.
3. Develop rapport with several managers who supervise positions considered to be attractive target repatriation positions.
4. Maintain visibility through e-mail, regular phone calls, and the like.
5. Visit HQ frequently during the overseas assignment to renew contacts.
6. Be aware of the dangers of leaving your fate in the hands of the HR system alone; actively manage your own career while on expatriate assignment.

● **Support and Coping**   In addition to the job-related strategies discussed above, there are other components of a good repatriation system that focus more on social and emotional support to expatriates and their families. The more social support available to an expatriate on return, the easier the reentry will be. Returnees who engage in behaviors focused on taking advantage of opportunities and avoiding threats in the new situation will adjust more easily to reentry than those who use primarily emotional coping behaviors, such as drinking, smoking, and sleeping. Individuals should seek out support for their return before they arrive and let colleagues know that they will want their help after they return. They should talk with former expatriates who have made the transition back home successfully to identify likely problems that will arise and get ideas for dealing with these problems. Organizations can aid expatriates in this aspect of repatriation. For example, Unocal provides a day-long debriefing session for expatriates and their family. The session focuses on common repatriation difficulties and ways of coping with them. The returnees watch videos of other repatriates and their families discussing their experiences. These taped discussions lead to a live discussion with repatriates, which usually ends with the "old hands" sharing tips that have been helpful to them in making the adjustment back home. Many repatriates have suggested that new returnees keep a journal because it helps them identify the source of their frustrations and aids in the problem-solving process.[98]

In summarizing this section of repatriation, one thing is extremely clear: HQ-based HR managers can handle the myriad problems associated with selecting, training, appraising, and paying expatriates successfully. Expatriates can be highly successful in their foreign assignment. However, unless both the organization and the individual take care to ensure a successful reentry for the expatriate into the domestic organization, the company may lose the skills and experience that the employee has gained during the foreign assignment and the employee may suffer the frustration of a career cut short and the stress of having to leave the firm within only a short time after returning home.

IHRM: ADDING VALUE IN THE GLOBAL BUSINESS ENVIRONMENT?

In each chapter of this text we have provided ideas about how to assess whether HRM activities add value to the organization, either by measuring the dollar costs and benefits of those activities or by assessing other nonfinancial inputs and outcomes. To a significant extent, assessing the value added by international HRM activities can be accomplished using indices similar to those used in domestic situations. The process of determining the costs and benefits of cross-cultural training programs is essentially the same as that used to assess training for domestic managers. Measures used in assessing stakeholder perceptions of changes in domestic pay packages may be equally applicable to determining reactions to expatriate pay policies.

As noted earlier in this chapter, one of the major differences between domestic and international IIRM is the level of risk inherent in IHRM activities. Thus, while the basic types of costs associated with expatriate failure may be similar to the costs when a domestic manager fails, the level of those costs in the international context may be much greater. If a domestic manager fails in an assignment (e.g., alienates a prospective client and loses a potential contract), this represents a cost to the organization—a customer not gained. In the international arena, however, if a manager alienates a potential customer, it may be more likely that the firm's reputation will be damaged more widely in the foreign market than it would be in a domestic context. If the firm were to terminate the failed domestic manager, there would be various separation and replacement costs. In the case of an international manager, these separation costs would likely be much greater. For example, separation costs would likely include having to ship the failed international manager and his or her family back to the home country along with all their possessions. A less dramatic example would be in the difference in costs between supplying a domestic versus international training program. For both programs, the costs would include program development, trainer salary for the time involved, trainer travel costs, trainee salary for the time spent being trained, trainee travel costs, facilities, materials, accommodations, and the like. In the international context, training materials might be much more expensive due to the need to have them translated into another language. Travel costs likely would be greater. Facilities could be more costly due to limited availability in the foreign location—and thus premium prices for those facilities that do exist.

There are, however, some HR activities that should be assessed on a "value-added" basis that are unique to IHRM. Examples of these include the following:[99]

- The costs and benefits of repatriation programs
- The ability of IHRM policies to provide an appropriate mix of PCN, HCN, and TCN managers for optimal organizational efficiency and effectiveness
- The costs and subsequent benefits of localization programs (reducing expatriate and increasing local employees) in foreign subsidiaries
- The costs and benefits of customizing HR activities to suit particular national cultures and legal systems
- The costs and benefits of HR programs developed to deal with the special problems of foreign taxation and social security systems

This list is not intended to be exhaustive. It does, however, exemplify the need for international human resource managers to be vigilant in identifying the unique aspects of HR programs in an international business environment that may add to the costs and benefits of such programs.

Summary of Key Points

International human resource management is distinct from domestic human resource management because of its broader perspective, greater scope of activities, and higher level of risk. Multinational corporations may take any one of a number of different approaches to HRM, with the choice of approach depending on political issues and legal regulations; the level of managerial, educational, and technological development in the host country; technology and the nature of the product; the stage of the organization's life cycle; and differences between the home and host cultures.

HR managers located in an MNC's foreign subsidiaries have many tasks. Often they must deal with labor markets that lack the level of skill needed for technical and managerial positions in their subsidiaries. Selection, training, and appraisal systems used at the headquarters of the MNC may be inappropriate for local use. Pay systems must conform to local laws and customs while fitting into global MNC policies.

The HQ-based manager must coordinate IHRM operations in a variety of countries, each with its own local cultural, legal, and traditional influences. Headquarters policies must be flexible enough to allow for these local variations. However, policies also must be developed to help achieve the overall strategic global objectives of the MNC.

One important IHRM activity is the management of expatriate and inpatriate managers. MNCs often select expatriates based primarily on technical competence, although research shows that many other factors are important in determining expatriate success. The ability of an expatriate's spouse and family to adapt to the new location is a significant determinant of expatriate success or failure. The expatriate's ability to establish personal relationships and understand the behavior of people from a foreign culture is a critical factor. Training, both before and after the foreign assignment begins, plays a crucial role in determining how expatriates perform. Extensive training is required when the job and culture to which the individual is being sent are very different from the person's current job and cultural background. In addition, programs to help dual-career couples deal with the special problems associated with the "trailing spouse" should be part of any effective program for preparing and managing expatriates abroad.

MNCs often underestimate the desirability of sending female employees to foreign assignments. They believe that women will not be accepted by businesspersons in many cultures. However, research contradicts this view and indicates that female expatriates can perform extremely well.

Care must be taken in developing performance appraisal systems for expatriates. Physical distance, the nature of the expatriate's tasks, and a variety of environmental factors make accurate assessment of expatriate performance very difficult. The development and coordination of compensation systems for expatriates also constitute a complex task. Expatriate pay systems that attempt to balance the living costs of home and foreign assignments also must be integrated into the overall MNC compensation system. Besides managing expatriates while they are abroad, the company also must design programs to effectively reintegrate the expatriates on their return so that it can make maximum use of the skills and experience that these employees have gained in their international assignments.

In assessing the costs and benefits of international HR programs, the basic natures of the factors that contribute to the value added are the same as for domestic HR activities. However, the magnitude of these costs and potential benefits may be considerably different in the international context. In addition, there are some HR activities that should be assessed for value added that are not typically found in domestic HR operations.

The Manager's Vocabulary

balance sheet approach
better of home or host model
closed hybrid model
cultural assimilator
cultural toughness
culture shock phase of training
developmental assignments
differentiation
dual-career couple
ethnocentric approach
expatriate managers
geocentric approach
global corporation
global manager
hardship premium
host-country/local-market package
host-country national (HCN)
HQ-based model

inpatriate
integration
international citizen's approach
international human resource management
    (IHRM)
management oversight assignments
modified home-country model
multinational corporation (MNC)
open hybrid model
operational performance
others-oriented dimension
parent-country national (PCN)
perceptual dimension
polycentric approach
postarrival training
project assignments
regiocentric approach
regional coordination assignments
reinforcement substitution
relationship development
self-oriented dimension
social security systems
standard index
strategic performance
stress reduction
technical competence
technology transfer assignments
third-country national (TCN)
trailing spouse
willingness to communicate
worldwide oversight assignments

Questions for Discussion

1. What are the differences between international and domestic human resource management?
2. What are some of the different approaches that MNCs take to managing human resources? What factors determine which approach an MNC is likely to take?
3. How can culture affect HR planning, staffing, training, and performance appraisal in a subsidiary?
4. Suppose your firm was about to set up a subsidiary in Thailand. What factors would be important in determining the type of compensation system the firm set up for local Thai workers?

5. You are planning to set up a subsidiary in India and are trying to decide whether the managing director of the new facility should be a local Indian manager, an expatriate manager from your firm's home country, or a third-country manager from elsewhere in your worldwide operations. On what basis would you make the decision?

6. Several researchers have identified the factors that seem to make it easier or more difficult for expatriates to adjust to foreign assignments. What are these factors, and which of them do you think are the most important?

7. Defend or refute this statement: "It is not a good idea to send female managers to countries that are very masculine in nature."

8. What is an inpatriate? What are the advantages and disadvantages of using inpatriate managers in an MNC?

9. What methods of cross-cultural training would you use to prepare an American manager for foreign assignment in China? Why?

10. What is a "trailing spouse." Why should MNCs be concerned about trailing spouses? How have some firms attempted to deal effectively with dual-career couples and the trailing spouse issue?

11. What is the difference between operational and strategic performance appraisal?

12. What are the components of an expatriate compensation system? What purposes do these components serve?

13. Suppose that you were an expatriate about to complete a foreign assignment in France. What steps would you take to get ready to return to a position in your home country? What would you have done before you left for the French assignment?

14. You are the IHRM director of an MNC. Your boss has just asked you to prepare a program for repatriating a manager who has been on a foreign assignment. Describe that program.

● ## Case 17.1
The Office Equipment Company

The Office Equipment Company (OEC) must identify a manager to help set up and run a new manufacturing facility located in India. The position will have a minimum duration of three years. OEC manufactures office equipment such as copying machines, recording machines, mail scales, and paper shredders in eight different countries. OEC's products are distributed and sold worldwide.

Currently, OEC has no manufacturing facilities in India but has been selling and servicing products in Thailand, the Philippines, and several European and Latin American countries since the early 1970s. OEC sells its products in Thailand and the Philippines through independent importers but is now convinced that it needs to expand its operations into the rapidly growing Indian economy. OEC believes that it must have a local manufacturing facility in India in order to enhance its competitive advantage in relation to both foreign and local competitors.

OEC hopes to begin constructing a factory in India within the next six months. This factory would import product components and assemble them. The construction of the assembly plant would be supervised by a U.S. technical team, and a U.S. expatriate would be assigned to direct the production. This expatriate manager would report directly to the U.S. headquarters of OEC.

The option of filling the managing director position with someone from outside the firm is alien to OEC's policy. Otherwise, the options are fairly open. OEC uses a combination of home-country, host-country, and third-country nationals in top positions in foreign countries. It is not uncommon for managers to rotate among foreign and U.S. domestic locations. In fact, it is increasingly evident that international experience is an important factor in deciding who will be appointed to top corporate positions. The sales and service operations in Thailand and the Philippines have been controlled through OEC's Asia regional office located in Manila. A committee at the Asia regional office has quickly narrowed its choice to the following five candidates.

Tom Zimmerman   Zimmerman joined the firm thirty years ago and is well versed in all the technical aspects required by the job. Zimmerman is a specialist in start-up projects and has supervised the construction of new manufacturing facilities in four countries. He has never been assigned to work abroad permanently. His assignments usually have been in European countries and for periods of less than six months. He is considered to be extremely competent in the duties he has performed during the years and will retire in about four and a half years. Neither he nor his wife speaks any language other than English; their children are grown and living with their own children in the United States. Zimmerman is currently in charge of an operation about the size that the one in India will be after the factory begins operating. However, that operation is being merged with another, so his present position will become redundant.

Brett Harrison   At age forty, Brett has spent fifteen years with OEC. He is considered highly competent and capable of moving into upper-level management within the next few years. He has never been based abroad but has traveled frequently to Latin America. Both he and his wife speak Spanish adequately. Their two children, ages fourteen and fifteen, are just beginning to study Spanish. His wife is a professional as well, holding a responsible marketing position with a pharmaceutical company.

Carolyn Moyer   Carolyn joined OEC after getting her B.S. in engineering from Purdue University and an M.B.A. from the prestigious Bond University in Australia. At age thirty-seven she has already moved between staff and line positions of growing responsibility. For two years she was second-in-command of a manufacturing plant in Texas about the size of the new operation in India. Her performance in that post was considered excellent. Currently she works as a member of a staff production

planning team. When she joined OEC, she had indicated her eventual interest in international responsibilities because of a belief that it would help her advancement. She speaks French well and is not married.

Francis Abhrams   Francis is currently one of the assistant managing directors in a large Argentinian operation, which produces and sells for the Argentinian market. He is a New Yorker who has worked for OEC in Argentina for five years. He holds an M.B.A. from New York University and is considered to be one of the likely candidates to head OEC's operation in Chile when the present managing director retires in four years. He is thirty-five, married with four children (ages two to seven). He speaks Spanish adequately. His wife does not work outside the home and speaks only English.

Leon Smith   At thirty, Leon is assistant to the managing director at the Athens manufacturing facility, a position he assumed when he joined OEC after completing his undergraduate studies in the United States seven years ago. He is considered competent, especially in production operations, but lacking in managerial experience. He was successful in increasing OEC's production output in Athens. During his tenure in Athens, Leon traveled extensively in Pakistan and India. He went to college with a number of students from Pakistan and India. These individuals came from prominent political and business families in their countries, and Leon has visited them during his travels. He thus has the advantage of being reasonably well connected with influential families in the region. He is not married.

1. Whom should the committee choose for the assignment and why?
2. What problems might each individual encounter in the position?
3. How might OEC go about minimizing the problems that the chosen person would have in managing the Indian operations?

Source: International Business: Environments and Operations, 7/e, by Daniels/Radeburgh, © 1995. Reprinted by permission of Pearson Education, Inc., Upper Saddle River, NJ.

● **Exercise 17.1**
Cultural Clues in the Entertainment World

Divide into groups of three or four. If there are foreign students in the class—particularly if they have a common culture—they should be placed in groups of their own.

The students in each group should identify books, short stories, newspaper stories, films/videos, and so forth that provide information about important cultural values in their society. The groups should note the important cultural characteristics that these informational vehicles present and that an expatriate should be aware of when ac-

cepting a job assignment in that culture. Groups could bring passages from the books or clips from the films/videos to class and share them with their classmates—providing an appropriate cultural analysis of their materials as they present them. For example, the film *Dirty Harry* with Clint Eastwood would provide an excellent example of Americans' love of the "rugged individualist," along with important information about some Americans' preoccupation with firearms.

● **Exercise 17.2**
Bicycles to New Zealand—Help from the World Wide Web

You are the assistant human resource director of a medium-sized firm that has been exporting bicycles to New Zealand. The bicycle market in New Zealand has expanded significantly in the past three years, and your firm is planning to open a small manufacturing facility in Wellington. Although you have hired a New Zealand national to run your facility, the initial construction and operation of the plant will be co-managed by both the New Zealand manager and one of your home-country executives.

Since your firm has not manufactured in New Zealand before, your home-country managers have no knowledge of many common human resource issues such as occupational safety and health laws, union practices and legislation, and pay rates and systems. Although the New Zealand manager will

handle most of these issues, you have been asked to develop a briefing paper for the home-country manager on health and safety, unions, and pay systems in New Zealand. This paper will not make the manager an expert but will at least give the individual a general knowledge of the HR environment in which the plant will operate. Rather than "reinventing the wheel," you decide that the best way for the manager to get acquainted with these issues is through the World Wide Web.

Your task is to search the Internet for web sites that will provide the home country manager with useful information about occupational health and safety, unions, and pay systems in New Zealand.

Note: You may focus on another country rather than New Zealand if you wish.

Answers to International Perspective Questions on pages 806–807

1. c. Studies have shown that when engaging in normal social conversation, Americans like to stand about one arm's length from one another.

2. b. Japanese do not like to say "no" directly, even if they do not like something. The word

"yes" has a much broader meaning in Japan; it is often used to acknowledge understanding of a point rather than agreement with it.

3. c. In Arab countries, if you disagree with something, you usually remain silent. You must encourage the manager to express his opinions.

If possible, ask the senior managers for their opinion about an issue. Once they have spoken, others will feel more free to speak up.

4. b. Authority and status are important in China. A promotion will give the supervisor higher status, salary, and authority.

5. d. Japanese generally dislike being singled out for recognition because this may disrupt group harmony. Acknowledging their efforts and encouraging them to help their company become even more competitive is the best response.

6. c. Arabs value friendship and relationships. A direct appeal to friendship is most likely the best approach. The person will also expect you to reciprocate the favor in the future.

7. c. This makes sure Betty does not lose face *and* helps her maintain her confidence. This may lead her to come to you with questions later.

8. a. Respect for age, seniority, education, and the like is high in Japan. Asking the senior person

first would limit any further responses. Going around the room or asking for volunteers would put the juniors in a difficult situation.

9. c. Don't mix status levels in these kinds of situations. Train the section engineers, who will in turn train their technicians.

10. a. Managers should be aware of family and personal issues as well as job performance. The manager should already know what the employee wants.

11. d. Performance is a continuous, measurable process. The group is always aware if performance falters.

12. c. Group harmony is less important than individual achievement. Business is separate from relationships. The United States is a highly individualistic, achievement-oriented society.

Source: Answers adapted from discussions of intercultural skills found in Farid Elashmawi and Philip Harris, *Multicultural Management: New Skills for Global Success* (Houston: Gulf Publishing Company, 1993), pp. 98–160.

Notes and References

1. Arvind V. Phatak, *Managing Multinational Corporations* (New York: Praeger, 1978), pp. 21–22.

2. Organization for Economic Cooperation and Development (OECD), *Monthly Trade Statistics.* (Available at: http://www.oecd.org/std/tradhome.htm)

3. Rosalie L. Tung, *The New Expatriates: Managing Human Resources Abroad* (Cambridge, Mass.: Ballinger, 1988), p. 1.

4. C. A. Bartlett and S. Ghoshal, *Managing Across Borders: The Transnational Solution* (London: Century Business, 1989).

5. Randall Schuler, Peter Dowling, and Helen DeCieri, "An Integrative Framework of Strategic International Human Resource Management," *Journal of Management*, Vol. 19 (2), 1991, p. 430; Patrick V. Morgan, "International HRM: Fact or Fiction," *Personnel Administrator*, Vol. 31 (9), 1986, pp. 43–47; Peter Dowling and Denise E. Welch, "The Strategic Adaptation Process in International Human Resource Management: A Case Study," *Human Resource Planning*, Vol. 14 (1), 1991, pp. 61–69; and Jaap Paauwe and Philip Dewe, "Human Resource Management in Multinational Corporations: Theories and Models," in *International Human Resource Management: An Integrated Approach,* ed. Anne-Wil Harzing and Joris Van Ruysseveldt (London: Sage, 1995), pp. 75–98.

6. Morgan, "International HRM."

7. Charlene Solomon, "Danger Below! Spot Failing Global Assignments," *Personnel Journal*, Vol. 75 (11), 1996, pp. 78–85.

8. Michael Harvey, "A Survey of Corporate Programs for Managing Terrorist Threats," *Journal of International Business Studies,* Vol. 24 (3), 1993, pp. 465–478.

9. J. Stewart Black and Hal Gregersen, "The Right Way to Manage Expats," *Harvard Business Review,* March–April, 1999, pp. 52–63.

10. Allan Bird, Sull Taylor, and Schon Beechler, "A Typology of International Human Resource Management in Japanese Multinational Corporations: Organizational Implications," *Human Resource Management*, Vol. 37 (2), 1998, pp. 152–172.

11. Ibid.

12. D. Heenan and H. V. Perlmutter, *Multinational Organization Development* (Reading, Mass.: Addison-Wesley, 1979); Ken Kamoche, "The Integration–Differentiation Puzzle: A Resource-Capability Perspective in International Human Resource Management," *The International Journal of Human Resource Management*, Vol. 7 (1), 1996, pp. 230–244; and Sully Taylor, Schon Beecher, and Nancy Napier, "Toward an Integrative Model of Strategic International Human Resource Management," *Academy of Management Review*, Vol. 21 (4), 1996, pp. 959–985.

13. Zeynep Aycan, Rabindra Kanungo, Manuel Mendonca, Kaicheng Yu, Jurgen Deller, Gunter Stahl, and Anwar Kurshid, "Impact of Culture on Human Resource Management Practices: A 10-Country Comparison," *Applied Psychology: An International Review*, Vol. 49 (1), 2000, pp. 192–221; John F. Milliman and Mary Ann Von Glinow, "A Life Cycle Approach to Strategic International Human Resource Management in MNCs," in *Research in Personnel and Human Resource Management: Supplement 2*, ed. James B. Shaw, John E. Beck, Gerald R. Ferris, and Kendrith M. Rowland (Greenwich, Conn.: JAI Press, 1990), pp. 21–36; Philip Rosenzweig and Nitin Nohria, "Influence on

Human Resource Management Practices in Multinational Corporations," *Journal of International Business Studies*, Vol. 25 (2), 1994, pp. 229–251; Randall Schuler, Peter Dowling, and Helen De Cieri, "An Integrative Framework of Strategic International Human Resource Management," *The International Journal of Human Resource Management*, Vol. 4 (4), 1993, pp. 717–764; and Taylor, Beecher, and Napier, "Toward an Integrative Model of Strategic International Human Resource Management."

14. Rosenzweig and Nohria, "Influences on Human Resource Management Practices in Multinational Corporations."

15. Tung, *The New Expatriates*; Richard Peterson, Nancy Napier, and Won Shul Shim, "Expatriate Management—The Differential Role of National Multinational Corporation Ownership," *The International Executive*, Vol. 38 (4), 1996, pp. 543–562.

16. Barry Staw, Lance E. Sandelands, and Jane Dutton, "Threat-Rigidity Effects in Organizational Behavior: A Multilevel Analysis," *Administrative Sciences Quarterly,* Vol. 26, 1981, pp. 501–524.

17. Aycan, Kanungo, Mendonca, Yu, Deller, Stahl, and Kurshid, "Impact of Culture on Human Resource Management Practices: A 10-Country Comparison."

18. Milliman and Von Glinow, "A Life Cycle Approach"; N. Adler and F. Ghadar, "Globalization and Human Resource Management," in *Research in Global Strategic Management: A Canadian Perspective,* ed. A. Rugman (Greenwich, Conn.: JAI Press, 1990), pp. 179–205; and L. Baird and I. Meshoulam, "Managing Two Fits of Strategic Human Resource Management," *Academy of Management Review*, Vol. 13 (1), 1988, pp. 116–128.

19. Adler and Ghadar, "Globalization and Human Resource Management."

20. Cited in Charlene Solomon, "Big Mac's McGlobal HR Secrets," *Personnel Journal*, Vol. 75 (4), 1996, pp. 46–54.

21. Peterson, Napier, and Shim, "Expatriate Management—The Differential Role of National Multinational Corporation Ownership"; Tony Morden, "International Culture and Management," *Management Decision*, Vol. 33 (2), 1995, pp. 16–21; and Mark Easterby-Smith, Danusia Malina, and Lu Yuan, "How Culture-Sensitive Is HRM? A Comparative Analysis of Practice in Chinese and UK Companies," *The International Journal of Human Resource Management*, Vol. 6 (1), 1994, pp. 32–59.

22. Tung, *The New Expatriates*; and Wayne F. Cascio, *Human Resource Planning, Employment and Placement* (Washington, D.C.: BNA Books, 1989).

23. Personal communication from George Hanna, human resource manager for a cement manufacturing firm in Vietnam.

24. R. L. Desatnick and M. L. Bennet, *Human Resource Management in the Multinational Company* (New York: Nichols, 1978).

25. Paul S. Kirkbride, S. F. Y. Tang, and W. C. Shae, "The Transferability of Management Training and Development: The Case of Hong Kong," *Asia Pacific Human Resource Management*, Vol. 27 (1), 1989, pp. 7–20.

26. Solomon, "Big Mac's McGlobal HR Secrets"; and Charlene Solomon, "Learning to Manage Host-Country Nationals," *Personnel Journal*, Vol. 74 (3), 1995, pp. 60–67.

27. Easterby-Smith, Malina, and Yuan, "How Culture-Sensitive is HRM?"

28. Morden, "International Culture and Management."

29. Peter J. Dowling and Randall S. Schuler, *International Dimensions of Human Resource Management* (Boston: PWS-Kent, 1990), pp. 131–134.

30. Kenneth Chilton, "Lincoln Electric's Incentive System: Can It Be Transferred Overseas?" *Compensation & Benefits Review*, November–December 1993, pp. 21–30.

31. Luis Gomez-Mejia and Theresa Wellbourne, "Compensation Strategies in a Global Context," *Human Resource Planning*, Vol. 14 (1), 1991, pp. 29–41.

32. Vladimir Pucik and Tania Saba, "Selecting and Developing the Global vs the Expatriate Manager: A Review of the State-of-the-Art," *Human Resource Planning*, Vol. 21 (4), 1998, pp. 40–55; quote from p. 41.

33. Michael Harvey and Ronald Buckley, "Managing Inpatriates: Building a Global Core Competency," *Journal of World Business*, Vol. 32 (1), 1997, pp. 35–52.

34. Reyer Swaak, "Expatriate Management: The Search for Best Practices," *Compensation & Benefits Review*, Vol. 27 (2), 1995, pp. 21–29.

35. Denise Welch and Lawrence Welch, "Linking Operation Mode Diversity and IHRM," *The International Journal of Human Resource Management*, Vol. 5 (4), 1994, pp. 911–926.

36. Clifford Hebard, "Managing Effectively in Asia," *Training & Development*, April 1996, p. 35.

37. Michael Harvey, "The Selection of Managers for Foreign Assignments: A Planning Perspective," *Columbia Journal of World Business*, Vol. 31 (4), 1996, pp. 102–118.

38. Myrtle Bell and David Harrison, "Using Intra-National Diversity for International Assignments: Model of Bicultural Competence and Expatriate Adjustment," *Human Resource Management Review*, Vol. 6 (1), 1996, pp. 47–74; and Nick Forster, "The Persistent Myth of High Expatriate Failure Rates: A Reappraisal," *The International Journal of Human Resource Management*, Vol. 8 (4), 1997, pp. 414–433.

39. Rita Bennett, quoted in Solomon, "Danger Below! Spot Failing Global Assignments."

40. Rita Bennett and Heidi O'Gorman, "Benchmark with the Best," *HRMagazine*, Vol. 43 (5), 1998, pp. 19–22; Carolyn Gould, "The Impact of Headquarters Location on Expatriate Policy," *HRMagazine*, Vol. 43 (5), 1998, pp. 8–12; and Carla Joinson, "Why HR Managers Need to Think Globally," *HRMagazine*, Vol. 43 (5), 1998, pp. 2–7.

41. Rochelle Kopp, "International Human Resource Policies and Practices in Japanese, European, and United States Multinationals," *Human Resource Management*, Vol. 33 (4), 1994, pp. 581–599.

42. Pucik and Saba, "Selecting and Developing the Global vs the Expatriate Manager."

43. Harvey, "The Selection of Managers for Foreign Assignments."

44. J. Stewart Black, Hal Gregersen, and Mark Mendenhall, *Global Assignments: Successfully Expatriating and Repatriating International Managers* (San Francisco: Jossey-Bass, 1992); Harvey, "The Selection of Managers for Foreign Assignments": and Reyer Swaak, "Expatriate Failures: Too Many, Too Much Cost, Too Little Planning," *Compensation & Benefits Review*, Vol. 27 (6), 1995, pp. 47–55.

45. Rosalie Tung, "Selection and Training of Personnel for Overseas Assignments," *Columbia Journal of World Business*,

Vol. 16 (1), 1981, pp. 68–78; and Mark Mendenhall and Gary Oddou, "The Dimensions of Expatriate Acculturation: A Review," *Academy of Management Review,* Vol. 10 (1), 1985, pp. 39–47.

46. Simcha Ronen, "Training the International Assignee," in *Training and Development in Organizations,* ed. L. L. Goldstein et al. (San Francisco: Jossey-Bass, 1989).

47. K. Barham and D. Oates, *The International Manager* (London: Business Books, 1991); C. Coulson-Thomas, *Creating the Global Company* (Maidenhead, England: McGraw-Hill, 1992); Winfred Arthur Jr. and Winston Bennett Jr. "The International Assignee: The Relative Importance of Factors Perceived to Contribute to Success," *Personnel Psychology,* Vol. 48 (1), 1995, pp. 99–114; David Birchall, Tan Jing Hee, and Keith Gray, "Competencies for International Management," *Singapore Management Review,* January 1996, pp. 1–13; and Alan Fish and Jack Wood, "Cross-Cultural Competence in Australian Business Enterprises," *Asia Pacific Journal of Human Resources,* Vol. 35 (1), 1997, pp. 37–52.

48. Swaak, "Expatriate Failures."

49. Black and Gregersen, "The Right Way to Manage Expats," p. 58.

50. Kreicker's comments are found on p. 91 of Charlene Solomon, "Staff Selection Impacts Global Success," *Personnel Journal,* Vol. 73 (1), 1994, pp. 88–101.

51. Pucik and Saba, "Selecting and Developing the Global vs the Expatriate Manager: A Review of the State-of-the-Art," p. 41.

52. Patricia Borstorff, Stanley Harris, Hubert Field, and William Giles, "Who'll Go? A Review of Factors Associated with Employee Willingness to Work Overseas," *Human Resource Planning,* Vol. 20 (3), 1997, pp. 29–41; Victor Haines and Tania Saba, "Understanding Reactions to International Mobility Policies and Practices," *Human Resource Planning,* Vol. 22 (3), 1999, pp. 40–52; and Charlene Solomon, "Expats Say: Help Make Us Global," *Personnel Journal,* Vol. 75 (7), 1996, pp. 47–52.

53. Sully Taylor and Nancy Napier, "Working in Japan: Lessons from Women Expatriates," *Sloan Management Review,* Vol. 37 (3), 1996, pp. 76–84.

54. Dowling and Schuler, *International Dimensions of Human Resource Management,* p. 64.

55. Mariann Jelinek and Nancy J. Adler, "Women: World-Class Managers for Global Competition," *Academy of Management Executive,* Vol. 2 (1), 1988, pp. 11–19; Nancy J. Adler, "Pacific-Basin Managers: A Gaijin, Not a Woman," *Human Resource Management,* Vol. 26 (2), 1987, pp. 169–192; and Taylor and Napier, "Working in Japan."

56. Micahel G. Harvey, Milorad M. Novicevic, and Cheri Speier, "An Innovative Global Management Staffing System: A Competency-Based Perspective, " *Human Resource Management,* Vol. 39 (4), 2000, pp. 381–394.

57. Allan Bird and May Mukuda, "Expatriate in Their Own Home: A New Twist in the Human Resource Management Strategies of Japanese MNCs," *Human Resource Management,* Vol. 28 (4), 1989, pp. 437–453; Michael Harvey, Milorad Novicevic, and Cheri Speier, "Inpatriate Managers: How to Increase the Probability of Success," *Human Resource Management Review,* Vol. 9 (1), 1999, pp. 51–81; and Michael Harvey, Cheri Speier, and Milorad Novicevic, "The Role of Inpatriates in Globalization Strategy and Challenges Associated with the Inpatriation

Process," *Human Resource Planning,* Vol. 22 (1), 1999, pp. 39–50.

58. J. Stewart Black, Mark Mendenhall, and Gary Oddou, "Toward a Comprehensive Model of International Adjustment: An Integration of Multiple Theoretical Perspectives," *Academy of Management Review,* Vol. 16 (2), 1991, pp. 291–317.

59. Kerstin Baumgarten, "Training and Development of International Staff," in Harzing and Van Ruysseveldt (eds.), *International Human Resource Management,* pp. 205–228.

60. Personal story related to the third author of this text by a student in the author's graduate-level international management course.

61. J. Stewart Black and Mark Mendenhall, "Cross-Cultural Training Effectiveness: A Review and Theoretical Framework for Future Research," *Academy of Management Review,* Vol. 15 (1), 1990, pp. 113–136; J. Kline Harrison, "Developing Successful Expatriate Managers: A Framework for the Structural Design and Strategic Alignment of Cross-Cultural Training Programs," *Human Resource Planning,* Vol. 17 (3), 1994, pp. 17–34.

62. P. Christopher Early, "Intercultural Training for Managers: A Comparison of Documentary and Interpersonal Methods," *Academy of Management Journal,* Vol. 30 (4), 1987, pp. 684–698.

63. Rita Bennett, Anne Aston, and Tracy Colquhon, "Cross-Cultural Training: A Critical Step in Ensuring the Success of International Assignments," *Human Resource Management,* Vol. 39 (2 & 3), 2000, pp. 239–250.

64. Harrison, "Developing Successful Expatriate Managers."

65. Black, Gregersen, and Mendenhall, *Global Assignments.*

66. The following discussion is based on information on contingency training models described in Dowling and Schuler, *International Dimensions of Human Resource Management;* J. Stewart Black and Mark Mendenhall, "A Practical but Theory-Based Framework for Selecting Cross-Cultural Training Methods," *Human Resource Management,* Vol. 28 (4), 1989, pp. 511–539; Black, Gregersen, and Mendenhall, *Global Assignments;* and Tung, *The New Expatriates,* p. 25.

67. Pucik and Saba, "Selecting and Developing the Global vs the Expatriate Manager."

68. Baumgarten, "Training and Development of International Staff"; and Jan Selmer, Ingemar Torbiorn, and Corrina T. de Leon, "Sequential Cross-Cultural Training for Expatriate Business Managers: Pre-Departure and Post-Arrival," *The International Journal of Human Resource Management,* Vol. 9 (5), 1998, pp. 831–840.

69. Black, Gregersen, and Mendenhall, *Global Assignments,* p. 100.

70. Ibid., p. 109.

71. Ibid.

72. Tung, *The New Expatriates,* p. 158.

73. Selmer, Torbiorn, and de Leon, "Sequential Cross-Cultural Training for Expatriate Business Managers."

74. Michael Harvey and Ronald Buckley, "The Process for Developing an International Program for Dual-Career Couples," *Human Resource Management Review,* Vol. 8, No. 1, 1998, pp. 99–123.

75. Charlene Solomon, "One Assignment, Two Lives," *Personnel Journal,* Vol. 75 (5), 1996, pp. 36–47.

76. Mark. E. Mendenhall and Gunter K. Stahl, "Expatriate Training and Development: Where Do We Go from Here?" *Human Resource Management,* Vol. 39 (2 & 3), 2000, pp. 251–265.

77. Gary Oddou, Mark. E. Mendenhall, and J. Bonner Ritchie, "Leveraging Travel as a Tool for Global Leadership Development," *Human Resource Management,* Vol. 39 (2 & 3), 2000, pp. 159–172.

78. Dowling and Schuler, *International Dimensions of Human Resource Management*, pp. 80–82.

79. Swaak, "Expatriate Management."

80. Dowling and Schuler, *International Dimensions of Human Resource Management*.

81. Charlene Solomon, "How Does Your Global Talent Measure Up?" *Personnel Journal*, Vol. 73 (10), 1994, pp. 96–108.

82. Gould, "The Impact of Headquarters Location on Expatriate Policy."

83. Kenton Klaus, "How to Establish an Effective Expatriate Program—Best Practices in International Assignment Administration," *Employment Relations Today*, Vol. 22 (1), 1995, pp. 59–70.

84. Kimberly Freeman and Jeffrey Kane, "An Alternative Approach to Expatriate Allowances: An 'International Citizen,'" *The International Executive*, Vol. 37 (3), 1995, pp. 245–259.

85. Ibid.

86. Leigh Ann Collins Allard, "Managing Globe Trotting Expats," *Management Review*, Vol. 85 (5), 1996, pp. 38–43.

87. Black and Gregersen, "The Right Way to Manage Expats." p. 60.

88. J. Stewart Black, Hal Gregersen, and Mark Mendenhall, "Toward a Theoretical Framework of Repatriation Adjustment," *Journal of International Business Studies*, Vol. 23 (4), 1992, pp. 737–760.

89. Michael C. Harvey, "Repatriation of Corporate Executives: An Empirical Study," *Journal of International Business Studies*, Vol. 20, 1989, pp. 131–144; and D. W. Kendall, "Repatriation: An Ending and a Beginning," *Business Horizons*, Vol. 24 (6), 1981, pp. 21–25.

90. Borstorff, Harris, Field, and Giles, "Who'll Go?"

91. Douglas Allen and Sharon Alvarez, "Empowering Expatriates and Organizations to Improve Repatriation Effectiveness," *Human Resource Planning*, Vol. 21 (4), 1998, pp. 29–39.

92. Andrea C. Poe "Welcome Back," *HRMagazine*, Vol. 45 (3), 2000, pp. 94–102.

93. Allen and Alvarez, "Empowering Expatriates and Organizations to Improve Repatriation Effectiveness."

94. Andrea C. Poe, "Destination Everywhere," *HRMagazine*, Vol. 45 (10), 2000, pp. 67–75.

95. Pucik and Saba, "Selecting and Developing the Global vs the Expatriate Manager"

96. Poe "Welcome Back."

97. Black and Gregersen, "The Right Way to Manage Expats."

98. Ibid.

99. Gary Florkowski and Randall Schuler, "Auditing Human Resource Management in the Global Environment," *The International Journal of Human Resource Management*, Vol. 5 (4), 1994, pp. 827–851.

Company Index

Author Index

Subject Index

Human Resource Management Model

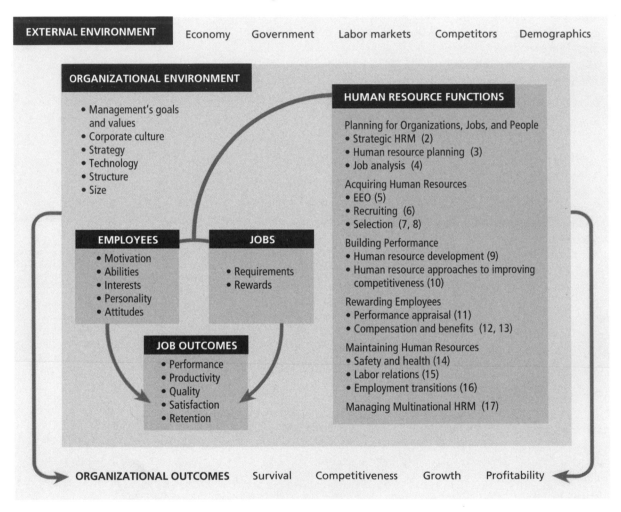

EXTERNAL ENVIRONMENT   Economy   Government   Labor markets   Competitors   Demographics

ORGANIZATIONAL ENVIRONMENT

- Management's goals and values
- Corporate culture
- Strategy
- Technology
- Structure
- Size

HUMAN RESOURCE FUNCTIONS

Planning for Organizations, Jobs, and People
- Strategic HRM (2)
- Human resource planning (3)
- Job analysis (4)

Acquiring Human Resources
- EEO (5)
- Recruiting (6)
- Selection (7, 8)

Building Performance
- Human resource development (9)
- Human resource approaches to improving competitiveness (10)

Rewarding Employees
- Performance appraisal (11)
- Compensation and benefits (12, 13)

Maintaining Human Resources
- Safety and health (14)
- Labor relations (15)
- Employment transitions (16)

Managing Multinational HRM (17)

EMPLOYEES
- Motivation
- Abilities
- Interests
- Personality
- Attitudes

JOBS
- Requirements
- Rewards

JOB OUTCOMES
- Performance
- Productivity
- Quality
- Satisfaction
- Retention

ORGANIZATIONAL OUTCOMES   Survival   Competitiveness   Growth   Profitability